Tavenner Publishing Company
406 Sutton Place
Anderson, South Carolina 29621

E-mail: tavpubco@charter.net

ISBN: 978-1-937435-20-2

Contents

Chapter 1

Economics:

What It's All About

When you graduate from college, will it be difficult or easy for you to find a job? How will changes in the prices of things you want to buy affect your standard of living? Will you be able to qualify for a car loan or a mortgage? What impact will federal budget deficits have on your future well-being as your tax funds are used to pay interest on the national debt? Will foreign competition deprive you of a job?

As these questions make clear, economics is about you: student, employee, consumer, and taxpayer. Economics is about the constraints you face, the choices you make, and your interdependence with others for survival.

In economics, you'll study the opportunities and obstacles you'll confront as you seek to make a living and to satisfy your desires for both the necessities and luxuries of life. As you learn economic principles, you'll develop a systematic way of thinking about the consequences of human behavior and the way the economy functions. You'll also gain insights into social problems and various approaches to resolving or alleviating them. The emphasis in this text is on how you can *use* economics as a practical tool to comprehend and deal responsibly with personal, business, and social issues.

Concept Preview

After reading this chapter, you should be able to

1. Describe the mechanism of the economy and the discipline of economics.
2. Understand the concepts of scarcity and opportunity cost.
3. Discuss major branches of economic inquiry: microeconomics, macroeconomics, positive analysis, and normative analysis.
4. Understand the concept of an economic model and its uses.
5. Explain *rational behavior* and *marginal analysis*, a method of analyzing the way we make decisions.

Some Basic Definitions

1 The economy is the mechanism through which the use of labor, land, structures, vehicles, equipment, and natural resources is organized to satisfy the desires of those who live in a society. The rules, institutions, and traditions used to coordinate economic activity differ considerably among nations, but all societies must deal with similar economic issues.

The discipline of economics is concerned with the use of available productive resources in a society to satisfy what often are conflicting desires and demands. Economics is concerned with *choices:* with evaluating and selecting among alternatives, realizing that each time we make a choice we also forgo an opportunity. One goal of this text is to help you develop an understanding of the issues of scarcity and choice within the context of the way modern economies function.

The Basic Task of an Economy: Grappling with Scarcity

The economy is a dynamic, constantly changing mechanism. The natural resources, workers, managers, innovators, equipment, structures, and technical know-how available to produce useful goods and services are all in some way limited. The wants we seek to satisfy, however, are seemingly unlimited. We all have biological needs for minimum amounts of food, clothing, and other basic goods—but few of us are content with minimum amounts of these items. We want amenities, comfort, and luxuries.

2 The fundamental economic problem is scarcity, the imbalance between our desires and the means of satisfying those desires. It is a problem faced by rich as well as poor societies—even the vast wealth of the United States is inadequate to satisfy all the desires of its people. The importance of scarcity as a unifying topic in economics is highlighted by the fact that many economists would define their discipline in the following way:

Economics is the study of how human beings make choices to use scarce resources as they seek to satisfy their seemingly unlimited wants.

Opportunity Cost

When scarcity exists, we know we must sacrifice something of value to obtain more of any scarce good or service. The limited availability of resources such as land, skilled labor, structures, and equipment means that the more resources are used for one purpose, the less will be available for other purposes. The opportunity cost of choosing to use resources for one purpose is the sacrifice of the next best alternative for the use of those resources. For example, if your next best alternative to studying for an hour is an hour of swimming, then the opportunity cost of studying is the hour of swimming you sacrifice when you choose to study. If you're considering the choice between a bicycle and new stereo speakers, then the opportunity cost of choosing to buy the bike is the speakers, and vice versa.

The concept of opportunity cost is vital because opportunity cost is a measure of everything you sacrifice to attain a given objective. When you make a decision, you want to consider carefully its opportunity cost before deciding whether the gain is worth the sacrifice you must make. For example, the actual opportunity cost of attending college is more than the sacrifice of the goods and services you could buy with the sum of money, say $12,000 per year, you must give up to pay for tuition, books, and equipment. Suppose attending college requires that you devote full time to your studies so that you forgo the opportunity of a paying job. If the next best use of your time is a job that would pay $18,000 over the college year, you must add the value of this forgone opportunity to your other annual money costs of attending college.

Your actual opportunity cost of attending college is the goods and services you could have bought with the $30,000 per year you sacrifice to go to college. You can now weigh the full opportunity cost of attending college against the gains you expect from doing so. The gains include possible higher future income and improvement in the quality of your life, as well as the chance to socialize with fellow students and to participate in sports and other activities.

Three Basic Economic Decisions

The concepts of scarcity and opportunity cost are vital to understanding how the economy works. In the face of the inevitable imbalance between limited productive capability and limitless wants, the following questions need to be considered:

1. *What will be produced?* The productive potential of an economy can't be used to do everything for everybody. Decisions must be made about what to produce and how much of each item to produce with the limited resources available. These decisions are political in nature, and they involve balancing needs and wants of various groups. For example, an increase in the use of productive capacity to provide military equipment inevitably reduces the availability of consumer goods such as cameras, microwaves, and automobiles. Choices must be made about which goods and services to make available and which to forgo.

2. *How will goods and services be produced?* There's more than one way to accomplish any given objective. For example, a certain quantity of iceberg lettuce can be produced on a large tract of land without the use of pesticides or fertilizers. However, the same amount of lettuce can be grown on less land with chemical agents. Goods and services can be produced by business firms or by government or nonprofit enterprises. Crops can be harvested by many workers using hand tools or with specialized machines and fewer workers. Textiles can be loomed and finished by hand or in automated plants where machines rather than workers perform many of the required tasks. Machines or other products (such as chemicals) can be substituted for labor or land when producing any mix of goods. Productive methods that squeeze the most out of available means allow the greatest possible material well-being from limited resources.

3. *To whom will goods and services be distributed?* Are they to be distributed equally to everyone so that each of us lives in the same type of house, eats the same amount and kinds of food, and wears the same clothes? Or are goods to be sold to those willing and able to pay? Under the latter method, people with higher incomes will enjoy more and better products and services than people with lower incomes. Will some of us be given special privileges to enjoy goods and services regardless of our ability to pay for those items? What rules will be used to decide who gets what?

The distribution of material well-being is never perfectly equal. Some people have the financial resources to enjoy great quantities of goods and services of the highest quality. Others, even in a nation with the vast productive potential of the United States, live in poverty. No society has yet discovered how to provide equally for the needs and wants of everyone while still offering the incentives that encourage high-quality production and technological innovation.

Microeconomics versus Macroeconomics

3 Economic analysis is divided into two main branches: microeconomics and macroeconomics. Both are important in dealing with the problem of scarcity.

Microeconomics takes a close-up view of the economy by concentrating on the choices made by individual participants in the economy such as consumers, workers, business managers, and investors. Macroeconomics looks at the economy from a broader perspective by considering its overall performance and the way various sectors of the economy relate to one another. The performance of the economy is gauged by the total value of annual production, the capacity of the economy to provide jobs, changes in the purchasing power of money, and the growth of employment and output.

Microeconomics

Microeconomics analyzes the ways individuals choose among various courses of action by weighing the benefits and costs of alternatives available to them. It emphasizes the role of prices in business and personal decisions. One of its major goals is to understand how the prices of particular goods and services are determined and how prices influence decisions. Because of its preoccupation with prices and the trading of goods and services, microeconomics is sometimes called *price theory.*

Microeconomics studies the actions of individuals as they buy and sell in market transactions. As you know, some services, such as education and police protection, are provided by government agencies rather than being sold in markets. What are the advantages and disadvantages of alternatives to markets as a means of accomplishing the basic tasks of the economy? What role does government play in the economy? How do political choices influence the economy's functions and performance? You'll find that microeconomic analysis provides a useful point of view about human behavior that will give you insights into important social and political issues.

Macroeconomics

Macroeconomics examines changes in total national production and consumption, averages of the prices of broad groups of goods and services, and the employment of workers in the economy. Macroeconomists seek to explain the causes of economic fluctuations and to suggest policies that will make the fluctuations less abrupt, with the aim of preventing excessive unemployment and rapid price increases.

In macroeconomics we place special emphasis on understanding the causes of unemployment. The *unemployment rate* is the number of jobless workers who are actively looking for work or who have been laid off from a job and are looking for work, expressed as a percentage of the total labor force. Unemployment is often a major issue in congressional and presidential elections. In fact, the federal government is required by law to pursue policies that seek to keep unemployment from becoming too high. If such policies are to succeed, the individuals who develop them must have a keen understanding of how the economy works.

Inflation is another highly charged political issue studied in macroeconomics. *Inflation* is a general yearly increase in the average level of prices for a broad spectrum of goods and services. Inflation erodes the purchasing power of money. It can create economic instability in a nation by harming the competitiveness of firms seeking to sell products in foreign markets and by distorting economic choices as people try to unload money today that they think will be worth less tomorrow. During the late 1970s inflation was a severely disrupting influence in the U.S. economy, rising to double-digit levels along with escalating interest rates. Macroeconomics seeks to understand the causes of inflation and to help government authorities pursue policies aimed at keeping the inflation rate low and within fairly predictable bounds. Stable and predictable prices facilitate planning for the future and reduce the uncertainty associated with market transactions.

In studying aggregate production in the economy and its fluctuations, macroeconomists seek to uncover the basic influences that cause national production to increase. The key to prosperity in an economy is steady growth in national output. When growth in a nation's output exceeds growth in its population, the output per person in the economy will grow, thus improving the well-being of the population on average.

Positive Analysis versus Normative Analysis

In the field of economics, we're concerned with more than understanding *how* the economy functions. We also look at ways of improving the outcomes that emerge as the economy accomplishes its tasks of producing and distributing goods and services. The operation of the economy isn't flawless, nor does it please all of us. As individuals, we differ in our opinions about the goals for which resources in the economy should be used. We also disagree about the appropriate nature and extent of government involvement in the economy, and through political channels we express our views about which groups government should help. Because we understand the concept of opportunity cost, we know that if a government action benefits one group, it inevitably imposes a cost on another group.

Positive Analysis

In evaluating economic policies, we must understand the basic functioning of the economy before we can predict the impact of those policies on the economy. Positive analysis is a way to forecast the impact of changes in economic policies or conditions on observable items such as production, sales, prices, and personal incomes. It then tries to determine who gains and who loses as a result of the changes. Positive analysis makes statements of the "if ...then" type that can be supported or refuted by empirical evidence. For example, "*If* electronics import quotas are imposed, *then* the prices of DVD players for U.S. consumers will increase." Or "*If* the federal government deficit is reduced, *then* interest rates will fall." We can accept or reject these statements by observing whether evidence exists that changes in prices, incomes, or interest rates actually do occur as a direct result of the policy changes.

Because no one completely understands how the economy works, economists often disagree about actual cause-and-effect relationships. Such disagreements must be resolved through examination of the facts that uses statistical methods to test the relationships.

Normative Analysis

Positive analysis cannot be used to evaluate an outcome. For example, positive analysis of government welfare programs can look at the impact of such programs on the incentives of recipients to work and on national production, but it cannot determine whether the programs are good or bad. To evaluate the performance of these programs, we must establish criteria or norms against which we will compare their actual outcomes.

We use normative analysis as a way to evaluate the desirability of alternative outcomes according to underlying *value judgments*. A normative statement presents a point of view about what a policy *should* accomplish. For example, "Families of four with incomes below $25,000 per year should be exempted from federal income taxes." Or "Tariffs and other restrictions that impede free international trade should be eliminated."

The normative approach used by many economists is based on an underlying value judgment that evaluates well-being in a nation only in terms of the well-being of individuals. The normative approach makes recommendations regarding *what ought to be*. It's used to *prescribe* changes in policy and the use of productive capacity in an economy as well as to evaluate performance.

Gains and Losses from Economic Policies

Economic policies and other changes affecting the way the economy functions usually result in gains to some groups and losses to others. In making judgments about whether an outcome is good or bad, we must weigh the gains against the losses. For example, protecting the American automobile industry from foreign competition can benefit you as an auto company owner or employee. However, as a consumer of domestic autos you can lose as a result of such protection because the prices of cars produced by this industry are likely to be higher than they would be if foreign competition were unrestricted.

Economists don't always share the same values. In particular, they hold many different opinions about the way the success of the economy in distributing material well-being should be evaluated. Opinions about the fairness of outcomes influence the recommendations economists make about alternative policies. For example, economists often support policies recommending that tax revenues be used to provide income to the poor. However, using tax revenues in this way can have unfavorable effects on the economy by reducing productive capacity. We use positive analysis to show the effects on production and on the incomes of the poor, while we use normative analysis to make judgments about the results.

Normative analysis is used to evaluate policies and outcomes in terms of specific goals. It does, however, benefit from positive analysis. For example, even if we agree that it's good to support policies that reduce poverty, we still need to know whether a particular program designed to aid the poor *can* achieve its objective. Positive analysis can help us choose intelligently among proposed policies whose predicted outcomes are in accord with our value judgments.

The Economic Way of Reasoning: Models and Marginal Analysis

4 What makes you behave the way you do? Given a number of alternatives from which to choose, why do you take one course of action while your roommate or your best friend takes a completely different course?

In the discipline of economics, we seek to isolate relationships of cause and effect in the economy as we study the behavior of human beings. To accomplish this objective, we gather information that will help us make generalizations about production, technology, and human behavior.

A chief goal of economic analysis is to help us understand the functions of the economy and the forces influencing the choices people make under the constraints they face. Much of economic theory is based on the premise that our behavior is quite predictable. Economists often assume that we systematically pursue certain objectives, such as seeking the greatest satisfaction from our purchases or the highest profit from the sale of a product.

A method economists use to study decision making, marginal analysis, is based on the idea that it's possible for you to gain from engaging in more of an activity if the extra benefits exceed the extra costs of doing so. You'll discover that marginal analysis is more than a technique for studying decisions—it can actually guide you in decision making. In fact, you can regard marginal analysis as applied common sense because it involves a systematic comparison of the benefits and costs of actions. By studying marginal analysis, you can understand how gains are sought as you and others make business and personal choices. For example, you decide whether to take additional courses in a semester based on whether the additional benefits of doing so outweigh the additional costs. Among the benefits are the possibility of graduating earlier or having a lighter course load next semester. The costs include the dollar expense of adding courses and the extra time you'll have to spend studying instead of socializing and participating in sports or other leisure activities. If you have a job, your employer decided to hire you by comparing the expected benefits of doing so—the value of your services—with the cost of having you on the payroll and the time needed to train and supervise you. As you study this chapter, you'll discover how often you already use marginal analysis in your personal affairs.

Although we can observe actions and their consequences, observation and description are not sufficient to understand and, ultimately, to predict actions. We need to establish cause-and-effect relationships so we can understand the basic economic forces and the way individuals cope with the problem of scarcity. Therefore, we use theories to interpret actions and outcomes. A theory is a framework that helps us understand the relationships between cause and effect. It is a simplification of actual relationships. The purpose of theory in all scientific analysis is to *explain* the causes of phenomena we observe. To conduct economic analysis, we frequently need to make assumptions about the economic environment and human motivation. Economic variables are quantities or dollar amounts that can have more than one value. For example, the price of an item is an economic variable representing what we must give up in exchange for each unit of that item. Price is an economic variable because it can go up or down as changes occur in the economy. The number of unemployed workers is another economic variable that fluctuates. We develop economic theories to explain such important economic variables as the production, prices, and consumption of goods and services; the employment of workers; and levels of saving and investment.

Economic Models

Just as you can't cure a disease if you don't know its cause, it's essential to understand *how* the economy works if you're interested in changing economic outcomes you consider undesirable. For example, if a goal of your economic policy is to reduce unemployment, the methods you propose will be more effective if you understand the causes of unemployment. A policy can fail miserably in achieving its objectives or can have unanticipated adverse effects if policymakers don't understand the impact of their policies on the economy. For example, economic theory can show that government policies designed to benefit consumers by controlling prices of basic goods inevitably result in shortages of those goods. If the objective of such policies is to increase the incomes of certain persons, economic theory can help policymakers consider other methods that don't result in shortages.

An economic model is a simplified way of expressing how some sector of the economy functions. It contains assumptions that establish relationships among economic variables. It uses logic, graphs, or mathematics to determine the consequences of the assumptions. In this way the model can make predictions about the changes in decisions affecting economic variables that result from a change in economic conditions.

A good economic model is comparable to a schematic drawing showing that when you jiggle a certain lever, you set off a series of reactions that result in the movement of certain gears. Just as the drawing fails to capture the texture and intricacy of the actual machine, so too an economic model fails to mirror the complexity of the real-life sector of the economy it seeks to explain. A model is a tool we can use to understand the consequences of a theory. A good model can also accurately predict changes in the economic variables it is set up to explain.

One model may seek to explain how changes in the rate of increase or decrease of the prices of goods and services affect interest rates in the economy by assuming that lenders seek to maximize the profit they make from loans. Another model may examine the way an improvement in technology that lowers the cost of producing computers affects the price of computers, assuming that businesses seek to maximize profit.

An economic model is abstract because it doesn't attempt to capture all of the relevant influences on behavior. For example, an economic model set up to explain the rates of marriage and divorce may assume that the earnings differences between males and females have an effect on marriage and divorce. The model may assume that as the gap between earnings is reduced, the gains from marriage decline. This implies that as more women pursue careers and their earning potential reaches that of men, the marriage rate will decline and the divorce rate will go up. Similarly, an assumption that sellers seek to maximize profit from the sale of their product may not capture the full complexity of business motivation. Business owners may have other goals in addition to earning profit.

They may also be concerned with their public image, their sales revenue, or the dividends they pay their stockholders. However, by concentrating on only one goal, even though this is not realistic, a model can more clearly unveil basic forces of cause and effect.

Suppose we construct a theory about the relationship between population growth and the apartment rents tenants pay in a certain city. We hypothesize that an increase in population growth in a booming area like Raleigh, North Carolina, will increase rents for apartments, other things being equal. The phrase *other things being equal*, or its Latin equivalent, *ceteris paribus*, is used to acknowledge that influences other than the one whose effect is being analyzed must be controlled for testing the hypothesis.

The hypothesis and the theory aren't necessarily refuted by the facts if other things *are not* equal. For example, in 2003 and 2004, in Raleigh, despite the growth of population that had been occurring, monthly rents for apartments didn't rise, on average, and in many cases for specific apartments, rents actually fell! Does this mean that the theory linking population growth with increases in apartment rents is incorrect? Before we scrap the theory, we need to determine whether *other influences* on the monthly rents changed at the same time population surged. In fact, there was also a significant increase in the number of new apartments being offered in the area as the result of a building boom. The reputation of Raleigh as a high-growth housing market for the Research Triangle area of North Carolina attracted builders and investors to supply more housing to the rental market at the same time the population was growing. The increased availability of apartments put downward pressure on monthly rents, which offset the upward pressure resulting from surging population.

When constructing economic models to explain the values of economic variables, economists seek to understand all the important determinants of these values. However, in concentrating on cause-and-effect relationships among particular variables, economists ignore the influence of other determinants on the values of variables by making the "other things being equal" assumption. Unlike physical scientists, who can conduct controlled laboratory experiments, economists are concerned with social relationships. In testing hypotheses, economists must therefore attempt to account for the influence of many simultaneous changes in economic conditions on data by using statistical methods. Support for hypotheses and theories from actual data is often elusive and subject to debate because in the real world other things are seldom equal.

Rational Behavior

5 A key component of any economic model is the assumptions it makes about the way people behave. Behavioral assumptions establish the motivations of individuals so we can understand cause-and-effect relationships among economic variables. For example, it's typically assumed that the owners of business firms seek to maximize their annual profits from the sale of a product. Once we make this assumption, we can use a model to trace out the impact of a change in an economic variable, such as the wages paid to a firm's employees, on the quantity of a product the firm is willing to sell. It's also commonly assumed that consumers act to obtain the most satisfaction possible from purchasing goods and services. We can use this assumption to examine how changes in such economic variables as the price of an item affect the quantity consumers are willing and able to purchase.

When you seek to gain by undertaking actions for which the extra benefit exceeds the associated extra cost, you're engaging in rational behavior. For example, your behavior will be considered rational if you choose to take additional courses each semester as long as the extra benefit you associate with those courses exceeds the extra cost you incur when you take them. You evaluate the benefits of actions subjectively in relation to your personal objectives. The cost of an action you take is the value you place on the sacrifice you must make to enjoy the benefits of the action. Scarcity implies that you can obtain a benefit only at the cost of forgoing an alternative opportunity. Thus, if you want to act in the dramatic society's new play and begin training for the cross-country squad and the two activities are scheduled at the same time, you decide to bask in the glow of the footlights at the cost of the chance to win glory on foot. You behave rationally when you actively pursue your self-interest, as you evaluate it, by trying to get the greatest possible well-being from the resources you have. In this case you've decided that you'll make the best (and perhaps most enjoyable) use of your resource, time, by acting instead of sprinting.

The assumption of rational behavior is a key component in many economic models. The term *rational* as used in economics implies nothing about a person's sanity. It merely supposes that each of us has certain objectives. You're regarded as rational in the economic sense if you systematically undertake actions to achieve your desired objectives. Those objectives may be good or bad from another person's point of view. For example, a burglar's objective may be to become rich by breaking into homes and stores each month. A burglar is rational if he or she chooses the monthly number of burglaries in a way that considers both the personal benefits (such as the value of goods stolen) and the personal costs (such as tools, the value of time in its next best use, and the possibility of being caught and having to pay a penalty). Likewise, altruistic motives are entirely consistent with rational behavior. A person who is altruistic receives benefit when the person uses resources to provide material or emotional gains to others. There's nothing irrational about parents feeding and caring for their children! Parents receive benefits from these activities and consider those benefits as well as the associated costs when choosing to have children. When economists say we are rational, they neither deny the fact that we differ in our objectives nor make any judgments that applaud or condemn those objectives.

Marginal Analysis of Rational Behavior

Marginal analysis is a step-by-step way of determining how people engaging in rational behavior make choices. Marginal analysis of your decision to buy music CDs would look at the benefits and costs associated with your purchase of each *extra* CD starting from zero. If the additional benefit you obtain from buying another CD exceeds its price, you'll be better off buying it than keeping your money to spend on something else. The dollar value you place on the satisfaction you obtain from another unit of an item is its marginal benefit. The marginal benefit of an item in dollars represents the maximum sum of money you're willing and able to give up to obtain one more unit of the item without becoming worse off or better off by doing so. The marginal cost of an item is the sacrifice you must make to obtain each extra unit. The marginal cost of buying another CD is what you forgo to obtain it. If you choose to buy one that costs $11.99, you forgo the opportunity to use that sum to purchase another item.

The graph in Box 1 shows how the marginal benefit of an item is likely to vary as you buy more of it during the period of a month. The extra satisfaction you get from each extra unit tends to decline because you tend to tire of the item.

Suppose the price of a CD is currently $11.99. In Box 1 this is represented by a horizontal line drawn from $11.99 on the vertical axis. This line shows that each additional CD will cost you $11.99 of expenditure on other items. The line therefore represents the marginal cost of each CD to you. Will you buy that first CD? To answer the question, you must begin using the economic way of reasoning through marginal analysis. What is the marginal benefit of the first CD? The graph indicates that it's $20. As long as the marginal benefit exceeds the marginal cost, you'll enjoy a net gain by making the purchase. In the graph the marginal benefit of $20 exceeds the marginal cost of $11.99. The net gain from exchanging your cash for the first CD will be $20 −$11.99 = $8.01. Marginal analysis therefore concludes that you'll purchase the first CD because its marginal benefit to you exceeds its marginal cost. The shaded portion of the bar *above* the price line represents the net gain of $8.01 from the first CD you buy each month.

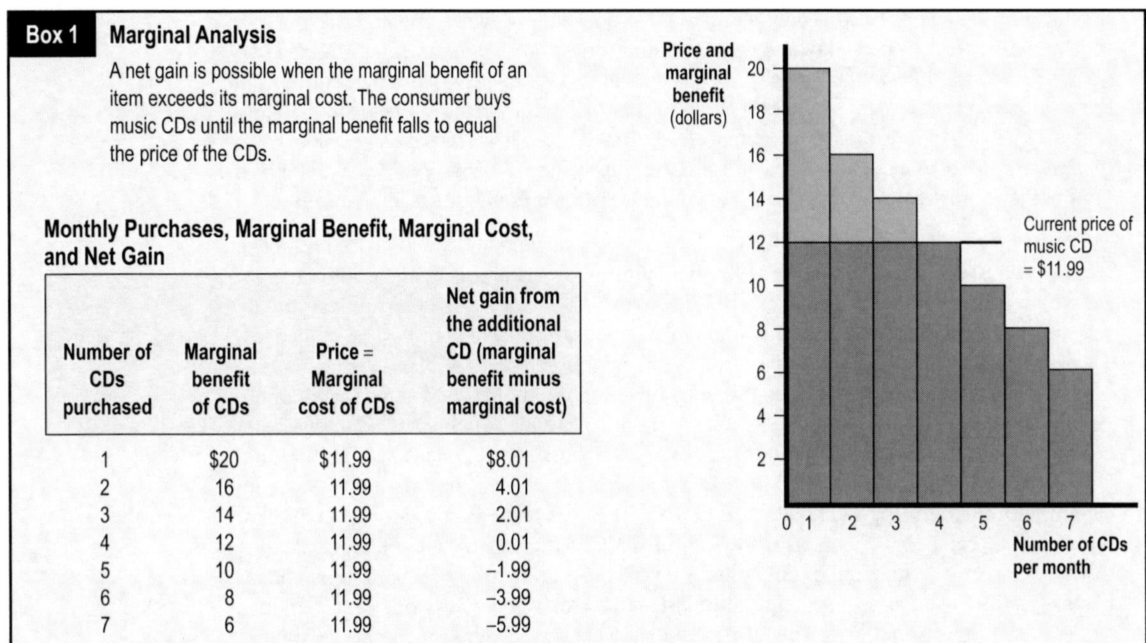

Box 1 Marginal Analysis

A net gain is possible when the marginal benefit of an item exceeds its marginal cost. The consumer buys music CDs until the marginal benefit falls to equal the price of the CDs.

Monthly Purchases, Marginal Benefit, Marginal Cost, and Net Gain

Number of CDs purchased	Marginal benefit of CDs	Price = Marginal cost of CDs	Net gain from the additional CD (marginal benefit minus marginal cost)
1	$20	$11.99	$8.01
2	16	11.99	4.01
3	14	11.99	2.01
4	12	11.99	0.01
5	10	11.99	–1.99
6	8	11.99	–3.99
7	6	11.99	–5.99

The second bar indicates that the marginal benefit of a second CD is $16 when you've already bought one CD that month. Similarly, the marginal benefit of a third CD is $14 when you've already bought two that month. The marginal benefit of a fourth CD is $12 when you've already bought three that month. The graph indicates that the marginal benefit of a fifth CD in the month is only $10 when you've already purchased four. Similarly, the marginal benefit of the sixth and seventh CD also declines.

How many CD will you buy in a month? *A rational person continues purchasing an item up to the point at which there is no additional net gain.* It's easy to see that this condition isn't met until you've bought four CD. This is because the marginal benefit of the second CD exceeds its marginal cost, as does the marginal benefit of the third and fourth CDs. As shown in the table, the net gain from purchasing a second CD is $4.01 ($16 –$11.99 = $4.01). The net gain from purchasing a third CD is $2.01. However, the marginal benefit of the fourth CD is just barely above the price. You buy the fourth CD that month because you enjoy an additional net gain of 1 cent by doing so.

Why will you not buy five CDs that month? Look at the graph and notice that the marginal benefit of the fifth CD is only $10. This falls short of the marginal cost of $11.99. As shown in the table, the net gain from a fifth CD per month is -$1.99. The net gain is negative because the marginal benefit of the CD falls short of its marginal cost. The negative net gain implies that purchasing that CD will make you worse off. If you're rational, you therefore buy no more than four CDs per month. As shown in the table, no positive net gain is possible from purchasing more than four CDs per month.

This simple economic model makes us aware of important influences on decisions to buy an item. We can reach the following conclusions from the model:

1. *The price of an item is an important influence on the amount of it that a buyer will choose to purchase.* This is because the price affects the net gain possible from buying a certain item. Each time you purchase it, you give up the opportunity to use the sum of dollars equal to the item's price to buy something else. If the price of music CDs falls, then, assuming nothing else changes, the net gains possible from buying more CDs increase. For example, suppose the price of CDs falls to $7.99. Just substitute $7.99 for $11.99 in the third column of the table in Box 1, and you'll see the change in the numbers in the last column. When the price of CDs is $7.99, you will buy six CDs per month because net gains from buying a fifth and a sixth CD each month are now possible. Given all the other influences on a person's decision to buy an item, the lower the price, the greater the net gain associated with any given amount. Lower prices allow additional net gains from additional amounts bought. Changes in the price of an item change the marginal cost of buying it and affect the amounts rational people purchase.

2. *A person's buying decision depends on the marginal benefit from purchasing an item and on the way marginal benefit varies with the amount bought.* Suppose you buy a new CD player that gives you much better sound than your old player. This may increase the marginal benefit you get from CDs. If the marginal benefit of each quantity purchased per month were to double, so would the height of each bar in the graph in Box 1. The increased marginal benefit will increase the net gain from each CD purchased and lead you to buy more CDs per month. To see this, double the marginal benefit for each quantity in the table in Box 1 and recalculate the net gain possible for each additional CD, assuming the price is still $11.99. You will see that net gains are now possible from buying up to seven CDs per month. Changes in the marginal benefit of buying an item therefore affect the quantities of the item that rational people choose to buy.

If you've mastered the logic of this simple model, you are well on your way to using the economic way of reasoning. You can see how changes that affect the marginal benefit and marginal cost of an activity (such as buying something) influence decisions to engage in that activity. You can also see how the assumption that rational people seek net gains helps us reach conclusions about the way they behave.

Rational behavior means that in deciding on any course of action, such as buying another unit of a good in a market, you compare the marginal benefit of that action with its marginal cost. As a rational person, you undertake actions as long as the marginal cost doesn't exceed the marginal benefit. By behaving in this way, you undertake all activities that provide you with additional net gains in well-being and you avoid all activities for which additional net gain would be negative.

The assumption that we are all rational decision makers relentlessly pursuing goals intended to improve our well-being has proved to be particularly fruitful in building economic models whose hypotheses are supported by facts. Not everyone agrees with this assumption. In fact, some of us don't consistently do what is in our best interest. However, the underlying assumptions of a model needn't be either realistic or without exception to be useful. Remember, the test of the usefulness of an economic model is the validity of the principles we can derive from it.

Graphs: An Aid to Understanding Economics

If you were offered a guaranteed way to enhance your grasp of economic concepts, you'd leap at it, wouldn't you? The Chapter 1 Supplement, *Graphs: A Basic Tool for Analyzing Economic Relationships*, provides a step-by-step guide to constructing, reading, and understanding graphs, a key component in the study of economics. When you've mastered the material in this supplement, you'll realize how graphs can simplify key economic relationships that might take paragraphs to explain. You'll be able to draw and label your own graphs and to interpret the graphs you'll find in almost every chapter of this text. If you take some time to become comfortable with graphs, you can be sure they'll serve you well throughout the course.

Summary

1. Economics is concerned with the use of available productive resources to satisfy the desires and demands of people in a society.
2. The fundamental economic problem of scarcity is the imbalance between the desires of members of a society and the means of satisfying those desires.
3. The opportunity cost of choosing to use resources for one purpose is the sacrifice of the next best alternative for the use of those resources.
4. There are two main branches of economics. *Microeconomics* views the economy from the perspective of its individual participants. *Macroeconomics* considers the overall performance of the economy and the way its various sectors relate to one another.
5. *Positive analysis* seeks to predict the impact of changes in economic policy on observable items such as production and income, then tries to determine who gains and who loses as a result of the changes. *Normative analysis* evaluates the desirability of alternative outcomes according to value judgments about what is good or bad.
6. Economic theories are designed to establish cause-and-effect relationships to help explain how economies function.
7. An economic model is a simplified way of expressing how a sector of the economy functions. Economic models can be used to develop hypotheses about the relationships among economic variables. These hypotheses represent implications of economic models that can be supported or refuted by examining facts.
8. Economic theories based on rational behavior assume that persons consider the marginal benefits and marginal costs of their actions. Net gains are possible when the marginal benefit of additional activity exceeds the associated marginal costs. Rational persons seek out net gains by choosing to undertake more of an activity when its marginal benefit exceeds its marginal cost.

Concept Review*

(1) What functions does the U.S. economy accomplish?

(2) How are the concepts of opportunity cost and scarcity related to each other?

(3) Give examples of a microeconomic issue and a macroeconomic issue for which we can conduct a positive analysis.

(4) What is the purpose of an economic model?

(5) How can marginal analysis be used to explain rational behavior?

Problems and Applications

1. Suppose an economic theory sets up a model that implies that, *other things being equal*, an increase in interest rates will reduce the growth of national production. How can you test the validity of the theory? (4)
2. An economic model to explain sales of cars establishes a relationship between the price of cars and the quantity buyers are willing to purchase. A hypothesis developed from the model postulates that whenever the price of cars goes up, the quantity buyers will buy goes down. During the year consumer income increases as the price of cars goes up. The quantity of cars sold also increases. Does this invalidate the theory establishing the relationship between the price of cars and the quantity consumers are willing and able to purchase? (4)
3. In what ways do economic theories and models abstract from reality? Why are unrealistic models useful? (4)
4. Give an example of a behavioral assumption in an economic model. What is the purpose of using behavioral assumptions in economic models? (4)
5. In what sense can an insane person or a criminal be regarded as engaging in rational behavior? (5)
6. A person makes decisions by habit. This person considers neither the benefits nor the costs of his or her actions. Can the person be considered rational? (5)

*If you need additional help, the concept symbol refers you to the appropriate text discussion.

7. Suppose the marginal benefit to you of acquiring another suit this year is $200. If the price of suits is $250 and you are rational, will you buy one? 5

8. You currently choose to buy two DVDs of new releases per month with your income. The current price is $29.99. Other things being equal, explain why a drop in the price to $25.99 next month is likely to increase the quantity you'll buy. 5

9. The following table shows how the marginal benefit of shoes of given quality varies with the number Jill purchases each year. As shown, the price of shoes is $29.99 per pair.

Pairs purchased per year	Marginal benefit	Price
1	$50	$29.99
2	40	29.99
3	30	29.99
4	20	29.99
5	10	29.99

a. Assuming that Jill is rational and the price of shoes accurately reflects the marginal cost to her, how many pairs of shoes will Jill buy per year?

b. Suppose the price of shoes increases to $39.99 per year. Assuming that nothing else changes, how many pairs will Jill now buy? 5

10. Suppose that the marginal benefit of a pair of shoes for Joe is exactly double the marginal benefit indicated for Jill in the previous example. If the price of shoes for Joe is also $29.99 and Joe is rational, how many pairs of shoes per year will Joe buy? 5

Chapter Supplement

Graphs: A Basic Tool for Analyzing Economic Relationships

Do graphs make you nervous? If so, relax—you're about to discover how helpful they'll be as you study economics.

Economists often use graphs to express relationships, such as the way the maximum possible production of one item is affected by the production of another item. Graphic analysis is a tool to aid you in learning economics and using it to reach important conclusions. Graphs show how the value of one variable changes as the value of some other variable is increased or decreased.

Plotting Points on a Set of Axes

A two-dimensional graph has a vertical axis along which one variable, designated in general by the symbol *Y*, is measured. Another variable, the *X* variable, is measured on the horizontal axis. As the value of *X* changes, so does the value of *Y*.

The origin of the axes is the point, designated by 0, at which both *X* and *Y* take on the value of zero. The axes drawn for most economic data are at a right angle to each other, with measurement scales drawn horizontally and vertically from the origin, because most of the data used in economics are positive rather than negative. If, however, *Y* were to take on negative values, the vertical axis would extend downward below the origin to accommodate those values. Similarly, if *X* were to take on negative values, the horizontal axis would extend to the left of the origin to accommodate them.

The table in Box 1 shows a relationship between *X* and *Y*. The second column gives the value of *Y* for each value of *X* in the first column. The pairs of numbers on each line of the table denote a *functional relationship* between *X* and *Y*. The functional relationship implies that the value of the *Y* variable changes as the value of the *X* variable increases or decreases. In this sense the value of *Y depends on* or is a *function* of the value of *X*. You can use the table to find the value of *Y* for each value of *X*, or vice versa.

Box 1 **A Curve Showing a Positive Relationship between *X* and *Y***

The curve shown is based on the data in the table below. The value of *Y* increases as the value of *X* increases, indicating a positive relationship between the two variables.

A Positive Relationship between *X* and *Y*

Value of *X*	Corresponding value of *Y*	Point on graph
1	2	A_1
2	3	A_2
3	4	A_3
4	5	A_4
5	6	A_5

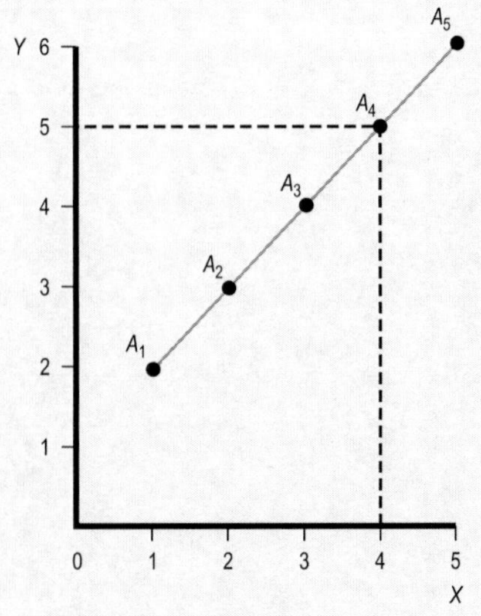

The data from the table in Box 1 are plotted on the set of axes shown in the graph next to the table. Each line of the table has been designated with a letter *A* followed by a number to identify the points on the graph. The point A_1 corresponds to the pair of values $X = 1$, $Y = 2$. When plotted, these numbers are called the coordinates of point A_1. Similarly, when *X* is equal to 2, *Y* is equal to 3. These coordinates correspond to point A_2 on the graph. Point A_3 on the graph is the point at which *X* is equal to 3 and *Y* is equal to 4. Similarly, points A_4 and A_5 from the table are plotted on the axes, and a line is drawn connecting each point. This line connecting the points corresponding to the coordinates of *X* and *Y* from the table depicts the relationship between *X* and *Y*. Such a line is called a curve even when its shape is not actually curvy. Many of the curves depicting economic relationships in this text will be straight lines.

Along the curve drawn in the graph in Box 1, there is a positive or direct relationship between *X* and *Y*, meaning that *Y increases* whenever *X increases*. For example, suppose the *Y* variable in Box 1 indicates the cost of producing each microcomputer in a factory. The *X* variable could be the number of computers produced per month. Assume that the numbers for both these variables could be estimated and the functional relationship established to draw up a table like the one in Box 1. An upward-sloping curve, as in the graph in the box (with different numbers, of course), would mean that there was a positive relationship between the unit cost of the computers and the number produced each month in the factory.

The curve drawn in any graph is used to find the value of *Y* for any possible value of *X*. For example, in the graph in Box 1, for the value of *X* equal to 4, follow the dashed line for the point on the horizontal axis corresponding to 4 *just up to the curve*. From that point, follow the dashed horizontal line from the curve to the vertical axis to find the corresponding value of *Y*, which is 5 in this case.

The data in the table of Box 2 depict a negative or inverse relationship between *X* and *Y*, showing that when the value of *X* increases, the corresponding value of *Y*, indicated in the second column, *decreases*. The graph in Box 2 plots the points that show the value of *Y* corresponding to each value of *X*. The points are labeled to correspond to the *B* letters followed by numbers in the last column of the table. The curve shows that whenever the value of *X* increases, the corresponding value of *Y* decreases.

Negative relationships between economic variables are quite common. For example, the *Y* variable may be the price of a VCR and the *X* variable may be the number of VCRs that buyers in a market are willing and able to purchase during a certain period. A curve like

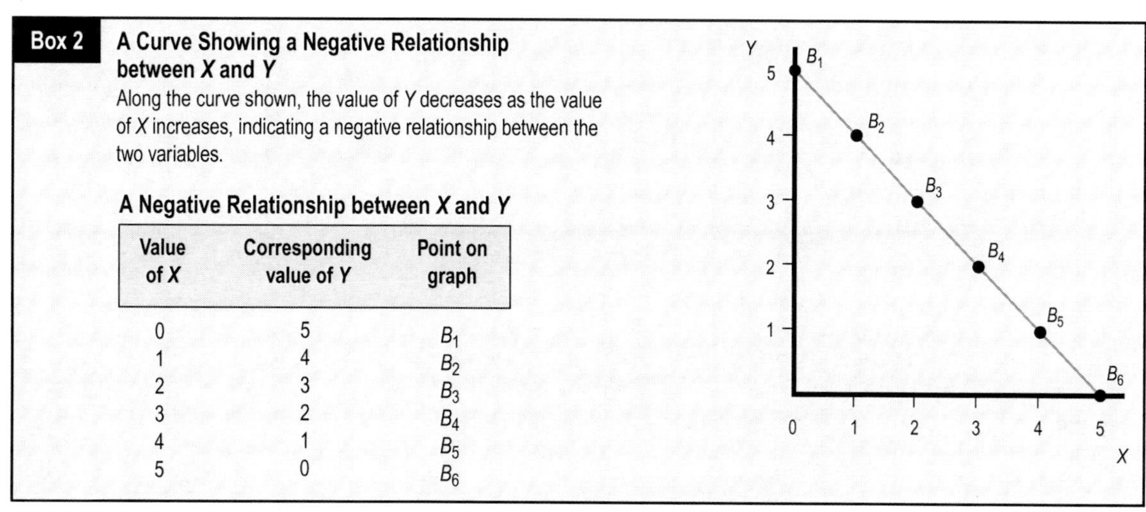

Box 2 **A Curve Showing a Negative Relationship between *X* and *Y***

Along the curve shown, the value of *Y* decreases as the value of *X* increases, indicating a negative relationship between the two variables.

A Negative Relationship between *X* and *Y*

Value of *X*	Corresponding value of *Y*	Point on graph
0	5	B_1
1	4	B_2
2	3	B_3
3	2	B_4
4	1	B_5
5	0	B_6

the one drawn in the graph indicates that the lower the price of the VCR, the greater the number of units buyers are willing and able to buy over the given period. In other words, the graph indicates a negative relationship between the price of a VCR and the quantity buyers will purchase over a period.

The Concept of Slope and Its Uses in Economics

The slope of a curve measures the rate at which the *Y* variable, on the vertical axis, rises or falls as the *X* variable, on the horizontal axis, increases. The slope of a line or curve is $\Delta Y/\Delta X$, where the Greek symbol Δ (delta) represents the amount of an increase (or decrease) in the value of each variable along the line or curve.

A curve or line that is upward sloping has positive slope. For example, along the upward-sloping line in graph **A** in Box 3, *Y increases* as *X* increases. For each one-unit increase in *X* along the line, the value of *Y* increases by two units. The slope of the line at any point is therefore $2/1 = 2$.

A curve or line that is downward sloping has negative slope. Along the downward-sloping line in graph **B**, *Y decreases* as *X* increases. For each one-unit increase in *X* along the line drawn in the graph, *Y* decreases by one unit. The slope of this line at any point is therefore $-1/1 = -1$. A downward-sloping curve has negative slope because ΔY is always negative when ΔX is positive.

A line with zero slope is, as you might expect, flat. Along the flat line in graph C, there is no increase in *Y* as *X* increases. It follows that $\Delta Y = 0$ for any ΔX, so that $\Delta Y/\Delta X = 0$.

The standard equation for a linear curve is

$$Y = mX + b$$

where *m* is the slope of the line and *b* is the value of *Y* that would prevail if the value of *X* were zero. The *b* of the equation represents the intercept of the line with the vertical axis. The intercept can be either a positive or a negative number.

Box 3 Curves with Positive Slope, Negative Slope, or Zero Slope

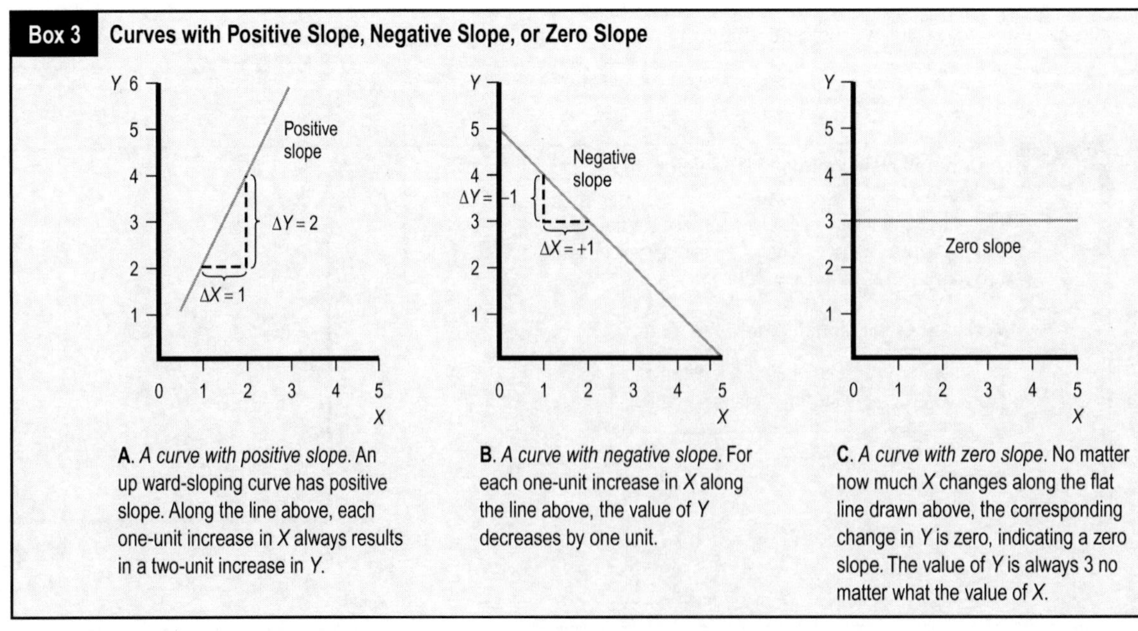

A. *A curve with positive slope.* An up ward-sloping curve has positive slope. Along the line above, each one-unit increase in *X* always results in a two-unit increase in *Y*.

B. *A curve with negative slope.* For each one-unit increase in *X* along the line above, the value of *Y* decreases by one unit.

C. *A curve with zero slope.* No matter how much *X* changes along the flat line drawn above, the corresponding change in *Y* is zero, indicating a zero slope. The value of *Y* is always 3 no matter what the value of *X*.

For example, the value of m in graph **B** would be equal to –1, while the value of b in would be 5. The equation corresponding to the curve drawn in graph **B** would therefore be

$$Y = 5 - x$$

This equation says that the value of Y is equal to 5 when X is zero and that each time X increases by one unit, the value of Y falls by one unit. If X were equal to 4, the value of Y would therefore be 1.

Similarly, the equation for the curve shown in graph **C** is

$$Y = 3$$

because the slope of the curve is 0 and its intercept on the Y axis is 3. This equation tells you that Y is equal to 3 no matter what the value of X.

Changes in Slope along a Curve

Nonlinear curves are those for which the slope changes from point to point. In Box 4, graph **A** shows a curve that has negative slope throughout but becomes steeper as X increases. Graph **B** shows a curve that also has negative slope throughout but whose slope becomes less negative, and therefore closer to zero, as X increases. When viewed from the origin, the curve in **A** has a *concave* shape, while the one in **B** has a *convex* shape.

Box 5 shows two curves, each with positive slope throughout, for which the slope changes as X increases. In **A** the slope of the curve increases as X increases. In **B** the slope of the curve decreases as X increases. When viewed from the origin, the curve in **A** is convex and the curve in **B** is concave.

Slope and Extreme Values of Variables

Many of the most important curves drawn in economic analysis have negative, zero, and positive slope depending on the value of the X variable. For example, graph **A** in Box 6 shows a curve that has positive slope at first and then, for just the value at which X equals 5, has zero slope. Thereafter the slope of the curve is negative because Y decreases as X increases beyond the value of 5. The point labeled M, at which the slope of the curve in graph **A** is just equal to zero as the slope shifts from being positive to being negative, is of great significance. The coordinates of that point give the value of X for which the corresponding value of Y is at its *maximum* value. The distinguishing feature of that point is that the slope is *zero*.

Box 4 Concave and Convex Curves with Negative Slope

Both curves have negative slope at all points. Viewing each curve from the origin, the curve in **A** isconcave, whereas the curve in **B** is convex.

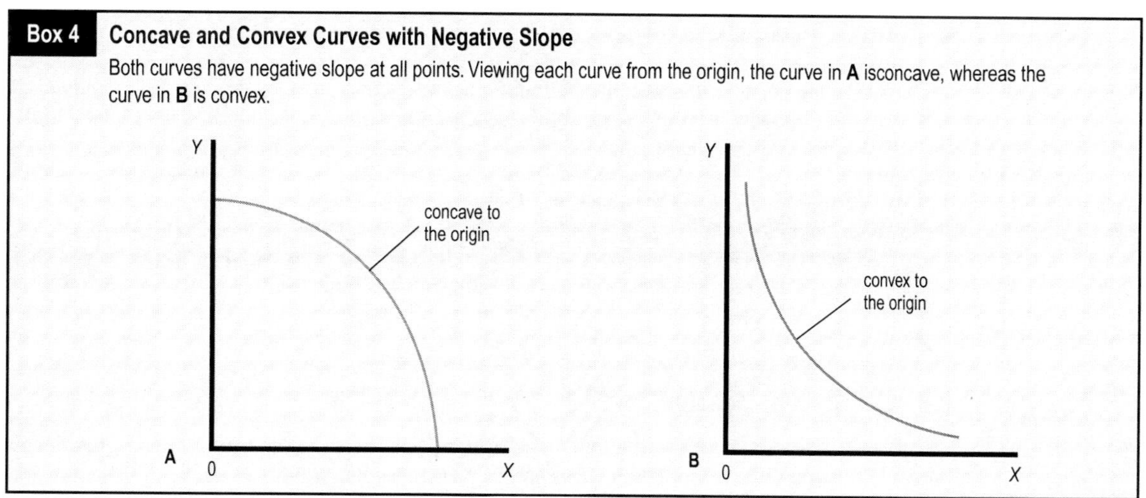

Box 5 Concave and Convex Curves with Positive Slope

Both curves have positive slope. The curve in **A** has a slope that increases as *X* increases. The slope of the curve in **B** decreases as *X* increases.

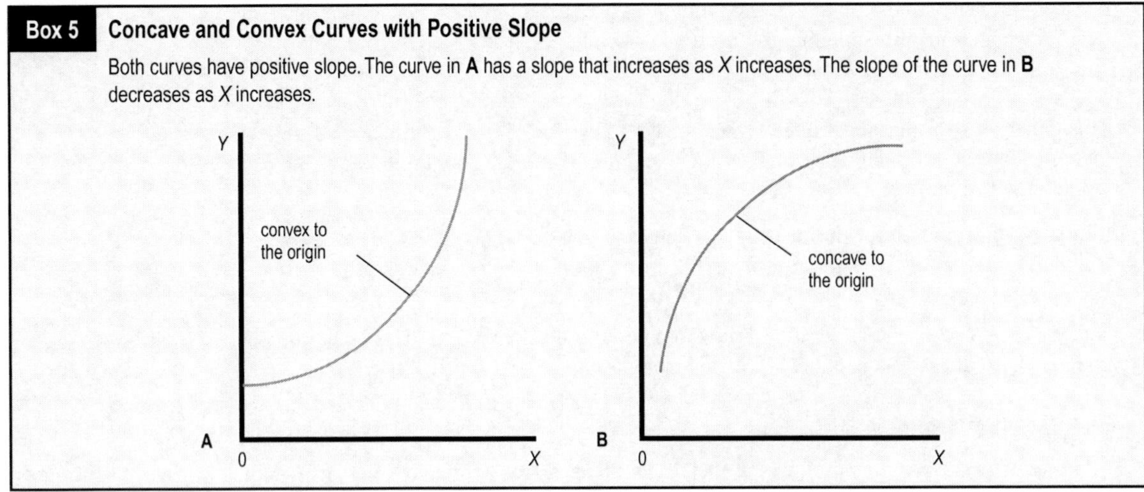

Box 6 Maximum and Minimum Values for *Y*

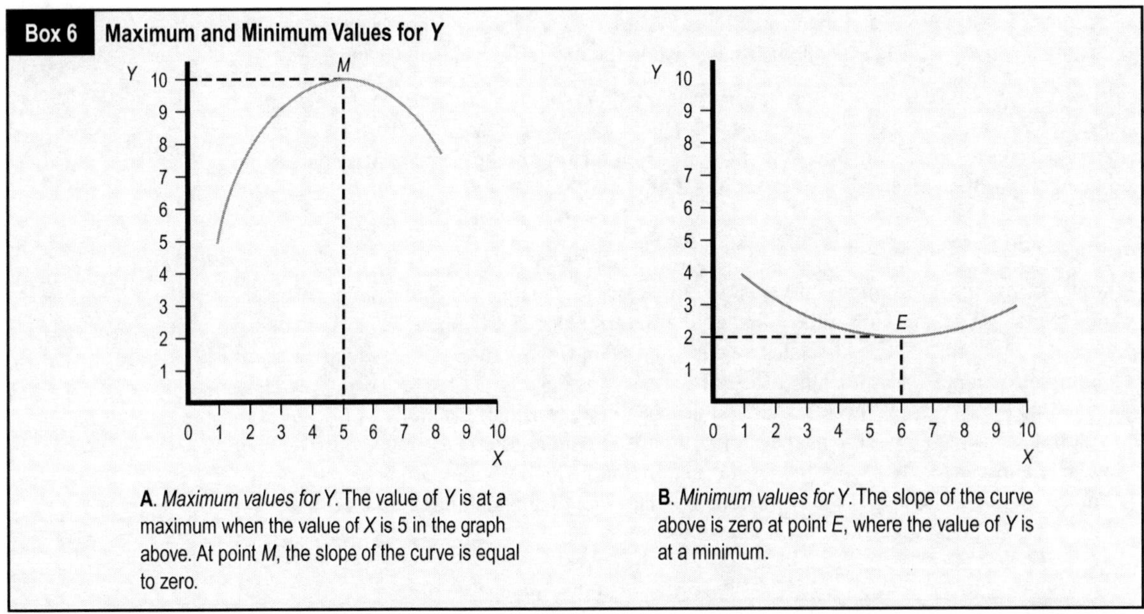

A. *Maximum values for Y.* The value of *Y* is at a maximum when the value of *X* is 5 in the graph above. At point *M*, the slope of the curve is equal to zero.

B. *Minimum values for Y.* The slope of the curve above is zero at point *E*, where the value of *Y* is at a minimum.

A zero slope can also indicate a minimum value of a variable. For example, in graph **B** the coordinates of point *E* give the value of *X* for which the value of *Y* is at a *minimum*. For values greater than 6, the slope is positive. When *X* equals 6, the slope just equals zero.

Be sure you understand the meaning of the concept of slope, because you'll find it very useful in economic analysis. Throughout this text, we make assumptions about the way the slope of a curve varies as one variable is increased in value and a related variable responds. We'll use these assumptions to reach important conclusions about economic behavior and relationships.

Units of Measurement

When discussing economic relationships, we need to specify units of measurement. Suppose the *Y* variable for graph **A** in Box 6 is profits. Its units would be measured in dollars.

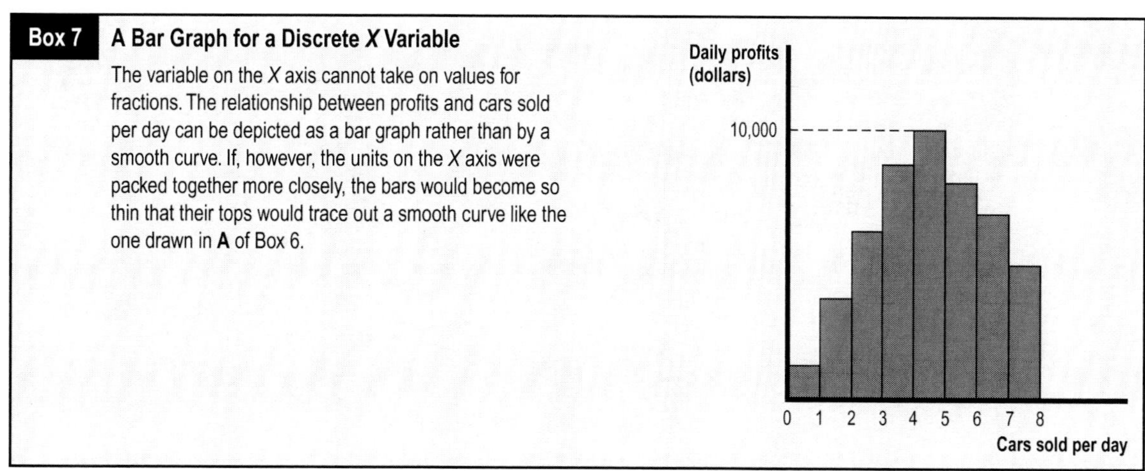

Box 7
A Bar Graph for a Discrete X Variable
The variable on the X axis cannot take on values for fractions. The relationship between profits and cars sold per day can be depicted as a bar graph rather than by a smooth curve. If, however, the units on the X axis were packed together more closely, the bars would become so thin that their tops would trace out a smooth curve like the one drawn in A of Box 6.
Daily profits (dollars)
10,000
0 1 2 3 4 5 6 7 8
Cars sold per day

The *X* variable could be number of cars sold per day by an auto dealer. The curve would therefore represent the relationship between profits and daily sales. It shows that the dealer would maximize profits by selling five cars per day.

The smoothness of a curve depends on how compact the units of measurement are along an axis and on whether it makes sense to talk about fractions of units. For example, an auto dealer can't sell half or one-quarter of a car. Therefore, points on a graph between 1 and 2 or any other two integers really don't exist. In actuality, profits are likely to change substantially rather than only minutely when each car is sold. A bar graph shows the value of a *Y* variable as the height of a bar for each corresponding value of *X*. In Box 7 the height of each bar shows profits for each number of cars sold. The first bar shows profit when only one car per day is sold. The second bar shows how profit jumps when two cars per day are sold.

Variables that cannot vary by fractions of units are called discrete variables. Variables that can realistically and meaningfully take on minute fractions of values are called continuous variables. For example, any variable measured in dollars can be regarded as a more or less continuous variable because each dollar can be broken down into hundredths.

Economists often draw graphs of economic relationships in which actual discrete variables are regarded as continuous. Little is lost by doing so because the main point of drawing curves is to analyze the way one variable depends on another. The curves are meant to show positive or negative relationships rather than to realistically depict actual variation of the discrete units. You should also note that graphs of relationships between discrete variables can have smooth curves if the scale of measurement along the axes is very compact. For example, suppose a graph shows the relationship between profits of all automakers and number of cars sold per day. If the *X* axis depicts the variation in cars sold from zero to 8 million per year, the distance on the *X* axis between any number of cars sold and *one more car* sold will be microscopic for a graph drawn on the page of a book. Similarly, the change in profits when one more car is sold will be quite small on the vertical axis when the scale of measurement is designed to accommodate millions of dollars for the millions of cars sold each year. The resulting graph of the economic relationship is therefore likely to be like the smooth curve in Box 6 rather than the bar graph in Box 7. In most of the cases in this text, smooth curves are drawn to show economic relationships. However, on occasion, when the variables are clearly discrete or the scale of measurement is not very compact between integers, bar graphs like the one in Box 7 are drawn, as was done for the graph in Box 1 of this chapter.

Box 8 Intersections

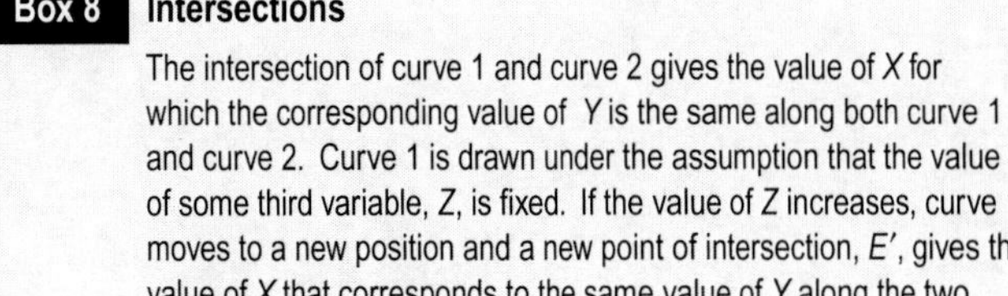
The intersection of curve 1 and curve 2 gives the value of *X* for which the corresponding value of *Y* is the same along both curve 1 and curve 2. Curve 1 is drawn under the assumption that the value of some third variable, *Z*, is fixed. If the value of *Z* increases, curve 1 moves to a new position and a new point of intersection, *E′*, gives the value of *X* that corresponds to the same value of *Y* along the two curves.

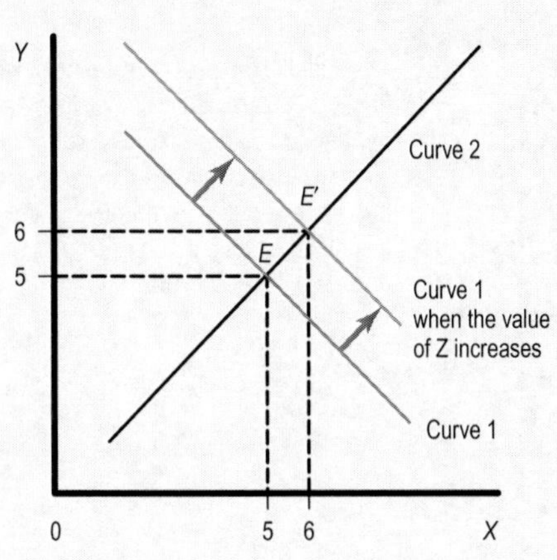

Intersections and Tangencies

The graphs used in this text are two-dimensional. This means they plot values for two variables. In many cases, however, a third variable can be introduced in a two-dimensional graph by showing how changes in its value affect the values of the two initial variables.

Intersections

In many graphs drawn to facilitate economic analysis, *two* curves are drawn on the same set of axes. The intersection of two curves is the point at which they cross. An intersection usually reveals important economic information. The graph in Box 8 shows the intersection of two curves at point *E*. The value of *X* at this point is such that the corresponding value of *Y* is the same for the relationship indicated by curve 1 and that indicated by curve 2.

When graphs are drawn in this way, the effect of a third variable other than *X* or *Y* can be investigated. To do this, we can hypothesize the impact of the third variable, *Z*, on the relationship represented by curve 1. If the change in this variable has no effect on the relationship between *X* and *Y* depicted by the upward-sloping curve labeled curve 2, then only the downward-sloping curve will move as the value of *Z* changes. If, for example, curve 1 shifts outward as *Z* increases, there will be a new point of intersection, *E′*. The role of economic analysis would then be to interpret the new point of intersection.

Tangencies

A tangency between two curves is a point at which the two curves just touch each other *but do not intersect. At a point of tangency, the slopes of two curves are equal.* Box 9 shows the tangency between a straight line and a convex curve. The slope of the convex curve varies from point to point. At the point of tangency, *T*, the slope of the convex curve is precisely equal to the slope of the straight line. The straight line has a slope equal to −1 at all points. It follows that the slope of the convex curve is equal to −1 at point *T*. The corresponding value of *X* is 4. For all values of *X* less than 4, the slope of the convex curve is more negative than −1. For values of *X* greater than 4, the slope of the convex curve is less negative, that is, closer to zero, than −1.

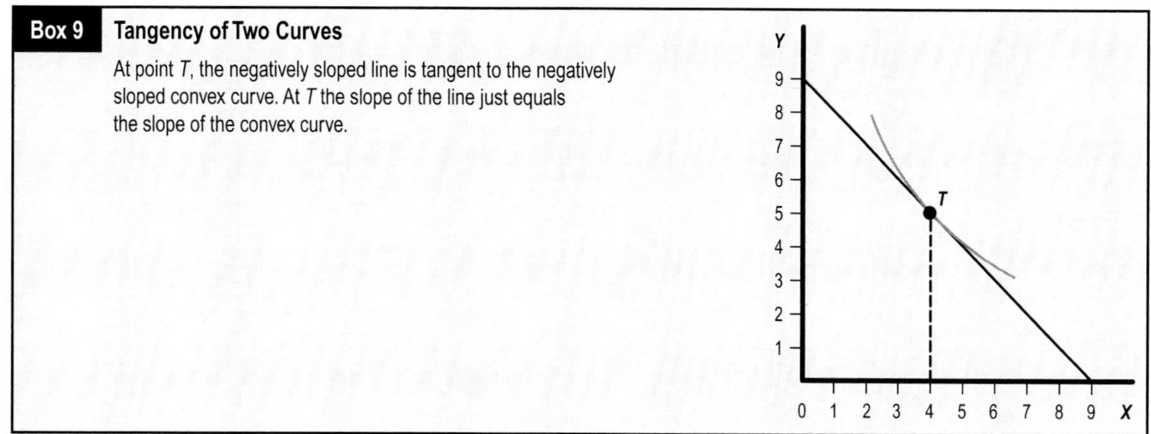

Box 9 **Tangency of Two Curves**

At point *T*, the negatively sloped line is tangent to the negatively sloped convex curve. At *T* the slope of the line just equals the slope of the convex curve.

Descriptive Graphs

Most of the graphs in this text are designed to illustrate functional relationships. In many cases these graphs aren't based on actual data. Their purpose may be simply to show the consequences of a positive or negative relationship and to aid in predicting the values of certain key economic variables. In other cases, graphs are drawn simply to describe how actual variables vary over time without trying to interpret the trend depicted. Most *descriptive graphs* are plots of time series data. For example, the graph in Box 10 shows how unemployment in a nation fluctuates over time. This graph shows trends between 1950 and 2003, but it doesn't necessarily illustrate a functional relationship. Graphs like this will be drawn in the text to describe what actually happened to a variable. However, understanding what causes fluctuations like those illustrated in the Box 10 graph requires the kind of economic analysis that allows functional relations to be established. The chapter Production Possibilities and Opportunity Cost shows how economists seek to establish the functional relationships that are used to obtain such insights.

Some Words of Advice

Many students have difficulty using graphs and interpreting the relationships curves are designed to explain. The way to avoid this difficulty yourself is to practice using graphs. You'll find it helpful to refer to this supplement whenever you have a problem with a graph. Also, a few basic points should make it easier for you to deal with the graphs you'll encounter:

1. *Make sure you know the economic variables that are being graphed.* You'll have a great deal of difficulty in understanding a graph if you simply memorize the shape of the curve but forget the names or units of measurement of the economic variables!

2. *Remember that the main point of drawing a curve on a set of axes is to depict an economic relationship. Make sure that the purpose of trying to understand that relationship is clear to you.* For example, is the purpose of the graph to find the minimum value or the maximum value of an economic variable? Is the graph supposed to show how quantities purchased vary with the price of a good? Is it designed to show how unemployment fluctuates with interest rates? Is its purpose to show how the average level of prices in the economy varies with the amount of money in circulation?

3. *Always try to understand the significance of the positive or negative relationships depicted by graphs.* Practice drawing graphs yourself from the information given in the

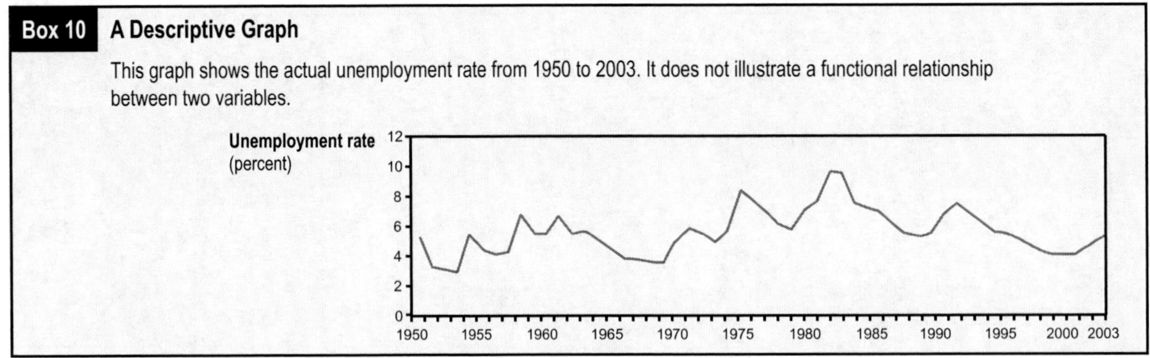

Box 10 A Descriptive Graph

This graph shows the actual unemployment rate from 1950 to 2003. It does not illustrate a functional relationship between two variables.

text. Make sure you label your axes and follow the common sense of the relationship the given graph is designed to illuminate.

4. *Make sure you understand how economic relationships depicted by curves change when there are changes in other variables that are not explicitly drawn on the set of axes.* For example, suppose a curve shows how consumer spending varies with income. This curve may shift if interest rates or tax rates change.

5. *Make sure you can interpret points of intersection or tangency between two curves.* These points almost always have great significance in economic analysis.

Remember that graphs represent a shortcut to reasoning. Use them as a tool. If you practice with them, you'll find that they save you a great deal of time and enable you to reach conclusions that would be much more difficult to reach with purely verbal reasoning.

Problems and Applications

1. The following table gives a relationship between *X* and *Y*:

Value of X	Corresponding value of *Y*
1	4
2	6
3	8
4	10
5	12

Plot the coordinates of *X* and *Y* on a graph, and draw a line through the points to show the relationship between the two variables.

2. Indicate whether the graph you've drawn in Problem 1 shows a positive or negative relationship between *X* and *Y*. Calculate the slope of the line you've drawn.

3. Draw up a table, like the one in Problem 1, that shows a negative relationship between *X* and *Y* Choose your numbers so that a curve with constant slope can be drawn through the coordinates. Calculate the slope of your line.

4. Weekly sales of computers are unaffected by the temperature of the outside air. Draw a curve that shows the absence of a relationship between temperature and sales of PCs. Let *Y* be PC sales, and let *X* be temperature. What is the slope of the curve?

5. The owner of a factory producing rugby shirts can sell as many shirts as he wishes at a price of $20. The total revenue he receives is equal to the price of shirts multiplied by the number of shirts shipped. Draw a graph that shows how his monthly revenue will vary with monthly shipments of shirts. Calculate the slope of the curve you have drawn, and interpret its meaning from an economic point of view.

6. Suppose the owner of the rugby shirt factory notices that his total costs of producing and shipping shirts form a concave curve similar to the one drawn as graph **A** in Box 5. His monthly profit is the difference between monthly revenue and monthly cost. Draw the cost curve on the same set of axes you used to draw the revenue curve, and then draw another curve that shows how monthly profit will vary with shirt production. Locate the point of maximum profits.

7. The following table shows how the unit cost of producing denim jackets varies with monthly output in a certain factory:

Monthly number of jackets produced	Cost per jacket
1,000	$80
2,000	70
3,000	60
4,000	70
5,000	80

Plot the points from the table and trace a curve through them. Describe the relationship between cost per denim jacket and number of jackets produced per month. What is the slope of the curve at the point at which the cost per jacket is at a minimum?

8. Draw a bar graph that shows the relationship between *X* and *Y* using the data from Problem 1.

9. The following equation describes a relationship between the price of running shoes and the quantity buyers will buy per month:

$$\text{Quantity buyers will buy} = 300 - 3P$$

The quantity sellers will sell is related to the price of running shoes in the following way:

$$\text{Quantity sellers will sell} = 2P$$

where *P* is the price per pair of running shoes.

Plot the graphs for the two preceding equations using the following values for *P*: $30, $40, $50, $60, $70, $80. Identify the value of *P* at which the two curves intersect, and indicate the corresponding number of pairs of running shoes that will be bought and sold.

10. A curve showing the relationship between *X* and *Y* has a slope of −2 at all points. Draw this line, and then draw a convex curve that's tangent to it. What is the slope of the convex curve at the point of tangency?

Protectionism versus Free International Trade: Who Gains and Who Loses?

Now let's use positive analysis to examine a key issue in U.S. foreign trade policy--protection of domestic industries from foreign competition. Increased foreign competition has led to intense lobbying for protection by U.S. industries whose sales have been hurt by it. Concern about the impact of increased foreign competition on employment opportunities in manufacturing has led to still more calls to protect U.S. industries from foreign competition. Both import quotas and tariffs have been used to protect U.S. industries from foreign competition.

Import quotas are annual limits to the amount of goods that can be brought into a nation through international trade. *Tariffs* are taxes on imported goods designed to raise the prices of those goods to domestic consumers.

Since 1962, the U.S. government has also provided trade adjustment assistance that cushions the impact of foreign competition on workers, businesses, and regions adversely affected by imports. Such assistance has very stringent eligibility requirements, and cash payments have been limited.

The issue of protection involves conflict between consumers and suppliers of specialized inputs, including labor, in industries whose profits and revenues are adversely affected by foreign competition. The political choice that must be made is between providing direct or indirect subsidies to these industries to keep them afloat or allowing them to go under if they can't compete. In the latter case, the resources released from these industries would then have to find employment in other industries. Because the search for employment can take time, this implies increased unemployment and declines in income until the transition has been made.

The conflict between avoiding economic dislocation from foreign trade and protecting consumers is clear from studies of the effects of previous protectionist measures:

1. The Smoot-Hawley Tariff Act of 1930, which raised tariffs in the United States by about 60 percent, was widely credited with helping induce a worldwide depression by reducing income in foreign nations as U.S. purchases of their exports plummeted.[1]

2. An estimate of the impact of U.S. restrictions on imports of sugar, clothing, and automobiles in 1984 indicated that these measures cost low-income consumers twice as much as they cost upper-income consumers, suggesting that trade

restrictions harm the poor more than the rich.[2]

3. Import quotas for Japanese cars from 1981 through 1983 increased the prices of those cars by an estimated $1,000 per vehicle and resulted in increased expenditure estimated at about $2 billion by consumers of Japanese cars. The quotas also contributed to a $370 per car price increase on average for American cars over the same period. The U.S. auto industry and its employees gained as a result of the quotas, while buyers of both U.S. and Japanese cars lost.[3]

4. An estimate of the impact of seven temporary protection actions found that they raised prices to such a degree as to cost consumers $340,000 per job saved.[4]

5. The combined effect of U.S. tariffs and import quotas on apparel in the late 1980s was equivalent to a whopping 46 percent tax on imported clothing! Although protection of the U.S. apparel industry saved jobs and raised the wages of textile workers, it cost us $52,000 per year to save these jobs, which paid on average less than $20,000 per year.[5]

Protectionism in the 1980s contributed to higher prices for clothing. The imported suit or outfit that would have cost $200 in the absence of protective tariffs and import quotas cost $292 instead, as a result of protectionism. The benefits of protectionism to workers often fall short of its cost to consumers. The total increase in the amounts paid for clothing as a result of tariffs and import quotas is often greater than the earnings of workers whose jobs are protected.

In the early 1990s, the forces of protectionism suffered a number of setbacks. First, in 1993, Congress approved the North American Free Trade Agreement (NAFTA), which reduced tariffs and liberalized trading regulations for the United States, Mexico, and Canada. In 1994, Congress approved a major new world trade agreement to slash tariffs worldwide by 40 percent over a 10-year period and cut import quotas on textiles, apparel, sugar, peanuts, and dairy products.

As of 2005, tariffs had been completely eliminated on beer, construction equipment, distilled spirits, farm machinery, furniture, medical equipment, paper, pharmaceuticals, steel, and toys. Bans on rice imports in Japan and South Korea that kept those markets closed to the United States and other foreign rice producers were eliminated. There has also been progress in eliminating government subsidies that give some nations unfair competitive advantages in international markets for such products as electronics and farm produce. Tariffs on information technology products have been eliminated. The World Trade Organization estimates that the value of imported industrial products that receive duty-free treatment increased from 20 percent in 1995 to 44 percent in 2005. The decline in tariffs has contributed to lower prices for consumers throughout the world and has improved living standards.

In January 2005, all import quotas on textiles and apparel were eliminated throughout the world. Imports of textile products from China into the United States increased by 75 percent in the first months of that year. The increased supply of imported clothing contributed to lower prices. As of 2005, that outfit of clothing that cost $292 in 1995 could very well be had for only $200. In fact, between 1995 and 2005, apparel prices in the U.S. actually declined, on average, by about 10 percent, while, on average, prices for all items in the budget of a typical consumer increased by nearly 30 percent. Liberalized free international trade and the elimination of tariffs and quotas have been responsible for much of this decline.[6]

Of course, U.S. jobs in industries subject to fierce international competition have declined as a result of reduced protection. There have been sharp drops in employment in U.S. textile industries since tariffs and import quotas were eliminated. However, new jobs have been created in other U.S. industries that have expanded to take advantage of the opening of new markets abroad, as protection barriers have made our exports more competitive in some areas of the world. Many other displaced workers have found jobs in service industries, such as health care, where output and job opportunities have been increasing. The advantages to consumers from liberalized trade are likely to outweigh the temporary disadvantages of workers who lose their jobs and eventually find new ones.

[1]See F. W. Taussig, *The Tariff History of the United States*, 8th ed. (New York: G. P. Putnam, 1931), pp. 490-500.
[2]Susan Hickok, "Consumer Cost of U.S. Trade Restraints," *Federal Reserve Bank of New York Quarterly Review* 10 (Summer 1985), p. 10.
[3]Robert W. Crandall, "Import Quotas and the Automobile Industry: The Cost of Protectionism," *Brookings Review* 2, no. 4 (Summer 1984), pp. 8-16.
[4]Gary Clyde Hufbauer, Diane T. Berliner, and Kimberly Ann Elliott, *Trade Protection in the United States: Thirty-one Case Studies* (Washington, D.C.: Institute for International Economics, 1980).
[5]See Congress of the United States, Congressional Budget Office, *Trade Restraints and the Competitive Status of the Textile, Apparel, and Nonrubber-Footwear Industries* (Washington, D.C.: Congress of the United States, December 1991).
[6]For discussion of the progress of trade liberalization, see *World Trade Report 2005* (Geneva: World Trade Organization, 2005). This report is published annually.

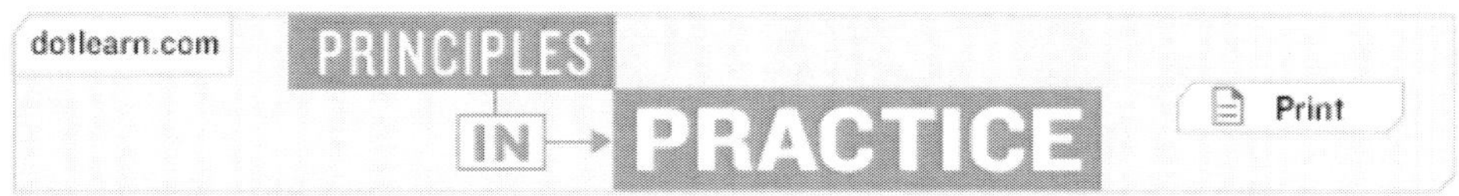

Policy Perspective: The Economics of Drinking, Driving, and Highway Deaths - An Example of Positive Analysis

What does drunken driving have to do with economics? The answer is "a whole lot," according to positive analysis of the impact on fatal motor vehicle accidents of raising the drinking age and taxing beer.

For people in the United States between the ages of 16 and 24, automobile accidents are a leading cause of death. Evidence suggests that policies increasing the cost of obtaining alcoholic beverages also reduce highway deaths. For example, taxes on beer increase the price of beer and tend to decrease its consumption. Similarly, raising the drinking age to 21 makes it more difficult for persons under that age to obtain alcoholic beverages.

Since 1984, all 50 states have raised their minimum drinking age to 21. Positive analysis by economists of the impact of the increased drinking age has concluded that it would reduce nighttime fatal crash involvements by 13 percent.[1]

Most young drinkers haven't been drinking long enough to become habitual alcohol users, and they typically have low incomes. Because a tax on beer will cause its price to increase, it's likely to induce young drinkers with low incomes to cut back their consumption of beer. Positive analysis of the impact of taxes on beer suggests that these too can save lives. Economists estimated that if beer taxes in the United States had increased faster than they actually did between 1975 and 1982, over 1,000 lives of youths between the ages of 18 and 20 could have been saved annually![2]

A follow-up study in 1994 indicated that raising the tax on beer to the level that prevailed in 1951, adjusted for inflation, would have decreased traffic fatalities by 32 percent per year between 1992 and 1988, saving 1,669 lives per year.[3] However, establishing causation is very difficult in economics, and some other studies using more current data since 1991 found little or no impact of increased beer taxes on drunk driving by teenagers.[4]

You may have your own views about the legal drinking age or increased taxes on beer. You may very well change your views in response to positive analysis of the economics of drinking and driving.

[1]William Du Mouchel, Allan F. Williams, and Paul Zador, "Raising the Alcohol Purchase Age: Its Effects on Fatal Motor Vehicle Crashes in Twenty-six States,"

Journal of Legal Studies 16, no. 1 (January 1987), pp.249-66.

[2]Michael Grossman and Henry Saffer, "Beer Taxes, the Legal Drinking Age, and Youth Motor Vehicle Fatalities," National Bureau of Economic Research, Working Paper no. 1914, May 1986.

[3]Michael Grossman, Frank J. Chaloupka, Henry Saffer, and Adit Laixuthai, "Effects of Alcohol Price Policy on Youth: A Summary of Economic Research, *Journal of Research on Adolescence* 4, no. 2 (1994), pp. 347-364.

[4]For example, see Thomas S. Dee, "State Alcohol Policies, Teen Drinking, and Traffic Fatalities, *Journal of Public Economics* 72 (1999), pp. 289-315.

Chapter 2

Production Possibilities and Opportunity Cost

Scarcity, the ever-present imbalance between desires and the ability to satisfy them, is the fundamental economic problem households, businesses, governments, and society at large face. In this chapter, we look at influences on a society's production possibilities. We use the concept of *opportunity cost* to show how choices involve sacrifices. In this way we paint a picture of the economic environment and the constraints we face daily in our personal and business lives.

We deal with the problem of scarcity and the reality of opportunity cost every time we make choices about the ways to spend our money. The greater our incomes, the wider the range of goods and services we can choose from; but the more we buy of one item, the less we can buy of other items. Rich or poor, each of us must face the problem of scarcity and consider the opportunity cost of our choices.

Similarly, the better endowed a nation is with productive resources, the more opportunities its citizens have. However, no matter how rich in resources a nation may be, the basic economic problem of scarcity remains. This is because all resources are in some way limited, so that in choosing to use resources for one purpose, we sacrifice the opportunity to use them for alternative purposes.

Concept Preview

After reading this chapter, you should be able to

1. Explain how limited available technology and scarce resources imply limited production possibilities over a period of time.
2. Show how the use of productive capacity to make more of one good or service available involves sacrificing the opportunity to make more of other items available.
3. Understand the concept of productive efficiency and discuss its significance.
4. Discuss the basic determinants of a nation's production possibilities and how these possibilities can expand over time.
5. Explain how trade can allow citizens consumption possibilities that exceed their nation's domestic production possibilities.

Resources, Technology, and Production Possibilities

Production is the process of using the services of labor and other resources to make goods and services available. (These goods and services are called *outputs*.) **Economic resources** are the *inputs* used in the process of production. They are divided into four broad categories:

1. Labor represents the services of human beings in the production of goods and services. Both physical and mental effort are included in this category. The number of workers; their general education, training, and skills; and their motivation to work are prime determinants of a nation's productive capability. The services of factory workers, truck drivers, salespeople, college professors, police officers, and physicians are all part of a nation's labor resources.

2. Capital is the equipment, tools, structures, machinery, vehicles, materials, and skills created to help produce goods and services.[1] Don't confuse capital resources with financial resources. Firms often raise funds to acquire new capital by borrowing money or issuing new corporate stock. However, the funds acquired in this way are not an input into production. They merely represent the purchasing power needed to build or purchase new capital.

3. Natural resources include land used as sites for structures, ports, and other facilities, as well as the natural materials that are used in crude form in production. Examples of land and other natural resources are farmland, industrial sites, deposits of minerals and petroleum, harbors, navigable rivers, sources of hydroelectric power, timber, the advantages of a region's climate, and environmental quality.

4. Entrepreneurship is the talent to develop products and processes and to organize production to make goods and services available. Entrepreneurs are innovators and risk-takers. Entrepreneurs in business seek to earn profits by satisfying the desires of consumers and by developing better and less costly ways of satisfying those desires. They undertake the tasks necessary to get the process of production started and make the decisions relating to the use of inputs.

The United States is a very rich country in the sense that it has many natural resources, a highly skilled labor force, and a great deal of capital. Many nations lack the skilled labor force, entrepreneurial ability, and capital equipment necessary to enjoy even a fraction of the goods and services per person that we take for granted in the United States. Scarcity is therefore a matter of degree. It is, however, ever present in rich and poor nations alike, given our tendency as human beings to want more than we have.

Technology

Technology, which helps us alleviate scarcity, is the knowledge of how to produce goods and services. Improved technology can streamline production or allow more goods and services to be produced from a given quantity of economic resources. Advances in technology help us cope with the problems of scarcity by making workers, capital, and land more productive. For example, technological advances in agriculture, including the use of farm machinery, improved seed varieties, fertilizer, and chemical control agents, have increased the productivity of U.S. farms. According to calculations by the U.S. Department of Agriculture, output per agricultural worker rose tenfold from 1930 to 2000. Over the same period, U.S. agricultural production quadrupled, without any increase in inputs (land, labor, and capital) allocated to agriculture. In fact, the number of workers in agriculture has declined significantly since the 1930s, when over 30 percent of the labor force was engaged directly in agriculture. Because of technological change, fewer farmers can actually produce more food. As of 2008, less than 2 percent of the labor force in the

[1]Capital inputs can be physical or human. A portion of the labor used in production includes human capital, which represents skills acquired for the purpose of producing medical, engineering, legal, and other services. Another portion includes physical capital—machinery and tools.

United States was directly employed in agriculture. Similarly, the commonplace technology of modern life, including computers, the Internet, and information technology, has made workers more productive. In the automobile industry, application of automated production techniques and new machinery has substantially decreased the amount of labor hours required to assemble cars.

The Production Possibilities Curve

1 You'll see the problem of scarcity more clearly with the aid of a simple model whose purpose is to examine the relationship between the production of goods and services and the availability and use of resources. In the analysis we make the following assumptions:

1. *The quantity and quality of economic resources available for use during the year are fixed.* There is a given amount of available labor, capital, natural resources, and entrepreneurial ability. This limits the extent to which our desires for goods and services can be satisfied during the year.

2. *There are two broad classes of outputs we can produce with available economic resources: food and clothing.* We make the assumption of only two products to simplify the analysis while showing the basic trade-offs we must consider while coping with the problem of scarcity.

3. *Some inputs are better adapted to the production of one good than to the production of another.* A pickup truck can as easily be used to transport materials needed to produce clothing as to transport materials needed to produce food. However, a loom that's used to weave cloth is virtually useless in the production of food. The loom may be dismantled and its parts used in agricultural machinery, but it's much more productive when used to manufacture clothing. Similarly, some workers have skills that are better adapted to one use than another. Transferring a skilled tailor from clothing to food production will cause a greater loss in output of clothing than transferring a truck driver from delivering clothing to delivering food. Transferring the labor of an experienced farmer from agricultural to clothing production results in a greater loss in food output than does transferring the labor of a crop picker. The more specialized a worker, the higher the opportunity cost of transferring him or her to another type of work.

4. *Technology is fixed and does not advance during the year.* In general, advances in technology take more than one year to develop. In assuming fixed technology, we're implying that the productiveness of inputs doesn't change during the year as a result of improved knowledge or technical advances.

Given available resources, their quality, and current technology, there is a limited amount of any one good that can be produced in an economy given the output of other goods. A production possibilities curve shows the maximum possible output of one good that can be produced with available resources, given the output of the alternative good over a period. A production possibilities curve for food and clothing shows the maximum number of garments that can be produced each year given each possible level of food production. The curve shows the *options* available to produce various combinations of goods and services under current technology during a year, assuming the available resources are fully utilized.

Given the assumptions we just made, we can derive a production possibilities curve using hypothetical data. The table in Box 1 shows that if all resources were used to produce food during the year, the maximum possible output would be 55,000 tons that year. This corresponds to production possibility *I* in the table, for which clothing output is zero and food output is 55,000 tons. Alternatively, we might interpret production possibility *I* as implying that if food output were 55,000 tons, the maximum possible clothing output during the year would be zero. The graph in Box 1 plots this production possibility, labeled *I*, on a set of axes on which food output is measured on the vertical axis and clothing output is measured on the horizontal axis.

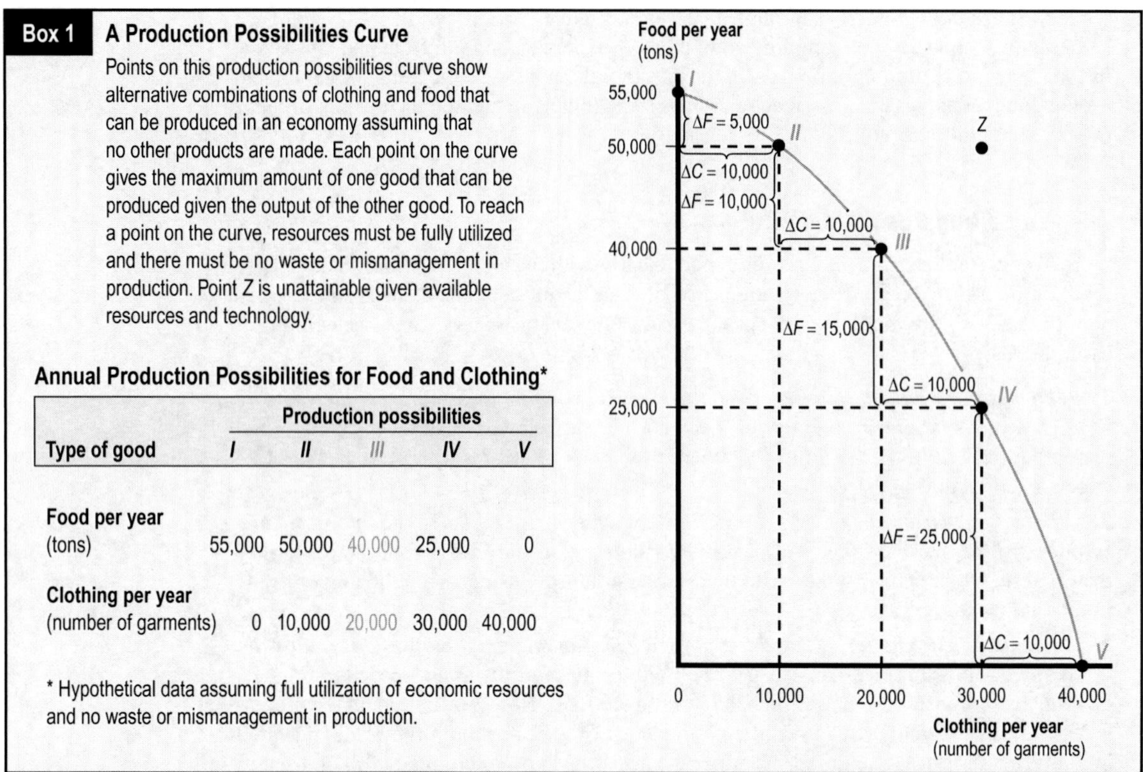

Box 1 **A Production Possibilities Curve**

Points on this production possibilities curve show alternative combinations of clothing and food that can be produced in an economy assuming that no other products are made. Each point on the curve gives the maximum amount of one good that can be produced given the output of the other good. To reach a point on the curve, resources must be fully utilized and there must be no waste or mismanagement in production. Point *Z* is unattainable given available resources and technology.

Annual Production Possibilities for Food and Clothing*

Type of good	Production possibilities *I*	*II*	*III*	*IV*	*V*
Food per year (tons)	55,000	50,000	40,000	25,000	0
Clothing per year (number of garments)	0	10,000	20,000	30,000	40,000

* Hypothetical data assuming full utilization of economic resources and no waste or mismanagement in production.

Now let's consider the option of producing less food and more clothing for the year. Because resources are scarce, increasing the annual output of clothing means we must sacrifice some of the annual output of food. Production possibility *II* consists of 10,000 garments and 50,000 tons of food per year. The opportunity cost of producing 10,000 garments per year is the 5,000 tons of food we must sacrifice to make that number of garments available. Production possibility *II* is labeled as point *II* in the graph.

Production possibility *III* shows the option available if 20,000 garments are produced per year. This option would require us to divert more resources away from food production and to allocate them to clothing production. If we chose this option, maximum possible food output would only be 40,000 tons per year. Notice that increasing clothing production by an additional 10,000 garments per year results in a 10,000-ton reduction in food output; this exceeds the 5,000-ton reduction that was required to produce the first 10,000 garments. The opportunity cost of the second 10,000 garments exceeds the opportunity cost of the first 10,000 garments.

This pattern of increasing opportunity cost continues as we allocate more resources away from food production and toward clothing production. At production possibility *IV*, increasing the output of clothing from 20,000 to 30,000 garments per year means we sacrifice an additional 15,000 tons of food per year. Finally, production possibility *V* shows that the output of food would fall to zero if we used our resources to produce 40,000 garments per year. The opportunity cost of increasing the production of clothing from 30,000 to 40,000 garments per year is the 25,000 tons of food we must sacrifice.

The points corresponding to production possibilities *III*, *IV*, and *V* are also plotted in the graph in Box 1. A smooth line has been drawn through the points corresponding to production possibilities *I* to *V*. The result is a production possibilities curve showing the maximum possible output of food for each possible output of clothing during the year, given available resources and technology. Points such as *Z*, which lie outside the area enclosed by the production possibilities curve and the two axes, represent unattainable combinations of food and clothing per year. Point *Z* corresponds to 50,000 tons of food and 30,000 garments per year. The economy lacks the resources or technology to produce the annual combinations of food and clothing represented by points like *Z*. When resources are used to produce 50,000 tons of food, the maximum amount of clothing that can be produced during the year is 10,000 garments.

All points on or within the production possibilities curve represent annual combinations of goods that can be produced. However, points *within* the area bounded by the curve and the two axes represent combinations of the two goods that correspond to *less than* the maximum possible annual production of one of the goods given the annual production of the other. Our economy might end up at a point within the area bounded by the curve and the axes if it did not utilize all the productive resources available or if resources were wasted or mismanaged.

The production possibilities curve therefore illustrates the idea of scarcity in two important ways. First, it shows that only a limited number of production possibilities exist over a year given available resources and technology. The possibilities are represented by points within and on the curve. Second, it shows that once the maximum amount of any one good is produced per year, given the output of the other good per year, additional annual production of the first good requires an annual reduction in the output of the other.

The Law of Increasing Costs

2 Box 2 shows the economy's opportunity cost for each 10,000-garment batch of clothing production. The first column of the table shows the annual output of clothing. The second column shows the increase in clothing output. The delta (Δ) shows *change in* the variable *C*. In this case *C* stands for clothing. When output increases from zero to 10,000 garments per year, the change in clothing production is $\Delta C = 10{,}000$. Now let's return briefly to Box 1. To obtain that increase in the output of clothing, the opportunity cost is 5,000 tons of food per year. The change in food output as the economy moves from point *I* to point *II* on the production possibilities curve is $\Delta F = 5{,}000$ tons, as shown in the last column of the table in Box 2. By sacrificing 5,000 tons of food per year, the economy moves from point *I* to point *II* on its production possibilities curve in Box 1.

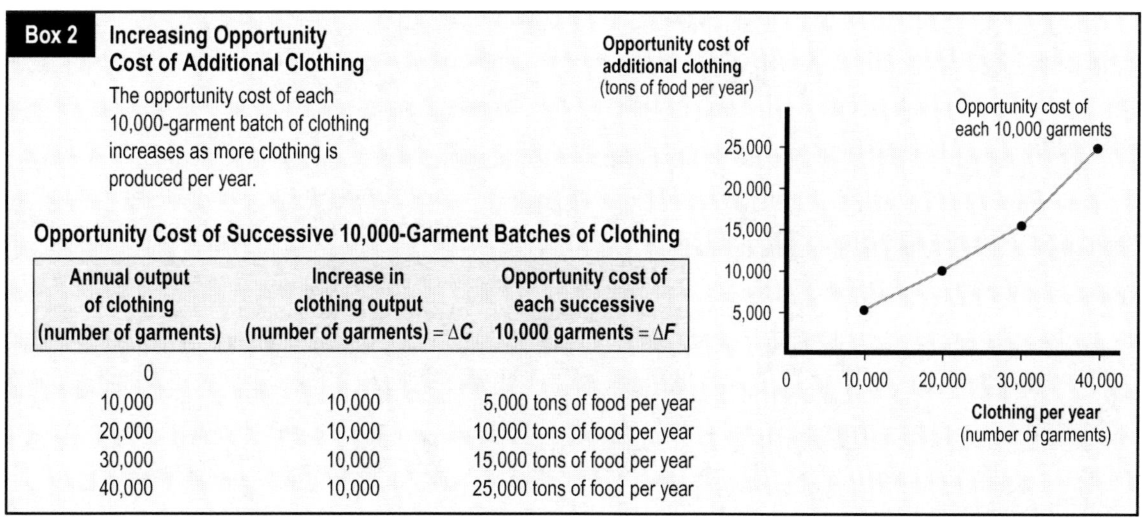

Box 2 Increasing Opportunity Cost of Additional Clothing

The opportunity cost of each 10,000-garment batch of clothing increases as more clothing is produced per year.

Opportunity Cost of Successive 10,000-Garment Batches of Clothing

Annual output of clothing (number of garments)	Increase in clothing output (number of garments) = ΔC	Opportunity cost of each successive 10,000 garments = ΔF
0		
10,000	10,000	5,000 tons of food per year
20,000	10,000	10,000 tons of food per year
30,000	10,000	15,000 tons of food per year
40,000	10,000	25,000 tons of food per year

The last column of the table in Box 2 shows how the opportunity cost of each successive batch of 10,000 garments per year increases as we allocate more resources from food to clothing production during the year. The graph plots the opportunity cost of each 10,000-garment batch of clot in terms of food sacrificed for each level of annual clothing production.[2] An upward-sloping curve has been fitted through the points to show how the opportunity costs of additional clothing production increase.

A basic reason that costs increase with successive units of output is the existence of specialized inputs that are more productive in a particular use. As we increase clothing production during the year, we have to sacrifice more and more food for each successive increment in the number of garments produced per year. You can see this by concentrating on the land that would have to be reallocated to build clothing factories and grow the fibers used to make cloth. At first the land least specialized for growing food can be reallocated to clothing production. As more fertile food land is transferred for successive increments in the annual production of clothing, the loss per acre transferred increases simply because the land more adapted to food production produces more food per acre than the less specialized land.

Similarly, at first the vehicles and equipment least specialized in the production of food, such as trucks and tractors, can be transferred at low opportunity cost to clothing production. However, as we produce more clothing, we must adapt more specialized agricultural machinery, such as combines, for use in clothing production. Because this type of machinery is more productive in food than in clothing production, the opportunity cost of additional clothing increases in terms of food sacrificed. Likewise, as clothing output increases, at first the workers least specialized in agricultural production are transferred to clothing production. As more and more workers are required to produce additional clothing, the more skilled and, therefore, more productive workers must be transferred out of food production. This increases the amount of food we must sacrifice to produce extra units of clothing.

The law of increasing costs states that the opportunity cost of each additional unit of output of a good over a period increases as more of that good is produced. This law is an implication of the assumption that some economic resources are more suited than others to the production of particular goods. Because this implication has been widely supported by empirical evidence, it is called a "law."

The concave shape of the production possibilities curve in Box 2 reflects the law of increasing costs. The slope of the curve at any point is $\Delta F/\Delta C$, where ΔF is the annual reduction in food output necessary for each extra garment per year. As you move from point *I* toward point *V*, the curve becomes steeper, reflecting the increase in the sacrifice of food, ΔF, required for each additional one-unit increase in clothing output.

Generalizing the Concepts: Trade-Offs and Increasing Costs

The economic concepts of production possibilities curve and the law of increasing costs are relevant to the world we live in. Consider the production possibilities between two broad classes of goods: military goods and all other goods. The production possibilities curve in the left panel of Box 3 shows that the more of our resources we devote to production of military goods for national defense, the less of other goods (such as cars, televisions, and housing) we will have. For example, during 1943, at the peak of World War II, the United States devoted over 40 percent of its productive resources to production of military goods and services. That year no private automobiles were produced because all automobile factories were under contract to the government to produce military vehicles. Similarly, in 1944 new consumer goods, such as housing and clothing, were very

[2]The opportunity cost of each 10,000-garment batch of clothing is the marginal cost of clothing when the units of clothing are 10,000-garment packages.

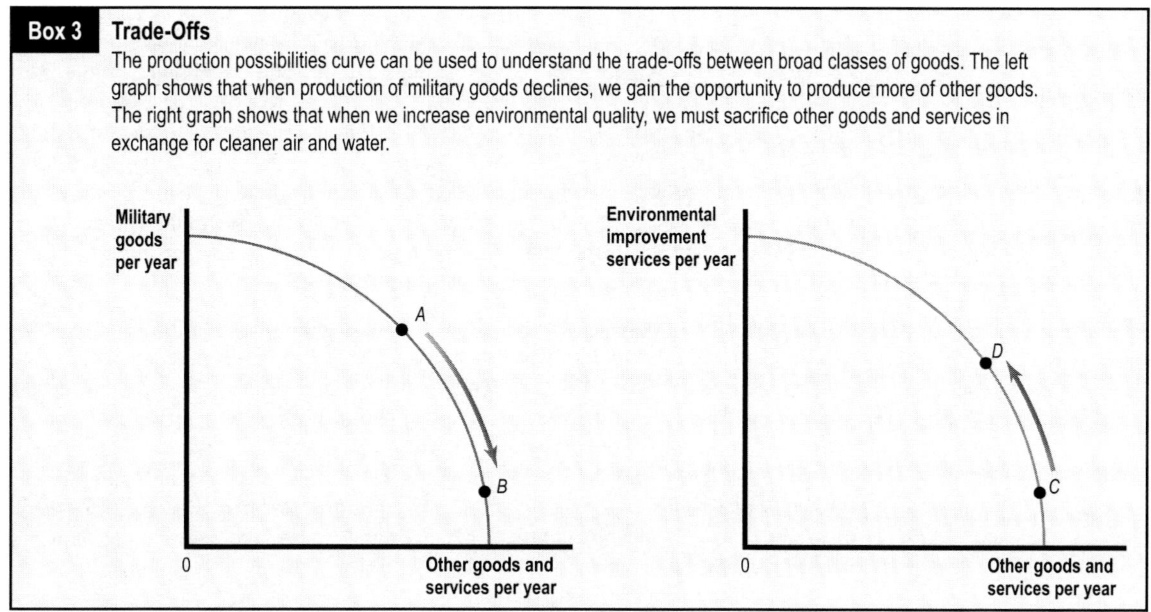

Box 3 Trade-Offs

The production possibilities curve can be used to understand the trade-offs between broad classes of goods. The left graph shows that when production of military goods declines, we gain the opportunity to produce more of other goods. The right graph shows that when we increase environmental quality, we must sacrifice other goods and services in exchange for cleaner air and water.

scarce, as was gasoline for private use. In 1944 the United States was at a point like *A* on its production possibilities curve in Box 3.

As of 1992, the United States was at a point like *B* on its production possibilities curve, allocating only about 5 percent of production to military purchases and thus allowing considerably more resources to be used to produce other goods and services than was possible at the peak of World War II. The demise of the Soviet Union and the end of the cold war offered us the possibility of further reallocating resources from defense to nondefense uses. However, because of the law of increasing costs, the gain in additional nondefense production per unit reduction in military production is much smaller at point *B* than at point *A*, where a lot of resources were devoted to defense. Therefore, it's unreasonable to expect relatively big gains in the capability of producing more of other goods (the "peace dividend") as the United States scales back its military purchases. By 2001, the United States was allocating 4 percent of total production to military goods—only one percentage point of production less than in 1992. So the peace dividend from the demise of the Soviet Union has proven to be quite small.

The terrorist attack on the United States on September 11, 2001, and military operations in Afghanistan and Iraq, caused a shift back toward allocation of more resources to national defense. Because of the attacks, the United States government and American businesses had to revamp their plans for security. A new cabinet-level Office of Homeland Security was established, and the trend toward declining government expenditures for military goods, which yielded peace dividends for the U.S. economy throughout the 1990s, was reversed. The increased vigilance now required because of the threat of new attacks will affect the mix of goods and services to be produced in the United States for many years to come.

The opportunity cost of increased homeland security is the alternative goods and services we must sacrifice. As we devote more and more resources to security, the law of increasing costs implies that each additional unit of protection will involve an increased amount of alternative goods that must be sacrificed. Increased allocation to goods and services that provide homeland security, including military operations abroad, surveillance, police protection, airline passenger screening, and other activities, in any given year moves the economy from a point like *B* to a point like *A*. Immediately after the September 11 attack, the U.S. Congress enacted the 2001 Emergency Supplemental Appropriations Act for Recovery from and Response to Terrorist Attacks on the United States. This legislation provided $40 billion to fund assistance to victims of the attacks and deal with its consequences. Also enacted was the Air Transportation Safety and Systems Stabilization Act, which provided assistance to the airline industry and funded improved air travel security programs. By 2008, defense spending in the United States had increased to 5 percent of the value of total production—up a full percentage point from 2001.

Private businesses will also spend billions of dollars more each year for security. Annual spending for security could absorb as much as an additional 1 percent of the value of production in future years. As the economy grows, some of that growth in the capacity to produce goods and services will have to go to national security. For example, if the U.S. economy's production potential grows in future years as it has in the past, on average at 3 percent, and we must allocate 1 percent of that to security, our growth in other goods and services will be only 2 percent. Assuming an additional one percent per year of the value of production goes to homeland security, living standards will grow more slowly than would have otherwise been the case.

Productive Efficiency

3 We can use the production possibilities curve to show the consequences of underutilizing or mismanaging economic resources in a nation. For example, suppose the labor force is underutilized in production, a situation that generally occurs when the unemployment rate is excessively high. Some unemployment is normal because people who have just entered the labor force or lost their previous job take time to search for jobs. However, excessive unemployment is a matter of concern to all of us and not just to those unfortunate enough to be out of work.

Excessive unemployment or failure to fully utilize capital and natural resources implies that an economy is operating at a point *within* rather than *on* its production possibilities curve. You can see this in the graph in Box 4. If the economy were not fully utilizing its economic resources, actual annual production of food and clothing might correspond to a point like *R*. At that point we could produce more food by moving to point *II* without sacrificing any clothing each year. Alternatively, we could produce more clothing without sacrificing any food each year by moving to point *III*. If resources were not fully utilized, we could attain all combinations of the two goods within the shaded triangular area enclosed by the points *R*, *II*, and *III* without acquiring more resources or without an advance in technology.

Mismanagement of economic resources also causes the economy to operate within its production possibilities curve. Suppose all economic resources are being utilized in production but aren't managed so that we obtain the maximum amount of any one good given the output of other goods under existing technology. In the graph in Box 4, mismanaging resources would result in a point like *R*. As was the case for excessive unemployment, all the combinations of clothing and food represented by points within the shaded triangular area are possible without additional resources or improvement in technical know-how. Sloppy management therefore also prevents an economy from attaining production possibilities for which it has the capability.

Productive efficiency is attained when the maximum possible output of any one good, given the output of the other goods, is produced. Attainment of productive efficiency means we can't reallocate economic resources to increase the output of any good or service without decreasing the output of some other good or service. Points on a

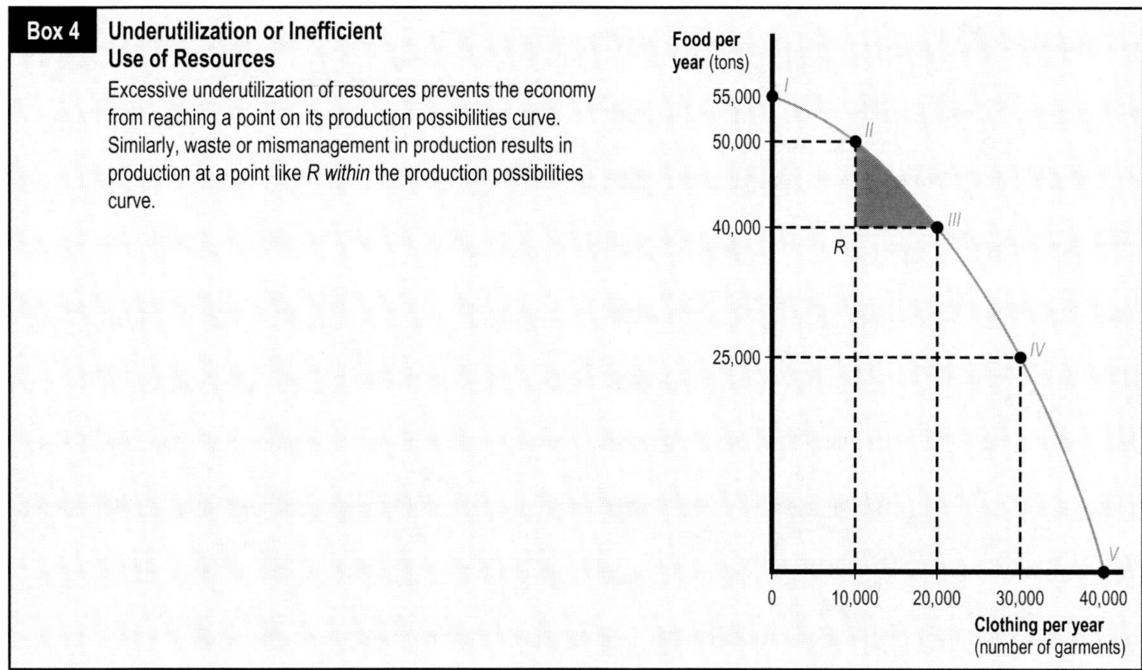
Box 4
Underutilization or Inefficient Use of Resources
Excessive underutilization of resources prevents the economy from reaching a point on its production possibilities curve. Similarly, waste or mismanagement in production results in production at a point like R within the production possibilities curve.
Food per year (tons)
55,000
50,000
40,000
25,000
0
10,000
20,000
30,000
40,000
Clothing per year (number of garments)
I
II
III
IV
V
R

production possibilities curve represent efficient use of productive resources because once we are on the curve, it's impossible to increase the output of one good without reducing the output of the other.

Division of Labor and Productive Efficiency

One factor that contributes to productive efficiency is division of labor, which is the breakdown of a larger process into particular tasks performed by workers who specialize in those tasks. By specializing, workers become more proficient at their jobs. Division of labor lets factories use mass production techniques that allow workers to produce more.

By dividing tasks, a factory obtains much more output per worker than it would obtain if each worker had to build each unit of an entire finished product alone. For example, suppose you had to build an automobile by yourself. You'd have to mold the steel; assemble the body, chassis, and motor; and do all interior assembly. You'd have to be an expert in welding, electrical wiring, painting, and upholstering. Even if you were skilled in all these operations, it might take you as long as a year to produce a finished car.

With division of labor, the numerous tasks involved would be assigned to many workers, each specializing in one task. By dividing tasks managers can use sophisticated machinery and equipment and produce many more cars than could be produced if each worker tried to do all the tasks. Division of labor exists in a broader sense throughout the economy. For example, people with specialized skills function as physicians, police officers, architects, musicians, and farmers.

Economic Growth: Expanding Production Possibilities

4 From year to year, growth in available supplies of economic resources, improvements in resource quality, and advances in technology can expand production possibilities in a society. Economic growth is the expansion of production possibilities that results from increased availability and increased productivity of

economic resources. When economic growth occurs over time, the production possibilities curve shifts outward. This means that the economy is able to produce more of all goods. In this section we'll consider three sources of economic growth:

1. Increased quantities of economic resources.
2. Improved quality of economic resources.
3. Advances in technology.

Annual Growth in Available Resources

An increase in available economic resources allows us to produce more. Other things being equal, the more workers willing and able to work, the more capital, and the more land, the greater the production possibilities. This means the production possibilities curve shifts outward in response to an increase in available economic resources, as you can see in the graph in Box 5. Production possibilities previously unattainable are now feasible. Increases in economic resources available for production therefore result in a new production possibilities curve. The shaded area in the graph represents previously unattainable combinations of food and clothing that become feasible when resources become more plentiful or their quality improves.

The availability of new capital is especially effective in pushing the production possibilities curve outward because new capital often complements labor, land, and other natural resources. This means that additional capital tends to increase the *productivity* of available labor and land. For example, supplying workers with more and better equipment increases the *output per worker*. Similarly, using more capital per acre of farmland can be very effective in increasing the production of *food per acre*. Growth in capital is an especially important determinant of our well-being as individuals because increases in capital per worker result in more goods per person, thereby increasing the material well-being of each of us.

By the same token, the destruction of economic resources in a nation moves the production possibilities curve inward. For example, a war destroys both human and physical resources, causing the production possibilities curve to shrink inward. A sudden decrease in the availability of a key input into production can also cause the production possibilities curve to shift inward. For example, if the United States found its fuel supplies cut in half because of difficulty in obtaining crude oil, our production possibilities curve would shift inward, making some previously attainable production possibilities no longer feasible.

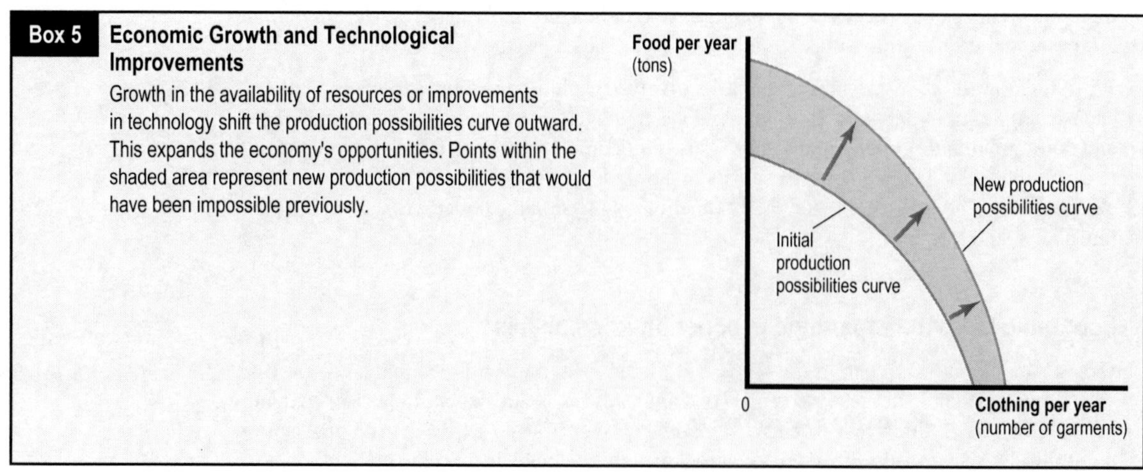

Box 5 Economic Growth and Technological Improvements

Growth in the availability of resources or improvements in technology shift the production possibilities curve outward. This expands the economy's opportunities. Points within the shaded area represent new production possibilities that would have been impossible previously.

Improved Quality of Inputs

Improvement in skills, education, or training of the labor force can also increase the output obtainable from any given combination of inputs. Devoting more economic resources to education and job training in the current year pays off in the future in terms of greater production possibilities. However, those of us who pursue more education must forgo current opportunities to work full-time. The opportunity cost to the economy of more education is the production lost when you and others attend college rather than immediately entering the work force after high school. The loss in current output from more education is often more than made up by an increase in future output, assuming that college graduates are more productive than high school graduates.

Similarly, the quality of capital also improves as new machines that can accomplish more tasks or accomplish tasks more quickly or more accurately are introduced. Improvements in the quality of capital require advances in technology, which is the next source of economic growth we'll consider.

Improvements in Technology

Like improvements in the quality of inputs, increased productive potential resulting from the development of new technologies is a very important source of economic growth. For example, technological improvements that increase the speed of computers mean that a given quantity of computers can process more information. One worker operating a more advanced computer can do the job of two or more workers. Similarly, improvements in agricultural technology mean that a given quantity of land, labor, and capital can produce more food and fiber.

As with improvements in worker skills, a cost is associated with the development of new technologies. To conduct research and development to advance technology, we must withdraw resources from production of goods for immediate consumption. By sacrificing current consumption opportunities, however, we gain future production possibilities.

Surprisingly, technological advances in one sector of the economy cause gains in production possibilities in other sectors as well. For example, suppose there's a technological advance in the food sector of the economy but not in the clothing sector. Improved technology in food production means that for any given quantity of food output, *more* economic resources are now available for clothing production, other things being equal. For any given quantity of food output, we can produce more clothing output than

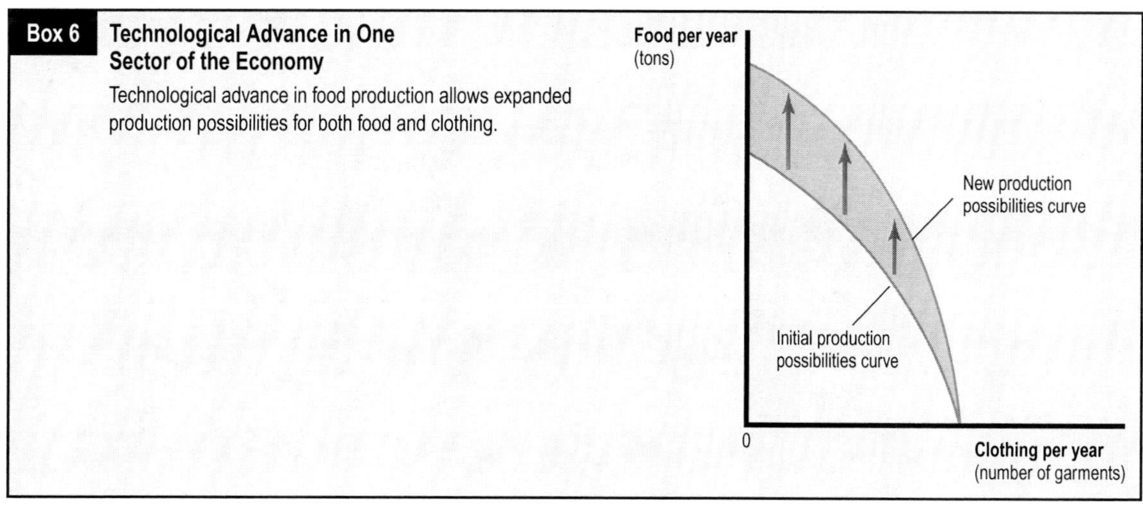

Box 6 Technological Advance in One Sector of the Economy

Technological advance in food production allows expanded production possibilities for both food and clothing.

before. You can see this effect in the graph in Box 6, where the production possibilities curve moves upward, but its intercept on the clothing axis doesn't change. In other words, if we were to devote all of our resources to clothing production after the advance in technology in food production, we wouldn't be able to produce more clothing than before. However, the advance in food technology means we can devote more of our available resources to clothing production for any given amount of food produced. As a result, the maximum amount of clothing corresponding to any given amount of food output is now greater. The shaded area in the graph represents the production possibilities of both food *and* clothing gained from a technological advance in food production. In fact, improvements in agricultural technology in the United States and other nations have freed labor so it can be employed in the production of other goods and services.

Technological Change in Manufacturing and Production Possibilities

Technological advance in the manufacturing sector of the economy has outpaced that of many other sectors in the U.S. economy. You may be familiar with the unfortunate side effect of what is popularly called corporate downsizing—loss of jobs in manufacturing. However, this loss of jobs really means that the manufacturing sector can produce the same and often *more* output with less labor because of technological change and other improvements in the production process. As this occurs U.S. manufacturing becomes more competitive in world markets because the same or more output than before can be produced with less labor. Cost per unit of output falls provided that wages do not rise (as has been the case in U.S. manufacturing). This enables U.S. firms to sell their products at lower prices in global markets.

The loss in jobs in manufacturing does not mean a permanent reduction in employment. Using your knowledge of production possibilities, you know that when labor is reduced in one use it becomes available for other uses. Faster technological change in manufacturing shifted out our production possibilities curve between manufacturing (plotted on the vertical axis) and all other goods (plotted on the horizontal axis) in the same way as the production possibilities curve between food and clothing shifted in Box 6. This means we can still produce the same amount of manufactured products with fewer workers, freeing labor for other important uses in the economy. Eventually workers who lose their jobs as a result of corporate downsizing will find employment in other occupations. As we can satisfy demands for manufactured products with less labor, more labor becomes available for employment in health care, environmental protection, and service industries to perform important social functions. Many so-called victims of corporate downsizing have found well-paying and satisfying jobs in other areas. Many of the executives forced to take early retirement from such large firms as IBM often open their own consulting firms or start other businesses, using their managerial skills to provide new socially useful services.

Production for the Present versus Production for the Future: A Basic Economic Choice

In each economy decisions must be made about how to allocate currently available resources between uses that provide goods for current consumption and uses that provide goods for future consumption. Education, new structures and equipment to be used in production, and research for and development of new technologies are *investments* in future production possibilities. The gain from these investments is the expansion in production possibilities they allow in the future.

Expansion of production possibilities results when workers have more and better capital (think of capital as "tools") and improved technology. Similarly, education increases workers' skills, allowing more output per worker.

The graphs in Box 7 show how future production possibilities are affected by the choice to allocate available economic resources to production of current consumption goods instead of investments. Suppose the current production possibilities for these two alternative uses of available resources are identical in the two nations. However, nation A chooses point *A* on its initial production possibilities curve, sacrificing ΔC_A units of consumption goods to produce I_A units of investment goods. The citizens in nation B end up choosing point *B* on their production possibilities curve in the current year. They sacrifice a smaller amount of consumption goods, ΔC_B, which is less than ΔC_A, but produce only I_B units of investment goods, which is less than I_A. In the future, citizens of nation A are rewarded for their sacrifice of current consumption possibilities with a greater outward shift of their production possibilities curve than citizens of nation B enjoy.

In addition to deciding what to produce, how to produce it, and who will receive it, each economy must also decide what and how much it will sacrifice today to make investments that expand future production possibilities.

Production, Specialization, and the Gains from Trade

5 In modern industrial economies, we cope with scarcity, in part, by specializing in what we do best. No one is self-sufficient in our complex modern economies. We earn our income by engaging in a particular occupation providing goods or services to others. Our specialized activities provide us with the means to buy goods and services from others. For example, your father might be an insurance agent earning a salary from his company and, possibly, commissions from the sale of polices, and your mother might be a high school teacher. Because they spend the bulk of their time engaging in their specialized activities, they can hardly be expected to grow food for you and your family or spin fiber into cloth so they can make your clothes. Instead, you and your family are dependent on others to supply you food and clothing in markets. Similarly, you don't generate your own electricity to run the air conditioner, computer, and other appliances you use in your daily activities. Instead, your family purchases electricity from the local electric power generating company.

Box 7 Consumption, Investment, and Economic Growth

The more investment in the current year, the greater the growth in production possibilities in future years. Nation A invested more than nation B and, as a result, nation A's production possibilities curve shifts out farther in the future than nation B's.

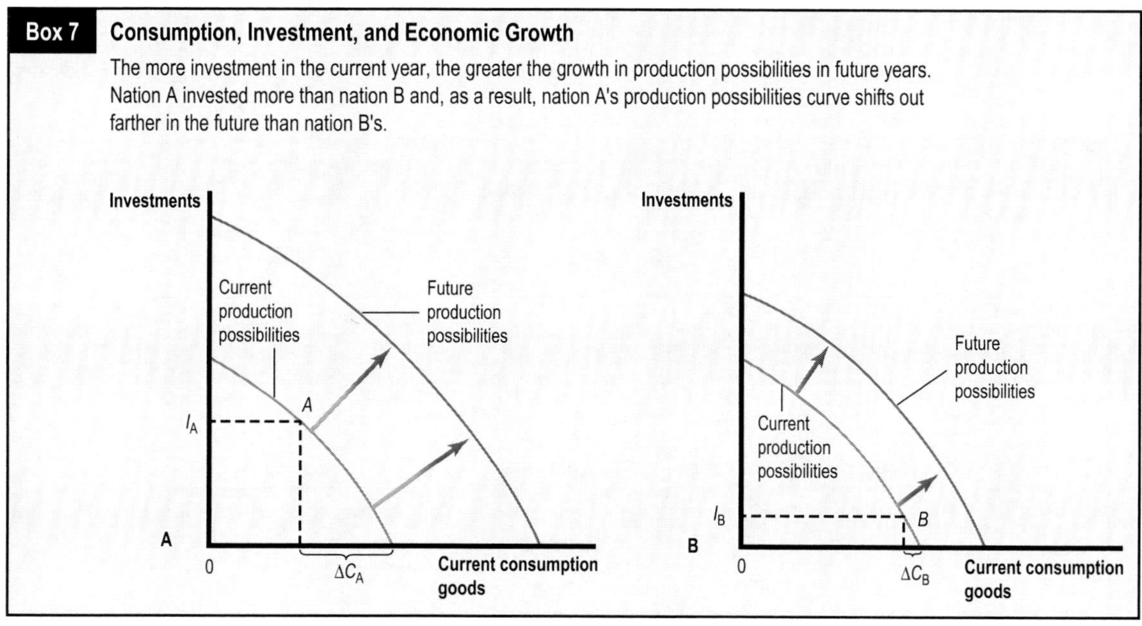

Specialization and trade allow us to economize on resources and permit each of us to consume more than we possibly could if we tried to produce every conceivable item we desire for ourselves. To see the benefits of specialization and the gains possible from trade among ourselves, we'll set up a simple model of life in a simpler time.

Let's go back to the frontier. Assume that two families live in an isolated western mountain region far from any city or market. Ordering from the Internet isn't an option, because UPS, FedEx, and even the U.S. Postal Service aren't available, and computers haven't been invented yet. Suppose Ms. Wheaton is the head of one family and Mr. Tailor is the head of another. As we begin our story of the Old West, both families are self-sufficient, producing their own clothing and food—mainly, grain.

Ms. Wheaton is a very talented lady. She has the skills necessary to produce clothing. If she were to spend all of her working hours during the year engaged in the production of clothing, she could make 200 outfits per year. But she's also a skilled farmer. If she were to work full time in farming, she could produce 10 tons of grain per year, from which she could make bread, pasta, and even a bit of beer.

Ms. Wheaton's neighbor, Mr. Tailor, can also produce clothing and grain. However, he's not quite as skilled as Ms. Wheaton in either of these pursuits; therefore, he can't quite match her output of either clothing or grain. Suppose that, if he works full time producing clothing, the maximum number of outfits he could make per year would be 180. If he were to devote full time to farming, the most he would be able to produce would be 5 tons of grain.

Box 8 shows the production possibilities for both Ms. Wheaton and Mr. Tailor, assuming they both work full time (say, 40 hours per week) during the year and devote all their working time to either production of clothing or production of grain.

Notice that Ms. Wheaton could produce more of *each of the two* products per year than Mr. Tailor can, working full time and specializing in one or the other. A producer has an absolute advantage over other producers when he or she can produce more of any good over a given period, with a given amount of resources, than others can. It's clear that when devoting all of her labor resources full time to clothing production, Ms. Wheaton can produce more than Mr. Tailor can when he devotes all of his resources to clothing production. Ms. Wheaton, therefore, has the absolute advantage in clothing production. But Ms. Wheaton can also produce more grain when devoting all her labor resources to grain cultivation during the year than Mr. Tailor can when he devotes the same amount of

Box 8

Hypothetical Production Possibilities for Two Frontier Neighbors (Output per Year, Full-Time Work)

Wheaton (annual output)	Tailor (annual output)
200 outfits and no grain	180 outfits and no grain
or	or
10 tons of grain and no outfits	5 tons of grain and no outfits

Opportunity cost (assuming constant costs)	Wheaton (per year)	Tailor (per year)
Each ton of grain costs	20 outfits	36 outfits
Each outfit costs	0.05 tons of grain	0.028 tons of grain

hours to grain production. Ms. Wheaton, therefore, also has an absolute advantage over Mr. Tailor in grain production.

Because Ms. Wheaton has the absolute advantage in both goods, you might argue she should produce both goods for herself. However, it's easy to show that, provided the opportunity costs of the two alternative products are different for the two producers, they would each be better off specializing in the production of one of the goods and exchanging some of their output for the other good. First, let's calculate the opportunity costs of both grain and clothing for each of the two producers. In making this calculation, we'll assume each ton of grain produced involves the sacrifice of a constant number of outfits per year, and vice versa. In effect, this presumes that labor, and any capital and land, used by the producers in making the alternative good is equally suited for the production of each. This will mean that the law of increasing costs won't hold, and production will take place at constant opportunity cost. Because Ms. Wheaton can produce either 200 outfits or 10 tons of grain per year, the opportunity costs of devoting all her labor to grain production will be the 200 outfits she must give up by doing so. Assuming constant costs, this means that the opportunity cost of each ton of grain is 20 outfits of clothing. We obtain this figure by dividing the 200 outfits sacrificed by the 10 tons of grain obtained by doing so.

By specializing in farming, Mr. Tailor will lose the opportunity to produce 180 outfits per year and get only 5 tons of grain by reallocating all his labor to grain production. The opportunity cost of specializing in grain production expressed as outfits per ton will be 36 outfits per ton of grain. This is obtained by dividing the 180 outfits sacrificed by the 5 tons of grain obtained by doing so. Assuming constant costs, notice that *the opportunity cost of grain is higher for Mr. Tailor than it is for Ms. Wheaton.* Grain production costs Tailor 16 outfits more for each ton than it costs Wheaton.

Now, calculate the opportunity cost for each of the producers if specializing in clothing production. If Ms. Wheaton were to spend all her time each year making clothes, she would forego the opportunity to produce 10 tons of grain. The opportunity cost of each outfit is, therefore, 10 tons of grain divided by 200 outfits, which equals 0.05 tons of grain per outfit. Performing the same calculation for Mr. Tailor shows that the opportunity cost of an outfit will be 5 tons of grain divided by 180 outfits, which equals 0.028 tons of grain per outfit, assuming constant costs. *The opportunity cost of an outfit in terms of tons of grain sacrificed per year is higher for Ms. Wheaton than it is for Mr. Tailor.* The data on opportunity costs is summarized in Box 8.

A producer has a comparative advantage in the production of an item if the producer can produce it at a lower opportunity cost than other producers can. Using the data from Box 8, we can now say that Wheaton has a comparative advantage in grain production over Tailor. However, Tailor has a comparative advantage in clothing production over Wheaton. Even though Wheaton has an absolute advantage in both products, she only has a comparative advantage in one of them—grain.

Differences in comparative advantage among traders make mutual gains from specialization and exchange possible. To see this, suppose Mr. Tailor takes the initiative to visit Ms. Wheaton after figuring out that he has the comparative advantage in clothing production. He points out to her that, although she's quite skilled in the production of both clothing and grain, the opportunity cost of each outfit of clothing is high relative to the cost he incurs. To produce each outfit of clothing, she must allocate her labor away from the production of grain. Each outfit produced will cause her to forego 0.05 tons, or 100 pounds, of grain per year. Pushing his luck, Mr. Tailor suggests that she simply specialize in grain production and, whenever she wants a new outfit of clothing for herself or a member of her family, she trade 100 pounds of grain to Mr. Tailor in exchange for a new outfit. This would naturally be a great deal for Tailor, because an outfit of clothing only costs him the sacrifice of 0.028 tons, or 56 pounds, of grain. He would get 100 pounds of grain for an outfit whose opportunity cost is only 56 pounds of grain! Unfortunately for Tailor, Wheaton is unlikely to accept that offer. Why should she? She'd be no better off in that case than if she produced the grain herself, because it would cost her, in trade, as much as the 100 pounds of grain she'd have to give up by using her own labor to make the outfit.

If she knows Mr. Tailor's opportunity cost is 56 pounds of grain per outfit, she might counteroffer that amount in exchange for the outfit. In this case, Tailor would just cover his opportunity cost for the outfit, but wouldn't gain. For mutual gains to be possible, the price of the outfit in terms of grain would have to be somewhere between 100 pounds and 56 pounds. For example, if the agreed-upon terms of exchange were 80 pounds of grain per outfit, Wheaton would gain because she'd be able to get each outfit for 20 pounds of grain less than it would cost her if she tried to produce the clothing herself. Similarly, Tailor would get 80 pounds of grain for each outfit—an amount equal to 24 more pounds of grain than the outfit costs him. *Living standards for both the Wheaton and Tailor families will increase, because they'll each be able to enjoy both more clothing and more grain than they would if each remained self-sufficient.* Each specializes in the product for which she or he has a comparative advantage, and trades with the other for the alternative product. *Specialization according to comparative advantage, coupled with exchange, allows mutual gains from trade for both parties to the exchange.*

The same result would occur if Ms. Wheaton, instead of Mr. Tailor, initiated the bargaining process. Suppose Ms. Wheaton visits Mr. Tailor and offers to trade grain for outfits. She knows that Tailor sacrifices 36 outfits for each ton of grain when he reallocates his labor from clothing to grain production. However, a ton of grain costs Wheaton only 20 outfits. If she were to offer to trade a ton of grain for 36 outfits, she'd gain by getting 16 more outfits than she'd be able to produce by reallocating her labor from grain to clothing production. But that offer wouldn't make Mr. Tailor any better off, and he's likely to refuse it. An agreement must be reached that allows mutual gains. An agreement to exchange grain for clothing that will give Wheaton more than 20 outfits per ton of grain, but less than 36 outfits per ton, would allow mutual gains. If such an agreement is reached, say, at 28 outfits per ton of grain, mutual gains will be achieved, and it would pay each of the parties to specialize in the production of the good for which they enjoy a comparative advantage.

Data from this example can also be used to show how specialization and exchange according to comparative advantage can allow consumption possibilities that exceed production possibilities. In this way, specialization and exchange can squeeze more output from resources and improve living standards. To see this, suppose the two parties remain self-sufficient. Ms. Wheaton devotes half her working hours each year to producing clothing and the other half to producing grain, instead of specializing in grain production and trading with Tailor. Based on the data in Box 8, she and her family would be able to consume 100 outfits and 5 tons of grain per year, assuming that cutting the work devoted to each activity in half will also cut the output in half (as implied by constant opportunity costs). If, under the same assumptions, suppose Mr. Tailor devotes two-thirds of his yearly work hours to grain production and one-third of his yearly work hours to clothing production. By remaining self-sufficient and allocating his work this way, he'd produce 60 outfits and 3 1/3 tons of grain for his family to consume. *The combined output of the two producers would be 8 1/3 tons of grain and 160 outfits per year when neither specializes according to his or her comparative advantage and allocates her or his work effort the way we described in this paragraph.*

The potential gains from specialization and trade can now be easily demonstrated. When Ms. Wheaton specializes in grain production, she produces 10 tons per year. When Mr. Tailor specializes in clothing production, he produces 180 outfits per year. *By specializing according to each one's comparative advantage, the two workers together can produce*

1 2/3 tons more of grain per year and 20 more outfits per year than would be possible if they were to try to be self-sufficient and allocate their time as described in the paragraph above. They can then trade among themselves for items they want for which they don't enjoy a comparative advantage. In this way, they can consume more, enjoying higher living standards than if they remained self-sufficient!

The principle of comparative advantage has wide applicability. For example, suppose Charles Compton, CEO of the Compton Computer Company, is a whiz at corporate planning and innovation, and also at data entry. He can input words and numbers on the computer keyboard more quickly and accurately than anyone else within the company. Does this imply he should do his own data entry? Well, he does have an absolute advantage in both corporate planning and keyboard skills. But, most likely, his comparative advantage is in corporate planning. The opportunity cost of using an hour of his time for data entry is probably much higher for the company than it is for using an hour of any other employee. According to the principle of comparative advantage, therefore, the CEO should specialize in corporate planning and leave the typing to the data entry specialists, whose comparative advantage lies in that domain, to use company resources as efficiently as possible.

The principle of comparative advantage also has applicability to economies in general. We'll now examine its role in global specialization and international trade.

The Gains from International Trade

The production possibilities curve can be used to show how we gain from foreign trade. Consumers gain when the United States trades with other nations to obtain goods that it can't produce itself. Less obviously, consumers also gain when the United States imports an item that it can produce itself. In general, if the opportunity cost of importing an item is lower than the opportunity cost of producing it domestically, a nation can enjoy a net gain from international trade.

Suppose a small nation is capable of producing both digital video recorders (DVRs) and wheat. Box 9 shows the nation of Atlantica's production possibilities curve for wheat and DVRs. At any point on the curve, the opportunity cost of an extra DVR is at least 1 ton of

Box 9 Illustrating the Gains Possible from International Trade

The graph shows the production possibilities curve for Atlantica when Atlantica can grow wheat at lower opportunity cost (measured in terms of sacrifice of DVRs) than its trading partner, Pacifica. By specializing in wheat, Atlantica can enjoy consuming 50,000 DVRs per year and 225,000 tons of wheat per year at point *T*, which lies above its production possibilities curve. It gets to point *T* by producing 250,000 tons of wheat and exporting 25,000 tons of that to Pacifica in exchange for 50,000 DVRs.

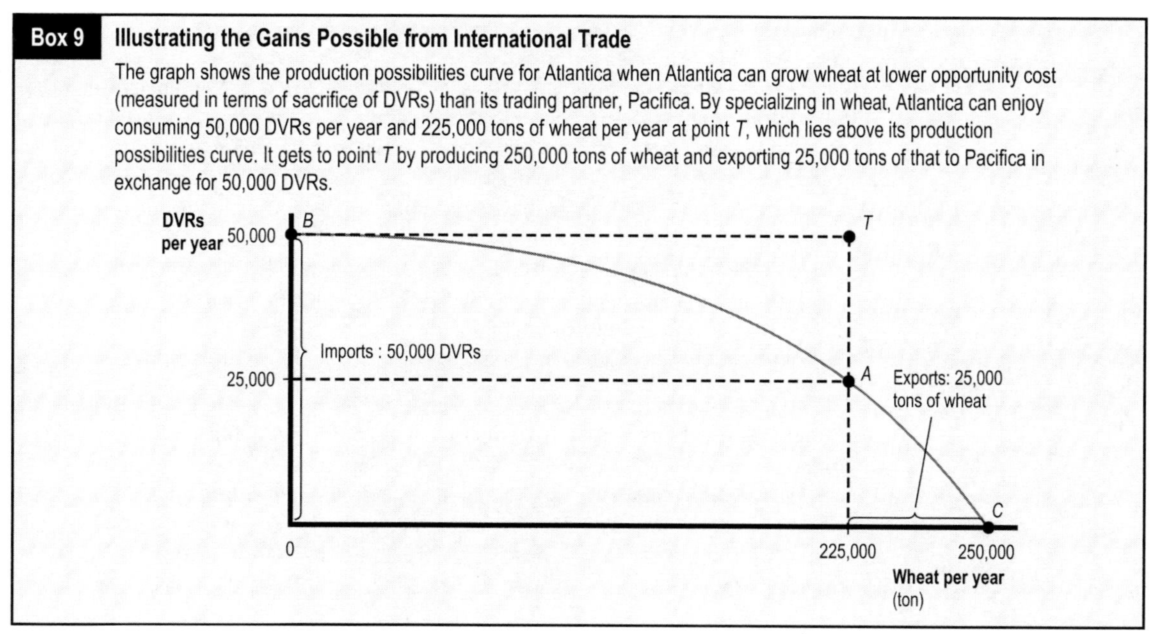

wheat. For example, an additional 25,000 DVRs per year at point *A* would require that Atlantica give up production of 225,000 tons of wheat. Each DVR would cost an average 9 tons of wheat if the nation reallocated resources to move from point *A* to point *B*.

Atlantica is now at point *A* on its production possibilities curve, where it grows 225,000 tons of wheat and makes 25,000 DVRs per year. Wouldn't it be nice to get to point *T*, where its citizens could enjoy 225,000 tons of wheat and 50,000 DVRs? Alas, that's not possible if Atlantica tries to produce both goods, as point *T* lies outside its production possibilities curve.

Suppose producers in the nation of Pacifica (where wheat costs more to produce than in Atlantica) will trade at the rate of one DVR for each one-half ton of wheat. Atlantica could then obtain DVRs through international trade at a much lower opportunity cost than is possible through domestic production.

Suppose now that Atlantica decides to specialize in wheat and uses all its resources to produce 250,000 tons per year at point *C*. It then exports 25,000 tons to Pacifica in exchange for DVRs. Because Pacifica is willing to trade at the rate of one-half ton of wheat for each DVR, the exported 25,000 tons of wheat buy 50,000 DVRs. By exporting 25,000 tons of wheat, Atlantica can therefore get to point *T*, where its citizens enjoy 225,000 tons of domestically grown wheat and 50,000 imported DVRs per year, even though no DVRs are domestically produced.

International trade is like magic! It allows a nation's citizens to enjoy consumption possibilities (like point *T*) that go beyond its production possibilities (like point *A*).

This simple example illustrates how the *principle of comparative advantage* applies to nations engaging in international trade. Citizens of a nation can gain consumption possibilities by specializing in goods that can be produced domestically at lower opportunity cost than that of its trading partners. There are *mutual gains* to trading partners when they specialize in producing items for which they enjoy a comparative advantage and then engage in international trade for other goods and services. Elsewhere in this text, we say more about the principle of comparative advantage and its implications for international trade.

This is a highly simplified example designed to illustrate the basic idea behind the gains from trade. In actuality, it's unlikely that a nation will completely specialize in the production of a single product when the law of increasing costs holds. For example, it's more likely that Atlantica will produce very few DVRs and import the bulk of them, and that Pacifica will produce some wheat but import the bulk of its supplies from Atlantica. Full specialization will occur only when production can take place at constant, rather than increasing, costs. Also, in actuality, goods aren't bartered for goods in the real world. Instead, currencies are exchanged among citizens and businesses of trading nations to engage in international transactions. Consumption possibilities expand over production possibilities as increased supplies of imported goods and services cause the prices of these items to fall. As this occurs, consumers in trading nations find that their incomes can be stretched further to buy more than would be possible in the absence of international trade. The mutual gains from international trade thereby contribute to higher living standards by allowing a nation's incomes to buy more than would otherwise be possible.

It's possible to determine the items for which producers in a nation enjoy a comparative advantage by delving into actual international trade transactions. If the exports of a product substantially exceed its imports in a nation, we can infer that the domestic producers have comparative advantage in that item. For example, in the 2004-2005 marketing year, United States producers marketed nearly 60 metric tons of wheat. Of this total, 29 million metric tons—nearly half the total output—was exported. In fact, U.S. producers export more wheat than any other country in the world. Its share of global wheat exports is about 29 percent. With highly efficient large farms in the Midwestern states, U.S. producers use capital-intensive methods to produce and harvest wheat, giving them a comparative advantage in its production over many foreign competitors. On the other hand, as of 2005, imported crude oil accounted for more than 60 percent of the total amount used in refineries in the United States, indicating that the U.S. doesn't have a comparative advantage in the production of crude oil. As of 2003-2005, other products the United States exported more than it imported included many chemicals, civilian aircraft and aircraft engines, and semiconductors, suggesting that U.S. producers had a comparative advantage in the production of those items. The United States imports more clothing than it exports and is unlikely to have a comparative advantage in production of apparel. Given its large exports of apparel, China most definitely has a comparative advantage in clothing production.

Scarcity and Trade-Offs

We deal every day with the trade-offs implied by scarcity. Both production possibilities for a society and options for us as individuals to spend our available income are limited over any given period. In the chapter Economics: What It's All About, we discuss the questions of what to produce, how to produce it, and to whom goods and services will be distributed. You can understand these questions better within the context of the constraints a nation faces. The problem of *what to produce* involves making decisions that eventually result in achievement of a particular production possibility. The problem of *how to produce it* affects the ability of participants in an economy to get to a point on their production possibilities curve. If efficient methods are employed to produce any given output and economic resources are fully utilized, then the maximum possible output of any one good, given the output of other goods, will be attained. Given current prices for goods and services, *who gets what is produced* depends on the way income is distributed among those of us in an economy. Naturally, the greater our income, the greater our options for consumption.

Summary

1. Production is the process of using economic resources to make goods and services available.
2. A production possibilities curve shows the maximum possible output of any one good that can be produced over a period of time with available economic resources and existing technology, given the output of other goods.
3. The law of increasing costs implies that the opportunity costs of extra production of any one good in any economy will increase as more and more specialized resources best suited for the production of other goods are reallocated away from their best use.
4. Not fully utilizing or mismanaging economic resources prevents the economy from achieving its full output potential and results in attainment of a point below the production possibilities curve.
5. Increased availability of labor, capital, and natural resources, as well as improvements in technology or in worker skills, can shift a nation's production possibilities curve outward.
6. A budget line shows the combinations of goods and services a consumer with limited income can purchase over a period, given the prices of the goods and services desired. The opportunity cost of consuming more of any one good is the quantity of the next best alternative good that is sacrificed.
7. A nation can gain consumption possibilities that exceed its production possibilities by engaging in international trade. This results when a nation specializes in goods and services that it can produce at lower opportunity cost than that of other nations and exports some of these goods and services in exchange for other items. A nation has a comparative advantage in the production of an item if it can produce it at lower opportunity cost than that of its trading partners. There are mutual gains from international trade when trading partners specialize in the production of items for which they enjoy a comparative advantage and then engage in international trade to obtain other items.

Concept Review

1. How are production possibilities influenced by technology and resource availability?
2. Explain how we would determine the opportunity cost of moving between two points on a production possibilities curve.
3. Explain why an economy that does not attain productive efficiency operates at a point below its production possibilities curve.
4. How can we use a production possibilities curve to show the impact of advances in technology and growth in resource availability on the economy?
5. How can trade allow us to consume combinations of goods and services that are above points on our production possibilities curve?

Problems and Applications

1. The United States is a rich and powerful nation with a skilled, productive labor force and a great deal of capital. Some less developed nations have few skilled workers and little capital. Why is scarcity an economic problem in rich and poor nations alike? (1)
2. Make a list of the economic resources required to operate a restaurant. How is the number of meals per day that can be served limited by available economic resources and current technology for meal preparation and service? (1)
3. The small nation whose annual production possibilities for food and clothing are illustrated in the table and graph in Box 1 receives a gift of new machines for use in clothing production and agriculture. The new machines allow the nation to produce twice as much food and clothing with the same number of workers and natural resources. Draw the new production possibilities curve for the nation, and show how the gift of capital expands its production possibilities. (1)

4. Referring again to Box 1, suppose the nation receives a gift of new agricultural machinery that doubles the maximum quantity of food that can be produced for any given quantity of clothing produced. Draw the new production possibilities curve, and show why the gift expands the production possibilities of the nation to allow it to consume more food *and* clothing. Shade in the new combinations of food and clothing made possible by the gift. 1, 4

5. A civil war erupts in the small nation whose production possibilities curve is shown in Box 1. The war results in the destruction of capital and natural resources, and causes casualties that reduce the supply of labor available for production of food and clothing. Show the impact of the war on the nation's production possibilities curve for food and clothing. 1, 4

6. Suppose the production possibilities curve for the production of trucks and cars in a two-product factory has a constant slope equal to –2 when weekly car production is plotted on the vertical axis and weekly truck production is plotted on the horizontal axis. Draw the production possibilities curve, and explain why the law of increasing costs doesn't hold for the production of cars and trucks in the factory. 1

7. Suppose you own and run a small business. You spend 40 hours per week managing the operation. By managing the business, you forgo your next best alternative, which is working at a job for someone else that pays $10 per hour. An accountant calculates all the money costs and revenues from the business and tells you you're making a $300 profit per week. However, the accountant doesn't include the opportunity cost of your time as part of the money costs because you don't incur any cash outlay to pay for your time. Does it make sense for you to continue in business? Explain your answer. 2

8. Imagine you're the manager of a small textile factory that has two product lines: flannel and corduroy. Some workers and some machines are specialized in the production of only one of these goods. The maximum amount of flannel that can be produced when 1,000 yards of corduroy are also produced is 1,500 yards per month, with 10,000 labor hours per month. You can't vary the number of machines or amount of floor space in the factory. Suppose you're currently producing at an efficient level. If monthly orders drop to 1,000 yards of corduroy and 1,000 yards of flannel, what could you do to reduce costs during the month? Explain your answer using a production possibilities curve. 2, 3

9. Your younger sister receives a weekly allowance of $20, which she spends entirely on nail polish and candy bars. Nail polish costs $4 per bottle, and candy bars are $1. Draw your sister's budget line. What is the opportunity cost of a bottle of nail polish? Would the opportunity cost of nail polish change if the prices of nail polish and candy bars doubled?

   Show how the budget line will shift for each of the following changes. Calculate the opportunity cost of each item for each of the changes.

   a. An increase in the weekly allowance to $24

   b. A decrease in the weekly allowance to $12

   c. A reduction in the price of a bottle of nail polish to $2

   d. An increase in the price of candy bars to $2

10. Suppose that each digital camera produced in the United States involves the sacrifice of 100 pounds of beef and that in Japan each digital camera produced involves the sacrifice of 50 pounds of beef. Use production possibilities curves to demonstrate how both Japan and the United States can gain from specializing in the production of one of these goods and engaging in international trade to obtain the other. 5

Production Possibilities in the U.S. Automobile Industry: Coping with Change

Since the mid-1990s, the major United States automobile producers, General Motors (GM), Ford, and Chrysler, have relied on the production of trucks and sport-utility vehicles (SUVs) for the bulk of their revenues and profits. The three companies invested billions of dollars to construct and modify plants to produce these large and profitable vehicles. By 2004 various types of trucks, including truck-based vehicles, such as SUVs, accounted for 62 percent of the output of the U.S. motor vehicle manufacturers.

In 2004 gasoline prices started to increase, and by 2008 prices more than doubled, from the levels that prevailed in 2000, to $4 a gallon. As the price of gasoline soared, sales of trucks and truck-based vehicles like SUVs plummeted. This was compounded in 2008 with the onset of a serious recession in the U.S. economy that reduced income and further reduced sales of vehicles produced by the Big Three American automotive companies. It became clear to the financially strapped companies that, to survive in the future, they would have to shift their productive capacity away from trucks and SUVs toward cars and more fuel-efficient utility vehicles. In 2008 and 2009, both GM and Chrysler had to ask Congress to approve government loans to allow them to pay their suppliers and avoid declaring bankruptcy. As of the spring of 2009, these two companies were still struggling and bankruptcy was a distinct possibility as a means to allow the companies to reorganize, so as to be more competitive. Ford did not ask for financial assistance from the government, in part because it had already taken measures to shift the production mix away from trucks and SUVs toward cars and more fuel-efficient trucks. Although the price of gasoline fell in 2009, it remained clear that future sales prospects for truck-based vehicles remained impaired and that significant change was required in the American automobile industry.

Although the problems of the U.S. automobile industry are complex, we can use a production possibilities curve to help understand some of the issues that must be confronted if the Big Three automobile manufacturers are to survive. The graph below shows production possibilities for two broad classes of vehicles for the U.S. companies—trucks (pickups, vans, and truck-based SUVs) and cars—with points for the product mix prevailing for each of the Big Three at the beginning of 2008.

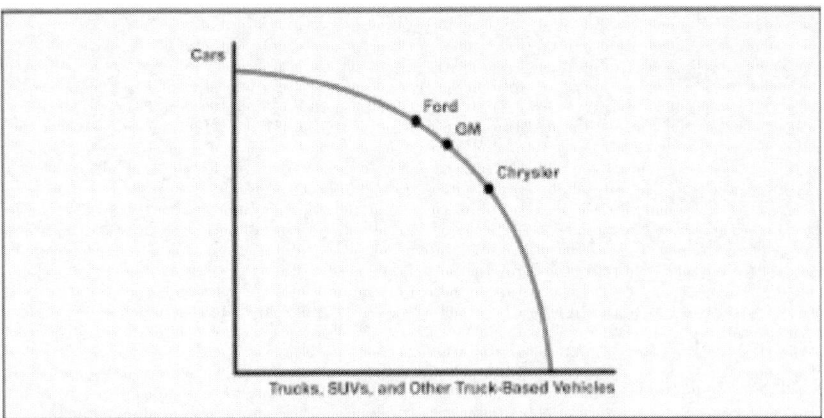

The mix of output for the companies varied between two-thirds trucks and 45 percent trucks. For example, Chrysler's North American production in plants located in the United States, Canada, and Mexico was two-thirds trucks and truck-based vehicles, and only one-third cars. In 2007 Chrysler's bestseller was the full-size Dodge Ram pickup, which accounted for nearly 20 percent of its total production! Naturally, when the price of gasoline went up and the recession hit (which hit the construction industry—one that uses a lot of pickup trucks—hard), sales of the Ram and other truck-based vehicles plummeted. The financial crisis in the United States at that time was also responsible for the decline in sales as many prospective buyers had trouble getting loans to purchase vehicles. In late 2008 sales of vehicles in the United States were down nearly 40 percent, compared to the same period a year earlier, and Chrysler, with its heavy mix of trucks, saw its sales plummet by nearly 50 percent.

As 2009 approached, Chrysler announced it would stop all production of both cars and trucks for at least one month and shut down all 30 of its North American plants. GM was in a slightly better position than Chrysler, with about half of its production allocated to trucks. Nonetheless, GM also idled about 30 percent of its productive capacity, reducing production by an estimated 250,000 vehicles. By mid-2009 both Chrysler and GM had declared bankruptcy, and were reorganizing as much smaller companies, with sharply reduced productive capacity.

Of the Big Three automobile manufacturers, Ford seemed to be in the best shape, because the company had planned in advance to shift the product mix away from truck-based vehicles to more fuel-efficient cars. Ford planned to reduce overall production in 2008, and to produce more cars and crossover SUVs by allocating more labor to production of cars while reducing labor allocated to truck-based vehicles. It also planned to convert some truck-producing plants to car-producing plants and to rapidly introduce new models with better fuel economy. Ford succeeded in dropping the share of truck-based vehicles in its product mix from 60 percent in 2004 to 45 percent in 2008.

Using the production possibilities curve to show the mix of production capacity, you can see that, in 2008, Ford was producing at a point corresponding to the greatest mix of cars, while Chrysler had the largest share of its productive capacity allocated to trucks. Given the slowdown in sales, each of the three producers was likely operating at a point below the respective points on their production possibilities curve in 2008 and 2009, indicating that significant labor and capital was idle in the industry. All three companies were planning to move further along their production possibilities curves in the future by changing the mix even more toward cars and by producing more fuel-efficient vehicles.

One decision the companies will also have to make in the future, if their sales decline and loss of market share to competing producers, such as Toyota, is permanent, is whether or not they want to reduce their productive capacity. If they choose to shut down plants and reduce the size of their labor force, the production possibilities curve for each of the three will shift inward.

The production possibilities curve is not only applicable to understanding societal problems relating to resource allocation and scarcity, but it is also relevant to understanding managerial problems faced on a day-to-day basis by business firms.

Personal Budgeting and the Opportunity Cost of Choices

Now that you understand the basic constraints the economy faces, let's focus on the constraints we as individuals face in satisfying our desires. Few of us have enough income to buy everything we want each month. Scarcity of both resources and time to satisfy all wants is a common personal problem. Most students have tight budgets that allow them to buy only a small portion of what they want. For example, suppose your parents give you a $100 monthly allowance that you spend entirely on gas and DVDs. The rest of your living expenses (such as room and board) are paid directly by your parents. In this simple example, you therefore have only two alternatives in which you're interested in spending your available income--gas and DVDs.

Suppose the price of gas is $2 per gallon and DVDs cost $10 each. It's now possible to derive the combinations of these two goods that you can afford with your $100 monthly income. The table shows five possible combinations of gas and DVDs you can buy if you spend all of your $100 monthly income on these two items. For example, it's feasible to consume 50 gallons of gas per month. However, because gas costs $2 per gallon, you'd spend all your monthly income on gas and forego the opportunity to buy DVDs. This option, labeled C_1, is plotted on the graph. The monthly quantity of gas is measured on the vertical axis, while the monthly quantity of DVDs is measured on the horizontal axis. You also have the opportunity to choose the option labeled C_5, where you'd be consuming 10 DVDs per month but would have no income left to buy gas.

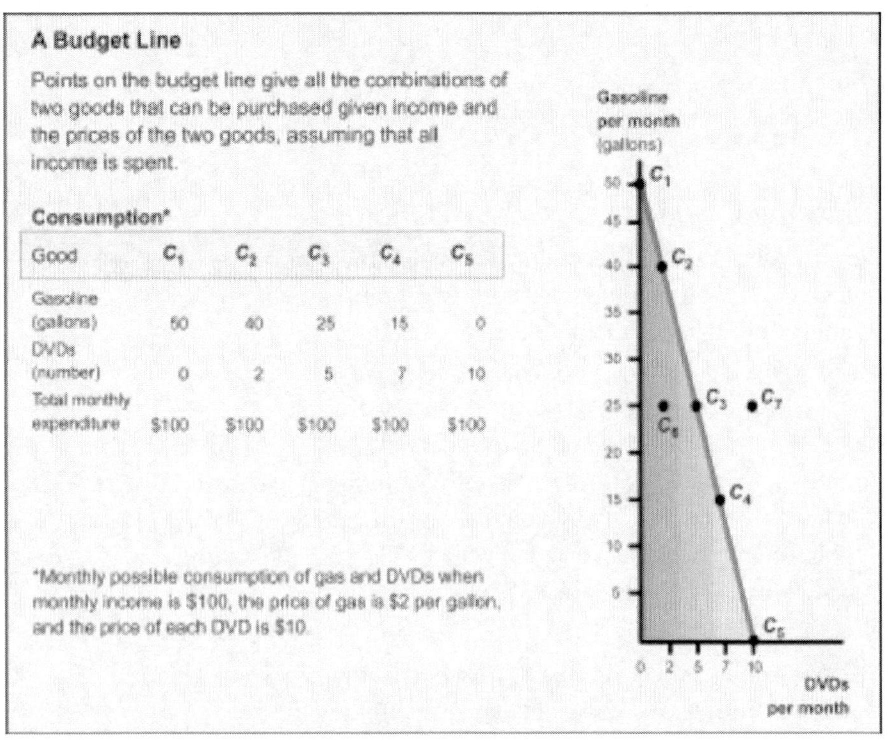

A Budget Line

Points on the budget line give all the combinations of two goods that can be purchased given income and the prices of the two goods, assuming that all income is spent.

Consumption*

Good	C_1	C_2	C_3	C_4	C_5
Gasoline (gallons)	50	40	25	15	0
DVDs (number)	0	2	5	7	10
Total monthly expenditure	$100	$100	$100	$100	$100

*Monthly possible consumption of gas and DVDs when monthly income is $100, the price of gas is $2 per gallon, and the price of each DVD is $10.

The options for spending your income corresponding to points C_2, C_3, and C_4 have also been plotted on the graph. The monthly *budget line* shows your opportunities to purchase two items, such as gas and DVDs, if you spend all your monthly income on these two items at their current prices. With your current income and at current prices, it's possible to buy all combinations of DVDs and gas on or below the budget line. Of course, if you choose a point below the line, you'll have some of your monthly income left over to save or spend on other items. If you choose a point like C_6, corresponding to 25 gallons of gas and two DVDs per month, you'll be spending $50 on gas and $20 on DVDs for a total monthly outlay of $70, leaving $30 to save or to spend on other items.

On the other hand, a point like C_7 is unattainable with your current monthly income, given the current prices of gas and DVDs. Point C_7 corresponds to 10 DVDs, which would cost $100, and 25 gallons of gas, which would cost $50. This combination is infeasible because it requires a monthly expenditure of $150, which exceeds your $100 income.

The budget line therefore shows certain combinations of items that are unattainable given your limited income and the prices of the items. The shaded area represents your monthly opportunities to purchase gas and DVDs. Of course, an increase in your income shifts the budget line outward, given the prices of the two items. To see this, recalculate your possible consumption options when your income increases to $200 per month. A decrease in the prices of both items would shift the curve outward by increasing the quantities of the items you could buy with your $100 monthly income. To see this, recalculate the points on your budget line when the price of gas is only $1 per gallon and the price of DVDs is $5. Conversely, a decrease in income or an increase in the prices of both items shifts the budget line inward. Inflation in the prices of goods consumed decreases the opportunities available to consumers with fixed money income. This is one of the harmful effects of inflation.

So what does the budget line tell you about opportunity costs? If you move along the budget line from C_1 to C_5, each extra DVD you buy will absorb $10 of your monthly income. Because the price of gas is $2 per gallon, each extra DVD involves the sacrifice of 5 gallons of gas. *The opportunity cost of each extra DVD is therefore always 5 gallons of gas at the current prices of these two items.*

In general the opportunity cost of a DVD or any other item depends on its price relative to the price of the item you give up. For example, if the price of DVDs were $10 each and the price of gas were $2 per gallon, the opportunity cost of each DVD would be 5 gallons of gas. If, instead, the price of DVDs were $20 each and the price of gas were $4 per gallon, the opportunity cost of DVDs would *still* be 5 gallons of gas. This might surprise you, because the money cost of units of both items went up. However, the opportunity cost of an item depends on the *quantity* of the alternative item you forego when you purchase more of the item you choose. When the price of gas is $4 and the price of a DVD is $20, each DVD you buy results in the sacrifice of 5 gallons of gas because you could have used the $20 to buy that amount of gas. Similarly, the opportunity cost of each gallon of gas is one-fifth of a DVD when the price of gas is $2 per gallon and the price of a DVD is $10. For each 5 gallons of gas you buy each month, you sacrifice the opportunity to buy one DVD.

Chapter 3

Market Transactions:

Basic Supply and Demand Analysis

Have you ever realized how much your life is influenced by prices? Your wardrobe, the kind of car you drive, and where you live were probably affected by the prices of the items available in the marketplace. Wouldn't you live in a better apartment or perhaps a better home if housing prices and interest rates to finance purchase of these items were lower? Who wouldn't drive a newer or better car if new car prices came tumbling down? Even your choice of a career is dependent on price—many students choose to enter fields such as engineering, law, or medicine, in part because of the price of the services of people with these skills.

Producers are also influenced by prices. For example, between 2001 and 2005, price per square foot of construction of houses, apartments, commercial and industrial buildings, and government facilities, such as schools, was rising. The rising prices increased profitability for general construction contractors, and more people were attracted into the industry to supply building services. Prices act as signals to producers, and they respond to price changes by increasing the allocation of resources to production of goods that consumers desire. Increased construction activity also affected employment opportunities for those engaged in various construction trades, such as carpentry, roofing, plumbing, painting, and electrical work. As the building industry grew, so did job opportunities and incomes for construction workers. In 2007 housing prices started to decline, and, as this occurred, building new homes became less profitable. The decline in housing prices decreased both job opportunities and incomes in the home-building industry from 2007 through 2009. As a result, construction of new homes declined.

In the chapter Production Possibilities and Opportunity Cost, you see how a production possibilities curve can show feasible options and the opportunity cost of changing from one option to another. In most economies today market prices influence the mix of products that gets produced over any given period. Market prices influence not only what we produce, but also how we choose to produce those products and to whom the products are distributed. For example, increases in the price of labor in agriculture have induced farmers in the United States to use mechanized means of both harvesting and planting their crops. Decreases in wages earned by unskilled workers in manufacturing and service industries in the United States since the 1970s have decreased the living standards of unskilled workers without a college degree relative to workers who do have such a degree.

This chapter introduces supply and demand analysis of market transactions, which shows how prices are established by the competition among buyers for goods and services offered by competing sellers. In addition to influencing choices, market prices play a vital role in coping with the problems of scarcity because they ration available goods and services.

Concept Preview

After reading this chapter, you should be able to

1. Discuss the purposes and functions of markets.
2. Explain how a demand curve illustrates the law of demand and distinguish between a change in demand and a change in quantity demanded.
3. Show how a supply curve illustrates the law of supply and distinguish between a change in supply and a change in quantity supplied.
4. Describe the conditions required for market equilibrium and locate the equilibrium point on a supply and demand diagram.
5. Explain the consequences of shortages and surpluses in markets and how prices adjust in a free and unregulated competitive market to eliminate shortages or surpluses.
6. Show how changes in demand and supply affect market equilibrium.

Markets: Purposes and Functions

No matter how independent we may be in spirit, none of us is truly self-sufficient. Think of how we rely on others for our basic needs. We go to the supermarket for food. A local power company provides our electricity. The road we drive on is built and maintained by the government and financed with taxes. Few people, even farmers, produce all the food and fiber they need to feed and clothe themselves.

Even those of us who have the skill to grow our own food, make our own clothes, build our own homes, and repair our own cars rarely, if ever, find it in our interest to be self-sufficient. Instead, we benefit from a complex division of labor and specialization in economic activities. Specialized firms and agencies provide particular goods and services to consumers, investors, and governments. In order to purchase these goods, buyers seek out sellers in markets. A market's purpose is to provide information on the goods and services sellers want to sell and buyers want to buy.

This chapter introduces you to supply and demand analysis of market transactions, which shows how prices are established by the competition among buyers for goods offered by competing sellers. Market prices play a vital role in coping with the problem of scarcity because they ration available amounts of goods and services.

1 A **market** is an arrangement through which buyers and sellers meet or communicate in order to trade goods or services. It's a way in which buyers and sellers can do business together. For example, a local electronics store is a place that displays the range of computers, digital cameras, DVD players, and cell phones offered by various manufacturers. A flea market has both buyers and sellers: One person can offer to sell a used bicycle or car stereo and, at the same time, look for old records or find a couch.

Many market transactions are conducted without buyers and sellers actually meeting. For example, buyers can look through catalogs and then order merchandise online or by telephone, without face-to-face contact with sellers. Buyers can also hire intermediaries to carry out transactions for them, such as travel agents, who will check the fares of all airlines and make the best deals for their clients, as will most Internet travel services.

As a means of communication between buyers and sellers, the Internet has revolutionized markets. Consumers routinely order merchandise online from Amazon.com and a host of other retailers. Searches can easily be run using the services of such companies as Google to locate sellers of items we want to buy. Businesses also use the Internet regularly to order materials, equipment, and supplies. eBay has become an online flea market for used goods.

Supply and demand analysis explains how prices are established in markets through competition among buyers and sellers and how those prices affect quantities traded. In a *competitive* or *free* market, many sellers compete for sales to many buyers who compete for available goods and services. In such a market, all those who wish to sell and all those who wish to buy can do so.

To analyze the way markets operate, you first must understand the concepts of supply and demand.

Demand

The amount of an item buyers actually purchase in a market over a given period is influenced by a number of important determinants:

1. Its price.
2. Buyers' available income.

3. Buyers' wealth (the value of assets such as stocks, bonds, homes and other real estate, and business property).

4. Expectations of future price changes.

5. The prices of alternative items.

6. Tastes or current fashions.

7. The population served by the market.

In analyzing the behavior of buyers in markets, we concentrate on the effect of each of these determinants, one at a time. We pay special attention to the relationship between the price of an item and the quantities buyers purchase. The quantity demanded of an item is the amount that buyers are willing and able to purchase over a period at a certain price, *given all other influences on their decision to buy.*

Demand is a relationship between the price of an item and the quantity demanded. The term *demand* as used in economics is not a fixed number. It signifies how the quantity buyers purchase varies with price, assuming that *all other influences on the amount buyers buy other than the price of the item* are held fixed. For example, the demand for cars over a year indicates how the annual quantity demanded varies as the price of cars changes, *other things being equal.* The other things held constant are all influences on the decision to buy *other than* the price of cars, such as income available for spending, wealth, or consumer preferences. Similarly, the demand for subway rides in a city isolates the relationship between the price of a ride and the number of rides demanded over a given period.

The Law of Demand and the Market Demand Curve

The law of demand states that, in general, other things being equal, the lower the price of a good, the greater the quantity of that good buyers will purchase over a given period. Conversely, the law implies that buyers will purchase less of a good over any given period if its price increases while nothing else changes. The law is relevant to all goods and services. For example, the lower the price of subway rides, other things being equal, the greater the quantity demanded. Lower prices make goods more attractive to us as consumers and increase our willingness to buy. To see this, just visit a store that's running a sale and watch how much more quickly goods leave the shelf!

The law of demand can be derived as an implication of an economic model based on rational behavior. It's also generally supported by empirical evidence. Other things being equal, lower prices induce us to buy more of an item over a period because we enjoy additional net gains that weren't possible at the higher prices.

Examine your own behavior as a buyer to convince yourself that the law of demand is quite reasonable. If you're like most people, you buy more electronic equipment, more clothing, and more of most items over any given period when their prices decline and nothing else changes. When the prices of these items rise, you tend to buy less of them. If the price of a movie increased from $8 to $12, you'd probably attend movies less often and look for other forms of entertainment. Other consumers like you behave the same way.

2 A demand schedule is a table that shows how an item's quantity demanded would vary with price, other things being equal. The table in Box 1 shows a hypothetical demand schedule for grade A eggs sold per week in a local farmers' market. The first column of the table shows possible prices per dozen eggs. The quantity demanded, shown in the second column, represents the weekly amount of eggs that buyers are willing to purchase at each price. The schedule is based on the assumption that there's no change in any other demand influence except price. The schedule shows a number of possible outcomes in the market. The actual quantity purchased over the period depends on the price of eggs, given all the other determinants of the amount buyers will buy.

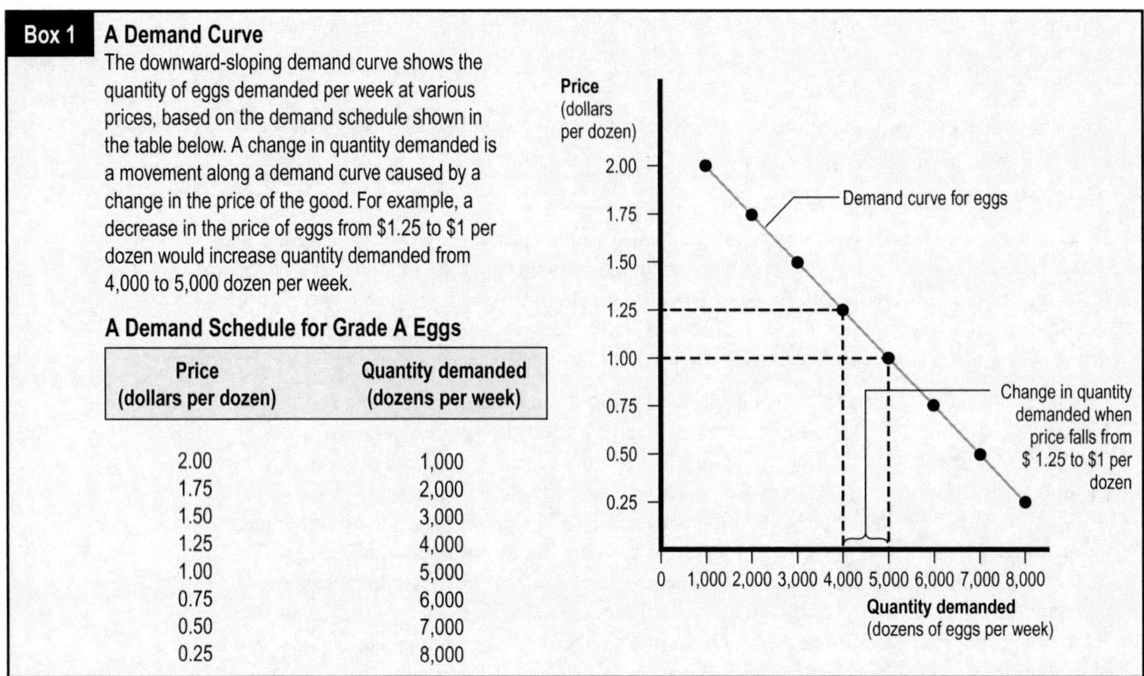

Box 1 A Demand Curve

The downward-sloping demand curve shows the quantity of eggs demanded per week at various prices, based on the demand schedule shown in the table below. A change in quantity demanded is a movement along a demand curve caused by a change in the price of the good. For example, a decrease in the price of eggs from $1.25 to $1 per dozen would increase quantity demanded from 4,000 to 5,000 dozen per week.

A Demand Schedule for Grade A Eggs

Price (dollars per dozen)	Quantity demanded (dozens per week)
2.00	1,000
1.75	2,000
1.50	3,000
1.25	4,000
1.00	5,000
0.75	6,000
0.50	7,000
0.25	8,000

The data in the hypothetical demand schedule indicate an inverse relationship between price and quantity demanded. When price goes down, the quantity demanded goes up. For example, at a price of $2 per dozen, the quantity of eggs demanded per week is only 1,000 dozen. At a price of $1.50 per dozen, quantity demanded is 3,000 dozen eggs per week.

A demand curve is a graph of the data comprised by a demand schedule. The graph in Box 1 shows the weekly demand curve for eggs by plotting the data from the table. Price is represented by points on the vertical axis, while quantity demanded is represented by points on the horizontal axis. To see how the curve is plotted, look at the demand schedule. Note that, if the price of grade A eggs is $1 per dozen, the quantity demanded is 5,000 dozen per week. A horizontal line drawn from the point corresponding to $1 on the price axis intersects the demand curve at the point that corresponds to 5,000 dozen eggs per week on the horizontal axis.

The downward slope of the demand curve reflects the law of demand. It's also useful to interpret points on a demand curve as indicating how the willingness of buyers to pay varies with the quantity of an item actually available in a market over a period of time. The demand curve indicates that the smaller the amount of eggs offered for sale each month, the more buyers are willing to pay. Conversely, the greater the amount of eggs available, the less buyers are willing to pay.

You can see the relationship between quantity available and price by examining your own experience in markets. If you've ever bought a car, you know that, during periods in which car dealers have few cars in stock, buyers are willing to pay higher prices. This is because buyers who are willing and able to pay the price for cars compete with one another for those available. They're willing to pay more rather than lose the opportunity to buy to a competing buyer.

Changes in Relative Price

The price of an item is usually measured as a sum of money. However, the money price of an item isn't always the best indication of what we must give up to obtain a unit of the item, because the purchasing power of money can change over time. For example, when an average of the prices of all the goods available in an economy increases by 5 percent over a year, each dollar will buy on average a smaller *quantity* of goods. This means that the purchasing power of the dollar is less.

A change in relative price of a good is an increase or decrease in the price of that good relative to the average change in the prices of all goods. The relative price of a good may not always change when its money price changes. For example, suppose an average of the money prices of all goods goes up by 3 percent over a year. If the money price of cars also goes up by that amount, the relative price of cars will be unchanged. If college tuition increases by 10 percent over the same year, its relative price will have risen because its money price has increased by a percentage that exceeds the average. Similarly, if the money price of athletic shoes increases by only 1 percent, the relative price of athletic shoes will have fallen over the year even though the money price has gone up.

When the purchasing power of money isn't constant, changes in relative prices of goods measure changes in the opportunity cost of a purchase better than changes in money prices. Strictly speaking, the law of demand expresses a relationship between changes in the *relative price* of a good and resulting changes in the quantities demanded.

Changes in Quantity Demanded

In general, the demand curve is *downward-sloping*. The negative slope reflects the inverse relationship between price and quantity demanded according to the law of demand. Although the demand curve in Box 1 has been drawn as a straight line, it could also be curvilinear. Along the demand curve, quantity demanded increases as the price of the good decreases. A change in quantity demanded is a change in the amount of a good buyers are willing and able to buy in response to a change in the price of the good. *A change in quantity demanded is represented by a movement along a given demand curve caused by an increase or decrease in the price of the good.*

For example, for the demand curve depicted in Box 1, an increase in the price of eggs from $1 to $1.25 per dozen would result in a decrease in weekly quantity demanded from 5,000 dozen to 4,000 dozen. The 1,000-dozen decline in the quantity buyers are willing to purchase as the price of eggs increases is called a *decrease in quantity demanded.* Similarly, if the price declined from $1 to $0.75 per dozen, there would be an *increase in quantity demanded* from 5,000 dozen to 6,000 dozen per week.

Changes in Demand

As we observed earlier, the relationship between the price of a good and the quantity of the good demanded over a given period also depends on such influences as income available for spending, wealth, prices of related goods, expectations of future prices, consumer preferences, and the number of buyers in the market. The quantity of a good that consumers are willing and able to buy at any given price changes if any one of these influences changes. A change in demand is a change in the relationship between the price of a good and the quantity demanded caused by a change in something other than the price of the good.

A change in demand implies a movement of an entire demand curve for a good. A new demand schedule must be drawn up, because the quantity demanded by consumers *at each price* changes. *(Be careful not to confuse a change in demand with a change in quantity demanded. A change in demand is a response to a change in a demand influence other than the price of the good, while a change in quantity demanded is a response to a change in a good's own price.)*

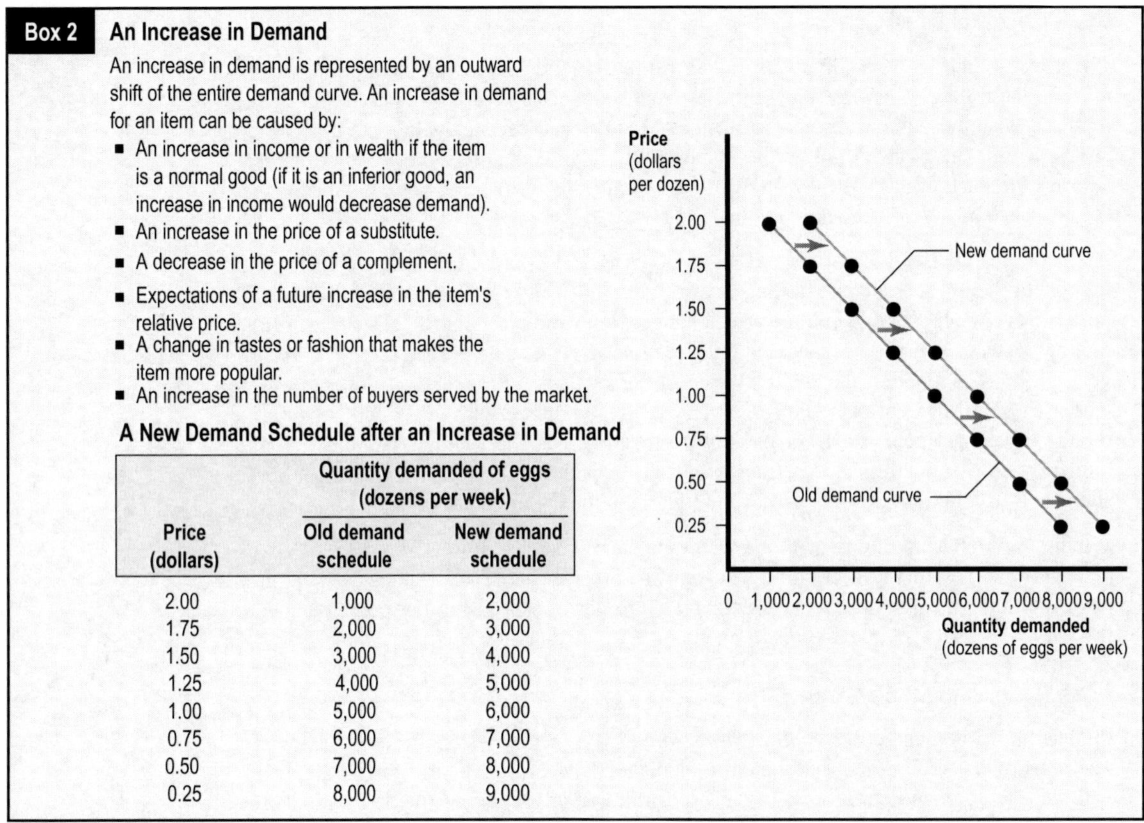

Box 2 An Increase in Demand

An increase in demand is represented by an outward shift of the entire demand curve. An increase in demand for an item can be caused by:

- An increase in income or in wealth if the item is a normal good (if it is an inferior good, an increase in income would decrease demand).
- An increase in the price of a substitute.
- A decrease in the price of a complement.
- Expectations of a future increase in the item's relative price.
- A change in tastes or fashion that makes the item more popular.
- An increase in the number of buyers served by the market.

A New Demand Schedule after an Increase in Demand

Price (dollars)	Quantity demanded of eggs (dozens per week): Old demand schedule	Quantity demanded of eggs (dozens per week): New demand schedule
2.00	1,000	2,000
1.75	2,000	3,000
1.50	3,000	4,000
1.25	4,000	5,000
1.00	5,000	6,000
0.75	6,000	7,000
0.50	7,000	8,000
0.25	8,000	9,000

The table in Box 2 shows not only the old demand schedule, but also a new demand schedule resulting from an increase in demand. You'll notice that the quantity demanded in the new schedule is greater than the quantity demanded in the old schedule at *each possible price*. The graph uses the data in the adjacent table to plot the new demand curve on the same set of axes as the old demand curve. The increase in demand is represented by a shift *outward* of the demand curve.

The graph in Box 3 illustrates a decrease in demand as an inward shift of the entire demand curve. At each possible price, the quantity demanded by consumers declines. Note that the new demand curve need not be parallel to the old demand curve.

Using logic and observation, we can make hypotheses about the possible impact of changes in various influences on the demand for a good:

1. *Changes in consumer income*. An increase in available income increases the *ability* of consumers to buy an item. Increases in income tend to increase the demand for most goods, while decreases in income tend to decrease the demand for most goods.

Although the demand for most goods increases as income goes up, there are some exceptions. The demand for less expensive cuts of meat, low-quality clothing, and secondhand furniture declines for many people as their income goes up. Goods whose demand declines as income increases are called inferior goods. Goods whose demand increases when income goes up are called normal goods.

2. *Changes in wealth*. Wealth is the net accumulated savings in a nation. Wealth includes such assets as real estate, stocks and bonds, money in the bank, and other financial assets

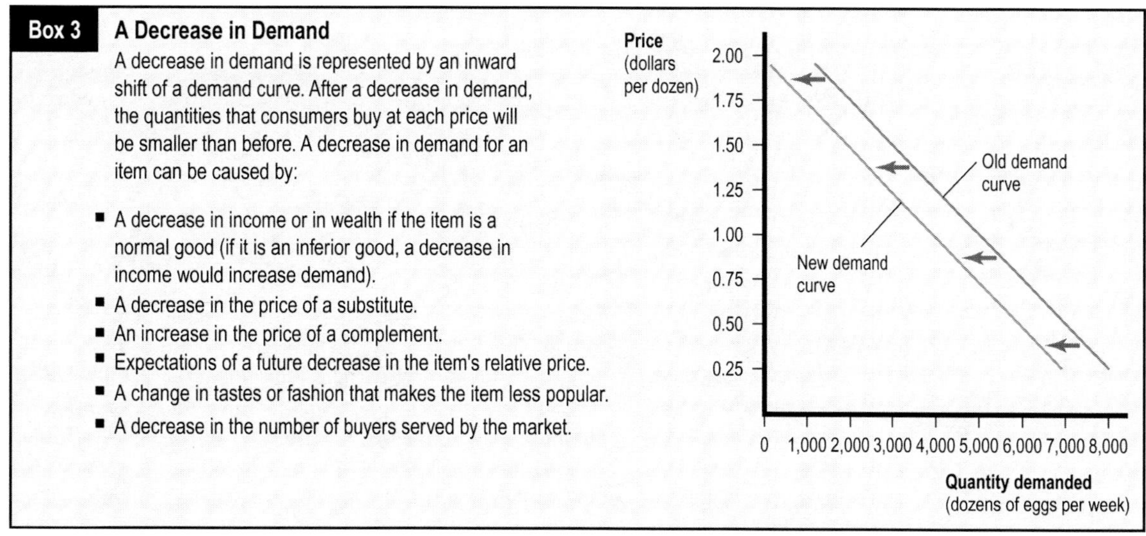
Box 3
A Decrease in Demand
A decrease in demand is represented by an inward shift of a demand curve. After a decrease in demand, the quantities that consumers buy at each price will be smaller than before. A decrease in demand for an item can be caused by:
■ A decrease in income or in wealth if the item is a normal good (if it is an inferior good, a decrease in income would increase demand).
■ A decrease in the price of a substitute.
■ An increase in the price of a complement.
■ Expectations of a future decrease in the item's relative price.
■ A change in tastes or fashion that makes the item less popular.
■ A decrease in the number of buyers served by the market.
Price (dollars per dozen)
2.00
1.75
1.50
1.25
1.00
0.75
0.50
0.25
Old demand curve
New demand curve
0 1,000 2,000 3,000 4,000 5,000 6,000 7,000 8,000
Quantity demanded
(dozens of eggs per week)

such as mutual funds. Declines in real estate values and in the values of stocks in 1990 and in 2008 caused a decrease in wealth that made many people cut back on spending and reduced the demand for such goods as new homes, furniture, and cars.

Some goods are relatively insensitive to wealth changes. Demand for bathroom tissue, for example, is unlikely to be affected by changes in wealth. The demand for other goods may actually increase in response to a decline in wealth. For example, people whose wealth declines may increase their demand for cars in the midprice range because they can no longer afford luxury cars.

3. *Changes in the prices of other goods.* Our willingness to buy a particular item also depends on the prices of related items. Alternatives, items that serve a purpose similar to that of a given item are **substitutes** for that item. An increase in the price of bagels is likely to increase the demand for English muffins because you can substitute English muffins for bagels at breakfast. Conversely, a decrease in the price of bagels may decrease the demand for English muffins. Similarly, an increase in the price of off-campus housing near your school may increase the demand for dormitory rooms.

The demand for a good can also be influenced by a change in the price of its complements. Complements are goods whose use together enhances the satisfaction a consumer obtains from each of them. For example, a decrease in the price of DVDs is likely to increase the demand for DVD players because these two goods complement each other. Similarly, if the price of gas goes up significantly, the demand for cars may go down because cars and gas are complements.

4. *Changes in expectations of future prices.* The demand for an item also depends on expectations buyers have about future events. In particular, if you as a buyer expect the price of an item to increase next week, you're likely to buy more of the item this week. If an item can be stored, as is the case for shampoo or socks, you'll increase your demand and stock up. Expectations of future price increases therefore tend to shift current demand curves outward. By the same token, expectations of price declines for an item tend to decrease current demand. If you expect the price of personal computers to decline next month, you'll be less willing to buy a PC this month. The expectation of a price decline therefore tends to decrease current demand and shift the demand curve for the product inward.

5. *Changes in tastes or fashion.* The general appeal of an item to buyers can change from time to time. If your taste for an item changes, your demand for it may decrease because you're less willing to buy it at any price. For example, the demand for long-playing records has decreased in recent years as you and other buyers have been attracted by the superior sound quality of CDs. You're also well aware of the influence of fashion on the demand for clothing. As styles change, you become more reluctant to buy certain items no matter how low the price. Even at a price of only 25 cents, you're not likely to buy a pair of plaid polyester pants unless you're planning to attend a costume party.

6. *Changes in the number of buyers served by the market.* The total quantity of any item demanded at any price also depends on the *number* of buyers interested in buying the item at that price. Higher population tends to be associated with increases in demand for goods. The number of buyers can also change when buyers in foreign countries become willing and able to purchase an item. For example, if Europeans become more willing and able to buy American cars, the demand for them will increase, other things being equal. A breakdown of trade barriers allowing U.S. firms to sell more beef in Japan will increase the demand for U.S. beef. An increase in the number of buyers in a market tends to increase demand, shifting the demand curve outward. A decrease in the number of buyers in a market tends to decrease the demand for a good, shifting the demand curve inward.

In addition to the influences we've just examined, the demand for particular goods can be influenced by weather, demographic trends, or government subsidies or taxes. For example, a cold winter can increase the demand for sleds and warm clothing. An increase in the proportion of Americans over the age of 65 has been increasing the demand for retirement residences and nursing homes.

Supply

The quantity of a good or service sellers are willing to sell in a market is affected by a number of important influences:

1. Its price.
2. Current prices of inputs needed to produce and market the good.
3. Current technology available to produce and market the good.
4. Prices of other goods that can be produced with inputs used or owned by the sellers.
5. Expectations about future prices.
6. The number of sellers serving the market.

In analyzing the quantity of a good made available for sale in a given period, we must isolate the effects of each of the separate influences. We'll pay special attention to the influence of price on the quantity sellers are willing to sell. The quantity supplied is the quantity of a good sellers are willing and able to make available in the market over a given period at a certain price, *other things being equal.* In this case the *other things* being held equal are all the previously listed supply influences other than the price of the good itself.

The concept of supply as used in economics is a relationship between the price of an item and the quantity supplied. Like demand, supply is not a fixed quantity. Instead, it signifies how the quantity sellers offer varies with price. The amount sellers bring to the market over any given period depends on the price of the product and the other supply influences.

The Law of Supply and the Market Supply Curve

3 The price is the payment a seller receives for each unit of a good sold. Just as changes in relative price influence incentives to buy a good, so do changes in relative

price influence incentives to sell a good. Naturally, the higher the price per unit of a good, other things being equal, the greater the potential gain from supplying it. The law of supply states that, in general, other things being equal, the higher the price of a good, the greater the quantity of that good sellers are willing and able to make available over a given period.

The law of supply is an implication of a model based on the assumption that sellers seek to maximize net gains from their activities. The law represents a hypothesis that is widely supported by empirical evidence. Let's sketch out the idea underlying the law of supply by using an example. Over any given period, say a week, there are a given number of suppliers of stone-washed denims in the United States. Each supplier can make only a certain number of pairs of jeans available. Some inputs, such as factory space and machinery, can't easily be increased over such a short period. As sellers try to make more jeans available by hiring more labor and increasing other inputs that can be more easily obtained, their operations become less efficient. Workers overutilize machines, which tends to make them break down more often. As the limit of productive capacity is approached, the costs per pair of jeans tend to rise, as does the marginal cost of making the jeans available to prospective buyers. These increasing marginal costs imply that sellers are unwilling to make more stone-washed denims available unless higher prices prevail to cover their increasing costs. Unless prices rise, sellers can't enjoy a net gain (profit) from producing more jeans. At higher prices each seller is likely to want to make more pairs of jeans available over a given period.

The table in Box 4 provides hypothetical data for the price and quantity of eggs supplied in a local farmers' market each week. (Other supply influences are assumed not to change as price changes.) The data constitute the supply schedule, which shows how quantity supplied is related to the price. The first column of the table shows possible prices per dozen eggs. The second column shows the quantities supplied per week at each possible price. The data indicate a direct relationship between price and quantity supplied: the higher the price, the greater the quantity supplied. For example, as the price of eggs increases from $1 to $1.25 per dozen, the weekly quantity supplied increases from 5,000 dozen to 6,000 dozen.

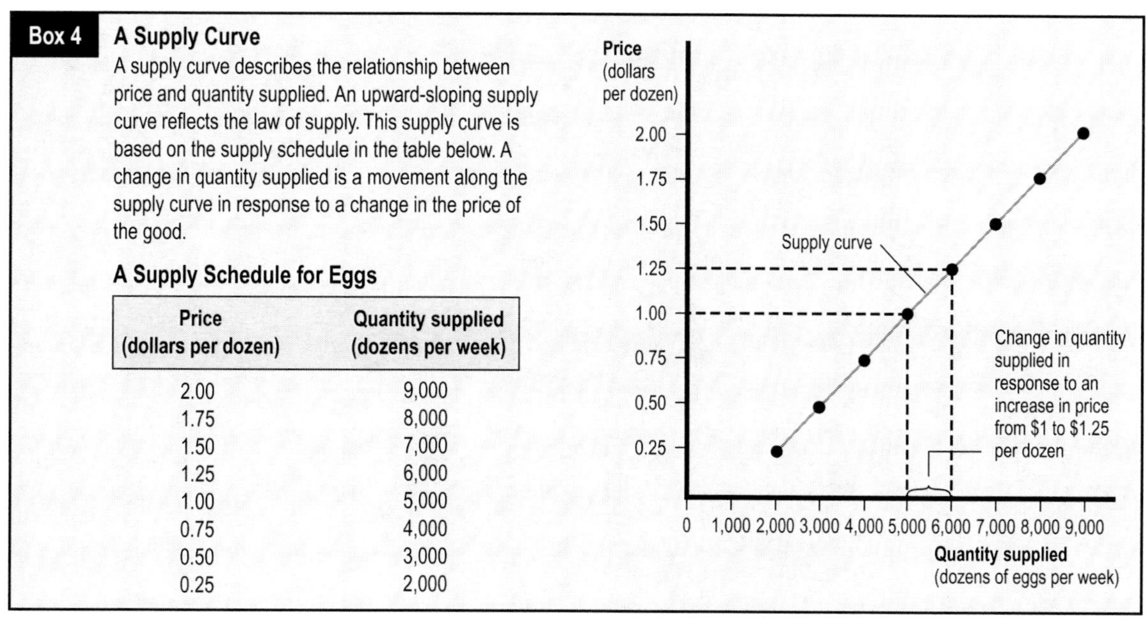

Box 4 **A Supply Curve**

A supply curve describes the relationship between price and quantity supplied. An upward-sloping supply curve reflects the law of supply. This supply curve is based on the supply schedule in the table below. A change in quantity supplied is a movement along the supply curve in response to a change in the price of the good.

A Supply Schedule for Eggs

Price (dollars per dozen)	Quantity supplied (dozens per week)
2.00	9,000
1.75	8,000
1.50	7,000
1.25	6,000
1.00	5,000
0.75	4,000
0.50	3,000
0.25	2,000

A supply curve is a graph of the data from a supply schedule that shows how quantity supplied varies with price. The graph in Box 4 plots the weekly supply curve for eggs based on the data in the table. Price is plotted on the vertical axis, while quantity supplied corresponds to points on the horizontal axis. For example, if the price were $2 per dozen, suppliers would be willing to make 9,000 dozen eggs available to the market. To see this, find the point on the price axis corresponding to $2 and draw a horizontal line across to the supply curve. Then draw a vertical line to the quantity axis that will intersect this axis at a quantity supplied of 9,000 dozen eggs per week. Assume that if the price fell below 25 cents per dozen, no one would be willing to sell eggs, so the quantity supplied would fall to zero. Understandably, sellers require a minimum price to cover their costs before they'll make goods available to buyers.

Note that you can also interpret points on a supply curve as indicating the price sellers will accept to make each possible quantity available to buyers. The greater the quantity buyers want to purchase, the higher the price necessary to induce sellers to make the desired quantity available.

Changes in Quantity Supplied

The upward slope of the supply curve reflects the law of supply. As the price increases, the quantity supplied over a period goes up. A change in quantity supplied is a change in the amount sellers are willing to sell over a period in response to a change in the price of the good. Changes in quantity supplied represent movements along a given supply curve in response to price changes while all other factors affecting the willingness of sellers to sell are unchanged. For example, if the price of eggs declined from $2 to $1.75 per dozen, there would be a *decrease in quantity supplied* and the quantity sellers would make available to the market would decline from 9,000 dozen to 8,000 dozen per week. Similarly, if the price increased from $1 to $1.25 per dozen, there would be an *increase in quantity supplied* as sellers would be willing to increase the quantity available for sale from 5,000 dozen to 6,000 dozen per week.

Changes in Supply

A change in supply is a change in the relationship between the price of a good and the quantity supplied in response to a change in a supply determinant other than the price of the good. A change in supply implies a shift of the entire supply curve. A new supply schedule must be drawn up because the quantity supplied by sellers at each price will change. For example, in the table in Box 5, a change in supply means that the data in the second column will change.

Among the important changes in economic conditions that can cause changes in supply are the following:

1. *Changes in the prices of the inputs necessary to produce and sell a good.* The possible profit at any given price depends on the prices a seller must pay for the economic resources to produce a good. Increases in input prices and costs associated with selling the good result in less profit for selling any given quantity. This decreases the supply of the good. Conversely, a decrease in input prices increases the profitability of selling the good and results in an increase in supply. Suppose, for example, that there's an increase in the price of chicken feed. This is likely to decrease the willingness of egg producers to make eggs available at a given price because it is now more expensive to produce any given quantity of eggs. The table in Box 5 shows that the quantity supplied *at each price* is now less than was the case when the old supply schedule prevailed. The graph in Box 5 plots the new supply curve alongside the old one. The new supply curve, corresponding to the data in the table, is closer to the vertical axis at each possible price. A *decrease in supply* is therefore represented by an *inward* shift of the entire supply curve. Similarly, an *increase in supply* is represented by an *outward* shift of the entire supply curve, illustrated by the graph in Box 6. Note that the new supply curves do not have to be parallel to the old ones.

Box 5 A Decrease in Supply

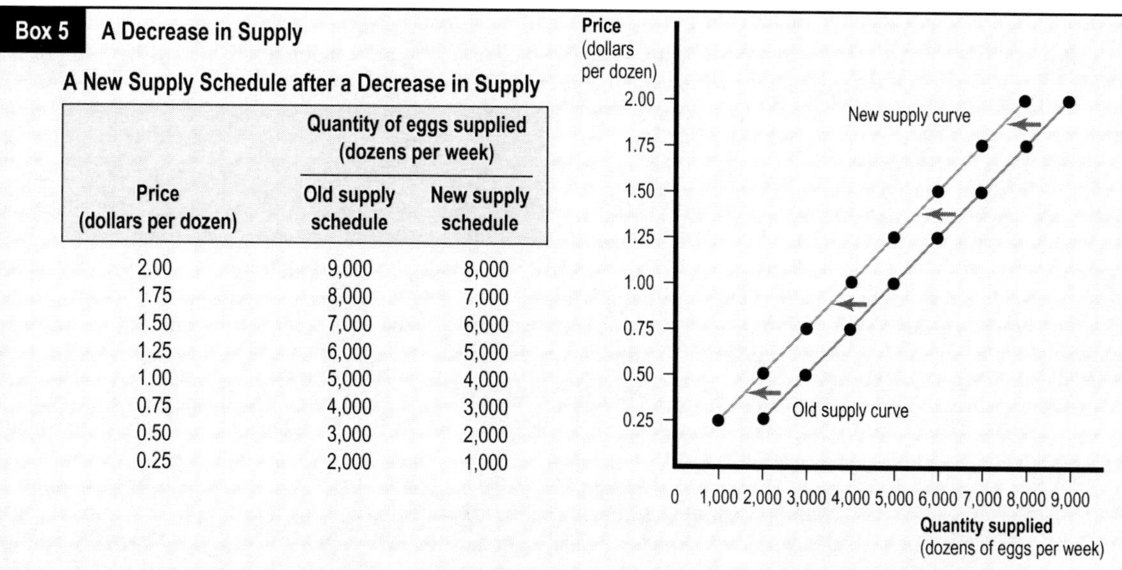

A New Supply Schedule after a Decrease in Supply

Price (dollars per dozen)	Quantity of eggs supplied (dozens per week)	
	Old supply schedule	New supply schedule
2.00	9,000	8,000
1.75	8,000	7,000
1.50	7,000	6,000
1.25	6,000	5,000
1.00	5,000	4,000
0.75	4,000	3,000
0.50	3,000	2,000
0.25	2,000	1,000

A decrease in supply is represented by an inward shift of the supply curve. A change in supply of an item can be caused by:

- A change in the prices of inputs used to produce it: an increase in input prices decreases supply, while a decrease in input prices increases supply.
- A change in technology: an improvement in technology increases supply, while the unlikely event of a deterioration in technology (caused by some catastrophe) would decrease supply.
- A change in the prices of other items: an increase in the relative price of an alternative item that can be produced with the same resources decreases supply of the first item, while a decrease in the relative price of the alternative item would increase supply of the first item.
- A change in the number of sellers serving the market: a decrease in the number of sellers decreases supply, while an increase in the number of sellers increases supply.

Box 6 An Increase in Supply

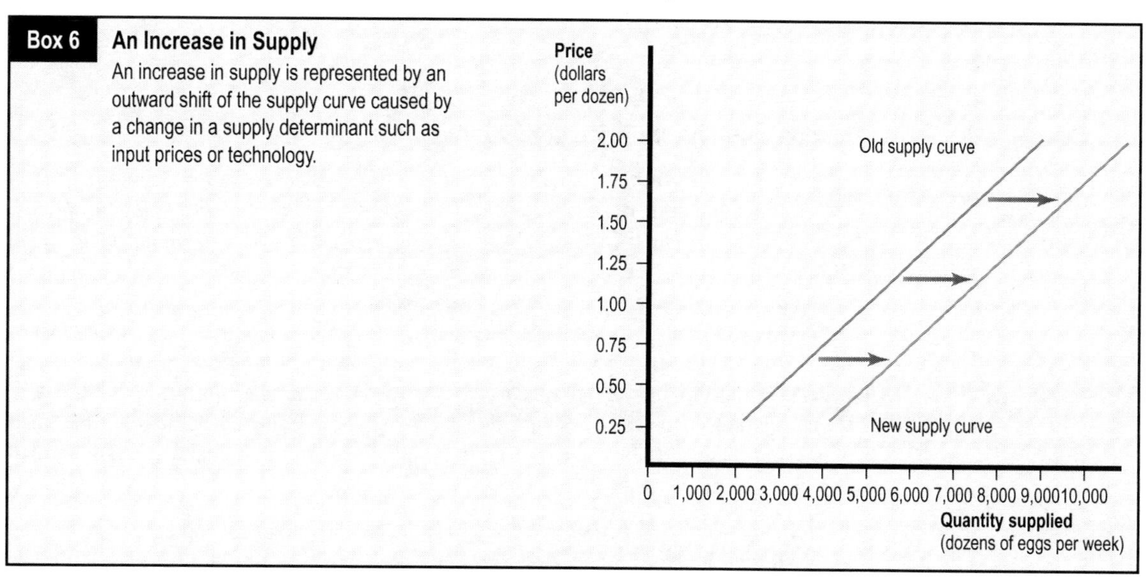

An increase in supply is represented by an outward shift of the supply curve caused by a change in a supply determinant such as input prices or technology.

2. *Changes in the technology available to produce a good.* Improvements in technology tend to increase the output from economic resources used to produce a good. Assuming that input prices are unchanged, advances in technology lower the cost per unit of output and tend to increase the profit possible from selling the good at various prices. For example, an improvement in the technology of producing CD players lowers the unit and marginal costs of making CD players available. The lower costs increase the potential profit and thus encourage existing sellers to supply more CD players while attracting new sellers to the market. Improvements in technology shift the supply curve to the right, as you can see in Box 6. Similarly, improvements in technology and innovations allowing individuals to inexpensively download MP3 files increases the supply of recordings available online, through such services as iTunes. And, as improved technology allows the development of MP3 players, such as the iPod, at lower cost per unit, the supply of both MP3 players and online music services increases.

3. *Changes in the prices of other goods that can be produced with the seller's resources.* The opportunity cost of producing and selling any one good is the sacrifice of the opportunity to sell some other good. Changes in the prices of alternative goods change the opportunity cost of producing a given good, resulting in changes in its supply. For example, given the price of T-shirts, an increase in the price of sweatshirts could decrease the supply of T-shirts if manufacturers use their facilities to produce more sweatshirts and fewer T-shirts. This would shift the supply curve for T-shirts to the left. Similarly, a decrease in the price of sweatshirts could increase the supply of T-shirts, shifting the supply curve for this item to the right.

4. *Changes in the number of sellers serving the market.* Other things being equal, an increase in the number of sellers increases the supply of a good. For example, an increase in the number of firms producing laser printers increases the number of printers available at any given price. Over long periods of time, changes in the number of sellers in a market are a very important determinant of supply. The number of sellers in a market changes with the profitability of producing a good.

Other important determinants can also affect the supply of particular goods. For example, weather can affect the supply of agricultural commodities. A frost in Florida that ruins the citrus crop can decrease the supply of oranges in the market over a year. Expectations about future prices of goods and services and inputs can also affect current supply, as can taxes and subsidies.

Market Equilibrium Price and Quantity

4 An equilibrium prevails when economic forces balance so that economic variables neither increase nor decrease. Market equilibrium is attained when the price of a good adjusts so that the quantity buyers will buy at that price is equal to the quantity sellers will sell. When a market equilibrium has been attained, forces of supply and demand balance so that there's no tendency for the market price or quantity to change over a given period. The equilibrium price acts to ration the good so that everyone who wants to buy the good will find it available. Similarly, at the equilibrium price, everyone who wants to sell the good will be able to do so successfully. For example, equilibrium in the personal stereo market requires that the price of personal stereos be such that the quantity demanded equals the quantity supplied. When quantity demanded equals quantity supplied, the market is said to *clear.*

A shortage exists in a market when the quantity demanded of a good exceeds the quantity supplied over a given period. For example, there will be a monthly shortage of compact disc players if at the current market price the monthly number of players that sellers will make available falls short of the monthly number that buyers will purchase.

A surplus exists in a market when the quantity supplied of a good exceeds the quantity demanded over a given period. There would be a monthly surplus of gas if the monthly quantity supplied by sellers exceeded the monthly quantity demanded by buyers at a certain price. At the market equilibrium price of a good, there can be neither surpluses nor shortages in the market. When a market clears, the good is rationed, because there are neither surpluses nor shortages.

Graphic Depiction of Market Equilibrium

The graph in Box 7 plots the demand curve for eggs on the same set of axes as the supply curve. Suppose the price of eggs is $2 per dozen. At that price the weekly quantity supplied by sellers would be 9,000 dozen, the weekly quantity demanded by buyers would be 1,000 dozen, and there would be a surplus of 8,000 dozen. *It follows that the price of $2 per dozen cannot result in a market equilibrium because at that price quantity supplied exceeds quantity demanded.*

Now suppose instead that the price of eggs is 50 cents per dozen. Will this price result in a market equilibrium? To find out, just draw a horizontal line from that price to the demand and supply curves. The quantity demanded at a price of 50 cents per dozen is 7,000 dozen. However, the weekly quantity supplied at that price is 3,000 dozen. Because the quantity demanded exceeds the quantity supplied by 4,000 dozen, it's clear from the graph that at a price of 50 cents per dozen there will be a weekly shortage of eggs in the market. *It follows that the price of 50 cents per dozen cannot result in a market equilibrium because at that price the weekly quantity of eggs demanded exceeds the weekly quantity supplied.*

Finally, let's look at the price of $1 per dozen. Draw a horizontal line from that price to both curves. Note that this line just touches the demand curve and the supply curve where the two curves intersect (point *E*). At $1 per dozen, the weekly quantity supplied will be 5,000 dozen and the weekly quantity demanded will also be 5,000 dozen. *Because the weekly quantity demanded equals the weekly quantity supplied, it follows that the $1 price will result in a market equilibrium. At that price there is neither a weekly surplus nor a weekly shortage of eggs on the market.* Note that, given all other influences on demand and supply, the $1 per dozen price is the *only* price that will result in market equilibrium.

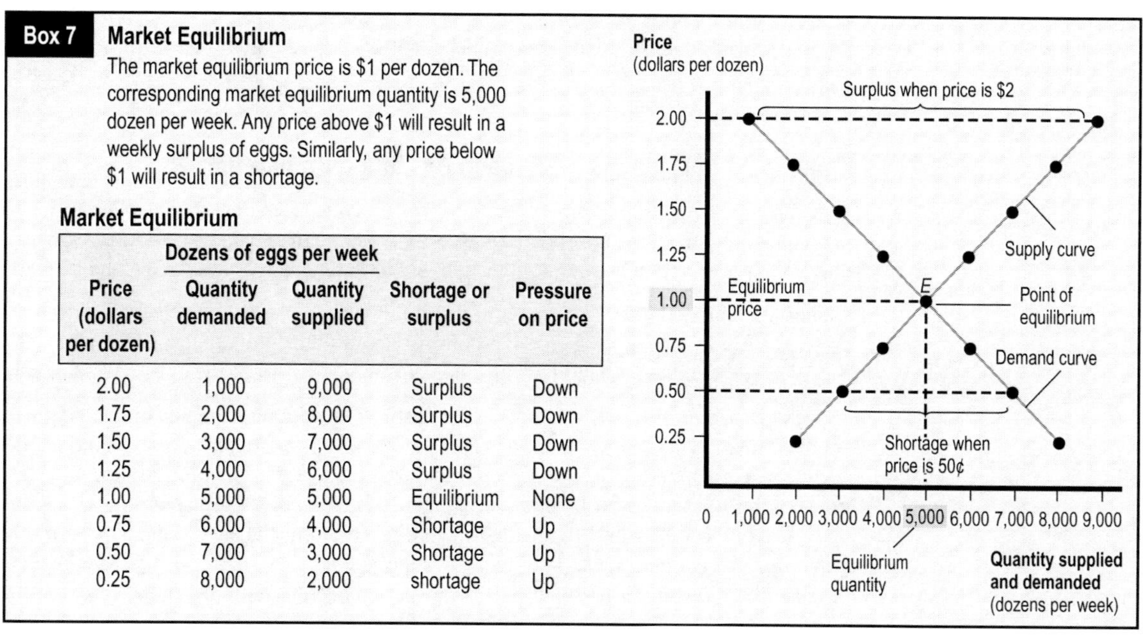

Box 7 Market Equilibrium

The market equilibrium price is $1 per dozen. The corresponding market equilibrium quantity is 5,000 dozen per week. Any price above $1 will result in a weekly surplus of eggs. Similarly, any price below $1 will result in a shortage.

Market Equilibrium

Price (dollars per dozen)	Dozens of eggs per week: Quantity demanded	Quantity supplied	Shortage or surplus	Pressure on price
2.00	1,000	9,000	Surplus	Down
1.75	2,000	8,000	Surplus	Down
1.50	3,000	7,000	Surplus	Down
1.25	4,000	6,000	Surplus	Down
1.00	5,000	5,000	Equilibrium	None
0.75	6,000	4,000	Shortage	Up
0.50	7,000	3,000	Shortage	Up
0.25	8,000	2,000	shortage	Up

To check your understanding, examine the relationship between quantity demanded and quantity supplied at any other price. You'll see that any price other than $1 per dozen will result in either a weekly shortage or a weekly surplus of eggs.

Self-Equilibrating Markets

5 If the equilibrium price is not initially established in a market, competition among buyers for goods, and among sellers for sales, will set up forces that cause the price to change. Whenever price exceeds its equilibrium level, there will be a surplus of goods on the market. Goods brought to market will go unsold. Sellers of eggs will accept lower prices rather than allow their weekly supply of eggs to spoil. In the case of goods whose quality doesn't deteriorate over time, sellers will accept lower prices to avoid the costs of maintaining inventory or transporting goods back to the point of production. *A surplus results in downward pressure on price.* As price falls, weekly quantity supplied declines and weekly quantity demanded increases, serving to eliminate the surplus. The weekly surplus in the egg market will be completely eliminated when the price reaches the equilibrium level, where quantity demanded equals quantity supplied each week.

A shortage implies that some buyers willing and able to pay the price of a good will find the good unavailable in the market. Although eggs seem to be a bargain when their price is below the market equilibrium level, there aren't enough of them to go around! Competition among consumers for the available weekly quantity of eggs supplied will inevitably increase the price. Some consumers will be willing to pay more than the prevailing price rather than go without eggs. *A shortage therefore results in upward pressure on market price.* As market price increases, weekly quantity supplied will also increase, while weekly quantity demanded will decline. This will continue until quantity demanded once again equals quantity supplied at the market equilibrium price and the shortage has been eliminated.

As you can see, a competitive market tends to be self-equilibrating as a result of the competition among many buyers and sellers. The competition among buyers for available goods and among sellers for sales ensures that prices will adjust to achieve an equilibrium.

The table in Box 7 summarizes the relationship between quantities demanded and supplied at various prices. The table shows that only at the equilibrium price of $1 per dozen is there neither upward nor downward pressure on price. The $1 price is the only price at which quantity demanded equals quantity supplied, given the current demand and supply curves.

The Impact of Changes in Demand on Market Equilibrium

6 Changes in either demand or supply can change market equilibrium prices and quantities. You can now begin to use supply and demand analysis to forecast what will happen to prices and quantities sold in response to these changes in demand and supply.

Changes in demand affect market equilibrium. For example, suppose there's a decrease in demand for eggs because of growing concern about their high cholesterol content. Recall that a decrease in the demand for eggs means an inward shift of the entire demand curve.

The graph in Box 8 shows the impact of a decrease in demand for eggs on the egg market. As the demand curve shifts inward, the old price of $1 and quantity of 5,000 dozen eggs per week, corresponding to point E_1, no longer represent market equilibrium. To see why, move along the dotted horizontal line drawn from the point corresponding to $1 on the vertical axis. The quantity demanded at that price along the new demand curve is now 3,000 dozen eggs per week. The quantity supplied at that price is still 5,000 dozen eggs because there has been no change in supply. If the price remains at $1, there will be a

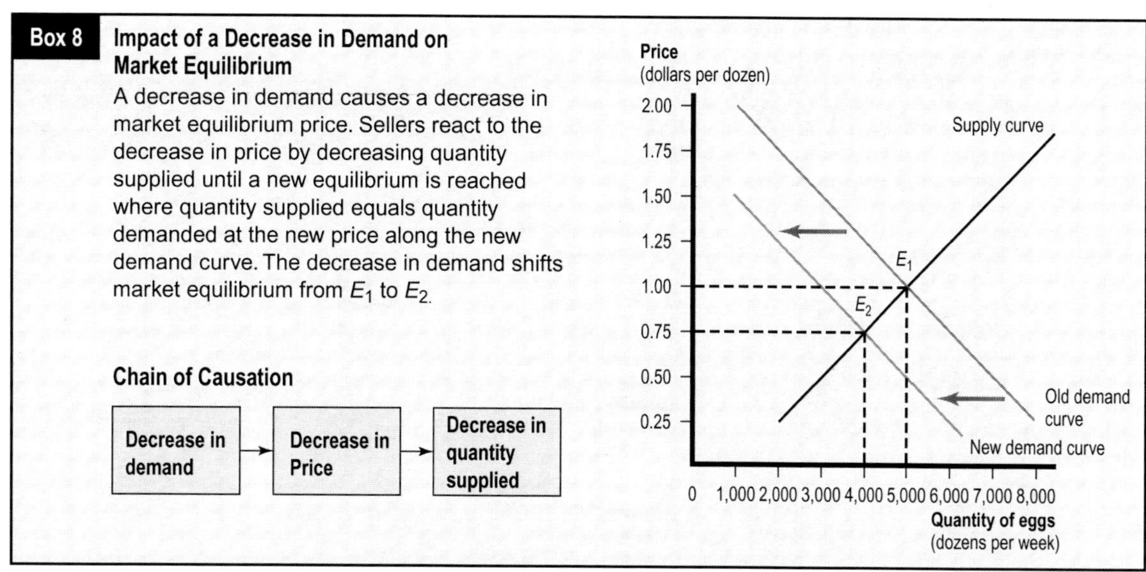
Box 8
Impact of a Decrease in Demand on Market Equilibrium
A decrease in demand causes a decrease in market equilibrium price. Sellers react to the decrease in price by decreasing quantity supplied until a new equilibrium is reached where quantity supplied equals quantity demanded at the new price along the new demand curve. The decrease in demand shifts market equilibrium from E_1 to E_2.
Chain of Causation
Decrease in demand
Decrease in Price
Decrease in quantity supplied
Price
(dollars per dozen)
2.00
1.75
1.50
1.25
1.00
0.75
0.50
0.25
Supply curve
E_1
E_2
Old demand curve
New demand curve
0
1,000
2,000
3,000
4,000
5,000
6,000
7,000
8,000
Quantity of eggs
(dozens per week)

weekly surplus of 2,000 dozen eggs. The market attains a new equilibrium in response to the decrease in demand as price declines to eliminate the surplus. The new market equilibrium corresponds to point E_2, at which the new demand curve intersects the supply curve. The price corresponding to that point is 75 cents per dozen. At the lower price the quantity supplied by sellers declines to 4,000 dozen per week, which exactly equals the quantity demanded by buyers along the new demand curve at that price.

The decrease in demand, other things remaining unchanged, sets up the following chain of events in the market. First, the price declines as a surplus develops at the original price. Second, sellers *respond* to the decrease in price by decreasing the quantity supplied. Finally, as the quantity supplied declines, a new equilibrium is attained at a price for which quantity demanded on the new demand curve equals quantity supplied on the existing supply curve. *Notice that sellers do not respond directly to the decrease in demand. Instead, they respond to the decline in price caused by the decrease in demand.* This illustrates the role of price as a *signal* through which buyers communicate a change in their desires to sellers.

Since the mid-20th century, demand for eggs has, in fact, fallen in the United States. Egg consumption per capita fell from a high of about 400 per person per year in 1945 to a low of 234 per person per year in 1991. Concern about the health effects of eating eggs (such as its effect on cholesterol) and life-style changes over the period contributed to this decrease in demand. In the 1980s, the decrease in the demand for eggs contributed to a 35-percent decrease in the market equilibrium price of the product. Since 1993, the demand for eggs has been rebounding, as medical evidence seems to indicate eggs are more healthful than was previously thought. Per-capita consumption in the United States increased from 234 in 1993 to 257 in 2004, a 10-percent increase over the period. The rebound in egg demand has helped increase the price of eggs in recent years. By early 2008 egg prices were averaging more than $1.50 per dozen in the United States. A combination of increased demand for eggs, resulting from increased per-capita consumption, and a decrease in supply, caused by higher feed and transportation costs, resulted in sharp increases in the market equilibrium price for eggs—up by more than 50 percent during 2007. Declines in the value of the dollar lowered the price of U.S. eggs to foreign buyers, which also contributed to increased demand. New government

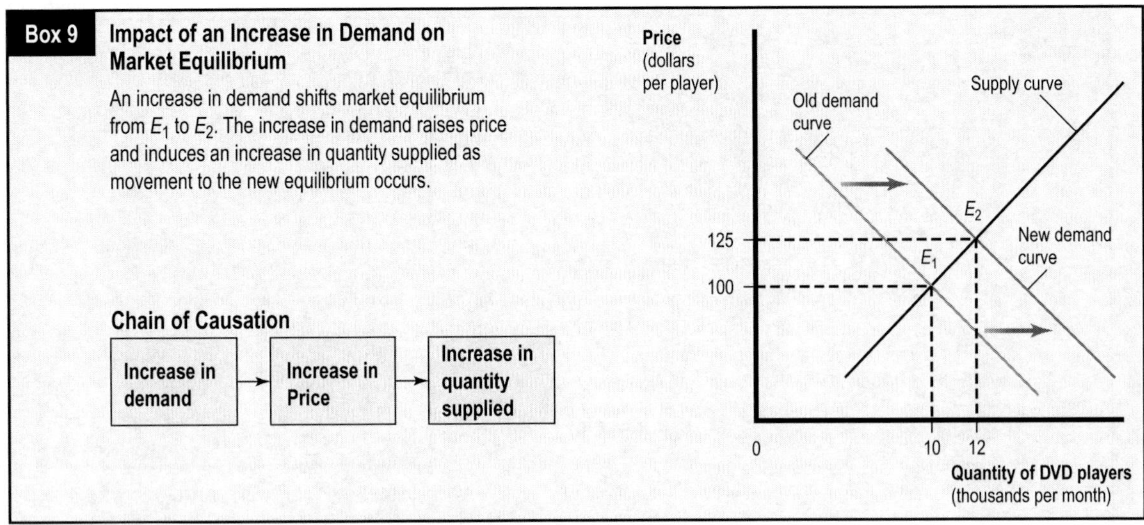

regulations regarding animal welfare increased cage space per hen, which contributed to a decrease in supply, as did summer heat and drought in southeastern states during 2007.

The reasoning for an increase in demand is exactly the reverse. Suppose an increase in income causes an increase in the demand for DVD players. An increase in demand is a shift of the entire demand curve outward. The graph in Box 9 shows that an increase in demand for DVD players will increase the market equilibrium price. As the price increases, there's a corresponding increase in quantity supplied until quantity demanded, on the new demand curve, once again equals quantity supplied. In the graph the initial equilibrium corresponds to point E_1, at which the price of a standard-quality player is \$100, and 10,000 DVD players are sold per month. After the increase in demand, the new equilibrium corresponds to point E_2, at which the price is \$125 per player, and the quantity supplied is 12,000 per month. The increase in price is a signal that induces sellers to increase the quantity supplied.

The Impact of Changes in Supply on Market Equilibrium

Remember that a change in the supply of a good is represented by a shift of the entire supply curve caused by a change in some influence other than price. For example, an increase in the price of chicken feed is likely to decrease the supply of eggs. The graph in Box 10 shows how a decrease in supply affects market equilibrium. Assume that the initial market equilibrium, corresponding to point E_1 on the graph, is once again a price of \$1 per dozen and that 5,000 dozen eggs are sold per week at that price. As the supply curve shifts inward, the initial price can no longer result in an equilibrium. This is because the quantity supplied at that price along the new supply curve is now only 3,000 dozen per week. Because there's been no change in demand, the quantity demanded at that price is still 5,000 dozen per week. There will therefore be a weekly market shortage of eggs if the price remains at \$1 per dozen. Competition among buyers eliminates the shortage and raises the price. As the price increases, quantity demanded declines until it equals quantity supplied. The new market equilibrium corresponds to point E_2, at which market price is \$1.25 per dozen and quantity sold is 4,000 dozen per week. This is the point at which the new supply curve intersects the original demand curve. Note that *buyers do not respond directly to the decrease in supply. Instead, they respond to the increase in market price caused by the decrease in supply.* Once again,

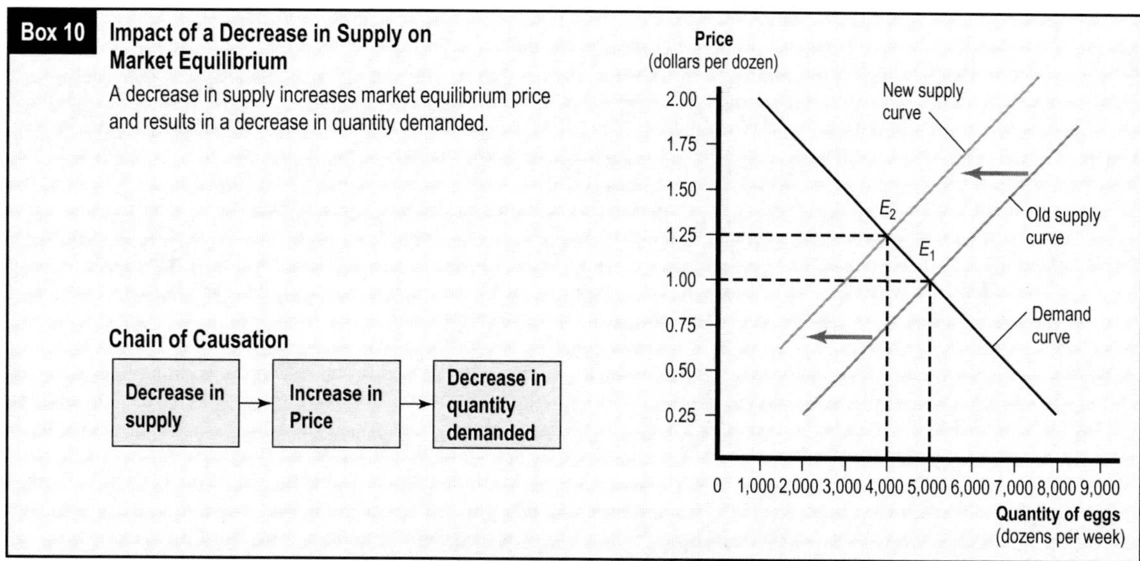

you can see how price serves as communication between buyers and sellers. Buyers are motivated to reduce the quantity demanded in response to the higher price caused by the decrease in supply.

The reasoning is similar for an increase in supply. For example, a number of years ago the equilibrium price for a standard 19-inch color TV was about \$300. As advances in technology increased supply, there was downward pressure on the price of TVs. The graph in Box 11 shows the impact of an increase in supply on market equilibrium. Start out once again at point E_1, at which the original demand curve intersects the original supply curve. At that point the market price of TVs is \$300 and the quantity sold per year is 4 million. The increase in supply means that the original supply curve shifts outward. The new market equilibrium corresponds to point E_2, at which the new supply curve intersects the original demand curve. If market price remains at \$300 per set, there will be an annual surplus of TVs on the shelves of retailers. The price must fall to clear the market. The new equilibrium price is now \$200 per TV. Quantity demanded at that price is 5 million TVs per year, which exactly equals the quantity sellers are willing to

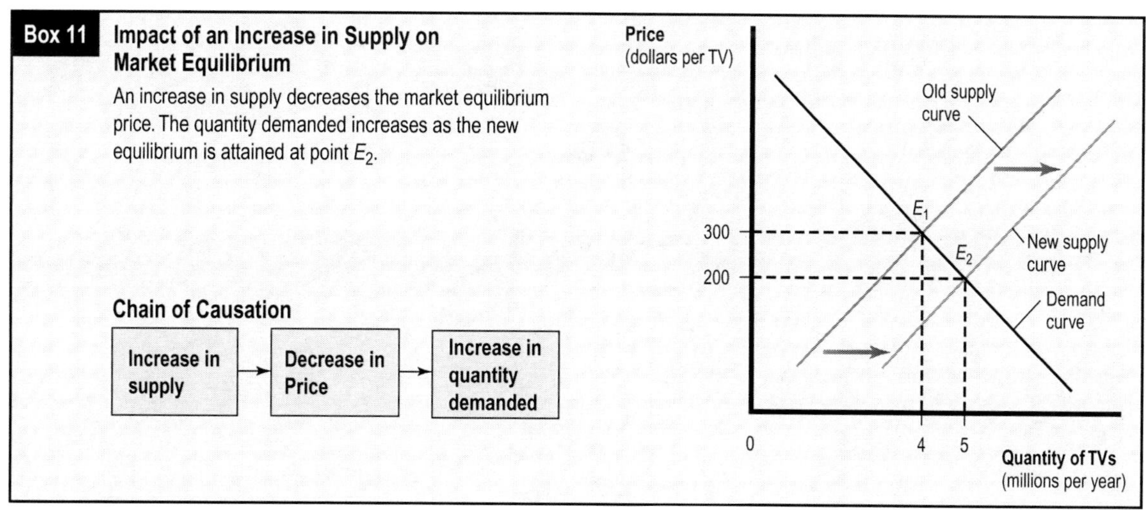

supply at that price along the new supply curve. An improvement in technology therefore tends to lower the market price of a good and to increase the quantity demanded.

Mastering the Art of Supply and Demand Analysis

The forces of supply and demand determine prices in competitive markets. If you thoroughly understand how buyers and sellers respond to changes in opportunities for gains in markets and how market equilibrium prices serve to equate quantity demanded with quantity supplied, you're on your way to understanding the most basic of economic relationships.

Supply and demand analysis is relevant to all goods and services exchanged in markets. You must understand how to manipulate supply and demand curves so that, in other chapters, you'll be able to explain changes in product prices, interest rates, wages, and rents.

You'll also want to keep in mind that supply and demand influences are constantly changing. We usually base our analysis of a market on a "snapshot" of the market at a single point in time. We then make hypotheses about the way market equilibrium would change if a certain demand or supply influence were to change. In actuality, many changes occur simultaneously in a market. Supply and demand curves are constantly shifting. Perhaps the best example of this is the stock market, where prices can move quickly and often erratically over a short period of time as conditions in that market change. However, you'll gain little understanding of the relationship between price and other variables by trying to analyze all variables at the same time. You'll find that the best way to understand the process of price determination in markets is to study one variable at a time. This will help you isolate the impact of important influences on price and quantities traded.

Part of the art of supply and demand analysis is knowing the relevant influences affecting the decisions of buyers and sellers in a market and their ability to purchase or sell goods. You need to understand the causes of changes in supply or demand so you can forecast market prices and trading. For example, weather is likely to be an important supply influence on an agricultural market, but it has little effect on the market for computers. Interest rates are likely to be an important influence on the net gains we can enjoy from buying homes and cars, and thus interest rates affect demand for those items. Improvements in technology are a major influence on the supply of electronic goods such as digital cameras, microwave ovens, and personal computers.

Summary

1. Markets are arrangements through which buyers and sellers can communicate and conduct transactions to enjoy mutual gains.
2. The law of demand states that, in general, other things being equal, there is a negative relationship between the price of a good and the willingness and ability of buyers to purchase it.
3. A demand curve illustrates the relationship between price and quantity demanded.
4. A change in quantity demanded is represented by a movement along a demand curve in response to a change in a good's price. A change in demand is a response to a change in something other than price that shifts an entire demand curve. Changes in demand can be caused by changes in consumer income, prices of other goods, expectations, tastes, or population.
5. The law of supply states that, in general, other things being equal, there is a positive relationship between price and the amount of a good sellers will make available.
6. A supply curve shows how quantity supplied varies with the price of a good.
7. A change in quantity supplied is represented by a movement along a given supply curve caused by a change in a good's price. A change in supply implies a shift of an entire supply curve caused by a change in something other than the price of a good that affects the willingness and ability of sellers to make the good available. Changes in supply can be caused by changes in input prices, improvements in technology, changes in the prices of other goods that can be produced with the sellers' resources, and changes in sellers' expectations about the future.
8. A market equilibrium is attained when the price of a good adjusts so that the quantity of the good demanded equals the quantity supplied. If price of the good is above the market equilibrium level, a surplus will prevail. If price is below the market equilibrium level, a shortage will prevail. Surpluses put downward pressure on prices, while shortages put upward pressure on prices.
9. Market equilibrium prices ration goods by ensuring that everyone who wants to buy a good will find it available, while everyone who wants to sell a good will do so successfully. Prices accomplish this objective because they influence the personal gains possible from buying and selling goods.
10. Changes in demand or supply result in new market equilibrium prices. A change in demand affects the market equilibrium price of a good. A change in market price affects the gains possible from selling the good and causes sellers to respond by adjusting the quantity they supply. A change in supply also affects the market equilibrium price of a good. The resulting change in price affects the gains possible from purchasing the good and therefore causes buyers to respond by adjusting quantity demanded.

Concept Review

1. Give an example of a market, and discuss how it functions.
2. What can cause a change in quantity demanded? What can cause a change in demand?
3. What can cause a change in quantity supplied? What can cause a change in supply?
4. How can you tell whether a market is in equilibrium?
5. Under what circumstances would there be a shortage in a market?
6. How will an increase in demand affect market equilibrium price and quantity supplied? How will a decrease in supply affect market equilibrium price and quantity demanded?

Problems and Applications

1. Imagine that a new report by the surgeon general on the harmful effects of cholesterol decreases the demand for eggs. Suppose the resulting decrease in demand reduces by 50 percent the quantities buyers are willing to buy each week at each possible price for the demand schedule in Box 1. Graph the new demand schedule, and show the decrease in demand by drawing both the old and new demand curves. 6

2. An improvement in the technology of egg laying doubles the number of eggs each chicken can lay per week. Assuming that the improvement doubles the weekly quantity supplied at each price in the table in Box 4, graph the new supply schedule. Draw both the old and new supply curves to illustrate the change in supply. 6

3. Assuming that both the decrease in demand for eggs and the increase in supply of eggs described in Problems 1 and 2 occur simultaneously, use a graph to show the impact on the market equilibrium price of eggs and on the quantity sold per week. 6

4. Suppose the market for coffee is currently in equilibrium at a price of $3 per pound. An early frost in coffee-growing nations decreases the supply of coffee. Use supply and demand analysis to forecast the impact of the freeze on the market equilibrium price and quantity of coffee. 4, 6

5. Suppose the market rate of interest on car loans declines substantially. Use supply and demand analysis to predict the impact of the interest rate decline on the prices of cars and the quantity sold. 6

6. Suppose you want to buy a popular brand of digital camera. Every store in town is out of stock. You are willing and able to pay the market price of $300 for a camera, but you can't find any available. Is the market for this digital camera in equilibrium? Use supply and demand analysis to explain your answer. 4

7. The federal government announces that it will pay $3 a loaf for all the bread that can't be sold in a competitive market at that price. At the end of each week, the government purchases 1 million loaves of bread. Use supply and demand analysis to show on a graph that the market equilibrium price is less than $3 per loaf. Why doesn't the market price fall in this case? 5

8. Using your graph in Problem 7, show how a decrease in the supply of bread can raise its market equilibrium price above $3 a loaf. How much bread would the government buy each week under these circumstances? 4, 5

9. Assume the market price of Mustang convertibles is $20,000. At that price the quantity demanded is 1 million per year, while the quantity supplied is only 500,000 per year. Is the market in equilibrium? Explain your answer. 4

10. A decrease in demand for computers results in a market surplus of PCs. Explain how market forces will act to eliminate the surplus. 4, 5, 6

The Dollar Has Its Price Too: Demand for and Supply of the Dollar in Foreign Exchange Markets

The dollar has its price in terms of foreign currencies—a price that fluctuates with changes in supply and demand. Demand for dollars is generated from foreigners' desires to purchase them so they can buy U.S. goods and services or acquire U.S. assets. The supply of dollars to the market is generated by the desires of U.S. households and businesses to acquire foreign currencies so that they can purchase foreign goods, services, and assets. There are markets for the dollar in exchange for many foreign currencies, but in this example we concentrate on the market for dollars in exchange for Japanese yen.

The price of one nation's money in terms of another country's money is called its *exchange rate*. In early 1985 the exchange rate of the dollar for Japanese yen was 261.5 yen. This means that the Japanese would have had to give up 261.5 yen to buy each dollar's worth of U.S. goods or services. By early 1988 a dollar could be bought for less than half the amount of yen hat was required in 1985 as the exchange rate fell to 125 yen per dollar. By 1995 the exchange rate plummeted to a mere 80 yen per dollar! In early 2001 the price of the dollar in Japanese yen was running in the range of 120 yen. However, by early 2009 the price of the dollar was once again down to 90 yen in foreign exchange markets. As you can see, the dollar's price fluctuates considerably over time. You might want to look up its current price. (You can find foreign exchange quotes in *The Wall Street Journal*, perhaps your local daily newspaper, or online.)

The graph in Box 12 shows the supply and demand curves for the dollar in international markets. The vertical axis shows the price of a dollar in terms of Japanese yen. The horizontal axis shows the number of dollars exchanged for yen per day. Like the demand curve for almost any commodity, that for dollars is downward-sloping. Similarly, the higher the price of dollars in terms of yen (the exchange rate), the greater the quantity of dollars supplied in exchange for yen, indicating an upward-sloping supply curve.

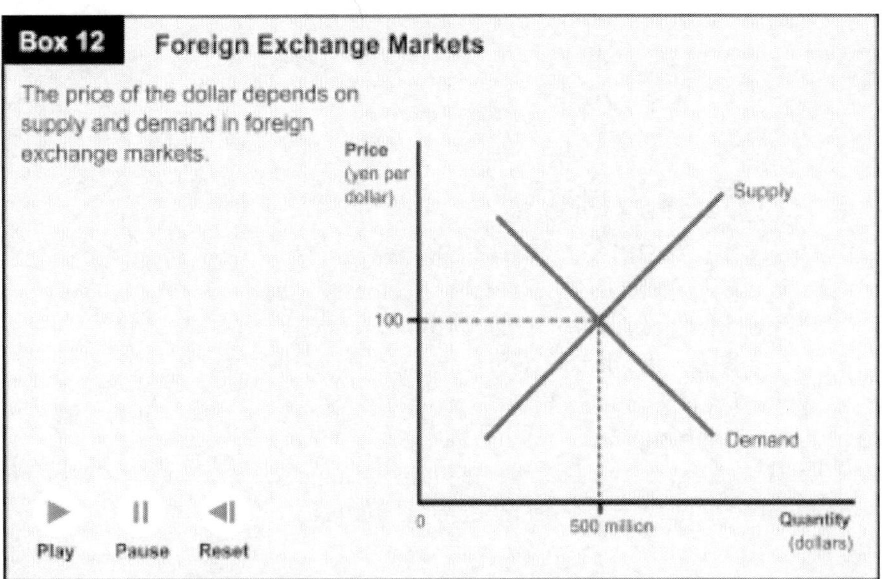

You can understand why the laws of supply and demand hold for dollars if you examine the consequences of changes in the exchange rate. Suppose the cost of production and the minimum acceptable profit for both Japanese and U.S. goods are given. The price U.S. farmers will accept for each bushel of wheat is $2. The price Japanese camera companies will accept for each camera is 50,000 yen. Suppose the current equilibrium price of the dollar is 125 yen. You can now use the equilibrium exchange rate to convert the price of wheat into yen and the price of cameras into dollars

Case 1: $1	=	**125 yen**
Price of wheat in yen	=	$2 (125 yen/$1) = 250 yen
Price of cameras in dollars	=	50,000 yen ($1/125 yen)
	=	$400

Now, suppose the price of the dollar falls to 80 yen. *Assuming there is no change in the prices sellers of these goods will accept in terms of their own currencies:*

Case 2: $1	=	**80 yen**
Price of wheat in yen	=	$2 (80 yen/$1) = 160 yen
Price of cameras in dollars	=	50,000 yen ($1/80 yen)
	=	$625

The *decrease* in the price of the dollar makes Japanese goods more expensive in dollars and makes U.S. goods less expensive in yen. This means that, other things being equal, the Japanese will be more eager to buy U.S. wheat and other goods when the price of the dollar falls. The increase in the demand for U.S. goods caused by the decrease in the price of the dollar induces holders of yen to increase the number of dollars demanded. Similarly, because a decrease in the price of the dollar makes Japanese goods more expensive in terms of dollars, the number of dollars supplied in exchange for yen will decrease as the price of the dollar falls.

The next obvious question is, What causes the demand for and supply of dollars offered for yen to change over time?

1. *Interest rates in the United States and Japan affect the Japanese demand for dollars.* The higher interest rates are in the United States relative to those in Japan, the greater the demand for dollars by the Japanese. This is because, when interest rates are high on assets denominated in U.S. dollars, Japanese holders of yen can earn more by acquiring dollars to buy U.S. assets than by using yen to invest in Japanese assets. Relatively high interest rates in the United States therefore raise the price of the dollar by increasing Japanese demand for dollars. On the other hand, a decline in U.S. interest rates relative to those in Japan (as occurred between 2002 and 2005) decreases the Japanese demand for dollars and puts downward pressure on the dollar's price in terms of the yen. During the period 2002 to 2005, when interest rates were falling in the United States, the value of the dollar in terms of the yen fell by more than 15 percent.

2. *The prices on domestic currencies that sellers in Japan and the United States will accept for products offered in international trade affect the supply of and demand for dollars.* An increase in the prices (in yen) Japanese automobile producers will accept for cars they want to export to the United States will, other things being equal, make those cars less attractive to U.S. citizens. An increase in Japanese prices in yen relative to those of competing U.S. products therefore decreases the supply of dollars offered in exchange for yen. The decrease in the supply of dollars tends to increase the price of the dollar in terms of the yen.

Sometimes a government steps in and buys and sells its own currency. The purpose is to adjust the price of the currency in terms of foreign exchange in order to improve the balance of exports and imports.

Changes in foreign exchange markets can affect you. For example, as the exchange rate of the dollar for yen declined from 1993 to 1995, the prices of a host of Japanese products sold in the United States soared for American buyers paying in dollars. At your local jewelry store, cultured pearls from Japan which could have been bought for a mere $900 in the mid-1980s were selling for over $3000 in 1995. Nikon cameras were priced out of the reach of many U.S. buyers as the dollar fell. A Nikon lens that could have been bought for $750 in 1992 was selling for well over $1000 by 1995. A similar decline in the exchange rate of the dollar for yen over the period 2007-2009 also put upward pressure on the prices of Japanese imports in the United States.

The higher yen hasn't done much for the competitiveness of cars produced in Japan. The average price of a Japanese-produced car rose by more than $2000 in the early 1990s, causing sales of these models to plummet as many U.S. buyers substituted cheaper U.S.-made cars for their favorite Japanese models. Japanese automobile executives were scurrying to shift more production operations to the United States so as to avoid some of the devastating effects of the lower exchange rate of the dollar on their sales.

The lower value of the dollar was great for soybean growers in the United States, who watched with glee as the price of their crops fell to Japanese buyers paying in yen and as sales increased.

The foreign exchange value of the dollar fell against the yen again in 2003 and 2005. By early 2009, the dollar was trading for 98 yen on foreign exchange markets. The weaker dollar was putting upward pressure on imported Japanese goods and increasing the cost of travel expenses for Americans visiting Japan.

E-Commerce: How the Internet Has Changed the Marketplace

A market is a means by which buyers and sellers can communicate for the purpose of engaging in commerce and trade. As a means of disseminating information and communication, the World Wide Web has revolutionized commerce and markets. Today, people routinely buy and sell manufactured goods, airline tickets, vacation packages, educational services, and just about anything else you can imagine by swiftly moving from Web site to Web site.

Much of e-commerce involves business-to-business transactions, For example, a business that produces metal frames and boilers in Poland regularly bids on specialized orders from American industries for equipment, and is prospering by winning those bids and shipping products abroad. Other transactions on the Internet involve travel services, financial services, babysitting, and almost everything else. Computer sales through such online merchants as Dell and Gateway account for a big chunk of e-commerce. Amazon.com originally was set up as an online bookseller, but, as its methods for marketing and selling online were developed and refined, it gradually turned into a department-store-type retailer, selling everything from tools to new cars!

The Internet has changed the market for secondhand goods and antiques. In 1995, AuctionWeb went online as a new experiment in Internet commerce. Auction services set up rules for buying and selling online through a bidding process, and earn profits from the fees and commissions they charge to their clients. As online auctions grew, they turned the market for antiques, collectibles, and just about anything people dared to offer for sale into a worldwide bazaar, where traders from anywhere on earth could engage in transactions. The services of eBay became a global flea market. By the late 1990s, eBay had already conducted over 10 million auctions, and was taking in millions of dollars in revenue by charging users for listing items and taking a percentage of the sales. By the year 2000, eBay's market sales were approaching $50 billion. Other Internet auction houses, like priceline.com, allowed participants to name their price and closed transactions if sellers accepted their bids. Many online sellers use such services as those offered by eBay as their sole market.

The Internet auction markets haven't been without controversy. The auction of a human kidney through eBay drew bids of more than $5 million, until the company banned sale of human organs through its facilities. However, there have also been sales of military weapons and other items that many have found objectionable. Amazon.com also runs auctions, and many business-to-business sites have been set up to auction equipment.

The modern world bazaar isn't located in a particular place. Instead of traveling to a location where sellers have set up shop to sell their wares and services, the modern bargain hunter just has to sit down and go online to become a buyer. Similarly, sellers can stay at one location, yet, at the same time, become worldwide merchants. The 21st century marketplace is a far cry from the weekly markets in the center of medieval cities!

The Market for Medical Services: How Health Insurance and Asymmetric Information Increase Spending on Health Care

Americans devote a whopping 13 percent of the value of annual output to health care. U.S. households spent more than $1.2 trillion on medical services in 2000. Most of that amount was paid to vendors of health care services through insurance programs. U.S. businesses now pay an average of more than $4,000 per employee in health insurance costs, and a major portion of government budgets in the United States is now allocated to pay for health care to the aged, the poor, and other groups, including veterans. More than 15 percent of the federal government's outlays are for medical payments and health care. Health care spending in the United States is projected to rise to 16 percent of the value of annual output and amount to $2.6 trillion by 2010.

Between 80 and 85 percent of the U.S. population is covered by health insurance or government programs that pay nearly three-quarters of personal health care costs in the United States. The major government programs that pay for health care are Medicare (a government-subsidized system of health insurance for the elderly) and Medicaid (which pays medical bills for the poor). When an insured person requires medical services, all but a small portion (if any) of the bill is usually paid by the insurance company. Most insurance plans require the patient to incur a certain modest amount of expenditures (called the "deductible") for medical services before the plan starts paying. When the patient incurs the deductible expense, the plan usually pays between 80 percent and all of the additional medical expenses each year.

Let's extend our use of supply and demand analysis to see how the system of health insurance in the United States has affected the expenditures for medical services. The bulk of payments for medical services in the United States is made by a *third party* other than the buyer or seller of the services. That third party is, of course, the health insurer or the government. The graph shows the supply and demand curves for medical services. In the absence of any third-party payments, the equilibrium price, on average, for medical services is P_1 and the equilibrium quantity is Q_1. As a result of third-party payments, the price per unit of service (on average) to the patient falls from P_1 to P_B because the insurance company picks up most of the bill for doctors' visits, surgery, and hospital stays. As a result of the fall in the price per unit of service, the quantity demanded increases from Q_1 to Q_B as we move along the market demand curve to point *A*. As the quantity demanded of medical services increases, the quantity supplied must also increase to prevent shortages. This means that the price paid to medical suppliers must increase to P_S to induce suppliers to move from point E to point B on the supply curve. From the suppliers' point of view, the third-party payments increase the demand for medical services. The new market equilibrium is at point B, where medical service suppliers receive a price of P_S as the combined payment from both patients and insurers.

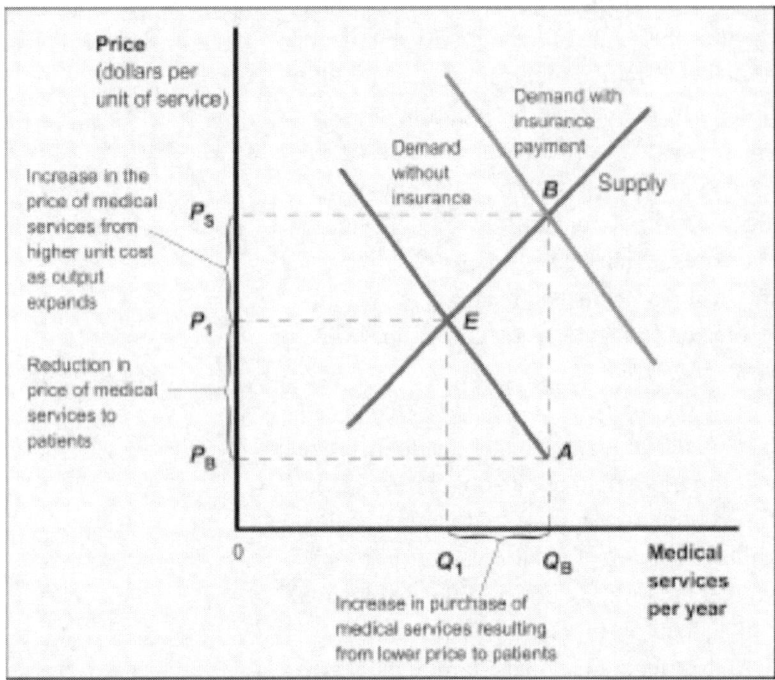

People do not choose to get sick more often because they have health insurance. However, in many cases, insurance results in people not being as careful to avoid medical problems as they might be if they knew they had to pay the full price of medical services. (This is called the "moral hazard" problem.) Insurance also induces people to visit physicians for more minor ailments (such as the common cold) than they would if they had to pay the full price of each visit. Medical practitioners often have the incentive to prescribe more tests and medical procedures when they know a third party will pay.

Third-party payments for medical services therefore provide incentives for individuals to increase the quantity of medical services demanded. Also, because providers are compensated for their costs at a higher rate, such payments attract more resources into the provision of health care. Naturally, as expenditures on health care have increased, so have health insurance premiums used to finance private insurance and taxes used to finance Medicare and Medicaid. Because of third-party payments, both consumption and the price paid to medical service suppliers rise. Total expenditure on medical care also increases as both the price and the quantity provided increase. Even though the price of a unit of medical services is now P_S, buyers pay only P_B and the insurance companies pay the remainder.

Many insurers are now increasing the portion of medical services (called the copayment) that the patient must pay. Some insurers also limit their payments for certain kinds of services and require patients to get second, and even third, opinions before agreeing to pay for costly medical procedures. Other insurers seek to control costs by requiring their insured employees to obtain their medical care from an approved health maintenance organization.

Health care spending may also be encouraged by asymmetric information in the health care market. In that market, physicians and other health care providers are better informed about the benefits and costs of medical services than are the consumers of those services.

Decision making in the market for health care is dominated by physicians who know about medical procedures and control access to medical technology. Patients find it difficult to obtain information about alternatives to those prescribed by their physicians and therefore find it difficult to evaluate the benefits of procedures relative to the costs. The not-for-profit Foundation for Informed Medical Decision Making produces videos designed to inform patients of the options available for dealing with some common health problems such as: prostate disease, low back pain, high blood pressure, early-stage breast cancer, etc. The videos describe treatments and their risks. At one medical office where the videos were used, the information they provided apparently convinced many patients that the benefits of some medical procedures were not worth the costs. For example, prostate surgery was reduced by as much as 60 percent after patients started using the videos. Information of this kind can be a good way of reducing the growth of medical costs.

Business Brief: The Stock Market – How It Works

On Monday, October 19, 1987, a wave of selling triggered widespread price declines in stock markets from New York to Australia. On that day, now infamous as "Black Monday," over 600 million shares were traded on the New York Stock Exchange—more than twice the NYSE's average sales volume. The Dow Jones Industrial Average of the prices of 30 stocks of major U.S. companies lost 22.6 percent of its value on that memorable day, plunging 508 points in the panicky rush to sell.

What is the stock market, and how is it affected by the forces of supply and demand? The stock market is the means through which previously issued corporate stocks, shares of ownership in a corporation, are traded. Stock exchanges are organizations whose members act as intermediaries to buy and sell stocks for their clients.

How are stock prices determined? The answer, as you might expect, is by supply and demand. However, the forces influencing the prices of corporate stocks are quite different from those influencing the prices of goods and services. People and organizations that buy and hold stocks do so for the incomes they hope to earn. The incomes depend on dividends paid to stockholders, changes in the price of stocks over time, and the expected return compared to the return on alternative investments.

On any given day in the stock market, there are orders to buy and orders to sell. The orders to buy constitute the quantity of stocks demanded at the current (or anticipated) prices per share, while the orders to sell constitute the quantity supplied at those prices. The chief influence on both the supply of and demand for stocks is the income potential of holding the stocks compared to the income potential of holding alternative assets such as bonds, other types of securities, or real property such as buildings and land.

The way in which the forces of supply and demand actually influence stock prices depends on the trading rules of the particular stock exchange. For example, the Paris stock exchange uses a "call market" method. Under this method, brokers have time to accumulate their orders to buy and sell specific stocks. When there's a call for a stock, a clerk acts like an auctioneer to establish an equilibrium price at the time of the call. The clerk may begin by calling out the most recent trading price of the stock. If after the call all the selling orders are filled and brokers still have orders to buy, the clerk will call out a higher price. Similarly, if at the initial price all the orders to sell aren't matched by orders to buy, the clerk will call out a lower price. In this way, the clerk acts to adjust price until quantity demanded equals quantity supplied at the call session. Naturally, if there are more sell orders than buy orders at the current price, the price of the stock will tumble during the call.

On the New York Stock Exchange, trading in all stocks is continuous. A specialist is assigned to oversee trading in each stock. This specialist is a "broker's broker" who tries to adjust the price of the stock so that quantity demanded equals quantity supplied. However, the specialist is also allowed to purchase the stock to hold as a personal investment if no buyer can be found. In this way, the specialist can exert some influence on the supply of and demand for stocks, and will do so if it's profitable. Much of the trading and pricing on the New York Stock Exchange is done electronically, through computer networks. All the trading and pricing on the NASDAQ stock exchange is handled electronically, through a large computer network.

When the orders to sell far outnumber the orders to buy, specialists and call clerks in the market must lower prices to equate quantity demanded with quantity supplied. On October 19, 1987, there were hardly any buy orders and the markets were flooded with sell orders. Because of the tremendous surplus of stocks at the prevailing prices, specialists and call clerks lowered prices until quantity demanded equaled quantity supplied. When Black Monday finally reeled to a close, many a portfolio had lost over a fifth of the value it had at the end of the previous trading day. The dollar value of outstanding stocks in the United States declined by a whopping $500 billion! In terms of supply and demand, the graph shows that the Crash of 1987 resulted from a sharp increase in the supply of stocks coupled with a decrease in demand.

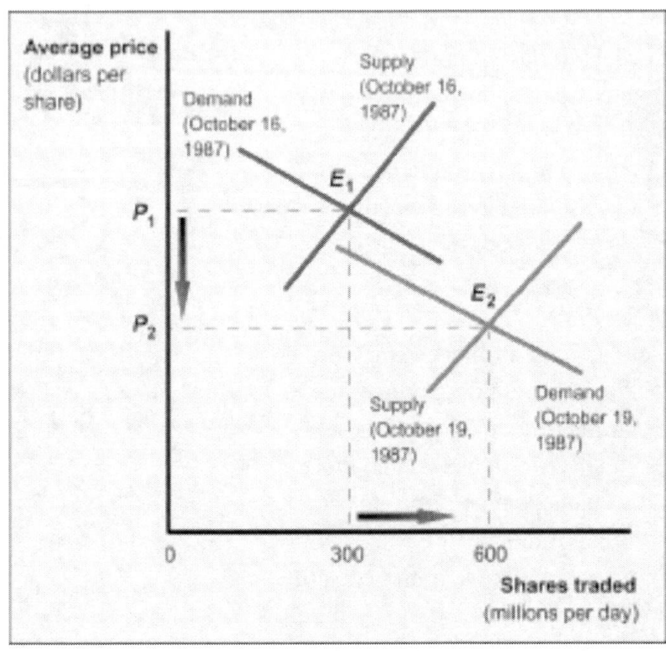

In the late 1990s, the demand for stocks, particularly those in the technology and Internet sectors, soared and prices skyrocketed. The stock market boom was fueled by optimistic profit expectations in these sectors. By 2001, the speculative bubble in technology stocks burst and demands for stocks declined as the economy slowed down and profit forecasts were revised downward for many companies. Investors increased supplies of stock for sale in the markets. By early 2001, stock prices were down sharply and the prices of some of the high-flying stocks of the late 1990s had lost upwards of 70 percent of the peak values of only a year before.

Stock prices ran up again after 2001, with the Dow Jones Industrial Average peaking at 14,000 in October 2007. However, demand for stock shares declined substantially in 2008 and 2009 as a result of a financial crisis and a recession that adversely affected the corporate profit outlook. By early 2009 stocks had lost over half their market value, on average, compared to the October 2007 peak, as the Dow Jones average fell to a level below 7,000.

Chapter 4

Using Supply and Demand Analysis

What are the prospects for profitably marketing a new product? Will an increase in interest rates bring on an economic recession? Should the federal government continue to subsidize farmers by guaranteeing them minimum prices for their crops? Should landlords be bound by laws that place a ceiling on the rents they can charge?

Each of these actions or policies has predictable results we can forecast using supply and demand analysis. In this chapter you'll have more opportunities to use supply and demand analysis and to understand its relevance to a wide range of business, political, and social issues.

As you'll see after reading the chapter, the laws of supply and demand can't be repealed. Because so many goods and services are bought and sold in markets, market outcomes influence our daily lives. Changes in supply and demand conditions change market prices. Changes in prices inevitably affect the gains possible from buying and selling goods and, thereby, change the choices we make.

Concept Preview

After reading this chapter, you should be able to

1. Demonstrate how market equilibrium prices deal with the problem of scarcity by rationing goods and services, and explain why prices would be zero for nonscarce goods.
2. Explain how supply and demand conditions affect the price and sales potential of new products.
3. Show how wages and interest rates are determined in competitive markets.
4. Use supply and demand analysis to show how government control of prices in competitive markets can result in shortages or surpluses.

Prices, Scarcity, and Marketing Prospects

Imagine that you could shop at all your favorite stores, pick out every item your heart desired, and sail right by the checkout counter without paying a dime. In this consumer's dream you could have the pleasure of acquiring at zero price as much as you wanted of any good or service: designer fashions, an expensive home entertainment system, a home gym, a chauffeur-driven limousine. Surely, you'd obtain more and better goods and services in this fantasy world than you do when confronted with the reality of market prices and limited income.

Suppose *everyone* were given the privilege of bypassing the checkout counter at the local car dealer. How would the available Jeeps, BMWs, and Mustangs be allocated among the hordes of eager consumers clamoring for them? Would customers obediently wait in line, or would they be more likely to turn into an unruly and perhaps violent mob, fighting over automobiles on the lot? Who would make the cars available?

If business firms couldn't charge for their goods, they wouldn't make a profit. If they couldn't cover their production and distribution costs and make a profit, they wouldn't make products available to consumers. If you're looking for a sleek Corvette at zero price, you probably know you're out of luck! This fantasy of a giveaway world should make it clear to you how prices are necessary to cope with scarcity.

Nonscarce Goods

There's only one case in which zero prices for goods will not create hopeless shortages. This is the rather improbable case of a good that's not actually scarce. A nonscarce (or free) good is one for which the quantity demanded does not exceed the quantity supplied at zero price. In other words, a nonscarce good is available in amounts that result in no shortage even if the price of the good is zero.

Of course, few, if any, goods can be described as nonscarce. However, we can fantasize about situations in which nonscarcity might prevail. For example, coconuts might be so plentiful in an island nation that its few people could enjoy all they wished at zero price. (Assume that no resident of this island paradise thinks about exporting the coconuts to other areas of the world where the fruit is scarce in relation to desires to use it.) The graph in Box 1 shows you the demand and supply curves for coconuts in such a paradise. You'll notice that the demand curve intersects the horizontal axis without intersecting the supply curve first. At zero price 10 tons of coconuts per season are demanded. At zero price the quantity of coconuts available is 20 tons per season. Because at zero price the quantity supplied exceeds the quantity demanded, there's a surplus of coconuts even when they're available free. Anyone who tries to sell coconuts on the island will be unable to find any buyers, because at zero price the availability of the fruit exceeds the amount desired.

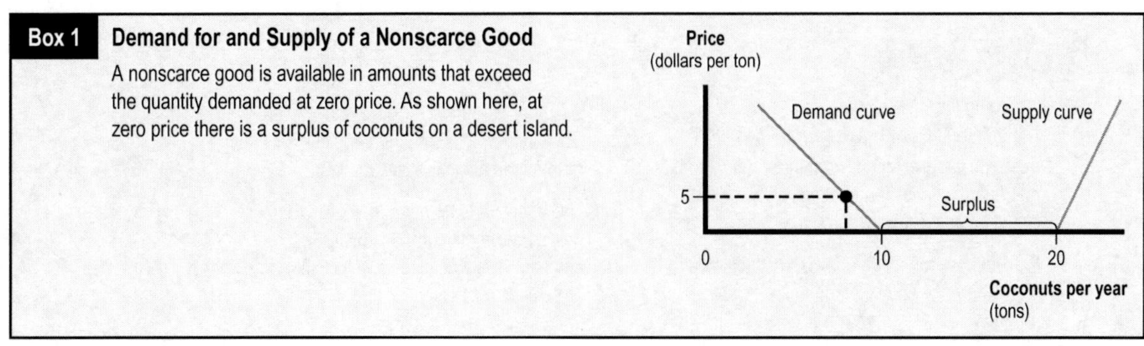

Box 1 Demand for and Supply of a Nonscarce Good

A nonscarce good is available in amounts that exceed the quantity demanded at zero price. As shown here, at zero price there is a surplus of coconuts on a desert island.

However, the laws of supply and demand are still relevant. The higher the price of coconuts on the island, the lower the quantity demanded, as you can see by the downward-sloping demand curve. For example, if the price were $5 per ton, as shown in the graph, the quantity demanded would fall below 10 tons per year. Similarly, the higher the price of coconuts on the island, the greater the quantity supplied as residents of other coconut-rich islands make their coconuts available. However, the quantity available at zero price exceeds the quantity demanded at that price, making it impossible for people with coconuts to sell them at a positive price.

Garbage is a negatively valued item that we pay someone to take away. However, with changes in either demand or supply items we currently toss away as garbage can become scarce goods. For example, the current quantity of plastic soft-drink bottles at zero price exceeds the quantity demanded. In the future, however, the supply curve for today's empty bottles will move to the left and the demand curve for such bottles by collectors will move to the right. If the supply and demand curves continue to shift in this way, they'll intersect at a positive price. Today's trash can end up being tomorrow's treasures—something you already know if your parents threw out your shoe box of baseball cards!

How Demand and Supply Conditions Affect the Success of New Products

We can use supply and demand analysis to evaluate the prospects for marketing new products profitably. The price of a new product influences the quantity demanded. Firms must be able to sell new products at prices that exceed costs sufficiently to allow a profit.

2 Suppose you're considering investing in a company that plans to market a product that utilizes a new and improved method of reproducing recorded sound. The company estimates that when it first puts the product on the market, the minimum price it can accept is $5,000 per unit. Will the product sell at that price? To find out, we need to guess how the supply and demand curves for the product look.

The demand curve for the product is like the one illustrated in the graph in Box 2. A number of supply curves are also drawn in the graph. Suppose the product is the flat-panel LCD television. The first supply curve shows the supply of flat-panel LCD TVs in 1995, when the technology for the product wasn't fully developed. However, let's assume that a prototype of the product could have been marketed at that time. The supply curve for 1995 hits the price axis at $5,000. The demand curve for that year hits the price axis at about $2,200. This implies that the minimum price sellers would accept to make only one LCD TV available per year exceeds the maximum price that any buyer would buy. *Using*

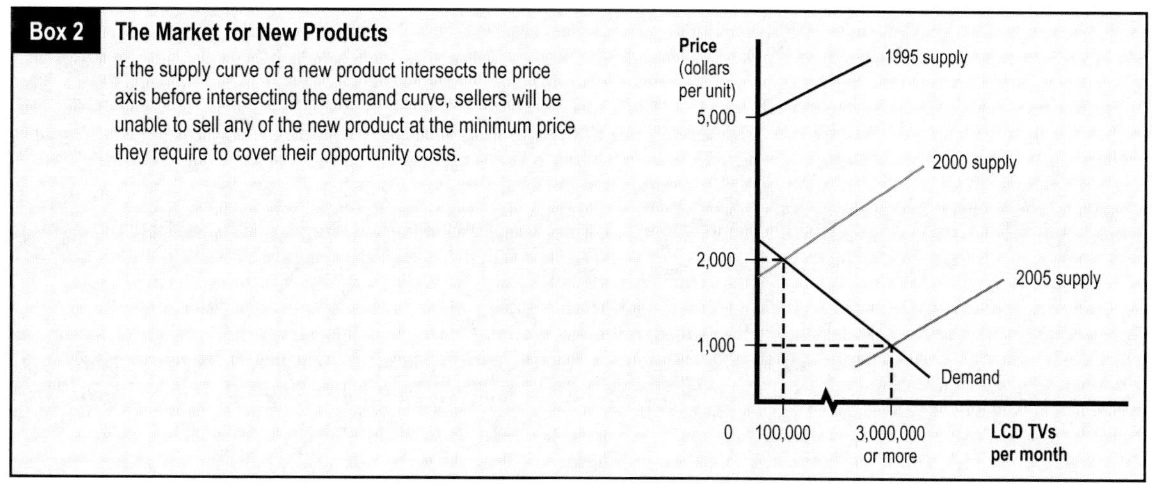

Box 2 The Market for New Products

If the supply curve of a new product intersects the price axis before intersecting the demand curve, sellers will be unable to sell any of the new product at the minimum price they require to cover their opportunity costs.

business jargon, this means that there's no market for the product. The supply and demand curves don't intersect at a positive quantity.

Rapid improvement in the technology of flat-screen LCD TVs has both enhanced the quality of their performance and images, and sharply reduced production costs and market equilibrium prices. Shipments of LCD TVs from producers in Japan increased from virtually zero in 1998 to nearly 3 million units in 2005. As improved technology lowered unit costs of production, shipments from major producers in Korea and China also increased. In 2004, Chinese producers announced major investments in factories producing flat-panel LCD TVs and a 300-percent increase in production. As supplies increased in 2004 and 2005, market equilibrium prices plummeted and it was possible to purchase a 20-inch HDTV-ready LCD TV for less than $700. The LCD TV was rapidly replacing older CRTs (cathode ray tubes), as consumers increased quantities demanded for the lightweight, flat-panel TVs in response to lower prices and improved quality.

The analysis in Box 2 assumes a fixed demand, while supply increases. Increases in demand would dampen some of the downward pressure on prices caused by increases in supply. In the graph, supply increases and market quantity demanded increases as equilibrium price falls. By 2005, abundant supply and low market equilibrium prices expanded quantity demanded to well over 3 million units per year.

In 2007 sales of LCD TVs in the United States surpassed those of CRT TVs for the first time. In that year an estimated 80 million LCD TVs were sold! And the prices kept tumbling. By early 2009 a 20-inch LCD TV could be purchased for a price in the range of $200. And if you wanted to move up to a bigger screen, you could buy a Sony Bravia 32-inch LCD HDTV-ready television for less than $600.

The expansion of market quantity demanded as a result of improved technology and price reduction has been common for electronic products in recent years. The lap-top computers, MP3 players, cell phones, Internet access, and DVD players that most of us take for granted were all unheard of 40 years ago. Today, thanks to improved technology, these products are readily available at affordable prices.

Markets for Labor and Credit

3 We can also apply supply and demand analysis to markets for *economic resources*, such as the services of labor. Many macroeconomic issues deal with analysis of prices and employment of productive resources. To understand these issues, you need to understand how the laws of supply and demand operate in markets for economic resources.

Labor Markets

In modern economies workers sell their services to employers in labor markets. In a competitive labor market many workers independently offer skills of a given quality to many employers who compete for the workers' services. As is the case in product markets, wages, the prices paid for labor services on an hourly or yearly basis, are important determinants of the amount of labor demanded and supplied over a given period.

It's reasonable to expect the laws of demand and supply to prevail in labor markets as they do in product markets. The lower the wage, the greater the quantity of labor services demanded by employers. The demand curve for labor services is therefore downward sloping because employers substitute other inputs, such as machines, for labor services as wages go up, while substituting labor services for other inputs as wages go down.

The higher the wage, the greater the quantity of labor services generally supplied. At higher wages individual workers are usually willing to work more hours per week. In addition, higher wages are likely to induce workers not currently looking for work, such as students, retirees, and homemakers, to enter the job market. Also, an increase in wages in one part of the country is likely to attract workers from other parts of the country who are looking for jobs at the higher wages.

The graph in Box 3 shows the demand and supply curves for labor services in a market for unskilled labor. Employers have no reason to prefer the services of one worker over another in such a market because labor services are standardized. In the graph the equilibrium wage is $8 per hour. At that wage 3 million labor hours per week are employed.

Our economy includes a multitude of labor markets for services that require many kinds of skills. There are, for example, markets for economics professors, heart surgeons, plumbers, musicians, grape pickers, and cruise directors. In each market workers have similar skills. Wages, of course, differ widely in these markets, depending on the value employers place on workers' skills and on the factors influencing the supply of each type of labor.

Notice how the market equilibrium wage rations the available number of labor hours per month. At the equilibrium wage of $8 per hour, the quantity of labor hours demanded just equals the quantity supplied. This means that all workers willing and able to work will find jobs, while all employers willing and able to hire workers at that wage will find them available. There's neither a shortage of labor services nor a surplus.

The demand for labor is derived from the demand for the products that labor produces. When a business enjoys an increase in orders, it will have to hire more labor to fill those orders. Consider the workers whose labor market is illustrated in Box 3. An increase in demand for labor caused by increased orders will increase wages. An increase in wages will make work more attractive to workers and cause an increase in the number of labor hours supplied per month.

You can see the effect of an increase in demand for labor services by looking at the graph in Box 4. The increase in demand for workers increases the wage from $8 to $10 per hour. If the wage were to remain at $8 after the increase in demand, the quantity demanded would be 4 million hours per month, while the quantity supplied would remain at 3 million hours per month. There would therefore be a shortage of workers.

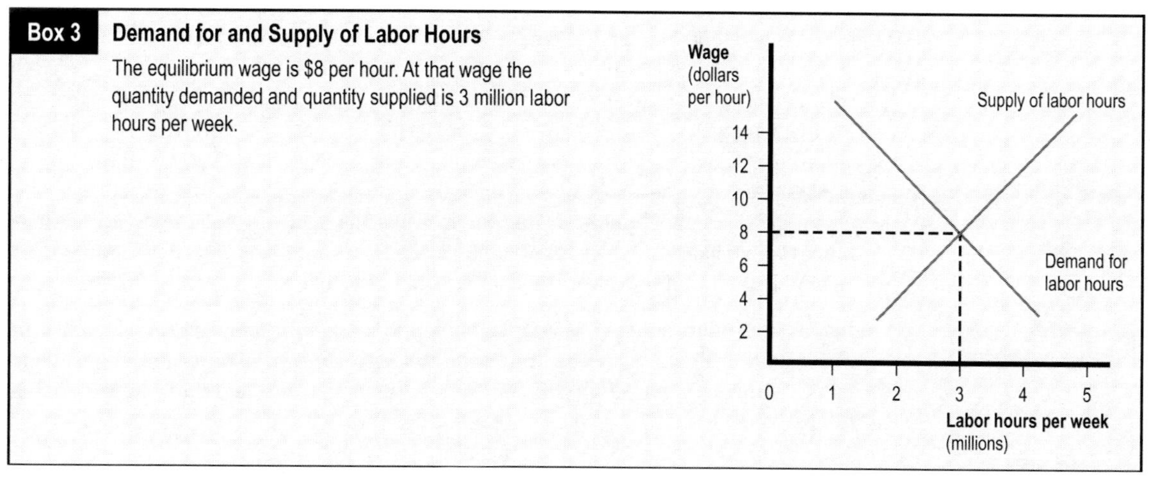

Box 3 Demand for and Supply of Labor Hours

The equilibrium wage is $8 per hour. At that wage the quantity demanded and quantity supplied is 3 million labor hours per week.

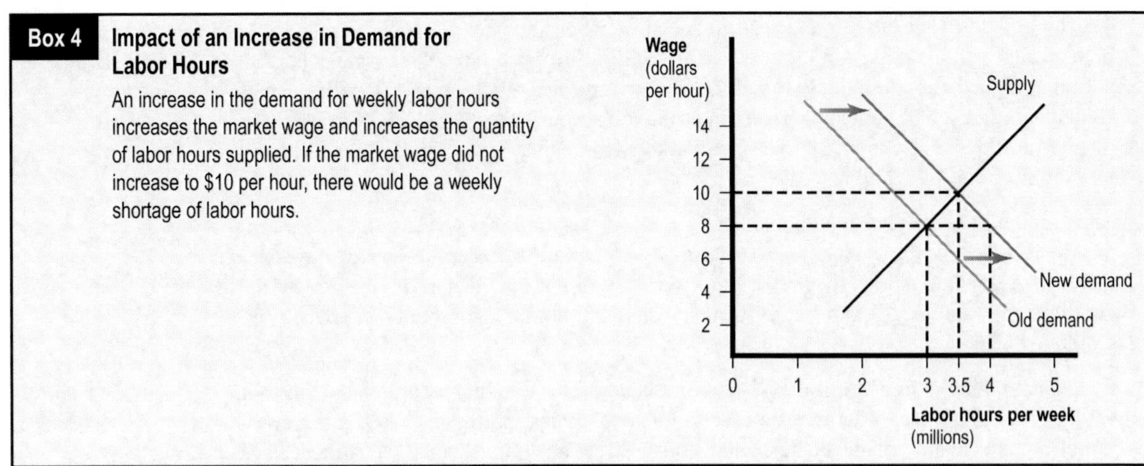

Box 4
Impact of an Increase in Demand for Labor Hours
An increase in the demand for weekly labor hours increases the market wage and increases the quantity of labor hours supplied. If the market wage did not increase to $10 per hour, there would be a weekly shortage of labor hours.
Wage (dollars per hour)
14
12
10
8
6
4
2
Supply
New demand
Old demand
0
1
2
3
3.5
4
5
Labor hours per week (millions)

Competition among employers would put upward pressure on wages. As the wage increases from $8 to $10, the quantity of labor hours supplied increases. A new labor market equilibrium is achieved, and 3.5 million labor hours per month are employed. As in product markets, the price of labor services (in this case, wages) acts as a signal to workers by increasing the gains possible from additional work. Workers respond to higher wages by increasing the quantity of labor supplied.

Conversely, a decrease in orders for products will cause a decrease in the demand for labor. Suppose the bicycle industry in the United States experiences a decline in orders because bikers are buying, as substitutes, inexpensive, foreign-produced bikes. The decrease in demand for American-made bikes will decrease the demand for bicycle workers. This will put downward pressure on workers' wages and thus decrease the quantity of labor supplied.

An increase in the supply of labor hours caused by, say, an increase in the working-age population will also affect labor market equilibrium. An increase in the supply of workers, other things unchanged, puts downward pressure on wages. As shown in the graph in Box 5, if market wages remain at $8 per hour after an increase in labor supply, there will be a surplus of labor hours at that wage. The surplus causes market wages to decline to $6 per hour, and the number of labor hours demanded by employers per month increases.

Credit Markets: The Demand for and Supply of Loanable Funds

We can use supply and demand analysis to analyze markets for credit just as we used it to analyze labor markets. Credit is the use of loanable funds supplied by lenders to borrowers who agree to pay back the borrowed funds according to an agreed-upon schedule. The price for the use of loanable funds, called interest, is usually expressed as a percentage per dollar of funds borrowed. This percentage is referred to as the *interest rate*. For example, if you borrow money from a bank to buy a car, the bank is the creditor and you, as the debtor, will make monthly payments that include an interest charge. If you deposit money in an interest-bearing account, you are, in effect, lending money to the bank and the bank will pay interest to you. Most of us conduct transactions as both lenders and borrowers, and so we both earn and pay interest.

Interest is a price, and its level depends on the demand for and supply of loanable funds in financial markets where credit is available. The demand for loanable funds depends on the willingness and ability of consumers, business firms, and governments to borrow funds. Among the factors these potential borrowers consider are the general business

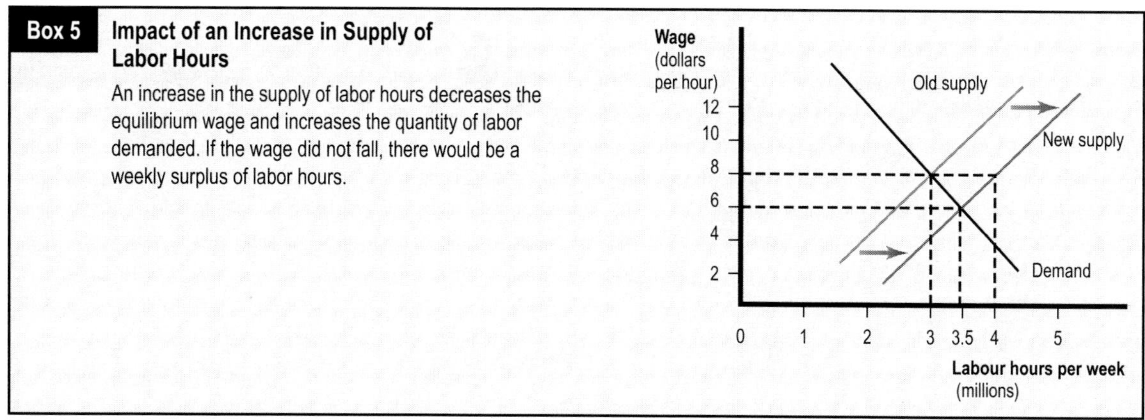

Box 5 Impact of an Increase in Supply of Labor Hours

An increase in the supply of labor hours decreases the equilibrium wage and increases the quantity of labor demanded. If the wage did not fall, there would be a weekly surplus of labor hours.

outlook, the expected profitability of business investment, and the level of consumer income. As you'd expect, the total quantity of loanable funds demanded in any year depends on the interest rate. You can see the demand curve in the graph in Box 6. The lower the interest rate, other things being equal, the greater the quantity of loanable funds demanded.

The supply of loanable funds depends on the willingness and ability of lenders to make funds available to borrowers. In general, the gains possible from lending funds depend on the interest rate paid for the use of funds. The higher the interest rate, the greater the gains. The supply curve of loanable funds as shown in Box 6 is therefore assumed to be upward sloping. In general, the supply of loanable funds depends on the willingness and ability of individuals, businesses, and governments to save rather than spend all their current income in the current year. Such factors as consumer income, expectations of future price levels, population, and average age of people in the population affect the supply of loanable funds.

The graph in Box 6 shows the equilibrium in the market for loanable funds. The equilibrium market rate of interest is 8 percent, and at that rate $1,000 billion of funds are loaned out. The equilibrium interest rate rations available credit by adjusting to equate the quantity of loanable funds demanded with the quantity supplied.

Changes in conditions affecting the demand for or supply of loanable funds will result in shifts of either the demand curve or the supply curve. This will cause changes in the market rate of interest. For example, an increase in the demand for credit by consumers

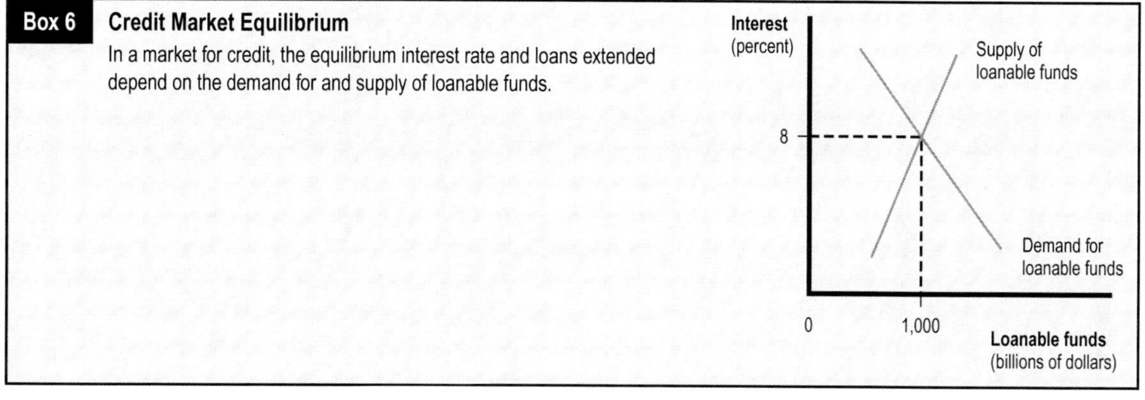

Box 6 Credit Market Equilibrium

In a market for credit, the equilibrium interest rate and loans extended depend on the demand for and supply of loanable funds.

caused, say, by confidence that future income will increase will move the demand curve outward. As shown in the graph in Box 7, this will, other things unchanged, result in an increase in the market equilibrium interest rate. Lenders will respond by increasing the quantity of loanable funds supplied.

Upward pressure on interest rates can also result from increased business demand for credit and from government borrowing. Many economists argue that the enormous federal budget deficits of the 1980s were a significant factor in pushing interest rates up at that time. When federal tax revenues fall short of expenditures, the U.S. Treasury must borrow in financial markets, which increases the demand for credit and could bid up market equilibrium interest rates. For example, a federal government budget deficit in excess of $1 trillion was anticipated for 2010, and the borrowing to cover that deficit could increase the demand for credit, causing interest rates to rise substantially.

Make sure you can also use supply and demand analysis to show that a decrease in the demand for credit will decrease the market interest rate and the quantity of loanable funds supplied. An increase in the supply of loanable funds will put downward pressure on interest rates by shifting the supply curve outward. Finally, a decrease in the supply of loanable funds will shift the supply curve inward and put upward pressure on interest rates. As you can see, forecasting movements in interest rates in competitive markets requires a solid understanding of the forces influencing both the supply of and demand for loanable funds.

Price Ceilings: Using Supply and Demand Analysis to Forecast Their Effects in Markets

4 Not all of us are satisfied with market outcomes. Undoubtedly, you'd like prices to be lower than actual equilibrium prices. You probably wouldn't complain if a law were enacted that would cut your monthly rent in half, provided you weren't adversely affected in any other way.

People dissatisfied with outcomes in unregulated markets often organize politically and seek legislation that allows government authorities to control or set prices in markets. A price ceiling is a maximum price that can legally be charged for a good or service. A price

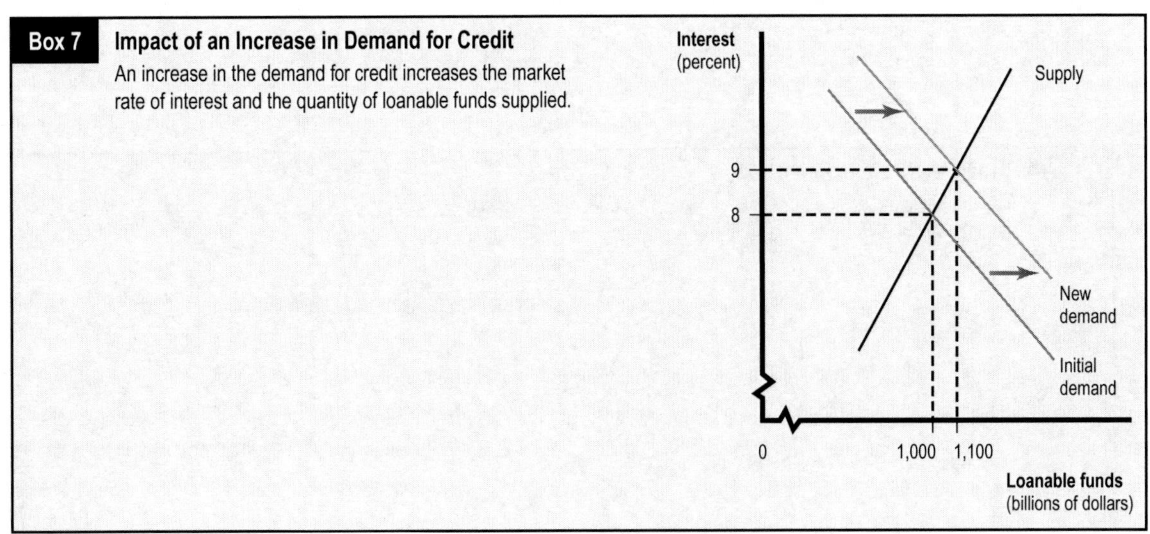

Box 7 Impact of an Increase in Demand for Credit

An increase in the demand for credit increases the market rate of interest and the quantity of loanable funds supplied.

ceiling is said to be *effective* if it is set below the price that would otherwise emerge as the market equilibrium price.

Government control of prices inevitably prevents the market system from performing its function of rationing goods and services. In this section we'll look at the consequences of price control policies. As you'll see, the laws of supply and demand can't be repealed even by government action!

Rent Control

Rent control is a price ceiling that government authorities sometimes use for rental housing. Rent control can prevent housing markets from reaching equilibrium only when rents are set *below* market equilibrium rents. After the end of World War II, when there was a sharp increase in the demand for housing, many cities instituted rent controls to prevent the spectacular increases in rents that were anticipated. Rent controls were abandoned by most cities in the 1950s but have regained popularity, particularly in cities on the West Coast where rents have risen rapidly.

Typically, rent controls limit increases in monthly rental rates or establish rules used to determine "fair" monthly rental rates for housing of varying kinds and quality. They seek to keep rents lower than those that would prevail in equilibrium in a competitive market. Many supporters of rent controls believe that these controls benefit lower-income people who would otherwise have to pay higher percentages of their income for rent. There's no doubt that those fortunate enough to snare rent-controlled apartments do benefit; however, the beneficiaries aren't always in the low-income bracket.

Rent controls cause shortages. The graph in Box 8 uses supply and demand analysis to show how rent controls cause housing shortages when the rents set by law are below the market equilibrium rents. Suppose the market equilibrium rent per room in a certain city would normally be $100 and that at this rent 8,000 rooms per year would be rented.

Now suppose a local rent control ordinance establishes a ceiling of $50 per room. Because the controlled rent is below the market equilibrium rent, the result is a shortage of housing. At the $50 per room rent the number of rooms demanded per year is 10,000, while the number supplied is only 6,000, resulting in an annual shortage of 4,000 rooms. The shortage arises from an increase in the quantity of housing demanded over the quantity

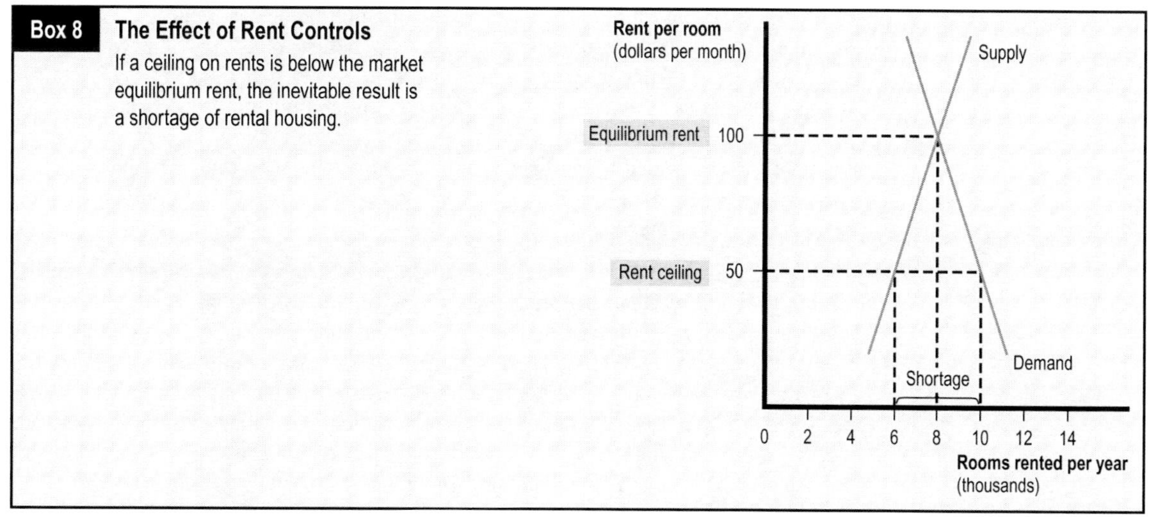

Box 8 The Effect of Rent Controls

If a ceiling on rents is below the market equilibrium rent, the inevitable result is a shortage of rental housing.

that would prevail at the equilibrium rent and from a decrease in the quantity of housing space supplied below the quantity that would prevail at the equilibrium rent.

Rent controls do make rental housing less expensive to tenants. Landlords respond to the reduction in possible gain by decreasing the quantity and often the quality of rental housing supplied. The inevitable result is a shortage of rental housing. The gainers are those fortunate enough to have found rent-controlled apartments, many of whom are in the middle- and upper-middle-income brackets. The losers are often people just starting out who seek a rent-controlled apartment but fail to find one because the established tenants with rent-controlled apartments don't give up their leases.

Nonprice Rationing of Shortages Resulting from Price Ceilings

Price ceilings inevitably result in shortages when they are set below market equilibrium prices. Because prices can't increase to ration a shortage when a ceiling is enforced, other means must be developed to distribute available supplies to those willing and able to pay. These means often reflect a high degree of human ingenuity. Nonprice rationing devices distribute available goods and services on a basis other than willingness to pay. Many people argue that nonprice rationing gives lower-income people the opportunity to consume a good they otherwise wouldn't be able to afford. Although this is true in some cases, the poor aren't always the ones fortunate enough to obtain available supplies when there's a shortage.

The simplest form of nonprice rationing is the use of a "first come, first served" rule. Available supplies of a good are rationed by time spent waiting in line. There's no way of knowing whether low-income people will be first in line or last. The waiting rations the good by doling out supplies only as they become available. Of course, waiting in line is time-consuming and annoying. People often choose to do without a good if the gain they expect from it is less than the price they must pay plus the value of their time and the annoyance of waiting.

Another method of rationing scarce goods is the use of eligibility criteria to select from a pool of people who are willing and able to pay the controlled price. This requires people to fill out forms to establish their eligibility. Government officials then decide who gets served first on the basis of predetermined criteria. For example, if price controls resulted in a shortage of milk, authorities might decide that families with children would get first priority to purchase available supplies. Similarly, if there were a shortage of housing, families might get priority over single people.

Prices are typically controlled in wartime, and the price ceilings result in shortages. A common method of rationing scarce goods is the use of special stamps, a certain number of which are issued to consumers each week. The stamps are usually valid for only a week to prevent people from hoarding them. Prices for goods are stated in both money and stamps. Under this system of nonprice rationing, it isn't enough to be willing and able to pay the money price. A person must also have the stamps. During World War II, for example, stamps issued to civilians limited gasoline consumption to 3 gallons per week. Other stamps limited food, and a system of "points" was used to limit purchases of scarce items such as meat and sugar.

With price ceilings and nonprice rationing there are always dissatisfied potential buyers willing to pay more than the legal price to get the goods or services they want. Selling goods at prices higher than those legally set is punishable by fines or even imprisonment. Nonetheless, there are always sellers willing to risk charging more than the ceiling prices. A market in which sellers sell goods to buyers for more than the legal prices is called a black market. In a black market, prices are invariably higher than those that would prevail if the controlled market were allowed to reach equilibrium. For example, it's not uncommon for eager people searching for housing in rent-controlled markets to make illegal payments in order to obtain choice apartments. In some cases these payments are outright bribes. In other cases they take the form of exorbitant security deposits or purchases of apartment improvements at greatly inflated prices.

Price Floors: Supply and Demand Analysis of Their Effects

The opposite of a price ceiling is a price floor, a minimum price established by law. Two commonly used price floors are minimum wages and agricultural price supports. Minimum wages prohibit employers from paying less than a certain stipulated wage. Agricultural price supports guarantee farmers a minimum price for their crops. As with price ceilings, providing benefits in this way impairs the rationing function of prices. When price floors are set *above* market equilibrium prices, the inevitable result is a surplus on the market. Again, we can use supply and demand analysis to see how such surpluses arise and to identify who gains and who loses as a result of the price floor.

Minimum Wages

Minimum wages are an example of a price floor that governments establish for labor services. Governments enforce minimum-wage laws by penalizing employers who pay less than the stipulated hourly wage.

In modern industrial nations, skilled workers and people employed in factories typically earn equilibrium wages that exceed the minimum wage. However, equilibrium wages for unskilled workers are usually lower than the minimum wage. The graph in Box 9 shows you the effect of a minimum wage in a market for unskilled labor.

The market equilibrium wage for the services of unskilled workers is $4 per hour. At that wage the quantity of labor services demanded per week just equals the quantity supplied of 3 million hours. The minimum wage is set at $5 per hour. At that floor the quantity of labor supplied is 4 million hours per week, while the quantity demanded is only 2 million hours. There is therefore a weekly surplus of 2 million labor hours. This means that some workers seeking employment at the minimum wage will be unable to find jobs, an inevitable situation when minimum wages are set above market equilibrium wages. Of course, if the wage floor were set below or equal to the market wage, it would have no effect on the market equilibrium, because employers would pay more than the minimum wage to avoid labor shortages.

Minimum wages benefit workers who are fortunate enough to find work at wage levels that exceed the equilibrium wage. However, they harm workers who seek employment at the higher wage but can't find jobs. Evidence has linked minimum-wage laws with teenage unemployment. Each 10 percent increase in the minimum wage appears to be

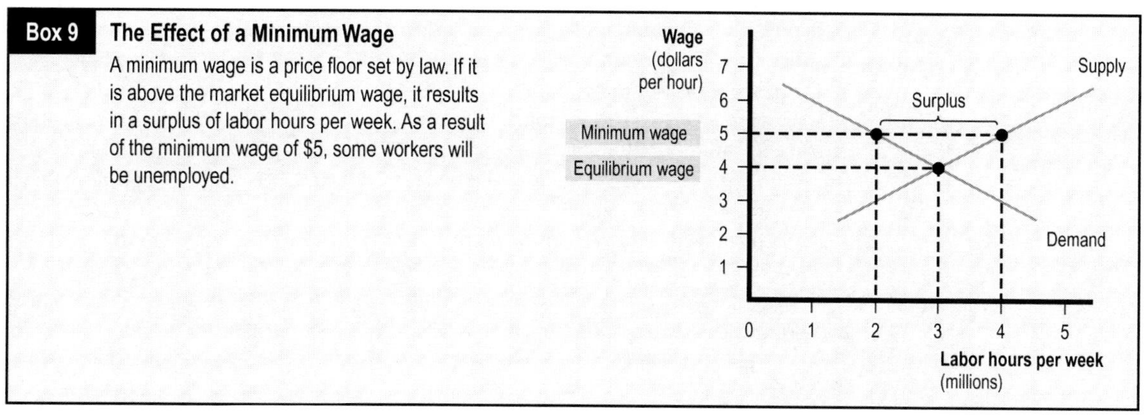

Box 9 The Effect of a Minimum Wage

A minimum wage is a price floor set by law. If it is above the market equilibrium wage, it results in a surplus of labor hours per week. As a result of the minimum wage of $5, some workers will be unemployed.

associated with about a 1 percent to 3 percent reduction in total teenage employment. Minimum wages also appear to reduce employment of young adults aged 20 to 24 and of the elderly. Some studies, however, have found that the minimum wage increases employment of some adults, particularly women, between the ages of 25 and 55.[1]

As you might expect, minimum wages have the most adverse effects on employment in low-wage industries such as retail sales. Employers often react to increases in minimum wages by decreasing the quality of working conditions and reducing fringe benefits. As minimum wages rise, the pace of work is increased and the number of vacation days tends to decline.[2]

Despite the adverse effects of minimum wages on employment opportunities for teenagers and on working conditions for workers in low-wage industries, many politicians and economists argue that minimum wages are an effective way of benefiting the working poor. Of course, employers whose marginal costs increase because of an increase in the minimum wage are likely to respond by decreasing the supply of their products in markets. Consequently, the prices of goods and services produced with unskilled labor will rise, and consumers will pay part of the cost of the minimum wage.

As of August 2008, the federal minimum wage was set at $6.55 per hour and was scheduled to rise to $7.25 per hour on July 24, 2009. In addition, many state governments have enacted minimum wage laws for workers, with legislated minimum wages in excess of the federal minimum wage. In 2008 the highest minimum wage was in the state of Washington, where it was set at $8.07. In California and Massachusetts, the minimum wage was set at $8.00 per hour. Other states with minimum wages in excess of $7.00 per hour in 2008 included Alaska, Colorado, Connecticut, Delaware, the District of Columbia, Hawaii, Illinois, Iowa, Maine, Michigan, New Jersey, New York, Ohio, Oregon, Pennsylvania, Rhode Island, Vermont, and West Virginia.

Agricultural Price Supports

Agricultural price supports are another example of a price floor. These supports, which are common in the United States, are a direct benefit to farmers. However, when the supports are established above equilibrium prices, the inevitable result is a surplus of agricultural commodities. Usually the federal government acquires such surpluses (at taxpayer cost) and holds them in storage. Limited amounts are given away as foreign aid. You may wonder why the government doesn't simply give all the surplus commodities away, in light of the great need for food in famine-stricken Third World countries. The reason is that this would increase world food supplies tremendously and sharply reduce prices. This would create political problems as the plummeting prices reduced incomes of farmers in other countries.

Let's briefly sketch how the price floor works for one farm commodity—milk. For many years dairy farmers have benefited from price supports for milk set by the U.S. Department of Agriculture. Dairy farmers decide how much milk to supply on the basis of the price floor. The graph in Box 10 shows how a surplus of milk results when the actual market price turns out to be less than the price floor. Suppose that the price floor is $2 per gallon, while the market equilibrium price would be $1.50 per gallon. Dairy farmers produce 11 billion gallons of milk per year, which corresponds to point *L* on the supply curve. At a price of $2 per gallon, the quantity demanded is only 10 billion gallons per year (point *M* on the demand curve). As a result, there's a surplus of 1 billion gallons per year. To prevent this surplus from putting downward pressure on price, the government

[1]For a summary of these studies, see Charles Brown, Curtis Gilroy, and Andrew Kohen, "The Effect of the Minimum Wage on Employment and Unemployment." *Journal of Economic Literature* 20, no. 2 (June 1982), pp. 487–528.

[2]Walter J. Wessels, *Minimum Wages: Fringe Benefits,* and *Working Conditions* (Washington, D.C.: American Enterprise Institute for Public Policy Research, 1980).

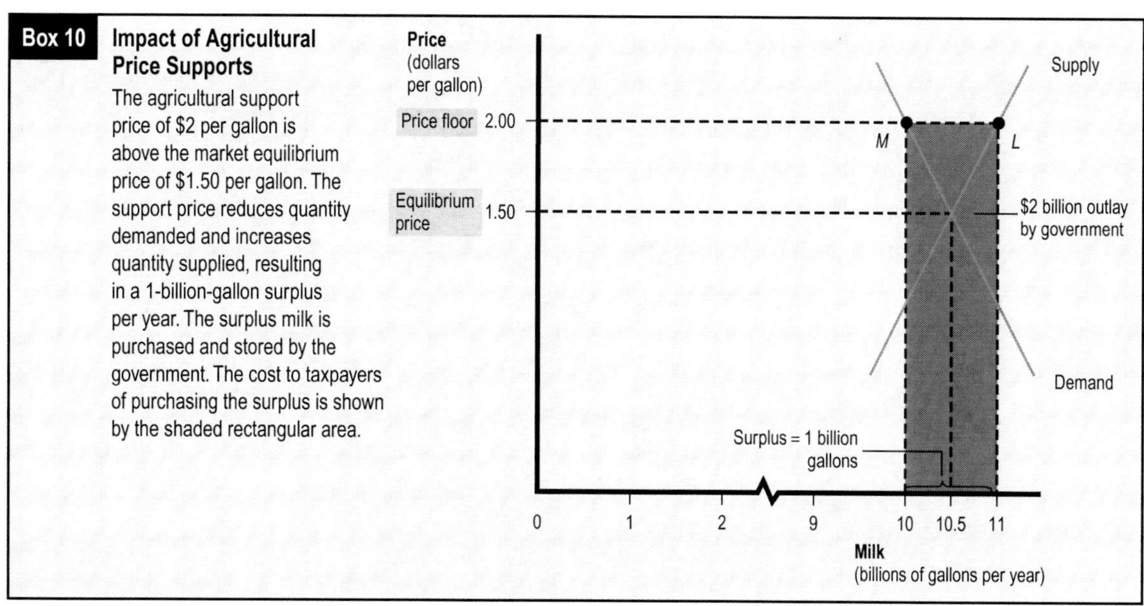
Box 10
Impact of Agricultural Price Supports
The agricultural support price of $2 per gallon is above the market equilibrium price of $1.50 per gallon. The support price reduces quantity demanded and increases quantity supplied, resulting in a 1-billion-gallon surplus per year. The surplus milk is purchased and stored by the government. The cost to taxpayers of purchasing the surplus is shown by the shaded rectangular area.
Price (dollars per gallon)
Price floor 2.00
Equilibrium price 1.50
Supply
M
L
$2 billion outlay by government
Demand
Surplus = 1 billion gallons
0
1
2
9
10
10.5
11
Milk (billions of gallons per year)

buys the 1-billion-gallon surplus at the official price floor each year and stores it. The shaded rectangle shows you the total cost of the program to taxpayers, which in this case is $2 billion. In addition, consumers pay $2 per gallon of milk rather than the $1.50 per gallon market equilibrium price. At the higher price the quantity demanded by consumers is 10 billion gallons per year instead of the 10.5 billion gallons per year that would be demanded if there were no government-established price floor.

You can note these important results of the price support policy:

1. The prices consumers pay for milk (and other agricultural commodities whose prices are supported by government programs) increase when the price floor is higher than the market equilibrium price.

2. Taxpayers foot the bill for purchase and storage of surplus commodities that result from the price floor. However, the government acquires the commodities as assets that it can sell later to generate revenue.

3. Farmers' incomes are higher when the government-established price floors exceed the equilibrium prices of the commodities they sell. As a result of the price supports, they can sell more output than they could otherwise and they receive higher prices than those that would prevail in free markets.

Price Controls: The Cost of Government Intervention

Price ceilings and price floors prevent the price system from rationing goods and services. Seeking to provide benefits to certain groups through regulation of the market mechanism therefore always impairs the function of prices in allocating goods and services. Government intervention in otherwise competitive markets often has unfortunate consequences. In the case of price ceilings, otherwise honest people are often tempted to enter into illegal transactions to obtain scarce goods or services. When price controls cause severe shortages, the costs of preventing illegal transactions are often very high. Price ceilings can also cause the quality of goods to deteriorate as sellers who can't cover their opportunity costs at the controlled prices provide shoddier products.

In the case of price floors, inefficient, high-cost producers can still make profits as a result of government support of prices. The costs of dealing with stored surplus commodities purchased by the government can be quite high. Taxpayers end up subsidizing farmers as tax money is used to purchase and store surplus crops. Finally, consumers of products or services protected by price floors are made worse off because they must pay higher prices than would prevail without the floors.

As you can see, interference with the functioning of free and competitive markets is likely to result in resource allocation problems and reduced efficiency. However, you shouldn't conclude that government intervention in markets is never justified. Making a judgment on the desirability of government intervention clearly depends on your point of view and your goals. In all the cases we've discussed, there were gainers as well as losers. Elimination of price controls always causes some business firms to fail as prices move to equilibrium levels. Obviously, you might rationally support rent control, minimum wages, interest rate ceilings, and agricultural price supports if you and people you care about gained as a result. *However, the important question is whether the gainers could have been made just as well off in other ways that didn't impair the rationing function of market prices.*

Finally, remember that the analysis in this chapter assumed that markets were in fact freely competitive. In many cases markets are not competitive, nor are buyers and sellers the only people who gain or lose when they transact their business. In such cases we must reassess the role of government in modifying market outcomes.

Summary

1. Prices serve to ration scarce goods sold in competitive markets by preventing shortages and surpluses.
2. A nonscarce good is one for which quantity demanded will not exceed quantity supplied at zero price.
3. Successful marketing of a new item depends on conditions of supply and demand for the item. If the minimum price sellers will accept exceeds the maximum price buyers will pay for the first unit made available, the item is not marketable. Changes in technology lower the minimum prices sellers can accept for items and expand markets for these goods.
4. Wages and hours worked in competitive labor markets depend on the demand for and supply of labor. Similarly, interest rates and credit extended in competitive financial markets depend on the demand for and supply of loanable funds.
5. Price ceilings, maximum prices that can legally be charged in competitive markets, result in shortages when they are below market equilibrium prices. Rent control laws are examples of price ceilings.
6. Nonprice rationing distributes available amounts of goods and services on a basis other than willingness to pay when shortages caused by price ceilings exist in competitive markets. The most common nonprice rationing device is "first come, first served."
7. Price ceilings usually result in illegal transactions in black markets at prices that exceed the legal limits.
8. Price floors establish minimum prices, which can result in surpluses when these prices exceed equilibrium prices in competitive markets. Minimum wages and agricultural price supports are common examples of price floor programs.
9. Price ceilings and price floors benefit certain groups but impair the rationing of goods and services by the price system in competitive markets.

Concept Review

(1) Why would a world in which scarce goods are free be chaotic?

(2) Under what circumstances would the equilibrium quantity of a good be zero in a market?

(3) Explain why downward rigidity of wages can result in surpluses of labor (excessive unemployment) during a recession when the demand for labor declines.

(4) Why do rent controls result in shortages of housing?

Problems and Applications

1. A local music store advertises it will give away Bruce Springsteen CDs from 8 A.M. to 5 P.M., on Saturday. What's likely to happen? Why might you be better off waiting until Monday to buy your CD at the market price? (1)
2. Residents on an island in which coconuts are a nonscarce good discover that people in the rest of the world don't consider coconuts nonscarce and will pay high prices to obtain them. Explain what's likely to happen to the demand for coconuts as island residents discover they can export the fruit to foreign markets. (1)
3. The price of personal computers was well over $5,000 when they were introduced in the early 1980s. Since then, the price has fallen drastically. Use supply and demand analysis to explain the likely cause of this fall. What was the effect of decreasing prices on the quantity demanded of this good? (2)
4. Rising enrollment in college accounting curricula causes a sharp increase in the supply of accountants four years later. Other things being equal, use supply and demand analysis to forecast the impact of the increase in the supply of accountants on annual salaries of accounting graduates. (3)
5. A drop in profits for oil companies results in a sharp decrease in the demand for chemical engineers. Use supply and demand analysis to predict the effect on salaries paid to chemical engineers and on the quantity of their labor supplied. (3)
6. Suppose the federal government finally balances the budget. The decrease in demand for loanable funds to cover the deficit is likely to have

a significant effect on credit markets. Use supply and demand analysis to forecast, other things being equal, the impact of a decrease in government demand for loanable funds on interest rates and on borrowing by business firms and consumers. (3)

7. The market equilibrium rent per room in a small city is $100. A rent control law is passed that establishes a price ceiling of exactly $100 per room. What will be the impact of the law on the market for rental housing? How will your answer change if, immediately after the rent controls have been passed, a major corporation announces it will build a new factory employing 10,000 workers? The new plant is expected to sharply increase the demand for housing. (4)

8. A $1.50-per-gallon price ceiling is established for gasoline. As a result of the ceiling, a weekly shortage of 10,000 gallons develops. How can the shortage be rationed? (4)

9. Although minimum wages prevent labor markets from rationing unskilled labor services, they're widely praised by labor leaders and are regarded as good by most people. How can you explain the political support for minimum wages? (4)

10. How could agricultural surpluses be eliminated in the United States? Use supply and demand analysis to show how agricultural price floors cause surpluses and how taxpayers pay the cost of the surpluses. Who would gain and who would lose if agricultural price support programs were phased out? (4)

The Transition to Free Markets in the Former Communist Nations

A hallmark of communism was price controls for everything. Throughout much of the 20th century, the economies of Eastern Europe and the republics of the former Soviet Union lacked free markets. Under communism, a cumbersome system of central planning prevailed through which governments determined what was produced and how it was produced, and influenced living standards by controlling wages and salaries. The economies of Eastern Europe and the former Soviet Union were characterized by government ownership or control of productive resources. Under central planning, these economies were managed by governing authorities who set prices and production targets to achieve political goals. All business was controlled by the government, and markets as means for the free exchange of goods and services were a rarity.

We can use our analysis of price controls to understand how the old system of central planning worked and some of the difficulties involved in the transition to free markets in the formerly communist nations. In most of these nations, central planning allocated a disproportionate amount of resources to heavy industries, such as steel, to support a vast military establishment. Production of consumer goods wasn't given high priority by the planners. The prices of food and other basic items were kept low. The government, which owned many of the farms, and all of the bakeries and food production facilities, often sold food below the costs of production as a way of subsidizing workers whose low wage levels were set by it.

Unfortunately, the low prices for such items as bread were well below equilibrium levels and vast shortages were common. Citizens of Eastern Europe and the former Soviet Union were accustomed to waiting in lines for many hours to obtain bread.

The graph below shows the effect of setting prices below equilibrium levels, under central planning. The supply of an item was usually determined at the beginning of the year by the planning authorities, and the amount made available each month was therefore fixed and independent of price. At the price set by the planners, quantity demanded far exceeded quantity supplied.

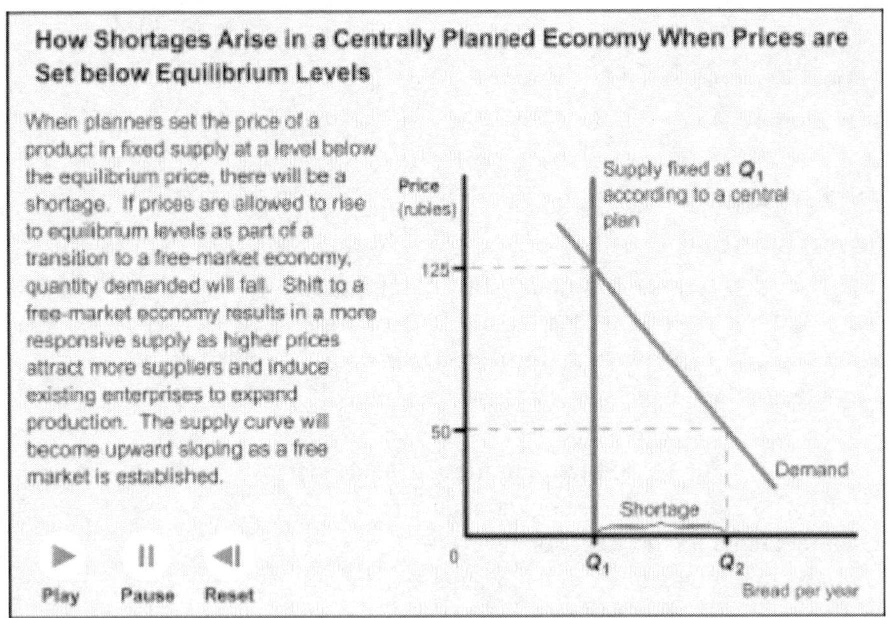

The prices set by the planners didn't result only in shortages--they also resulted in waste. Bread was so cheap that farmers often used it instead of raw grain to feed pigs! There was also waste, because many items, such as unpopular, frumpy clothing, were priced above equilibrium levels and were therefore in surplus. Despite the surpluses, because of the rigid system of central planning, these items continued to be produced.

As communism ended, food prices were allowed to rise to equilibrium levels. In the early 1990s, for example, Poland was feeling the effects of the move to free markets. The food shops were well stocked with meat, bread, and cakes. There were no lines. Individual entrepreneurs set up makeshift markets selling goods they had acquired directly from factories in Poland. Others took advantage of newly opened borders and the freedom to acquire foreign currency. They traveled abroad, where they bought fresh produce to sell to eager Polish consumers with the ability to pay.

As prices rose, quantities demanded fell. The Polish people could now find what they wanted in the shops, but most people couldn't afford these items! The Poles were poor before the prices were allowed to rise--under the first come, first served principle, however, some of them were able to obtain basic goods in short supply *if they were lucky*. Now, it took hard cash rather than time in line to obtain sausage.

To complete the move to free markets, the governments of the formerly communist nations must transfer their property rights in productive resources to private interests. "Privatizing" former government enterprises means selling them to domestic or foreign buyers who will operate them as business firms. The privatization process will result in the shutdown of unprofitable enterprises. As private ownership becomes the norm, the owners of firms will become independent suppliers of products to a system of markets in which prices are determined by supply and demand. Eventually, the rigid fixed-supply curves, such as that for bread illustrated in the graph above, will become upward-sloping as profit-seeking entrepreneurs become responsive to price changes. When the economies of the formerly communist nations complete their transition to free markets, prices will serve as signals of scarcity and profitability to the new private enterprises that will supply goods and services.

However, the transition to free markets isn't painless. As old, inefficient state enterprises are privatized or shut down, many workers lose their jobs and have to seek new ones, while the prices of many of the products they need rise. Higher prices eliminate shortages, but also reduce the purchasing power of already low incomes. Unemployment, reduced living standards, and soaring prices are the unfortunate consequences of the painful transition to free markets that, eventually, improves resource use and raises incomes in the formerly communist nations. From 2001 to 2008, economic growth was strong for many economies in transition. And, for such nations as Russia, Poland, the Czech Republic and China, the transition to free markets was bearing fruit. Although the gains from growth weren't evenly distributed among all and income inequality was increasing, living standards, on average, improved substantially over the days of the old centrally planned systems.

Operation of Labor Markets in the United States

In practice, market wages don't always instantaneously adjust to eliminate surpluses and shortages of labor. For example, during a recession the demand for factory workers typically declines as the demand for factory output decreases. If wages were to adjust immediately after the decline in demand, the quantity of labor demanded would equal the quantity supplied at a lower wage, as shown in the graph.

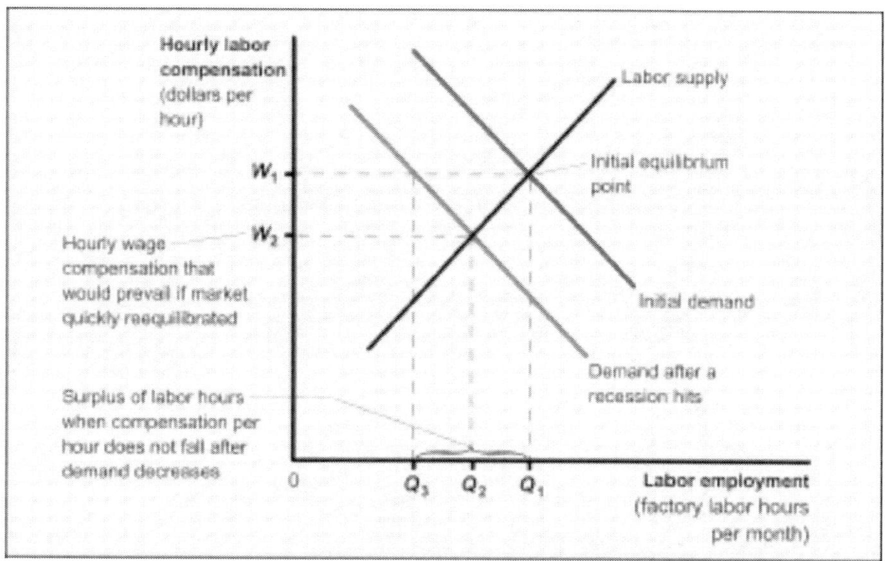

However, the data on wage adjustment in the united States during recessions since the end of World War II indicate that wages adjusted for the effects of inflation actually *rise* slightly during recessions! This suggests that labor markets don't adjust quickly to temporary declines in labor demand. During a typical recession in the United States, the unemployment rate rises about 2 to 4 percentage points.*

As a result of downward rigidity in wages during recessions, employment declines by more than would otherwise be the case. In the graph, employment would fall from Q_1 to Q_2 during a recession if wages fell in response to the decrease in labor demand. However, when wages don't fall quickly in response to the decline in demand, employment falls to Q_3. Rigid wages therefore result in a surplus of labor and excessive unemployment during a recession. However, workers who keep their jobs during recessions don't suffer a decline in income. The way U.S. Labor markets operate, the workers with the greatest seniority are laid off last during a recession. This implies that much of the loss of income caused by layoffs in a recession is borne by younger workers.

*See Thomas J. Kniesner and Arthur H. Goldsmith, "A Survey of Alternative Models of the Aggregate U.S. Labor Market," *Journal of Economic Literature* 25, no. 3 (September 1987), pp. 1241-80.

Policy Perspective: Rent Control in New York City

Rent control has been used in New York City since 1943. Nearly two-thirds of the city's population lives in rental units, and more than one million of these units is subject to some form of rent control. Because rent control applies to units of housing and isn't based on the income or needs of individuals, its benefits extend to rich and poor alike. Ironically, many of the beneficiaries of rent control are middle-income and upper-middle income families.

Rent controls in New York City prevented rents from rising from 1965 to 1975, a period of increasing housing maintenance costs. This contributed to the loss of nearly 200,000 housing units through abandonment during that period. Although tenants in rent-controlled apartments pay lower rents, the quality of their housing is often lower than that enjoyed by people whose units aren't under rent control. Vacancy rates in New York City for rental housing have consistently been below those of cities without rent controls, suggesting that the controls have in fact contributed to housing shortages.[1]

Rent control is a government-mandated subsidy from landlords to tenants. One study estimates the value of this subsidy in New York City at $20 billion between 1943 and 1976. Many of the landlords whose income is reduced as a result of rent control are small investors of modest means.[2]

One way landlords in New York City can avoid the unfavorable effects of rent control on their incomes is to convert rental housing to industrial and commercial property, for which rents are not controlled. During the 1980s, landlords frequently responded to rent regulations by converting rental housing to condominiums, which they could then sell at the market price.

When a rent-controlled apartment becomes vacant, the landlord often chooses not to rerent it. (In 1987, it was estimated that as many as 90,000 of the city's 1.2 million rent-regulated apartments were being held off the market. Landlords were "warehousing" the units to avoid legal difficulties in converting them to condominiums.) Warehousing aggravates the shortage of rental units caused by controls in the first place. The landlords argue it's their right to choose not to rent apartments they own. Critics of warehousing argue that it should be outlawed.

You can easily understand the motivation for warehousing if you look at some of the costs landlords incur in converting rental units to salable owner-occupied condominium units. When a building in New York City is converted to condominiums, the tenants in rent-regulated apartments are protected by law against eviction. Tenants have three options: retain the right to rent (and to renew the lease at a modest increase in rent), buy their apartments at discounted "insider" prices, or accept payments from the landlord in return for giving up their tenant rights. Before a condominium conversion can begin in New York City, a certain minimum number of apartments must be vacant or tenants must agree to vacate or purchase their units. Landlords gladly offer tenants discounts and payments to induce them to give up their legal rights to rent-controlled units.

One Manhattan tenant was given the option to purchase the apartment he currently leased at a price of $72,000, which represented a 28 percent discount from the outsider price. Alternatively, the landlord would have happily paid the tenant $36,000 to give up his tenant rights. This tenant chose to keep renting the apartment at the current regulated rent of about $400 a month. The tenant wasn't acting irrationally. The controlled rent was a good deal compared to the other alternatives. Had the tenant accepted the payment and bought the apartment, his monthly housing costs would probably have tripled![3] About two-thirds of the tenants in condominium conversions in New York City find keeping their rent-controlled apartments the best alternative compared to accepting payments to vacate or buying their apartments at the insider price.

The boom in condominium conversions in New York City came to a halt in 1990 as an economic slowdown in the city sharply reduced the demand for housing. As real estate values and rents began to fall, and maintenance costs rose, many landlords found it difficult to earn profits whether they rented apartments or tried to sell them as condos. In some cases in early 1990, market equilibrium rents fell enough so that rent-controlled apartments could not be rented for the legally authorized rents! There is little incentive to convert apartments to condominiums when rent controls are no longer effective.

However, as the city's economy began to recover in the early 1990s, rent control became an issue again, with particular concern about its benefits to upper income groups. But, as of 1995, rent control remained entrenched in New York City, despite the reign of a mayor who ran on a platform of free markets and reduced government activity. The popularity of rent control in New York City stems in part from these facts: 85 percent of Manhattan residents are tenants, and 69 percent of the apartments they rent are rent-regulated by the city.[4] Even a free-market politician is cautious about changing a law that provides benefits to that many voters--despite the fact that the city forgoes an estimated $100 million in property taxes annually as depressed rents hold down the value of residential property. However, the state legislature (whose constituents are not so dependent on city voters) recently stepped in to take rent control benefits away from tenants earning more than $250,000 per year provided that their rent exceeds $2,000 per month.

Many of the benefits of rent control in the city have accrued to upper-income tenants who could easily afford to pay more for the apartments at prime locations in Manhattan. For example, in 1994, the director of the Metropolitan Museum of Art was paying $1,985 per month for a seven-room Fifth Avenue apartment that would rent for $6,000 if it were available on the free market. The choicest apartments are rent-controlled units that were built before 1947. There are 47,000 of these units that, in 1994, were occupied by the original 1947 tenants or their close relatives. The actress Mia Farrow lives in a 10-room Central Park West apartment for which her mother, the actress Maureen O'Sullivan, signed a lease more than 40 years ago. Because she lived in the apartment as a child, she's still eligible for rent control, and she pays a monthly rent of $2,900 for the 10 rooms--much below the rent the apartment would command on a free and competitive market.[5] "Rent-stabilized" apartments in New York City tend to be newer than the rent-controlled units and have higher rents, but those rents are still below market equilibrium levels.

As of 2004, rent control and stabilization remained entrenched in New York City. About 60,000 apartments in the City are still classified as rent-controlled. These are units located in buildings constructed before 1947 and currently occupied by a tenant (or family member of the tenant) who has occupied it since 1971. The apartment becomes “decontrolled” only if those tenants move from the premises and no relative assumes the lease. A rent regulation board allows annual increases in the rents of these units each year. In 2004, the rent increase was 7.5 percent. Tenants naturally complain when their rents rise. However, landlords say that, in 2003, their operating costs for the rent-controlled apartments went up 17 percent, so the increase doesn't make them better off and provides little incentive to improve the units.

When a rent-controlled apartment is decontrolled in New York, it becomes rent-stabilized. There are currently about one million rent-stabilized apartments in New York City. A “legal rent,” which has no relation to a market equilibrium rent, is established for rent-stabilized apartments. Rent increases for these apartments are regulated, but they can be raised as much as 20 percent if an existing tenant moves out. However, under state law, vacated rent-stabilized apartments are phased out of the system once (if ever) their rents increase to $2,000 per month. Because tenants lose their subsidies when they move, the incentive is, of course, to stay put. Under current rules, however, households with incomes in excess of $175, 000 per year are not allowed to lease rent-stabilized apartments (although they're not barred from occupying rent-controlled units). As of 2004, it was estimated that 13 percent of the households occupying rent-controlled units had incomes in excess of $70,000 per year. Despite reforms, the system still doesn't clearly target low-income tenants and still discourages landlords from making quality improvements in controlled or stabilized apartments.

[1]See Frank S. Kristof, "The Effects of Rent Control and Rent Stabilization in New York City," in *Rent Control: Myths and Realities*, ed. Walter Block and Edgar Olsen (Vancouver, B.C.: Fraser Institute, 1981).

[2]Ibid.

[3]See Michael de Courcy Hinds, "For New Yorkers, Is There Life after Rent Regulation?" *The New York Times*, Real Estate, October 26, 1986, p.2.

[4]See Laurie P. Cohen, "Home Free: Some Rich and Famous of New York City Bask in the Shelter of Rent Law," *The Wall Street Journal*, March 21, 1994, p. 1.

[5]Cohen, "Home Free."

Subsidies and the Milk Surplus

Fueled by an increase in worldwide demand for milk products, U.S. dairy farmers were enjoying a price of $20 per hundredweight (cwt) of raw milk in early 2008. Then came a deep recession in 2008 and 2009 that sharply decreased demand for milk products, and the price of milk plummeted to $14 per cwt. At the retail level, the price of powdered milk fell from a peak of $2.20 per pound in mid-2007 to a mere 80 cents per pound.

As the price of powdered milk collapsed, federal government price support programs kicked in. To keep the price of milk at the support level, the federal government had to commit to buying a surplus at the support price. As of early 2009, the U.S. Department of Agriculture was committed to purchasing about 112 million pounds of milk powder from U.S. producers at a support price of 80 cents per pound and at an estimated cost of $91 million to taxpayers.*

Dairy farmers had been benefiting from the boom in demand for dairy products, as the need for such items as cheese, ice cream, and milk shakes soared worldwide. Increased income in nations such as China resulted in more westernized diets, including pizza and ice cream. U.S. exports of dairy products to China, Indonesia, Mexico, as well as many middle-eastern countries, soared. But as demand shrank and the U.S. dairy industry faced more competition from producers in New Zealand and Australia, prices fell drastically.

Dairy farmers warned that unless they continued to receive price supports and unless those price supports were expanded to include dairy products other than powered milk, such as cheese, hundreds of producers would be forced to reduce the size of their herds or leave the dairy business.

The price supports will moderate income declines in the dairy industry and keep the supply of dairy products stable, but will also keep dairy prices higher for domestic consumers than would otherwise be the case. And taxpayers will also be paying for the purchase and storage of surplus dairy products for some time into the future, unless prices recover or the government can sell the surplus without adversely affecting milk prices.

*See Andrew Martin, "As Recession Deepens, So Does Milk Surplus," *The New York Times*, January 2, 2009.

Chapter 5

The Price System and the Mixed Economy

In this chapter, we'll look at how prices guide economic decisions in a system of markets under which business firms seek to profit by supplying products that satisfy market demands. We'll examine the basic components of a capitalist economy, and how production of goods and services in such an economy generates the income necessary to buy these products.

The production or consumption of many products sold in markets often has undesirable side effects, such as pollution. Governments often intervene in markets to reduce or eliminate such effects. International trade plays an important role in modern economies by allowing consumers to enjoy a greater variety of products and to obtain products at lower prices. To completely understand how modern economies function, it's therefore necessary to look at both government activity and the process of international trade.

Concept Preview

After reading this chapter, you should be able to

1. Examine the framework of a pure market economy, and show how the circular flow of income and expenditure in a capitalist economy keeps it functioning.
2. Explain the price system as a means of allocating resources in terms of what is produced, how it is produced, and how it is distributed.
3. Identify the defects of a pure market system.
4. Briefly outline the functioning of the modern mixed and open economy, including the role of government and principles of taxation.

Capitalism and the Market Economy

1 Capitalism is an economic system characterized by private ownership of economic resources and freedom of enterprise in which owners of factories and other capital hire workers to produce goods and services. Under capitalism, anyone is free to use economic resources to start a business and sell a product in a market. In a purely capitalist economy government's role is quite limited, and the economy relies on the pursuit of profit through market sales to make goods and services available.

In most modern nations, however, governments control many resources, and criteria other than personal gain and business profit are used to decide how resources will be employed. Most modern nations have a mixed economy, where governments as well as business firms provide goods and services. In such economies governments supply roads, defense, pensions, and schooling directly to citizens. In modern economies governments also commonly intervene in markets to control prices and correct for the shortcomings of a system in which prices and the pursuit of personal gain influence resource use and incomes.

Let's look first at how resources would be allocated in an economy in which all useful goods and services are traded in competitive markets. In such an economy, prices would act as signals that influence the possibilities for gain. The price system is a mechanism by which resource use in a market economy is guided by prices. In such a system, changes in prices caused by changes in demand and supply affect opportunities for profit and personal gain and cause changes in resource use.

The driving force behind a capitalist economy is the pursuit of personal gain by both sellers and buyers who seek to get the most satisfaction from their income. In such an economy, people are free to organize business firms for the purpose of selling goods and services at a profit. There are few restrictions on what can be bought or sold. The people who manage and assume the risks of business enterprises are called *entrepreneurs.* They are innovators who develop new products and processes or reorganize production in ways that reduce costs or better satisfy consumers. Profit is both the reward and the incentive that motivates them.

The owners and managers of business firms acquire capital equipment and inventories of materials and negotiate contracts to hire workers who produce goods and services for sale in markets. The private ownership of capital and other resources is a dominant feature of capitalism. In the capitalist system *freedom of enterprise* is the right of business firm owners to employ private economic resources for whatever purpose they want.

Capitalism is also characterized by *economic rivalry,* a situation in which large numbers of buyers are competing for available supplies of goods and services offered by large numbers of sellers. Economic rivalry implies a diffusion of economic power, so that no single buyer or seller can make a good significantly more abundant or scarce. Free markets exist when there are no restrictions that prevent either buyers or sellers from entering or exiting a market. No one is forced to enter into market transactions; therefore, only those transactions that provide mutual gains to buyers and sellers will be pursued. Finally, another key institution of capitalism is property rights, established and enforced by law, to the exclusive use of goods and services. These property rights lubricate the wheels of market exchange by allowing prices to be established in markets and by providing incentives to use resources in the most socially productive ways.

Specialization and Exchange

Specialization and division of labor mean that workers and entrepreneurs devote most of their time to producing one or a few goods and services. These specialists sell the goods or services they specialize in and then use their incomes to buy goods and services they want that are offered for sale by other specialists. In this way specialization and voluntary exchange allow people to enjoy additional gains from existing production. Such exchange involves *mutual gains* to the traders. If no one else is harmed when people specialize and trade in goods and services and there is no deception, then more benefit can be obtained from an existing amount of production. For example, suppose a farmer produces more food than he can use. This farmer can gain if he is allowed to exchange the food that results from specialization for another item that he values more, such as clothing. Similarly, a tailor who produces more clothing that he needs can gain by exchanging some of the clothing for food. Even if both the tailor and the farmer produce their products without waste, they can both enjoy further gains by exchanging their food and clothing in a market trade.

This process of exchanging goods (or services) for goods (or services) is known as barter. In a barter economy a farmer can truck his produce into a market and trade it for clothing offered by a tailor. Barter is an inconvenient means of exchange because it requires *double coincidence of wants,* which means that to exchange an item a trader must truck items around to find someone else who both wants what the trader offers and has what he or she desires. For example, suppose you have accounting skills. This week you want to buy a new digital camera. To exchange your accounting services for a camera, you'll need to find someone willing to exchange the camera you want for your accounting services. Making this exchange can require a time-consuming search. You may find someone who has the kind of camera you want but who has absolutely no desire for your accounting services. You may also find people who want your accounting services but don't have anything you want. With a barter system of exchange, each trader must seek out people who have the desired goods and want the goods offered in exchange for them.

Money exchange doesn't require this double coincidence of wants. All you have to do is sell your accounting services to anyone willing to pay for them. When you've earned enough money income, you go to the store and exchange it for a stereo system. *Money,* usually issued only by governments, is what sellers generally accept as payment for goods and services. The characteristics of money are so important that an entire chapter can be devoted to its functions. At this point you should realize that a generally accepted medium of exchange serving as money greatly facilitates specialization and market exchange of goods and services.

How Production Generates Income in the Market Economy: Circular Flow of Income and Expenditure

Imagine an economy in which all goods and services are made available through markets. Business firms acquire resources from households, whose members provide labor services, entrepreneurial talent, and funds to acquire new capital. Household members also provide natural resources if they own land. The diagram in Box 1 gives you a simplified overview of a pure market economy.

In such an economy, business firms are buyers of resources offered for sale in input markets. Households supply economic resources as sellers in these input markets. The competition among the many buyers and sellers of inputs then results in market prices for labor, the use of funds, capital, and natural resources. The prices depend on conditions of supply and demand in each input market.

The sale of input services provides a flow of income in the form of wages, rent, interest, and profit to the members of each household supplying resources or owning businesses. For example, people in one household may earn wages as department store employees. They may also own land and buildings that they allow a business to use in exchange for rent. Income from both wages and rent flows into the household. Household members also earn interest income from bank deposits or bonds. If they own corporate stock, they may receive a flow of income as dividends on the stock. They may run a small business that generates profits. The flow of payments for labor and resource use plus distribution of

Box 1 The Circular Flow of Income and Expenditure in a Market Economy

Business firms acquire resources from households in input markets. The income earned by households is then spent on goods and services offered for sale in product markets by business firms.

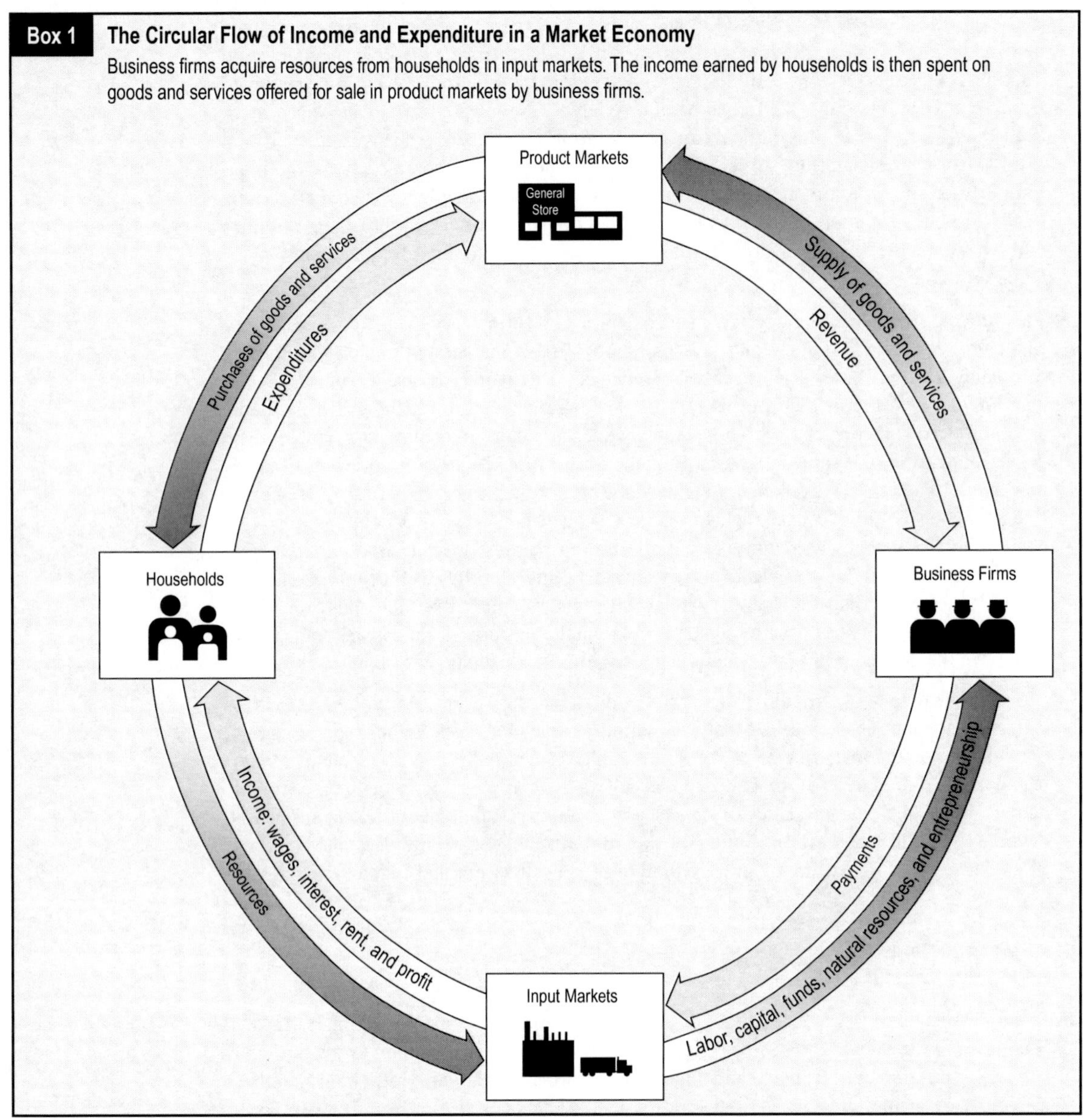

profit to the members of households who own businesses equals the income earned in the economy.

Household members use the money income they earn to express their demand for goods and services. Firms respond to that demand by producing a variety of goods and services. The price of each good and service is determined by its supply and demand in product markets. Consumers' expenditures constitute revenue for firms that they use to finance outlays for inputs (wages to staff, purchases of inventories, rent) and profit payments to owners of the firms.

The picture of the economy as a set of interrelated markets in which income and expenditure move in a circular flow between business firms and households is a simplified but enlightening view of a pure market economy. It points out that both households and business firms meet in two sets of markets—households are sellers in input markets and buyers in product markets; business firms are buyers in input markets and sellers in output markets. Money lubricates the wheels of exchange. It is paid out as income to households that they in turn spend on products. It then becomes revenue to business firms that they use to pay for the items they need in order to make goods available. These payments provide income as the cycle goes on and on. Business firms also employ a steady flow of resources that are used to supply goods and services each day to households. The clockwise flow of expenditures, revenue, payments, and income fuels the counterclockwise flow of goods and services and resources in the circular flow diagram in Box 1.

The production of goods and services therefore generates income. The income then becomes the means by which households purchase the products produced by business firms. As production grows, so will income payments to households.

Box 1 does not show that business firms conduct market transactions among themselves. Some of the products firms purchase, such as machinery, structures, and vehicles, are intended for final use in production and will not be resold to consumers or governments. Others are used as materials and parts that will be incorporated into other products sold to final users. The diagram also ignores the role of government in the economy, since government has only a minor role in an economy where all useful goods and services are provided through markets. Finally, the circular flow analysis does not consider the effects of international trade. We will soon show how both government and international trade affect the flow of income and expenditure in the modern mixed economy.

The Price System: How It Works

2 We need to elaborate on the diagram in Box 1 to show you how the price system works and when it fails. Within the box labeled "households," you and other individuals constantly weigh the costs and benefits of working or enjoying leisure, of using land for personal purposes or renting it out for use by others, and of providing funds for business firms to expand or spending those funds on consumer goods. Within the box labeled "business firms," managers decide how to employ resources and what to produce. *The unifying feature of all these decisions is that they are influenced by prices determined by free play of the forces of supply and demand in competitive markets.*

How the Price System Influences What Is Produced

No one directs a market economy. Instead, the prices established in markets act as signals for personal gain and profit to which households and business managers respond. *What* gets produced in a market economy is determined chiefly by profitability. When demand for a particular good increases, so does its price. For example, other things being equal, an increase in the demand for exercise bikes increases their price. The higher price increases the profitability of producing them. Because entrepreneurs seek out profits and avoid losses, when more profits are possible from making exercise bikes than from making cars, entrepreneurs will reallocate their resources from cars to exercise bikes. In this way, through the price system, suppliers respond to demand by producing the products that consumers want to purchase.

Box 2 shows how the price system responds to an increase in demand. Graph **A** shows that, given the initial demand and supply, at the market price of $300, 1 million exercise bikes per year are sold. An increase in demand increases the market price of exercise bikes to $350 and results in an increase in quantity supplied over the year to 1.2 million. This increase occurs as existing firms hire more workers and use material in existing factories to respond to the profit opportunities that arise when the price increases.

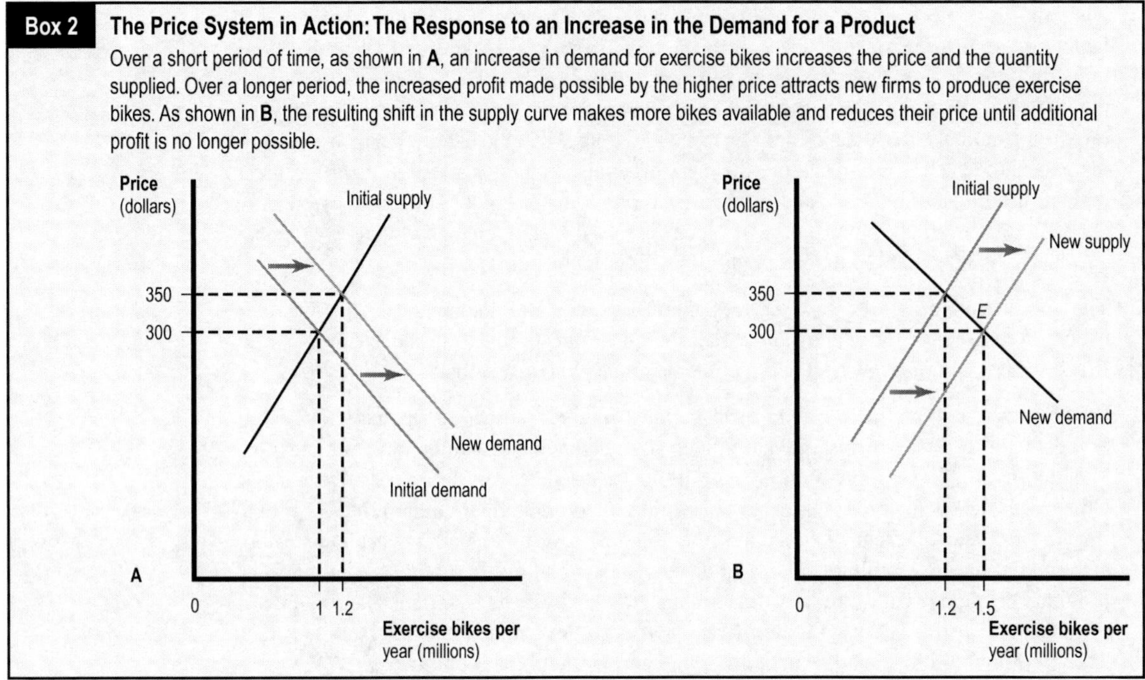

Box 2 The Price System in Action: The Response to an Increase in the Demand for a Product

Over a short period of time, as shown in **A**, an increase in demand for exercise bikes increases the price and the quantity supplied. Over a longer period, the increased profit made possible by the higher price attracts new firms to produce exercise bikes. As shown in **B**, the resulting shift in the supply curve makes more bikes available and reduces their price until additional profit is no longer possible.

Over a longer period of time, the higher price makes it profitable for entrepreneurs to start new factories specializing in the production of exercise bikes. More resources are devoted to producing exercise bikes over time. As shown in graph **B**, this increases the supply of exercise bikes. The final equilibrium is at point *E* in graph **B**, at which the new supply curve intersects the new demand curve. The quantity of exercise bikes sold increases to 1.5 million per year, and the price falls from $350 to $300. No single person planned the increase in the supply of exercise bikes. Instead, competition among entrepreneurs for profit opportunities caused the increase in supply that ultimately lowered prices and made more exercise bikes available.

Adjustments like this occur all the time in markets. For example, in 2004 and 2005, the demand for flat-panel LCD TVs was increasing. However, sellers anticipated this increased demand and sharply increased supply. In China alone, new factories were opened to more than triple the supply of TVs produced. Seeing the opportunity to increase profits by producing LCD TVs, firms expanded their capacity to satisfy the increased demand. The supply of flat-panel LCD TVs increased substantially in 2005, putting downward pressure on prices. Meanwhile, the market for older CRT (cathode ray tube) TVs was also affected, as demand for these sets declined, and the price and quantity supplied fell. The older CRT TVs commanded smaller and smaller shares of the market in 2005, and it was just a matter of time before TVs using this older technology would be extinct.

We can conduct a similar analysis for a decrease in demand for a product. By 2005, digital cameras and digital imaging were changing the market for photographic products. As more and more people started using digital cameras and digital imaging processes, the demand for film, photographic cameras that use film, and silver-based photographic papers that use chemicals for development of images declined. Sale of traditional silver-halide film dropped 30 percent in 2005. The decrease in demand for traditional photographic papers and films resulted in downward pressures on their prices and sharp declines in quantities supplied. The decrease in profitability of supplying these items resulted in the closing of production facilities. In 2005, the Eastman Kodak Company announced it was in the process of emphasizing digital imaging products and it would sharply curtail production of traditional photographic papers. The production of photographic films was also being cut in response to the decrease in the demand for these products. Kodak closed production facilities in Rochester, NY, and West Virginia, and announced it was scaling back production in plants it operated in China. The decline in film and paper sales, and the decrease in their prices and profitability of production, set up a process of adjustment through which producers reallocated resources away from traditional photographic products toward digital products.

The decrease in demand for traditional photographic films and papers affected other markets as well. Nearly 40 percent of all the silver mined in the United States was used in the production of photographic films and papers in 2002. As the demand for traditional photographic films and papers declined, so did the demand for silver. In 2003, silver production declined by 7 percent in the United States, as the events in the photographic markets were putting downward pressure on sales and prices of silver. As you can see, the events in one market can have repercussions in other related markets.

Similarly, changes in resource prices can affect the profitability of producing certain items. For example, a decrease in the cost of fuel can make supplying air travel more profitable, causing a reallocation of resources toward air travel services. As shown in Box 3, a decrease in fuel prices increases the supply of air travel offered between two points—New York and San Francisco. The increase in supply lowers the price, and the decrease in input prices allows more profits to be made on this route. As firms compete for the extra profit, supply increases. In Box 3 you can see that the increase in supply lowers the airfare from $300 to $200. As a result of the lower price, the number of passenger-miles of travel demanded on this route increases from 3 million to 4 million per year.

Changes in price signal changes in scarcity or demand, and both business firms and households respond by altering their choices. To gain more insight into the workings of the price system, we study the decisions made by business managers selling in competitive markets elsewhere in the text.

How the Price System Influences Production Methods

The pursuit of profit also influences *how* goods and services are produced. Business firms can earn more profit by producing any given quantity of goods and services at lower cost. Managers therefore try to use the *least costly* techniques to supply a given quantity of

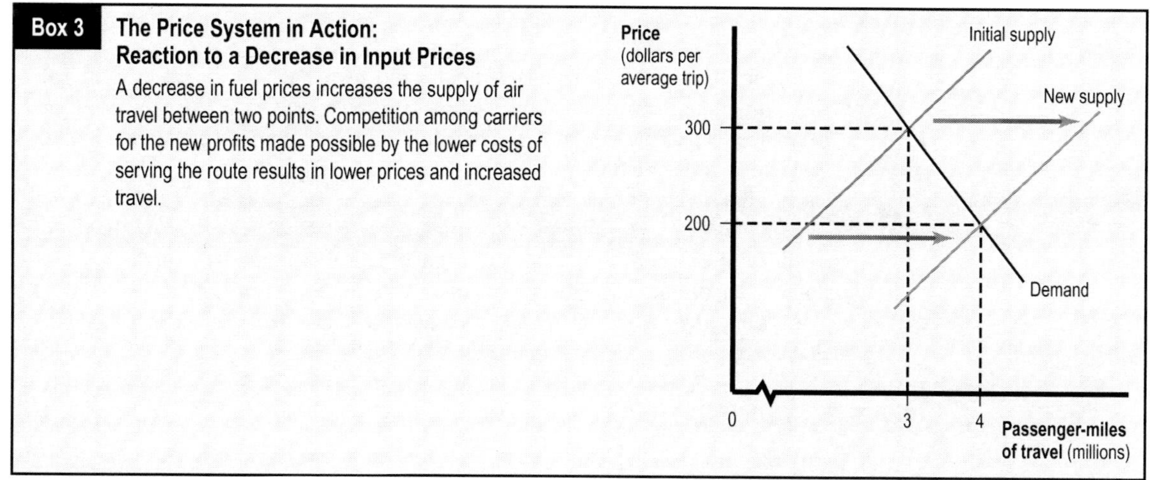

Box 3 The Price System in Action: Reaction to a Decrease in Input Prices

A decrease in fuel prices increases the supply of air travel between two points. Competition among carriers for the new profits made possible by the lower costs of serving the route results in lower prices and increased travel.

goods. If they don't, their competitors will, resulting in lower costs that will enable rival firms to profitably increase supply. There will then be downward pressure on prices, which will make it more difficult for a firm using older techniques to enjoy a profit.

Entrepreneurs seek opportunities for profit by developing new techniques that lower costs in much the same way that they seize opportunities to earn additional profit by responding to changes in consumer demands. Once again, prices, in this case those of inputs, play an important role in entrepreneurial and managerial decisions. For example, an increase in the price of labor services is likely to induce firms to look for ways to reduce labor use. If wages paid to farm workers increase, farm operators will find it more attractive to switch to mechanized harvesting and cultivation. Around 2000, the demand for pharmaceutical prescriptions was soaring, as were the salaries paid to pharmacists and other pharmaceutical workers. To cope with the increased costs of dispensing drugs, in 2005, many pharmacies were using robotic systems. These systems sharply increased the number of prescriptions a worker could dispense over a given period, often allowing workers to fill 150 or more prescriptions per hour. Hospitals were also using the new computerized systems to cut costs, in response to the increased volume of prescriptions and the increased salaries of pharmacists.

Entrepreneurs can also make more profit by devising less costly methods of production. For example, Henry Ford developed mass production techniques that enabled him to sell automobiles at much lower prices than those of his competitors. These innovative methods expanded the market for automobiles, and soon competing sellers adopted similar techniques. In this way innovation in production methods resulted in the allocation of more resources to the production of automobiles. Similarly, in the 1980s some steelmakers in the United States began using scrap steel instead of blast furnaces to produce steel directly from iron ore and coal. This method, used in small mills, allowed cost reductions in steel production. As a result, there was more investment in the so-called mini-mills and less investment in the larger "integrated" steel mills as profit opportunities in the mini-mills expanded.

Who Gets the Goods and Services?

Who gets what in the capitalist system? Remember that in such a system your income is determined by your labor skills and the other economic resources you possess and choose to sell at market prices. Your ability to buy goods and services in product markets therefore depends on your ability to register a demand for products. Remember also that demand is much more than the desire for an item. Demand is desire that can be *backed up* with the willingness and ability to pay. It is on this basis that the price system allocates goods and services among consumers. Your ability to pay in turn depends chiefly on your money income.

People who are poorly skilled, lack funds, and own no land or capital will have low incomes in a pure market economy. They will receive low wages for their labor and will have no other economic resources to provide them with income to buy goods and services. People whose skills are highly valued will earn high wages. People who have accumulated funds through saving or inheritance, and are fortunate enough to own land and capital, will enjoy nonlabor income. Entrepreneurs often earn spectacular incomes if their profitable innovations allow them to accumulate a great deal of capital. The market system can't guarantee support and sustenance to people who don't (or can't) work and who have no economic resources aside from their own labor. As you can see, income inequality is a likely occurrence in a market economy.

A Recap: The Price System in Motion

Given the ownership of economic resources, the market system is driven by prices. Changes in prices or technology signal changes in opportunities for private gain. The market system is dynamic in the sense that the pursuit of gain results in changes in resource use as economic conditions change. Profits and personal gain fuel the system, while competition keeps it on course. Profitable innovations are inevitably copied. As long as profit is possible from making more of a good available in a market, supply will increase and prices will fall. The competition for profit eventually lowers prices and results in the elimination of profits. Competition eliminates profits after they have served the purpose of allocating resources to uses that are in the greatest demand.

Some Common Defects in the Price System

3 The picture of the pure market economy painted earlier assumes that all useful goods and services can be sold in markets for a profit. However, such services as environmental protection, national defense, and police and fire protection are hard to sell by the unit in a market. You can't buy cleaner air and national security the way you can buy bread by the loaf! If we relied on competing sellers to produce these useful goods for profit in a competitive market, it's possible that none of them would be made available. For this reason people often find it convenient to have goods like national defense made available through government. The quantity and means of financing these goods are then determined politically by voters.

Public Goods and Externalities

Public goods are those consumed equally by all of us, whether we pay or not. Environmental protection and national security are good examples of public goods because they benefit all of us, regardless of whether we pay. Because we can't rely on competing sellers to provide public goods, revenue to make them available can be obtained only through a sharing arrangement such as taxation. In the modern mixed economy we rely on government to provide roads, military defense, air traffic control, and many other public goods. In fact, purchases of economic resources by governments to provide various services amount to 20 percent of the value of all goods and services produced in the United States.

In a nutshell, one common problem in a pure market economy is that not all the goods we want and are willing to pay for can easily be sold in neat packages that can be priced. The market often fails to provide public goods even though net gains are possible from doing so.

A related problem with the price system is that production or consumption of goods and services often results in costs or benefits to people other than the buyers and sellers. For example, if a firm disposes of wastes in a stream, it imposes costs on people who want to use the stream for swimming, fishing, and drinking water. It's not easy to put a price on economic resources like streams, the ocean, and the atmosphere when these resources are used as convenient receptacles for industrial wastes. When natural resources that no single person owns are used to dispose of harmful waste products, the result is pollution. The inability to charge for the use of the environment as a waste dump often results in the degradation of air and water quality.

Externalities are costs or benefits of market transactions that are not reflected in the prices buyers and sellers use to make their decisions. For example, aircraft noise in a neighborhood near an airport is a *negative* externality (or external cost) of the transaction between airlines and their passengers. Insofar as you and other college students make all members of society better off by improving the quality of life, transactions between college students and the university result in *positive* externalities (external benefits) to third parties. Externalities prevail because the use of resources like streams and the air, or the external benefits resulting from education, can't easily be priced. To understand the failure of the price system to allocate resources efficiently when externalities exist, we first need to examine the prerequisites for market exchange.

Externalities and Resource Use

Buyers and sellers in competitive markets seek personal gains through market transactions. If no one other than the buyers and sellers is harmed or benefited by these transactions, then those personal gains will be the only gains in the society at large. However, when externalities prevail, there are *third parties* in addition to the buyers or sellers who are affected by market transactions. For example, suppose pollution from the purchase and use of gasoline makes people other than the buyers or sellers worse off by impairing their health. Part of the cost of making gasoline available is the impaired health of those harmed by pollution. The market prices of gasoline are *too low* because they are not based on *all* the costs of making gasoline available. In this case the price system fails to price a valuable environmental resource, and consequently a negative externality prevails.

Similarly, you might not consider the fact that when you buy a particular item you benefit some third party other than you and the seller. For example, if you buy a smoke detector, you benefit your neighbors by reducing the risk of fire that can spread to their homes. The third parties in this case benefit from your purchase of the good but aren't charged for the benefit they receive. In this case the price system fails to price a benefit to third parties to a market transaction.

When a negative externality prevails, the unit and marginal costs that sellers consider in deciding quantity supplied are lower than the actual marginal costs because the sellers aren't charged for the damage they cause to third parties. As a result, the sellers produce more than they would if they were charged for the external costs they impose. If it were possible to price the use of the resources that are used free of charge, such as air or water, the marginal cost of any given output would increase. This increase in cost would cause sellers to decrease the supply of the product, and as a result price would increase. As a consequence of the higher price, the quantity of the good demanded would decline. For example, if the emissions of harmful pollutants resulting from the production of gasoline could be measured, sellers could be charged according to the damage the emissions cause. These charges would increase the sellers' marginal cost and would therefore decrease supply, resulting in an increase in price. The charges would also induce the sellers to change their productive methods to reduce the harmful emissions.

In the Box 4 graph you can see how charges for emitting damaging wastes affect the market for goods whose production or use causes such emissions. Suppose that when the externality prevails, the market equilibrium for gasoline corresponds to point E_1. At that equilibrium the price is $1 per gallon and 5 million gallons are sold. When sellers are charged for the damage they cause to third parties, they now have to include a previously unpriced input (the air) as part of the cost of producing and using gasoline. This results in a decrease in supply. The new market equilibrium is now at E_2, and the price of gasoline rises to $1.40 per gallon. As a consequence, quantity demanded declines to 4 million gallons per year. Reducing the emissions provides benefits to third parties and results in more efficient resource use. Sellers must consider the marginal cost of emissions as well as other costs when choosing output. However, because they're now charged for the emissions, the price of gasoline goes up. Without such charges, the price of the product doesn't reflect the entire cost of producing it or using it, and more of the product is sold than would be sold if the price reflected all the costs.

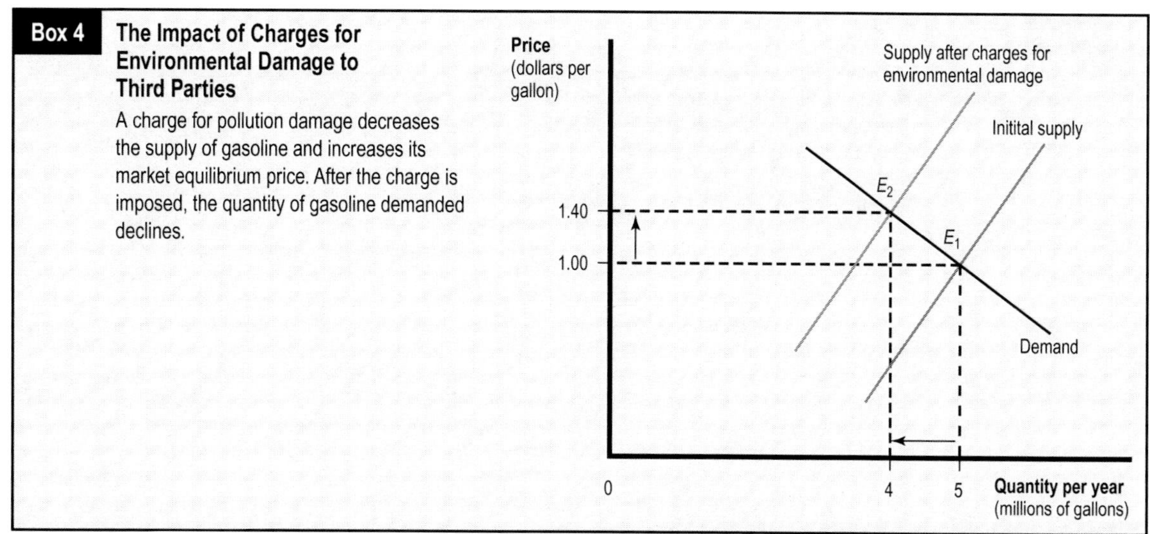

Box 4 The Impact of Charges for Environmental Damage to Third Parties

A charge for pollution damage decreases the supply of gasoline and increases its market equilibrium price. After the charge is imposed, the quantity of gasoline demanded declines.

Similarly, when a positive externality prevails, the sale of a good benefits someone other than the buyer or seller. If it were possible to charge these third parties for the benefit they receive, the seller could use the funds obtained to reduce the cost of making the good available. Such a subsidy to output would increase the gain from selling it and result in an increase in supply. The increase in supply would lower the price to buyers and increase the quantity demanded. For example, tuition is subsidized by citizens' taxes at state-supported schools. Taxpaying residents are third parties who eventually enjoy external benefits from students' education. Their tax dollars are used to lower tuition costs and increase the supply of higher-education services.

Box 5 shows you the impact of subsidies to encourage consumption of a good whose use results in a positive externality. When there are no means for third parties to contribute to the cost of higher education, the market equilibrium corresponds to point E_1. The corresponding tuition per year is \$15,000, and the number of students enrolling in colleges and universities is 10 million. After third-party subsidies to higher education (such as the tax revenues a state government gives its colleges), the supply of higher-education services increases and the new market equilibrium corresponds to E_2. At that point the tuition per student declines to \$5,000 per year and the number of students enrolled increases to 12 million per year. In the absence of any means for third parties to contribute toward the cost of higher education from which they benefit, the market devotes less than the efficient amount of resources to higher education.

Other Common Problems in a Market System

Other problems are also common in a market system. Three of the most important are lack of competition, income inequality and poverty, and instability.

Lack of Competition Markets are not always free and competitive. In noncompetitive markets barriers prevent gains from being achieved. For example, suppose there's only one seller of eggs in a market and it's impossible for additional sellers to enter the market. Buyers now have only one source of supply. Additional sellers who might be able to gain by making more eggs available at the profitable price set by the single seller are prevented from doing so. Under these conditions, the seller who monopolizes the supply can control the price to buyers who have no other source of supply.

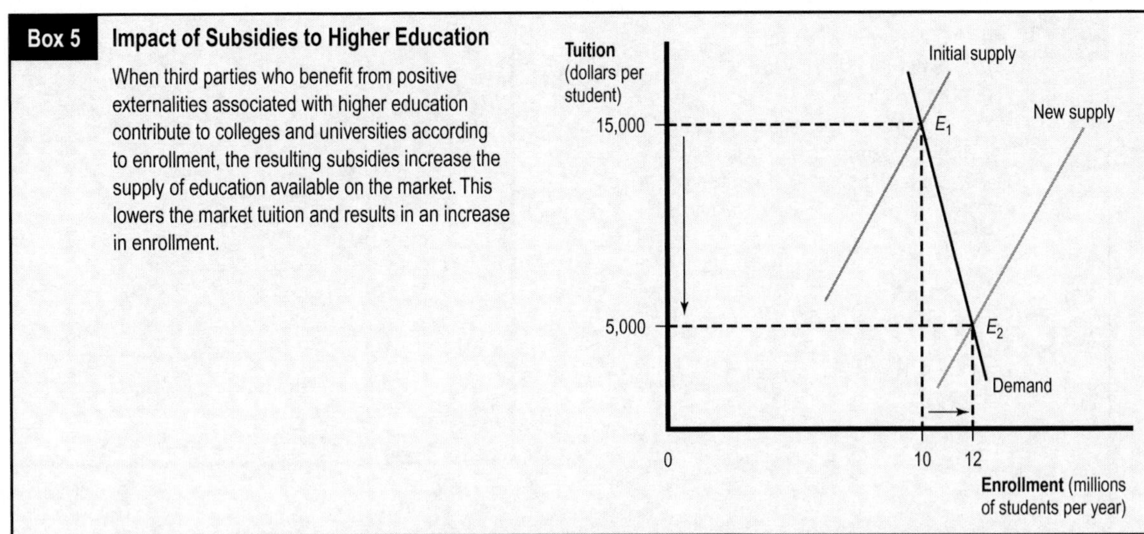

Box 5 Impact of Subsidies to Higher Education

When third parties who benefit from positive externalities associated with higher education contribute to colleges and universities according to enrollment, the resulting subsidies increase the supply of education available on the market. This lowers the market tuition and results in an increase in enrollment.

Lack of adequate competition impairs the ability of the price system to respond to changes in demand. Monopolization of supply prevents profits from serving as a signal for entry of new firms and more output in markets in which additional output would be profitable.

Income Inequality and Poverty In a pure market economy income depends entirely on the quantity, quality, and types of resources people are willing and able to sell. Income influences willingness and ability to pay for goods. People with very low incomes may be unable to buy the minimal amounts of goods and services required for their survival. If a large number of people in the economy lack the skills that would enable them to earn labor income and the ownership of capital and land is concentrated in the hands of a few wealthy individuals, the masses will be poor, while an elite class will earn most of the income.

In the United States, for example, the top 20 percent of families ranked according to income account for nearly half of all the income earned each year. On the other hand, the poorest 20 percent earn less than 4 percent of the nation's annual income. As you can see, the gap between the rich and the poor is vast.

Many critics of the pure market economy argue that its outcomes can't be given high marks on the basis of normative criteria for evaluating income distribution, even when the results of market exchange rank high in terms of efficiency criteria. The paradox of poverty in the midst of wealth is a common criticism of the performance of the capitalist economy. In 2007, an astounding 12.5 percent of the U.S. population was estimated to have money income inadequate to attain minimum acceptable living standards.

Instability When markets react to changes in demand or supply, it often takes a considerable amount of time for them to achieve equilibrium again. For example, fluctuations in the demand for products result in fluctuations in the demand for labor. A decrease in demand for labor is likely during a recession. Market wages don't always decline quickly enough to eliminate the labor surplus that occurs at the initial wage after the decrease in demand. As a result, during recessions there is excessive unemployment.

Similarly, prices are sometimes quite unstable and subject to sharp and unpredictable increases. Unpredictable inflation of the price level can make planning for the future difficult and can result in price changes that distort the way we conduct our daily affairs. For example, fear of future price increases can cause us to stock up on certain items. By stocking up, we further increase the demand for those items, thereby putting more upward pressure on prices.

Fluctuations in demand and supply and consequent periods of market disequilibrium are an inherent problem that results from lack of coordination of decision making in the price system. Governments often regulate markets and seek to influence the demand for products and loanable funds in attempts to correct market instability.

The Modern Mixed and Open Economy

4 The shortcomings of a pure market economy have led to the evolution of the modern mixed economy. When markets do a poor job of allocating resources, we look to government to improve matters. The impact of government on resource use and income distribution is a controversial question that we address in many parts of the text. However, the fact is that neither the United States nor any other nation can be regarded as having a purely capitalist economy.

In the United States the federal, state, and local governments levy taxes on both businesses and households to finance the provision of public goods and services. Governments also borrow funds to help meet their expenses. Finally, governments intervene in decisions made by households and business managers to protect environmental resources, prevent restraints on competition in markets, and correct for failures of the price system to account for the property rights of third parties to market transactions.

Governments in the United States acquire resources to provide hospital and health services, provide free and compulsory elementary and secondary education, assist the poor in maintaining minimum standards of living, provide for the national defense, and make pension and insurance services available to the elderly and other groups. About 20 percent of all workers in the United States are employed by governments.

The U.S. government supports the prices of some agricultural products. Government regulations influence the quality of such products as automobiles and new drugs, and through various taxes governments affect the prices of gasoline, cigarettes, and alcoholic beverages. Governments provide the legal structure that facilitates market transactions. Finally, governments seek to stabilize the general level of economic activity to correct for the difficulty that the price system often encounters in maintaining stable prices and full employment of labor and other economic resources.

Government and the Economy

Box 6 shows how government fits into the circular flow of expenditure and income. Governments participate in input markets by purchasing labor services and other productive resources. They borrow funds from credit markets when their expenditures exceed their tax revenues. Governments also participate in product markets to purchase the output of business firms. They purchase such goods as paper, aircraft, and machinery, and they contract with construction firms to build roads and structures. The vertical arrows in Box 6 show how governments participate in markets and provide income to workers, resource owners, and business firms.

The horizontal arrows show how governments tax households and businesses to obtain the funds necessary to purchase products and hire input services. The inputs and products are used to provide government goods and services that benefit both households and business firms. Governments provide national defense, education, police and fire protection, and a host of other services to the public at no direct charge. Most government

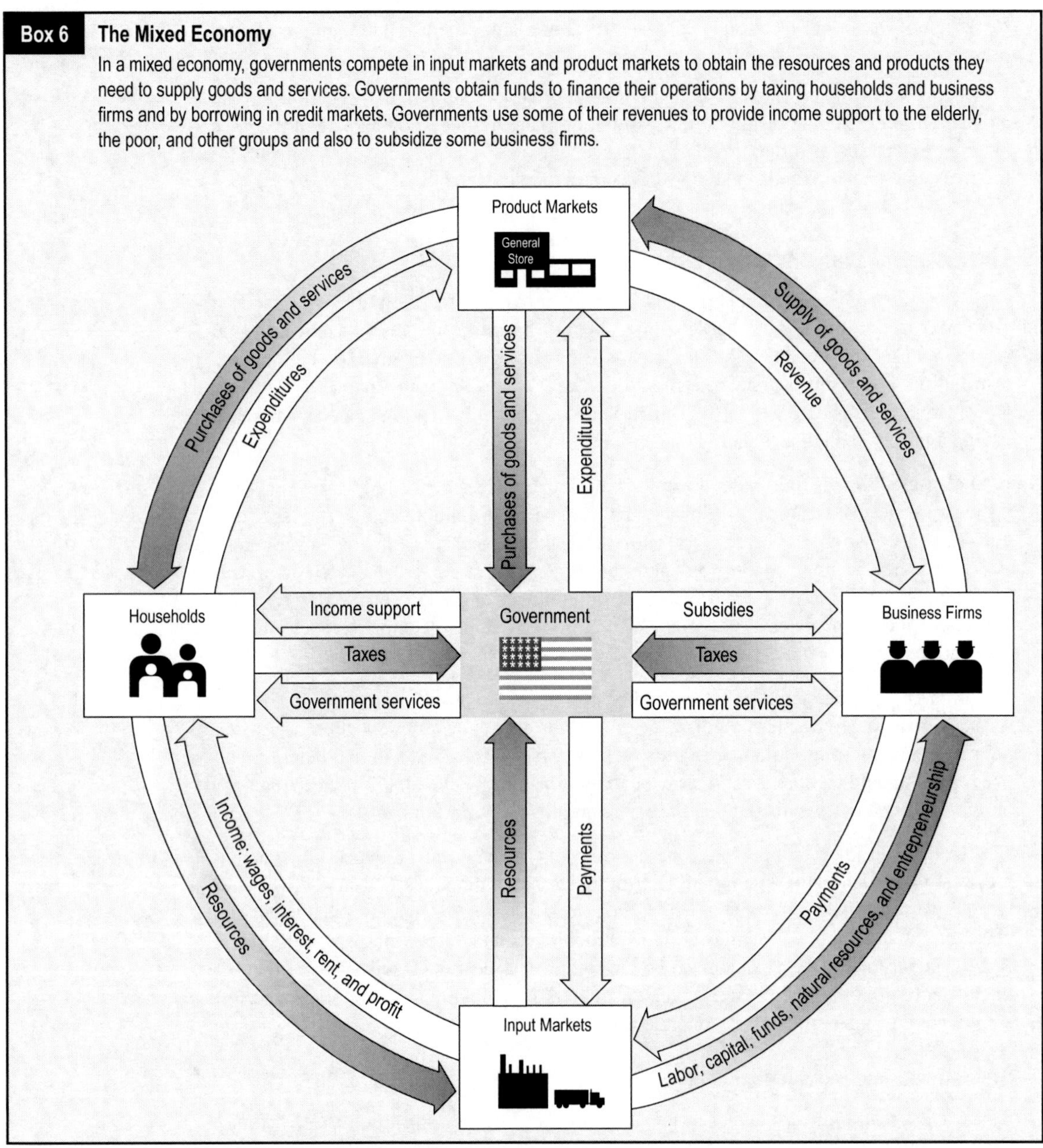

Box 6 The Mixed Economy

In a mixed economy, governments compete in input markets and product markets to obtain the resources and products they need to supply goods and services. Governments obtain funds to finance their operations by taxing households and business firms and by borrowing in credit markets. Governments use some of their revenues to provide income support to the elderly, the poor, and other groups and also to subsidize some business firms.

goods and services are not sold by the unit in markets. Instead, governments make their goods and services available freely as public goods or establish criteria for the eligibility of individuals to obtain certain services. For example, government funds are used to provide income support to eligible persons. Social Security pensions, welfare payments to the poor, veterans' benefits, payments for medical care, and unemployment insurance payments are examples of government income-support programs financed by taxation. Finally, governments provide subsidies to business firms such as price support payments to farmers and loan guarantees.

By bidding for resources, providing income support for the elderly, the poor, and veterans, subsidizing certain activities, and taxing businesses and households, governments influence market demand and affect prices. Thus, in the mixed economy governments, as well as households and business firms, influence resource allocation.

Shaping the Role of Government

Over the past 50 years government expenditures and activities have broadened and expanded. Under a system of majority rule, voters have consented to more and more government programs. It's difficult to evaluate whether the current allocation of resources between government goods and services and other goods and services is efficient. Many government programs are approved simply to redistribute income among citizens. In addition, government taxes result in losses of efficiency in markets by distorting choices in ways that reduce net benefits from national production.

Although government seeks to correct for defects in the price system, it also has an impact on resource use. When voters approve programs for which marginal costs exceed marginal benefits, a government failure exists because resources are allocated to uses for which the net gain is negative. The efficiency of government expenditures can be improved if we as voters are provided with accurate information on both the marginal costs and the marginal benefits of proposed programs.

Governments are a major force in economies. Both business firms and households rely on the federal government, the 50 state governments, and thousands of local governments to provide them with essential services. The United States has a federal system of government, a system in which numerous levels of government, each with its own powers, provide services and regulate private affairs. Over the years a division of responsibility has evolved among the levels of government in the United States. For example, the federal, or central, government has as its major functions the provision of national defense and social insurance programs. State and local governments have primary responsibility for education, roads and other transportation facilities, and hospitals and other health services.

The basic functions of government are the following:

1. *Establishment of rights to use productive resources and the regulation of private actions.* Government guarantees rights and enforces contracts. Disputes between private citizens concerning property rights and the contractual obligations are resolved through the government judicial system. In effect, government serves as a rule maker and a rule enforcer in the economy.

Government rules facilitate trade in markets. Government also uses its powers to regulate how goods and services are produced and what can or cannot be sold in markets.

2. *Provision of goods and services.* Government purchases input services to provide national defense, education, roads and health services. About one-fifth of the work force in the United States is employed by government.

3. *Redistribution of income.* Government establishes and administers programs that redistribute income among citizens. Welfare programs provide assistance to the poor. Government Social Security pensions redistribute income from workers to retirees. Government also subsidizes workers and producers in certain industries, such as agriculture, to stabilize supplies and put floors on incomes.

Government transfers are payments made directly to certain people or organizations that do not provide a good or service in return at that time. Social Security pensions are transfers from workers who pay Social Security taxes to retired workers and their dependents. Welfare payments to the poor are government transfers from taxpayers to eligible low-income people.

4. *Stabilization of the economy.* The federal government pursues policies designed to affect the overall level of demand and supply in the economy so as to control economic fluctuations. This is accomplished through control of the government's spending and taxation and through control of the nation's supply of money and credit.

Categorizing Government-Provided Goods

Government goods and services can be divided into two broad types:

1. *Goods that are made available to all citizens free of charge, the costs of which are financed by taxes or borrowings.* Included in this category are national defense, police and fire protection, public health, sanitation services, roads, bridges, national parks, and museums. Some of these goods, such as roads, bridges, and some recreational and health services, can be priced. For example, we pay a toll to use some roads and bridges and we pay admission for the right to enter government-provided recreational and cultural facilities.

2. *Goods and services that are tax-financed but are available only to individuals who meet predetermined eligibility criteria.* Public education is provided only to people in a certain age group. To be eligible for a Social Security pension, you must have worked in a job covered by Social Security for about 10 years and have attained a specified minimum age or become disabled.

In many cases government provides services that private firms also provide, such as pensions. Public and private schools and universities exist side by side, and people are free to choose between them, assuming they're able to pay the higher costs of private education.

Many government transfer programs, such as Social Security and the various welfare programs, are designed primarily to help particular people rather than provide a service to everyone. However, these programs do provide a public good because any of us, if and when we become eligible, can take advantage of their benefits. Also, by placing a floor under the incomes of many people, the programs decrease poverty, thus providing a public good to everyone in the form of a more stable and humane society. Total government spending in the United States averaged about one-third of the value of national output in the 1990s. This includes spending for such services as police, national defense, and roads, as well as spending on such transfer payments as Social Security and income support for the poor.

Principles of Taxation

The bulk of government spending is financed by taxes, compulsory payments associated with income, consumption, or wealth that individuals and corporations are required to make each year to governments. Taxes have become one of the most important items in the budgets of most households in the United States. On average, U.S. citizens allocate 25 percent of their annual incomes to help finance government goods and services.

Nobody enjoys paying taxes. Unlike prices, which are paid for the right to acquire or consume a good or service, taxes are compulsory payments that aren't a prerequisite to the right to consume a good. Naturally, everybody would like to pay as little tax as possible while still receiving the benefits of government goods and services.

Most of us have some idea of what we consider a fair distribution. Taxes are therefore usually evaluated according to fairness or *equity*. However, they also affect our incentives to work, save, invest and buy goods and services. The fairest taxes aren't always those that are the most efficient in terms of affecting incentives.

Tax Equity: Different Points of View

There are many different points of view about the way to evaluate tax equity. Many people believe taxes should be levied according to a person's ability to pay.

In fact, taxes are commonly evaluated by the way they vary with respect to income. A regressive tax is one for which the fraction of income used to pay it decreases as income increases. For example, the federal payroll tax used to finance Social Security pensions and Medicare can be regarded as a regressive tax. This is because it's levied as a flat percentage of labor income only up to a certain maximum. The combined employee-employer tax rate on worker earnings was 15.3 percent in 2009, but worker earnings in excess of $106,800 were taxed at only 2.9 percent. If your father had labor income of $60,000 in 2009, the total tax on those earnings would have been $9,180, half of which would have been paid by your father and the other half by his employer.

Suppose your uncle was the CEO of a large corporation in 2009, and his salary was $1 million per year. The total payroll tax on the first $106,800 of his wages would have been $15,340, which is 15.3 percent of $106,800. Again, the corporation that employed him would have paid half of that and the remainder would have been deducted from his salary. The payroll tax on the remaining $893,200 of his income would have been only 2.9 percent, or $2,590, which would also have been split between the employer and the employee. The total payroll tax on his salary would have been only $17,930--1.79 percent of his total income--compared to the 15.3 percent your father paid! Because the fraction of income paid in payroll taxes declines as income rises above $106,800 per year, such taxes are regarded as regressive.

A progressive tax is one for which the fraction of income used to pay it increases as income increases. The federal income tax is a progressive tax because its rates tend to rise as income rises. Under the federal income tax, income is taxed at a 15 percent rate until it reaches a certain level. Income above that level is taxed at higher rates. Because the tax rates increase with income, upper-income people pay higher percentages of their income in taxes that lower-income people.

A proportional tax is one for which the percentage of income paid in taxes is the same no matter what the taxpayer's income. A flat 20 percent tax rate on all income would be a proportional tax. Note, however, that a proportional tax results in people with higher income paying more in taxes than people with lower income. Under a 20 percent flat-rate income tax, for example, your cousin with an annual income of $10,000 would pay only $2,000 per year in taxes, while your aunt with $100,000 annual income would pay $20,000 per year in taxes.

We also evaluate taxes by looking at the amounts paid by people with similar abilities to pay. If income measures ability to pay, then people with the same income should pay the same amounts in taxes.

Another common criterion used to evaluate taxes holds that taxes should vary with the benefits received from government services. This principle is very hard to administer because of the difficulties involved in allocating the benefits of government services to individual taxpayers. However, the federal gasoline tax is earmarked to finance roads and other transportation services. The idea here is that the benefits we receive from transportation services vary with the amount of gasoline we consume. By taxing gasoline, the government establishes a rough linkage between the use of roads and the taxes paid to build and maintain them.

Tax Rates: Average and Marginal

When discussing taxes, it's important to be clear about the meaning of *tax rate*. The average tax rate is the amount of taxes paid divided by the dollar value of the item taxed.

For example, suppose your income is \$25,000 per year. If you pay \$5,000 per year in income tax, your average tax is

$$\frac{\text{Income taxes paid}}{\text{Income}} = \frac{\$5,\ 000}{\$25,\ 000} = 20\%$$

The average tax rate is an important factor in evaluating the fairness of a tax because it shows how taxes vary as a percentage of income among taxpayers with different incomes.

The marginal tax rate is the *extra* tax paid on extra income or the extra dollar value of any other taxed item. As of 2004, the federal income tax had five positive marginal tax brackets for most taxpayers. Under a flat-rate tax, there's no difference between the marginal and average tax rates. For example, if income is subject to a flat 20 percent tax rate, total taxes paid divided by total income will always be 20 percent. Under a flat-rate tax, the average and marginal tax rates are the same. However, when a progressive tax structure is used, the marginal tax rate often exceeds the average tax rate. For example, if you were a single person earning exactly \$7,150 in 2004 from your summer job, after all exemptions, exclusions, and deductions, you would have paid \$715 in federal income tax. Your average tax rate expressed as a percentage of your taxable income would therefore have been 10 percent. However, the marginal tax rate *increased* to 15 percent on taxable income in excess of \$7,150. This means that, for each dollar of taxable income over \$7,150, you would have paid 15 cents rather than 10 cents in taxes. Also, under the federal income tax law for 2004, if your taxable income exceeded \$29,050, you would have paid a 25 percent marginal tax rate on the portion of your income above \$29,050. There were also higher marginal tax rates for still higher income—up to a maximum of 35% in 2004.

Naturally, when deciding whether to work or engage in any other activity that increases your income, you look at your *marginal* tax rate rather than your average tax rate. This is because your marginal tax rate tells you how much of your *extra* earnings subject to tax you can keep.

Taxes and Efficiency

Taxes distort choices. For example, an income tax is likely to distort the choice between work and leisure by affecting the *net wage* you can keep after payment of taxes. As you certainly know if you work, you don't receive the full amount of your salary because of the payroll and income taxes withheld from your paycheck. When you decide how many hours to work per week or year, you look at your net wage, which will vary with your marginal tax rate. For example, if your marginal tax rate were 28 percent, you'd get to keep only 72 percent of the additional gross wages you earned.

Because they reduce net wages, income taxes can cause us to make choices that differ from those we would have made if our wages weren't subject to those taxes. If you're subject to a high marginal tax rate, you may choose to work less than you would have worked otherwise. The high rate causes a substitution of leisure for work and results in a loss of efficiency in labor markets. This decreases production in the economy and results in less output from available resources. Taxes on interest income can also result in efficiency losses. If you earn 10 percent interest and are subject to a 15 percent marginal tax rate, you'll receive net interest of only 8.5 percent after taxes. This lower interest rate may induce you to substitute spending for saving, reducing the funds available for investment. Fewer investment funds will ultimately reduce the economy's production potential.

Of course, the actual reduction in efficiency depends on how responsive we are as taxpayers to tax-induced changes in net wages, net interest rates, and other prices. The actual impact on taxes on efficiency is therefore a subject for empirical investigation.

A tax's excess burden is the loss in net benefits from resource use caused by the tax-induced distortion in choices. For example, suppose that the revenue collected from the federal income tax is $300 billion. In addition, suppose that as a result of reduced output, the tax indirectly causes losses in net benefits estimated to be $10 billion per year. This amount is the excess burden of the tax over and above the $300 billion it raises.

A tax levied on goods that are unresponsive to price changes, such as a tax on basic food items, is likely to have a low excess burden. Many people oppose such a tax on the grounds that it is regressive. This is because the percentage of income we spend on basic food items tends to decline as your income rises. As we observed earlier, the most efficient taxes aren't always the most equitable ones.

Summary

1. Capitalism is characterized by private ownership of economic resources and freedom of enterprise in competitive markets. The people who manage and assume the risks of business enterprises in a capitalist economy are its entrepreneurs.
2. Under capitalism, economic rivalry tempers market power. When economic rivalry prevails, large numbers of buyers compete for available supplies of goods and services offered by large numbers of sellers. No single buyer or seller can make an item significantly more abundant or scarce so as to influence its price in a market. Free markets have no restrictions to prevent the entry or exit of buyers or sellers.
3. In modern economies people tend to specialize in specific productive endeavors. The resulting division of labor makes people dependent on each other to obtain items that they choose not to produce for themselves.
4. Mutual gains from exchange are possible when the minimum amount of goods or money a person will accept in trade for an item is less than the maximum amount a trading partner will surrender in exchange for that item.
5. In modern economies most exchange involves trades of money for goods (or services) rather than barter of goods for goods (or services). Barter is inconvenient because it requires double coincidence of wants.
6. In a market economy there is a circular flow of income and expenditure. Business firms employ economic resources offered for sale in input markets. The payments they make for the resources constitute income to members of the economy's households. Households use their income to buy goods and services offered for sale in markets by business firms.
7. The price system is the mechanism by which resource use is guided by prices in a market economy. Price changes occur in response to shifts in demand and supply. They affect the opportunities for personal gain in market transactions and result in resource reallocation until no further gain is possible. In this way prices guide what is produced and influence business managers' choice of production methods.
8. The amounts of goods and services you can enjoy depend on your money income, which you use to back up your desire for goods and services insofar as your income influences your ability to pay. Your money income is determined by the prices of the services or economic resources you have and are willing to sell.
9. Public goods are those consumed equally by all of us, whether we pay or not.
10. The price system fails when some goods people want and are willing to pay for can't be easily packaged into units that can be priced. Market exchange is feasible only for items for which property rights can be guaranteed and easily exchanged.
11. Externalities are costs or benefits of market transactions not reflected in market prices. Externalities are indicative of market failure to price the use of valuable resources.
12. Markets are not always competitive. For example, one or several buyers or sellers can control price in a market if entry into the market is limited. This can prevent the market from achieving allocative efficiency.
13. A market economy often results in significant poverty if the distribution of skills and ownership of capital is unequal. People with low incomes because of lack of marketable resources will live in poverty unless they receive assistance from charities or government authorities. In 2007, in the United States, 12.5 percent of the population was classified as living in poverty.
14. In the modern mixed economy, governments supply goods and services and can use their power to attempt to correct for the shortcomings of the price system.
15. An open economy is linked to the rest of the world through international trade. International trade has become increasingly more important for the U.S. economy since 1980. Both exports and imports have grown.
16. Annual spending by all levels of government in the United States accounts for about one-third of the value of national production.
17. Taxes represent the bulk of revenues raised by governments in the United States.
18. Taxes affect our incentives to work, save, invest, and purchase goods and services. We evaluate taxes in terms of their fairness or equity, as well as in terms of the distortions they cause in resource use.
19. A *progressive tax* collects higher fractions of income from taxpayers as their income rises. A *proportional tax* collects the same fraction of income no matter what the taxpayer's income. A *regressive tax* collects

smaller fractions of income from high-income taxpayers than it does from low-income taxpayers.

20. The average tax rate is the amount of taxes paid over a certain period divided by the dollar value of the item taxed. The marginal tax rate is the extra tax paid on a dollar of additional income or an extra dollar's worth of any other taxed item. The average tax rate is useful in evaluating the equity of a tax because it indicates the proportion of a person's income paid in taxes. The marginal tax rate is useful in evaluating the impact of a tax on incentives because it shows how much extra earnings (or extra dollars' worth of other activities) a person has to give up to pay the tax.

21. Taxes distort choices and the ability of the price system to allocate resources efficiently because they cause decisions to be made on the basis of prices distorted by taxes. The excess burden of a tax is the loss in net benefits from production caused by the distortion in choices induced by the tax.

Concept Review

(1) How do specialization and exchange in markets contribute to providing additional gains from an existing amount of production?

(2) How do prices and profit act in a capitalist economy as signals to allocate resources to the uses in which they are of highest value?

(3) Why are public goods unlikely to be supplied in free markets?

(4) What do we mean when we describe the United States as a mixed and open economy? How can taxes prevent efficient outcomes in markets and affect incentives to engage in work?

Problems and Applications

1. Suppose you start a new business distributing software. The business proves to be extremely profitable. Explain how freedom of enterprise and economic rivalry are likely to come into play in a market economy in a way that will eventually reduce the profits of your business. (1)

2. The marginal benefit of a good represents the sum of money a consumer is willing and able to pay for one more unit of the good. The marginal cost of a good represents the minimum sum of money a seller is willing to accept to make more of the good available. Suppose the marginal benefit of televisions is \$200, while the marginal cost is only \$100. Assuming that the marginal benefit of TVs declines and the marginal cost increases as more are made available, show that more TVs must be sold to achieve all possible mutual gains from exchange. (1)

3. Use supply and demand analysis to show how an increase in the demand for SUVs, accompanied by a decrease in the demand for standard full-size passenger cars, will affect resource allocation in the automobile industry. (2)

4. During the energy crisis of the early 1970s, the price of smaller cars actually increased above the price of gas guzzling full-size models. How did the American automobile industry react to the change in prices? What do you expect will happen to the kinds of cars made available if the supply of gas increases substantially to push the price down, permanently, to an average of 75 cents per gallon? (2)

5. Use supply and demand analysis to trace out the impact of a sharp reduction in the price of electronic components on the price, use, and profitability of producing goods that use electronic components as inputs. What effect is the change in price likely to have on production techniques? (2)

6. Your parents own 1,000 acres of land. The land is on the flight path to an airport, and planes regularly fly over it as they make their approach to the airport. Why can't your parents charge the airlines for using their airspace? (3)

7. You plan to sell your bicycle at the end of the year when you graduate. You'd like to get \$100 for it. List the transaction costs you must incur to find a buyer. Under what circumstances might you be better off giving the bike away, instead of trying to sell it? (2), (3)

8. A firm that manufactures paper products dumps its wastes into a stream and doesn't pay for the right to do so. The stream is used by fishermen and boaters as a source of recreational enjoyment. The waste products dumped into the stream make it less useful

for recreation. Explain why an externality exists, and identify the groups involved in the externality. In what sense is there a failure of the price system in this case? 3

9. A flat-rate income tax of 20 percent is levied on all citizens, with no allowable tax preferences. Show that both the average and marginal tax rate equal 20 percent. How would you evaluate the equity of this tax? 4

10. Suppose the following tax schedule is used to collect an income tax:

Annual income	**Marginal tax rate (%)**
0–$4,000	0
$4,000–$29,000	15
$29,000–$70,000	25
Above $70,000	35

Calculate the average tax rate for people with annual incomes of $4,000, $29,000, and $70,000. Is this tax progressive, regressive, or proportional? 4

International Trade

We have one more building block to set in place to get a full view of the modern economy. An *open economy* is one that is linked to the rest of the world through international input, product, foreign exchange, and credit markets. The United States and virtually all other nations today have open economies, although most nations place at least some government restrictions on international trade. Business firms export some of their products to buyers in the rest of the world. Similarly, American households, businesses, and even governments buy imported products. American businesses also own and operate production facilities abroad and regularly purchase foreign assets. At the same time, foreign businesses and individuals own and operate production facilities in the United States and regularly supply funds to American credit markets. The graphic below provides a schematic view of the international links between the United States and the rest of the world. No nation today is self-sufficient. International linkages are becoming more and more important to the functioning of the U.S. economy.

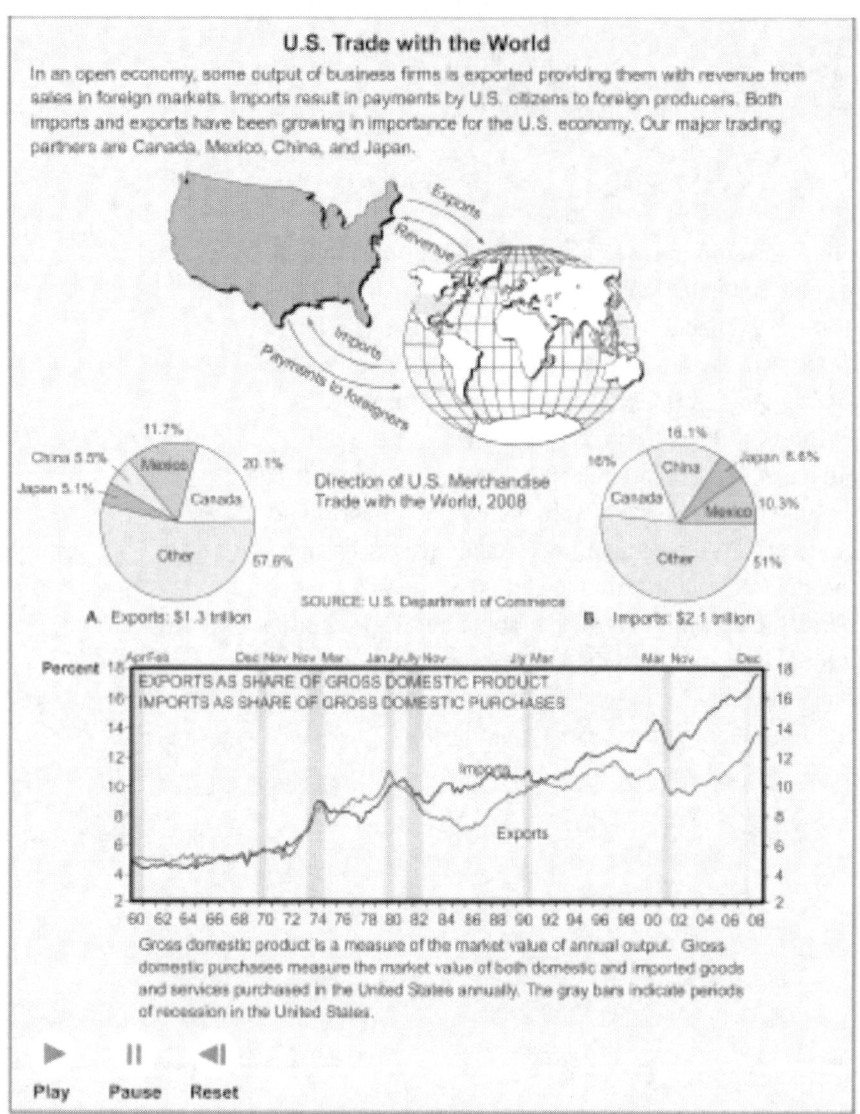

U.S. Trade with the World
In an open economy, some output of business firms is exported providing them with revenue from sales in foreign markets. Imports result in payments by U.S. citizens to foreign producers. Both imports and exports have been growing in importance for the U.S. economy. Our major trading partners are Canada, Mexico, China, and Japan.
Exports
Revenue
Imports
Payments to foreigners
11.7%
China 5.5%
Mexico
20.1%
Japan 5.1%
Canada
Other
57.6%
Direction of U.S. Merchandise
Trade with the World, 2008
16.1%
China
Japan
Canada
Mexico
10.3%
Other
51%
SOURCE: U.S. Department of Commerce
A. Exports: $1.3 trillion
B. Imports: $2.1 trillion
Percent
EXPORTS AS SHARE OF GROSS DOMESTIC PRODUCT
IMPORTS AS SHARE OF GROSS DOMESTIC PURCHASES
Imports
Exports
60 62 64 66 68 70 72 74 76 78 80 82 84 86 88 90 92 94 96 98 00 02 04 06 08
Gross domestic product is a measure of the market value of annual output. Gross domestic purchases measure the market value of both domestic and imported goods and services purchased in the United States annually. The gray bars indicate periods of recession in the United States.
Play
Pause
Reset

Exports are a source of revenue for American business firms. They provide income to workers and other resource owners whose services are used to produce exported goods and services. When we import goods and services, we place dollars in the hands of foreigners. When we import a greater dollar volume of products than we export, we place more dollars in the hands of foreigners than they return to us, and there will be a deficit in the balance of trade. Under such circumstances, foreign holders of dollars choose to save or invest those funds in the United States by acquiring U.S. assets such as real estate, bonds, and bank deposits denominated in dollars. In effect, if we import more than we export, as has been the case in recent years, we must borrow from foreigners to make up the difference. Foreign saving and investment in the United States grew rapidly in the 1980s and 1990s, mainly as a result of a persistent balance-of-trade deficit in goods over that period.

Of course, it's also possible for a nation to incur a balance-of-trade surplus. In this instance, the value of goods and services exported exceeds the value of imports. If the United States were to have a balance-of-trade surplus, it would earn more foreign currency than it used to import goods and services during the year. The excess foreign currency would be saved and invested in foreign nations. In effect, the United States would be a net lender to the rest of the world.

Shown in the graph above is the upward trend in U.S. exports and imports as a share of gross domestic production and gross domestic purchases, respectively, from 1959 to 2008. The total share of domestic U.S. production exported has grown from a mere 4 percent in 1959 to 14 percent in 2008. Imports now account for 18 percent of domestic purchases--up from a bit more than 4 percent in 1959. Imports exceeded exports from 1980 to 2008. Foreigners also increased their holdings of U.S. assets over that period. Canada, Mexico, China, and Japan are major customers for U.S. goods, accounting for a bit more than 40 percent of the dollar value of exports in 2008, and about half of our imports came from this same group of nations. The pie charts above show the direction of our trade with various trading partners.

The total share of both domestic production exported and of domestic income used to purchase imports has increased substantially in the United States since 1960. Also, because we have had a chronic balance-of-trade deficit for a number of years, foreigners have increased their holdings of U.S. assets. We will discuss international linkages between the U.S. economy and the rest of the world regularly throughout the text.

Property Rights, Transaction Costs, and Pricing

As a buyer, you have an incentive to buy something only if you're assured that you'll get certain benefits when you actually pay the price to purchase it. *Property rights* are privileges to use or own goods, services, and economic resources. As a consumer, you acquire property rights when you make market purchases. Similarly, sellers are induced to offer items for sale because they know they have the right to transfer the items in exchange for payments from buyers. *Markets can be established only for items for which property rights can be guaranteed and easily exchanged.* If you know you can enjoy the right to cleaner air and other public goods without purchasing that right from someone else, you have little incentive to pay a price for them. You'd scoff at an opportunity to buy the Brooklyn Bridge or an acre of the ocean because you know those items can't be bought. You'll engage in market transactions only when you can gain by obtaining something of value. Similarly, you'd be unwilling to invest in the production of a good if those who refused to pay for the good could obtain property rights of use or ownership. For example, the incentives to produce cable television programming for sale are affected by the ease with which those who don't pay can be prevented from benefiting from its availability. If all viewers can receive the programs even if they don't pay, sellers will have no incentive to make cable TV available.

If people are to be motivated to engage in market transactions, resources must be devoted to establishing and enforcing property rights. *Transaction costs* are those incurred in enforcing property rights, locating trading partners, and actually carrying out the transactions. Transaction costs are associated with exchanging, rather than producing, goods and services. One transaction cost to enforce property rights is the cost of scrambling satellite transmissions of television programs by firms like HBO. Examples of transaction costs to locate trading partners and carry out transactions are advertising and brokerage fees, the salaries of sales personnel, and the costs of transporting goods to and from the point of sale.

High transaction costs can prevent markets from being organized for the exchange of items. For example, the right to use the ocean for fishing is rarely sold in a market. Exclusive ownership rights to the use of the ocean can't be granted to a particular seller in ways that allow the ocean to be rented out to others for payment. Even if such rights were granted, the ocean is so vast that the seller would have to invest in a fleet of sophisticated vessels to monitor use. The high cost of actually enforcing these rights would make it infeasible to actually sell them in a market.

The concepts of property rights and transaction costs are intertwined. The establishment of property rights to own or use goods or services depends on the transaction costs of guaranteeing those rights. Government plays an important role in markets by using its power to guarantee and enforce agreements to exchange property rights. In effect, the government is the silent partner in all market transactions, because its system of courts and police power is used to guarantee property rights acquired in market exchanges and to settle disputes concerning such exchanges. The effectiveness of government in establishing and facilitating the exchange of property rights is crucial to the smooth functioning of markets.

In addition, changes in technology often reduce transaction costs, thereby providing gains from market exchanges of new goods and services. For example, the right to park on city streets wasn't priced until the development of the parking meter.

There are other examples of pricing previously "unpriceable" activities. In 1995, the EPA gave electric power generating plants limited rights to emit sulfur dioxide into the atmosphere. The EPA then issued "emission allowances" to the electric power plants, but the total amount issued were less than the amount of emissions at the time--with the goal of reducing sulfur dioxide emissions by 10 million tons from the amounts prevailing over a 10-year period. One emissions allowance was required for each ton of emissions per year. The allowances were sellable, and a market was established at the Chicago Board of Trade for trading the rights. In 2005, emissions rights were selling in the range of $200. The EPA audits firms each year, and, if they've emitted more than their allowances permit, they're required to either purchase more allowances or pay a fine of about $2,000 per ton! As there are a relatively small number of power plants in the United States, it's easy to measure emissions to enforce the program. Power plants that can reduce emissions at less than the market price of the emissions allowance can sell their rights to others and increase their profits by doing so. Power plants that find the cost of reducing emissions greater than the price of the allowances will want to purchase them. By the stroke of a pen, Congress was able to establish a workable market for buying and selling the right to emit sulfur dioxides that has effectively reduced emissions of these chemicals (a major source of acid rain), while minimizing the costs of that reduction to power plants.

Also, the technology now exists to price the use of road services to motorists. Such a plan was proposed in 2005 in California and is also under consideration for use in the United Kingdom. The system would use global positioning devices installed in cars to keep track of mileage. Government authorities would establish a fee per mile. Every time drivers fill up their tanks with gas, a computer in the pump would communicate with the driver's odometer and calculate the bill that would be added to the cost of gas. It would also be possible to use this system to charge higher fees per mile during rush hours to encourage drivers to stay off the roads, if possible, at those times. The pricing scheme would ration use of the roads, and generate funds governments can use to maintain existing roads and construct new ones.

The Entrepreneurial Spirit in American Capitalism

In the United States, entrepreneurs often attain the status of folk heroes. Entrepreneurs are opportunists, seeking to exploit the right moment for an innovation in products or processes. When successful, they are rewarded with spectacular profits that enable them to accumulate vast fortunes. Entrepreneurs are the dynamic and driving spirits who start businesses, satisfy demands for resources or products, and prosper from doing so.

Who are the great entrepreneurs of American history? Thomas Edison, the inventor of electric lighting and the phonograph, was foremost an entrepreneur interested in marketing his inventions. To make his inventions profitable, Edison had to acquire funds to purchase the necessary capital. He acted as an entrepreneur in doing so and capped his skill as an inventor with equal skills as an entrepreneur to translate his ideas into revenue and profit.* He engineered a profitable way to deliver electrical power to homes and businesses. The delivery system was the key, because electricity had to be *priceable* for it to be profitable. The Edison Electric Illuminating Company of New York was organized in 1880 to provide street lighting. By 1883, it was supplying electricity to more than 700 private customers.

Fred Smith is a modern-day entrepreneur who envisioned a profitable opportunity for a firm specializing in overnight delivery of small packages. Unlike Edison, Smith was not an inventor, but he too saw a demand and organized the resources needed to satisfy that demand. What Smith saw was an economy with dispersed production and service facilities that needed a quick and reliable means of shipping documents, drugs, discs and tapes, and small electronic components among those facilities.

In 1970, no one was providing such shipments. The U.S. Postal Service had a monoopoly on the shipment of first-class mail. The performance of the Postal Service wasn't reliable enough for business firms that needed guaranteed 24-hour delivery. Private freight services likewise were incapable of providing guaranteed overnight delivery. Airmail and air freight were carried by a number of airlines, but the inevitable delays involved in loading and unloading made overnight delivery infeasible. In a term paper Smith wrote when he was a junior at Yale, he outlined his idea. The professor gave the paper a grade of "C."

In 1971, Smith began to put his idea into action. He succeeded in raising $90 million to start up his company, which he called Federal Express. He purchased 33 small Dassault Falcon jets and developed a hub at Memphis, Tennessee, for sorting packages, which were restricted in size and weight. All packages picked up during the day were sent to the Memphis hub for sorting. They were shipped out the same night to their ultimate destination for delivery the next morning. The company invested considerable resources in developing its distinctive logo and its reputation for reliability. When Federal Express began in 1973, it served 22 cities. It wasn't immediately profitable. In fact, it didn't turn a profit until 1976. After that time, changes in government regulations enabled it to expand more easily and to operate larger aircraft. In 1977, Federal Express earned $20 million. In 1980, it took in nearly $600 million in revenue and earned $60 million.

As happens with most successful enterprises, competition stiffened. By the 1980s, many other firms, such as Purolator, United Parcel Service, Airborne, and even the U.S. Postal Service, were offering overnight delivery service for small parcels. As you can see, the price system works in the long run both to create entrepreneurs and to encourage other firms to emulate the innovations of successful ones.

*For a more detailed account of Edison's achievements, see Robert Sobel and David B. Sicilia, *The Entrepreneurs: An American Adventure* (Boston: Houghton Mifflin, 1986), pp. 7-16.

Chapter 6

Elasticity of Demand and Supply

Suppose you're the owner of a popular pizzeria. You're considering raising the price of your double-cheese deluxe by $1—but how will your customers react? You know that, according to the law of demand, when a good's price rises, quantity demanded generally falls. But what you really need to know is the *extent* to which the quantity demanded of your deluxe pizzas will fall if you boost the price by $1.

To forecast the effect of price changes on their revenues, businesses need a measure of buyer sensitivity to changes in price called the *elasticity of demand.* In this chapter, we'll look at the conceptual problems involved in measuring elasticity of demand along points on the demand curve for a good. We'll also develop measures of demand sensitivity to changes in such important demand determinants as consumer income and prices of substitutes and complements. Knowledge of demand sensitivity to income and the prices of related goods helps businesses market their products and manage resource use. For example, a retailer of casual clothing who knows the sensitivity of demand for jackets to fluctuations in consumer income can manage her inventory to avoid running short of jackets or incurring high costs for storing and financing stocks of the jackets.

Elasticity of supply is a measure of the sensitivity of quantities supplied to changes in prices. As you'll learn, knowledge of the supply elasticity of products is very useful in forecasting the impact of policies designed to influence quantities supplied by sellers in markets. You'll also learn how knowledge of elasticity of both supply and demand is crucial in forecasting the impact of taxes and changes in tax rates on prices and government tax collections.

Concept Preview

After reading this chapter, you should be able to

1. Explain the uses of the concept of price elasticity of demand and show how it can be calculated for points on a given demand curve.
2. Use information on price elasticity of demand to forecast changes in total expenditure on an item and total revenue from its sale when its price changes.
3. Explain how to use other elasticity measures, including the income elasticity of demand, the cross-elasticity of demand, and the price elasticity of supply.
4. Show how the price elasticities of supply and demand are relevant to explaining the impact of taxes on market prices of goods and services.

Price Elasticity of Demand

1 Price elasticity of demand is a number representing the percentage change in quantity demanded resulting from each 1 percent change in the price of a good. This number is used to gauge the sensitivity of quantity demanded of a good to percentage changes in the price of that good. Price elasticity of demand is a measure of the responsiveness of quantity demanded to price changes along a given demand curve.

Price elasticity is calculated by dividing the percentage change in quantity demanded of a good by the percentage change in price that caused it, other things being equal:

$$\text{Price elasticity of demand} = \frac{\text{\% change in quantity demanded}}{\text{\% change in price}}$$

For example, suppose the price of cars went up by 1 percent this year and the resulting decline in cars purchased was 2 percent. The price elasticity of demand would be

$$\frac{-2\%}{1\%} = -2$$

Note that price elasticity of demand is a number without units of measurement because it's obtained by dividing two percentage changes. Also note that price elasticity of demand is a negative number. This is because an increase in price will generally result in a decrease in quantity demanded, other things being equal. Therefore, if the percentage change in price is positive, the percentage change in quantity demanded will be negative, as shown in the calculation just presented. Similarly, if price were to decline, the percentage change in price would be negative and the percentage change in quantity demanded would be positive. For example, suppose the price of gasoline declines by 2 percent and the annual increase in gasoline sales attributable to this price decline is also 2 percent. The price elasticity of demand for that price decline would therefore be

$$\frac{2\%}{-2\%} = -1$$

How to Use Price Elasticity of Demand to Make Market Forecasts

You've just learned how to calculate price elasticity of demand from percentage changes in quantities demanded that result from certain percentage changes in price. Suppose instead you have a good estimate of the price elasticity of demand for the product you sell. Now you can work backward and use the concept of elasticity to make predictions of changes in quantity demanded in response to price changes.

For example, imagine you run a car dealership. Last year you sold 10,000 cars. This year you know that the price of each car you sell will go up by 10 percent. You know the law of demand implies that, other things unchanged, you'll sell fewer cars this year; but the law gives no hint of *how many* fewer you'll sell. You can now see the relevance of the concept of price elasticity of demand. You know from past experience that the price elasticity of demand for the cars you sell is –2. Because you know the percentage change in price and the price elasticity of demand for your product, you can easily calculate the percentage change in quantity demanded:

$$\frac{\text{\% change in quantity demanded}}{10\%} = -2$$

Therefore,

$$\text{\% change in quantity demanded} = -20\%$$

You therefore expect a 20 percent reduction in sales as a result of the price increase. This means you can expect to sell only 8,000 cars instead of 10,000 this year, assuming that your estimate of price elasticity of demand is accurate and that nothing else changes that might affect car sales. You can use this estimate of reduced sales volume to cut back on your orders for cars from the manufacturer and avoid tying up your funds in a large inventory of unsold cars.

You can also use price elasticity of demand to formulate pricing strategies if you own a firm that can control its prices. For example, suppose you manage an electronics store and you want to increase your annual quantity of home entertainment systems sold by 20 percent. You estimate that the price elasticity of demand for your systems is –4. One obvious way to increase the quantities you sell is to lower prices. Other things being equal, how much must you cut prices to increase sales by 20 percent? The answer is easy because you know the price elasticity of demand for your systems and you know the percentage increase in quantity demanded. To calculate the necessary percentage reduction in price, simply use the formula for price elasticity of demand:

$$\frac{20\%}{\%\text{ change in price}} = -4$$

Therefore,

$$\%\text{ change in price} = -5\%$$

In this case you'd need to reduce prices by 5 percent to achieve your desired increase in home entertainment system sales volume.

Categorizing Price Elasticity of Demand as Elastic or Inelastic

In categorizing demand as more or less elastic, it's convenient to *ignore the minus sign* in front of the number measuring the elasticity of demand. The larger the number after the minus sign, the more elastic the demand. In other words, the larger the *absolute value* of the price elasticity of demand, the more elastic the demand. For example, if the elasticity of demand for cars is –2, while the elasticity of demand for bread is – 0.5, the demand for cars is more elastic than the demand for bread.

An elastic demand prevails if a good's price elasticity of demand turns out to exceed 1, ignoring the minus sign. For example, if the price elasticity of demand for fur coats were – 5, the demand for fur coats would be elastic. If the price elasticity of demand for sweatshirts were –2, their demand would also be elastic. However, note that the demand for fur coats would be more elastic than the corresponding demand for sweatshirts. If demand is elastic, the percentage change in quantity demanded caused by a price increase will exceed the percentage change in the price (ignoring the direction of change).

A good has an inelastic demand if its price elasticity of demand is equal to or greater than 0 but less than 1, ignoring the minus sign. The smaller the number after the minus sign, the more inelastic the demand for the good. For example, demand for milk would be categorized as inelastic if its price elasticity of demand were –0.8 because 0.8 is less than 1. If the price elasticity of demand of aspirin were –0.5, its demand would be considered more inelastic than the demand for milk because 0.5 is less than 0.8. Ignoring the direction of change, the percentage change in quantity demanded will be less than the percentage change in price that caused it when demand is inelastic. If the price elasticity of demand for a good were 0, this would imply that consumers wouldn't respond at all to price changes and demand would be considered *perfectly* inelastic.

Finally, a good has a unit elastic demand if its price elasticity of demand is exactly equal to 1 when the minus sign is ignored. If demand for a good is unit elastic, the percentage change in its quantity demanded caused by a price change will equal the percentage

Box 1 Price Elasticity of Demand as a Gauge of Demand Responsiveness

Demand response	% change in quantity demanded relative to % change in price (ignoring direction of change)	Value of elasticity of demand (ignoring minus sign)
Inelastic	% change in quantity demanded is *less than* % change in price	Equal to or greater than 0 but less than 1
Unit elastic	% change in quantity demanded *equals* % change in price	1
Elastic	% change in quantity demanded is *greater than* % change in price.	Greater than 1

change in price, again ignoring the direction of change. For example, if each 1 percent increase in the price of milk resulted in a 1 percent decline in the quantity demanded, demand for milk would be unit elastic.

Box 1 summarizes the range of variation for price elasticity of demand and the various ways of categorizing the demand for a product according to its price elasticity. Remember, the larger the number after the minus sign, the more elastic the demand.

Determinants of Price Elasticity of Demand

A number of factors can influence the price elasticity of demand for an item. These factors include the following:

1. *The availability of substitutes.* Remember that a substitute for a good is one that serves the same general purpose. In general, the more and better substitutes that exist for an item, the more elastic its demand. For example, it's quite likely that diabetics' demand for insulin is extremely inelastic because insulin has few, if any, substitutes. However, the demand for a particular car brand is likely to be very elastic because many substitute brands are available in the market.

2. *Time.* In general, demand tends to become more elastic with time because we find more substitutes for goods over longer periods. Over longer periods we also have more time to adjust our consumption patterns in response to price changes, which also contributes to a more elastic demand. For example, within a period of a month or two there may be little that we as drivers can do to react to an increase in gas prices. However, over several years we can seek out more fuel-efficient cars and buy them to replace our older gas guzzlers. We can also move closer to work. Also, over a period of several years more substitutes are developed for goods whose prices go up. For example, a sharp permanent increase in the price of gas might lead to the development of substitute fuels.

3. *The proportion of income consumers spend on the good.* As consumers, we tend to spend high proportions of our income on housing and cars. A 10 percent increase in the prices of these goods is likely to reduce substantially our ability to buy them and to result in sharp percentage declines in quantities demanded. The demand for goods on which we spend large percentages of our income is likely to be quite elastic. On the other hand, a 10 percent increase in the price of pencils will have little effect on the purchasing power of our income and is unlikely to result in sharp percentage declines in quantities demanded. Of course, there are exceptions to this rule. We might spend only a small portion of our income on oysters, but the demand for oysters might be elastic because oysters are considered dispensable luxuries. In general, other things being equal, the smaller the percentage of income spent on a good, the less elastic the demand unless the good is considered a dispensable luxury.

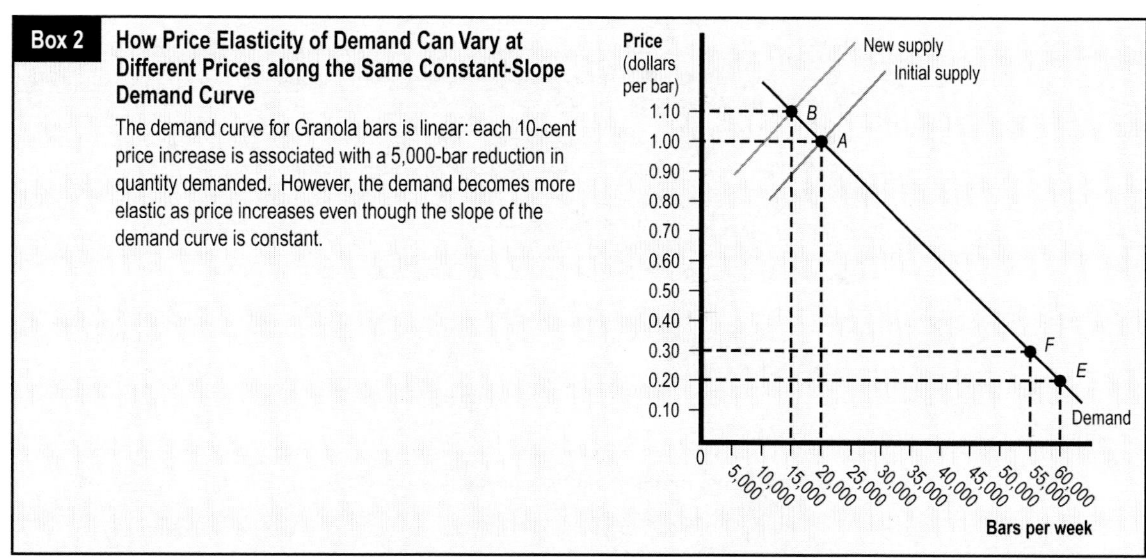

Box 2 How Price Elasticity of Demand Can Vary at Different Prices along the Same Constant-Slope Demand Curve

The demand curve for Granola bars is linear: each 10-cent price increase is associated with a 5,000-bar reduction in quantity demanded. However, the demand becomes more elastic as price increases even though the slope of the demand curve is constant.

Calculating Price Elasticity of Demand from Two Points on a Demand Curve

We can use the concept of price elasticity of demand together with the demand curve to reach some interesting conclusions. The graph in Box 2 shows a downward-sloping linear demand curve for Granola bars. Suppose the equilibrium price of Granola bars is currently \$1 and 20,000 bars are sold at that price each week. This corresponds to point *A* on the demand curve. Now suppose, as a result of a decrease in the supply, the price of Granola bars increases to \$1.10 and the quantity demanded falls to 15,000 per week as the equilibrium moves from point *A* to point *B* on the demand curve. To calculate the price elasticity of demand for the data, we follow these steps:

1. Calculate the change in price (ΔP) and the change in quantity demanded (ΔQ). In this case the change in price is $\Delta P = 10$ cents and the resulting change in quantity demanded is $\Delta Q = -5{,}000$.

2. Calculate the *percentage change* in price caused by the decrease in supply. Here a slight problem occurs when the change in price or quantity demanded is substantial. The 10-cent increase in price is 10 percent of the initial price (P_1) of \$1 but is only 9.1 percent of the *new price* (P_2) of \$1.10. To see this, divide the 10-cent change in price by the new price. This will give you the following result: \$0.10/\$1.10 = 0.091. To convert this to a percentage, multiply the result by 100 percent, which gives you 9.1 percent.

Because you'll get a different percentage change depending on whether you use the initial or new market price to make your calculation, economists often use the *average* of the initial and new prices to calculate a compromise percentage change. In this case the average price will be (\$1.00 + \$1.10)/2, which equals \$1.05. The percentage change in price can therefore be calculated as (\$0.10/\$1.05)(100%) = 9.5%.

In symbolic terms, the percentage change in price can be written as

$$\left[\frac{\Delta P}{\frac{1}{2}(P_1 + P_2)}\right] 100\%$$

where P_1 is the initial price and P_2 is the new price.

3. Calculate the percentage change in quantity demanded caused by the price increase. Here the change in quantity demanded is –5,000 Granola bars per week. This is equal to 25 percent of the initial quantity demanded (Q_1) of 20,000 bars and 33 percent of the *new* quantity demanded (Q_2) of 15,000 bars after the price increase. To resolve the ambiguity, once again calculate the percentage change on the basis of the average of the initial and new quantities demanded. The average quantity demanded is (20,000 + 15,000)/2 = 17,500 Granola bars per week. The percentage change in quantity demanded will therefore be (–5,000/17,500)(100%) = –28.6%.

In symbols, the percentage change in quantity demanded is

$$\left[\frac{\Delta Q}{\frac{1}{2}(Q_1 + Q_2)}\right]100\%$$

where Q_1 is the initial quantity demanded and Q_2 is the new quantity demanded.

4. Divide the percentage change in quantity demanded by the percentage change in price to get the price elasticity of demand:

$$\text{Price elasticity of demand} = \frac{-28.6\%}{9.5\%} = -3.01$$

Because the number after the minus sign exceeds 1, the demand for Granola bars can be categorized as *elastic*.

The formula for calculating the price elasticity of demand between two points on a demand curve can be written as

$$\text{Price elasticity of demand} = \frac{\Delta Q/\ (Q_1 + Q_2)}{\Delta P/\ (P_1 + P_2)}$$

which is obtained simply by dividing the expression for the percentage change in quantity demanded just shown by the expression for the percentage change in price.

How Price Elasticity Can Vary along a Demand Curve

From the calculation you just made, can you conclude that the price elasticity of demand for Granola bars will *always* be –3.01 no matter what the price? The answer is no. In fact, we can easily show that the price elasticity of demand varies continuously at different points on a downward-sloping linear demand curve. To see why this is so, suppose the initial price of Granola bars was 20 cents instead of $1. Of course, at a price that much lower, the quantity of Granola bars demanded would be substantially higher. The graph in Box 2 shows that the quantity demanded is 60,000 bars per week when the price is 20 cents. This corresponds to point E on the demand curve drawn in the graph. Now suppose the price of Granola bars goes up by 10 cents as before. The percentage increase in this case, based on the average of the initial price of 20 cents and the new price of 30 cents, is 40 percent. Because the downward-sloping demand curve is *linear*, the reduction in quantity demanded for each 10-cent increase in price is the same as before: 5,000 bars. A linear demand curve is one with constant slope: Each 10-cent increase in price results in a 5,000-bar reduction in weekly quantity demanded, no matter what the initial price and quantity demanded. After the price increases from 20 cents to 30 cents, we find that the change in quantity demanded expressed as a percentage of the average of initial quantity demanded (60,000) and new quantity demanded (55,000) equals –9 percent. The price elasticity of demand is therefore

$$\frac{-9\%}{40\%} = -0.23$$

Because the number after the minus sign is less than 1, we'd now categorize the demand for Granola bars as *inelastic*.

If you use elasticity estimates to make forecasts, heed this warning: If the demand curve for your product is linear, like the one drawn in Box 2, then price elasticity of demand will change as price changes. When using past data based on previous price changes, be very careful to calculate the *current* price elasticity of demand for your product. *Assuming that the demand curve for your product is linear (or almost linear) like the one in Box 2, the demand for your product will tend to be more elastic at higher prices than at lower prices.* We can also state this proposition in a slightly different way: The greater the quantity demanded along a given linear demand curve, the more inelastic the demand in response to further price declines.

We can apply this proposition directly to the marketing of products. When a new product is introduced at a relatively high price, demand is likely to be quite elastic. This means sellers can expect consumers to be quite responsive to price declines for a new product. For example, when the personal computer was introduced in the early 1980s, increases in supply resulted in small percentage declines in price, but much larger percentage increases in quantity demanded. By the late 1980s, the market became saturated with computers, meaning that the quantity sold per year was quite large as prices fell drastically in response to increased supply. When a market becomes saturated, sellers find that further price declines result in only modest percentage increases in quantity demanded and demand becomes much more inelastic. By 2009 the market for personal computers was very saturated and demand appeared to be extremely inelastic. Many manufacturers were relying on innovations, such as smaller and faster computers, and new products, such as phone-based computers, rather than price cuts, to generate more sales and revenue.

Here's a simple way to understand why price elasticity along a linear demand curve changes as price changes: When the initial price is low rather than high, a 10-cent change in price is a higher percentage of the average of the initial and final prices. Also, when the initial price is low, the quantity demanded will be high. Along a linear demand curve, each given change in price will result in the same change in quantity demanded. So even though the quantity demanded is high at low prices, each 10-cent increase in price will still result in a 5,000-bar reduction in the weekly quantity of Granola bars demanded. Naturally, the 5,000-bar change in quantity demanded is a smaller percentage of the average of the initial and final quantities demanded at low prices (when quantity demanded is high) than at high prices (when quantity demanded is lower). As price increases over time in 10-cent increments along a linear demand curve, therefore, the percentage change in price decreases, while the percentage change in quantity demanded tends to increase. Price elasticity of demand will move further away from zero as price increases along a linear demand curve, meaning that demand becomes more elastic. (See the graph in Box 2.)

In summary:

1. Even though a linear demand curve has constant slope, its elasticity varies from point to point. The slope of the demand curve in Box 2 can be expressed as –$0.10/5,000 Granola bars because each 10-cent change in price is associated with a 5,000-bar change (in the opposite direction) in quantity demanded. This number can be expressed only as a ratio of dollars to Granola bars and is therefore a cumbersome measure of responsiveness that varies with units of measurement. The price elasticity of demand is, however, a negative number with no units of measurement.

2. Along a downward-sloping linear demand curve, demand is very elastic at high prices but becomes less elastic as price declines. Demand becomes inelastic at relatively low prices, and it approaches zero as prices get lower and lower.

3. Don't judge the price elasticity of demand at points on different demand curves by looking at their slopes. To calculate price elasticity of demand for points on each demand curve, you need to calculate percentage changes in prices and quantities demanded. These percentage changes will vary with the actual price and quantity demanded.[1]

Perfectly Inelastic and Perfectly Elastic Demand Curves

Suppose the price elasticity of demand for a good were *always* zero, no matter what the price. What would its demand curve look like? If the price elasticity of demand is zero, the percentage change in quantity of the good demanded will always be zero, no matter what the price or how much the price changes. For this to be the case, the quantity demanded of the good would have to be completely insensitive to changes in price. A demand curve that corresponds to such a situation is drawn in graph **A** in Box 3. This demand curve is a vertical line, indicating that if the price changes, there's no change in quantity demanded. The percentage change in quantity demanded along this demand curve is therefore zero, and the price elasticity at all points is 0/Percentage change in price = 0.

It's doubtful that any good has a perfectly inelastic demand curve. For this to be the case, the good would have to have virtually no substitutes or it would have to be a good on which consumers spend only minute fractions of their income. In most cases we'd expect the demand curve for a good to have at least some downward slope. Diabetics' demand curve for insulin might be close to a vertical line because insulin has few, if any, substitutes. However, higher prices for insulin could induce diabetics to watch their diet

Box 3 Perfectly Inelastic and Perfectly Elastic Demand Curves

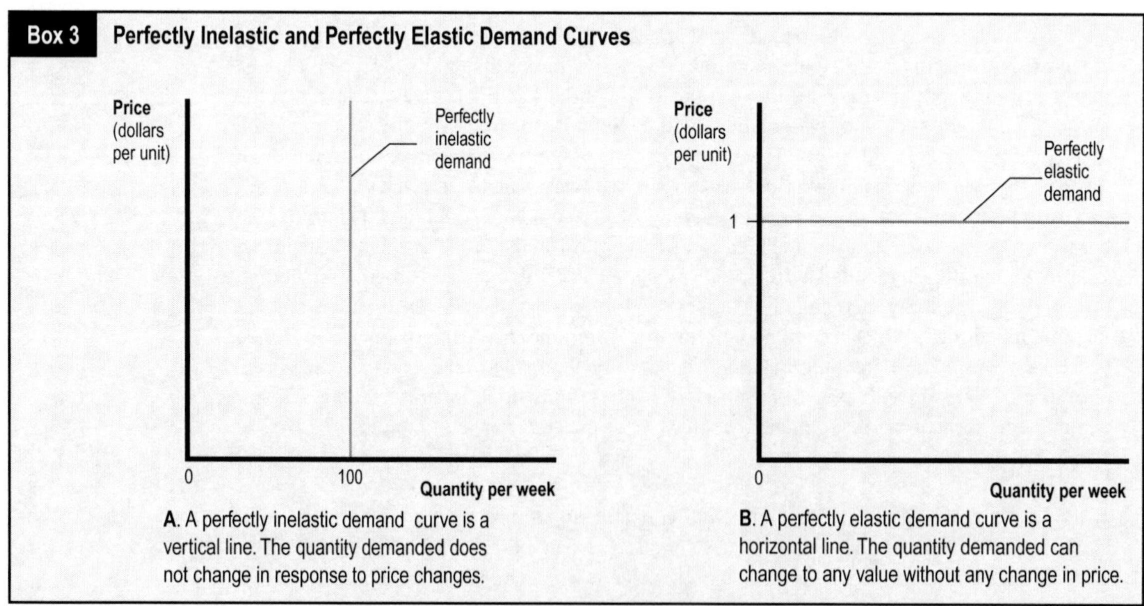

A. A perfectly inelastic demand curve is a vertical line. The quantity demanded does not change in response to price changes.

B. A perfectly elastic demand curve is a horizontal line. The quantity demanded can change to any value without any change in price.

[1] When the price change is very small, there will be little difference between the initial and final prices and quantities. For points on a demand curve, the formula for price elasticity of demand can be written as

$$\frac{\Delta Q/\ Q)100\%}{\Delta P/\ P)100\%} = \frac{(\Delta Q/\ Q)}{(\Delta P/\ P)} = \frac{P\Delta Q}{Q\Delta P}$$

for any given *P* or *Q*. As *Q* approaches zero, price elasticity of demand approaches an infinitely large negative number. As *P* approaches zero, price elasticity of demand also approaches zero.

more carefully and to pursue other measures that might affect the frequency with which they take insulin.

In Box 3, graph **B** illustrates a demand curve that can be regarded as infinitely elastic at all prices. This demand curve is flat. You can think of such a demand curve as one that is approached when a downward-sloping demand curve becomes so flat that it can't be distinguished from a horizontal line. An almost flat downward-sloping demand curve implies that the most minute change in the price of a good will result in an infinite change in the quantity demanded. You can also understand why the demand curve shown in graph **B** is considered perfectly elastic by reasoning that along the curve no change in price is necessary to change quantity demanded.

An infinitely elastic demand curve would prevail for a product that has a great many perfect substitutes. In fact, such a demand curve can be regarded as existing for a particular seller in a competitive market. For example, suppose you're one of a million sellers of eggs in the egg market. Because eggs are a standardized product, buyers will view your eggs as a perfect substitute for those of any other seller. You could sell all the eggs you wanted at the market price of $1 per dozen, and the demand curve for *your* eggs would be perfectly elastic, like the one shown in **B** in Box 3.

Using Price Elasticity of Demand to Forecast Changes in Total Expenditure and Total Revenue When Prices Change

Total Expenditure and Total Revenue

In 1991 Apple Computer, Inc., slashed the prices on its Macintosh computers by as much as 50 percent on some models. The market response to the price cuts was phenomenal—by the end of the year, Apple reported an 85 percent jump in the sale of its Macs and the company's revenues had soared. The price elasticity of demand for Macintosh computers was even more elastic than the company's managers had estimated. Apple continued to cut prices in 1992, and by the end of that year revenues had again increased, contributing to higher profits for the company.

2 Price elasticity of demand is a vital factor when business people estimate the total revenue they can expect to make. All sellers are interested in the amounts consumers will spend on an item because consumer expenditure is an important determinant of their profits. Expenditures by consumers represent the total revenue sellers take in from selling their products.

Total expenditure by consumers over any given period is the number of units of a product purchased over that period, Q, multiplied by the price of the product, P:

$$\text{Total expenditure} = PQ = \text{Total revenue}$$

This equation shows that PQ, price times quantity, over any period equals *both* the total expenditure on that product by consumers *and* the total revenue sellers receive from selling the product.

For example, if the price of ground beef averaged $1.50 per pound and 20 million pounds were sold last month, total expenditure on ground beef was $30 million. This sum also equals the total revenue received that month by sellers in the market.

Box 4 shows the demand for and supply of ground beef assuming a $1.50 per pound equilibrium price and an equilibrium quantity of 20 million pounds per month. Consumers' total expenditure can be represented as the rectangular area $0AEQ$ on the

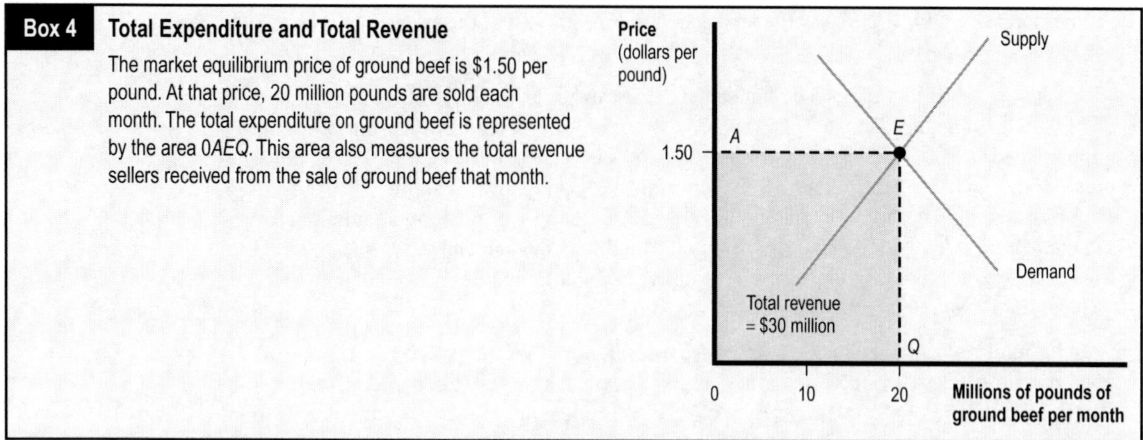
Box 4
Total Expenditure and Total Revenue
The market equilibrium price of ground beef is $1.50 per pound. At that price, 20 million pounds are sold each month. The total expenditure on ground beef is represented by the area 0AEQ. This area also measures the total revenue sellers received from the sale of ground beef that month.
Price (dollars per pound)
Supply
E
A
1.50
Demand
Total revenue = $30 million
Q
0
10
20
Millions of pounds of ground beef per month

graph. The width of this rectangle is the $1.50 price per pound represented by the distance 0*A* on the vertical axis. The length of the rectangle is the 20 million pounds sold per month, represented by the distance 0*Q* on the horizontal axis. Multiplying the length by the width gives the rectangle 0*AEQ*, which represents $30 million per month. This area represents both the total expenditure by consumers and the total revenue of sellers.

Predicting Changes in Total Expenditure and Revenue in Response to Price Increases

Suppose there's a decrease in the supply of ground beef. Box 5 shows how such a decrease in supply affects the price of ground beef and the quantity demanded. As a result of the decrease in supply, the market equilibrium price of ground beef increases from $1.50 per pound to a new price, P_2. The increase in price causes the quantity demanded per month to decline to Q_2. What effect will the increase in price have on consumer expenditure on ground beef and on the total revenue of sellers?

There's no clear-cut answer to this question. The increase in the price of ground beef acts to increase total consumer expenditure by increasing the *P* component of *PQ*. However, the law of demand indicates that as price goes up, the quantity of ground beef demanded

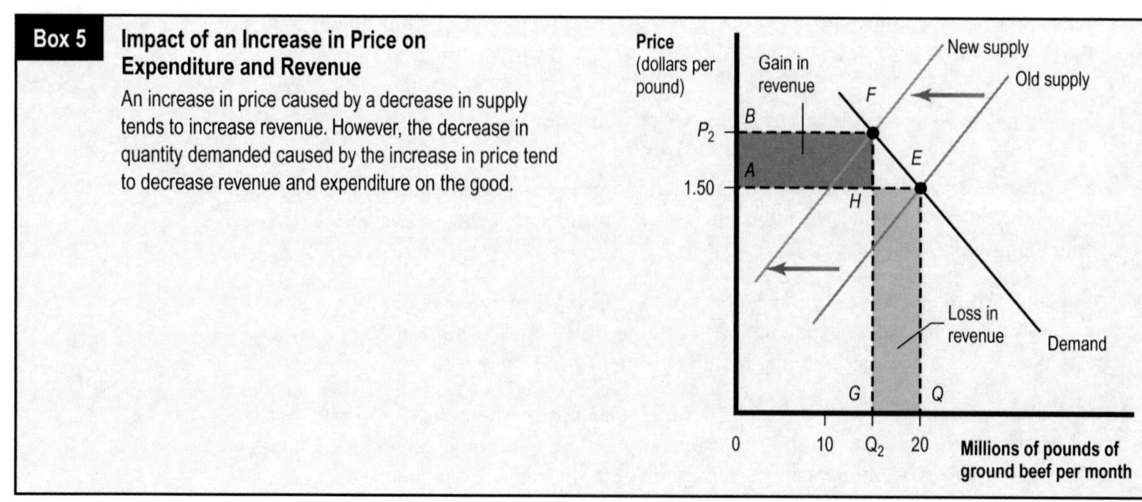
Box 5
Impact of an Increase in Price on Expenditure and Revenue
An increase in price caused by a decrease in supply tends to increase revenue. However, the decrease in quantity demanded caused by the increase in price tend to decrease revenue and expenditure on the good.
Price (dollars per pound)
Gain in revenue
New supply
Old supply
F
B
P2
E
A
1.50
H
Loss in revenue
Demand
G
Q
0
10
Q2
20
Millions of pounds of ground beef per month

will go down. The Q component of PQ thus will decrease whenever price goes up. There are therefore two forces that influence PQ when price goes up, and they act in opposite directions. If we know the price elasticity of demand for ground beef, however, we can forecast the change in PQ. This is because we can use price elasticity of demand to predict the relative magnitudes of the upward and downward forces influencing expenditure and revenue. Thus, sellers can use price elasticity of demand to predict changes in their total revenue when prices change.

Suppose the demand for ground beef is *inelastic*. This means the percentage reduction in quantity demanded caused by the price increase will be *smaller* (ignoring the direction of change) than the percentage increase in price that caused it. Under such circumstances, the *upward* influence on the price increase on revenue is stronger than the *depressing* effect of the reduction in quantity demanded on revenue. For example, if a 10 percent price increase results in only a 5 percent decline in quantity demanded, as would be the case if the elasticity of demand for ground beef were –0.5, total revenue will *increase* as a result of the price increase. *An inelastic demand therefore implies that total revenue and total expenditure on a good will increase when price rises.*

In the graph in Box 5, the gain in revenue as a result of the price increase is represented by the area $ABFH$. This represents the increase in revenue from the Q_2 pounds of ground beef sold at the higher price. The loss of revenue from the reduction in quantity demanded is represented by the area $GHEQ$. This represents revenue that sellers would have enjoyed by selling more units had the price remained at \$1.50 per pound. *When demand is inelastic, the gain in revenue from the price increase will exceed the loss in revenue from the decline in sales volume.* At the extreme, suppose the price elasticity of demand for a good were 0. This implies that an increase in price would have no effect on the quantity demanded. If this were the case, the total revenue taken in by sellers would increase by the percentage increase in price.

Now suppose demand were *elastic*. This implies that the percentage reduction in quantity demanded (ignoring the direction of change) would exceed the percentage increase in price that caused it. In this case the upward pressure on revenue caused by the price increase would be more than offset by the downward pressure on revenue resulting from the reduction in quantity demanded. As a consequence, total revenue, and therefore total expenditure, would decline. For example, if the demand for ground beef were equal to –1.50, indicating an elastic demand, sellers could expect the price increase to adversely affect their revenue.

Finally, if the demand for a product is unit elastic, any given percentage change in price will result in an equal but opposite percentage change in quantity demanded. The net effect would be no change in total revenue because the upward force on revenue would be exactly offset by the downward force. For example, estimates of the demand for housing indicate that its price elasticity is about –1. This implies that consumers tend to spend constant amounts on housing irrespective of its price.

Price Decreases, Total Expenditures, and Total Revenue

When price falls, it exerts downward pressure on total expenditure that can be offset by increases in quantity demanded. The net effect on revenue or expenditure of a price decrease depends on the relationship between the percentage decrease in price and the percentage increase in quantity demanded. Why would a decrease in price have a favorable effect on the total revenue from sale of a good whose demand is elastic but an unfavorable effect on the total revenue from sale of a good with inelastic demand? Elastic demand implies that the percentage increase in quantity demanded is greater than the percentage decrease in price that caused it. The downward pressure on total revenue caused by the price decline would therefore be more than offset by the upward pressure on total revenue resulting from the increase in quantity demanded.

Similarly, a decrease in the price of ground beef would decrease sellers' total revenue if the demand for ground beef were inelastic. For example, assuming the price elasticity of demand for ground beef is –0.5, a 10 percent decline in the price of ground beef would result in only a 5 percent increase in the quantity demanded by consumers. The 5 percent increase in purchases wouldn't offset the 10 percent decline in price, and *PQ* would decline.

Of course, if demand is unit elastic, a decrease in price will have no effect on either total revenue or total expenditure. This is because the downward pressure of the price decline would be exactly offset by the upward pressure of the increase in quantity demanded as price fell.

Box 6 summarizes the relationship between price elasticity of demand and total revenue or expenditure.

Other Demand Elasticity Measures

3 In addition to price elasticity of demand, income elasticity of demand and cross-elasticity of demand provide useful information. Income elasticity of demand is a number that measures the sensitivity of consumer purchases to given percentage changes in income. Cross-elasticity of demand is a number used to measure the sensitivity of consumer purchases of one good to percentage changes in the price of a substitute or complementary good.

Income Elasticity of Demand

Income elasticity of demand measures the percentage change in the number of units of a good consumers demand, other things being equal, resulting from each 1 percent change in income. We calculate income elasticity by dividing the percentage change in the quantity of a good purchased by a corresponding percentage change in income, assuming that only income and no other demand determinant changes:[2]

$$\text{Income elasticity of demand} = \frac{\text{\% change in number of units consumers demand}}{\text{\% change in income}}$$

For example, an income elasticity of 3 for foreign travel means that a 1 percent increase in income will result in a 3 percent increase in consumer trips overseas.

Box 6 Price Elasticity of Demand and Total Revenue or Expenditure

Price elasticity	Implication (ignoring direction of change)	Change in *P·Q* for price decrease	Change in *P·Q* for the price increase
Elastic	% change in quantity demanded exceeds % change in price	+	–
Unitary	% change in quantity demanded equals % change in price	0	0
Inelastic	% change in quantity demanded is less than % change in price	–	+

[2]For small changes in income, the income elasticity of demand is $\frac{\Delta Q/\ Q}{\Delta I/\ I}$, where *Q* is the initial consumers' demand and *I* is the initial income.

Income elasticity of demand for a good may be positive or negative. A positive income elasticity implies that increases in income (other things being equal) are associated with increases in the quantity of a good purchased. Normal goods have positive income elasticity of demand. The quantity of such goods that consumers demand is positively associated with consumer income. A good whose income elasticity is greater than 1 is sometimes called a "luxury good." Foreign travel in fact has an estimated elasticity of about 3, indicating that it can be considered a luxury good. Goods with income elasticities between 0 and 1 are considered necessities.

A negative income elasticity of demand implies an inverse relationship between income and the amounts of a good purchased. Goods with negative income elasticities are those that consumers will eventually stop buying as their incomes increase. For example, if income elasticity of demand for bus travel is negative, bus travel can be expected to decline as income increases. Inferior goods have negative income elasticity of demand. These are goods we tend to consume less of as our income increases. You'd expect such goods as poor cuts of meat, second-hand clothing, and used cars to have negative income elasticity of demand.

Using market data, we can estimate income elasticity of demand to get an indication of the sensitivity of consumer purchases of an item to fluctuations in consumer income. For current and potential sellers, income elasticity of demand is an extremely important number. For example, if you believe Americans will become more affluent in the future, you'll probably want to market products with income elasticities greater than 1—luxury items like yachts, Rolls-Royces, and world tours.

The income elasticity of food, on the other hand, is usually estimated to be less than 1. This means that the percentage increase in the demand for food is likely to be less than the percentage increase in income over time. Thus, if you're a dairy farmer, you can expect the demand for your milk to grow less quickly than the nation's income grows.

Cross-Elasticity of Demand

Another useful price elasticity concept is cross-elasticity of demand, which measures the sensitivity of purchases of one good to changes in the price of *another good*. For example, the cross-elasticity of demand for beef with respect to the price of pork would measure the percentage change in purchases of beef resulting from a 1 percent change in the *price of pork*, other things being equal. The formula for the cross-elasticity of demand between the demand for good *X* and the price of some other good, *Y*, is[3]

$$\text{Cross-elasticity of demand} = \frac{\text{\% change in number of units of X consumers demand}}{\text{\% change in price of Y}}$$

Cross-elasticity of demand may be positive or negative. A positive cross-elasticity of demand implies that the two goods are substitutes. Whenever the price of one good changes, other things being equal, the demand for the other moves in the same direction. This means that a price increase for one of the goods leads to an increase in the amounts purchased of the other. Suppose the cross-elasticity of demand between chicken and the price of pork is 0.3. Since this is a positive cross-elasticity, it indicates that consumers treat these two meats as substitutes. In general, the greater the substitutability between two goods, the higher the value of their cross-elasticities of demand. A zero cross-elasticity of demand means that the consumption of one good is independent of the price of the other.

The cross-elasticity of demand between two competing brands, such as Coke and Pepsi, is likely to be quite high. The same is probably true for any two brands of 25-inch

[3] The cross-elasticity of demand for small changes in the price of good Y is $\frac{\Delta Q_X/Q_X}{\Delta P_Y/P_Y}$ where Q_X is the number of units of X consumers demand and P_Y is the price of good Y.

televisions. However, the cross-elasticity of demand for unrelated goods, such as ice cream and computers, is likely to be 0.

Goods that are complements have a negative cross-elasticity of demand. Coffee and nondairy creamer are complements. An increase in the price of coffee is likely to decrease the demand for nondairy creamer. We'd therefore expect the cross-elasticity of demand between nondairy creamer and the price of coffee to be negative.

Estimates of the cross-elasticity of demand for a product are important for business planning. For example, suppose a sharp increase in natural gas prices is expected. This is likely to increase demand for electricity because the two are regarded as substitutes for heating, cooking, and other uses. Electric companies can plan to meet the increased demand for their product if they know its cross-elasticity with respect to the price of natural gas. For example, if the cross-elasticity of demand for electricity with respect to the price of natural gas is 0.29, then a 20 percent increase in the price of natural gas can be expected to result in a 5.8 percent increase in the number of kilowatt-hours that consumers demand per year.

Price Elasticity of Supply

The concept of price elasticity of supply is similar to the concept of price elasticity of demand. The price elasticity of supply is a number used to measure the sensitivity of changes in quantity supplied to given percentage changes in the price of a good, other things being equal. Price elasticity of supply indicates the percentage change in quantity supplied resulting from each 1 percent change in price. It can be calculated by dividing the percentage change in quantity supplied by the percentage change in price that caused it, given all other supply determinants:[4]

$$\text{Price elasticity of supply} = \frac{\text{\% change in quantity supplied}}{\text{\% change in price}}$$

For example, if a 10 percent increase in price results in a 20 percent increase in quantity supplied, the price elasticity of supply is

$$\frac{20\%}{10\%} = 2$$

Since supply curves generally slope upward, supply elasticity tends to be positive. An increase in price tends to generate an increase in quantity supplied, while a decrease in price tends to generate a decrease in quantity supplied. In the equation for price elasticity of supply, the signs of the numerator and the denominator are the same. The ratio therefore has a positive sign.

As with demand, be sure you remember that the slope of a supply curve is an unreliable measure of its elasticity. The price elasticity of supply is related to but isn't the same as the slope of the supply curve.

The price elasticity of supply ranges from 0 to infinity. An elastic supply prevails when the price elasticity of supply is greater than 1. If the price elasticity of supply is equal to or greater than 0 but less than 1, an inelastic supply prevails. Finally, when the price elasticity of supply is just equal to 1, a unit elastic supply prevails. Box 7 summarizes the relationship between percentage changes in price and quantity supplied for various cases.

[4]For small changes in price, the price elasticity of supply can be expressed as $\frac{\Delta Q_S/\ Q_S}{\Delta P/\ P} = \frac{P\Delta Q_S}{Q_S\Delta P}$ where Q_S is quantity supplied.

Box 7 Price Elasticity of Supply as a Gauge of Supply Responsiveness

Supply response	% change in quantity suppplied relative to % change in quantity demanded	Value of elasticity of supply
Inelastic	% change in quantity suppplied is *less than* % change in price	Equal to or greater than 0 but less than 1
Unit elastic	% change in quantity suppplied *equals* % change in price	1
Elastic	% change in quantity suppplied is *greater than* % change in price	Greater than 1

The greater the price elasticity of supply of an item, the more responsive, or elastic, is the quantity supplied to given percentage price changes.

Determinants of Price Elasticity of Supply

In general, a good's price elasticity of supply depends on the extent to which costs per unit rise as sellers increase output. If unit costs of production rise only slightly as output expands, small percentage increases in price will result in large percentage increases in quantity supplied. Under such circumstances, supply will be very elastic because small increases in price will allow sellers the possibility of large additional gains.

When the price of an item increases. not only do existing firms tend to produce more, but additional firms are attracted to production of the item. However, it often takes a considerable amount of time for new firms to start producing an item. For this reason, supply tends to become more elastic over time as the lure of profits attracts more sellers.

For example, rising petroleum prices in the 1970s led to new exploration and development of previously unprofitable sources of oil. Over time, the quantity of petroleum products supplied increased substantially. After the sharp increase in the price of crude oil in 1973, oil reserves from the North Sea, Alaska, and Mexico were slowly developed. High oil prices slowly, but surely and massively, resulted in a response by suppliers. The sharp increase in crude oil prices that occurred between 2005 and 2008 encouraged more oil exploration and development of new technology for extracting known oil reserves over a long period of time. The high oil prices provide incentives to develop new technologies and alternative sources of energy. Higher gasoline prices lead to investment in new refineries. However, an immediate response is impossible because of the time required to develop new petroleum resources and energy alternatives. And when oil prices fall, as they did in late 2008 and early 2009, incentives to make investments in development of new energy sources also is diminished. The time necessary to gear up and make new supplies available varies from industry to industry. This variation in response time is an important determinant of variations in the price elasticity of supply among industries.

The supply of housing also tends to become more elastic over time. For example, suppose rent controls, like those described in the chapter Using Supply and Demand Analysis, reduce market rents to 20 percent lower than they would be without the controls. Over a short period the rental housing supply is likely to be quite inelastic, say 0.7. We can easily calculate the reduction in rental housing in the short run caused by the 20 percent reduction in market rents:

$$0.7 = \frac{\text{\% change in quantity supplied}}{-20\%}$$

$$\text{\% change in quantity supplied} = -14\%$$

Let's assume that over 10 years the price elasticity of supply of rental housing is higher, say equal to 2. In this case the percentage reduction in the quantity of rental housing supplied ultimately resulting from the 20 percent decline in rents will be

$$2 = \frac{\text{\% change in quantity supplied}}{-20\%}$$

$$\text{\% change in quantity supplied} = -40\%$$

Landlords' reaction to rent controls will therefore intensify as time goes by. This implies that the shortage resulting from rent controls will become more acute over time.

Perfectly Inelastic and Perfectly Elastic Supply

When supply is fixed, sellers have no opportunity to vary the quantity they can offer. A perfectly inelastic supply curve for a good is a vertical line above a certain minimum price necessary to induce sellers to make the good available for sale. No matter what the percentage change in price above this minimum price, the percentage change in quantity supplied is always 0. Price elasticity of supply is always 0 along such a curve. Note that the supply curve doesn't hit the horizontal axis. This is because sellers require a minimum price before they'll make the item available for sale in a market. The supply of land in the United States is close to perfectly inelastic. No matter how much the price of land changes, there's unlikely to be any appreciable change in the total amount of usable land in the country.

The elasticities of supply of many goods are likely to be close to zero for very short periods. For example, the supply of fresh fish on a given day after the fishing fleet has brought in its catch will be perfectly inelastic. It takes time to catch more. Over time the supply of fish will be more elastic as higher prices induce fishers to catch more. As you can see in graph **A** in Box 8, when supply is perfectly inelastic, an increase in demand results in an increase in market price but has no effect on quantity supplied. However, if the price were below P_0, fishers wouldn't go out fishing and the quantity supplied would be zero.

A perfectly elastic supply curve is a horizontal line such as that in graph **B** in Box 8. Price elasticity of supply is infinite on this line. You can think of such a supply curve as meaning that the slightest change in price would result in an infinite change in quantity supplied. The horizontal line also means that any change in demand results in a change in quantity supplied, but no change in price is necessary to induce sellers to supply more.

In effect, the supply curve of cheeseburgers to you in a McDonald's is probably shaped like the one drawn in graph **B**. You can buy all the cheeseburgers you want at the established price without causing the price to go up. In effect, to any particular buyer in a competitive market, the supply curve of a good will be perfectly elastic.

Another example of perfectly elastic supply would be an industry where over a long period the prices of inputs necessary to produce output don't increase as output increases. This means that no price increases would be required to increase quantities supplied because costs per unit of the good wouldn't increase as more was made available. There's evidence that the supply of new residential construction is nearly infinitely elastic over the long run.[5] Other things being equal, this implies that any increases in the price of new construction per square foot over short periods will eventually be balanced by future price declines. Over a long period an increase in demand results in an increase in quantity supplied but no increase in market price. Temporary price increases tend to attract new

---

[5]James R. Follain, Jr., "The Price Elasticity of the Long-Run Supply of New Housing Construction," *Land Economics* (May 1979), pp. 190–99.

Box 8 Perfectly Inelastic and Perfectly Elastic Supply Curves

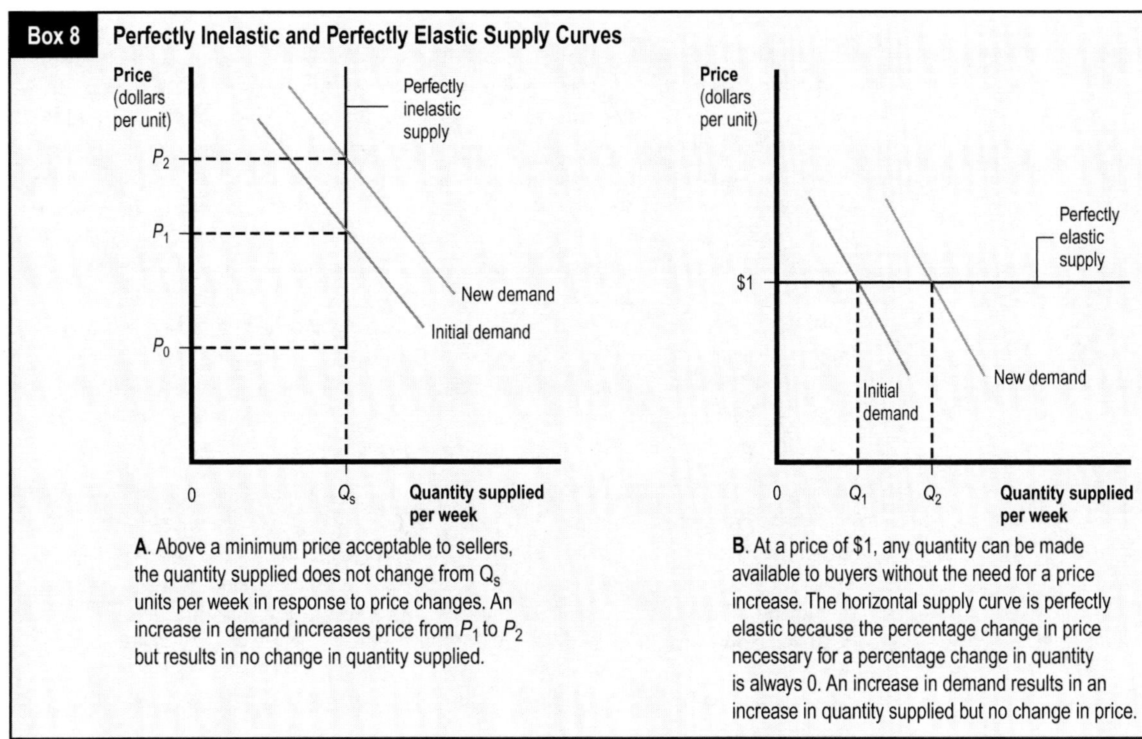

A. Above a minimum price acceptable to sellers, the quantity supplied does not change from Q_s units per week in response to price changes. An increase in demand increases price from P_1 to P_2 but results in no change in quantity supplied.

B. At a price of $1, any quantity can be made available to buyers without the need for a price increase. The horizontal supply curve is perfectly elastic because the percentage change in price necessary for a percentage change in quantity is always 0. An increase in demand results in an increase in quantity supplied but no change in price.

firms into the construction industry. The resulting increase in supply acts to decrease price over a longer period.

Tax Shifting

4 The concepts of price elasticity of demand and supply are relevant to the analysis of taxes levied on sellers of such goods as gasoline, cigarettes, and alcoholic beverages. Even though these taxes are collected from sellers, buyers are often harmed by them because they can result in shifts in supply that cause prices to rise. Tax shifting occurs when a tax levied on sellers of a good causes the market price of the good to increase. Under certain circumstances, the price of a good can increase by exactly enough to cover the tax levied on each unit of the good. If we know the price elasticities of demand and supply of a taxed good, we can forecast the impact of the tax on the good's market price.

To find out how a tax affects market price, we need to analyze its impact on supply and demand conditions. Assume the government collects from sellers a 10-cent tax per gallon of gasoline. *From the sellers' standpoint, this means that the cost of each gallon of gasoline sold will go up exactly 10 cents.* The effect of the tax is exactly the same as the effect of having the price of an input used to produce gasoline go up 10 cents. The minimum price that sellers will accept for each gallon of gas will be increased by the amount of the tax. The supply curve for gasoline will therefore shift upward 10 cents for each quantity of gasoline sold. In effect, the tax causes a decrease in the supply of gasoline by reducing the gain obtained from selling each gallon.

Full Shifting

The graphs in Box 9 show two cases in which a supply decrease caused by the gasoline tax will cause the market price per gallon to increase by the *full amount* of the tax. In **A**, gas demand is perfectly inelastic. Here, as the supply decreases, buyers don't respond by decreasing the quantity demanded. The quantity demanded is 1 million gallons per month before and after the tax. The initial price is $1 per gallon. After the tax shifts the supply curve upward by 10 cents for any quantity, the price increases by exactly the amount of the tax per unit. The tax will collect $100,000 per month in this case, which equals the 10- cent per gallon tax multiplied by the 1 million gallons sold each month. The tax revenue is represented by the shaded area in **A**. *In effect, consumers pay the entire tax in the form of a 10-cent increase in the price of gasoline*. After the tax has been imposed, the market price buyers pay increases to $1.10. After paying the tax of 10 cents per gallon, sellers receive a net price of $1 per gallon, which is exactly the price they received before the tax was imposed. *When the demand for gasoline is perfectly inelastic, a tax collected from gas sellers is fully shifted to gas buyers as the gas price rises to cover the tax per unit.*

Sellers would also succeed in shifting the entire tax per unit to buyers if the *supply* of gasoline were perfectly elastic. In **B** in Box 9, the gas supply is assumed to be a horizontal line, implying a perfectly elastic supply. As before, the tax would shift the supply curve upward by 10 cents per gallon. In this case, however, the demand curve is assumed to be downward sloping, as is normally the case. As a result, the monthly quantity demanded declines from 1 million gallons to 750,000 gallons. However, the new supply curve intersects the demand curve at a price exactly 10 cents higher than the initial price of $1. At any price lower than that, sellers would be unable to cover their costs and would reduce production until price increased.

When the supply of gasoline is perfectly elastic at the $1 per gallon price before the tax has been imposed, sellers will be unwilling to make gas available at any price below $1 per gallon. The market price must rise to $1.10 per gallon for sellers to receive a net price of $1 per gallon after paying the 10-cent per gallon tax. Here, as in the first case, the price of gas goes up by the full amount of the tax per gallon. In this case, however, quantity demanded does decline; as a result, the tax collects only $75,000 per month, which is

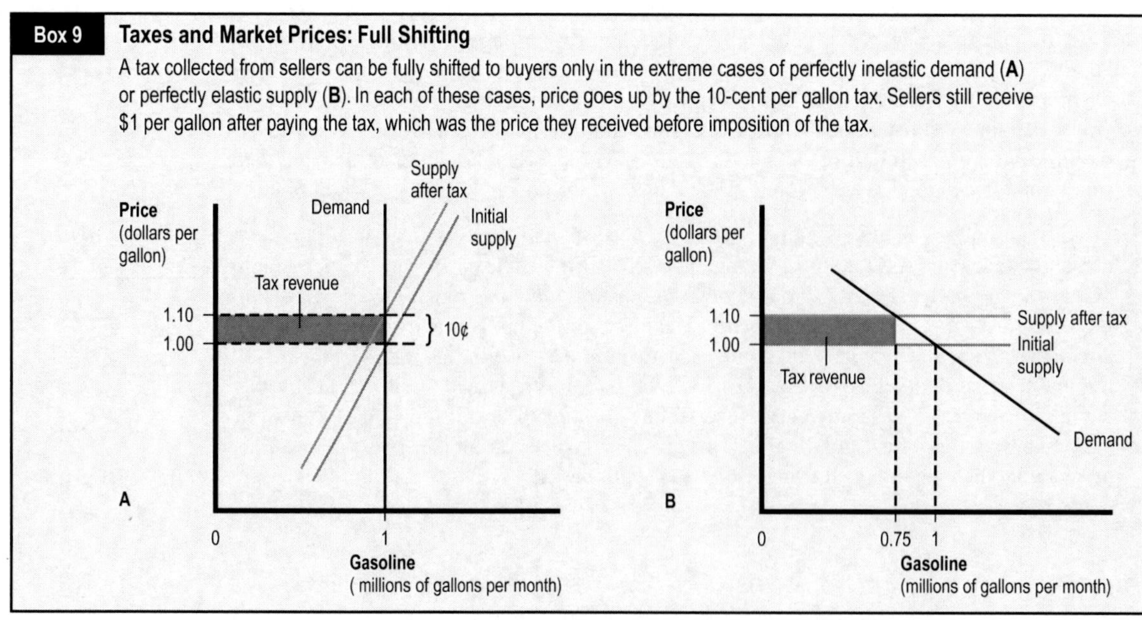

Box 9 **Taxes and Market Prices: Full Shifting**

A tax collected from sellers can be fully shifted to buyers only in the extreme cases of perfectly inelastic demand (**A**) or perfectly elastic supply (**B**). In each of these cases, price goes up by the 10-cent per gallon tax. Sellers still receive $1 per gallon after paying the tax, which was the price they received before imposition of the tax.

represented by the shaded area in **B** in Box 10. Nonetheless, the tax collected from sellers is still fully paid by buyers because the gas price increases by just enough to cover the tax. In general, if a good's supply is infinitely elastic, sellers can shift any tax collected from them to buyers by reducing the amount they supply until price increases by the full amount of the tax.

Partial Shifting

In reality, it's highly improbable that the price elasticity of demand for a good will be zero. Although the price elasticity of supply can be close to infinity over long periods, this too is highly improbable over short periods. Suppose, then, that neither the price elasticity of demand nor the price elasticity of supply takes on the extreme values of zero or infinity. In this case we can easily show that the tax will be *shared* by the buyers and sellers of the good. The case is illustrated in Box 10. The initial market equilibrium is at point *E*, which corresponds to a market price of $1 per gallon and monthly sales of 1 million gallons. As before, the tax shifts the supply curve up by 10 cents per gallon. The new market equilibrium corresponds to point *E'*, at which the market price paid by sellers increases to $1.04 and the quantity demanded declines to 850,000 gallons per month. After sellers pay the 10-cent-per-gallon tax, the net price they receive is $1.04–$0.10 = $0.94. Total tax revenue collected is $85,000 per month, which is equal to the 10-cent-per-gallon tax multiplied by the 850,000 gallons sold per month. In effect, sellers pay 6 cents of the 10-cent-per-gallon tax because the price they receive per gallon falls from $1 to 94 cents after the tax has been imposed. The remaining 4 cents is shifted to buyers as a 4-cent-per-gallon increase in the market price.

What would happen if sellers tried to shift the full 10-cent-per-gallon tax to buyers by increasing price to $1.10? To find out, go to the graph in Box 10 and follow the dashed line from the price axis at $1.10 to the demand curve and the supply curve that prevail after the tax has been imposed. Note that the quantity demanded at that price would be only 630,000 gallons per month, while the quantity supplied would be 1 million gallons per month. There would therefore be a gas surplus that would push the market price down until it reached $1.04 per gallon.

The conclusion of this analysis is straightforward: *Sellers in competitive markets are subject to the laws of supply and demand when it comes to shifting taxes. Only in the unlikely case when demand is perfectly inelastic or when supply is perfectly elastic will sellers succeed in raising the price by the full amount of the tax.*

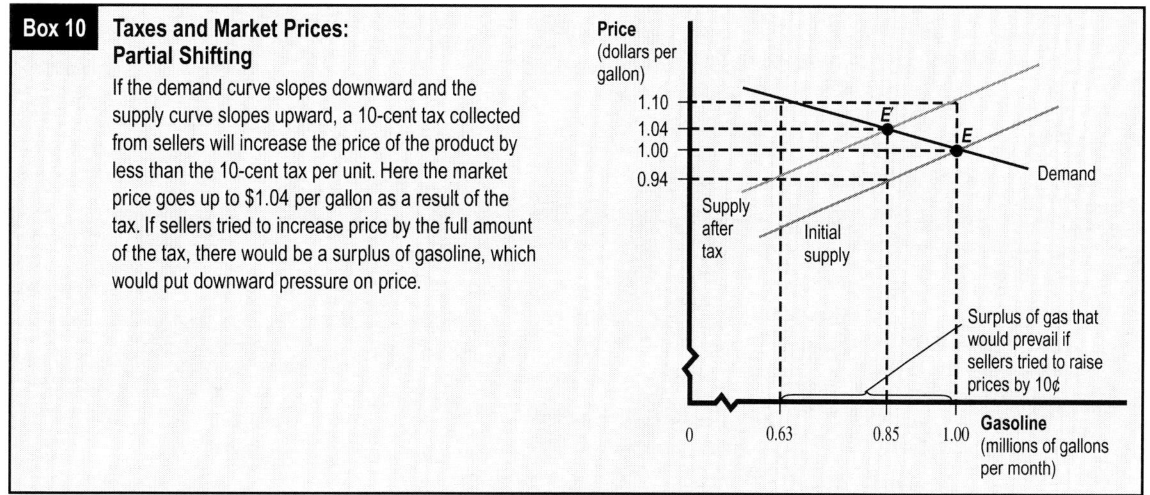

Box 10 Taxes and Market Prices: Partial Shifting

If the demand curve slopes downward and the supply curve slopes upward, a 10-cent tax collected from sellers will increase the price of the product by less than the 10-cent tax per unit. Here the market price goes up to $1.04 per gallon as a result of the tax. If sellers tried to increase price by the full amount of the tax, there would be a surplus of gasoline, which would put downward pressure on price.

Summary

1. Price elasticity of demand, a number that gauges the sensitivity of quantity demanded of a good to each 1 percent change in its price, is calculated by dividing the percentage change in quantity demanded by the percentage change in price that caused it.
2. Price elasticity of demand can range from 0 to an infinitely large negative number. Demand for a good is inelastic if the number indicating its price elasticity is less than 1, ignoring the minus sign. Demand for a good is unit elastic if the number indicating its price elasticity is exactly equal to 1, ignoring the minus sign. Demand for a good is elastic if the number indicating its price elasticity exceeds 1, ignoring the minus sign.
3. The price elasticity of demand for a good is influenced by the availability of substitutes for it, the proportion of their income consumers spend on it, and time.
4. Price elasticity of demand cannot be easily gauged from the slope of demand curves. For example, a downward-sloping demand curve with constant slope at all points will become more elastic as price increases.
5. A perfectly inelastic demand curve is a vertical line, while a perfectly elastic demand curve is a horizontal line.
6. The way consumers' total expenditure and sellers' total revenue change as price changes can be forecast if the price elasticity of demand for the good is known. If demand is elastic, price increases will decrease total revenue. If demand is inelastic, price increases will increase total revenue.
7. Income elasticity of demand gauges the sensitivity of demand for a good to changes in consumer income. Cross-elasticity of demand measures the sensitivity of demand for a good to changes in the prices of related goods.
8. Price elasticity of supply measures the sensitivity of changes in quantity supplied to each 1 percent change in the price of a good. It is calculated by dividing the percentage change in quantity supplied of a good by the percentage change in price that caused it.
9. When price elasticity of supply is greater than 1, supply is elastic. When the number is equal to or greater than 0 but less than 1, supply is inelastic. When the number is 1, supply is unit elastic.
10. A perfectly inelastic supply curve is a vertical line, while a perfectly elastic supply curve is a horizontal line.

Concept Review

1. How is the price elasticity of demand for a product calculated? Under what circumstances is the demand for a product categorized as "elastic" or "inelastic?"
2. Why is information on the price elasticity of demand for a product required to forecast the effect of an increase in the price of the product on the total revenue earned by business firms selling it?
3. List some possible uses of each of the following concepts: income elasticity of demand, cross-elasticity of demand, and price elasticity of supply.
4. Under what circumstances would a tax collected from sellers of a product be shifted entirely to buyers in the form of a price increase? Why are excise taxes likely to be shared by buyers and sellers of the taxed product?

Problems and Applications

1. The price elasticity of demand for furniture you sell is estimated to be –3. What will be the effect on the quantity you sell if you lower your prices by 10 percent next month? What will happen to the total revenue you take in next month as a result of the price cut? 1, 2
2. The price elasticity of demand for Brussels sprouts is estimated to be –0.5. Government authorities want to increase Brussels sprouts consumption by 15 percent. By what percentage must the price to consumers fall to achieve this objective? What will happen to total consumer expenditure on Brussels sprouts as a result of the price cut? 1, 2
3. The price of a package of Reese's Peanut Butter Cups rises from $1 to $1.25. As a result, the weekly quantity of Reese's demanded falls from 10,000 to

9,000 packages. Calculate the price elasticity of demand using the average of the initial and new prices and quantities as the basis for figuring the percentage changes. ①

4. Suppose that, for each 25-cent increase in the price of Reese's Peanut Butter Cups, the demand curve is such that the quantity demanded falls by 1,000 packages per week. Plot the demand curve for Reese's on a set of axes. Show that demand for Reese's becomes more elastic as price increases. ①

5. Suppose Susan decides she'll spend $30 per month on Taco Supremes, no matter what the price. Assuming she sticks to her decision, show that her demand for Taco Supremes is unit elastic at all possible prices. ①, ②

6. Draw the demand curve for a good that has a unit elastic demand at all possible prices. ①

7. The supply of pencils decreases, but there's no change in the quantity demanded. Draw the demand curve for pencils, and comment on its price elasticity. What will happen to total expenditure on pencils as the price of pencils increases? ①, ②

8. The income elasticity of demand for furniture is 3. A recession reduces consumer income by 10 percent. What will happen to furniture sales? Explain why the demand for soap will be much less responsive to a reduction in income than the demand for furniture if the income elasticity of demand for soap is only 0.2. ③

9. The cross-elasticity of demand for bacon with respect to the price of eggs is –2. What does this tell you about the way consumers perceive the relationship between bacon and eggs? ③

10. The price elasticity of demand for cigarettes is –1.2. The price elasticity of supply for cigarettes is estimated to be 1. Will a 15-cent tax per pack of cigarettes increase the price of cigarettes by 15 cents per pack? ④

Import Quotas: How They Affect Supplies

Import quotas are restrictions on the quantity of foreign goods that can be sold in a nation. Such quotas are often used to protect domestic industries from foreign competition. (See The Global Economy feature Protection versus Free International Trade in the chapter Economics: What It's All About.) People who support import quotas argue that they merely limit quantities and don't necessarily raise prices for consumers. Using a bit of supply and demand analysis, along with the concept of price elasticity of supply, will convince you that import quotas are likely to result in price increases both for imports and for the domestic goods that are substituted for the imports!

For example, suppose a limit is placed on the number of Japanese cars that can be imported into the United States. Such an import quota was in effect during 1983 as part of a "voluntary export restraint" agreement negotiated by the U.S. and Japanese governments. The quota, set at 1.85 million cars for 1983, was designed to protect the U.S. auto industry that year and to encourage U.S. producers to invest in new facilities.

The effect of an import quota is to make the supply of the imported good perfectly inelastic after a certain number of units have been sold. The supply curve for imported Japanese cars in the United States in 1983 is shown in the graph below. The curve is upward-sloping up to point *A* and becomes vertical after point *A*. Point *A* corresponds to the import limit of 1.85 million cars.

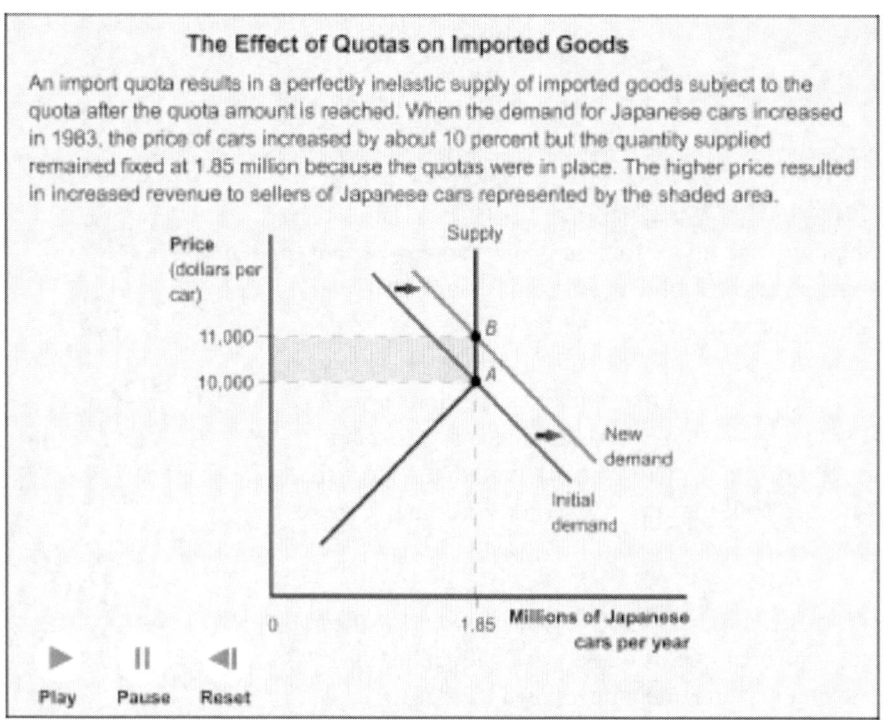
The Effect of Quotas on Imported Goods
An import quota results in a perfectly inelastic supply of imported goods subject to the quota after the quota amount is reached. When the demand for Japanese cars increased in 1983, the price of cars increased by about 10 percent but the quantity supplied remained fixed at 1.85 million because the quotas were in place. The higher price resulted in increased revenue to sellers of Japanese cars represented by the shaded area.
Price (dollars per car)
Supply
11,000
10,000
B
A
New demand
Initial demand
0
1.85
Millions of Japanese cars per year
Play
Pause
Reset

The effect of a quota on the price of imported Japanese cars depends on the level of demand. If the demand curve intersects the supply at or below point *A*, the quota will neither reduce the quantity of cars purchased nor raise the price of the cars. If, however, demand is stronger, so that it intersects the supply curve at a point like *B*, the price of Japanese cars would rise as a result of the quota, but sales would remain fixed at the quota of 1.85 million units. In 1983, there was a surge in the demand for Japanese cars, because consumer incomes were rising as the U.S. economy pulled out of a severe recession. As illustrated in the graph, the impact of the quota with the higher level of demand was to increase the price of Japanese cars by $1,000.

It has been estimated that quotas on Japanese car imports had the effect of raising the price of these cars by about $1,000, on average.[1] As illustrated in the graph, the $1,000 price increase also added $1.85 billion in revenue, represented by the shaded rectangle, to producers of imported cars and their dealers. Although quotas limit sales of imports, they add to the revenues of foreign suppliers by raising the price at which they can sell their products. For that reason, Japanese car manufacturers don't complain much about quotas.

What effect do quotas have on domestic producers? Because quotas tend to increase the price of foreign substitutes for domestic products, they tend to increase demand for domestic products. In the early 1980s, import quotas on Japanese cars contributed to an increase in demand for domestic cars that raised their price by an estimated $370 per unit, on average. The higher price increased the quantity of domestic cars supplied and, therefore, helped the U.S. automobile industry.

But what was the cost of this gain in U.S. production? The total increase in the cost of buying both domestic and imported cars resulting from the quotas in the early 1980s came to over $4 billion. This cost was incurred to save an estimated 26,000 jobs in the U.S. auto industry. The total cost of the jobs saved when the quotas were in effect amounted to over $150,000 per worker per year, which was a lot more than the annual salaries earned by those workers![2] Do you think the benefits were worth the costs?

Quotas can also result in shortages if prices don't rise quickly in markets and if domestic producers can't respond quickly to increased demands for their products. For example, U.S. quotas on steel imports during the late 1980s contributed to shortages of unfinished steel. These shortages induced domestic users to import more expensive finished-steel products to meet their demands, because the finished products were not subject to quotas.[3] In the United States, import quotas also contribute to higher prices for many textile products and agricultural commodities. These measures preserve jobs in U.S. industries at the cost of higher prices for consumers.

By 2005, most tariffs and import quotas on textile products were eliminated. The supply of inexpensive clothing imported from China increased substantially that year and put downward pressure on prices. Although jobs were lost in domestic textile industries, consumers benefited from the lower prices.

[1]Robert W. Crandall, "Import Quotas and the Automobile Industry: The Cost of Protectionism," *Brookings Review* 2, no. 4 (Summer 1984), pp. 8-16.

[2]Crandall, "Import Quotas and the Automobile Industry," p. 16.

[3]*Economic Report of the President, 1989* (Washington, D.C.: U.S. Government Printing Office, 1989), pp. 169-70.

How to Maximize Revenue: Pricing Theater Tickets during Off-Peak Hours

Suppose you manage a movie theater and want to maximize profits for midweek screenings. Demand is slack during midweek, and it's likely to take a price much lower than the $8 weekend admission to fill the theater. You know that, once you open the theater and screen a movie, your costs are independent of the number of admissions you sell. Under these circumstances, you can maximize your profit from the sale of tickets when you maximize revenue from admissions.

Assuming the demand curve for admissions to your midweek screenings is linear, it's easy to apply the analysis in this chapter to choose the price that maximizes revenue. Graph **A** shows the demand curve for midweek screenings. Along the linear demand curve, each 1-cent reduction in ticket prices results in the sale of two more tickets. The theater's capacity is 600 people.

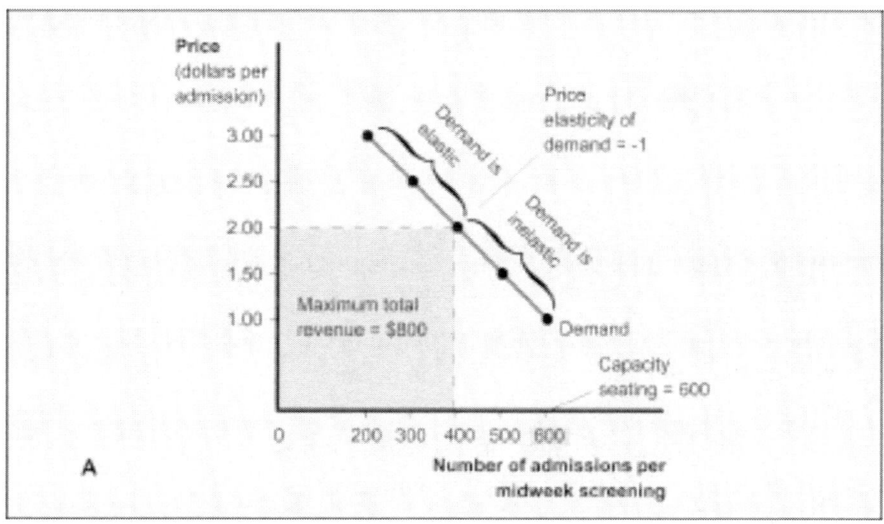

The demand curve indicates that, if you choose a ticket price of $3, the number of admissions demanded would be 200. Total revenue would be $600 for the evening (the $3 ticket price multiplied by the 200 admissions). But at $3, demand for theater admissions is elastic. This means that, if you were to lower the price, your total revenue would increase. You can verify this by choosing a lower price, such as $2.50, and remembering that each 1-cent reduction in price results in two more admissions. It follows that, if price were $2.50, the number of admissions demanded would increase by 100, to 300, and your total revenue would be $750 per screening.

Total revenue will continue to increase as long as demand remains elastic and will begin to decline just at the point at which price is reduced to make demand inelastic. For example, if you reduced the price to $2 per admission, the number of admissions demanded would be 400 and your total revenue would be $800 for the evening. At a price of $2, demand is unit elastic, because, if price were reduced an additional 1 cent, to $1.99, admissions would increase to 402 and total revenue would decline to $799.98. If the price were reduced to $1.50, the quantity demanded would go up to 500, but total revenue would decline still further, to $750, because demand would be inelastic. Graph **B** shows how total revenue varies with the number of admissions when the demand curve shown in graph **A** prevails.

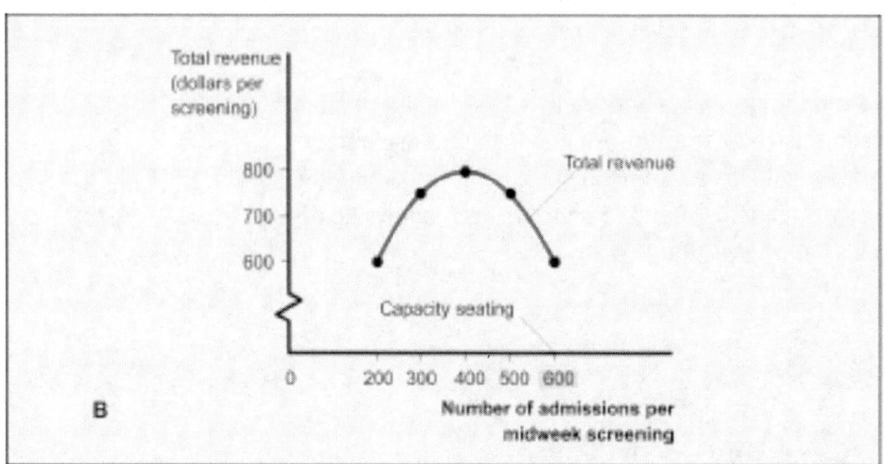

Also note, from the table and graph **A,** that you could fill up the theater if you charged $1 for admission. At that price, you'd fill all of your 600 seats for each screening, but your total revenue would be only $600! To maximize revenue, you'd therefore choose to price your tickets at $2 and be content with filling only two-thirds of your seating capacity, but enjoying $800 revenue for the evening.

The point of this example is that, if a business wants to maximize revenue, it must choose the price at which demand just becomes inelastic. This is the price for which demand is unit elastic.

Demand and Total Revenue per Midweek Screening

Price (dollars)	Number of admissions demanded	Total revenue	Price elasticity of demand
3.00	200	600	Elastic
2.50	300	750	Elastic
2.00	400	800	Unit elastic
1.50	500	750	Inelastic

1.00	600	600	Inelastic

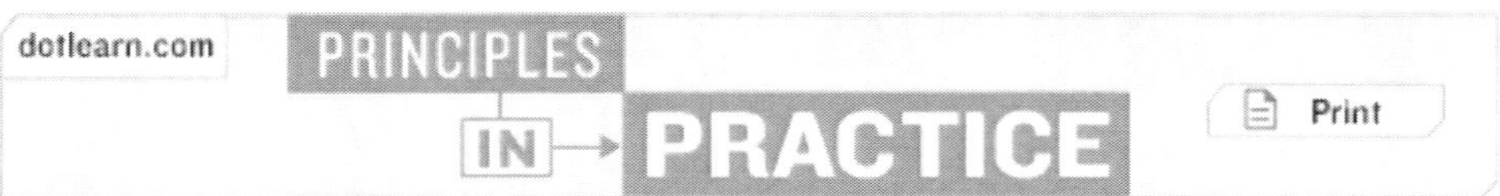

Empirical Estimates of Demand Elasticities

The key to understanding market demand for products often lies in estimating the relevant elasticities of demand. Firms and governments are well aware of this and spend large sums of money each year to estimate these elasticities for products. Economists regularly estimate demand elasticities as part of their research. The three tables below show estimated demand elasticities for various goods and services. Table A shows both short-run and long-run estimated price elasticities. For most goods, demand is more elastic with respect to price over longer periods of time than over the short run. Over longer periods, consumers have more time to find substitutes for goods whose prices increase. In addition, more substitutes are developed and made available by sellers in the long run.

A. Estimated Price Elasticities of Demand

Item	Short run	Long run
Food Items[1]:		
Beef	−0.35	-
Pork	−0.69	-
Poultry	−0.64	-
Fish	−0.39	-
Dairy	−0.79	-
Bread	−0.35	-
Vegetables	−0.72	-
Fruit	−0.72	-
Other Items:		
Military housing[2]	−0.28	-
Bus transit use[3]	−0.36	-
New Vehicles[4]:		
Compact Cars	−8.5	-
Luxury cars	−9.7	-
SUVs	−10.0	-
Pickup trucks	−11.1	-
Jewelry and watches	−0.41	−0.67
Gasoline[5,6]	−0.40	−1.50
Foreign travel by U.S. residents	−0.14	−1.77
Civilian housing	−0.30	−1.88
Household electricity use	−0.13	−1.89
Tobacco products	−0.46	−1.89
Household natural gas use[7]	−1.40	−2.10
China, glassware, tableware	−1.54	−2.55
Toilet articles and preparations	−0.20	−3.04
Movies	−0.87	−3.67
Electricity	-	−1.39

Note that estimated short-run price elasticity of demand for food items, housing, and bus transit indicates inelastic demand. However, the demand for new cars is quite elastic with respect to price in the short run. In general, estimated long-run price elasticities indicate more elastic demand than in the short run.

Table B presents empirical estimates of income elasticities for various goods and services. Estimated income elasticities for automobiles, foreign travel by U.S. citizens, and household appliances are quite high (greater than 1) and positive. These are goods whose demands are quite responsive to changes in income and increase when income goes up.

B. Estimated Income Elasticities of Demand

Item	Short run	Long run
Potatoes[8]	N.A.	−0.81
Pork[9]	0.27	0.18
Beef[9]	0.51	0.45
Furniture	2.60	0.53
China, glassware, tableware	0.47	0.77
Dental services	0.38	1.00
Chicken[9]	0.49	1.06
Automobiles	5.50	1.07
Spectator sports	0.46	1.07
Physician services	0.28	1.15
Clothing	0.95	1.17
Gasoline and oil	0.55	1.36
Household appliances	2.72	1.40
Shoes	0.90	1.50
Jewelry and watches	1.00	1.60
Owner-occupied housing	0.07	2.45
Foreign travel by U.S. citizens	0.24	3.09
Toilet articles and preparations	0.25	3.74
Electricity	–	0.97

Both short-run and long-run estimates of income elasticities are presented in Table B. In most cases, as we'd expect, long-run elasticity exceeds short-run elasticity. Notable exceptions are household appliances, furniture, and automobiles. These are durable goods. Consumers don't always replace them as their incomes increase. Note that the income elasticity of demand for potatoes is negative, indicating that consumers tend to reduce purchases of potatoes as their incomes increase.

Table C presents some estimated long-run cross-elasticities. The estimates indicate that consumers regard margarine and butter, pork and beef, and natural gas and electricity as substitutes for each other. The estimated cross-elasticities for these goods are positive.

C. Estimated Cross-Elasticities of Demand

Item	Estimate
Margarine with respect to price of butter[8]	1.53
Pork with respect to price of beef[8]	0.40
Chicken with respect to price of pork[8]	0.29
Electricity with respect to price of natural gas[10]	0.29

[1]All food item estimates are from Kuo S. Huang and Biing-Hwan Lin, "Estimation of Food Demand and Nutrient Elasticities from Household Survey Data" (Washington, DC: United States Department of Agriculture, Economic Research Service, Technical Bulletin Number 1887, August 2000).

[2]Congressional Budget Office, "Housing Prices, Housing Choices, and Military Housing Allowances" (Washington, DC: Congressional Budget Office, October 1998). The number reported is an average from data for E-1, E-2, E-3, O-1, and O-2 pay-grade personnel.

[3]Todd Litman, "Transit Price Elasticities and Cross-Elasticities," *Journal of Public Transportation*, 7(2), 2004. The bus transit estimate is for large cities with populations more than 1 million.

[4]Adam Copeland, Wendy Dunn, and George Hall, "Prices, Production, and Inventories over the Automotive Model Year," *NBER Working Paper No. 11257*, April 2005. Estimates are for the first quarter of the new model year.

[5]Robert Archibald and Robert Gillingham, "An Analysis of the Short-Run Consumer Demand for Gasoline Using Household Survey Data," *Review of Economics and Statistics* 62 (November 1980), pp. 622-28.

[6]J. M. Griffin, *Energy Conservation in the OECD, 1980-2000* (Cambridge, MA: Ballinger, 1979).

[7]G. R. Lakshmanan and William Anderson, "Residential Energy Demand in the United States," *Regional Science and Urban Economics* 10 (August 1980), pp. 371-86.

[8]Dale M. Helen, "The Structure of Food Demand: Interrelatedness and Duality," *American Journal of Agricultural Economics* 64, no. 2 (May 1982), pp. 213-21.

[9]M. K. Wohlgenant and W. F. Hahn, "Dynamic Adjustment in Monthly Consumer Demand for Meats," *American Journal of Agricultural Economics* 64, no. 3 (August 1982), pp. 553-57.

[10]Hui S. Chang and Yu Hsing, "The Demand for Residential Electricity: New Evidence on Time-Varying Elasticities," *Applied Economics*, 1991, 23, pp. 1251-56. The figure given is an estimate of the elasticity in 1987.

NOTE: Unless otherwise indicated, estimates are from Hendrik S. Houthakker and Lester D. Taylor, *Consumer Demand in the United States: Analyses and Projections* (Cambridge, MA: Harvard University Press, 1970). This is a classic study of demand and its elasticity in the United States.

Chapter 8

The Business Firm:

A Prologue to the Theory of Market Supply

Do you work part time or have a summer job? If so, you know you don't work just for the fun of it. You may enjoy your job, and it may be enabling you to acquire skills that will be valuable to you in your postcollege career. But whether you need income to meet college expenses or to provide yourself with extras, because you're a rational person, your primary objective in working is to earn income.

By the same token, businesses don't make goods and services available in markets for the pleasure of doing good deeds. Instead, their purpose is to earn income for their owners. Like your personal goals, the goals of a business can be multifaceted. However, much of economic theory about the behavior of businesses assumes their primary goal is to make profits—just as your primary goal as a rational consumer is to maximize your satisfaction.

In their quest for profits, business owners often face many competitors. Just think how many companies manufacture jeans, DVDs, or hair care products! A firm's opportunities to make profits depend on demand for its product, its competition, and its cost of making products available. In this chapter, we examine the characteristics of businesses and the way profit is measured. We discuss the functions of the firm and its organization, and we consider the simplifications necessary to construct a model that explains the firm's behavior. From a practical standpoint, we also look at the advantages and disadvantages of different forms of business organization.

Concept Preview

After reading this chapter, you should be able to

1. Outline the advantages of alternative forms of business organization: the sole proprietorship, the partnership, and the corporation.
2. Explain the functions of firms, and how various aspects of production and distribution are integrated within a single firm.
3. Present a simplified view of the firm that's useful in constructing a model that explains market supply.
4. Show how the concept of opportunity cost must be applied to accurately measure the profit of a firm.

The Business Firm

A business firm is an organization under one management set up for the purpose of earning profits for its owner by making one or more items available for sale in markets. The terms *firm, business*, and *enterprise* are often used interchangeably to mean the same thing.

As of 2001, there were more than 25 million business firms operating in the United States. Firms operate out of one or more plants, physical structures or locations at which a firm's owners or employees conduct business. For a manufacturing firm like General Motors, the plant is one or more factories. For a restaurant like Taco Bell, the plant is the structure where employees produce meals and serve them to customers. A farmer operates an agricultural firm, whose plant is the location or locations where the farmer has fields, barns, tractors, and other equipment.

Some firms (Walden Bookstores, JCPenney, and a chain of bakeries, for example) operate many similar or identical plants. Some large firms operate different plants for various stages of production. For example, your supermarket might own a dairy and a bakery and sell their products in its stores. A firm producing petroleum products, such as gasoline and lubricants, might own oil wells and supertankers. The ownership by a single firm of plants used in various stages of its production is called vertical integration. Such firms operate different kinds of plants to provide themselves with the raw materials, parts, and services they need to produce their final product. Finally, many modern business firms operate plants that produce very different kinds of goods. For example, Sony produces televisions, compact discs, and various other kinds of goods. A firm operating plants that produce many different kinds of goods and services is called a conglomerate.

Industries

An industry is a group of firms that sell a similar product in a market. For example, Ford, Chrysler, and General Motors are part of the auto industry.

However, drawing neat industry lines isn't always easy. For example, should firms that specialize in producing athletic footwear be placed in the same industry as firms that specialize in producing leather shoes? Should fast-food restaurants be placed in the same industry as full-service luxury restaurants serving gourmet dishes and fine wines? Defining a group of firms as an industry requires arbitrary judgments.

Corporate versus Noncorporate Firms

1 Not only are there different types of industries, but there are also different forms of business organization. The most basic type of business organization is the sole proprietorship, a business owned by one person. Not all sole proprietorships are small. Some are large firms with many employees and hired managers.

The sole proprietorship is the most popular form of business in the United States, accounting for nearly three-quarters of all business firms in the country. However, even though there were over 18 million sole proprietorships in 2001, they only accounted for a mere 5 percent of total business revenue that year. This is because, on average, sole proprietorships are smaller than other types of business, such as corporations.

A partnership is a business owned by two or more persons, each of whom receives a portion of any profits. Sometimes one of the persons is actually an organization, such as a corporation or an estate. Partnerships allow two or more persons to pool their resources. Because more than one person is involved, a partnership has more opportunity to expand than a sole proprietorship, in which one person is responsible for raising all the money and assumes all the risks of the enterprise. However, partnerships are the least popular form of business organization in the United States, accounting for approximately 8 percent of all firms and 6 percent of annual sales revenue.

In both sole proprietorships and partnerships, the owners are personally liable for the firm's debts and for any judgments imposed by a court of law. There's no limit to these owners' liability, and both their personal and business assets are exposed to it.

The alternative to sole proprietorships and partnerships is the corporation. A corporation is a business legally established under state laws that grant it an identity separate from that of its owners. A corporation is a *legal fiction*. This term is used by lawyers to describe a preposterous or impossible state of affairs that everyone accepts. From a legal standpoint a corporation *is* a person. By incorporating, owners of a firm create an organization that can legally own property and incur debts and is granted many of the other legal rights of a citizen, including the right to engage in litigation. Any group of people can form a corporation by obtaining a corporate charter from one of the 50 states. This requires paying a fee and filing the appropriate forms.

There are more than 5 million active corporations conducting business in the United States. Although these corporations represent 20 percent of all firms in the nation, they account for nearly 85 percent of the total sales revenue of all U.S. firms.

The bar graphs in Box 1 show how U.S. businesses were organized in 2001. In **A** you can see the breakdown by number of firms, while **B** shows the breakdown by percentage of annual sales revenue.

The form of organization can affect the cost of running a business and thus influence its profits. To understand why the corporate form might be preferable to other forms of business organization, we need to analyze the impact of incorporation on the costs of production and transactions.

The Corporate Form of Business

The corporate form of business has a number of distinctive features that set it apart from sole proprietorships and partnerships:

Box 1 Business Organizations

Although the dominant form of business in the United States in terms of numbers is the sole proprietorship, the corporate firm accounts for 90 percent of sales revenue of all business firms in the United States.

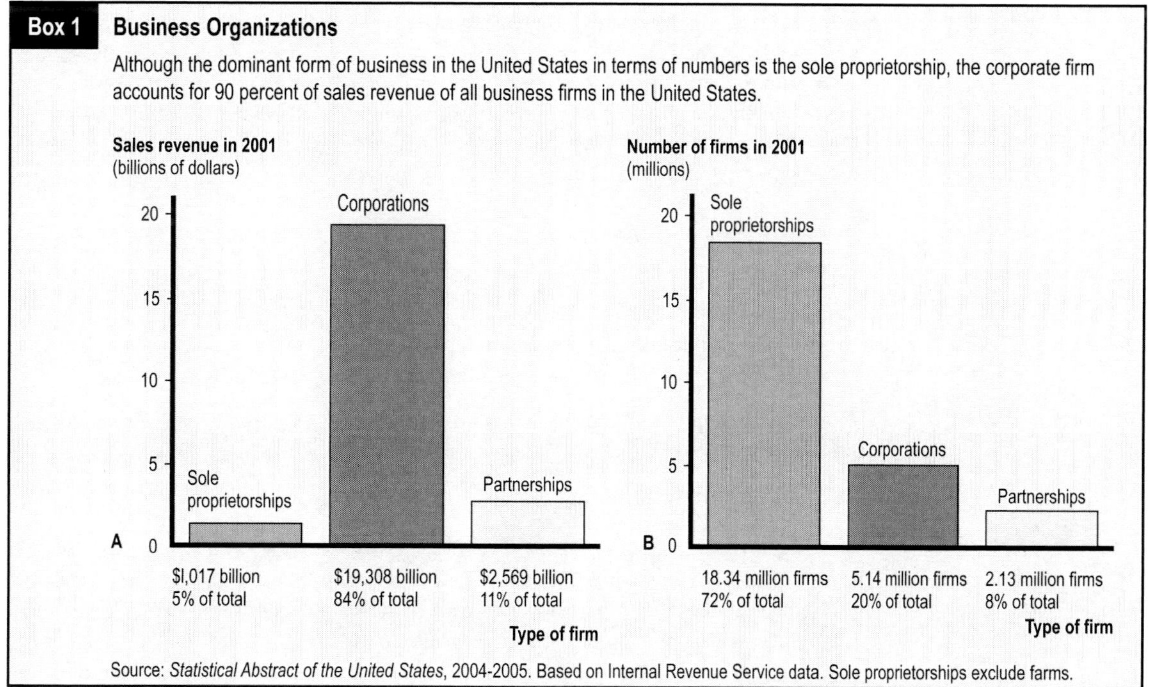

Source: *Statistical Abstract of the United States*, 2004-2005. Based on Internal Revenue Service data. Sole proprietorships exclude farms.

1. *The corporation is owned entirely by its stockholders, who have purchased shares of ownership in it.* These shares are called *stocks*. For example, suppose a corporation has 10,000 shares of stock. If you own 1,000 shares, your share of ownership in the corporation is 10 percent. Stockholders, as the owners of the corporation, have certain rights. They can vote for the directors of the corporation, who manage it, and on other issues. The number of votes a stockholder can cast depends on the number of shares owned.

2. *As owners of shares of a corporation, stockholders are entitled to a share of the corporation's income.* The portion of any corporate profits paid to its stockholders is called dividends. Dividends are paid to stockholders on a per share basis. The corporation typically retains a portion of its profits as a source of funds to make investments and expand its capacity to earn income. The portion of corporate profits not paid out as dividends is called retained earnings. A corporation isn't required to pay dividends each year and always has the option of retaining all of its earnings.

3. *Stockholders cannot be held personally liable for the debts of the corporation.* Limited liability is a legal provision that protects the owners of a corporation (its stockholders) by putting a ceiling equal to the purchase price of their stock on their liability for debts of the corporation. If a corporation goes bankrupt, no stockholder can lose any more than he or she has invested in it.

Limited liability reduces the risk of investing in a corporation and makes it easier for such firms to raise large sums of money. Limited liability isn't available to owners of sole proprietorships and partnerships, who place their personal assets (such as their homes) at stake when they start a business.

4. *Everyone who works for a corporation is an employee.* The concept of the owner-operator isn't applicable to a corporation. Everyone, from the president down to the janitors, is on the corporation's payroll. The ownership and management of a corporation are clearly separate. This isn't always the case in sole proprietorships and partnerships, where it's common for the owners to act as managers without actually receiving a salary. As owner-operators, they earn profits if they are successful.

The officers, directors, and managers of a corporation serve at the pleasure of its stockholders. They can be—and sometimes are—voted out of a job. Typically, executives own some stock in the corporation, but this is usually a small percentage. The existence of many stockholders makes it difficult for any single stockholder to control a corporation's day-to-day management decisions. Sometimes there are conflicts between the interests of a corporation's officers and those of its stockholders.

Pros and Cons of Corporate versus Noncorporate Business

Most big businesses in the United States are corporations. Although sole proprietorships outnumber corporations by about four to one, corporate business revenues in a typical year exceed the revenues of sole proprietorships by almost 20 times! Big business is corporate business. How can we explain the popularity of the corporate form of business?

There are both pros and cons to organizing a business as a corporation. For large firms the pros often outweigh the cons. The opposite is frequently true of small firms.

The pros include the following:

1. *The corporate form of business allows the firm to issue both stocks and bonds as a means of raising revenue.* Remember, a corporation has many of the rights of an individual citizen. It can borrow in its own name rather than in the names of its owners. Corporations can borrow directly from banks or issue corporate bonds that are sold to investors. (A bond is a promise by a corporation to pay the bondholder a certain amount of money by a specified future date and to pay interest to the bondholder.) In addition, a

corporation can obtain funds to finance its operations and expansion by selling more stock. By issuing stocks and bonds, a corporation can obtain large sums of money that a noncorporate firm would have difficulty in raising.

2. *The owners of a corporation, its stockholders, have limited liability.* Because they risk no more than the funds they invest in the corporation, they're more willing to supply those funds. Once again, this enables corporations to raise the large sums of money they need to expand. Owners of noncorporate businesses have unlimited liability for debts because their *personal* as well as business assets are at risk.

3. *It's relatively easy for stockholders to sell their rights of ownership.* Corporate stocks are sold in the stock market. This gives investors in corporations more flexibility than is enjoyed by investors in sole proprietorships and partnerships.

The cons include the following:

1. *The separation of owners from managers in the corporate structure has the potential for conflicts of interest between these two groups.* Sometimes managers of a corporation try to protect their jobs at the expense of stockholders' profits. Of course, this can also be a problem for a sole proprietorship or partnership if an absentee owner hires a manager to run the business. However, the large number of owners in a corporation increases the costs associated with remedying such conflict.

2. *In the United States corporations are subject to a separate income tax.* The corporate income tax subjects profits earned by corporations to double taxation. Those profits are taxed annually. In addition, the portion of profits paid out as dividends is taxable as personal income to stockholders. Moreover, when stockholders sell their shares, they pay a tax on the difference between the selling price and the purchase price.

Do the Pros Outweigh the Cons?

The major advantage of the corporate form of business over the noncorporate forms is its ability to raise funds. To conduct its business and grow, a large firm needs a way to raise large sums of money. The costs and risks of raising money are greatly reduced by incorporation. For this reason the corporation is the dominant form of business enterprise for large firms. This also explains why large corporations dominate business in the United States, employing about 25 percent of the labor force and accounting for nearly 90 percent of business revenue.

The Functions of Business Firms

2 Whether they make microwave pizzas or space shuttles, all firms are first organizations of *people*. As such, they must make daily decisions about how to deal with other firms that supply them with goods and services and with workers they hire. They must also decide how to market their products.

Production of Goods and Services to Be Sold

A **manager** is a person who coordinates decisions *within* a firm. Managers make decisions about methods of producing goods and services. They also decide *what* and *how much* to produce and how the firm will adapt to change and new technology. They hire workers and assign them various tasks, and they must decide which tasks to have the firm's workers perform and which tasks to fulfill by purchase (or contract) with other firms. As the manager of a restaurant, for example, you might buy equipment and hire workers to launder tablecloths, napkins, and uniforms, or you might send these items out to a laundry.

Assignment of Tasks to Workers versus Contracting with Other Firms: Determining the Degree of Vertical Integration

A fully *vertically integrated firm* doesn't purchase the goods or services of any other firms in the process of making its products available to consumers. Such a firm supplies itself with all the materials and services it needs. A fully vertically integrated firm is a rarity. Managers of most firms find it cheaper to rely on specialized firms for at least some materials and services.

A key factor in determining the degree of a firm's vertical integration is the transaction costs involved in contracting with other firms to provide services needed to produce or market the firm's output. Firms try to keep their transaction costs, as well as their production costs, as low as possible to earn a higher profit. Managers are always looking for ways to lower the costs of operating the firm. For example, a department store manager can hire and train workers as security guards or obtain guard services under contract with a specialized firm. To a great extent she'll base her choice on the costs of these two methods.

It stands to reason that a firm's own employees perform some tasks more reliably, more conveniently, and, most important, at lower cost than outsiders. This is why there's at least some degree of vertical integration within firms. However, conditions change over time, and managers are always on the alert for ways to increase profits by reducing costs and possibly by providing new services to other firms.

When a firm is vertically integrated, it has divisions that do the same jobs as independent businesses existing elsewhere in the economy. There are a number of reasons why a firm may choose to integrate operations that could be performed by other firms:

1. *To ensure a reliable flow of materials and services as inputs.* By controlling its own production, a manufacturer can reduce or eliminate delays that might prevent it from shipping its orders on time. Of course, each firm has to calculate whether integration actually reduces uncertainties in input supply.

2. *To put rival firms at a disadvantage by controlling a key input.* For example, if an aluminum manufacturer acquires all of the bauxite mines, it gains control of a key input into the production of aluminum. Control of this input could prevent rival firms from producing aluminum.

3. *To improve communication in ways that might reduce costs or enhance the quality of output.* For example, many managers believe that integrating their advertising operations rather than purchasing advertising services from another firm results in higher-quality advertising. Many managers also believe the firm can keep its own advertising people informed about the development of new products at a lower cost than would be possible if it used an outside advertising agency.

4. *To adapt more easily to changing technology.* Changes in the technology of producing parts and components can have a significant effect on the way a firm assembles its output. By constantly communicating with an integrated division supplying materials, the firm's managers might more easily keep abreast of these changes.

What's the most desirable degree of vertical integration for a firm? It boils down to a question of cost and quality of product. The advantages of vertical integration are likely to differ from industry to industry and from firm to firm. It's not unusual to see firms with varying degrees of vertical integration competing with one another in the same industry. When deciding whether to obtain inputs from other firms or from divisions within the firm, owners and managers consider the costs of searching for the best price, negotiating contracts with suppliers, taking on risks associated with contractual arrangements, and other transaction costs.

Some Simplifications

3 It's clear from the preceding analysis that the organization and functions of the modern business firm are multifaceted and complex. To analyze the behavior of businesses, we need to make a number of simplifications so we can concentrate on the essential features of a firm's activities. The economic model of the firm we develop in detail in the two chapters Production and Cost and The Profit-Maximizing Competitive Firm and Market Supply involves quite a bit of abstraction from reality. The simplified firm of economic theory is one that produces only one product and seeks to maximize profits.

In reality, the modern business firm produces more than one product. For example, a pharmaceuticals company might have thousands of *product lines*. In addition to prescription and over-the-counter drugs, it might produce cosmetics, perfume, and toothbrushes. A multiproduct firm is one that produces several different items for sale in markets. An important problem faced by the management of a multiproduct firm is the allocation of scarce productive resources among the various product lines.

The economic model of the firm we use in the two chapters referenced above is based on a single-product firm, a firm that produces only one type of item for sale. By analyzing the operations of a single-product firm, we can understand most of the important managerial decisions relating to production, resource use, and profits.

Profit is the difference between the revenue a firm takes in over any given period and the costs incurred in operating the firm over the same period. To explain how firms supply products and obtain inputs, the behavioral assumption usually made is that firms seek to maximize profits. Of course, the owners or managers may have other goals as well. They may be concerned about the firm's image, its sales, the price of its stock, or the dividends it pays to stockholders. Managers may be concerned about their salary and prestige, and they may have goals that conflict with those of the firm's owners.

Economists recognize that firms are complex organizations and that their owners or managers can have more than one goal. They also realize that a great deal of risk and uncertainty is involved in making business decisions. Managers don't have crystal balls that tell them whether their decisions will achieve the intended objectives. Nevertheless, models based on the assumption that those who operate firms seek to maximize profits have proved to be very fruitful. These models have consistently yielded hypotheses that empirical evidence has supported. Models based on the assumption that firms maximize profits have also been useful in explaining the law of supply and possible exceptions to it.

Measuring Cost and Profit

4 Because of the importance assigned to profit as a motivating force for business firms, our first step in analyzing market supply is to carefully analyze the way profits are measured. To do this, we need to analyze the differences in the way economists measure costs and the way costs are currently measured according to standard accounting practices. Total cost is obtained by summing the value of all inputs used to make a good available to buyers. In making this calculation, we must be careful to include the monetary value of inputs supplied by the firm's owners rather than purchased.

Economic Cost versus Accounting Cost

Economic cost is the monetary value of *all inputs* used in a particular activity or enterprise over a given period, say a year. The idea behind economic cost is that the sum of dollars representing the value of resources used must accurately reflect the opportunity cost of those resources. Remember, the opportunity cost of a resource used in a particular activity is its value in its next best use. When firms hire or purchase inputs in markets, the market price in most cases reflects the value of these resources to others. Owners of firms give up funds to buy these resources; and if they're rational, they consider the opportunity cost of not using those funds in their next best uses.

However, in many cases owners of firms use *their own resources* in producing goods and services instead of purchasing these goods and services from others in markets. For example, the owner of a firm might work 40 hours a week managing his business. Similarly, a large corporation typically owns structures, equipment, vehicles, and land. Owner-supplied inputs aren't purchased from others in markets. However, these input services must be valued in dollar terms at their highest value in their next best use so the firm can accurately measure its economic costs. The costs of nonpurchased inputs are called implicit costs. These are costs to which a cash value must be imputed (estimated and assigned) because the inputs aren't purchased in a market transaction.

For example, the implicit cost of the labor hours the owner of a business devotes to running it are the earnings he forgoes by not working for someone else or the value he places on the leisure time he gives up—whichever is higher. The implicit cost measures the opportunity cost of the owner's time spent working for his own business.

The implicit cost of tying up funds in a business enterprise is the highest return that could have been earned on those funds had they been invested elsewhere. For example, running a bicycle manufacturing business requires materials, machines, and other capital equipment. Suppose the owner uses her own funds instead of borrowing to acquire these assets. The opportunity cost of money used in this way is the return she could earn by investing these funds in the next best alternative, say, corporate stocks. Suppose the owner ties up $50,000 of her own funds in the business and forgoes the opportunity to earn a 10 percent annual return on the funds in the stock market. The annual opportunity cost of those funds would therefore be $5,000. To calculate the economic cost of the enterprise, we have to add implicit costs of $5,000 to the firm's actual cash outlays that year.

Costs as measured by accountants don't include the opportunity cost of inputs supplied by a firm's owners. Accounting cost measures the explicit costs of operating a business. Explicit costs don't include the value of nonpurchased inputs. Accounting cost provides valuable information. Those who own businesses, however, are aware of the shortcomings of this measure and actually base their decisions on economic cost, including implicit costs, to accurately measure their opportunity costs. Business owners always compare the desirability of remaining in a particular enterprise with what they forgo by doing so. Economists therefore assume that decisions made by business firms are always based on economic cost, which is a complete measure of the opportunity cost of using economic resources in a business.

Because there are no owner-supplied labor services in a corporation, the implicit cost of a corporation is represented by forgone interest on funds tied up in the corporation by stockholders and any rental income on equipment, land, and structures that's forgone when the corporation uses these inputs. The equity of a corporation is the difference between the value of its assets (including the cash that could be obtained if its equipment and real estate were sold rather than rented) and its debt. For example, if a corporation has equity of $1 million and the interest rate is 10 percent, the implicit cost of funds tied up in the corporation will be $100,000 per year.

Opportunity Costs versus Accounting Costs: An Example

Accounting costs are only part of opportunity costs because accounting costs don't include the value of the services of inputs owned by the business firm. Accounting costs include only explicit costs involving monetary outlays. An example will make the distinction between economic cost and accounting cost clearer. Suppose Melissa owns a monogramming and embossing store and devotes 40 hours a week to personalizing and decorating sweaters, sweatshirts, and T-shirts. At the end of the year, her accountant provides information on the costs of operating the firm.

The information supplied by the accountant is summarized in Box 2. Melissa has two full-time employees, to whom she has paid $40,000 in wages during the year. She has also borrowed money from the bank to finance her purchase of equipment. She incurs total interest payments of $10,000 per year. The original cost of this capital equipment was $100,000. Its current market value is estimated to be $80,000.

In computing the annual cost of this capital, the accountant spreads the original purchase price over a number of years. This accounting practice is called *depreciation*. The accountant assumes the capital equipment will last five years before it has to be replaced. He therefore takes one-fifth (20 percent) of its purchase price as depreciation. This is $20,000.

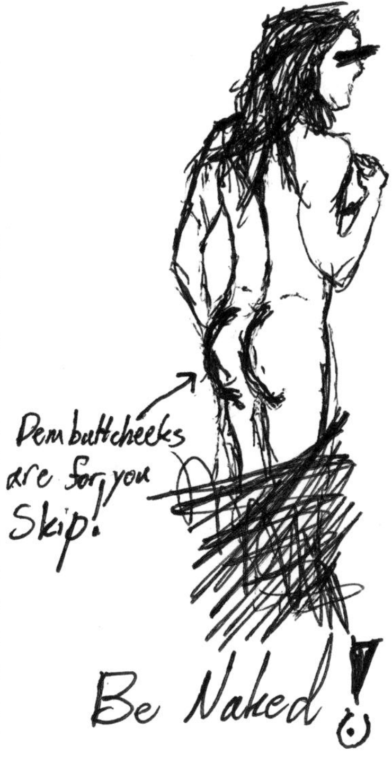

In measuring cost, the accountant also includes all other cash outlays such as those for insurance, materials, and utilities. These outlays as measured by the accountant amount to $20,000. Total accounting costs are therefore $90,000, as shown in Box 2.

Melissa appreciates the information supplied by the accountant. However, she's more concerned with the economic cost of running her shop than with the accounting cost. To find the economic cost, Melissa estimates implicit costs. Her next best alternative other than running her shop is to work as a monogrammer for someone else. She figures she could earn $30,000 per year managing someone else's shop. She includes this as her implicit wage. She must also impute a wage to her husband, who works 20 hours a week in the shop. Her husband's next best alternative for the 20 hours per week would pay $10,000 annually. This is her husband's implicit wage.

Melissa also forgoes the opportunity of renting her store to someone else when she uses it herself. If the annual market rent on her store is $40,000, she forgoes that amount by using the store herself. This opportunity cost of using the store for her own business represents the implicit rent.

Finally, the market value of Melissa's equipment is $80,000. She owes the bank $50,000. If Melissa were to sell her equipment and pay off her bank loans, she'd have $30,000 in cash left over. By remaining in her business, she forgoes the opportunity of investing these funds elsewhere. If she could earn 10 percent on these funds in her next best investment, their opportunity cost is $3,000 per year. This $3,000 is included in costs as

Box 2 Accounting Cost versus Economic Cost: An Example

Item	Accounting cost	Economic cost
Wages and salaries	$40,000	$40,000
Interest paid	10,000	10,000
Depreciation (1/5 of the value of capital)	20,000	20,000
Miscellaneous (garments, transfers, acrylic paints, thread, etc.)	20,000	20,000
Implicit wage of owner	0	30,000
Implicit wage of owner's spouse	0	10,000
Implicit rent	0	40,000
Implicit interest of owner's equity	0	3,000
Total cost	$90,000	$173,000

implicit interest. This must be added to the depreciation expense calculated by the accountant to get the full cost of capital.

Adding all implicit costs to those figured by the accountant gives the opportunity cost, or economic cost, of Melissa's annual operation. As shown in Box 2, Melissa's total economic cost for the year is $173,000, which is almost double the accounting cost.

The extent to which opportunity costs diverge from accounting costs varies with the amounts and kinds of inputs supplied to a firm by its owners. Typically, large corporations pay all employees wages even if those employees are also stockholders. It's rare, therefore, to have implicit wages in corporations. However, corporations usually have considerable amounts of cash tied up in capital equipment and land. The costs of these corporate funds are implicit interest and implicit rents.

Normal Profit versus Economic Profit

Economic profit is the difference between total revenue and the cost of all inputs used by a firm over a given period. The equation for a firm's economic profit over a certain period can be written as follows:

$$\text{Economic profit} = \text{Total revenue} - \text{Total cost}$$

The total revenue for a single-product firm is the total units of output sold over the period multiplied by the price per unit:

$$\text{Total revenue} = \text{Price} \times \text{Quantity sold}$$

Total cost is the economic cost of inputs used over the period. Total profit is therefore the difference between total revenue and the sum of accounting cost and the implicit cost of owner-supplied inputs. *Throughout this text, when a firm is said to be earning profits, this means that its revenues exceed the sum of its accounting cost and the implicit cost of owner-supplied inputs.*

Normal profit is a term economists use to indicate that portion of a firm's costs that isn't included in accounting costs. Normal profit is therefore a measure of the implicit costs of owner-supplied resources in a firm over a given period. When a firm earns zero economic profit, it covers both its accounting cost and its implicit costs. If a firm takes in enough revenue to pay all its accounting costs during the period and still has enough left over to cover its implicit costs, it is earning a normal profit.

For example, suppose the only owner-supplied input to a corporation is $1 million worth of capital net of debt. If the owners of the firm can earn 10 percent by investing that $1 million elsewhere, the normal profit would be $100,000. If total revenue exceeds accounting costs by $100,000, the owners of the firm are earning zero economic profit. However, because they took in enough revenue to cover their implicit costs, they can also be said to just be earning the normal profit. *A firm earning zero economic profit is said to be earning the normal profit.* This means that the firm earns just enough to cover the opportunity cost of remaining in business.

When earning a normal profit in a business, the owners of the business cannot improve their well-being by using the resources they supply to the firm in another activity. It follows that when a firm earns zero economic profit, its owners can do no better in any other activity, so their best alternative is to keep the firm operating.

If a firm is earning negative economic profit, it is incurring an economic loss. Under such circumstances, its owners can't cover their implicit costs. They are therefore earning less than the normal profit, which implies that they can do better by transferring the resources they own to another activity.

Because current accounting practice doesn't include implicit costs of owner-supplied inputs, accounting costs, as we've shown, underestimate economic costs. As a result, accounting profits based on accounting costs overestimate profits by underestimating costs. For example, suppose Melissa's annual sales revenue in the preceding example were $200,000. Because annual accounting cost was $90,000, the accountant would report an annual profit of $110,000! Melissa, being shrewd, would realize that her actual economic profit was only $27,000 that year. The normal profit for Melissa's store is $83,000, the opportunity cost of her owner-supplied inputs. Suppose her annual sales revenue was instead only $100,000. The accountant would report a $10,000 annual profit. However, Melissa would realize that she actually lost $73,000 based on her economic costs that year! She would go out of business as soon as possible if she didn't expect an improvement in sales.

Because economists always measure costs as opportunity costs, normal profit is always included as a cost of operating the firm. When measuring costs, remember that the normal profit is included in those costs because it's a measure of the value of owner-supplied resources.

Summary

1. A business firm is an organization under one management set up for the purpose of earning profits for its owners by making one or more items available for sale in markets.
2. Business firms can be grouped according to industries selling similar products. Each firm might operate more than one physical facility, called a plant.
3. Sole proprietorships, partnerships, and corporations are different types of business organizations. Sole proprietorships and partnerships are owned by individuals, while corporations have a legal identity separate from that of their owners. A corporation is owned by its stockholders.
4. Limited liability is a legal provision that protects stockholders by limiting their liability for debts of a corporation to the amount of funds they invested by purchasing its stock.
5. Firms that supply themselves with all materials and services used at all stages of production are vertically integrated. A firm's degree of vertical integration is influenced by the transaction costs of contracting with other firms for materials and services.
6. In analyzing the behavior of firms, it's useful to simplify by assuming that they produce a single product and seek to maximize profits.
7. Profit is the difference between a firm's total revenue and total cost over a certain period.
8. Economic cost is the monetary value of all the inputs used in a particular activity or enterprise over a given period. Economic cost exceeds accounting cost by the value of the services of owner-supplied inputs. The value of the services of owner-supplied inputs is called *implicit cost* (or *normal profit*). Economic profits are always based on economic costs.

Concept Review

(1) How does a corporation differ from a sole proprietorship and a partnership? Why are most large business firms in the United States corporations?

(2) List the functions of business firms, and explain how a vertically integrated firm differs from a firm that is not vertically integrated.

(3) What simplifications are usually made by economists to construct a model of supply by a business firm?

(4) Why is the opportunity cost of using some resources in a business not included in cost as measured by accountants? Why must implicit costs be added to accounting cost to accurately measure economic profit?

Problems and Applications

1. How would you group firms into industries? How can you use the concept of elasticity of demand to help establish industry groups? (1), (2)
2. Suppose you're a management analyst for a fast-food chain selling meals similar to those at McDonald's. Make a list of the firm's inputs and outputs. (2)
3. A major auto producer hires you to evaluate the desirability of acquiring a firm that produces tires. The firm would be vertically integrated into the auto firm and would produce tires *only* for use in new cars it manufactures. What factors would you consider when evaluating the acquisition? (1)
4. Write an equation to calculate total revenue for a single-product firm. How would you calculate total revenue for a multiproduct firm? How would you calculate total profit for both of these firms? (3)
5. A corporation earns \$100,000 profit. None of this profit is paid out as dividends to stockholders. What does the corporation do with the profit? (1)
6. A corporation has assets valued at \$5 million. It also has debts of \$2 million. What is the corporate equity? The next best use of funds tied up in the corporation is an investment that would earn a 10 percent annual return. What is the normal profit for the corporation? (1), (4)
7. If you were starting a new business, what factors would you consider before choosing to organize as a sole proprietorship or a partnership? (1)
8. Your firm's accountant calculates that its annual profit is \$10,000. Under what circumstances would the firm's economic profit also be \$10,000? (4)

9. You own a small retail clothing store that you manage yourself. You rent your facilities, but you have $30,000 of your own funds tied up in the firm after making allowance for your debts. How would you calculate your implicit costs? How would you use these costs to supplement information provided to you on accounting costs? 4

10. "Normal profit is really a cost. That's why it isn't included in economic profit." Do you agree with these statements? Why or why not? What can cause normal profit to differ among firms? 4

Total Quality Management:
The Emphasis on Quality by U.S. Businesses

Quality control was invented by American management experts. However, their techniques were most eagerly and most successfully adopted by Japanese businesses after World War II. Now, quality is again a buzzword of U.S. businesses. These businesses discovered that an emphasis on improving the quality of products and services can increase output per worker, reduce production costs, and improve sales by raising the confidence of customers in the products and services they purchase.*

Techniques involve the joint efforts of workers and management to find better ways to carry out their functions and to produce products with fewer defects. Let's look at the concept of *total quality management* and how it's being used by businesses.

Total quality management (TQM) is a set of techniques applied to all of a company's activities to improve the quality of its products and services. TQM seeks not only to improve the quality of products a company offers its customers, but also to improve the quality of services one division of a company (such as the marketing department) offers another division (such as the product development staff).

The techniques of TQM were originally developed by J.M. Juran, who called them *total quality control*. Juran applied his techniques to everyone in a firm, and his goal was to involve all employees at all levels in the management process. The other guru of the quality control movements has been W. Edwards Deming, who developed a technique he called *statistical quality control* to eliminate quality defects in production by changing productive techniques, rather than by improving inspection. Both Deming and Juran had a great influence on Japanese management after World War II.

TQM seeks to change both the productive and managerial processes of the firm to achieve acceptable quality levels that are agreed on by managers. The "six-sigma quality" criterion is a goal of 3.4 defects per million parts made. One of the TQM techniques is to examine a product for potential sources of defects *while it's in the design stage* and to eliminate controllable problems at that stage. For example, suppose the design of a car headlamp is such that it could be installed upside down. To prevent this from happening, the design could be changed so that it's impossible for the headlamp to be installed unless it's right side up. TQM also involves working with suppliers to reduce defects in purchased components of a product, so that delivery will be reliable and costs can be cut.

Many U.S. companies have adopted TQM as a management tool. Eastman Kodak Company was able to increase the number of patents issued to it simply by doubling the number of its patent attorneys and locating them right in its research labs. IBM involves workers in the production process at its Research Triangle Park location in North Carolina by employing agents who specialize in helping employees who feel that the company's bureaucracy is impeding improvements in the production process. TQM techniques have also been employed by U.S. automobile manufacturers, and quality defects in cars have decreased considerably.

*For an excellent discussion of quality issues in business, see *Business Week*, Special 1991 Bonus Issue: "The Quality Imperative." Many of the examples here are based on information appearing in this issue.

Chapter

9

Production and Cost

Have you ever had a brilliant idea for a product or service that would make you a millionaire? Chances are, if you took your idea beyond the fantasy stage, you would find that when it comes to producing an item, there's no free lunch. Whether it's a hot new bumper-sticker slogan or a way to make delicious ice cream without calories, the hard reality is that getting your product to consumers has a cost.

In this chapter we'll examine the process of supply in markets by looking at the production and cost of goods and services. We'll see how supply decisions made by the managers of firms are influenced by production and cost considerations that affect the profitability of making goods available to consumers.

Cost is a measure of the value of alternatives forgone when we use inputs to make goods or services. Cost depends partly on input prices, such as wages, rental rates for equipment, and unit prices of materials. But cost also depends on how output varies with input use. The productivity of inputs is a key factor in the cost per unit output. In deciding how much to produce, managers consider the output they can get from using various combinations of inputs and the prices of those inputs.

The production process involves using inputs to create products. Products can be tangible goods like digital cameras and frozen pizzas or intangible services like education and insurance. Economic theory assumes that no matter what's produced—aircraft or hairstyling services—certain basic principles of production govern how output varies with inputs used. The most famous principle of production may be *diminishing marginal returns*, which we'll discuss in this chapter.

Concept Preview

After reading this chapter, you should be able to

1. Show how the law of diminishing marginal returns implies a certain pattern of variation in output in the short run when the use of some inputs can't be varied.
2. Distinguish between variable cost and fixed cost and describe the variation in total cost and other costs as a single-product firm varies production.
3. Explain the relationship between the cost and productivity of inputs and input prices.
4. Derive a long-run average cost curve from short-run average cost curves.

Production Relationships

Production is the process of using the services of labor and equipment together with other inputs to make goods and services available. Inputs are the labor, capital, land, natural resources, and entrepreneurship that are combined to produce any output—cars, insurance policies, hairstyling, hamburgers. To produce a concert, for example, the inputs would include the concert hall, electricity, and the services of promoters, musicians, sound technicians, equipment transporters, security guards, ticket takers, ushers, and refreshment stand workers. To produce pizzas, the inputs would include the cooks' labor, pizza ingredients, pans, ovens, boxes, delivery vans, and drivers.

The relationship between any combination of input services and the maximum output obtainable from that combination is described by a production function. Production functions are defined for a given technology. An improvement in technology increases the maximum output obtainable from any combination of inputs and therefore results in a new production function.

The Period of Production

The short run is a period of production during which some inputs cannot be varied. A variable input is one whose quantity can be changed over the short run. For example, because factory managers can hire more or fewer workers to produce compact discs, labor is a variable input. A fixed input is one whose quantity cannot be changed over the short run. For example, if a factory has a certain number of machines occupying a specified amount of floor space that can't be changed over a short period, the machines and floor space are a fixed input.

The short run can best be thought of as a period of production during which the firm is confined to a given plant. It has some flexibility to vary input use within that plant, but it can't vary *all* inputs simultaneously. Typically, labor inputs are more variable in the short run than are capital inputs, such as structures. A firm can work a factory around the clock in periods of peak demand by using both day-shift and night-shift workers. However, it takes more time than is available in the short run to increase plant size by building additions to existing facilities or constructing new facilities. *In effect, in the short run there's a limit to production because there's only limited plant capacity available.*

The long run is a period of production that gives managers adequate time to vary *all* the inputs used to produce a good. In the long run there are no fixed inputs. It's clear that producers have more flexibility in the long run than they have in the short run.

The actual period of time encompassing the long run is likely to vary from one industry to another. For example, the owner of a hot-dog stand might be able to increase all of its inputs in a month. However, an oil company might take years to increase the capital inputs, such as refineries, required to produce more output. We can think of the long run as a planning period in which managers contemplate future changes in the use of currently fixed inputs. For example, in the long run the manager of a waterbed factory can consider expanding by acquiring more floor space and machinery.

Production in the Short Run: The Law of Diminishing Marginal Returns

1 Before you can understand the relationships between output and cost, you first need to understand the physical relationships between inputs used and outputs. To begin the analysis, we'll examine the relationship between the quantity of one variable input used and the quantity of output. You can think of managers as being confined to one plant of given size with a given number of machines.

The law of diminishing marginal returns states that the extra production obtained from increases in a variable input will eventually decline as more of the variable input is used together with the fixed inputs. This law implies that there's a certain predictable pattern of variation in output as more of a variable input is used in the short run.

The law of diminishing marginal returns means, for example, that in a factory with a given amount of space and a given number of machines, there's a limit to the extra production that can be obtained by hiring more workers. Eventually, the extra output obtained over any period from an extra worker peters down to near zero. You can actually reach a point where adding another worker would result in a decrease rather than an increase in output! This might occur because the worker has no equipment to work with and his presence actually impairs the functioning of other workers.

The Total Product Curve and the Marginal Product Curve

A total product curve describes how output varies in the short run as more of any one input is used together with fixed amounts of other inputs under current technology. Points on a total product curve give the output that's obtainable, given current technology, from any quantity of the variable input used with the fixed inputs.

The data in the Box 1 table show how weekly output is likely to vary in the short run as a firm hires more workers (each working a 40-hour week) to operate a given amount of equipment in a plant of given size. Suppose a factory produces running shoes and you're the manager. The total product of a variable input, such as labor services, is the amount of output produced over any given period when that input is used along with other fixed inputs. The first column of the table shows the number of workers employed per week in your factory. The second column shows the greatest possible output that can be produced with that number of workers, assuming nothing else is varied when more workers are employed.

The first line of the table shows that if no workers were employed, your factory's weekly output would be zero. You need at least some workers before the equipment and other facilities of your factory can be productively utilized. When you hire one worker to put in a 40-hour week, the total product of labor is 7 pairs of running shoes each week. Hiring a second worker results in a sharp increase in weekly output, from 7 to 18 pairs of shoes.

The marginal product of an input is the increase in output from one more unit of that input when the quantity of all other inputs is unchanged. The marginal product of labor (MP_1) is 7 pairs of shoes per week when you hire one worker because production increases from zero to 7 units when you hire the first worker. The marginal product of labor when you hire two workers per week is 18 – 7 = 11 pairs of shoes per week. In other words, by hiring a second worker, your factory adds 11 units of output to its weekly production. Hiring a third worker to put in a 40-hour week increases output to 33 pairs per week. The marginal product of labor when three workers are employed, as shown in the third column of the table, is 15 pairs of shoes per week.

Now notice what happens when you hire the fourth worker: Weekly output increases to 46 pairs of shoes; however, the marginal product of labor declines to 13 pairs per week. Thereafter, the data in the table show that as your factory continues to hire more workers, the marginal product of labor continually declines. In fact, hiring a 10th worker doesn't increase weekly production at all! The marginal product of labor when 10 workers are employed per week is zero. If you were to hire more than 10 workers, the data show that your factory's weekly production would actually decline. The marginal product of labor when more than 10 workers per week are hired would be negative!

Graph **A** in Box 1 plots the data for the total product of labor from the table in Box 1. The vertical axis corresponds to the total output of running shoes per week. The horizontal axis shows the number of workers hired per week. A smooth curve is drawn through the

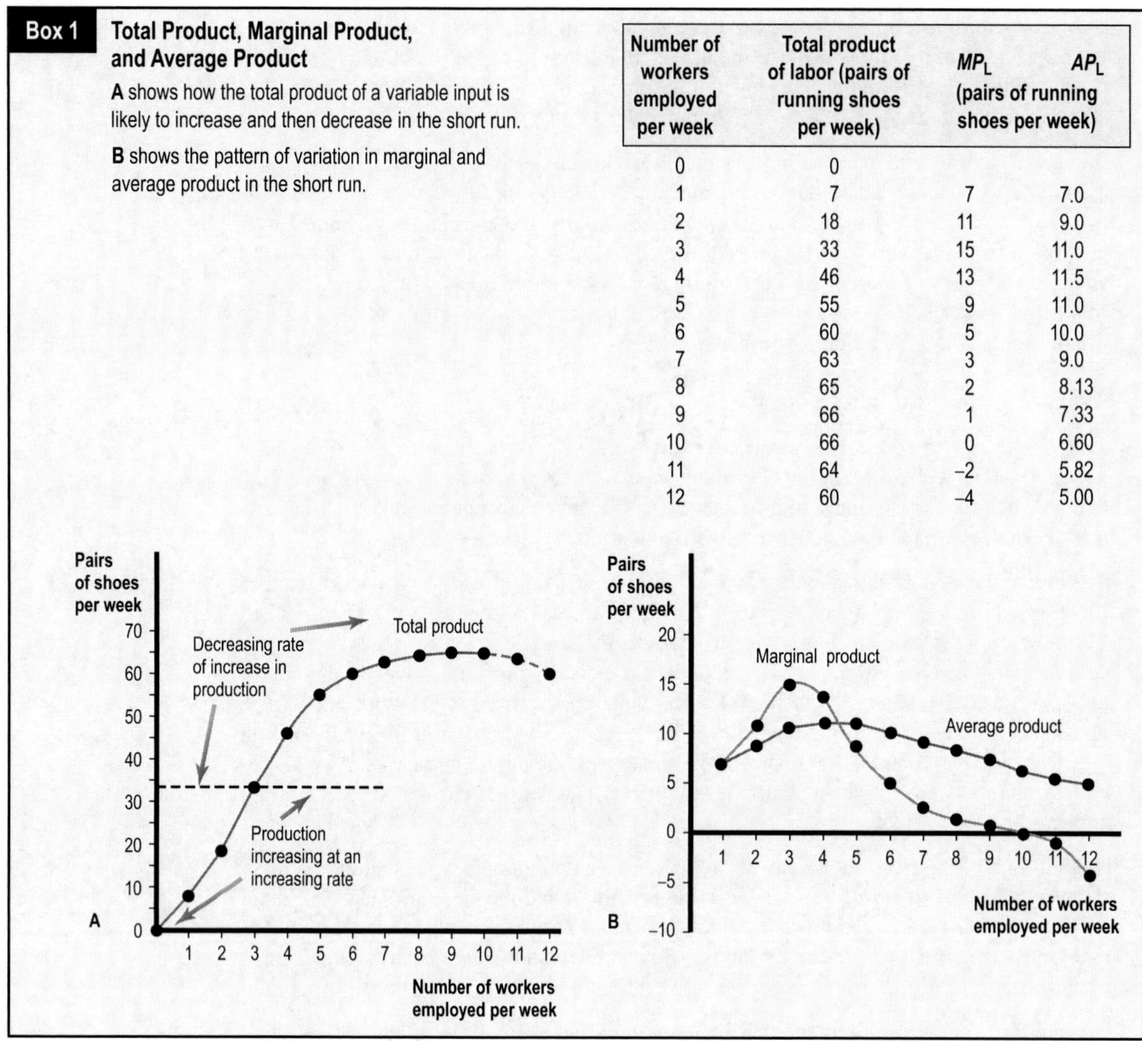

Box 1 Total Product, Marginal Product, and Average Product

A shows how the total product of a variable input is likely to increase and then decrease in the short run.

B shows the pattern of variation in marginal and average product in the short run.

Number of workers employed per week	Total product of labor (pairs of running shoes per week)	MP_L (pairs of running shoes per week)	AP_L (pairs of running shoes per week)
0	0		
1	7	7	7.0
2	18	11	9.0
3	33	15	11.0
4	46	13	11.5
5	55	9	11.0
6	60	5	10.0
7	63	3	9.0
8	65	2	8.13
9	66	1	7.33
10	66	0	6.60
11	64	–2	5.82
12	60	–4	5.00

points showing the pattern of variation in weekly output as labor input is increased while all other inputs are held constant. Notice how production initially increases at an increasing rate as the curve becomes steeper, up to the point at which three workers are hired per week. When more than three workers are hired per week, the rate of increase in output decreases. You can see this from the fact that the curve becomes flatter as more workers are hired. Eventually, when ten workers are hired, the rate of increase in output is zero. At this point the total product curve is at a maximum. This implies that there's a maximum amount of weekly output you can squeeze out of your plant. Thereafter, hiring additional workers would actually decrease output. This is shown in the dotted portion of the total product curve. As a manager who seeks to maximize profits, you'll *never* operate your plant in the downward-sloping portion of the total product curve. If you did so, you'd be paying additional workers to *decrease* total production. This implies higher costs *and* less output to sell, and therefore less revenue. The increase in costs and the decrease in revenue would both act to reduce your profits.

Graph **B** in Box 1 plots the marginal product of labor from the data in the table. You'll notice that marginal product increases at first and then decreases. You can also see that when marginal product is decreasing, the rate of increase in total product is declining. This is because the marginal product of labor *is* the slope of the total product curve. Marginal product (MP_L) is

$$MP_L = \frac{\Delta TP}{\Delta L}$$

where ΔTP is the change in the total product of labor and ΔL is the increase in the number of workers hired per week. When the marginal product of labor is zero, total product is at its maximum weekly value. This is because at the point where MP_L is zero, hiring another worker doesn't add to production, and hiring still another worker would begin to reduce output. When marginal product is *negative*, additional workers *decrease* weekly production.

Average Product

The average product of an input is the total output produced over a given period divided by the number of units of that input used. We can calculate the average product of labor from the data in the Box 1 table simply by dividing the total weekly output of running shoes by the number of workers. The average product of labor is therefore total product (*TP*) divided by number of workers (*L*):

$$\text{Average product of labor} = \frac{TP}{L}$$

The average product measures output per worker, which indicates the *productivity* of the workers in a plant. The average product of labor is shown in the last column of the Box 1 table.

The pattern of variation in the average product of labor is similar to that in the marginal product of labor. The average product of labor increases at first, reaches a maximum, and then decreases. Although the average product of labor becomes smaller and smaller, it never reaches zero.

The Relationship between Average and Marginal Products of a Variable Input

Graph **B** in Box 1 plots the average product of labor and the marginal product of labor on the same set of axes. You'll notice that when the marginal product exceeds the average product, the average product increases. This is because the marginal product is the *last number* added in to compute the average product. When the marginal product exceeds the average product, the average product has to go up. A good way to understand this is to think about your average of test grades. Until the end of the semester, your average changes each time you take another test. The grade on each extra test is your *marginal* grade. Suppose you have an 80 average on the first two tests. What happens to your average if you get an 85 on the third test? Your average will increase because the last number, your grade on the third test, exceeds your previous average. By the same token, your average will fall if you get a grade of less than 80 on the last test.

Graph **B** in Box 1 reflects this relationship between average and marginal numbers for an average that is continually recomputed as the number of workers is increased. Average product increases when marginal product is above it. Average product declines when marginal product is below it. Finally, this implies that the marginal product curve must intersect the average product curve at the latter's maximum point.

How Product Curves Illustrate the Law of Diminishing Marginal Returns

The total, marginal, and average product curves drawn in Box 1 reflect the law of diminishing marginal returns. It's possible for the marginal product of labor to increase for a while when the amount of labor used is low. *However, the law of diminishing marginal returns implies that the marginal product eventually declines.* The point of diminishing returns corresponds to the level of use of a variable input at which its marginal product begins to decline. In Box 1, the point of diminishing returns occurs after three workers have been hired per week because hiring more than three workers results in a decline in the marginal product of labor. The marginal product of labor could actually become zero and even negative, as shown in Box 1.

Because the marginal product of a variable input will approach zero, it will eventually fall below the average product of the variable input. *Remember that when the marginal product falls below the average product of an input, the average product declines. Thus, the law of diminishing marginal returns also implies that the average product of a variable input will eventually decline as more of that input is used together with fixed inputs.* The average product of labor in a factory of given size inevitably declines as more workers are hired, unless more space, equipment, and other inputs can be supplied to complement the extra labor services.

Reasons for Diminishing Marginal Returns

It's easy to comprehend the reasons for the law of eventually diminishing marginal returns. Inputs complement one another. You can't increase production indefinitely by hiring more workers to work with a fixed number of machines and a fixed amount of materials in a facility of given size. Eventually, you'll have too many workers relative to other inputs. Some workers will have nothing to do because they'll lack space or equipment to do their jobs. You'll soon cram so many workers into a given amount of space that they might actually impair each other's productivity by bumping into or distracting each other. This could result in a negative marginal product of labor. On the other hand, when you hire too few workers relative to the equipment and space available in your factory, it isn't possible to assign workers specialized tasks that contribute to increased productivity. In effect, when too few workers are hired relative to a plant's capacity, capital equipment and space are wasted. This is why the productivity of workers increases in early stages of production when output is low and plant facilities are underutilized.

You can also understand the implications of the law by asking yourself what the consequences would be if it didn't hold. For example, if marginal returns didn't eventually decline from using more labor to farm an acre of land, there would be no limit to the amount of food that workers could produce on an acre. Adding more workers to farm the acre would increase output under any given technology. It would therefore be feasible to produce the entire world supply of food on a single acre. This, of course, is impossible. As you can see, the hypothesis of diminishing marginal returns is quite reasonable. Throughout the text, we assume that this law holds.

Short-Run Cost Curves

2 Our next step is to examine how costs of production vary with output over any given period. *Cost measures the dollar value of inputs used over any given period to produce an item.* Remember that economic cost also includes the implicit cost of nonpurchased inputs. (See the chapter on the business firm.) Actual cost depends on the prices of the input services hired (or the monetary value of input services supplied by the firm itself), the quantity of the inputs used, and the productivity of those inputs. In this section, we analyze the variation of cost with inputs in the short run, when some inputs are variable while others are fixed.

Variable Costs, Fixed Costs, and Total Cost

In the short run, costs are divided into two basic categories. Fixed costs (FC) are those that don't vary as a firm varies its output. Managers often refer to their fixed costs as *overhead costs*. These are costs that must be incurred in the short run even if the firm doesn't produce anything. Examples of fixed costs are rents on leased property, interest on borrowed funds, salaries of managers (who must be employed to oversee the affairs of the firm even if the firm shuts down and produces no output for a short period), and depreciation on capital equipment. The monthly value of fixed inputs is a firm's monthly fixed cost.

Variable costs (VC) are those that change with output. These are the costs of variable inputs. Examples of variable costs are the monetary value of the services of most workers, fuel, materials, and machinery or equipment that is rented on a monthly or hourly basis. To produce more goods and services per month, a firm requires more of the services of these variable inputs. As it hires more of these inputs, its variable costs will increase. Variable cost is therefore dependent on weekly or monthly output.

Total cost (TC) is the sum of the value of *all* inputs used over any given period to produce goods. Total cost is the sum of fixed costs and variable costs:

$$TC = VC + FC$$

Input Substitution and Variable Cost: The Equimarginal Principle

In using variable inputs, managers of a firm must choose the combination of inputs that will produce any given output at the lowest possible variable cost. Remember that there's usually more than one way to accomplish any production objective. For example, as the manager of a running-shoe factory, you could produce a certain number of shoes of given quality with a great deal of labor, using hand tools and very little machinery. Alternatively, you could produce the same number of shoes with lots of machinery and very little labor. *To produce efficiently, managers seek to produce any given output using the combination of variable inputs that costs the least.* In choosing inputs in this way, managers must consider both the price and the marginal product of each input.

The appendix to this chapter provides a technical analysis of how managers choose inputs so as to minimize variable cost. However, we can easily use a numerical example to illustrate the general principle involved in choosing input combinations that will keep the total cost of a given output as low as possible. Suppose your objective as manager is to fill orders for a certain number of running shoes per month. If some inputs were variable and could be substituted for each other to perform similar tasks, you'd have to examine how costs could be reduced by, say, substituting machines for workers.

For example, suppose you can rent an extra machine for \$100 per hour. Assume the machine could replace 10 workers who currently produce 20 pairs of shoes per week. Each worker gets paid \$20 per hour. By renting the machine, you could replace the 10 workers without any reduction in weekly output. Because the 10 workers cost a total of \$200 per hour and the machine can be rented for only \$100 per hour, the firm's costs will fall by \$100 per hour if you substitute the machine for the 10 workers. The reduction in hourly costs would reduce the total cost of producing shoes.

The actual cost saving from substituting capital for labor depends in part on the hourly rental rate for the machine compared to the hourly wage of workers. For example, if the workers were paid \$5 per hour, the total hourly labor cost for 10 workers would be only \$50. In this case it would *not* pay you to rent the machine and dismiss the workers, because the \$100 per hour cost of the machine would now exceed the \$50 per hour cost of workers who can produce the same 20 pairs of shoes.

The marginal products of the machine and the workers are important in your choice of the input combination. If each machine could produce only 10 pairs of shoes per week instead of 20, you'd need two machines to do the work of the 10 workers. If the machine still rents for \$100 per hour, you'd now have to incur hourly costs of \$200 to replace the 10 workers. If they're paid \$20 per hour, you'd enjoy no cost saving from replacing the workers with two machines. This is because the \$200 hourly cost for the two machines would just equal the \$200 hourly cost for the 10 workers.

We can generalize the principle involved in choosing the combination of variable inputs that minimizes the cost of producing any given output. Think of the manager of the firm as examining the cost of producing the last unit of output in various ways. Suppose that labor and capital equipment are variable inputs for the manager of the firm. The cost of producing the last unit of a given amount of output with more labor will be

$$\frac{P_L}{MP_L} = \text{Dollar cost per unit of additional output from hiring more labor}$$

where P_L is the price of labor (wages) and MP_L is the marginal product of labor.

The cost of producing the last unit of a given amount of output with more capital will be

$$\frac{P_K}{MP_K} = \text{The dollar cost of producing the additional output by hiring more capital equipment}$$

where P_K is the price (rental rate) of capital equipment and MP_K is the marginal product of capital.

For example, if the price of labor is \$4 per hour and one hour of labor is necessary to produce another unit of output, then the last unit of output will cost \$4 when produced with labor. Suppose that an hour of capital equipment costs \$6 but with an hour of capital equipment you can get 2 units of output. The dollar cost of producing the last units of output with more capital would then be \$6/2 = \$3 per unit. Now it's easy to see that the firm can reduce the variable costs of producing its output by renting more capital equipment while hiring less labor. By making this reallocation of input use, the firm will reduce the cost of producing the last unit from \$4 to \$3, resulting in a net reduction in variable costs of \$1, as shown in Box 2.

As the firm substitutes capital for labor, the marginal product of capital will fall (because more of it is used), while the marginal product of labor will rise (because less of it is used). Given the prices of labor and capital, this causes the cost of producing the last unit of output with capital to rise, while the cost of producing the last unit of output with labor falls.

Box 2 Illustrating the Equimarginal Principle for Production: Two Variable Inputs—Labor and Capital

Cost of producing the last unit of output with more labor: P_L/MP_L	Cost of producing the last unit of output with more capital: P_K/MP_K	Net reduction in variable costs possible
\$4	\$3	By using more capital and less labor the variable cost can be reduced by \$1
3.5	3.5	No reduction possible
3	4	By using more labor and less capital the variable cost can be reduced by \$1

General condition for minimizing variable costs of producing a given output:

$P_L/MP_L = P_K/MP_K$ where L and K are any two pair of variable inputs

or

$MP_L/P_L = MP_K/P_K$ which is the equimarginal principle for production

Box 2 shows that as long as the cost of producing the last unit of output by using more of one input is not equal to the cost of producing that last unit by using more of an alternative variable input, the firm can reduce the variable costs of production. Only when the costs of producing the last unit of output by using either more labor or more capital are exactly the same will the variable cost of producing total output be as low as possible.

We can express the condition for minimizing the variable cost of producing any given quantity of output as follows:

$$\frac{P_L}{MP_L} = \frac{P_K}{MP_K}$$

This condition can also be expressed as an equimarginal principle:

$$\frac{MP_L}{P_L} = \frac{MP_K}{P_K}$$

This condition states that the variable cost of producing any given output will be minimized when the marginal product *per dollar* is the same for any two pairs of variable inputs used in production.

As you can see, managers must look at the marginal product and the price per unit of inputs to decide which combination to use. In our analysis of costs we always assume that managers choose the lowest-cost combination of variable inputs to produce a given output.

Average Cost

Average cost (AC) is total cost divided by the number of units of output produced over a given period. It's also called *average total cost.* Managers often refer to average cost as their *unit cost*:

$$AC = \frac{TC}{Q}$$

Average variable cost (AVC) is variable cost divided by the number of units of output produced over a given period:

$$AVC = \frac{VC}{Q}$$

Average fixed cost (AFC) is fixed cost divided by the number of units of output produced over a given period:

$$AFC = \frac{FC}{Q}$$

It's easy to show that average cost is the sum of average variable cost and average fixed cost. Remember that total cost is the sum of variable cost and fixed cost. It follows that

$$\frac{TC}{Q} = \frac{VC}{Q} + \frac{FC}{Q}$$

because dividing both sides of an equation by the same variable doesn't disturb the equality. The first term of the equation just given is *AC*. The two terms on the other side of the equal sign are *AVC* and *AFC*, respectively. It follows that

$$AC = AVC + AFC$$

The Relationship between the Total Cost Curve and the Total Product Curve

3 It's now possible to derive a total cost curve for your running-shoe firm, whose total product curve was drawn in Box 1, by making a few simplifying assumptions. First, let's assume your firm uses only two inputs in the short run: labor (a variable input) and

capital (a fixed input). Lumped into capital are the services of all machines, structures, land, the inventory of materials the firm keeps on hand, and any other equipment. Assume that the monthly cost of all capital is $500. This is your firm's monthly fixed cost.

The only variable input is labor services. Assume that as the firm's manager you can hire all the workers you desire at the going market wage of $300 a week. It's now possible for us to use the data on production in the Box 1 table to calculate the firm's total cost and to show how that cost varies with output in the short run. Box 3 shows how costs vary with output as your firm produces more by hiring more workers. The first column shows the number of workers, and the second column shows the output per week that can be produced with that number of workers and the fixed inputs. These data are identical to the data in the Box 1 table. The third column of the table in Box 3 shows the fixed costs of production: $500 per week no matter how much is produced. For example, the first entry in the third column shows that fixed costs are $500 *even if the factory shuts down for the week* by laying off all workers and producing no running shoes.

The fourth column shows the variable costs of production. In this case the only variable cost is the cost of hiring workers. To obtain the variable cost, we simply multiply the number of workers hired per week by the weekly wage of $300. For example, weekly variable cost is $300 when only one worker is hired. As more output is produced and more workers are hired, weekly variable cost increases by $300 for each extra worker. (Of course, you could hire part-time workers for added flexibility in the production process.) Finally, the last column in Box 3 shows total cost, which we obtain simply by adding variable cost and fixed cost for each row of the table.

The graph in Box 4 plots the variable cost data. The vertical axis measures the variable cost, while the horizontal axis measures the corresponding weekly output of running shoes. It's easy to show how the variable cost curve is related to the total product curve drawn in *A* in Box 1. The total product curve shows how output varies with the number of workers hired per week and reflects the law of diminishing marginal returns. The variable cost curve shows the relationship between labor cost and output produced. Because the weekly wage doesn't change as more workers are hired, the variable cost curve reflects the way output varies with labor input. *The shape of the variable cost curve mirrors the shape of the total product curve.*

Notice in Box 1 that your factory's maximum possible output of running shoes is 66 pairs per week. Accordingly, if you tried to hire more labor to produce more than 66 pairs per

Box 3 Calculating Total Cost

Number of workers employed	Total output (pairs of running shoes per week)	Fixed cost	Variable cost	Total cost
0	0	$500	$ 0	$ 500
1	7	500	300	800
2	18	500	600	1,100
3	33	500	900	1,400
4	46	500	1,200	1,700
5	55	500	1,500	2,000
6	60	500	1,800	2,300
7	63	500	2,100	2,600
8	65	500	2,400	2,900
9	66	500	2,700	3,200
10	66	500	3,000	3,500
11	64	500	3,300	3,800
12	60	500	3,600	4,100

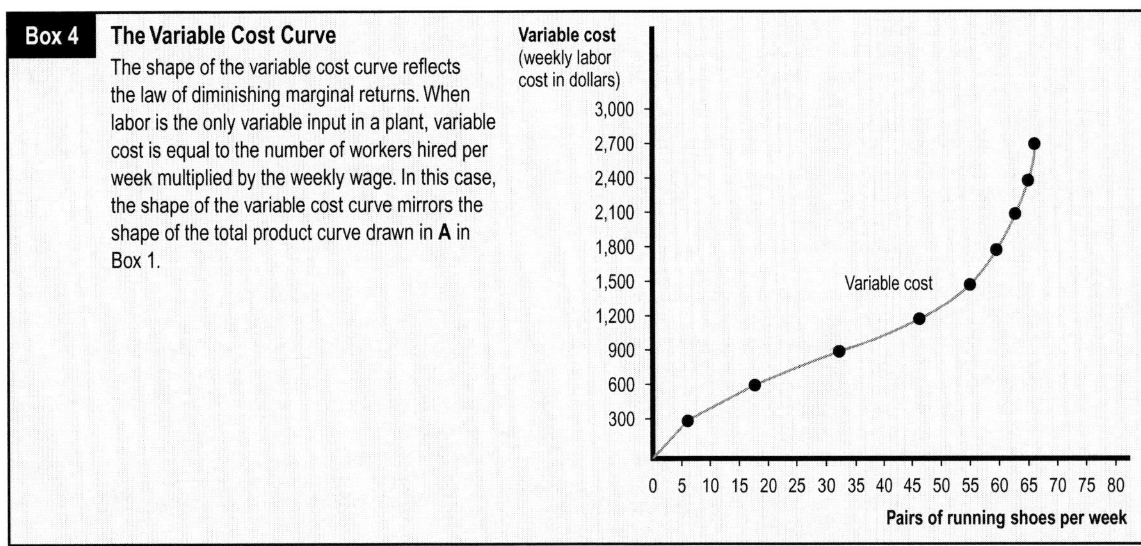
Box 4
The Variable Cost Curve
The shape of the variable cost curve reflects the law of diminishing marginal returns. When labor is the only variable input in a plant, variable cost is equal to the number of workers hired per week multiplied by the weekly wage. In this case, the shape of the variable cost curve mirrors the shape of the total product curve drawn in A in Box 1.
Variable cost (weekly labor cost in dollars)
3,000
2,700
2,400
2,100
1,800
1,500
1,200
900
600
300
Variable cost
0 5 10 15 20 25 30 35 40 45 50 55 60 65 70 75 80
Pairs of running shoes per week

week, variable cost would increase, but output could not increase. As a manager who seeks to maximize profit, you won't hire more labor if you can't increase salable output by doing so. Therefore, the variable cost curve in Box 4 isn't extended upward after your firm has reached a weekly output of 66 pairs of shoes.

The pattern of variation in variable costs reflects the pattern of variation in the total product of labor in the short run. In general, when there's more than one variable input, the shape of the variable cost curve will reflect the variation in the total product of all these inputs.

To obtain the total cost curve from variable cost, simply add fixed costs to variable costs. Because fixed costs are always \$500 per week, no matter how much your firm produces or how many workers it employs, total costs will always be \$500 more than variable costs. Box 5 shows the fixed cost curve as a horizontal line intersecting the vertical axis at the point corresponding to \$500.

As you can see, the total cost curve has exactly the same shape as the variable cost curve but is higher up on the axes. Also note that both total cost and variable cost increase at a *decreasing rate* at first but then increase at an *increasing rate* as weekly output increases.

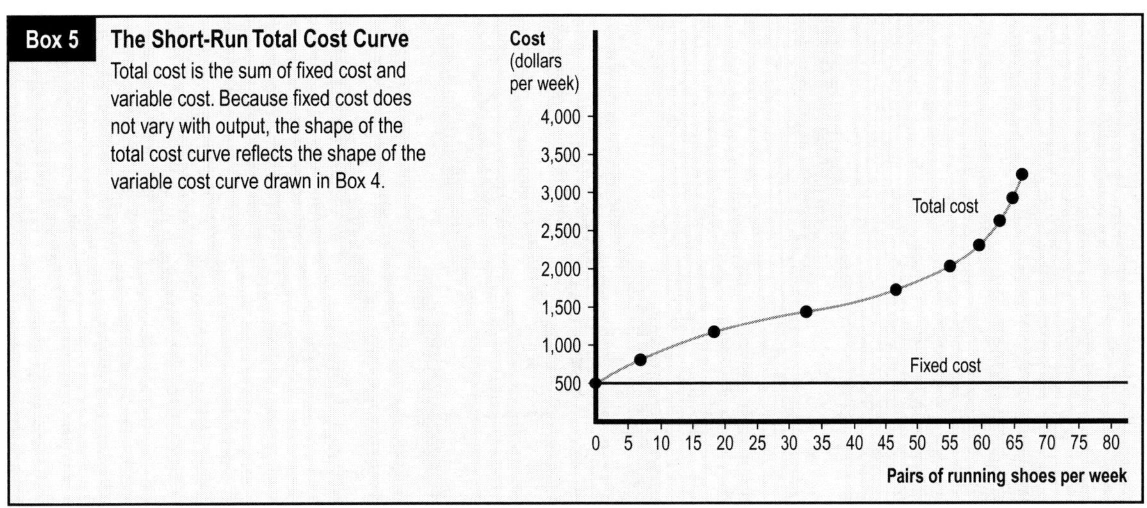
Box 5
The Short-Run Total Cost Curve
Total cost is the sum of fixed cost and variable cost. Because fixed cost does not vary with output, the shape of the total cost curve reflects the shape of the variable cost curve drawn in Box 4.
Cost (dollars per week)
4,000
3,500
3,000
2,500
2,000
1,500
1,000
500
Total cost
Fixed cost
0 5 10 15 20 25 30 35 40 45 50 55 60 65 70 75 80
Pairs of running shoes per week

Deriving Average Cost Curves

The table in Box 6 shows how average fixed cost, average variable cost, and average cost can be calculated from the data in Box 3. In drawing up the table, we assume that no rational manager would hire more than nine workers per week because additional workers beyond that number don't increase weekly output above 66 pairs of running shoes. We obtain average fixed cost simply by dividing the $500 weekly fixed cost by the number of pairs of running shoes produced per week. Similarly, dividing the data for variable cost and total cost in Box 3 by weekly output gives us the average variable cost and average cost, respectively. Note that the sum of average fixed cost and average variable cost is equal to average cost in all cases.

Box 6 shows the average fixed cost, average variable cost, and average cost curves on the same set of axes. Smooth curves have been fitted on the axes from the data. First, note the shape of the average fixed cost curve. *As more output is produced per week, average fixed cost continually declines.* Business managers sometimes refer to this phenomenon as *spreading of overhead costs.* Because fixed costs (overhead costs) don't vary with output, it's inevitable that the amount of these costs per unit of output will decline as weekly output goes up.

Both average variable cost and average cost decline at first as weekly production increases after reaching a minimum level. They then increase, giving each a U shape. Note that the average variable cost curve reaches its minimum before the average cost curve reaches its minimum.

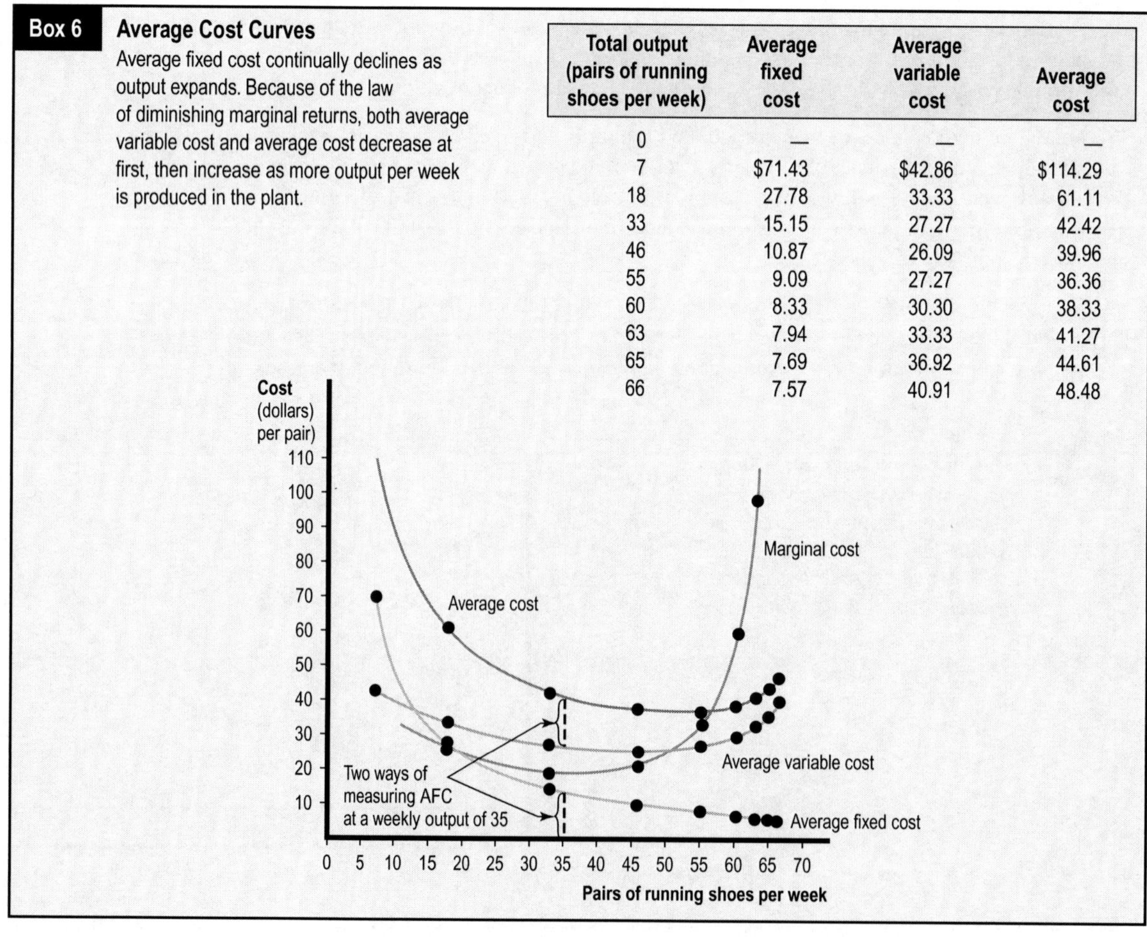

Box 6 Average Cost Curves

Average fixed cost continually declines as output expands. Because of the law of diminishing marginal returns, both average variable cost and average cost decrease at first, then increase as more output per week is produced in the plant.

Total output (pairs of running shoes per week)	Average fixed cost	Average variable cost	Average cost
0	—	—	—
7	$71.43	$42.86	$114.29
18	27.78	33.33	61.11
33	15.15	27.27	42.42
46	10.87	26.09	39.96
55	9.09	27.27	36.36
60	8.33	30.30	38.33
63	7.94	33.33	41.27
65	7.69	36.92	44.61
66	7.57	40.91	48.48

Marginal Cost

Marginal cost (MC) is the extra cost of producing one more unit of output. There is no accounting concept that parallels marginal cost. However, all good business managers have an idea of their marginal cost and use their estimates of marginal cost of production to make decisions.

We can calculate marginal cost from the data in Box 7. As is common in many businesses, the data show increases in weekly output associated with additional workers rather than increases in cost for *each unit* of output. However, we can approximate marginal cost from the data by recalling that marginal cost can be thought of as the change in cost associated with any given change in output. Marginal cost for the batch of output associated with each extra worker can be calculated from the following formula:

$$MC = \frac{\Delta TC}{\Delta Q}$$

where ΔTC is the change in total cost associated with any given change in weekly output, ΔQ.

Box 7 calculates marginal cost from the data on total cost and output in Box 3. The second column in Box 7 shows the change in total cost associated with each change in output as more workers are hired. For example, the change in total cost when the first worker is hired is ΔTC = \$800 – \$500 = \$300. The change in output is $\Delta Q = 7 - 0 = 7$. Marginal cost for the batch of running shoes produced by the first worker is therefore approximated as \$300/7 = \$42.86. Note that marginal cost depends *only* on changes in variable cost.

Because fixed cost doesn't change as output changes, fixed cost doesn't influence marginal cost. Marginal cost is influenced only by variable cost. For example, here fixed cost is \$500. As output increases, fixed cost remains \$500. Only labor cost, which is the variable cost, increases as output increases.

Marginal cost decreases at first and then increases. The eventually increasing marginal cost of output reflects the law of diminishing marginal returns. As more of the variable input is hired, the extra output obtained eventually becomes smaller and smaller. This means that it eventually takes more and more of the variable input to produce each extra unit of output. Given the price per unit of the variable input, this implies increasing marginal cost.

The marginal cost curve is plotted in Box 6 together with the average cost and average variable cost curves. Note that the marginal cost curve must intersect *both* the average

Box 7 Calculating Marginal Cost

Output (pairs of shoes per week)	Change in total cost (ΔTC) (dollars)	Change in output (ΔQ) (pairs of shoes per week)	Marginal cost = $\frac{\Delta TC}{\Delta Q}$ (dollars per pair)
7	800 – 500 = 300	7 – 0 = 7	300/ 7 = 42.86
18	1,100 – 800 = 300	18 – 7 = 11	300/11 = 27.27
33	1,400 –1,100 = 300	33 – 18 = 15	300/15 = 20.00
46	1,700 –1,400 = 300	46 – 33 = 13	300/13 = 23.08
55	2,000 –1,700 = 300	55 – 46 = 9	300/ 9 = 33.33
60	2,300 –2,000 = 300	60 – 55 = 5	300/ 5 = 60
63	2,900 –2,300 = 300	63 – 60 = 3	300/ 3 = 100
65	2,600 –2,600 = 300	65 – 63 = 2	300/ 2 = 150
66	3,200 –2,900 = 300	66 – 65 = 1	300/ 1 = 300

variable cost curve and the average cost curve at their minimum points. This is because the marginal cost is the last number added into both *AVC* and *AC* when each of these averages is calculated. When *MC* is below either of these averages, the average will decline. Similarly, when it's above either of these averages, the average will increase. This means that the *AVC* curve must reach its minimum before the *AC* curve reaches its minimum. This is because when *AVC* = *MC*, *MC* is *below AC* because *AVC* is always less than *AC* by an amount equal to *AFC*. Average cost must therefore still be falling to its minimum when average variable cost begins above its minimum. You can see this in Box 6.

A Recap: How the Shapes of Average and Marginal Cost Curves Reflect the Law of Diminishing Marginal Returns

Box 8 shows the general shapes of the average cost, average variable cost, and marginal cost curves likely to prevail for all enterprises in the short run. Study these curves to make sure you understand the logical relationships of each curve to the others. To help you remember the basic ideas, a number of significant points are shown in Box 8.

Point *A* is the level of output where marginal cost begins to increase. This corresponds to the *point of diminishing returns*. After this level of output has been reached, the marginal product of variable input begins to decline. The declining marginal product contributes to increasing marginal costs of production because the firm gets less output for each extra unit of variable input used beyond that point.

Point *B* is the minimum possible average variable cost. At the level of output corresponding to point *B*, marginal cost rises to equal average variable cost. Point *C* is the minimum possible average cost. At the level of output corresponding to this point, marginal cost just equals average cost. The output level corresponding to minimum possible average cost is of special significance for the firm—it represents the output, q^*, at which the plant operates most efficiently.

The U-shaped average cost curve reflects the law of eventually diminishing marginal returns. Think of the plant as being designed to operate most efficiently at the weekly level of output q^*, for which average cost is minimized. If the plant operates below that level, some of its space and machines won't be fully utilized, and average cost of production will be relatively high. If the plant strains to produce more than q^* units of output, then machines and space will be over utilized, and the resulting increase in marginal costs will pull average costs of production up quickly. As the plant approaches the physical limit to production over the time period, average variable cost and average

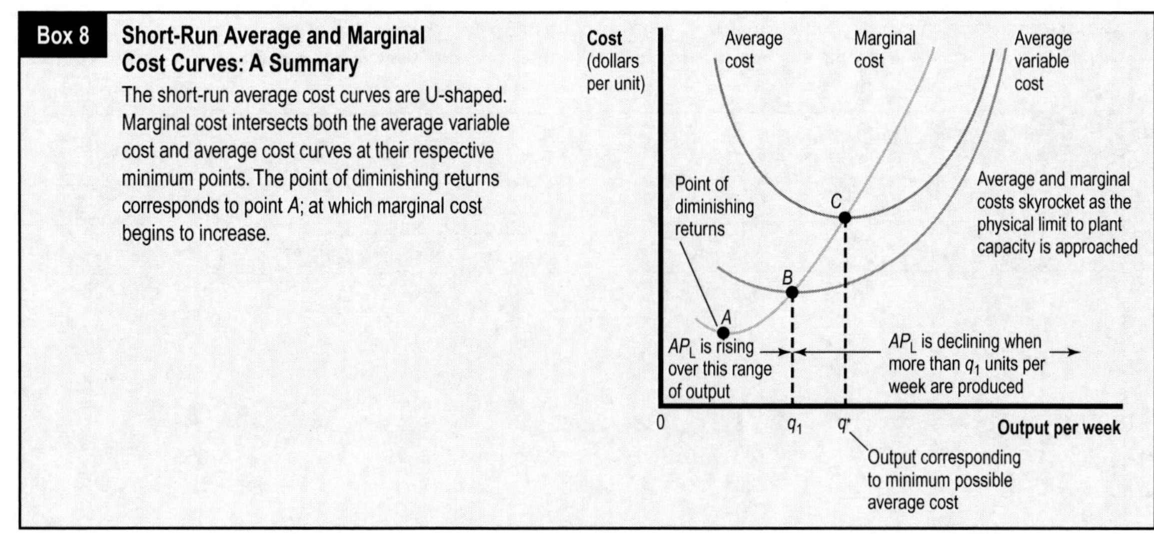

Box 8 Short-Run Average and Marginal Cost Curves: A Summary

The short-run average cost curves are U-shaped. Marginal cost intersects both the average variable cost and average cost curves at their respective minimum points. The point of diminishing returns corresponds to point *A*; at which marginal cost begins to increase.

cost skyrocket. Note how the distance between the *AC* and *AVC* curves decreases as more output is produced, reflecting the "spreading of overhead" and the consequent decline in average fixed cost.

You can also think of the U-shaped average cost curves as reflecting the way the average product of variable input increases at first and then begins to decrease as more variable input is employed. To see this, assume that labor is the only variable input. Remember that the average product of labor is output, *Q*, divided by the number of workers employed, *L*:

$$\text{Average product of labor} = \frac{\text{Output}}{\text{Number of workers}}$$

Because in this example the only variable cost in the plant is labor cost, average variable cost is simply labor cost divided by output. Weekly labor costs are obtained by multiplying the number of workers by the weekly wage. Average variable cost is

$$AVC = \frac{\text{(Weekly wage) (Number of workers)}}{\text{Output}}$$

Because the average product of labor is output divided by the number of workers, the expression for average variable cost can also be written as

$$\begin{aligned} AVC &= \frac{\text{Wages per time period}}{\text{Output/Number of workers}} = \frac{\text{Wages per time period}}{\text{Average product of labor}} \\ &= VC/Q = (wL)/Q \\ &= w/(Q/L) = w/AP_L \end{aligned}$$

where *w* is the wage per time period (for example, per hour or per week). Using the data in Box 1, note that if your firm uses three workers per week, it will produce 33 pairs of running shoes per week. The average product of labor will be 11 pairs of running shoes per week. Using the formula just given, and noting that the weekly wage is \$300, we find that average variable cost is \$300/11 = \$27.27, which agrees with the data in Box 6.

With the formulas just presented, we can also show how data on labor productivity can be used to calculate average variable cost and average cost at varying wage rates. For example, suppose data for a steel mill show that it takes six hours of labor to produce 1 ton of steel. This represents the variable input (labor) per unit of output, which is the inverse of the average product of labor. If the wage is \$20 per hour and labor is the only variable input, then variable cost per ton of steel will be \$120, which is the hourly wage multiplied by the labor it takes to produce a ton of steel. If fixed cost per ton of steel is \$1,000, then average cost will be \$1,120, which is the sum of average variable cost and average fixed cost. In general, when labor is the only variable output:

$$\begin{aligned} \text{Average cost} &= w(\text{Labor per unit of output}) + \text{Average fixed cost} \\ &= w/(AP_L) + AFC \end{aligned}$$

It's now easy to see why the *AC* curve must fall at first and then increase if the law of diminishing returns holds. This is because as you hire more workers to produce more output in your plant, their average product increases at first, *decreasing* average variable cost, and then decreases, *increasing* average variable cost.

We can derive the average cost curve simply by adding average fixed cost to average variable cost. The vertical distance between the *AVC* and *AC* curves must get smaller and smaller as output is increased, reflecting the fact that average fixed cost gets smaller and smaller as output is increased. This is because the vertical distance between the two curves is average fixed cost.

Long-Run Cost Curves

4 Over the long run, production managers can think about expanding or contracting operations. They can move to larger plants or smaller plants by varying the amounts of *all* inputs. Remember, that in the long run, *all costs are variable*. At any given time, however, the firm is confined to a plant of given size. Within that plant, costs will vary according to the pattern described for the short run. At any given time, short-run costs are relevant.

The long-run cost of any given output is the minimum cost of producing that output when *all inputs are variable*. The basic difference between the long run and the short run is flexibility. In the long run, producers have options that aren't available in the short run. In the long run, managers can control output and costs, not only by varying a given plant's intensity of operation, but also by varying the *size* and *number* of plants operated.

Variation in Plant Size

Suppose your firm that manufactures running shoes can consider only five possible plant sizes. Your options as the firm's manager are plants designed to operate most efficiently at weekly outputs of 50, 100, 150, 200, and 250 pairs of running shoes.

Box 9 contains the short-run cost curves for each of the five plants. As a manager seeking to operate efficiently, you must determine the minimum possible level of average cost for each possible output. Points satisfying this requirement are shown on the long-run average cost curve.

Look at weekly outputs ranging from 0 to 70 pairs of running shoes. At any output below 70 pairs, your firm can produce at lower average cost in the first plant. For example, the average cost of a weekly output of 65 pairs is $21 in the first plant, whose short-run average cost curve is labeled AC_1. In the second plant, whose short-run average cost curve is labeled AC_2, it would cost $30 per unit to produce the same output. If you tried to produce this output in the second plant, much of its capital equipment would be underutilized. It's cheaper to produce the 65 pairs in the smaller plant.

At outputs below 70 pairs per week, the relevant points on the long-run average cost curve are those that fall on AC_1. Beyond the point where AC_1 and AC_2 intersect on the Box 9 graph, it becomes cheaper to produce in the second plant. Only points on the short-run average cost curves below these points of intersection will also be points on the long-run

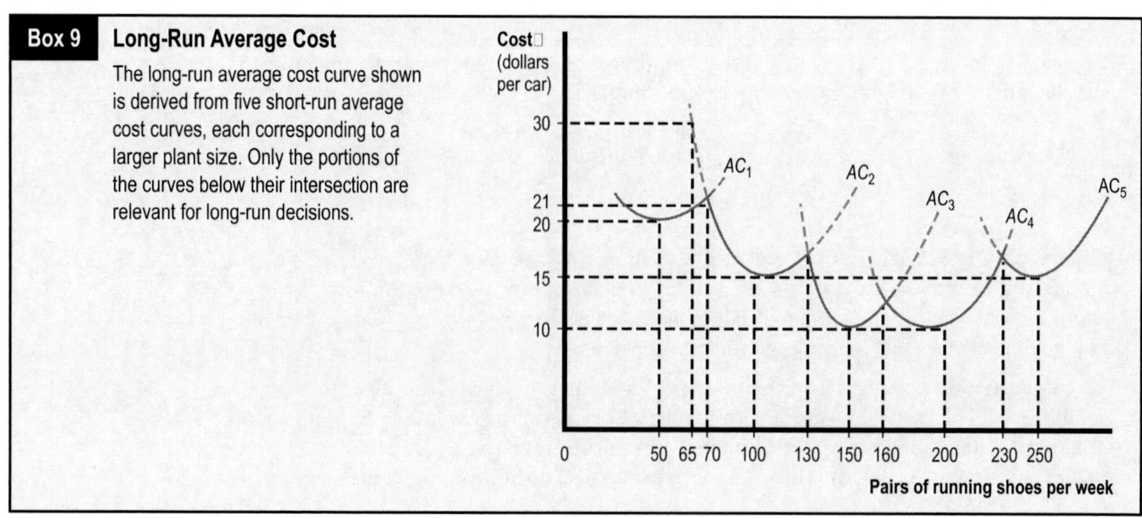

Box 9 Long-Run Average Cost

The long-run average cost curve shown is derived from five short-run average cost curves, each corresponding to a larger plant size. Only the portions of the curves below their intersection are relevant for long-run decisions.

average cost curve. This holds for all points of intersection on the curve. For example, beyond a monthly output of 130 pairs, corresponding to the point at which AC_2 and AC_3 intersect, it becomes cheaper to produce in the third plant. *The long-run average cost curve for all five possible plant sizes is the portion of all five short-run average cost curves below each point of intersection.* The dashed portions of each short-run average cost curve aren't included in the long-run average cost curve because they don't correspond to the *minimum* possible cost of producing output when all inputs are variable.

A smooth long-run average cost curve exists when it's possible to vary plant size so that the output corresponding to minimum possible average cost for each plant is one unit greater than the output of the previous plant. This would be the case if it were possible for you as manager to expand by adding one square foot and the smallest fraction of a machine hour whenever you wished. In the previous example we assumed that additional capital had to be acquired in large "lumps" that limited your options to only five plants of widely varying capacities.

When managers have more flexibility to expand to a greater variety of plant sizes, the long-run average cost curve becomes smooth rather than lumpy, as shown in Box 10. As the intersection points of the short-run average cost curves come closer and closer together, they trace out a smooth long-run average cost curve. Each point on the curve corresponds to a slightly larger plant. The graph shows some of the short-run average cost curves and how the long-run average cost curve touches each of them. The minimum possible long-run average cost is achieved when you choose the plant whose short-run average cost curve is AC^* and whose output is Q^* units per week.

Explaining the Shapes of Long-Run Average Cost Curves

In Box 10 the long-run average cost curve is U-shaped. The pattern of variation in average cost in the long run when all inputs are variable can't be explained by the law of diminishing marginal returns, which applies only when it's impossible to increase all inputs in the same proportion. However, we have a number of reasons to expect that average cost of production will decline and then increase when a firm expands in the long run.

Economies of scale (sometimes called *increasing returns to scale or economies of mass production*) are reductions in unit costs resulting from increased size of operations. The scale of a firm's operations increases as a firm operates out of larger plants. Economies of scale can result from increases in the productivity of inputs caused by increased specialization and division of labor as the firm builds more or bigger factories. This is

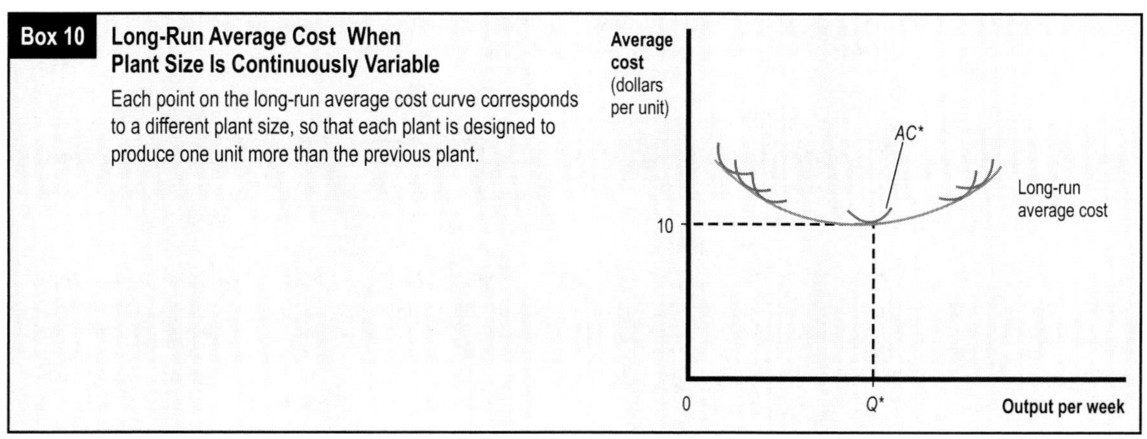

Box 10 Long-Run Average Cost When Plant Size Is Continuously Variable

Each point on the long-run average cost curve corresponds to a different plant size, so that each plant is designed to produce one unit more than the previous plant.

particularly common as a firm initially expands production. With only one worker and one machine, there's little opportunity to allocate specialized tasks to labor. With two workers and two machines, one worker can specialize in machine operations and the other can specialize in hand-finishing operations.

Economies of scale also result from the fact that a larger scale of operations doesn't require a proportionate increase in all inputs. For example, a farmer doesn't have to double the amount of fencing to double his grazing area. This is because the perimeter of the grazing area doesn't double when the grazing area doubles.

Finally, economies of scale can result from shifts in the method of production as a firm expands productive capacity in the long run. Expanding operations also permits use of more sophisticated machinery and allows workers to specialize in certain tasks. Some production processes aren't feasible when firms are small. However, as a firm grows in the long run, its greater productive capacity makes it economical to use production processes whose use is too expensive when output is low. Typically, a firm shifts to a more capital-intensive production process (meaning more equipment per worker) as it expands. The use of more capital per worker increases labor productivity and helps reduce cost per unit of output.

For example, a cabinet shop that can ship only 100 units per month might find it too expensive to use a machine that lacquers its cabinets. At low levels of output, the cheapest way to finish the cabinets is likely to be by hand. However, when the shop expands and can ship 1,000 units per month, the machine becomes the lowest-cost method of lacquering.

A firm may also be able to purchase certain inputs at lower prices per unit when it buys in greater volume. This helps reduce average costs of production.

Economies of scale are eventually exhausted in the long run. As a firm becomes large, it's likely to encounter diseconomies of scale (also called *decreasing returns to scale*), which are increases in average costs of operation resulting from problems in managing large-scale enterprises. It's hard to pinpoint the exact time at which diseconomies of scale set in or the reasons for their occurrence. However, as a firm expands, communication between managers and workers is often impaired and the firm can become more difficult to manage. Since the level of managerial skill varies from firm to firm, it's not at all certain that diseconomies of scale will occur in all enterprises.

Most businesses are likely to enjoy a fairly long range of output for which average costs neither increase nor decrease in the long run. Constant returns to scale prevail when economies of scale no longer exist and when average costs do not increase as a result of diseconomies of scale in the long run. If constant returns to scale prevailed at all possible outputs in the long run, the long-run average cost curve would be a horizontal line. The long-run average cost curve for the case of constant returns to scale is illustrated in Box 11. If constant returns to scale prevailed from zero output on, large-scale firms would have no cost advantage over small-scale firms.

Economies of Scale and the Size of the Firm

Economies of scale are an important determinant of the size of firms in various industries. When economies of scale exist, a firm can produce at lower average cost as it gets larger. This gives it a competitive edge. Because expansion reduces average cost, firms tend to expand until economies of scale have been exhausted. This is because lower average cost, other things being equal, increases profits. For example, in electric power generation, economies of scale exist over a long range of output. This explains why electric power companies tend to be very large.

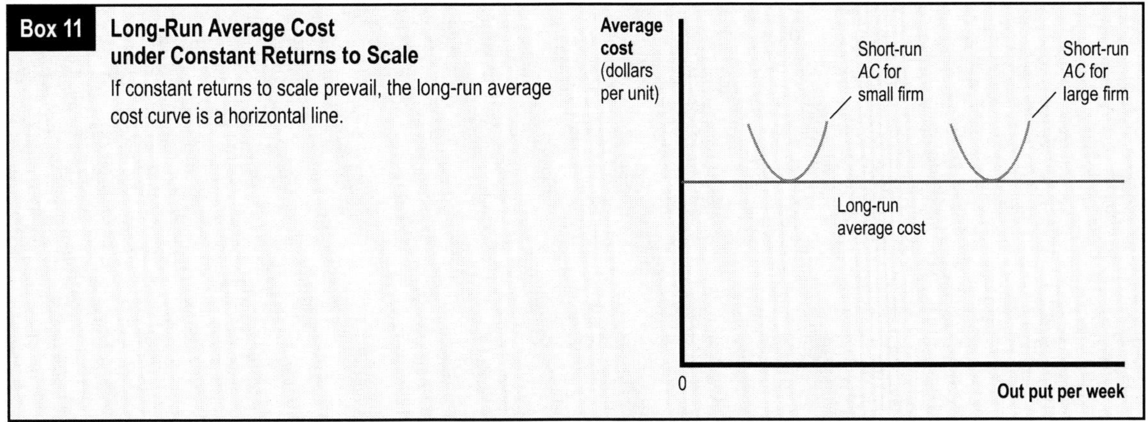

Box 11 Long-Run Average Cost under Constant Returns to Scale

If constant returns to scale prevail, the long-run average cost curve is a horizontal line.

If constant returns to scale are present for a long range of output before any diseconomies of scale increase average costs, an industry will comprise firms of various sizes. For example, if the long-run average cost curve looks like the one in Box 12, medium-sized firms will be able to produce at the same minimum possible average cost as large firms in the long run. This state of affairs is common in retailing, farming, and manufacturing of electronic components, clothing, and other goods. Many studies of manufacturing industries have shown that there's an extensive range of constant returns to scale.

In industries where economies of scale are quickly exhausted and diseconomies of scale set in rapidly, firms tend to be small. Examples of such industries are shoe repairing and dry cleaning.

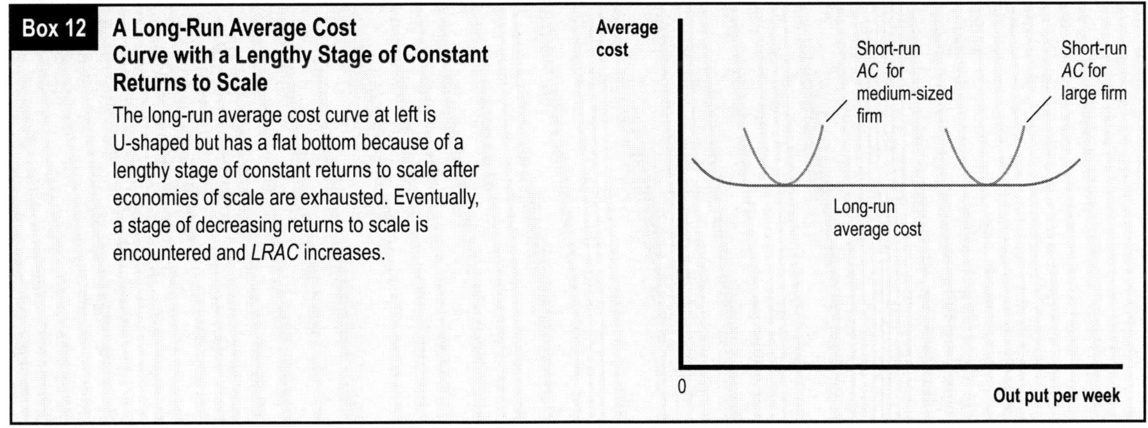

Box 12 A Long-Run Average Cost Curve with a Lengthy Stage of Constant Returns to Scale

The long-run average cost curve at left is U-shaped but has a flat bottom because of a lengthy stage of constant returns to scale after economies of scale are exhausted. Eventually, a stage of decreasing returns to scale is encountered and *LRAC* increases.

Summary

1. Production is the process of using inputs to make goods and services available. A production function is a relationship between any combination of inputs and the maximum output obtainable from that combination under current technology.

2. The short run is a period of production during which only some inputs are variable, while others are fixed. In the long run all inputs are variable.

3. The theory of production assumes that there's a limit to the increase in output that can be obtained by using more of any one input while other inputs and technology are fixed.

4. A total product curve describes the way output varies in the short run as more of any one variable input is used together with fixed amounts of other inputs. The average product of a variable input is the total output divided by the number of units of the variable input when that variable input is used together with a certain number of units of fixed input. The average product of labor is a measure of the productivity of labor expressed as output per worker or per labor hour. The marginal product of a variable input is the extra output that results from using an extra unit of the variable input.

5. According to the law of diminishing marginal returns, the average product and marginal product of a variable input will increase at first and then decrease. The marginal product of the input equals the average product of the input when the average product is at a maximum. When the marginal product of an input falls below its average product, this results in decreases in the average product (or productivity) of a variable input.

6. Cost measures the dollar value of inputs used over any given period to produce an item. Total cost is the sum of fixed cost and variable cost. Variable cost is the cost of variable inputs, while fixed cost measures inputs that don't change as the firm increases or decreases output in the short run. To produce efficiently, managers must seek to produce any given output with the lowest-cost combinations of variable inputs.

7. Average cost is total cost divided by total output. Average cost is the sum of average variable cost and average fixed cost in the short run.

8. Given input prices, the shape of cost curves reflects the fact that the marginal product of variable inputs eventually tends to decline as more are used. The U-shaped average cost curve and eventually increasing marginal cost reflect the law of diminishing marginal returns in the short run.

9. In the long run all costs are variable—there are no fixed costs. In the long run firms can build larger plants or duplicate existing plants at other locations. Economies of scale result in decreases in average cost in the long run, while diseconomies of scale increase average cost. When constant returns to scale prevail, expansion of output in the long run involves no increase or decrease in average cost.

Concept Review

1. Draw a total product curve, and explain how its shape reflects the law of diminishing marginal returns. Explain how the marginal product and average product of a variable input would change as more of the input is used in the short run. Identify the point of diminishing marginal returns.

2. Draw a total cost curve, and show how total cost is the sum of variable cost and fixed cost. How is the shape of a variable cost curve related to the shape of a total product curve?

3. Explain why, other things being equal, an increase in the average product of variable inputs used to produce an item will reduce the average cost of its production.

4. Why are only portions of a short-run average cost curve included in a firm's long-run average cost curve? How do economies of scale affect the shape of a firm's long-run average cost curve?

Problems and Applications

1. Suppose you run a retail stereo store. In operating the store, you have expenses for insurance, depreciation on business property, rent, and interest on borrowed funds. Explain why these payments represent prices for fixed inputs rather than variable inputs. List the variable inputs you're likely to use in operating the store. (1)

2. As the manager of a fast-food restaurant, you estimate that the total product of labor used to make meals available varies each day according to the following data

Number of workers per day	Total product of labor (meals per day)
1	30
2	70
3	100
4	120
5	130
6	135
7	140
8	140

Calculate the marginal product and the average product of labor as the number of workers increases. (1)

3. Plot the total product, average product, and marginal product curves for the data in the table in Problem 2. Explain why you'll never hire more than seven workers if you seek to maximize profits. How does the shape of the curve you've drawn illustrate the law of diminishing marginal returns? (1)

4. The average product of labor in a textile factory you manage is estimated to be 50 yards of fabric per labor hour. The marginal product of labor is estimated to be 60 yards of fabric per labor hour when the average product of labor is 50 yards. What will happen to the average product of labor if the factory uses additional labor? What would the relationship between the average and marginal product of labor have to be to maximize worker's productivity in the factory? (1)

5. Your T-shirt manufacturing plant currently produces 2,000 shirts per day. Fixed costs for the plant are \$10,000 a day. Variable costs are \$30,000 per day. Calculate total cost and average cost at the current output level. Calculate average fixed cost and average variable cost. (2)

6. As the owner of a dry-cleaning firm, you're considering the rental of a new pressing machine. The machine can be rented for \$200 per day and will press 200 garments per day. You currently pay \$40 per day to each worker who hand-presses 50 garments per day. Assuming that your firm seeks to press garments at the lowest possible cost, will you choose to rent the machine? Would your answer differ if the machine could be rented for only \$150 per day? Explain. (1), (2)

7. The average product of three hair stylists employed by the small beauty shop you manage is five haircuts per day. Assuming labor is the only variable input used in hair-styling and the hair stylists are paid \$20 per hour, calculate the average variable cost of a haircut. If your shop's daily fixed cost is \$100, calculate the minimum price that you must charge to cover its average cost when it schedules 15 appointments per day. (3)

8. As the owner of a firm producing towels, you estimate that the average cost of production in your factory is \$2. You also estimate that marginal cost is \$2 at the current level of output. Explain why average cost must be at a minimum but average variable cost must be increasing. (2)

9. Use the data in Box 3 to recalculate variable cost and total cost when the fixed cost in column 3 suddenly increases to \$1,200 per week. Recalculate marginal cost and average cost for the various levels of output. Show how the average cost, average variable cost, and marginal cost curves are affected by the increase in fixed cost. Why is marginal cost unaffected by the increase in fixed cost? (2), (3)

10. Your firm estimates that whenever it doubles the labor, capital, land, and any other inputs in the long run, its output also doubles. Assuming input prices don't increase or decrease as your firm expands, draw the firm's long-run average cost curve. (4)

Chapter Appendix

Isoquant Analysis: Choosing the Method of Production

What influences the input combination that a firm's managers choose in order to produce the items they sell? In other words, what forces determine *how* goods are produced?

Managers are well aware that there are alternative production methods. For example, the degree of mechanization used to produce furniture varies. A table can be produced entirely by a worker using hand tools. The same table can be produced in a highly mechanized factory with sophisticated machinery substituting for labor. A farmer can produce a crop of 10,000 pumpkins with relatively little land and labor and lots of fertilizer, machinery, and insecticide. He can produce the same crop with less machinery, fertilizer, and insecticide but with more labor and land substituted for those inputs.

In this appendix we'll develop a model for analyzing the choice of a production method for any given item. In developing the model, we make the behavioral assumption that producers seek to minimize the cost of producing any given amount of output over any given period.

Isoquants

The table in Box 1, drawn up by an industrial engineer, shows five alternative methods that can be used to produce a maximum of 300 pairs of western boots per month in a small factory. Thanks to your experience in managing the running-shoe factory in the chapter, you've just been named manager of the factory.

Method *I* involves the use of enough capital equipment to provide 600 hours of machine use. If this much capital is used, the 300 pairs of boots can be produced with only 100 hours of labor per month. This is a very *capital-intensive* method because it involves six hours of machine use for each hour of labor use. Alternatively, you could choose to use

Box 1 **An Isoquant**

An isoquant is a curve that shows alternative combinations of inputs that can be used to produce a given output.

Production Methods for 300 Pairs of Boots and the Marginal Rate of Technical Substitution of Labor for Capital

Method	Machine hours	Labor hours	ΔK (hours)	ΔL (hours)	$MRTS_{LK} = \frac{-\Delta K}{\Delta L}$ (machine hours per hour of labor)
I	600	100			
			−200	100	2
II	400	200			
			−100	100	1
III	300	300			
			−70	100	0.7
IV	230	400			
			−30	100	0.3
V	200	500			

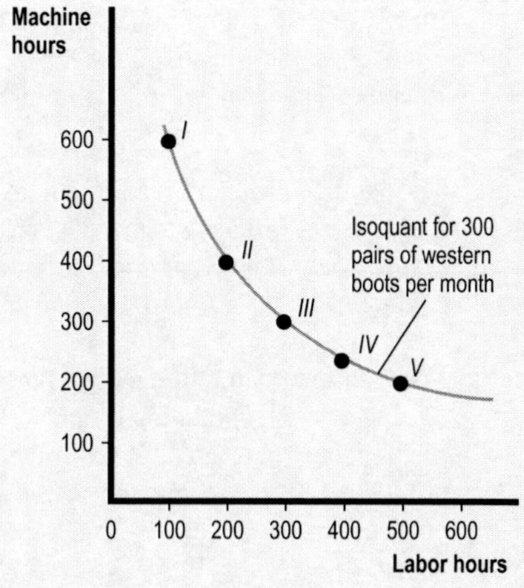

less capital and more labor to produce 300 pairs of boots per month. For example, method *II* involves the use of 400 machine hours and 200 labor hours per month. This is a less capital-intensive method of production than method *I* because only two machine hours are used together with each labor hour. You *substitute* 100 labor hours for 200 machine hours *without* reducing production when you switch from method *I* to method *II*. The table shows three other production methods capable of producing 300 pairs of boots per month.

An isoquant is a curve showing all combinations of variable inputs that can be used to produce a given quantity of output. The isoquant for 300 pairs of western boots is illustrated in Box 1. It is obtained by plotting the combination of labor and capital corresponding to each production method in the Box 1 table and tracing a smooth curve through the points. Points on the curve represent all the combinations of labor and capital that can produce a maximum of 300 pairs of boots per month given available technology.

The isoquant shows you that a given quantity of output can be produced in many ways. The highly mechanized production method *I* is represented by point *I* on the isoquant, which corresponds to 600 machine hours and only 100 labor hours per month. Point *V* corresponds to 500 labor hours and only 200 machine hours per month. As you move along the isoquant from point *I* to point *V*, labor is substituted for capital and there's a decline in the proportion of machine hours to labor hours.

Properties of Isoquants

Common sense and observation of actual production suggest that isoquants are likely to have certain properties. For example, you know that if you use fewer machine hours each month, other things being equal, production will fall. However, you can make up for the reduced use of capital by hiring more labor to prevent production from falling. For any reduction in capital input, $-\Delta K$, the corresponding change in labor input, ΔL, must be positive to prevent output from declining. It follows that along the isoquant, the slope, $\Delta K \Delta L$, must be negative because the signs of the numerator and the denominator are always opposite when labor is substituted for capital and output remains constant.

The marginal rate of technical substitution of labor for capital ($MRTS_{LK}$) is a measure of the amount of capital each unit of labor can replace without increasing or decreasing production. The marginal rate of technical substitution along the isoquant at any point is the slope at that point multiplied by minus one:

$$MRTS_{LK} = -\frac{\Delta K}{\Delta L}$$

The table in Box 1 calculates the marginal rate of technical substitution of labor for capital as labor is substituted for capital in 100-hour increments along the isoquant.[1] This calculation approximates $MRTS_{LK}$ based on 100-hour (rather than 1-hour) changes in labor use as labor is substituted for capital.

At first each hour of labor can replace two hours of capital while production is kept fixed at 300 pairs of boots per month. However, as labor use is increased and capital use is decreased, there is a decline in the number of machine hours that each labor hour can

[1]The marginal rate of technical substitution depends on the marginal products of labor and capital and on the way these marginal products vary. To remain on the same isoquant, the decline in machine hours must be replaced with enough labor hours to get back to a point on the original isoquant. The gain in production is ΔL, multiplied by its marginal product. Because the gain in production equals the loss in production, it follows that

$$\Delta L(MP_L) = -\Delta K(MP_K)$$

Solving for the slope of the isoquant

$$MRTS_{KL} = -\frac{\Delta K}{\Delta L} = \frac{MP_L}{MP_K}$$

when MP_K is the marginal product of capital and MP_L is the marginal product of labor.

replace. For example, when 400 labor hours are used with only 230 machine hours per month, it takes only 0.3 machine hour to replace each labor hour when labor use is increased to 500 hours. The marginal rate of technical substitution of labor for capital tends to decline as labor is substituted for capital.

You can think of diminishing marginal rates of technical substitution of labor for capital as implying that increasing numbers of machine hours are required to substitute for successive reduction in labor hours if output is to remain constant. Moving from point *V* to point *IV* on the isoquant in Box 1, you can see that only 30 machine hours will be required to make up the output lost by withdrawing 100 labor hours from production when the method of production currently used involves 200 machine hours and 500 labor hours per month. However, if you want to move from point *II* (where 400 machine hours and 200 labor hours are used to produce the same monthly output) to point *I* by withdrawing 100 labor hours from production, 200 machine hours will be required to make up the output lost by withdrawing the labor hours. The convex shape of the isoquant drawn in Box 1 reflects the declining marginal rate of technical substitution of labor for capital as labor is actually substituted for capital along an isoquant.

The reason for declining marginal rates of technical substitution is that inputs tend to complement each other. Each input has the capability of doing something the other either can't do or can do only imperfectly. In most activities labor and capital are not perfect substitutes for each other. When labor hours are reduced, each additional reduction requires progressively more machine hours to replace the lost workers. The curvature of the isoquants indicates the difficulty with which one input can be substituted for the other without sacrificing production. This varies from activity to activity. It may, for example, be relatively easy to substitute labor for machines in a boot factory, but it may be virtually impossible to substitute labor for capital in the production of complex chemicals such as antifreeze.

Isoquants can be drawn for 400 or 200 pairs of boots per month as well. Naturally, it will take more labor and capital to produce more output. Box 2 contains an isoquant map for western boot production that shows the combinations of labor and capital that can be used to produce three output levels. Isoquants farther from the origin correspond to higher output levels than those of isoquants closer to the origin. Each isoquant gives alternative combinations of the labor and capital inputs that can be used to produce the indicated output.

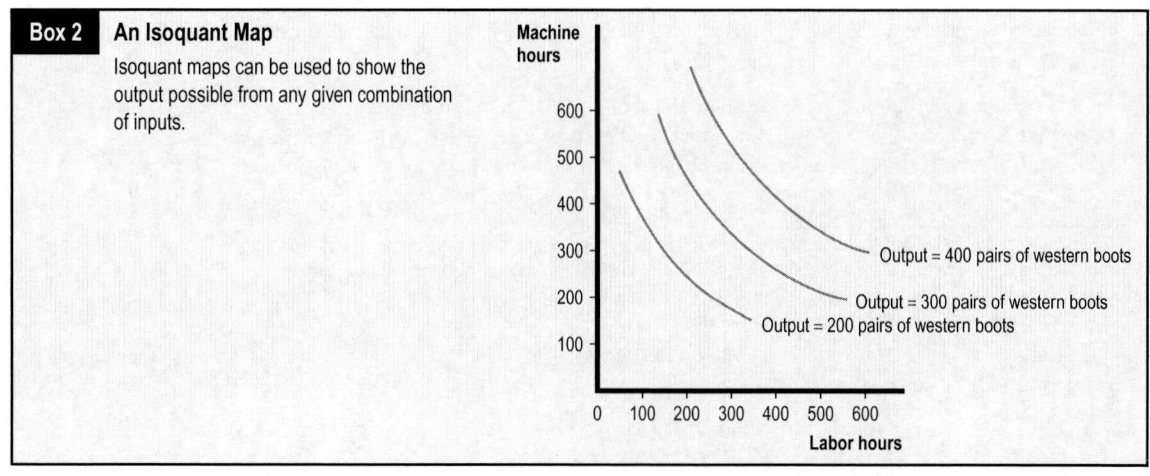

Isoquant maps can be used to show the output possible from any given combination of inputs.

Cost of Production

Assume that labor and capital are the only two variable inputs used and that the prices of their services per hour are P_L and P_K, respectively. The total cost, *TC*, of any amount of these two inputs is

$$TC = P_L L + P_K K$$

where *L* is measured as labor hours and *K* is measured as machine hours. P_L is the hourly wage of labor, and P_K is the hourly rental rate for machines. For example, if the price of labor were \$10 per hour and the price of capital were \$20 per hour, the total cost of production method *III* in Box 1, which uses 300 labor hours and 300 machine hours, would be

$$TC = \$10(300) + \$20(300) = \$9{,}000$$

Isocost Lines

An isocost line gives all combinations of labor and capital that are of equal total cost. Suppose, for example, that the price of labor services (wages) is \$10 per hour, whereas the price of capital services (the machine rental rate) is \$20 per hour. A monthly input combination consisting of 500 labor hours and 200 machine hours, corresponding to production process *V* in Box 1, would therefore cost \$9,000. This input combination lies on the same isocost line as the point corresponding to production process *III*. An isocost line can be drawn between the two points corresponding to production processes *III* and *V*, as is done in Box 3. Any other monthly input combination costing \$9,000 would lie on the isocost line drawn through points *III* and *V*.

There's a different isocost line for each level of total cost. This is shown in Box 3, where each line is labeled according to the cost of input combinations lying on it. Isocost lines farther from the origin involve more input use and therefore more cost than isocost lines closer to the origin.

The Slope of Isocost Lines Depends on Input Prices

When the price of labor is \$10 per hour and the price of capital is \$20 per hour, labor use must be reduced by two hours to free the \$20 necessary to purchase each machine hour. The slope of any isocost line in the family is:

Box 3 **Isocost Lines**

Points on a given isocost line show alternative production processes of equal cost. The family of isocost lines at right prevails when the price of a machine hour is \$20 and the price of a labor hour is \$10.

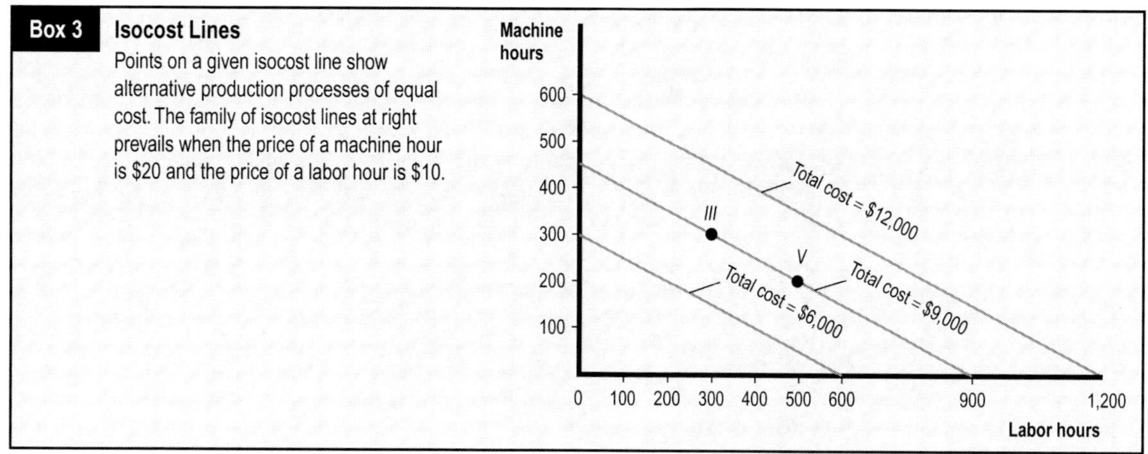

$$-\frac{\Delta K}{\Delta L}$$

When labor use is reduced by $-\Delta L = 2$ hours, the manager can rent one extra hour of machine use ($\Delta K = 1$) using the \$20 released without increasing total cost. It follows that along the isocost line:

$$-\frac{\Delta K}{\Delta L} = \frac{1}{2} = \frac{\$10}{\$20} = \frac{P_L}{P_K}$$

Note that $\Delta K/\Delta L$ is the slope of the isocost line, which in this case is $-1/2$. The slope of the isocost line therefore varies according to the price of labor relative to the price of capital.[2] The higher the ratio of the price of labor to the price of capital, the less labor use must be reduced to purchase each hour of capital without changing total cost, and the steeper the isocost line.

For example, if the price of labor were only \$5 per hour, it would take four hours of labor reduction to free the funds needed to rent one machine hour when a machine hour costs \$20. In this case the slope of the isocost line would be:

$$-\frac{\$5}{\$20} = -\frac{1}{4}$$

If labor and capital both cost \$20 per hour, only one labor hour would have to be sacrificed to buy an hour of capital without changing cost. In this case the slope of the isocost line would be

$$-\frac{\$20}{\$20} = -1$$

and the isocost line would be steeper than it was when the price of labor was only \$5 per hour.

A change in the price of either labor or capital changes the slope of a whole family of isocost lines. For example, an increase in the price of labor, given the price of capital, will make each of the isocost lines in the family steeper.

The Minimum-Cost Input Combination for a Given Output

Box 4 reproduces the isoquant for producing 300 pairs of western boots. The family of isocost lines corresponding to wages of \$10 per hour and an hourly machine rental rate of \$20 per hour is superimposed on the same set of axes as that used for the isoquant.

As manager of the boot factory, what production method will you choose if you want to produce the 300 pairs at the lowest possible total cost? The table in Box 4 shows the total cost of five possible production methods. You can see from the table that production method *IV*, which involves 230 machine hours and 400 labor hours per month, costs \$8,600, which is less than the cost of any of the other methods shown when the price of labor is \$10 per hour and the price of capital is \$20 per hour.

Using isoquant analysis, it's easy to show the influences on the choice of the least costly production method. The graph in Box 4 shows that method *I* isn't the least costly method, because it corresponds to a point on the isocost line for which total cost is \$13,000. By substituting labor for capital, you can move from point *I* to lower isocost lines without decreasing output. Similarly, production method *II*, which corresponds to a total cost of

[2]You can also see this by writing the equation for total cost in terms of K:

$$K = -\left(\frac{P_L}{P_K}\right)L + \frac{TC}{P_K}$$

In this case

$$\frac{P_L}{P_K} = \frac{\$10}{\$20} = \frac{1}{2}$$

The slope of the iscocost line is therefore – 1/2.

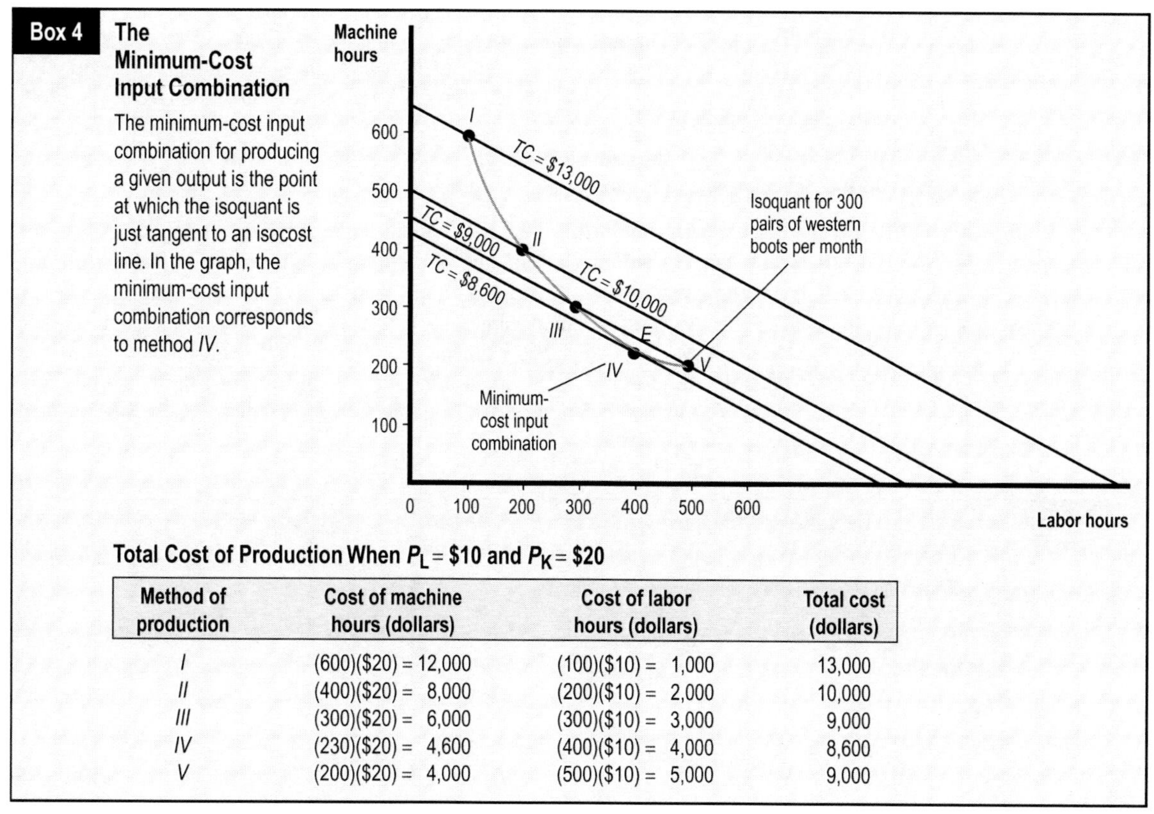

Box 4 The Minimum-Cost Input Combination

The minimum-cost input combination for producing a given output is the point at which the isoquant is just tangent to an isocost line. In the graph, the minimum-cost input combination corresponds to method *IV*.

Total Cost of Production When $P_L = \$10$ and $P_K = \$20$

Method of production	Cost of machine hours (dollars)	Cost of labor hours (dollars)	Total cost (dollars)
I	(600)($20) = 12,000	(100)($10) = 1,000	13,000
II	(400)($20) = 8,000	(200)($10) = 2,000	10,000
III	(300)($20) = 6,000	(300)($10) = 3,000	9,000
IV	(230)($20) = 4,600	(400)($10) = 4,000	8,600
V	(200)($20) = 4,000	(500)($10) = 5,000	9,000

$10,000, is not the least costly method because by further substituting labor for capital, you can move to a lower isocost line. By the same token, production method *V* is not the least costly method because you can move to a lower isocost line from point *V* by substituting machine use for labor use.

The minimum-cost production method corresponds to the point at which the isoquant for 300 pairs of boots is just tangent to an isocost line. This condition is met at point *E*, which corresponds to production method *IV*. At that point it's not possible to reduce cost by substituting one input for another.

A tangency of the isoquant and an isocost line implies that the slope of the isoquant equals the slope of the isocost line at that point. Because the slope of the isoquant is $-MRTS_{LK}$ and the slope of the isocost line is $-P_L/P_K$, the condition for minimizing the cost of producing a given output can be written as

$$\frac{P_L}{P_K} = MRTS_{LK}$$

This equation shows that, as manager, your choice of the least costly production method is influenced by the prices of variable inputs and by the marginal rate of technical substitution between variable inputs. The marginal rate of technical substitution associated with any given input combination on an isoquant depends on technology. However, you're free to substitute inputs for each other given technology by varying production methods until input use is adjusted to minimize cost. The actual production method you choose depends on *both* input prices and technology affecting the marginal rates of technical substitution. Changes in technology change the shape of the isoquants and cause movement to a new least costly production method.

Given the availability of the same technology to two nations, you wouldn't expect to see capital-intensive methods used to produce goods and services in nations where labor is cheap relative to capital, as is the case in China. On the other hand, in the United States labor is expensive, while capital equipment is relatively abundant. It's therefore not surprising to see highly mechanized apparel manufacturers in the United States, while in China clothes are produced with less capital-intensive techniques—even though both nations have access to the same technology.

Note that changes in the price of labor or capital will change the slope of the isocost lines. When this occurs, assuming no change in technology affects the shape of the isoquant, managers will respond by adjusting their production method until the isoquant is just tangent to one of the new isocost lines. For example, if the price of machine rental in China were to decrease relative to the price of labor, the isocost lines would become steeper and the minimum-cost production methods would become more capital intensive. The impact of a decrease in the price of capital relative to labor is shown in Box 5.

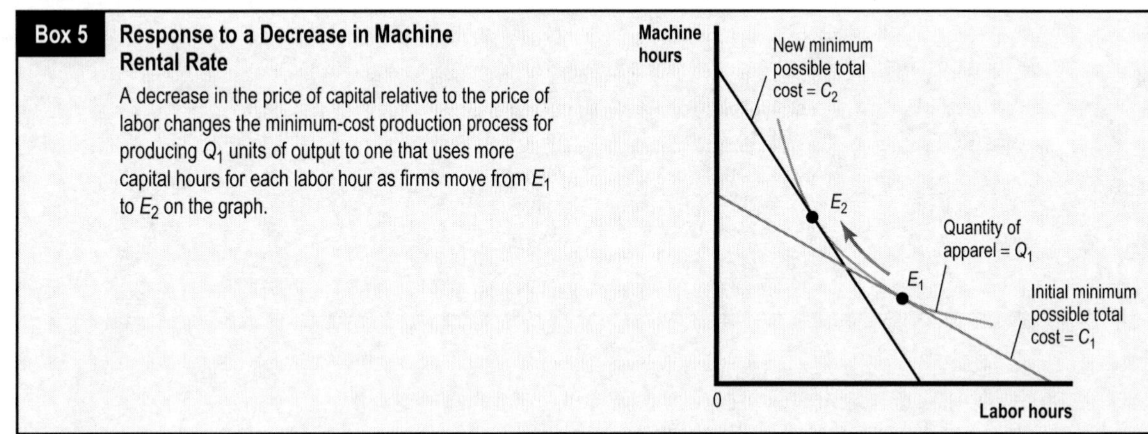

Box 5 Response to a Decrease in Machine Rental Rate

A decrease in the price of capital relative to the price of labor changes the minimum-cost production process for producing Q_1 units of output to one that uses more capital hours for each labor hour as firms move from E_1 to E_2 on the graph.

Globalization of the Auto Industry: Productivity and Cost in Auto Manufacturing

International competition is putting relentless pressure on GM, Ford, and Chrysler to lower average costs so they can compete more effectively in global markets. In the past, U.S. auto manufacturers were complacent about cost. In the 1970s, for example, auto unions demanded and got wage increases, though U.S. auto workers' average productivity and marginal productivity didn't increase by the same percentage. The result was sharp increases in average variable costs of production for U.S. automakers. You can see this effect in the graph below.

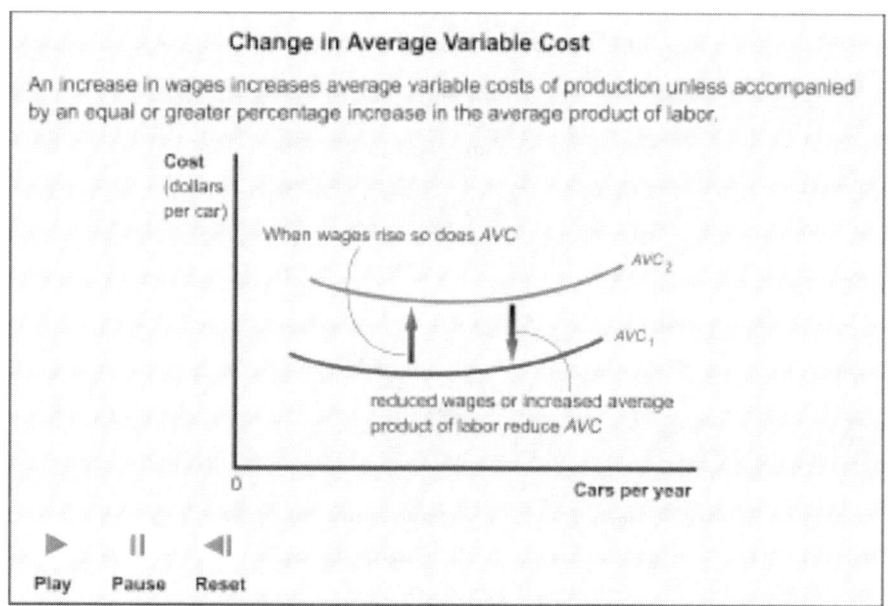

A wage increase shifts the average variable cost curve upward. However, increases in the average product of labor contribute to lower average variable costs. When wage increases are accompanied by increases in the average product of labor (i.e., increased productivity of the work force), average variable costs need not rise, despite the wage increases. In the 1967-80 period, labor compensation per worker in the U.S. auto industry increased *5 1/2 times faster than did workers' productivity*![1] As a result, average variable costs soared. GM and the other auto manufacturers simply passed the higher costs on to consumers when they didn't have to worry about foreign competition.

Today, the picture is different. With fierce international competition in what has become a global car market, U.S. firms are scrambling to reduce average costs of production. They're doing this by trying to reduce both average variable costs and average fixed costs of production. GM trimmed its enormous bureaucracy of white-collar workers by eliminating 40,000 clerical and professional jobs in the 1980s. Cost-cutting, plant closures, and elimination of positions continued through the 1990s and was still going on in 2009, as GM struggled and faced the prospect of bankruptcy. In 2008 and 2009, GM, Ford, and Chrysler reduced health and other benefits to retired workers and initiated further cuts in salaried workers. These measures reduced average fixed costs by reducing the fixed number of workers in the company and payments to retirees who didn't directly produce cars. U.S. automakers are now more resistant to demands for increased wages, and are trying desperately to modernize their plants and take other steps to increase the average product of labor. The number of labor hours required to assemble cars in the North American production plants owned by GM, Ford, and Chrysler has declined since 2001.

GM, Ford, and Chrysler all saw their market shares shrink as a recession cut the demand for new cars in 2008 and 2009. This put downward pressure on new car prices and contributed to further losses in the U.S. automobile industry, adding to the urgency to cut average costs of production. By mid-2009, both Chrysler and GM were in bankruptcy, and were reorganizing by taking measures to reduce both average costs of production and productive capacity.

The rush to reduce costs is not confined to U.S. automobile manufacturers. German and Japanese producers were buffeted by both increased wages and an increased value of their currencies in the early 1990s and, again, in 2003-2008. Prices of German and Japanese cars have consequently increased in terms of dollars and other currencies in foreign markets. These foreign manufacturers are also taking steps to reduce costs.

Mercedes-Benz vehicles, produced originally in Germany (where wages are among the highest in the world), are now manufactured all over the world. As high wages and a high-valued euro reduced both foreign sales and profit, Mercedes executives decided to build plants in foreign countries in an effort to reduce labor costs. Mercedes' U.S. plant in Tuscaloosa, Alabama, produces luxury SUVs. Mercedes follows its fellow German car manufacturer, BMW, which is operating a plant on a 900-acre site between Spartanburg and Greenville, South Carolina. Japanese manufacturers already have plants in Ohio, Kentucky, and Tennessee, and announced plans to build more auto plants in the United States. Toyota doubled the capacity of its Georgetown plant in Kentucky during the mid-1990s. Also during the mid-1990s, Mercedes built a plant in France to produce its new Smart car for the European market. And German workers have agreed to wage reductions to keep the prestige automaker from transferring more operations to non-German sites.

Globalization and increased competition in the auto market have increased pressures to use the latest technology, and to keep both fixed and variable production costs down. The beneficiary of the increased competition is ultimately the consumer, who can get better cars at lower prices than would be possible without pressure from foreign competition.

The U.S. worker also benefits. As U.S. cars become more competitive in world markets, exports are likely to increase. By 2004, Chrysler-brand vehicles--including minivans, jeeps, and the PT Cruiser--were being sold in 47 countries, and a lower-priced dollar was helping sales for vehicles with high U.S. part or labor content. Of course, foreign auto companies provide jobs for U.S. workers, and they may eventually export significant numbers of their U.S.-produced cars to foreign markets.

[1]See Walter Adams and James W. Brock, "The Automobile Industry," in *The Structure of American Industry*, 8th ed., ed. Walter Adams (New York: Macmillan, 1990), p. 114.
[2]See Gabriella Stern, "GM Launches Early-Retirement Plans," *The Wall Street Journal*, July 5, 1995, p. A3.

Measuring Fixed Cost: An Example

The common business term for fixed costs is *overhead costs*. Fixed, or overhead, costs are all costs that don't vary with output. The following data show how fixed cost can be measured. These data are based on cost estimates for a fish processing plant. The plant dresses mountain trout for shipment to urban fish markets. The plant will cost $67,782 to construct. Equipment cost will be $60,337. The cost of acquiring the land for the plant is $7,500. The plant is designed to produce 2,304 pounds of dressed trout per day.

Fixed costs include depreciation on plant and equipment, property taxes, insurance, repairs, maintenance, and forgone interest on cash invested. In addition, the plant manager's salary may be regarded as a fixed cost. Irrespective of the output level, he must be paid his salary to oversee operations or to manage the plant's affairs if it's to be shut down.

In calculating depreciation, we assume the plant has a 20-year life and the equipment has a 10-year life. A straight-line depreciation of these assets uses 1/20th of the plant cost and 1/10th of the equipment cost as a measure of annual capital cost. Forgone interest is estimated at 9 percent of one-half of the total investment in land, building, and equipment. Annual fixed, or overhead, costs are as follows:

Depreciation	
Plant	$ 3,389
Equipment	6,034
Total	9,423
Forgone interest	6,103
Property Tax	1,356
Insurance	1,239
Repairs and maintenance	1,922
Manager's salary	15,325
Total fixed cost	$35,368

Property taxes are estimated at 1 percent of investment in land, building, and equipment. Insurance is estimated at a bit less than 1 percent of investment in building and equipment, while repairs and maintenance are estimated at 1.5 percent of the same amount.

NOTE: Based on estimates by Professor J. E. Easley of North Carolina State University.

Chapter 10

The Profit-Maximizing Competitive Firm and Market Supply

People just like you have good product ideas every day. And the stroke of inspiration for the next hot craze could very well be yours. If you've already read the chapter Production and Cost, however, you're aware that manufacturing even a popular item like running shoes involves a lot of cost considerations.

This chapter shows how cost considerations influence a profit-maximizing firm's supply decisions. We use marginal analysis (which we introduce in the chapter Economics: What It's All About) to isolate the marginal benefit and cost of business decisions. By doing so, we can develop a rule for profit maximization. This rule will help us establish the cause-and-effect relationship between changes in price and changes in quantity supplied that's necessary to derive a supply curve. Once we've derived the individual firm's supply curve, it's easy to show how market supply curves are related to individual supply curves.

In the model we develop, we assume that firms produce a single product and that they *react to* (rather than control) their product's price. Such firms are usually small and sell their products in a market where many competing sellers offer identical products. A good example is your local farmers' market, where many sellers have similar tomatoes. In such a competitive market, if any one seller raises his price above the market price, buyers simply get their tomatoes from his competitors.

Concept Preview

After reading this chapter, you should be able to

1. Define perfect competition and explain why the demand curve for the product of a competitive firm is perfectly elastic at the market equilibrium price.
2. Use marginal analysis to explain how a firm chooses its output so as to maximize profits.
3. Use graphs to show what profits a firm actually earns and how a product's market price affects the firm's profitability.
4. Explain the conditions under which a firm will cease operations in the short run.
5. Show how a supply curve can be derived for a competitive firm that maximizes its profit from selling a single product and how the market supply curve can be derived from the supply curve of the individual firms in an industry.
6. Tell how changes in input prices affect supply curves in the short run.

Profit, Price, and Output in the Short Run for a Competitive Firm

Why do supply curves slope upward? The answer requires an analysis of how product prices influence the business choice of how much to produce and make available for sale. You'll soon see that a key reason for upward-sloping supply curves is the law of diminishing marginal returns.

To develop a theory of supply, we begin by making a number of simplifying assumptions. Although these assumptions are unrealistic, they allow us to develop a model of the basic forces that underlie supply to markets by profit-maximizing firms. In this instance, as is the case for all economic models, you'll find that unrealistic assumptions yield useful insights into the way the economy actually functions. The purpose of the model we'll develop in this chapter is to allow us to use marginal analysis to explain how quantity supplied to a market in the short run is related to a product's price, assuming that sellers maximize profit.

Perfect Competition

1 The theory of supply is based on the simplifying assumption of "perfect" competition in a market for a product. A perfectly competitive market exists when the following conditions prevail:

1. There are *many sellers* in the market competing to sell a product to many buyers. In a perfectly competitive market the number of sellers usually exceeds 100 and is often in the thousands.

2. The products sold in the market are *homogeneous*, which means that each seller's product is identical to that of other sellers. A homogeneous product is one that is standardized. Grade A eggs are an example, as are bushels of soybeans of a given quality. Buyers view one seller's product as a perfect substitute for that of any other seller.

3. Each firm has a *very small market share* of total sales. Market share is a single seller's percentage of total sales over any period. Generally, in a perfectly competitive market no seller's market share exceeds 1 percent.

4. No seller in the market regards competing sellers as a threat to its market share. *Firms are therefore unconcerned about their competitors' marketing or production decisions.*

5. *Information is freely available* on prices, technology, and profit opportunities. Also, resources are mobile.

6. There is *freedom of entry and exit* by sellers of the standardized good. This means there are no restraints preventing firms from entering the market, nor are there difficulties in ceasing operations.

In a perfectly competitive market an *individual* seller cannot influence the market price of its product. Because each seller's product is a perfect substitute for that of any other seller in the market, buyers have no reason to prefer the product of one seller to that of any other. A firm that tries to charge more than the going market price for its product will lose all its customers to competing sellers.

In a perfectly competitive market no individual firm can shift the market supply sufficiently to make a good scarcer or more abundant. Even if one firm withholds its entire production from the market, this won't cause the good to become scarcer and therefore won't result in an increase in the market price. If a firm floods the market with its output, the good won't become sufficiently more abundant to put downward pressure on market price. This means that no seller in the market can affect the price of the good by offering to sell either more or less of it.

A competitive firm is one that sells its product in a perfectly competitive market. *A competitive firm is characterized as a "price taker" because it can only react to the market price and cannot by itself cause the market price to go up or down.* In a perfectly competitive market the number of sellers depends on the profitability of selling the product. Free entry and mobility of resources ensure that the number of sellers, and therefore market supply, will increase when it's profitable to sell a product in a market.

The key idea underlying the notion of perfect competition is that individual firms *react to* rather than influence the prices of the products they sell. The model is relevant to markets in which prices are set largely by impersonal forces of supply and demand and firms take the market price as more or less given.

In many agricultural markets (such as the wheat market), the conditions of standardized products, many sellers, and small market shares are often approximated. For example, there are nearly half a million wheat sellers in the United States. Even though a small percentage of wheat farms account for about half of total wheat production, the top 3 percent or so of wheat producers amount to many thousands of independent firms.

Demand as Seen by a Competitive Firm

The market demand curve is downward sloping for a competitive *industry* composed of many firms selling a homogeneous product. Market price is determined by demand and supply in the competitive market, in which prices adjust until quantity demanded by the many buyers equals quantity supplied by the many sellers.

For example, suppose you run a small firm that weaves fabric sold by the yard. Suppose that 1,000 firms in your industry produce a standard woven fabric sold throughout the nation in a competitive market and that consumers regard the product of any one of these firms as a perfect substitute for the product of any other firm. The market in which these firms sell their fabric is perfectly competitive, and each firm can be considered a price taker. Each firm in the industry is very small and operates out of a very small plant in which it can produce a small amount of fabric each day.

In Box 1, graph **A** shows how the market price is determined by supply and demand and how this influences the demand as seen by any single competitive firm in the industry. The market demand and supply curves for the fabric intersect at point *E*. The corresponding market equilibrium price is $100 per yard, and the equilibrium quantity sold per day at that price is 8,000 yards.

Graph **B** shows the demand curve as seen by any firm in the industry. This curve is a horizontal line. We can easily understand why by considering the short-run productive capacity of each firm in the industry. Suppose each firm can produce no more than 10 yards of fabric per day in its existing plant. The most any one firm can add to (or subtract from) market supply is therefore 10 yards per day. Even if any one firm adds or subtracts this maximum amount, the shift in the supply curve will be imperceptible. There would therefore be no perceptible effect on market price. To see this, go to **A** in Box 1 and note that removing 10 yards per day from the market quantity supplied of 8,000 at the $100 price won't noticeably change the quantity supplied. No firm has the capacity to make the good appreciably scarcer or more abundant. This means that any firm can sell all it wants to at the market equilibrium price. This being the case, there's no incentive to sell at any price lower than the market price. A firm that lowers its price won't be able to sell more than it would have sold otherwise. The price decrease would therefore lower revenue but have no effect on the quantity sold and the cost of production. Thus, selling at a price below the market equilibrium price would decrease a firm's profit.

The standardized product sold by any one competitive firm is a perfect substitute for that of any other competing seller. The horizontal demand curve of each firm in a competitive industry is perfectly elastic at the market price. (See the chapter Elasticity of Demand and Supply for an explanation of why a horizontal demand curve is perfectly elastic.)

Box 1 Market Price and the Demand for the Output of a Competitive Firm

The market price of fabric is $100. A competitive firm can sell all the fabric it wishes at that price. The demand for a competitive firm's output is infinitely elastic at the market price. The output of any one firm is a perfect substitute for that of any other firm.

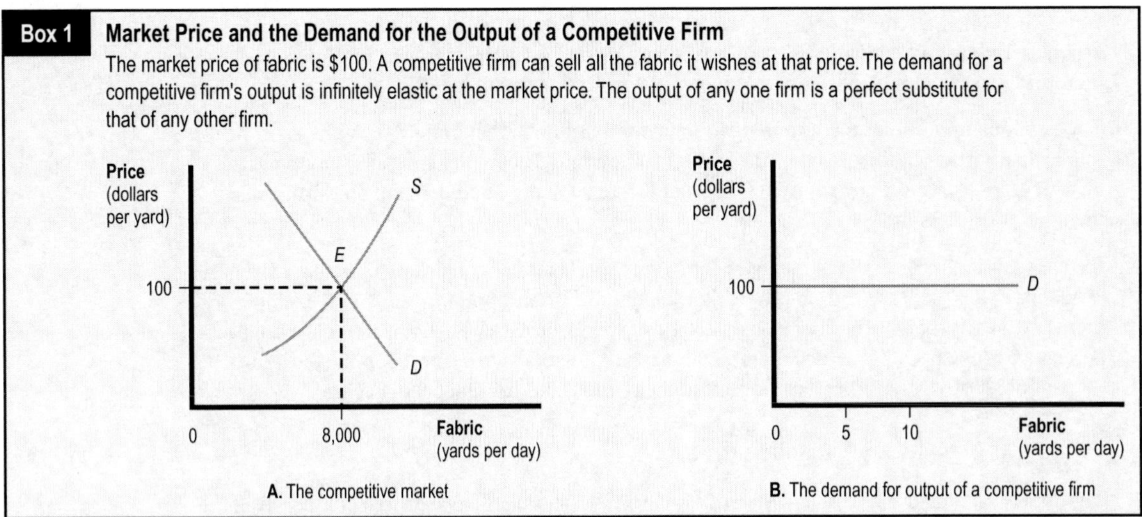

How Profit Varies as a Competitive Firm Increases Output

In the chapter The Business Firm, we see that economic profit can be calculated as the difference between total revenue (*TR*) and total cost (*TC*) per sales period:

$$\text{Economic profit} = TR - TC$$

Total revenue is the price (*P*) of the good sold multiplied by the amount of the good produced (*Q*). The total cost of production includes all implicit costs.

Price is beyond the influence of a competitive firm. Therefore, the only way a competitive firm can influence its revenues is by varying the amount it produces. However, as output changes, so does cost. The current market price of the fabric is $100 per yard. That price can also be expressed as total revenue divided by output. Total revenue *per unit* of a good sold is called the average revenue of the good. It's easy to show that average revenue is just another name for the price of a good:

$$\text{Average revenue} = \frac{\text{Total revenue}}{Q}$$

where *Q* is output. Because total revenue is $P \times Q$, it follows that

$$\text{Average revenue} = \frac{PQ}{Q} = P$$

Therefore, average revenue, or revenue per unit, *is* the price of a product.

The table in Box 2 provides hypothetical data on output, revenue, cost, and profits for a typical weaving firm selling in a competitive market. Let's call the firm Weaving Works, and let's appoint you as its manager. We assume the firm has fixed costs of $100 per day and the pattern of variation of short-run costs reflects the law of diminishing marginal returns we discussed in the previous chapter.

The first column of the table shows the daily output of fabric ranging from 0 to 10 yards per day. To obtain the total revenue from that output, just multiply output by market price, which is assumed to be $100 per yard. The second column shows the total revenue, *PQ*, of all the output levels shown. The third column shows total cost. Notice that your firm incurs $100 in fixed cost even if its output is zero. Finally, profit is shown in the

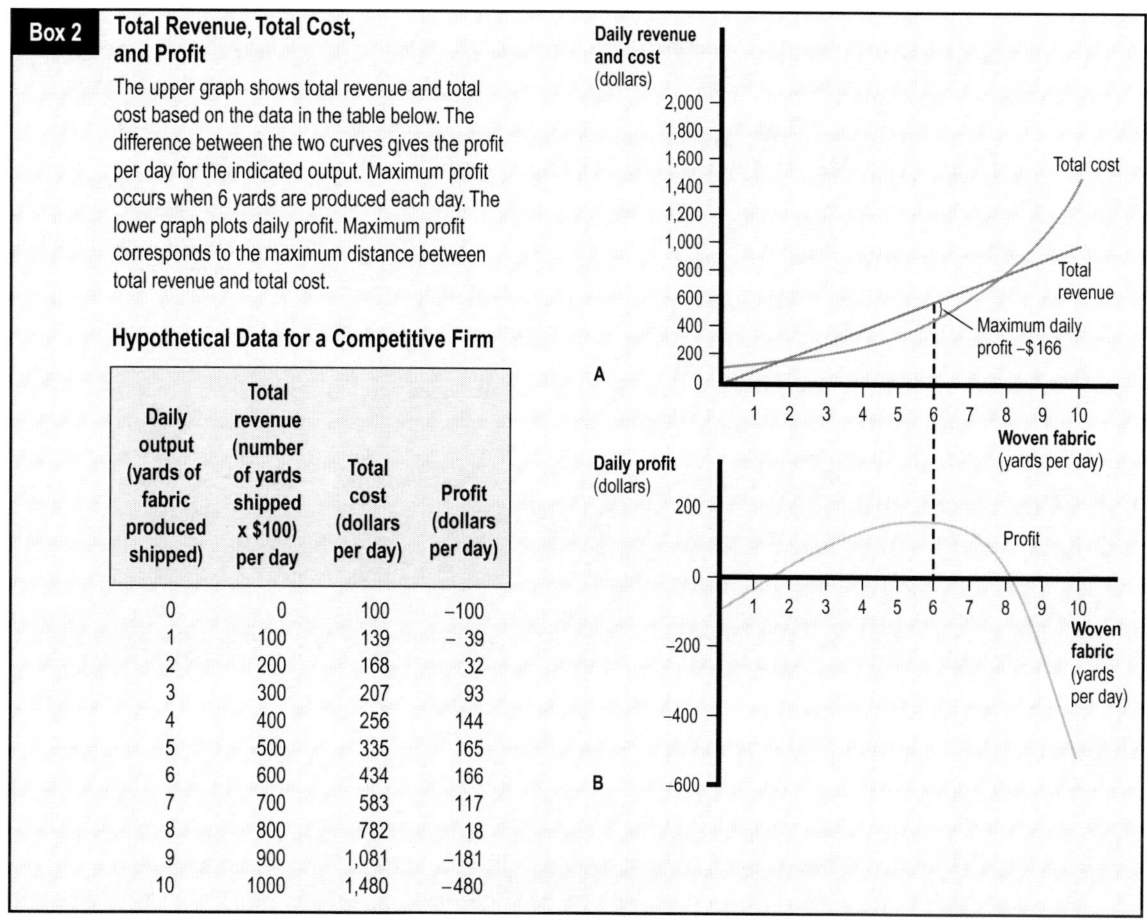

Box 2 Total Revenue, Total Cost, and Profit

The upper graph shows total revenue and total cost based on the data in the table below. The difference between the two curves gives the profit per day for the indicated output. Maximum profit occurs when 6 yards are produced each day. The lower graph plots daily profit. Maximum profit corresponds to the maximum distance between total revenue and total cost.

Hypothetical Data for a Competitive Firm

Daily output (yards of fabric produced shipped)	Total revenue (number of yards shipped x $100) per day	Total cost (dollars per day)	Profit (dollars per day)
0	0	100	–100
1	100	139	– 39
2	200	168	32
3	300	207	93
4	400	256	144
5	500	335	165
6	600	434	166
7	700	583	117
8	800	782	18
9	900	1,081	–181
10	1000	1,480	–480

fourth column. Profit is simply the difference between total revenue and total cost at each possible output level.

Graph **A** in Box 2 plots the total revenue and total cost curves for the data in Box 2 and shows profit graphically as the difference between the two curves. Graph **B** plots daily profit. Total revenue increases by $100 each time an extra yard of fabric is sold. The graph of total revenue is a straight line through the origin of the two axes because the change in total revenue (ΔTR) is always $100 when another yard is sold. The total cost curve has the shape typically assumed to exist in the short run. Its shape reflects the law of diminishing marginal returns. *The vertical distance between the total revenue and total cost curves gives profit at each level of production.* This difference is plotted directly below the total revenue and total cost curves.

You'll note that at low levels of output, Weaving Works would incur losses. *If it were to produce nothing, its losses would equal its fixed costs.* As production begins, profits increase, eventually reaching a maximum level. Maximum possible daily profits are earned when the firm sells 6 yards of woven fabric per day. If the firm were to produce more than 6 yards per day, profits would steadily decline and eventually become negative again. Given the price of its product and the way its cost varies as more is produced, the competitive firm therefore finds that its profit varies as it produces more and more per day. At low levels of output, it can expect to incur losses because it will earn little revenue but still incur fixed costs. As output increases, profits tend to rise at first but then tend to fall as the law of diminishing marginal returns comes into play. As the firm approaches its capacity to produce woven fabric, the rapid increase in costs tends to decrease profits.

Using Marginal Analysis to Choose the Profit-Maximizing Output: The Theory of Short-Run Supply

2 Business managers are seldom confronted with a neat graph like the one in Box 2 showing how profit varies with output. Managers usually grope for maximum profits by comparing the extra gains possible from additional production with the additional costs they incur. Marginal analysis is ideally suited to show how the benefits of actions are compared with their costs to achieve certain objectives. In this case your objective as the manager of Weaving Works is assumed to be the maximization of profit each day. To achieve this objective, as a rational manager you must compare the gain from producing and shipping more fabric with the cost of doing so. The gain to your firm of selling more fabric is the *extra revenue* from selling an additional yard of fabric. The cost of doing so is the *extra cost* of making the yard of fabric available.

Marginal Revenue, Marginal Cost, and Marginal Profit

The extra revenue obtained from selling an additional unit of a good is called the marginal revenue (MR) of output. We can compute marginal revenue for any given output by calculating the change in total revenue (ΔTR) associated with any given change in output sold (ΔQ):

$$MR = \frac{\Delta TR}{\Delta Q}$$

Because a competitive firm can sell all the output it wishes at the market price, it's easy to show that its marginal revenue will *always* equal the price of its product and therefore its average revenue. For example, if weavers can sell all the fabric they wish at the market price of $100 per yard, the extra revenue they'll take in for each extra yard they sell will be $100. As long as price is unaffected by the amount the firm sells, the marginal revenue of selling an additional yard of fabric will be its price. Because price is also average revenue, this means that for a competitive firm, $P = AR = MR$. It follows that the additional gain (*marginal revenue*) a competitive firm enjoys from selling output is measured by the market price of its product. In this case the marginal revenue is always $100.

Box 3 shows daily output, total revenue, and marginal revenue, assuming the price of a yard of fabric is $100. You can now convince yourself that marginal revenue equals price by observing that total revenue increases by $100 each time an additional yard is sold.

The *marginal cost* is the extra cost of selling an additional unit of a good. In the table in Box 4, the marginal cost is obtained by calculating the extra cost associated with each extra yard of fabric produced and shipped. Notice how marginal cost decreases at first but then steadily increases as the firm approaches its short-run maximum output of 10 yards per day. This pattern of variation in marginal cost reflects the law of diminishing marginal returns as the firm tries to produce more in the short run.

In Box 4, the marginal cost of each output is measured by calculating the increase in total cost incurred to increase output to that level. For example, total costs rise by $39 with production of the first yard of fabric as $39 in variable costs are incurred in addition to the $100 fixed cost per day. The marginal cost of the first unit is therefore $39. Similarly, the marginal cost of any given output level can be calculated by determining the increase in total costs incurred when output is increased by one unit to that amount. The marginal cost of 5 yards is therefore the total cost incurred to produce 5 yards less the total cost incurred when only 4 yards are produced. This is equal to $335 minus $256, which is $79. Accordingly, the table lists $79 as the marginal cost of 5 yards of fabric per day.

Box 3 Output, Total Revenue, and Marginal Revenue for a Competitive Firm (Hypothetical Data)

Daily output (yards of fabric produced and shipped)	Total revenue (dollars per day)	Marginal revenue (dollars per yard)
0	0	100
1	100	100
2	200	100
3	300	100
4	400	100
5	500	100
6	600	100
7	700	100
8	800	100
9	900	100
10	1,000	100

Box 4 Marginal Cost Calculated from Total Cost for a Competitive Firm (Hypothetical Data)

Daily output (yards of fabric produced and shipped)	Total cost (dollars per day)	Marginal cost = $\frac{\Delta TC}{\Delta Q}$ (dollars per yard)
0	100	—
1	139	39
2	168	29
3	207	39
4	256	49
5	335	79
6	434	99
7	583	149
8	782	199
9	1,081	299
10	1,480	399

In choosing the profit-maximizing output, managers can be thought of as comparing the marginal cost with the marginal revenue for each extra yard of fabric sold. When marginal revenue exceeds marginal cost, selling an additional yard will increase profits. The marginal cost influences the willingness of firms to sell more. When marginal revenue falls short of marginal cost, sale of an additional yard will decrease profits.

The marginal profit is the change in profit from selling an additional unit of a good, representing the difference between the marginal revenue from that unit and its marginal cost. The marginal profit represents the firm's net gain from making an additional unit available. When the marginal profit is positive, Weaving Works adds to total profits by selling more fabric. When the marginal profit is negative, Weaving Works would reduce its profits if it sold more fabric.

Profit Maximization: Choosing the Output

Box 5, which is based on the data in previous tables, shows how marginal revenue, marginal cost, and marginal profit vary as more output is made available for sale. The next to last column of the table calculates marginal profit from the following formula:

$$\text{Marginal profit} = MR - MC$$

Box 5 Marginal Analysis for Profit Maximization

Daily output (yards of fabric produced and shipped)	Marginal revenue = Price (dollars per yard)	Marginal cost (dollars per yard)	Marginal profit (dollars per yard)	Total Profit (dollars per yard)
0	0	—	—	–100
1	100	39	61	–39
2	100	29	71	32
3	100	39	61	93
4	100	49	51	144
5	100	79	21	165
6	100	99	1	166
7	100	149	–49	117
8	100	199	–90	18
9	100	299	–199	–181
10	100	399	–299	–480

A firm maximizes profits by continuing to produce up to the point at which marginal revenue just equals marginal cost. The condition for maximum profit is therefore

$$MR = MC$$

Whenever marginal revenue exceeds marginal cost, producing more will result in extra revenue that exceeds the extra cost. This causes increases in profit, so marginal profit will be positive. Whenever marginal cost exceeds marginal revenue, the extra output will cost more than the revenue it brings in, so profit will fall. Marginal profit in this case will be negative. *Marginal analysis therefore shows that a firm can continue to increase profits up to the point at which marginal revenue equals marginal cost.*

Because price (P) is equal to marginal revenue for a competitive firm, maximum profits for such firms occur when output has been adjusted to the point at which

$$P = MC$$

Any output below this level means that the firm can increase profits by producing more. Any output above the point at which marginal cost equals the product price means that the firm can increase profits by producing less.

Box 5 shows that Weaving Works can continue to increase profits by producing more fabric until it produces 6 yards per day. Up to that point the $100 marginal revenue from selling fabric exceeds the marginal cost of making the fabric available. If the firm produces a seventh yard per day, its marginal cost rises to $149. This exceeds the marginal revenue of $100 that could be obtained from selling that final yard. The firm would therefore reduce its profits by selling the seventh yard. The last column of the table shows that profit would fall from the maximum of $166 per day to $117 per day if the firm were to produce and sell a seventh yard. Notice how the firm's choice of output depends *both* on the market price of fabric and on the way the marginal cost of making fabric available to buyers varies as more fabric is actually produced.

In Box 6, graph **A** shows Weaving Works's choice of the profit-maximizing output. Along the firm's demand curve, $P = MR =$ \$100. The marginal cost curve intersects the firm's demand curve at point B. Equilibrium output corresponding to that level of marginal cost is 6 yards per day. If the firm were to produce one unit more than 6 yards per day, marginal cost would exceed marginal revenue and profit would decline. In Box 6, graph **B** shows the profit curve based on the data in Box 5. Notice how maximum profit is achieved at the point where 6 yards per day are produced.

Box 6

Profit Maximization by a Competitive Firm

At the profit-maximizing output, $P = MC$. The firm earns economic profits equal to the shaded area *ABCD*.

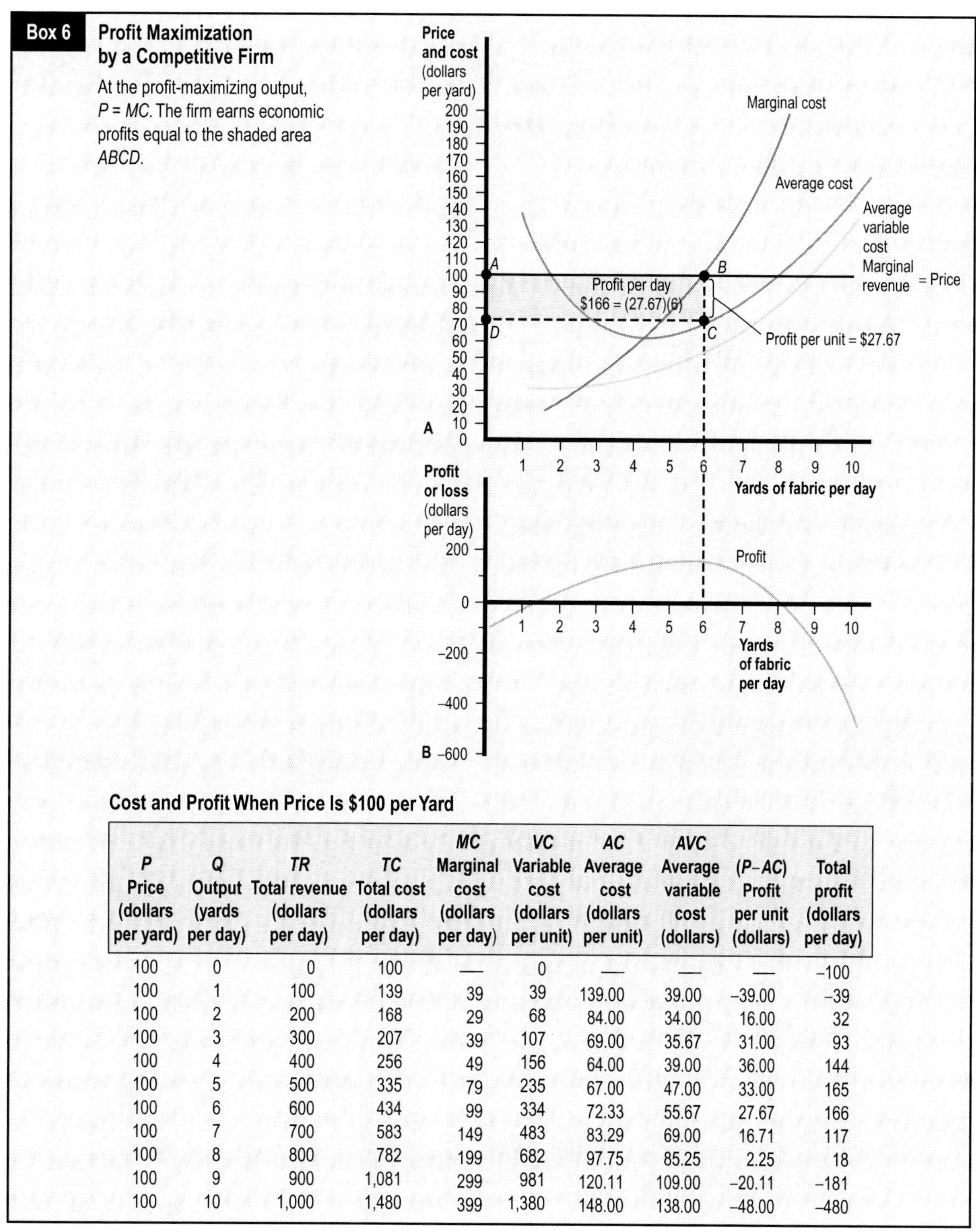

Cost and Profit When Price Is $100 per Yard

P Price (dollars per yard)	*Q* Output (yards per day)	*TR* Total revenue (dollars per day)	*TC* Total cost (dollars per day)	*MC* Marginal cost (dollars per day)	*VC* Variable cost (dollars per unit)	*AC* Average cost (dollars per unit)	*AVC* Average variable cost (dollars)	(*P–AC*) Profit per unit (dollars)	Total profit (dollars per day)
100	0	0	100	—	0	—	—	—	–100
100	1	100	139	39	39	139.00	39.00	–39.00	–39
100	2	200	168	29	68	84.00	34.00	16.00	32
100	3	300	207	39	107	69.00	35.67	31.00	93
100	4	400	256	49	156	64.00	39.00	36.00	144
100	5	500	335	79	235	67.00	47.00	33.00	165
100	6	600	434	99	334	72.33	55.67	27.67	166
100	7	700	583	149	483	83.29	69.00	16.71	117
100	8	800	782	199	682	97.75	85.25	2.25	18
100	9	900	1,081	299	981	120.11	109.00	–20.11	–181
100	10	1,000	1,480	399	1,380	148.00	138.00	–48.00	–480

Profit per Unit versus Total Profit

Box 6, based on the data in Box 2, shows how average cost, average variable cost, and profit per unit of output vary as your firm produces more fabric. The firm's daily profit at the equilibrium output is represented by the area of the rectangle *ABCD* in Box 6. The height of the rectangle, $P - AC$, is the profit per unit of output sold, where P is the price of the product and AC is the average cost of production. The width of the rectangle is the quantity produced. Total profit equals profit per unit multiplied by the number of units sold:

$$\text{Total profit} = (\text{Profit per unit})(\text{Output sold}) = (P - AC)Q$$

3 According to the data in the Box 6 table, at a price of $100 per yard, the profit per yard is $27.67 at the profit-maximizing output. Selling 6 yards per day at this price gives Weaving Works a total profit of $166 per day. Notice that the profit-maximizing output is *not* the output for which *profit per unit* is highest. It would be a mistake, therefore, for managers of a profit-maximizing firm to use profit per unit as an indication of total profit. For the data in the table, maximum profit per unit is $36, which occurs when a daily output of only 4 yards is sold. Note that maximum profit per unit corresponds to the output for which average cost is at a minimum. However, at the point of actual maximum profits, profit per unit is only about $27.67 and output is 6 yards per day. *This shows that the output at which profits are maximized is not necessarily the output at which the plant achieves the minimum possible average cost of production.* To maximize profits, a business manager must carefully gauge marginal costs. Comparing average cost instead of marginal cost with marginal revenue doesn't guide the manager to the point of maximum profit.

How Maximum Possible Profit Depends on Market Price

When the market price is greater than the average cost of production at the profit-maximizing output, as is the case in the Box 6 graphs, the firm earns economic profits. Suppose instead that the price of the product is lower. For example, suppose a decrease in the market demand for the standardized fabric produced by Weaving Works causes its price to fall to $63. Assume nothing else changes that might affect the firm's cost curves. The data in Box 6 reveal that minimum possible average cost is a bit less than $64. To understand why, notice that the marginal cost of 4 yards of fabric is $49, while the average cost of the 4 yards is $64. Because marginal cost is below average cost, it follows that average cost must still be declining. However, when output is increased to 5 yards per day, marginal cost rises to $79, while average cost goes up to $67. We know that when marginal cost is above average cost, average cost will rise. From this information we can infer that Weaving Works' minimum possible average cost of production is less than $64 and that it occurs when between 4 and 5 yards of fabric are produced per day. Let's assume the minimum possible average cost of production is $63 per yard and that it occurs when Weaving Works produces 4.5 yards of fabric per day.

Marginal cost must equal average cost when average cost is at a minimum. As shown in Box 7, if the price were to fall to $63 per yard, the profit-maximizing output would correspond to 4.5 yards per day, where marginal cost just equals $63. At that output the firm earns zero economic profit because profit per unit ($P - AC$) is zero. Here the best the firm's owners can do is to cover all of their explicit and implicit costs.

Economic profit is the difference between a firm's total revenue and its total economic cost. A firm earns zero economic profit when it takes in just enough revenue to cover its explicit and implicit costs. When price falls to the minimum possible average cost, the firm's owners are earning just as much as they could in their next best alternative.

Remember that economic costs differ from accounting costs when some inputs are supplied by owners of the firm. It's therefore possible for profits as measured by an accountant to be positive when economic profits are zero. The difference between total revenue and accounting costs is the implicit costs of owner-supplied inputs. The implicit costs that show up as profit on the accountant's books are sometimes called *normal profit*.

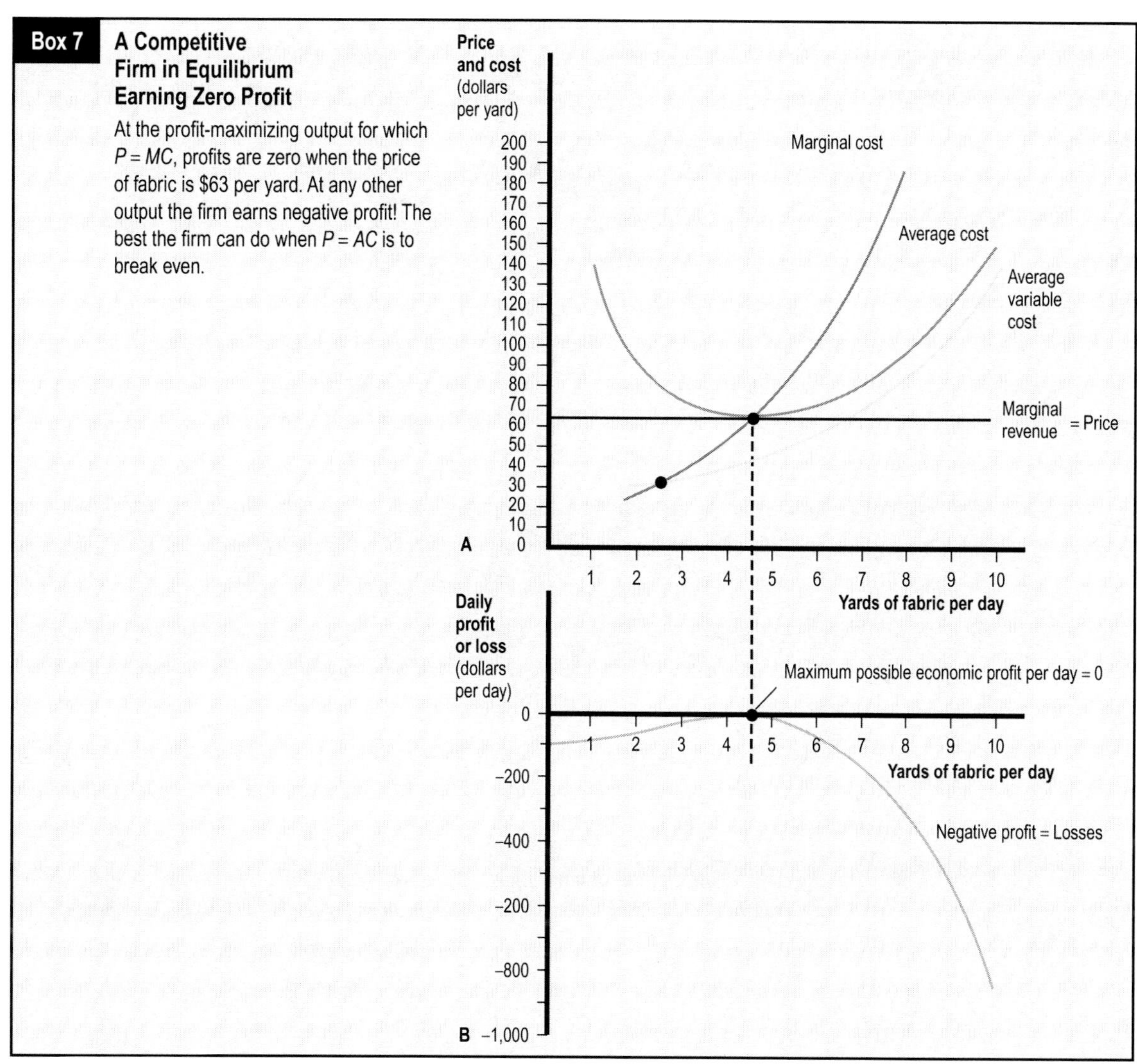
Box 7
A Competitive Firm in Equilibrium Earning Zero Profit
At the profit-maximizing output for which P = MC, profits are zero when the price of fabric is $63 per yard. At any other output the firm earns negative profit! The best the firm can do when P = AC is to break even.
Price and cost (dollars per yard)
Marginal cost
Average cost
Average variable cost
Marginal revenue = Price
A
Yards of fabric per day
Daily profit or loss (dollars per day)
Maximum possible economic profit per day = 0
Yards of fabric per day
Negative profit = Losses
B

When economic profit is zero, a firm's owners therefore earn a normal profit, which is just enough to keep them from transferring their resources to an alternative use in the long run. When economists use the term *profit*, they always mean *economic profit.*

The actual market price influences the maximum possible profits a firm can earn. A market price above the minimum possible average cost of production will allow the firm to enjoy economic profits. If price falls to the minimum possible average cost, the firm will just cover its economic cost and not earn any profit at the equilibrium output. The profit a firm earns always varies with output no matter what the market price of its product. However, the level of the market price for the product sold by the competitive firm affects the *level* of actual profits at the output for which marginal revenue just equals marginal cost.

Box 7 illustrates the case of a firm earning zero economic profit. This firm is earning just enough revenue to cover all of its economic costs. Since price equals average cost, the profit per unit is equal to zero. The area $(P - AC)Q$ also becomes zero. Because marginal cost equals average cost at the latter's minimum point, $P = MC = AC$ at the point of minimum average cost. Graph **A** in Box 7 therefore shows that a competitive firm, one for which the demand curve is horizontal, breaks even (meaning that it earns enough revenue to cover all of its costs) at the level of output corresponding to minimum average cost. Graph **B** in Box 7 shows how profits vary with output when the market price is $63. At any output other than the equilibrium output, profit will be negative! At the $63 price the best Weaving Works can do is make zero profits. If it were to produce more, its profits would evaporate into losses. If it were to produce less, its profits would become negative as well. *The marginal analysis remains foolproof: The level of output for which MR = MC still gives maximum profits. In the case for which price also equals minimum possible average cost, maximum possible profits are zero.*

Using Marginal Analysis to Choose Output When Market Price Is below Minimum Possible Average Cost

What happens if price falls below the level corresponding to the minimum possible average cost of production? For example, if the market price of fabric were to fall below the minimum possible average cost of $63, what would you as manager of Weaving Works choose to do? At any price below $63, you couldn't cover your economic costs. This means you'll incur losses rather than profits at the level of output for which marginal revenue equals marginal cost. You can earn more by employing your inputs elsewhere. In the short run, however, producers often find they lose less by remaining in business than by shutting down! A shut-down firm produces nothing but still incurs fixed costs in the short run.

The graphs in Box 8 show the case of a firm in the unfortunate position of incurring losses at the market price of its output. At a price of $40 per yard, the firm incurs economic losses because that price is below the minimum possible average cost of $63. By still producing up to the output level at which *MR* = *MC*, it can *minimize* those losses. The output corresponding to the point of minimum loss is 3 yards of fabric per day. The loss at that level of output is represented by the area *ABED* in graph **A** in Box 8. Graph **B** shows that positive profits aren't possible at any output when the price is at such a low level. The firm would incur greater losses if it produced any output greater or less than the one for which marginal revenue just equals marginal cost. *When positive profits are not possible, marginal analysis can be used to pick the option that results in the smallest losses!*

If the Weaving Works produces 3 yards of fabric per day that it sells at a price of $40 per yard, it generates $120 in revenue per day. Its total cost of producing the fabric (from Box 6) is $207. The loss it incurs is therefore $87 per day. If it produces any other quantity of fabric, the firm loses still more per day, as you can see in **B** in Box 8.

If you choose to shut down the factory, you'll have zero variable cost and produce zero output. However, you'll still incur losses in the short run because you'll have to pay the firm's fixed cost until its leases and other commitments expire. In this case fixed cost per day is $100.

If you were to shut down, you'd have no revenue to offset your $100 fixed cost. Your losses would therefore be $100 per day. If, on the other hand, you continue to operate, producing the output for which *MR* = *MC*, you will generate enough revenue to cover *all* of your variable cost and some of your fixed cost. Your loss will be only $87 if you continue to operate. For a profit-maximizing firm, losing $87 a day is a better alternative than losing $100 a day! You therefore continue to operate.

The Decision to Shut Down in the Short Run

4 As long as the market price exceeds the minimum possible average variable cost of production, Weaving Works will continue to operate even at a loss in the short run rather than shut down. To see this, recall that the vertical distance between the *AC* and *AVC* curves is average fixed cost (*AFC*). Therefore, at an output of 3 yards per day, fixed

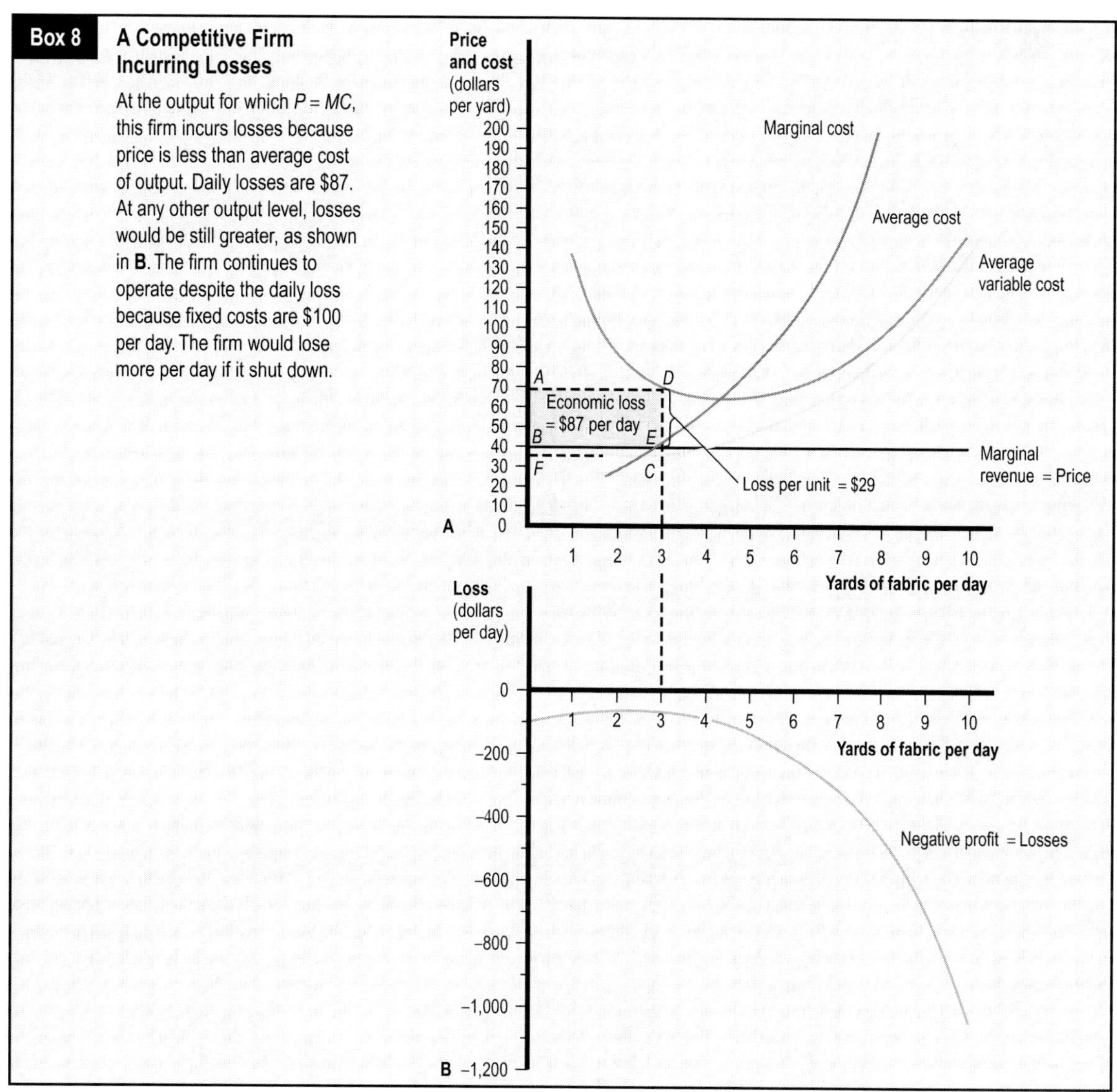
Box 8
A Competitive Firm Incurring Losses
At the output for which $P = MC$, this firm incurs losses because price is less than average cost of output. Daily losses are $87. At any other output level, losses would be still greater, as shown in B. The firm continues to operate despite the daily loss because fixed costs are $100 per day. The firm would lose more per day if it shut down.
Price and cost (dollars per yard)
Marginal cost
Average cost
Average variable cost
Economic loss = $87 per day
Loss per unit = $29
Marginal revenue = Price
Yards of fabric per day
Loss (dollars per day)
Negative profit = Losses
A
B
C
D
E
F

cost can be represented by the rectangle *AFCD* in Box 8. The height of this rectangle is average fixed cost, while its length is the equilibrium quantity of output (Q). By shutting down, Weaving Works would generate no revenue to offset its fixed costs. Short-run losses would therefore be equal to fixed costs if the firm ceased operations.

By continuing to operate, Weaving Works would lose the amount represented by the area *ABED* in Box 8. The distance *DE* represents ($AC - P$), the daily loss per unit of output. The distance *BE* is the output. Multiplying these two distances gives total losses. As long as price is greater than the average variable cost at the output for which $MR = MC$, the loss from remaining in business will be less than fixed cost, which is the short-run loss incurred by shutting down.

The graph in Box 9 shows that if price falls below the minimum possible average variable cost, Weaving Works will shut down immediately. When price has fallen to a level below that which just allows the firm to cover its minimum possible average variable cost, the firm is at the shutdown point. When price has fallen to minimum possible average variable

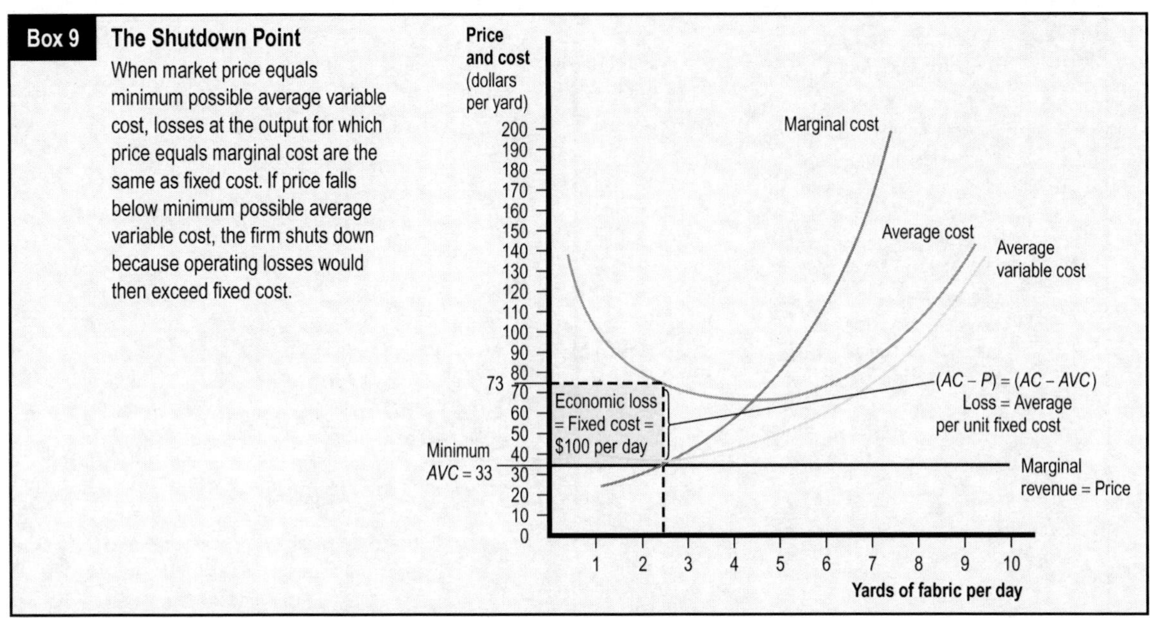

Box 9 The Shutdown Point

When market price equals minimum possible average variable cost, losses at the output for which price equals marginal cost are the same as fixed cost. If price falls below minimum possible average variable cost, the firm shuts down because operating losses would then exceed fixed cost.

cost, the loss per unit is equal to average fixed cost. The loss from continuing to operate will exactly equal fixed cost.

If price were to fall below the minimum possible *AVC*, the losses from remaining in operation would exceed fixed cost and Weaving Works would cease operating. At any price below the minimum possible *AVC*, the loss per unit (*AC* – *P*) would exceed average fixed cost. This is because the vertical distance between the firm's demand curve and its average cost curve would exceed the vertical distance between *AC* and *AVC*.

The data in Box 6 reveal that the minimum possible average variable cost occurs when between 2 and 3 yards of fabric are produced daily. You can infer this because marginal cost is below average variable cost when 2 yards are produced daily at an average variable cost of $34. As output is increased to 3 yards, however, average variable cost rises to $35.67 per yard and marginal cost begins to exceed average variable cost. It follows that the minimum possible average variable cost occurs when the plant is operated to produce more than 2 but less than 3 yards of fabric per day. Assume that minimum possible average variable cost is $33 per yard and that this occurs when output is 2.5 yards per day.

At an output of 2.5 yards per day, marginal cost is also just equal to $33 per yard because marginal cost must equal average variable cost at the minimum point of the *AVC* curve. If price were to fall to $33 per yard, you would therefore choose to produce 2.5 yards as the output that would minimize economic losses. Box 9 shows that the average cost of 2.5 yards of output would be $73. You would therefore lose $40 per yard at that output and your total economic loss for the 2.5 yards of output would be $100. Your economic loss at this output is *exactly equal to your fixed costs*. If price were to fall below this level, you would choose to shut down because operating losses would exceed fixed costs.

For example, suppose price were to fall to $30. At that price the best you could do is produce 2 yards of output at a marginal cost of $29. You would take in $60 of revenue daily and incur total costs of $168. (See the second column of Box 4 for total cost data.) Your minimum possible economic loss would therefore be $108 if price were $30. Because this exceeds your fixed costs of $100, you would lose less by shutting down than by continuing to operate Weaving Works.

To sum up, the firm elects to continue operating at a loss in the short run only if total revenue exceeds variable costs. This allows the firm to generate revenue to cover some of its fixed costs.

The Competitive Firm's Short-Run Supply Curve

5 Next we'll look at how the supply curve relates to the various cost curves. As you know, a supply curve shows a relationship between price and quantity supplied. To maximize profits, a competitive firm always adjusts output until price is equal to marginal cost. The marginal cost curve therefore gives the relationship between price and the quantity supplied by the competitive firm. Price must exceed minimum possible average variable cost of production; otherwise, the firm will cease operations. The quantity supplied by the firm at any price below minimum possible *AVC* will be zero. *The competitive firm's* short-run supply curve *is therefore that portion of its marginal cost curve above the minimum point of its average variable cost curve.* This is illustrated in Box 10.

Short-run supply curves slope upward because the firm's marginal costs tend to increase as output is increased. When firms operate within a fixed plant or facility, marginal cost eventually increases. To induce a profit-maximizing firm to supply more output, market price must rise to cover increased marginal cost as the firm increases output. Of course, marginal costs increase as a consequence of the law of diminishing marginal returns. It follows that the underlying cause of upward-sloping supply curves in the short run is diminishing marginal returns to the use of variable inputs.

To determine quantity supplied by the competitive firm at any price, draw a horizontal line from that price to the marginal cost curve. At any price below minimum possible *AVC*, quantity supplied in the short run is zero. At a price P_1, for example, quantity supplied is Q_1. At a higher price, P_2, quantity supplied is Q_2. You can see this in Box 10.

Market Supply

Let's turn from a single company's supply curve to an industrywide supply curve. A market supply curve gives the sum of the quantities supplied by all firms producing a product at each possible price over a given period. Such a curve can be derived from the supply curves of competitive firms. To do this, assume that input prices and technology are given. In particular, assume that prices of variable inputs used to produce the product are independent of the total quantity produced by all sellers. If this is the case, the market

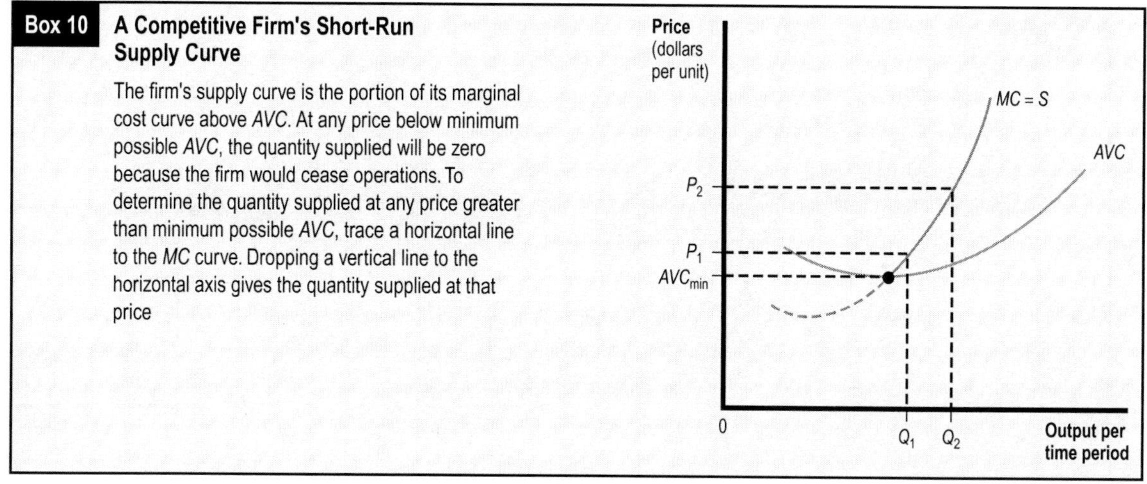

Box 10 A Competitive Firm's Short-Run Supply Curve

The firm's supply curve is the portion of its marginal cost curve above *AVC*. At any price below minimum possible *AVC*, the quantity supplied will be zero because the firm would cease operations. To determine the quantity supplied at any price greater than minimum possible *AVC*, trace a horizontal line to the *MC* curve. Dropping a vertical line to the horizontal axis gives the quantity supplied at that price

supply curve is the horizontal summation of the marginal cost curves of all firms producing the standardized product.

Assume there are 1,000 small firms producing exactly the same standardized woven fabric. Assume as well, for simplicity, that all these firms are the same size and have exactly the same cost curves. At a price of $100 per yard, each firm will supply 6 yards per day. Total quantity supplied at that price will be 6(1,000), or 6,000, yards per day, corresponding to point *E* on the market supply curve in Box 11, where the market demand curve intersects the market supply curve. Similarly, to find the market quantity supplied at any other price, find the quantity supplied by each firm at that price and multiply that quantity by the number of firms selling in the market. To maximize profits under perfect competition, each firm adjusts output until price equals marginal cost of production. The market supply curve is upward sloping because each firm's individual supply curve slopes upward.

When firms are of equal size and have exactly the same cost curves, we obtain the quantity supplied to the market by multiplying the output of a typical firm by the number of firms supplying the product. If firms are not of equal size or have different marginal cost curves, simply add the quantity supplied by all firms to obtain the quantity supplied to the market at each price.

The determinants of market supply are

1. The number of firms in the industry selling in the market.
2. The average size of firms in the industry measured by the average productive capacity of individual firms.
3. The prices of the variable inputs used by firms in the industry.
4. The technology employed by firms in the industry.

The last three determinants affect the marginal cost of individual firms. For example, larger firms employ more fixed inputs, which means their physical production facilities are designed to produce higher output. This means larger firms achieve the minimum possible average cost and the minimum possible average variable cost at a higher output level than do smaller firms. As a result, the marginal cost curves lie farther out from the origin for larger firms than for smaller firms. Accordingly, the larger a firm, the greater the quantity supplied at any given price. Therefore, the greater the average size of firms supplying a product to a market, the greater the quantity supplied at any given price. The higher the prices of variable inputs, the higher the marginal cost associated with any given

Box 11 Market Supply

The market supply curve is the sum of the quantities supplied by all firms producing the good at each possible price. At a price of $P^* = \$100$ per yard, each producer will supply 6 yards per month. If there are 1,000 producers, market quantity supplied is 6,000 yards per month.

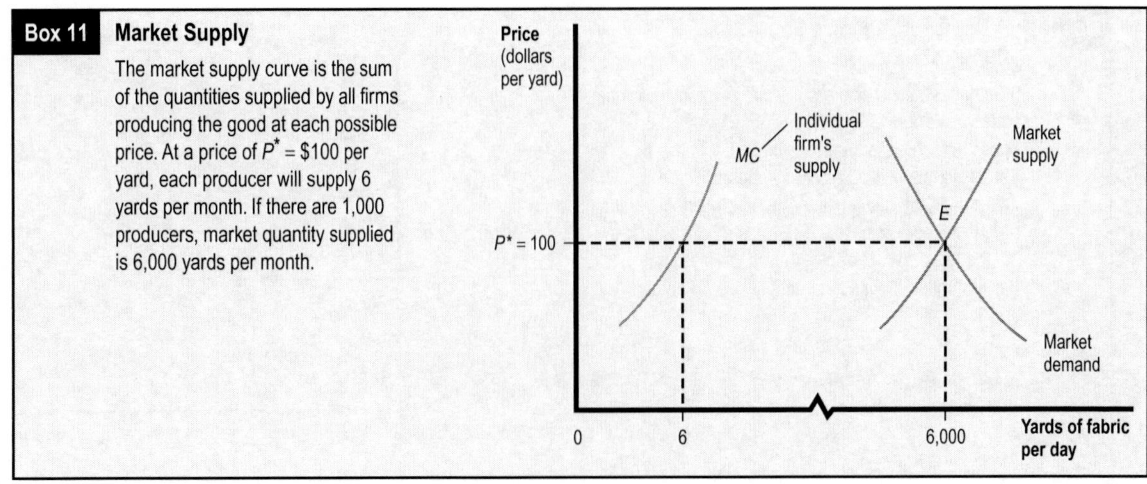

output. This means that an increase in the prices of variable inputs tends to shift the firms' marginal cost curves upward. As this occurs, firms will produce less output at a given price. It follows that an increase in the prices of variable inputs will decrease supply. Finally, when firms in an industry employ a new technology that reduces the marginal cost of production, each firm's marginal cost curve will shift downward. The downward shift in marginal cost will increase the quantity supplied by each firm at each price. An improvement in technology that shifts marginal cost curves downward for firms in a perfectly competitive market will therefore contribute to an increase in supply.

Using the Theory of Competitive Supply

A Reduction in the Price of a Variable Input: How a Decrease in Materials Prices Affects Market Supply and Market Price

6 A change in input prices will affect costs of production. This will affect both the competitive firm's supply curve and the market supply curve. Suppose the price of yarn used in the production of fabric declines. **A** decrease in the price of any variable input used by producers, other things being equal, decreases variable costs. The short-run effects of a decrease in the price of this variable input on the market price of fabric, and on the quantity produced, for a typical competitive firm are illustrated in Box 12.

The decrease in the price of the variable input causes a downward shift in average variable costs, average costs, and marginal costs. Graph **A** in Box 12 shows the impact of the decrease in the price of yarn on *AC* and *MC* for a typical competitive firm such as Weaving Works. The price decrease of the variable input shifts the average and marginal cost curves downward from MC_1 to MC_2 and from AC_1 to AC_2. If the market price were to remain at $100 a yard, its initial level, each competitive firm would increase production until MC_2 equaled $100. However, as all firms increase production in response to the decrease in marginal cost, the market supply increases from S_1 to S_2, as shown in graph **B** in Box 12. Given the level of demand, this results in a decrease in the market price of fabric from $100 to $80 a yard. In equilibrium at the new price, each firm produces the output corresponding to the point at which MC_2 equals $80. The output corresponding to

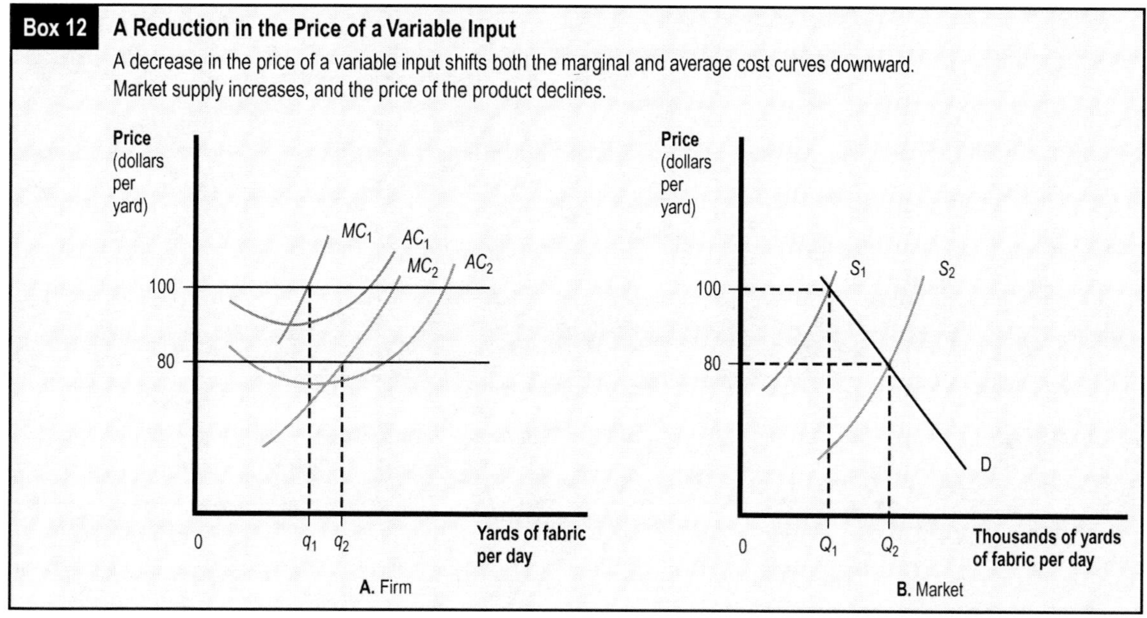

Box 12 A Reduction in the Price of a Variable Input

A decrease in the price of a variable input shifts both the marginal and average cost curves downward. Market supply increases, and the price of the product declines.

this is q_2. As all firms increase output, the market equilibrium quantity increases from Q_1 to Q_2, as shown in **B** in Box 12. A decrease in the price of a variable input for all producers therefore results in a decrease in market price as market supply increases.

A Change in the Price of a Fixed Input: The Short-Run Impact of License Fees and Fixed Annual Subsidies

Moving from variable inputs to fixed inputs, we see that a change in the price of a *fixed input* affects fixed costs and average costs. However, it has no effect on variable costs or marginal costs. As we'll see, this has some interesting implications for policies that affect the prices of fixed rather than variable inputs.

Suppose the market for contractors' services in your state is competitive. The state government, in an effort to raise extra revenue, decides to triple the contractor's annual license fee, raising it from $1,000 to $3,000. A license fee is a fixed input in the practice of an occupation or activity. It must be paid independent of the amount of services sold. In the short run, therefore, an increase in such fees is equivalent to an increase in fixed costs.

Graph **A** in Box 13 assumes that the price per square foot of construction was initially $50. At that price contractors just broke even, earning zero profit. Before the increase in the license fee, price was just equal to the minimum possible average cost, and firms just covered their economic costs at their equilibrium output at which $P = AC = MC$. The increase in the license fee has no effect on variable costs. It does, however, increase average costs. As the average cost curve shifts upward, the distance between the AVC curve and the AC curve increases, reflecting the increase in average fixed costs at any level of output. Because marginal cost depends only on variable cost, the increase in the license fee has no effect on that curve. The market supply curve doesn't shift because the license fee doesn't affect the marginal cost curve. The price of construction therefore remains at $50 per square foot, as shown in graph **B** in Box 13.

Each contractor continues to produce the same level of output, q_1 square feet per year, where MC = $50. Market equilibrium output remains Q_1 square feet per year. Nothing changes *except* the profit earned by contractors. The typical contractor was assumed to be just

Box 13 A Change in the Price of a Fixed Input

An increase in the price of a fixed input shifts the *AC* curve upward but has no effect on the *AVC* or *MC* curves. Because *MC* is not affected by the change in price, there is no change in supply and market price remains the same in the short run. If $P = AC$ before the increase in price of the fixed input, the firm will incur losses equal to the shaded area.

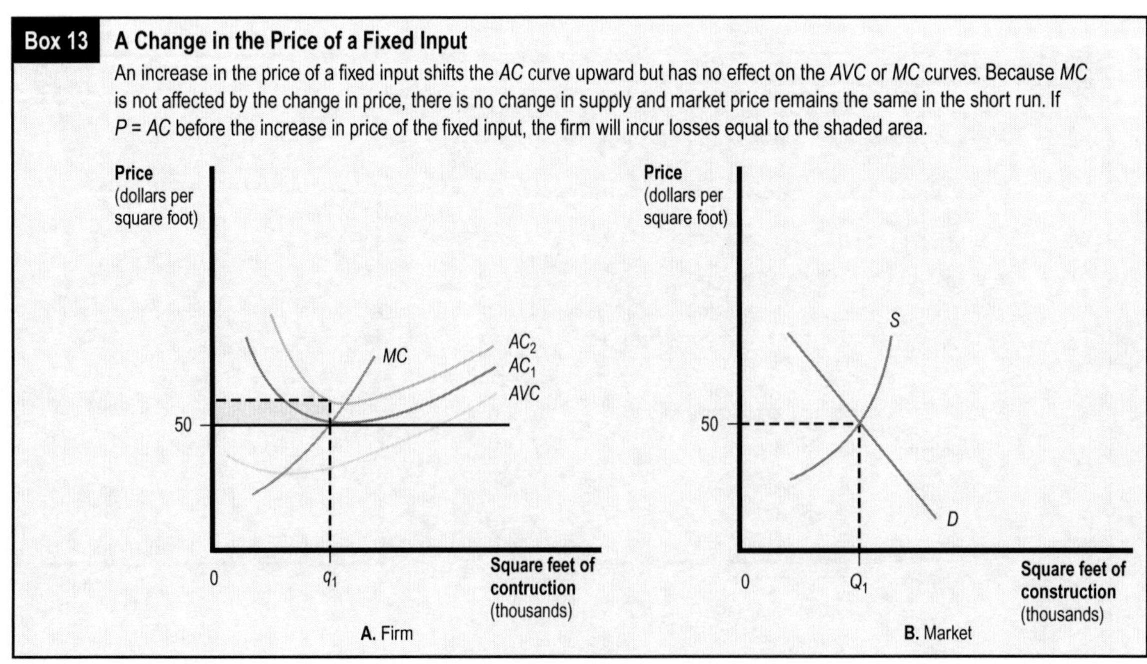

breaking even before the increase in *AC*. The increased fee therefore results in losses equal to the shaded area in **A** in Box 13. Price remains above *AVC* because neither *AVC* nor *MC* is affected by the license fee increase. The short-run impact of the increased license fee is therefore confined to the profits of contractors. Neither price nor marginal cost is affected.

A similar analysis holds for a *decrease* in fixed costs. Any factors decreasing fixed costs won't influence either price or supply in a competitive market in the short run. For example, if the government *reduces* license fees for the purpose of increasing construction, there will be no effect on the amount supplied in the short run. If authorities want a rapid increase in the amount of construction supplied, they must reduce the price of a *variable* input used by contractors.

For example, suppose a government offers farmers a fixed subsidy of $10,000 a year to get them to produce more food. This would be a windfall to farmers. It would decrease their average costs of operation while having no effect on their variable or marginal costs. Accordingly, their profits would increase, but there would be no increase in the quantity of food supplied in the short run. Over the long run, however, there would be an increase in supply as more individuals entered food-related businesses.

Marginal Analysis: Key Insights and Conclusions

Our marginal analysis of decisions made by profit-maximizing firms shows that, in the short run, market supply curves in competitive markets are upward sloping. The reason for this is rooted in the law of diminishing marginal returns, which implies that marginal costs of production eventually increase in the short run. Competitive firms are in equilibrium when they produce the output corresponding to the point at which price equals marginal cost, provided price is higher than average variable cost at that point. The price is the marginal revenue for a competitive firm. Because marginal cost tends to increase as more output is made available in the short run, the firm will increase quantity supplied only if price increases. The increase in price causes marginal revenue to exceed marginal cost at the existing output. This allows additional profits from increased quantity supplied. Firms then increase output until marginal cost increases to equal the higher price. Supply curves slope upward because marginal cost increases with increased output in the short run.

In gauging the profitability of producing more output, firms must estimate marginal costs. Knowing average cost down to the penny isn't enough. *Marginal cost is the relevant figure to calculate before deciding to increase or decrease output if the firm's goal is to maximize profit.* As is the case in most marginal analysis of behavior, the key to using it is to find out how changes in economic conditions affect marginal benefits and costs. Increases in market demand tend to increase market prices and thereby to increase marginal revenue, which is the marginal benefit, to sellers. To understand and forecast shifts in supply, we must forecast the impact on marginal cost of changes in such conditions as input prices and technology.

The theory of supply in perfectly competitive markets isolates the cause-and-effect relationship between price and quantity supplied. The simplifying assumptions of the perfect competition model are clearly unrealistic. Nonetheless, the model gives us useful insights in cases where a firm has enough competitors and sells a product very similar (but not identical) to those of its competitors. The model is relevant as long as it's reasonable to assume that firms largely react to prices set by broad forces of supply and demand in a market, without the ability to influence those prices appreciably by producing more or less by themselves. Hypotheses based on the perfect competition model are widely supported by evidence. As the price of a product such as personal computers goes up, the quantity supplied increases. Similarly, decreases in the variable costs of producing personal computers caused by improved technology tend to increase supply. The insights we obtain from the model of supply in perfectly competitive markets are therefore useful, despite the fact that few markets conform exactly to the model's assumptions.

Summary

1. Competitive firms react to prices. A competitive firm is a price taker in the sense that it considers the price of its output as beyond its influence.
2. A perfectly competitive market consists of many sellers and buyers. Each seller has a small market share and sells a standardized product that is also sold by many competing sellers in the market. Information is freely available in such a market, and both buyers and sellers can freely enter or exit the market as they choose.
3. The demand curve for the output of a perfectly competitive firm is perfectly elastic at the product's market price. However, the demand curve for the product of the industry to which the competitive firm belongs is downward sloping.
4. Marginal revenue is the extra revenue obtained from selling an additional unit of output. If a seller can sell all it wishes at the market price, as is the case for a competitive firm, marginal revenue is equal to price. Another term for price is average revenue, which is total revenue divided by the quantity of output sold.
5. A firm can increase total profit by selling more as long as marginal cost doesn't exceed marginal revenue. Marginal profit is zero when marginal revenue just equals marginal cost. At the point at which marginal revenue equals marginal cost, profit is at a maximum because additional sales would decrease profit. The equilibrium output of a profit-maximizing competitive firm corresponds to the output for which marginal revenue equals marginal cost.
6. A profit-maximizing firm will operate at a loss in the short run as long as the market price is greater than the minimum possible average variable cost. However, when price falls below minimum possible average variable cost, the firm will cease operating because at so low a price its losses would exceed its fixed costs at the output for which marginal revenue equals marginal cost. The firm is at the shutdown point when price equals the minimum possible average variable cost of production.
7. A firm's short-run supply curve is the portion of its marginal cost curve lying above its average variable cost curve. Short-run supply curves tend to be upward sloping because the marginal cost of production tends to increase as more goods are made available for sale in markets. Short-run market supply is obtained by adding the quantities supplied by all the sellers in a market at various prices.
8. Changes in the prices of variable inputs shift marginal cost curves and therefore result in changes in supply in the short run. However, because changes in the prices of fixed inputs don't affect variable costs, they do not shift marginal cost curves and therefore do not change supply in the short run.

Concept Review

1. List the characteristics of a perfectly competitive market, and explain why the demand curve as seen by an individual firm in such a market differs from the market demand curve.
2. Explain why adjusting output until marginal cost rises to equal price results in maximum profits for a business firm.
3. Draw the average and marginal cost curves of a firm earning economic profit. Show the profit-maximizing output, and use the graph to identify profit per unit and total profit.
4. Explain why a firm's losses from continuing to operate will exceed fixed costs when price falls below the minimum possible average cost of production for a product. Why will a competitive firm shut down in the short run only if price falls below minimum possible average cost of production?
5. Which portion of a competitive firm's marginal cost curve is its supply curve? How can a market supply curve be derived?
6. Explain why a change in the price of a variable input results in a change in supply in the short run, while a change in the price of a fixed input does not shift the supply curve.

Problems and Applications

1. The market equilibrium price of wheat is currently $2.50 a bushel. Assuming that wheat is produced by firms in a perfectly competitive industry, draw the industry demand and supply curves. Draw the demand curve for the wheat produced by a *single* wheat producer, and explain how it differs from the industry demand curve. 1

2. Draw a curve that shows how total revenue will vary as a typical wheat producer sells more wheat per season at the market equilibrium price of $2.50 per bushel. What is the average revenue from selling wheat? Assuming the wheat producer has fixed costs of $50,000 per season, draw a total cost curve. (Also assume input prices are constant and that the law of diminishing marginal returns governs the way cost increases with output.) Show how profit will vary with output as more wheat is sold per season. 1, 2

3. Suppose a farmer's marginal cost of producing wheat is $1 per bushel when 10 acres are planted. The farmer wants to maximize profits from selling wheat this season. Assuming that the market price is expected to be $2.50 per bushel, would you advise the farmer to plant more wheat this season? Explain. 2

4. Suppose the price of fabric in Box 2 increases to $200 per yard. Assuming that nothing else changes, recalculate profit at the daily output levels shown in the table. How much fabric will a profit-maximizing firm produce daily after the price increase? 2, 5

5. Given the price of a firm's product, show that profit per unit of output is always at a maximum when the average cost of producing the product is at a minimum. Prove that a profit-maximizing firm will choose to produce the output for which profit per unit is at a maximum only if the market equilibrium price just equals the minimum possible average cost. Show that, if this is the case, both the profit per unit and total profit will be zero! 3

6. The current market price of a standardized wire cable produced by a competitive firm is $1 per foot. The firm produces cable each month up to the point at which its marginal cost increases to $1 per foot of cable. At the output for which marginal cost equals $1, the average cost of the cable is $1.25 per foot. Draw the firm's cost curves and the demand curve for cable as seen by the firm. Show that the firm is losing money each month at the output for which marginal cost equals $1. Explain why a firm can incur losses while seeking to maximize profits and why it might fill orders for its product, even though it can't make profits by doing so. 3, 4

7. Suppose that, for the firm described in Problem 6, the minimum possible average variable cost of producing wire cable is $1.10 per foot. Under these circumstances, what would you advise the owner of the firm to do, assuming the price of cable is $1 per foot? Explain your answer. 3, 4

8. Suppose the current equilibrium price of housing construction is $50 per square foot, and new government subsidy program to encourage new housing construction promises to pay contractors $10 per square foot. Show how the subsidy will reduce the marginal cost of housing construction. Use graphic analysis to show how each individual contractor will want to increase housing construction per year after the subsidy. Show how the subsidy will affect market supply and the price of housing construction. 6

9. Instead of a subsidy paid per square foot of housing construction, suppose the government simply gives housing construction contractors a flat $1,000 per year subsidy. Explain why such a subsidy will be ineffective in increasing the supply of housing construction in the short run. 6

10. Suppose two table manufacturers in a perfectly competitive industry each operate a factory of the same size. One of these manufacturers is located close to a cheap source of hydroelectric power that results in lower variable costs of production. Prove that, other things being equal, the quantity of tables supplied by the manufacturer with lower variable costs will exceed that of the other manufacturer at any given price for tables. 5

Coping with Declining Prices in Retailing—Lord & Taylor and the Shutdown Point

Retailing has become an extremely competitive business in the United States. Retailers provide a service to consumers by offering a variety of goods and services for sale, at brick-and-mortar retail outlets and over the Internet. Department stores sell a multitude of items, and are found either in malls or in buildings located on streets within towns and cities. Retailers may specialize in "high-end" luxury items, catering to upper income consumers, or to the "mid" or "low end" of the market, catering to middle-income shoppers and low-income shoppers on tight budgets. The middle market has been highly competitive in recent years, as stores like Target, Wal-Mart, Kmart, and other major retailers have cut their costs and have been offering moderately priced merchandize at discounts to consumers. Prices at which companies like Lord & Taylor could sell items such as clothing, a mainstay of department store revenue, had fallen, as the chain had to compete with stores like Target, which sold also mid-quality products.

Lord & Taylor, formerly owned by the May Department Stores Company, has traditionally been regarded as a high-end retailer. However, when Lord & Taylor expanded into suburban shopping malls in recent years, its merchandize was closer to the middle part of the market. The strategy of trying to tap the middle of the market by offering moderately priced goods failed because of competition from discounters, like Target, which forced Lord & Taylor to price products at lower levels than anticipated.

In 2003 the May Company announced it would shut down 32 of its "underachieving" Lord & Taylor stores, in 15 states. The closed stores represented 38 percent of the chain's locations, but accounted for only 19 percent of revenue. However, as of 2004, these stores weren't yet at the shutdown point. Although increased supply of retailing services had pressured the stores to discount prices and, therefore, cut revenue, those prices had not fallen below AVC_{min}. The stores were still stuck with lease payments or interest and depreciation cost at many suburban malls, and it was expected to take between 12 and 24 months for the company to make arrangements to get out of its fixed cost commitments.

The stores would remain open only if it were possible to generate enough revenue to at least cover variable costs of production and, hopefully, a bit more to offset fixed costs. In the long run, May department stores would sell the spaces they owned to other department stores, back to the owners of the shopping malls, or to a third-party investor. Alternatively, they could lease facilities to other users, who would acquire the right to use a fully-fixtured store, ready for business. In cases in which the facilities were leased, the stores could be sublet to other tenants. In Colorado, there were other department store chains, including Marshall Field's and Macy's, that were considering entering the market by acquiring the properties Lord & Taylor were still operating.

The graph below shows how losses can be reduced by staying open, instead of shutting down, in the short run.

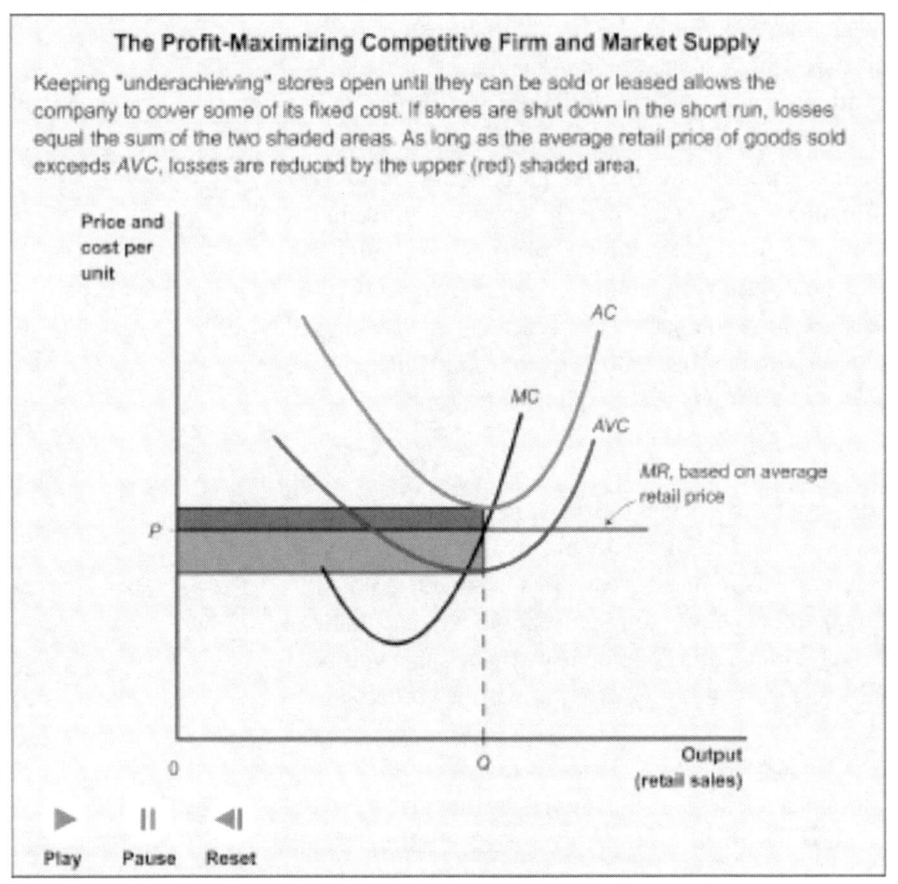

By 2006 most of the underachieving Lord & Taylor stores had been closed, as fixed commitments expired, and, in that year, a new owner acquired the company. The new owner was taking steps to restore the chain to its previous life as a luxury retailer, in the hopes of restoring it to profitability.

The severe recession that began in 2007, however, put pressure on other retailers to consider closing. In 2008 and 2009, the popular chain retailers Linens 'n Things and Circuit City closed their doors and many other retailers were considering shutting down, as downward pressures on price resulted in economic losses.

Chapter

11

Long-Run Supply in Competitive Markets

Suppose your college gets a surge in enrollment. To accommodate the larger student body, the college can hire more instructors and schedule more classes in the afternoon and evening. However, over a short period, it can't add more classrooms. Over a longer period it can build more facilities to handle the increase. Like a college, a firm has more flexibility in supplying goods and services in the long run than in the short run. Its limited ability to respond to price changes in the short run makes supply relatively inelastic compared to the long run.

In this chapter, we analyze long-run supply in competitive markets. In the long run, a good's market supply is more responsive, chiefly because the number of sellers can change when markets are free and competitive. Profits and losses are signals firm owners respond to in ways that, in the long run, change supply. Supply changes caused by opportunities to earn profits or actions taken to avoid losses cause changes in product prices that, in the long run, eliminate those profits or losses. A system of competitive markets is fueled by profits in the long run.

For example, increased demand for exercise bicycles creates profit opportunities. In the long run new manufacturers are likely to enter the market, attracted by the chance to earn profits. This competition increases the supply of exercise bikes, which eventually pulls price down. As the price falls, so do profits. As you'll see, profits plant the seeds of their own destruction when free entry exists in a market, as it does under perfect competition.

Concept Preview

After reading this chapter, you should be able to

1. Describe the conditions that exist when *long-run competitive equilibrium* has been achieved in a market.
2. Show how profits and losses act as signals that cause shifts in market supply over the long run.
3. Derive long-run supply curves for products sold in perfectly competitive markets and show how long-run supply differs from short-run supply.
4. Analyze the long-run impact of technological advances, taxes, and subsidies on prices and quantities traded in perfectly competitive markets.
5. Show how allocative efficiency is achieved in competitive markets.

Long-Run Competitive Equilibrium

1 In the short run a firm is confined to a plant of fixed size. Managers of a single-product firm can adjust production in the plant to achieve the goal of maximum profits. However, the plant's limited capacity eventually causes average and marginal costs to increase sharply as the firm tries to produce more and more. In the long run the firm's managers have the flexibility to build larger or additional plants if they can increase their profits by doing so. Moreover, the opportunity to earn profits lures new firms into a market. By the same token, established firms tend to leave a market if losses prevail.

A long-run competitive equilibrium exists in an industry when there is no tendency for firms to enter or leave the industry or to expand or contract the scale of their operations. New firms will enter the industry if profits are possible, and existing firms will leave the industry if they can't cover their opportunity costs. Similarly, firms tend to expand if they can thus increase their profits. All opportunities to earn profits or eliminate losses must be exhausted for an industry to attain a long-run competitive equilibrium. When economic profits are zero, firms just cover all their economic costs. When firms cover their opportunity cost, they can't earn more in their next best alternative, so they have no incentive to leave the market. New firms won't enter the market because they can't earn more by doing so than they currently earn in their existing enterprises.

Moving toward Long-Run Equilibrium

The process by which long-run competitive equilibrium is attained can be illustrated with a simple example. Suppose the market for bicycles is perfectly competitive. The current price of bicycles is $200 each. To simplify the analysis, assume that 100 firms are currently selling standardized bikes in the market. Assume also that the long-run costs of producing bicycles are the same for all producers in the industry and that new entrants into the industry can easily acquire the machinery and labor needed to produce bikes at the same cost as existing firms. Finally, assume that at the current price, all sellers in the industry are enjoying economic profits. The price of bikes therefore exceeds their current average cost of production.

The graphs in Box 1 show the average and marginal cost curves prevailing over the short run, along with the market demand and supply curves. As you can see in graph **A,** each bicycle seller currently maximizes profit by producing the number of bikes annually for which price equals marginal cost. The annual output that maximizes profit is 1,000 units for each seller. Because there are 100 sellers in the market, each maximizing annual profit, industry output is 100,000 bikes per year. Graph **B** shows the market demand curve and the existing *short-run* market supply curve. At the current market equilibrium price of $200, the equilibrium quantity is 100,000 bikes per year. Remember that the short-run supply curve reflects the marginal cost of producing bikes. At a $200 price the marginal cost of bikes is also $200 for each seller.

The graphs in Box 1 also show that firms in the industry earn profits. The average cost of producing bicycles is only $150 at the output for which price is equal to marginal cost. Each firm earns a profit of $50 on each bike sold. The $50 represents the difference between the market price of a bike and the average cost of producing it. Because each firm sells 1,000 bikes per year, its annual profit is $50,000, which is represented by the shaded area in graph **A.**

2 Now it's easy to illustrate the process by which a competitive industry moves toward equilibrium in the long run. Because the opportunity to earn profit exists in the bicycle industry, new firms will be attracted into it. These firms have to acquire machinery and workers and to build the plants they need to start producing bicycles. The increased demand for these inputs could increase their prices. However, if these inputs are used in industries other than the bicycle industry, it's unlikely that bike producers will have a

Box 1 Short-Run Equilibrium in a Profitable Market

At the current market price for bicycles of $200, firms in the industry can earn profit. The firm whose cost curves are illustrated above earns $50,000 per year economic profit by selling bicycles in the market. The industry has not reached long-run equilibrium because the profit will induce new firms to enter and existing firms to expand.

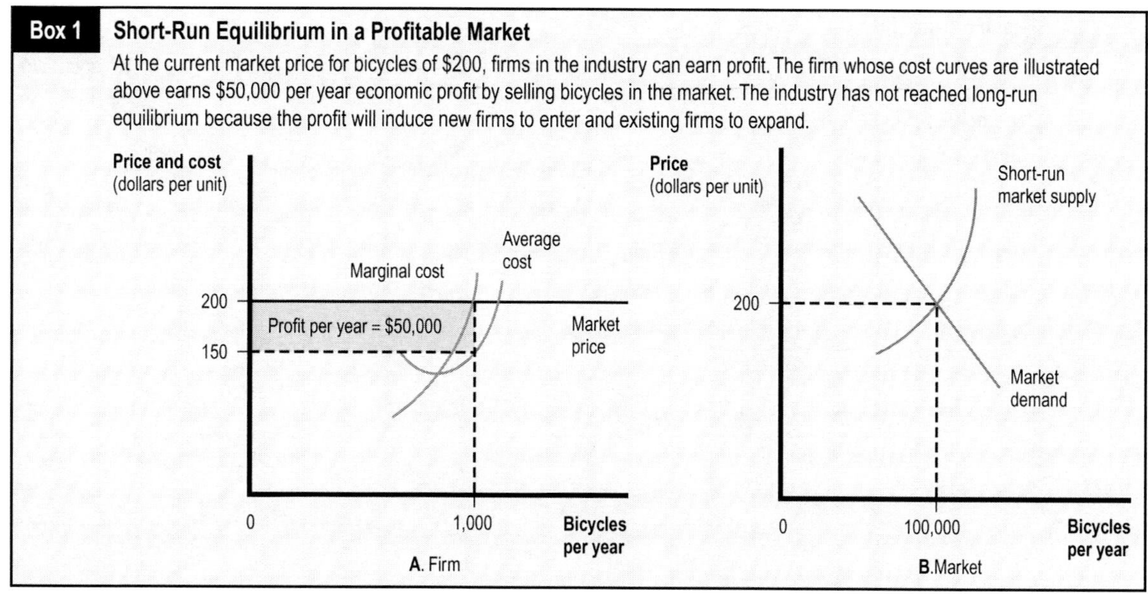

significant effect on overall market demand for them. If this is the case, the long-run average cost curves won't shift upward as new firms enter the bicycle industry because there will be no change in input prices. In other words, new bicycle sellers will have the same cost curves as those shown in Box 1.

However, the entry of new firms into the market as sellers will increase market supply, resulting in a new short-run market supply curve. The increase in market supply caused by the increased number of firms will put downward pressure on price. The graphs in Box 2 show how the increase in the number of firms selling the product shifts the short-run supply curve to the right as new firms enter, thereby increasing quantity supplied and decreasing market equilibrium price. But how far will market price fall?

Price Equals Minimum Possible Average Cost in Long-Run Equilibrium

As long as profit is possible in the bicycle industry, the number of firms will continue to increase or existing firms will expand. This means that the opportunity for profit will result in increases in supply that continually put downward pressure on price. This downward pressure will stop only when profit falls to zero—that is, when price has fallen to a level just allowing sellers to recover their average costs. When the profit per bike is zero, any further increases in supply will push price down to levels that result in losses. At the level for which price just equals average cost, total annual profit will therefore be zero for all sellers.[1] Firms remain in the industry even though they earn zero economic profit because they cover their implicit costs as well as their explicit costs by doing so.

The graphs in Box 2 show that profit per unit is zero only when price has fallen enough to equal the *minimum possible average cost of producing the good in the long run.* The minimum possible average cost of producing bicycles is $125. At any price greater than $125, price will exceed average cost, and this will allow profit opportunities for new sellers.

Graph **A** in Box 2 shows the short-run marginal and average cost curves for a plant that can produce bicycles at the minimum possible average cost of $125. It also shows the

[1]This assumes that the minimum possible average cost of production is the same for all sellers.

Box 2 Long-Run Competitive Equilibrium

In long-run competitive equilibrium, market price just equals marginal cost and minimum possible average cost. In response to profits, new firms enter, which increases market supply. As market supply increases, market price falls and quantity demanded increases.

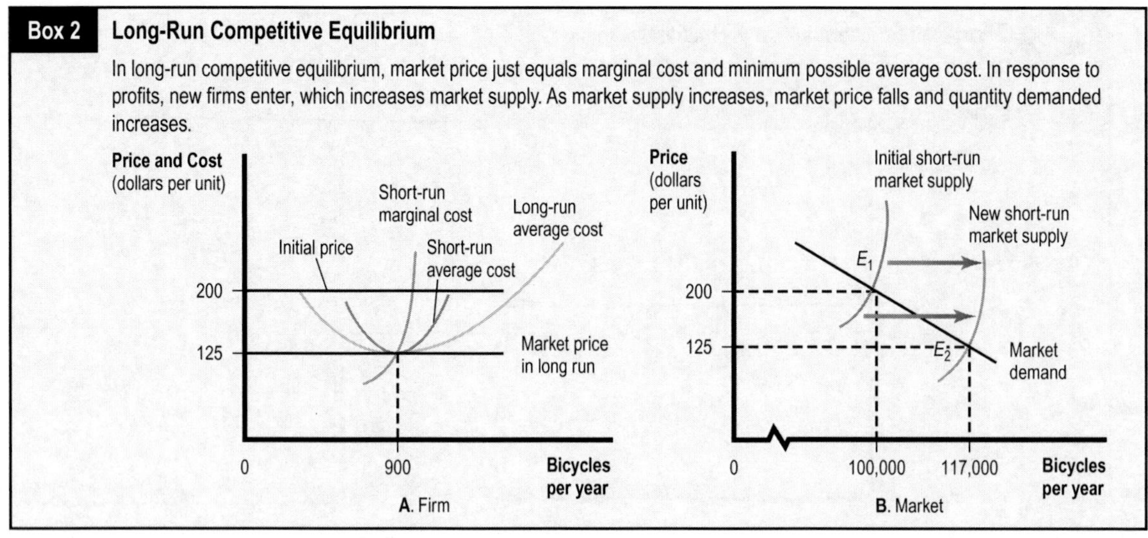

long-run average cost curve whose points correspond to various plant sizes. In the long-run equilibrium all firms operate out of plants that can produce bicycles at minimum possible average cost. If they were to operate out of larger or smaller plants, their minimum possible average cost would exceed the long-run equilibrium price and they would incur losses.

Entry of new firms into the bicycle industry will continue until price has fallen to the minimum possible average cost of making bicycles available in the long run. In graph **B**, the market supply has increased enough for the price of bikes to fall to \$125. At that price, profit per unit, and therefore total profit, equals zero for each firm.

Suppose the number of firms in the bicycle industry increases to 130 after the industry has attained its long-run competitive equilibrium. Notice in **B** that the market quantity supplied at the \$125 price is 117,000 bikes per year—an increase of 17,000 over the initial quantity supplied. Also notice that after enough firms have entered the market to push profits to zero, each firm produces *less* than it did initially. Output per firm falls from 1,000 to 900 units per year. However, total market output increases because the number of firms increases. Total industry output rises to 117,000 per year even though each firm in the industry now produces less than it did.

We can use the analysis for this example to reach a number of important conclusions about the characteristics of long-run competitive equilibrium.

1. In the long run, competitive equilibrium prices equal the minimum possible average cost of making the good available.

2. When prices equal minimum possible long-run average cost, they also equal marginal cost because marginal cost equals average cost when average cost is at a minimum. The maximum profit attainable for the competitive firm is therefore equal to zero when long-run equilibrium has been reached. This is because profit per unit equals zero at the profit-maximizing output (the one for which price equals marginal cost) for each firm when marginal cost equals average cost.

Long-Run Impact of Changes in Demand

Suppose the bicycle industry is initially in long-run equilibrium, as was illustrated in Box 2. How would the industry react to a decrease in the demand for bikes? Because bikes are currently being produced at the minimum possible average cost of \$125, the decrease in demand will cause prices to fall below average cost. The graphs in Box 3 show how the decrease in demand causes the price to fall to $105. Notice how in the short run there's a decrease in quantity supplied as the firms currently in the industry decrease quantities supplied by moving downward along the initial short-run supply curve. Each firm cuts back production to the point at which marginal cost declines to $105 in the plant with minimum possible average cost. The corresponding output for each firm is 800 bikes per year. Because there are 130 firms in the industry, total quantity supplied equals 104,000 bikes.

Graph **A** shows that firms in the industry can't cover their opportunity costs at the new price. Average cost of production for 800 bikes per year is $150. Each firm therefore loses $45 per bike sold, for a total annual loss of $36,000. In the long run firms will begin to leave this industry because they can earn more by selling their equipment and using the cash to set up other types of businesses.

As firms begin to leave the industry in the long run, the short-run market supply curve will shift to the left. Firms will continue to leave until supply has shifted just enough to push price back up to $125. The final long-run equilibrium therefore occurs, as illustrated in graph **B,** at the point at which the new short-run supply curve corresponding to the reduced industry size intercepts the new demand curve. At that price each firm in the industry is again producing 900 bikes per year, but the number of firms in the industry has declined, let's say to 110. Total industry output is now 99,000 bikes per year. Notice that as long as changes in the number of firms in the industry don't result in changes in input prices that cause the cost curves to shift, the price of bikes returns to its initial $125 level.

We can also trace the industry reaction to an increase in demand. Suppose that initially there are 130 firms in the industry, each producing 900 bikes per year, for a total industry output of 117,000 bikes at a market equilibrium price of $125 that just covers average cost of production, as shown in graph **A** in Box 4. The increase in demand increases market price to $175. In response to the increase in price, each of the 130 firms in the industry increases quantity supplied by producing more in its existing plants until marginal cost has increased to $175. This occurs when each firm produces 950 bikes per year for a total industry output of 123,500 per year, as shown in the graph. This corresponds to the point at which the new market demand curve intersects the existing short-run supply curve at point E_2 in graph **B.**

Box 3 **Reaction of Firms in a Competitive Industry to a Decrease in Demand**

At the initial market equilibrium at E_1, the industry is in equilibrium. In response to a decrease in demand, market equilibrium shifts to E_2, at which price falls to $105. At that price, firms in the industry incur losses. In the long run, firms in the industry leave the market. This decreases supply and results in a final equilibrium at E_3, at which price is $125 and firms earn zero economic profits.

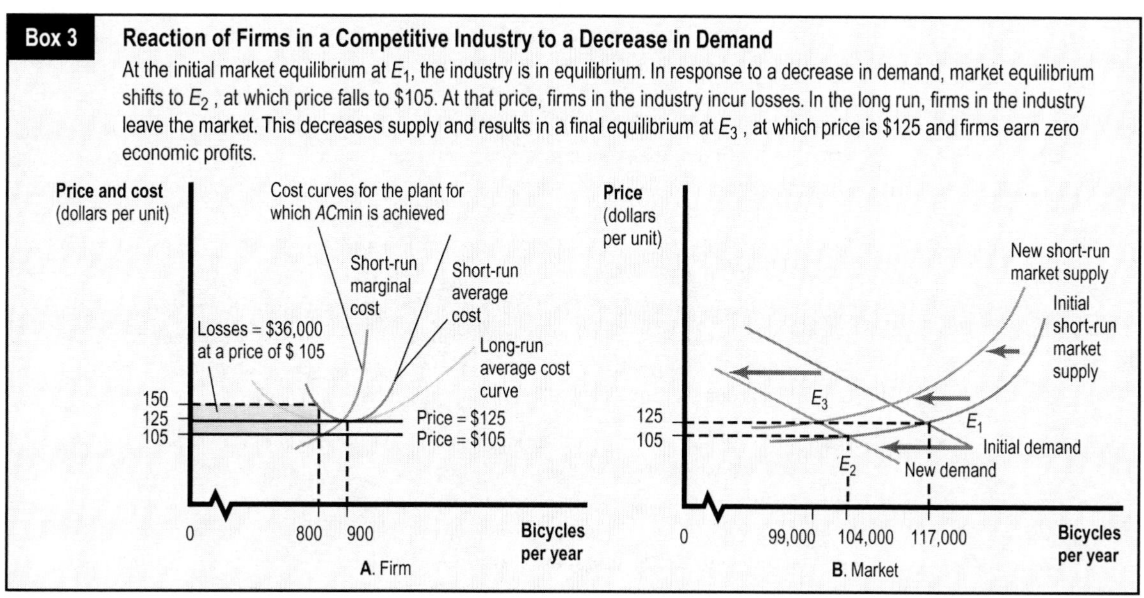

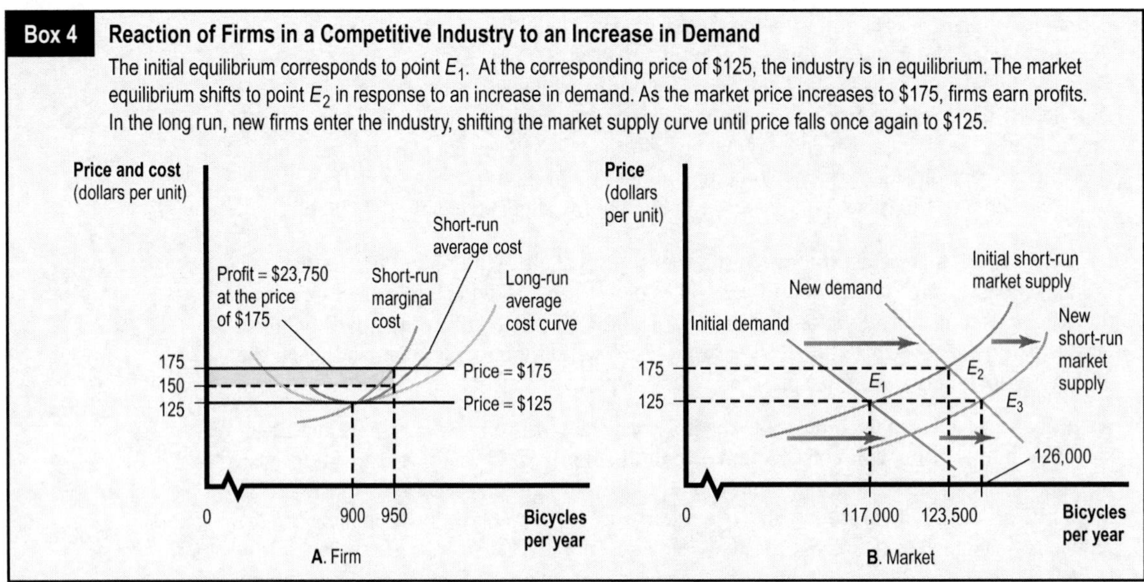

Box 4 Reaction of Firms in a Competitive Industry to an Increase in Demand

The initial equilibrium corresponds to point E_1. At the corresponding price of $125, the industry is in equilibrium. The market equilibrium shifts to point E_2 in response to an increase in demand. As the market price increases to $175, firms earn profits. In the long run, new firms enter the industry, shifting the market supply curve until price falls once again to $125.

At the new market price firms in the industry can earn profits. The average cost of producing 950 bikes per year is $150. This allows a $25 per unit profit, for a total profit of $23,750 per year. This profit will lure new firms into the industry. (Once again, assume no change in input prices resulting from the entry of new firms into the market in the long run.) As new firms enter, the short-run supply curve shifts to the right until price is again $125. At that level, price equals minimum possible average cost and the number of firms in the industry increases to 140, with each firm producing 900 bikes per year. Total industry output is therefore 126,000 bikes per year at the equilibrium price of $125. This corresponds to the point at which the new short-run supply curve intersects the new demand curve in graph **B.**

Profits, Losses, and Long-Run Supply

3 In the previous examples, notice how profits and losses are zero in the long run. Why do firms continue to produce if they can't earn profits in the long run? The answer to this question lies in the fact that when economic profits are zero, firms are still covering their explicit as well as their *implicit* costs. These implicit costs show up as accounting (or normal) profit on firms' income statements and reflect the opportunity cost of owner-supplied inputs. For example, suppose the only owner-supplied input for the bicycle firms is the capital used to make the bikes. Assume that the annual value of this capital, represented by the structures, machines, other equipment, and materials in inventory, is $1 million for each firm and that each firm has no current debt. If the opportunity cost of this capital is 10 percent in its next best use, each firm must earn 10 percent of $1 million, or $100,000 per year, when economic profits are zero. It follows that even though economic profits are zero in the long-run competitive equilibrium, firms earn an accounting or normal profit that just covers their opportunity costs of staying in the bicycle industry.

Be sure to notice another interesting result of the analysis of long-run equilibrium in the examples we've used. In all cases the price of bicycles returns to $125 in the long run. As long as nothing happens to change the minimum possible long-run average cost of producing bicycles as the number of firms in the industry changes, the market price will always return to $125. In general, minimum possible average cost will not change as the number of firms in the industry changes if input prices are not bid up or down as a result. A constant-costs industry is one for which input prices are unaffected by the quantity of a good produced or the number of firms in the industry. For such an industry, the minimum possible average cost of producing the good doesn't change as firms enter or leave the industry, other things being equal.

For a constant-costs industry, as the number of firms changes, price always returns to the same level in the long run. You can confirm this by reexamining the graphs in Boxes 3 and 4. In the long run, changes in the number of firms cause shifts in the short-run supply curves that change equilibrium output until price falls back to minimum possible average cost. Of course, changes in technology or changes in input prices that occur for reasons other than changes in the number of firms can affect minimum possible average cost. For an industry of constant costs, however, given technology and given influences on input prices other than the number of firms in the industry, minimum possible average cost will be unchanged as the industry expands or contracts in the long run.

The graph in Box 5 plots the points of long-run competitive equilibrium for the bicycle industry based on our previous examples. Connecting these points gives a long-run industry supply curve, a relationship between price and quantity supplied *for points where the industry is in long-run competitive equilibrium*. Each point on a long-run supply curve corresponds to the minimum possible average cost of producing the good. Point E_1 on the long-run supply curve corresponds to the initial long-run equilibrium first illustrated in Box 2. Point E_2 corresponds to the long-run equilibrium that resulted from the decrease in demand illustrated in Box 3. Finally, point E_3 corresponds to the long-run equilibrium that resulted from the increase in demand traced out in Box 4.

Notice that the long-run supply curve is a horizontal line for an industry of constant costs because the minimum possible average cost of producing the good doesn't change as the industry expands or contracts. Given input prices and technology, industry output is perfectly elastic at the price corresponding to minimum possible average cost for an industry of constant costs. Any price increases above minimum possible average cost can only result in temporary short-run equilibriums and won't be included as points on the long-run supply curve. Although increases in price are necessary to increase quantity supplied in all cases in the short run, the long-run supply curve for a constant-costs industry will be flat.

When Are Long-Run Supply Curves Upward-Sloping?

A long-run supply curve for an industry is upward sloping when input prices increase as a direct result of increases in the number of firms. This condition will prevail if firms buy a large proportion of the total supply of a particular input. For example, if the bicycle

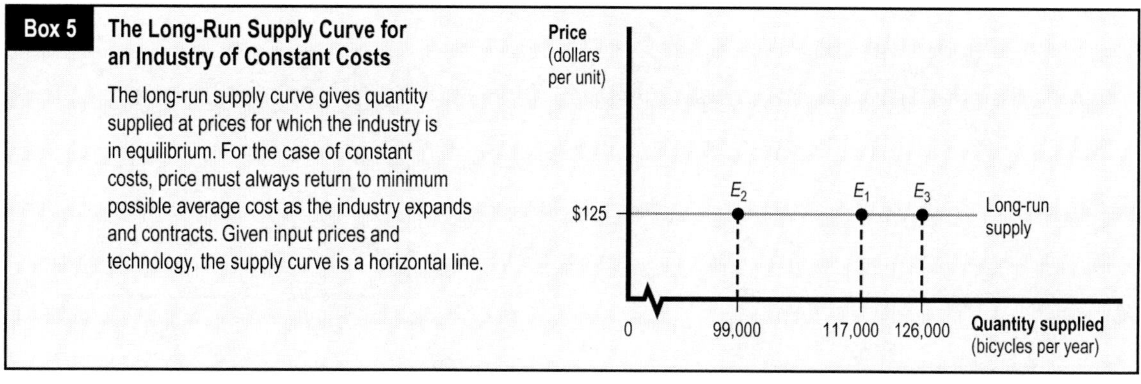

Box 5 The Long-Run Supply Curve for an Industry of Constant Costs

The long-run supply curve gives quantity supplied at prices for which the industry is in equilibrium. For the case of constant costs, price must always return to minimum possible average cost as the industry expands and contracts. Given input prices and technology, the supply curve is a horizontal line.

industry is the chief employer of certain skilled mechanics, then its expansion will tend to bid up the wages necessary to attract more mechanics. By the same token, a contraction of the bicycle industry will cause these mechanics' wages to decrease.

An increasing-costs industry is one for which the prices of at least some of the inputs used increase as a direct result of the industry's expansion. For such an industry, expansion will *increase* the minimum possible cost of producing the output, while contraction will *decrease* the minimum possible cost of producing the output. The long-run supply curve for an industry of increasing costs is upward sloping, as illustrated in Box 6. For example, suppose the initial price of bicycles is $125. An increase in demand increases their price in the short run, resulting in profits that will increase the number of firms in the bicycle industry in the long run. If the industry were one of increasing costs, the increased demand for specialized inputs would result in a price increase for these inputs. The increase in input prices would increase the minimum possible average cost of producing bicycles in the long run. If the new minimum possible average cost is $150, the competitive equilibrium price for bikes will have to increase to this level in the long run as the industry expands to reach its new equilibrium output.

The graph in Box 6 shows three points of long-run equilibrium for an industry of increasing costs: E_1, E_2, and E_3. Each point corresponds to a higher minimum possible average cost represented by the corresponding higher price.

Applications of the Model

4 Changes in technology and other changes affecting the minimum possible cost of making a good available to buyers in a market can disturb the equilibrium of a competitive industry. Firms will enter or exit an industry as changes in costs affect its profitability. The insights possible from the competitive model allow you to go behind the mechanism of supply and demand to better understand the process of adjustment to changes in the costs of making goods available in markets.

Improvements in Technology in a Competitive Industry

Many industries, particularly those producing electronic products, have experienced rapid technological improvements in recent years. These improvements have allowed sellers to produce their products at lower average costs. We can use the model of long-run competitive equilibrium to show how technology-induced cost decreases are passed on to consumers in the form of lower prices if perfect competition prevails.

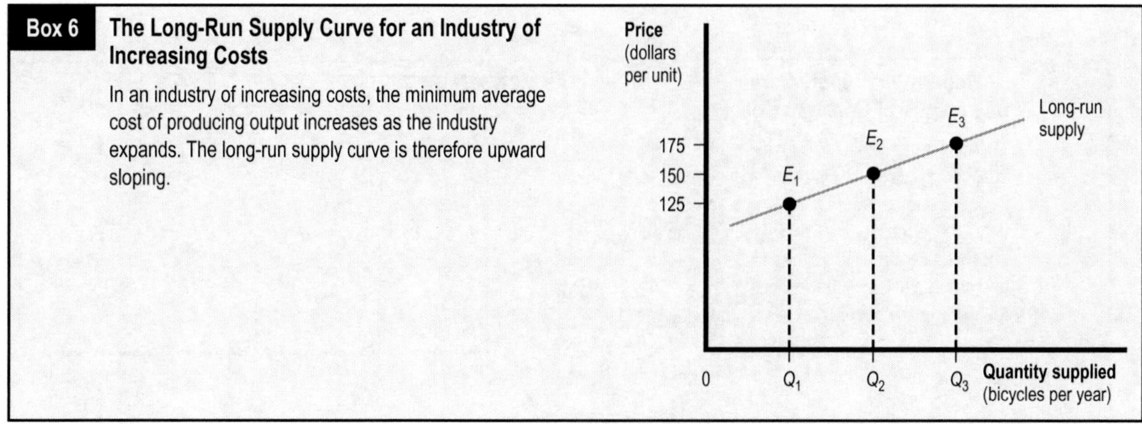

Box 6 The Long-Run Supply Curve for an Industry of Increasing Costs

In an industry of increasing costs, the minimum average cost of producing output increases as the industry expands. The long-run supply curve is therefore upward sloping.

The market for personal computers provides a useful illustration of how changes in technology affect market equilibrium. Today, personal computers are standardized products. There are also many sellers in the market, and free entry prevails, so the conditions of perfect competition are closely approximated. Suppose the current competitive equilibrium price is $2,000 per unit. At that price, each of the many firms in the personal computer industry earns zero economic profit. Graph **A** in Box 7 shows the cost curves of a typical firm in the industry. Assume that the industry is one of constant costs.

Now assume that an improvement in technology sharply lowers the cost of producing a standardized personal computer. The long-run average cost curve shown in **A** will then shift downward. Assume that the new minimum possible average cost is $1,500. *Any price above $1,500 per unit will encourage new firms to enter the industry.* It follows that short-run market supply, as shown in graph **B,** will increase until the quantity of personal computers available per year has increased sufficiently to drop the price to $1,500 per unit. At that lower price quantity demanded increases substantially. The assumption of constant costs means that the decline in average costs induced by the improvement in technology won't be offset in part by any increases in input prices as the number of firms in the industry increases. Entry of new firms under perfect competition therefore guarantees that consumers will benefit from the improvement in technology through lower prices for personal computers.

This conclusion can be generalized. Any change that *decreases* the minimum possible average cost of making a good available to consumers in markets will ultimately lower prices. In the long run, the decrease in minimum possible average cost will be passed on to consumers in the form of a decrease in the equilibrium price of the good in a competitive market.

We can also apply the insights of this analysis to the question of international competition. The reason improvements in technology lower the minimum possible average cost of production is that they increase the productivity of inputs. When more output can be

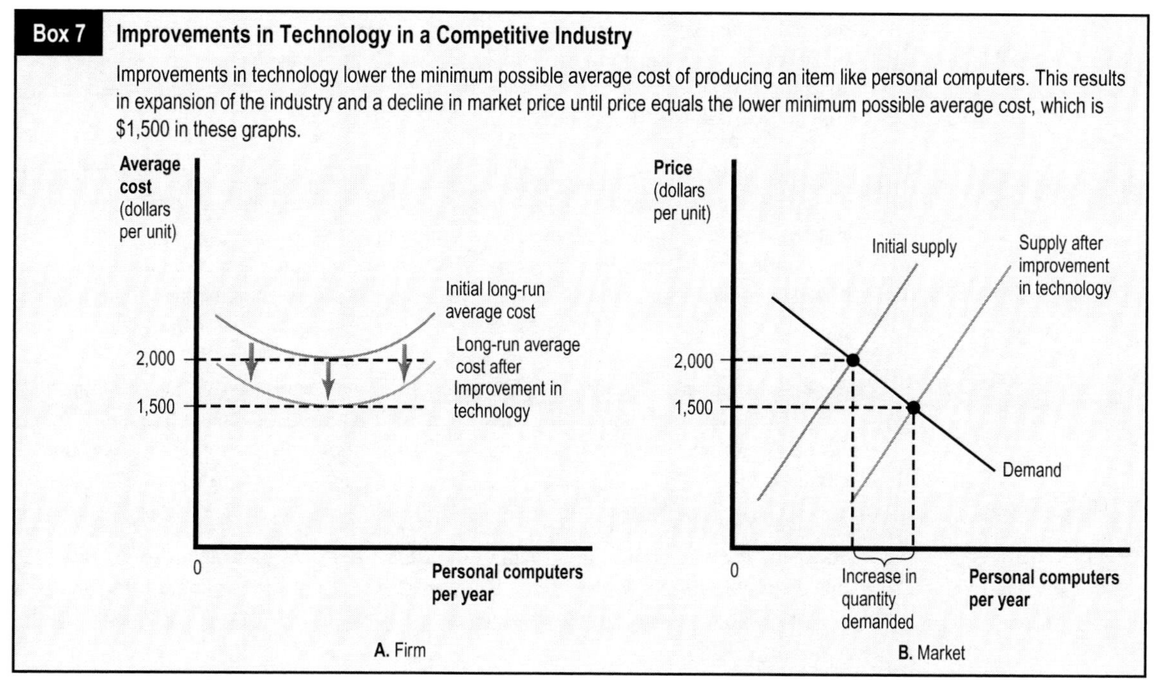
Box 7
Improvements in Technology in a Competitive Industry
Improvements in technology lower the minimum possible average cost of producing an item like personal computers. This results in expansion of the industry and a decline in market price until price equals the lower minimum possible average cost, which is $1,500 in these graphs.
Average cost (dollars per unit)
2,000
1,500
0
Initial long-run average cost
Long-run average cost after Improvement in technology
Personal computers per year
A. Firm
Price (dollars per unit)
Initial supply
Supply after improvement in technology
2,000
1,500
Demand
0
Increase in quantity demanded
Personal computers per year
B. Market

squeezed from a given combination of inputs of given cost, the cost *per unit* of output tends to decline. Failure to adapt quickly to new technology therefore means that industries forgo the opportunity to produce goods at lower cost. For example, if firms in the U.S. electronics industry compete with Japanese electronics firms in domestic and world markets, the U.S. firms won't have a competitive edge unless they keep up with technological change. If the Japanese develop and apply new technology before the U.S. firms do, they'll be able to sell at lower prices in world markets and thus increase their share of total sales at the expense of U.S. firms. The secret of remaining competitive in world markets is therefore quick response to changes in technology that allow firms to reduce average costs of production.

Taxing the Output of a Constant-Costs Competitive Industry

Any change that increases the minimum possible average cost of making an item available will set up a process that ultimately causes a competitive industry in equilibrium to achieve a new equilibrium at a higher price. Suppose the trucking industry is perfectly competitive and in equilibrium at a price of $1 per pound of freight shipped. A new tax equal to 10 cents per pound of freight shipped is then imposed on trucking firms. *From the truckers' point of view, the tax is equivalent to a 10-cent increase in the cost of each pound shipped.* The cost curves of all firms in the industry will therefore shift upward. Any change in the prices of inputs used in trucking (such as an increase in the price of fuel) will have a similar effect.

Because the trucking industry was initially in equilibrium, the increase in the minimum possible average cost caused by the tax will result in economic losses. In the long run firms will exit the industry. They will continue to do so until the supply of trucking services has decreased enough to increase price to the minimum possible average cost of production, including the tax per pound shipped. In the long run price rises to $1.10, which equals minimum long-run average cost, including the tax. *If the taxed industry is one of constant costs, the price per pound must rise by the amount of the tax.* This is because the increase in the minimum possible average cost is equal to the tax per pound shipped.

The graphs in Box 8 illustrate the long-run effect of the tax. Graph **A** shows that the trucking industry is initially in equilibrium at point E_1, where the demand for trucking services intersects the long-run supply curve. Each point on the initial long-run supply curve corresponds to the $1 minimum possible average cost. Initially, the price of freight shipped by truck is $1 per pound.

As shown in **B,** the minimum possible average cost of shipping freight increases to $1.10 per pound after the tax. As a consequence, the long-run supply curve shifts upward by 10 cents per pound shipped. The new long-run competitive equilibrium is at point E_2, where the quantity of freight shipped declines from Q_1 to Q_2 pounds per month and price rises to $1.10 per pound. The entire 10-cent per pound tax is reflected in the price paid by shippers in the long run. *If the price doesn't rise to $1.10 per pound to cover the full tax, it will fall short of minimum possible average cost.* After payment of the 10-cent per pound tax, trucking firms *must* receive $1 per pound to cover their average costs of production. Otherwise, they will leave the trucking industry until the long-run quantity supplied decreases enough to allow them to receive $1 per pound after payment of the 10-cent per pound tax. This requires that the price paid by shippers increase to $1.10 per pound.

The tax is fully reflected in the price paid by shippers only for the case of constant costs. If increasing costs prevail in the trucking industry, the prices of some of the inputs used by truckers would fall as firms exited. The decrease in input prices would offset the upward pressure of the tax on prices. In general, prices would rise by *less* than the tax in the increasing-costs case.

Box 8 Taxing an Industry of Constant Costs

A tax on the output of a constant-costs industry results in a price increase equal to the tax per unit of output. Unless the price increases to $1.10 in the long run, firms will incur economic losses and leave the industry.

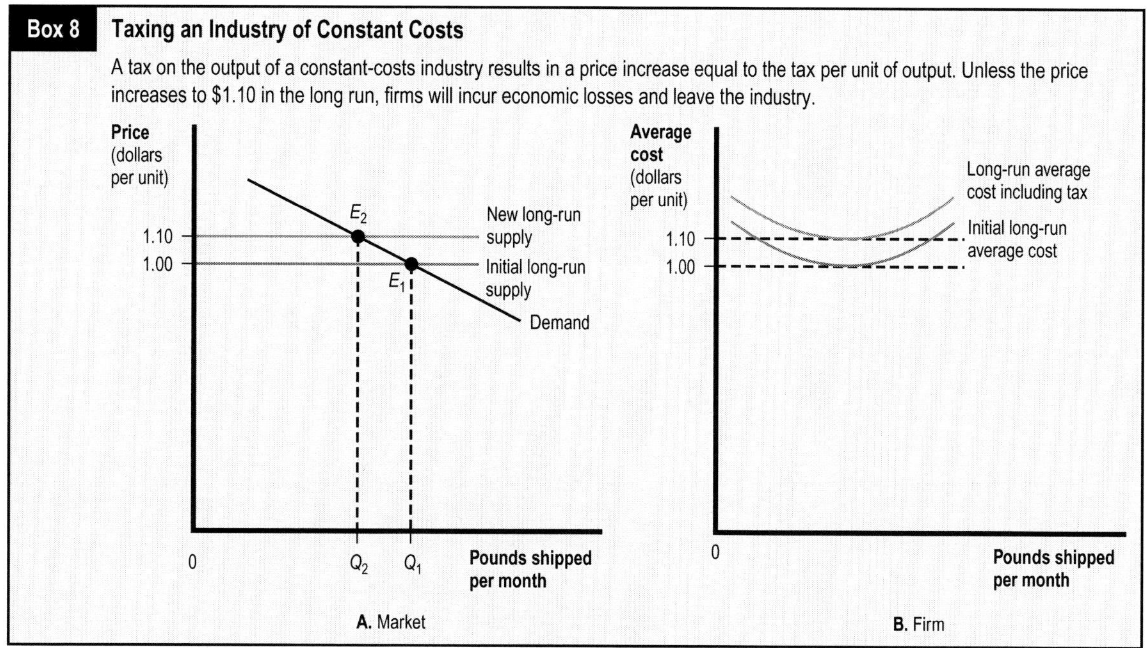

Long-Run Competitive Equilibrium and Allocative Efficiency

4 Allocative efficiency is a condition achieved when resources are allocated in ways allowing the maximum possible net benefit from their use. When an efficient allocation of resources has been attained, it's not possible to make any person in a society better off without making someone else worse off. No change in productive methods or further exchange of goods and services can result in additional net gains if resources are efficiently allocated.

It's easy to show that a system of competitive markets has the potential to achieve allocative efficiency. Concentrate on the single competitive industry that produces bread. A net gain is possible if the maximum price someone is willing to pay for more bread exceeds the minimum price a seller is willing to accept to make that bread available. You'll remember that the maximum price a buyer will pay for another unit of a good is the *marginal benefit* of the good. The minimum price a seller will accept for making another unit of the good available is its *marginal cost*. The marginal cost represents the value of the resources necessary to make one more unit of a good available. The marginal cost is the opportunity cost of making more of the good available.

The graph in Box 9 plots the marginal benefit of bread, together with the marginal cost of making it available. The marginal benefit is assumed to decline with consumption of bread, while the marginal cost is assumed to increase.

A net gain is possible from making more bread available as long as the marginal benefit of bread exceeds its marginal cost. Start at the point on the horizontal axis that corresponds to 50,000 loaves of bread per day. Follow the vertical dashed line from that quantity up to both the marginal benefit and marginal cost curves. This line intersects the marginal benefit curve at point *B* and intersects the marginal cost curve at point *A*. The marginal benefit of 50,000 loaves of bread per day is $3, and the marginal cost is $1.

It's now easy to show that net gains are possible from making more than 50,000 loaves of bread per day. The marginal benefit of bread exceeds its marginal cost at that daily output,

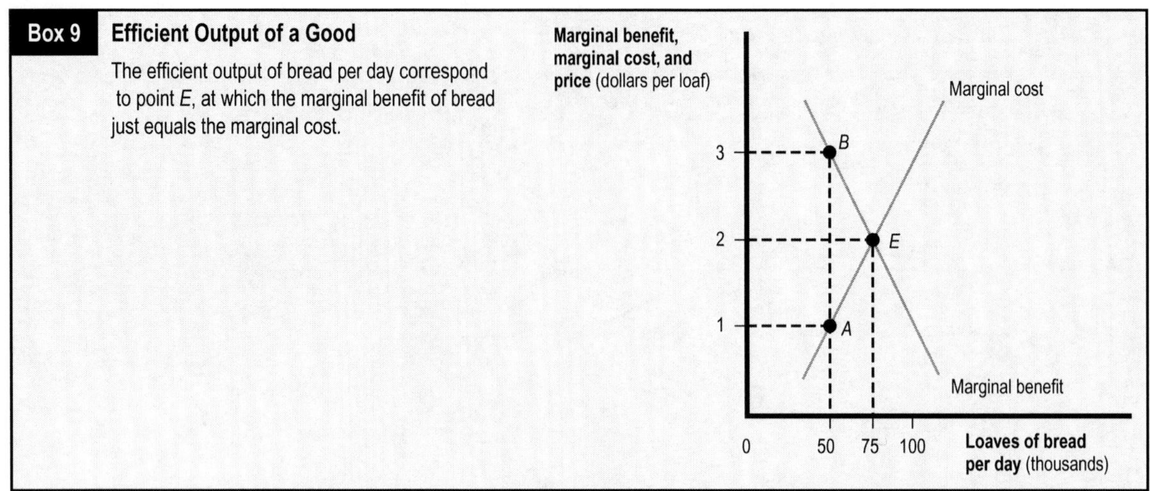

Box 9 Efficient Output of a Good

The efficient output of bread per day correspond to point *E*, at which the marginal benefit of bread just equals the marginal cost.

meaning that the maximum price consumers will pay exceeds the minimum sum of money needed to compensate the owners of resources for making that bread available. The difference between the marginal benefit of $3 and the marginal cost of $1 is the *net gain* from making another loaf of bread available when 50,000 loaves of bread per day are currently produced.

When one more loaf is produced, *that extra loaf is worth more to buyers than it is to those whose resources are used to make it available.* This is the basis for the gain from exchange. If consumers were to get the loaf for $3, they would be no worse off from exchanging their dollars for the bread. Those who made the bread available would be better off because they would receive more than the opportunity cost. Similarly, if the bread were made available for $1, those who made it available would just cover their opportunity cost and would be no worse off. Consumers, on the other hand, would now be better off because they would obtain bread they value at $3 for only $1.

If the bread were made available for a price anywhere between $1 and $3 when 50,000 loaves per day were produced, *mutual gains* would be possible. This is because consumers would get the bread at a price below the maximum they would be willing to pay. Similarly, those whose resources were used to produce the bread would receive a sum that exceeded the minimum they would accept. Additional mutual gains from exchange by producing more of a good are possible whenever the marginal benefit of the good exceeds its marginal cost. The output of 50,000 loaves per day is not efficient because, as our analysis has just shown, at that output it is possible to make consumers better off without harming producers. Similarly, our analysis has shown that at that output it is possible to make producers better off without harming consumers. Finally, because mutual gains from more daily output are possible, *both consumers and producers can be made better off by making more bread available each day.*

As long as the marginal benefit of bread exceeds its marginal cost, a net gain will be possible by making more bread available. *Efficiency requires that bread be produced just up to the point at which its marginal benefit equals its marginal cost.* In Box 9 the marginal benefit of bread just equals its marginal cost when 75,000 loaves per day are produced. The marginal cost of making more than this amount available would exceed the marginal benefit of the added amount. The maximum sum a consumer would pay for one more loaf would fall short of the value of the resources necessary to provide that loaf. The loaf couldn't be made available without making resource owners worse off. The efficient output of bread is therefore 75,000 loaves of bread per day.

We can generalize the results of this example: *Efficiency requires that all goods be made available just up to the point at which their marginal benefit equals their marginal cost.*

Competitive Markets and Efficiency

A system of competitive markets in which all useful goods and services are traded under conditions of perfect competition is capable of achieving efficiency. The market demand curve is the marginal benefit curve because each point on a market demand curve reflects the maximum sum a consumer will give up to get more of a good, given its current availability. The portion of the marginal cost curve lying above the average variable cost curve is the short-run market supply curve for bread produced by a competitive industry.

If bread were traded in a competitive market, the equilibrium would therefore occur at point *E* in graph **A** in Box 10. The marginal benefit and marginal cost curves intersect at that point. The market equilibrium price of bread would be $2 per loaf. The quantity of bread demanded at that price would equal the quantity supplied, which would be 75,000 loaves per day—which is also the efficient output!

The market price of a good in a competitive market equals both its marginal cost and its marginal benefit. To see this, remember that each seller can make more profits by producing more of a good whenever price exceeds marginal cost. Each seller therefore adjusts the output of bread until marginal cost rises to equal the good's market price:

Price = Marginal cost = $2

In this case the marginal cost equals $2.

Box 10 Efficiency in Competitive Markets

In competitive markets, prices equal the marginal benefit and marginal cost of goods. In addition, in the long run these prices also equal the minimum possible average cost.

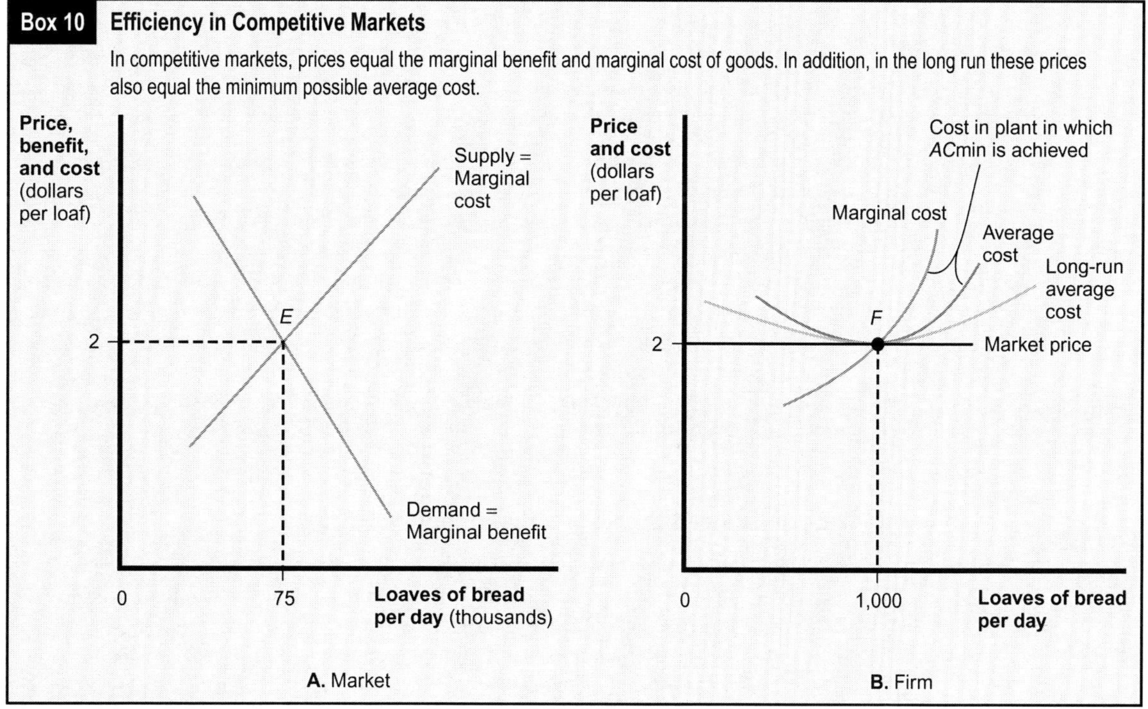

Similarly, buyers can gain whenever their marginal benefit exceeds a good's market price. Buyers therefore continue to purchase bread until the marginal benefit they receive falls to equal the market price:

Price = Marginal benefit = \$2

In this case the marginal benefit equals \$2. Because both the buyers and sellers adjust their respective marginal benefits and marginal costs to equal the \$2 market price, both marginal benefit and marginal cost will equal \$2, resulting in the efficient output of 75,000 loaves per day.

This leads us to an important conclusion: A system of competitive markets, rare though it may be, receives high marks on the basis of efficiency. A competitive market system is capable of squeezing the greatest net gain possible from making goods available, given the willingness of consumers to pay for them. Changes in the marginal benefit of goods caused by changes in tastes or changes in the way income is distributed will result in changes in demand. These changes in demand will change market prices and result in a new efficient resource allocation. In this sense a competitive market system is responsive to changes in the value consumers place on various goods. Similarly, changes in the marginal cost of making goods available will shift market supply curves. This will change the market prices of goods and again result in a new efficient resource allocation. A competitive market system is therefore also responsive to changes in the value of productive resources.

In a system of perfectly competitive markets, prices simultaneously equal the marginal cost and marginal benefit of goods in equilibrium in both the short and long run. Another desirable feature of such a system is attained only in the long run. As we have shown, in long-run competitive equilibrium prices also equal the *minimum possible average cost* of a good. Therefore, in the long run

Price = Minimum possible average cost = Marginal cost

Consumers can buy goods at the lowest possible price that covers both the average and marginal costs of production. A typical bread producer's cost curves are drawn in graph **B** in Box 10. The \$2 market price just covers both the marginal cost of bread and its minimum possible average cost at point *F*.

In a system of competitive markets, the greatest net benefit will be squeezed from available resources because the marginal benefit of each good equals its marginal cost. Finally, assuming that perfect competition prevails in markets for the production of each and every good, the price of each good will reflect its minimum possible average cost. The system will economize on resource use because *each good* will be produced at the minimum possible unit cost. This outcome is quite remarkable because it results from competition in a system in which each producer seeks nothing more than to maximize profits. However, the outcome is a resource allocation for which net benefits are the maximum possible from using available resources and prices are just high enough to cover the opportunity cost of sellers.

Perfect Competition: From Abstraction to Reality

Perfectly competitive markets are capable of achieving efficiency. For this reason economists take perfect competition as a benchmark against which to compare actual market performance. Although the model of perfect competition is an abstraction, it's useful not only as a benchmark but also as a basis for providing an understanding of the way actual markets function. The model shows how the pursuit of profit by sellers and of net benefits by consumers results in outcomes that maximize the total net gains possible from resource use. Adam Smith's "invisible hand" does its work superbly in perfectly competitive markets. Box 11 summarizes the long-run outcomes when perfect competition prevails in a market.

But alas, the world seldom conforms to theoretical ideals. We must therefore evaluate actual market performance and outcomes on an ad hoc basis. As you'll see, there are many cases in which markets fail to achieve outcomes that measure up to the standard of efficiency. When this is the case, government policies can often result in additional net gains that wouldn't be possible otherwise.

Box 11 Long-Run Competitive Equilibrium

Variable	Outcome
Product prices	$P = MC =$ minimum AC
	Prices are equal to marginal cost and are also equal to minimum possible average cost of production in the long run.
Output	Output is adjusted until $MB = MC$ and allocative efficiency is achieved.
	No additional net gains are possible from adjusting output, assuming that all the marginal benefit of output accrues to buyers and sellers incur all the marginal cost of output.
Profit	Economic profit is zero.
	Owners of firms earn a normal profit that is just enough to keep them in the industry because they cannot earn more in any other activity.
	Profit acts as a signal to shift supplies in response to changes in cost and demand but ultimately falls to zero in the long run.

Summary

1. A long-run competitive equilibrium exists in an industry when there's no tendency for firms to enter or leave or to expand or contract the scale of their operations.
2. In the long run new firms will enter an industry whenever the market price for a good produced by that industry exceeds the minimum possible average cost of producing the good. When price is above minimum possible average cost, new firms can earn more than their opportunity costs by entering the industry. Similarly, when price is below minimum possible average cost, existing firms will leave the industry because they can earn more by using their resources elsewhere.
3. In the long run in a competitive industry, prices equal the minimum possible average cost of producing goods, and economic profits are zero at the output for which price equals marginal cost for each firm. In the long run firms just cover their opportunity costs, which include normal profit.
4. A long-run industry supply curve shows a relationship between price and quantity supplied for prices at which an industry is in long-run competitive equilibrium. The long-run supply curve for a constant-costs industry is a flat line that's infinitely elastic at the price equal to the industry's minimum possible average cost of producing its product. Long-run supply curves are upward sloping for industries of increasing costs. An increasing-costs industry is one for which input prices increase as a result of the industry's expansion. A constant-costs industry can purchase all the input services it demands without affecting input prices.
5. Improvements in technology lower the minimum possible average cost of producing goods and services. This results in lower product prices in the long run as the industry expands and supply increases in response to the profit opportunities created by lower costs.
6. Efficiency prevails in an economy when all net gains from resource use have been achieved. Efficient resource allocation requires that each good be made available up to the point at which its marginal benefit equals its marginal cost. When efficiency has been attained, it's not possible to make any individual better off without harming another individual.
7. Competitive markets can achieve efficiency because firms make goods available up to the point at which marginal costs rise to equal market prices. Buyers adjust to the same market prices that sellers face and consume goods up to the point at which marginal benefits decline to equal market prices. In addition, resource use is economized because in the long run market prices in such markets also equal the minimum possible average costs of production.

Concept Review

1. What are the desirable features of long-run competitive equilibrium from the point of view of consumers?
2. In what sense do profits in a competitive market set up forces that eventually result in their elimination? Why do firms remain in business in a competitive market when they earn zero economic profits?
3. Why is the long-run supply curve of a constant-costs industry perfectly elastic at a price corresponding to the minimum possible average cost of its product?
4. Explain why a subsidy of 10 cents per bushel of wheat to farmers in a perfectly competitive constant-costs industry will cause the price of wheat to fall by 10 cents in the long run.
5. Show how competitive markets can result in allocative efficiency.

Problems and Applications

1. An industrial engineer calculates that, under current technology, the minimum possible average cost of producing roach poison is $10 per gallon. The current market price of roach poison is $15 per gallon. Assuming the roach poison is produced under conditions of perfect competition, use graphic analysis to show what will happen to its market supply and price in the long run. 1, 2

2. Suppose a sharp decrease in the demand for roach poison lowers its price to $8 per gallon. Using the data from Problem 1, and assuming the industry is initially in equilibrium, trace the industry's response. What will the price of roach poison be in the long run, assuming a constant-costs industry? 1, 2

3. Suppose wheat is produced under conditions of perfect competition. Assume the wheat industry has attained long-run competitive equilibrium at a price of $3 per bushel. What are the average and marginal costs of producing wheat? If a typical wheat farmer has $200,000 of capital equipment, and this is the only owner-supplied input, calculate the wheat farmer's economic and accounting profits, assuming the opportunity cost of capital invested in wheat farming is 10 percent. 1

4. The industry that produces computer cable is perfectly competitive. Firms in this industry can obtain all the inputs they demand without affecting the market prices of those inputs. Derive three points on the industry's long-run supply curve by using graphs to show the long-run equilibrium points in response to increases and decreases in demand. Assume that the minimum possible average cost of producing cable is 5 cents per foot. 3

5. A firm's short-run supply curve is the portion of its marginal cost curve lying above its average variable cost curve. Explain why points on a long-run supply curve for a competitive market equal *both* the marginal cost and the minimum possible average cost of making the product available. 3

6. Suppose the trucking industry is perfectly competitive and in equilibrium. A new procedure is then introduced that lowers the minimum possible average cost of shipping freight by truck from 2 cents per pound each mile to 1 cent per pound each mile. Show how the procedure will affect the price of shipping freight if the trucking industry is one of increasing costs. 2, 4

7. Suppose both U.S. and Japanese firms compete in perfectly competitive markets to sell digital cameras. The U.S. firms adopt a new technology that permits them to produce more cameras without increasing costs. Show that, in the long run, U.S. firms will be able to sell the cameras at lower prices than Japanese firms, assuming the new technology isn't available in Japan. 2

8. Show that a 10-cent per gallon subsidy to gasoline sellers will ultimately reduce the price of gasoline to consumers by 10 cents per gallon if gasoline is sold in perfectly competitive markets and the gasoline industry is one of constant costs. 4

9. Suppose the marginal benefit of automobiles is currently $15,000, but their marginal cost is only $10,000. Is the efficient quantity of automobiles being sold? 5

10. Currently, the market price of a standardized microwave cart produced by firms in a perfectly competitive industry is $100. A $10 tax is levied on the sale of each cart. The tax increases the market price of microwave carts, in the long run, to $106. The net price received by sellers after paying the tax is, therefore, $96. Show that efficiency isn't attained in the competitive market for microwave carts after the tax is introduced. 4, 5

Economic Integration in Europe: The Promise and the Problems in the European Union

The year 1992 marked the beginning of a remarkable change in the economic environment of Western Europe. By 1995, the European Union's 15 member nations (Austria, Belgium, France, Germany, Finland, Greece, Italy, Luxembourg, the Netherlands, Denmark, Ireland, the United Kingdom, Portugal, Spain, and Sweden) eliminated most of the economic barriers that hindered trade and investment among themselves. This elimination of barriers makes the nations of the European Union (EU) more like the states of the United States, from an economic point of view. Businesses in the EU member nations are able to move capital, labor, and products among these nations, just as businesses in the United States are able to transport goods and make production decisions among the states. As of 2007, the EU had expanded to 27 nations, as Bulgaria, Cyprus, the Czech Republic, Estonia, Hungary, Latvia, Lithuania, Malta, Poland, Romania, Slovakia, and Slovenia became member states.

Economic integration in Europe removes numerous barriers to doing business across nations' borders, such as the following:

1. Differences in industrial standards and regulations (including health and safety regulations) that increase the costs of operating businesses in more than one European nation.

2. Delays at borders for customs checks that increase the costs of moving goods and services between nations.

3. Restrictions on sales to governments that prevent business firms in one EU nation from bidding on contracts for the sale of goods and services to the governments of other EU nations.

4. Restrictions that have made it difficult or impossible for many service firms in one EU nation, especially firms that provide banking and other financial services, from competing in other EU nations.

Economic integration in Europe puts downward pressure on production costs and prices by increasing competition among firms. Prices for similar goods and services varied widely among the EU nations in the past, because many firms in one EU nation were insulated against competition from firms in other EU nations. Now, all of the firms in the EU nations are able to make locational decisions that take advantage of the unique features of each EU nation. For example, labor-intensive operations can now move to Portugal or Greece, where labor costs are significantly lower than those in other EU nations.

We can use the model of long-run competitive equilibrium to illustrate the effects of economic integration in Europe. Allowing firms to sell and locate their operations without constraint in all EU nations (much as American firms are free to operate plants and sell in all 50 states) pushes down average costs of production. As this occurs in given industries, new firms enter and prices fall. Under a new long-run equilibrium, more goods and services are sold at lower prices, generating jobs and increases in the purchasing power of income. The graphs below show how economic integration is likely to lower average costs and increase the supply of output in the European Union over the long run.

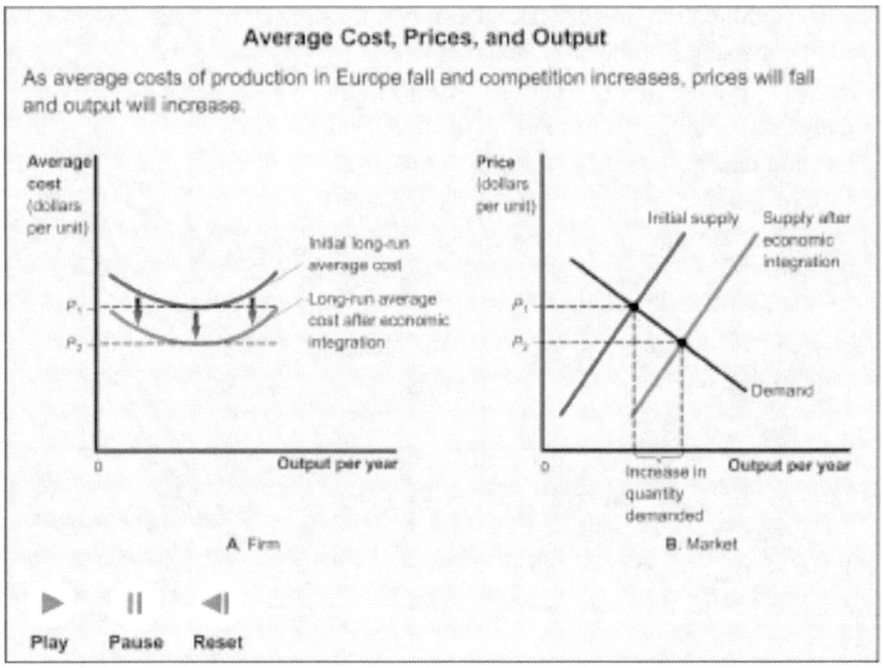

The benefits of economic integration are likely to be substantial, perhaps adding as much as 1 percent to the annual growth rate of production and income in the EU nations. The more competitive environment created by economic integration forces all European firms to keep production costs as low as possible or risk being forced out of business by new entrants using the latest technology. Inefficient firms that were previously protected from competition have to modernize their operations and improve their management or be forced out of business. Increased competition among financial services firms increases the supply of loanable funds for all EU nations, putting downward pressure on interest rates. As interest rates fall, investment increases. Finally, the cost of government services is also likely to be reduced, as increased competition in bidding for government contracts puts downward pressure on the cost of producing such services.

What does economic integration in Europe mean to American business? If, as expected, Europe prospers as a result of economic integration, income in EU markets will increase. An integrated Europe (with a population of 340 million people) will have income rivaling that of the United States. Europeans will demand more goods, including more goods from America. However, U.S. firms will also have to keep production costs low to compete effectively, both at home and abroad, with increasingly efficient European producers.

A majority of EU nations now use a common currency (the euro), coordinate their economic policies for the common benefit, and hope to have a formal constitution for instituting changes in government policy affecting all EU nations. Unfortunately, political forces in a more united Europe may increase pressures for protecting the EU nations against competition from suppliers in other nations. If new barriers to trade result, those nations may retaliate with barriers that make it difficult for firms in the EU nations to export their products.

In practice, the road to economic integration since 1992 has proven to be rocky. Also, some of the benefits low-wage nations had hoped to gain from integration have proven elusive. Under fierce competition in global markets, European producers have been forced to transfer operations to nations out of the EU, particularly to Eastern European nations, where labor costs are lower than in the lowest-wage EU nations and where employers have more flexibility in using workers.

Cultural, legal, and tax differences that inhibit trade remain among European Union nations. Strong labor unions in such nations as Spain make it difficult to fire workers and costly to lay off workers. The high government-mandated payments for workers for generous pensions, health benefits, and vacations contribute to high labor costs throughout the EU. And materials costs and costs for such services as communications remain higher in Europe than they are in the United States or Japan. Improvements in productivity of workers in EU nations have lagged behind those of U.S. workers. On average, productivity is lower in Europe than either in Japan or the United States, while wages are as high or, in the case of Germany, higher than they are in the United States.

As a result of all these problems, producers haven't been successful, since 1992, in significantly lowering costs of production in EU nations. Job creation has also suffered. Because of high labor costs in EU nations, many companies have looked eastward to the former communist nations of Europe and to Asia to locate new production facilities. For example, a major German garment company has reduced its production operations in Germany and has opened plants in Sri Lanka and Poland. This large company has only 40 percent of its employees located in European Union nations. Western European nations find Eastern Europe especially attractive as a means of lowering average costs of production, because the labor force is highly skilled and equilibrium wages are well below those prevailing in any EU nation. These nations are also located closer to Western European markets than are Portugal, Spain, and Greece, the low-wage EU nations.

European Union producers are lowering their costs and becoming more competitive, as they must be in the modern global economy; however, they 're *not* doing so by moving operations around EU nations. Instead, they're reducing production in the EU and increasing it in non-EU nations. The end result is high unemployment in the EU, where unemployment averaged 11 percent in the 1990s. Between 1970 and 1990, employment in EU nations increased by only 10 percent, compared to a 52 percent increase in the United States. From 1990 and through 2008, employment growth has lagged in EU nations, compared to the United States, and unemployment rates in EU nations have remained consistently higher than in the United States, particularly for younger workers.

In short, the good news for Europe is that European Union nations are lowering their average cost of production and becoming more competitive. The bad news is that much of that cost reduction is not the result of economic integration. The European Union has a long way to go before the promise that elimination of borders brings can be associated with increased employment.

Long-Run Competitive Equilibrium for U.S. Industries Facing International Competition from Low-Cost Suppliers: The Case of Furniture*

The U.S. furniture industry is highly competitive. As of 2002, there were more than 1,000 domestic manufacturers of case goods--wood furniture typically shipped in crates. These products consist of cabinets, dressers, wall units, media centers, bedroom sets, and dining room sets, as well as other wood furniture. The items use a capital-intensive production process, and are often customized and hand-finished. There are only 3 domestic manufacturers with more than a 1-percent share of the market, and the biggest of these has only a bit more than 4 percent of the market.

There's free entry into the market. From 1994 to 2001, imports from Chinese manufacturers more than tripled. More than 40 percent of imported furniture entering the United States was produced in China in 2001. There are more than 50,000 furniture-manufacturing companies in China. Many U.S. furniture producers are now sourcing their products in China and closing their U.S.-based operations. Domestic production by one of the largest U.S. furniture manufacturers, La-Z-Boy, has declined by 45 percent since 2001.

Increased furniture supply from China at lower average costs of production has caused furniture prices to fall and, as a result, many firms in the United States have become unprofitable. The largest 4 furniture-manufacturing firms in the United States shut down 6.5 million square feet of factory space in 2001. As firms fail or outsource their production to China, employment in the industry naturally declines. Chinese furniture manufacturers are also expanding rapidly, adding capacity at an estimated 25 to 30 percent per year. Chinese wages in furniture manufacturing run between 50 and 75 cents per hour and, although the work force is quite skilled, many Chinese products aren't up to the quality of U.S. goods. Remaining domestic producers can retain market share by concentrating on high-quality goods. However, quality of Chinese furniture manufacturing is improving.

Shipping adds about 23 percent to the costs of selling Chinese furniture in the United States. However, even when shipping is added to average production cost of these imports, they can still be profitably sold at prices 20 to 30 percent lower than comparable U.S. goods.

There's no doubt that the size of the domestic furniture industry will shrink as it moves to a new equilibrium. To remain competitive, firms will have to reduce their average costs of production by either increasing worker productivity or lowering overhead costs. They can also concentrate on high-quality premium furniture, with designs that cater to American consumers.

The graph below show how equilibrium of the furniture industry is affected by increased supply of low-cost Chinese imports.

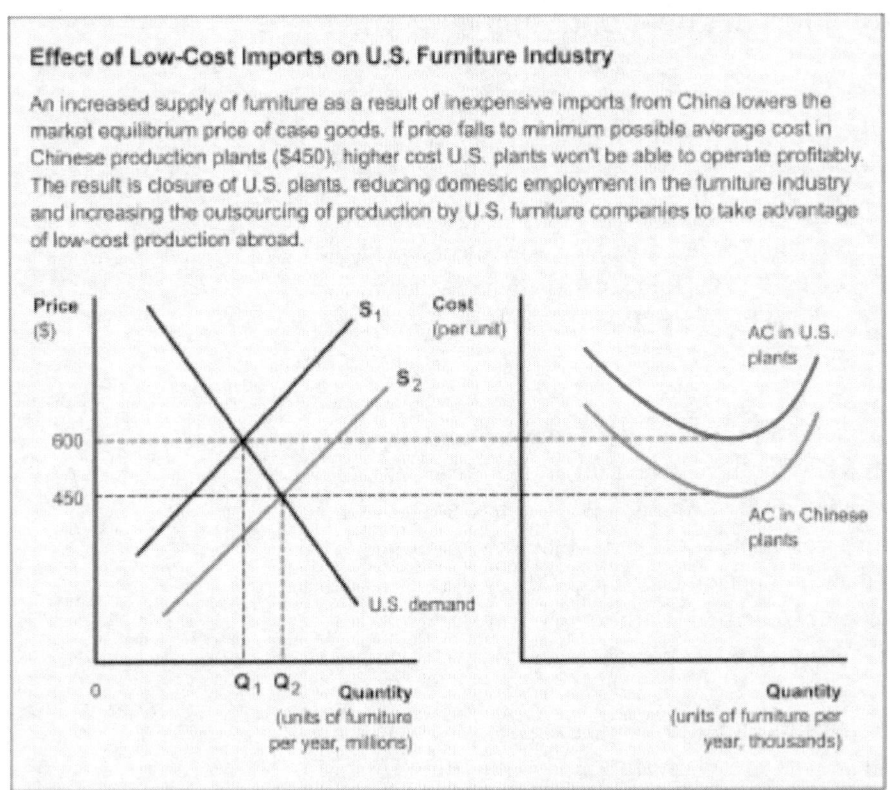
Effect of Low-Cost Imports on U.S. Furniture Industry
An increased supply of furniture as a result of inexpensive imports from China lowers the market equilibrium price of case goods. If price falls to minimum possible average cost in Chinese production plants ($450), higher cost U.S. plants won't be able to operate profitably. The result is closure of U.S. plants, reducing domestic employment in the furniture industry and increasing the outsourcing of production by U.S. furniture companies to take advantage of low-cost production abroad.
Price ($)
S1
S2
600
450
U.S. demand
0
Q1 Q2
Quantity (units of furniture per year, millions)
Cost (per unit)
AC in U.S. plants
AC in Chinese plants
Quantity (units of furniture per year, thousands)

*See Virginia Bryson, Gianni Lanzillotti, Josh Myerberg, Elisabeth Miller, and Fred Tian, *The Furniture Industry (Case Goods): The Future of the Industry, United States versus China*, UNC at Chapel Hill, Kenan-Flagler Business School, March 7, 2003. Available at http://www.kenan-flagler.unc.edu/assets/documents/furn_paper.pdf. The information in this *Principles in Practice* is based on this report.

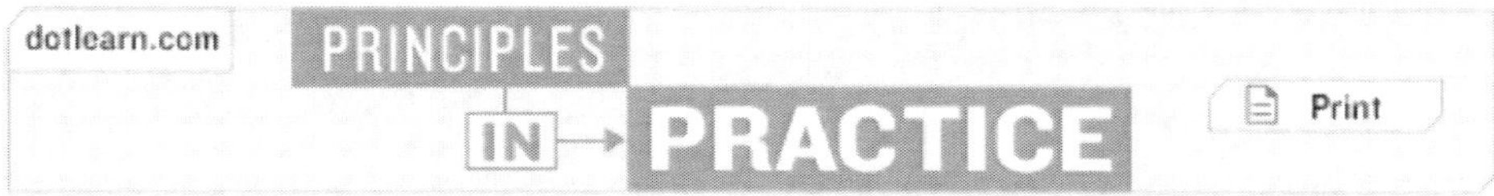

How Limits to Entry Affect a Competitive Industry: The Case of Taxis in New York City and the Soaring Price of Taxi Medallions

The taxi industry is one that seems to meet many of the requirements for perfect competition.The service is more or less standardized. In large cities, there are usually thousands of independent firms offering taxi service, and it's rare for one of these firms to have a large market share. However, in many cities, entry into the taxi industry is restricted by government controls.

If you've ever hailed a cab on the streets of New York City, you may have noticed the metal medallion affixed to the hood of the vehicle. The taxi medallion is the license that gives the taxi owner the right to pick up street passengers. Every vehicle used as a taxi to pick up street passengers on demand must have this medallion on its hood. The medallion licenses the car as a taxi.

A taxi medallion is a transferable license to operate a taxi in New York City. In the late 1930s, the city auctioned off nearly 12,000 medallions for $10 each, one per cab, to people already in the business. The market price of a New York City taxi medallion was $300,000 as of 1999. The price of a medallion fell between 2000 and 2003, to about $200,000, but soon started to climb again. The price was in the range of $250,000 in 2004. By January 2009, the price of a medallion for use by an individual taxi had climbed to $600,000 and the price of a medallion for a taxi used in a corporate fleet was selling for $750,000.

In 2003, a plan allowed the creation of 900 new taxi medallions, to be sold at the rate of 300 a year for three years. The sale of the new medallions would raise revenue for the City. The total medallions available as of 2004 were 12,187, including 400 that were issued in 1996 and 1997. The 900 new medallions resulted in a 7 percent increase in taxis available in the City. Some medallion owners were concerned that the increased supply of medallions would lower the market value of their existing medallions. However, this could be offset by a fare increase. As of 2009, enough new medallions were issued to allow 13,200 medallion taxis to cruise the streets of New York.

A medallion can be thought of as a government-created fixed input required to engage in the sale of taxi service. Its purpose is to provide a stable supply of such service over time. Before the medallion system was implemented in New York City, the supply of taxi service would decrease sharply during economic expansions, when the opportunity cost of operating a taxi was high in terms of forgone wages in other jobs. Conversely, the supply of taxi service would increase in periods of recession, when the opportunity cost of using time to operate a taxi was low for those who would have otherwise been unemployed.

The fixed costs of operating a taxi are very low. The vehicle itself has alternative uses to its owner and can easily be withdrawn from the industry on short notice, with little loss. By the same token, it's at least theoretically easy to enter the taxi industry, because most people have the requisite fixed input--a passenger car.

Because the supply of medallions is *perfectly inelastic*, their price is determined solely by the level of demand, as shown in the graph below. The demand, of course, depends on the profitability of selling taxi service.

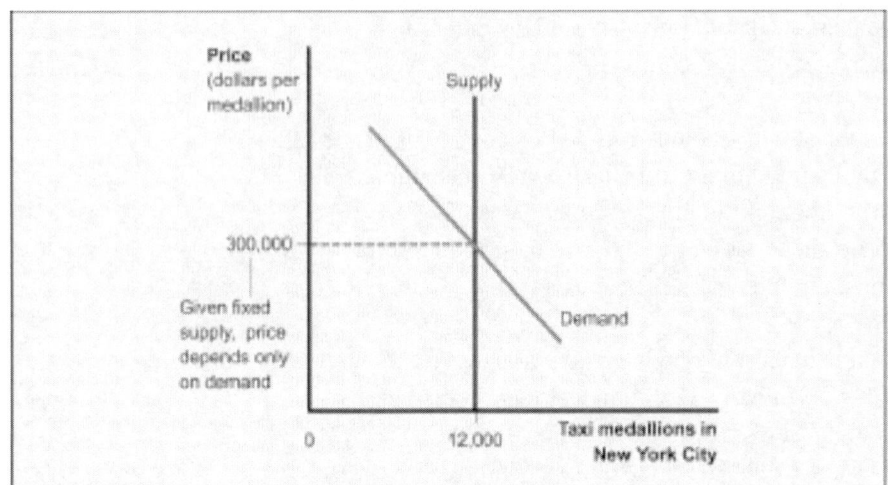

It's easy to see how the medallion increases the fixed costs of operating a taxi. After acquiring a medallion, its owner is also required to pay a $150 fee each year to maintain the right to operate a cab. However, the real opportunity cost of the medallion is the forgone interest on its market price. If, for example, the owner of a medallion forgoes 8 percent interest by holding a medallion with a market value of $600,000, the opportunity cost is 8 percent of $600,000, or $36,000 per year. The cost becomes part of the fixed costs of operating a taxi.

The medallion system is an effective limit on entry into the taxi industry that strictly controls the number of taxis on the street. The profits can't act as a lure to increase the supply of taxi service, because the number of taxis is limited by the fixed number of medallions. However, this doesn't mean taxi owners will enjoy tremendous economic profits, because, as the profitability of taxi service increases, the market price of a medallion goes up. The opportunity cost increases in terms of forgone interest income, thereby increasing the costs of operating a taxi. This contributes to higher prices for taxi service--but not to higher profits.

Of course, the medallion owners benefit from the increased profitability of taxi service by having the option of selling their medallion for much more than they paid for it. Someone who bought a medallion in the 1930s for $10 would have done quite well by selling it in 2009 for $600,000!

In recent years, many people have bought medallions as investments, rather than to operate cabs themselves. They lease the right to use their medallions to someone else, thereby earning a cash flow. They hope to be able to sell the medallions at a good profit in the future. In fact, if you had bought a medallion in early 1986 for $75,000, you could have sold it three months later for $100,000, a 33 percent return in three months, or an annual return of 132 percent.

Chapter 12

Monopoly

If you attend college in a small town, you might find only one store where you can buy fresh fruit and vegetables. In such a case, you and your fellow students are rival buyers in a market in which there's only *one* seller. You can expect to pay higher prices for fresh produce than if there were more competition in the market.

Markets often have only a few sellers, and free entry of additional sellers into such markets is sometimes impossible. In this chapter, we examine outcomes in markets in which there is only a *single* seller and entry of additional sellers isn't possible. In such markets the sale of the product is *monopolized* by a single firm. As you'll see, markets in which a single profit-maximizing firm monopolizes the supply are unlikely to result in the efficient outcomes we expect in perfectly competitive markets.

Firms that control the entire market supply of a good can also control the price of that good because they can make the good significantly scarcer or more abundant. They can therefore influence the price buyers are willing to pay. Absence of free entry into a market controlled by a monopoly prevents prices from falling to the minimum possible average cost in the long run because the number of sellers and supply in the market won't increase in the long run if the single seller earns profits.

Concept Preview

After reading this chapter, you should be able to

1. Define *pure monopoly*, discuss how it can be maintained in a market, and show that the demand curve for a product sold by a monopoly implies that the monopoly can control the market price of the product.
2. Show that the marginal revenue from a monopolist's output is less than the price the monopolist charges for its product.
3. Explain how a profit-maximizing monopoly seller chooses how much of its product to make available to buyers, and demonstrate that the decision of how much to sell is inseparable from the decision of how much to charge.
4. Compare market outcomes under pure monopoly with those that would prevail under perfect competition, and discuss the social cost and possible social benefit of monopoly.
5. Discuss government regulation of natural monopoly.
6. Understand why firms with monopoly power sometimes engage in price discrimination.

Pure Monopoly

1 A pure monopoly occurs when there's a single seller of a product that has no close substitutes. Buyers then have only one source of supply for that product. Perfect competition is characterized by the inability of individual sellers to control price. No individual firm produces a large enough share of the total market supply to affect price. Monopoly, on the contrary, is characterized by concentration of supply in the hands of a single firm.

A firm has monopoly power if it can influence the market price of its product by making more or less of the product available to buyers. Although pure monopoly is very rare, monopoly power is quite common.

Local monopolies are more common than national monopolies, and local markets are often served by single sellers. However, few, if any, products have no substitutes. A local electric power company may be the sole seller of electricity in an area, but electricity has substitutes. Natural gas and oil furnaces are good substitutes for electric heat.

In most regions where local monopolies provide public utility services, the seller can't set the price it charges for service. Most local monopolies that provide electricity, natural gas, and transportation services are regulated by state and local government agencies. In evaluating the rates charged by utility monopolies, these agencies are influenced by political as well as profit considerations. In fact, in many cases, utility monopolies are actually owned and operated by government agencies. The undesirable outcomes we expect when a pure monopoly is free to set its price lead to political intervention to control its pricing policies.

How Monopoly Is Maintained: Barriers to Entry

Our discussion of long-run competitive equilibrium shows how profits serve as a signal to attract new suppliers in competitive markets. If free entry into monopolistic markets were possible, the economic profits earned by monopoly firms would attract new sellers. Supply would increase, as would the number of sellers. The monopolists' control over price would disappear as the markets became competitive. A barrier to entry is a constraint that prevents additional sellers from entering a monopoly firm's market. The major barriers to entry in a monopoly market are discussed in the following sections.

Government Franchises and Licenses Some barriers to entry are the result of government policies that grant single-seller status to firms. For example, local governments commonly give the right to install cable television systems to a single firm. Governments typically establish monopolies for the rights to sell electric power, and transportation, water, sewer, and natural gas service. In many cases in the United States, the most notable being the U.S. Postal Service, government-supported enterprises act as monopolists. Many states run monopoly liquor stores, and, in some states, the sole legal source of gambling is state-run lotteries.

Patents and Copyrights Patents and copyrights are another government-supported barrier to entry. They give creators of new products and works of literature, art, and music exclusive rights to sell or license the use of their inventions and creations. For example, many popular pharmaceutical prescription drugs, such as Crestor, used for treating high cholesterol, are patented. Amazon.com has a patent for its "one-click ordering" process of storing customer information for online orders. Patents and copyrights provide monopoly protection for only a specified number of years. After a patent or copyright expires, the barrier to entry is removed.

The idea behind patents and copyrights is to encourage firms and individuals to innovate and produce new products by guaranteeing exclusive rights to the profits through monopoly supply for limited periods.

Ownership of the Entire Supply of a Resource A monopoly can also be maintained by owning the entire source of supply of a particular input. De Beers had monopoly power in the diamond market because it controlled the sale of up to 90 percent of uncut gem diamonds in the 1980s through its Central Selling Organization. The Aluminum Company of America had a monopoly in the U.S. aluminum market until the end of World War II. Its monopoly was based on its control of bauxite ore, the source of aluminum, and its control of a few excellent sources of low-cost power.

Unique ability or knowledge can also create a monopoly. Talented singers, artists, athletes, and the "cream of the crop" of any profession have monopolies on the use of their services. Firms with secret processes or technologies have monopolies if other firms can't duplicate those techniques.

Cost Advantages of Large-Scale Operations and the Emergence of Monopolies *Economies of scale* are cost savings that result from large-scale production. Such cost savings favor the establishment of monopolies because bigger firms in industries for which economies of scale prevail can produce at lower average cost than smaller competitors.

If firms can continually reduce average costs of production and profits by expanding in the long run, one firm will eventually emerge as the dominant supplier. Under such circumstances, much higher average costs of production would result under perfect competition, which requires many small firms with small market shares. If perfect competition existed initially, it would end as soon as existing firms merged or one firm purchased their assets and consolidated them to achieve lower average costs. Eventually, one firm would dominate. Once it does, new firms can't enter because they are too small initially to achieve the low average costs that the dominant firm enjoys by virtue of producing the entire market supply in very large plants.

The term natural monopoly is sometimes used to describe a situation in which a firm emerges as the single seller in a market because of cost or technological advantages that lower the average cost of production. Competition among firms in such a market results in one large firm supplying the entire market demand at a lower average cost than that of two or more smaller firms. A natural monopoly can produce the entire quantity demanded by buyers at any price at a lower average cost than would be possible for each firm in its industry if more than one firm existed. For example, a local electric company is a natural monopoly if the average cost of producing the quantity of electricity currently demanded is higher when more than one firm sells electricity.

The Demand for a Monopolist's Product

A common mistake made by people who criticize monopoly is to assume that the demand for a monopolist's product is perfectly inelastic. Consumers always have the alternative of doing without a monopolist's product when its price is increased. For example, if your local electric monopoly raises its price, you and other consumers can use your air conditioners less or be more careful about turning out lights.

If there were only one seller of automobiles in the United States, we'd still react by buying more cars when the monopoly seller lowered prices and buying fewer when it increased prices. The managers of a monopoly firm know that the amount they'll sell depends on the price they choose. Because there's only one firm in a pure monopoly market, there's no distinction between the market demand curve and the demand curve for the firm's product. The output of a pure monopoly firm *is* the market output. *The demand curve for the pure monopolist's product is the downward-sloping market demand curve that would be faced by an entire competitive industry.* For this reason the monopolist's pricing decision is inseparable from its decision about the amount to offer for sale. The higher the price it sets, the lower the quantity it will sell.

The Monopolist's Marginal Revenue

2 For a competitive firm marginal revenue is the same as price. For example, if bread is sold by many rival firms in a competitive market, each individual seller can sell as much as it wishes each day without reducing price. If the price of bread is $2 a loaf, any one firm will take in an extra $2 each time it sells an additional loaf. A monopolist, on the other hand, must *decrease* the price of the product to sell more. This follows because the demand curve for a monopolist's product is downward sloping. The marginal revenue of additional sales is therefore always less than the price.

Let's use a numerical example to illustrate how marginal revenue is related to price for a monopoly. Suppose you're a popular entertainer on a par with Bon Jovi or Beyoncé. You're the single seller of live concerts in which you are the principal performer. Your fans see no close substitute for your voice and appearance. They're crazy about you. You are, in short, a monopolist in the sale of your services. You can set your price for a concert.

The table in Box 1 provides data on the price per performance and the number of appearances you can sell at each price per year. The price you charge can also be thought of as the *average revenue* per performance. Average revenue is total revenue (*PQ*) divided by quantity (*Q*). At a price of $1 million per performance, only one concert hall will buy your services. Thus, your total output of concerts per year will be one and your total revenue per year will be $1 million. Remember that marginal revenue is the *extra revenue* for each *extra* unit of output. It's the *change* in total revenue divided by the *change* in quantity sold. The third column calculates annual total revenue from the sale of your services to the concert halls. Your marginal revenue is simply the change in total revenue for each extra concert.

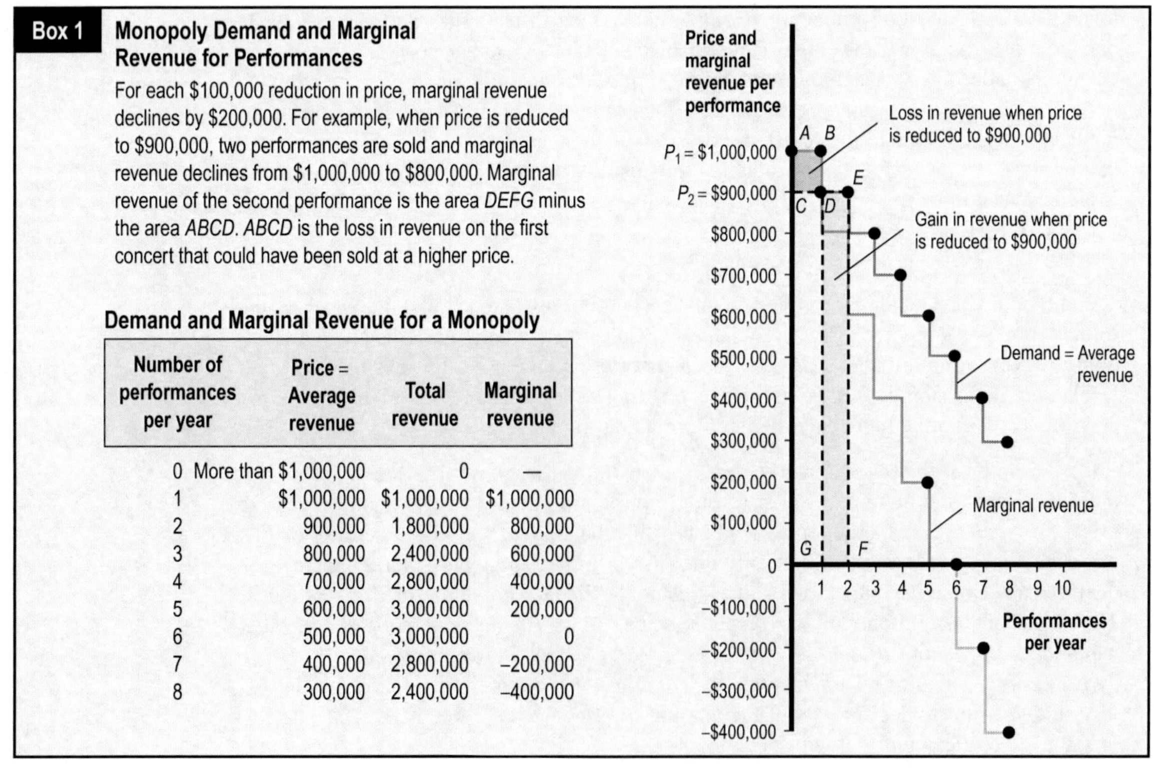

Box 1 Monopoly Demand and Marginal Revenue for Performances

For each $100,000 reduction in price, marginal revenue declines by $200,000. For example, when price is reduced to $900,000, two performances are sold and marginal revenue declines from $1,000,000 to $800,000. Marginal revenue of the second performance is the area *DEFG* minus the area *ABCD*. *ABCD* is the loss in revenue on the first concert that could have been sold at a higher price.

Demand and Marginal Revenue for a Monopoly

Number of performances per year	Price = Average revenue	Total revenue	Marginal revenue
0	More than $1,000,000	0	—
1	$1,000,000	$1,000,000	$1,000,000
2	900,000	1,800,000	800,000
3	800,000	2,400,000	600,000
4	700,000	2,800,000	400,000
5	600,000	3,000,000	200,000
6	500,000	3,000,000	0
7	400,000	2,800,000	−200,000
8	300,000	2,400,000	−400,000

$$\text{Marginal revenue} = \frac{\text{Change in total revenue}}{\text{Change in number of concerts}}$$

The marginal revenue of your first concert is $1 million because you'd have zero revenue if you gave zero concerts. If you want to give two concerts per year, you must lower your price to $900,000 per concert. Your total revenue will then be $1,800,000 per year. The marginal revenue of the second concert is therefore $1,800,000 minus $1 million, which equals $800,000. The marginal revenue of the second concert is $100,000 less than the price you received. (Unlike a competitive firm, a monopoly firm experiences a fall in marginal revenue below average revenue as it sells more.) Notice that you must announce your price in advance. Assuming that you don't have the option of charging $1 million for the first concert and $900,000 for the second, the only way the quantity of your services demanded will increase to two concerts per year is if you lower the price you're willing to accept for *each* concert.

The decrease in price results in downward pressure on your revenue because you lose the opportunity to sell one concert at $1 million. However, the extra sales resulting from the lower price result in upward pressure on revenue. *The marginal revenue is the difference between the loss in revenue due to the lower price and the gain in revenue due to the increase in the quantity sold.* Lowering your price gives you $900,000 in revenue from the second concert that you wouldn't have had the opportunity to give had you kept your price at $1 million. The graph in Box 1 shows your gain in revenue from the extra concert. It also shows the loss of the $100,000 you could have earned from the first concert had you kept your price at $1 million. The net gain in revenue is therefore $900,000 less the $100,000 forgone on the first concert. Your marginal revenue from the second concert is $800,000.

The table in Box 1 calculates marginal revenue for each price and quantity. After the first concert successive reductions increase the difference between price and marginal revenue. At $500,000 per concert, marginal revenue becomes zero. At any price below $500,000, marginal revenue is negative. Giving more than six concerts per year will decrease rather than increase your total revenue!

A monopoly seller can be regarded as *a price maker rather than a price taker* whether or not it wants to be! The fact is that a pure monopolist *must* lower its price if it wants to sell more because its demand curve is the entire market demand curve.

Profit Maximization by Monopoly Firms

3 A competitive firm, which can't influence the price of its product, maximizes profit by merely adjusting the amount it produces at the market price until marginal revenue equals marginal cost. Although a monopoly seller can influence the market price of its product, the principle of profit maximization is the same. Maximization of profit implies that marginal revenue must equal marginal cost at the output produced. *However, the marginal revenue of additional output for a monopolist is less than the price at which that output is sold.*

The table in Box 2 provides data on the costs incurred for your concert performances. The total cost per year of all your performances is shown in the third column of the table. The fourth column shows the average cost of each performance. The marginal cost is calculated in the fifth column as the change in the total cost for each extra performance. The sixth column shows your total revenue, while the seventh column reproduces data on marginal revenue from the table in Box 1.

Marginal cost rises with output because additional concerts mean more wear and tear on equipment (more annual repair costs) and on the performer. The hassle of more travel wears down even the most dedicated performer, and you could be looking at extra medical

Box 2 Costs and Determination of Profit-Maximizing Monopoly Output

Price	Output (performances per year)	Total cost (*TC*) per year ($)	Average cost ($ per performance)	Marginal cost (*MC*) ($ per performance)	Total revenue (*TR*) per year ($)	Marginal revenue (*MR*) ($ per performance)	Total profit (*TR*–*TC*) ($ per year)	Marginal profit (*MR*–*MC*)
More than $1,000,000	0	$ 100,000	—	—	0	—	$ -100,000	—
$1,000,000	1	500,000	$500,000	$ 400,000	$1,000,000	$1,000,000	500,000	$ 600,000
900,000	2	1,000,000	500,000	500,000	1,800,000	800,000	800,000	300,000
800,000	3	1,550,000	516,666	550,000	2,400,000	600,000	850,000	50,000
700,000	4	2,250,000	562,500	700,000	2,800,000	400,000	550,000	-300,000
600,000	5	3,150,000	630,000	900,000	3,000,000	200,000	–150,000	-700,000
500,000	6	4,150,000	691,666	1,000,000	3,000,000	0	–1,150,000	–1,000,000
400,000	7	5,550,000	792,857	1,400,000	2,800,000	–200,000	–2,750,000	–1,600,000
300,000	8	7,550,000	943,750	2,000,000	2,400,000	–400,000	–5,150,000	–2,400,000

expenses. Also, the implicit wage that you pay yourself rises when you perform more, because you are giving up more and more of your leisure. Fatigue from overperforming can impair the quality of your performance and ruin your reputation. After all, show business is a tough life! The rising marginal cost in the fifth column of the table reflects these additional costs that can be associated with increasing the number of concerts per year.

Your fixed costs are $100,000 per year. These consist of depreciation and interest on capital equipment, such as musical instruments, sound equipment, costumes, and the vehicles used to transport you and your entourage (including bodyguards) to each performance. Even if you give no concerts in a year, you still incur these costs. The next to last column, total profit, thus shows that you'll lose $100,000 per year if you choose not to give any concerts. If you price your performances at over $1 million each, there will be no buyers. You'll therefore lose an amount equal to your fixed costs.

If your price is $1 million, you'll find a buyer for one concert per year. Your total costs will be $500,000, so you'll make a $500,000 profit on that concert. The marginal cost of the first concert is $400,000. This is equal to the average variable cost of that concert. It consists of wages paid to your assistants, accompanying musicians, bodyguards who protect you while on the road, and fuel for the vehicles that get you from location to location. The marginal revenue of the first concert is $1 million. Marginal profit, shown in the last column of the table, is therefore $600,000. Recall that marginal profit is the difference between marginal revenue and marginal cost.

After the first concert marginal revenue falls below price because you must lower your asking price to have the opportunity of giving more performances. You must price your concerts at $900,000 each if you want to sell two per year to the promoters. The total revenue of two concerts is $1.8 million. The total cost of two concerts is $1 million. The marginal cost of the second concert is therefore $1 million less $500,000, divided by 1. Because the marginal revenue of the second concert is $800,000, your marginal profit is positive. In this case your marginal profit is $300,000 and your total profit increases from $500,000 to $800,000 per year.

As long as marginal revenue exceeds the marginal cost of a concert, your profits will increase. The marginal cost of the third concert is $550,000, while its marginal revenue is $600,000. Your marginal profit is therefore $50,000, and your total profits increase to $850,000 per year. If you want to give three concerts per year, you have to price each concert at $800,000.

Will you be interested in reducing your price below $800,000? If you cut your price to $700,000, you can give four concerts per year, but it won't be worth it! The marginal cost of the fourth concert is $700,000 and its marginal revenue is only $400,000. Your marginal profit is therefore –$300,000. By cutting your price to $700,000, you'd actually reduce your profits from $850,000 to $550,000 per year.

As the table in Box 2 shows, any output greater than three concerts per year will cost more than it brings in. Your equilibrium price is therefore $800,000 per concert. The equilibrium quantity demanded at that price is three concerts. Any price above or below $800,000 per concert will result in either more or less than the profit-maximizing number of concerts.

Your profits at that price are $850,000 per year. The marginal cost of concerts at that output is $550,000. *At the equilibrium output, therefore, marginal cost is less than price.* This follows because marginal revenue is less than price under monopoly.

The price set by the monopoly firm determines the quantity demanded. For example, a monopoly electric company can't easily increase or decrease the availability of electricity. However, it can influence the quantity demanded by manipulating its price until quantity demanded adjusts to the level at which marginal cost just equals marginal revenue.

As long as the price exceeds the average cost at the output for which marginal revenue equals marginal cost, a monopoly will be profitable. The monopoly price of a concert was $800,000. The average cost was a bit less than $516,666 (the average cost shown in Box 2 has been rounded to the nearest dollar) when you gave three concerts per year. Profit per concert, which is the difference between price and average cost, was therefore $283,334. Multiplying this by 3 gives approximately $850,000.

How much profit a monopolist actually makes depends on both costs and the demand for the product. Having a monopoly doesn't guarantee that you'll earn profits. Monopolists can and do go out of business when the demand for their product declines. Owning the only factory that produces vinyl records won't be profitable if no one is willing to buy vinyl records anymore. If demand and marginal revenue decline, it can be impossible to make a profit.

The graph in Box 3 draws the cost curves, the demand curve, and the marginal revenue curve for a profit-earning monopolist. Suppose this firm monopolizes the supply of bread

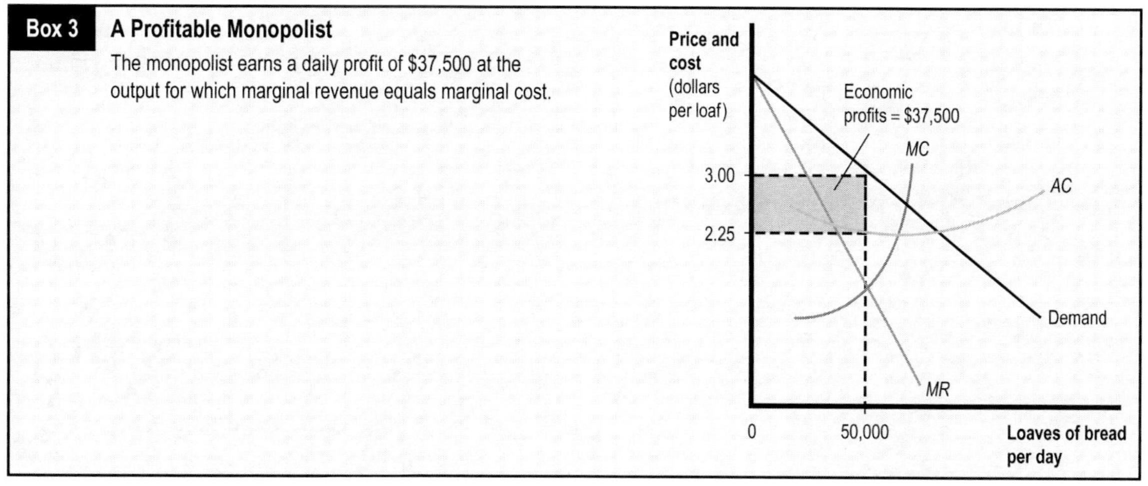

A Profitable Monopolist

The monopolist earns a daily profit of $37,500 at the output for which marginal revenue equals marginal cost.

in a nation. The output for which marginal revenue equals marginal cost is 50,000 loaves per day. The monopolist prices bread at $3 per loaf to sell that amount. The average cost of producing 50,000 loaves per day is $2.25. The monopolist therefore earns a daily profit of 75 cents per loaf. At the daily output of 50,000 loaves, total profit is $37,500 per day, shown as the shaded area of the graph in Box 3.

The graph in Box 4 shows a monopoly producer of vinyl records that incurs losses at the profit-maximizing output corresponding to the point at which marginal revenue equals marginal cost. The profit-maximizing output for the records is 50 per day, and the corresponding price is $5. However, the average cost of 50 records per day is $10. Because average cost exceeds price at the profit-maximizing output, the monopoly incurs losses of $250 per day. *It follows that having a pure monopoly doesn't always guarantee that the monopoly will be profitable!*

Notice that it's not in the interest of a monopoly firm to charge the highest possible price. The monopolist that maximizes profits realizes that it loses sales by increasing price. *Monopoly firms maximize profits by always setting price to achieve the output over any period for which marginal revenue equals marginal cost.*

Elasticity of Demand and Monopoly Pricing

The graph in Box 5 shows a linear demand curve and the corresponding marginal revenue curve for a monopoly firm. Demand is elastic when a decrease in price results in an increase in total revenue. (See the chapter Elasticity of Demand and Supply.) If total revenue increases when price decreases, marginal revenue must be positive. We can therefore conclude that, whenever the marginal revenue resulting from a price decrease is positive, demand is elastic. By the same token, if the marginal revenue from the extra sales resulting from a price decrease is negative, it follows that demand must be inelastic. This is because negative marginal revenue implies that the price decline results in a decrease in total revenue. Finally, when marginal revenue is zero, a change in price doesn't change total revenue and demand is unit elastic. The lower part of the graph in Box 5 shows how total revenue for the monopoly firm varies as price is reduced. *Maximum total revenue occurs where marginal revenue is equal to zero.* At that point on the linear demand curve, demand is unit elastic.

Monopolists are assumed to maximize profits instead of revenue. Therefore, they must produce the output corresponding to the point at which marginal revenue equals marginal cost. Marginal cost, of course, is always positive because more resources must always be used to produce additional output. It follows that marginal revenue at the profit-maximizing

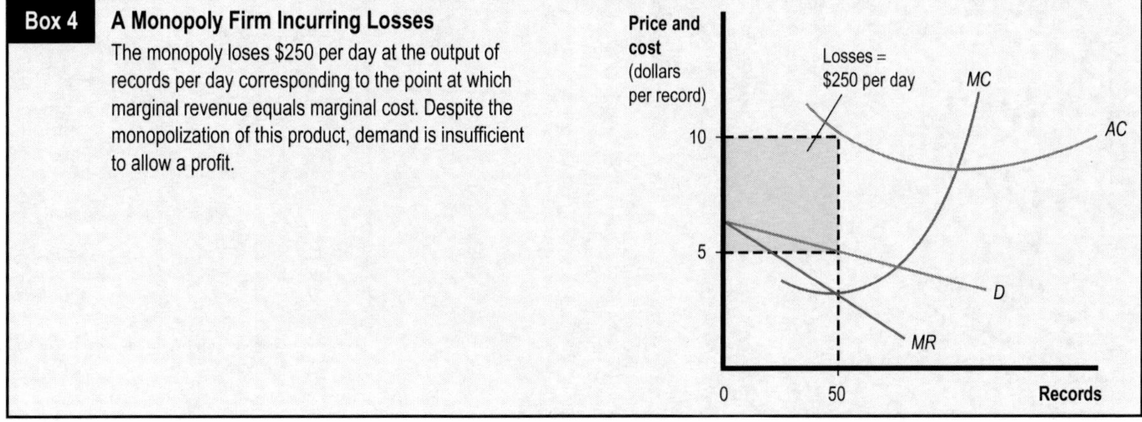

Box 4 A Monopoly Firm Incurring Losses
The monopoly loses $250 per day at the output of records per day corresponding to the point at which marginal revenue equals marginal cost. Despite the monopolization of this product, demand is insufficient to allow a profit.

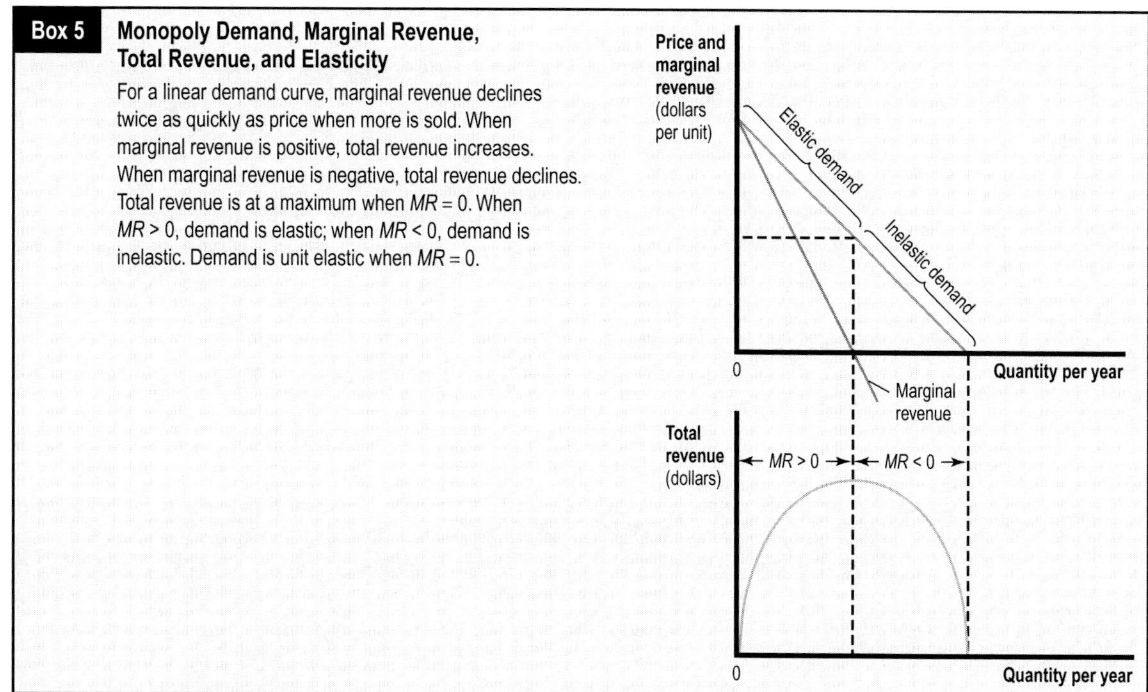

Box 5 Monopoly Demand, Marginal Revenue, Total Revenue, and Elasticity

For a linear demand curve, marginal revenue declines twice as quickly as price when more is sold. When marginal revenue is positive, total revenue increases. When marginal revenue is negative, total revenue declines. Total revenue is at a maximum when $MR = 0$. When $MR > 0$, demand is elastic; when $MR < 0$, demand is inelastic. Demand is unit elastic when $MR = 0$.

output must also be positive. A positive marginal revenue means that demand for the product is elastic. *A monopoly firm will always price its product to ensure that demand is elastic.*

Monopoly Supply

A supply curve shows a relationship between price and the quantity supplied by a firm or an industry. Competitive firms simply react to prices. A monopolist, however, is a price maker. It decides how much to produce on the basis of the information it has on the demand for its product. Given this information, it prices its product so that marginal revenue equals marginal cost.

Even though a monopoly firm has an upward-sloping marginal cost curve at any point in time, it doesn't necessarily increase quantity supplied when the demand for its product increases. Sometimes a monopoly firm reacts to an increase in demand by raising the price of its product rather than increasing quantity supplied. The change in the quantity supplied by a monopoly firm depends on the shift in its marginal revenue curve when demand increases. In deciding how to respond to an increase in demand, the monopolist examines the way the price elasticity of demand has changed to calculate the new marginal revenue associated with each possible output. It then adjusts price to maximize profit, given the new marginal revenue curve, by choosing the price that allows sale of the output for which under the new demand $MR = MC$.

Evaluating Market Outcomes under Pure Monopoly

4 The differences in market outcomes in the long run under monopoly and perfect competition can be illustrated by making a few simplifying assumptions. Suppose that, in the long run, the average cost and marginal cost of producing raisin bread are constant and equal to $2 per loaf. Small firms as well as large firms can produce at that average and marginal cost. This means that no inherent cost advantage is available to a

single firm serving the entire market demand. If raisin bread were produced under perfect competition, the long-run supply curve would be a horizontal line that intersects the price axis at $2, as illustrated in the graph in Box 6. This line corresponds to both the average and marginal cost of bread.

Suppose the market is currently served by 1,000 small, independently owned and operated bakeries. Each bakery sells raisin bread in a perfectly competitive national market in which the forces of supply and demand determine price. In Box 6, the long-run market equilibrium corresponds to point *E*, at which the market demand curve intersects the market supply curve. The equilibrium output is 100,000 loaves of raisin bread per day, and the equilibrium price is $2 per loaf. The price of raisin bread equals both the average and marginal cost of raisin bread. If the price exceeds $2, new firms will enter the market, and, over the long run, quantity supplied will increase until price falls to $2, the minimum possible average cost.

Now suppose that, in a dramatic move, all of the 1,000 independent bakeries are taken over by a single seller that now monopolizes the sale of raisin bread. Naturally, the new monopoly seeks to maximize profits. To do so, it estimates the marginal revenue obtainable from selling raisin bread. (See Box 6 for the marginal revenue curve corresponding to market demand.) The new monopoly's marginal cost of producing raisin bread is always $2, as it was when the industry was competitive. The marginal revenue of selling raisin bread equals the marginal cost of raisin bread at point *A*, which corresponds to an output of 50,000 loaves per day. To maximize profits over the long run, the monopolist therefore has to cut back output to half of the level that prevailed in the competitive market! The reduced availability of raisin bread will result in a higher price in the long run. At a daily output of 50,000 loaves, competition among buyers will result in a market price of $3 per loaf, corresponding to point *M* on the market demand curve.

At the $3 price, the monopolist will enjoy a daily profit of $1 per loaf (the average cost of raisin bread remains $2 after output has been cut). Given the daily output of 50,000 loaves, the monopolist earns a profit of $50,000 per day, shown by the shaded rectangular area in Box 6. Under perfect competition, each of the 1,000 independent bakeries just covered its opportunity costs of remaining in business and earned zero economic profits. The monopoly, on the other hand, raises the price above the average cost of raisin bread and earns a handsome profit each day at the expense of consumers, who now pay more.

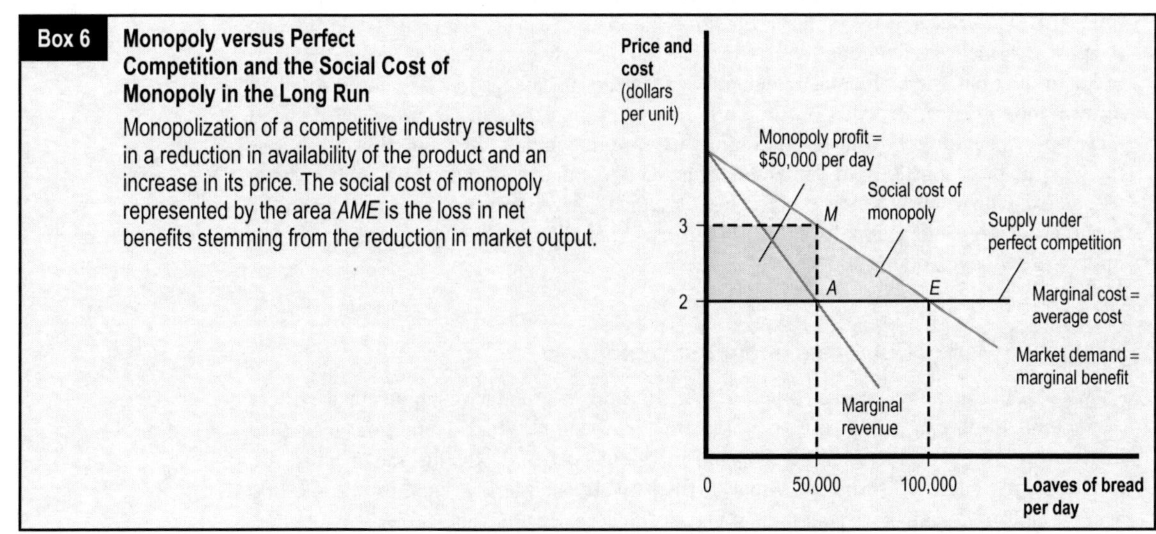

Box 6 Monopoly versus Perfect Competition and the Social Cost of Monopoly in the Long Run

Monopolization of a competitive industry results in a reduction in availability of the product and an increase in its price. The social cost of monopoly represented by the area *AME* is the loss in net benefits stemming from the reduction in market output.

To reduce output, the monopolist is likely to close plants in the long run. It will dismiss workers and sell off land and equipment. It will eventually close a substantial number of the 1,000 bakeries it acquired in the takeover. The remaining bakeries will be operated at the minimum possible cost of $2 per loaf, producing a total daily output of 50,000 loaves.

Now note the following differences between the monopoly equilibrium and the perfectly competitive equilibrium:

1. *The monopoly price exceeds the competitive price, and the monopoly output falls short of the competitive equilibrium output.*

2. *The price set by the monopolist exceeds the marginal cost of its product.* Price always exceeds the monopolist's marginal revenue. When the monopolist chooses the output that sets marginal revenue equal to marginal cost, price will also exceed marginal cost.

3. *The monopoly firm earns economic profit by charging a price that exceeds the minimum possible average cost of production.* The absence of free entry into the market ensures that supply won't increase, thereby causing price to fall. The monopoly firm enjoys economic profits, whereas firms in competitive equilibrium earn no economic profits.

To sum up: Monopolists produce less and price their products higher than do firms in competitive equilibrium. The higher prices paid under monopoly enrich monopoly owners at the expense of consumers, who, other than consuming less, have no alternative but to pay. In short, monopoly control over price is used to redistribute income from consumers to monopoly owners.

The Social Cost of Monopoly

Profit-maximizing monopolies can prevent efficiency from being achieved. Remember that points on a demand curve represent the marginal benefit of various quantities of a good to consumers. The efficient output is the one at which the marginal benefit of a good just equals its marginal cost. At that output it's impossible to make consumers better off by producing more of a good without harming those whose resources are used to make more of the good available. At the efficient output the net gains from making the good available are at a maximum. The efficient output of raisin bread is 100,000 loaves per day in Box 6. This corresponds to point *E* on the graph, at which the marginal cost and benefit curves intersect.

The monopoly market fails to achieve the efficient output of 100,000 loaves per day in the long run. At the monopoly output of 50,000 loaves per day, the marginal benefit of bread is $3 and the marginal cost is only $2. Because the marginal benefit exceeds the marginal cost at the monopoly output, less than the efficient output of bread is made available each day.

The social cost of monopoly is a measure of the loss in potential net benefits that results from monopoly control of price and supply. The graph in Box 6 shows how the social cost of monopoly can be measured. Because the marginal benefit exceeds the marginal cost at the monopoly output, additional net benefit is possible from producing more raisin bread each day. This net benefit can accrue either to buyers of bread or to resource owners whose inputs are used to produce bread. For example, if one loaf of bread more than 50,000 per day were made available, the maximum price that a buyer would pay for the loaf would be $3. This is the marginal benefit of raisin bread corresponding to point *M* in Box 6. The minimum price necessary to cover the opportunity cost of making that loaf available is $2. This is the marginal cost of raisin bread corresponding to point *A* on the graph. This means either the buyers can be made better off without harming sellers or that sellers of additional raisin bread can cover their opportunity cost while buyers are made better off.

The sum of the additional net gains possible from increases in the daily output of raisin bread from 50,000 to 100,000 loaves, the efficient output, is shown in area *AME* in Box 6. *This area represents potential net gains to buyers or additional sellers of raisin bread that are prevented by the monopoly control over supply and price.* The area *AME* therefore represents the social cost of monopoly. If barriers to entry were removed and the single seller of raisin bread were replaced by many competing sellers, price would fall to the competitive level of $2 per loaf, and these potential net gains would be realized.

There have been attempts to measure the actual social cost of monopoly in particular industries. In the 1960s the automobile market in the United States was dominated by General Motors, which accounted for nearly 50 percent of domestic production at a time when imports had a very small share of the U.S. market. One study estimated that the social cost of GM's monopoly control over price at the time amounted to over $1 billion per year.[1] This amount was about 4 percent of the value of GM's revenues per year. Assuming the estimate was accurate, the exercise of monopoly influence on price amounted to a 4 percent tax on consumers that was added to GM's profits. As of 2009, GM accounted for less than 20 percent of U.S. automobile sales, a sharp reduction compared to its market share in the 1960s. Increased competition in the U.S. automobile market has substantially diminished the company's ability to influence market prices. And in 2009, decreased demand for cars and high production cost relative to competing suppliers in the market had both GM and Chrysler fighting for their survival.

Are There Any Benefits from Monopoly?

In some cases a firm attains a monopoly position in the market for a good because of technological or cost advantages that aren't possible if many smaller firms supply the good. Under these circumstances, benefits associated with monopoly offset part of the social cost of its control over supply and price. Price is still higher than the marginal cost and minimum possible average cost of production in this case, assuming that the monopoly firm maximizes profits. However, the level of average cost is lower.

It's also sometimes argued that monopolists protected against competition from new entrants tend to be more innovative than sellers with many rivals because the monopolists know that in the long run they won't lose profits to competitors. More innovation means more technological progress, which in turn means lower average costs of production and lower product prices. However, many innovations are made in highly competitive industries. In many cases new entrants to industries are the most creative innovators.[2]

Regulation of Pricing: The Case of Natural Monopoly

5 You'll recall that a *natural monopoly* occurs when a firm can supply the entire market demand for a product at lower average cost than would be possible if two or more smaller firms supplied the market demand. Natural monopolies can prevail for the local provision of electric power, gas, and telephone services. The industries that provide these services are sometimes called *public utilities*.

Changes in technology can change cost conditions. For example, long-distance telephone service was once regarded as a natural monopoly, but changes in technology, such as satellite communication systems, now make it possible for a number of firms to compete for long-distance business.

[1]Keith C. Cowling and Dennis C. Mueller, "The Social Costs of Monopoly Power," *Economic Journal* 88 (December 1978), pp. 722–48.

[2]For a discussion of evidence both supporting and rejecting the hypothesis that monopoly or large market share tends to result in more innovation, see F. M. Scherer, *Industrial Market Structure and Economic Performance*, 2nd ed. (Boston: Houghton Mifflin, 1980), pp. 421–38.

Cost Curves and the Profit-Maximizing Output for a Natural Monopoly

The cost curves for a natural monopoly firm are shown in Box 7. Assume that in the absence of any government intervention in the market, the monopoly firm will try to set a price that allows it to earn maximum profit. Given the demand for its product, the profit-maximizing monopoly firm produces the output for which marginal revenue equals marginal cost. The profit-maximizing monopoly output is Q_M, and the monopoly firm selects a price of P_M to induce its customers to buy that amount annually. For example, if the natural monopoly firm is a power company, it will select a price per kilowatt-hour that induces its customers to purchase Q_M kilowatt-hours of electricity per month.

The monopoly firm earns economic profits equal to the shaded area in Box 7. Notice that the firm can lower average costs of production further by producing beyond Q_M. Its objective, however, is to maximize profits, not to continually reduce average costs. You should also note that allocative efficiency isn't attained when the monopoly sets its price to maximize profits. Remember, efficiency requires that output be made available up to the point at which its marginal benefit just equals its marginal cost. When the monopolist charges price P_M for a good, consumers buy the good until their marginal benefit just equals P_M. However, the marginal cost of the corresponding quantity demanded, Q_M, is less than P_M. You can see this by following the dashed line running from Q_M to the marginal cost curve. The output is inefficient because the price the monopolist sets to maximize profits exceeds the marginal cost of making that output available.

The Problem: Marginal-Cost Pricing Results in Losses for a Natural Monopoly

Natural monopolies and government-franchised monopolies are commonly subject to the authority of government commissions that regulate prices for the services of monopoly suppliers in their jurisdiction. In determining what price they allow a monopoly to charge for its product, such commissions usually consider the input prices paid by the monopoly and the interests of consumers.

Suppose government intervenes to get a monopoly firm to produce an efficient output. This will require an increase in output until the marginal cost of the service and its marginal benefit to consumers fall to the point at which the two are equal. Monthly output will have to increase to the quantity labeled Q_C, for which the demand curve just intersects the marginal cost curve. To induce consumers to buy Q_C, the monopoly firm will have to charge price P_C. If government intervened to require the firm to set a price of P_C, efficiency would be attained. This is because at that price the quantity sold would be Q_C,

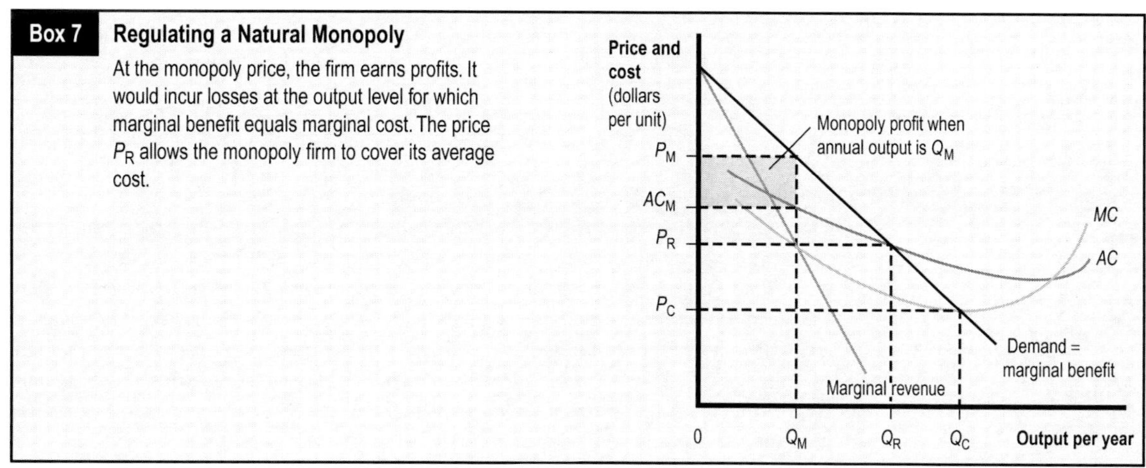

Box 7 Regulating a Natural Monopoly

At the monopoly price, the firm earns profits. It would incur losses at the output level for which marginal benefit equals marginal cost. The price P_R allows the monopoly firm to cover its average cost.

for which both the marginal cost and the marginal benefit would also be P_C. Remember that points on the demand curve reflect the marginal benefit, or the maximum price that buyers will pay for available quantities. Government intervention in the market to help attain efficiency therefore requires that price be controlled to equal the marginal cost of output at the point at which marginal benefit has declined to equal marginal cost.

The policy of marginal-cost pricing to achieve efficiency, however, runs into a snag because at Q_C average cost exceeds marginal cost. Setting price equal to marginal cost therefore results in losses for the seller. If a natural monopoly were forced to charge a price equal to its marginal cost, it would need a government subsidy to remain in business. Alternatively, the government could nationalize the monopoly, as is done quite often, and absorb the loss itself.

Regulators seeking to achieve efficiency in the market know that breaking up the monopoly into smaller firms isn't the solution because average cost and marginal cost of production will rise as a result. They also know the monopoly firm won't cover its opportunity cost, and thus won't voluntarily serve the market, if it is forced to charge a price low enough to induce consumers to buy an efficient quantity. What should the regulators do to solve the problem?

A Solution: Average-Cost Pricing

Regulatory commissions rarely attempt to make public utilities establish a price that equals a service's marginal cost and marginal benefit. Such commissions generally try to let the monopoly firm at least cover its accounting costs and the opportunity costs of invested capital.

Suppose a commission approves a price that allows the owners of a natural monopoly to just cover their opportunity costs. The graph in Box 7 shows that the price allowing zero economic profits is P_R. This price corresponds to the point where the demand curve intersects the average cost curve. When the price is P_R, the quantity demanded is Q_R. The price approved by the commission is P_R, which equals the average cost corresponding to the quantity Q_R. At this price economic profits are zero because the profit per unit is zero. However, price exceeds marginal cost. Any price lower than P_R will result in economic losses for the natural monopoly. *P_R is therefore the minimum price that will allow the monopoly firm to operate privately without subsidy.* Because average costs are lower, consumers are better off than they would be if there were more competition in the industry. However, they aren't as well off as they would be if price were set lower until it fell to equal marginal cost and marginal benefit at the output Q_C.

Note that the firm's owners would be better off if they could charge P_M, corresponding to the output where marginal revenue equals marginal cost. If the commission selects this price, the owners of the monopoly can earn maximum economic profits. Similarly, a price above P_R and below P_M will permit the firm's owners to enjoy more than the normal profit.

Average-cost pricing seeks to allow the owners of a monopoly to earn a "fair rate of return" just equal to the normal profit. Remember that the normal profit is a cost of production equal to the value of owner-supplied inputs. Because most large natural monopolies, such as electric power companies, are corporations, their main owner-supplied input is capital. To figure the fair rate of return, regulators measure the value of that capital. For example, suppose an electric company has $100 million of capital. Suppose its stockholders could on average earn 10 percent in their next best investment. The opportunity cost of holding on to their share of the monopoly's capital is 10 percent of $100 million, which is $10 million per year. The regulators would add all the accounting costs of the electric company and then include the $10 million fair return before computing the average cost of the output.

Government Regulation of Natural Monopolies in Practice

Implementing a policy that allows natural monopoly firms to just cover their costs is easier said than done. Regulators don't have neat graphs like the one in Box 7 with which to calculate average cost, Q_R, and P_R. Accurately determining average production costs at the level of output for which price equals average cost is difficult. In recent years, critics of the regulatory process have argued that consumers are being forced to pay for poor management decisions that result in higher average costs of production. The alleged management blunders include overinvestment in nuclear power plants and overexpansion of facilities.

By increasing the amount of capital it uses, the natural monopoly can increase the dollar amount of its normal profits. Some economists have argued that this results in more capital-intensive production techniques than would prevail in the absence of regulation. The choice of relatively inefficient capital-intensive production methods results in average costs higher than those that would otherwise prevail.[3]

The average-cost pricing rule provides no incentives for utilities to minimize their cost of production. They face no competitors, and any increase in cost resulting from blunders won't affect the rate of profit they earn on their investment as long as the regulatory commission sets a price that allows them a normal profit. In recent years, opponents of average-cost pricing have attempted to shift at least part of the burden of mismanagement from consumers to stockholders. Managers of natural monopolies counter such efforts by contending that if their firms can't make a normal profit, they'll have difficulty in attracting additional investors. These managers claim that service quality will decline or rates will increase still more to cover interest costs as their firms are forced to borrow because they find fewer buyers for their stock.

Critics of the regulatory process have also argued that political interests favorable to the natural monopolies tend to gain control of the regulatory commissions. When this is the case, the prices set by such commissions often allow the natural monopoly to come close to enjoying the price it would set to maximize its profits.

Price Discrimination

6 In some cases, a profit-maximizing monopoly firm charges different buyers different prices for the same good or service. When this is the case, some lucky consumers are able to purchase the monopolist's product at a price that's just equal to the marginal cost of the good!

The practice of selling a certain product of given quality and cost per unit at different prices to different buyers is called price discrimination. Public utilities charge businesses higher rates than they charge household users. Many drugstores, restaurants, and movie theaters offer discounts to senior citizens. Airlines are notorious price discriminators, as is shown by the multitude of fares available for similar seats on a given flight.

To engage in price discrimination, a seller must meet the following conditions:

1. *The seller must be able to control the price of its product.* A monopoly firm can engage in price discrimination because it can control prices.

2. *The product that's sold at more than one price must not be resalable.* It isn't possible to charge different prices to different buyers if a good is resalable. If a good is resalable, individuals who buy it at low prices can resell it to people who will pay higher prices.

[3]Harvey Averch and Leland L. Johnson, "The Behavior of the Firm under Regulatory Constraint," *American Economic Review* 52 (December 1961), pp. 1053–69.

Eventually, this process will lead to the establishment of a single price in the market because resale will continue until those who buy at a low price can no longer resell at a higher price. Automobiles, for example, are resalable products. People who can buy cars at low prices will turn around and resell them to people who will pay high prices. Medical services are nonresalable. If you get a deal on your appendectomy, you can't turn around and sell it to your friend at a higher price!

3. *The seller must be able to determine how willingness and ability to pay vary among prospective buyers.* Price discrimination will result in some people paying more and some paying less than would be the case if one price were charged for the product. The seller must be able to distinguish among buyers in a way that allows it to charge higher prices only to buyers whose marginal benefit from the product would exceed the single price.

Monopolists engage in price discrimination when they can increase their profits by doing so. A simple example will convince you that a monopoly seller that meets the conditions required for price discrimination can in fact increase its profits by engaging in the practice.

Price Discrimination in the Sale of Personal Services

Suppose that only one neurosurgeon in the world is capable of performing a rare brain operation. Anyone wanting the operation must come to this surgeon. The surgeon is therefore a monopolist. The medical service is clearly nonresalable. Also suppose that the surgeon requires all of the people who want the operation to fill out an elaborate questionnaire that enables him to determine the maximum amount each of them would pay for it.

Box 8 shows the demand curve for operations along with the marginal revenue curve. For simplicity we assume that the marginal cost of the operation is constant and equal to $40,000. If the surgeon behaves like a regular profit-maximizing monopolist, he'll want to do 20 operations a year because this is the quantity for which the marginal revenue would just equal the marginal cost of operations (at point *C*). The market price he would have to announce to get quantity demanded equal to 20 operations per year is $50,000. Because marginal cost equals average cost when marginal cost is constant, the average cost of an operation is $40,000. The surgeon would therefore earn a $10,000 profit per operation for a total annual profit of $200,000.

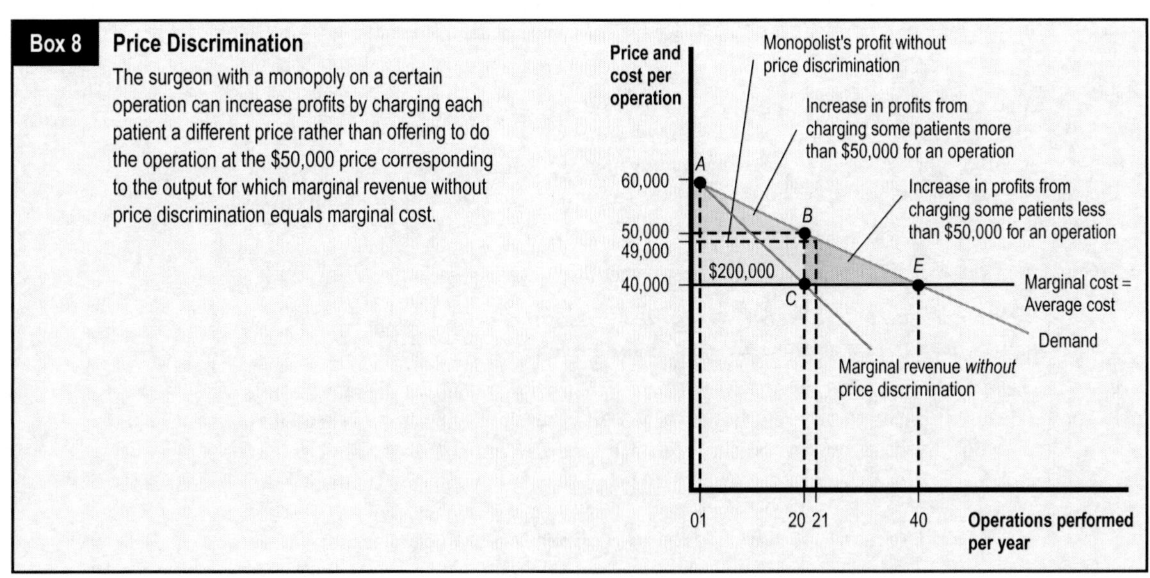

Box 8 Price Discrimination

The surgeon with a monopoly on a certain operation can increase profits by charging each patient a different price rather than offering to do the operation at the $50,000 price corresponding to the output for which marginal revenue without price discrimination equals marginal cost.

But the surgeon can earn more profits by engaging in price discrimination. For example, go to the point on the horizontal axis corresponding to one operation per year. The marginal benefit of that first operation to some patient is $60,000 (point *A*). Someone would be willing to pay that much to have the operation. Because the surgeon's elaborate questionnaire identifies this patient, he can charge the patient $60,000. The profit on the operation is $20,000 instead of $10,000. Similarly, the surgeon can charge more than $50,000 for all the other patients whose marginal benefit exceeds that amount. By doing so, the surgeon can increase profits by the indicated triangular area in Box 8.

Will the surgeon charge any patients *less than* $50,000? To find out, ask yourself whether he can increase his profits by doing so. For example, going to the point on the demand curve corresponding to 20 operations per year shows you that some patients would be willing to pay $49,000 for the operation after the surgeon has already performed 20 operations on those willing to pay more than $50,000. Because the marginal cost of the operation is still $40,000, the surgeon can increase his profits by $9,000 per year by performing the 21st operation. Similarly, as long as the marginal benefit of the operation exceeds $40,000, the surgeon can increase his profits by charging the patient a price equal to the patient's marginal benefit. This would increase the surgeon's profits by the indicated triangular area in Box 8.

The marginal benefit of the operation declines to the $40,000 marginal cost when 40 operations are performed per year. At that output the surgeon can't increase his profits by performing more operations, because the maximum price anyone else would pay falls short of the $40,000 marginal cost.

The output increases to the point at which its marginal benefit equals its marginal cost. This output is the same as the output that would be produced under competitive equilibrium. *However, only the last buyer gets the operation at the price of $40,000 that would prevail under perfect competition. All other buyers pay higher prices.*

Block Pricing

Sometimes a monopolist does not have enough information on willingness to pay to charge each consumer a different price. Under these circumstances the seller could price its product in blocks, charging different prices for the service depending on *how much* the buyer purchases over a given period. For example, an electric power company may have a rate structure under which different rates are charged per kilowatt-hour depending on how much electricity is consumed per month. In this way the monopolist takes advantage of the fact that the marginal benefit of electricity, and therefore the willingness to pay for it, declines as more electricity is consumed.

Box 9 shows how this form of price discrimination would work in the pricing of electricity. Your price per kilowatt-hour (kwh) would depend on the amount of electricity you consumed per month. The electric company would price its output in "blocks." The first 500 kwh that you consumed per month might be priced at nine cents per kwh; the second 500, at seven cents per kwh; and the third 500, at five cents per kwh. The pricing schedule would give you a price break if you consumed more electricity per month.

Box 9 shows how this pricing schedule enables a monopoly to capture some, but not all, of the consumer surplus from its customers. If the monopoly charged a single price corresponding to the quantity at which $MR = MC$ in the graph, the price would be six cents per kwh. But because the monopoly engages in block pricing, customers who consume relatively little electricity each month pay more than six cents per kwh, and very big customers, such as industrial users, pay less than six cents per kwh. As the graph shows, the monopoly earns more by engaging in price discrimination than it would earn if

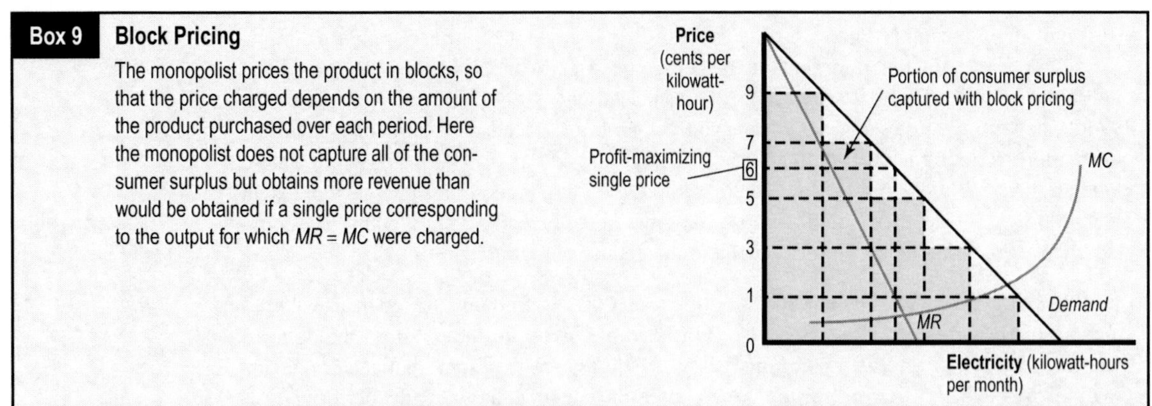

Box 9 Block Pricing

The monopolist prices the product in blocks, so that the price charged depends on the amount of the product purchased over each period. Here the monopolist does not capture all of the consumer surplus but obtains more revenue than would be obtained if a single price corresponding to the output for which $MR = MC$ were charged.

it charged a single price. However, because it doesn't price each unit at a different rate, it doesn't capture the entire consumer surplus. Many gas and electric companies have similar rate structures and can be regarded as engaging in second-degree price discrimination.

Price Discrimination in Segmented Markets

A segmented market is one in which two or more classes of buyers with differing responsiveness to price changes can be identified by certain characteristics. By charging different prices to each of these classes of buyers, the monopolist can increase its profits.

This type of price discrimination is common in airline travel. Airlines with monopoly power often perceive two classes of passengers: tourists and business travelers. Tourists have more elastic travel demands than business travelers. The business market is segmented from the tourist market by the duration of trips. Tourists on vacation tend to take trips that last one to three weeks and usually spend at least one weekend at their destination. Business travelers, on the other hand, tend to take very short or very long trips. On short trips they rarely spend a weekend at their destination. Accordingly, airlines have the opportunity to charge tourists and business travelers different prices by discriminating according to the duration of trips. The fare differential is often substantial. A business traveler sitting next to a tourist on a flight may be paying twice the tourist fare. The tourist fare is increased if the tourist ticket is used for a trip of any other duration. A tourist who extends her vacation beyond 28 days (or 45 days, if that's the cutoff) and attempts to use the ticket on her return trip is in for a rude surprise when she checks in for her departure. She will have to pay the differential between the tourist rate and the business rate. Travel agents now use complex computer programs to keep up with the discount fares, their advance booking requirements, and the penalties associated with violating their conditions.

Box 10 shows how a monopoly airline can increase profits through price discrimination. **A** shows the total demand curve for air travel on one of the airline's routes. That demand curve has a "kink" in it at the point at which tourists enter the market. At prices above the kink, only business travelers buy tickets. At prices below the kink, tourists start buying tickets. If there's no price discrimination, the airline charges the monopoly price, P_M, and sells Q_M miles of air travel per year on the route. The monopoly price is the one corresponding to the output for which $MR = MC$. Marginal revenue rises sharply when tourists start buying tickets. Assume that marginal costs are constant and, therefore, equal to average costs at all output levels.

B and **C** show the business and tourist segments of the market. At any price tourist demand is more elastic than business demand. Tourist demand begins at the price corresponding to the kink in the total demand curve.

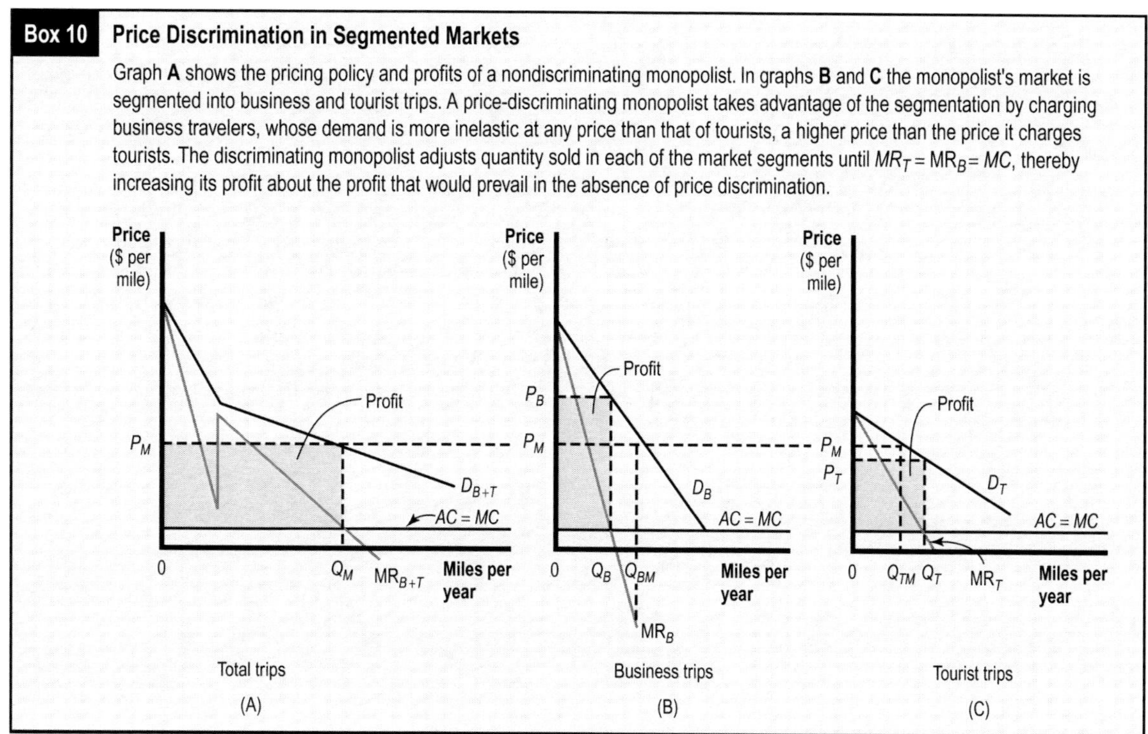

Box 10 Price Discrimination in Segmented Markets

Graph **A** shows the pricing policy and profits of a nondiscriminating monopolist. In graphs **B** and **C** the monopolist's market is segmented into business and tourist trips. A price-discriminating monopolist takes advantage of the segmentation by charging business travelers, whose demand is more inelastic at any price than that of tourists, a higher price than the price it charges tourists. The discriminating monopolist adjusts quantity sold in each of the market segments until $MR_T = MR_B = MC$, thereby increasing its profit about the profit that would prevail in the absence of price discrimination.

The airline can increase its profit by price discrimination. At the single monopoly price, P_{M}, business travelers would consume Q_{BM} miles per year and tourists would consume Q_{TM} miles per year. **B** and **C** show that, at those output levels, marginal revenue is negative in the business segment and positive in the tourist segment.

Because marginal revenue in the tourist segment (MR_{TM}) exceeds that in the business market (MR_{BM}), the airline can increase its profit by selling fewer tickets to business travelers and more tickets to tourists. It accomplishes this by raising business fares and reducing tourist fares. It can continue to increase its profit until

$$MR_{\text{TM}} = MR_{\text{BM}}$$

assuming that MC is independent of the mix of sales to tourists and business travelers.

Total profit, the shaded area in **B** and **C** is now the sum of the profit from tourist trips and business trips. This profit exceeds the profit that could have been earned at P_{M}, the single monopoly price.

Price Discrimination in Practice

In reality, firms with monopoly power use a variety of ingenious price discrimination techniques to increase their profits. Firms in the airline industry, as we just pointed out, use a variety of fares based on length of trip, day of departure, and one-way or round-trip service. Firms in other industries have also developed ways to divide buyers into groups with elastic and inelastic demands. For example, large food companies such as Nabisco and General Foods often distribute coupons through advertising that allow customers to purchase products at a discounted price. You're all familiar with these coupons, and you may have even used them to get rebates on various items or direct price reductions at the checkout counter.

Lower-income customers, who place a lower value on their time than do higher-income customers, usually clip and collect the coupons. These customers tend to have more elastic demands for many nonessential food products. By lowering the price only to customers who bother to clip and use the coupons, the food companies are able to segment their market and sell more to customers with more elastic demands.

Sellers of products that can be marketed in different formats, such as books, can also price-discriminate. For example, book publishers can market a book in a hardback or softcover edition. Typically, they first produce a high-priced hardback edition of a new book. They assume that the people most eager to read the book have the most inelastic demands and will pay a higher price for it. However, they also know that many additional readers whose demands are more elastic also want to buy the book. These people are willing to wait for the book. Book publishers usually issue a low-priced paperback edition after the high-priced hardback edition has fully tapped the market of eager readers with inelastic demands.

Summary

1. A pure monopoly is a single seller of a product that has no close substitutes.
2. In a market in which a profitable monopoly firm sells a product, a barrier to entry must prevent additional sellers from entering to compete for sales. Monopolies often arise among larger firms possessing cost or technological advantages that aren't enjoyed by smaller firms. A natural monopoly is a firm that attains its position as the single seller in a market by virtue of cost advantages.
3. A monopolist's demand curve is the market demand curve. Monopolists can expect to sell more by lowering the price of their product. When they increase the price of their product, they can expect to sell less. Unlike a perfectly competitive firm, a monopolist can't sell all it wishes at a given price. The price the monopolist receives depends on the amount of its product that it makes available.
4. Marginal revenue is the extra revenue a monopolist receives for selling additional output. For any amount sold, the marginal revenue received by a monopolist is less than the price it receives for its product.
5. A monopolist maximizes profits by setting the price that allows it to sell the amount of its product for which marginal revenue equals marginal cost over any period. Marginal revenue is positive only when demand for the monopolist's product is elastic. A monopoly firm never sells in a market in which demand for its product is inelastic because sales in such a market will decrease rather than increase revenue.
6. The price set by a profit-maximizing monopoly firm exceeds the marginal cost and minimum possible average cost of its product in the long run. A monopoly firm that can't earn profit at the output for which marginal revenue equals marginal cost goes out of business in the long run. Monopolization of a competitive industry results in an increase in product prices and a reduction in quantities supplied to buyers.
7. The social cost of monopoly is the loss of net gains to buyers and additional sellers of a product resulting from the control of supply and price by the monopoly firm. Monopolists prevent efficiency from being attained by pricing their product at a level that exceeds its marginal cost.
8. A natural monopoly is a firm that can supply the entire market for a product at lower average cost than would be possible if two or more smaller firms supplied the market. The average cost of production for a natural monopoly tends to fall as more output is produced.
9. A natural monopoly won't be able to cover its average cost of production if it produces an output large enough to result in a market price that falls to equal its marginal cost of production. This is because when average cost is declining, it exceeds marginal cost.
10. Firms franchised to serve the entire market, such as electric power or natural gas companies, are commonly regulated by government commissions. These commissions generally seek to control pricing so as to allow such a monopoly supplier to cover its accounting costs and earn a "fair rate of return" equal to the opportunity cost of the capital invested in it. In practice, average-cost pricing policies may provide monopoly suppliers with little incentive to control costs and with substantial incentives to overinvest in capital inputs.
11. Monopolists sometimes find it profitable to engage in price discrimination by selling the same product at different prices to different buyers, even though the cost per unit is the same. When monopolists engage in price discrimination, they sell more than would be possible if they charged all buyers a single price.

Concept Review

1. Explain why a monopoly can influence the market price of its product and why a competitive firm cannot do so.

2. Why does a monopolist's ability to influence the market price of its product imply that the marginal revenue of any given quantity will be less than its price?

3. A monopoly producer of computers in a small nation sets a price of $4,000 for its computers. Assuming the producer maximizes profits, what can you say about the marginal cost of the computers?

4. What would happen to prices, output, and employment in a competitive building supply industry if the industry were taken over by a profit-maximizing monopoly?

5. Why do regulatory commissions avoid setting prices for the natural monopolies they supervise at levels equal to the marginal cost of market output?

6. Give some examples of price discrimination by monopolies.

Problems and Applications

1. The average cost of a kilowatt-hour of electricity is lower if a single plant is designed to serve 100,000 customers than if two plants serve the same market, with each plant serving 50,000 customers. Draw the long-run average cost curve for firms producing electricity, and explain why a single seller building a single plant in a city of 100,000 is likely to emerge as a natural monopoly. 1

2. A Mercedes-Benz dealership in a small city enjoys a monopoly. The following table gives the market demand schedule for the Mercedes:

Price (dollars)	Quantity demanded per month
120,000	1
110,000	2
100,000	3
90,000	4
80,000	5
70,000	6
60,000	7
50,000	8

Calculate the total revenue and the marginal revenue obtained from selling Mercedes-Benz cars. 1, 2

3. Using the data from the demand schedule in Problem 2, draw the demand curve, the marginal revenue curve, and the total revenue curve. For each price, indicate whether the demand is elastic, inelastic, or unit elastic. 2

4. The dealership in Problem 2 estimates that the marginal cost of selling Mercedes-Benz cars each month varies according to the following schedule. The marginal cost consists of the wholesale cost of each Mercedes plus the cost of other variable inputs such as salespersons' salaries, advertising, and other expenses necessary to sell additional vehicles each month.

Quantity sold per month	Marginal cost (dollars)
1	70,000
2	75,000
3	80,000
4	85,000
5	90,000
6	100,000
7	120,000
8	150,000

Assuming the dealership seeks to maximize profits, predict what price it will set for the Mercedes and indicate the quantity it will succeed in selling at that price. 3

5. Suppose the marginal cost of selling any given quantity of Mercedes-Benz cars doubles. What will the monopoly dealership do? 3

6. Currently, bubble gum is supplied by many competing producers in a nation. The market for bubble gum is perfectly competitive. In a massive takeover effort, a large conglomerate corporation buys out all the assets of the current bubble gum producers and establishes a monopoly. Draw the market demand and supply curves for bubble gum prior to the takeover, assuming the market equilibrium price of bubble gum is $1 per pack and the equilibrium quantity supplied is 5 million packs per month. Show what will happen to the price of bubble gum and the quantity supplied as a result of the takeover, assuming the new bubble gum monopoly maximizes prof-

its. Show the social cost of the monopoly takeover. 4

7. Suppose the average cost of producing electric power declines continually as more electric power is made available to buyers. If an electric company can be induced to charge a price of 2 cents per kilowatt-hour, the quantity demanded would be great enough to allow a reduction in marginal cost to 2 cents. Use a graph to show that the electric company wouldn't cover its opportunity cost at that price. 5

8. Use the graph you drew in answer to Problem 6 to show how a tax of 10 cents per pack collected from bubble gum sellers will result in a smaller monthly decrease in quantity sold when the bubble gum industry is a monopoly than would be the case if the industry were competitive. 4

9. List goods and services for which price discrimination is possible. Under what circumstances will a monopoly firm engage in price discrimination? 6

10. Prove that no buyer in the market for a medical procedure that can be purchased only once in a lifetime will earn any consumer surplus when a monopolist engages in price discrimination and charges each buyer an amount equal to that buyer's marginal benefit from the procedure. (See the chapter Consumer Choice and the Theory of Demand for the definition of consumer surplus.) 6

How a Global Organization Monopolized the Sale of Diamonds and How Its Monopoly Is Eroding

De Beers SA is an enormous diamond producer that runs mines in Botswana, Namibia, and South Africa. For a good part of the 20th century, the company controlled much of the supply of rough diamonds throughout the world, with a cartel-like arrangement managed by its Central Selling Organization (CSO), headquartered in London. Until recently, the CSO (now called the Diamond Trading Company) effectively monopolized the supply of diamonds with its cartel.

Sir Ernest Oppenheimer established the CSO in the 1930s to control the market supply of diamonds. The CSO bought as well as sold diamonds. By holding on to stockpiles of the gems, it was able to threaten to dump diamonds on the market to lower prices and thus ruin any independent sellers. For example, in 1981, Zaire (now called the Democratic Republic of the Congo) attempted to market its diamonds independently. The CSO reacted by flooding the market with diamonds similar to those sold by Zaire. The price Zaire was obtaining for its diamonds plummeted, and Zaire ceased to sell its diamonds independently.

The CSO acted to control the price of diamonds in order to maximize the profits of its members. In the early 1980s, when the price of diamonds plunged because of flagging demand, the CSO bought many of the gems unloaded by speculators to prevent the price of diamonds from falling too steeply. In 1994, excess supplies of diamonds in the marketplace were putting downward pressure on prices. That year, De Beers entered the market again as a buyer to stockpile more and more diamonds. In doing so, De Beers was able to keep diamonds scarce and keep the price from falling. During 1994, it was estimated that De Beers spent nearly $790 million to increase its diamond inventories to an amount double that of 1984.

The De Beers monopoly on diamonds faced serious challenges in the 1990s, when its share of the diamond market fell from 80 percent in the early 1990s to 63 percent in 2000. First, in 1992, thousands of independent prospectors flocked into Angola, taking advantage of its political instability to search for and sell diamonds independent of De Beers. Diamond smuggling was on the rise in the former Soviet Union, and large batches of diamonds from Russia turned up in Belgian diamond markets without having gone through the CSO. Independent sellers of diamonds in the former Soviet Union disregarded government agreements with De Beers.

Russia now ranks second after Botswana as the world's largest diamond producer. Under pressure to raise foreign currency, Russian producers sold huge amounts of rough, uncut diamonds, independent of De Beers, throughout the 1990s. De Beers's contract with Russia as of 1995 allowed it to sell 95 percent of Russian diamond exports. However, it was clear that Russia wasn't abiding by the agreement. Russia's independent sale of diamonds was estimated at $800 million in the first 8 months of 1994. These sales were largely responsible for De Beers's market share to decline by 75 percent.[1]

By 2009, De Beers's market share had fallen to 40 percent of total sales of rough stones. It's clear that the company's grip on the global diamond market has weakened.[2] In recent years, new mines have been operating in Australia, Canada, and Russia, and new high-quality synthetic diamonds for gems and industrial uses have been developed. More and more sellers of rough diamonds have chosen to sell their products independently rather than going through the CSO run by De Beers. Lev Leviev Diamond, a major diamond cutting and polishing firm, is revolutionizing the way business is done in the diamond market. This company is seeking to integrate diamond mining and processing by channeling stones it produces or purchases directly from mining companies (other than those run by De Beers) directly to diamond cutting and polishing businesses, without going through the CSO. As of 2009, such operations were underway in Russia, Namibia, and Angola, independent of any control by De Beers.

De Beers is still a force in the diamond markets. It spends close to $200 million on advertising each year to encourage the purchase of gem-quality diamonds. However, by 1999, shareholder pressure caused De Beers to drop its policy of buying surplus diamonds to keep prices high. That year, it began selling diamonds from its $4 billion stockpile to raise cash.

For the 21st century, De Beers appears to be developing an entirely new strategy and is abandoning attempts to monopolize industry supply through its cartel. Its new strategy is to more aggressively market and sell its own brand-name gems and jewelry made from De Beers rough diamonds (under the *De Beers* and *A diamond is forever* trademarks).

In preparation for its new strategy and greater presence in the U.S. retail jewelry market, the company had to settle an old lawsuit filed against it by the U.S. Department of Justice. In 1994, the Justice Department charged De Beers with conspiring with the General Electric Company to fix the prices for industrial diamonds used for cutting and polishing. General Electric was acquitted of the charges, but De Beers still had charges pending. The legal problems made it impossible for De Beers executives to enter the United States without running the risk of being arrested. On July 14, 2004, De Beers pleaded guilty to the price-fixing charges in an Ohio court and agreed to pay $10 million to settle the indictment. One year later, in the summer of 2005, De Beers opened a flagship retail store at 703 Fifth Avenue in Manhattan to sell products made with stones mined by the company or marketed through the CSO. The company now appears more intent on establishing a "mystique" about its brand to raise prices, rather than on controlling all the world's diamonds.

This is good news for diamond buyers. The breakup of the cartel and more competition in the market will increase the supply of diamonds. If you're thinking about making a "gift of love" to your sweetheart, it will soon be less costly to do so--provided you stay away from the De Beers brand. A diamond may be forever, but it looks like cartels are not.

In 2008, De Beers settled a class-action lawsuit that alleged antitrust violations and false advertising by the company. De Beers agreed to pay up to $300 million to those who purchased diamonds in the United States between January 1, 1994, and March 31, 2006. Those who filed the required forms before May 19, 2008, were eligible to receive refunds on their purchases between 6 and 60 percent of the original price.

De Beers was facing new challenges in 2009, as a severe recession sharply reduced the demands for diamonds. De Beers' sales were down by more than 20 percent, and prices for its diamonds were also plunging. When demand falls, even a firm with monopoly power must reduce prices to maximize profits!

[1]See Neil Behrmann, "De Beers's Diamond Cartel Shows Flaws," *The Wall Street Journal*, October 31, 1994.

[2]See "The Diamond Cartel: The cartel isn't forever," *Economist.com*, Print Edition Special Report, July 15, 2004.

Why Do Electric Companies Want You to Use *Less* Electricity?

Back in the 1960s, electric companies throughout the country were encouraging their customers to consume *more* electricity. Many local companies offered free installation of power lines to "all-electric" homes that heated and powered appliances with electricity. Going a step further, some companies advertised electrical appliances and urged customers to buy the latest kilowatt-consuming contraptions. In those halcyon days, power was not only plentiful, but also delightfully cheap.

Expecting sharp increases in the demand for electricity in the 1970s and 1980s, many electric companies invested heavily in nuclear power plants. They expected to sell lots of electricity to an ever more affluent population. This scenario turned out to be far too optimistic.

In the projections they made in the 1960s, the power companies assumed electricity would remain cheap and expansion of capacity would lower average costs. However, steep hikes in the prices of oil and coal in the 1970s, accompanied by safety woes and new regulations that significantly increased the costs of building nuclear power plants, markedly raised the average cost of electricity. Consumers responded by conserving power. Houses were built to be energy efficient. Thus, many power companies found themselves saddled with expensive nuclear plants that generated more electricity than was demanded. These companies petitioned their regulatory commissions for rate increases to cover their higher-than-expected capital costs. The resulting rate hikes aggravated the problem by further decreasing the quantity of electricity demanded.

Although nuclear power plants have fixed costs because of their extensive capital requirements, the marginal cost of generating electricity in such plants is quite low. In a typical nuclear plant, electricity can be generated at a cost of less than 1 cent per kilowatt-hour. In some of the older nonnuclear plants, electricity costs over 12 cents per kilowatt-hour! When demand increases beyond the capacity of a nuclear plant, most power companies have computerized controls that automatically turn on the more expensive nonnuclear sources of power. Naturally, profits go down when the price per kilowatt-hour is fixed by a regulatory commission and the company shifts to a higher-cost source. For a typical company with at least one nuclear power plant, the marginal cost of electricity can rise quite sharply with peak demand, as older plants are put into operation to meet the demand.

Many power companies believe the solution to this problem is demand management. They offer low-interest loans to households that install storm windows and other energy-saving devices. Some power companies offer a discount to homes that are fully insulated.

Power companies have also petitioned regulatory commissions to allow "peak load" pricing that will increase the price per kilowatt-hour as marginal costs increase. Some power companies use a time-of-use policy that gives customers a discount on electricity used during hours of the day when demand is usually slack.

Despite these changes in policy, many electric companies are still in financial difficulty because of past investment decisions. Should the regulatory commissions make customers pay higher prices to allow a fair rate of return on investments that didn't pan out as expected? Or should the stockholders of the electric companies take the loss? If this route is chosen, it may be more difficult for electric companies to raise funds for future expansion and maintenance through the issuance of corporate stock. On the other hand, should consumers be forced to pay for decisions in which they had no voice?

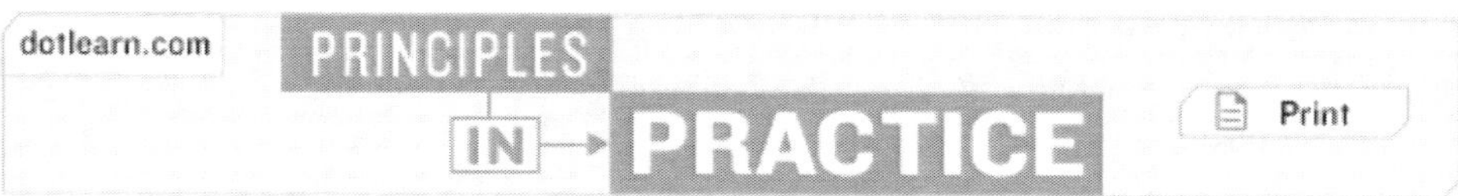

Business Brief: Monopoly Pricing Methods--Two-Part Tariffs

Monopolies have shown quite a bit of ingenuity in taking advantage of their power to set prices so as to maximize profits. One of their techniques requires buyers to pay a fee for the right to purchase their product and then to pay a regular price per unit of the product. For example, your cable TV company charges you a base fee for hooking into its system and then charges you extra for pay-per-view transmissions.

The fee for privilege of service plus prices for services consumed is called a two-part tariff. Theme parks sometimes employ such a pricing scheme to increase their profits. To see how the scheme works, suppose you operate a theme park and have a local monopoly. The graph below shows the demand for rides at your theme park by any given tourist, along with the marginal revenue and marginal cost of the rides. If you charge a single monopoly price, your rides will be priced at $6 each, and each tourist will consume four rides per visit, spending $24.

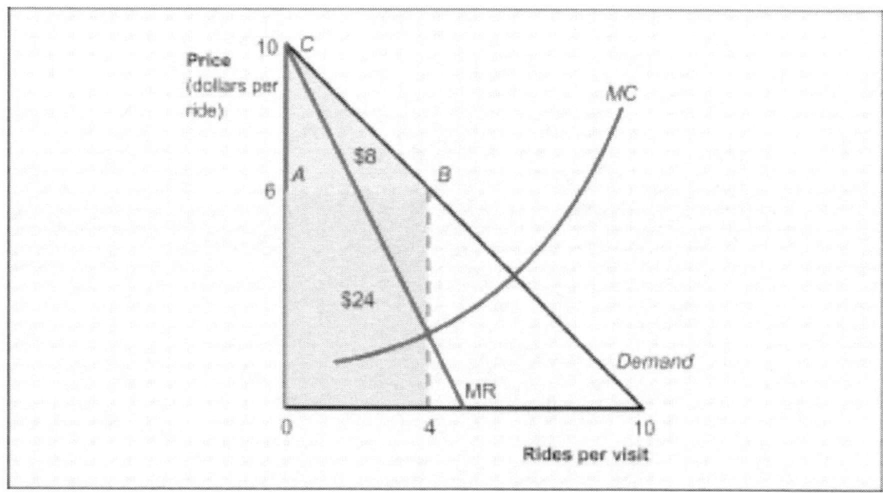

Now, let's see if a bit more can be extracted from each tourist. Given the demand curve drawn, each tourist would be willing to pay more than $24 to enter your theme park and take four rides. If you know the demand curve for rides, you know that the typical tourist is enjoying a consumer surplus of $8, corresponding to the area of triangle *ABC* in the graph (area $ABC = 1/2 \times 4 \times 4$). Therefore, if you charge an entry fee of $8, in addition to $6 per ride, you can add $8 per tourist to your profit.

Given the demand curve of a typical tourist, you can add still more to your revenue from each tourist if you simply eliminate the price per ride and just charge an admission fee equal to consumer surplus at zero price per ride. For example, if the price per ride were zero, a tourist would go on 10 rides per visit and you would get revenue of $50 per tourist--0.5($10)(10)--instead of the $32 you would get from the two-part pricing scheme. But be careful. With more rides, your marginal costs will increase, and, thus, your profit might not increase. Also, if you extract the entire consumer surplus with a single entry fee, you increase the tourists' cost per visit, so the total number of admissions will fall.

A two-part tariff is often a good way to increase profit by extracting some, but not all, of the consumer surplus from a monopolist's clients. Monopolists usually experiment with various two-part tariff pricing schemes before hitting on the one that gives them maximum profit.

Chapter

21

Gross Domestic Product and the Performance of the National Economy

If you follow the news about the economy, you know there are periods during which it appears to be bursting at the seams. At those times, business firms can't keep up with orders. At other times, the economy's performance is sluggish, so that inventories of unsold goods build up. When production declines in the economy, factories and offices aren't fully utilized, workers are laid off, and incomes fall. The fact is your job prospects, your income, and the purchasing power of your hard-earned dollars all depend on the performance of the economy as a whole.

This part of the text shows how we measure the economy's growth and explains why a slowdown in growth, excessive unemployment, or inflation can be serious problems. In the part of the text on aggregate demand/aggregate supply, we analyze the forces that influence the performance of the economy.

In this chapter, we'll show how an economy's output is measured and how the elaborate National Income and Product Accounts of the United States keep track of how resources and income are used. By tracing the flows of expenditure and income through the economy, we'll see how its various sectors and markets fit together and how decisions to save, invest, and allocate resources to government use influence production and income. We'll also show how the U.S. economy is tied to the rest of the world through international trade.

Concept Preview

After reading this chapter, you should be able to

1. Explain what GDP is, how it can be viewed as the value added to intermediate products, and how real GDP differs from nominal GDP.
2. Understand why GDP must equal the sum of consumption, investment, government purchases, and net exports and how expenditure on the nation's output results in income to resource owners.
3. Explain how the concepts of gross national product, net national product, national income, personal income, and disposable income can be derived from GDP.
4. Understand how spending and income circulate among business firms, households, and governments and how international trade affects the economy.
5. Explain how national saving is computed, and show how net foreign saving in the United States has helped finance domestic investment in recent years.

Looking at the Economy from a Macroeconomic Perspective

Macroeconomics is the study of the overall performance of the economy and the way various sectors of the economy relate to one another. Our goal in studying macroeconomics is to analyze the big issues relating to employment opportunities, inflation, and economic growth. But before we can accomplish that goal, we must have a means of measuring the performance of the economy so we can tell how well it is doing and whether economic conditions are improving or deteriorating.

The performance of the economy depends on decisions made by millions of individuals. In macroeconomics we focus on the total value of a nation's production, ranging from safety pins to oil-drilling rigs and from haircuts to coronary bypass surgeries. Rather than looking at the purchases of one household or business firm alone, we examine influences on the total purchases of all households and all business firms. Rather than looking at production for sale in a specific market, we add up the total value of products produced during the year and offered for sale in all markets. We then show how changes in conditions of demand and supply can affect employment of workers, inflation, and growth of production and income.

During the 1930s, when the U.S. economy was performing dismally, economist Simon Kuznets helped create a system that became the basis for charting the course of the economy, for which he was later awarded a Nobel prize. The National Income and Product Accounts (NIPA) are the official system used for measuring economic activity in product and input markets in the United States. Our system of National Income and Product Accounts focuses on aggregates, which are broad totals of economic variables such as production, consumption, and investment.

The NIPA also provide information on what we're producing and which groups are reaping the rewards for producing those goods and services. They provide us with information about how much output is produced, how much income results from production, and what types of products are produced. You may be surprised to read that the bulk of the income resulting from production goes to workers and that only a very small share ends up as rents. It may not surprise you, however, to read that the United States devotes the bulk of its vast productive capability to satisfying the desires of consumers who save very little of their income.

The NIPA not only measure economic activity; they also show how households, business firms, and governments affect the flow of expenditure and income in product and input markets. We can use the accounts to discover how production influences income and how consumer spending, business investment, government policies, and international trade affect current and future output.

Measuring Aggregate Output: Gross Domestic Product

1 In reading the newspapers and watching television news reports, you've probably been exposed to the term *gross domestic product*, the cornerstone of our system of National Income and Product Accounts. Gross domestic product (GDP) is the market value of the final goods and services produced by workers and other resources located within the borders of a nation over a period of one year. United States GDP in 2008 was $14.26 trillion. The goods and services whose values are included in GDP are the nation's final products that are sold to final users and not used as materials, parts, or services to be incorporated in the value of other items that are to be resold. Included in GDP is the value of domestic output produced by foreign workers with jobs in the United States and by foreign-owned property located within the borders of the nation. For example, the cars produced in a Japanese-owned Toyota factory located in Kentucky are part of America's

GDP. By the same token, computers produced by a U.S.-owned Apple Computer factory in Singapore are included in the GDP of Singapore.

Gross domestic product is a key economic variable that is closely watched in gauging the performance of the economy. Both job opportunities and earnings in a nation are linked to production. When the output of final products in the economy grows, so too will income and job opportunities. More production means greater use of inputs; and as more inputs are used, the earnings of those who supply them goes up—as do the opportunities for employment. Conversely, if GDP falls, fewer resources will be used, and income in the nation will also fall.

How GDP Is Calculated

GDP is calculated by multiplying the quantity of each individual type of final product by its market price. The dollar values of all final products derived in this way are then added to obtain a sum that equals the market value of the economy's aggregate production of final products. We aggregate the value of loaves of bread, computers, tickets to football games, pizzas, televisions, new homes, new cars, bulldozers, drill presses, aircraft, insurance, medical services, and other items produced over a year to measure GDP.

Because GDP is a measure of the market value of aggregate production, transactions that don't involve production aren't included in it. For example, the value of sales of stocks and bonds is *not* part of GDP because these and other purely financial transactions don't involve actual production of goods and services. Changes in the value of existing assets are also excluded from GDP because they don't represent production of new goods and services. Likewise, the value of used goods sold during the year is not part of GDP because the value of these goods was counted in prior years. Finally, in most cases goods and services not sold through markets are not reflected in GDP. For example, if you clean your own apartment or cook your own meals, the value of these productive services you provide to yourself instead of purchasing them in a market will not be included in GDP.

By placing dollar values on output based on the market prices of final products, we measure the worth of those products to buyers. We also avoid the difficulties involved in adding up goods and services measured in different units. Does aggregate production go up or down, for example, if the economy produces 50,000 fewer cars and 100,000 more insurance policies in a given year? To answer this question, simply compare the market value of the 50,000 cars and the 100,000 insurance policies. If the market value of the insurance policies exceeds the market value of the cars, we would say that aggregate output has increased.

Intermediate Products and Value Added

In measuring GDP, it's important to exclude the market value of production that is not for final use to avoid overestimating aggregate production. Intermediate products are those produced by business firms for resale by other firms or for use as materials or services that will be included in the value of resold goods. For example, steel purchased by General Motors from the United States Steel Corporation is an intermediate product because the steel will be used by General Motors as an input in the production of automobiles. If the value of the steel and the value of the automobile it is used in are *both* counted in GDP, the value of the steel will be counted twice.

During the process of production, business firms add worth to the intermediate products they purchase from other firms. Value added is the extra worth that a business firm adds to intermediate products. It is measured by the difference between the market value of a firm's sales and the market value of the intermediate products that the firm purchases.

Value added comes from such inputs as labor, capital, land, and entrepreneurial expertise. Firms combine these inputs with intermediate products that they purchase from other firms. A carmaker buys steel, glass, tires, and other products from other firms and uses its workers, capital, and managerial expertise to produce a vehicle. Naturally, the vehicle is worth more than the intermediate products that the carmaker purchased from other firms.

Total value added in a nation is the difference between the market value of *all* products of business firms and the market value of all intermediate products.

Total value added in a nation (GDP)	=	Market value of all products	–	Market value of intermediate products

The market value of all products includes the value of both final and intermediate products. Therefore, when the value of intermediate products is subtracted from this sum, the result is the market value of the nation's final products. *Because the market value of final products is GDP, it follows that GDP can be viewed as total value added in a nation over a year.*

A simple example about the production of blue jeans (see Box 1) will show you how value added is computed at each stage of production and how it is related to the receipts and payments of a business firm.

1. To make a pair of blue jeans available in product markets, cotton is first grown by farmers. If you assume that farmers produce cotton without purchasing any materials or services from other firms, the value added by farmers equals the market value of their sales of cotton. (The value of the intermediate products is zero.)

Suppose annual sales of the cotton to be used in producing blue jeans are $1 million. The value of these sales must be fully accounted for by the sum of the farmers' profit and costs incurred. Because the farmers are not purchasing anything from other firms, the value of wages paid to workers, rent paid to land and equipment owners, and interest paid to lenders are the only costs reflected in the $1 million sales receipts. Therefore, any part of the $1 million not accounted for by these costs is the profit. *The value added of the farmers is the income generated by the sale of cotton.*

2. Next weavers who convert the cotton to cloth purchase the cotton from the farmers. The weavers' only intermediate purchase is that of the $1 million worth of cotton they obtain from farmers. After processing the cotton into cloth, the weavers sell the cloth for $2 million to a manufacturer of jeans. The value added by the weavers is therefore the $2 million in sales less the $1 million purchase of cotton.

Box 1 Computing Value Added

Sales transactions	Intermediate purchases	Value added (Sales receipts- Intermediate purchases)
1. $1 million sale of cotton by farmers to weavers	None	$1 million
2. $2 million sale of cloth by weavers to manufacturer of blue jeans	$1 million of cotton	$1 million
3. $4 million sale of blue jeans by blue jean manufacturer to consumers	$2 million of cloth	$2 million

Market value of all products	–	Market value of intermediate products	=	Total value added
$7 million	–	$3 million	=	$4 million

The logic of the concept of value added should be clear to you now. *Value added at each stage of production is the difference between the value of the product at that stage and the cost of products purchased from other firms for use as inputs.* The value added by the weavers is the worth they have added to the cotton by processing it into cloth. This worth must reflect the value of the inputs used to process the cotton into cloth that are *not* purchased from other firms.

3. The manufacturer of blue jeans sells the product it produces with the cloth to consumers who wear the jeans. Assume that the only intermediate purchase made by the blue jean manufacturer is the $2 million purchase of cloth. If the total market value of the jeans produced by the manufacturer is $4 million, then the value added at this final stage of production is $4 million less $2 million, which equals $2 million. Once again, the $2 million value added by the blue jean maker must equal the sum of incomes of workers and other input owners whose resources are used to produce the blue jeans, plus the manufacturer's profit.

The table in Box 1 shows how we arrived at total value added. Line 1 shows the sales transactions of farmers. The sum of product sales, including those of intermediate products, is $7 million, which is obtained by adding the numbers in Column 1. The sum of the market value of all intermediate purchases is $3 million, obtained by summing the dollar values of sales in Column 2. The sum of value added is $4 million (Column 3). *The sum of the value added associated with the production of blue jeans at its various stages exactly equals the market value of the final product sold by the blue jean makers to consumers.*

To summarize: GDP can be viewed as the sum of value added in all transactions involving new production in a nation over a year. Value added also equals the sum of payments to the owners of all resources used to produce the goods and services included in GDP and the profit of business firms because value added at each stage represents the sum of payments to labor, capital, land, and all other inputs. When value added goes up in a nation, so will income.

Nominal GDP and Real GDP

Nominal GDP is the market value of a nation's final output based on *current prices* for the goods and services produced during the year. Nominal GDP is of only limited use in measuring changes in aggregate production over time. This is because nominal GDP can rise from one year to the next as a result of increases in the market prices of goods even when the nation's aggregate production of final products does not increase. In fact, nominal GDP can increase as a result of substantial increases in a broad array of market prices even when the nation's aggregate production of final output actually declines! Similarly, if market prices fall substantially during a year, nominal GDP might fall even if the nation's aggregate production goes up.

Real GDP is an estimate of the value of a nation's final products adjusted for changes in prices since a certain base year. Real GDP approximates the expenditure in dollars necessary to buy the economy's final products during a given year had there been no change in prices since the base year. The base year for estimating real GDP in the United States is 2000. Real GDP is a more accurate measure of changes in the value of aggregate production in the economy over time than nominal GDP because it removes the effects of rising prices when valuing output.

Prior to 1996 the U.S. Department of Commerce calculated real GDP simply by valuing current output at base year dollars. Up until the end of 1995 the National Income and Product Accounts published a constant dollar estimate of real GDP by valuing current output at prices prevailing in a 1987 base year. This method tended to overstate growth of real GDP since the base period by placing too high a value on products (such as computers) whose prices fell since the base period. Now, the U.S. Department of Commerce estimates real GDP by first calculating an output index for the economy. As of 2008, the year 2000 is used as the base and the output index for that year is set at 100. A "chain-type annual-weighted output index" is used to estimate growth in output for the economy by averaging prices in the current year and the past year for each year. Real GDP is then estimated by multiplying 2000 nominal GDP by the chain-type annual-weighted output index and dividing the result by 100. Both nominal GDP and real GDP for the base year 2000 are the same because the output index is equal to 100 in 2000.

The table in Box 2 shows how real GDP is calculated for the U.S. economy. First, start with nominal GDP for the 2000 base year, which was $9,817 billion. The chain-weighted output index for 2008 was 118.7, which means that, after adjustment for increases in prices since 2000, output increased 18.7 percent since the base period. Multiplying the 2000 nominal GDP by the output index and dividing the result by 100 gives us real GDP, which is output measured in 2000 dollars. These dollars are "chained" or averaged in each year since the base year to adjust for changing valuations of output at different prices each year as prices change. Measured in 2000 chained dollars, real GDP in the year 2008 was $11,652 billion, compared to the nominal GDP of $14,264 billion.

Real GDP per Capita: A Measure of Living Standards

We can divide real GDP by the population of a country to get a measure of the market value of goods and services per person adjusted for changes in prices from the base year. Because real GDP per capita is a measure of goods and services produced on average for each person in the nation, it is generally used as a measure of material well-being or living standards in a nation. Real GDP per capita in the United States amounted to $38,265 in 2008. The graph in Box 3 shows how real GDP per capita has grown in the United States since 1960. In 1960, GDP per capita was a mere $14,000. Because production of goods and services has grown more rapidly than population, output, measured by real GDP, per person has nearly tripled in the United States since 1960. The more rapid growth of real GDP relative to growth in population is the key to improving living standards in a nation.

Real Gross Domestic Product in the United States, on average, grew at a rate of about 3 percent per year in the 20th century. This positive growth rate is reflected in the upward trend in real GDP per capita shown in Box 3. However, there are periods in which real GDP declines. During these periods, output falls and living standards are sometimes set back temporarily, as unemployment rates increase and both production and income decline. In Box 3, gray bars depict these periods of recession for the economy. During a recession, the upward trend in living standards stalls. Between 1960 and 2008, there were 8 periods of recession for the U.S. economy. The most recent recession began in the last quarter of 2007, and its beginning is marked by a vertical line on the graph in Box 3.

Box 2 Calculating Real GDP Using the Chain-Weighted Output Index

Real GDP is calculated for the United States by using an index number for output which is set equal to 100 for the 2000 base year. The index number exceeds 100 for years after 2000 and is less than 100 for years before 2000. The table below shows the steps used to calculate 2008 real GDP in the United States:

Step 1: 2000 Base Year Nominal GDP = $9,817 billion

Step 2: 2008 Chain-Type Annual-Weighted Output Index, 2000 Base = 118.7

$$\text{Step 3: Real GDP} = \frac{\text{(2000 Nominal GDP)(Chain-Type Annual-Weighted Output Index)}}{100}$$

$$\text{2008 Real GDP} = \frac{(\$9{,}817 \text{ billion})(118.7)}{100}$$

2008 Real GDP = $11,652 billion

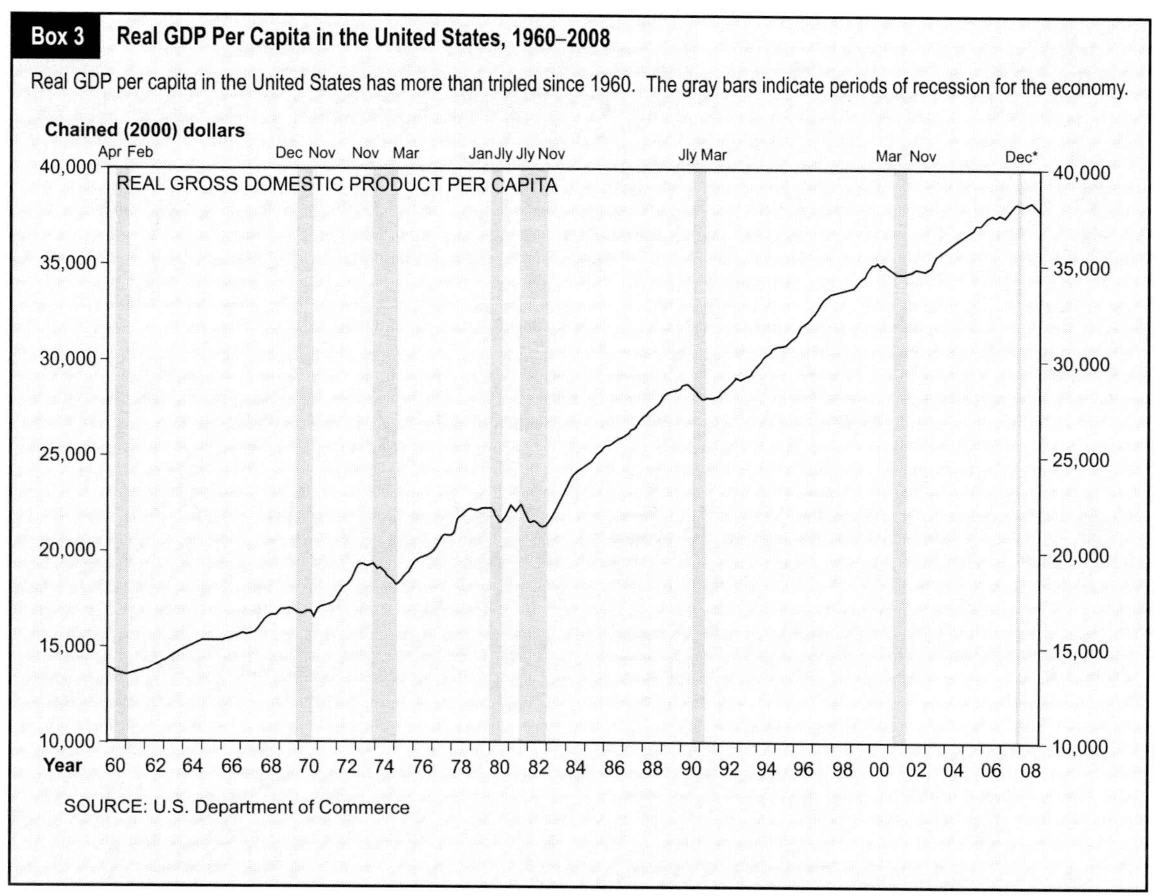

Box 3 Real GDP Per Capita in the United States, 1960–2008

Real GDP per capita in the United States has more than tripled since 1960. The gray bars indicate periods of recession for the economy.

How Good Is GDP as a Measure of National Well-Being?

How does GDP rate as a measure of the overall well-being of Americans? How does exclusion of nonmarket services affect the accuracy of GDP as an index of national well-being? Does GDP account for *decreases* in the quality of the environment that result from pollution? In this section we discuss important items affecting our well-being that are not included in GDP.

1. *Nonmarket production.* Many useful services are produced by members of households for the benefit of themselves or their families. Husbands and wives perform useful services for themselves and their families when they prepare meals, make household repairs, and handle their own financial affairs. The value of these services is *not* included in GDP because they do not represent services purchased through market transactions. Perhaps you can see this more graphically if you imagine each husband paying his wife for her services and each wife paying her husband for his services. These services would now become market services and would be included in GDP. Similarly, if more people remain single and hire housekeepers to do work that spouses would normally do without monetary compensation, GDP will increase!

Some nonmarket transactions, however, are included in GDP. For example, homeowners who live in their own homes enjoy the housing services their homes provide. In the National Income and Product Accounts, these owner-occupiers are viewed as being in the business of renting their homes to themselves. An estimate of the value of housing services enjoyed in this way *is included in GDP.*

In addition, GDP accountants impute values to farm products consumed on farms and food, clothing, and lodging furnished to employees. The imputed market values of these goods and services are also included in GDP. Of course, the goods and services made available by governments, such as national defense, are not sold in markets. However, their value is reflected in GDP because government purchases of labor and products are a component of GDP.

2. *The value of leisure*. All of you place some value on your time. You sell some of your time to employers for labor income; however, you retain much of it for your own use as leisure. Some of this leisure is used to produce household services that, as we discussed earlier, escape inclusion in GDP. The satisfaction you get from recreational activities and other uses of your leisure time also escapes inclusion in GDP.

3. *Cost of environmental damage*. We Americans may be able to enjoy more and better goods and services each year, but we must also put up with more congestion, dirty air, polluted waters, and other environmental costs that decrease the quality of our lives. Costs are associated with pollution and other aspects of industrial activity that damage the environment. The costs of environmental damage are not subtracted from the market value of final products when GDP is calculated. Some economists therefore believe that GDP overestimates the value of output by failing to account for environmental costs of production.

4. *The underground economy*. The United States has a vast underground economy. This economy consists of transactions that are never reported to tax and other government authorities. It includes transactions involving illegal goods and services, such as narcotics, gambling, and prostitution. These illegal goods and services are final products that are not included in GDP!

The transactions of the underground economy also include activities by people who don't comply with tax laws, immigration laws, or government regulations and who don't report their income to authorities. For example, a person might obtain a job and be paid in cash without paying any Social Security taxes or income taxes. Such transactions are not reported to the Internal Revenue Service, and because no record of the transactions is transmitted to governing authorities, the final product of the transactions often goes unvalued in GDP.

The Expenditure and Income Components of GDP

2 A major task of any economy is creating a mechanism for determining *what* is produced. The National Income and Product Accounts were designed not only to provide information on the total value of the final products produced over a year but also to keep track of the *kinds* of output produced. GDP can be broken down into components that show how much of our productive resources is being allocated to satisfy consumers' demands, to produce investment goods such as new machinery, to be used by governments, and to produce goods for export. It can also provide us with information about how much of our income we use to purchase imported products.

We can show how the receipts from the sale of final products are used to reward those who produce the output, thereby dividing GDP into income components. You will see that most of the receipts that businesses receive for selling their products are allocated to paying their workers.

The Expenditure Components of GDP

GDP provides information on what we use our resources to produce by dividing expenditure on final products into components showing how much of our production we devote to consumption, investment, government activity, and exports.

Let's examine the kinds of output that are included in GDP and show how these aggregates are measured in the National Income and Product Accounts.

1. *Consumption.* If you were to browse through the National Income and Product Accounts, you could find out how much consumers spend on haircuts, beer, cosmetics, or anything else. Personal consumption expenditures are purchases of final products (except new homes) by households and individuals. The NIPA treat the purchase of a new home as an investment purchase (as opposed to a consumption purchase). Personal consumption consists of the purchase of both durable and nondurable goods and services by people like you. Durable goods are items that last for a number of years, such as automobiles, kitchen appliances, and furniture. Nondurable goods are items that consumers use up soon after purchase, such as food and fuel. Services are nonmaterial items, such as the services of physicians and hospitals, lawyers, mechanics, banks, insurance companies, hotels, and educational institutions. Included in expenditures on services are housing rents, transportation costs, and household operating expenses for electricity, gas, and water. In recent years, services have become the dominant component of consumption in the United States, accounting for more than half the dollar value of consumption expenditures.

Personal consumption expenditures in the United States typically account for two-thirds or more of GDP. A reduction in consumer spending can spell trouble for the economy because the reduced consumer demand for goods and services can reduce production and job opportunities.

2. *Investment.* Investment is the purchase of final products by business firms for use in production or as additions to inventories and the purchase of new homes by households. Investment involves the production of new capital goods by businesses, including changes in inventories of unsold goods, materials, and parts over the year.

Gross private domestic investment includes purchases of new machinery, equipment, and structures by businesses, purchases of new homes by households, and the change in business inventories during the year. When inventories increase from one year to the next, they are added to investment. Reductions in business inventories during the year are treated as negative investment. Increases in business inventories represent goods that have been produced during the year but have not been sold to buyers in the market. These inventory accumulations must be included in GDP to accurately measure current production. In effect, the NIPA treat increases in business inventories as a final use of goods by businesses during the year. Similarly, when inventories decline during a year, the decline represents goods that were produced in previous years but sold during the current year. To accurately measure current GDP, the decline in inventories must be subtracted from investment.

Investment is *domestic* because it includes only that which takes place in the United States. For example, if IBM invests by building a new plant in Mexico, this investment is not part of U.S. GDP except to the extent that IBM purchases machinery in the United States for use in its Mexican plant.

Investment is *gross* because it doesn't deduct the amount of purchases necessary to replace capital that wears out or becomes obsolete during the year. Depreciation (also called *consumption of fixed capital*) is an estimate of the value of capital goods that wear out or become obsolete during the year. Net private domestic investment is gross investment less depreciation. If gross investment were just equal to depreciation, net investment would be zero and there would be no net addition to the value of capital during the year.

Gross private domestic investment fluctuates quite a bit, but it typically accounts for between 12 and 15 percent of GDP in the United States.

3. *Government purchases.* A significant amount of resources are devoted to government use each year, and government also purchases final products from business firms.

Government purchases of goods and services include expenditure on final products of business firms and all input costs, including labor costs, incurred by all levels of government in the United States. Each paper clip, computer, fighter plane, and filing cabinet purchased by government is included in the government purchases component of GDP. Also included is the entire payroll of all governments in the United States (local, state, and federal), representing purchases of labor services by governments.

Governments themselves produce valuable goods and services, such as national defense, police and fire protection, roads, bridges, schooling, and environmental protection. However, government services are not sold in the marketplace. Such government services as national defense, public education, and garbage pickup are indirectly valued in computing GDP because the costs (including labor) of making these services available are included in the government purchases component of GDP.

Not all government expenditures represent purchases of final products. Governments often incur expenditures that disburse payments to individuals without requiring any services in return. Transfer payments are payments for which no good or service is currently received in return. Expenditures by governments for Social Security pensions, welfare payments to the poor, and subsidies to agriculture and industry are examples of transfer payments. These transfer payments constitute a source of income for the recipients and, when spent, show up as consumption or possibly as investment in the GDP accounts. In effect, transfer payments are negative taxes representing payments by governments to individuals instead of payments by individuals to governments. Government expenditures (which include transfer payments) far exceed government purchases.

The treatment of the government sector of the economy in the NIPA has been criticized for not providing sufficient information on the way governments affect both current and future economic performance. Governments also add worth to intermediate products by using labor and other inputs. There is no way to determine the worth added to intermediate products by government's use of labor and other inputs because government output is not typically sold in the marketplace. The types of investments made by governments include roads, bridges, airports, structures, water resources development, sewers, mass transit, and other items referred to as the nation's *infrastructure*. Government purchases account for about 19 percent of GDP in the United States. Since 1996, government purchases in the NIPA are divided into government consumption and government investment to better measure the government sector's contribution to current and future output.

4. *Net exports*. Exports represent expenditure on U.S. final products by foreigners and show us how much of our total production is sold abroad. Imports represent the value of goods and services produced abroad and purchased by Americans. Net exports represent the excess of expenditure on exports over imports.

Total dollar values for consumption, investment, and government purchases include spending on both domestically produced *and* imported goods and services. In measuring GDP, expenditure on imports by consumers, businesses, and governments must be subtracted from their total expenditures to avoid counting the value of other nations' production in the U.S. GDP. Exports must then be added to account for the portion of our domestic production that is sold to foreigners.

When exports exceed imports, net exports are positive and foreign trade adds to GDP. When net exports are negative, imports exceed exports. In recent years U.S. imports have exceeded U.S. exports, and net exports have been a negative component of GDP that is subtracted from the sum of consumption, investment, and government purchases to arrive at GDP.

Since 1980, we have been spending more than the value of what we produce in the United States. As you'll see, when a nation spends more than the value of its production, it must borrow from foreigners to make up the difference. In recent years, the United States has, in fact, been a net borrower from the rest of the world.

Aggregate Expenditure The sum of consumption expenditures (C), expenditures on investment goods (I), government purchases (G), and net exports (NE) during the year is aggregate expenditure. This represents the dollar value of the nation's final production and is therefore equivalent to GDP:

$$GDP = C + I + G + NE = \text{Aggregate expenditure}$$

Whenever some goods produced during the year are not sold and are added to inventory, the NIPA treat them as investment expenditures by businesses. In this way the accounts must always balance because the value of aggregate production (GDP) will always, by definition, equal aggregate expenditure.

When the expenditure components of GDP are valued at base year market prices, aggregate expenditure measures real GDP.

The Income Side of GDP

Expenditure on output in product markets provides the funds for business firms to meet such expenses as wages, interest, and rents. You can therefore think of gross domestic product as also measuring *gross domestic income*, which is the costs incurred to pay for resources and profits earned in production of items included in GDP. Gross domestic income is the aggregate income earned annually from production. Aggregate expenditure on final products becomes the aggregate income of the nation. Every dollar spent on final products produced during the year ends up as income to either businesses or households.

The total income generated from production of final products is therefore equal to the value of those final products, which, as you saw in the previous section, is also equal to the value added to intermediate products by productive resources in the nation. Real GDP represents the value of final products produced during the year after adjustment for inflation. You can now see that real GDP also represents the aggregate real income of a nation, which is its nominal (money) income adjusted for inflation since the base year used to measure real GDP. If real GDP falls, so too will aggregate real income. If income, and living standards, in a nation are to grow, real GDP must also grow.

One of the reasons economists are so concerned about gross domestic product and its rate of growth is that production generates income. The more production in a given year, the more jobs. More jobs mean more income for workers.

Dividing GDP into Income Components Who earns the income that results from the production of goods and services in the economy? How much of that income is saved? How much goes to pay the taxes that finance government purchases and government transfer payments? The National Income and Product Accounts help us answer questions like these by keeping tabs on the way our aggregate expenditure on goods and services is channeled through the economy to businesses, resources owners, and governments.

Let's examine the income side of GDP by tracing out the uses of the receipts businesses take in during the year. Some receipts of business firms are used to pay sales taxes on output, such as gasoline taxes and state and local sales taxes, and some are plowed back into the businesses to finance investment. Most of the remainder is paid out as wages and salaries, interest on borrowings, and rents. Whatever is left over after making these payments is the profit of business firms.

The income components of GDP show how the receipts of business firms are allocated to pay for the resources used to produce final products during the year. The major income components of GDP are discussed here.

1. *Compensation of employees.* Employee compensation is the income from the sale of labor services during the year. It includes wages, salaries, and fringe benefits, such as employer-provided insurance and employer contributions to pension funds. Compensation of employees is the labor cost of producing final products and is by far the largest income component of GDP. It accounts for between 55 and 60 percent of the value of final products produced each year.

2. *Net interest.* The portion of business receipts used to pay for borrowed funds that finance investment purchases is called *net interest.* Interest payments provide earnings for savers and other suppliers of loanable funds for investment purchases. Interest paid by governments is not included in this category because it is financed by taxes rather than out of revenue from the sale of final products.

3. *Rental income.* Rental income is earned by those who supply the services of land, mineral rights, and buildings for use by others. Also included in rental income is an estimate of the imputed rent earned by homeowners who live in their own homes less the expenses of maintaining their homes. Rental income is a very small share of GDP, accounting for about 1.5 percent.

4. *Profits.* Before we can calculate the profit of corporations and unincorporated businesses, we have to make two additional deductions from business receipts in addition to payments for the use of productive resources:

a. Taxes on production and imports. Taxes levied on sales of final products that are reflected in the market value of goods and services sold by business firms are called indirect business taxes. These taxes include sales taxes, excise taxes, and other taxes that business firms treat as costs. Indirect business taxes account for about 7 to 8 percent of the value of receipts taken in from the sale of final products each year. They are really the portion of the receipts collected by business firms that are claimed by governments rather than used to pay for input costs or to be included as profit.

b. Consumption of fixed capital. A surprisingly large portion of the receipts from the sale of final products is set aside by business firms as allowances for consumption of fixed capital. As we pointed out in our discussion of investments, this allowance accounts roughly for the value of capital goods that are "used up" in production during the year. Allowance for consumption of fixed capital accounts for about 8 to 12 percent of GDP and represents the second largest use of business receipts after compensation of employees. Capital consumption allowances are a major portion of *business saving*, which represents business receipts that are neither paid out to resource owners nor used to pay taxes or add to profits.

After deductions from business receipts for indirect business taxes, capital consumption allowances, and costs for compensation of employees, net interest, and rents paid, the remainder is profit. Profit represents the income earned by owners of unincorporated corporate business (proprietors' income). Profit can be positive or negative. If costs exceed the receipts from the sale of final products, profit will be negative—implying that in the aggregate business firms incur losses during the year. As you know, the rate of profit is a very important determinant of the incentive firms have to supply goods and services.

The Economy's Income Statement

For the national economy we can use an income statement to show how receipts are allocated to pay expenses over a period. Such a statement shows how the receipts from expenditure on final products are accounted for by earnings of owners of resources and by other payments. Box 4 shows the *income statement* for the national economy in 2008.

The value of the final products represented by the sum C + I + G + NE must be accounted for as the flow of income and other payments generated by their sale. The left side of the income statement in Box 4 shows how GDP is measured by aggregate expenditure. The

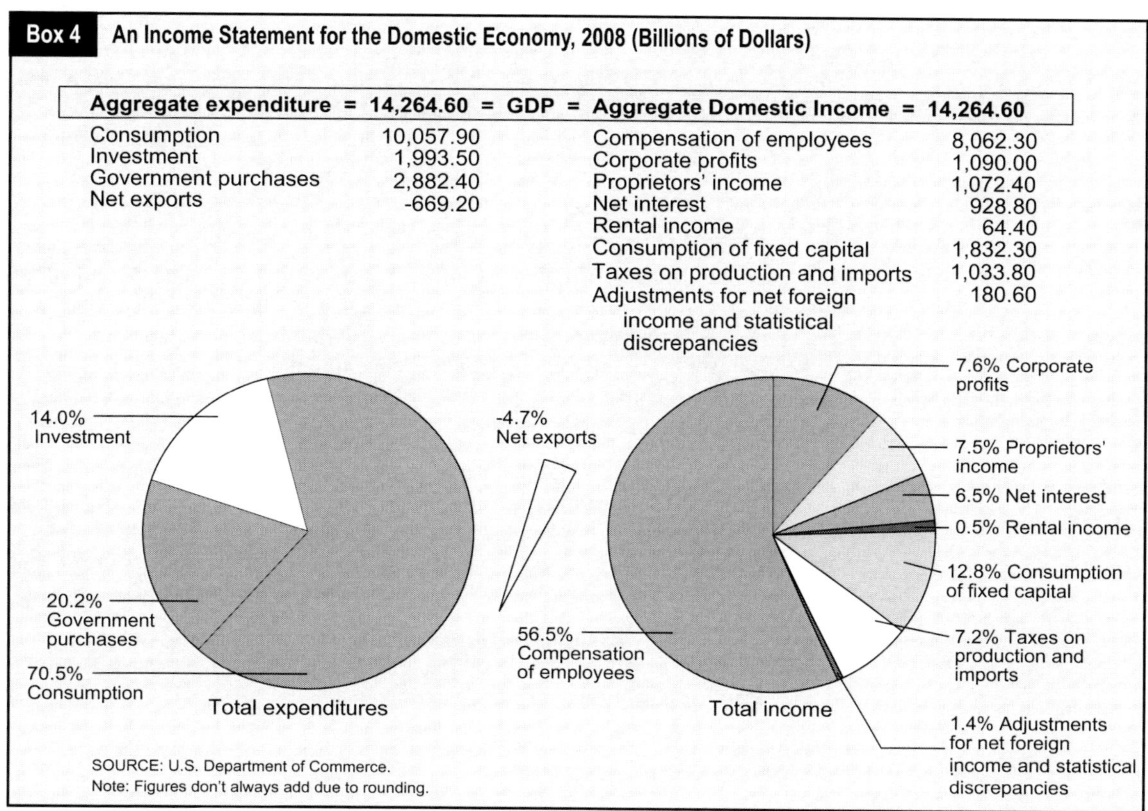

Box 4 An Income Statement for the Domestic Economy, 2008 (Billions of Dollars)

Aggregate expenditure = 14,264.60 = GDP		= Aggregate Domestic Income = 14,264.60	
Consumption	10,057.90	Compensation of employees	8,062.30
Investment	1,993.50	Corporate profits	1,090.00
Government purchases	2,882.40	Proprietors' income	1,072.40
Net exports	-669.20	Net interest	928.80
		Rental income	64.40
		Consumption of fixed capital	1,832.30
		Taxes on production and imports	1,033.80
		Adjustments for net foreign income and statistical discrepancies	180.60

SOURCE: U.S. Department of Commerce.
Note: Figures don't always add due to rounding.

right side of the income statement shows how receipts taken in from sales of final products are allocated to reward resource owners and to fund capital consumption allowances and pay indirect business taxes.

In effect, the economy is viewed as an enormous household in the NIPA. Aggregate expenditure must equal aggregate income.

Other Measures of Aggregate Expenditure and Income

3 The National Income and Product Accounts include other measures of expenditure and income that are used to keep tabs on the performance of the economy. This section discusses how gross national product, net national product, national income, personal income, and disposable income are related to GDP and how these accounting concepts are used.

Gross Domestic Purchases When the U.S. Department of Commerce measures consumption, investment, and government purchases, imported goods and services are also included in these expenditures. The car or computer purchased in the United States this year may have been manufactured domestically, but it may include components imported from abroad. So, some domestic products have imported products embodied within. To measure GDP the Commerce Department first measures total consumption, investment, and government purchases, which includes imported products, adds exported domestic production, and then subtracts all imports whose value are included in the sum of C + I + G. If exports are subtracted from GDP, we are left with a measure called gross domestic purchases, which is equivalent to all purchases made domestically, both of goods and services produced in the United States and those imported from other nations. Because gross domestic purchases are the sum of consumption, investment, and government purchases, they will exceed gross domestic product when net exports are negative. For example, in 2008, gross domestic purchases amounted to $14,933.8 billion, which exceeded the GDP that year of $14,264.6 billion. When this is the case, Americans spend more than the value of their production and income and must borrow from abroad. When gross domestic purchases exceed gross domestic product, we are putting more dollars in the hands of foreigners than they use to buy our goods and services. The difference ends up as foreign saving in the United States and is used to accumulate such assets as bank deposits, stocks, bonds or real estate by foreigners.

Gross National Product GDP is the primary measure used to gauge the growth of the domestic economy. However, a portion of the value of final output included in GDP reflects the worth of foreign resources employed within the boundaries of the United States. Moreover, GDP does not include the value of output produced by U.S. labor and property employed abroad. Let's now look at a NIPA concept that measures the value of output produced by U.S.-owned resources.

Gross national product (GNP) is the market value of final output produced annually by all labor and property supplied by a nation's households, no matter where those resources are employed. GNP includes U.S. income from foreign sources (such as Ford's earnings on its foreign investments) but excludes the income of foreigners from work or investments in the United States (such as Toyota's profits from its U.S. production facilities).

GNP is calculated by adding to GDP income that U.S. households earn from work or investments in other nations and by subtracting from GDP income earned by foreigners from work or investments in the United States:

$$\text{GNP} = \text{GDP} + \begin{array}{c}\text{Foreign source}\\ \text{income of}\\ \text{U.S. households}\end{array} - \begin{array}{c}\text{Income earned}\\ \text{by foreigners in}\\ \text{the United States}\end{array}$$

Because GNP measures the total value of output produced by resources that U.S. households supply, it is the best measure of the aggregate income of Americans.

In 2008, the U.S. gross domestic product of $14,264.6 billion included $665.1 billion of income foreigners earned by working or owning property in the United States. In the same year, Americans earned $798.3 billion from employment of their resources in foreign nations. Using the above formula, we can now calculate GNP for 2008:

$$\text{GNP} = \$14{,}264.6\text{ billion} + \$798.3\text{ billion} - \$665.1\text{ billion} = \$14{,}397.8\text{ billion}$$

Because earnings from U.S. resources supplied abroad exceeded the earnings of foreign resources employed in the United States, GNP was greater than GDP in 2008. If a nation's foreign earnings were less than the earnings of foreigners in that nation, its GNP would be less than its GDP.

Net National Product GNP includes investment purchases reflecting replacement of existing capital goods (including residential structures) that have worn out or become obsolete. To account for *net* new additions to capital stock, a measure of the depreciation of existing capital stock must be deducted from the estimate of gross investment. Net national product (NNP) is GNP less capital consumption allowances (officially called "consumption of fixed capital" in the NIPA), which estimate depreciation:

$$\text{NNP} = \text{GNP} - \text{Consumption of fixed capital}$$

Net national product is a measure of national production that includes only net additions to capital and excludes any purchases for replacement of worn-out or obsolete capital.

Similarly, by deducting an estimate of depreciation of existing capital stock from gross domestic product, we would obtain *net domestic product.*

Because capital consumption allowances are only very rough estimates of actual depreciation, most economists believe that NNP is not a very reliable indicator of net production. NNP is rarely used in economic analysis because of the dubious accuracy of the NIPA estimate of depreciation.

National Income Some of the receipts shown on the income side of the statement in Box 5, such as capital consumption allowances, are not paid out to owners of productive resources. We can, however, make some adjustments to better gauge how much of the value of final products is actually paid out to those whose resources are used in production.

National income is a measure of household and business earnings from the use of productive resources over a period of one year. It can be calculated by subtracting capital consumption allowances and a statistical discrepancy from GNP:

$$\text{National income} = \text{GNP} - \text{Consumption of fixed capital} - \text{Statistical discrepancy}$$

It can also be calculated by summing the compensation of employees, rental income, net interest income earned by those who make loans to finance production, and profits.[1]

Personal Income How much income do households actually have available to spend before paying personal taxes? Personal income is the NIPA measure of the income

Box 5 From GDP to Personal Income, 2008

	Billions of dollars
Step 1 Gross Domestic Product	14,264.60
Plus: Receipts of foreign income	798.30
Less: Payments of income to foreigners	665.10
Equals: Gross National Product	14,397.80
Step 2 Gross National Product	14,397.80
Less: Consumption of fixed capital	1,832.30
Equals: Net National Product	12,565.50
Step 3 Net National Product	12,565.50
Less: Statistical discrepency	135.80
Equals: National Income	12,221.00
Step 4 National Income	12,429.70
Less: Social Security payroll taxes and taxes on production and imports+	
Corporate profits+	
Net interest paid+	
Misc. adjustments	
Plus: Government transfer payments+	
Personal interest, dividends, and other transfers	
Net Adjustment	327.10
Equals: Personal income	12,102.60
Step 5 Personal income	12,102.60
Less: Personal taxes	1,460.60
Equals: Disposable income	10,642.00

SOURCE: U.S. Department of Commerce.

Note: Figures don't always add due to rounding.

[1]Revisions of the NIPA in 2003 changed the definition of national income. Prior to 2003, indirect business taxes were also subtracted from GNP to obtain national income. Indirect business taxes (also called "taxes on production and imports") are now included in national income.

available to households in a given year. To obtain personal income, the following subtractions from and additions to national income are required:

1. Subtract all net interest and corporate profits from national income because these accrue to businesses rather than to households.

2. Subtract Social Security (payroll) taxes. These taxes are not paid out to individuals and therefore are not available for households to spend. Also subtract taxes on production and imports, less any subsidies.

3. Add all personal interest income. This income exceeds the net interest that is initially subtracted because much of the interest earned by individuals is not used to finance production. Included in personal interest income is the interest paid by government to individuals who own government securities.

4. Add personal dividend payments, the portion of corporate profits that is paid to individuals.

5. Add all payments that individuals receive through government transfers (such as Social Security pensions) and business transfers (such as pensions).

After these adjustments have been made, the result is a measure of the income from production that actually gets paid out to households during the year along with income that does not necessarily reflect the sale of productive services. Note that personal income exceeds national income because the additions we make to national income to derive it exceed the subtractions.

Personal income is a useful measure of the ability of households to make purchases, save, and pay taxes. Retail sales forecasters eagerly await the monthly release of personal income estimates because they consider trends in personal income to be of great importance in influencing consumption.

Disposable Income The income that individuals have to spend or save after payment of personal taxes is called disposable income. Officially designated *disposable personal income* in the NIPA, it is obtained by deducting personal tax and nontax payments to governments from personal income. Disposable income is closely watched by forecasters as a key determinant of consumers' ability to spend and save.

The table in Box 5 shows how GDP is related to NNP, national income, personal income, and disposable income. By moving from the first line to the bottom line, you can see how disposable income is derived from GDP in the 2005 National Income and Product Accounts.

The Circular Flow of Expenditure and Income: A Macroeconomic Perspective

4 National income and product accounting demonstrates that expenditure on final products generates income; but this is not a onetime affair. Instead, the income in turn generates purchases of final products, which then result in more income as the process goes on and on. We can illustrate the continued flow of expenditure and income with a *circular flow diagram* similar to the one used in the chapter The Price System and the Mixed Economy. However, with our enhanced knowledge of the NIPA accounts, we can now further investigate the relationship between the sources and uses of income by showing how the financial system, governments, and international trade affect the economy.

The enhanced circular flow diagram is drawn in Box 6. The upper loop of the big circle represents expenditures on final products, while the lower loop represents a flow of income generated by the purchases. Where does the expenditure that generates income originate? To find out, let's start at the box marked "Households."

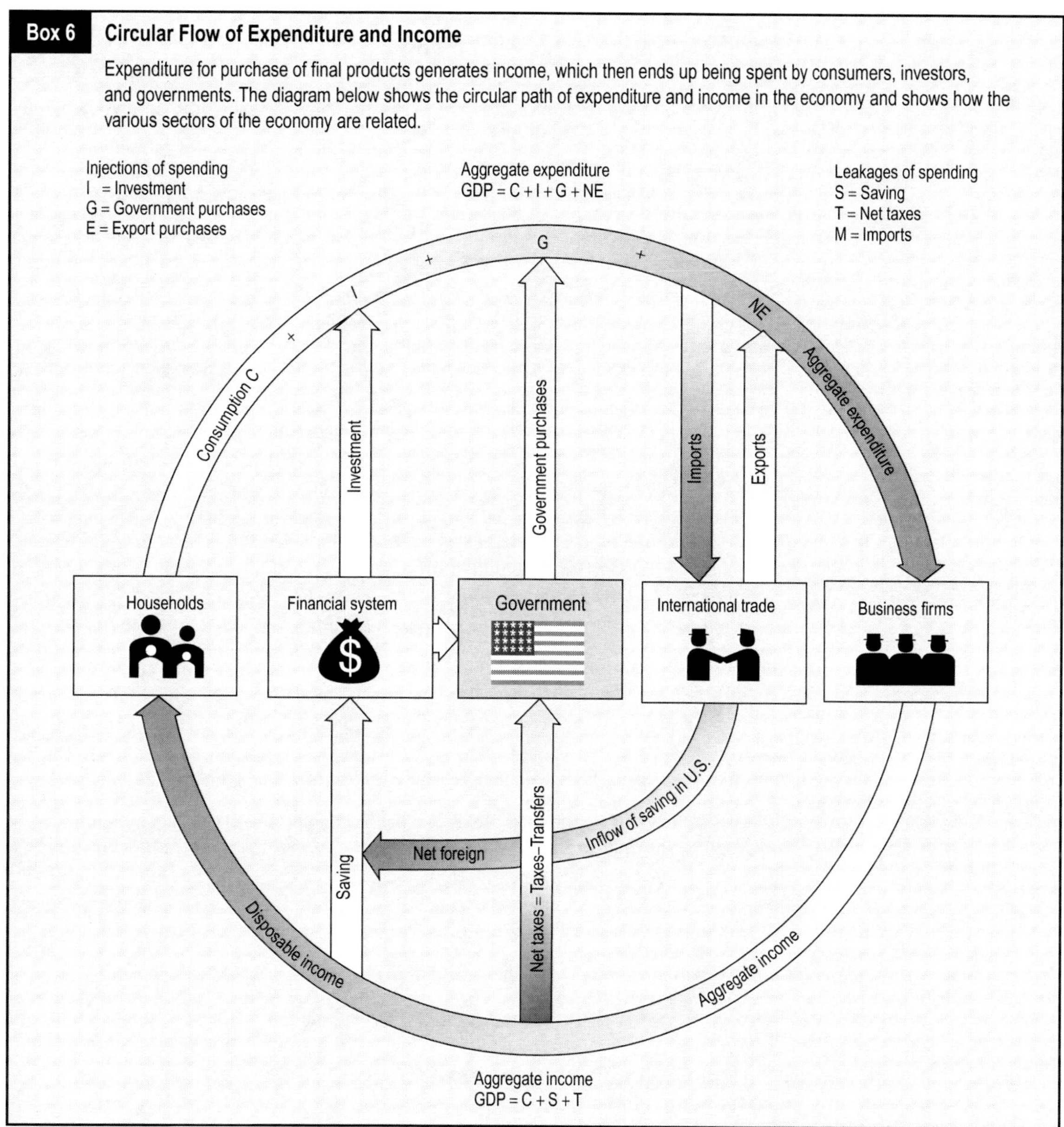

Box 6 **Circular Flow of Expenditure and Income**

Expenditure for purchase of final products generates income, which then ends up being spent by consumers, investors, and governments. The diagram below shows the circular path of expenditure and income in the economy and shows how the various sectors of the economy are related.

Household consumption (C) in the United States accounts for about two-thirds of GDP. Now move along the upper loop and notice that investment purchases (I) add to the flow of expenditures as funds from the nation's financial system are used to finance acquisition of machinery, new structures, and other investment goods. As you reach the top of the loop, government purchases (G) represent another addition to the flow of spending. Finally, moving down along the upper loop toward the box marked "business firms," notice that some spending is for import purchases (M) from international trade. Expenditures by U.S. buyers for such goods as Japanese computers and televisions, German automobiles, and Korean shoes end up as receipts to foreign sellers rather than to U.S. businesses. The spending for imports is therefore removed from the circular flow and does not end up as income to U.S. businesses and households. However, U.S. exports (E) are foreign purchases of U.S. products that help generate income in the United States from international trade. The difference E – M represents net exports (NE). By the time you get to the box marked "business firms," the total spending has grown to the sum C + I + G + NE, which you now know represents GDP expressed as the sum of its expenditure components.

The expenditure on final products generates the aggregate income earned by owners of business firms and members of households. This income is paid out as compensation to employees, net interest on funds borrowed, and rents, and a portion is set aside (saved) by business firms as capital consumption allowances. The remainder is profit.

We can now trace the uses of income by moving along the lower loop of the circle. Some of the income earned "leaks out" of the lower loop to pay taxes to governments. A portion of the taxes paid by U.S. households and businesses is used to finance transfers that are added to income and thus become available for spending. However, net taxes, which are the difference between taxes and transfer payments, are positive because taxes exceed transfers. Net taxes (T) are then used to finance government purchases, which were shown in the upper loop. Finally, a portion of income earned also flows out of the lower loop as saving, which is channeled to the financial system to provide funds for investment purchases. Some business saving (capital consumption allowances) is channeled to financial markets. Personal saving is the portion of household income that is not used to make purchases or pay taxes over the year. Governments also absorb some of the saving during the year when they run a budget deficit. When this is the case, the government must borrow through the financial system, as shown by the flow of funds from the financial system to government. In the early 1990s the federal government was absorbing over $200 billion of annual savings to finance its enormous deficits.

Some funds are supplied to the financial system by foreigners saving in the United States. When foreigners acquire more dollars during the year than they spend on U.S. products, the excess dollars end up as dollar deposits in U.S. banks. These dollars then enter the U.S. financial system as net foreign saving in the United States. (See Box 6.) When the net export component of GDP is negative, the United States runs a *balance of trade deficit*.[2]

Now you're back to the box marked "Households," and the process begins all over again. Expenditure on final products during the year has provided households with the income necessary to finance their consumption. Income is used for consumption purchases (C), household and business savings (S), or payment of the difference between taxes and government transfers (net taxes = T).

GDP expressed as the sum of income uses is

$$GDP = C + S + T$$

Leakages and Injections of Purchasing Power and the Demand for U.S. Final Products

A leakage of spending represents a portion of income that is not used to purchase domestically produced products during the year. There are three types of leakage of spending power from the circular flow:

1. Net taxes—the difference between total taxes paid to governments and transfer payments made by governments.
2. Saving.
3. Import purchases.

[2] Net foreign saving in the United States typically exceeds the balance of trade deficit for goods and services. This is because foreign holders of dollars also earn interest income on their U.S. investments and because some foreigners also receive transfer payments from governments in the United States. For example, in 2003 the balance of trade deficit was $464.1 billion, but in that year the excess of dollars earned by foreigners over their expenditure on U.S. products was $465.4 billion.

Leakages of spending from the circular flow cause decreases in the current demand for U.S. final products. Other things being equal, the more saving, the greater the difference between taxes and transfers, and the greater the import purchases, the less national income is used to buy U.S. goods and services during the year.

An injection of spending is a purchase made by business firms, governments, or foreign buyers that increases the flow of income in a nation. Injections of purchasing power for purposes other than consumption by U.S. households increase demand in the economy. The injections illustrated in the circular flow diagram are

1. Investment.
2. Government purchases.
3. Exports.

A reduction in business investment purchases during the year or a decline in export purchases could spell trouble for the economy by reducing current income. On the other hand, an increase in government purchases increases the demand for goods and services.

You can think of real GDP as a volume of liquid flowing through the tubes of the circular flow diagram in Box 6. When the injections of spending exceed the leakages of spending, the volume of liquid in the tubes will increase, meaning that current real GDP will increase. On the other hand, when the injections of spending fall short of the leakages of spending, the volume of liquid in the tubes will decline, meaning that current real GDP or the price level will decrease. The task of macroeconomic theory is to understand the economic forces that influence these leakages and injections in order to forecast changes in real GDP and to develop policies that minimize fluctuations in real GDP.

Flows of Saving and Investment in the United States: Do We Save Enough?

5 A nation's *future* production possibilities depend on investment. Individuals in the economy must refrain from devoting all of their resources to purchases of consumption goods so that some resources can be devoted to investment. When we save rather than consume, we can allocate some of our resources to the production of new machinery, equipment, education, research and development, and other uses that help us provide more output in the future. The more we save, the more of our resources we can devote to investment and the greater will be our output in the future. How does the United States shape up against other nations in terms of its recent saving and investment performance?

National saving is the sum of household saving, business saving, and government saving. Box 7 shows how national saving has varied as a percentage of GNP (used here as a measure of aggregate income) since 1960. The U.S. saving rate has dropped substantially since 1960, when it was 22 percent of GNP. In 2008, national savings amounted to less than 11.9 percent of GNP, which is the best measure of gross national income.

Now let's examine the saving rate of three sectors of the domestic economy: households, businesses, and government. Notice that virtually all of national saving in 2007 and 2008 (about 12 percent) is accounted for by business firms, mainly in the form of capital consumption allowances and undistributed corporate profits. Next, look at how household (or personal) saving declined substantially from 5 percent of GNP in 1960 to about zero in 2007. However, personal saving increased somewhat in 2008, to about 2.5 percent of gross national income. The government sector of the economy had negative saving for almost all of the period from 1981 to 1995. This was due mainly to large federal government deficits that resulted in heavy borrowing by the federal government over this period. On net, the government sector absorbs rather than adds to saving when it must

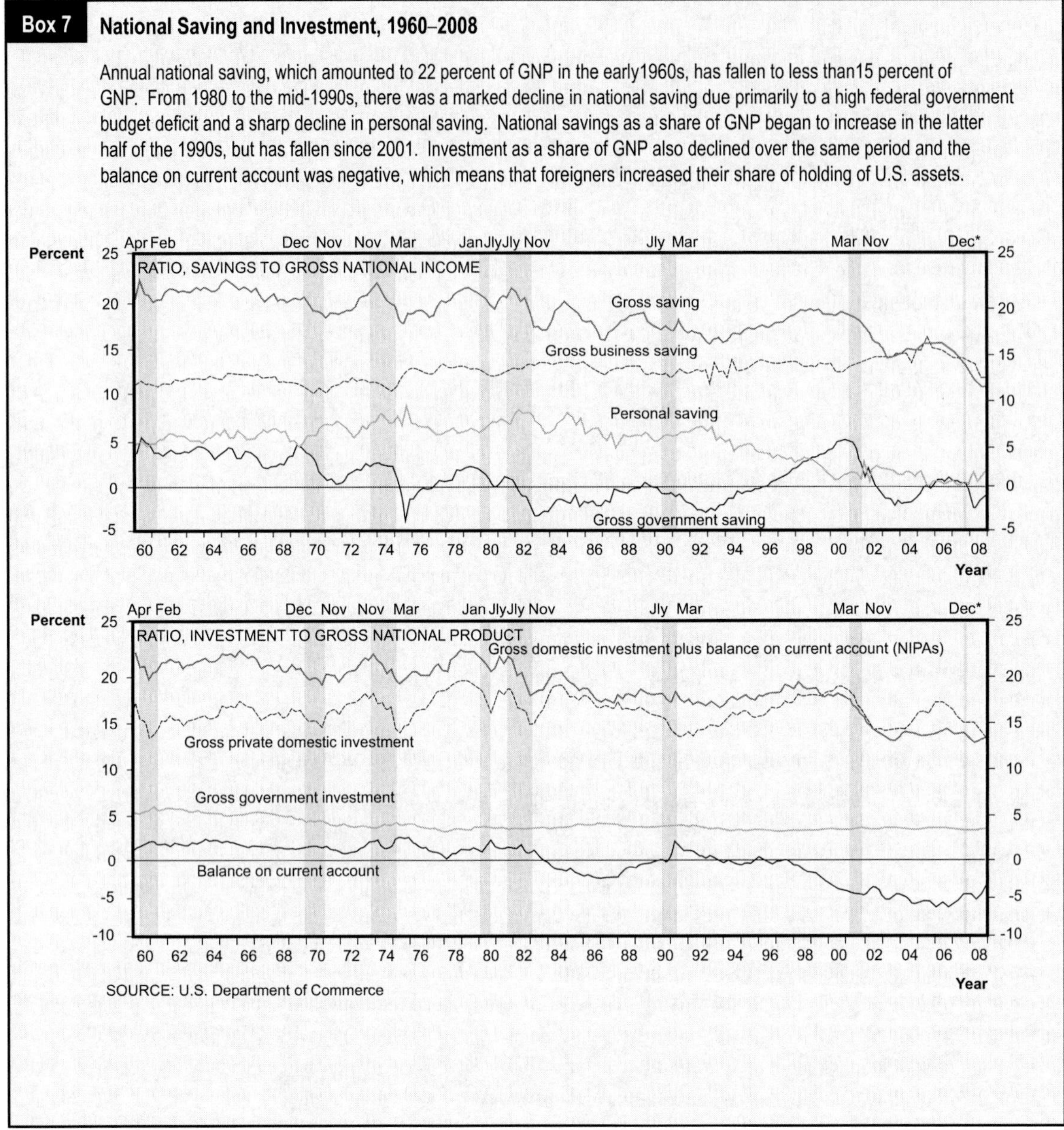

Box 7 **National Saving and Investment, 1960–2008**

Annual national saving, which amounted to 22 percent of GNP in the early1960s, has fallen to less than15 percent of GNP. From 1980 to the mid-1990s, there was a marked decline in national saving due primarily to a high federal government budget deficit and a sharp decline in personal saving. National savings as a share of GNP began to increase in the latter half of the 1990s, but has fallen since 2001. Investment as a share of GNP also declined over the same period and the balance on current account was negative, which means that foreigners increased their share of holding of U.S. assets.

borrow to cover expenses not financed by taxes, fees or charges. The saving rate of the government sector averaged -2.5 percent from 1980 to 1991 and a whopping -3.2 percent of GNP between 1992 and 1994. This negative saving was primarily due to the federal budget deficit, because state and local governments actually ran surpluses during this period. Between 1995 and 2001, government saving turned positive, as the federal budget swung from deficit to surplus in 1998 and state government surpluses increased between 1995 and 1999. Since 2000, in part as a result of federal government budget deficits, government saving has fallen and was once again negative in 2007 and 2008. As the upper graph in Box 7 shows, national saving increased in the latter half of the 1990s. But national saving fell from a peak of nearly 20 percent of GNP in 2000 to less than 15 percent of GNP by 2002. The lower graph in Box 7 shows that gross investment remained fairly steady in the 1990s, at around 18 percent of GNP. However, gross private domestic investment did increase substantially in the 1990s, from around 13 percent to nearly 20 percent of GNP, as foreign investment in the U.S. increased over this period. By 2008, gross investment had fallen to less than 15 percent of GNP.

Because saving is the key to improving economic growth and future living standards, higher savings rates can mean a better future for Americans, on average. More domestic investment means that U.S. workers are equipped with more and better tools, which contributes to higher productivity and higher incomes.

How Foreigners Helped Finance U.S. Investment

Americans have not saved enough in recent years to finance investment purchases by U.S. businesses. This shortfall in national saving has been overcome by the net inflow of foreign saving. Foreigners save in the United States when they use the dollars they acquire during the year in foreign exchange markets to purchase U.S. assets instead of spending those dollars on U.S. exports. *Net foreign saving in the United States* is the difference between total foreign saving in the United States and U.S. saving abroad and is positive whenever we have a balance of trade deficit. In Box 7, net foreign saving in the United States is measured by the negative balance on the current account of international trade.

The net inflow from foreign saving in the United States averaged 1.5 percent of U.S. GNP from 1980 to 1994. In 2008, foreign saving in the United States amounted to 4 percent of GNP. When these funds are added to national saving, total saving in the United States exactly equals gross private investment. Total saving in the United States is the sum of national saving and net foreign saving in the United States. The circular flow diagram in Box 6 shows how foreign saving in the United States is added to national saving to help finance investment purchases.

You have probably read quite a bit about foreign saving in the United States. Some of it takes the form of direct investment in the United States, as is the case when foreign savers use dollars they have acquired in foreign exchange markets to buy U.S. real estate and U.S. businesses. Most foreign saving in the United States, however, involves the acquisition of paper assets, such as stocks, bonds, and certificates of deposit. In recent years foreign saving, including the portion of such saving that is direct investment in the United States, has served a valuable function in the U.S. economy by allowing the rate of investment to exceed the national saving rate.

Because of foreign saving, we have been able to create more jobs and we are likely to have more rapid economic growth in the future than would otherwise have been possible. In effect, foreign saving in the United States since 1980 has allowed U.S. spending to exceed U.S. income! The low supply of savings from U.S. households makes funds for investment scarce and puts upward pressure on interest rates. Foreign saving offsets the low rate of U.S. saving and puts downward pressure on interest rates by increasing the supply of loanable funds. By purchasing U.S. government securities such as Treasury bonds, notes, and bills, foreign savers keep the huge federal budget deficit from exerting still more upward pressure on interest rates.

By making direct investments in U.S. industries, which is what foreigners do when they acquire U.S. firms and plants, foreigners will in the long run enable U.S. firms to compete in international markets. This is because the new equipment and technology that U.S. firms acquire with funds supplied by foreign investors will enable these firms to produce at lower cost in the future. And foreign producers are finding it in their interest to use the U.S. dollars they acquire in trade to build their own plants in the United States. The Toyota Camry you buy may very well have been produced in Georgetown, Kentucky, where Toyota has a plant. Honda also has plants in the United States. Since 1982 manufacturing costs per unit have fallen in the United States, while they have risen in other nations. This makes direct investment in the United States a good deal for foreign producers, who find that in many cases they could *reduce* their labor costs by producing in the United States instead of at home! On the flip side, the more U.S. assets owned by foreigners, the more income earned in the United States will accrue to foreign citizens instead of U.S. citizens in the future. In perspective, the United States owns lots of foreign assets. For example, a substantial portion of the Canadian economy consists of assets owned by U.S. businesses and households. In recent years U.S. businesses and individuals have invested heavily in such nations as Switzerland, the United Kingdom, and the Netherlands. It's all part of increased globalization of business—a trend that shows no signs of subsiding.

Summary

1. Macroeconomics is the study of the overall performance of the economy and the way its various sectors are related.

2. The National Income and Product Accounts represent the official system of national accounting in the United States. Statistics on these accounts are published quarterly by the U.S. Department of Commerce and are used to measure the performance of the national economy.

3. Gross domestic product is the market value of the final goods and services produced in a nation over a period of one year.

4. Nominal GDP is the market value of a nation's aggregate production of final goods and services based on current prices, while real GDP measures the value of aggregate production adjusted for changes in prices since a base year. Changes in real GDP reflect changes in aggregate production over time more accurately than do changes in nominal GDP.

5. Total value added in a nation over the year is the difference between the market value of all products of business firms and the market value of all intermediate products and is equivalent to GDP. Value added at each stage of production is the worth added to items purchased from other firms.

6. From the expenditure standpoint, GDP is the sum of consumption, investment, government purchases, and net exports. Net exports are the difference between exports and imports of goods and services over the year.

7. From the income standpoint, GDP is the sum of annual compensation of employees, profits, net interest, rental income, capital consumption allowances, and indirect business taxes. Capital consumption allowances are a form of business saving. Capital consumption allowances, indirect business taxes, and corporate profits taxes are not paid out as income to members of households.

8. The circular flow of expenditure and income in an economy stems from the fact that expenditures on final products end up as income, which is then used to make purchases. Disposable income is the income available to households for spending or saving after payment of taxes.

9. In the circular flow of income and expenditure, the financial system acts to channel savings so that they can be used to finance investment purchases. The government collects taxes and makes transfers of income among citizens. Net taxes are the difference between taxes and transfers. Net taxes finance government purchases. Some income earned during the year is used to purchase imports, and U.S. businesses export some of their products through international trade. When net exports are negative, a net inflow of foreign saving into the United States helps finance investment purchases.

10. National saving is the sum of household saving, business saving, and government saving.

11. In recent years national saving in the United States has fallen short of gross private domestic investment. The national saving rate is lower in the United States than in other advanced nations.

Concept Review

1. Explain how GDP is measured and how nominal GDP differs from real GDP.

2. Suppose that personal consumption expenditures are $3 trillion, gross private domestic investment is $1 trillion, and government purchases are $2 trillion. If GDP is $5 trillion, what is the value of net exports?

3. What is the best NIPA measure of income earned by owners of productive resources? What is the best NIPA measure of after-tax income available for household spending?

4. How does expenditure on final products end up as income to households and businesses?

5. What is national saving, and how does it differ from total saving in the United States?

Problems and Applications

1. During the year a small nation produces the following final products: 1 million automobiles, 5 million clothing outfits, 10 million pounds of food, rental of 2 million dwelling units, 1 million hours of attorneys' services to households, and 2 million hours of medical services to households. The current market price for these products are:

   $10,000 per automobile

   $100 per clothing outfit

   $2 per pound of food

   $4,000 per year per dwelling unit

   $20 per hour of attorneys' services

   $30 per hour of medical services

   Calculate the nation's nominal gross domestic product. 1

2. Suppose nominal GDP in the U.S. economy increases from $5,000 billion to $5,500 billion. Can you conclude that aggregate production, income, and job opportunities have increased as well? Explain your answer. 1

3. Explain why GDP would be overestimated if the market values of both final products and intermediate products were included in it. 1

4. Suppose the market value of all sales in an economy, including those of intermediate products, is $10,000 billion. If the market value of intermediate products is $6,000 billion, what is the total value added in the nation? Why is the value added equal to gross domestic product? 1

5. Suppose GDP is currently equal to $4,500 billion. Consumption is $3,000 billion, and government purchases are $1,000 billion. If net exports are zero, how much is gross private domestic investment? What are the major components of gross private domestic investment? Under what circumstances would net private domestic investment be negative? 2

6. Suppose total government expenditures in the United States amount to $1,400 billion. In the same year, the government purchases component of GDP is only $815 billion. Explain why the government purchases component of GDP falls short of actual government expenditures. List some of the important government expenditures that are not included in the government purchases component of GDP. What is the logic of excluding these expenditures? 2

7. Assume GDP is $5,000 billion in the current year. During the year, employee compensation is $3,000 billion, net interest earned is $300 billion, and rental income is $50 billion. Calculate the sum of corporate profits and proprietors' income, assuming that capital consumption allowances are $400 billion and indirect business taxes are $300 billion. 3

8. Suppose investment, government purchases, and exports are expected to decline this year. Can you conclude that real GDP will also decline? Why would you look at growth in disposable income to predict changes in consumer spending? 4

9. Suppose gross private domestic investment is $900 billion. Personal saving is $250 billion, business saving is $650 billion, and the government sector runs a $200 billion budget deficit. Calculate national saving. What is the net inflow of foreign saving into the United States? 4, 5

10. Suppose that gross domestic purchases, which are the sum of consumption, investment, and government purchases, are equal to $6,000 billion. Gross domestic product is equal to $5,500 billion in the same year. Calculate net exports. How can an increase in the government budget deficit contribute to a balance of trade deficit? 5

The Growing Importance of Exports and Imports for the U.S. Economy

How many Japanese or other foreign cars were on the American roads 50 years ago? Practically none. Likewise, there were few foreign TV sets, shoes, or cameras in comparison to what's available today.

In recent years, the U.S. economy has become increasingly linked with the rest of the world through international trade. Americans have enjoyed gains from foreign trade because foreign trade has enabled them to buy quality goods at lower prices than would have otherwise been possible. In the 1980s and 1990s, the growth in the value of imported products exceeded the growth in the value of exported products, which contributed to huge balance of trade deficits in the United States. The trade deficit remained with us in 2008.

The graph below documents the spectacular rise in the importance of exports and imports for the U.S. economy since 1960. In 1960, exports amounted to 4.5 percent of real GDP. By 2008, nearly 14 percent of U.S. output was exported. A similar trend is observed for imports, which grew from a bit more than 4 percent of GDP in 1960 to a whopping 18 percent of real GDP in 2008. Both imports and exports fluctuate from year to year as a result of changes in economic conditions. For example, both imports and exports are responsive to changes in the international value of the dollar. A rise in the value of the dollar in terms of foreign currency from 1980 to 1986 was responsible, in part, for the sharp decline in real exports as a share of real GDP in the United States over that period. During the same period, the higher-valued dollar caused the price of imports to fall to U.S. buyers, and we observed a sharp increase in imports as a share of real GDP from 1980 to 1986.

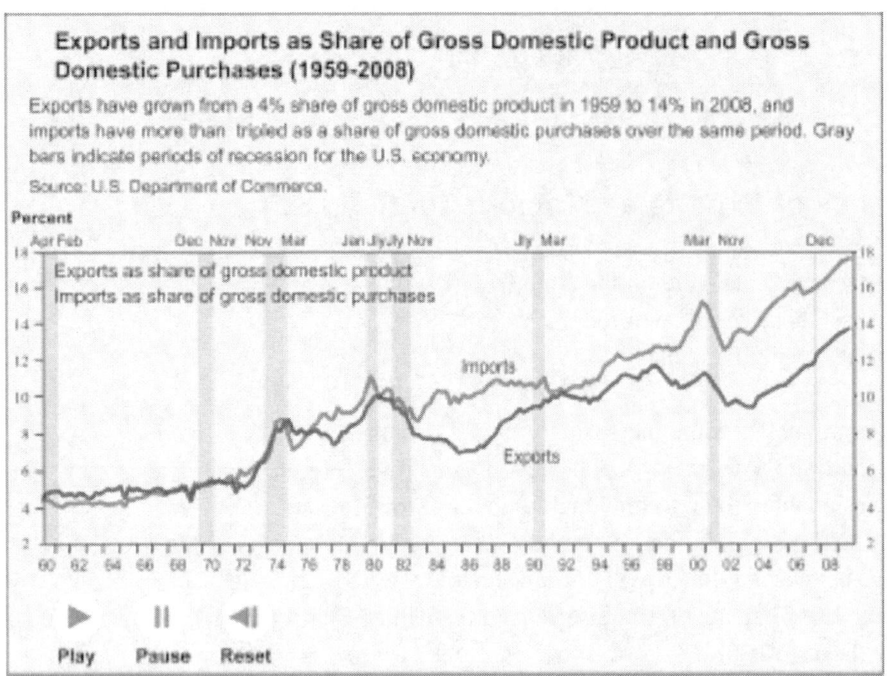
Exports and Imports as Share of Gross Domestic Product and Gross Domestic Purchases (1959-2008)
Exports have grown from a 4% share of gross domestic product in 1959 to 14% in 2008, and imports have more than tripled as a share of gross domestic purchases over the same period. Gray bars indicate periods of recession for the U.S. economy.
Source: U.S. Department of Commerce.
Percent
Exports as share of gross domestic product
Imports as share of gross domestic purchases
Imports
Exports
Play
Pause
Reset

The U.S. economy is now enmeshed in the global economy through the strong appetite of U.S. buyers for imports and through the reliance of U.S. industry on export demand as a source of revenue. More income is now generated from the sale of exports, and more income is spent on imported goods and services.

As we've just demonstrated, the negative net export position of the United States has enabled foreigners to increase their holding of U.S. assets. Our balance of trade deficit is mirrored by a net inflow of foreign saving in the United States. Of course, if the United States were to begin exporting more than it imported, it would convert the balance of trade deficit into a *balance of trade surplus*, as a result of which the net inflow of foreign saving into the United States would become negative and foreign ownership of U.S. assets would decline.

Exports have been a driving force of the U.S. economy in recent years. The U.S. share of world exports rose from 15.3 percent in 1986 to 22 percent in 1992. By 2000, export of U.S. goods was up to 30 percent of industrial output. Investment goods (such as machinery) and industrial supplies (such as chemicals, paper, and metals) have accounted for much of the growth in U.S. exports in recent years. However, exports of consumer goods, food, and even automobiles have also increased. Among the products foreigners have been buying in increased volume from American sellers are pharmaceuticals, tobacco products, toys, sporting goods, kitchen appliances, and electronic items. Markets for U.S. exports have been growing in Europe, Latin America, and Asia. Even the beleaguered General Motors Corporation has been increasing its exports by selling more full-size cars in Europe and the Middle East.

In recent years, the improved export performance of the U.S. economy has contributed to GDP growth and reduced balance of trade deficits. However, increased reliance on exports for growth of jobs and income also means that the U.S. economy is increasingly subject to fluctuations in foreign demand. Recessions in Germany and other European nations, along with a slowdown in Japanese economic growth, could dampen growth in the United States.

The Value-Added Tax:
A New Way to Tax GDP or Its Components

From the hallowed halls of Congress to the local diner, there's an ongoing debate about government spending and income taxes. Should we cut spending? Raise income taxes? Neither? Both?

Amid all the controversy, a new source of government revenue is being considered--the value-added tax. What is it? Where is it being used? And how does it work?

In European nations, it's common to tax value added. Value-added taxes account for over 20 percent of tax revenue in European Union nations. Such a tax has often been proposed as a means of providing additional revenue for the federal government without raising income tax rates. The tax is also used in Canada and in Japan.

A value-added tax (VAT) is sometimes called a *national sales tax*, because it's levied on every transaction as both intermediate and final products are sold. Under the value-added tax used in European nations, almost every transaction in the economy is subject to tax. Sellers must add the tax to the value of the goods they sell at each stage of production. Business firms that collect the tax then make tax payments quarterly on their value added over the period.

In European nations, the "invoice method" is used to collect the tax. Under this method, no taxpayer has to compute value added (or understand what it is)! Each firm adds up the tax it has collected during the period as recorded on its sales invoices, where the tax is itemized. At the same time, the firm gathers all the invoices for the purchases it made from other firms during the period. The value-added taxes on these transactions are also itemized on the bills the firm has paid. The firm's accountants then sum the amounts of tax it *paid* on intermediate purchases from other firms. The firm's tax liability is the difference between the tax it collected from sales to other firms and the tax it paid on purchases from its suppliers.

Tax liability = Tax payable on sales - Tax paid on purchases from other firms

If the tax rate on each transaction is 20 percent, then the firm's tax liability is

20% (Sales receipts - Purchases from other firms).

Because the difference between a firm's sales receipts and its purchases of materials, parts, and services from other firms is its value added, the tax liability will be 20 percent of its value added.

Tax liability = 20% of value added

If *every* purchase is taxed at 20 percent, the government will collect 20 percent of GDP in tax revenue. Even the federal government's own purchases will be subject to the value-added tax. In other words, if a value-added tax is levied on all the components of expenditure in GDP, the federal government will collect the tax from itself, as well as from state and local governments. The buyers of the final products will find that the price they pay for goods increases by 20 percent, because the 20 percent tax is levied on all final sales, as well as on intermediate sales. The tax will therefore collect 20 percent of the market value of the nation's final products, which is 20 percent of GDP.

In practice, the value-added tax as used in most European nations is not levied on most investment purchases and government purchases. In this case, the value-added tax is really a tax on purchases of consumption goods! If the European version of the value-added tax were introduced in the United States, it would be equivalent to a national sales tax on consumption goods.

Viewing GDP as total value added in a nation thus helps us understand how a VAT would affect the economy. If a VAT that excludes investment and government purchases from taxation were introduced in the United States, those who allocate high percentages of their income to consumption would end up paying higher percentages of their income in taxes.

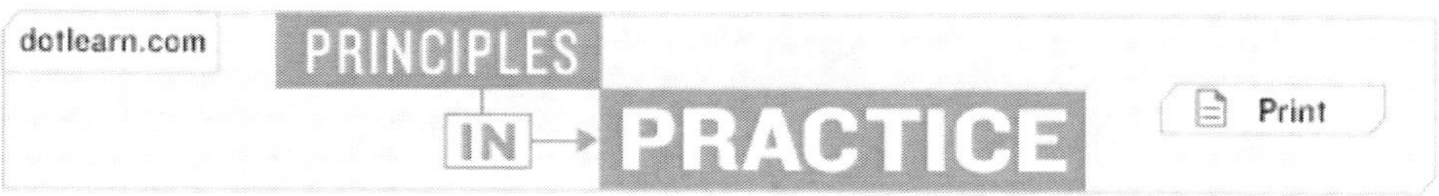

Real GDP: The Department of Commerce's Method for Estimating Output Changes

In the marketplace, producers are always introducing new and better products. The government statisticians who work for the Bureau of Economic Analysis (BEA) of the U.S. Department of Commerce also like to improve their products. In January 1996, BEA proudly unveiled a new and improved method of estimating real GDP and its rate of growth. Here's how the newer system works and how it improves our ability to gauge the performance of the U.S. economy.

When computing nominal GDP, we weight current outputs by current price and then add up the market value of all products to obtain a total. In the case of real GDP, the Department of Commerce has weighted current output by base year prices. In the past, BEA economists have changed the base year every five years and recomputed real GDP for every year over history using the new base year prices.

Using a single base year results in some distortions in measuring economic growth when there are significant changes in the relative prices of some products. For example, between 1987 and 1995, the prices of mainframe and personal computers fell significantly compared to an average of all prices. As a result of lower prices, the share of computers in total output has increased since 1987. However, when we value (weight) those computers by their relatively high 1987 price in computing real GDP, we overestimate their current market worth and the value of resources that go into producing them.

In general, output growth tends to be fastest for products whose prices are falling relative to prices on average. For example, over the 1982-87 period computer prices fell at an average annual rate of 17 percent. Over the same period, computer output increased at a whopping 34 percent per year. However, by using base year prices as much as five years in the past to weight outputs, we give *too high a weight* to products whose output is growing fast relative to the value of the resources used to produce those products. The resulting measure of real GDP tends to *overstate growth of output* for periods after the base year, while *understating growth of output* for periods before the base year. In the past, BEA would correct for this problem by changing the base year every five years. Now, they have an alternative solution.

A simple example will show how the new system works.[1] The table shows output of oranges and apples in a simple two-product economy for two consecutive years.

Year 1: 2006

Final product	2006 price	Market value
30 oranges	10¢	\$3.00
10 apples	20¢	\$2.00
Nominal 2006 GDP	=	\$5.00

Year 2: 2007

Final product	2007 price	Market value
20 oranges	20¢	\$4.00
20 apples	20¢	\$5.00
Nominal 2007 GDP	=	\$9.00

Nominal GDP in 2007 is nearly twice nominal GDP in 2006. Of course, this overstates output growth, because both prices and outputs have increased. To adjust for this, we need to use one set of prices to value output in both years.

The choice of the base year is an arbitrary decision. We could use 2006 prices to value 2007 output, or we could use 2007 prices to value 2006 output. In both cases, we eliminate the effect of price changes in comparing the two years. However, the measure of growth of real GDP is sensitive to the choice of the base year. To see this, first use 2006 as the base year to calculate real GDP in 2007.

Calculation 1: 2006 Base Year

Use 2006 prices to "deflate" 2007 output so that it can be compared with 2006 output:

Real GDP = 2007 output of oranges
weighted by 2006 prices + 2007 output
of apples weighted by 2006 prices

(20 x 10¢) + (20 x 20¢) = \$6.00

Now, to obtain an index of real GDP using 2006 as the base year, simply divide real GDP by nominal GDP:

Year 1 base index = \$6.00/\$5.00
= 1.20

This index tells us that real GDP, an estimate of output, in 2007 is 1.2 times output in 2006--a 20 percent increase!

Calculation 2: 2007 Base Year

Now, let's use 2007 as the base year and "inflate" 2006 output so that it can be compared with 2007 output.

Real GDP = 2006 output of oranges weighted by 2007 prices + 2006 output of apples weighted by 2007 prices

(30 x 20¢) + (10 x 25¢) = $8.50

Now, to obtain an index of real GDP using 2007 as the base year, simply divide nominal GDP in 2007 by real GDP in 2006:

Year 2 base index = $9.00/8.50
= 1.06

This index tells us that real GDP, an estimate of output, in 2007 is 1.06 times output in 2006--only a 6 percent increase! By arbitrarily choosing a base year, we affect the measure of economic growth when prices of goods don't all change in the same proportion. One solution to this problem is to *average* the two measures we've calculated. For example, if we average the two index numbers in this example, we get 1.13.[2]

The method illustrated above is called a *chain-type annual weighted index* to compute real GDP. This index measures real GDP by using the current and immediate past year as alternative bases to calculate indexes, as we did in this example, and then takes an average of the two numbers. A chain is created in this way, because each year the weights will be different--always adjacent years. The new featured measure of GDP growth is based on this index and doesn't have a fixed base year.

The new featured measure of real GDP provides a more accurate measure of growth in the economy of time by minimizing the effect of using old prices to value products, like computers, whose output has increased, in part, because of falling prices. Output is valued by prices closer to the current period in all years so that, in cases in which prices fall, the measure of current output will more closely reflect the current worth of those products.

[1]This example is based on analysis in "Preview of the Comprehensive Revision of the National Income and Product Accounts: BEA's New Featured Measures of Output and Prices," *Survey of Current Business* 75, 7, July 1995 (Washington,

D.C.), U.S. Department of Commerce: pp. 31-38.

[2]This is a simple arithmetic average. BEA uses a geometric average to compute the index, which multiplies indexes for adjacent years together and then takes the square root. In this example, there's little difference between the geometric and arithmetic mean.

How the Bureau of Economic Analysis Calculates GDP Every Three Months

There are two teams and a match. But there's no competition. The teams are composed of staff members of the Bureau of Economic Analysis of the U.S. Department of Commerce. One team measures GDP from the expenditure side, while the other measures it from the income side. When the two teams finish their independent work, the staff of the two groups meets to reconcile the two estimates. Aggregate expenditures on final products must equal aggregate income earned. On occasion the results don't match, and, when the economists can't explain the source of the difference, it shows up as a statistical discrepancy on the GDP accounts.

The team that estimates GDP from the expenditure side uses data collected by the U.S. Bureau of the Census and other organizations. The team that estimates GDP from the income side uses the results of a number of income surveys.

The Bureau of Economic Analysis takes its first stab at estimating GDP for each quarter during the month following the end of that quarter. For example, the first, or "advance," estimate of the GDP at a seasonally adjusted annual rate for the third quarter is released toward the end of October. A revised estimate is issued the next month as more data become available. Finally, one month later, the bureau issues its "final" estimate of GDP for the third quarter. The final estimate of GDP for the third quarter would therefore not be available until December. The president and his economic advisers are privileged to obtain each GDP estimate one day before its official release.

Chapter 22

Business Cycles, Unemployment, and Economic Growth

You've undoubtedly heard the terms *recession* and *unemployment* talked about on the nightly news. In 1990, the United States fell into a recession, and the consequences for the economy were increased unemployment and declining incomes. By early 1991, unemployment rates were moving upward throughout the country and businesses were complaining about sluggish sales. After the 1990 recession, the U.S. economy enjoyed 10 years of unprecedented and uninterrupted growth. But in March of 2001, another recession occurred. During 2007, after six years of expansion, the U.S. economy's growth rate began to slow. As new housing construction declined and consumer spending weakened, growth turned negative in the fourth quarter of 2007, as the U.S. economy entered into a new recession that continued throughout 2008. By late 2008, amid a financial crisis and declining aggregate demand, real GDP was declining at an annual rate of 6.2 percent for the last quarter of the year. The recession continued through 2009, with a loss of millions of jobs (since late 2007) and an unemployment rate that had soared to over 8 percent by March 2009.

A major goal of this chapter is to discuss the history of fluctuations and growth of real GDP, and show the links among real GDP growth, employment of workers, and living standards. The chapter will show how unemployment is measured and will explain why some unemployment is normal in a dynamic economy that doesn't instantaneously adjust to change.

When excessive numbers of workers are unemployed, it's difficult for new entrants into the labor force to find jobs and more people have difficulty meeting their expenses. Excessive unemployment is wasteful because the labor services of idle workers are not being used to produce goods and services. Lack of employment can disrupt the lives of families and threaten the social fabric of a nation. For this reason, the United States pursues policies designed to minimize unemployment and reduce its cost.

Concept Preview

After reading this chapter, you should be able to

1. Discuss the business cycle, and give examples of recent periods of recession and expansion of the U.S. economy.
2. Explain how unemployment is measured, and how the unemployment rate can be viewed as the sum of frictional, structural, and cyclical unemployment.
3. Define the concept of *full employment* and show how it's related to the natural rate of unemployment.
4. Explain *potential real GDP* and the difficulties involved in estimating it.
5. Discuss the social costs of unemployment and the programs designed to cushion these costs.
6. Discuss the record and sources of economic growth in the United States.

Fluctuations in Real GDP: The Historical Record

Increases in real GDP from one year to the next indicate that the economy's aggregate production of final products has also increased. More production means more goods and services available for people to consume. Given a growing population, increases in real GDP are necessary to maintain the standard of living as measured by the average of goods and services per person. When real GDP falls from one year to the next, final output per person will also fall, implying a reduced average standard of living. When output falls from one year to the next, employers won't use as much input as they did the year before. This means some workers will lose their jobs, and new entrants into the labor force will have difficulty finding jobs. *Declines in real GDP therefore also imply declines in income, employment opportunities, and the standard of living on average in a nation as output per person falls in the economy.*

The Business Cycle

1 Real GDP is estimated quarterly by the U.S. Department of Commerce. The quarterly estimate is then multiplied by 4 (after adjusting for normal seasonal variation) to obtain the annual rate of GDP over the three-month period.[1] Unfortunately, real GDP doesn't always steadily increase. There are irregular fluctuations in real GDP over time that have consequences for you and for everyone else.

Business cycle is the term used to describe the fluctuations in aggregate production as measured by the ups and downs of real GDP. The fluctuations, although not subject to easy predictability or regularity, can be readily identified. Box 1 contains a stylized graph depicting the recurrent business cycle that shows the periodic ups and downs of real GDP.

The business cycle is characterized by peaks and troughs and periods of contraction or expansion:

1. *Peak.* The *peak* is the highest level of real GDP in the cycle. Each peak (two are illustrated in the graph) indicates an economy operating at close to full capacity, so that national product and national income correspond to a very high degree of utilization of labor,

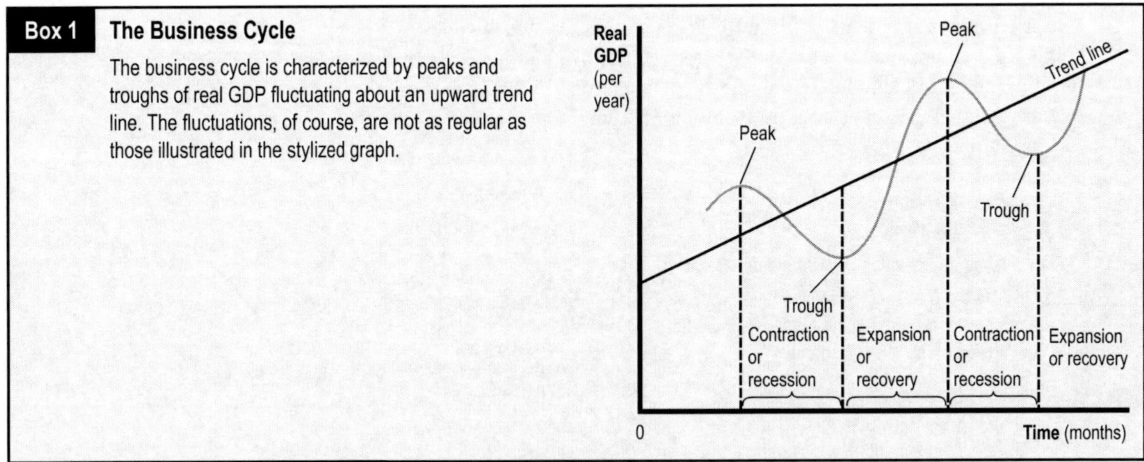

Box 1 The Business Cycle

The business cycle is characterized by peaks and troughs of real GDP fluctuating about an upward trend line. The fluctuations, of course, are not as regular as those illustrated in the stylized graph.

[1] In some quarters real GDP is normally expected to be higher because of seasonal production patterns. To avoid overestimating the *annual* rate of GDP during quarters when GDP is higher because of seasonal increases, actual data are adjusted downward before multiplying by 4 to obtain annual real GDP. A similar upward adjustment is made for quarters during which real GDP is normally expected to be lower.

factories, and offices. During a peak of the cycle, there are likely to be shortages of labor, parts, and materials in certain markets. On occasion the economy booms to such a degree that factories and offices are utilized around the clock, with two or more shifts of labor.

2. *Contraction or recession.* A contraction is a downturn from peak economic activity during which real GDP declines from its previous value. During a contraction, real GDP and therefore earnings also decline. Business profits also typically decline. As profitability falls, so does business demand for investment goods.

Sometimes the decline in real GDP that occurs during a contraction is particularly severe or prolonged. The U.S. Department of Commerce usually considers a contraction to be a recession when the decline in real GDP measured at an annual rate occurs for two consecutive three-month reporting periods. In 1982, which was a recession year, real GDP fell by 2 percent of its 1981 value. Real GDP fell by 0.5 percent during the 1991 recession. During the 2001 recession, the U.S. economy had negative growth in real GDP, averaging minus 1 percent for the first three quarters of the year. As a consequence of a decline in real GDP, the percentage of the work force classified as unemployed usually rises by anywhere from 2 to 4 percentage points. In a typical nonrecession year, only 4 percent to 6 percent of the labor force may be unemployed, while during a recession the unemployment rate may rise to 8, 9, or even 10 percent.

During recessions (which, since the end of World War II, have typically lasted for 10 to 12 months, although the two since 1990 have been of shorter duration), increased unemployment can turn families topsy-turvy. As earnings fall, so do living standards. Work routines are broken up, and the idleness that goes with joblessness often leads to mental illness. Divorces and suicides increase along with the increase in unemployment. From an economic standpoint, the waste of labor and other resources capable of both producing goods and services and earning incomes for their suppliers is lamentable.

3. *Trough.* A *trough* is the lowest level of real GDP observed over the business cycle. A trough is reached when the economy begins to pull out of a contraction or recession. During this time there is an excessive amount of unemployment and idle productive capacity. Businesses are more likely to fail because of low demand for their products.

Although a trough is the pits, it's also the point at which things start looking up. Once a trough has been reached, things can't get much worse, and the economic health of the nation begins to take a turn for the better.

4. *Expansion or recovery.* An expansion is an upturn of economic activity between a trough and a peak during which real GDP increases. During an expansion, demand for goods and services increases and real GDP rises as firms expand production, hire more workers, and purchase more investment goods. Employment opportunities increase during an expansion. The expansion in economic activity after a trough is called a recovery if it follows a period of contraction severe enough to be classified as a recession. During an expansion the economy moves toward a new peak, at which the cycle begins again.

The cycle of peak-contraction-trough-expansion-peak is never as regular and predictable as in the graph shown in Box 1. However, the fluctuations in real GDP actually occur even if they don't do so in a clear pattern. Notice that an upward-sloping trend line has been fitted through the peaks and troughs of the cyclical pattern of real GDP. This line shows that, although real annual GDP fluctuates, the trend is upward over the long run.

Actual Fluctuations and Trend of Real GDP in the United States

The graph in Box 2 shows the variation in real GDP over time. A trend line has been fitted through the data to reflect the average rate of increase in real GDP since 1900.

The general upward trend in real GDP is clear in Box 2. On average, real GDP has grown by 3.1 percent per year since 1900. *Real GDP has increased more than tenfold since 1900.* However, the growth has not been steady. There are clearly ups and downs in real GDP

Box 2 The Ups and Downs of U.S. Real GDP

The top graph shows that, although real GDP has had its ups and downs since 1900, the trend on average has been upward. The average annual growth rate of real GDP since 1900 has been 3.1 percent. A number of historical periods are shown on the graph. The scale used to measure real GDP uses the same vertical distance for each doubling of real GDP.

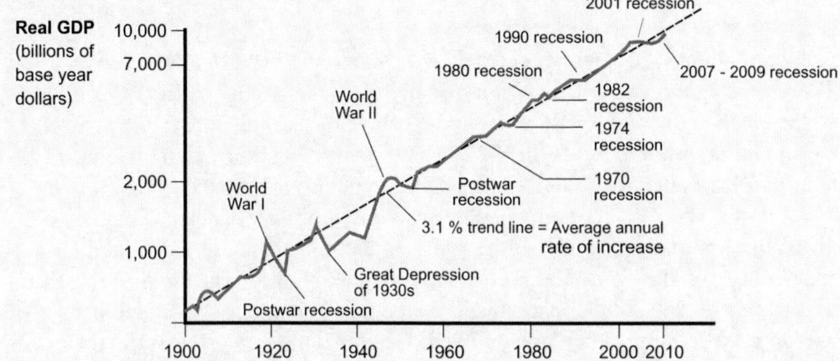

SOURCE: *Historical Chart Book*, Board of Governors of the Federal Reserve System; and U.S. Department of Commerce.

The bottom graph shows the annual growth rates for the U.S. economy since 1900. Notice how the ups and downs were much more pronounced prior to 1950 than they were after 1950. Since 1950, the U.S. economy has been relatively more stable than in the past. Although there have been 8 recessions in the United States since 1950, all have involved much smaller percentage declines in real GDP than was the case for the period 1900 to 1950.

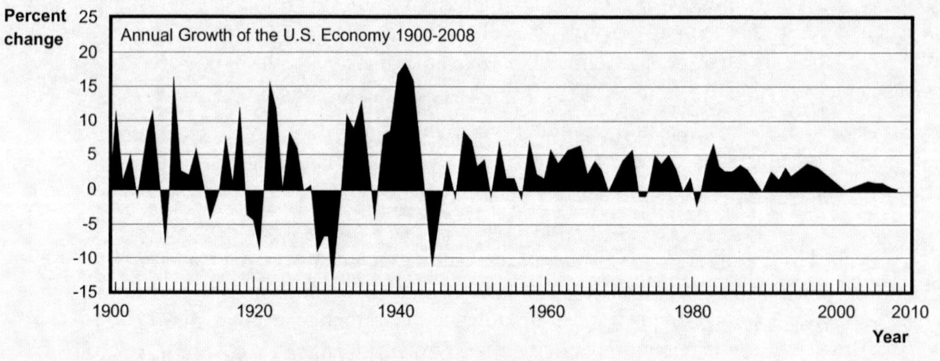

that can be identified as peaks, contractions, troughs, and expansions, although they're not as regular as those shown in the stylized graph in Box 1. A number of historical periods have been identified on the Box 2 graph.

1. *The Great Depression.* The Great Depression of the 1930s is clearly identifiable as a prolonged recession with a deep trough. It was unquestionably the trough of troughs.

The Great Depression hit in 1929 as a stock market crash late that year wiped out a substantial portion of the nation's accumulated savings. From the end of 1929 through 1933, real GDP fell by nearly one-third of its 1929 value. During many severe recessions it isn't uncommon for prices to fall on average. From the end of 1929 through 1933, prices fell to only 75 percent of their 1929 level. Those who could spare a dime in 1933 knew it was worth more then than it had been in 1929.

During the Great Depression there were virtually no business investment purchases. The decline in aggregate real income made the prospects for selling goods bleak. Given the gloomy outlook, few investors were willing to build new plants or purchase new equipment.

But the worst part of the Great Depression was the unemployment. One out of every four workers in the labor force was jobless in 1933. Imagine the terrible waste of having one-quarter of the able-bodied workers in the nation without jobs. You can also imagine the plight of the unemployed at a time when our nation didn't have the unemployment insurance and welfare programs we take for granted today. If you think there are a lot of street people today, you should have been around in the 1930s. The increased unemployment of the early 1930s is all the more dramatic when you realize that in 1929 only 3 percent of the labor force had been unemployed.

To anyone who lived through it, the Great Depression was a period of social unrest as well as economic contraction. The depression was worldwide, and the social instability it caused in Europe helped spawn the Nazi party and bring Hitler to power. As you can see in the aggregate demand/aggregate supply chapters, the Great Depression also affected the thinking of economists, most of whom prior to the 1930s thought that recessions would quickly cure themselves without assistance from the government. Their revised views led to the birth of macroeconomics—a policy-oriented branch of economics that would help formulate government programs to prevent severe recessions.

2. *Wartime prosperity and the post-World War II expansions.* The peaks, just before the 1920s and the early 1940s, when the economy was working at full steam producing goods for the war efforts, have also been clearly marked in Box 2. Notice that after World War I and World War II ended, there was a recession as the economy readjusted.

The 1950s were a period of prolonged and markedly steady growth in real GDP. However, the postwar expansion wasn't entirely uninterrupted by contractions and recessions. There was a recession immediately after World War II, and there were also recessions in 1949, 1954, 1958, and 1961. However, these five recessions were remarkably mild and much shorter than earlier recessions.

3. *The booming 60s.* After the recession of 1961 ended, the economy moved into a period of expansion. The 1960s were a period of military expansion and the Vietnam conflict. The increase in government purchases fueled the economy and also resulted in rising inflation.

4. *The curious 70s.* The 1970s came in with a recession. Although the recovery began in 1971, something strange happened in the economy in 1973. At that time the Organization of Petroleum Exporting Countries (OPEC) instituted an embargo on oil shipments to the United States and other nations. Inflation increased, and the price of petroleum products skyrocketed. Not only did inflation go up in the 1970s, but, curiously, so did unemployment! By 1974 the economy was buffeted by double-digit inflation and a severe recession. This was viewed as highly unusual. In the past inflation had usually eased up during a recession and sometimes prices had actually fallen, as was the case during the Great Depression. Real GDP fell substantially between 1973 and 1975, and unemployment soared to 9 percent of the labor force. It was all over by the end of 1975, when the economy recovered, and an expansion led to a 5 percent growth in real GDP in 1976. Inflation continued at a rampant rate during the remainder of the 1970s, but the nation avoided another recession.

5. *The expanding 80s.* Like the 1970s, the 1980s came in with a recession. The recession of 1980 was brief, lasting only six months, but extraordinary because it took place when inflation was still in double digits. As was the case for the 1974 recession, inflation and high unemployment sat side by side. The recession of 1980 was quite mild, with real GDP declining by only 0.5 percent that year. However, inflation remained a serious problem for the economy, running at 10 percent annual rates. At the end of 1981, the economy was plunged into the deepest recession it had experienced since the Great Depression of the 1930s. In that year real GDP fell by 2.2 percent and the unemployment rate soared to 11 percent.

The recession ended in late 1982, and the economy was well on its way to recovery. Starting in November 1982 and continuing to the end of the decade, the U.S. economy enjoyed a period of unprecedented peacetime expansion. In March 1989 the unemployment rate bottomed out at 5 percent—the lowest level that had been achieved since the early 1970s. Despite a major crash of the stock market in 1987, the economy remained resilient and continued to expand. Nearly 20 million new jobs were created during this period, and aggregate real income grew in a generally prosperous economy.

6. *The booming "high-tech" 90s.* The 1990s began with a distinct slowdown in the growth rate of real GDP. By the second quarter of 1990, real GDP growth had slowed to a 0.4 percent seasonally adjusted annual rate. The economy was buffeted by declines in real estate values, bank failures, and a growing federal budget deficit. Declining profits in a heavily debt-burdened corporate sector contributed to a market slowdown in hiring. Unemployment rates began to creep up from their low of 5 percent in March 1990.

In August 1990 Iraq invaded Kuwait. The crisis sent oil prices soaring from less than $20 a barrel to as much as $40 a barrel. The increased oil prices caused gasoline prices and other prices to increase. The resulting increase in the price level adversely affected real incomes and caused a general decrease in the demand for a variety of goods and services. The oil price increase came at a time when the economy was already suffering from slowing growth. By September 1990 it was becoming very clear that the economy was slipping into a recession. During the last three months of 1990, real GDP in the United States fell at an annual rate of nearly 2 percent. As the expansion of the 1980s ended, the unemployment rate increased to over 7 percent of the labor force. In the aftermath of the Gulf War, however, oil prices fell to less than $20 a barrel, which helped stimulate the sluggish U.S. economy. The recession of 1990–91 officially ended in March 1991. The recession was mild by historical standards, but it was followed by an uncharacteristically weak recovery. Throughout 1991 and 1992 real GDP grew at a relatively slow rate, and there was no surge in job creation to help the unemployment rate decline. By early 1993, as the Clinton administration took power, unemployment rates were still in the range of 7 percent and economic growth was improving, but the expansion was still sluggish compared to other postrecession periods. However, the recovery continued, and in 1993 real GDP grew at an annual rate of 3.1 percent. By 1994 the economy was booming; real GDP grew at 4.1 percent in that year. By the end of 1994 the unemployment rate in the United States fell to 5.4 percent, and the economy seemed to be expanding at a healthy rate.

The last half of the 1990s was a period of strong economic expansion for the U.S. economy. Fueled by rapid application of new technology and the explosive development of the Internet for both commerce and information transfer, the economy grew rapidly without significant inflation. Labor productivity increased as computer technology was applied, and unemployment rates dropped. Real GDP grew at an average annual rate of 4.32 percent between 1996 and 2000. Inflation averaged a mere 2.5 percent per year over this period despite a booming economy that was clearly operating at full employment. The unemployment rate in 2000 was 4 percent.

7. *The new millennium and the recession of 2001.* As the new millennium began, the U.S. economy appeared to be nearing the end of the all-time record expansion it had enjoyed beginning in 1991. The economy continued to boom in 2000, with real GDP growth of an impressive 5 percent that year. However, inflation was beginning to rear its ugly head and, with the rate of increase of prices accelerating, interest rates began to creep up. By the end of 2000, the great stock market boom was starting to falter, and stock market prices fell

substantially during the first quarter of 2001. The economy's growth rate had slowed substantially in the last quarter of 2000 and, by early 2001, corporate profits, particularly in the technology sector of the economy, were plummeting. Inventories started to build up in some sectors and workers were beginning to be laid off.

The Business Cycle Dating Committee of the National Bureau of Economic Research (NBER) officially declared that a recession arrived in the United States in March 2001. Industrial production had peaked in June of 2000 and, by March of 2001, employment started to decline. As real GDP growth slowed down, unemployment rates began to rise. The terrorist attack of September 11, 2001, further pushed the economy into a tailspin, and it was clear that the stock market bubble that had fueled so much spending had clearly burst and an enormous amount of wealth had disintegrated. Real GDP declined during the first three quarters of 2001. The recession of 2001 ended in November of that year, only eight months after it began, and the economy started to recover during the fourth quarter of 2001. Real GDP growth was 2.4 percent during 2002, compared with total growth of only 0.3 percent in 2001.

Despite positive economic growth throughout 2002, averaging close to 3 percent, job growth was anemic that year and unemployment rates hovered around 6 percent for the U.S. economy. The economy continued to grow in 2003, at a rate of 3.1 percent, in spite of fears of a "double dip" recession. However, growth in 2003 was moderate, averaging less than 2 percent for the first half of the year. The labor markets in 2002 and 2003 were stagnant, with slow job growth, and wages and salaries growing more slowly than the rate of inflation of prices in most sectors of the economy. The hiring slump affected a broad sector of the population—factory workers, white-collar workers, and professionals. The labor market was particularly dismal for new college graduates in 2003, with job offers by graduation day running in the range of half the usual rate. So, you can see, when the economy falls into recession, everyone can be affected. However, by mid-2004, the economy appeared to be expanding at a healthy rate and job growth was increasing. Economic growth remained solid throughout 2004, growing at a rate of 4.2 percent that year. By 2005, economic growth had slowed to 3.5 percent.

8. *The mortgage debt crisis and the 2007-2009 recession.* By early 2008, it was clear that the 6-year expansion of the U.S. economy since the 2001 recession was slowing down, and that the economy was possibly beginning to contract and enter into its first recession since 2001. A recession was officially declared as beginning in the fourth quarter of 2007. Problems in the mortgage market, due to defaults in subprime mortgage lending, caused widespread losses to financial institutions that had purchased mortgage-backed securities. Tightening of credit standards in the mortgage credit markets resulted in a sharp slowdown in housing demand and new construction. Housing values in many regional markets began to decline, reducing wealth, in the form of home equity, for individuals who owned their own homes. As reduced real estate lending continued, the demand for construction workers and those employed in housing-related industries also declined. In early 2008, corporate stock prices declined sharply, further reducing wealth. By mid-year, consumer spending was declining, job growth in the economy was negative, and the unemployment rate had risen to 5.5 percent, from 4.6 percent in 2007. The recession continued throughout 2008 and into 2009, with millions of jobs lost. The unemployment rate rose to 8.5 percent, the highest level in 25 years, by March 2009.

Sharp increases in basic materials, oil and food prices, in 2008, reduced consumer spending on other goods, as more of a household's budget was absorbed by expenditures on gasoline and basic necessities. Demand for new automobiles and other discretionary retail spending was weak, as wage and salary increases began to lag behind price increases.

The price of oil and gasoline fell drastically in late 2008, as the recession spread to much of the rest of world and decreases in aggregate demand reduced the demand for oil products. The price of crude oil fell between the summer of 2008 and early 2009 from a peak of nearly $150 a barrel to less than $40 a barrel, and the price of gasoline also declined drastically.

A financial crisis that threatened the solvency of the banking system reduced the supply of credit and further decreased spending. Despite aggressive action by government authorities, the recession remained severe in 2009, with declining home and corporate stock values decreasing wealth and causing further declines in consumption, investment, and export demand.

The ups and downs of real GDP depend on changes in market conditions of supply and demand. In the aggregate demand/aggregate supply chapters, we begin to develop the economic theory that shows how the forces of aggregate supply and demand influence real GDP. You can see that changes in economic and political conditions, as well as changes in labor and other inputs, financial markets, and foreign exchange markets, affect the level of both real GDP and prices.

Unemployment

Increased unemployment is a major consequence of cyclical declines in real GDP during periods of contraction or recession. Workers in some industries are more apt to be unemployed during recessions than others. Those who produce producer-durable goods, consumer-durable goods, and construction are typically hard hit by economic contractions and recessions because investment purchases by businesses and purchases of durable goods by consumers decline. However, unemployment is not limited to a few industries. As unemployed workers cut back on their spending, other workers soon find their jobs in jeopardy.

Some unemployment naturally exists even during periods of peak economic activity. The portion of unemployment attributable to a cyclical downturn or to production below the economy's potential can, however, be identified once agreement has been reached on what constitutes "normal" unemployment. In this way the concept of "full" or high employment for the economy can be defined.

Macroeconomic stabilization policies seek to minimize excessive unemployment. However, to intelligently formulate such policies, it is first necessary to understand what unemployment is and how it is measured. This makes it possible to distinguish excessive or cyclical unemployment from normal unemployment.

The Unemployment Rate

2 The labor force is the number of people over the age of 16 who are either employed or actively seeking a job. The unemployment rate measures the ratio of the number of people classified as unemployed to the total labor force. An unemployed person is defined as one over the age of 16 who is available for work and has actively sought employment during the previous four weeks. Note that this definition excludes people who *choose not* to have or seek jobs and therefore are not part of the labor force. By definition, full-time students over the age of 16, people who choose to devote their time to household chores or to raising their children, retired people, people unable to work because of disability, and people in mental or correctional institutions, although not working for pay, are not part of the labor force.

The U.S. Department of Labor estimates the unemployment rate each month with a sample of about 60,000 households. The households in the sample are changed periodically. A person is classified as unemployed if he or she did not do any work during the previous week. Note that people who have suffered reductions in paid work *hours* because of employer work cut-backs are *not* counted as unemployed. For example, a person whose work hours were cut from 40 to 20 a week because of slack demand for the product his employer manufactures is not counted as unemployed. However, a 50 percent reduction in the paid hours of work of two such workers amounts to the loss of a 40-hour workweek for the economy! This type of work loss isn't picked up by the unemployment statistics. Because the statistics don't measure the "underemployment" of workers who are not working full time but would like to be, they tend to underestimate actual unemployment.

The U.S. Department of Labor's monthly survey asks those in the sample whether they are actively looking for work. Some of the people who answer no to this question would be looking for work if wages were higher. Similarly, some of those classified as unemployed because they answer yes to this question may have unrealistic ideas about the value of their services and the wages they can reasonably expect. They may therefore be holding out for a job that they are unlikely to ever be offered.

A discouraged worker is one who leaves the labor force (stops actively seeking a job) after unsuccessfully searching for a job. It's not unusual for more than 1 percent of those surveyed by the Department of Labor to respond that they aren't looking for a job because they don't believe one can be found. It's difficult to objectively determine why workers respond in this way. However, by not counting discouraged workers among the ranks of the unemployed, the official unemployment statistics tend to *underestimate* actual unemployment. Because of the way it treats part-time and discouraged workers, the official unemployment rate is an imperfect indicator of actual unemployment as a percentage of the labor force. For example, in March 2009, the official unemployment rate was 8.5 percent. However, if both discouraged workers and workers who are working part-time, but would rather be working full-time, are considered, the unemployment rate more broadly measured would be closer to 15 percent!

Frictional, Structural, and Cyclical Unemployment

When a worker quits a job, is fired, or is laid off, a *job separation* occurs. Unemployment would always be zero if the time between a job separation and the discovery of a new job were zero for each worker and if new entrants and reentrants into the labor force immediately found a job. The time, effort, and transaction costs required to find a new job guarantee that there will always be some unemployed workers looking for jobs. *Job search* is the process of looking for a suitable job either by those who have just entered the labor force or have just experienced a job separation. *Job finding* occurs when an unemployed worker accepts an offer of a new job.

Members of the labor force search for jobs that best suit their skills and preferences. It's normal for workers to leave jobs they find unsuitable and for employers to fire workers who aren't performing their tasks up to required standards. Frictional unemployment represents the usual amount of unemployment resulting from people who have left jobs that didn't work out and are searching for new employment, or people who are either entering or reentering the labor force to search for a job. For example, if you spent six months looking for the right job after graduation, you would have been counted among the frictionally unemployed during that period. If a worker who is dissatisfied with a job managing a fast-food restaurant quits and takes two months to find a new job, that worker would be among the frictionally unemployed during that period.

Structural unemployment is unemployment resulting from permanent shifts in the pattern of demand for goods and services or from changes in technology such as automation or computerization. Structurally unemployed workers have skills that are not in demand by employers because of permanent changes in the economy. Structural unemployment often requires that workers who lose their jobs as a result of such changes learn new skills or move to other locations to find satisfactory new jobs. For example, the automobile workers who lost their jobs in the 1980s as result of a permanent decline in the demand for U.S.-made cars and increased automation of production facilities would be counted among the structurally unemployed. A permanent decline in the demand for petroleum products that resulted from improved conservation methods and higher oil prices in the 1980s caused structural unemployment for oil field and refinery workers in the United States. In the 1990s structural unemployment increased as a result of a permanent reduction in defense-related spending by the federal government and of corporate "downsizing" of work forces to reduce costs and increase productivity in a more competitive environment. To regain employment, some workers in the pool of the structurally unemployed have to find jobs in other industries or learn new skills.

The economy is always in flux because the pattern of demand and technology changes almost monthly. Both the industrial and regional patterns of demand for workers also change, implying that some workers will lose their jobs and have to search for new ones as a result of normal changes in the economy.

It's inevitable that a certain percentage of the labor force will experience job separation over the year. Forcing workers to stay in their jobs forever and preventing employers from ever cutting back employment, going out of business, or firing or laying off workers would involve losses in efficiency just as surely as excessive unemployment would result in waste.

Some unemployment, however, is directly attributable to cyclical declines in real GDP. Cyclical unemployment is the amount of unemployment resulting from declines in real GDP during periods of contraction or recession or in any period when the economy fails to operate at its potential. In macroeconomic policy analysis, cyclical unemployment receives the greatest amount of attention because cyclical unemployment is viewed as controllable. Policies that help prevent cyclical declines in real GDP can limit cyclical unemployment.

Cyclical unemployment is characterized by layoffs. A layoff is the temporary suspension of employment without pay for a period of seven consecutive days or more. Workers who are on layoff are not fired. Instead, they are let go because of temporarily reduced demand for the product they are employed to produce. A worker who is laid off has some expectation of being recalled by his or her employer should business pick up again. Of course, a layoff may end up being permanent, in which case the worker must search for a new job to regain employment.

The total amount of unemployment in any month is the sum of frictional, structural, and cyclical unemployment. Frictional and structural unemployment result from natural and, perhaps, unavoidable occurrences in a dynamic economy. Cyclical unemployment, however, is the result of imbalances between aggregate purchases and the aggregate production corresponding to full employment.

The Natural Rate of Unemployment and Potential Real GDP

3 The natural rate of unemployment is the percentage of the labor force that can normally be expected to be unemployed for reasons other than cyclical fluctuations in real GDP. In other words, the natural rate of unemployment is the sum of the frictional and structural unemployment expected over the year. When the economy operates so that there is only structural and frictional unemployment, it is viewed as achieving the potential productive capacity normally expected at the peak of the business cycle.[2] When the actual rate of unemployment is no more than the natural rate of unemployment, the economy

operates at full employment. *Because the natural rate of unemployment is not zero, full employment does not mean zero unemployment!*[3]

In 1985, the natural rate of unemployment was generally believed to be about 6 percent. If this was the case, cyclical unemployment would have been 1.1 percent, because the actual unemployment rate that year, based on monthly averages, was 7.1 percent. In 1992, the natural rate of unemployment was estimated to be 5.5 percent. Because actual unemployment was 7.3 percent, on average, in 1992, there was cyclical unemployment of 1.8 percent that year. Of course, when the economy attains full employment, as it did in 1989, the actual unemployment rate is close to the natural rate of unemployment and cyclical unemployment is close to zero. In 2000, the Congressional Budget Office estimated that the natural rate of unemployment was 5.2 percent. That year, unemployment rates in the United States averaged 4 percent, indicating that cyclical unemployment in the economy that year was actually negative. In 2003, with unemployment rates averaging 5.8 percent, cyclical unemployment was 0.6 percent, based on a 5.2 percent estimated natural rate of unemployment. However, by 2005, the U.S. economy appeared close to full employment, with an unemployment rate in the range of 5.2 percent and virtually no cyclical unemployment. With an unemployment rate of 8.5 percent in March 2009, cyclical unemployment was positive at 3.3 percent, based on a 5.2 percent natural rate of unemployment.

4 Potential real GDP is the level of real GDP that would prevail if the economy achieved the natural rate of employment over a period of one year. When the economy's performance is below its potential, such as during recessions, the unemployment rate exceeds the natural rate of unemployment.

An overheated economy, on the other hand, is one for which the actual unemployment rate is *less* than the natural rate of unemployment. In an overheated economy factories are run around the clock and many workers put in overtime. Typically, unit costs of production rise rapidly and labor shortages occur, putting upward pressure on wages and labor costs. When actual GDP rises above potential real GDP, the typical result is rapidly rising prices. The higher prices tend to decrease the aggregate quantity of goods and services demanded and cause real GDP to decline. In 2000, U.S. potential real GDP was estimated to be $9.5 trillion. Because actual GDP that year was $9.8 trillion, the economy was a bit overheated and inflation rates began to accelerate. By 2003, actual GDP was running below potential real GDP, in the aftermath of a recession. The Congressional Budget Office estimated potential nominal GDP at $12,450 billion in 2005. This was about equal to actual GDP, indicating the economy had achieved full employment.

In 2008, potential real GDP was estimated to be $12 trillion. As of midyear, 2008 real GDP for the U.S. economy was running at an annual rate of about $11.7 trillion, indicating that the U.S. economy was operating below its potential. Real GDP declined at an annual rate of 6.2 percent in the fourth quarter of 2008, and, with the unemployment rate moving up in 2009 to over 8 percent, the U.S. economy was running well below its potential. For the last quarter of 2008, the Congressional Budget Office estimated potential real GDP to be $12 trillion, while actual real GDP was running at an annual rate of only $11.5 trillion.

---

[2]The *natural rate of unemployment* can also be defined as the unemployment rate that would prevail if all wages and prices were instantaneously adjustable to changes in market conditions.

[3]Actually, it's a matter of simple arithmetic to calculate the natural rate of unemployment when there are no movements of workers in or out of the labor force. The natural rate of unemployment, U, under these circumstances is the rate of job separation, s, divided by the sum of the rate of job finding, f, and the rate of job separation: $U = s / (f + s)$. For example, if 1 percent of the labor force experiences job separation during the year and 15 percent of the unemployed find jobs, the natural rate of unemployment is 0.01/0.16 = 6.2%. See Robert J. Barro, *Macroeconomics*, 3rd ed. (New York: John Wiley & Sons, 1990), pp. 256–59.

You should understand the following basic facts about potential real GDP:

1. *Potential real GDP is not the economy's "capacity" output.* The economy can produce *more* than potential real GDP when the actual unemployment rate falls below the natural unemployment rate. Even though capacity output exceeds potential real GDP, most economists believe that the economy cannot exceed potential real GDP for long periods without consequences that impair its future performance and ultimately cause actual real GDP to decline to its potential level.

2. *It's not easy to measure potential real GDP.* The natural rate of unemployment can vary from year to year. The number of hours worked per year when the natural rate of unemployment has been attained can also vary, depending on the mix of employment. In addition, it's hard to determine the level of output associated with the natural rate of unemployment because the output depends on the productivity of workers. It's often only possible to guess at the level of real GDP that corresponds to the natural rate of unemployment. When we discuss economic policy to stabilize the economy, you can see that if policies are based on erroneous estimates of potential real GDP, they can destabilize the economy instead. For example, if policymakers mistake an increase in the natural rate of unemployment for an increase in cyclical unemployment and seek to expand the economy to get back to full employment, they could cause the economy to overheat and start a process of inflation that would impair the functioning of the economy for several years.

3. *Potential real GDP grows over time.* Remember that the long-term growth rate of real GDP in the United States has been slightly greater than 3 percent per year since 1900. Potential real GDP also grows on average from year to year. In some years the economy may grow more slowly than the growth in potential real GDP, and in some years it may grow faster. Potential real GDP growth depends on growth in the labor force and other resources, improvements in technology, and general improvements in the quality of productive resources (such as those that result from improvements in the educational level of workers). Potential real GDP will also grow if labor market conditions lower the natural rate of unemployment. For example, there is currently some concern that the growth rate of potential real GDP will decline in the future because of declines in the growth rate of the labor force. However, a decline in the growth rate of the labor force can be offset by improvements in technology that will either increase labor productivity or reduce the natural rate of unemployment.

Potential real GDP is the benchmark we will use throughout our study of macroeconomics to gauge the performance of the economy. Ideally, we would like to see the economy operate most of the time at potential real GDP.

Cyclical Unemployment

Excessive unemployment is a sign that the economy is operating below its potential. When this is the case, there is cyclical unemployment. Not only is there idle labor, but machines and factories are also idle when real GDP is below its potential. The main cost is a reduction in output; when output falls, so does aggregate real income. The decline in income stems mainly from the workers who are unfortunate enough to lose their jobs. However, owners of other inputs, particularly capital, also experience declines in income because the profit rate of many businesses declines when the economy contracts. Some industries are more sensitive to cyclical declines in output than others. For example, income tends to fall sharply in the construction and automobile industries when there is a recession.

How Unemployment Varies with the Business Cycle

One source of unemployment is a predictable pattern of quits and layoffs. Layoffs tend to increase, as you would expect, during contractions and recessions. Typically, during a recession, a significant portion of the labor force will be unemployed because of layoffs. In 2004, a good year for the U.S. economy, with an unemployment rate of 5.5 percent, only 0.67 percent of the labor force was unemployed due to layoffs. However, in 1982, a severe recession year, about 3 percent of the labor force was unemployed because of layoffs. The unemployment rate in 1982 averaged more than 9 percent. The 1982 unemployment rate can be thought of as the sum of a natural rate of about 6 percent and the cyclical rate of 3 percent. Layoffs represent the cyclical component of the unemployment rate. In 2001, a mild recession year, 0.75 percent of the labor force was unemployed due to layoffs–somewhat higher than in 2004.

Unemployment resulting from quitting tends to drop during recessions but increases during expansions. Obviously, you wouldn't want to quit a job when the probability of finding another one is low, as it is during a recession. However, when times are good, you and many workers like you take the chance and quit to find a new job.

The pie charts in Box 3 show that during a peak in the business cycle, the percentage of unemployed workers who lost their jobs because of layoff is typically not more than 12 percent of the unemployed. The chart at the left shows that, during 1978, a year generally classified as one of peak economic activity, only 11.5 percent of the job losers were on layoff. During a peak year the percentage of the unemployed who quit their jobs (job leavers) also tends to increase. In 1978, 14.1 percent of the unemployed voluntarily left their jobs.

Box 3 Distribution of Unemployment by Reason: Peak and Recession Years

As the economy moves from peak economic activity to a recession, the percentage of the unemployed on layoff and other job losers typically rises, while the percentage who are unemployed because they voluntarily left their jobs (job leavers) goes down.

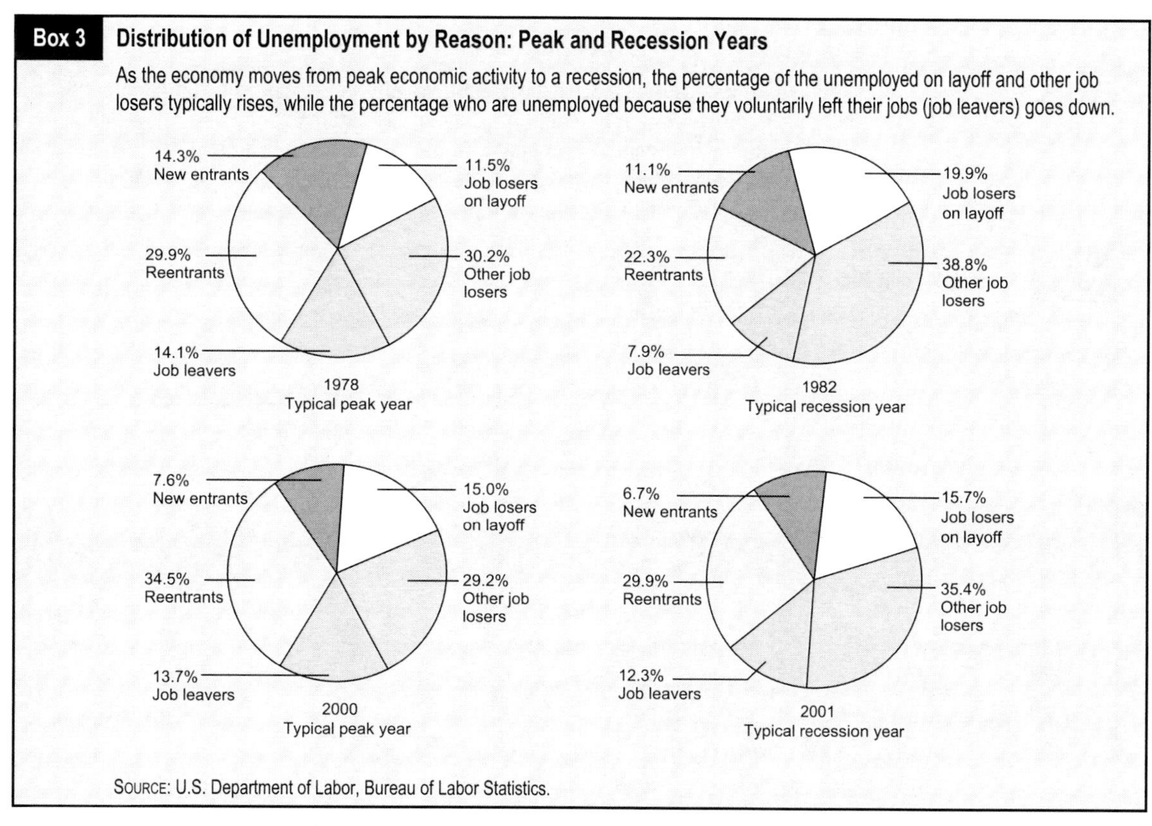

SOURCE: U.S. Department of Labor, Bureau of Labor Statistics.

During a recession year such as 1982 (a particularly severe period of recession), the proportion of unemployed who are on layoff approaches 20 percent. At such times people who have voluntarily left their jobs account for a much smaller percentage of the unemployed. In 1982 only 7.9 percent of the unemployed were people who left their jobs voluntarily. Similar patterns are also seen between the peak year 2000 and the recession year 2001, with layoffs and other job losses rising as the recession occurs, while the rate at which workers voluntarily leave their jobs declines. The United States has suffered only two mild recessions since 1982. In both the recession of 1990 and the recession of 2001, layoffs weren't as pronounced as they were during the 1982 recession. Box 4 shows how U.S. unemployment rates have varied since 1950.

The Costs of Unemployment

5 Unemployment means a drop in national production. This implies a reduction in income for the nation. When business receipts decline and firms have unused capacity, profits decline. When workers lose their jobs, they also lose the labor income they would have otherwise earned. The loss in wages and profits is part of the costs of unemployment. As income and business revenues decline during a recession, governments also suffer because they experience a decline in their tax revenues.

But still more costs are associated with unemployment. Unemployment can be a depressing experience. Research provides evidence that increases in the cyclical unemployment rate are associated with increased suicide, crime, mental illness, and physical illness.[4] During recessions the average period of unemployment tends to double from the normal two-month duration. During recessions it's also more probable that in many families both spouses will lose their jobs. This tends to compound the stress and other social problems stemming from unemployment.

Cushioning Unemployment Costs

Unemployment insurance benefits available to eligible workers cushion the loss of income associated with temporary unemployment. These benefits vary from state to state, but they average about 35 percent of previous earnings. Usually the benefits last for a maximum of 26 weeks. Because the average duration of unemployment is only about 18 weeks, workers seldom collect for the full period. In a recession, however, the duration of

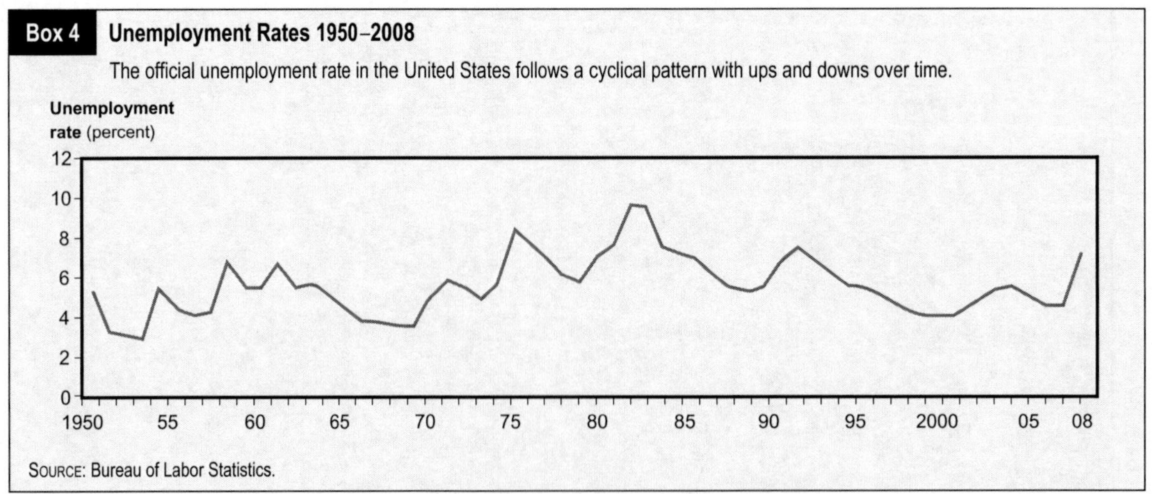

Box 4 Unemployment Rates 1950–2008

The official unemployment rate in the United States follows a cyclical pattern with ups and downs over time.

SOURCE: Bureau of Labor Statistics.

[4]See Barry Bluestone and Bennett Harrison, *The Deindustrialization of America* (New York: Basic Books, 1982), chap. 3.

unemployment increases dramatically to more than four months. In periods of unusually high unemployment, Congress can extend unemployment insurance benefits.

Unemployment insurance was established in the United States as part of the Social Security Act of 1935. The program is managed by individual states, each of which has a separate trust fund used to support unemployment insurance benefits. The unemployment insurance tax is collected from employers by the federal government, which returns most of the funds to the states for deposit in their trust funds.

Unemployment insurance puts a floor on income and eases the costs of unemployment, but unemployment insurance is not available to all the unemployed. Eligibility varies from state to state. However, in all states only *covered* workers are eligible. How does a worker obtain coverage under unemployment insurance? He or she must have worked for a specified period at a job for which an employer paid the payroll tax for unemployment insurance.

New entrants and reentrants into the labor force are *not* eligible. For example, if it takes you six months to find a job after graduating from college, don't count on getting unemployment insurance to tide you over until you gain employment! Job quitters almost without exception are not eligible, nor in most cases are people who are fired because of poor performance. Who, then, gets the benefits? The answer is mainly people who lose their jobs temporarily because of layoffs or permanently because of shutdowns of business firms or contractions in business operations. In other words, the insurance alleviates the costs of cyclical and structural unemployment.

Finally, to remain eligible for benefits, an unemployed worker must be actively looking for a new job and cannot reject an offer of a suitable job. This last provision, however, is hard to enforce.

Recently, there has been a significant decline in the proportion of the unemployed receiving unemployment insurance benefits. Between 1990 and 2005, on average, only about one-third of the unemployed were receiving unemployment checks, compared to 75 percent of the unemployed in 1975. To reduce the tax bill for unemployment insurance, most state governments now require workers to work longer and earn more wages before they can qualify for unemployment insurance benefits. In addition, today's work force comprises more service workers, many of whom are part-timers and some of whom change jobs frequently. These workers are less likely to be eligible for unemployment insurance benefits.

During the recession of 2001, many workers found it difficult to collect unemployment insurance benefits. Because eligibility is based on earnings over the 12- to 18-month period prior to losing a job, many low-wage workers and part-time workers found they had insufficient earnings to qualify. Similarly, recently hired workers and workers who quit their jobs because new shifts or other changes in scheduling interfered with family obligations found they couldn't get benefits. In most states, only full-time workers who held their jobs at least one year before being laid off were guaranteed benefits.

Unemployment insurance benefits have not kept pace with inflation. The average benefits paid have declined from half of previous earnings in the 1970s to only a bit more than one-third of previous earnings today. There are concerns among many that unemployment insurance has become a less effective cushion against the costs of unemployment than it once was.

Economic Growth and Its Sources

6 Over the long run, the ability of the economy to create job opportunities for a growing population depends on its rate of growth. There are always periods of

recession, but their effects tend to be offset occasionally by boom periods during which the economy exceeds its potential. Over a long period, real GDP *on average* grows along with growth in potential real GDP. However, because of the tendency of prices to rise more in expansion periods than they fall during contraction periods, the price level rises along with the growth in real GDP.

Economic growth in a nation is measured by the annual percentage increase in its level of real GDP. Economic growth is the key to improvements in a nation's standard of living. Since 1900 real GDP growth in the United States has averaged 3.1 percent per year. Thus the nation's ability to produce goods and services has increased at slightly more than 3 percent per year since 1900. The table in Box 5 shows the growth rates of real output in the United States for each year from 1959 to 2008.

Box 5 Annual Growth Rate of Real GDP in the United States, 1959–2008 (Percent Change from Previous Year)

Year	Growth rate
1959	7.1
1960	2.5
1961	2.3
1962	6.1
1963	4.4
1964	5.8
1965	6.4
1966	6.5
1967	2.5
1968	4.8
1969	3.1
1970	0.2
1971	3.4
1972	5.3
1973	5.8
1974	–0.5
1975	–0.2
1976	5.3
1977	4.6
1978	5.6
1979	3.2
1980	–0.2
1981	2.5
1982	–1.9
1983	4.5
1984	7.2
1985	4.1
1986	3.5
1987	3.4
1988	4.1
1989	3.5
1990	1.9
1991	–0.2
1992	3.3
1993	2.7
1994	4.0
1995	2.5
1996	3.7
1997	4.5
1998	4.2
1999	4.5
2000	3.7
2001	0.8
2002	1.6
2003	2.5
2004	3.6
2005	3.1
2006	2.9
2007	2.0
2008	1.1

SOURCE: U.S. Department of Commerce

The Sources of Growth

Ultimately, actual economic growth depends on the growth of the potential of the economy to produce goods and services. Actual real GDP may fluctuate around potential real GDP, but over a long period the economy on average comes reasonably close to producing a potential real GDP. As potential real GDP grows, so too do employment opportunities and potential aggregate real income. To understand the process of economic growth, therefore, we must understand the important influences on a nation's potential real GDP.

The major influences on a nation's potential to produce goods and services are as follows:

1. *The productive resources available to the nation.* The labor, capital equipment, natural resources, and other inputs available in any year influence productive potential. The more workers and equipment available, given a nation's population and natural resources, the greater the nation's productive potential.

The U.S. labor force has grown considerably over the past 40 years. In recent years immigration, maturation of the baby boom generation, and increased employment of women have contributed to economic growth. In 2004, 59.2 percent of working-age women participated in the labor force, compared to only 34 percent in 1950. However, in 2004, labor force participation for males in the United States was 74.7 percent, so females remain less likely than males to be in the labor force.

2. *The quality of productive resources available to the nation.* The quality of a productive resource is measured by its productivity, which is a measure of output per unit of input. The more productive workers, natural resources (such as agricultural land), and capital equipment, the greater the real GDP possible from a given amount of productive resources. Because labor is the dominant productive input, growth in labor productivity is a key to economic growth. When output per worker increases in a nation, output per person also tends to go up! Therefore, steady growth in a nation's labor productivity ensures steady growth in final products per person and in the material well-being of individuals in the nation.

The skills of a nation's labor force represent "human capital." The quality of a nation's human capital depends on the education and experience of its workers. Years and quality of schooling and on-the-job experience increase both output per worker and wages. Recent concerns about the quality of education in the United States reflect the fact that education is a key influence on worker productivity and living standards.

3. *Improvements in technology.* As technology advances, the output available from a given quantity of productive resources increases. Technological progress requires investment in research and development.

4. *Improvements in the efficiency with which available inputs are used.* Policies that promote efficiency in resource use allow the economy to obtain the greatest possible output of final products from available resources. Changes in management or policies that reduce waste in production and conserve resources can therefore contribute to increases in the economy's productive potential.

A favorable change in any of the preceding factors can be viewed as shifting the nation's production possibilities curve outward. As the nation enjoys improvements in the quality of resources, the quantity available, or technology, its potential to produce any combination of goods also increases. The production possibilities curve drawn in Box 6 illustrates the economy's potential to produce two broad classes of goods: private goods available to individuals and business firms for their exclusive use and government goods whose benefits are shared by all. You can see that growth helps deal with the problem of scarcity by allowing an increase in both government goods and private goods as the economy moves from point *A* to point *B*.

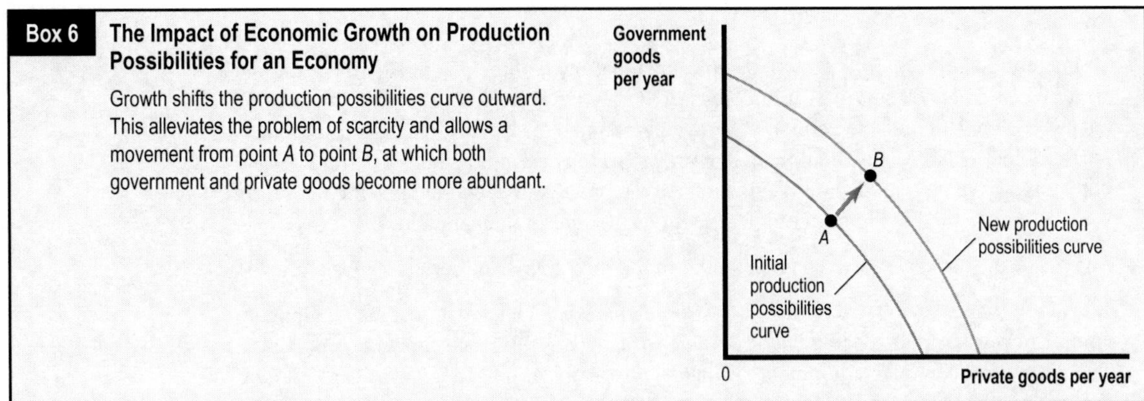

Box 6 The Impact of Economic Growth on Production Possibilities for an Economy

Growth shifts the production possibilities curve outward. This alleviates the problem of scarcity and allows a movement from point *A* to point *B*, at which both government and private goods become more abundant.

Improvements in Productivity

As suggested earlier, a key to the growth process is annual improvements in labor productivity. Output per worker goes up when worker skills or education improves or when workers have improved tools to work with. Because workers gain more experience as they spend more time on their jobs, productivity growth is also influenced by the age composition of the labor force. When the percentage of younger workers in the labor force increases, the influx of inexperienced workers can adversely affect productivity.

Improvements in technology allow a given amount of capital or natural resources to be more productive when used by a labor force of given size. The sources of growth just listed are therefore not independent. Steady improvements in the quality of resources depend on steady improvements in technology and steady growth in capital per worker. Improvements in the quality of management can also improve the productivity of workers. Better productive management can improve the division of labor in ways that generate more output from a given work force. Improvements in personnel management procedures can give workers incentives to acquire more skills and to produce more efficiently. Economic growth has an important *allocative* component that is influenced by both business management techniques and public policies. In any given year growth is greater when resources are used in ways that allow maximum output to be squeezed from available inputs. Improvements in labor productivity accounted for over two-thirds of the growth in real GDP over the period 1929 to 1982.[5] Increases in the quantity of available labor accounted for the remaining third. Research by Edward Denison, in a classic study, indicates that the most important factor influencing improvements in labor productivity over that period was technological advance. Improvements in the technology of production and of management in the United States have been estimated to account for nearly 40 percent of the improvement in labor productivity. Keep in mind that it takes considerable business investment to create new technology, so technological advance and investment are not unrelated. Technological improvements result in new and better equipment, machines, and techniques that enhance worker productivity. New computers, machines, and modes of transportation have made workers much more productive in recent years.

Increases in the amount of capital available to workers, according to Denison, account for nearly 30 percent of the increase in labor productivity. Another 21 percent is accounted for by improved education and training. The bulk of the gains in labor productivity are therefore accounted for by improvements in technology, growth of capital equipment, and better education and training.

[5]Edward F. Denison, *Trends in American Economic Growth, 1929–1982* (Washington, D.C.: Brookings Institution, 1985).

Box 7 shows trends in productivity growth from 1959-2008. Labor productivity growth was relatively low from 1975-1994 in the United States, but it has risen since 1995, in part as a result of the application of new technology.

Saving, Investment, and Economic Growth

A nation's growth rate is influenced by the portion of national income that is invested. The process of investment involves the sacrifice of current consumption so that resources can be devoted to creating new capital, technology, or skills that will increase productivity and income in the future.

Business investment requires the outlay of funds that are obtained through financial markets or through capital consumption allowances or retained earnings. Capital consumption allowances (depreciation) are a form of saving through which businesses finance investment by setting aside earnings to replace worn-out or obsolete capital. Retained earnings are corporate savings used to finance the acquisition of capital goods.

Personal savings are also used to finance investment. They are channeled through financial markets to investors who borrow funds to make investments.

Investment in *human* capital often requires that people forgo opportunities for current income by attending colleges, universities, or training institutes. When people study to obtain new skills, they give up opportunities for current consumption in the hope that the extra education and skills they acquire in school will allow them to enjoy more annual future consumption.

The Trade-Off between Current and Future Consumption

The process of economic growth depends on the willingness of people in a nation to give up current consumption in exchange for the possibility of greater future consumption. The funds and labor hours allocated to investment can be used to develop new technology, new factories and equipment, and more productive labor that will increase future real GDP. Of course, all investment entails risks, and the actual payoff to investment is uncertain.

A nation with a higher saving rate is more likely to have a higher growth rate of output per capita over the long run than a nation with a lower saving rate. But a high saving rate can exert downward pressure on aggregate demand in a given year when the business outlook is poor and saving exceeds intended investment. High saving can thus exert downward pressure on equilibrium real GDP in some years because it detracts from demand. Over the long run, however, when the ups and downs of the business cycle average out, high saving rates will be matched by high investment rates. High saving over the long run will contribute to growth in productive capacity for the nation and increased future output per capita.

Box 7 **Annual Average Growth Rates in Labor Productivity 1959-2008**
(Average annual change in output per hour, all workers in the business sector)

Period	Labor productivity growth (percent)
1959–1974	2.96
1975–1989	1.67
1990–1994	1.62
1995–1999	2.30
2000–2008	2.50

SOURCE: *Economic Report of the President* and U.S. Bureau of Labor Statistics.

Summary

1. The material well-being of a nation's citizens depends on real GDP. Declines in real GDP reduce both national production and national income. In a nation with a growing population, declines in real GDP result in decreases in final production per person.

2. The business cycle describes the periodic fluctuations in national production as measured by the ups and downs of real GDP.

3. The business cycle consists of movements from peaks to contractions and occasional recessions, then to troughs, and then expansions and recoveries from recessions. A recession is a decline in real GDP that occurs over at least a six-month (two consecutive quarters) reporting period.

4. Despite the ups and downs of the business cycle, there has been a general upward trend in real GDP since 1900. On average, real GDP HAS grown at the rate of 3.1 percent per year in the United States since 1900.

5. A consequence of declines in real GDP is excessive unemployment. The unemployment rate measures the ratio of the number of people classified as unemployed to the total labor force, which consists of the sum of employed and unemployed people over the age of 16. An *unemployed person* is a person over the age of 16 who is available for work and has actively sought employment during the past four weeks. The unemployment rate is estimated each month from a sample of 60,000 households. Not included in the ranks of the unemployed are people who suffer reductions in hours worked but are employed part time during a period because of production cutbacks.

6. A layoff is a temporary suspension of employment without pay for a period of seven days or more.

7. A job separation occurs whenever a worker quits, is fired, or is laid off. Job separations are normal occurrences resulting from poor matches of workers to jobs and from changes in the pattern of demand for goods and services. *Frictional unemployment* is the usual amount of unemployment that occurs when people have left jobs and are searching for new employment or are entering the labor force. *Structural unemployment* is the unemployment that results from permanent shifts in the pattern of demand for goods and services or from changes in technology that affect the profitability of hiring workers in specific industries. *Cyclical unemployment* is the unemployment that results from declines in real GDP when the economy fails to operate at its potential. The excessive unemployment observed during a recession is cyclical unemployment. Layoffs are the major source of cyclical unemployment.

8. The natural rate of unemployment is the percentage of the labor force that can normally be expected to be unemployed for reasons other than cyclical fluctuations in real GDP. Natural unemployment is the sum of frictional and structural unemployment. The economy is viewed as operating at full employment when cyclical unemployment is zero. At full employment the actual unemployment rate is not zero because some frictional and structural unemployment is normal even when the economy is operating at its potential. The natural rate of unemployment varies, but in March 2009, it was 8.5 percent.

9. Potential real GDP is an estimate of the level of production that would prevail in an economy if the natural rate of unemployment were achieved.

10. The costs of unemployment include a reduction in national output and tax revenues. Increases in unemployment appear to be associated with increased mental and physical illness and other social problems. Unemployment insurance cushions the declines in well-being that result from excessive unemployment.

11. Economic growth is measured by the annual percentage change in a nation's real GDP. The most important sources of economic growth are increases in the quantity and quality of economic resources, improvements in technology, and more efficient resource use.

12. Improvement in labor productivity is a driving force behind economic growth. Improvements in workers' skills or education or the capital that workers use can improve their productivity.

13. The process of investment involves the sacrifice of current consumption so that resources can be devoted to creating new capital, technology, or skills that will in the future increase productivity and therefore real GDP and real income.

Concept Review

1. What is the business cycle?

2. How is the unemployment rate measured in the United States?

3. Explain why the unemployment rate is not zero when the economy achieves "full employment."

4. How is the concept of potential real GDP related to the natural rate of unemployment and the economy's "capacity" output?

5. How does the system of unemployment insurance operate in the United States?

6. What could cause a slowdown in the rate of economic growth in the United States?

Problems and Applications

1. Following are seasonally adjusted data for real GDP for each of 10 quarters:

Period	Quarterly real GDP (billions of seasonally adjusted dollars)
1st quarter, year 1	1,000
2nd quarter, year 1	900
3rd quarter, year 1	800
4th quarter, year 1	700
1st quarter, year 2	700
2nd quarter, year 2	750
3rd quarter, year 2	850
4th quarter, year 2	1,100
1st quarter, year 3	1,150
2nd quarter, year 3	1,100

Calculate the real GDP at an annual rate for each quarter, and plot the points associated with each quarter. Trace a curve through the points to illustrate the phases of the business cycle. Was there a recession over the period covered by the data? How would you calculate the long-term trend in growth in real GDP over that period? (2)

2. Can real GDP decline even though there is no recession? What are the consequences for the economy of declines in real GDP? (1), (2)

3. In January there are 60 million employed workers and 2 million unemployed workers in the economy. Calculate the January unemployment rate. (2)

4. Why can the official unemployment rate be criticized for underestimating actual unemployment in the economy? (2)

5. Explain why it is unreasonable to expect an economy's unemployment rate ever to fall to zero. Why can unemployment be decreased by an improvement in the job search process that decreases the time required for job finding? (3)

6. Suppose the natural rate of unemployment in 2008 is 6 percent and corresponds to 320 billion hours of labor for the year. When that unemployment rate has been achieved, output per labor hour is $20 measured in base year prices. Calculate potential real GDP for 2008. (4)

7. Assume the current unemployment rate is 7 percent. If the sum of structural and frictional unemployment is 6 percent, how much cyclical unemployment prevails? (3)

8. Explain how the pattern of quits and layoffs varies predictably with the business cycle. (3), (5)

9. Why does a slowdown in the rate of economic growth imply that future living standards may deteriorate? (6)

10. Why is the rate of productivity growth in a nation likely to be tied to the rate of saving and investment in the nation? (6)

What's a Recession, and Who Can Predict When One Will Arrive?

Who decides whether the United States is in a recession. The Business Cycle Dating Committee, which meets under the auspices of the National Bureau of Economic Research (NBER), dates the beginnings and ends of recessions after they've actually occurred. The committee consists of a panel of seven experts that meets periodically to assess business conditions.

A recession is usually defined as a period in which output, income, and employment decline nationally over a period of at least six months. During a recession, there's a widespread contraction of economic activity affecting many sectors of the economy. Orders for new plants and equipment, and for materials and inventories, typically plummet. Real GDP, industrial production, and personal income usually decline, while unemployment increases. Almost all recessions are preceded by a decline in stock market prices, but not all declines in stock market prices are followed by a recession.

Predicting when a recession will start isn't easy. Most forecasters failed to predict the worst recessions of the 1970s and 1980s--the recessions of 1974-75 and 1981-82. However, the recession that began during 1990 was widely anticipated. In fact, the Dating Committee of the NBER, in a rare early ruling, declared that a recession "probably" began in August 1990. However, the official designation of the beginning of the recession wasn't made until 1991. The committee waited until late 1992 before designating March 1991 as the end of the 1990-91 recession. In 2001, it waited until November to designate March 2001 as the beginning of a recession. Although the end of the recession was finally pegged at November 2001, the committee waited until July of 2003 to make the final assessment, announcing that the recession had ended nearly two years prior!

What do you look for when trying to determine whether a recession is brewing? Most economists regard overexpansion of business investment--overstocks of parts and materials--as a prelude to contraction. Sudden increases in the prices of key inputs, such as oil, can also precipitate a recession.

Experts who try to forecast changes in real GDP keep a close watch on various sectors of the economy. *Leading economic indicators* are economic variables whose values are normally expected to decline prior to a decline in real GDP and to rise prior to a rise in real GDP. In other words, leading economic indicators can sometimes (but not always) be useful in forecasting economic contractions or expansions. Among the important leading economic indicators watched in the United States are these:

1. Average workweek of production workers in manufacturing.
2. Average weekly initial claims for unemployment insurance.
3. New orders for manufacturing, consumer goods, and materials.
4. A measure of vendors reporting slower deliveries.
5. Plant and equipment contracts and orders
6. Building permits for new residential housing.
7. Common stock prices (an index of 500 stock prices).
8. Checking deposits, currency in circulation, and certain liquid assets.
9. Interest rate spread between 10-year government bonds and short-term bank loans.
10. An index of consumer expectations about the future.

A composite index of these 10 leading indicators is published monthly. The year 1996 is used as a benchmark year, so its indicators are set equal to 100. Other years are then compared with 1996. Some of the indicators enter negatively in the index. For example, an increase in initial claims for unemployment insurance forebodes a decline in real GDP, so the index will go down whenever such claims go up. Similarly, a decline in materials prices will decrease unit costs of production and, thus, will cause the index to go up. Other components of the index can signify increases in economic activity and real GDP, for fairly obvious reasons. For example, an upturn in the average workweek, building permits, bank deposits and other liquid assets, or the number of new contracts and orders implies more demand for final products and upward pressure on real GDP. Similarly, if vendor companies have difficulty getting deliveries of parts and equipment, a peak level of economic activity may be approaching.

Other components of the composite index are more difficult to interpret. For example, declines in stock prices decrease wealth and can adversely affect demand. Declines in stock prices can also mean reductions in future business profits. However, stock prices change in response to investors' perception of the profitability of holding stocks compared to other assets.

The index of leading indicators does occasionally decline without a subsequent decline in real GDP, so it must be used with caution. Forecasting the ups and downs of real GDP is riddled with pitfalls.

The graph below shows the percentage change in real GDP from 1959 to 2003. The gray bars show periods of recession, when real GDP declined. The index tends to turn downward just prior to each recession. It begins to rise again after the recession has run its course and an expansion begins. However, you should also note that, in some cases, the index declines for an extended period, as long as one year, before a recession occurs. In other cases, such as in 1984, declines in the index aren't followed by a recession. Typically, once a recession does hit, the index plummets. For example, the index dropped sharply during the 1974 and 1982 recessions.

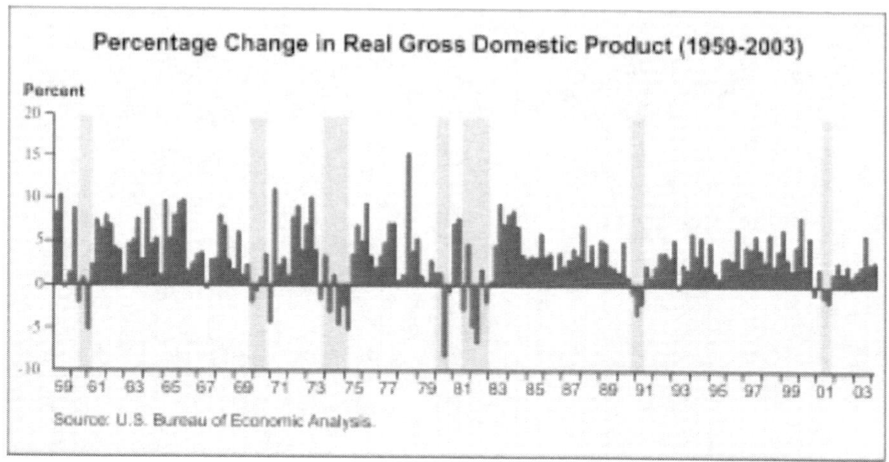

Like any measure employed in forecasting, the index of leading economic indicators is useful, but not infallible.

What Influences the Natural Rate of Unemployment?

Changes in the natural rate of unemployment can easily be mistaken for cyclical unemployment. For this reason, it's important to understand the forces influencing the natural rate of unemployment in an economy. The natural rate of unemployment is related to the willingness of workers to voluntarily separate from their jobs, job loss, the duration of unemployment periods, the rate of change in the pattern of demand, and changes in technology.

Younger workers are more likely to quit their jobs than older workers. It takes some time for them to match their skills with their employment. It's therefore reasonable to assume that the younger the average age of workers in the labor force, the higher the natural rate of unemployment, because frictional unemployment increases when job separations increase. Teenagers, in particular, are likely to quit their jobs after only a short period. The higher the percentage of teenagers in the labor force, therefore, the higher the natural rate of unemployment.

The high unemployment rates observed in the United States in the late 1970s were partly the result of the entry of a disproportionately high number of younger workers into the labor force. At that time, the baby boomers were in their 20s. These younger workers had higher quit rates than did older workers. The natural rate of unemployment fell in the 1990s as the bulk of the baby boomers hit 40 and were snugly matched to the right jobs. Workers over 40 are much less likely than younger workers to quit their jobs.

Increased fluctuation in the pattern of demand for domestic goods increases structural unemployment and, in turn, contributes to a higher natural rate of unemployment. For example, the increase in energy prices that occurred in the mid-1970s disrupted hiring in many U.S. industries. Increased foreign competition also hurt the U.S. automobile and steel industries at that time. One researcher estimated that the changes in the structure of demand in the late 1970s increased the natural rate of unemployment by 1 to 2 percentage points.[1]

Rapid changes in technology designed to cut costs can also result in greater job separation. In an effort to compete more effectively with foreign firms, many U.S. firms have shifted to new technology that requires fewer workers per plant and results in slower hiring of new workers.

In recent years, the number of married women in the labor force has increased sharply, thereby increasing the number of two-earner families. The existence of a second income prevents income from falling to zero when one of the spouses quits a job to search for a better one. Also, the second income allows a longer period to find a new job than would otherwise be possible. Thus, an increase in the number of two-earner families increases the natural rate of unemployment, because it increases job separation through quitting and the duration of unemployment.

Tendencies toward moving in and out of the labor force can also affect the natural rate of unemployment, because such movement can affect the rate of job separation and job finding in the future. Workers who frequently move in and out of the work force have a high rate of job separation because they're less experienced than other workers. As a result, they're more likely to quit or be fired from a job.

In the early 1990s, structural unemployment increased, due to reductions in defense spending and corporate downsizing. These changes increased the natural rate of unemployment. By the late 1990s, the U.S. economy had adapted well to structural change, while, at the same time, aging of the work force contributed to a decline in frictional unemployment. As of 2001, the natural rate of unemployment for the U.S. economy was estimated to be around 5.2 percent of the labor force--down from an estimated 5.9 percent in 1990.[2]

[1]David M. Lilien, "Sectoral Shifts and Cyclical Unemployment," *Journal of Political Economy* 90, no. 4 (August 1982), pp. 777-93.

[2]Congress of the United States, Congressional Budget Office, "The Budget and Economic Outlook: Fiscal Years 2001-2011," January 2001 (Washington, D.C.: U.S. Government Printing Office), p. 139.

Rewriting History: New Measures of Economic Growth

The new chain-type index now used by the Bureau of Economic Analysis (BEA) of the U.S. Department of Commerce is providing a new picture of the growth of the U.S. economy in recent years. The new method values output changes at prices that prevailed at the time they took place, rather than using base year prices that can be many years distant from that time. The older method of measuring growth was believed to make recessions look less severe than they really were and to distort the picture of long-term growth. The use of the new measures of economic growth has rewritten history. BEA believes that chain-type indexes of real GDP provide a more accurate picture of the strength of expansions and the depth of contractions. The new indexes value output at prices that more accurately reflect the value of resources used to produce goods and services.

Here is a sampling of conclusions about economic growth in recent years that have emerged as the new method of measuring real GDP has been applied by BEA:

1. The recession of 1991 was slightly more severe than previously estimated, using older methods of valuing output loss.
2. Since the recession of 1991, average annual real GDP growth has been *overstated*, on average, by about 0.5 percent per year. This is because much of the growth in output was due to growth in output of products like computers, whose prices had fallen significantly compared to prices on average.
3. For the five economic expansions between 1960 and 1990, economic growth was *understated* by an average of about 0.5 percent per year.
4. The average rate of decline in real GDP during the six contractions between 1960 and 1991 has been understated by an average of 0.3 percentage points.

According to BEA analysis, therefore, the U.S. economy of the 1990s ran at a slower pace than previously believed, compared to its historical performance. In rewriting history, BEA has given us more to worry about. The U.S. economy has been slowing down more than we've realized!

The chart shows economic growth rates for the U.S. economy from 1959 to 1994, using both fixed 1987 weights (standard real GDP) and chain-type weights (the new featured measure of growth now used by BEA).

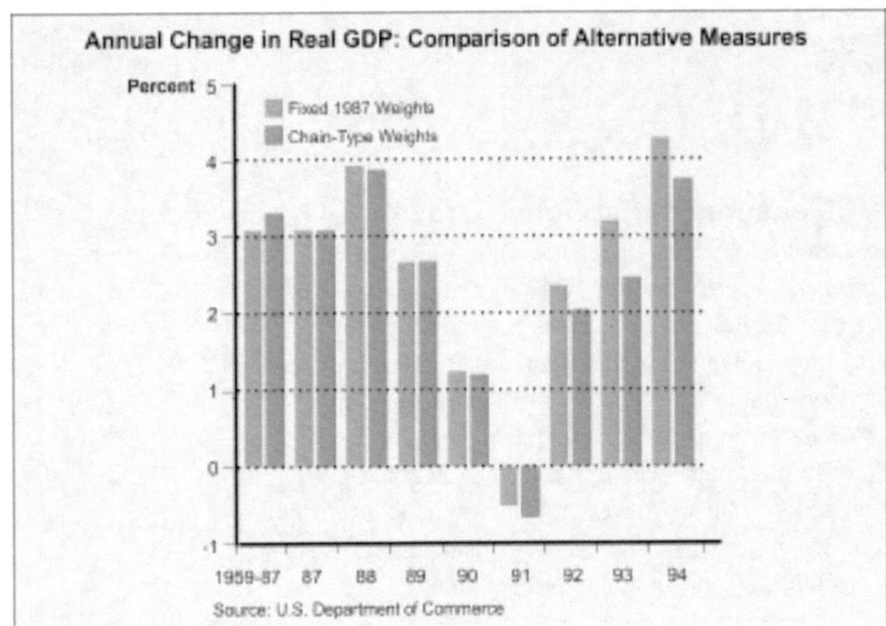
Annual Change in Real GDP: Comparison of Alternative Measures
Percent
Fixed 1987 Weights
Chain-Type Weights
5
4
3
2
1
0
-1
1959-87
87
88
89
90
91
92
93
94
Source: U.S. Department of Commerce

The Costs versus the Benefits of Economic Growth

Can economic growth in a nation be anything other than a positive development? Can it actually have a down side? Let's see why the answers to these questions are yes by examining some of the negative consequences of economic growth.

Increases in output per capita benefit people in a nation by allowing higher average levels of material well-being over the long run. Such growth means more job opportunities for workers. It causes an outward shift of a nation's production possibilities curve that allows a nation the luxury of using government services to deal with social problems without increasing tax rates.

But what about the costs of economic growth? More output each year can mean more pollution, more stress, and the development of a materialistic philosophy. Preoccupation with economic growth can prevent social progress that improves job safety and human health. Growth-oriented politicians are likely to oppose social programs that increase business costs if these programs slow growth in output.

Many of the amenities of life aren't included in real GDP. In fact, some of the costs of economic growth require expenditures of funds to solve such problems as congestion and pollution. These expenditures to offset the side effects of economic growth are actually included in real GDP.

It's clear that social programs designed to cope with pollution, congestion, income inequality, and abuse of workers' rights do slow down the rate of economic growth. Estimates in a classic study by Edward F. Denison conclude that improvements in the legal and human environment stemming from government regulations and other measures to control the social costs of economic growth contributed to a decline in such growth in 1973 and 1976.* A trade-off clearly exists between economic growth and policies to correct its undesirable effects. People must decide whether they're willing to give up some of the material benefits of economic growth in exchange for increased allocation of resources to correct the social problems of a growing economy.

*Edward F. Denison, *Trends in American Economic Growth, 1929-1982* (Washington, D.C.: Brookings Institution, 1985).

Chapter

23

The Price Level and Inflation

In 1975, you could buy a hot dog for 65 cents. Nowadays, try to find a decent hot dog for less than $2. Just think about how much more you could buy with your allowance or earnings if prices were what they were when you were a kid. A pair of jeans priced at $50 today would cost only $24 if it were still available at the price that prevailed 10 years ago. In fact, prices on average have more than quintupled in the United States since 1970!

Inflation can make it difficult to plan for the future and can adversely affect the purchasing power of our income and savings. When the prices of goods and services we buy are subject to erratic increases, the result is distortions in resource use as we seek ways to protect the purchasing power of our dollars.

In this chapter, we'll show how the economy's price level and inflation are measured and how inflation can damage the functioning of the economy by affecting incentives to save, invest, and allocate resources. We'll also examine who loses and who gains as a result of inflation. Our goal will be to understand the impact of fluctuations in the average level of prices on the economy and on people. In other parts of the text, we consider the causes of inflation and evaluate policies designed to keep it under control.

Concept Preview

After reading this chapter, you should be able to

1. Understand how price indexes are used to measure the price level and inflation.
2. Deflate nominal income using a price index to derive real income, and know the distinction between real and nominal wages.
3. Explain how inflation affects workers, employers, creditors, and debtors.
4. Explain how inflation affects interest rates, and know the distinction between real and nominal interest rates.
5. Explain how inflation affects economic decisions and the functioning of the economy.

The Price Level and Inflation

1 Before discussing inflation, we need to define what we mean by the level of prices in the economy in a given year. The price level is an indicator of how high or low prices are in a certain year compared to average prices in a certain *base period.* Given the bewildering variety of goods and services available in markets, the government chooses a representative group (or aggregate) of goods and services, called a *market basket*, and calculates the cost of purchasing the items in the basket. The cost of the market basket of goods and services in the current year is then compared with the cost of the same market basket in a certain base year.

A price index is a number used to measure the price level. The value of the index is set at 100 in the base year or period. If the price index in a given year exceeds 100, the price level in that year is higher than it was in the base year. Similarly, a price index of less than 100 for a given year means the price level in that year is lower than it was in the base year.

Inflation is the rate of upward movement in the price level for an aggregate of goods and services. Inflation occurs when prices on average are increasing over the year. Of course, not all prices increase at the same rate during periods of inflation, and it's quite common for some items to fall in price even during periods when prices are generally rising. Rising prices make it difficult to plan for the future and cause distortions in decisions as people seek to protect themselves against the effect of inflation on the purchasing power of their money income and savings.

Although you're accustomed to a rising price level, there have been periods when the price level actually declined. During the Great Depression of the 1930s, for example, there was a sharp decline in prices. Deflation is the rate of downward movement in the price level for an aggregate of goods and services.

The Consumer Price Index

A price index measures how the cost of purchasing a standard market basket of goods and services varies from the cost of purchasing the same market basket in the base period. It is calculated as the ratio of the current cost of a given market basket to the cost of the same market basket in the base period multiplied by 100:

$$\text{Price index} = \left(\frac{\text{Cost of a market basket of products at current prices}}{\left[\begin{array}{c} \text{Cost of the same basket of products} \\ \text{at prices prevailing over the base period} \end{array} \right]} \right) 100$$

The value of the index is always 100 in the base period because the numerator and denominator of the equation are the same in the base period.

The consumer price index (CPI) is the price index most commonly used to measure the impact of inflation on households. This index is based on a standard market basket of goods and services purchased by a typical urban family. The CPI market basket does not include exported goods, investment goods, or items purchased by governments. However, changes in the prices of imported goods purchased by the typical urban family are considered when the CPI is calculated.

The goods in the CPI market basket are based on a survey conducted once a decade by the Bureau of Labor Statistics. Since 1988 an average of prices for the years 1982 to 1984 has been used in calculating the base period cost of the market basket.

The CPI is actually a *weighted average* of a number of component price indexes. Price indexes for such items as housing, transportation, food and beverages, and other broad categories for expenditure are computed separately. Then the price index for each item receives a weight that indicates the relative importance of the item in consumer spending.

For example, housing is presumed to account for 42 cents of each dollar spent by the urban family, based on weights used in 2009. The index measuring the aggregate price level of housing services is therefore multiplied by 0.42 when calculating the "all items" CPI. Apparel is currently assumed to absorb 4 cents of each dollar spent. The price index for apparel is therefore multiplied by 0.04 when calculating the "all items" index.

Because the weight attached to housing exceeds the weight attached to apparel, a given percentage increase in the price of housing will have a much greater impact on the CPI than the same percentage increase in the price of apparel. For the current CPI, a 4 percent increase in the aggregate price level of housing services will receive nearly 10 times as much weight in calculating the "all items" CPI as a 4 percent increase in the aggregate price level of apparel.

Measuring Inflation

Annual rates of inflation are measured by the percentage change in a price index, such as the CPI, from one year to the next. For example, the monthly average of the CPI in 2005, using the average of prices between 1982 and 1984 as the base, was 195.3. In 2004, the monthly average of the CPI was 188.9. To calculate the percentage change in the CPI, first take the change in the price index over the year, which in this case is (195.3 – 188.9). Next, divide the change in the price index by its value in the initial year, 2004, and multiply the result by 100 percent to convert to a percentage increase. The rate of inflation between 2004 and 2005 was therefore

$$\left(\frac{\text{CPI in 2005} - \text{CPI in 2004}}{\text{CPI in 2004}}\right) \times 100\%$$

$$\left(\frac{195.3 - 188.9}{188.9}\right) \times 100\% = 3.4\%$$

You can also use the CPI to calculate inflation from one month to another over a span of time. Measuring inflation between February 2008, when the CPI was 211.693, and February 2009, when the CPI was 212.193, shows that the inflation rate over this period was less than 0.1 percent.

Changes in the Price Level versus Changes in Relative Prices

You should always keep in mind that the official inflation rate is a measure of the average rate of change in the prices of a broad aggregate of products. For example, in 2005, when the official inflation rate was 3.4 percent measured by the percentage change in the CPI, energy prices *rose* by 17 percent, which helped pull the average of all prices up. However, that year food prices rose by only 2.4 percent and the price of medical care rose by 4.8 percent. The economy rarely experiences pure inflation, during which the prices of *all* goods rise by the same percentage over the year.

The *change in the relative price of a good* is a change in its price relative to the prices of an average of all goods. If the economy experienced pure inflation, there would be no changes in the relative prices of goods because the price of every good would rise by the same percentage. Under pure inflation, the price of any one good does not change more or less than the average rate. This means that over the year no particular good becomes any cheaper or more expensive relative to other goods than it was at the beginning of the year. Pure inflation therefore does not provide consumers with any incentive to substitute one good for another in their budget, nor does it change the profitability for sellers of one good rather than another. On the other hand, changes in the relative prices of goods in the economy are signals that provide incentives to adapt to changing conditions.

The GDP Deflator

The CPI is the best measure of the price level for determining changes in the cost of living for typical urban households in the United States. Sometimes, however, we want to use a broader measure of the price level to determine the effects of inflation on producers' incentives to supply all goods and services. Remember, GDP does not include only consumption goods–it also includes goods and services produced for use as final products by businesses, governments, and foreign buyers that demand our exports. A broader index of inflation would include the effects of changes in the prices of all investment goods, government purchases, and net exports.

The GDP deflator is the ratio of nominal GDP to real GDP (multiplied by 100); it is an index of the average of the prices implicitly used to deflate nominal GDP. Remember that nominal GDP measures aggregate production of final products valued at their current market prices. Real GDP measures aggregate production of final products adjusted for inflation since a base year. The Department of Commerce currently uses 2000 as the base year in calculating real GDP. The GDP deflator is therefore calculated as follows:

$$\text{Implicit GDP deflator} = (\text{Nominal GDP}/\text{Real GDP})100$$

For example, at the end of 2008, the GDP deflator stood at 123, which implies that, *on average*, final products priced at $100 in 2000 would have been priced at $123 in 2008.

The GDP deflator will also change with the mix of products in the current GDP. Unlike the CPI, the GDP deflator does not measure the change in the cost of a standard market basket of a given combination of products. In 2008, inflation measured by the GDP deflator was 2.2 percent.

A History of the Consumer Price Level and Inflation

The graph in Box 1 shows fluctuations in the consumer price index from 1913 to 2008. The base period is 1982–84. As you can see in the graph, consumer prices rose sharply during World War I. Immediately after the war there was a period of deflation followed by price stability during the 1920s. Consumer prices plummeted, however, during the Great Depression of the 1930s. Prices began to increase again in 1933, but at a very slow rate.

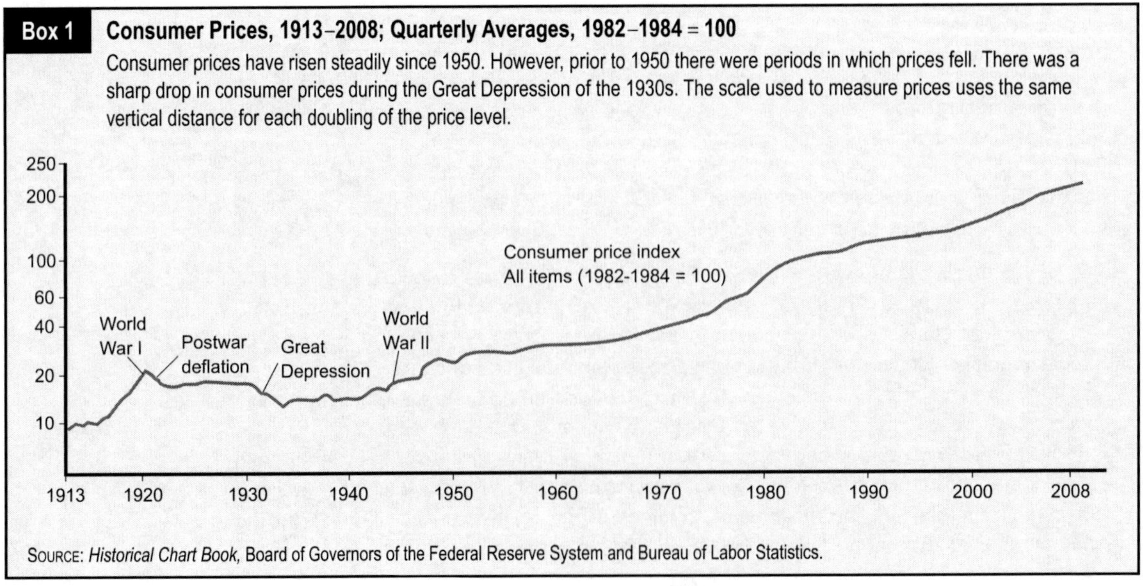

Box 1 Consumer Prices, 1913–2008; Quarterly Averages, 1982–1984 = 100

Consumer prices have risen steadily since 1950. However, prior to 1950 there were periods in which prices fell. There was a sharp drop in consumer prices during the Great Depression of the 1930s. The scale used to measure prices uses the same vertical distance for each doubling of the price level.

SOURCE: *Historical Chart Book,* Board of Governors of the Federal Reserve System and Bureau of Labor Statistics.

Box 2 Quarterly Percentage Changes in the Consumer Price Index: Seasonally Adjusted Annual Rates 1950-2009

Since 1950 the pattern of inflation has been erratic. Inflation was very high during the period 1974-1975 and between 1978 and 1981.

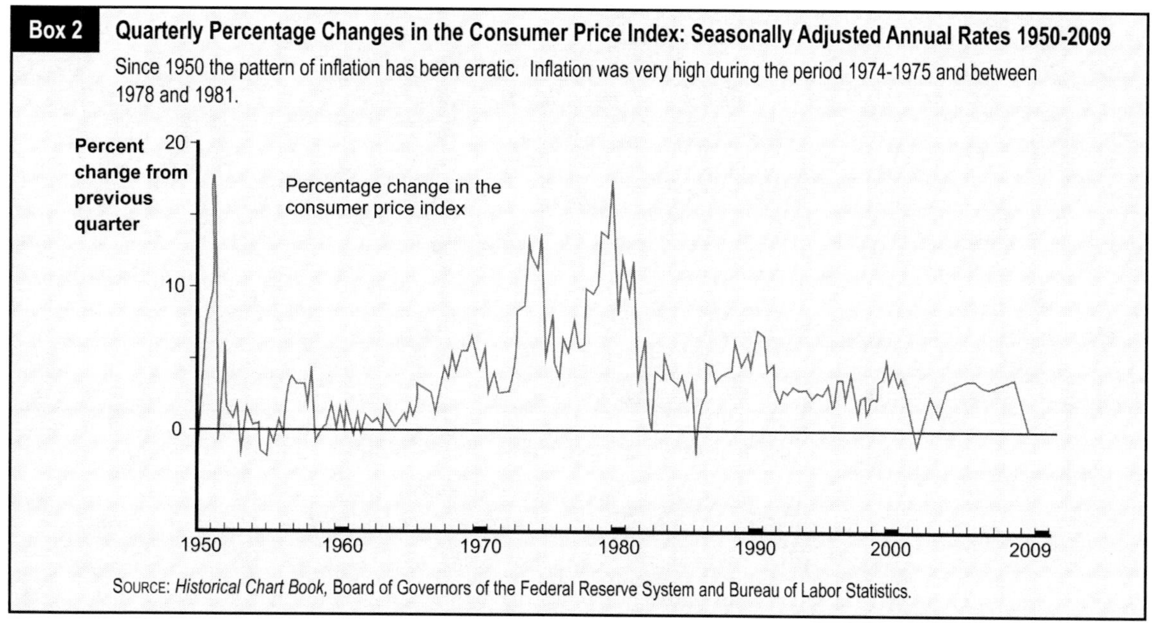

SOURCE: *Historical Chart Book*, Board of Governors of the Federal Reserve System and Bureau of Labor Statistics.

After World War II began, the price level shot up again. There was a mild deflation of the price level in 1948.

Since 1948 consumer prices have risen. The rate of increase was greatest in the 1970s. During the 1980s prices continued to rise, but at a much slower rate than during the 1970s. The rate of increase of the CPI leveled off still more in the 1990s.

The graph in Box 2 shows the quarterly percentage changes in the consumer price index from 1950 to 2009. As you can see, the pattern of inflation measured by the annual percentage changes in the CPI has been quite erratic since 1950. After a sharp increase in the inflation rate in the early 1950s, during the Korean War, the price level was relatively stable, with inflation seldom exceeding 5 percent per year. There was even a brief period of deflation. However, the 1970s were a period of high and erratic inflation. The average annual rate of inflation ranged between 3.3 percent and 11.3 percent. In 1980 inflation was roaring at an average annual rate of 13.5 percent.

From 1983 to 1989, inflation averaged 3.64 percent per year based on year-to-year percentage changes in the CPI. In fact, mainly because of sharp drops in the prices of gasoline and other energy-related products, there was even deflation of the price level in some months during 1986. In 1999, the rate of inflation was only 2.2 percent, but it increased to 3.4 percent in 2000. In 2002, inflation was a mere 1.6 percent, but the rate had crept up to 3.4 percent by 2005. Since 2005, inflation has remained in the range of 3 to 4 percent. However, with the effects of a recession in 2008 and 2009 putting downward pressure on prices, by early 2009, inflation was close to zero.

Box 3 shows the average annual rate of inflation for consumer prices during periods from 1960 to 2008. As you can see, inflation was quite low in the early 1960s, when it averaged 1.26 percent per year. It peaked in 1975 to 1979, when it averaged 8 percent per year. Between 1980 and 1984, inflation averaged 7.5 percent per year, and, between 1985 and 1989, inflation averaged 3.6 percent per year. Inflation averaged 3.5 percent per year from 1990 to 1994 and only 2.55 percent per year between 1995 and 2005 Between 2006 and 2008, inflation averaged 3.36 percent per year.

Box 3 **Average Annual Rate of Inflation, 1960 - 2008**

Period	Average annual percentage change in consumer price index
1960–1964	1.26
1965–1969	3.46
1970–1974	6.10
1975–1979	8.06
1980–1984	7.50
1985–1989	3.60
1990–1994	3.50
1995–2005	2.55
2006–2008	3.36

SOURCE: *Economic Report of the President* and Bureau of Labor Statistics.

The Distortions and Costs of Price Instability

Why all the concern about price instability? Who gains and who loses as a result of inflation or deflation? What distortions in decision making are associated with price instability?

Inflation can significantly affect the national standard of living. It can also cause changes in behavior that can have serious effects on resource use and the functioning of the economy. To analyze the costs of inflation, we must examine its effects on both incomes and decisions. There are always gainers and losers from inflation, but it is not always easy to predict who will lose and who will gain.

Real Income: Using the CPI to Deflate Nominal Income

2 Fluctuations in the price level affect the quantity of goods and services that can be purchased with a given sum of money. The purchasing power of a dollar (or any other unit of currency) is a measure of how much it can buy. An increase in the price level means a decrease in the purchasing power of a dollar. For example, if the price level were to double over a year, the purchasing power of a dollar would be cut in half because it would take $2 to buy what a year earlier could have been bought for $1. In any given year, the greater the rate of inflation, the greater the decline in the purchasing power of a dollar for the year.

To measure changes in the purchasing power of income over time, it is necessary to adjust nominal income for changes in the price level. Nominal income is the actual number of dollars of income received over a year. Real income is the purchasing power of nominal income. Real income is usually expressed in terms of the market value of the final products it can purchase when those products are valued in *base period* prices rather than current period prices.

Real income is obtained by deflating nominal income by the current CPI to adjust for rises in the price level since the base period. To deflate nominal income, divide it by the current CPI/100:

$$\text{Real Income} = \frac{\text{Nominal income}}{\text{Current CPI}/\ 100}$$

For example, suppose your nominal income in 2008 was $30,000. To find out what your *real* income was in 2008, first divide the 2008 CPI, which was equal to 215.3, by 100, which gives 2.153. This tells you that the price of a market basket of goods purchased by a typical urban family was 2.153 times higher in 2008 than it was, on average, between 1982 and 1984. Your real income is:

$$2008 \text{ real income} = \frac{\$30{,}000}{2.153} = \$13{,}930.$$

Real income measures income in base period (in this case 1982–84) dollars rather than current dollars. Your $30,000 nominal income for 2008 had the same purchasing power that $13,930 had on average between 1982 and 1984! A person who earned $30,000 in 2008 had the same purchasing power as a person who earned about half of that amount in 1983, when the CPI was 99.6.

You can also use the preceding formula to deflate $1 to find out the purchasing power of a current dollar after adjusting for inflation since the base year:

$$\text{Purchasing power of a current dollar} = \frac{\$1}{\text{CPI}/\ 100}$$

In 2008, the purchasing power of a dollar was

$$\frac{\$1}{2.153} = 46 \text{ cents.}$$

On average, each dollar in 2008 bought what could have been purchased for only about 46 cents at the prices that prevailed, on average, over the period 1982–84.

The graph in Box 4 shows how the purchasing power of a dollar varied from 1960 to 2005. Because the price level has increased substantially since 1960, the purchasing power of a dollar has fallen. The more rapid the rate of inflation in a given year, the greater the decline in the purchasing power of a dollar.

Of course, conclusions about the impact of inflation on the purchasing power of a dollar for particular consumers must be qualified. Not all consumers buy exactly the same mix of goods. If you spend more of your income than the average urban consumer on goods

Box 4 Purchasing Power of the Dollar, 1960–2008

As the price level has risen, the purchasing power of the dollar has declined.

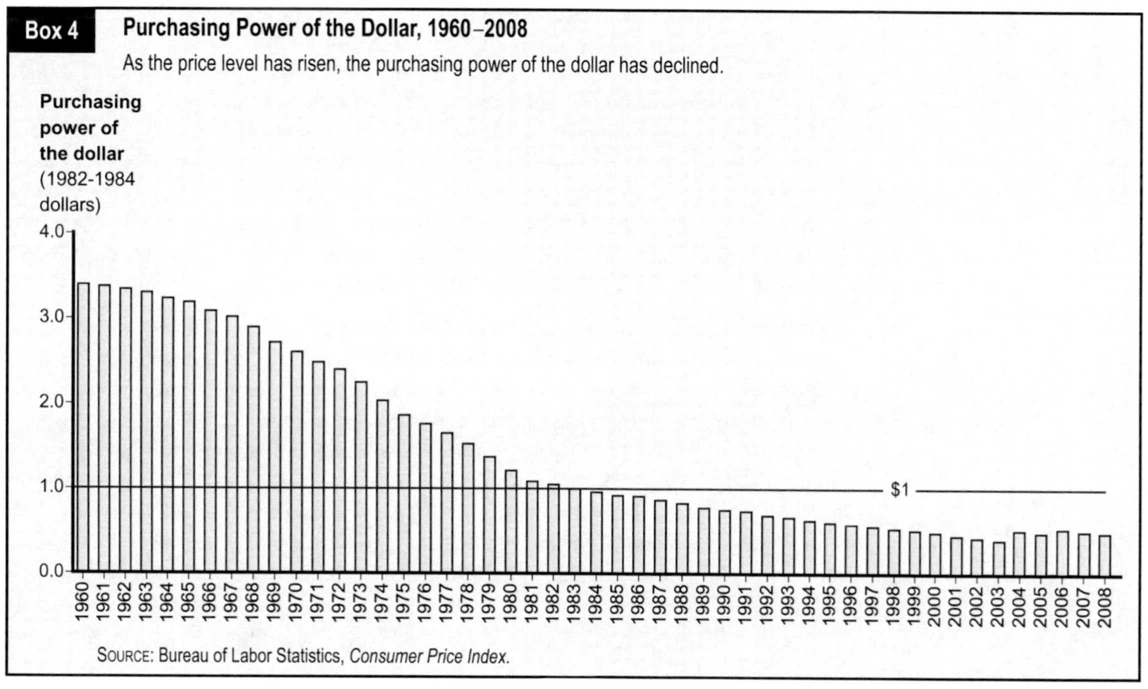

SOURCE: Bureau of Labor Statistics, *Consumer Price Index*.

whose prices have not increased as fast as the average, such as televisions, inflation is less of a problem for you than for the typical urban consumer. Also, because not all prices rise by the same percentage during inflationary periods, consumers adjust their buying habits in response to changes in prices. They buy more goods whose prices have increased less than the average and fewer goods whose prices have increased more than the average. To say that the purchasing power of a dollar in 2005 was 51 percent of what it was in 1983 means that a dollar bought only 51 percent as many goods in 2005 as it did in 1983 *for the consumer who bought exactly the same goods in the CPI market basket year after year.*

When the rate of inflation of consumer prices exceeds the rate of increase of a person's nominal income, a person buying the standard market basket of goods used to calculate the CPI will find that his money income buys less this year than it bought the year before. *When a person's annual rate of increase in nominal income lags behind the annual rate of increase in the price level, the person's real income declines.* A decline in a person's real income implies a decline in his standard of living as measured by the quantity of goods and services his income can buy. To find out the effect of inflation on a person's standard of living, we must therefore analyze its impact on that person's real income. As you'll soon see, inflation can have some rather capricious and unpredictable effects on the distribution of real income. Inflation affects everyone, but not equally!

Nominal Wages versus Real Wages

3 Wages are a measure of both hourly payments for labor services by business firms and hourly compensation to workers. Nominal wages are hourly payments to workers in current dollars. Real wages are nominal wages deflated to adjust for changes in the purchasing power of a dollar since a certain base period. Real wages give hourly compensation in terms of base period dollars. For example, suppose nominal hourly wages in 2006, including the hourly dollar value of fringe benefits, are $20. If the consumer price index is 200 in 2006 (and 1982–84 is the base), then the purchasing power of a 2006 dollar is only one-half the purchasing power of a 1982–84 dollar. It follows that the real wage expressed in terms of base period dollars is only $10.

The graph in Box 5 shows the percentage changes in consumer prices and the percentage changes in hourly employee compensation (the hourly nominal wage and the nominal value of hourly fringe benefits) from 1960 to 2008. In most years, the percentage change in hourly employee compensation exceeds the percentage change in prices. In most years, therefore, the growth rate of nominal wages (including the value of fringe benefits) exceeds inflation because employers compensate workers not only for changes in the price level but also for changes in productivity. The graph shows that, on average, competition for labor services has resulted in a nominal wage growth exceeding the inflation rate. On average, real wages in the United States have increased each year. The increase in the real wage reflects increases in labor productivity.

You should also observe that the annual percentage change in labor compensation and the inflation rate move together. However, there's often a lag between the increase in consumer prices and the increase in nominal hourly labor compensation. During periods of rapid inflation, the rate of increase in consumer prices often exceeds the rate of increase in nominal hourly labor compensation. For example, during the periods of rapid inflation from 1973 to 1975 and from 1979 to 1981, inflation outstripped increases in hourly labor compensation. Real wages therefore fell over that period. Similarly, in 1984 inflation outstripped the growth of nominal wages, resulting in a decline in real wages. In the late 1990s, low inflation and increased productivity of workers resulted in net gains for workers as hourly compensation increased more rapidly than prices. However, in 2008, changes in labor compensation were just equal to the rate of increase of consumer prices, so real wages did not increase in that year.

During periods of rapid inflation, when real wages decline, workers' hourly compensation falls. Who gains? The answer is employers, who end up paying less in hourly labor costs. *As a result, during periods in which inflation exceeds the percentage increase in nominal wages (hourly labor compensation), there is a redistribution of income from workers to their employers.* This is one of the capricious effects of inflation on the distribution of income.

Workers consider inflation when engaging in contract negotiations that set wages. By and large, the growth in nominal wages and inflation move together because workers demand increases to offset the effects of inflation. Nominal increases in hourly compensation lag behind inflation only in periods when inflation heats up rapidly.

How Inflation Can Redistribute Income and Wealth from Creditors to Debtors

Inflation is great for people who are in debt because the purchasing power of dollars will decline over the life of their loans. Debtors will therefore pay back principal and interest in dollars that are worth less each year in terms of purchasing power. *Inflation tends to decrease the burden of paying off loans because debtors make payments in dollars that have less purchasing power than the dollars they borrowed!*

Inflation decreases the wealth of creditors, who experience a reduction in the purchasing power of the outstanding balances on the loans they carry on their books as assets. For example, suppose you borrowed mortgage money in 1967. Assume the outstanding balance on your loan in 1987 was $10,000. Because the purchasing power of a dollar in 1987 was only about one-third of its purchasing power in 1967, the outstanding balance valued in 1967 dollars (when you borrowed money to buy the house) was only $3,333. In this way inflation redistributes wealth (asset values) from creditors to debtors.

In effect, savers can be regarded as creditors. Those who have savings accounts in banks, such as 10-year certificates of deposit, are harmed by inflation because the purchasing power of their savings will be eroded unless the interest they earn is high enough to

Box 5 Annual Percentage Changes in Hourly Labor Compensation and in Consumer Prices 1960–2008

Changes in annual consumer prices and annual hourly labor compensation move together. In some years, however, increases in the prices of consumer products do exceed increases in labor compensation.

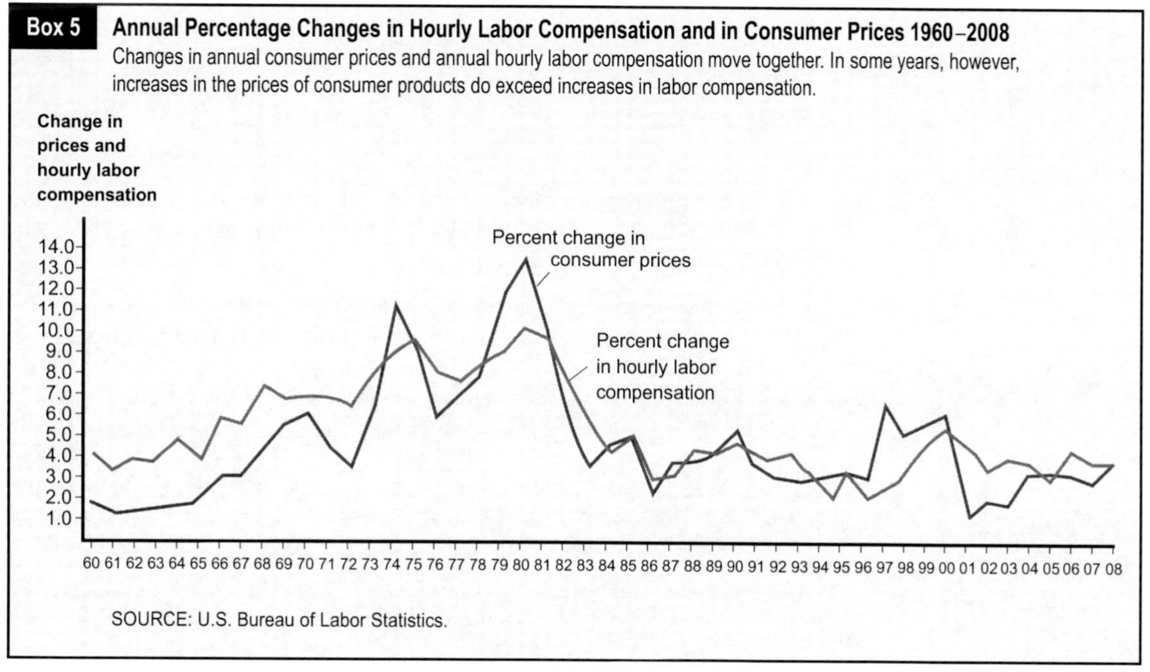

SOURCE: U.S. Bureau of Labor Statistics.

compensate them for the effects of inflation. For example, suppose you purchase a five-year certificate of deposit that yields 10 percent interest per year. If inflation is 20 percent per year, you'll lose purchasing power on your savings each year. Although the balance will go up by 10 percent per year because of interest payments, the 20 percent inflation will outstrip the interest payments. The net effect will be a fall in the purchasing power of your savings.

Nominal Interest Rates versus Real Interest Rates

4 The preceding analysis of the impact of inflation on debtors and creditors assumes that the interest rate doesn't adjust for the effects of inflation. You should recall the analysis of the impact of inflation on wages. Inflation is considered in the bargains struck between workers and employers. By the same token, inflation is considered in the bargains struck between borrowers and lenders. Lenders are less willing to make loans when they see inflation coming because they know that inflation will reduce the purchasing power of the dollars that will be repaid. As lenders anticipate the adverse effects of inflation on the profitability of lending, they decrease the supply of loanable funds and thus put upward pressure on interest rates.

The nominal interest rate is the annual percentage amount of money that is earned on a sum loaned by or deposited in a bank. The nominal interest rate is the contract interest on the face of the loan or deposit and is always positive. For example, if you buy a $5,000 certificate of deposit that yields 10 percent annual interest, you are a creditor who loans the bank that sum for a period of time at a 10 percent nominal annual rate of interest. The real interest rate[1] is the actual annual percentage change in the *purchasing power of interest income* earned on a sum of money that is loaned out. When inflation is present, the real rate of interest will be less than the nominal rate. The real rate of interest is the nominal rate adjusted for the decrease in purchasing power that results from inflation.

The earned real rate of interest can be thought of as the nominal interest rate minus the rate of inflation.[2] For example, suppose the nominal interest rate you earned over a one-year period on a $5,000 certificate of deposit was 9 percent. If inflation averaged 6 percent over the same period, then the real interest rate you earned was 3 percent.

Real interest earned on a loan over its life		Nominal interest rate per year		Inflation rate per year
3%	=	9%	–	6%

The $5,000 principal plus the interest it earned over the period that the bank held it, after adjustment for inflation, was worth only 3 percent more than it was worth when you deposited it.

Although nominal interest rates are always positive, real interest rates are negative when the actual rate of inflation exceeds the nominal interest rate. Lenders will incur losses on loans during periods when the nominal interest rate on the loans is less than the rate of inflation. Of course, given the nominal interest rate, lenders need not incur losses in future

[1] The definition refers to the "earned" or *ex post* real interest rate. In contrast, the *ex ante* real interest rate is the nominal interest rate minus the anticipated rate of inflation. The "earned" real interest rate is important for calculating the actual real return on an outstanding loan. The *ex ante* real interest rate is important when parties are considering a new loan or investment.

[2] The real interest rate can be shown to equal the nominal interest rate minus the rate of inflation plus the product of the rate of inflation and the nominal interest rate. However, when both inflation and the nominal interest rate are less than 20 percent, the product of inflation and the nominal interest rate is so low that it can be ignored.

years on loans made when real interest rates are negative. Changes in the inflation rate over the life of the loans will affect the real interest rate earned in future years.

Despite the fact that nominal interest rates soared to double digits in the late 1970s, borrowing was a good deal at that time because roaring inflation actually resulted in negative real interest rates! In 1978, for example, the real interest rate on three-month Treasury bills, which represent short-term borrowing by the federal government, was estimated to be –1.5 percent. In such periods, when nominal interest rates increase less rapidly than prices, borrowers benefit greatly while lenders are harmed.

Naturally, creditors seek to anticipate the rate of inflation when lending funds over a long period. If creditors expect inflation to heat up in the future, they are going to be very cautious about making long-term loans. This decreases the supply of long-term credit in the markets for loanable funds and pushes up nominal interest rates in those markets to compensate for expected inflation. Because market forces tend to adjust nominal interest rates in response to inflationary expectations, it is difficult to conclude whether creditors or debtors gain as a result of inflation. For example, if actual inflation turns out to be less than is anticipated by the creditors when they make long-term loans, the debtors could be harmed by inflation because they will end up paying relatively high real interest rates over the life of their loans.

If all long-term contracts involving loanable funds had clauses allowing automatic adjustment for inflation, no redistribution of income from creditors to debtors would arise from changes in the inflation rate. In fact, after the rapid unanticipated inflation of the 1970s, many banks became reluctant to make long-term loans (such as mortgages) at fixed interest rates. Instead, they made long-term loans with variable interest rates tied to current interest rates. Both individual consumers and business managers learn from their mistakes!

How Price Instability Affects the Performance of the Economy

5 Price instability, or, more accurately, the actions taken in anticipation of it, can adversely affect the performance of the economy. When buyers and sellers try to guess what price instability will do to the purchasing power of the dollar in the future, they also base their decisions in part on the gains or losses they might incur as a result of inflation (or deflation). The resulting shifts in supply and demand in individual markets cause distortions in market prices. For example, suppose everyone thought that inflation would erode the real value of savings. This would cause the supply of savings to decrease, which would make interest rates higher than they would be in the absence of these inflationary expectations.

Anticipated Inflation and Economic Decisions

You've undoubtedly become used to the fact of inflation over your lifetime. If you're like most people, you've probably made purchases that you might otherwise have put off because you *anticipated* that inflation would increase the prices of the product. For example, if you anticipate a 10 percent price increase in the home entertainment system you want to have next year, when you move out of your dorm into an apartment, you might choose to buy it now rather than next year. Similarly, when signing a lease for an apartment or borrowing money, you've probably considered what inflation would do to rent or interest charges.

Inflation makes it hard to collect information about what constitutes a reasonable price for an item. You never know whether the price of an item has gone up because of shifts in the supply of and demand for that item or because of general inflation. This makes it difficult to decide what to buy and when to buy it.

Anticipated inflation affects the choices we make as individuals. Those who correctly anticipate the impact of inflation on their incomes can avoid the reduction in real income and wealth that inflation will cause. For example, if lenders correctly anticipate inflation, they can avoid its undesirable effect on their real income by attaching an inflation "premium" to the nominal interest rate they charge for new loans. Businesses consider inflation when placing orders. For example, businesses that expect future price increases may stock up on parts and raw materials.

When inflation is steady and predictable, many people correctly anticipate its effects on the purchasing power of the dollar. However, when inflation is erratic, fewer people succeed in anticipating its effects. The actual impact of inflation on the distribution of income between workers and their employers and between borrowers and lenders will depend on how accurately inflation is anticipated by each of these groups.

Inflationary Distortions in Saving and Investment

Erratic inflation is particularly troublesome for long-term contracts. It increases the risk involved in estimating the returns on investment projects by making it difficult to anticipate future input and output prices. This may lead to distortions in decisions to save and invest and cause investment to be reduced below the efficient level.

Let's first look at how inflation can reduce investment by increasing the cost of acquiring new plants and equipment. Capital consumption allowances (depreciation) represent a cost of production that can be deducted from business income before taxes are computed. The sum of capital consumption allowances deducted over the life of an asset equals its purchase price. The *real value* of capital consumption allowances falls as a result of inflation. This means the tax deduction that business firms get for purchasing capital is worth less, and businesses will pay more in taxes. The higher the rate of inflation, the less will be the gain in after-tax profits for businesses from purchasing investment goods. Inflation therefore reduces the incentives of businesses to make investments and could adversely affect the economy's growth rate.

Now let's look at how inflation can reduce the supply of saving to fund investment. Remember that inflation erodes the value of bank deposits and other assets that are fixed in monetary value, such as funds. If inflation soars, savers may liquidate their financial assets and purchase land or antiques and other collectibles because when inflation soars, the prices of land and collectibles are also likely to soar. This makes fewer funds available for productive investments such as new factories that ensure future increases in labor productivity and employment opportunities for workers. This puts further upward pressure on interest rates.

Inflation not only distorts current choices but also can decrease confidence in the nation's financial markets, thereby adversely affecting future opportunities as the amount of saving channeled into productive investment is reduced. A nation's real GDP growth rate can be adversely affected if inflation reduces business investment.

When inflation reaches excessive levels, the central banking authorities of a nation, such as the Board of Governors of the Federal Reserve System in the United States, are usually obliged to take action to raise interest rates and reduce the supply of credit. If monetary authorities tighten credit severely to achieve their objective of reducing the rate of inflation, the result could be a recession. This has happened in the past. For example, the recession of 1982 in the United States was a direct result of economic policies designed to reduce the rate of inflation.

The Disastrous Effects of Hyperinflation

Extraordinarily high rates of inflation are likely to be more costly than modest rates of inflation. If people expect very high inflation, they'll try to spend their earnings as quickly as possible so as to avoid holding money whose purchasing power will be quickly eroded. For example, if you anticipate that prices will rise 10 percent per week, you'll be eager to be paid once or twice a day so you can spend your earnings before the purchasing power of the dollar deteriorates!

During the 1920s inflation in the German Weimar Republic reached such astronomical rates that it was dubbed hyperinflation, defined by the International Monetary Fund now as inflation at an annual rate of 200 percent or more prevailing in a nation for at least one year. In 1922 the annual inflation rate in Germany exceeded 5,000 percent because the Weimar government sought to pay its bills by printing money. In 1922 the money stock in Germany grew by about 30 percent per month. Prices rose almost hourly! German currency became worthless and was used as kindling for stoves. Once people began to anticipate the inflation, they tried to unload cash balances, which caused further inflationary pressures by increasing the demand for goods and services.

The cost to Germany was tremendous. Credit markets virtually collapsed, as no one was willing to take the risk of lending money. A massive redistribution of income wiped out the savings of millions and benefited people who were heavily in debt. Employees demanded to be paid at least once a day and spent an inordinate amount of time each day trying to unload their earnings before the price level rose again! The ultimate solution for Germany was a monetary reform in 1923 that changed the currency and limited printing of the new currency.

Hyperinflation is not a historic relic. In 1985 the rate of inflation in Bolivia was 11,749 percent! An item that sold for the equivalent of 50 cents at the beginning of 1985 cost more than $5,000 at the end of the year! In 1989 prices in Argentina increased by over 5,000 percent, and in some months of 1989 the annual rate of inflation was over 12,000 percent. The result was social chaos and a collapse of monetary and financial markets. After some bitter medicine of cutting back government spending and controlling the growth of money and credit, however, both Argentina and Bolivia managed to control their inflation in the 1990s. In fact, as of mid-1995 inflation was virtually nonexistent in Argentina.

Despite a global trend toward reduced inflation in the mid-1990s a few nations had very high inflation rates in 1995. Prices were rising at an annual rate of 100 percent in Turkey in that year, and in 1995 the inflation rate in Venezuela was in the range of 60 percent. Since 2000, both countries have significantly reduced their inflation rates. Between 2002 and 2005, the inflation rate in Turkey fell from 44 percent to 9.5 percent. Venezuela's inflation rate has also been reduced, but it's still relatively high, running at 15 percent as of 2005. Russia too has inflation running at a fairly high rate–12.5 percent as of 2005.

Deflation

The preceding discussion concentrated on only one aspect of price instability: inflation. What about deflation, which occurs when prices are unstable on the down side? What are the consequences of reductions in the price level? As is the case for inflation, the impact of deflation on income depends on how that income varies when the price level falls.

The Great Depression of the 1930s was also a period of deflation. Between 1928 and 1933 the CPI declined 29 percent while nominal wages fell by only 18 percent in manufacturing and 21 percent overall. As a result, real wages during this period increased by 8 percent and by 11 percent in manufacturing.[3] However, we can't conclude from this that workers gained from deflation because high unemployment rates during the Depression years of 1929–1933 reduced labor income in the aggregate despite the increase in real wages.

Deflation *increases* the purchasing power of a dollar over time. Deflation benefits creditors because the dollars they receive as loan payments have higher purchasing power than those they lent. During periods of deflation, real interest rates tend to soar.

In 2003, there were concerns that deflation could become a problem for the U.S. economy. Inflation rates were actually negative for some months, and nominal interest rates had fallen to record low numbers. However, by 2004, it was clear that deflation wasn't an issue and there were concerns that the rate of inflation was increasing. By 2009, a major recession was putting downward pressure on prices, and some economists became concerned that deflation might become a problem for the U.S. economy.

Deflation can really cause problems for the economy if it gets built into expectations. If people think prices will be lower in the future than they are currently, they'll put off purchases they would normally make today. This could decrease demand for goods and services, and cause a recession. As prices fall, so can wages, as the demand for labor declines. A deflationary spiral could further escalate if asset prices fall and interest rates approach zero. Japan has been suffering from deflation in recent years, which has contributed to recurrent recessions in that nation.

[3] See Martin N. Baily, "The Labor Market in the 1930s," in *Macroeconomics, Prices and Quantities*, James Tobin, ed. (Washington, D.C.: Brookings Institution, 1983), pp. 21–61.

Summary

1. Inflation is the rate at which the general price level increases for goods and services produced in a nation. When inflation exists, the purchasing power of a nation's currency declines over time. A dollar buys fewer goods and services over time as a result of increases in the price level. Deflation is the opposite of inflation. When deflation exists, the price level declines and the purchasing power of a dollar increases.

2. The percentage change in the consumer price index (CPI) over a year is the most common measure of inflation. The CPI is a weighted average of the prices of a market basket of goods purchased by a typical urban family relative to a weighted average of the prices of the same basket of goods in a base period. Measured in this way, inflation is an average of the increases in the prices of all goods in the CPI market basket. The greater the weight attached to an item in the CPI, the greater the impact of a change in its price on the CPI.

3. Some goods can actually decrease in price even when inflation is positive. Pure inflation prevails in an economy if the prices of all goods rise by the same percentage over the year. The relative price of a good increases when its price rises at a more rapid rate than the prices of all goods.

4. Nominal income is the number of dollars received as income during a year. Real income is the purchasing power of nominal income measured by the quantity of goods and services that can be bought with that income. Real income is measured in base period prices and is obtained by dividing nominal income by the CPI/100. When there is inflation in an economy, increases in nominal income do not necessarily imply increases in real income.

5. When the rate of inflation exceeds the growth rate of nominal income, real income declines. The real wage for an hour of work declines if the nominal wage increases at a rate less than the rate of inflation. In the U.S. economy nominal wages tend to increase with inflation. However, there is a lag between increases in the price level and increases in nominal wages, particularly during periods of rapid inflation. Under those circumstances, workers suffer temporary reductions in real wages.

6. Inflation can result in a redistribution of income and wealth from creditors to debtors. As a result of inflation, borrowers can pay back loans in dollars that have less purchasing power than the dollars they borrowed. This makes debtors better off at the expense of creditors, who are repaid in dollars that are worth less than those they lent. Inflation can also harm savers, who, in effect, are creditors, because the purchasing power of dollars in savings decreases as a result of inflation.

7. The effect of inflation on debtors and creditors also depends on how much the nominal interest rate adjusts for inflation. The real interest rate on a loan is the annual percentage change in the purchasing power of interest income earned on a sum of money loaned out. As a result of inflation, the real interest rate is less than the nominal interest rate. The real interest rate earned on a loan can be thought of as the annual nominal interest rate less the annual inflation rate over the life of the loan. Real interest rates can be negative.

8. Actions taken in anticipation of inflation can adversely affect the performance of the economy. When buyers and sellers try to anticipate inflation, they base their economic decisions, in part, on the gains or losses they expect to incur. This can affect the supply of and demand for particular goods and services, thereby distorting market prices.

9. Anticipated inflation can distort consumer choices by causing buyers to purchase goods now that they might otherwise prefer to purchase in the future. Hyperinflation seriously impairs the functioning of the economy by causing credit markets to collapse and by wiping out the purchasing power of accumulated savings.

10. Inflation is a distorter of choices and a capricious redistributor of income. Erratic inflation has both gainers and losers, but it is difficult to predict who will gain and who will lose.

Concept Review

1 What is the consumer price index (CPI)?

2 How can the CPI be used to deflate nominal income to real income measured in base year dollars?

3 How can inflation harm workers and creditors (including savers)?

4 How do real interest rates differ from nominal interest rates?

5 How can very high and erratic inflation reduce an economy's rate of growth?

Problems and Applications

1. Suppose the consumer price index is 200 this year. Assuming an average of prices for 1982–84 is the base, explain the implication of the CPI for prices and the cost of living this year as compared to the 1982–84 average. 1

2. Suppose nominal income for managers averaged $30,000 per year in 1982–84 and $50,000 per year in 2004. Using 1982–84 as the base period, calculate the real 2004 income of an average manager measured in base period dollars, assuming the CPI was 200 in 2004. 2

3. Suppose the rate of inflation is 5 percent. Does this mean that all the goods you purchase will cost 5 percent more than they did the year before? How would you determine the rate of inflation for goods and services that are included in your personal budget? What can cause a decline in the relative price of a good? 1

4. Suppose the consumer price index goes up from 300 to 310 during the year. At the beginning of the year, your nominal wage is $10 per hour. At the beginning of the following year, you get a raise that increases your nominal wage to $11 per hour. Calculate your real wage in each year, and indicate whether your real wage has gone up or down. 2

5. How are real wages in the United States affected by inflation on average over a period of several years? What is the implication of a decline in real wages for both workers and their employers? Under what circumstances does inflation redistribute income from workers to employers? 2, 3

6. A borrower negotiates a $20,000 loan at 3 percent interest in 2004, when the value of the consumer price index is 100. In 2011, the outstanding balance on the loan is $10,000. If the CPI is 200 in 2011, how much is the outstanding balance of the loan in 2004 dollars? How has inflation since 2004 affected the borrower? 2, 3

7. In what sense does inflation redistribute income from the holders of the federal debt to current taxpayers? 3

8. Suppose the nominal interest rate on bank deposits is 6 percent. During the year the inflation rate is 3 percent. What is the real interest rate earned on bank deposits that year? Suppose depositors and banks anticipated 4 percent inflation during the year. How did real interest rates differ from those anticipated, and how did the difference between actual and expected inflation affect the distribution of well-being between borrowers and lenders? 4

9. The nominal interest rate in a certain nation is not permitted to exceed 10 percent. During the year most lenders anticipate 14 percent inflation. Predict the impact of these expectations on decisions to lend funds. 4, 5

10. Suppose you live in a nation where hyperinflation prevails. If you are given a choice between two jobs, both paying the same wage and having the same fringe benefits, explain why you would be more likely to choose the job that pays you every week instead of the one that pays you every month. 5

Worldwide Disinflation

Disinflation is a term coined to describe the process of reducing a nation's rate of inflation. Since 1995, the process of disinflation has worked itself out throughout the world. By 2004, inflation had fallen considerably. According to the Organization of Economic Cooperation and Development (OECD), average inflation during the years 1996-2004 was down in the United States, Europe (the euro currency area), the United Kingdom, and Canada, compared to the period 1984-1995. The table below shows average inflation rates for these nations based on their CPIs.

Nation	**Average inflation, 1996-2004 (percent/year)**
United States	2.42
Canada	2.01
Euro Area	1.88
United Kingdom	1.34
Japan	−0.04

Even nations in which hyperinflation has been a problem have been showing signs of disinflation. For example, Turkey's inflation rate, which was at 44.1 percent in 2002, was down to 9.9 percent in 2004--and OECD forecasts indicated it would fall to 6.2 percent by 2006. Nations that still had inflation rates above or close to 10 percent in 2005 included Venezuela, Russia, Argentina, Brazil, and Indonesia.

In some countries, the problem of *deflation* has been more of a worry than that of inflation. Deflation has been a serious problem in Japan. Asset values, including those of corporate stocks, land, and homes, have fallen. Land prices in major cities in Japan in 2001 had fallen by 65 percent of their peak 1991 values. Consumer prices, excluding those for food, fell by 1.1 percent in 2000. Deflation is causing severe problems for homeowners, many of whom purchased their dwellings at inflated prices in the early and mid-1990s. Now, for many of these homeowners, selling their home would result in an economic loss. As wealth evaporates as a result of widespread deflation, Japanese consumers have been reluctant to spend, and the decline in consumer spending is plunging Japan into recessions.

With incomes, in many cases, falling faster than prices, the outlook for Japan was bleak in 2001. Wages were being cut and nominal interest rates plunged to zero. Some Japanese economists were arguing that the Japanese economy was headed for the unique prospect of "hyperdeflation!" The deflation was wiping out fortunes, particularly in real estate, and contributing to lower stock prices. Some banks were in danger of failing as the value of their assets plummeted, and companies were starting to eliminate jobs as falling prices squeezed their profit rates. Notice in the table above that prices in Japan have been falling, on average, from 1996 through 2004. However, as of 2005, the deflation problem seemed to be dissipating--but still causing concern--in Japan. Interest rates as of 2005 were running at zero!

There have been numerous explanations for the surprising disinflation of the period 1996-2004. For one thing, liberalized international trade put downward pressure on prices. Lower-priced products coming out of such low-wage nations as China and India have contributed to reduced inflation. Increased international competition has provided incentives for businesses to cut costs and inflicts a bitter blow on the incomes of nations whose prices are above those of international competitors. Inflation-fighting central bankers are the norm today, and they don't hesitate to put the brakes on money and credit supply at the first hint of rising inflation.

The global trend to disinflation put downward pressure on interest rates throughout the world. And, when interest rates fall in the United States or Germany, closely linked global credit markets tend to spread the decline throughout the world. However, by 2005, there were concerns that inflation was once again rearing its ugly head in the United States and other nations. There was growing anxiety about inflation becoming a problem in China. In the United States, the central bankers engaged in an aggressive campaign to stave off inflation by steadily putting upward pressure on short-term interest rates.

Chapter

24

Aggregate Demand and Aggregate Supply

What causes excessive unemployment and inflation? Is it possible to avoid recessions and the cyclical unemployment that goes hand in hand with economic contractions? Can the ravages of inflation be kept under control? How can we explain why an economy suffers simultaneously from both high unemployment and high inflation, as was the case during the recessions of the 1970s and 1980s? In this chapter, we begin an investigation of these questions.

Supply and demand analysis can be used to explain prices and quantities exchanged in individual markets. In macroeconomics, the basic tools of supply and demand are adapted to explain fluctuations in and growth of aggregate production (real GDP) and fluctuations in the price level.

Concept Preview

After reading this chapter, you should be able to

1. Distinguish an aggregate demand curve from a market demand curve and discuss changes in aggregate demand.
2. Distinguish an aggregate supply curve from a market supply curve and discuss changes in aggregate supply.
3. Use aggregate supply and demand analysis to show how the equilibrium level of real GDP and the price level over a given year are determined.
4. Use aggregate supply and demand analysis to show how changes in aggregate demand and aggregate supply affect the equilibrium levels of real GDP and the price level for a given year, and to explain the causes of recessions, excessive unemployment, and inflation.

Aggregate Demand and Aggregate Supply

In macroeconomics, supply and demand analysis is used to help us understand how changes in the economy can result in expansions or contractions and price instability. Instead of trying to explain the quantity of an individual item produced over a certain period, macroeconomics tries to explain the forces that influence *aggregate* production, measured by real GDP. Similarly, instead of trying to explain how the price of one good is established in a market, macroeconomics tries to explain how the price *level*, measured by a price index such as the GDP deflator or the CPI, is established.

When you understand the forces influencing demand and supply in the aggregate, you'll be in a better position to make your own forecasts about where the economy is headed. You will better understand the mysteries of inflation, recession, and why the economy sometimes suffers simultaneously from both excessive inflation and increasing unemployment. You'll then be able to comprehend newspaper articles and evening news reports more clearly to formulate your own ideas about what the government and banking authorities should do to help stabilize the economy.

Aggregate Demand

1 The demand for goods and services is an important influence on the performance of the economy. Aggregate demand depends on the willingness and ability of consumers, business firms, and governments to purchase the goods and services produced nationally and made available for sale in domestic and foreign markets.

The amount of the final products that will be demanded in any given year depends on a variety of factors, including the price level, consumer confidence, wealth, and the availability of credit. In analyzing the overall demand for final products in the economy, we first isolate the relationship between the amount that will be demanded and the general level of prices for products, holding all other influences on demand fixed. The amount of final products (measured as real GDP) that buyers will purchase at a given price level is called the aggregate quantity demanded.

Aggregate demand is a relationship between aggregate quantity demanded and the economy's price level. In macroeconomics we depict this relationship using an aggregate demand curve, a graph that shows how aggregate quantity demanded varies with the price level for the economy. A downward-sloping aggregate demand curve implies that the lower the price level, the greater the aggregate quantity demanded, other things being equal.

The graph in Box 1 shows the aggregate demand curve prevailing for a given year. The vertical axis measures the price level for the aggregate of final goods and services included in real GDP. The horizontal axis measures the quantity of final products demanded measured in base year dollars, representing the quantity of aggregate production that will be demanded for the year at each possible price level.

Although the aggregate demand curve may look like a market demand curve, it's really quite different. It describes a relationship between an *index* of prices and an *aggregate* of the final products demanded in a nation instead of a relationship between the price and quantity of a single good. For example, when you move down an aggregate demand curve, there is an increase in an *aggregate* of the goods and services demanded in the nation. When the price level falls, it means that the cost of purchasing an *aggregate* (or "market basket") of many products falls. Some individual prices may actually rise when the price level falls, and vice versa.

Because changes in real GDP mean changes in input use in the nation, income earned in the nation also changes when you move along an aggregate demand curve. Therefore,

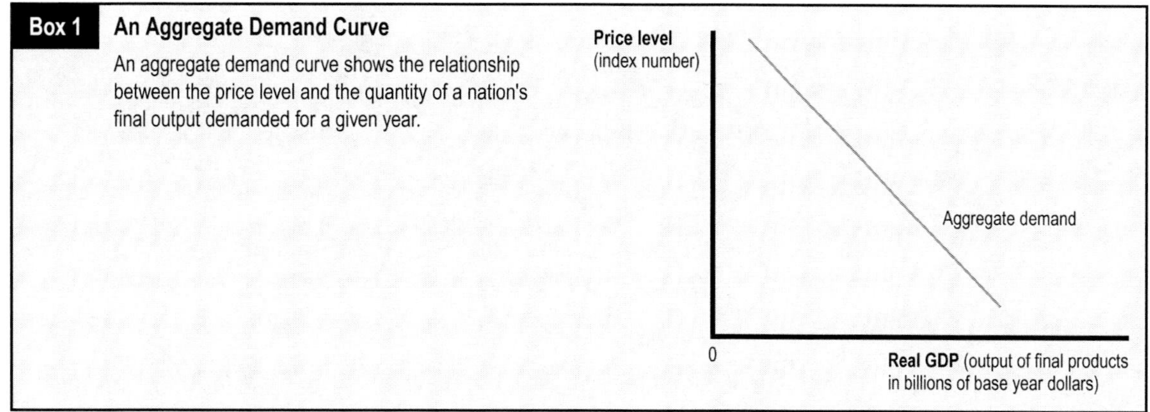
Box 1
An Aggregate Demand Curve
An aggregate demand curve shows the relationship between the price level and the quantity of a nation's final output demanded for a given year.
Price level
(index number)
Aggregate demand
0
Real GDP (output of final products in billions of base year dollars)

income is not held constant as you move along an aggregate demand curve as it is held constant when you move along the market demand curve for a single product.

The downward-sloping aggregate demand curve means that an increase in the price level will decrease the willingness and ability of at least some buyers to purchase the products included in real GDP. The reasons for the downward slope of an aggregate demand curve are much more complex than those that explain downward-sloping market demand curves for a single product. Here are three basic reasons for the inverse relationship between the aggregate quantity demanded and the price level:

1. *The real wealth effect: A higher price level can decrease real wealth in a nation and reduce consumer spending on final products.* The purchasing power of accumulated savings denominated in fixed dollar amounts declines when the price level goes up. For example, suppose you have $100 in cash in a cookie jar in your apartment. If the price level rises, the real value of this currency falls. The reduction in purchasing power associated with the rise in the price level will make you less wealthy and can decrease your willingness and ability to purchase final goods and services. The aggregate reduction in wealth caused by an increase in the price level is likely to decrease the willingness and ability of all consumers to purchase currently produced final products during the year.

A higher price level can also increase saving. If savers have specific goals, such as accumulating enough funds to make a down payment on a house or to finance their children's college education, an increase in the price level can induce them to save more of their current income for those purposes. When the price level rises, they must accumulate more dollars to achieve the same goal. For example, if the goal is to save enough to pay a child's college tuition costs, an increase in the price level that includes an increase in tuition costs means that more dollars must be saved to achieve that goal. As saving increases because of the higher price level, consumer purchases in the *current year* decrease, resulting in a decrease in the aggregate quantity demanded.

2. *The real interest rate effect: A higher price level can increase interest rates, making credit more expensive and reducing the quantity of investment goods demanded.* The ability of business firms and households to purchase goods and services produced depends on the cost of credit, which is measured by the real interest rate. Naturally, at a higher price level the dollar amount of credit necessary to purchase any given quantity of goods and services also increases. However, at a higher price level, households and businesses want to hold more cash in their bank accounts to finance their larger dollar volume of transactions. The increased desire to hold cash decreases the supply of loanable funds, thereby putting upward pressure on real interest rates when people need more credit to finance their daily business. As real interest rates rise, business firms cut back their purchase of investment goods and households cut back their spending. These actions decrease the aggregate quantity of goods and services demanded.

3. *The foreign trade effect: A higher price level reduces foreign demand for U.S. exports and increases domestic demand for imports.* Because the higher domestic price level implies that U.S. goods become more expensive relative to foreign goods, consumers in the United States tend to substitute imported goods for domestic goods. For example, rapid increases in the price level over the year mean an increase in the price of domestically produced cars. Assuming the increase in the price level in the United States has little effect on the dollar prices Korean sellers are willing to accept for cars they export to the United States, there will be a decrease in the quantity of U.S. cars demanded and an increase in the demand for Korean cars.

The increase in the price of U.S. items also decreases the quantity of U.S. exports demanded, other things being equal. The net effect of the increase in the price level is therefore a decline in the demand for the final products of U.S. firms in foreign markets and a further decline in the quantity of final products of U.S. firms demanded in domestic markets as buyers substitute foreign goods for domestic goods. Both the increase in U.S. demand for foreign products and the decrease in demand for U.S. products abroad contribute to a decline in the aggregate quantity of U.S. final products demanded during the year.[1]

Changes in Aggregate Demand

The amount of final products demanded does not depend on the price level alone. Aggregate demand is also influenced by such economic variables as wealth, interest rates, foreign exchange rates, and expectations about the future. A change in aggregate demand is a change in the amount of a nation's final products that will be purchased caused by something other than a change in the price level.

A change in aggregate demand is represented by an inward or outward shift of the economy's aggregate demand curve. The distinction between a *change in aggregate demand* and a *change in aggregate quantity demanded* is similar to the distinction between change in demand and change in quantity demanded for market demand curves. A change in aggregate quantity demanded is a movement along a given aggregate demand curve that occurs in response to a change in the price level. *A change in aggregate demand, however, implies a movement of the entire aggregate demand curve.* When aggregate demand increases or decreases, the relationship between the price level and aggregate quantity demanded is altered. The graphs in Boxes 2 and 3 illustrate changes in aggregate demand. An increase in aggregate demand implies an outward shift of the aggregate demand curve, while a decrease in aggregate demand implies an inward shift of the curve.

Influences on Aggregate Demand

Changes in the economy cause changes in aggregate demand by affecting the willingness of consumers to spend their income on the final products of domestic producers. Business demand for investment goods fluctuates, as do government purchases. Similarly, changes in the demand for our exports can influence aggregate demand for the products of domestic producers.

[1]This analysis assumes that the exchange rate of the dollar for foreign currency does not immediately adjust to cancel out the effect of the increase in the domestic price level. In practice many foreign nations manipulate the demand for and supply of their currencies in ways that prevent the exchange rate of those currencies from changing immediately in response to changes in the U.S. price level.

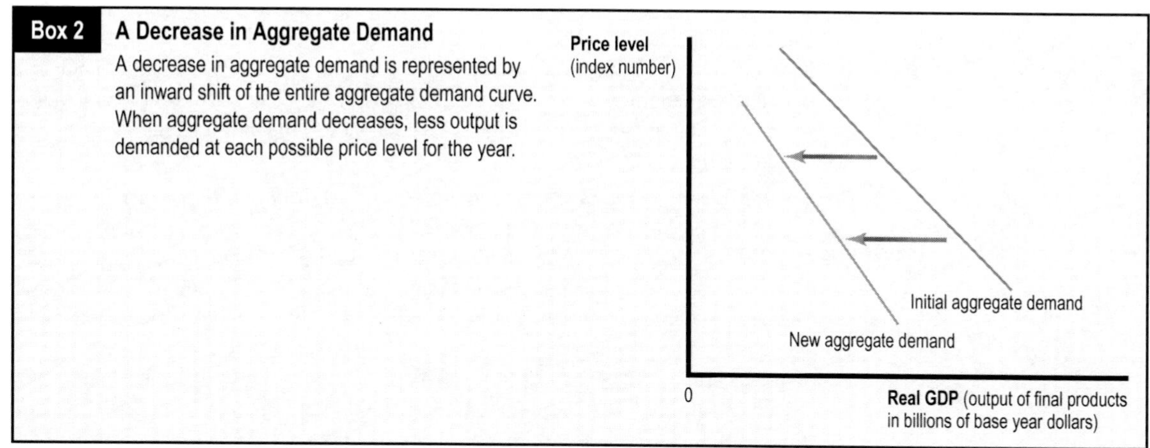
Box 2
A Decrease in Aggregate Demand
A decrease in aggregate demand is represented by an inward shift of the entire aggregate demand curve. When aggregate demand decreases, less output is demanded at each possible price level for the year.
Price level
(index number)
Initial aggregate demand
New aggregate demand
0
Real GDP (output of final products in billions of base year dollars)

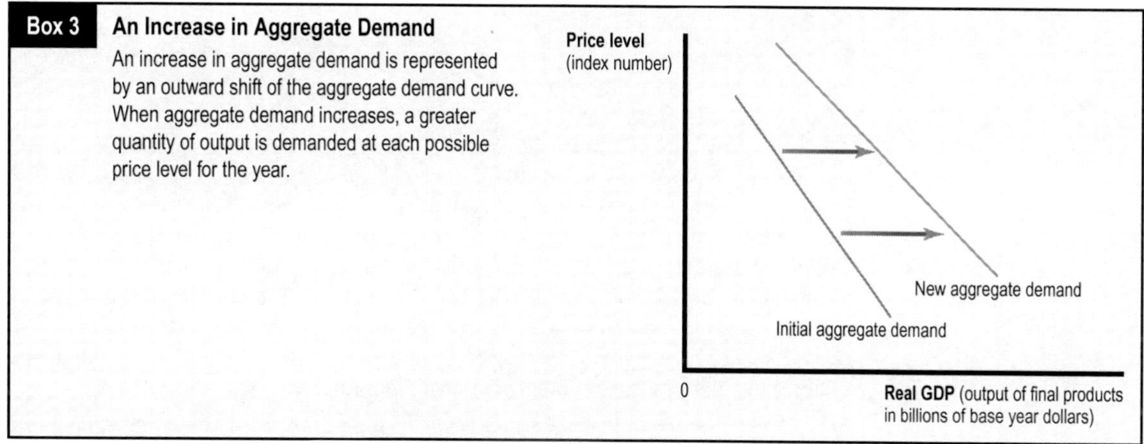
Box 3
An Increase in Aggregate Demand
An increase in aggregate demand is represented by an outward shift of the aggregate demand curve. When aggregate demand increases, a greater quantity of output is demanded at each possible price level for the year.
Price level
(index number)
New aggregate demand
Initial aggregate demand
0
Real GDP (output of final products in billions of base year dollars)

Much of the macroeconomic analysis in the text examines, in depth, the various influences on aggregate demand. At this point, we'll briefly list them.

1. *Real interest rates.* When real interest rates go up, businesses cut back on their plans to buy new equipment and structures, and households find they cannot afford the monthly payments necessary to buy such items as furniture, cars, and new homes. An increase in real interest rates therefore causes a decrease in aggregate demand, while a decrease in real interest rates causes an increase in aggregate demand.

2. *The quantity of money in circulation.* Suppose the government were to suddenly declare that each dollar people held in their pockets as currency or on deposit in banks was now worth two dollars. As a result, aggregate demand would increase because people would have more money to spend. On the other hand, a decrease in the quantity of money would decrease aggregate demand. Unrestrained increases in the quantity of money in circulation are a major cause of inflation and hyperinflation.

3. *Changes in the international value of the dollar.* As the price of the dollar goes up in terms of foreign currencies, our exports become more expensive in foreign markets, while imports become cheaper (other things being equal) to U.S. buyers. A higher dollar decreases aggregate demand by decreasing the demand for our exports and stimulating domestic demand for imports. As the price of the dollar goes down, the prices of our exports fall in terms of foreign currencies, stimulating demand for them, while the prices of imports go up in dollars, thereby encouraging U.S. consumers to substitute domestic products for imports. A decrease in the price of the dollar therefore results in an increase in aggregate demand. Changes in foreign exchange rates can have a major impact on an economy like that of the United States, where increasing proportions of spending are accounted for by imports and exports.

4. *Wealth.* Wealth consists of assets that can be sold, if necessary, to provide money for spending, such as stocks, bonds, and real estate. When stock prices are high, consumers who hold stocks are likely to be more willing to spend their current income rather than save it. Conversely, when the prices of stocks and other assets (such as land and homes) fall, aggregate demand can decrease. For example, when stock prices fell in 1929, aggregate demand plummeted as the savings of millions of stockholders were wiped out. However, the link between short-term changes in wealth and aggregate demand is not always clear-cut. In 1987, when there was another major stock market crash, many economists predicted a sharp cutback in aggregate demand. The effects, however, proved negligible, and aggregate demand continued to increase in 1987 and 1988. By 1990, however, declining real estate values and increased debt burdens did contribute to a decline in aggregate demand.

In 2007, real estate prices began to decline again and, by the end of that year, the defaults on mortgages and declines in the values of mortgage-backed securities decreased the supply of credit. Home prices in the United States began to decline significantly. The supply of credit then further decreased as banks began to be concerned about loan defaults. By the last quarter of 2008, the stock market began a significant nosedive, as confidence in the nation's financial system was weakened. As of early 2009, the major stock market indices indicated that, on average, the value of corporate stocks in the United States had declined to half their peak value, prevailing in October of 2007. This time, there was no doubt that the massive decline in wealth caused by both sharp drops in real estate and corporate stock prices was having a major impact on aggregate demand in the United States. As aggregate demand decreased, in part as a result of decline in wealth, the nation plunged into a deep recession that continued through 2008 and 2009.

5. *Government purchases, taxes, and transfers.* An increase in government purchases of goods and services increases aggregate demand, while a decrease in such purchases decreases aggregate demand. Taxes take a portion of income earned by households and businesses out of the spending stream. An increase in tax rates, other things being equal, decreases disposable income to households and is likely to decrease aggregate demand. Conversely, a decrease in tax rates is likely to increase aggregate demand because it increases disposable income. Transfer payments are a source of income to millions of Americans on Social Security pensions and to those who depend on welfare or unemployment benefits. Transfers influence consumption expenditures, and when they increase, aggregate demand also increases. For example, when the unemployment rate goes up, aggregate demand tends to decrease because labor earnings decline. However, unemployment insurance compensation (which is a transfer) goes up when the unemployment rate increases. The increase in transfer payments from unemployment insurance acts to increase aggregate demand, thereby cushioning the impact of increased cyclical unemployment on the economy.

6. *Expectations about the future.* If the outlook for future increases in disposable income is bleak, consumers are likely to cut back on spending. The decrease in aggregate demand resulting from a decline in the demand for consumption goods can reduce the demand of business firms for investment goods. If business firms do not think they can sell all their current production, they are unlikely to purchase more inventory, machines, or equipment or to plan new plants. When expectations turn up, aggregate demand is also likely to increase.

7. *Income and other economic conditions affecting demand in foreign countries.* When income goes up in foreign nations, their demand for such U.S. products as aircraft, beef, and lumber also goes up. This will increase aggregate demand in the United States. Conversely, if income in the rest of the world declines, there will be a decrease in the demand for U.S. exports, and the aggregate demand curve will shift inward.

Box 4 summarizes the major factors that can result in a change in aggregate demand.

Aggregate Supply

2 Sellers, like buyers, respond to incentives. How much they are willing to produce in a given year depends on their assessments of the profitability of selling their products. The amount sellers are willing and able to supply to product markets is influenced by the price of their products and by such considerations as wages, other input prices, and technology. In macroeconomic analysis we begin by isolating the influence of product prices on production decisions. The aggregate quantity supplied is the quantity of final products (measured by real GDP) that will be supplied by producers at a given price level. Aggregate supply is a relationship between the price level and aggregate quantity supplied.

An aggregate supply curve shows the aggregate quantity supplied for each possible price level over a given period. When drawing an aggregate supply curve, we assume that all input prices and the general availability and quality of productive resources in the economy are fixed. We also assume that technology does not advance over the given period.

An upward-sloping aggregate supply curve, illustrated in Box 5, implies that an increase in the price level will increase the aggregate of the final products, measured by real GDP, that domestic business firms will produce. As was the case for aggregate demand, the shape of the aggregate supply curve cannot be as easily explained as that of a market supply curve for a particular item. A market supply curve slopes upward because higher prices imply greater opportunities for profit, thereby attracting new sellers to enter the market over the long run. When we discuss aggregate supply, the number of sellers and the resources available during the year are more or less fixed, so it's not possible to explain the increase in output in terms of the attraction of additional sellers or resources into production.

Box 4 **Factors Influencing Changes in Aggregate Demand**

Changes in aggregate demand are caused by changes in the demand for domestically produced consumption goods or investment goods, changes in the demand for exports or imports, and changes in government purchases.

Changes that can cause an increase in aggregate demand	Changes that can cause a decrease in aggregate demand
■ A decrease in real interest rates.	■ An increase in real interest rates.
■ An increase in the quantity of money in circulation.	■ A decrease in the quantity of money in circulation.
■ A decrease in the international value of the dollar.	■ An increase in the international value of the dollar.
■ An increase in the general level of wealth.	■ A decrease in the general level of wealth.
■ An increase in government purchases.	■ A decrease in government purchases.
■ A decrease in tax rates.	■ An increase in tax rates.
■ An increase in government transfers.	■ A decrease in government transfers.
■ Improved expectations about the future.	■ Deteriorating expectations about the future.
■ Higher income and improvements in economic conditions in foreign nations.	■ Lower income and worsening economic conditions in foreign nations.

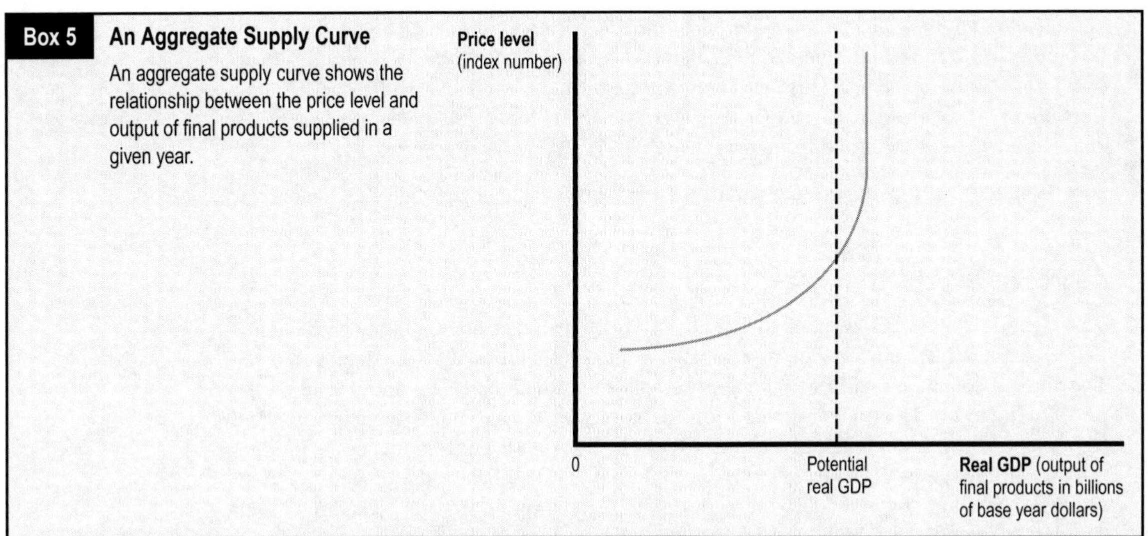

Box 5
An Aggregate Supply Curve
An aggregate supply curve shows the relationship between the price level and output of final products supplied in a given year.
Price level (index number)
0
Potential real GDP
Real GDP (output of final products in billions of base year dollars)

However, there's reason to believe that profit opportunities from supplying more output do increase in the aggregate, at least over a period of a year, when the price level rises. Over a short period a higher price level increases the amount businesses receive from selling additional output, *while input prices stay the same*. Naturally, if product prices rise but *input* prices remain constant, opportunities arise for additional profit from producing more. This leads producers to produce more until the costs of additional output rise to match the higher prices. (This is the marginal cost of output.) The costs of additional output eventually rise because firms must work their existing facilities more intensely and must hire less experienced workers to produce more. As this occurs, unit costs of production tend to rise because of overuse of facilities and because of the lower skill and productivity of less experienced workers. If you've already studied microeconomics, you know that the marginal cost of output for a firm tends to increase as more output is supplied.

In the graph in Box 5, the level of real GDP corresponding to potential real GDP is indicated on the horizontal axis. Potential real GDP is the level of real GDP that would be produced if the economy were at full employment. As potential real GDP for the economy is approached, factories, offices, and other productive facilities are pushed beyond the levels at which the unit cost of production is at a minimum. This impairs the overall efficiency of operation. These factors contribute to the higher unit production costs that occur, even though input prices are constant.

In addition, as an economy's potential real GDP is approached, businesses often have difficulty in obtaining all of the input they require. To operate facilities around the clock, firms must use overtime labor, which is often difficult to obtain without paying bonuses. The aggregate supply curve becomes steeper as output increases, because the costs of producing the additional units increase as potential real GDP is approached.[2]

Notice that the aggregate supply curve goes through the line corresponding to potential real GDP. The economy can produce more than the amount of final products corresponding to potential real GDP when the actual unemployment rate falls below the natural rate of unemployment. However, there's a physical limit to the amount of output that can be produced in a given year. When the economy surpasses potential real GDP,

[2]Just as the marginal cost of output for an individual producer increases when output goes up, so too does the marginal cost of real GDP for the economy increase as the economy approaches full employment.

firms hire less experienced workers and work their plants around the clock. As this occurs, unit costs of production tend to soar. These higher costs are reflected in the steeply rising aggregate supply curve beyond the level of real GDP corresponding to the natural rate of unemployment.

The aggregate supply curve eventually becomes vertical. (See Box 5.) The level of real GDP corresponding to that point is the physical limit of production for the economy for the year. At that point, it's virtually impossible to obtain the labor and other inputs necessary to increase output anymore.

Segments of the Aggregate Supply Curve

The slope of the aggregate supply curve differs depending on how much slack there is in the economy at the beginning of a year (or any other production period). The aggregate supply curve drawn in Box 6 has been divided into three distinct segments for corresponding levels of real GDP:

Segment 1: *The economy is operating well below its potential, with considerable cyclical unemployment.* When actual real GDP is considerably below the level that corresponds to potential real GDP, there will be cyclical unemployment and idle capacity. Under these circumstances, aggregate production can increase without much upward pressure on unit costs. If the economy is operating in this segment, business firms can easily produce more by bringing idle plant capacity and equipment back into service. It's also easy for business firms to obtain materials and labor under these circumstances, so they can increase output without increasing the costs of additional units of output. In this segment there is considerable slack in the economy and, other things being equal, little or no increase in the price level will suffice to increase aggregate quantity supplied.

Segment 2: *The economy is close to full employment.* As idle capacity is eliminated and the economy is approaching the level of aggregate production corresponding to potential real GDP, costs of additional units of output begin to rise more quickly. Under these circumstances, more substantial increases in the price level are necessary to induce firms to increase aggregate quantity supplied. It follows that as the economy approaches full employment, inflation will heat up if aggregate quantity supplied increases further.

Segment 3: *The economy is overheated.* The aggregate quantity supplied will exceed potential real GDP. Unit costs of production will rise very rapidly, and much higher prices

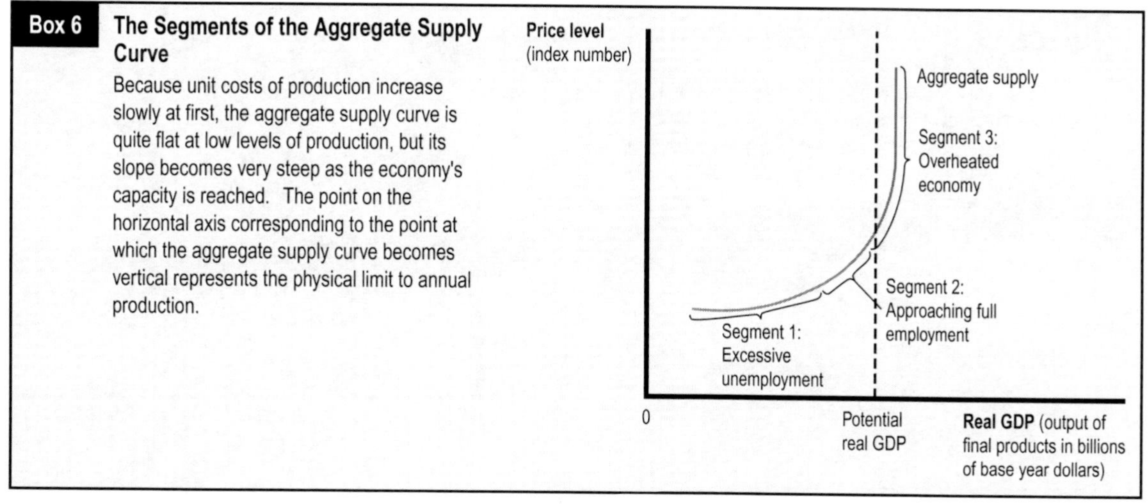

Box 6 The Segments of the Aggregate Supply Curve

Because unit costs of production increase slowly at first, the aggregate supply curve is quite flat at low levels of production, but its slope becomes very steep as the economy's capacity is reached. The point on the horizontal axis corresponding to the point at which the aggregate supply curve becomes vertical represents the physical limit to annual production.

will be necessary to cover those higher unit costs if the economy is to produce more. An economy operating at the beginning of the year in the nearly vertical portion of its aggregate supply curve will be bursting at the seams through overproduction.

Changes in Aggregate Supply

The amount that sellers will produce does not depend on the price level alone. Changes in wages and other input prices, changes in the quality and quantity of resources available, and advances in technology will change the aggregate quantity supplied at each possible price level. A change in aggregate supply is a change in the amount of national production resulting from something other than a change in the price level. A change in aggregate supply implies a shift of the economy's aggregate supply curve. Remember that the aggregate supply curve is drawn under the assumption that the level of all input prices, including the price of labor (nominal wages), the availability and quality of inputs, and technology are fixed. A decrease in aggregate supply is represented by an *inward* shift of the aggregate supply curve, and an increase in aggregate supply is represented by an *outward* shift of the aggregate supply curve.

How Changes in Input Prices Affect Aggregate Supply Some changes in the economy that change aggregate supply have little impact on the level of real GDP that corresponds to potential real GDP and the nation's physical limit to output for the year. Consider the impact of a change in nominal wages on aggregate supply. As nominal wages go up, the unit and marginal costs of production also go up, decreasing the profitability of selling output at any given price level. Because firms now require higher prices to make any given level of output available, the aggregate supply curve shifts inward, just as a market supply curve shifts inward in response to an increase in wages. However, the wage increase itself affects neither the economy's potential real GDP nor the level of output corresponding to the economy's physical limit to production.

The graph in Box 7 illustrates a decrease in aggregate supply that results from an increase in nominal wages or an increase in other input prices (such as fuel prices). Notice that the curve shifts inward but that the level of output for which the curve becomes vertical does not change. The level of output corresponding to potential real GDP and the economy's physical limit to output does not change.

A decrease in nominal wages or a decrease in fuel prices would increase aggregate supply without affecting potential real GDP or the level of real GDP corresponding to the

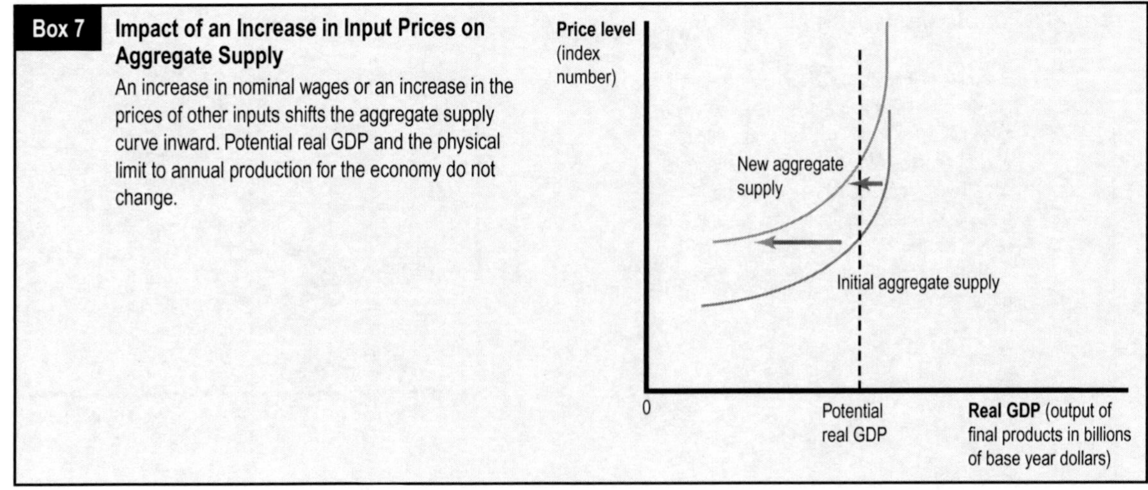

Box 7 **Impact of an Increase in Input Prices on Aggregate Supply**

An increase in nominal wages or an increase in the prices of other inputs shifts the aggregate supply curve inward. Potential real GDP and the physical limit to annual production for the economy do not change.

economy's capacity output. Lower input prices increase profit opportunities and induce businesses to increase the aggregate quantity supplied at each possible price level. The graph in Box 8 shows how a decrease in input prices affects the aggregate supply curve. For example, suppose the price of oil, a key input used in production, falls by 20 percent during the year. This means the unit and marginal costs of production will also fall. This induces businesses to increase the aggregate quantity supplied at any given price level. The decrease in oil prices itself, however, does not change the level of real GDP corresponding to potential real GDP or to the physical limit to output during the year.

How Changes in the Quantity or Productivity of Inputs Affect Aggregate Supply Changes in the availability or productivity of resources and advances in technology increase or decrease aggregate supply and also change the levels of output corresponding to potential real GDP and the nation's capacity output. The graph in Box 9 shows an increase in aggregate supply that results when changes in the economy affect the nation's potential real GDP and the level of real GDP corresponding to capacity output. For

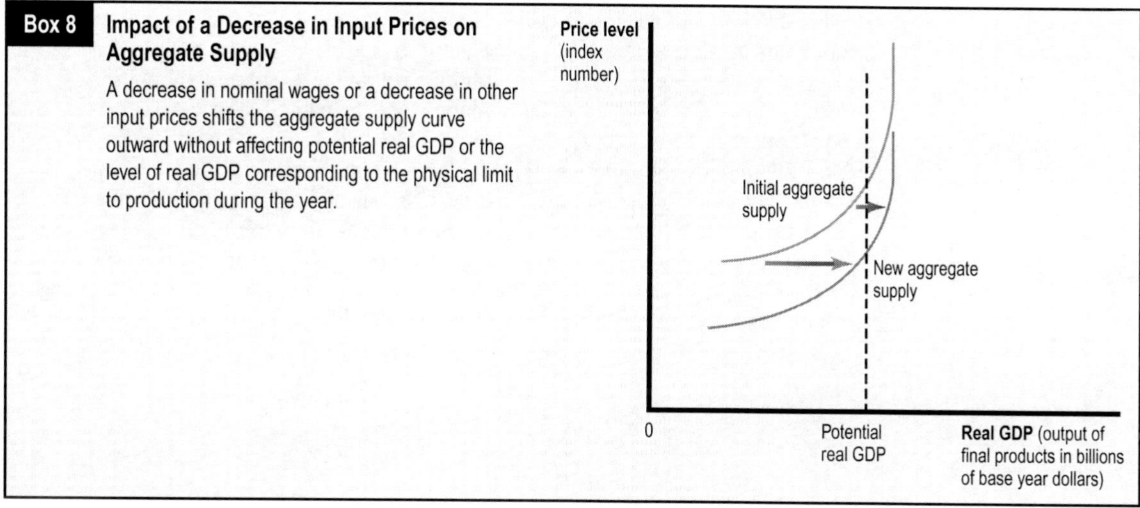
Box 8
Impact of a Decrease in Input Prices on Aggregate Supply
A decrease in nominal wages or a decrease in other input prices shifts the aggregate supply curve outward without affecting potential real GDP or the level of real GDP corresponding to the physical limit to production during the year.
Price level (index number)
Initial aggregate supply
New aggregate supply
0
Potential real GDP
Real GDP (output of final products in billions of base year dollars)

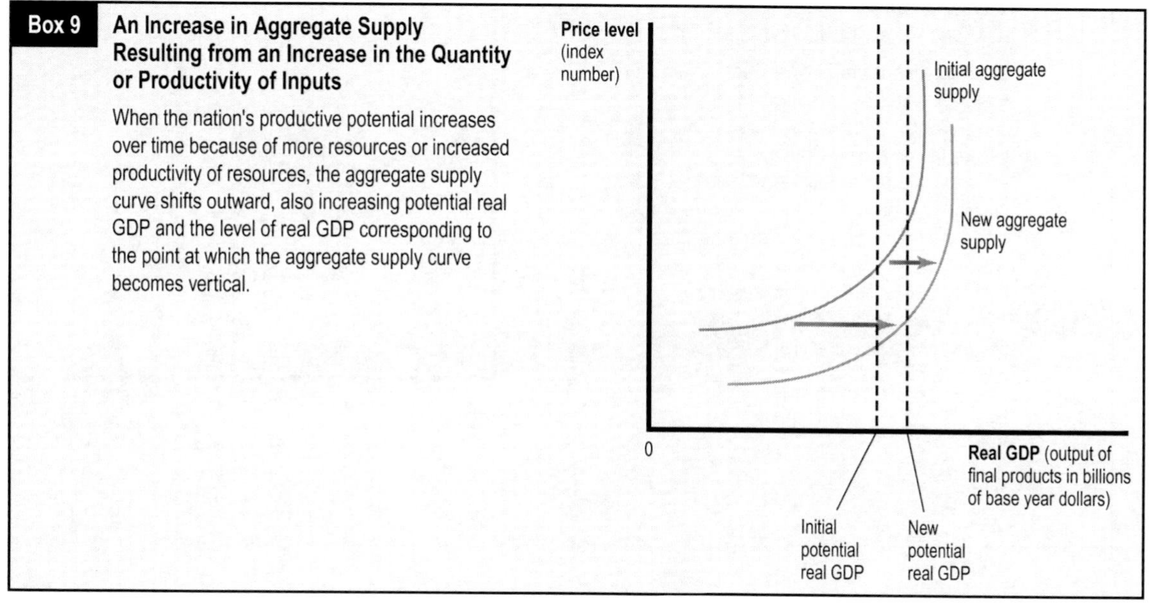
Box 9
An Increase in Aggregate Supply Resulting from an Increase in the Quantity or Productivity of Inputs
When the nation's productive potential increases over time because of more resources or increased productivity of resources, the aggregate supply curve shifts outward, also increasing potential real GDP and the level of real GDP corresponding to the point at which the aggregate supply curve becomes vertical.
Price level (index number)
Initial aggregate supply
New aggregate supply
0
Real GDP (output of final products in billions of base year dollars)
Initial potential real GDP
New potential real GDP

example, an increase in the size of the labor force means that more labor hours are available for production. Because of the increased labor, potential real GDP is greater, and so too is the capacity of the economy to produce goods and services. Similarly, an increase in the nation's capital stock will increase aggregate supply because more capital means that a given labor force has more tools with which to work. Naturally, with more tools labor will be more productive. The graph in Box 9 shows that as a result of the increase in the availability of inputs, both potential real GDP and the level of real GDP corresponding to the physical limit to production (for which the aggregate supply curve becomes vertical) increase as aggregate supply increases.

An increase in the availability of raw materials can also increase aggregate supply, as illustrated in Box 9. Improvement in the *quality* of inputs is another important cause of increases in aggregate supply that also increase potential real GDP. For example, improvement of the educational level of the labor force is a major cause of such increases in aggregate supply. Advances in technology, such as new and faster computers and automated production techniques, also contribute to such outward shifts in aggregate supply.

Although it is normal for aggregate supply to increase over time as the availability and productivity of resources increase, natural or social catastrophes occasionally result in decreases in aggregate supply. For example, in 1988 a severe drought in the United States resulted in a decrease in aggregate supply. Wars and natural disasters, such as earthquakes and hurricanes, can destroy productive resources and decrease aggregate supply. The sharp cutoff in imported supplies of oil that occurred in the 1970s in the United States as a result of the OPEC oil embargo caused a decrease in aggregate supply. Similarly, in 2005, decreased availability of crude oil due to hurricanes along the Texas and Louisiana coasts on the Gulf of Mexico resulted in higher oil prices and higher fuel prices, which caused decreases in aggregate supply for the U.S. economy. Box 10 shows a decrease in aggregate supply resulting from a decrease in resource availability; it also shows how both potential real GDP and the nation's capacity output decline as a consequence.

Box 10 **A Decrease in Aggregate Supply Resulting from a Decrease in the Quantity or Productivity of Inputs**

In some cases natural or other catastrophes can result in inward shifts in the aggregate supply curve. A war, an earthquake, or a hurricane could destroy human and physical resources. A change in climate (such as a drought) could also decrease aggregate supply by decreasing the productivity of inputs such as land. When there is a decrease in aggregate supply because of decreases in the quantity or productivity of inputs, potential real GDP and the nation's physical limit to production for the year also decrease.

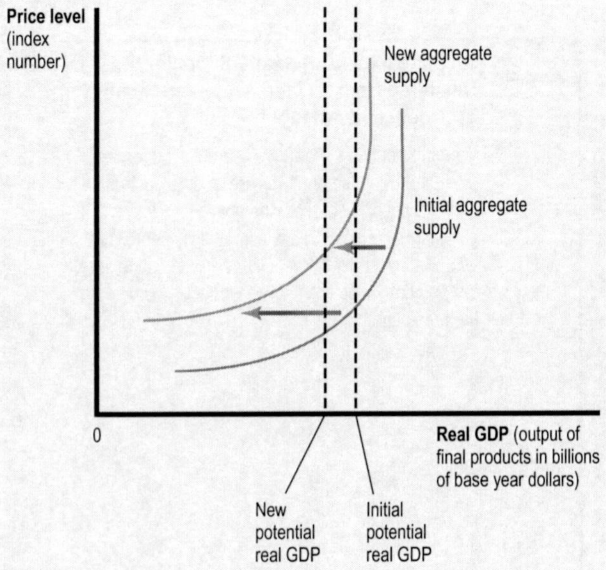

Macroeconomic Equilibrium

3 The preceding analysis of aggregate demand and aggregate supply shows that both the amounts buyers are willing to buy and the amounts sellers are willing to produce depend on the price level. But what determines the actual price level and the level of real GDP that will prevail over a given period? Will actual real GDP be equal to potential real GDP over that period? Will increases in aggregate demand result in inflation that sends the price level skyrocketing, or will they merely result in an increase in aggregate production? How will an oil embargo affect real GDP and the price level over the period?

To answer these questions, we have to examine whether the spending plans of buyers match the production plans of sellers over the given period. We must also examine how changes in aggregate demand and aggregate supply will affect the balance between aggregate quantity demanded and aggregate quantity supplied. In this way we can forecast how changes in the economy will affect unemployment and inflation. We can also examine the way government stabilization policies can affect the economy through their impact on the balance between aggregate quantities demanded and supplied.

A **macroeconomic equilibrium** is attained when the aggregate quantity demanded equals the aggregate quantity supplied. When aggregate supply and demand balance at the equilibrium price level, there is neither widespread unplanned buildup of product inventories nor an unexpected rapid reduction in inventories because businesses cannot fill orders quickly enough. When a macroeconomic equilibrium is achieved, the aggregate production made available for sale over a given period is, on average, willingly purchased in markets at the prevailing price level.

The phrase *on average* is important when discussing macroeconomic equilibrium because both the price level and real GDP are aggregates. Some *individual* markets can be out of equilibrium even when a macroeconomic equilibrium is attained. For example, the demand for digital cameras may fall, resulting in a surplus of cameras and an unanticipated buildup of inventories. At the same time, an increase in the demand for DVRs may result in an unanticipated depletion of producer inventories. There would therefore be downward pressure on the price of digital cameras and upward pressure on the price of DVRs as these markets move to a new equilibrium.

When a macroeconomic equilibrium exists, there may be shortages in some product markets and surpluses in other product markets. *In the aggregate*, however, there is neither upward nor downward pressure on the price level or the level of real GDP once macroeconomic equilibrium is attained.

The graph in Box 11 illustrates the concept of macroeconomic equilibrium, using the aggregate demand and aggregate supply curves prevailing for a given year. The macroeconomic equilibrium corresponds to the point at which the aggregate demand and aggregate supply curves intersect. The equilibrium level of real GDP corresponding to the point of intersection, *E*, is $5,000 billion. Aggregate production of $5,000 billion (measured in base year dollars) also corresponds to the quantity of final products demanded at the equilibrium price level of 120 as measured by a price index such as the GDP deflator. Because the entire aggregate quantity supplied of $5,000 billion is willingly purchased at the current price level of 120, there is, on average, no upward or downward pressure on prices or production.

The Results of Unintended Inventory Changes

Suppose the quantity of final products demanded fell short of aggregate quantity supplied at the existing price level during the year. Under these circumstances, there would be an abundance of unsold goods. Many industries would experience slack demand for the final products they produced during the year. Manufacturing firms would find that their orders

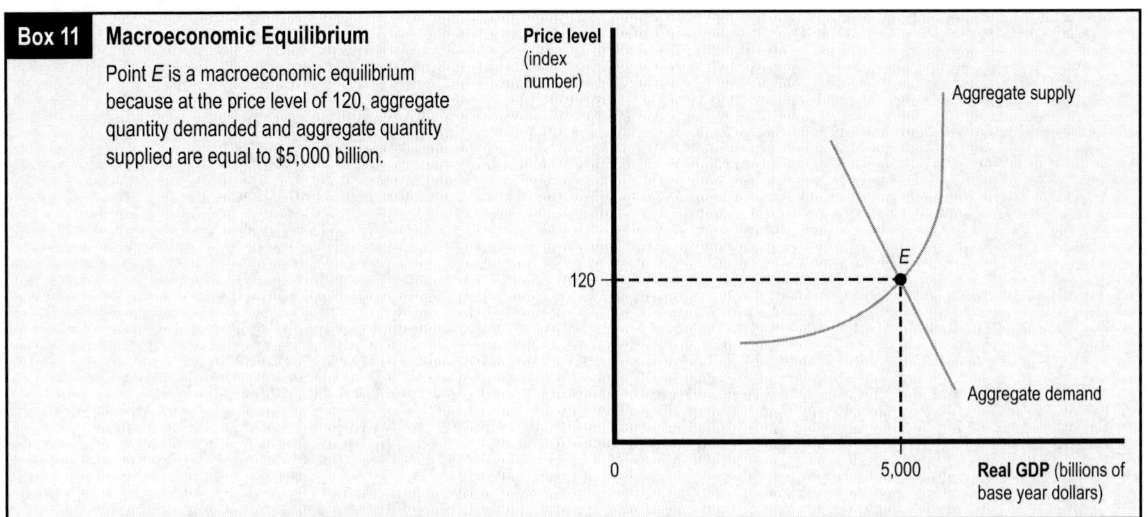
Box 11
Macroeconomic Equilibrium
Point E is a macroeconomic equilibrium because at the price level of 120, aggregate quantity demanded and aggregate quantity supplied are equal to $5,000 billion.
Price level (index number)
Aggregate supply
E
120
Aggregate demand
0
5,000
Real GDP (billions of base year dollars)

were less than anticipated. As inventories built up, these firms would lay off workers and cut back on orders for materials. Service firms, such as banks, insurance companies, and brokerage houses, would find that their staffs were excessive for the volume of their business, and they too would lay off workers. Production and employment would begin to fall, and there would be downward pressure on the price level.

Now imagine a scenario in which the quantity of final products demanded exceeded aggregate quantity supplied. Inventories would be rapidly drawn down. Manufacturing firms would experience difficulty in keeping up with orders. These firms would hire more workers or work their plants around the clock with existing workers as goods were reordered. Service firms would expand their staffs or offer overtime bonuses to existing workers. There would be upward pressure on the price level and upward pressure on the output of final products as the economy moved to a macroeconomic equilibrium.[3]

In a market economy no one coordinates the production decisions of business firms with the purchase decisions of buyers. For example, business firms may anticipate a strong holiday selling season. Then an unanticipated event, such as a sharp increase in real interest rates or a stock market collapse, may cause buyers to buy less than anticipated. As a result of the unexpected decline in sales, business firms that are stuck with lots of inventory cancel their orders for more goods. Business firms may also reduce their investment purchases. As orders are canceled, aggregate production and aggregate real income will decline. There might also be downward pressure on the price level as sellers stuck with inventories of unsold goods lower prices. Real GDP, and possibly the price level, will adjust until an equilibrium is attained. On the other hand, if sellers *underestimate* the aggregate quantity demanded during a period, there will be upward pressure on real GDP and the price level as reorders of goods and additional hiring of workers increase aggregate quantity supplied and aggregate real income.

How a Decrease in Aggregate Demand Can Affect the Economy

4 A decrease in aggregate demand can result in a decrease in equilibrium real GDP and a consequent decrease in earnings and employment in the economy. If the decrease in

[3]In the National Income and Product Accounts, final sales are a measure of the quantity of final products actually purchased in markets. Changes in business inventory at the end of the year are treated as an investment purchase by the firms holding the inventory, even though they don't actually buy the goods from themselves.

aggregate demand is severe enough, it can cause the economy to operate well below its potential and thereby result in excessive unemployment. If the decline in aggregate demand is prolonged, it pushes the economy into a recession.

The graph in Box 12 shows the impact of a decrease in aggregate demand in an economy. Suppose the economy is initially in equilibrium at point E_1, at which the price level is 120 and real GDP is at the full-employment level of $5,000 billion. When aggregate demand decreases, the economy moves to an equilibrium at point E_2, at which real GDP declines to $4,500 billion and the price level falls to 115. The decline in aggregate demand during the year means that a level of output corresponding to $5,000 billion real GDP cannot be sustained because at the new level of aggregate demand it is not possible to sell that much output. As inventories build up unexpectedly during the year, firms cut back orders, and both real GDP and employment decline as the economy moves to the new equilibrium at point E_2. The decline in real GDP means the economy moves into a contraction as a result of the decrease in aggregate demand. *A decline in aggregate demand is a possible cause of contractions or recessions and can explain increases in cyclical unemployment.* We can now begin to unravel the mysteries of the causes of excessive unemployment and recessions.

Recessionary GDP Gap

A macroeconomic equilibrium need not occur at a level of real GDP that corresponds to potential real GDP. If potential real GDP were attained, the economy would be at full employment. However, in Box 12 the level of new aggregate demand is not high enough to generate full employment. The equilibrium level of real GDP is $500 billion below potential real GDP, implying that there is some cyclical unemployment in the economy. In other words, if the level of real GDP corresponding to full employment were attained, the result would be a widespread buildup of inventory, which would set up forces that cause production to decline and move the economy to equilibrium at point E_2. The difference between the equilibrium level of real GDP and potential real GDP when the economy is operating at less than full employment is called a recessionary GDP gap. The recessionary GDP gap in Box 12 amounts to $500 billion.

It's quite possible for the aggregate demand curve to intersect the aggregate supply curve along the latter's flat portion. In this case the macroeconomic equilibrium would correspond to considerable unemployment of workers and idle capacity in the economy.

Box 12 Impact of a Decrease in Aggregate Demand

Other things being equal, a decrease in aggregate demand reduces the equilibrium price level and real GDP. The decrease in aggregate demand shown causes the economy to contract. Equilibrium real GDP falls below potential real GDP, opening up a recessionary GDP gap.

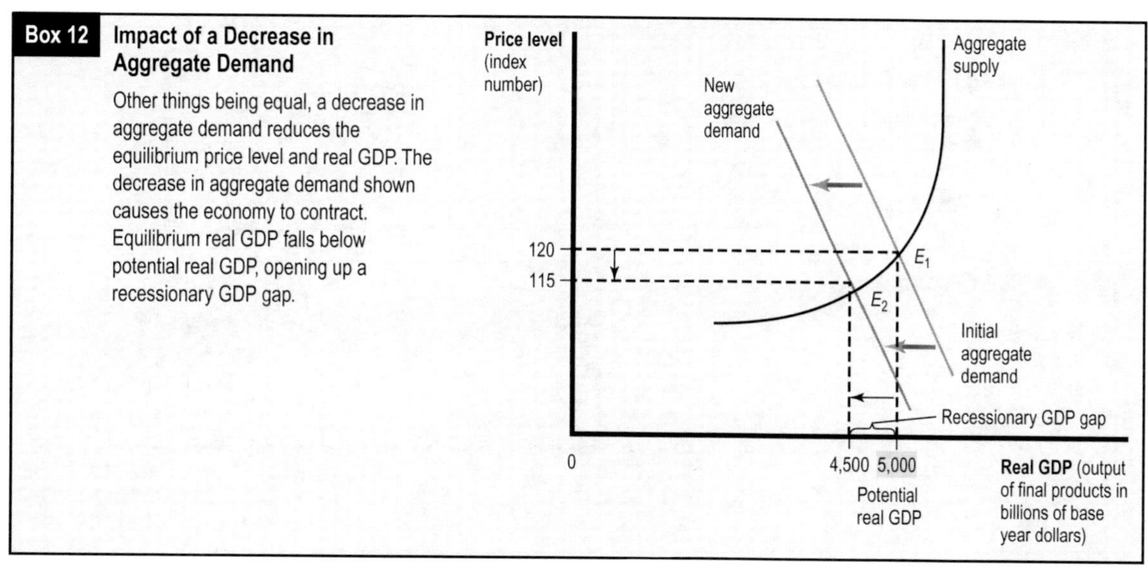

How an Increase in Aggregate Demand Can Affect the Economy

An increase in aggregate demand puts upward pressure on equilibrium real GDP and the price level. The graph in Box 13 shows how an increase in aggregate demand moves the economy to a new macroeconomic equilibrium corresponding to point E_2, at which both real GDP and the price level are higher than at the initial equilibrium, corresponding to point E_1. The increase in aggregate demand is sufficient to overheat the economy. As a result, equilibrium real GDP rises above potential real GDP, creating an inflationary GDP gap, which is the difference between equilibrium real GDP and potential real GDP when the economy is overheated.

Demand-pull inflation is inflation caused by increases in aggregate demand. When, given aggregate supply, the aggregate demand curve continually shifts outward, the result is upward pressure on prices, which means inflation. A general increase in the availability of money and credit in the economy is a common cause of demand-pull inflation that we'll investigate later on. Increases in the stock of money measured by currency in circulation and bank deposits can cause inflation through their impact on aggregate demand.

The extent to which changes in aggregate demand cause changes in aggregate production and the price level depends on how close the economy is to the level of real GDP that corresponds to full employment. Suppose the economy starts the year operating in segment 3 of its aggregate supply curve. Factories and offices are already operating around the clock, and there is little unemployment. Under these circumstances, the main impact of the increase in aggregate demand will be upward pressure on the price level. There will be little, if any, effect on equilibrium real GDP. The economy will move along the portion of its aggregate supply curve that is nearly vertical, as shown in graph **A** in Box 14. Demand-pull inflation will be a very serious problem. When the economy is operating in equilibrium above potential real GDP, steady increases in aggregate demand will surely put sharp, steady upward pressure on the price level. On the other hand, if there is considerable unused capacity in the economy and excessive unemployment during the year, then the main effect of the increase in aggregate demand will be an increase in real GDP, with little upward pressure on the price level. For example, government stabilization policies that seek to increase real GDP by increasing aggregate demand can do so with little fear of generating inflation in an economy operating in segment 1 of its aggregate

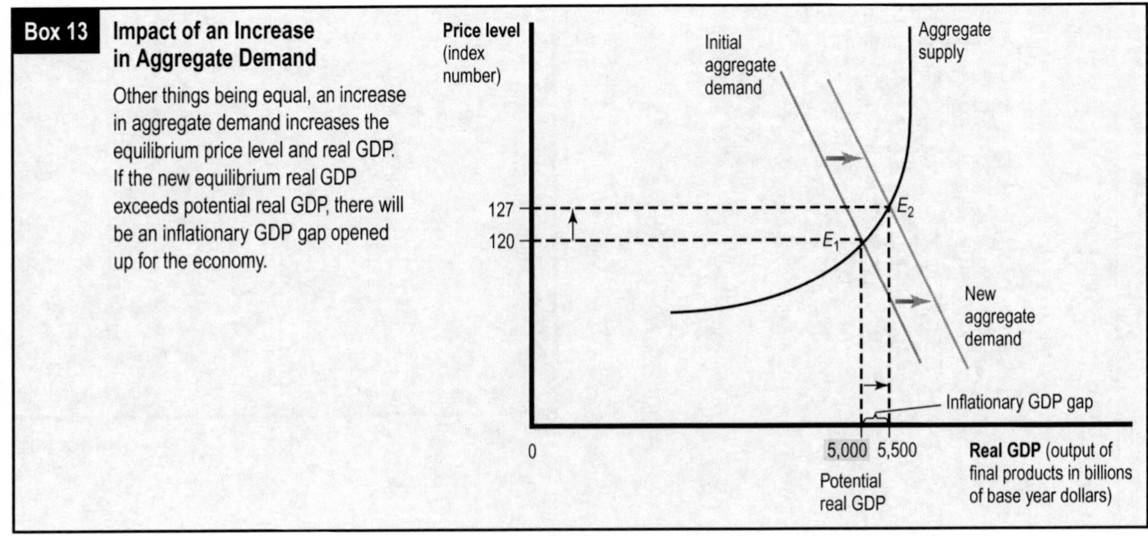

Box 13 Impact of an Increase in Aggregate Demand

Other things being equal, an increase in aggregate demand increases the equilibrium price level and real GDP. If the new equilibrium real GDP exceeds potential real GDP, there will be an inflationary GDP gap opened up for the economy.

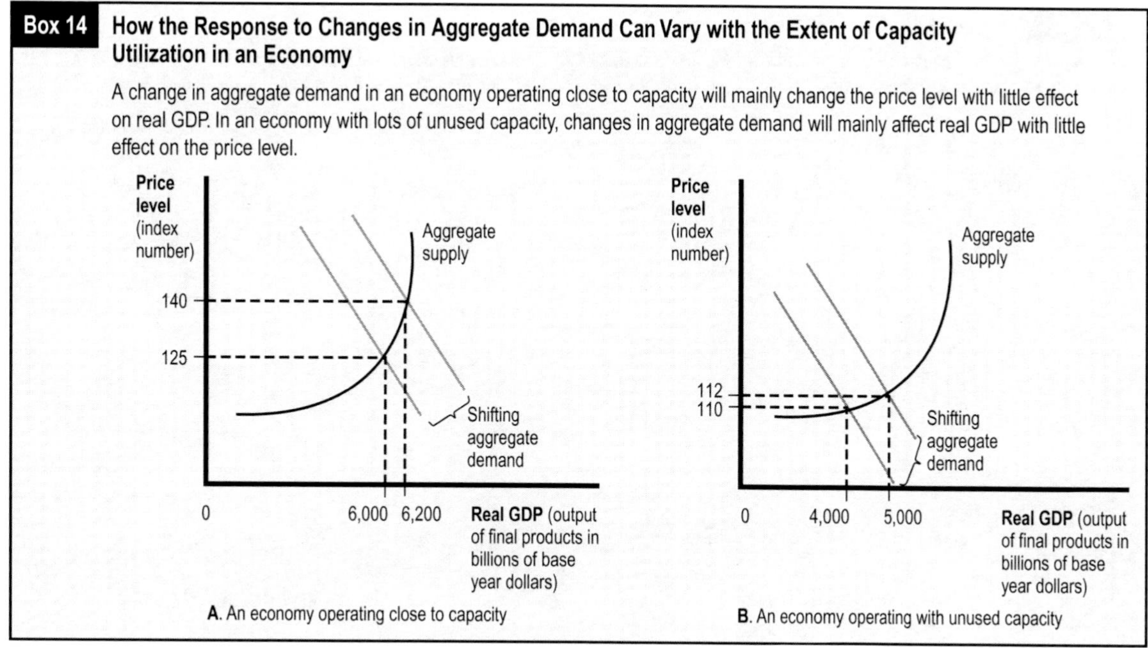

Box 14 How the Response to Changes in Aggregate Demand Can Vary with the Extent of Capacity Utilization in an Economy

A change in aggregate demand in an economy operating close to capacity will mainly change the price level with little effect on real GDP. In an economy with lots of unused capacity, changes in aggregate demand will mainly affect real GDP with little effect on the price level.

A. An economy operating close to capacity

B. An economy operating with unused capacity

supply curve. In such a case, the increase in aggregate demand moves the economy along the relatively flat portion of its aggregate supply curve, as shown in graph **B** of Box 14.

If the economy is in equilibrium at a level of real GDP at which factories and offices are utilized well below capacity levels and there is excessive unemployment, a decrease in aggregate demand will decrease real GDP with little downward pressure on the price level.

How a Decrease in Aggregate Supply Can Affect the Economy

Suppose there's a decrease in aggregate supply resulting from an increase in the general level of nominal wages not matched by productivity increases or from a sharp increase in the price of a key input such as oil. The decrease in aggregate supply shown in graph **A** in Box 15 moves the economy from its initial equilibrium at point E_1 to a new equilibrium at point E_2.

Note that, at the new equilibrium, real GDP is lower than it was initially and the price level is higher. Decreases in aggregate supply are particularly harmful because they result in *both* decreased production and upward pressure on the price level. Thus, a decrease in aggregate supply can simultaneously contribute to increased unemployment *and* to increases in the price level that erode the purchasing power of income! So recessions can be caused not only by decreases in aggregate demand but also by decreases in aggregate supply. For example, the soaring price of oil in 1990, triggered by Iraq's invasion of Kuwait, caused a decrease in aggregate supply that increased the price level and cut job growth in the United States.

Inflation caused by *continual* decreases in aggregate supply is called cost-push inflation. Cost-push inflation is usually found in an overheated economy whose actual unemployment rate has fallen below the natural rate of unemployment. Except for cases in which the economy overheats, cost-push inflation is relatively rare. In most cases a decrease in aggregate supply results in a *onetime* increase in the price level that increases the rate of inflation only during the year the decrease in aggregate supply occurs. In later years, unless aggregate supply decreases again, there is no acceleration in the rate of inflation.

Box 15 Changes in Aggregate Supply

A decrease in aggregate supply will raise the price level and reduce equilibrium real GDP. An increase in aggregate supply will affect macroeconomic equilibrium by reducing the price level and increasing real GDP, other things being equal.

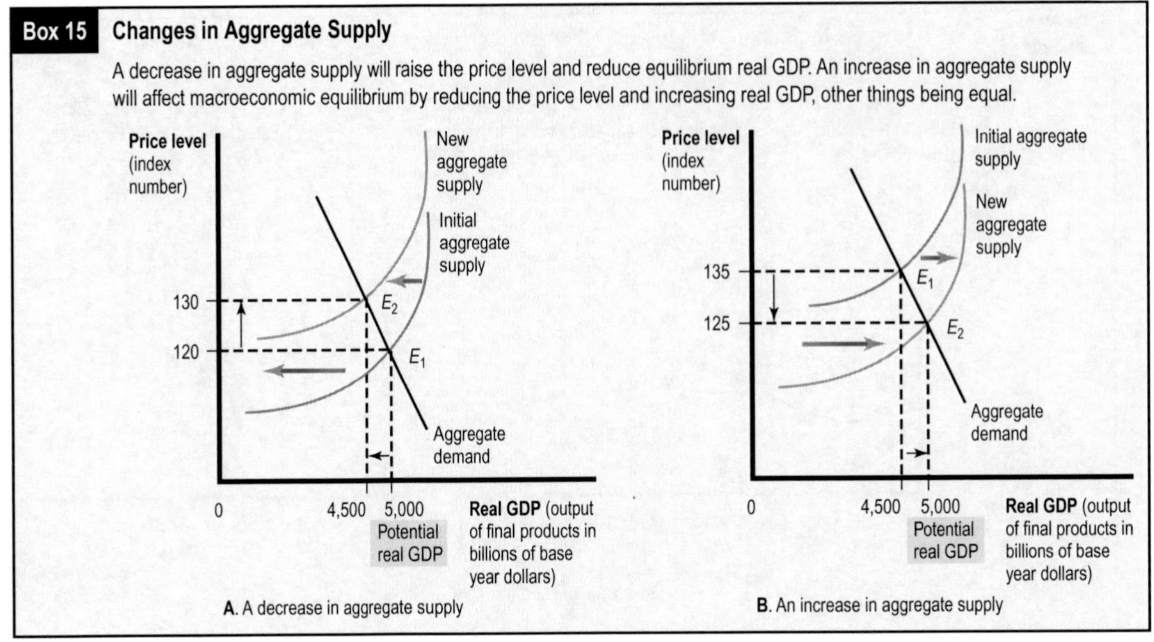

A. A decrease in aggregate supply

B. An increase in aggregate supply

How an Increase in Aggregate Supply Can Affect the Economy: Resource and Labor Markets

An increase in aggregate supply can improve the performance of the economy by simultaneously increasing production and putting downward pressure on the price level. In graph **B** of Box 15, the economy is in equilibrium at point E_1, at which real GDP is $4,500 billion and the price level is 135. As aggregate supply increases, the economy moves to a new equilibrium at point E_2. Real GDP is equal to $5,000 billion, its potential level, while during the year the price level falls to 125.

Increases in aggregate supply are particularly desirable for the economy because they can reduce cyclical unemployment and keep inflationary pressures down. In early 1988, for example, news of decreasing oil prices was greeted very favorably by the people who evaluate the economy. Because a decrease in aggregate demand was feared at that time, the forecast of a likely increase in aggregate supply was viewed as reducing the likelihood that there would be a recession in 1988. An increase in aggregate supply also occurred as a result of a decrease in oil prices in 1991, after it became clear that the conflict in the Persian Gulf could not disrupt oil supplies.

Increases in aggregate supply also result from resource growth, increased productivity, and technological advance in the economy. As an economy grows because of increased labor force participation, improvements in the quality of economic resources, increased capital stock, and advances in technology, its potential real GDP also increases. For the U.S. economy in the middle to late 1990s, the common estimate for the rate of growth for potential real GDP was in the range of 2.5 percent per year. Increases in aggregate supply due to resource growth also help increase output, while putting downward pressure on the price level.

Labor market conditions in the United States helped accommodate this growth in potential real GDP, with only modest growth in nominal wages, on average, in the 1980s and 1990s. The U.S. economy accommodated an increased supply of workers between 1973 and 1994 by creating 37 million additional jobs. Over the same period, there was slow productivity growth for labor and, in part as a result of lagging productivity growth, nominal wages of workers in the U.S. also grew slowly. Real hourly labor compensation in the United States grew more slowly than in other industrial nations. But, perhaps because of the slow growth in real labor compensation, the U.S. economy continued to expand to absorb a growing labor force without the high chronic unemployment rates that have plagued some nations, particularly in Europe.

Between 1990 and 2000, total average labor compensation in the United States rose at an annual rate of 3.9 percent. The rise in labor compensation is roughly equal to the rate of increase in the price level. This means that there was little or no increase in real labor costs for business during the 1990s. The increase in aggregate supply and potential real GDP resulting from resource growth and technological change wasn't offset by wage increases that could decrease short-run aggregate supply. As a result, since the end of the 1990 recession, the U.S. economy has enjoyed moderate economic growth, with little inflation. The slow growth in wages has contributed to increased profit opportunities for U.S. business, and producers have responded by increasing output and hiring more workers.

The graph in Box 16 shows how demand and supply conditions in U.S. labor markets have allowed increased job creation while wage increases have been modest. As the demand for labor increased in the 1990s, supply of labor also increased. A new equilibrium was achieved that allowed the increase in workers to be accommodated with only a moderate increase in hourly labor compensation. Many of the new entrants in the labor force were low-skilled, which contributed to the downward pressure on the average wage levels. Decreased labor union power in manufacturing occupations also contributed to increased labor supply and helped keep hourly wage growth low. As the economy performed at or close to its potential in 2006 and 2007, average hourly labor compensation increased and exceeded annual inflation in consumer prices. However, by the end of 2007, the demand for labor began to decrease as aggregate demand started to decline. The decline in the demand for labor persisted throughout 2008 and 2009, and job growth turned negative. In 2008 average hourly labor compensation barely kept up with inflation. Between the last

Box 16 **U.S. Labor Market Performance 1991–2007**

As the demand for labor has increased, so has labor supply. Since 1991 U.S. labor markets have created enough jobs to accommodate growing labor supply. On average wage increases have been modest, which has allowed new workers to be absorbed without upward pressure on the price level. The performance of U.S. labor markets has allowed the U.S. economy to operate near its potential in the 1990s and after the recovery from the recession of 2001 by contributing to increased aggregate supply.

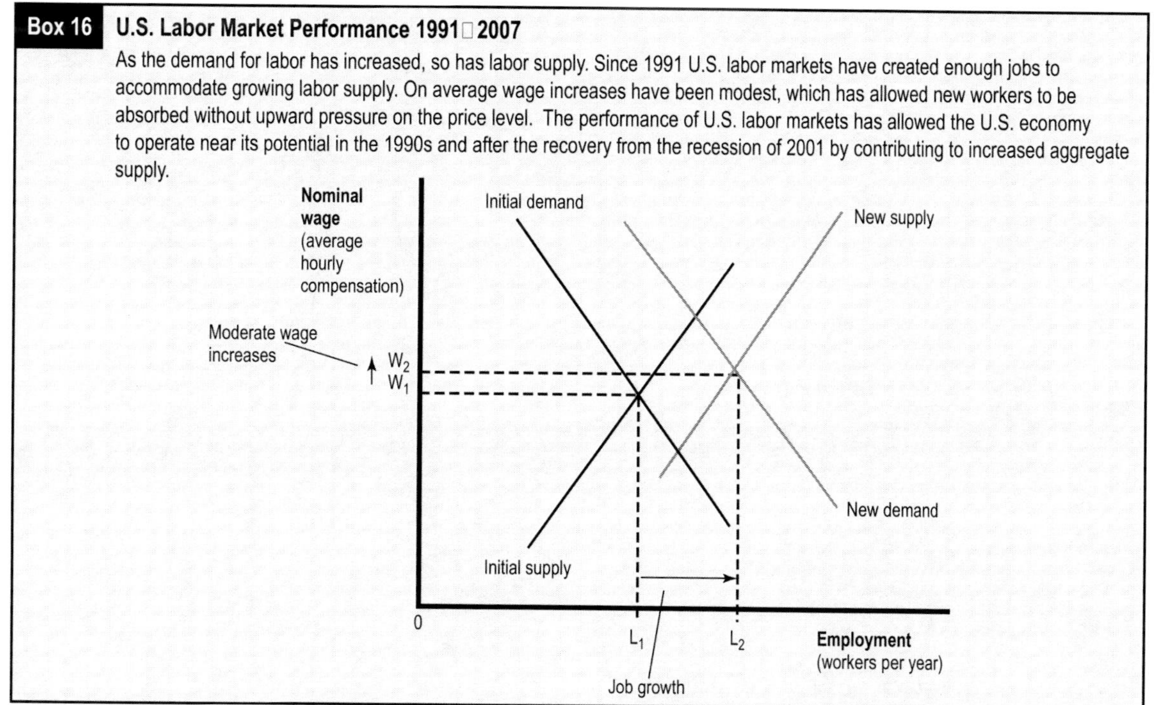

quarter of 2007 and the first quarter of 2009, over 5 million jobs evaporated in the United States and labor compensation in some sectors of the economy, hard-hit by the decline in aggregate demand, was declining. So, when the demand for labor fails to keep up with the growth in the supply of labor, we can also have job losses and wage declines in the economy.

A Recap: Economic Fluctuations and Their Causes

Recessions can be caused by *both* decreases in aggregate supply and decreases in aggregate demand. A recession induced by a decrease in aggregate supply is likely to be accompanied by *both* inflation and excessive unemployment. A recession caused by a decrease in aggregate demand will result in both excessive unemployment and some downward pressure on the price level. Except for very severe economic contractions (such as the Great Depression of the 1930s), there's usually little, if any, decline in the price level during a typical recession.

Inflation can be explained by either increases in aggregate demand or decreases in aggregate supply. Both demand-pull and cost-push inflation occur, and sometimes both occur simultaneously.

In other chapters, we carefully examine the underlying forces that cause aggregate demand and aggregate supply to fluctuate. A good understanding of these forces is essential in formulating macroeconomic stabilization policies.

Summary

1. Aggregate demand is a relationship between the price level and the aggregate quantity of final products demanded that is depicted by an aggregate demand curve. Aggregate supply is a relationship between the price level and the aggregate quantity of final products supplied that is depicted by an aggregate supply curve.
2. An aggregate demand curve slopes downward because increases in the price level can result in decreases in real wealth, increases in real interest rates, and changes in prices of exports and imports that decrease people's willingness and ability to purchase a nation's aggregate output of final products.
3. An aggregate supply curve slopes upward because the unit costs of additional production tend to increase as more is produced over a given year. The aggregate supply curve is quite flat when the economy has considerable slack, but it is very steep when the economy is operating above the level of aggregate production corresponding to potential real GDP.
4. A change in aggregate demand is a change in the relationship between the price level and aggregate quantity demanded caused by something other than a change in the price level. An increase in aggregate demand is represented by an outward shift of the aggregate demand curve, while a decrease in aggregate demand is represented by an inward shift of the aggregate demand curve. Aggregate demand can change in response to changes in real interest rates; the quantity of money in circulation; the foreign exchange rate of the dollar; government purchases, taxes, or transfers; and factors influencing the demand for exports.
5. A change in aggregate supply is a change in the relationship between the price level and aggregate quantity supplied caused by something other than a change in the price level. An increase in aggregate supply is represented by an outward shift of the aggregate supply curve, while a decrease in aggregate supply is represented by an inward shift of the aggregate supply curve. Changes in aggregate supply result from changes in input prices, changes in the quantity and quality of inputs, and advances in technology.
6. A macroeconomic equilibrium is attained for the economy when the aggregate quantity demanded equals the aggregate quantity supplied at the prevailing price level. Under macroeconomic equilibrium, there are no unintended inventory changes that can cause changes in business orders for new goods or services.
7. Equilibrium real GDP can differ from potential real GDP. When equilibrium GDP is less than potential real GDP, a recessionary GDP gap equal to the difference exists. When equilibrium real GDP exceeds potential real GDP, an inflationary GDP gap equal to the difference exists.
8. Decreases in aggregate demand put downward pressure on real GDP and the price level, while increases in aggregate demand put upward pressure on real GDP and the price level. A recession can be caused by a decrease in aggregate demand or a decrease in aggregate supply.
9. Inflation can be caused by continual increases in aggregate demand (demand-pull inflation) or by continual decreases in aggregate supply (cost-push inflation).
10. Decreases in aggregate supply exert upward pressure on the price level and downward pressure on real GDP, while increases in aggregate supply exert downward pressure on the price level and upward pressure on real GDP.

Concept Review

1. What is aggregate demand, and how is it depicted by an aggregate demand curve? List some major influences on aggregate demand that can cause it to increase or decrease.
2. Explain the shape of an aggregate supply curve, and list the major influences that can cause aggregate supply to change.
3. Under what circumstances will an economy be in macroeconomic equilibrium?
4. Other things being equal, how will an increase in aggregate demand affect the economy? How is the economy affected by an increase in aggregate supply?

Problems and Applications

1. An increase in aggregate demand occurs. Under what circumstances would you expect the increase in aggregate demand to increase real GDP while having little or no effect on the price level of the economy? 1, 4

2. Suppose potential real GDP in the current quarter is $5,000 billion and equilibrium real GDP in the current quarter is also $5,000 billion. There's a sharp increase in the demand for U.S. exports during the year. Other things being equal, forecast the effect of that increase on unemployment and inflation in the economy. 1, 4

3. Assume that an economy exists in which all assets held by the public are automatically adjusted for inflation or deflation whenever the price level changes, there's no international trade, and real interest rates don't change when the price level changes. What would the aggregate demand curve for such an economy look like? 1

4. Imagine that the economy is currently operating at full employment. At the beginning of the year, all nuclear power plants are shut down because of protests about the risk of environmental contamination. As power companies shift to more expensive sources of electricity, the price of electricity triples. Predict the effect of the power plant closings on macroeconomic equilibrium. 2, 4

5. Suppose that, after a period of labor unrest, the workers in a nation succeed in getting governing authorities to order a 25 percent increase in nominal hourly wages. Other things being equal, predict the impact of this settlement on macroeconomic equilibrium for the economy. Under what circumstances will the increase in the wage level reduce labor earnings? 2, 4

6. Suppose the economy is in a deep recession. After extensive negotiations, labor unions and all other workers agree to a 25 percent cut in nominal wages at the beginning of the next year. Use a graph to show the impact of the wage cut on macroeconomic equilibrium. 3, 4

7. Suppose the aggregate supply curve for an economy is a flat line. What would this imply about the relationship between real GDP and the price level? Show how a decrease in aggregate demand will affect the economy if the aggregate supply curve is a flat line. 2, 4

8. Suppose the economy is currently in a deep recession. The Federal Reserve System, which influences the supply of credit, takes actions to lower real interest rates. As real interest rates fall, business firms increase their demand for investment goods. Use a graph to show how the increase in demand can pull the economy out of the recession with little or no resulting inflation. 4

9. Suppose there's a severe drought in a nation whose agricultural output accounts for a large percentage of real GDP. Show the impact of the drought on the nation's aggregate supply curve and its macroeconomic equilibrium. Why is the drought likely to result in both inflation and a recession? 3, 4

10. Typically, there are increases in both aggregate demand and aggregate supply for a growing economy. Use aggregate demand—aggregate supply analysis to show how aggregate demand can increase in an economy without causing inflation if the quantity and productivity of resources are also growing. 3, 4

What Caused the Recession of 1990-1991?

In July 1990, the longest peacetime expansion in the history of the United States came to an abrupt halt. It was followed by eight months of declining real GDP and a relatively weak recovery that began in March 1991. During the first 12 months of the recovery, economic growth averaged less than 2 percent per year.

Although the beginning of the recession coincided with the beginning of the Gulf War and a consequent temporary run-up in the price of oil, it is now clear that the fundamental cause of the recession was a decline in aggregate demand. The following factors contributed to decreasing aggregate demand in 1990 and 1991.

1. *Growing corporate and household debt and new tax laws that increased borrowing costs.* The 1980s left a legacy of large debt burdens for consumers and corporations that decreased their willingness to spend or to take on new debt. The ratio of household interest payments to income had climbed to 18 percent by 1989. Many corporations had borrowed heavily in the late 1980s to restructure their operations. Moreover, tax law changes that were enacted in 1986 increased the cost of borrowing to consumers by limiting the deductibility of interest payments and to investors by changing the depreciation rules.

2. *A credit crunch.* Because of an increase in bank failures and more stringent regulatory standards for banks, financing for new business ventures became more difficult by 1990. The growing reluctance of banks to make loans constrained the growth of aggregate demand.

3. *Declining spending for defense and constraints on the growth of government spending.* The end of the cold war in the early 1990s resulted in significant reductions in defense spending that had particularly adverse effects in the states of Connecticut, Virginia, Massachusetts, and California, whose economies had many defense-related industries. In addition, demands that the federal budget deficit be kept under control led to federal tax increases in 1991 and prevented new government spending from adding significantly to aggregate demand. In many states, slowdowns led to tax increases and reductions in state and local government spending that also adversely affected aggregate demand.

4. *Industry restructuring.* Because of increased global competition, many industries were compelled to restructure in the early 1990s so as to remain profitable and survive. The restructuring involved attempts to increase productivity by reorganizing, adapting to changing technology, and reducing the size of their work forces. The restructuring contributed to job losses and to a decline in the rate of formation of new jobs. There was also a slowdown in the

construction industry, as a combination of demographic changes and tax law changes decreased the demand for new homes. Overbuilding of office space in the 1980s resulted in a decrease in commercial construction as markets worked off the surplus of space. As the demand for new homes and new office space declined, so too did the demand for furniture and other durable goods.

The effects of all these events were to decrease aggregate demand in 1990 and early 1991, while contributing to a slow recovery through most of 1992. When the recovery finally gained steam in early 1993, much of the growth in real GDP came as a result of an increase in productivity rather than an increase in jobs. Corporate downsizing resulted in the retention of the most productive workers and thus increased worker productivity. However, unemployment rates remained stubbornly high in late 1992 and 1993 because many large corporations were still downsizing. The recovery from the recession of 1990-1991 was going down as one of the weakest recoveries in history.

Chapter

25

Aggregate Demand—Aggregate Supply Analysis of Economic Fluctuations and Growth

How resilient is the U.S. economy—can it automatically stay on a steady path of growth, close to full employment? What would happen to the economy if the stock market were to crash again, as it did in 1929? Can there be another depression as serious and as long-lived as the Great Depression of the 1930s? Between 2007 and 2009, there was, in fact, a major recession that some were referring to as the first "great recession" of the 21st century. However, despite a substantial decline in aggregate demand, unemployment rates in 2009 were not nearly as high as those of the 1930s depression, when one out of every four workers was jobless. Why are we likely to be in for an unfortunate combination of both inflation and increased unemployment if the economy overheats? What effect will a rise or fall in the international value of the dollar have on the economy? Why is economic growth important in increasing living standards and keeping inflation under control? We're now ready to use macroeconomic analysis to answer questions like these.

In this chapter, we'll use aggregate demand—aggregate supply analysis to understand why the economy is sometimes in macroeconomic equilibrium at levels of real GDP that either fall short of or exceed potential real GDP. We'll also show how the economy is affected by increases or decreases in nominal wages or fluctuations in the price of fuel, and how these changes can affect the inflation rate and employment. We'll also examine how changes in the foreign exchange rate of the dollar can affect macroeconomic equilibrium. Finally, we'll use the analysis to further understand economic growth and its impact on living standards.

Concept Preview

After reading this chapter, you should be able to

1. Understand the classical model of macroeconomic equilibrium and explain why the self-correction mechanism implied by the model doesn't always work quickly and reliably.
2. Discuss the Keynesian model of macroeconomic equilibrium and explain why Keynes thought the economy could stagnate in equilibrium at a level of real GDP well below potential real GDP.
3. Discuss the process of self-correction in an overheated economy, and explain how that process results in a wage-price spiral and a period of stagflation.
4. Explain how supply-side shocks affect the economy and understand the consequences of a supply-side recession.
5. Use aggregate demand–aggregate supply analysis to explain how changes in the international value of the dollar affect macroeconomic equilibrium.
6. Discuss the process of economic growth using aggregate demand–aggregate supply analysis.

Macroeconomic Equilibrium: The Classical Model versus the Keynesian Model

The classical economists of 19th-century England were inspired by Adam Smith's concept of the "invisible hand," which implied that individuals pursuing their own self-interest would unintentionally contribute to the general interest. David Ricardo, Thomas R. Malthus, John Stuart Mill, and other classical economists believed that prices for both products and resources would adjust quickly in markets to avoid general shortages or surpluses of goods. They also believed that the production of goods and services generated enough income to buy all the output produced—that supply created its own demand (based on the ideas of J. B. Say). According to the classical economists, if the economy was not in equilibrium at full employment, changes in prices would eventually adjust market outcomes to get the economy back to full employment without any need for government intervention to stimulate aggregate demand. The economy would self-correct to assure equilibrium at potential real GDP.

The views of the classical economists were naturally subject to criticism during the Great Depression of the 1930s, when much of the world appeared hopelessly stuck in macroeconomic equilibrium at a level of real GDP much lower than potential real GDP. At the trough of the Great Depression in the United States, one out of every four workers was unemployed. It was during this period that the great English economist John Maynard Keynes (1883–1946) developed a new theory of macroeconomic equilibrium. Keynes (pronounced "Kains") presented reasons for believing that the economy could stagnate in equilibrium at a level of output well below the level that could provide full employment. He argued that, during a recession, government should use its powers to increase aggregate demand so as to restore full employment.

The controversy between the Keynesian (pronounced "Kainsian") and classical views of the economy still rages. Many modern economists believe that the powers of the economy to regulate itself have become stronger in recent years. These economists argue that attempts to stabilize the economy through changes in government spending or tax policy, or changes in the supply of money and credit, often do more to destabilize the economy than to stabilize it.

The Classical Model of Macroeconomic Equilibrium

1 When an economy is in macroeconomic equilibrium with excessive unemployment, why don't the markets where there are excess supplies reequilibrate to eliminate the surpluses? In other words, how is it that an economy can stay locked in a deep depression, as it did during the Great Depression of the 1930s? This problem perplexed economists for much of the 19th and early 20th centuries.

Economists of the 19th century believed that, when the level of aggregate demand was insufficient to purchase the output of final products that would provide full employment, the resulting surpluses in input markets would cause input prices to decline. The declines in nominal wages, interest rates, rents, and other input prices would then increase aggregate supply to increase equilibrium real GDP. The model of macroeconomic equilibrium of the 19th-century classical economists maintained that price flexibility in the economy would prevent it from stagnating in a macroeconomic equilibrium with excessive unemployment.

The classical model of macroeconomic equilibrium implied that excessive unemployment and unused productive capacity would set up market forces that would eventually increase real GDP and eliminate cyclical unemployment. In other words, the economy has a self-correcting mechanism that keeps it working at full employment most of the time. A key assumption of the classical model is that in response to decreases in aggregate demand causing cyclical unemployment, nominal wages and other input prices fall sufficiently to shift aggregate supply outward enough to restore full employment quickly.

Think about why a decrease in aggregate demand reduces equilibrium real GDP and causes unemployment to increase. Given the level of input prices, a decline in aggregate demand reduces the profitability of supplying final products in markets. The decline in profitability causes firms to reduce output. A decrease in aggregate demand moves the economy to a new macroeconomic equilibrium at which real GDP is lower. Of course, the decrease in real GDP that occurs in response to the decrease in aggregate demand also implies a decrease in the demand for labor and other inputs used to make products available. What would happen if nominal wages and other input prices (measured by some index of *input* prices) *also* fell when the price level fell? Such declines would reduce the unit costs of any given level of aggregate production and would, therefore, make it more profitable for firms to supply output.

Declines in nominal wages and other input prices cause the aggregate supply curve to shift outward. For example, suppose a decrease in aggregate demand moves an economy initially in equilibrium at potential real GDP (implying full employment) to a new equilibrium along the initial aggregate supply curve. As shown in Box 1, the economy moves from point E_1 to point E'. According to the classical economists, the equilibrium at point E' is only temporary. The decrease in aggregate demand that caused real GDP to decline below potential real GDP results in cyclical unemployment. The resulting surplus of labor then causes nominal wages to decline. As this happens, the aggregate supply curve shifts out. The increase in aggregate supply continues until nominal wages decline enough to restore full employment. Downward flexibility of nominal wages and other input prices, including interest rates, ensures that the economy will soon return to a new equilibrium at point E_2.

The increase in aggregate supply in response to the decrease in nominal wages and other input prices (including interest rates) puts upward pressure on real GDP and further downward pressure on the price level. This counteracts the unfavorable effects on real GDP of the initial decrease in aggregate demand.

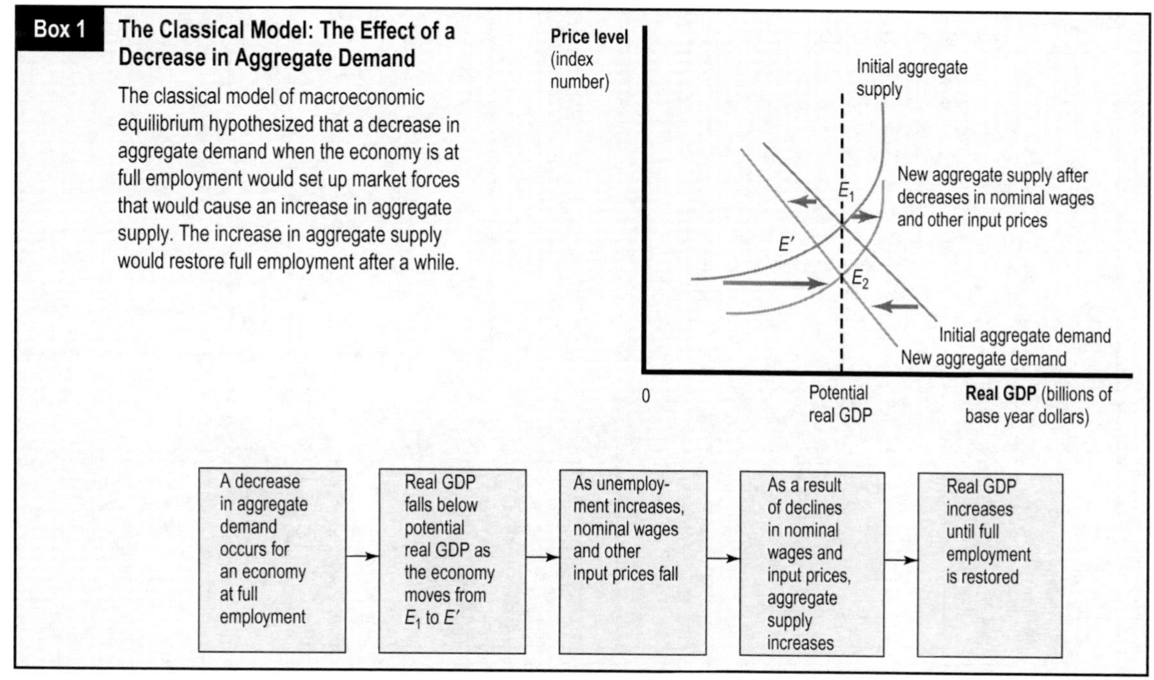

Box 1
The Classical Model: The Effect of a Decrease in Aggregate Demand
The classical model of macroeconomic equilibrium hypothesized that a decrease in aggregate demand when the economy is at full employment would set up market forces that would cause an increase in aggregate supply. The increase in aggregate supply would restore full employment after a while.
Price level (index number)
Initial aggregate supply
New aggregate supply after decreases in nominal wages and other input prices
E1
E'
E2
Initial aggregate demand
New aggregate demand
0
Potential real GDP
Real GDP (billions of base year dollars)
A decrease in aggregate demand occurs for an economy at full employment
Real GDP falls below potential real GDP as the economy moves from E1 to E'
As unemployment increases, nominal wages and other input prices fall
As a result of declines in nominal wages and input prices, aggregate supply increases
Real GDP increases until full employment is restored

The logical conclusion of the classical model is that equilibrium real GDP can never deviate for long below the level that corresponds to the full employment of labor and all other economic resources, as long as product prices, input prices, and interest rates are flexible. As long as nominal wages are flexible, they must fall enough to eliminate cyclical unemployment.

The key to the classical model is the assumption that *prices and quantities in all markets are flexible*. The classical economists presumed that price flexibility would eliminate all surpluses or shortages in markets and that markets were competitive enough to adjust to changes in economic conditions. If markets quickly adjusted to changes in economic conditions, widespread surpluses of labor would be rare and excessive unemployment would be unlikely.

The classical model also implies that an *increase* in aggregate demand will put upward pressure on real GDP only temporarily if the increase causes the economy to overheat. An increase in aggregate demand can cause the economy to exceed its potential real GDP as overtime labor is used and physical facilities are operated around the clock. This will, of course, put upward pressure on the price level. An increase in aggregate demand moves the economy to a temporary equilibrium at a level of real GDP that exceeds the level for which full employment is attained. Because of the increase in aggregate demand, the economy becomes temporarily overheated. As shown in Box 2, the economy moves along its initial aggregate supply curve from point E_1 to point E' . The resulting increase in demand for labor puts upward pressure on nominal wages (and other input prices). Temporary shortages occur in labor markets until nominal wages rise sufficiently. The wage increase continues shifting the aggregate supply curve inward until labor shortages have been eliminated. The aggregate supply curve shifts inward until equilibrium is attained at point E_2, at which equilibrium real GDP has declined to potential real GDP corresponding to full employment. At the final equilibrium at point E_2, both nominal wages and the price level have increased.

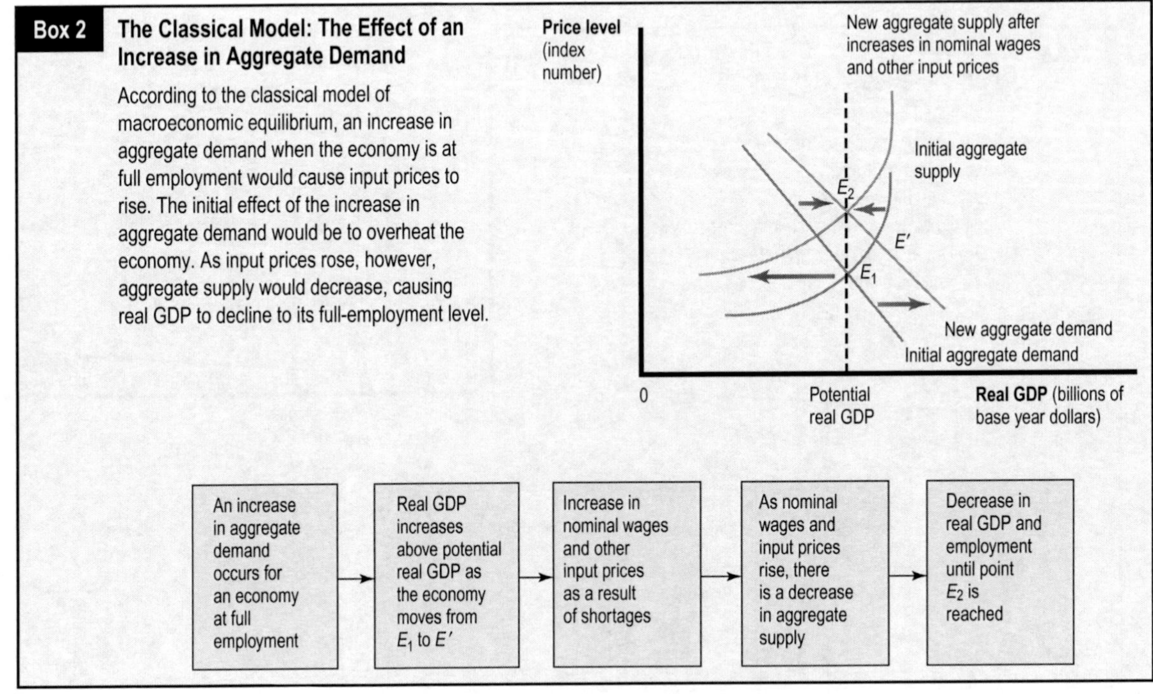

The Classical Model: The Effect of an Increase in Aggregate Demand

According to the classical model of macroeconomic equilibrium, an increase in aggregate demand when the economy is at full employment would cause input prices to rise. The initial effect of the increase in aggregate demand would be to overheat the economy. As input prices rose, however, aggregate supply would decrease, causing real GDP to decline to its full-employment level.

The Classical Long-Run Aggregate Supply Curve

According to the classical economists, equilibrium real GDP can deviate from potential real GDP only temporarily. Any recessionary or inflationary real GDP gaps are quickly eliminated through changes in aggregate supply that eliminate the discrepancy between equilibrium and potential real GDP. The classical economists therefore argued that except for short-lived episodes the economy could be expected to achieve equilibrium at full employment. The long-run aggregate supply curve (LRAS) shows the relationship between the aggregate quantity supplied and the price level that would be observed if nominal wages and other money prices were flexible enough to allow the classical self-correction mechanism to work. Because equilibrium real GDP over the long run would equal potential real GDP if all prices were flexible, the long-run aggregate supply curve would be a vertical line corresponding to potential (full-employment) real GDP.

The graph in Box 3 shows the long-run aggregate supply curve for the economy. This curve can be thought of as simply indicating the economy's potential real GDP at any point in time. Points on the long-run aggregate supply curve correspond to full employment. Points of temporary equilibrium (such as *E′* in Boxes 1 and 2) are not points on the LRAS.

In the long run, an increase in real GDP is possible only if potential real GDP increases. When potential GDP increases, the long-run aggregate supply curve shifts outward. In the long run, increases in productive potential arise from improvements in productivity, resource availability, technology, and other supply-side forces. Although the economy occasionally produces more than potential GDP over the short run when aggregate demand increases, an increase in aggregate demand cannot permanently increase output beyond potential GDP over the long run. Temporary inflationary GDP gaps are eventually eliminated by increases in wages and prices.

Outward shifts of the long-run aggregate supply curve imply growth in potential and equilibrium real GDP on average over time. Increases in aggregate demand contribute to short-term economic growth because such increases give businesses the confidence necessary to make investments that expand the economy's productive capacity. Annual shifts in aggregate demand therefore exert an influence on the year-to-year performance of the economy. Ultimately, however, the growth of an economy depends on the expansion of its productive capacity and is therefore a supply-side phenomenon. Growth in aggregate demand can prevent an economy from falling into a recession and can occasionally cause the economy to exceed its potential temporarily, but the real engine of economic growth is an outward-shifting long-run aggregate supply curve.

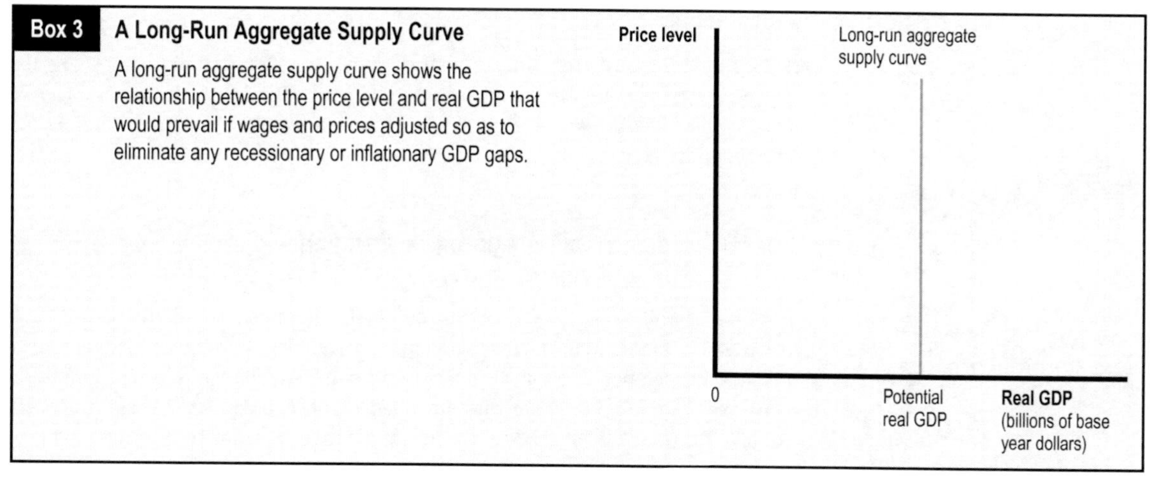

Box 3 A Long-Run Aggregate Supply Curve

A long-run aggregate supply curve shows the relationship between the price level and real GDP that would prevail if wages and prices adjusted so as to eliminate any recessionary or inflationary GDP gaps.

The Keynesian Model of Macroeconomic Equilibrium

2 Although the logic of the classical model is correct, the evidence indicates that nominal wage levels, which measure unit labor costs (an important determinant of aggregate supply because they constitute more than 70 percent of production costs) are quite inflexible over a period of one year. This is not to say that nominal wages never fall in response to sharp declines in aggregate demand. Based on past evidence, however, nominal wages don't appear to fall *enough* to increase the profitability of production and aggregate supply sufficiently to restore full employment when the U.S. economy operates below potential real GDP. As a consequence, declines in aggregate demand tend to reduce real GDP in the United States without setting up a process of rapid self-correction. For example, although there was a 21 percent decrease in nominal wages between the end of 1929 and 1933, that decrease wasn't sufficient to shift the aggregate supply curve outward enough to restore full employment.

The reason for downwardly inflexible nominal wages isn't completely understood. However, it's believed that labor market characteristics, such as long-term wage contracts and seniority rules dictating which workers are laid off first, prevent wages from falling quickly in response to declines in labor demand. Whatever the reasons for downward rigidity of the nominal wage level in the United States and other economies, the phenomenon is well-documented.

Downward nominal wage rigidity plays an important role in the theory of macroeconomic equilibrium developed by John Maynard Keynes. Keynes believed that an economy could become locked in a macroeconomic equilibrium with high cyclical unemployment, and that the classical self-correcting mechanism wouldn't work. The Keynesian model of macroeconomic equilibrium assumes that, because of rigid nominal wages, the economy's self-correction mechanism can't be expected to automatically restore full employment when aggregate demand declines. The Keynesian model implies that corrective measures are necessary to restore aggregate demand to the level that ensures full employment and to avoid declines in aggregate real income and employment opportunities. Therefore, government policies influencing aggregate demand are necessary. When there's considerable slack in the economy, increases in aggregate demand result primarily in increases in real GDP, with little upward pressure on the price level.

Reductions in aggregate demand may never reduce the price level enough to get to points on the long-run aggregate supply curve! Even over relatively long periods, downward rigidity in prices and wages can prevent the economy's self-correcting mechanism from working. This situation is what Keynes had in mind when he said, "In the long run we are all dead." Recessions often require short-run action to increase aggregate demand, because the long-run self-correcting mechanism of the economy doesn't work well in the downward direction.

Modern Keynesians also believe that because of the way labor contracts are negotiated, over a period of one year nominal wages tend to be upwardly inflexible as well. This tends to reduce the effectiveness of the economy's self-correcting mechanism during periods in which the economy is overheated.

The Great Depression: Using Aggregate Demand—Aggregate Supply Analysis to Understand What Happened

The Great Depression hit the U.S. economy suddenly and unexpectedly. In early 1929, the economy was operating at full employment, with an unemployment rate of only 3.2 percent. Then, in October 1929, the stock market crashed. The value of corporate stocks plunged to two-thirds of the value that prevailed early in the year. Panicky traders sold stocks to meet the demands of creditors who wanted their loans paid off. Many loans were uncollectible, and thousands of banks failed. In an era without federal deposit insurance, households lost their savings when banks could not meet demands for withdrawals. The end result of the decline in wealth was a massive decline in aggregate demand, which was particularly acute for housing and construction. Thousands of firms in the building industry were forced out of business.

A number of mistakes made by policymakers aggravated the decline in aggregate demand and prevented the economy from recovering. The supply of money in circulation was sharply reduced as a result of bank failures, and the nation's monetary authorities made no effort to reverse the trend. As the money supply declined, spending declined. Interest rates remained high as the supply of loanable funds dried up.

Box 4 shows the aggregate demand and aggregate supply curves prevailing in early 1929, prior to the stock market crash, and then in 1933 at the trough of the Great Depression. The initial equilibrium at point E_1 corresponds to potential real GDP in 1929. After the decline in aggregate demand, the unemployment rate soared, and a substantial recessionary GDP gap opened up. The price level fell in 1930. In response to the general decline in the demand for inputs, there was some decline in input prices—just as the classical economists would have predicted. As nominal wages, land prices, and other input prices declined, there was an increase in the aggregate supply, as suggested in the classical model of macroeconomic equilibrium. However, the increase in aggregate supply was *not* sufficient to restore full employment. In 1933 the economy was in equilibrium at point E_2, at a level of real GDP well below potential real GDP.

By 1933 one out of every four workers was unemployed, and real GDP was only 73 percent of its 1929 value. The price level had fallen to about 75 percent of its 1929 value. The classical self-correcting mechanism failed to restore full employment, and for most of the 1930s the economy stagnated in equilibrium at well below potential real GDP.

By 1933 the amount of money in circulation declined by 20 percent of the amount available in 1929, and prices of real estate and other assets fell. More policy blunders were

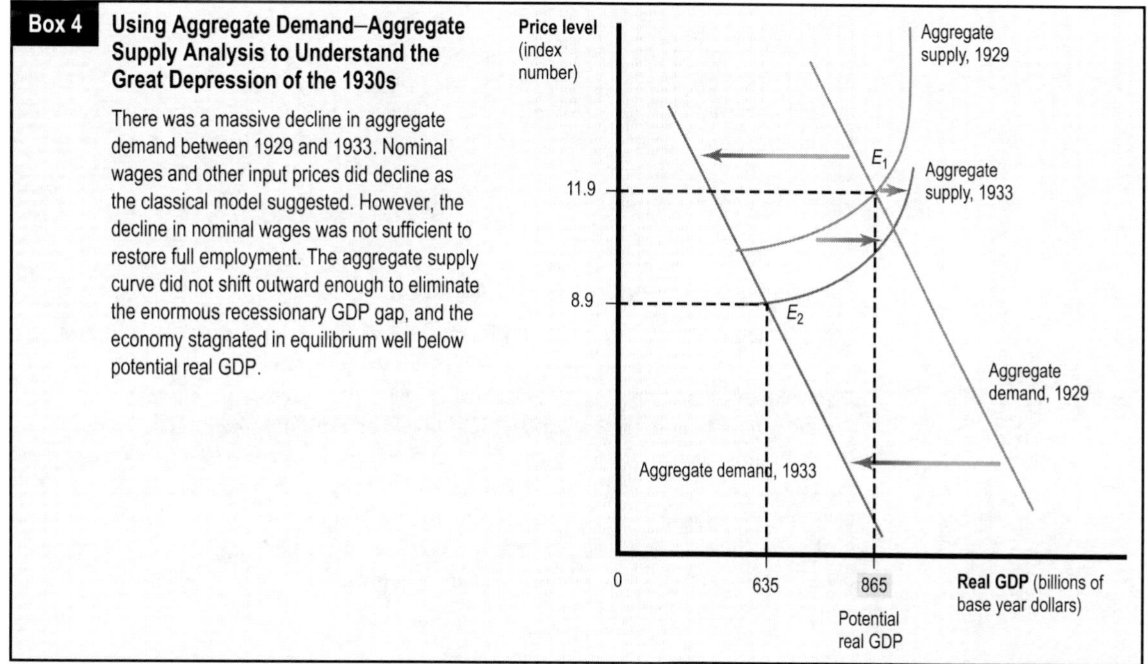

Box 4 Using Aggregate Demand–Aggregate Supply Analysis to Understand the Great Depression of the 1930s

There was a massive decline in aggregate demand between 1929 and 1933. Nominal wages and other input prices did decline as the classical model suggested. However, the decline in nominal wages was not sufficient to restore full employment. The aggregate supply curve did not shift outward enough to eliminate the enormous recessionary GDP gap, and the economy stagnated in equilibrium well below potential real GDP.

made that made the contraction worse. Congress passed the Smoot-Hawley tariff, which was designed to stimulate U.S. industry by protecting it from foreign competition. Instead, the tariff had the opposite effect. By depriving the rest of the world of an enormous export market in the United States, it spread the recession around the world. As income and aggregate demand declined in European nations, so too did their demand for American products. The decline contributed to a further decline in aggregate demand in the United States, thus further reducing real GDP and the price level.

It was in the environment of the 1930s that Keynes developed his model of macroeconomic equilibrium, offering a unique solution to the problem of an economy stagnating in equilibrium at a level of real GDP below full employment. Keynes recommended that the government increase its purchases, even if it had to borrow to do so. Keynes reasoned that, if the government purchases component of real GDP were increased without increasing taxes, aggregate demand would increase so that the economy could move toward full employment.

Why Another Great Depression Is Unlikely

We've learned a great deal from the Great Depression, and it's unlikely that such a massive contraction can occur again. It's no longer possible to borrow extensively to purchase corporate stocks. This restraint has eased speculation in the stock market and reduced the risk of overinflated stock prices. The monetary authorities are now more careful about assuring an adequate supply of money and credit in times of financial stress. When stock prices collapsed in 1987, Alan Greenspan, the chairman of the Board of Governors of the Federal Reserve System, was careful to assure banks and the financial community that the system would provide the money and credit banks needed to meet their withdrawal demands. Similarly, during the financial crisis of 2007-2009, the Federal Reserve System was taking measures to extend credit by purchasing asset-backed securities and government bonds, and pumping money into the banking system.

Despite the increase in bank failures in more recent years, bank deposits are insured so that household savings aren't wiped out if banks fail. However, bailing out failed banks has increased the federal budget deficit, as the government has had to increase borrowings to pay deposit insurance claims and purchase bank assets. In addition, the government purchases component of real GDP is much larger than it was in 1929. Government purchases are a much more stable component of aggregate expenditures than investment, exports, or even consumption. When we study stabilization policies, you see that the federal government budget contains built-in stabilizers, such as unemployment insurance, that maintain private spending even when earnings decline. Because of both institutional changes in the economy and improved methods of stabilization in times of crisis, aggregate demand is much less likely to decline as sharply as it did in the period 1930–33.

An Overheated Economy and Stagflation

3 Sometimes aggregate demand increases enough so that, at the equilibrium level of real GDP, aggregate quantity supplied exceeds potential real GDP. When that happens, the economy booms and inflationary pressures build up. An economy can produce more than its potential real GDP in a year. An *inflationary GDP gap* prevails for the economy when equilibrium real GDP exceeds potential real GDP. The inflationary gap puts upward pressure on the price level, which then reduces aggregate quantity demanded as a new equilibrium is attained. Eventually, the inflationary gap is eliminated. Now, by analyzing shifts in aggregate supply, we can obtain greater insight into what is likely to occur in the economy when an inflationary gap prevails.

The process of reequilibration that results when an inflationary gap prevails involves shifts in aggregate supply that can cause the economy to experience stagnation or declines in the growth of real GDP at the same time that the price level rises. If the price level increases enough during the year, business firms find it profitable to increase production to levels that actually *exceed* the economy's potential. An economy *overheats* when it operates beyond its potential in much the same way that an engine overheats when it's run faster than its potential. When an economy is overheated, factories and offices are worked around the clock. Under these circumstances, total labor hours used during the year exceed the level that corresponds to the natural rate of unemployment. This occurs as workers put in overtime and some workers normally out of the labor force are induced to enter it.

The graph in Box 5 shows the process by which an overheated economy reequilibrates to eventually eliminate an inflationary gap. At the beginning of the year, the economy is in equilibrium at a price level of 120 and a real GDP level of $5,500 billion. Assume that potential real GDP is $5,000 billion. There is now an *inflationary* GDP gap, measured by the difference between the equilibrium real GDP of $5,500 billion and the potential real GDP level of $5,000 billion. This $500 billion inflationary GDP gap is illustrated along the horizontal axis. The current equilibrium corresponds to point *E*. Assume that during the past year the price level has increased from 112 to 120, implying inflation of just over 7 percent.

As a result of the higher prices caused by the increase in aggregate demand, workers whose wages have lagged behind the rate of inflation during the pst year are likely to demand wage increases when contract talks are opened up again. The labor market is likely to be tight when the economy is overheated, and workers will be in short supply. Under these conditions, employers are likely to grant worker demands for wage increases that at least keep pace with inflation. Similarly, materials will be in short supply in an overheated economy, and the prices of these inputs will rise over the year. *Because of increases in wages and other input prices that take place over the year in an overheated economy, the aggregate supply curve will shift inward.* As this process occurs, the economy will move toward an equilibrium, given the aggregate demand curve, at point

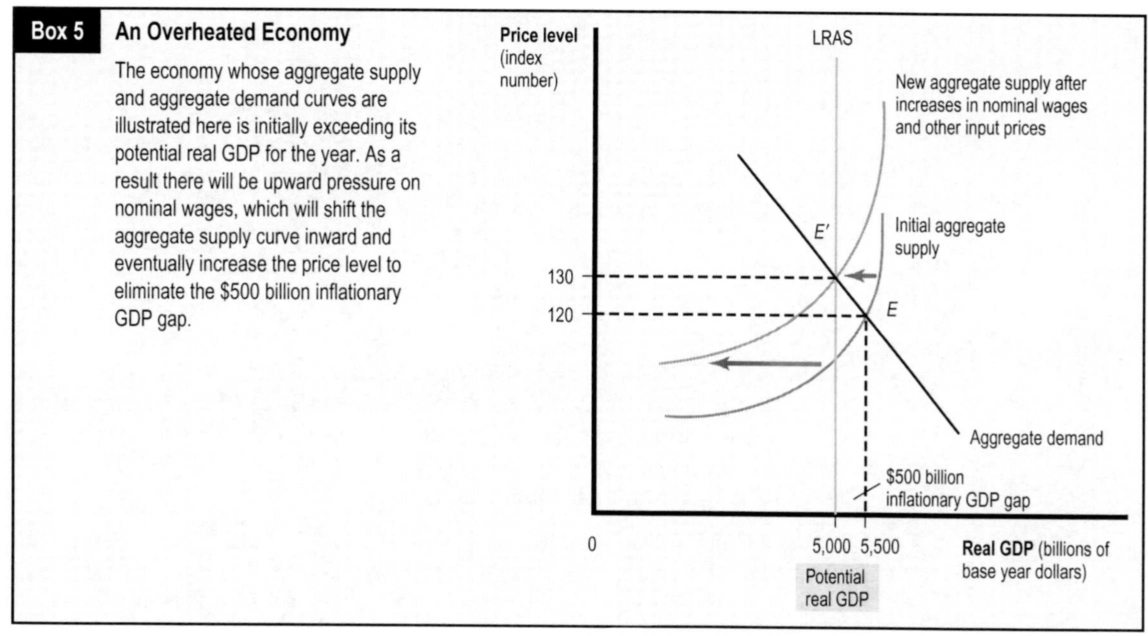

Box 5 An Overheated Economy

The economy whose aggregate supply and aggregate demand curves are illustrated here is initially exceeding its potential real GDP for the year. As a result there will be upward pressure on nominal wages, which will shift the aggregate supply curve inward and eventually increase the price level to eliminate the $500 billion inflationary GDP gap.

E' , at which real GDP falls to its potential level. But the decrease in aggregate supply *also* further increases the price level during the year! Eventually, real GDP will decline by $500 billion and the price level will increase from 120 to 130, implying 8 percent inflation. The preceding year's inflation caused the economy to stretch beyond its potential. The wage increases negotiated by workers to keep up with inflation then resulted in cost-push inflation in the following year as the aggregate supply curve steadily shifted inward.

Wage-Price Spirals in an Overheated Economy

Whenever aggregate demand is so excessive that is causes an economy to overheat, the result is an inflationary process. In some cases an economy can remain overheated for a number of years. For example, the U.S. economy was overheated between 1966 and 1968, when the government was engaged in a military buildup for the Vietnam conflict. During those years, when equilibrium real GDP exceeded potential real GDP, a process of demand-pull inflation followed by cost-push inflation had the economy in its grip. Between 1965 and 1970 inflation surged. Relatively high inflation continued in 1969 and 1970 despite a brief recession that hit the economy in 1969.

A wage-price spiral exists in the economy when higher product prices result in higher wages, which in turn increase prices still further through a decrease in aggregate supply. When a wage-price spiral exists, increases in aggregate demand cause an inflationary GDP gap, which in turn causes wages to increase. The resulting decrease in aggregate supply causes further increases in the price level. Further increases in aggregate demand then cause the price level to increase again, and the process starts all over. The process continues until the inflationary gap has been eliminated.

The U.S. economy was caught in a wage-price spiral exactly like this during the period from 1966 to 1970. From the beginning of 1966 to the end of 1969, the economy was clearly overheated, with the official unemployment rates over that four-year period averaging only 3.6 percent. Workers were in short supply, and it's likely that the economy was exceeding its potential. Inflation increased from a mere 2 percent per year in 1965 to nearly 6 percent per year in 1970. Each year workers negotiated labor contracts that pushed wages higher. In fact, workers began to anticipate inflation and usually demanded a little more in wages so their nominal wages wouldn't lose purchasing power over the next year. The result was a wage-price spiral. Cost-push inflation followed from the demand-pull inflation that overheated the economy.

Stagflation

Stagflation is the term that has been coined to describe an economy in which real GDP stagnates at a given level or actually declines from one period to the next while inflation ensues at relatively high rates. Stagflation is a combination of stagnation of economic growth in real GDP and rising prices. The process described in Box 6, as the economy moves from an equilibrium at point E to the one at E' , was one of stagflation. After the economy overheated, the consequence was a decrease in aggregate supply, which in turn caused a decrease in real GDP and an increase in the price level.

When workers start to anticipate the effect of inflation on their real wages and succeed in getting large nominal wage increases, the aggregate supply curve can shift inward enough to cause equilibrium real GDP to be below potential real GDP. This effect can be compounded, as you'll soon see, when other changes in economic conditions result in further inward shifts of the aggregate supply curve.

Stagflation implies that an economy, after overheating, can suffer from both a recession and inflation. For example, during the period 1974–75 the U.S. economy experienced a recession after achieving huge increases of 5 percent in real GDP in both 1972 and 1973.

In 1974 real GDP declined by 0.5 percent of its 1973 value, and in 1975 real GDP fell by nearly 1 percent of its 1974 value. The unemployment rate soared to 8.3 percent of the labor force in 1975. At the same time, however, inflation roared at record levels. The rate of inflation measured by the annual percentage change in the consumer price index was 11 percent in 1974 and 9.1 percent in 1975.

Stagflation occurred again in 1980, when real GDP suffered a slight decline and inflation was in high gear at an annual rate of 13.5 percent. Then, during the severe 1982 recession, real GDP fell by 2.5 percent, and in 1983 unemployment rose to 9.5 percent while inflation still continued at an annual rate of 6.1 percent.

Stagflation is particularly harmful to consumers because at the same time real GDP declines, so does the purchasing power of the dollar. As people seek to protect themselves against inflation, decision-making is distorted.

Supply-Side Shocks

4 In some cases, a supply-side shock, a sudden and unexpected shift of the aggregate supply curve, occurs. In 1973, as the economy was reequilibrating from an inflationary gap, it also got socked with a supply-side shock in the form of the OPEC oil embargo that sent the price of a key input skyrocketing. The result was an inward shift of the economy's aggregate supply curve. In 1979 higher oil prices caused another unexpected and unfavorable supply-side shock that raised prices and decreased real GDP. In August 1990, the price of crude oil skyrocketed after Iraq's invasion of Kuwait. This shock caused the price level to rise and put downward pressure on real GDP just when aggregate demand was beginning to slow its rate of outward growth.

Supply-side shocks result from either increases in input prices or decreases in the availability of resources. In the chapter Aggregate Demand and Aggregate Supply, we trace the effect of a price shock in which aggregate supply decreases as a result of an unexpected increase in the price of a key input. Let's examine the effect of a supply-side shock that results from a decrease in the availability of a key input—perhaps because of a cutoff (as opposed to a simple price increase) in the supply of oil or a disaster (an earthquake or a war) that destroys human life and capital.

The graph in Box 6 shows how the economy reacts to an unfavorable supply-side shock. Suppose the economy is initially in equilibrium at point *E* at a real GDP of $5,000 billion and a price level of 120. As aggregate supply decreases because of the reduced availability

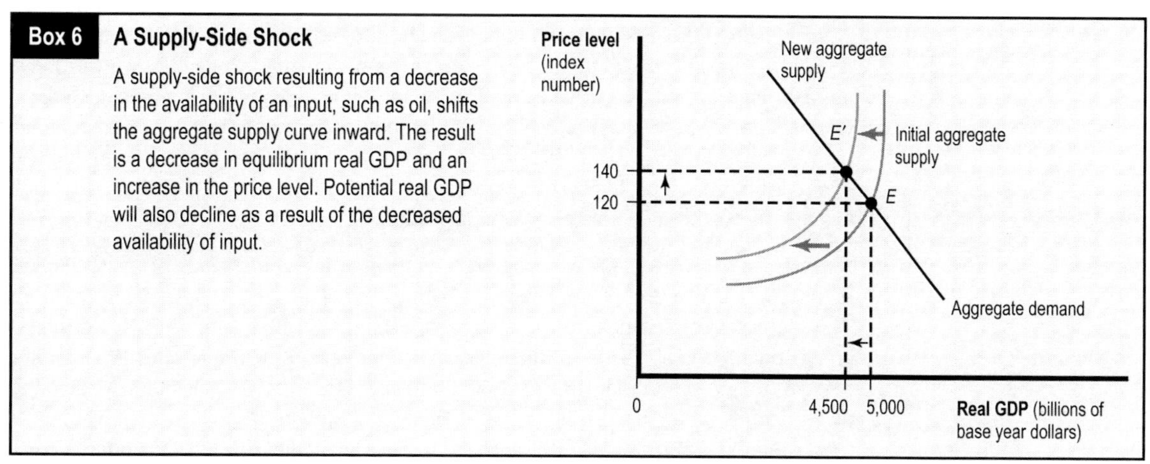

Box 6 A Supply-Side Shock

A supply-side shock resulting from a decrease in the availability of an input, such as oil, shifts the aggregate supply curve inward. The result is a decrease in equilibrium real GDP and an increase in the price level. Potential real GDP will also decline as a result of the decreased availability of input.

of resources, both potential real GDP and the level of real GDP corresponding to the economy's capacity output also decrease. The economy adjusts during the year by moving to a new equilibrium at point E' . At the new equilibrium the price level increases to 140. Notice that the effect of the shock is a *onetime* increase in the price level. Because the shock is a onetime event, it doesn't add to the inflation rate in the following year. In other words, a supply-side shock doesn't start an inflationary process in the same way as it would in an overheated economy. Note also that a supply-side shock that results from a decrease in the availability of input also reduces potential real GDP and the capacity output of the economy.

Exchange Rates and Macroeconomic Equilibrium

5 As imports and exports have increased in importance for the U.S. economy since 1960, macroeconomic equilibrium has become more sensitive to changes in the international value of the dollar. In our discussion of exchange rates in Market Transactions: Basic Supply and Demand Analysis, we see that the price of the dollar affects the selling price of our exports to foreigners, who must buy dollars to buy our goods. Other things being equal, the higher the price (the foreign exchange rate) of the dollar, the higher the price of our exports in terms of foreign currency. When the exchange rate of the dollar changes, so does the price of imported goods. For example, as the price of the dollar in terms of Japanese yen increased in 1990, Japanese imports became cheaper for American buyers. Similarly, when the price of the dollar in terms of Japanese yen fell in 1994 and 1995, Japanese imports became more expensive for Americans. The impact of changes in the international value of the dollar on macroeconomic equilibrium can be traced using aggregate demand-aggregate supply analysis.

Impact of a Higher Dollar on Aggregate Demand

When the exchange rate of the dollar increases, our exports, other things being equal, will become more expensive to foreigners, while imported goods will become less expensive for us (although there's sometimes a lag in the change in the prices of imports). Other things being equal, we expect increases in the exchange rate of the dollar against a broad group of currencies to contribute to lower net exports. As net exports decline, there is a reduction in employment in export industries and in industries facing strong competition from foreign suppliers.

An increase in exchange rates therefore decreases aggregate demand, with the extent of the decrease depending on the size of the economy's export sector and the extent to which domestic industries must compete with foreign sellers at home. A decrease in aggregate demand caused by an increase in the exchange rate of the dollar is illustrated in the graph in Box 7. As you can see, the decrease in aggregate demand results in downward pressure on both real GDP and the price level. The unemployment resulting from the decline in real GDP is concentrated in export industries and industries facing strong foreign competition from imports. From 1981 to 1985, for example, the U.S. automobile and textile industries were particularly hard hit by the high price of the dollar. U.S. agriculture, which relies heavily on export sales, was also adversely affected.

Similarly, a decrease in the exchange rate of the dollar can increase aggregate demand by increasing the demand for U.S. exports while decreasing the U.S. demand for imports. This increases employment in U.S. export industries and, after a lag, in U.S. industries that compete with imports. The decline in the exchange rate of the dollar after 1985 resulted in a boom in U.S. export industries in 1987 and 1988. However, because of the delayed effect of the decline on import prices, import demand was slow to respond, which dampened the expansionary effect. Since 2001 sharp declines in the value of the U.S. dollar against the

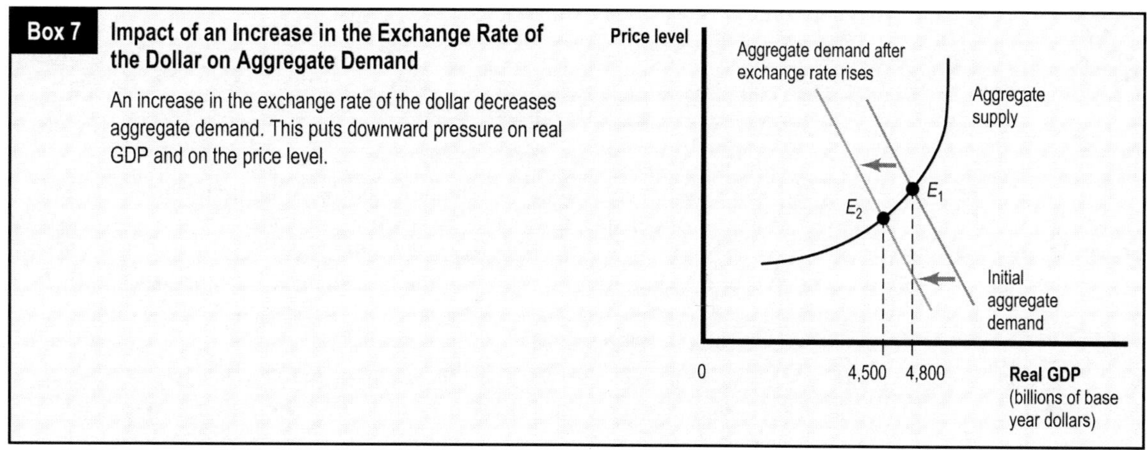
Box 7
Impact of an Increase in the Exchange Rate of the Dollar on Aggregate Demand
An increase in the exchange rate of the dollar decreases aggregate demand. This puts downward pressure on real GDP and on the price level.
Price level
Aggregate demand after exchange rate rises
Aggregate supply
E1
E2
Initial aggregate demand
0
4,500
4,800
Real GDP (billions of base year dollars)

euro, the Japanese yen, the British pound, and other currencies has contributed to an increase in the demand for U.S. exports abroad. However, despite the decline in the value of the dollar, relatively inelastic demand for imports in the United States, especially crude oil, and lags in price increases for imported products, the dollar value of U.S. imports did not substantially decline.

Impact of Changes in Exchange Rates on Aggregate Supply

Changes in exchange rates can also affect macroeconomic equilibrium through effects on aggregate supply. The United States and many other nations import substantial amounts of raw materials and machinery. An increase in the exchange rate of the dollar means that the prices of imported inputs, after adjustment for inflation, will decline. A higher-priced dollar can therefore contribute to lower input prices and cause the aggregate supply curve to shift outward, as shown in the graph in Box 8.

The increase in aggregate supply that results from a higher exchange rate of the dollar puts upward pressure on real GDP and downward pressure on the price level. A higher-valued dollar therefore contributes to both increased employment and lower inflation through its impact on aggregate supply. On the other hand, a decline in the exchange rate of the dollar contributes to a decrease in aggregate supply by raising the prices of imported inputs. The decrease in aggregate supply is a contractionary influence on the economy and puts

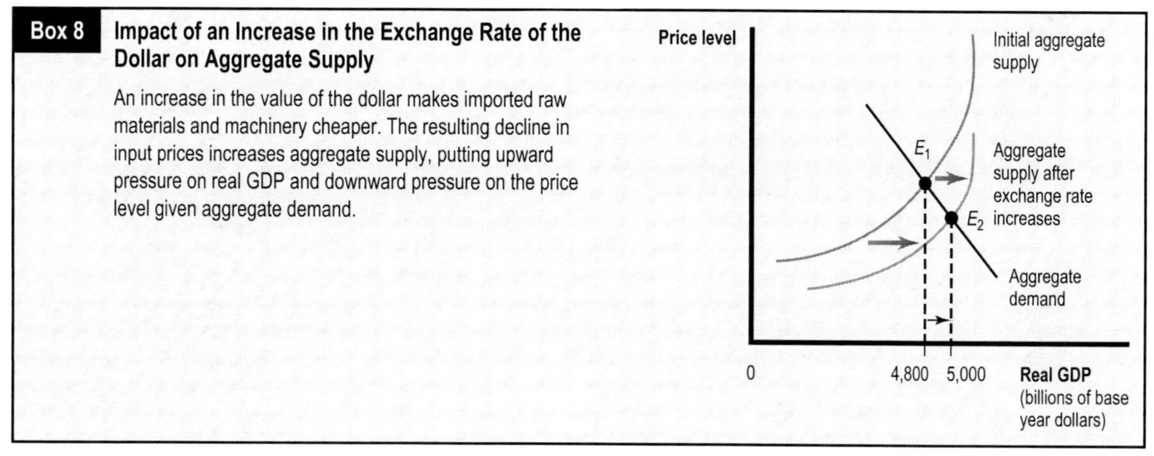
Box 8
Impact of an Increase in the Exchange Rate of the Dollar on Aggregate Supply
An increase in the value of the dollar makes imported raw materials and machinery cheaper. The resulting decline in input prices increases aggregate supply, putting upward pressure on real GDP and downward pressure on the price level given aggregate demand.
Price level
Initial aggregate supply
E1
Aggregate supply after exchange rate increases
E2
Aggregate demand
0
4,800
5,000
Real GDP (billions of base year dollars)

upward pressure on the price level. Of course, the magnitude of the supply-side effects will depend on the importance of imported inputs in production.

Conclusion: The Impact of Changes in Foreign Exchange Rates on Macroeconomic Equilibrium

As you can see from the preceding analysis, changes in exchange rates have a complex impact on macroeconomic equilibrium in the economy. A higher-priced dollar, through its effect on aggregate demand, is a contractionary influence on the economy. But through its effects on aggregate supply, the higher-priced dollar is an expansionary influence on the economy because it lowers the prices of imported inputs. Depending on whether the demand-side or supply-side effects are stronger, a higher-priced dollar can either increase or decrease equilibrium real GDP.

However, there's no doubt that a higher-priced dollar will moderate inflationary pressures in the U.S. economy. The reason for this is that both the demand-side and supply-side effects of the increase in the exchange rate put downward pressure on the equilibrium price level.

There's one other complication in the analysis that we must consider. If you've already studied the analysis of the circular flow of income and expenditure, you know that whenever net exports are negative, foreign saving in the United States must increase. An increase in the exchange rate of the dollar that contributes to a further deterioration of the U.S. balance of trade, therefore, increases the supply of foreign saving in the United States. This puts downward pressure on real interest rates by increasing the supply of loanable funds in U.S. credit markets. The lower real interest rates can increase the quantity of investment goods demanded by U.S. businesses, which increases aggregate demand in the United States. This interest rate effect moderates the contractionary influence of the negative net exports on U.S. real GDP.

The graph in Box 9 shows a case where a higher exchange rate acts to decrease equilibrium real GDP. The aggregate demand curve shifts inward in response to lower net export demand by a greater amount than the aggregate supply curve shifts outward in response to lower input prices. As real GDP declines, there's an increase in the unemployment rate in the economy.

We can analyze the impact of a decrease in the exchange rate of the dollar in a similar fashion. You know that, other things being equal, a lower-priced dollar increases demand for U.S. exports and decreases U.S. demand for imports. This tends to increase aggregate demand, putting upward pressure on U.S. real GDP and the price level. Similarly, a lower-priced dollar contributes to higher input prices as a result of increases in the prices of

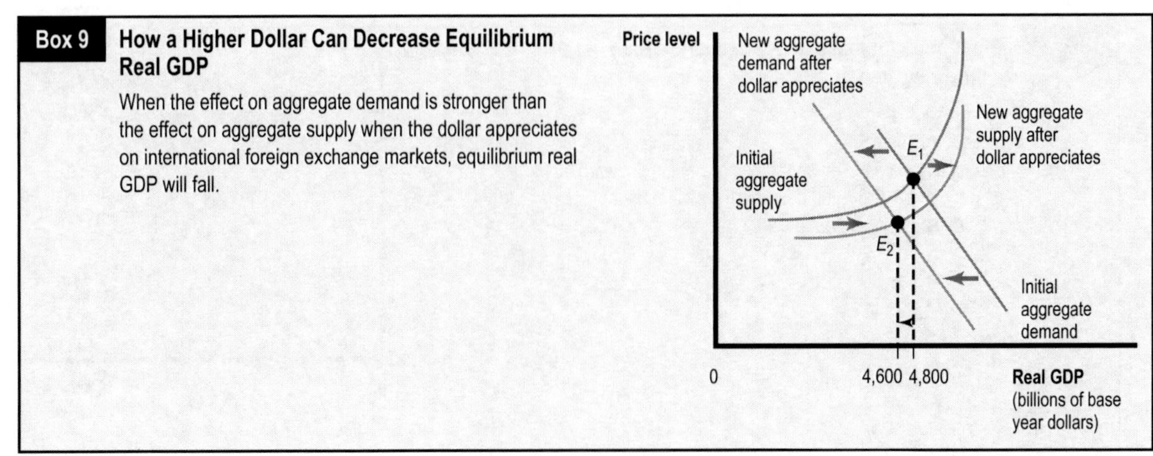
Box 9
How a Higher Dollar Can Decrease Equilibrium Real GDP
When the effect on aggregate demand is stronger than the effect on aggregate supply when the dollar appreciates on international foreign exchange markets, equilibrium real GDP will fall.
Price level
New aggregate demand after dollar appreciates
New aggregate supply after dollar appreciates
Initial aggregate supply
E1
E2
Initial aggregate demand
0
4,600 4,800
Real GDP (billions of base year dollars)

imported raw materials and machinery. As this occurs, aggregate supply will decrease, which in turn puts downward pressure on real GDP and upward pressure on the price level. We can conclude that a decrease in the exchange rate of the dollar contributes to inflationary pressures in the United States and either increases or decreases real GDP, depending on whether the demand-side or supply-side effects are stronger. As the exchange rate of the dollar declined in 1987 and 1988, the demand for U.S. exports boomed. The demand-side effects were quite strong at that time, and real GDP increased, as did inflationary pressures in the economy. The graph in Box 10 shows how a decline in the exchange rate of the dollar can result in an increase in equilibrium real GDP. In 1994 and 1995, declines in the exchange rate of the dollar also contributed to an increase in aggregate demand that helped push the U.S. economy to full employment levels in early 1995. Exports as a share of U.S. domestic production of goods increased from 22 percent in the beginning of 1994 to more than 23 percent at the beginning of 1995.

Finally, a lower-priced dollar means that foreign saving in the United States will decline as the U.S. balance of trade improves. There will be upward pressure on real interest rates in the United States in response to a decrease in the foreign supply of loanable funds in credit markets.

Macroeconomic Equilibrium in a Growing Economy

6 In a growing economy both the aggregate demand and aggregate supply curves shift outward yearly. Normally, assuming that there are no supply-side shocks, the process of economic growth results in fairly steady increases in aggregate supply. There are, of course, occasional cyclical downturns in aggregate demand. However, as population and income grow, aggregate demand on average also increases as the increased aggregate income in the economy results in more purchases by households, businesses, and government.

In any given year, the changes in equilibrium real GDP and the price level depend on how far out aggregate demand shifts relative to the outward shift in aggregate supply (from increases in the labor force or increases in labor productivity). This situation is illustrated in the graph in Box 11. If aggregate supply were fixed, the increase in aggregate demand that occurred during the year would increase the price level from 120 to 126, and equilibrium real GDP would increase from $5,000 billion to $5,200 billion. However, because aggregate supply also shifts outward, the price level ends up increasing to only 124 during the year, and real GDP increases to $5,300 billion. As you can see, outward

Box 10 **How a Lower Dollar Can Increase Equilibrium Real GDP**

When the impact of the lower dollar on aggregate demand is stronger than its effect on aggregate supply, real GDP will increase. In 1987 and 1988 the strong increase in aggregate demand resulting from increased exports dominated the U.S. economy and acted to increase equilibrium real GDP, as shown in the graph, while at the same time putting upward pressure on the price level.

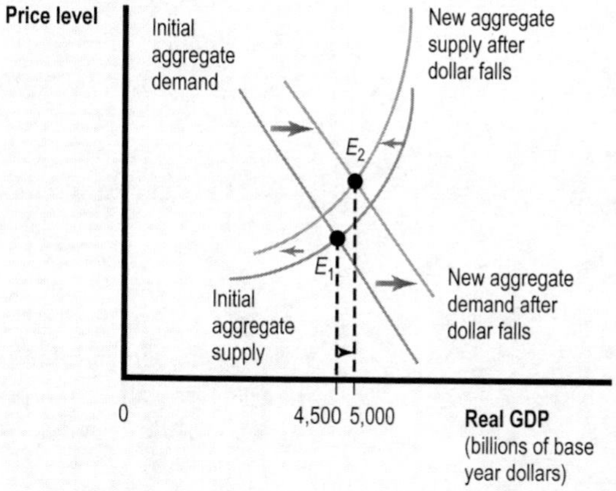

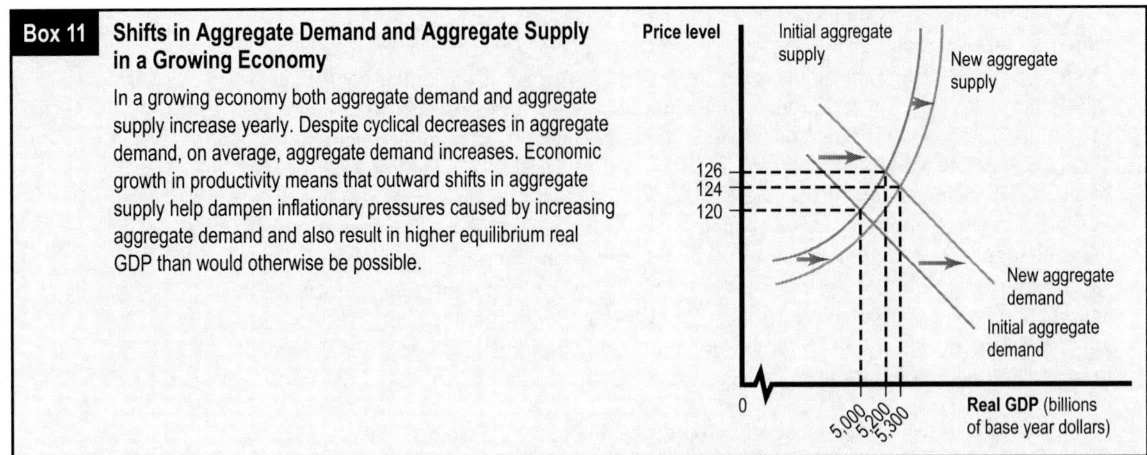
Box 11
Shifts in Aggregate Demand and Aggregate Supply in a Growing Economy
In a growing economy both aggregate demand and aggregate supply increase yearly. Despite cyclical decreases in aggregate demand, on average, aggregate demand increases. Economic growth in productivity means that outward shifts in aggregate supply help dampen inflationary pressures caused by increasing aggregate demand and also result in higher equilibrium real GDP than would otherwise be possible.
Price level
Initial aggregate supply
New aggregate supply
126
124
120
New aggregate demand
Initial aggregate demand
0
5,000
5,200
5,300
Real GDP (billions of base year dollars)

shifts in aggregate supply resulting from normal economic growth have favorable effects on macroeconomic equilibrium.

1. Supply-side shifts from economic growth moderate inflationary pressures as outward shifts in aggregate supply offset the upward pressure on the price level resulting from outward shifts in aggregate demand.

2. Supply-side shifts from economic growth increase real GDP beyond the equilibrium level that results from normal increases in aggregate demand.

Of course, in a given year what actually happens to aggregate demand depends on the spending plans of households, businesses, and governments. In some years aggregate demand shifts outward more quickly than does aggregate supply. When that is the case, the inflationary pressures from increased aggregate demand are strong. In years when there is little economic growth, increases in aggregate demand can result in substantial inflationary pressure that can overheat the economy. Given the rate of growth in aggregate supply, the more rapid the outward shift of the aggregate demand curve for the economy, the greater is the rate of inflation and the more likely it is that the economy will overheat.

Increases in productivity and the labor force also tend to increase potential real GDP. When increases in productivity and other positive supply-side influences are shifting the aggregate supply curve outward, it's less likely that an increase in aggregate demand will overheat the economy.

Noninflationary Growth

The situation depicted in Box 11 is a good representation of economic growth in the U.S. economy since the end of World War II. Real GDP has increased at a rate of about 3 percent per year on average, but growth in real GDP has also been accompanied by inflation of the price level. Real GDP increased by 188 percent from 1970 to 2004, while over the same period the price level increased by over 300 percent.

It is, however, possible to have noninflationary growth. Box 12 shows the case of an economy enjoying noninflationary growth. In this economy the growth that results from supply-side influences is strong enough to counter the inflationary effects of increases in aggregate demand that occur over time. As a result, this economy achieves equilibrium year after year at the price level of 120. At the same time, real GDP increases. For the economy illustrated in Box 12, equilibrium occurs at potential real GDP.

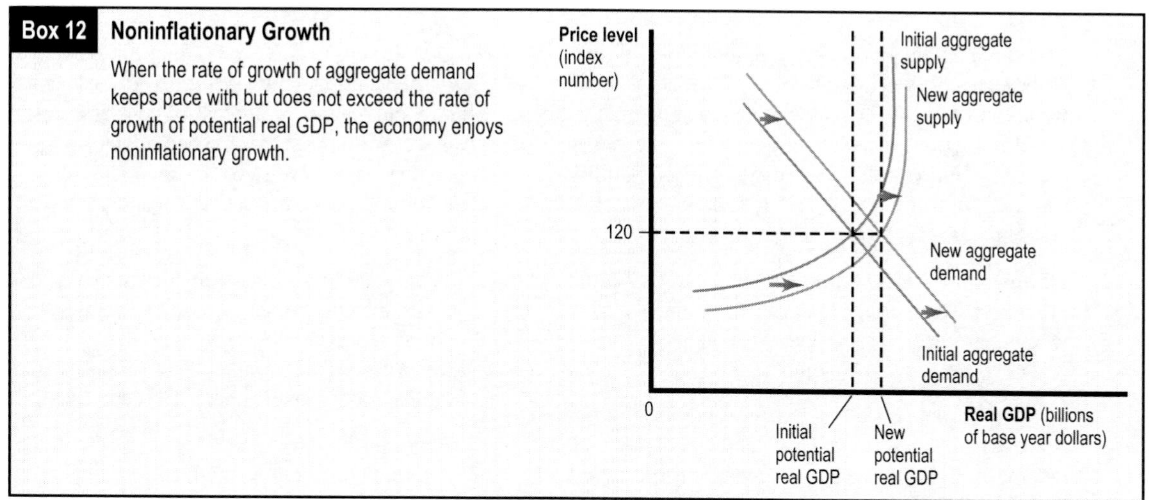

Box 12 Noninflationary Growth

When the rate of growth of aggregate demand keeps pace with but does not exceed the rate of growth of potential real GDP, the economy enjoys noninflationary growth.

Noninflationary growth is possible when economic policies restrain aggregate demand and keep it from becoming excessive. For example, controlling the growth rate of money and credit to keep it in line with the growth rate of potential real GDP is one way of achieving noninflationary growth. This policy was quite effective in West Germany from 1983 to 1989, when that nation enjoyed annual real GDP growth rates of nearly 3 percent while inflation rates were less than 1.5 percent.

In 1994 and 1995, the U.S. economy succeeded in expanding to a level of full employment while keeping inflationary pressures minimal. Increased productivity contributed to increased aggregate supply at the time. For example, in 1994, the U.S. economy grew at a healthy 4 percent, while inflation remained low at only 2.8 percent. Throughout the late 1990s, the U.S. economy was able to grow with only moderate inflation. Despite a healthy growth rate of 4.4 percent in real GDP in 2004, inflation remained in the range of 3 percent that year. Inflation remained in the range of 3 percent or less from 2004 through 2008 and, with the onset of the recession inflation during early 2009, was close to zero.

Summary

1. The classical model of macroeconomic equilibrium is based on an assumption of flexible nominal wages and prices. The classical model suggests that a self-correcting mechanism guarantees the return of the economy to full employment when equilibrium GDP moves temporarily above or below potential real GDP.
2. Downwardly rigid wages can prevent the economy's self-correcting mechanism from working when aggregate demand decreases and equilibrium real GDP falls below potential real GDP.
3. The Keynesian model of macroeconomic equilibrium explains how real GDP and aggregate real income are determined in an economy in which there is downward rigidity in nominal wages.
4. The long-run aggregate supply curve shows the relationship between the price level and real GDP that prevails if wages and prices adjust in order to eliminate any recessionary or inflationary GDP gaps. The long-run aggregate supply curve is a vertical line that intersects the horizontal axis at potential real GDP.
5. When the economy produces beyond its potential, an inflationary GDP gap prevails. When the economy overheats in this way and workers are in short supply, wage levels are likely to be renegotiated. As wage levels and other input prices increase, the aggregate supply curve prevailing for the year shifts inward. Continual inward shifts of the aggregate supply curve cause a process of cost-push inflation. A wage-price spiral exists when higher prices result in higher wage levels, which then shift the aggregate supply curve inward and result in still higher prices.
6. A supply-side shock is a sudden and unexpected shift of the prevailing aggregate supply curve. A decrease in aggregate supply caused by an increase in the price or a decrease in the availability of a key input can throw the economy into a recession.
7. Changes in the international value of the dollar can cause both the aggregate demand curve and the aggregate supply curve to shift. When the price of the dollar falls, the demand for exports increases and the demand for imports decreases, causing an outward shift of the aggregate demand curve. A fall in the price of the dollar causes aggregate supply to decrease because it increases the price of imported inputs. The overall effect is an increase in the price level, but equilibrium real GDP can either increase or decrease.
8. In a growing economy annual increases in aggregate supply help moderate inflationary pressures by counteracting the effect of increases in demand on the price level.

Concept Review

(1) Briefly summarize the implications of the classical model of macroeconomic equilibrium.

(2) Briefly summarize the implications of the Keynesian model of macroeconomic equilibrium.

(3) Why is the rate of inflation in an overheated economy likely to accelerate while real GDP declines?

(4) Give an example of a supply-side shock, and trace out its effects on the economy.

(5) Forecast what is likely to happen to the equilibrium price level and real GDP if the foreign exchange rate of the dollar falls against all other currencies.

(6) How does economic growth affect aggregate supply and macroeconomic equilibrium?

Problems and Applications

1. What is the underlying logic of the classical model of macroeconomic equilibrium? Explain why this model doesn't fit the facts for the U.S. economy very well when aggregate demand decreases. (1), (2)
2. Assume an economy in which all input and output prices instantaneously adjust whenever there are shortages or surpluses in markets. Draw the aggregate supply curve for such an economy. (1)
3. Suppose real GDP is currently $4,500 billion, and potential GDP is $4,600 billion. At the beginning of the year, new labor contracts are negotiated that increase the general level of wages in the economy by 10 percent. Other things being equal, show the impact of the new labor contracts on the aggregate

supply curve. What effect will the shift in the aggregate supply curve have on macroeconomic equilibrium? 1

4. Imagine that an improvement in technology increases labor productivity in the economy. Show the impact of the improvement on the economy's long-run aggregate supply curve. Why is the economy less likely to overheat in response to an increase in aggregate demand after the improvement in technology is adopted? 3, 6

5. In the next 10 years the average age of the labor force will increase. Workers are expected to be more experienced and better educated. What effects are the improvements in the quality of the labor force likely to have on aggregate supply and macroeconomic equilibrium? 6

6. Assume the economy is operating with a recessionary GDP gap of about $500 billion. Under what circumstances can economic policies designed to eliminate the recessionary gap cause a wage-price spiral? 3

7. Suppose potential real GDP is $5,000 billion per year. A surge in aggregate demand causes the equilibrium level of real GDP to equal $5,500 billion for the year. Show how the resulting inflationary gap is eliminated over time by a shift of the aggregate supply curve. 1, 3

8. Suppose an international disturbance disrupts the shipment of petroleum products into the United States. As a consequence, the prices of energy resources increase sharply. Forecast the impact of the increase in energy prices on aggregate supply and macroeconomic equilibrium. Show how, if the price increases are severe enough, they can cause a recession coupled with very high inflation. Why does a nation like Japan have to be very concerned about supply-side shocks resulting from increases in the price of petroleum? 4

9. Suppose the price of the dollar soars next year. Trace out the possible effects of the higher dollar on the equilibrium level of real GDP and the rate of inflation for the year. 5

10. Explain why both aggregate demand and aggregate supply tend to increase yearly. Use aggregate demand and supply analysis to show how an increase in the rate of outward shift of the economy's aggregate supply curve prevailing each year helps keep inflation down while putting upward pressure on equilibrium real GDP and potential real GDP. 6

Labor Markets in Western Europe: High, Inflexible Wages and Labor Surpluses

Wage and labor inflexibility in the European Union contributes to very high unemployment rates throughout Western Europe. In 2008, unemployment rates were 7.2 percent in Germany, and ranged between 7 and 8 percent of the labor force in France and Italy. In Spain, unemployment rates hovered around 15 percent of the labor force. Unemployment rates among younger workers are typically higher than average in many European nations, typically 15 to 20 percent or higher, with the youth unemployment rate in France running at close to 20 percent of the younger portion of the labor force and an astounding 28 percent in Spain during 2008. Labor markets throughout much of Europe are very inflexible, with work rules that make it difficult both to hire new workers and fire existing workers.

We can use basic supply and demand analysis to illustrate the problem of high unemployment rates in Europe. It's clear that, given current levels of demand for labor and the supply of labor, current wages in many European nations are above equilibrium levels. In Germany, for example, wage levels average more than $25 per hour in manufacturing. This, coupled with long vacations for German workers and high payroll taxes paid by employers to finance government social insurance benefits, has resulted in large labor surpluses.

The graph below illustrates typical labor market conditions in Europe. The high hourly labor compensation (including costs for government-provided social security and health benefits, as well as fringe benefits like sick leave and vacations), say, 30 euros per hour, is above an equilibrium level of compensation of, say, 20 euros. At that wage level, the quantity of labor demanded exceeds the quantity supplied. The result is a surplus of labor (unemployment) that remains abnormally high unless wages fall to equilibrium levels. In Germany, as well as in other European nations, strong labor unions and difficulty in lowering payroll taxes that constitute part of the cost of labor for employers make wages inflexible in the downward direction, thereby contributing to high unemployment rates.

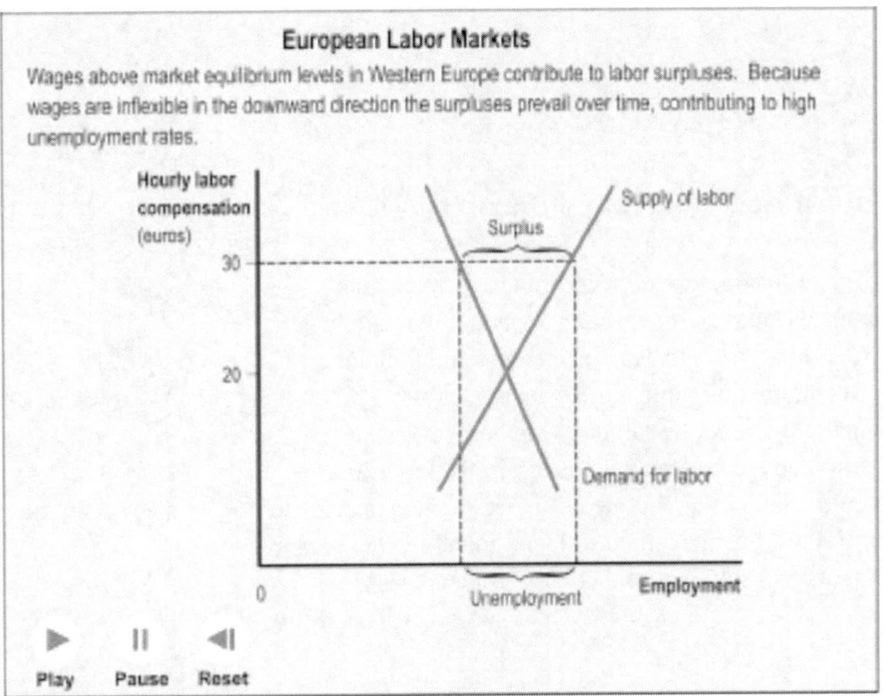

Much of the problem of wage inflexibility stems from the fact that nonwage costs European employers must pay for government social security and health insurance can't be reduced by the firms alone--this is a political decision. Nations such as Italy and Spain have been rocked by strikes and social protests against any cuts in these benefits. Similar resistance to such cuts exists in France and Germany. But, without cuts in labor compensation, private jobs will flee Europe and labor surpluses will continue to grow. Hardest hit by the dearth of jobs will be new entrants into the labor force--younger people.

Inflexible working rules also discourage foreign firms from building plants in some European nations and encourage domestic firms to look abroad for expanding operations. For example, labor rights laws in Spain make it extremely difficult and costly to lay off workers. It can take two years to negotiate layoffs with unions, and lump sum payments to dismissed workers can run into the thousands of dollars. With employers having the opportunity to operate in Eastern Europe, where wages are low, layoffs are easy, and payroll taxes not as burdensome as at home, while workers are just as productive, Europe might very well be pricing itself out of jobs!

Business Brief: How Long-Term Labor Contracts Prevent Wage Flexibility in the U.S.

Union workers in the United States today account for less than 15 percent of the labor force. Although the influence of organized labor on the U.S. economy has waned over the last several years, unions still exert considerable power over wage levels in the nation by negotiating long-term labor contracts with employers. Union wage levels tend to influence wages in non-union jobs as well. The existence of labor contracts prevents nominal (money) wages from fluctuating daily, as prices do in stock markets and commodity markets.

Because of long-term contracts, nominal wages are likely to be quite unresponsive to changes in the price level over a period of at least one year. Most union contracts are for a three-year period and sometimes contain inflation-linked, cost-of-living adjustments in wages--but such adjustments are usually made at the *end* of the contract year.

Why do workers agree to contracts that fix nominal wages over a period of a year? The reason lies in the costs of negotiating wages. A three-year contract that specifies yearly increases in wages economizes on the costs incurred in reaching wage agreements. Such a contract also reduces the losses incurred in strikes and lockouts by limiting their incidence to once every three years. For these reasons, both workers and employers gain when long-term contracts are negotiated, even though they run the risk that real wages will fluctuate over the contract period.

Rapid cost-of-living adjustments are rare in U.S. labor agreements. Firms fear that, as the price level increases, rapid automatic increases in nominal wages will force them to raise the prices of their products. This, they fear, will cause a large reduction in sales volume that will adversely affect their profits. Similarly, unions fear that a reduction in sales resulting from nominal wage increases will cut the demand for labor and increase unemployment. Both workers and employers prefer not to take the risks associated with automatic cost-of-living adjustments.

These labor market practices keep the aggregate supply curve from shifting inward rapidly when the U.S. economy overheats. Over a period of one year, nominal wages are not only inflexible in the downward direction, but also appear to be inflexible in the upward direction. The rigidity of wages in the U.S. economy implies that, over a relatively short period (say, one year), the economy's self-correcting mechanism is unlikely to operate to stabilize real GDP at its full-employment level.

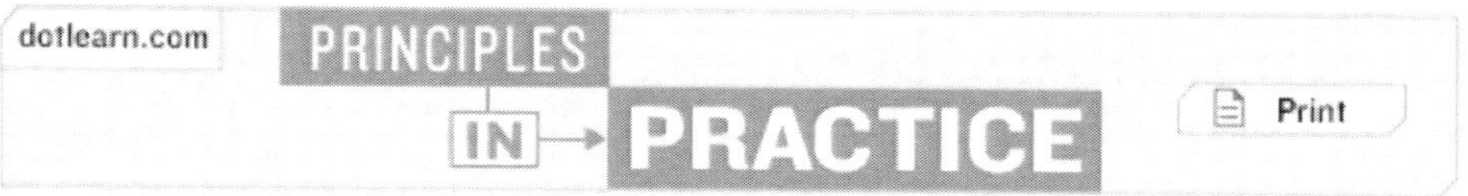

U.S. Macroeconomic Equilibrium, 1970-2008

Let's look at the actual equilibrium points for the U.S. economy from 1970 to 2008. Each point in the graph below is assumed to correspond to the intersection of the aggregate demand curve and the aggregate supply curve for the given year. (We've drawn in the curves corresponding to 1970 and 2008 for reference.) The points shown give the level of real GDP and the value of the GDP deflator for the year (assuming the economy is in equilibrium). As you can see, there were increases in both aggregate demand and aggregate supply since 1970, but the race was clearly won by aggregate demand, indicated by the more rapid rise in price level than in real GDP. Based on data up to 2008, real GDP doubled, while the GDP deflator tripled!

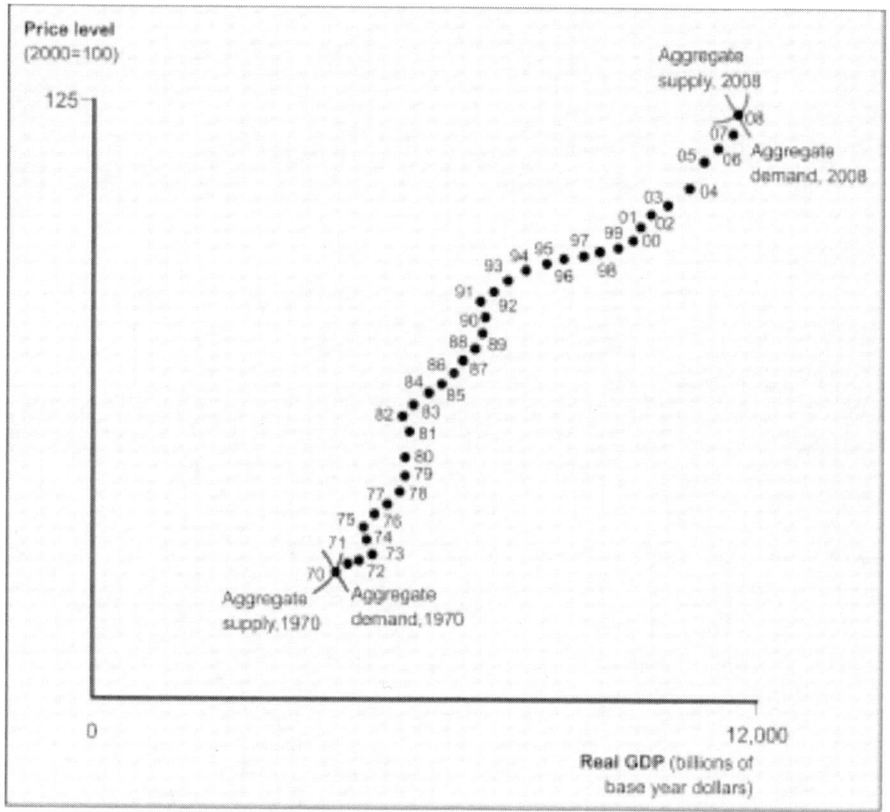

Follow the dots in the graph, and you'll take a ride on the economy! Each dot represents a snapshot of the economy for the given year. Notice how the economy expanded steadily, with only moderate inflation, from 1970 to 1973. Then, in 1973, it was hit by a massive decrease in aggregate supply, caused by sharply increased oil prices. The oil price increases decreased aggregate supply and resulted in sharp increases in the price level in 1974 and 1975. In 1975, inflation hit double-digit levels, mainly as a result of the decreases in aggregate supply, which also caused a recession in 1974. This was a supply-side-induced recession. The decrease in aggregate supply outpaced the normal increase in aggregate demand in 1974, and real GDP fell sharply.

From 1975 to 1982, real GDP grew only moderately, because productivity didn't increase greatly. Over the same period, there was strong inflation. That inflation was the result of both decreases in aggregate supply and increases in aggregate demand. The increases in oil prices over the period 1974-79 contributed to shifts in the aggregate supply curve that put upward pressure on the price level. The Federal Reserve System, the nation's central bank in charge of controlling the supply of money and credit, allowed the quantity of money in circulation to increase over the same period. This provided the public with the credit to buy higher-priced goods and services resulting from the higher oil prices. The increased supply of money and credit contributed to increased aggregate demand that allowed the economy to expand moderately (to avoid a recession), but also contributed to a high rate of inflation.

In 1979, the nation's central banking authorities decided to apply the brakes. From 1980 to 1981, the growth rate of aggregate demand slowed, but the price of oil and other raw materials continued to increase. The consequent continual decreases in aggregate supply resulted in strong inflation, while slow productivity growth prevented strong outward movement in aggregate supply. The slow growth rate of potential real GDP, coupled with slower growth in aggregate demand, meant that the growth rate of equilibrium real GDP slackened quite a bit between 1979 and 1981. However, inflation remained strong during these years because of the decreases in aggregate supply.

In 1982, the growth rate of aggregate demand was sharply curtailed by a slowdown in the growth rate of money and credit. This situation was engineered by Paul Volcker, Chairman of the Board of Governors of the Federal Reserve System. Because aggregate supply was still decreasing that year, due to increases in oil prices, inflation continued at a strong pace, and the economy was plunged into another supply-side recession. *Stagflation*, the unfortunate pairing of high inflation with high unemployment, was the outcome.

The recession of 1981-82, the most severe economic turndown the U.S. economy had experienced since the Great Depression of the 1930s, was bitter medicine for the U.S. economy. However, the recession managed to reduce the growth rate of aggregate demand enough to keep inflation under control. After 1983, oil prices increased more slowly. In fact, during the 1980s, they often declined! With increases in aggregate supply occurring more often than decreases, the economy prospered and inflation moderated. From 1983 to 1990, the economy enjoyed an uninterrupted period of economic expansion, with moderate growth in real GDP and moderate, but steady, inflation (in the range of 4-5 percent per year). From

1983 to 1990, steady increases in aggregate supply, coupled with steady but moderate increases in aggregate demand, contributed to expansion of real GDP and moderate inflation. In 1991, a decrease in aggregate demand reduced real GDP. After 1990, inflation was at moderate levels.

From 1993 to 2008, the United States economy expanded, but inflation increased only moderately, at a rate of less than 2 percent as measured by the GDP deflator. So, in the 1990s, the U.S. economy seemed to be coming close to achieving the goal of noninflationary growth. Over the period 2000 to 2004, inflation increased slightly over the rates of the late 1990s. However, in general, inflation remained contained, averaging close to between 2 and 4 percent. In 2009, the forces of a major recession held inflation down to close to zero and macroeconomic growth was stalled.

Chapter 28

The Functions of Money

Money may not make the world go round, but it surely lubricates the wheels of exchange. A financial crisis during 2008 and 2009 provides a jarring example of what happens to an economy when availability of new money and credit dry up. As the value of financial assets in the United States and many other nations declined in response to defaults on mortgage loans and decreasing home prices, banks became more cautious in extending credit. Consequently, the supply of new money and credit sharply decreased. The decreased availability of money caused the wheels of exchange to slow down, contributing to a major recession, both in the United States and abroad.

In this chapter we'll explore the functions of money and how the amount in circulation can be measured. We'll examine why people and businesses hold money as an asset rather than using it to make purchases of goods or financial assets such as stocks and bonds. The amount of money in circulation is important because it can affect credit availability, aggregate demand, and the price level in the economy. Finally, we'll see how changes in the supply of money can affect the performance of the economy by influencing interest rates over the short run and affecting aggregate demand and the price level over the long run. The Federal Reserve System, the nation's central banking authority, uses its control of the nation's money supply to stabilize the economy by influencing aggregate demand.

Historically, many commodities, ranging from precious metals to cigarettes, have been used as money. In most modern societies, however, commodities are rarely used as money. Instead, money consists mainly of paper currency issued by governments and deposits in checking accounts that are accepted as a means of making payments for goods and services.

Concept Preview

After reading this chapter, you should be able to

1. List the four major functions of money in the economy.
2. Discuss the major components of the money stock in an economy, the concept of *near money*, and the official measures of the U.S. money stock.
3. Discuss the determinants of the demand to hold money.
4. Explain how, given the demand for money, changes in the available money stock can affect credit and interest rates and influence spending decisions and how, given the stock of money, changes in money demand can affect interest rates.

What Is Money, and What Are Its Functions?

1 Money is something you've been familiar with throughout your life. In fact, you may already consider yourself an expert on the subject. You regularly use money to measure the value of things you own. You also have some of it (in the form of currency) in your pocket and in bank accounts. It may surprise you to learn that there's a great deal of disagreement among economists about what money is and how to measure it. Money serves a number of functions, and any definition of money must consider all of its functions.

The four major functions of money are to serve as a medium of exchange, a standard of value, a standard of deferred payment, and a store of value. It's useful to begin our analysis of the fascinating concept of money by looking into its functions.

1. *A medium of exchange.* As a generally accepted medium of exchange, money eliminates the need for *barter*, the direct exchange of one item for another. Barter is a very inconvenient means of trading because it requires the *double coincidence of wants.* A trader with a good or service to offer must search for a buyer who has exactly what the trader desires. Under a barter system, for example, if a baker wants meat, he must search for a butcher who wants bread. Because money is generally accepted as payment for any purchase, a baker who sells bread for money can use the money to buy meat or anything else the baker wants. Money facilitates specialization and the division of labor in an economy by avoiding the inconvenience of barter. As a generally accepted medium of exchange, money cuts down on the transaction costs of trading.

2. *A standard of value.* Money provides a unit of account (in the United States it's the dollar) that serves as a standard for the measure of value. The value of an item is a measure of what a person will sacrifice to obtain it. How much is a two-week vacation in Hawaii worth to you? If you're like most people, you'll probably answer this question by valuing the vacation in dollars—say, $3,000—rather than in terms of other things (such as your car). Whether or not you're conscious of it, you're constantly valuing items in dollars. You measure your income and the value of things you own in terms of dollars. You measure the opportunity cost of most of your purchases in terms of the dollar values of expenditure on other things. As a *standard of value*, money allows the addition of the values of such diverse items as automobiles and haircuts and of all other goods and services. The concept of GDP would be useless without a standard of value such as the dollar.

3. *A standard of deferred payment.* Many contracts involve promises to make payments in the future. The unit of account for *deferred payment* of debts is money. If you borrow money to buy a car, the loan contract specifies how much money you must pay back per month and the number of such payments that are required to satisfy your obligation. However, money serves its function as a standard of deferred payment only if its purchasing power remains fairly constant over time. If the price level rises, the purchasing power of money will decline over time. Similarly, a decrease in the price level will increase the future purchasing power of money.

4. *A store of value.* Money serves as a store of value that can be quickly converted into goods and services. As the actual medium of exchange, money is completely *liquid*, which means that it can be converted into goods and services without any inconvenience or cost. Other assets that serve as stores of value, such as stocks, bonds, or real estate, must first be liquidated (sold) to be converted into a generally accepted medium of exchange. Costs (such as brokerage fees) and inconvenience (a time delay) are often associated with the liquidation of other assets. Thus, holding money as a store of value can reduce the transaction costs involved in everyday business. When inflation is present, however, the purchasing power of money declines. In holding money as a store of value, we weigh the gains of doing so against the possibility of loss in its purchasing power from inflation.

A simple definition of money emphasizes its role as a medium of exchange. A more comprehensive definition of money emphasizes its four functions. Money is anything that is generally accepted as payment in exchange for goods or services. It also serves as a standard of value, a standard of deferred payment, and a store of value.

Commodity Money

When you think of money, you probably think of the green dollar bills and coins that are used as currency in the United States. Yet a variety of *commodities* have been used as money in the course of history. Commodity money is an item that serves the functions of money but also has *intrinsic* value as a marketable item in addition to its value as the medium of exchange. In the early days of America, tobacco, corn, and other agricultural commodities were accepted as payment for goods and services. Gold and silver were most commonly used by European and other nations as money throughout much of their history.

Many strange items have cropped up as commodity money. For example, in ancient Russia furs were used as money, and stamped pieces of leather were sometimes used as tokens of the furs and circulated as money. The Zulus of South Africa used cattle as money. The American Indians used *wampum*, a form of money consisting of trinkets made out of shells. In Rumania Kent cigarettes were used during the communist 1980s as money for black market transactions! It had to be Kent; no other brand would do. The packs were exchanged unopened; no one would dream of smoking the cigarettes. A Rumanian lighting up a Kent in the mid-1980s would have been considered as crazy as a person who burned dollar bills in the United States.

Fiat Money

Fiat money is money that is accepted as a medium of exchange because of government decree rather than because of its intrinsic value as a commodity. The dirty dollar bill in your pocket is really just a piece of high-quality 100 percent rag paper whose market value is virtually nil. You value it because you know that it will be accepted for a dollar's worth of goods and services at current prices.

In the past U.S. coins were made of silver. However, as the market price of silver increased, the market value of the silver in those coins increased to more than their face value. This meant that the silver in a 50-cent piece was worth more than 50 cents. Under these circumstances, it was profitable to melt down the coins into silver bullion because they were more valuable as raw silver than as money! Now the market value of the metal in a quarter is only a fraction of a cent.

Paper money was apparently invented by the Chinese in the 13th century. If you're fortunate enough to have paper money in your wallet, pull out a bill and look at it closely. You'll observe, on the dark-colored side, above a picture of a famous American, that the bill is a "Federal Reserve Note." This means it's issued by one of the 12 regional banks of the Federal Reserve System, the central banking system of the United States. Toward the upper left corner you'll see these words: "THIS NOTE IS LEGAL TENDER FOR ALL DEBTS, PUBLIC AND PRIVATE," a proclamation (or decree) by the government that this piece of paper is the legal medium of exchange in the United States. In effect, whenever you purchase an item, you incur a debt to the seller. You can pay off that debt immediately with Federal Reserve notes, which serve as fiat money in the United States.

Fiat money, like Federal Reserve notes, can serve the function of money simply because it's generally accepted in exchange for goods and services. Again, look at a Federal Reserve note. Nowhere on the note will you find any promise that the Federal Reserve banks will redeem it for gold, silver, or anything else. Of course, if you take a $20 bill to a Federal Reserve bank, you may be able to exchange it for two $10 bills. You can also use your money to *buy* gold or silver as you would use it to buy any other commodity.

Technically, Federal Reserve notes are a liability (or debt) of the Federal Reserve banks. You'll see in the chapter on the Federal Reserve System that the liabilities of the Federal Reserve banks are balanced by their assets, which include government bonds and some gold. However, by law the Federal Reserve banks are not required to exchange Federal Reserve notes held by the public for anything other than more currency (either paper money or coins).

Monetary authorities in central banks must be careful to keep confidence in money. When the public loses confidence in the official money of a nation, it seeks alternative forms of money. This impairs the functions of money as a medium of exchange, a standard and store of value, and a standard of deferred payment. If you expected rampant inflation, you wouldn't want to hold any money, and whenever you got some, you'd quickly exchange it for commodities whose value would keep up with the inflation rate.

Checkable Deposits as a Form of Money

Federal Reserve notes, along with the coins minted by the federal government, which constitute the nation's *currency*, are not the only means of paying off debts. A check serves the same function as currency because it can be used to pay for purchases and pay off debts. Checkable deposits are money deposited in bank accounts that can be used to write checks accepted to pay debts or that can easily be converted to currency. Paying by check has the advantage of safety. A check is made payable to a specific party and must be endorsed by that party before it can be converted to currency or before funds can be transferred from the payer's account to the recipient's account. Paying by check also avoids the risks associated with transporting sums of currency. Thieves find currency a more desirable target than checks, which require endorsement before they can be cashed or deposited. Checkable deposits can also be accessed electronically through computer payment systems that transfer funds among accounts to pay for purchases.

Checkable deposits are money because they are accepted as a means of payment for goods and services and also perform the other major functions of money. The convenience of paying by check (or electronic transfer of checkable deposits), particularly when large sums of money are involved, explains why the bulk of the money stock is held in the form of checkable deposits rather than currency.

Checkable deposit accounts are offered by various types of specialized firms called *depository institutions*. These institutions are commonly called "banks" and include commercial banks, savings and loan associations, savings banks, and credit unions. Commercial banks are firms that acquire funds by accepting checkable deposits and savings deposits from households and business firms and use these funds to make loans. Commercial banks, such as JPMorgan Chase and the Bank of America, make both short-term and long-term loans to businesses and individuals seeking credit. Such banks also extend credit to governments by purchasing government bonds. Thrift institutions are depository institutions that acquire funds by attracting savings deposits and have, in the past, specialized in mortgage loans and consumer credit. Thrift institutions are sometimes referred to as savings associations or savings banks, and many of them were formerly called "savings and loan associations" and "mutual savings banks." Credit unions are depository institutions whose depositors, called *members*, belong to a particular organization such as a business firm or government. Credit unions make loans only to their members for the purpose of financing homes or personal goods and services (such as cars). Savings and loan associations, mutual savings banks, and credit unions are called "thrift institutions" because they encourage saving by households and small businesses.

Prior to the late 1970s, checkable deposits in the United States were mainly available at commercial banks. Up to that time, funds in checkable deposits didn't earn interest. Since that time, changes and reforms in the U.S. financial industry have allowed thrift institutions to issue checkable deposits and have modified the restrictions on the types of loans that all depository institutions can make. Checkable deposits are now available at thrift institutions as well as commercial banks, and some checkable deposit accounts pay interest. For example, checkable deposits are available at savings and loan associations and mutual saving banks as *NOW* (negotiable order of withdrawal) *accounts*, which permit writing checks on the sums deposited in interest-bearing savings accounts.[1] Commercial banks offer *ATS* (automatic transfer of savings) *accounts*, which transfer funds from an interest-bearing savings account to a non-interest-bearing checking account when a check is written. The funds in an ATS account therefore earn interest until checks written on the checking account result in the transfer of funds from the savings account to the checking account. *Demand deposits* are non-interest-bearing checkable deposits held at commercial banks. Over two-thirds of demand deposits at commercial banks are held by business firms. These demand deposits largely represent the deposit accounts of corporations.

The nation's total checkable deposits are the sums in demand deposits, NOW accounts, ATS accounts, and other checkable deposits.

What Money Is Not

You should review the preceding discussions of money and its function and make sure you understand how the functions of money can be used to define *money* itself. Be careful not to confuse money with other important economic concepts. Although money is a store of value, it is not a productive input. Do not confuse money with capital. Money can be used to purchase investment goods that add to the nation's capital stock. However, this is simply because money is the medium of exchange. Also, do not confuse money with bonds and other debts of corporations. Bonds can be sold for money, but in themselves they are not a medium of exchange. Bonds are securities issued by corporations and governments representing the promise to make periodic payments of interest and to repay borrowed funds at a certain time.

Do not confuse money with income. Income is measured as a *flow* of dollars over a given period. It's convenient to measure income as a money sum because, after all, money is the standard of value. However, money itself is merely an asset that is held mainly in bank accounts and as currency in people's pockets and purses or in vaults.

Do not confuse credit cards with money. If you've ever used a credit card, you know it's accepted almost as readily as currency as a means of purchasing goods and services. However, when you make a purchase with a credit card, you are really incurring a debt that must be paid with money at a later time. Most credit card companies give you a specified period in which to repay your loan. After that period has elapsed, you must pay interest on your debt. You cannot use credit cards as a store of value. But credit cards have allowed many Americans to economize on the amount of money they hold. Rather than having to use money in checkable deposits *each day* for purchases, they can hold more bonds and other interest-bearing assets that they liquidate on a monthly rather than daily basis to pay their credit card bills.

Measuring the Stock of Money

2 Money is a stock rather than a flow. A *stock* is a variable that can be measured only at a given point in time. For example, the stock of money can be measured as the amount held by the public on a certain day. The stock of money can vary from day to day

[1]Credit unions issue checkable deposits similar to NOW accounts. Checkable deposits issued by credit unions are called *share draft accounts*.

with conditions of supply and demand. To delve further into the mysteries of money, let's examine the method used to measure the stock of money available at a given point in time.

Measuring the Money Stock: M1

The Federal Reserve System has developed several measures of the money stock. The narrowest measure includes only items that serve as a medium of exchange. M1 is a measure of the money stock that includes only currency and account balances commonly used in payment for purchases of goods and services. M1 is the sum of the currency, traveler's checks, and checkable deposits held by the public.

Box 1 shows the components of the money stock, measured as M1, based on daily averages of the dollar amounts outstanding during January 2009. An estimated 60 percent of the currency component of M1 circulates abroad in foreign nations. Although, technically, currency constituted about half of the M1 money stock in January 2009, only 40 percent of that currency actually circulated domestically. If the portion of currency circulating abroad is removed from M1, then currency accounts for 31.5 percent of

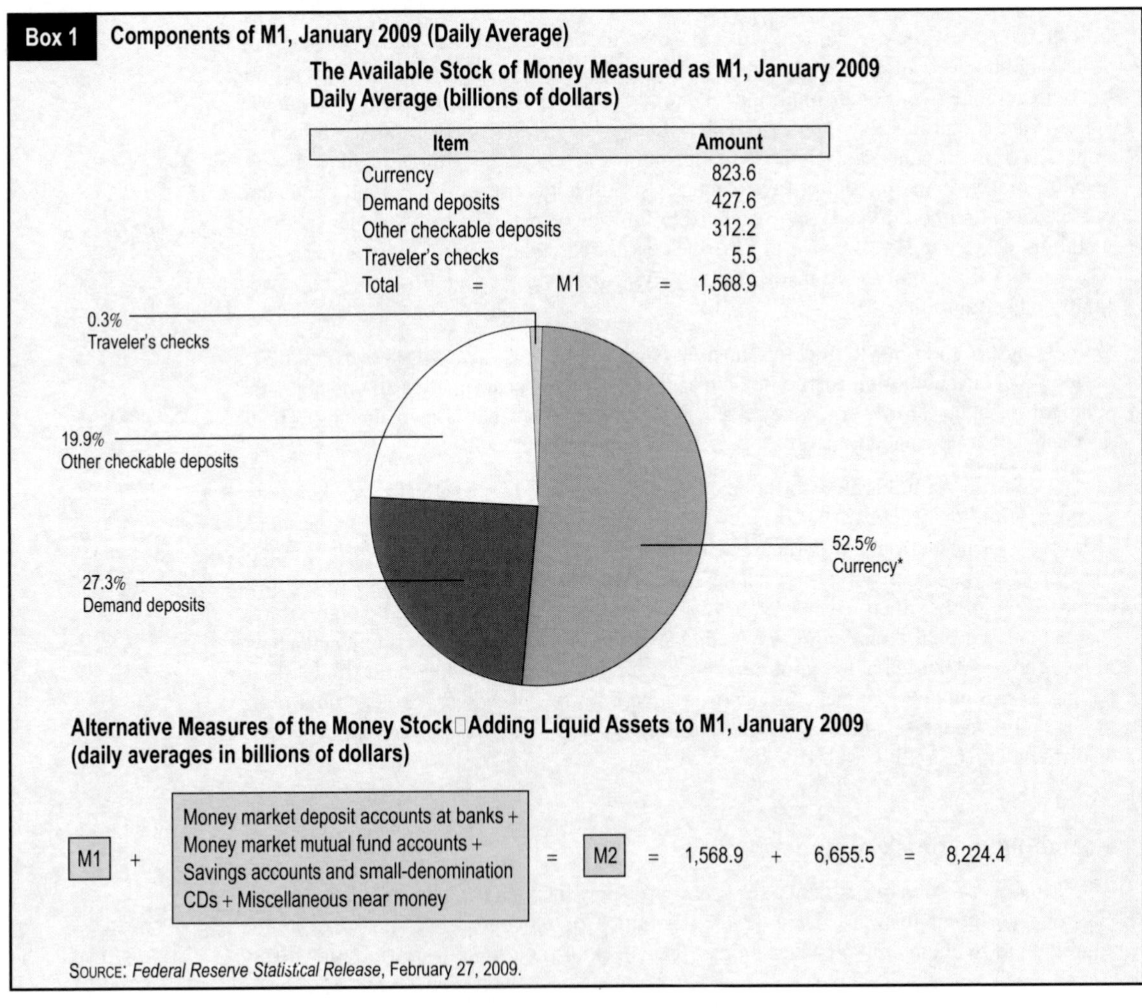

Box 1 Components of M1, January 2009 (Daily Average)

The Available Stock of Money Measured as M1, January 2009 Daily Average (billions of dollars)

Item	Amount
Currency	823.6
Demand deposits	427.6
Other checkable deposits	312.2
Traveler's checks	5.5
Total = M1 =	1,568.9

SOURCE: *Federal Reserve Statistical Release*, February 27, 2009.

domestic M1. You may be surprised to learn that currency constitutes less than one-third of the available dollars used as a means of payment within U.S. borders. Checkable deposits are by far the most important component of the available stock of money. Demand deposits at commercial banks and other checkable deposits, mainly NOW and ATS accounts held at commercial banks and thrift institutions, accounted for more than half of the money stock. Traveler's checks outstanding (such as those issued by the American Express Company) are a very small part of M1, accounting for less than 1 percent of the money stock.

Adding Near Money to M1: M2

Deposits in noncheckable savings accounts, certificates of deposit, bonds, and other types of financial assets are usually not considered to be money because they cannot readily be used to make payments. These assets must be *liquidated* into currency or demand deposits before the sum they represent can be used to make payments. Near monies are assets that are easily converted into money because they can be liquidated at low cost and little risk of loss.

Because near monies can be easily converted into money, some economists prefer to include them in a measure of the nation's stock of liquid assets available to make purchases. The Federal Reserve System measures the sum of M1 and certain near monies to obtain a measure of liquid assets held by the public that constitute a store of readily available purchasing power. M2 is a broader measure of money than M1. It includes M1 and liquid assets that cannot be used directly as a medium of exchange but can be easily converted into checkable deposits or other components of M1. M2 is the sum of M1 and certain near monies:

M2 = M1 + Money market deposit accounts at banks + Money market mutual fund accounts + Savings accounts and small-denomination certificates of deposit + Certain other near monies

Money market mutual fund accounts, offered by investment companies, give owners a share in financial assets and allow them limited check-writing privileges on their accounts. Savings accounts are noncheckable savings deposits. Certificates of deposit (CDs) are deposits made in banks for a specified time, with a penalty charged for early withdrawal. Savings deposits and certificates of deposit are examples of time deposits, which are interest-bearing accounts at a commercial bank or a thrift institution for which the bank can legally request a 30-day notice before paying out the funds. In practice, banks rarely ask for the 30-day notice, but they do have the legal right to do so. Only insured certificates of deposit in amounts less than $100,000 are included in M2. Certificates of deposit in excess of $100,000 are not insured by an agency of the federal government. The other near monies mainly include certain types of debts issued by commercial banks. The table in Box 1 shows the relationship between M1 and M2. In January 2009, average daily balances of funds included in M2 amounted to about 5.25 times M1.

In recent years, M2 has increased significantly relative to M1, as corporations and individuals sought ways of earning interest on their cash balances. M1 and M2 are measured at the end of the business day for Federal Reserve authorities. Towards the end of the day, money managers tend to move their balances, as much as is feasible, out of non-interest bearing checkable deposits into other accounts that yield interest. Further, the currency component of M1 increased from about one-third to nearly one-half. Some of this may be explained by exports of currency for use in foreign nations where U.S. dollars are preferred to domestic currencies, because of inflation and other reasons. Another explanation for the rise in currency is the fact that people have learned to economize on the balances in their checkable deposits as new technology has made it easier to shift funds between accounts included in M2 and M3, and checkable deposits.

The Demand for Money

3 Why do people desire to hold demand deposits and currency? After all, holding these two forms of money deprives them of the opportunity to earn interest on the sum held. Similarly, money held in the form of interest-bearing checkable deposits usually earns less interest than can be earned on near monies, bonds, and other less liquid assets that can be purchased with money.

The *opportunity cost* of holding a dollar in money over the year is the interest income that is forgone. For example, if you can earn 8 percent per year in a savings account, the opportunity cost of holding a dollar in cash is 8 cents over the year, assuming interest is computed once annually. The higher the interest rate you can earn in the next best alternative you have, such as investing in bonds or certificates of deposit, the greater the opportunity cost of holding money.

People hold money because they receive benefits from doing so. In deciding how much to hold, people consider both the benefits and the costs of holding money. In the following sections we analyze the benefits of holding money and we look at various motives for choosing to hold money as an asset.

Transaction Demand for Money

At any given level of interest rates, people demand a certain amount of money to carry out the basic transactions associated with everyday business. The level of interest rates is an average of a broad array of interest rates that can be earned on a variety of assets. The greater the dollar volume of transactions during the year, the greater the sum of money that is willingly held each day over the year at each possible level of interest rates.

By holding money, you avoid the inconvenience and the possible embarrassment of settling your debts late. You also avoid the need to incur other costs involved in liquidating assets to make payments. For example, suppose you have both a savings account and a checking account. To pay for your periodic purchases, you must be sure to have at least a minimum amount of currency and checkable deposits on hand. Your savings deposits do you little good as a means of payment unless you go to the bank and transfer some of these funds to your checking account or withdraw them as currency. The transaction demand for money is the sum of money people want to hold per day as a convenience in paying their everyday bills. The benefit of holding money in this form is the avoidance of the transaction costs of converting other assets into currency and checkable deposits.

Suppose you're paid once a month, your expenses require daily expenditure of money, and you don't borrow to meet any of your expenses. You can deposit *all* of your monthly money income in a savings account on the day you're paid to avoid the loss in interest income associated with holding it. However, every time you need to pay for an item, you'll have to go to the bank and wait in line to convert some of your savings deposits into checkable deposits or currency. In some cases you may incur penalties for early withdrawal that reduce your interest income. The time (the trip to the bank, for example) and the money costs involved in liquidating the savings deposits are your transaction costs. In managing the money you keep for transactions, you must weigh these transaction costs against the income you forgo by holding money instead of interest-bearing assets. You may decide to always keep a certain sum each month as checkable deposits and currency rather than as less liquid assets. The interest you forgo by doing so is worth less to you than the inconvenience of having to liquidate those assets to make payments every day.

The yearly transaction demand for money at any given level of interest rates depends on the dollar volume of transactions over the year. In general, the greater the level of nominal GDP over the year, the greater the transaction demand for money. After all, if your monthly bills increase from $1,000 to $1,500 this year, you'll need to hold more money to make payments. Similarly, when nominal GDP increases from $6,000 billion to $7,000 billion per year, the transaction demand for money in the economy also increases even if interest rates don't change.

Money as an Asset

Money is one of many alternative assets people can choose to hold as a store of purchasing power. In deciding how much money to hold, people weigh the opportunity cost of holding it against the purchasing power of the interest income they forgo by doing so. However, benefits are associated with holding money rather than holding alternative assets. In deciding how much of a money stock to hold, people weigh the marginal benefits of holding additional money against the marginal cost of doing so.

The main advantage of money over alternative assets is its liquidity. Many people usually find that the benefits of holding money are worth the opportunity cost of doing so. By holding money, they have an asset they can quickly and conveniently draw upon to make payments when emergencies arise. People also hold money because of uncertainty about future flows of income and required payments. They hold it as a *precaution* against lack of synchronization between inflow of income and outflow of payments. You never know when your income over a certain period will fall short of the bills you must meet over that period. Holding money allows you to make payments quickly even when your income falls short of your expenditures. Would you run the risk of letting your checking account balance run down to zero and encountering embarrassing delays in meeting your bills?

Business firms have a similar precautionary motive for holding money. They do so to ensure a way of quickly paying their bills even when their cash receipts from sales are abnormally low. Because receipts of income and the due dates of bills are rarely synchronized, no household or business firm can expect to have income readily available to pay bills exactly at the time the bills come due.

Another reason why people hold money has to do with uncertainty about the future level of prices and interest rates in the economy. Although financial assets such as stocks and bonds yield income, the prices of these assets fluctuate with economic conditions. Therefore, people evaluate the riskiness of stocks, bonds, and other assets by trying to forecast movements in their prices. Considering economic conditions, people often find money an attractive alternative to stocks and bonds. In periods during which bond prices are expected to fall, other things being equal, the stock of money that people want to hold is likely to increase. Uncertainty concerning the future prices of stocks and bonds leads to a *speculative* motive for holding money.

For example, suppose that people expect stock and bond prices to fall in the future. In that case they may hold money instead of stocks and bonds. A modest positive return on money may be better than a negative return on stocks and bonds! Typically, the speculative demand for money increases when the prices of such assets as stock, bonds, or real estate are expected to fall. When the speculative demand for money increases, people try to hold more money and fewer alternative assets. Conversely, when it is generally believed that the prices of assets such as stock, bonds, and real estate will rise in the future, the speculative demand for money decreases. When the speculative demand for money decreases, people seek to hold less money and increase their demand for alternative assets.

The Money Demand Curve

The demand for money is the relationship between the sums of money that people willingly hold and the level of interest rates in the economy, given *all other influences* on the desirability of holding money instead of other assets. Among the other influences on the demand for money, aside from the level of nominal interest rates in the economy, are all the factors that affect the transaction, precautionary, and speculative demand for money. Among these factors are the degree to which payments and receipts can be synchronized in the economy, expectations about future levels of interest rates, stock and bond prices, inflation, and the level of nominal GDP.

A money demand curve shows a relationship between the level of interest rates in the economy and the stock of money demanded at a given point in time. In effect, the cost of holding a dollar is measured by the interest rate because the interest forgone on money balances is the opportunity cost of holding money. The higher the level of interest rates in the economy, the greater the opportunity cost of holding money and the lower the quantity of money demanded.

The graph in Box 2 shows a money demand curve that illustrates how the stock of money demanded on a given day varies inversely with the level of interest rates. The lower the interest rate, the lower the opportunity cost of holding money and the greater the quantity of money demanded on any given day as balances in checkable deposits or as currency. The actual responsiveness of the desired stock of money to changes in the level of interest rates is hotly debated among economists. Some economists believe the money demand curve looks like the one in Box 2. Other economists believe the money demand curve is nearly vertical, which implies that changes in the level of interest rates have little effect on the quantity of money demanded.

Changes in Money Demand

A change in money demand is a change, caused by a change in economic conditions, in the relationship between the level of interest rates and the stock of money demanded in the economy. When there's a change in money demand, the entire demand curve for money shifts inward or outward. A change in the transaction demand for money at any given interest rate level results in a change in money demand. As pointed out earlier, a change in nominal GDP results in a change in the transaction demand for money. Nominal GDP increases when either real GDP or the price level goes up. It follows that either an increase in real GDP or an increase in the price level shifts the money demand curve outward, as shown in graph **A** in Box 3. Similarly, a decrease in real GDP or a decrease in the price level shifts the money demand curve inward, as shown in graph **B**.

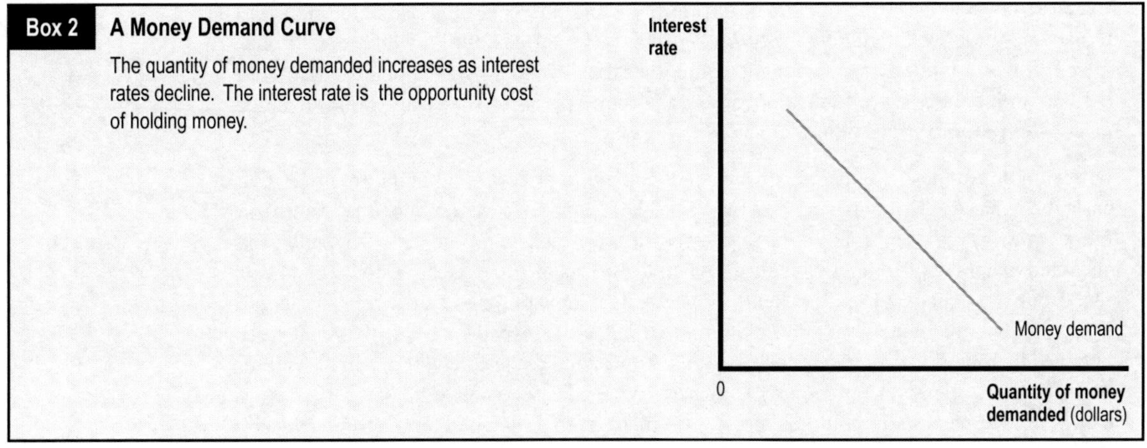

Box 2 A Money Demand Curve

The quantity of money demanded increases as interest rates decline. The interest rate is the opportunity cost of holding money.

Box 3 Increases and Decreases in Money Demand

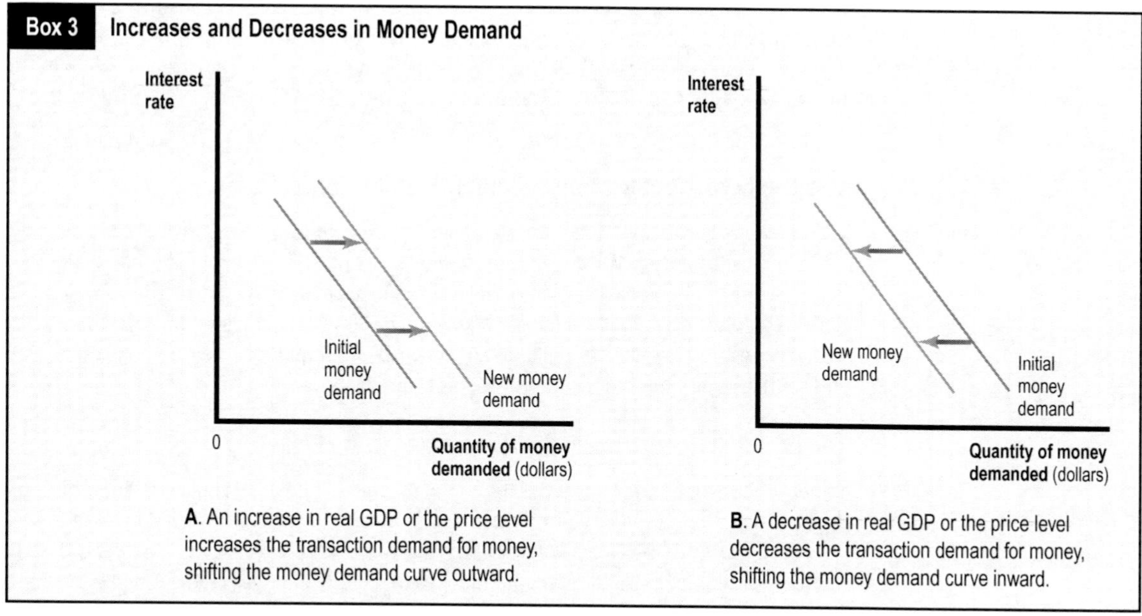

A. An increase in real GDP or the price level increases the transaction demand for money, shifting the money demand curve outward.

B. A decrease in real GDP or the price level decreases the transaction demand for money, shifting the money demand curve inward.

Given the price level, it's therefore reasonable to expect an increase in real GDP to increase money demand. During periods of economic expansion, the money demand curve shifts outward. Similarly, given the price level, decreases in real GDP imply decreases in the demand for money. During periods of contraction or recession, it's therefore reasonable to expect the demand for money to decrease.

The money demand curve can also shift in response to other changes in economic conditions. For example, the invention of automatic teller machines has reduced the transaction cost of obtaining currency. You can now easily obtain currency from your savings account even when banks are closed. This innovation has probably affected your demand to hold currency and checkable deposits.

The proliferation of credit cards is another financial innovation that has affected the demand for money. With a credit card you can consolidate many bills into one bill that you can pay each month, and if you pay it in full, you'll incur no interest expense. By using a credit card, you can hold less money in checkable deposits and more in savings accounts or money market accounts that yield interest. You can then withdraw funds from these accounts as needed to meet credit card bills.

A decrease in the transaction cost of converting near money into money decreases the demand for money. The cost of converting bonds, savings deposits, and other assets into currency and checkable deposits falls when the time required to do so or the penalties involved in doing so are reduced. People hold less money when the transaction costs of converting near money into money fall, because it's then less advantageous to hold money. They therefore shift some of their wealth to bonds and near money. A decrease in the transaction cost of converting near money into money thus shifts the money demand curve inward. Similarly, an increase in the transaction cost of converting near money into money shifts the money demand curve outward.

The demand for money also changes with changes in the risk associated with holding assets other than money. For example, in periods when bond prices are expected to rise, the demand for money is likely to decline as people seek to hold lower money balances at any given interest rate so they can acquire more bonds. If, however, bond prices are expected to fall, the demand for money is likely to increase because money becomes a more attractive asset as the probability increases of incurring a loss from holding bonds. The demand curve for money therefore shifts inward when bond prices are expected to rise and shifts outward when bond prices are expected to fall.

The Stock of Money, Money Demand, and Interest Rates

4 Given the demand for money, changes in the money stock available can affect the interest rate level for the economy over short periods of time. To understand the link between the available stock of money and interest rates each day, assume the price level, real GDP, and all the other determinants of money demand are fixed in the short run. These assumptions simplify the analysis by ensuring that the money demand curve doesn't shift at the same time the available stock of money shifts.

The Effect of an Increase in the Available Money Stock

Suppose the stock of money available on average each day in January is $600 billion, and this is exactly equal to the quantity demanded at the current interest rate level of 8 percent. In March the available stock of money is up to $700 billion on average each day. If the interest rate remains at 8 percent, there will be no change in the quantity of money demanded. This means that the $700 billion stock of money available will exceed the $600 billion demanded at the 8 percent interest rate level.

The graph in Box 4 shows the excess stock of money at the 8 percent interest rate. What will holders of the excess $100 billion worth of money seek to do with it? They could put the extra funds in savings accounts or use them to buy bonds. Everyone tries to get rid of the excess money, but like a hot potato it ends up in someone's hands or checking account whenever it's used to buy bonds. As banks find they have more funds on deposit than they had before the money stock increased, the supply of funds available for loans increases. The increased supply of loanable funds puts downward pressure on interest rates. At lower interest rates, the opportunity cost of holding money is also lower, and the existing larger stock is willingly held. In the graph in Box 4, the increase in the available stock of money will be willingly held only if the market rate of interest falls to 7 percent. Other things being equal, an increase in the available stock of money must increase the supply of credit and put downward pressure on the level of interest rates. Over a short period, therefore, given the level of nominal GDP, the price level, and the other determinants of money demand, the

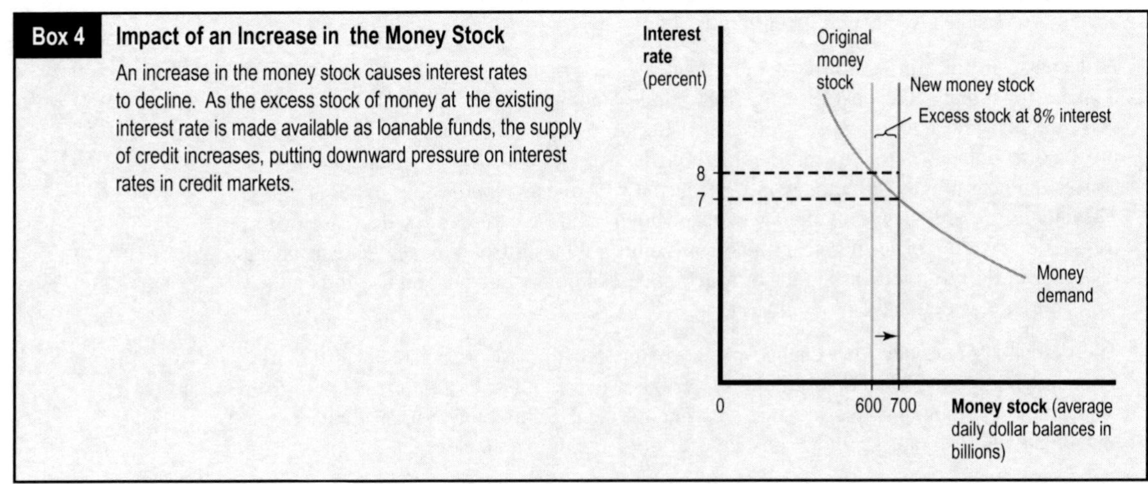

Box 4 Impact of an Increase in the Money Stock

An increase in the money stock causes interest rates to decline. As the excess stock of money at the existing interest rate is made available as loanable funds, the supply of credit increases, putting downward pressure on interest rates in credit markets.

immediate effect of an increase in the available supply of money is a decrease in interest rates in the economy. The lower interest rates will encourage more purchases of investment goods and thus will increase aggregate demand and put upward pressure on real GDP.[2]

The Effect of a Decrease in the Available Money Stock

Other things being equal, a decrease in the available stock of money puts upward pressure on the interest rate in the short run. Given the money demand curve, a decrease in the available stock of money results in a shortage (excess demand) of money available at the current interest rate. The graph in Box 5 shows the impact of a decrease in the supply of money from $600 billion per day to $500 billion per day. The initial equilibrium interest rate is 8 percent. As the available stock of money decreases, the quantity available at the 8 percent interest rate will fall short of the quantity demanded. There will be a $100 billion excess demand for money. How will the difference between the quantity the public wants to hold and the quantity available be made up? Individuals and corporations will seek to liquidate near money such as bonds so as to add funds to their money balances. As the public tries to increase its holdings of money, the funds available for credit and new bonds will decrease. The decrease in the supply of loanable funds will then put upward pressure on interest rates, which will continue to rise until the reduced money stock is willingly held without further liquidation of near monies. In the graph, interest rates must rise to 9 percent before the quantity demanded declines to equal the $500 billion of available money per day. Decreases in the stock of money therefore put upward pressure on interest rates in the short run. The higher interest rates reduce the availability of credit in the economy. This is likely to put downward pressure on aggregate demand over a longer period and therefore tends to reduce real GDP.

How Shifts in Money Demand Can Affect Interest Rates

Given the available stock of money, an increase in money demand puts upward pressure on interest rates. An increase in money demand can be caused by an increase in real GDP,

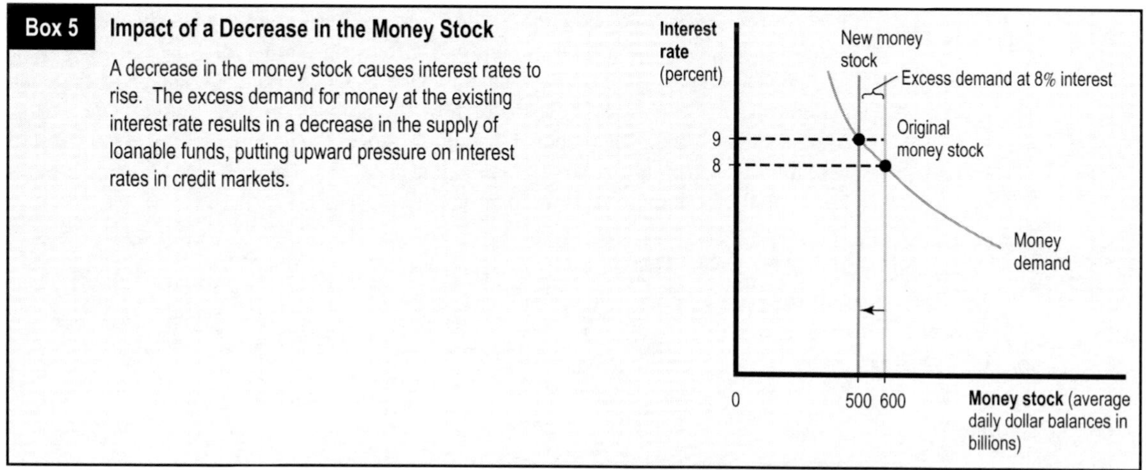
Box 5
Impact of a Decrease in the Money Stock
A decrease in the money stock causes interest rates to rise. The excess demand for money at the existing interest rate results in a decrease in the supply of loanable funds, putting upward pressure on interest rates in credit markets.
Interest rate (percent)
New money stock
Excess demand at 8% interest
Original money stock
9
8
Money demand
0
500 600
Money stock (average daily dollar balances in billions)

[2]As you'll see in the chapter entitled "Stabilization of the Economy through Monetary Policy," the long-run effects of an increase in the available supply of money are more complex because over longer periods of time the added money stock could also increase the price level.

the price level, or the transaction costs of converting other assets into money or by expectations that the prices of bonds and other assets will fall.

The graph in Box 6 illustrates the effect of an increase in money demand on interest rates, assuming a fixed stock of money. As the money demand curve shifts outward, interest rates tend to rise, other things being equal. For example, an expanding economy in which real GDP is increasing is likely to be characterized by upward pressure on interest rates because the transaction demand for money increases during the expansion. An increasing price level will also increase money demand and puts upward pressure on interest rates.

You can expect downward pressure on interest rates as an economy moves into a recession because a decline in real GDP reduces the transaction demand for money and shifts the money demand curve inward. If there is no change in the money stock, the interest rate will fall, as shown in the graph in Box 7. Similarly, a decrease in the transaction costs of converting near money into money puts downward pressure on interest rates over a short period because the decrease in these transaction costs means the demand curve for money shifts inward.

The Need to Understand Changes in the Money Stock

As you can see, the demand for money and the available stock of money exert an important influence on interest rates in the economy. The impact of changes in the money stock on the economy is complex because changes in interest rates are likely to affect aggregate demand. Consumers find it more attractive to borrow as interest rates decline, so they spend more on homes, cars, and other durable goods. Similarly, business firms find it more attractive to make investments as interest rates decline. As a result, over longer periods, changes in the national money stock are likely to affect nominal GDP. As nominal GDP changes, so does the demand for money.

The next step in our quest to understand how the economy works is to examine the process by which the money stock changes in the economy. To do this, we need to begin an in-depth look at the nation's financial system and to learn how banks conduct their business. We also need to examine how the Federal Reserve System, the central bank of the United States, regulates the financial system and affects the ability of financial institutions to make loans and provide credit in financial markets. Once you understand how the financial system operates, you can begin to see how the policies pursued by the Federal Reserve System can influence macroeconomic equilibrium in the nation. Our goal is to develop the necessary background for an economic analysis of the impact on real GDP and the price level of policies that affect the money supply.

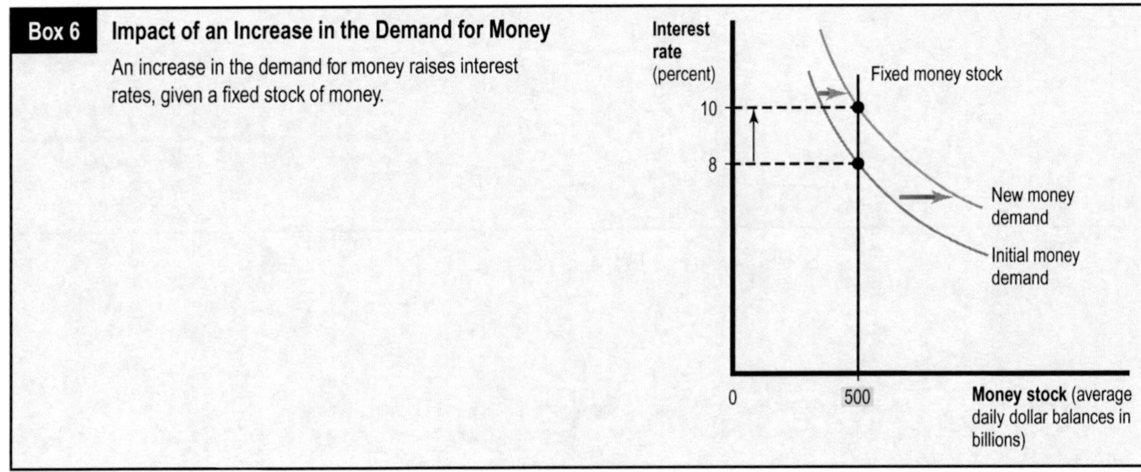

Box 6 Impact of an Increase in the Demand for Money

An increase in the demand for money raises interest rates, given a fixed stock of money.

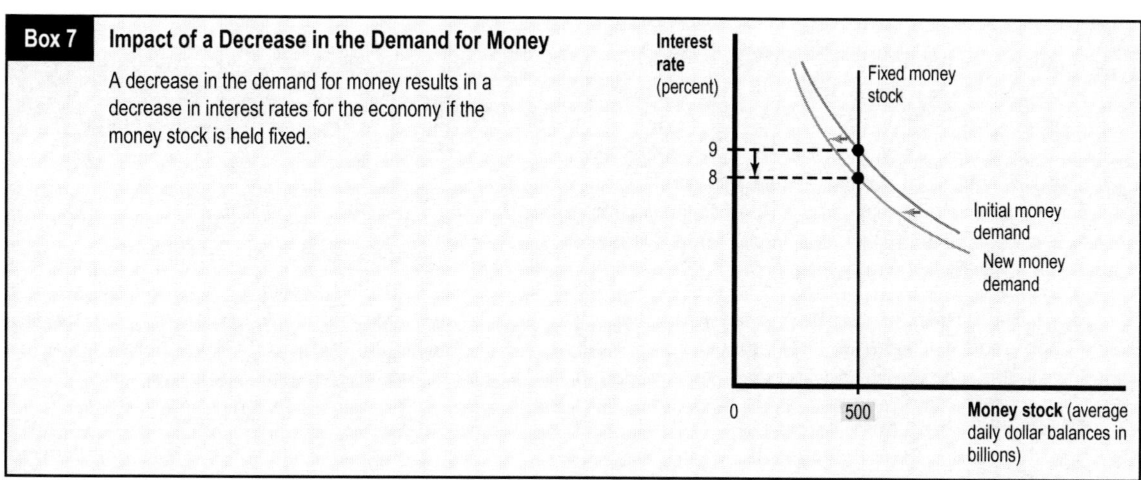
Box 7
Impact of a Decrease in the Demand for Money
A decrease in the demand for money results in a decrease in interest rates for the economy if the money stock is held fixed.
Interest rate (percent)
Fixed money stock
9
8
Initial money demand
New money demand
0
500
Money stock (average daily dollar balances in billions)

Summary

1. Money serves four basic functions—medium of exchange, standard of deferred payment, and store of value. Currency is the paper money and coins that serve as a medium of exchange. Paper money in the United States is issued by Federal Reserve banks. Checkable deposits represent money held in checking accounts that can be used to pay debts or can be converted to currency.
2. M1 is a measure of the money stock that consists of the sum of checkable deposits and currency held by the public on average each day over a certain period.
3. Near monies are assets that can be liquidated at low cost and little risk of loss. An asset is liquidated when it is redeemed for currency or a checkable deposit. M2 is a broader measure of the money stock than M1, representing the sum of M1 and certain near monies.
4. The opportunity cost of holding a dollar of money over a year is the interest income that is forgone by doing so.
5. The demand for money is the relationship between the sums of money that people willingly hold and the level of interest rates, given all the other influences on the desirability of holding money instead of other assets. Money is held for precautionary and speculative motives and also to facilitate transactions. Money is part of the stock of wealth existing in the economy at a certain point in time.
6. A money demand curve shows a relationship between the level of interest rates in the economy and the stock of money demanded on a given day. The interest rate measures the cost of holding each dollar in terms of the annual interest income forgone.
7. The transaction demand for money is the sum that people wish to hold per day as a convenience in paying their everyday bills. Holding money economizes on the transaction costs of liquidating alternative assets to make payments. In general, the greater the nominal GDP over the year, the greater the transaction demand for money.
8. A decrease in the transaction costs of converting near money into money decreases the demand for money.
9. Changes in the available stock of money are likely to result in changes in the level of interest rates in the economy, given the demand for money. An increase in the stock of money is likely to increase the supply of loanable funds as holders of money use the excess supply of money at the current interest rate level to buy bonds and extend credit. This puts downward pressure on interest rates. Similarly, a decrease in the stock of money puts upward pressure on interest rates.
10. The level of interest rates in the economy can be affected by shifts in the demand for money. An increase in money demand puts upward pressure on interest rates, while a decrease in money demand puts downward pressure on interest rates.

Concept Review

1. What is money?
2. How does the M1 measure of the money stock differ from the M2 measure?
3. What can cause a change in money demand?
4. Explain why interest rates change when the demand for money changes while the stock of money is fixed.

Problems and Applications

1. What is the difference between commodity money and fiat money? Explain why U.S. currency is fiat money. 1
2. Explain how currency and checkable deposits fulfill the functions of money for the U.S. economy. What are some advantages of currency and checkable deposits over gold and silver as a form of money? What are some disadvantages of currency and checkable deposits compared to commodity money? 1
3. Suppose you open an account with a mutual fund composed of corporate bonds. The company managing the mutual fund gives you a checkbook that allows you to write checks against the market value of the bonds in the account. Is the value of the assets held in the mutual fund part of M1? 2

4. Suppose inflation is expected to heat up in the future. How does inflation affect the function of money as a medium of exchange, standard of value, and store of purchasing power? 1

5. What can U.S. currency be redeemed for if it is presented to the U.S. Treasury or a Federal Reserve bank? 1

6. Suppose the level of interest rates in the economy increases on average over the year from 6 percent to 8 percent. What effect will this change have on the quantity of money demanded? 3

7. Explain how a decrease in the level of interest rates affects the quantity of money demanded in the economy. 3

8. Suppose nominal GDP is $5,000 billion, and the average daily stock of money measured by M1 during the year is $1,000 billion. What is likely to happen to the demand for money and interest rates if, as a result of an increase in government purchases, nominal GDP increases to $5,500 billion and M1 is held fixed at $1,000 billion? 2, 4

9. Use a graph to show how a decrease in the demand for money will affect interest rates if the money stock is held fixed. 3

10. Suppose that, this year, there's a 10 percent reduction in the stock of money measured as M1. Use a graph to show how the reduction in the stock of money will affect the quantity of money demanded and the equilibrium level of interest rates in credit markets. How could such a sharp reduction in the money supply precipitate a recession? 4

Eurodollars: How the U.S. Dollar Circulates Overseas as a Medium of Exchange

The U.S. dollar is an *international reserve currency* that's often used by foreigners in international transactions not involving U.S. traders. Its status has created a huge "offshore" demand for U.S. currency and checkable deposits. For example, oil and coal are always priced in U.S. dollars when they're sold on international markets. An Italian firm buying crude oil from Saudi Arabia pays in dollars. The Saudis then hold the dollars as deposits in foreign or U.S. banks, until they're ready to spend them. Similarly, in nations in which the official foreign exchange rate of the national currency is set at artificially high levels or isn't freely convertible into other currencies, many international and domestic transactions involve trades of goods or services for U.S. dollars. Foreigners visiting Russia and Eastern European nations are often amazed by the amount of U.S. dollars circulating as money within those nations. The dollar is also heavily used in nations with high inflation.

Because a substantial demand for dollars exists overseas, an organized market has developed. *Eurodollars* are deposits denominated in U.S. dollars at banks and other financial institutions outside the United States. The name "Eurodollar" was coined because most of these foreign deposits of dollars were located at banks in Western Europe. Today, however, similar deposits held in other parts of the world are also referred to as Eurodollars. For example, a large French corporation creates a Eurodollar account when it deposits a $2 million check denominated in U.S. dollars in its Paris bank.

The Eurodollar market is a market in foreign nations for exchange of bank deposits denominated in U.S. dollars. The total amount of Eurodollars outstanding is over $1 trillion! The principal center for trading Eurodollars is London; however, Eurodollars are also traded extensively in Hong Kong, Singapore, and the Bahamas. Many U.S. banks with foreign branches in Europe actively compete for Eurodollars, which are easily transferred to the United States, where they can be used by U.S. banks to make loans. In recent years, Eurodollars have been used by U.S. banks to extend credit in the United States amounting to more than $100 billion per year.

The prime buyers in the Eurodollar market are large corporations that usually purchase a minimum of $1 million in each transaction. Foreigners can also purchase "Eurodollar bonds," which are bonds denominated in dollars and traded in Europe.

Eurodollars are not included in the M1 definition of the money stock. However, some Eurodollars held by U.S. residents are included in M2. The demand for Eurodollars adds to the overall demand for U.S. money. Changes in that demand can have some impact on U.S. interest rates.

The demand for Eurodollars depends, in part, on the stability of the dollar's price in terms of foreign currencies. In 1994 and 1995, the price of the dollar in terms of European currencies and Japanese yen plunged. As this occurred, holders of Eurodollars became nervous about holding assets in dollars. Similarly, during the period 2005-2007, a decline in the foreign exchange value of the U.S. dollar reduced the demand for Eurodollars.

The role of the dollar as an international currency can be jeopardized by continual fluctuations and fall in its foreign exchange rate.

Silver Coins in the United States: Good Money, Bad Money, and Gresham's Law

In the 1950s, in the United States, it was common for people to hand a teller or cashier a $1 bill, ask for "a dollar's worth of silver"--and get it. That's because, up until the 1960s, dimes, quarters, and half-dollars were actually made of silver.

Those days are gone. There's no silver in the dimes, quarters, and half-dollars used in everyday transactions. When the price of a precious metal rises above its face value as money, the metal becomes more valuable in alternative uses. Silver dimes, quarters, and half-dollars are no longer in circulation, because the silver in these coins is worth much more than the denominations of the coins. If such coins were still issued, an enterprising silver firm would find it cheaper to obtain silver by melting down coins than by buying it on the commodity market! Coins today are made of an alloy of nonprecious metal sandwiched around a layer of copper.

Gresham's Law, named after Sir Thomas Gresham, argues that "good money" is driven out of circulation by "bad money." Good money has higher value as a commodity than bad money.

Gresham, an Englishman, lived in the 16th century, when it was common for gold and silver coins to be *debased*. Governments did this by mixing nonprecious metals with the gold and silver. Governments could thus make a profit by issuing coins that had less precious metals than their face value indicated. Because different mintings of coins had varying amounts of gold and silver, even though they bore the same monetary denomination, some coins were *worth more* than others as *commodities*. People who dealt in gold and silver could easily see the difference between the "good money" and the "bad money." Even the common folk could get a rough idea about the value of coins by teasing their malleability. Because gold and silver are softer than other metals, this was a good test of the precious metal content of coins. Gresham observed that coins with a higher content of gold and silver were melted down for their precious metal or were hoarded, rather than being used in exchange.

In the mid-1960s, when the United States issued new coins to replace silver coins, Gresham's Law went right into action. Whenever a silver coin was found, it was hoarded or sold as silver rather than spent. Of course, old coins were also hoarded, because they became valuable as collector's items. In any event, it didn't take long for the new nonsilver coins to quickly replace the old coins. The "bad" alloy coins drove the "good" silver coins out of circulation, just as Gresham would have predicted!

Inflation always speeds up the action of Gresham's Law when both commodity money and paper money are used. When the price level rises, the money value of silver or gold rises as well. A bout of inflation, therefore, increases the rate at which gold and silver coins are hoarded. Today, few nations use gold and silver coins for money.

What's New in Money: An Electronic Revolution

Technology for putting money into and taking it out of your checkable deposit account is changing rapidly. In the future, your wallet may not contain wads of greenbacks, nor will you be jingling coins in your pockets. Instead, your wallet will contain small electronic devices about the size of a minicalculator and a card that looks like a credit card, but is really a minicomputer, that you can load up with dollar (or foreign currency) credits at an automatic teller machine (ATM) and use to pay for your purchases, just like cash. ATMs are now in use throughout the world and are linked to banking networks internationally via satellite.

We say that "checkable deposits" rather than "checks" are the major component of the money stock because these deposits can be accessed electronically, as well as by writing a check. A large portion of the work force already receives weekly or monthly pay in the form of an automatic transfer of funds from the employer's checkable deposit account to the employee's checkable deposit account. Many households enjoy the convenience of paying monthly bills by bank draft, or by accessing their bank accounts online and directly transferring funds to pay bills, rather than by writing checks. A bank draft is an automatic transfer from your checking account to that of a payee. You may already pay your car loan by bank draft. Thousands of people like you pay their monthly mortgage installments, electric and gas bills, and other bills through such automatic transfers of funds among banks. In effect, much of the nation's money stock is now automated, and our payments are made electronically through a computer network rather than by manual transfer!

You might already have a debit card. A debit card comes with a secret personal identity number (PIN) that can be used to get cash from an ATM or pay for groceries, like a credit card. However, unlike a credit card, payment with a debit card results in an instantaneous debit from your checkable deposit account, just as if you wrote a check on your account. As we use debit cards more, we'll need less currency to go about our daily business. Debit cards are readily accepted at most supermarkets, gas stations, and stores.

In the future, still more technological innovations in money are likely to come. Some companies are already experimenting with a cash card that has a built-in microchip. These cards can be loaded with cash credits from your checkable deposits at an ATM or through a specially adapted telephone. Merchants with special machines can then unload your cash when you make purchases and transfer it instantaneously into their checkable deposit accounts. There will also be electronic wallets that can store cash before it's actually loaded on the card. These wallets can also be used to make payments or to add cash to a depleted cash card. Ultimately, with satellite links among banks, you could use the card to make payments when you visit foreign countries, without the hassle of changing money at a foreign bank. You simply pay with the card. The conversion to euros or British pounds will be made automatically. Your checkable deposit account at home will be instantaneously debited for the dollar equivalent of your purchase via satellite, at the current exchange rate!

Many people already do their banking over the Internet using popular software supplied by banks. With such software, you can pay your bills electronically by transferring funds from your bank account to that of the person or firm to whom you owe money. You can even apply for a loan from your bank using the software; then, when the loan is approved, you can directly access the credit through your checkable deposit account to make payments.

In the future, money as you have known it may be extinct. It will have been transformed into checkable deposits that are activated only electronically to make payments.

Chapter 29

The Banking System

How old were you when you opened your first savings account? If you were grade-school age, you probably had a child's-eye view of the bank as a vast place where the coins and crumpled bills you handed the teller were deposited in the bank. In return, you received a brand new bank book, indicating the amount of your dollars the bank was holding for safekeeping. You also discovered that you could use the bank book to make additional deposits and that you could make withdrawals from your account, receiving the amount in either cash or as a check. The bank even paid for the use of your money by crediting your account with interest every month.

Modern banks are complex businesses that accept deposits from the public, facilitate payments, and actually create money by extending credit to their customers. The financial activities of private banks and the banking industry are vital to the smooth functioning of modern economies. During the period 2007-2009, a severe financial crisis that began with defaults on poor-quality mortgage loans, made by banks and other financial institutions, resulted in losses for many banking firms. As bank financial health deteriorated, the ability of the banking system to extend credit to businesses and households was impaired, and the result was a "credit crunch." Because businesses rely on credit from banks to finance their operations and households borrow from banks to acquire homes and cars, and make purchases with their credit cards, the decreased availability of credit caused a severe contraction of the economy, beginning in late 2007. In part, as a result of this credit crunch, the U.S. economy entered into a recession that continued throughout 2008 and 2009. During this period, many banks' financial health deteriorated to such a degree there was doubt some banks could meet all the demands of depositors if they wanted to withdraw funds. This led to a whole slew of government actions to help regain confidence in the banking system--many of which required taxpayer funding.

It is important to understand the role banks and the banking system play in the economy. In this chapter, we concentrate on the activities of banks. We will show how banks influence the money stock by extending credit. We will also analyze the balance sheets of banks to show what happens when the value of a bank's assets declines and how such a situation can cause a bank to become insolvent. In another chapter, we explicitly consider the role in the economy played by the central bank of the United States, the Federal Reserve System.

Concept Preview

After reading this chapter, you should be able to

1. Discuss the origins of banking and explain the concept of *fractional reserve banking*.
2. Examine the balance sheets of a bank and show how the balance sheets are affected when the bank makes loans.
3. Show how multiple expansion of the money stock can result from an inflow of excess reserves into banks and calculate the reserve multiplier.
4. Discuss bank portfolio management practices.

Banking

1 In the chapter The Functions of Money, we see that the bulk of the money stock, measured as M1, at any given point in time, is held as checkable deposits in depository institutions. Depository institutions are those that make loans and offer checkable deposit and time deposit accounts for use by households and business firms. They're members of a broad class of firms that seek to make profits by linking savers who supply loanable funds to investors and other borrowers.

Financial intermediaries are firms that specialize in borrowing funds from savers and lending those funds to investors and others. Depository institutions such as commercial banks, savings and loan associations, mutual savings banks, and credit unions are financial intermediaries. Brokerage houses, mutual fund companies, insurance companies, pension funds, and a host of other institutions and firms also provide financial intermediation services. However, only the banking system can actually create money.

Don't confuse depository institutions with another type of financial intermediary called an investment bank. Investment banks raise funds for their clients (which include institutions, such as corporations, pension funds, and insurance companies) and trade financial obligations in the form of securities, such as bonds and other assets that produce cash flows for investors. They also arrange for the sale of securities, such as newly issued stock or bonds of a corporation, or securities backed by such assets as mortgages, and guarantee their sale to investors--a process called underwriting. Investment banks do not issue checkable deposits, but do provide financial services, including assisting business in mergers and acquisitions, and selling securities in various financial markets.

Up until the late 1980s and 1990s, investment banks were separated from commercial banks, but in recent years, that separation has blurred and many commercial banks have acquired financial interests in investment banks. Since 1999, commercial banks in the United States have been allowed to underwrite securities and have, therefore, taken on some of the functions of investment banks. Also, the financial crisis in 2008 resulted in some famous Wall Street investment banks, such as Goldman Sachs and Morgan Stanley, choosing to convert to commercial banks to be eligible for such government programs as deposit insurance. In recent years, investment banks have played a leading role in structuring and selling risky financial instruments known as derivatives. During the financial crisis of 2007-2009, many of these assets lost value, leading to the failure of such investment banks as Lehman Brothers, in the United States.

The Evolution of Banking

In the Middle Ages, gold and silver were used as money in most European nations and for international trade. To avoid the inconvenience (and risk) of carrying around a wheelbarrow full of gold and coins, most merchants preferred to keep their money in a safe place. They usually left it with goldsmiths or money changers who first placed it on benches (or counters) so it could be examined and weighed. This practice evolved into what is now known as *banking*. The word *bank* is derived from the Italian word for bench, which is *banco*.

The goldsmiths of medieval England and the money changers of medieval Italy assessed the purity of the gold or coins before issuing depositors official receipts certifying the deposits. The depositors paid a fee for the storage service, just as you pay a fee for your checking account and other services at your bank. The deposit receipts soon began to circulate as a medium of exchange, which reduced the transaction costs by avoiding the inconvenience and risk of physically transporting gold in payment for goods and services. The holders of the receipts could at any time go to the goldsmiths and redeem the receipts for the stored gold. In effect, the receipts for the gold became paper currency.[1]

At first, the early bankers issued receipts for no more than the gold they had in the vault. If they stored 10,000 ounces, the total receipts in circulation were for no more than 10,000 ounces. However, some of the more astute goldsmiths observed that while receipts were presented each day for redemption of gold, new deposits of gold offset the decline from the outflow and resulted in the issuance of new receipts. *This meant the goldsmiths could either loan out a portion of the gold on deposit for the use of others or issue more gold receipts than the actual gold available in the vault.* On any given day the inflows and outflows of gold were quite predictable, and it was rare for more than 25 percent of the gold receipts outstanding to end up as net withdrawals on a given day. By making loans, the goldsmiths could add to profits but would run little risk of being unable to meet the demand for withdrawals.

The goldsmiths made loans by issuing receipts for more gold than the actual amount of gold in the vault. *Because the gold receipts circulated as money, the goldsmiths actually created money by issuing receipts to borrowers for more gold than was in the vault*!

Fractional Reserve Banking

The medieval goldsmiths and money changers were the first people to practice fractional reserve banking, in which a banking system creates checkable deposits by making loans in some multiple of the reserves it actually has on hand to pay withdrawals.

If goldsmiths had fully backed all their receipts (used 100 percent reserve banking), they would have been unable to issue gold receipts for more than the amount of gold in their vaults. They would have had to keep enough reserves on hand to pay out *all* their deposits in cash on a given day. But suppose the goldsmiths made loans equal to *all* the gold they had in their vaults. They would have created receipts for deposits even though the people receiving the loans would not have actually deposited gold in their vaults. If a goldsmith with 10,000 ounces of gold in the vault makes loans of 10,000 ounces to people who don't actually deposit gold, the goldsmith, who can now be called *a banker*, credits the accounts of the people receiving the loans with "deposits" of 10,000 ounces of gold even though those people don't actually deposit any gold. The borrowers are now free to use receipts for these "created" deposits as money in making purchases.

The fractional reserve ratio the banker is operating under is the ratio of actual cash reserves (which in this case is gold) in the vault to total receipts for deposits. In this case the fractional reserve ratio would be

$$\begin{aligned}\text{Fractional reserve ratio} &= \text{Cash reserves/receipts for deposits}\\ &= 10{,}000/20{,}000\\ &= 0.5\end{aligned}$$

The gold held in the vault is sufficient to pay out only half the actual receipts the banker has issued. The fractional reserve is only 50 percent of the actual deposit receipts. This sounds very risky, but it really isn't. The banker knows from experience that because of daily inflows of new deposits, the new outflow of the reserves is almost never more than 25 percent of the gold receipts that have been issued.

A banker who wants to earn even more interest income on loans may use a lower fractional reserve ratio. If it's highly unlikely that more than 20 percent of the receipts issued for deposits will be redeemed in gold on any given day, the banker may find it prudent and profitable to loan out *four times* as much gold as is actually in the vault! The fractional reserve ratio for this banker would be 0.20. The banker would issue receipts for the 10,000 ounces of gold on deposit plus receipts for an additional 40,000 ounces of

[1]For a discussion of the activities of goldsmiths in medieval England, see A. Andreades, *History of the Bank of England, 1640–1903*, 4th ed., with a new introduction by Paul Einzig (New York: Augustus M. Kelley, 1966), pp. 20–26 (first published in 1909).

loans for which no gold has been deposited. The fractional reserve ratio is therefore 10,000/50,000 = 0.20.

A banking system that held 100 percent cash reserves for currency deposited by its customers would be unable to create checkable deposits to make loans. The 100 percent reserve system would be very safe for a banking system because the system could meet its customers' demand for currency in the unlikely event that all customers simultaneously closed their accounts. But like most businesses, banks must weigh safety considerations against profitability. Banks therefore use a fractional reserve system and earn interest income on the checkable deposits they create when they make loans.

In the United States, banking operations and practices are closely supervised by the Federal Reserve System, the U.S. Comptroller of the Currency, the Federal Deposit Insurance Corporation, and a multitude of state regulatory agencies. The purpose is to maintain confidence in the banking system to prevent "panics" that might cause depositors to try to withdraw abnormally high percentages of the total deposits on a given day.

How Banks Make Loans and Create Checkable Deposits

2 The term bank generally refers to commercial banks and thrift institutions that offer checkable deposits. As of late 2008, the banking industry in the United States consisted of about 7,000 commercial banks, 1,200 thrift institutions (consisting of organizations such as savings and loan associations, and savings banks), and about 8,000 credit unions. Each of these institutions offers checkable deposits, time deposits, loans to businesses and households, credit to governments, and other financial services.

How a Bank Accepts Deposits and Makes Loans

To understand how the banking system of a modern nation operates, it's useful to begin by analyzing the operations of a single bank in a fractional reserve banking system. By examining the way a single bank accepts deposits and makes loans, you'll begin to understand how a modern banking system can actually create money in the same way the ancient goldsmiths created receipts.

The reserves of a modern bank in the United States consist of the balances the bank keeps on deposit with the Federal Reserve bank in its district or as currency in its vault. Each of the 12 regional Federal Reserve banks serves the function of a "banker's bank" in which banks have accounts, just as you have accounts at your bank. The Federal Reserve System seeks to control the money stock and, as you'll see shortly, *requires* banks to maintain a certain minimum fractional reserve ratio.

A bank's operations can be greatly clarified by examining its *balance sheet*, a statement of its assets and the claims against those assets. A balance sheet summarizes the financial position by showing the relationship between the bank's loans, property, and reserves and the claims that can be made on the bank by its creditors and owners. A bank's most important creditors are its depositors, who place their funds in the bank for safekeeping and have the right to withdraw those funds. The funds that depositors place in the bank are part of the bank's *liabilities*. They're debts of the bank to the depositors.

The bank's *assets* are property, cash, and debts owed to the bank, which include loans and any marketable securities the bank holds, such as Treasury bills and other notes of indebtedness. The *net worth* of the bank is the difference between its assets and its liabilities. Liabilities and net worth are two types of claims made against a bank's assets. The liabilities of a bank are the claims of its depositors and other creditors who aren't owners of the bank. The net worth of a bank is the claim the bank's owners have to its

Box 1 Bank Balance Sheet—End of Week 1: No Loans

Assets		Liabilities and net worth	
Reserves		Deposits	$10,000,000
Required	$2,000,000	Net worth	500,000
Excess	8,000,000		
Loans	0		
Property	500,000		
Total Assets	$10,500,000	Total liabilities and net worth	$10,500,000

assets after the claims of its creditors have been met. To understand how a bank can create money, we need to examine the relationship between its assets, liabilities, and net worth.

The function of a balance sheet is to divide the claims against assets into two mutually exclusive categories—liabilities and net worth. In other words, the bottom line of a balance sheet always shows that

$$\text{Assets} = \text{Liabilities} + \text{Net worth}.$$

The balance sheet equation is actually an *identity* because it must always hold by definition.

Box 1 shows the balance sheet of a bank that has just opened for business. After one week the bank has attracted $10 million in deposits. Assume these are all deposits of currency. The deposits don't actually increase the money stock. They simply convert currency into checkable deposits, which are the bank's liabilities. The bank has yet to extend any loans. The $10 million in currency that the bank accepts is deposited as reserves in the bank's own account at its district Federal Reserve bank. These reserves constitute part of the bank's assets because they are a sum of money owed to the bank. When the bank needs currency to meet the demands of its depositors, it can draw on its account at the Federal Reserve bank and request a delivery of currency. (Remember that currency is issued by the Federal Reserve banks.) The bank also has assets in the form of the structures and equipment that constitute its physical plant. Assume the value of the bank's property is $500,000.

As shown in Box 1, the bank's assets consist of $10 million of reserves and $500,000 of property. Its liabilities are $10 million of checkable deposits. Its net worth, which is the portion of its assets not owed to creditors or other nonowners, is $500,000. The total assets of $10.5 million exactly equal the sum of liabilities and net worth.

With reserves equal to its deposits, the bank is like the goldsmith who doesn't issue receipts for any more gold than the gold on deposit. The bank cannot make any loans as long as it keeps reserves equal to 100 percent of its deposits. Its only source of income will be the fees it charges its depositors for the services it provides.

Making Loans: Deposit Creation by a Single Bank

During the second week of business, the executives of the newly organized bank in this example will advertise their services and drum up some loan business. But how much can they loan out? Suppose the bank's managers believe it's safe to keep 20 percent reserves against its deposits. Also assume that the regulatory authorities overseeing bank operations will not permit bank reserves to fall below 20 percent of deposits. The regulators set a required reserve ratio, which is the minimum percentage of deposits that a bank must hold in reserves. *A bank can hold more than this minimum percentage of deposits in reserves, but it cannot hold less.* The required reserve ratio is one of the tools the Federal Reserve System uses to control the amount of money in circulation.[2]

Required reserves are the dollar value of the currency and deposits in Federal Reserve banks that a bank must hold to meet current regulations. For our example the bank's required reserves are $2 million, which equals 20 percent of current deposits. Excess reserves represent the difference between total reserves and required reserves against deposits. Our bank currently holds $8 million in excess reserves. This is the excess of its $10 million total reserves over its $2 million required reserves. *An individual bank can make loans in an amount up to the value of its excess reserves.* Our bank can therefore make up to $8 million in loans out of its initial deposits of $10 million when it operates under the 20 percent required reserve rule.

Many local business firms that want funds to finance expansion, inventories, new equipment, and other investments come to the bank and fill out applications for credit. The managers of the bank carefully examine the applications and choose the most creditworthy businesses as their loan clients. Bank managers must be concerned about the risk of default, which is nonrepayment of the principal and interest, on each of its loans. They must carefully balance the risk of default against the interest income the bank obtains from making any given loan.

After the bank sorts through the applications and makes its decisions, it creates deposits for the clients to whom it makes loans. Usually a bank requires that its loan clients have an account at the bank. When a loan is approved, the bank simply adds the amount of the loan as a checkable deposit to the client's account.

Assume that our bank actually lends out *all* of its excess reserves by creating deposits for its clients on the first day of business of its second week of operation. The resulting balance sheet is shown in Box 2. The bank now has $18 million in deposits, of which $8 million represents the proceeds of the loans it has just made. Because the newly created deposits didn't result from inflows of currency or from an increase in deposits in the bank's Federal Reserve account, reserves do not increase. Total reserves remain $10 million on the day the loans are made. The bottom line of *both sides* of the bank's balance sheet increases by $8 million on the first day of business of week 2 as the bank acquires assets in the form of $8 million of loans balanced by $8 million of newly created liabilities in the form of deposits. *By making loans in this way, the bank has created $8 million of checkable deposits. It has therefore created money equal to its initial amount of excess reserves.*

How Checks Drawn on Newly Created Deposits Affect an Individual Bank's Balance Sheet

If the $8 million of newly created deposits were to remain in the bank, the required reserves would be $1.6 million, and the bank would still have $6.4 million of excess reserves. However, the newly created deposits resulting from the $8 million in loans will be quickly withdrawn as the business firms use their loaned funds to finance their

Box 2 Bank Balance Sheet—Beginning of Week 2: $8 Million in Loans Not Yet Withdrawn

Assets		Liabilities and net worth	
Reserves	$10,000,000	Deposits	$18,000,000
Loans	8,000,000	Net worth	500,000
Property	500,000		
Total assets	$18,500,000	Total liabilities and net worth	$18,500,000

[2]As you can see in the chapter on the Federal Reserve System, the required reserve ratio is actually much less than 0.2 for most types of deposits at banks.

investments. *Because the banking system comprises many banks, spent loan proceeds are unlikely to be redeposited in the bank that initially created the checkable deposits.*

For example, suppose our bank is located in Denver and a firm receiving a loan of $1 million from it uses the funds to purchase a conveyor system from a firm in Detroit. The $1 million check that the firm writes to pay for the conveyor system is therefore deposited in a Detroit bank. The Detroit bank sends the check to its district Federal Reserve bank and requests that the check be deposited in its account there. The Federal Reserve bank then sends the check to the Denver bank's district Federal Reserve bank, where it will reduce the balance in the Denver bank's account by $1 million. When the Denver bank finally gets the check back, it will reduce by $1 million the sum in the account of the firm that wrote the check.

The process of transferring Federal Reserve deposits among banks as checks are paid is called check clearing. Because the Federal Reserve deposits held by banks constitute their reserves, the clearing of the $1 million check will reduce the Denver bank's reserves by $1 million and increase the Detroit bank's reserves by $1 million. Check clearing, which is handled by specialized firms and the Federal Reserve banks, usually takes a few days. The Denver bank can expect *all* of its $8 million of newly created deposits to clear through the banking system in this way and end up as deposits in *other* banks. Box 3 shows the Denver bank's balance sheet at the end of week 2 *after all its newly created deposits have been drawn on by the loan clients and the checks have cleared.*

Look at the liability side of the balance sheet. The bank now has only $10 million of deposits because its $8 million of newly created deposits has been drawn down and paid to other banks. Its net worth remains $500,000. Its assets now consist of $8 million in loans, $500,000 in property, *and only $2 million in reserves.* What happened to the $8 million in excess reserves that the bank had during its first week? These were paid out to *other* banks as the checks drawn on the loans cleared. The Denver bank's account at its district Federal Reserve bank was debited by $8 million after all of the checks written on the newly created checkable deposits were cleared. The bank no longer has any excess reserves, so it cannot make any more loans. When the excess reserves of a bank are zero, the bank is said to be *loaned up.* This bank will remain loaned up until it obtains more reserves from cash deposits or from deposits of checks drawn on other banks that increase the sums in its Federal Reserve account.

There's an important difference between the deposits that a single bank creates by making loans and those it obtains from customers who actually deposit cash or from checks drawn on other banks. Deposits of the latter type increase the bank's reserves, while created deposits do not. This bank cannot create any more checkable deposits by making loans until it receives more deposits that increase its reserves. In general, its reserves will go up if it receives deposits of cash or of checks drawn on other banks. Any type of deposit that

Box 3 Bank Balance Sheet—End of Week 2: All Newly Created Deposits Drawn and Paid to Other Banks

Assets		Liabilities and net worth	
Reserves		Deposits	$10,000,000
Required	$2,000,000	Net worth	500,000
Excess	0		
Loans	8,000,000		
Property	500,000		
Total assets	$10,500,000	Total liabilities and net worth	$10,500,000

increases the cash in the bank's vault or its deposits at its Federal Reserve bank will increase the bank's excess reserves and allow it to make more loans.

Multiple Expansion of the Money Stock for the Entire Banking System

3 A truly amazing fact is that the *entire* banking system can create checkable deposits by an amount equal to a multiple of existing reserves available to all banks. To see how this process works, we need to trace the progress of newly created checkable deposits resulting from loans as they filter their way down through many banks. Suppose the deposits that the Denver bank received during its first week of operation increase *total reserves* for the banking system by $10 million. This would be the case if the $10 million in new deposits consisted of currency from the mattresses of local misers! The $10 million in deposits would then increase excess reserves in the banking system by $8 million. In the previous section we saw how this $10 million in deposits supported $8 million of newly created checkable deposits as the Denver bank loaned out its excess reserves. To see how these initial deposits can support still *more* loans and more money creation, assume that *all* of the $8 million of new checkable deposits created by the Denver bank is deposited in the Detroit bank.

The table in Box 4 shows the changes in assets and liabilities of the Detroit bank. The $8 million increases the Detroit bank's liabilities by $8 million. As the deposited checks clear, the Detroit bank's reserves also increase by $8 million as $8 million in deposits at the Federal Reserve bank is transferred from the Denver bank's account to the Detroit bank's account. Remember that the deposits held by banks at their district Federal Reserve banks constitute the bulk of their reserves.

The Detroit bank must hold 20 percent of its new reserves as required reserves against its $8 million in new deposits. This amounts to $1.6 million. The remaining $6.4 million is excess reserves that can be loaned out. *The initial $10 million in deposits at the Denver bank that has already supported $8 million in loans can now be used to support an additional $6.4 million in loans.* As the Detroit bank makes these loans, it will create checkable deposits equal to $6.4 million for its clients, assuming it loans out of its excess reserves. The total expansion in the money stock as a result of the initial $10 million increase in bank reserves is now $8 million plus $6.4 million, which equals $14.4 million.

The process of expansion doesn't stop here! As the checkable deposits created by the Detroit bank are spent by the people who obtain the loans, they will be deposited in other banks, increasing the reserves of still more banks and allowing additional money creation. For example, suppose all of the $6.4 million is deposited in a New York bank. After the checks clear, the New York bank will find that both its deposits and its total reserves have increased by $6.4 million. This bank must keep 20 percent of these funds, or $1.28 million, in required reserves, and can loan out amounts up to the excess reserves of $5.12 million as newly created checkable deposits. The initial change in the New York bank's balance sheet is shown in Box 5. Assuming the New York bank loans out all its excess reserves, the money stock will increase by an additional $5.12 million.

Box 4 Changes in Assets and Liabilities—Detroit Bank

Changes in assets		Changes in liabilities	
Reserves	+ $8,000,000	Deposits	+ $8,000,000
Required	+ $1,600,000		
Excess	+ $6,400,000		

Box 5 Changes in Assets and Liabilities—New York Bank

Changes in assets		Changes in liabilities	
Reserves	+ $6,400,000	Deposits	+ $6,400,000
Required	+ $1,280,000		
Excess	+ $5,120,000		

The Money Creation Process

By now you can probably see how the process works. At each stage, as a result of new loans made by banks, the initial $10 million injection of reserve allows more money creation. At each stage, however, the loans that can be made become smaller because only 80 percent of the deposits created from new loans end up as excess reserves that can be used to make more loans. The increase in checkable deposits becomes smaller as the funds work their way through the banking system. Eventually the new loans that can be made approach zero.

The table in Box 6 shows how newly created checkable deposits decline at each stage, assuming that all excess reserves created at each stage of redeposit of loan proceeds are used to make new loans. It's also assumed, in the process of deposit and redeposit of checks among banks, that no reserves leak out of the banking system. For example, at each stage some of the people presenting checks to the banks may not deposit the full amount in their checking accounts. Instead, they may ask the bank to give them a portion of the funds in currency. If the currency is held by customers instead of being deposited in banks, the growth of excess reserves at each stage will be less, and the amount of new checkable deposits that can be created will also be less.

The sum of additional deposits eventually reaches a limit as the additional excess reserves for the banking system that result from redeposit of funds eventually approach zero. The table in Box 6 shows how additional checkable deposits fall to $4.10 million when the checks drawn on the New York bank's $5.12 million of deposits are deposited in a Chicago bank. The table also shows how the maximum amount of checkable deposits that can be created becomes smaller as the Chicago bank makes loans that are then deposited in a St. Louis bank. The last column traces out the process for a number of other stages

Box 6 Growth in Checkable Deposits from an Initial $10,000,000 of New Bank Reserves with a 0.2 Required Reserve Ratio (millions of dollars)

Stage	Bank	New reserves acquired	Required reserves	Excess reserves	Checkable deposits that can be created from new excess reserves
1	Denver	10.00	2.00	8.00	8.00
2	Detroit	8.00	1.60	6.40	6.40
3	New York	6.40	1.28	5.12	5.12
4	Chicago	5.12	1.02	4.10	4.10
5	St. Louis	4.10	0.82	3.28	3.28
6	San Francisco	3.28	0.66	2.62	2.62
7	Los Angeles	2.62	0.52	2.10	2.10
8	Seattle	2.10	0.42	1.68	1.68
9	Cleveland	1.68	0.34	1.34	1.34
10	All other				5.36
Total increase in money stock					40.00

and shows how the maximum sum of new checkable deposits that can be created approaches $40 million when banks find it profitable to loan out all the excess reserves they acquire at each stage of the process.

The Reserve Multiplier

For the entire banking system, an injection of $8 million in new excess reserves can be used to support a maximum of $40 million in new deposits when the required reserve ratio is 0.2! An individual bank can create no more checkable deposits than the amount of the excess reserves it acquires. However, the *entire banking system* can create new checkable deposits that amount to a *multiple* of the initial injection of excess reserves into the banking system. Any individual bank is likely to lose the excess reserves it acquires when it creates a checkable deposit for a loan customer. However, except for currency withdrawal, the excess reserves are not lost from the banking system. When the new checkable deposits are deposited in another bank, that bank also acquires reserves of which another 80 percent can be loaned out.

Notice that the money creation process is just like the one described for the multiplier effect in the chapter on Keynesian analysis. The maximum amount of new checkable deposits that can result from a new injection of excess reserve dollars into the banking system can be expressed as an infinite geometric progression. After the $8 million in initial deposits created by the initial injection of new excess reserves, $6.4 million is the second-stage maximum of new deposits that the Detroit bank can create. The $6.4 million can be expressed as (0.8)($8 million). Similarly, the $5.12 million maximum of new deposits that can be created at the third stage by the New York bank can be expressed as 0.8[0.8($8 million)], which equals $(0.8)^2$($8 million). In the same way the $4.10 million in maximum checkable deposits that the Chicago bank can create at the fourth stage, assuming it loans out all of its newly acquired excess reserves, can be expressed as $(0.8)^3$($8 million). The infinite geometric progression is

$$\begin{aligned}\text{Newly created checkable deposits} &= \$8\text{ million} + 0.8(\$8\text{ million})\\ &+ 0.8^2(\$8\text{ million}) + 0.8^3(\$8\text{ million})\\ &+ 0.8^4(\$8\text{ million}) + \ldots\end{aligned}$$

As the sum continues, each successive term becomes smaller because any number less than 1 becomes smaller when it is raised to a higher power. The maximum possible increase in checkable deposits, and hence the money stock (ΔM), resulting from the initial increase in excess reserves for the banking system can be calculated by using the following formula to solve for the sum of an infinite geometric progression:

$$\Delta M = \frac{\Delta ER}{(1-0.8)} = \frac{\Delta ER}{0.2}$$

where ΔER is the change in excess reserves for the banking system. In this example, ΔER is $8 million, which represents the increase in excess reserves resulting from an initial $10 million deposit of currency into the banking system. The maximum increase in the money stock resulting from new checkable deposits that can be created from this amount of excess reserves is therefore

$$\Delta M = \frac{\$8\text{ million}}{0.2} = \$40\text{ million}$$

When the required reserve ratio is 0.2, each dollar of excess reserves that enters the banking system can support *five times* as much in new checkable deposits when banks find it profitable to loan out all their excess reserves at each stage of the process. Under these circumstances, an injection of $8 million in *new excess reserves* into the banking system can therefore ultimately support \$40 million of new money stock in the form of checkable deposits.

The reserve multiplier is the maximum amount of new money stock that can be created from each dollar increase in the excess reserves available to the banking system. In the example just given, the reserve multiplier was 5. In general, the reserve multiplier can be calculated simply by dividing the number 1 by the required reserve ratio:

$$\text{Reserve multiplier} = \frac{1}{\text{Required reserve ratio}}$$

In this case the reserve multiplier is

$$\frac{1}{0.2} = 5$$

If the required reserve ratio were 0.1 instead of 0.2, the reserve multiplier would be increased to

$$\frac{1}{0.1} = 10$$

The maximum amount of new checkable deposits, ΔM, that can result from any increase in excess reserves can also be expressed as

$$\Delta M = \Delta ER(\text{Reserve multiplier})$$

This gives the amount of checkable deposits that the banking system can create from any increase in excess reserves when all excess reserves are loaned out and there is no withdrawal of currency from the banking system. In the previous example the maximum increase in checkable deposits is 5 times \$8 million, which is \$40 million.

Notice that the maximum possible increase in the money stock depends *both* on the excess reserves injected into the banking system and on the required reserve ratio. Other things being equal, the larger the increase in excess reserves or the lower the required reserve ratio, the greater the increase in the money stock. The *actual* increase in the money stock depends on the willingness of banks to lend out the excess reserves they acquire as a result of the money creation process and the amount of loan proceeds that end up in other banks (that is, the public's taste for currency). Thus, the preceding equation represents the maximum possible creation of deposits; in reality, the amount of money created will be less than is implied by the formula.

As a further illustration of the way to use the formula, suppose the Denver bank borrows \$5 million from its district Federal Reserve bank. When it does, the Denver bank's account at the district Federal Reserve bank will be credited by \$5 million. This \$5 million represents new bank assets in the form of reserves that are balanced by a liability in the form of a \$5 million debt to the Federal Reserve bank. Because no new deposits were acquired, the entire \$5 million becomes excess reserves for the Denver bank. Assuming a required reserve ratio of 0.1, the maximum increase in the money stock that can result from the Denver bank's loan from the Federal Reserve bank is

$$\Delta M = \frac{\$5\text{ million}}{0.1} = \$50\text{ million}$$

Assuming that banks find it profitable to loan out all their excess reserves at each stage of the money creation process, a \$5 million loan to a bank by the Federal Reserve bank will increase the money stock by \$50 million.

Deposit Contraction: The Process in Reverse

The banking system's capacity to create money by making loans is impaired if its reserves are reduced. Suppose misers decide to withdraw \$10 million in bank deposits and stuff the \$10 million into their mattresses. There will be no change in the money stock at first. The amount of checkable deposits will decline by \$10 million, but the amount of currency will increase by the same amount even if the currency stays in mattresses. However, bank reserves will also decline by \$10 million as a result of the withdrawal of currency that is not redeposited into the banking system. The \$10 million withdrawal from the banking system reduces excess reserves by \$8 million.

If the banking system is fully loaned up, to make up for its loss it will have to obtain more reserves or to reduce the amount of loans it has outstanding or the securities it holds. Certain types of loans can be called in. This means the bank tells the borrowers they must repay their loans. As loans are repaid, the banks in the system find that their deposits decline and the required reserves they must hold also decline. Of course, if there are excess reserves in the system, the decline in deposits will be less drastic than it would be otherwise.

In practice, banks rarely have to call in loans when reserves fall. There's a constant turnover of loans as old loans are paid off and new loans are negotiated. The decline in reserves caused by the \$10 million withdrawal will force the banks in the system to refuse to renew existing loans as their terms expire. As existing loans are paid off, the banks will also make fewer new loans than they would have otherwise. Finally, banks typically supply credit in an impersonal way by buying government securities and other notes of indebtedness. Banks can easily and quickly obtain additional reserves to meet their reserve requirements by selling securities they hold. If government securities are sold to the Federal Reserve banks, the banks will be credited with an increase in deposits that serve as reserves at the district Federal Reserve banks.

Assuming a required reserve ratio of 0.2, the maximum reduction in the money stock, ΔM, resulting from an \$8 million withdrawal of excess reserves from the banking system will be

$$\text{Maximum reduction in checkable deposits} = \frac{\text{Loss in excess reserves}}{\text{Required reserve ratio}}$$

$$\Delta M = \frac{-\$8\text{ million}}{0.2}$$

$$= -\$40\text{ million}$$

The maximum decline in the money stock that results from the \$10 million withdrawal from the banking system will therefore be \$40 million. Of course, the decline in checkable deposits will be less if the banking system has excess reserves than would be the case if it were fully loaned up.

Bank Demand for Excess Reserves

Why do banks give up the opportunity to earn interest income by holding excess reserves instead of using the reserves to create checkable deposits for loan customers? One reason is to meet expected deposit outflows. If banks anticipate a heavy net outflow of deposits, they may retain more excess reserves so they will be able to meet that demand without calling in loans, selling securities, or borrowing. When excess reserves are on hand, banks avoid the transaction costs of obtaining the funds they need in other ways. The savings realized by avoiding these transaction costs often more than offset the forgone interest income on the excess reserves. Banks also hold excess reserves when they perceive that making new loans or purchasing additional securities is risky, particularly if they have experienced losses on financial securities or defaults on loans.

A bank's opportunity cost of holding each dollar of excess reserves is the interest income it forgoes by not lending that dollar out. Naturally, the higher the interest rate, the lower the quantity of excess reserves demanded. The lower the interest rate, the greater the willingness of banks to hold excess reserves.

Remember that banks are motivated to make profits. During a recession, interest rates typically decline and business failures tend to rise. It's both less profitable and riskier for banks to make loans during periods of economic downturn than during periods of recovery, when aggregate demand and real GDP are increasing. Banks are therefore more likely to hold excess reserves during a recession, when lower interest rates and the increased risk of loan defaults make lending money less profitable. Similarly, they're less likely to hold excess reserves during a recovery, when interest rates increase and the risk of loan default declines. The graph in Box 7 illustrates the downward-sloping bank demand curve for excess reserves and shows how changes in the market rate of interest affect bank holdings of excess reserves.

The cyclical fluctuation in bank demand for excess reserves has important implications for the money stock. The more excess reserves banks hold, the less the amount of checkable deposits that banks create by making loans and therefore the smaller the money stock. For example, if the required reserve ratio is 0.1, each dollar increase in the excess reserves *held by banks* rather than used by them to make loans or buy securities will prevent the money stock from increasing by $10! During recessions, when banks seek to increase the excess reserves they hold, there is downward pressure on the money stock. Because, the available stock of money influences aggregate demand, the decline in the money stock could further decrease aggregate demand during the recession, thereby causing a further decline in real GDP. By the same token, the eagerness of banks to make loans with their excess reserves during periods of peak economic activity tends to increase the money stock. This puts upward pressure on aggregate demand and can contribute to inflation.

The profit-motivated banking system can therefore cause destabilizing swings in aggregate demand that exaggerate the ups and downs of the business cycle. In an attempt to minimize the swings, the Federal Reserve System seeks to manage the total reserves available to the banking system. The role of the Federal Reserve System in influencing the money stock in this way is the subject of the chapter The Federal Reserve System and Its Influence on Money and Credit.

Box 7 **Bank Demand for Excess Reserves**

The dollar amount of excess reserves banks desire to hold, other things being equal, increases with declines in the market level of interest rates. During an expansion, when interest rates typically rise, banks decrease holdings of excess reserves by extending more credit. This fuels the expansion and can cause inflation. During a contraction, when interest rates typically fall, banks increase their holdings of excess reserves by cutting back on credit extended, thereby decreasing aggregate demand and making the contraction more pronounced.

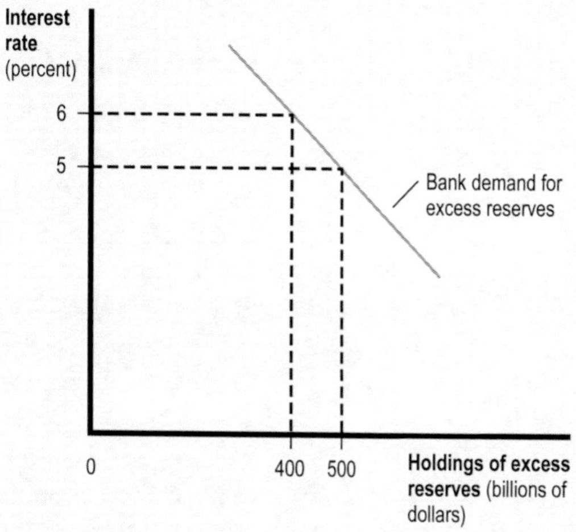

Interest rate (percent)
6
5
Bank demand for excess reserves
0
400 500
Holdings of excess reserves (billions of dollars)

The Federal Funds Market

In addition to holding excess reserves, banks lend these reserves to other banks that require reserves to support loans and security purchases. Banks with excess reserves often find it convenient to loan out these reserves to other banks on an overnight basis. Because these loans are repaid the following day, they allow the lending banks to maintain high liquidity. At the same time, they allow the lending banks to earn interest on their reserves, thereby reducing the opportunity cost of holding them. When excess reserves are lent out, the total reserves available to the banking system do not increase. However, the loan of excess reserves by one bank to another bank that uses the borrowed reserves to support loans to its customers acts to reduce the excess reserves in the banking system by converting the excess reserves of the lending bank into required reserves of the borrowing bank.

Federal funds are reserves loaned out by one bank to another bank on a short-term basis (usually overnight and rarely more than one week). Note that federal funds are funds belonging neither to the federal government nor to the Federal Reserve System. They are deposits that banks make at the Federal Reserve banks. Any bank that maintains a deposit account at a Federal Reserve bank can either lend or borrow federal funds. Special brokers arrange loans of federal funds among banks. When a loan is made, the Federal Reserve bank simply transfers deposits from the account of the lender to the account of the borrower. When the loan is repaid, the borrowing bank's Federal Reserve account is debited by the amount of the loan and an amount equal to the interest on the loan. That sum is then transferred to the account of the bank that lent the funds. Most transactions in the federal funds market are very large, involving transfers of-millions of dollars of reserves among banks.

The federal funds rate is the interest rate charged for the loan of reserves from one bank to another. This rate is a closely watched indicator of the availability of credit in the economy. It is published daily in such financial newspapers as *The Wall Street Journal*. Because the federal funds rate represents the market price of reserves to banks, its level varies with the scarcity of those reserves relative to the demand for their use to support loans. When reserves are scarce relative to demands for their use, the federal funds rate increases. On the other hand, when there is an increased availability of bank reserves relative to demands for their use and a consequent easing of credit conditions, the federal funds rate decreases. Because the federal funds market is very competitive, the federal funds rate fluctuates readily in response to changes in the demand or supply of bank reserves.

Bank Portfolio Management

4 The picture of bank deposit creation just presented is highly simplified. In actuality, banking is a very complex business. Banks must be concerned with both the *liquidity* and the *profitability* of their operations.

Banks earn profits because they can make loans at interest rates higher than the rates they pay to depositors. In fact, for most checkable deposit accounts, banks pay no interest to depositors. Instead, they charge fees for checking services and other financial services. For time deposit accounts, such as savings accounts and certificates of deposit, banks pay interest to compete with other financial intermediaries and attract deposits.

A bank whose management makes loans only to the least creditworthy applicants is able to charge higher interest rates than it could charge if it made safer loans. In this way the bank will make higher profits, provided the borrowers actually repay their loans. However, the bank risks the possibility that a high percentage of its loans will default. Loan default means the bank earns no interest and also loses the funds it lent out. Banks must balance their desire for increased profitability against the risk of default and the risk of having assets that cannot be easily converted into reserves to meet unexpected withdrawals. To do this, most banks are careful to have a diversified *portfolio*, or mix, of assets.

Typically, a bank will make some risky loans at high interest rates. The riskiest types of loans are those made in exchange for unsecured promises to repay. Consumer loans on credit card accounts are an example of such loans. Banks also make short-term loans to creditworthy businesses at lower interest rates than they charge consumers. The prime rate is the interest rate a bank charges its most creditworthy customers, usually large corporations, for short-term loans of less than one year.

A bank often demands collateral, which is an asset a borrower pledges to a lender in case of default. For example, if you borrow money to buy a car, the bank typically asks you to pledge the car as collateral. The bank usually has a formal *lien* on the car, which means you can't sell the car without the bank's permission or repayment of the loan. If you default on the loan, the bank can seize the car and sell it to obtain the outstanding balance on your loan. Similarly, a *mortgage* is a loan a bank makes to finance the purchase of a house or other real estate, with the loan secured by that asset as collateral. The interest rate a bank charges on a loan depends on the collateral offered by the customer, the customer's credit history (as rated by independent credit bureaus), and various other factors. In general, loans are not very liquid. Most loans cannot be easily called in to be converted into reserves when the need arises. However, very short-term loans—those made for a period of, say, one to three months—turn over quickly and give the bank some flexibility in adjusting the amount of loans outstanding when the need for reserves arises.

In the late 1980s and 1990s, there were some fundamental changes in bank portfolio management. In an attempt to add more liquidity to their portfolios, many banks shifted to securitized financial assets. Securitization is the process of combining a group of relatively illiquid assets, such as mortgages, together into a pool that's split into shares. The combined assets produce a cash flow accruing to the shares, as loan payments are made. Investors, such as banks, that purchase shares of these assets for their portfolios take on the risk that some of the loans will default and, therefore, payments will cease. If a significant number of loans backing the security default, the security's market value declines. Securitized loans are sometimes called asset-backed securities. The most common asset-backed security is the mortgage-backed security. However, securitization is also used to pool other assets, such as car loans, credit-card loans, and other types of credit, that are then sold in shares through financial markets. Sometimes, large securitized pools of assets are even cut up into slices (called tranches), with the underlying assets grouped according to risk.

Securitization began in the 1960s and was expanded in the 1980s for mortgage-backed securities. Two major government-sponsored enterprises, the Federal National Mortgage Association (Fannie Mae) and the Federal Home Loan Mortgage Corporation (Freddie Mac), engineered trillions of dollars worth of mortgage-backed securities to be sold to banks and other investors. By 2005 about half of all mortgage debt in the United States was bundled into mortgage-backed securities of varying risk. Many banks purchased these securitized assets in an effort to add liquidity to their portfolios. As housing values began to decline in the United States and many mortgage loans went into default, the value of the shares of the securitized debt began to plummet. Banks discovered that the price declines for these securities made shares much more difficult to sell, in part, because the complexity of the securitization process made it almost impossible to assess the riskiness of shares of the mortgage-backed assets. Tranches for so-called "subprime" mortgages, those backed by loans to borrowers with poor credit ratings, were particularly risky in 2007 and 2008, and, as a result of loan defaults and declining home values, the values of these tranches fell significantly. Some of these assets lost so much of their value that no one wanted to risk purchasing them. In fact, they were commonly referred to as "toxic assets," and a government program had to be enacted to use public funds to establish a more viable market for selling such assets.

The business of banking involves careful portfolio management to balance risks, profits, and liquidity. Most banks carry 10 percent to 20 percent of their assets in the form of government securities that can be sold quickly at very low transaction costs to obtain reserves when the bank needs them. Government securities are interest bearing debts of the federal government in the form of Treasury bills, Treasury notes, and Treasury bonds. The interest earned on these securities is typically lower than the interest the bank can earn on loans. However, their liquidity is worth the loss in profitability to the bank.

Commercial bank assets in the form of highly liquid government securities are often called secondary reserves. The sum of cash and government securities is the banking system's *liquidity base*, which is used to meet deposit withdrawal demands. About two-thirds of bank assets are in loans, the bulk of which is commercial and industrial credit.

Thrift institutions differ from commercial banks in that they specialize more in the provision of credit to real estate markets. As of 2008, nearly three-quarters of assets held by thrift institutions were for mortgages and other real-estate-related loans. Thrift institutions developed primarily to supply credit to homeowners and consumers rather than to commerce and industry. This legacy still dominates the balance sheets of these institutions, even though they have moved into other types of loans. The number of thrift institutions in the United States declined from a peak of over 4,800, in the late 1960s, to only 1,200 by the end of 2008. Many former thrift institutions have been acquired by commercial banks and other thrift institutions.

The bulk of the liabilities of commercial banks and thrift institutions is deposits, which account for over 70 percent of the sum of their liabilities and their net worth.

The Future of Banking

The banking industry is facing more challenges than ever before in credit markets. In the 1990s, large corporations, once the major clients of commercial banks, were borrowing directly from individual lenders by issuing commercial paper and raising more funds through direct issue of stock. When corporations did borrow from banks, many of the outstanding loans seemed in trouble, as some debt-ridden corporations faced bankruptcy.

In an effort to make banks more competitive in credit markets, new legislation in the United States enacted a number of reforms for the banking industry. The Riegel-Neal Interstate Banking and Branching Efficiency Act, enacted in 1994, encouraged bank mergers and more interstate banking. By 2003, widespread national branching networks, established by such large banks as Wachovia and the Bank of America, were resulting in cost efficiencies and a change in the U.S. banking structure. There were 3,517 bank mergers between 1994 and 2003, as banks sought to lower their operating and overhead costs, by sharing facilities, and to expand their market areas.

The Financial Services Modernization Act of 1999, also known as the Gramm-Leach-Bliley Act, removed restrictions on commercial banks to acquire businesses, such as investment banks and insurance companies, which had been prohibited since the 1930s by the Glass-Steagall Act. With the enactment of this legislation, commercial banks became bigger and more diversified, and acquired more outlets for extending credit and underwriting securities in financial markets. Huge commercial banks, such as Citibank, were able to acquire insurance companies and brokerage houses, and engage in investment bank activities in the credit markets. Between 2001 and 2008, as a result of mergers and acquisitions, the number of commercial banks in the United States fell from 8,200 to 7,000, and many banks became larger. As they became bigger and more diversified, the largest banks made fundamental changes in the way they conducted their operations. On the liability side, it became more common for banks to raise funds not only by accepting deposits, but also by borrowing in financial markets. Large banks issued bonds and other certificates of long- and short-term debt to help finance and expand their operations. For example, as of 2009, more than half of the liabilities of the three largest banks in the nation--Citigroup, Bank of America, and JPMorgan Chase--consisted of debts other than deposits.

There were also changes on the asset side of the balance sheet. As a result of securitization and the new bank legislation, many banks also began to take more risks in extending credit. Banking had become more impersonal, as direct interaction between individuals and bankers declined. Rather than directly originating mortgage loans within the local community, banks now purchased securitized mortgage-backed assets. Although banks were often able to reduce their costs by applying new technology and reducing the number of branches, the move to securities resulted in less investigation of the credit worthiness of borrowers. As standards for granting loans, particularly mortgage loans, became lax, bank portfolios became subject to more risk of default.

When housing values began to decline in 2007, many of the large banks found their portfolios had become less liquid and the value of their assets declined. Some of the large banks that had expanded into risky businesses and loans became close to insolvent, and some actually failed. (See the Principles in Practice Using Balance Sheets: Understanding How a Depository Institution Becomes Insolvent.) One of the largest commercial banks in the United States, Wachovia, had to be acquired by another large bank, Wells Fargo, to avoid the risk of failure.

As a result of the financial crisis and recession of 2007-2008, the future of banking in the United States is clouded. Many large banks have required government assistance (commonly called bailouts) to reduce the risk of insolvency. In 2008 there were 25 bank failures in the United States. The cost of bank failure is borne, to a large degree, by taxpayers, as deposit insurance is paid out. Of course, bank failure wipes out the net worth of the bank and stockholders suffer as well. Bank stocks lost much of their value in 2008 and 2009, contributing to sharp declines in major stock indices. Some of the deregulation of the 1990s is now being rethought, and it is likely that Congress will pass legislation to further regulate depository institutions in the United States.

Toward Understanding How the Money Supply Changes

The decisions made by the firms that constitute the nation's banking system exert an important influence on the money stock. In this chapter we've concentrated on the process by which the banking system actually creates money in the form of checkable deposits. As you have seen, the excess reserves available to the system and the willingness of banks to loan out these excess reserves are the major factors influencing daily money supplies.

To understand how the quantity of money available to the public changes, our next step is to examine how changes occur in the reserves available to the banking system. The Federal Reserve System manages the nation's money stock by determining the reserves available to the banking system and thus influencing the level of interest rates in the economy. To understand the role of money in the economy, we must analyze how the Federal Reserve System can control bank reserves and influence the willingness of banks to lend excess reserves.

In the chapter The Federal Reserve System and Its Influence on Money and Credit, we examine the operations of the Federal Reserve System. This examination gives you the necessary background to understand how the monetary policies pursued by the Federal Reserve System can influence macroeconomic equilibrium in the economy.

Summary

1. Financial intermediaries are firms that specialize in borrowing funds from savers and lending those funds to investors and others. The nation's banking system includes financial intermediaries that offer checkable deposits, such as commercial banks and thrift institutions.

2. Modern banking originated in the Middle Ages with the practice of issuing receipts for gold on deposit with goldsmiths and money changers. The receipts began to circulate as money. By observing inflows and outflows of gold deposits, the goldsmiths realized that only a small fraction of the gold on deposit was likely to be withdrawn on average each day. The issuers of gold receipts, who acted as bankers, ran little risk of running out of gold to meet depositors' demands for withdrawals. As a result, they could issue receipts for more than the actual amounts of gold they held in their vaults.

3. Fractional reserve banking allows a banking system to create checkable deposits by making loans in some multiple of the reserves that banks actually have on hand to meet withdrawals. The fractional reserve ratio is actual reserves divided by total deposits.

4. The banking industry in the United States consists of commercial banks and thrift institutions that offer checkable deposits. The reserves of modern banks consist of cash on hand and balances kept on deposit with the regional banks of the Federal Reserve System, the nation's central bank, which serves as a bank for bankers.

5. A bank balance sheet is a statement of its assets and the claims against those assets in the form of liabilities and net worth. A bank's liabilities consist mainly of deposit accounts, which represent the debt of the bank to depositors. A bank's major assets are its loans, government securities, and reserves in the form of cash on hand and deposits at a Federal Reserve bank. Its net worth is the difference between the value of its assets and the value of its liabilities.

6. The required reserve ratio for a bank is the legal minimum percentage of its deposits it must hold in reserves. Required reserves are the dollar value of the currency and deposits in a Federal Reserve bank that a bank must hold to meet current regulations. Excess reserves represent the difference between total reserves held against deposits and required reserves. A bank can use its excess reserves to make loans.

7. When a bank uses excess reserves to make a loan, it creates a deposit for the borrower. When the borrower spends the newly created deposit, excess reserves are likely to flow out of the borrower's bank and into another bank. The process of check clearing involves the transfer of deposits at the Federal Reserve banks. Excess reserves that one bank loses after making a loan are likely to end up as excess reserves for another bank in the banking system. A bank that uses up all of its excess reserves to make loans is said to be "loaned up." Banks typically hold at least some of their assets as excess reserves.

8. The banking system can create checkable deposits by an amount equal to a multiple of existing reserves available to all banks. As deposits created through loans are drawn down to make purchases, they increase deposits and reserves in other banks, which can use the excess reserves to make more loans. The reserve multiplier is the maximum number of new dollars in checkable deposits that can be created from each dollar increase in the excess reserve available to the banking system. The reserve multiplier is the inverse of the required reserve ratio.

9. Just as an increase in excess reserves can cause an increase in checkable deposits, a decrease in excess reserves can cause a decrease in checkable deposits. Because checkable deposits are the major component of the money stock, the excess reserves available to the banking system are an important influence on the money stock.

10. Banks choose to hold some of their assets as excess reserves instead of using those reserves to make loans. The opportunity cost of holding excess reserves depends on the interest that banks forgo by not using the funds to make loans. The demand for excess reserves typically increases during economic downturns and decreases during economic upturns. The greater the bank demand for excess reserves, the smaller the money stock.

11. Banks are motivated to make profits, but they must also maintain enough liquidity in their assets to permit adjustments in the composition of their asset portfolio as business conditions change. Banks are concerned about the riskiness of their assets and seek to minimize the risk of default on loans. Most banks hold 10 percent to 20 percent of their assets in government securities—assets that can be easily liquidated at low transaction cost. In their day-to-day operations, banks balance considerations of profitability, risk, and liquidity.

Concept Review

1. Why does fractional reserve banking give depository institutions the power to create money?
2. A bank has assets of $5 million and liabilities of $4 million. What is the net worth of the bank?
3. What is the reserve multiplier?
4. Under what circumstances does a bank become insolvent?

Problems and Applications

1. A banker operates under a 20 percent fractional reserve ratio. What amount of deposits can be supported by $5 million of reserves? In what form does a bank hold its reserves? Explain why a bank is unlikely to ever have to pay out all of its deposits in a single day. (1)

2. Suppose you deposit $3,000 in cash from your mattress in your local bank. Show the impact of your deposit on the bank's balance sheet. Explain why the bank cannot increase the loans it makes after it receives your deposit by more than a certain percentage of $3,000. If the required reserve ratio is 0.1, what is the maximum increase in checkable deposits that will result *in the entire banking system* as a result of your deposit? (1), (2), (3)

3. Suppose you have accounts at two banks. During a particular week you write a check on one of your accounts for $1,000 and deposit it in your account at the other bank. Will the money stock increase as a result of your transaction? (2)

4. Suppose the Federal Reserve bank lends funds to the First National Bank of Toledo. It does so by crediting the Toledo bank's account at the Federal Reserve by $2 million. Show the impact of the loan on the Toledo bank's balance sheet. What will happen to the Toledo bank's excess reserves as a result of the loan? If the required reserve ratio is 0.1, what is the maximum increase in the money stock that can result from the loan? (2), (3)

5. Suppose that during the holiday season households withdraw $10 billion from their accounts in banks to hold as cash in their pockets to facilitate shopping. What will happen to bank excess reserves and the capacity of the banking system to make loans as a result? (2), (3)

6. Suppose the required reserve ratio is 0.1, and current available bank reserves are $40 billion. Explain why checkable deposits in the banking system are likely to be less than the maximum possible $400 billion. (3)

7. Following is the balance sheet of the First National Bank of Jonesville:

Assets	Liabilities and net worth
Reserves, $100 million	Deposits, $180 million
Securities, $50 million	Net worth, $20 million
Loans, $50 million	

   If the required reserve ratio is 0.1, what is the amount of the bank's excess reserves? How many dollars' worth of additional loans or securities can the bank acquire as assets? How much of an increase in the money stock could the bank's excess reserves support if all banks in the banking system were to hold zero excess reserves? (2), (3)

8. Suppose the bank demand curve for excess reserves is a horizontal line. What will be the effect on the money stock of an increase in the amount of excess reserves available to the banking system? (3)

9. Explain why bank demand for excess reserves tends to increase during recessions. Why does the fact that bank demand for excess reserves varies with general business conditions tend to destabilize the economy? (3)

10. How do banks choose their portfolio of assets to balance considerations of profitability, liquidity, and risk? (4)

International Banking and the Global Economy

As the U.S. economy has become more integrated into the modern global economy, banking's international operations have increased. For example, as of 2009, Citibank operated 1,400 foreign branches. That same year, other large banks also had a significant presence in foreign nations--Bank of America operated in more than 150 foreign nations and JPMorgan Chase operated in over 100.

U.S. banks with international operations and branches in foreign nations assist U.S. business firms in exporting products. These banks also offer their customers international payment services that facilitate both importing and exporting. They serve as dealers in foreign exchange, earning a profit from exchanging the currency of one nation for that of another. By operating branches abroad, they can also compete for Eurodollars. Eurodollars, which aren't subject to any reserve requirements, can easily be transferred to the United States, where they can be used to support domestic credit demands and add to the profit of U.S. banks.

Banking laws in the United States provide certain special concessions to U.S. international banks. Since 1919, with the passage of the Edge Act, U.S. international banks that specialize in international financial services (Edge Act banks) have been granted the privilege of interstate banking, which is not generally available to other banks in the United States. International banking facilities (IBFs), other types of international banking operations within the United States, can accept deposits from and make loans to foreigners, and aren't subject to reserve requirements. IBFs are treated like foreign branches of U.S. banks, which are not subject to U.S. regulations or taxes.

Foreign banks maintain offices in the United States to assist their customers in export and import operations. An agency office of a foreign bank cannot accept deposits from domestic residents, but it is allowed to lend funds. In addition, some foreign banks operate subsidiaries within the United States. These banks offer all banking services and compete with American-owned banks. The International Banking Act of 1978 subjects these full-service foreign banks to the same rules and regulations as U.S.-owned banks, including taxation. Foreign banks can also operate full-service branches in the United States, subject to U.S. rules and regulations. Foreigners can also operate Edge Act and IBFs that compete with U.S.-owned and -operated counterparts.

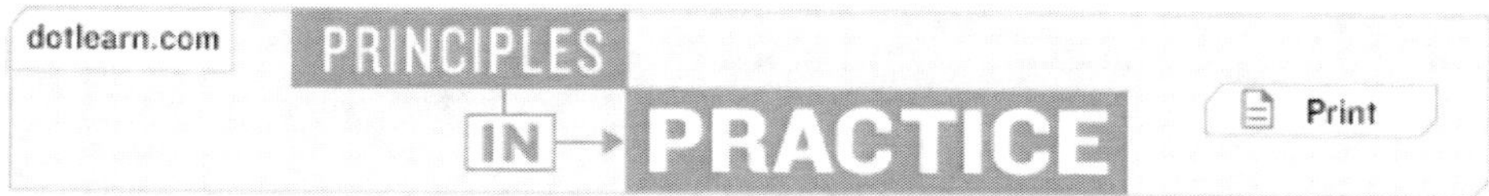

Business Brief: Nonbank Financial Intermediaries

All banks are financial intermediaries, but not all financial intermediaries are banks. What are nonbank financial intermediaries? How do they differ from banks, and what role do they play in the financial system?

Nonbank financial intermediaries are those that make loans and provide other financial services, but don't offer checkable deposits included in the M1 definition of money. These intermediaries channel funds from savers to borrowers. Some of them also help individuals and firms manage their cash balances in ways that are likely to affect the demand for money balances. Nonbank financial intermediaries include insurance companies, pension funds, mutual funds, and brokerage houses.

Insurance companies invest the premiums paid on policies in government securities, corporate stocks and bonds, mortgages, and real estate. Life insurance companies also allow their policy-holders to borrow funds against the cash value of life insurance.

Pension funds invest the contribution of employers and employees in various assets. In effect, these funds channel savings for the retirement of workers to finance investment by corporations and other businesses.

Finance companies that loan money to consumers and small businesses raise funds by borrowing on the open market and by issuing their own stocks and bonds. They use the funds they raise in this way to finance small loans. General Motors Acceptance Corporation is a finance company set up for the sole purpose of financing cars. Consumer finance companies such as Household Finance finance the purchase of such consumer durables as furniture and appliances. Business finance companies specialize in providing credit to business firms.

Mutual funds are financial intermediaries that channel the funds of savers into a variety of assets. These firms enable small investors to purchase part of a diversified portfolio of stocks, bonds, or other types of assets. One of the most significant developments in financial markets has been the organization of *money market mutual funds*. These funds invest in various kinds of short-term debt of business firms and governments, and also purchase bank certificates of deposit. They were first organized in the late 1970s. As of 2009, these funds had over $9 trillion in assets. A unique feature of money market mutual funds is that they often allow their investors to write checks on the balances in their mutual fund accounts! In other words, these funds are often as liquid as checkable deposits for the savers who invest in them. They're redeemable at a fixed price per share. However, most of the funds don't permit checks to be written for less than $500 or $1,000.

Money market accounts with check-writing privileges aren't considered legal checkable deposits. They aren't subject to reserve requirements. Money market funds enable small investors to earn interest on funds they would normally hold in checkable deposit accounts. By reducing average daily cash balances that households hold, the funds contribute to quicker turnover of the available money stock. In other words, they tend to decrease the demand for money represented by M1.

Deposit Insurance and Bank Failures

When he was asked why he robbed banks, outlaw Willie Sutton said, "Because that's where the money is!"

Perhaps because banks are where the money is, they're among the most regulated firms in the economy. The reason for stringent regulation by various state and federal agencies is to prevent the horrifying specter of a collapse of the banking system. A *bank failure* occurs when a depository institution cannot meet its obligations to depositors who want to withdraw funds. Because one bank often has deposits and loans at other banks, a major bank failure can set up a chain reaction that causes chaos in the financial payments system.

A loss of confidence in the banking system can cause a *bank panic* in which depositors flock to banks to convert their deposits to cash. The increase in withdrawals on a given day can deplete the banking system's reserves. During the Great Depression of the early 1930s, thousands of bank failures wiped out the savings of millions of people. In 1934, to prevent future bank failures and to maintain confidence in the banking system, the Federal Deposit Insurance Corporation (FDIC) was established to guarantee bank deposits. The FDIC insures all deposits, up to $250,000 per account in 2009, against loss as a result of bank failure. The National Credit Union Share Insurance Fund (NCUSIF), a federal fund backed by the full faith and credit of the United States government, insures deposits at most credit unions in the United States up to $250,000 per account, as of 2009. Because many corporations maintain deposit accounts well in excess of $250,000, this insurance provides protection mainly to households. If a bank should fail, the FDIC has the right to dismiss its management and take over the bank to oversee the sale of its assets to pay off depositors.

Like any insurance system, the FDIC works if there's a small, predictable number of bank failures in any year. The insurance fund held by the FDIC amounts to about 2 percent of insured deposits and only a fraction of a percent of total deposits. If a panic spread throughout the banking system, it would be difficult for the FDIC to meet all of its insurance obligations without help from the federal government, which would have to use tax revenues to bail out the banks.

In the 1980s, bank failures in the United States rose dramatically, placing a tremendous burden on the deposit insurance system. By 1989, the Federal Savings and Loan Insurance Corporation (FSLIC), which insured deposits at savings and loan associations, was insolvent, and the FDIC was running a loss. Major legislation was enacted by Congress to deal with a savings and loan (S&L) industry in which bank failure had become almost epidemic. The 1990 legislation

(1) established a new Office of Thrift Supervision to regulate thrift institutions, (2) transferred the insurance functions of the FSLIC to the FDIC (organizing the Savings Association Insurance Fund for S&Ls and the Bank Insurance Fund for commercial and savings banks), and (3) created two funds to deal with failed thrift institutions. The FSLIC Resolution Fund manages the remaining assets of S&Ls taken over prior to 1989, while the Resolution Trust Corporation manages the assets and liabilities of thrifts that became insolvent since 1989.

From 1989 to 1995, the Resolution Trust Corporation took over 747 thrifts with total assets of $394 billion, liquidated their assets, and paid off depositors. The bulk of the funds for the bailout, from the U.S. Treasury, were raised directly from taxpayers. Other funds were obtained from loans on which taxpayers would ultimately pay the interest.

To understand the causes of the savings and loan disaster, we have to go back to 1980. In that year, Congress enacted the Depository Institutions Deregulation and Monetary Control Act, which allowed savings and loan associations and other thrift institutions to issue checkable deposits and compete more aggressively for loanable funds. The increased competition caused a rise in the interest rates thrift institutions paid to attract loanable funds. Although most thrift institutions had previously specialized in low-yielding mortgage loans, they were now pressured to seek more lucrative loans to compensate for the low-interest loans in their portfolios. Many thrifts made riskier loans on which they charged higher interest rates. The Garn-St. Germain Act of 1982 increased the trouble by allowing S&Ls to expand their lending into commercial ventures and speculative land development.

In many ways, the deposit insurance provided by the FDIC and FSLIC contributed to the risk-taking of depository institutions and precipitated many of the bank failures in the late 1980s. Many depositors believed that amounts in excess of $100,000, the maximum amount (per account) insured at that time, would be protected in the event of a bank failure. Most of the people who supplied their loanable funds to the thrifts were fully protected by deposit insurance and, therefore, cared little about their bank's financial health or the way it was managed. The net worth of a poorly managed bank that becomes insolvent is negative. The bank's owners, therefore, have none of their own capital at risk and become more willing to take risks with the funds they obtain from insured depositors. In some notorious cases, officers of thrift institutions contributed to the insolvency of their institutions by using the funds of depositors for extravagant and sometimes fraudulent personal purposes.

Bank failures increased in 2007, and accelerated in 2008 and 2009, as declining real estate values, increases in mortgage loan defaults, and a major recession, which was expected to result in still more loan defaults, decreased the value of bank assets. A total of 25 banks failed in 2008 in the United States. More bank failures were expected, and outlays by the FDIC were increasing, especially after deposit insurance coverage was increased to $250,000 per account, in 2008 and 2009. In 2009 the FDIC estimated it would have to pay out $65 billion through 2013 to cover insured accounts and raised fees it charges banks for deposit insurance to cover the cost of insurance. Although taxpayers will not foot the bill for these fees, other programs designed to prevent bank failure, by using government funds to buy bank assets and bank stock, could cost taxpayers as much as $750,000 billion in the next few years, if the government cannot sell these assets at a later date for amounts close to their acquisition costs.

Using Balance Sheets: Understanding How a Depository Institution Becomes Insolvent

The net worth of a depository institution is the claim its owners have on its assets. Net worth measures how much the owners of the institution have, over and above the value of assets, to pay the claims of depositors. A bank's net worth (also called its "capital" or "equity") serves as a reserve to cushion against losses on the bank assets. In general, regulatory authorities in the United States worry that a bank is in danger of insolvency if its net worth falls below 5.5 percent of the value of its assets. Defaults on loans or decreases in the value of asset-backed securities held by a bank can reduce the value of the bank's net worth. If net worth approaches zero, the value of shares of the bank's stock will also approach zero. When investors sense a bank is running into difficulties that reduce the value of its assets, they often sell the bank's stock, pushing down the value of the bank's equity. Therefore, defaults on loans or general economic difficulties that hamper the abilities of clients to repay loans can quickly wipe out the meager net worth of a savings and loan institution, and even make it negative!

To see how this happens, let's take a look at the change in the balance sheets of a typical depository institution when a loan defaults or the market value of its asset-backed securities declines. Similarly, defaults on mortgage loans and declines in home values for mortgage-backed securities make those securities less marketable. This is reflected in a decline in the market value of the securities.

Assets	Liabilities and net worth
Reserves: No change	Deposits: No change
Loans and asset-backed securities: - $2 million	Other liabilities: No change
Government securities: No change	Net worth: - $1 million
Other assets at market value: + $1 million	

When a default takes place, the loan no longer produces a stream of income and becomes worthless. Beginning in 2007, an $8 trillion bubble in the U.S. housing market burst. Easy credit and lax lending standards had artificially inflated the demand for housing since 2001. The building boom eventually resulted in an oversupply of homes and housing prices began to decline. As home prices declined and interest rates on many adjustable rate mortgages began to rise, many homeowners defaulted on their loans and the value of mortgage-backed securities declined. Under these circumstances, if the borrower has pledged collateral for the loan, such as real estate, the bank can claim the right to sell the collateral. However, when the value of the collateral is less than the loan balance, as might be the case in a declining real estate market, the total asset value will decline.

For example, suppose a developer borrowed $2 million from a bank, using a shopping center as collateral. When building is finished, suppose the shopping center can't find any tenants willing to lease stores and the developer defaults on the loan. When the bank forecloses on the mortgage, it finds that the most it can get for the shopping center on the free market is $1 million. Therefore, the value of the loan declines by $2 million, while the value of other assets (property) increases by $1 million. The net decline of $1 million in assets must be matched by a $1 million decline in the sum of liabilities and net worth. Because deposits don't decline as a direct result of the foreclosure, the accountants debit the decline in assets against net worth. The balance sheet shows how the default causes the bank's net worth to decline by $1 million. If the depository institution's assets fall short of its liabilities, its net worth then becomes negative. When this situations occurs, it's declared insolvent.

When the economies of oil-producing states such as Texas, Louisiana, and Oklahoma went into a tailspin after 1985, hundreds of depository institutions in those states became insolvent. The difference between the value of their assets and their liabilities for insured deposits then became the responsibility of the deposit insurance agencies. The burden of making up the difference between the value of assets and liabilities is effectively transferred to taxpayers.

Notice that a bank whose net worth turns negative has nothing to lose by taking risks. It has none of its own funds at stake, because they've already been wiped out! Depositors care little about the fact than an institution has become insolvent, because they know that their deposits (up to the limit of $250,000 per account, in 2009) are insured by the federal government. As is always the case when someone else's money is at stake (in this case, that money belongs to taxpayers), managers and their creditors can afford to be more careless because they won't bear the costs of their mistakes! To avoid such perverse incentives, regulatory authorities will take over an insolvent bank when its net worth approaches zero. The authorities will try to pay off the bank's liabilities through deposit insurance and then sell the bank's assets to offset some of the costs to taxpayers. During the financial crisis of 2007-2009, legislation was enacted to allow the federal government to use funds to actually purchase bank stock, thereby increasing the bank's net worth and giving the government a claim on the bank's assets. Government funds were also used to buy some of banks' devalued mortgage-backed securities, to provide banks with more liquidity in support of deposits.

Chapter 30

The Federal Reserve System and Its Influence on Money and Credit

It's nicknamed "the Fed," and its chairman is a highly visible and powerful person whose pronouncements can change the course of the world's securities markets. It's the Federal Reserve System, and its policies and activities play a central role in the economies of the United States and the world.

As the nation's central banking system, the Fed engages in activities that influence the money stock available in the nation. The 12 regional Federal Reserve banks provide deposit accounts for commercial banks and thrift institutions and supply them with currency and check-clearing services. The Federal Reserve System charges banks fees for its services and earns interest on government securities it holds. However, unlike an ordinary bank, the Fed isn't motivated to maximize profits. It's an independent agency charged with promoting the public interest. In its efforts to promote economic stability, the Fed pursues policies that influence the stock of money in circulation, interest rates, and other macroeconomic variables.

In this chapter, we'll outline the organization and operations of the Federal Reserve System. Our main goal is to see how the Fed can influence the money stock and the level of interest rates in the economy. In the chapter Stabilization of the Economy through Monetary Policy, we examine how the Fed's activities can affect aggregate demand in the economy, and influence real GDP and the price level.

Concept Preview

After reading this chapter, you should be able to

1. Discuss the organization and structure of the Federal Reserve System.
2. Describe the techniques used by the Fed to influence the money supply.
3. Show how the Fed's open market operations affect bank reserves, securities prices, interest rates, and the money supply.
4. Analyze the nation's money supply curve and show how the desire of banks to hold excess reserves affects the quantity of money supplied.

The Federal Reserve System

1 The Federal Reserve Act of 1913 established the Federal Reserve System and the 12 regional Federal Reserve banks. The system was organized in response to a series of bank panics in the late 19th and early 20th centuries. One of the most serious of these panics occurred in 1907. The loss in savings resulting from bank failures at that time led to strong political support for a central banking authority. Since it was established in 1913, the Federal Reserve System has acted in the public interest to promote the stability of the nation's banking and monetary system. Its role in the economy has evolved gradually since its organization. Currently, the Fed's day-to-day operations constitute an essential mechanism in the functioning of the economy. To gain a complete understanding of how the economy operates, it's necessary to examine the organization and functions of the Federal Reserve System.

The Federal Reserve System: How It Is Organized

The Board of Governors of the Federal Reserve System, located in Washington, D.C., supervises the operation of the nation's banking system and acts as an authority to regulate the money supply. It consists of seven governors, each of whom is appointed by the president of the United States, after approval by the Senate, for a 14-year term. One of the governors serves as chairman of the Board. The chairman is appointed by the president for a four-year term.

The Board of Governors operates as an independent, self-supporting authority. It doesn't receive funding from Congress, and it doesn't take orders from the president or any other political official. The Board has broad policymaking functions. For example, within certain limits the Board makes decisions about reserve requirements for banks.

The regional Federal Reserve banks perform central banking functions for banks within each of 12 Federal Reserve districts. The regional Federal Reserve banks are located in San Francisco, Minneapolis, Kansas City, Dallas, Chicago, St. Louis, Atlanta, Cleveland, Richmond, Philadelphia, New York, and Boston. The maps in Box 1 show the boundaries of the 12 Federal Reserve districts.

Each of the regional Federal Reserve banks is a corporation. The stockholders in each of these corporations are the banks of the region that are members of the Federal Reserve System. All national banks—those with charters from the U.S. Office of the Comptroller of the Currency—must be members of the Federal Reserve System. Commercial banks whose charters are approved by state governments can choose to become members of the system. Currently, all depository institutions—both commercial banks and thrift institutions—are *required* to keep deposits at their regional Federal Reserve banks as reserves. Beginning in 2008, both required and excess reserves on deposit at regional Federal Reserve banks earn interest. The Fed can change this interest rate to influence incentives for the depository institutions to make loans. All depository institutions have the privilege of borrowing funds from the Fed. From the standpoint of the control the Fed exercises over banks, there's little distinction between member and nonmember banks.

The Federal Reserve banks are very unusual corporations. Member banks can neither sell their shares on the stock market nor expect to receive a large share of the Fed's profits, most of which are given to the U.S. Treasury. Member banks earn a 6 percent annual dividend on their stock no matter how much the Fed actually earns in a given year.

The regional Federal Reserve banks also issue currency. Although commercial banks and thrift institutions can't issue currency, they can draw down their deposit accounts at the Fed in exchange for crisp, clean dollar (or any other denomination) bills when they want to hold cash. Both currency and the deposits banks hold at their regional Federal Reserve banks are merely the liabilities issued by the Federal Reserve System.

Box 1 Boundaries of the 12 Federal Reserve Districts

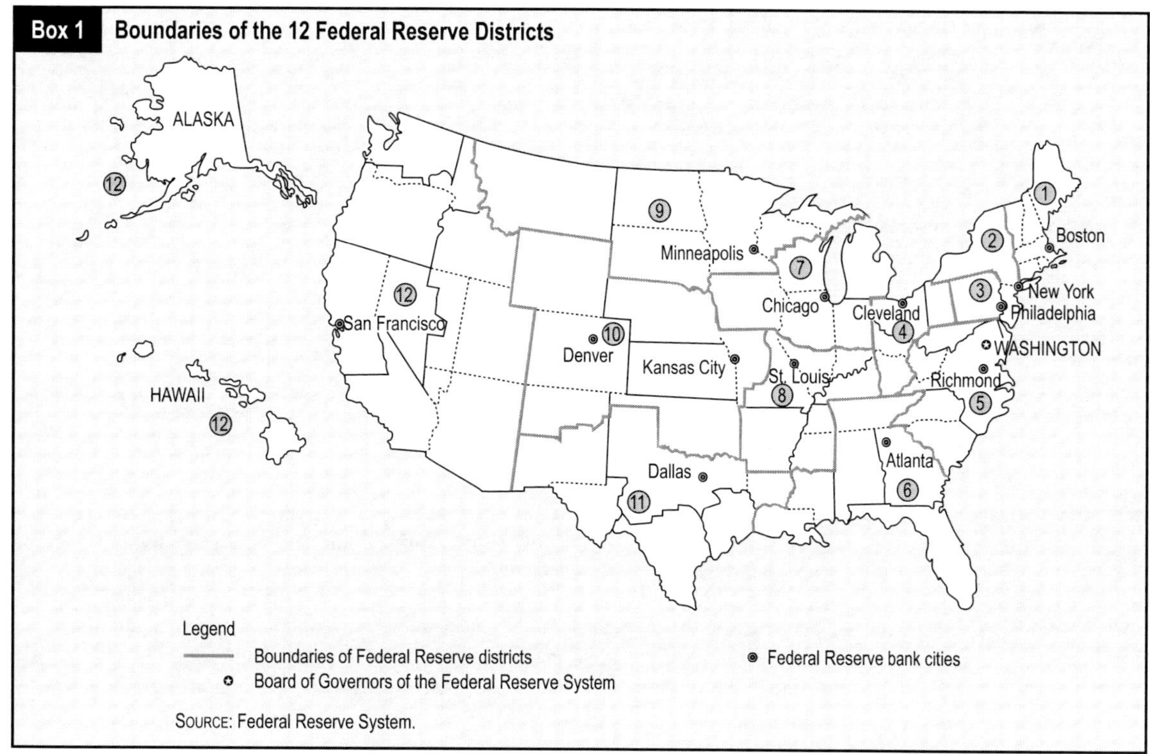

SOURCE: Federal Reserve System.

The most important policymaking component of the Fed is the Federal Open Market Committee (FOMC), which makes decisions that influence the amount of excess reserves available to banks. The FOMC is composed of the seven governors of the Federal Reserve System, the president of the Federal Reserve Bank of New York, and the presidents of four other Federal Reserve banks. The committee's decisions and their implementation are a major determinant of interest rates and the availability of credit each day. The committee issues directives to the Federal Reserve Bank of New York to buy or sell government securities on the open market. As you'll soon see, adjustments in the amount of government securities held by the Federal Reserve banks are the major means used by the Fed to influence the stock of money in circulation.

There's also the *Federal Advisory Council*, which represents the owners of the Fed—its member banks. This council, which consists of 12 bankers, has virtually no policymaking power. Its function is purely advisory, and its members have no direct influence on the Fed's day-to-day operations.

Box 2 contains a convenient chart that shows how the Federal Reserve System is organized.

Is the Fed Independent of Political Interference?

The intent of the original Federal Reserve Act of 1913 was to diffuse central banking power among the 12 regional Federal Reserve banks. However, the Federal Reserve System has evolved into an organization that's responsible for promoting economic stability. The Fed's Board of Governors now has a considerable degree of power in establishing policies that affect the performance of the economy. The Board can also influence the activities of the regional banks, and it has substantial input in the choice of the presidents of these banks. Thus, the Federal Reserve System has become a much more centralized decision-making organization than was originally intended.

Box 2 Major Components of the Federal Reserve System

Board of Governors of the Federal Reserve System

1. **Supervises the nation's banking system.**
2. **Regulates the money supply by setting reserve requirements and approving discount rate changes.**

Regional Federal Reserve Banks

1. **Perform central banking services for banks.**
2. **Issue currency and hold bank deposits to serve as reserves.**

Federal Open Market Committee

1. **Makes decisions that influence bank excess reserves by determining open market operations.**
2. **Is the policy arm of the Fed.**

The chairman of the Board of Governors wields considerable power. That power rests in his control over professional staff members and advisers to the system. This control enables the chairman to influence the information and analysis upon which policy decisions are based.

In an attempt to eliminate political pressures on the governors, each of the seven governors is appointed for a *nonrenewable* 14-year term. Therefore, the governors have little incentive to pursue policies that always please the president or senators. To avoid possible regional bias, each of the governors must be from a different Federal Reserve district. Finally, the Fed isn't dependent on Congress for funds. It earns interest income from its holdings of securities and from loans it makes to depository institutions. It earns, on average, more than $10 billion per year, but it returns the bulk of these earnings to the Treasury.

Despite the precautions that have been taken to ensure its political independence, the Fed is under constant and considerable political pressure. Congress can reduce the Fed's independence by changing the law. The threat of such legislative change can influence the Fed's behavior, thereby subjecting it to indirect and subtle political interference. In 1975, for example, Congress passed a resolution that requires the Fed to periodically announce its money supply growth targets. The Humphrey-Hawkins Bill, passed in 1978, requires the Fed to explain how its objectives coincide with the president's economic policies. The president can influence the Board of Governors by appointing governors and by his choice of the chairman. The president can also exert political pressure on the Fed in much the same way Congress can.

The issue of the Fed's political independence is highly controversial. Critics of an independent central bank argue that decisions affecting the functioning of the economy should be made by elected representatives rather than long-term appointees. However, those who favor an independent central banking authority argue that political control of the Fed can result in expansion of the money stock and credit in periods before elections to help the dominant political party win. Expansion of the money stock before an election may contribute to short-term increases in aggregate demand that result in expansion of the economy. If this causes the economy to overheat, there may be a period of inflation after the election.

The Fed's Influence on the Monetary Base

2 In the chapter The Banking System, we see that the banking system's potential to create money depends on the excess reserves available for loans. The Fed uses a

variety of techniques to control the excess reserves available to depository institutions. The monetary base is the sum of currency in circulation and total bank reserves outstanding at any given time. Note that both currency and bank reserves, which consist mainly of vault cash and bank deposits at the Federal Reserve banks, are *liabilities* of the Federal Reserve System. The Fed can vary the monetary base by adjusting its liabilities and assets and by regulating banks through control of reserve requirements.

By controlling the monetary base, the Fed can exert a strong influence on the equilibrium money stock. However, the equilibrium quantity of money held by the public at any point in time depends on a variety of factors, not just the actions taken by the Fed. An increase in the monetary base that increases bank excess reserves will increase the money stock only if banks choose to use those reserves to extend credit, thereby creating new deposits. The decisions made by profit-maximizing banks are therefore an important influence on the equilibrium money stock. The equilibrium money stock also depends on the public's demand for money balances. Shifts in the demand for money can affect interest rates and the desire of banks to create checkable deposits by extending credit.

In this section we concentrate only on the techniques available to the Fed to control the monetary base and, through that control, to influence excess reserves and the banking system's potential to create money. Once you understand how the Fed can achieve this, the next step is to show how Federal Reserve policies that control the monetary base also influence the equilibrium money stock and the equilibrium level of interest rates.

The Fed's major tools to control the monetary base are

1. Control of *required reserve ratios*, the legally mandated ratios of reserves to deposits for banks.

2. Control of the discount rate, the interest rate Federal Reserve banks charge member banks for loans. Beginning in 2008, the Fed can also influence the opportunity cost of lending out excess reserves by controlling the interest rate it pays on depository institution reserves, on deposit at Federal Reserve banks.

3. Open market operations, the Fed's purchases and sales of government securities on financial markets that affect the amount of excess reserves available to banks.

4. *Credit and liquidity programs*, the extension of credit in times of financial crisis to provide liquidity not only to banks, but also directly to borrowers and investors in key credit markets.

Control of Required Reserve Ratios

The Board of Governors of the Federal Reserve System sets reserve requirements for depository institutions. Within certain limits established by Congress, the Fed can raise or lower the required reserve ratio for checkable deposits, savings deposits, and time deposits. The table in Box 3 summarizes the reserve requirements for depository institutions in effect as of January 2005.

The maximum amount of checkable deposits supported by any given amount of bank reserves is inversely related to the required reserve ratio. If the average reserve requirement is, say, 10 percent, the maximum amount of checkable deposits can be computed by dividing the excess reserves by the required reserve ratio. If excess reserves are $20 billion and the required reserve ratio on average is 0.1, a maximum of $200 billion ($20 billion/0.1) in checkable deposits can be supported by those reserves. If the required reserve ratio were to fall to 0.05, the maximum amount of checkable deposits that could be supported by the available excess reserves would *double* to $400 billion ($20 billion/0.05).

Suppose checkable deposits at depository institutions are currently \$400 billion and the required reserve ratio is 0.1. An increase in the required reserve ratio of a mere 0.005 for these deposits would increase required reserves by a whopping \$2 billion (\$400 billion × 0.005). Excess reserves would fall by \$2 billion. If the required reserve ratio were 0.1005 after this increase, the potential decrease in the money supply resulting from the increase in the required reserve ratio would be

$$-\Delta M = \frac{-\Delta ER}{\text{Required reserve ratio}} = \frac{\$2 \text{ billion}}{0.1005} = \$19.9 \text{ billion}$$

The increase in required reserves would therefore have the potential to reduce the ability of the banking system to create checkable deposits by nearly \$20 billion, which is almost 5 percent of the amount outstanding prior to the increase in the required reserve ratio.

The effects of manipulating reserve requirements on excess reserves and the money supply are so powerful and pronounced that they prevent small adjustments in the money supply. A very small increase in reserve requirements can cause serious disruptions in the loan business of banks with low excess reserves because it may force them to call in loans or clamp down on new credit. However, the Fed occasionally reduces reserve requirements as a dramatic way of signaling its intention of following an expansionary monetary policy. In late 1990, for the first time since 1983, the Fed reduced the reserve requirement on business time deposits, from 3 percent to 0 percent, as it became clear that the economy was in a recession. This increased bank excess reserves by \$11.7 billion. Then, in April 1992, in response to a very sluggish recovery from the recession of 1990–91, the Fed reduced the reserve requirement for checkable deposits at large banks from 12 to 10 percent. Except for minor technical changes in reserve requirements, there were no significant adjustments in required reserve ratios between 1992 and 2005.

Discount Policy: The Fed as Lender of Last Resort

Bank borrowings from the Federal Reserve System are called discount loans or *advances*. These constitute a fraction of a percent of the assets of Federal Reserve banks usually amounting to less than 2 percent of the reserves of the banking system.

When Federal Reserve banks make loans to creditworthy institutions, they create deposits for those institutions. Because deposits at the Fed are part of the reserves of banks, these loans increase the reserves available to the banking system. Therefore, discount loans to banks have the potential to increase the money stock by a multiple of the amounts loaned. Increased willingness of the Federal Reserve System to loan funds to banks, as evidenced by a decrease in the discount rate, will increase excess reserves and the supply of loanable funds. By the same token, an increase in the discount rate will tend to decrease the potential supply of loanable funds.

Box 3 Reserve Requirements of Depository Institutions, January 2005

Type of deposit	Requirement as of January 2005
Checkable deposits	
\$0–\$7.0 million	0%
More than \$7.0 million to \$47.6 million	3%
More than \$47.6 million	10%
Business time and Eurocurrency deposits	0%

SOURCE: Board of Governors of the Federal Reserve System.

The Fed is very careful to regulate banks' use of the *discount window*, the Federal Reserve facility at which discount loans to banks are actually made. For example, if the discount rate is 8 percent and the market rate of interest that can be earned on three-month Treasury bills is 10 percent, banks will be tempted to borrow from the Fed to buy Treasury bills. They'll earn an easy and safe 2 percent on these transactions without risking any of their own funds. The Fed is well aware of this temptation, and it limits the frequency with which banks can avail themselves of the discount window loan facilities. By borrowing too much for short-term profit opportunities like investing in Treasury bills, a bank runs the risk of being turned down for credit in the future. Regulating the use of the discount window by refusing or discouraging borrowing is sometimes called *moral suasion* by the Fed. The Fed simply uses its discretionary power to say no to banks so that it can keep the supply of reserves down.

The discount window is also used by the Fed to maintain confidence in the banking system. The Fed lets it be known that it is the "lender of last resort." By creating new reserves for a bank when it is in danger of failing, the Fed can maintain confidence in the bank and prevent a bank run. For example, in 1970 the bankruptcy of the Penn Central Railroad rendered worthless much of that firm's short-term marketable loans, or *commercial paper.* Other companies that relied on short-term marketable loans as a means of raising funds had trouble selling their marketable loans in financial markets. The Fed solved this problem by announcing that it would gladly make discount loans to banks willing to make direct loans to firms that had difficulty in marketing their commercial paper. This avoided a chain reaction of bankruptcies that might have developed otherwise. Similarly, immediately after the stock market crash of 1987, the chairman of the Fed, Alan Greenspan, announced that the Fed would take measures to assure banks of access to the discount window. His motive was to bolster public confidence in the banking system's ability to obtain funds. Greenspan thereby hoped to prevent fears that banks that couldn't get quick repayment of loans to securities dealers would be unable to meet deposit withdrawal demands.

Changes in the discount rate don't always imply a change in Fed policy to influence the monetary base. Sometimes the Fed raises the discount rate simply because short-term market interest rates have risen. The Fed's objective may be merely to discourage overuse of the discount window for profit making rather than to slow down economic activity and decrease bank reserves.

How Open Market Sales of Government Securities by the Fed Affect Bank Reserves

3 The most flexible and most commonly used method of controlling the monetary base in the United States is Federal Reserve open market operations. These operations consist of daily sales and purchases of government securities by the Federal Reserve System. All open market operations are conducted through the Federal Reserve Bank of New York. The Fed's trading partners, 19 security dealers as of 2009 (many of which are banks), trade for their own accounts or act as agents for banks, for business firms, or for individuals who want to buy and sell government securities.

Any purchases of government securities by the Fed are purchases of securities *already outstanding* and held by the public. The Fed *does not* have the authority to purchase new Treasury issues of government securities.

Suppose, for example, that on a given day the Fed decides to reduce its holdings of government securities. It will sell securities on that day to dealers that are also depository institutions or through dealers that act as agents for such depository institutions (banks). To see how this affects the reserves available to the banking system, we need to examine both the balance sheet of the Federal Reserve banks and the consolidated balance sheet of all depository institutions.

Government securities held by the Federal Reserve banks are part of their assets. When they sell these securities to depository institutions, the Fed's asset holdings decline. As any accountant will tell you, when an entity's assets decline, its liabilities must also fall unless it acquires other assets to replace the ones that were sold. But how do the Fed's liabilities decline in this case? Well, the depository institutions pay for the purchases of government securities by drawing down their account balances (which serve as banking system reserves) at their district Federal Reserve banks. The Fed uses an electronic wire service (Fedwire) to simultaneously transfer securities to the banks and debit their accounts at their regional Federal Reserve banks. The Fed's liabilities therefore decline by the net sales of government securities. As a result, sales of government securities by the Fed to depository institutions will *decrease bank reserves. It follows that sales of government securities will decrease the monetary base and the potential of the banking system to create money.*

For example, a \$1 billion sale of government securities by the Fed to banks will reduce bank reserves by that \$1 billion. If the required reserve ratio is 0.1, the \$1 billion sale will reduce the potential amount of checkable deposits in the banking system by \$10 billion (\$1 billion/0.1). Box 4 shows the effect of the \$1 billion sale of securities on the balance sheets of the Federal Reserve banks and the banking system. For the Fed, the sale of securities reduces both its assets and liabilities by \$1 billion. For the banking system, \$1 billion of assets in the form of reserves are exchanged for \$1 billion of assets in the form of government securities. This decreases the reserves in the banking system and thus reduces the banking system's potential to extend credit. There is no direct change in the liabilities of the banking system as a result of the transaction.

As the supply of reserves in the banking system declines, the federal funds rate increases. In the chapter The Banking System, we learn that the federal funds rate is the interest rate charged for the loan of reserves from one bank to another. As bank reserves (the federal funds) become scarcer, the federal funds rate increases. This could also increase other short-term interest rates in the economy. The Federal Open Market Committee (FOMC) establishes the target rate for trading in the federal funds market. When it engages in open market sales of government securities, it monitors the federal funds rate, continuing to sell securities to primary dealers until reserves decrease enough to raise the federal funds rate to the targeted level.

Typically, the Fed will announce a target for the federal funds rate in a statement issued at the end of each FOMC meeting. If it wants to slow down economic activity, it announces an increase in the targeted federal funds rate and directs the President of the New York Federal Reserve Bank to engage in open market sales of securities until the federal funds rate rises to the target. For example, between 2005 and 2006, the federal funds rate target was increased each time the FOMC met. And, as bank reserves became scarcer as a result of Fed open market operations, the federal funds rate increased from 2.5 percent in February 2005 to 5.25 percent by June 2006.

How Open Market Purchases of Government Securities Affect Bank Reserves

It's easy to show that the Fed's *purchase* of government securities from banks or the public will increase the monetary base. For example, suppose the Fed acts through its dealers to buy \$1 billion of government securities from the portfolios of depository institutions. The Fed pays for the purchase by crediting the deposit accounts of these banks at regional Federal Reserve banks. These deposits, of course, are part of the banking system reserves. *The purchase of government securities from banks therefore increases the excess reserves of the banking system.* The creation of these excess reserves has the potential to allow multiple expansion of checkable deposits if the banks are willing to use the excess reserves to make loans. For example, if the required reserve ratio is 0.1, the $1 billion increase in excess reserves can support an increase of up to $10 billion in checkable deposits.

The table in Box 5 shows the impact of the Fed's purchase of government securities on its balance sheet and the consolidated balance sheet of the banking system. The purchase of $1 billion of government securities increases the Fed's assets by $1 billion. Of course, whenever assets increase, liabilities must increase by an equivalent amount unless other assets decline. The new liabilities for the Fed in this case are the $1 billion in bank reserves that the Fed creates when it credits the accounts of banks that have sold securities. The Fed can also pay for its purchase of government securities by issuing more Federal Reserve notes. This is another neat trick of the central bank—it can actually create currency. All the Fed needs to do is put in a call to the Bureau of Engraving and Printing and order a crisp, clean batch of new $10, $20, $50, and $100 bills to ship out to the banks in payment for the securities. The currency, of course, is just as much a liability of the Fed as the deposits it creates for banks.

Box 5 also shows the change in the balance sheet of the banking system. When the banks sell government securities to the Fed, their assets in the form of securities fall by $1 billion. In exchange, the banks receive new reserves in the form of the $1 billion that the Fed creates for them as deposits at regional Federal Reserve banks. These are now new excess reserves that the banks can use to make loans and create checkable deposits.

As bank reserves become more abundant as a result of the FOMC purchases of government securities, naturally, the federal funds rate falls. When engaging in an expansionary monetary policy, the FOMC usually establishes a targeted reduction in the federal funds rate after each of their meetings. As the federal funds rate declines, other short-term interest rates in the economy also, typically, decline.

For example, in response to the financial crisis and severe recession in 2008, the FOMC sharply lowered its target for the federal funds rate at each meeting. By December 2008, it reached an unprecedented target of between zero and 0.25 percent! Although bank reserves soared, the bankers were still reluctant to extend new credit, because of the risk they perceived in the credit markets. Although the Fed can supply banks with new excess

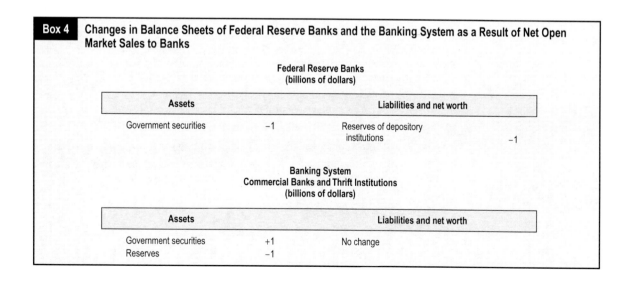

Box 4 Changes in Balance Sheets of Federal Reserve Banks and the Banking System as a Result of Net Open Market Sales to Banks

Federal Reserve Banks (billions of dollars)

Assets		Liabilities and net worth	
Government securities	−1	Reserves of depository institutions	−1

Banking System Commercial Banks and Thrift Institutions (billions of dollars)

Assets		Liabilities and net worth
Government securities	+1	No change
Reserves	−1	

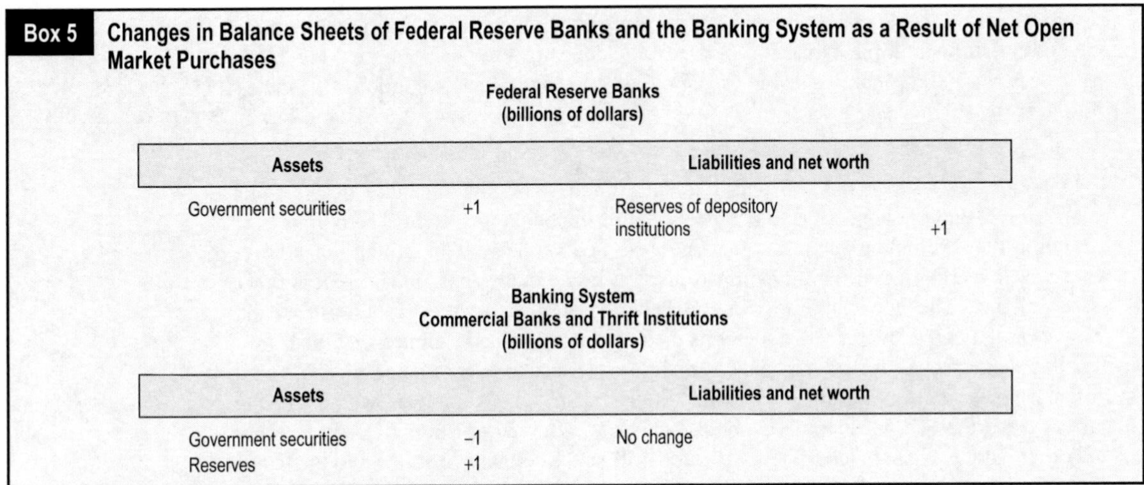

Box 5 Changes in Balance Sheets of Federal Reserve Banks and the Banking System as a Result of Net Open Market Purchases

Federal Reserve Banks (billions of dollars)

Assets		Liabilities and net worth	
Government securities	+1	Reserves of depository institutions	+1

Banking System Commercial Banks and Thrift Institutions (billions of dollars)

Assets		Liabilities and net worth	
Government securities	–1	No change	
Reserves	+1		

reserves, the decisions to use those reserves to expand the supply of money and credit remain those of the bankers.

A Recap: The Operations of the Federal Open Market Committee

The Federal Open Market Committee (FOMC) meets regularly (about once every six weeks) in Washington to decide on targets for the federal funds rate and bank reserves in an attempt to help stabilize economic fluctuations. The Fed might also monitor M1 (currency and checkable deposits). The FOMC directs the Federal Reserve Bank of New York, which is located in the center of the financial district in Manhattan, to buy or sell securities to achieve the Fed's objectives. The trading desk of the Federal Reserve Bank of New York (located on the eighth floor of the New York Fed, in case you want to visit) is the hub of the Fed's trading of government securities. The manager of the trading desk communicates daily with FOMC members to make sure their objectives are being achieved. If the objective on a given day is to increase bank reserves, thereby lowering the federal funds rate, the manager will purchase government securities from dealers who act as agents for the banks and the general public. If, instead, the objective is to decrease bank reserves, thereby raising the federal funds rate, the manager will sell government securities.

Open market operations are the most flexible and direct tool available to the Fed to influence bank reserves and the money supply. For example, open market operations are more direct than discount policy. A reduction in the discount rate doesn't necessarily increase bank reserves. Banks may not respond to the lower discount rate by borrowing significantly more. Another advantage of open market operations is that they are easily reversed. If the manager of the trading desk overshoots the target for bank reserves on a given day by buying too many securities, the manager can easily correct the mistake the following day by selling a bit more than would have been offered otherwise.

The chart in Box 6 summarizes the policies used by the Fed to influence the monetary base and shows how the impact of those policies on excess reserves affects bank loans and the money creation process.

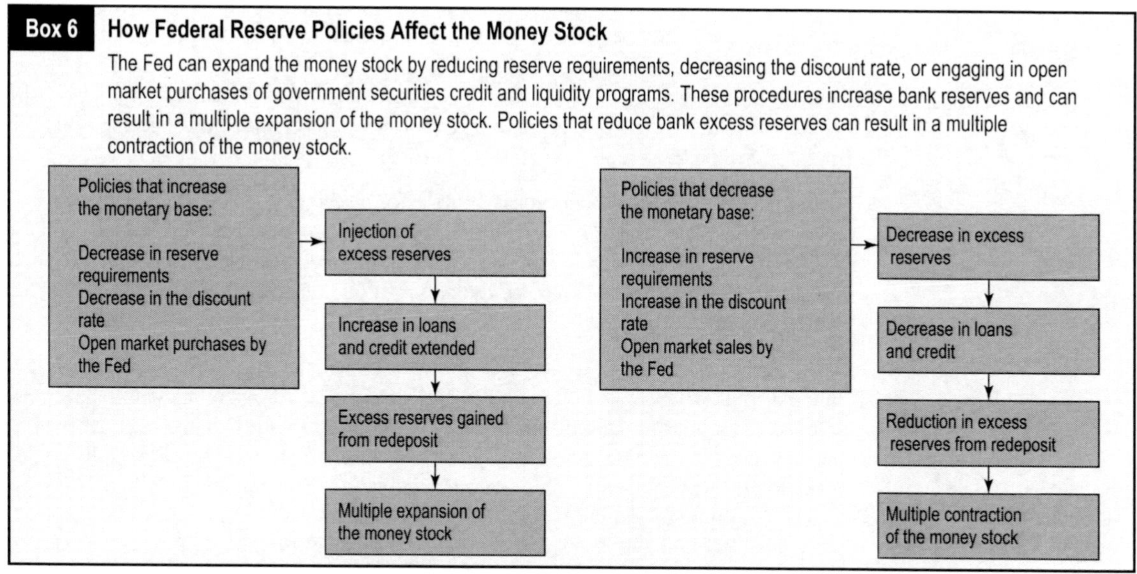

Box 6 How Federal Reserve Policies Affect the Money Stock

The Fed can expand the money stock by reducing reserve requirements, decreasing the discount rate, or engaging in open market purchases of government securities credit and liquidity programs. These procedures increase bank reserves and can result in a multiple expansion of the money stock. Policies that reduce bank excess reserves can result in a multiple contraction of the money stock.

Securities Prices, Interest Rates, and the Monetary Base

Here is one question that may have crossed your mind: How does the Fed get banks and the public to readily buy or sell securities so that the monetary base and bank reserve targets can be met? The answer lies in the price adjustments that allow securities markets, like all markets, to equilibrate. In fact, much of the trading that takes place is in short-term securities of the U.S. government that don't yield explicit interest. The return earned on these short-term assets depends on the difference between their purchase price and the price at which they can be redeemed when they mature. (A financial asset *matures* when its principal, or face value, is repaid by the borrower.)

Open market transactions of the Fed are usually trades of Treasury bills. (The Fed trades other government securities. In 2008 it announced it would also purchase longer-term securities, government-sponsored enterprise debt and agency mortgage-backed securities, in an effort to increase bank reserves and lending.) *Treasury bills* are short-term obligations of the U.S. government, with maturities of three months to one year, that are sold at auction without a stated rate of interest. If you buy a $10,000 one-year Treasury bill for $9,500 and hold it until it matures, you can redeem it for $10,000. Your effective interest is represented by the $500 *discount* you received from the face value when you bought the bill. In this case the effective annual interest rate would be 5.3 percent = ($500/$9,500)(100%).

When Treasury bill prices decline, their effective interest yield increases. For example, if you could buy a $10,000 one-year Treasury bill for $9,000, your annual interest would be the $1,000 discount from the face value of the bill. The annual interest rate on the bill would now be 11.1 percent = ($1,000/$9,000)(100%). A decrease in the auction price for Treasury bills therefore implies an increase in their effective interest yield. Similarly, an increase in the price of a security implies a decrease in its effective yield.

A similar relationship exists between securities prices and effective interest rates for Treasury notes and bonds with fixed yields. A *coupon bond* yields a certain stated percentage interest rate based on its face value. This interest rate is called the "coupon yield." For example, a bond with a $1,000 face value and a 10 percent coupon yield would pay $100 in interest over the year. If market prices of previously issued bonds decrease, the bonds sell at a *discount*. In addition to the coupon yield, the purchaser of a previously issued bond that sells at a discount will in effect earn additional interest when the bond is cashed in at maturity because of the discount in the bond price. For example, if you buy a one-year $1,000 bond with a 10 percent coupon yield for $900, you'll earn $100 per year interest plus an additional $100 (which was the discount on the bond) when you cash it in for its face value of $1,000 at maturity. Your effective yield if you hold the bond until it matures will be 22 percent = ($200/$900)(100%).

If the market price of a bond goes up, its effective yield goes down. For example, if the market price of a $1,000 bond with a 10 percent coupon yield were $1,050, you'd earn $100 interest on the bond. However, you'd still receive only $1,000 when the bond matures. The extra $50 you pay for the bond over its face value is a *premium* that reduces your effective yield on the bond.

With this bit of insight into the relationship between securities prices and their effective interest yields, you can better understand the impact of open market transactions on interest rates and the equilibrium quantity of securities held by banks and the public. On any given day, a certain amount of government securities (measured in dollar value) is available to banks and the public as financial assets. The amount held by the Fed is *not* available to the general public and banks as financial assets. The Fed holds such a large amount of government securities that it can influence the prices of these Treasury bills, bonds, and notes by selling or buying from its portfolio.

The graph in Box 7 shows the impact of the Fed's open market sales on the price of government securities. The sales by the Fed *increase* the supply of securities available for the public to hold. The increase in supply, other things being equal, lowers the prices. Therefore, the securities sell at a deeper discount than they did initially. In effect, this increases their yield and makes them more attractive assets for banks and the public to hold in their portfolios. Banks, securities dealers, and private investors are induced to buy the securities offered by the Fed because the price changes and yield changes caused by the increased supply serve to increase the quantity demanded. In Box 7 the supply curve for securities shifts outward and lowers the price of Treasury bonds, notes, and bills from P_1 on average to P_2 on average. The dollar value of quantity demanded increases accordingly from Q_1 to Q_2. The sales reduce the monetary base as banks and the public increase the quantity of securities they hold.

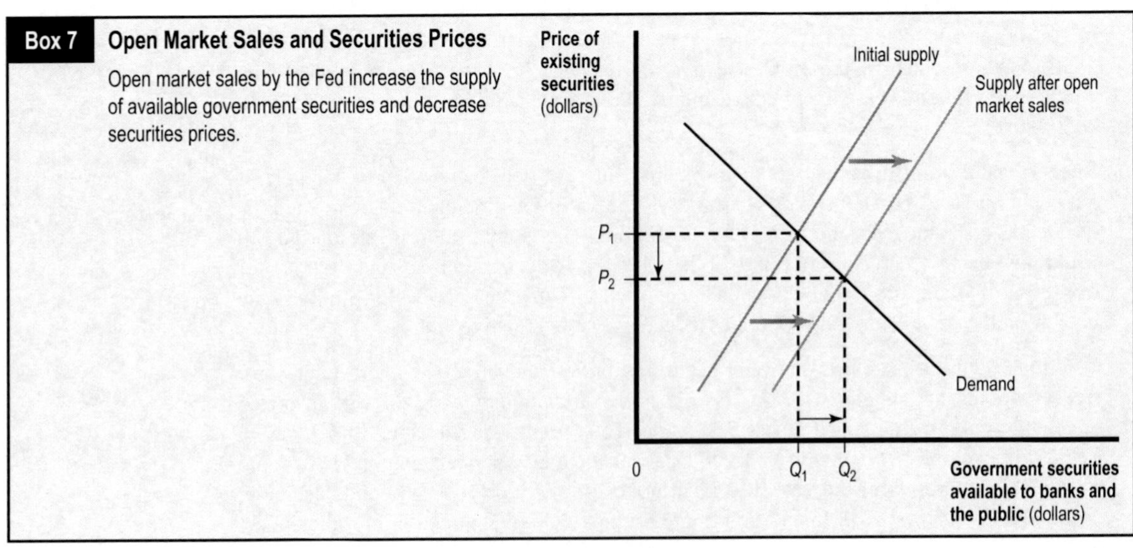

Similarly, open market purchases by the Fed reduce the supply of government securities available to banks and the public for their portfolios. The graph in Box 8 shows the impact of open market purchases. Once again, the initial equilibrium price and quantity are P_1 and Q_1, respectively. After open market purchases, the supply of government securities available to banks and the public decreases. This increases the price of the securities, which means the effective yield at maturity will fall. Government securities are now a less attractive financial asset to banks and the general public. The quantity demanded is therefore willingly reduced by the amount of the Fed's purchases. As the price of securities goes up to P_3 in Box 8, the quantity demanded declines to Q_3. As banks and the public willingly sell their securities to the Fed, the monetary base increases. Bank excess reserves also increase, allowing a potential multiple expansion of checkable deposits.

The Fed usually conducts its open market operations by buying and selling short-term government securities, such as Treasury bills. However, in March of 2009, it began also purchasing long-term government securities. As it did so, it bid up the prices of the 30-year Treasury bond. As bond prices rose, bond yields declined. However, it is much more difficult for the Fed to influence long-term interest rates than it is for it to influence short-term rates. This is because expectation of future inflation is a key influence on long-term interest rates. If participants in financial markets believe Fed policies will result in more inflation in the future, they will sell the longer-term securities, thereby lowering the price and increasing the yields.

This analysis points out an inevitable impact of the Fed's open market operations. As government securities are bought and sold, the equilibrium interest rates earned on them change. Because these securities are substitutes for loans and other financial assets held by banks and the public, a change in their interest rates will affect the demand for and supply of all types of financial assets. In effect, the Fed influences the general level of interest rates in the economy when it conducts its open market operations. The Fed therefore influences the economy in two ways through open market operations:

1. It affects excess reserves and the monetary base available to banks and the public directly through its open market sales and purchases.

2. It affects the equilibrium amounts of money holdings, spending, and investment through its impact on interest rates.

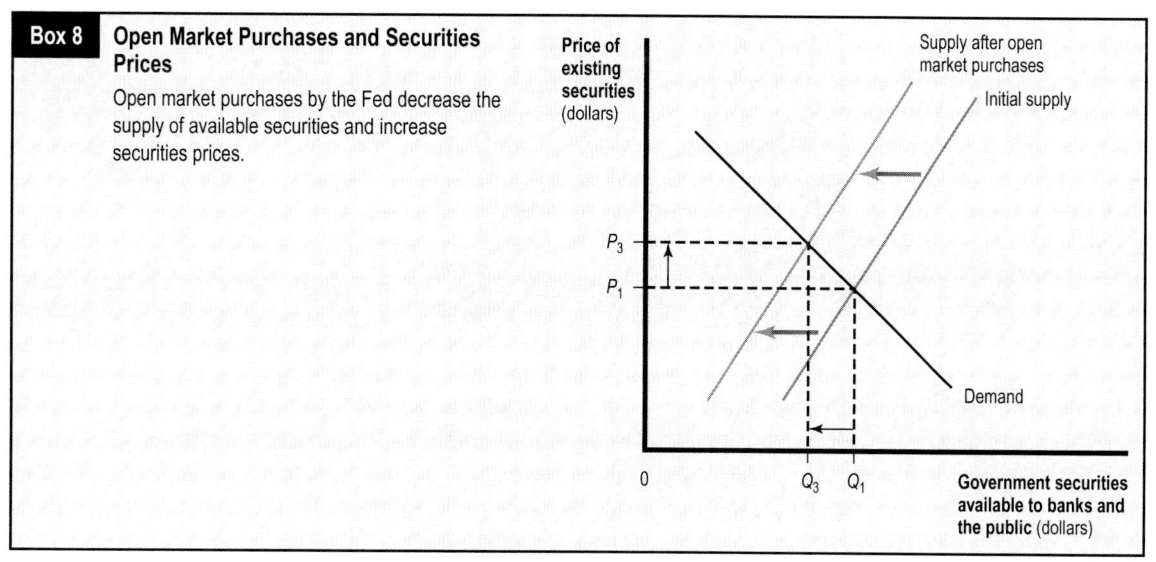

Box 8 Open Market Purchases and Securities Prices

Open market purchases by the Fed decrease the supply of available securities and increase securities prices.

Federal Reserve Credit and Liquidity Programs: Providing Funds Directly to Credit Markets

4 In response to the severe financial crisis of 2008, the Fed initiated a number of new programs designed to supply funds (liquidity) directly to investors and borrowers in financial markets. Many of these programs allowed distressed banks and other financial institutions to use illiquid assets, such as shares of mortgage-based securitized assets that had lost market value, as collateral to obtain loans from the Fed or to obtain more-liquid government securities in exchange for the illiquid assets. The programs, designed to keep financial institutions solvent, are linked to the Fed's role as the "lender of last resort."

When the Fed lends directly to participants in credit markets, it increases the monetary base by creating deposits at the Federal Reserve banks. When the borrowers spend the funds, they increase bank reserves, adding to the banking system's potential to extend credit.

The new programs included the Commercial Paper Funding Facility, the Asset-Backed Commercial Paper Money Market Mutual Fund Liquidity Facility, and the Money Market Investor Funding Facility--all designed mainly to provide liquidity to credit market financial institutions. For example, in 2008, the Fed lent $85 billion to the distressed American International Group (AIG) insurance company, in exchange for which it effectively became the largest investor in that company. It also lent hundreds of billions of dollars to a variety of financial institutions by accepting, as collateral, mortgage-backed securities that had depreciated in value because of loan defaults.

In March of 2009, the Fed initiated the Term Asset-Backed Securities Loan Facility (TALF). This new program committed the Federal Reserve Bank of New York to lend up to $200 billion to support consumer credit for automobile purchases, education loans, and credit card and other consumer debt finance. The program allowed finance companies and investors to use asset-backed securitized debt instruments that support consumer loans and small business loans as collateral for direct loans from the TALF. This program was designed to help increase consumer spending by making credit easier to obtain during the deep recession that plagued the U.S. economy in 2009.

As these programs injected credit into a troubled economy, the Fed's balance sheet ballooned from $1 trillion in assets, mainly in the form of Treasury bills and other government securities, to more than $2 trillion dollars in various assets. Just as the Fed's open market acquisition of government securities increases its liabilities by increasing bank reserves, so does its acquisition of such assets as mortgage-backed securities increase bank reserves. The new direct lending programs resulted in a net inflow of $1 trillion dollars in liquidity and bank reserves into the economy. In March 2009, the Fed announced it planned to acquire another $750 billion in government-guaranteed, mortgage-backed securities and $300 billion in longer-term Treasury securities (including 30-year government bonds), injecting that much more liquidity and bank reserves into the economy.

Despite the influx of bank reserves from both open market operations and direct lending, in 2008 and 2009, banks remained reluctant to extend new credit and bank excess reserves soared over this period. Between January 2008 and January 2009, the monetary base more than doubled, from $820 billion to $1.6 trillion, and bank excess reserves increased from a mere $1.6 billion to $674 billion!

Money Supply, Money Demand, and Equilibrium Interest Rates

5 The stock of money available on any given day must be willingly held by the public. The quantity of money demanded depends on the interest rate, the price level, real

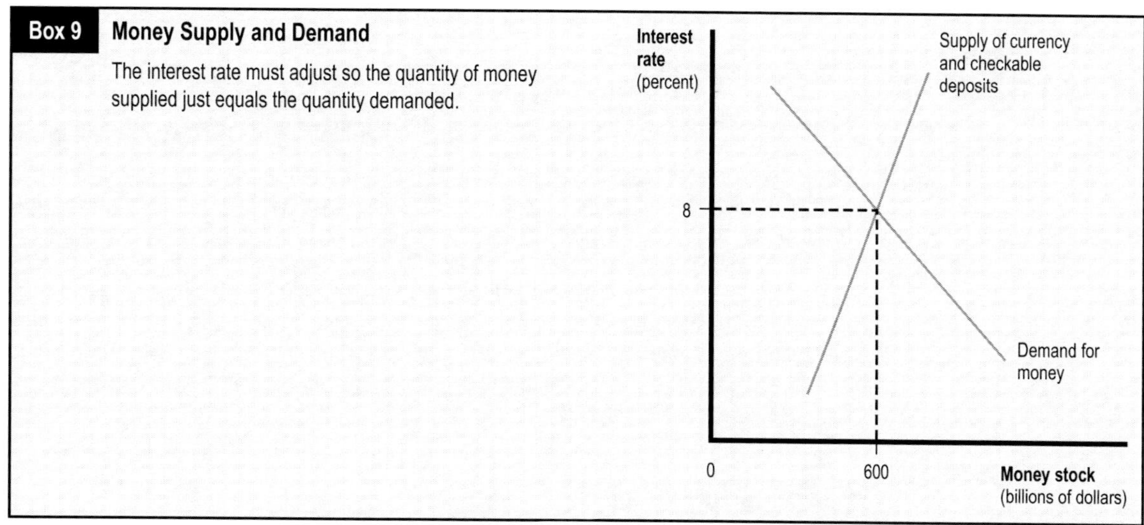

GDP, and other variables. In general, the lower the market rate of interest, the greater the quantity of money demanded. The higher the level of real GDP or the price level, the greater the demand for money. The graph in Box 9 depicts the demand for money as a downward-sloping function of the interest rate.

The money supply is a relationship between the quantity of money supplied in the form of currency and checkable deposits and the level of interest rates prevailing at a given point in time. An important influence on the money supply under the direct control of the Fed is the monetary base. One component of the monetary base, currency in circulation, is a part of the money stock. Bank reserves, the other component of the monetary base, aren't part of the money stock. However, each dollar of bank reserves has the potential to support many times that amount of checkable deposits, depending on the willingness of banks to create checkable deposits by extending credit. Although the Fed has direct control over the monetary base, the banking system's willingness to lend out excess reserves is a major determinant of the quantity of checkable deposits supplied.

The willingness of the banking system to create checkable deposits out of its available reserves is influenced by the prevailing level of interest rates. As pointed out in the chapter The Banking System, banks desire to hold more excess reserves at low interest rates than at high interest rates. It follows that, for any given available amount of bank reserves supplied by the Fed, the amount of checkable deposits made available by the banking system tends to increase as interest rates increase. This is because the profitability of making loans and extending credit in general tends to increase as interest rates rise. The total quantity of money supplied, therefore, tends to increase as market interest rates go up. The graph in Box 9 shows an upward-sloping money supply curve. The money supply curve shows the relationship between interest rates and the quantity of money supplied, given the monetary base and all the other influences on the willingness and ability of banks to extend credit.

In equilibrium, the interest rate must adjust so that the quantity of money demanded exactly equals the quantity supplied. The graph shows the demand for and supply of money balances. The equilibrium quantity of money balances is $600 billion at the equilibrium market interest rate (an average of all interest rates) of 8 percent. If the interest rate were higher than 8 percent, the quantity of money balances supplied would exceed the quantity demanded, and this would reduce interest rates. As interest rates fell, the quantity of money balances demanded would increase, while the quantity supplied by the banking system would decline. Similarly, if the interest rate were below 8 percent, the quantity of money balances demanded would exceed the quantity supplied and the interest rate would increase to 8 percent.

How the Fed Influences the Supply Curve of Money and the Equilibrium Interest Rate

The *equilibrium* quantity of money balances and the equilibrium interest rate level depend on the demand for and supply of money. The Fed can shift the money supply curve by influencing bank excess reserves, but it has no direct influence over the demand for money. Whenever the Fed engages in operations that increase bank reserves or currency in circulation, it shifts the money supply curve to the right. As shown in graph **A** of Box 10, the increase in the money supply puts downward pressure on interest rates, which fall until the quantity of money demanded once again equals the quantity supplied. Similarly, open market operations by the Fed that decrease the monetary base tend to put upward pressure on interest rates. (See graph **B**.)

The Power of the Fed

In this chapter, we've emphasized the mechanics of the Federal Reserve System's control of the monetary base and the money supply. The Fed's policies can affect both interest rates and the equilibrium money stock in ways that can influence real GDP and the price level in the economy. In the chapter Stabilization of the Economy through Monetary Policy, we analyze the impact of Fed actions that alter aggregate demand in the economy. To help you see how actions of the Fed affect the performance of the economy, we discuss the mechanism through which changes in interest rates and the equilibrium money stock affect aggregate demand curves.

Box 10 **The Monetary Base, Money Supply, and Interest Rates**

An increase in the monetary base increases money supply and results in a decline in interest rates, as shown in **A**. A decrease in the monetary base decreases the supply of money and increases the interest rate, as shown in **B**.

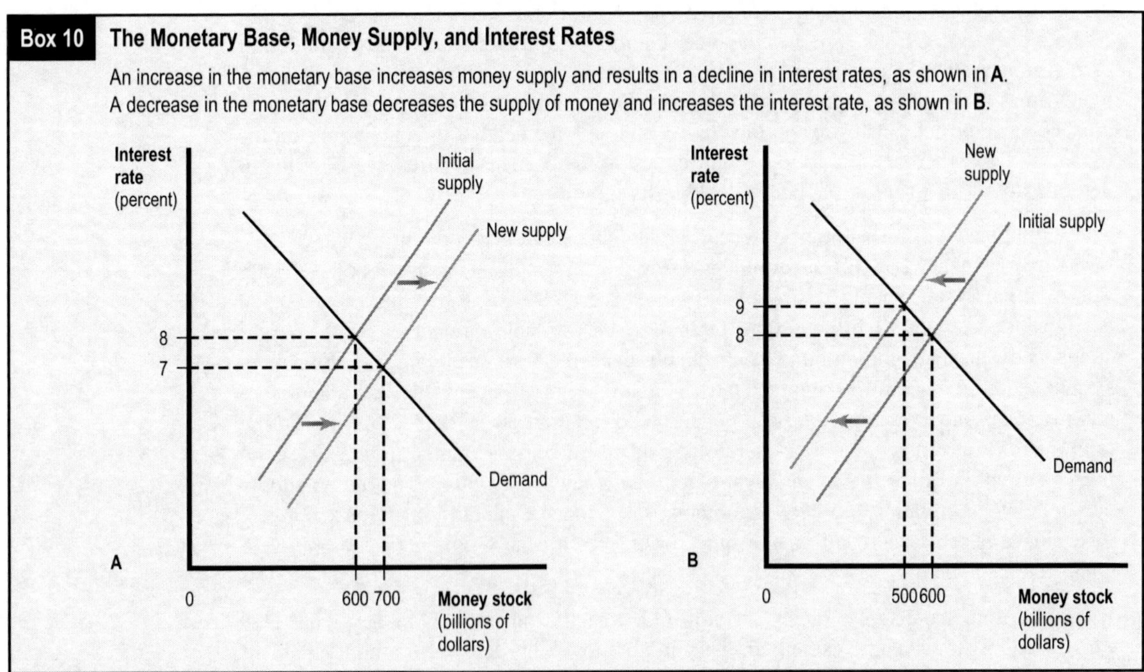

Summary

1. The Federal Reserve System, called *the Fed* for short, is the central banking system for the United States. The Fed consists of the Board of Governors of the Federal Reserve System and 12 regional Federal Reserve banks that perform central banking functions. The Federal Reserve banks are the "bankers' banks" that hold reserve deposits, issue currency, and provide check-clearing services for commercial banks and thrift institutions.
2. The Federal Reserve System operates as an independent authority that is not under the direct influence of the president or Congress. It earns income on government securities it holds as assets, and it does not receive any funding from Congress. The Fed also loans funds to banks.
3. The monetary base is the sum of currency in circulation and total bank reserves outstanding at any given time. The monetary base consists of liabilities of the Federal Reserve System. The Fed can vary the monetary base by adjusting its liabilities and assets and by regulating banks to control reserve requirements.
4. By controlling required reserve ratios, the Fed can influence the maximum amount of checkable deposits that can be supported by any given amount of bank reserves. An increase in the required reserve ratio decreases excess reserves and can result in a chain reaction that reduces the money supply. Similarly, a decrease in the required reserve ratio increases the excess reserves available from a given amount of reserves and can result in an expansion of the money supply.
5. The discount rate is the interest rate the Fed charges banks that borrow funds from the Federal Reserve banks. As the lender of last resort, the Fed can create bank reserves through discount loans for banks in danger of failing so as to maintain confidence in the banks and discourage bank runs. By making it easy to borrow to increase reserves, a decrease in the discount rate tends to be an expansionary influence on the money supply.
6. Open market operations by the Fed represent the major means of influencing bank reserves and the money supply. Open market operations consist of daily sales and purchases of government securities by Federal Reserve banks. Sales of government securities by the Fed absorb bank excess reserves and decrease the banking system's potential to create money. Fed purchases of government securities increase bank excess reserves and increase the banking system's potential to create money.
7. When the Fed sells government securities, it puts downward pressure on securities prices by increasing the amount available to the public. The lower prices of government securities mean that their yield to maturity increases. The public is induced to hold the larger supply of securities because their lower prices and higher yields make them more attractive as assets. Similarly, when the Fed buys government securities, it decreases the amount available to the public. This puts upward pressure on the prices of securities and lowers their yields to maturity. In this case the public willingly holds a smaller quantity of securities because their higher prices and lower yields make them less attractive as assets.
8. The money supply curve for the economy tends to be upward sloping. As the general level of interest rates increases, the quantity of money supplied by banks increases. This is because banks find it more profitable to make loans when interest rates rise. Higher interest rates therefore increase the quantity of checkable deposits created by the banking system.
9. The equilibrium quantity of money balances and the equilibrium level of interest rates adjust to equate the quantity of money demanded with the quantity supplied. The Fed can shift the money supply curve outward by increasing the monetary base, thereby putting downward pressure on interest rates. Similarly, a decrease in the monetary base shifts the money supply curve inward, putting upward pressure on interest rates. Although the Fed can influence money supply, it has no direct control over money demand. Actual money supply and interest rates depend on the interaction of the demand for and supply of money.

Concept Review

1. Briefly describe the organization and functions of the Federal Reserve System.
2. What are the major liabilities of the Federal Reserve banks?
3. How can the Fed influence the nation's monetary base and interest rates?
4. Describe the new programs the Fed initiated in 2008 and 2009.
5. What is the money supply?

Problems and Applications

1. In what sense is the Federal Reserve System independent of Congress and the president of the United States? How can the president influence the Fed's policies despite the fact that the president has no direct control over the central bank? (1)
2. The Fed increases its liabilities. Explain why this means that the monetary base will increase. How does the monetary base differ from the money stock? (2)
3. Suppose the Fed wishes to increase the money stock by $100 billion over the next three months. What techniques can it use to accomplish its objective? (3)
4. On a certain day the Fed buys $30 billion worth of government securities and sells $20 billion worth. Show the changes in the Fed's and the banking system's balance sheets. What effects will the Fed's operations have on securities prices and interest rates that day? (3)
5. Suppose on another day the Fed sells $80 billion worth of government securities and buys $30 billion worth. Show the changes in their balance sheets and the impact on securities prices and interest rates that day. (3)
6. When the economy moves into a recession, bank demand for excess reserves increases. How can the Fed use open market operations to increase the money supply under these circumstances? Use supply and demand analysis to show the impact of the Fed's policies, assuming the demand for money is given. (3)
7. The Fed decreases the monetary base. Show the impact of the Fed's action on the supply of money in the economy and the likely impact of the action on the level of interest rates. (3)
8. Under what circumstances will open market sales and purchases by the Fed have *no effect* on the level of interest rates in the economy? (3)
9. Suppose the demand for money increases. How can the Fed act to prevent the market rate of interest from increasing? (3)
10. Explain why Federal Reserve System open market operations can increase bank reserves but do not guarantee an increase in the money supply. (5)

International Operations of the Fed

The supply of and demand for the dollar in foreign exchange markets influence its price in terms of foreign currency. Changes in the price of the dollar affect the demand for U.S. exports and U.S. demand for imported goods, which in turn can influence real GDP and the price level.

Since the mid-1970s, when flexible foreign exchange rates became the norm, the Federal Reserve system has often intervened in foreign exchange markets to influence the price of the dollar. The Federal Open Market Committee (FOMC) of the Fed authorizes foreign currency purchases and sales, and a special manager for foreign operations is employed to supervise these operations. When the Fed buys and sells dollars and other foreign currencies on foreign exchange markets, it often does so in conjunction with similar operations by foreign central banks. In these ways, the Fed can affect the supply of and demand for dollars offered in foreign exchange, and thus can control the price of the dollar to achieve certain policy objectives.

Suppose the price of the dollar increases sharply in terms of a foreign currency, such as the yen. This increases the prices of U.S. exports in terms of foreign currency (yen) and reduces the quantity of U.S. exports demanded. The higher price of the dollar therefore decreases aggregate demand for U.S. products. To avoid this, the FOMC may instruct its manager for foreign operations to sell dollars on the foreign exchange markets. The increase in the supply of dollars on the foreign exchange markets puts downward pressure on the dollar's price in terns of the yen. In this way, the Fed can prevent the price of the dollar, in terms of the yen, from rising as much as it would otherwise.

Sometimes, the Fed acts to prevent the price of the dollar from falling excessively. When the price of the dollar declines, this puts upward pressure on the prices of imported raw materials and imported final products, which contributes to inflation in the United States. When the Fed wants to avoid such declines in the price of the dollar, it buys dollars, using its holdings of deposits denominated in foreign currencies. When the Fed buys dollars, it increases the demand for U.S. currency, thus putting upward pressure on the price of the dollar in terms of foreign currency. This prevents the price of the dollar from falling excessively.

By intervening in the foreign exchange markets in this way, the Fed acts to stabilize the price of the dollar.

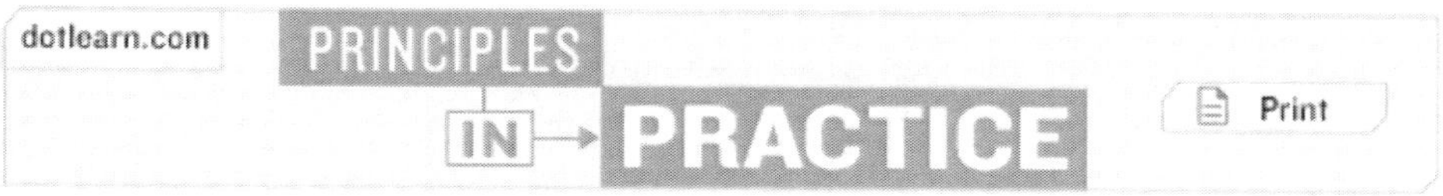

The Fed's Open Market Operations: A Visit to the Trading Desk

If you read *The Wall Street Journal,* you know that securities trading is a fast-paced, high-stakes business that demands keen minds and nerves of steel. You certainly need those qualities in abundance if you're in charge of trading for the Federal Open Market Committee (FOMC). Let's see what this job entails.

Policies of the FOMC are executed by the Federal Reserve Bank of New York. The responsibility for actually making the daily purchases and sales of government securities is that of the manager for domestic operations at the trading desk of the New York Fed. The manager supervises a staff of traders who telephone securities dealers to conduct transactions on the open market.

The Treasury securities that the trading desk of the New York Fed deals in are held in electronic book entry form. When transactions take place, ownership of securities is transferred through the electronic Fedwire system, and payment is also made through Fedwire. The volume of securities transfers that take place through Fedwire is very large, with transfers made into and out of the Fed's vast holdings of government securities. The trading desk moves around lots of cash and securities each day.

The manager keeps track of available reserves in the banking system and also watches the federal funds rate to get an idea of changes in bank demand for excess reserves. The federal funds rate is the interest rate banks charge for overnight loans of funds on deposit at Federal Reserve banks. The federal funds rate tends to fall when banks have increasing excess reserves, and it tends to rise when excess reserves are decreasing.

A day at the trading desk begins at 7:30 A.M., when staff members review changes in market conditions and analyze the effects of current economic reports on the demand for bank reserves.* Some staff members of the trading desk then meet with government securities dealers, who arrive at the Fed from their nearby Wall Street offices, to discuss forces at work in the financial markets that day. The manager of the System Open Market Account also confers with the staff of the Board of Governors and other Fed officials, via a telephone conference call, discussing forecasts for Federal Reserve bank balances. After due deliberation, the staff members develop a plan for open market operations for the day to hit the target for the federal funds rate. The decision is announced publicly to the markets at around 9:30 am, at which time the trading desk solicits offers from dealers.

At around 11:15 A.M., a conference call is put into the office of the director of the Division of Monetary Affairs at the Board of Governors of the Fed. This puts the staff of the trading desk in touch with members of the FOMC. The conference call, which usually lasts 15 to 20 minutes, gives the members a chance to comment on the trading plan for the day.

At around 11:30, the Fed begins executing its trading program by contacting dealers and making an announcement of its plan to the press. At that time, the traders on the eighth floor of the Federal Reserve bank begin making their telephone calls to dealers in government securities for price quotations. The Fed usually collects quotes on prices and makes all its trades by 12:15 P.M.

*For a full description of activities of the trading desk, see Ann-Marie Meulendyke, *U.S. Monetary Policy and Financial Markets* (New York: Federal Reserve Bank of New York, 1990), and M.A. Akhtar, *Understanding Open Market Operations* (New York: Federal Reserve Bank of New York, 1997). Also see *The Federal Reserve System: Purposes and Functions, 9th Edition*, (Washington, DC: Board of Governors of the Federal Reserve System, 2005).

Chapter 31

Stabilization of the Economy through Monetary Policy

In other chapters, we discuss the disruptive effects of cyclical unemployment and rampant inflation on the economy. In this chapter, we examine policies designed to stabilize the economy.

By studying the macroeconomic effects of monetary policy, you can see how changes in financial markets caused by shifts in the money supply are transmitted to the rest of the economy. Daily shifts in the money supply result in frequent changes in equilibrium interest rates. You'll now see that, over longer periods, changes in market interest rates and the equilibrium quantity of money affect the willingness and ability of buyers to spend.

The shifts in aggregate demand that result from changes in monetary policy also affect the demand for money in ways that further influence financial market equilibrium. In other words, there's a complex relationship among money, financial markets, and product markets we must understand to evaluate the ultimate impact of monetary policy.

Concept Preview

After reading this chapter, you should be able to

1. Discuss the mechanism through which monetary policy affects interest rates.
2. Show how an expansionary monetary policy shifts the economy's aggregate demand curve and affects macroeconomic equilibrium.
3. Show how a contractionary monetary policy shifts the economy's aggregate demand curve and affects macroeconomic equilibrium.
4. Discuss the quantity theory of money and the possible long-term effects of monetary policy on the price level.
5. Discuss the basic ideas and implications of monetarism for monetary policy.
6. Discuss monetary policy in the United States and some of the challenges the Fed faces in influencing interest rates in the modern global economy.

Stabilization and Monetary Policy

Stabilization policies are the procedures undertaken by governing authorities to maintain full employment and a reasonably stable price level. The federal government often seeks to stabilize the economy by using its expenditure and taxing powers to influence macroeconomic equilibrium. Central banks also use their powers to stabilize the economy through their influence on the money supply and the level of interest rates. In this chapter we concentrate on the ways central banking authorities seek to stabilize the economy and the difficulties they encounter in doing so. We also discuss how the growth rate of the equilibrium money stock can affect real GDP and the price level over the long run and how central banks seek to avoid the specter of hyperinflation.

Monetary policy consists of actions taken by central banks, such as the Fed, to influence the money supply or interest rates in attempts to stabilize the economy. Remember that there's a normal tendency for profit-motivated banks to increase loans during periods of economic expansion, when interest rates are rising. The expansion of credit and the quantity of money supplied during periods of peak economic activity tends to increase aggregate demand just when it needs to be restrained to prevent inflation from heating up. Similarly, during economic downturns, when interest rates are falling, there's a normal tendency for banks to cut back on loans and increase their holdings of excess reserves. As banks create fewer dollars of checkable deposits, the resulting reduction in the availability of credit and slowdown in the growth of the money stock could decrease aggregate demand and turn an economic contraction into a recession. By influencing the money supply, the Fed attempts to stabilize aggregate demand in ways that smooth out the swings of the business cycle.

A growing economy requires a growing money supply. Over time monetary policy is set to ensure that the banking system has adequate growth in excess reserves so that the long-term upward trend in real GDP isn't held down by inadequate monetary growth. However, monetary policymakers must also take care to avoid excessive monetary growth, which can cause high and continued rates of inflation.

Money and Short-Term Macroeconomic Equilibrium

1 Monetary policy affects the economy daily through its impact on investment spending, household spending, and international transactions. Economic stabilization is an art, not a science. No policymaker or economist has a flawless crystal ball that can foresee all the possible effects of a policy. Unexpected changes in an economy can frustrate the goals of the most carefully planned policies. The Federal Reserve System is one of two major forces acting to stabilize the U.S. economy. The other major force is the federal government itself, whose spending and taxing policies affect aggregate demand and, in some cases, attempt to influence aggregate supply over the long run.

Fiscal policy, which is the use of government spending and taxes to stabilize the economy, is the subject of the chapter Stabilization of the Economy through Fiscal Policy. In many ways, your understanding of the effects of fiscal policy on the economy will be enhanced if you first master the impact of monetary policy on economic performance. Studying monetary policy will help you understand the role of money in the economy and will enable you to see how the goals of fiscal policy must be coordinated with those of monetary policy. You'll then be better able to understand some of the controversies you often read about in the newspapers regarding the choice of appropriate policies to even out the swings of the business cycle.

Our first step in understanding how monetary policy affects the economy is to examine the mechanism through which changes in the monetary base (currency and bank reserves) by the Fed influence financial markets and aggregate demand on a day-to-day basis.

Short-Term Impact of Monetary Policy

In the chapter The Federal Reserve System and Its Influence on Money and Credit, we show how increases in excess reserves available to banks increase the capacity of the banking system to make loans. When the Fed supplies the banking system with new excess reserves, an expansion of the money supply results as banks use the new reserves to extend credit and, thereby, create new checkable deposits. The increased supply of money puts downward pressure on short-term interest rates and increases the quantity of credit demanded. The Fed also directly affects the level of short-term interest rates through the impact of its open market operations on securities prices. As interest rates fall, the opportunity cost of holding money falls, and the public willingly holds an expanded money stock created through new loans.

The chart and graphs in Box 1 summarize the immediate effects on interest rates of a decision by the Fed to adjust the excess reserves available to depository institutions. As you can see, a decrease in the money supply causes interest rates to rise, while an increase in the money supply causes interest rates to fall.[1] When the Fed increases the monetary base or its rate of growth by pumping excess reserves into the banking system, it's engaging in an expansionary monetary policy. When the Fed decreases the monetary base or its rate of growth by decreasing the excess reserves available to depository institutions, it's said to be engaging in a contractionary monetary policy.

Box 1 The Monetary Policy Transmission Mechanism: Immediate Effects

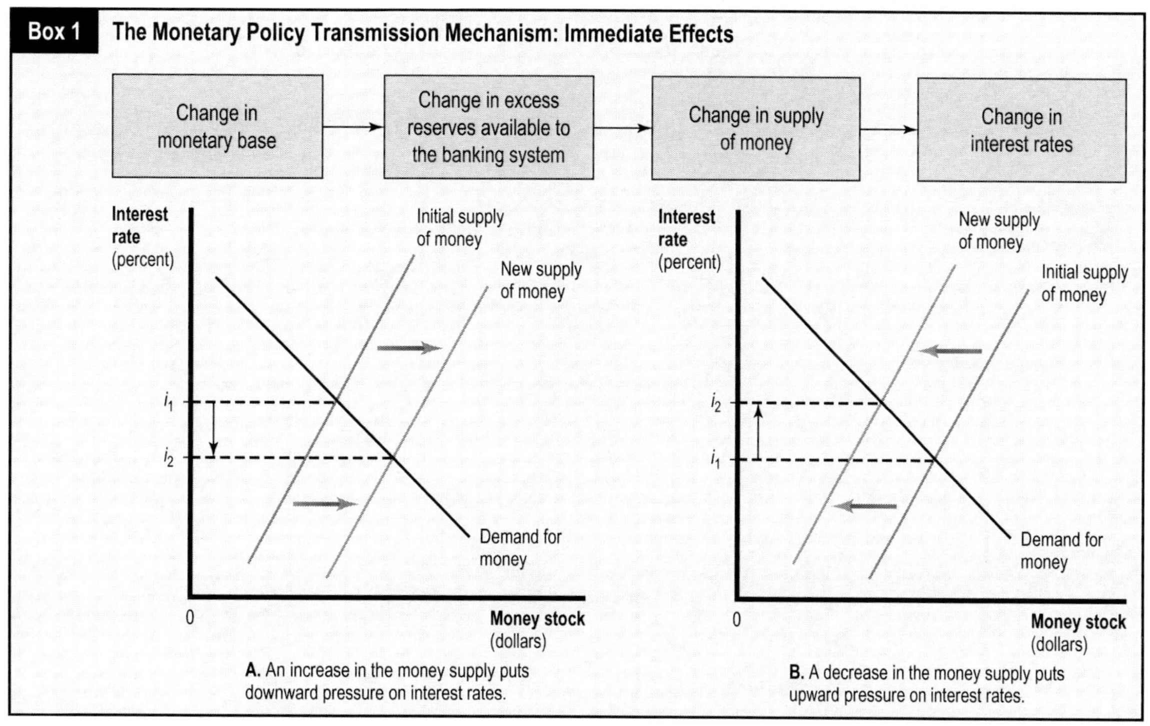

A. An increase in the money supply puts downward pressure on interest rates.

B. A decrease in the money supply puts upward pressure on interest rates.

[1]Note that changes in money demand can also affect interest rates in the economy. An increase in money demand puts upward pressure on interest rates in much the same way as is done by a decrease in money supply. By the same token, a decrease in money demand puts downward pressure on interest rates.

Interest Rates and Aggregate Demand

In studying the effects of monetary policies, we must investigate the relationship between changes in financial markets and changes in product markets. Our next step is, therefore, to show how changes in short-term interest rates caused by changes in the money supply affect aggregate demand.

When the Fed shifts the money supply, it influences nominal short-term interest rates. Spending decisions over the long term are influenced by real interest rates. The Fed must increase nominal interest rates relative to the inflation rate generally expected by the public if it wants to decrease aggregate demand over a longer period. Conversely, it must reduce nominal interest rates relative to the expected rate of inflation to increase aggregate demand.

Expected inflation is a subjective concept that the Fed can influence only indirectly. However, because spending decisions depend on the real interest rate, the Fed must make some estimate of expected inflation in formulating monetary policy. Its job is simplified if inflationary expectations are fixed or change very slowly because then an increase in the nominal interest rate will also increase the real interest rate. Many economists argue that a goal of both monetary and fiscal policy for the long run should be the creation of an economic environment that contributes to very stable expectations of changes in the price level.

The component of aggregate demand that is likely to be most responsive to changes in real interest rates is investment purchases, including purchases of homes. Lower real interest rates encourage increased investment purchases, while higher real interest rates cause business firms to scale back their planned investment expenditures. Of course, some consumer expenditures are also sensitive to changes in real interest rates because such changes affect the monthly payments associated with installment purchases. Here, to simplify the analysis, we will concentrate on the impact of changes in real interest rates on investment purchases.

Graph **A** in Box 2 draws the demand curve for investment goods in the economy. When, through the transmission mechanism we just discussed, the Fed causes real interest rates to

Box 2 Impact of an Expansionary Monetary Policy on Aggregate Demand

An expansionary monetary policy has the effect of lowering real interest rates. The decline in interest rates increases the quantity of investment goods demanded, as shown in **A**. An increase in orders for investment goods shifts the economy's aggregate purchases line upward, as shown in **B**. This implies an increase in aggregate demand, as shown in **C**.

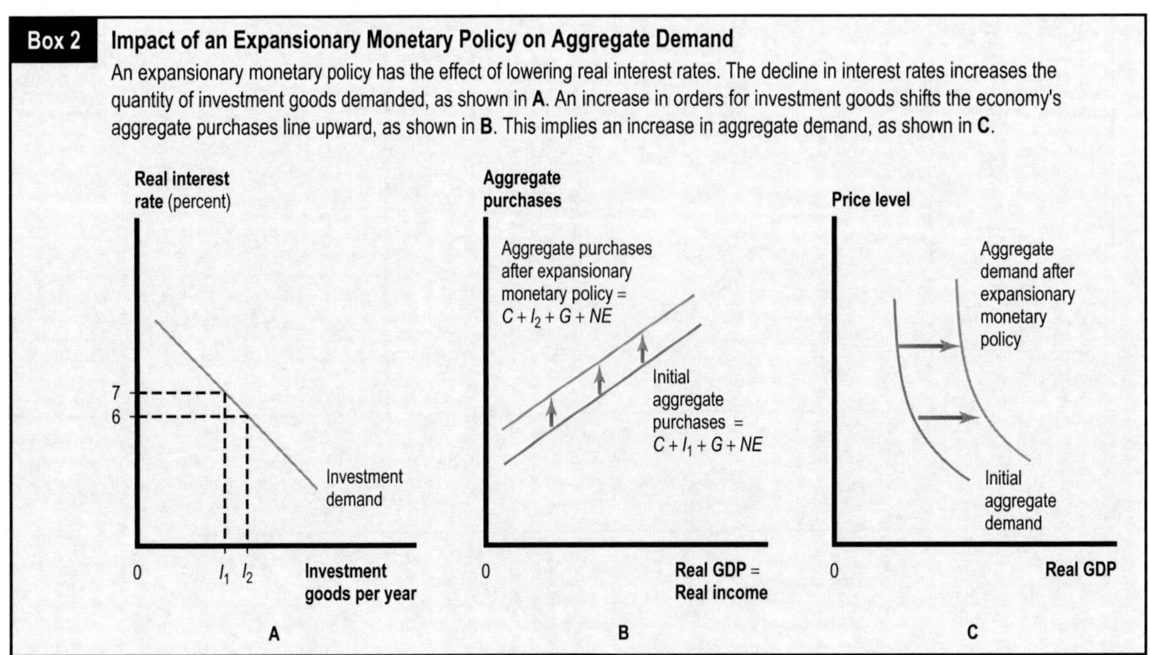

decline, the quantity of investment goods demanded increases. Other things being equal, the increase in investment purchases means the economy's aggregate purchases line will shift upward, as shown in graph **B**. An increase in aggregate purchases means the economy's aggregate demand curve will shift outward, as shown in graph **C**.

We can now begin to see how an expansionary monetary policy can affect macroeconomic equilibrium through shifts in aggregate demand. A decrease in interest rates caused by an expansionary monetary policy affects the investment component of aggregate demand. As aggregate demand increases, other things being equal, it puts upward pressure on real GDP and the price level. You can test your understanding of how monetary policy influences aggregate demand by working out the implications of a contractionary monetary policy for the economy. An increase in real interest rates resulting from a decrease in the money supply will decrease planned investment purchases. This will shift the economy's aggregate purchases line downward. A decrease in aggregate purchases at any given price level will shift the economy's aggregate demand curve inward, putting downward pressure on real GDP and the price level. The Fed can therefore act to restrain surging aggregate demand in periods of expansion by pursuing policies to increase the level of real interest rates in the economy. Now let's see how the Fed's use of an expansionary monetary policy can help pull the economy out of a contraction or a recession.

Using an Expansionary Monetary Policy to Eliminate a Recessionary GDP Gap

2 When the economy is operating at an equilibrium level of real GDP that falls short of potential real GDP, a recessionary GDP gap will prevail. Under these circumstances, there will be cyclical unemployment. Policies designed to stimulate aggregate demand can help restore full employment.

Assume the economy is initially in equilibrium at a real GDP level of $4,700 billion and a price level of 100. Potential real GDP, at which full employment will be achieved, is $5,000 billion. There is therefore a $300 billion recessionary GDP gap. The current level of aggregate demand is insufficient to result in an equilibrium real GDP equal to the economy's potential real GDP of $5,000 billion.

If you were chairman of the Board of Governors of the Federal Reserve System, what would you do to eliminate the recessionary GDP gap and restore full employment? Well, if you followed the line of reasoning just given, you know that the Fed can lower real interest rates by engaging in an expansionary monetary policy. The decline in real interest rates will then increase planned investment and other interest-sensitive purchases, which represent an important component of aggregate demand. As a result, the aggregate demand curve will shift outward.

The impact of just such a policy on macroeconomic equilibrium for the economy is illustrated in Box 3. After an expansionary monetary policy has increased aggregate demand, equilibrium real GDP will increase from $4,700 billion to $5,000 billion, eliminating the recessionary GDP gap. By acting to decrease real interest rates through its influence on bank excess reserves and the money supply, the Fed can stimulate aggregate demand and increase equilibrium real GDP to potential real GDP after a recession hits. But the Fed's policies also increase the price level. In the graph the price level goes up from 100 to 105 after the expansionary monetary policy has shifted aggregate demand. There is therefore 5 percent inflation during the year as a result of the expansionary monetary policy. The Fed must take care not to decrease the level of interest rates too much in order to avoid initiating a process of inflation that can result from steady increases in aggregate demand. Too much growth in excess reserves for the banking

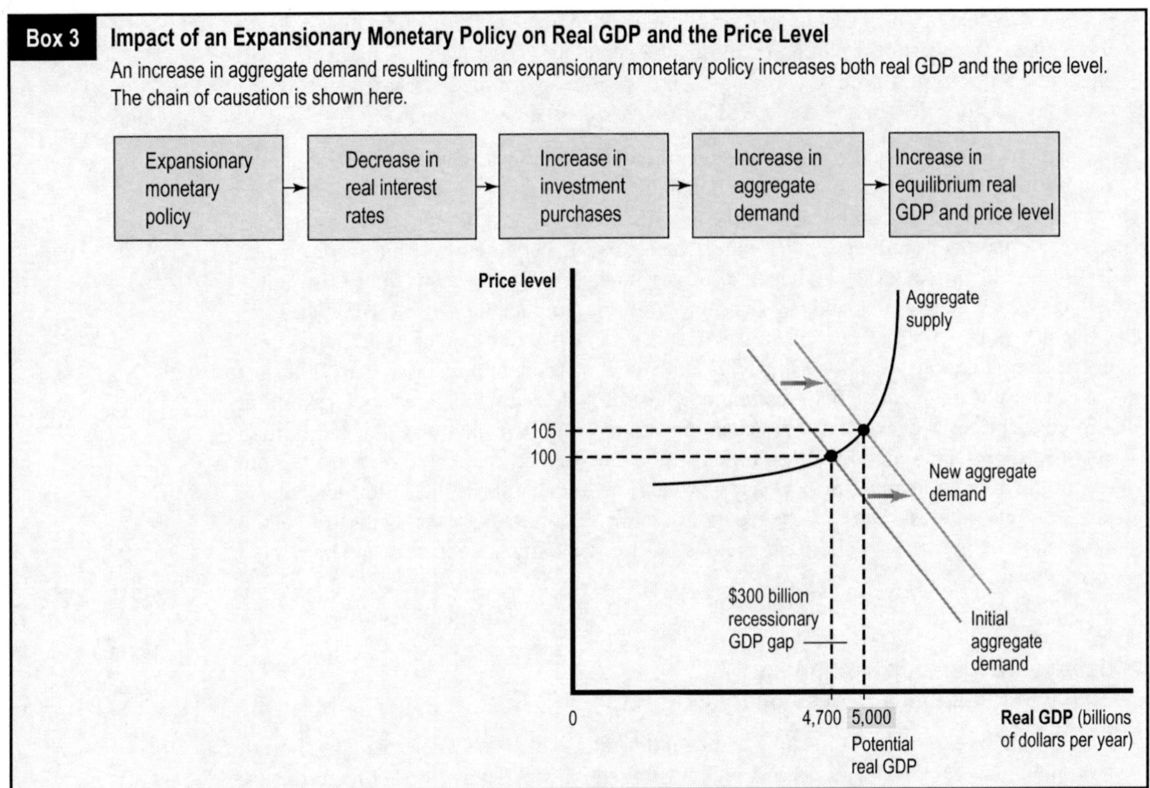

Box 3 Impact of an Expansionary Monetary Policy on Real GDP and the Price Level
An increase in aggregate demand resulting from an expansionary monetary policy increases both real GDP and the price level. The chain of causation is shown here.

system can result in shifts in money supply that can ultimately cause inflation to become a serious problem.

The risk of inflation from increases in aggregate demand depends on how close the economy is to full employment. If the economy is in a serious recession, it will be operating with considerable excess capacity and high cyclical unemployment. Under these circumstances, an expansionary monetary policy is likely to run little risk of starting an inflationary process because the economy will be operating in the flat portion of its aggregate supply curve. Increases in aggregate demand will therefore have little effect on the price level during a deep recession. The closer the economy is to full employment, however, the greater the risk that an expansionary policy designed to eliminate a recessionary GDP gap will start a process of demand-pull inflation.

How Effective Is Monetary Policy in Increasing Aggregate Demand?

Suppose you were a member of the Federal Open Market Committee. It would be nice to know exactly how much you would have to increase bank excess reserves in order to increase aggregate demand and eliminate a recessionary GDP gap. Unfortunately, monetary policy is not an exact science, and its effectiveness depends on how responsive both banks and investors are to changes in the monetary base and the level of real interest rates.

The effectiveness of an expansionary monetary policy in increasing aggregate demand depends on two factors:

1. The willingness of the banking system to create new checkable deposits by making loans using newly created excess reserves.

2. The responsiveness of investment and other credit-sensitive purchases to declines in interest rates.

Suppose the banking system *does* respond to an increase in excess reserves by making more loans. As this occurs, banks will create more checkable deposits for their customers and the supply of money will increase, putting downward pressure on interest rates. The effectiveness of an expansionary monetary policy in increasing aggregate demand will then hinge on the responsiveness of investment purchases to the change in interest rates. The more responsive investors are to declines in real interest rates, the greater the increase in investment purchases from any given decrease in real interest rates.

In periods of deep recession, the short-term business outlook may be so gloomy that banks may prefer to hold onto their excess reserves rather than extend credit. Under such circumstances, because of the high risk of default on bank loans, bank managers will hold liquid assets in the form of excess reserves. Therefore, the increase in excess reserves pumped into the banking system by the Fed will have little effect on the money supply, because the banks won't use them to extend credit and, thus, create checkable deposits. There will be no increase in the equilibrium money stock. As a consequence, there will be little downward pressure on interest rates in the first place. If interest rates don't fall, investment purchases won't increase in response to the increase in the monetary base.

John Maynard Keynes was quite pessimistic about the effectiveness of monetary policy as a means of pulling an economy out of a deep recession. He argued that, in a deep recession, banks would be unwilling to extend credit through loans or bond purchases because of fear of default or fear of a fall in bond prices. Under such circumstances, the Fed would have a hard time shifting the money supply curve to the right to lower interest rates.

Even if the Fed were effective in increasing the equilibrium money stock in a deep recession, Keynes argued that its effect on the market rate of interest might be negligible. This is because, during a deep recession, money is likely to be a very attractive asset for households and businesses compared to stocks and bonds. After all, inflation rates are low during a recession (or even negative, as was the case during the Great Depression). There would be little risk of loss in the dollar's purchasing power. As people try to increase the quantity of money they hold during a recession, the Fed's attempt to lower interest rates is stifled. The increased money stock ends up being held as currency or checkable deposits. As a result, there is little increase in the supply of loanable funds. Therefore, there's little downward pressure on the level of interest rates.

Sometimes unusual factors limit the effectiveness of monetary policy in stimulating demand in the short run. During the recession of 1990–91, for example, the Fed acted to increase bank reserves, which resulted in a substantial decline in short-term interest rates. At the same time, however, many banks were forced to raise their standards for approving loans because new laws were then enacted to reduce the exposure of banks to loan defaults. Regulators were pressuring banks to reduce the riskiness of their portfolios so as to reduce the rate of bank failure. The result was a "credit crunch" that had a strong impact on small businesses trying to get loans approved for new ventures. Between 1990 and 1992, banks used increased reserves to acquire relatively riskless government securities and reduced the volume of loans in their portfolios. All these factors combined to reduce the ability of the Fed's expansionary monetary policy to increase commercial credit and investment spending.

An even worse credit crunch developed beginning in July 2007. As real estate prices began to plummet and defaults on mortgages soared, the value of asset-backed securities held by many banks declined. As bank asset values fell, some banks approached insolvency and their net worth also plummeted. A recession developed over the period 2007-2009, in part, as a result of declining asset values, and difficulties for both consumers and businesses to obtain credit. The Fed responded to the recession with an aggressive expansionary monetary policy. From September 2007 to January 2009, the federal funds rate fell from 4.75 percent to zero, as reserves were pumped into the banking system. The Fed began a whole slew of new programs designed to provide liquidity directly to the credit markets, by allowing investors and financial institutions to use asset-backed securities as collateral for direct lending from the Fed. These programs also increased bank reserves, as the Fed created deposits at the Federal Reserve banks to finance these loans.

However, the new bank reserves resulting from this unprecedented expansion of the monetary base simply ended up as excess reserves on the balance sheet of many troubled banks, which remained cautious in extending new credit. Excess reserves of depository institutions rose from about $1.5 billion in late 2007 to about $800 billion in early spring 2009. Despite the enormous increase in the monetary base and innovative programs designed to directly support credit, the Fed was still having a difficult time increasing aggregate demand.

Using a Contractionary Monetary Policy to Prevent the Economy from Overheating

3 Now, let's turn the tables on you. As chairman of the Federal Reserve Board, suppose you're more worried about inflation than about unemployment. Suppose the current rate of unemployment is only 5.5 percent, and you have good reason to believe the economy is in danger of overheating. An overheated economy is one that's temporarily operating beyond its potential because of excessive aggregate demand. You know that, as the economy is approaching full employment, there's real danger that shifts in aggregate demand will trigger an inflationary process. You also know that demand-pull inflation at full employment can start a wage-price spiral. Demand-pull inflation can be followed by cost-push inflation as workers negotiate wage increases to keep up with anticipated inflation. As chairman of the Fed, you want to avoid such an inflationary scenario. You're likely to recommend that a contractionary monetary policy be pursued to prevent an inflationary process from beginning.

The graph in Box 4 shows an economy that is initially in equilibrium at point *E*, at which

Box 4 Using a Contractionary Monetary Policy to Restrain Aggregate Demand

Monetary policy can be used to prevent aggregate demand from increasing. This prevents the economy from moving to an equilibrium from *E* to *E′*, where an inflationary gap would exist as the economy overheats.

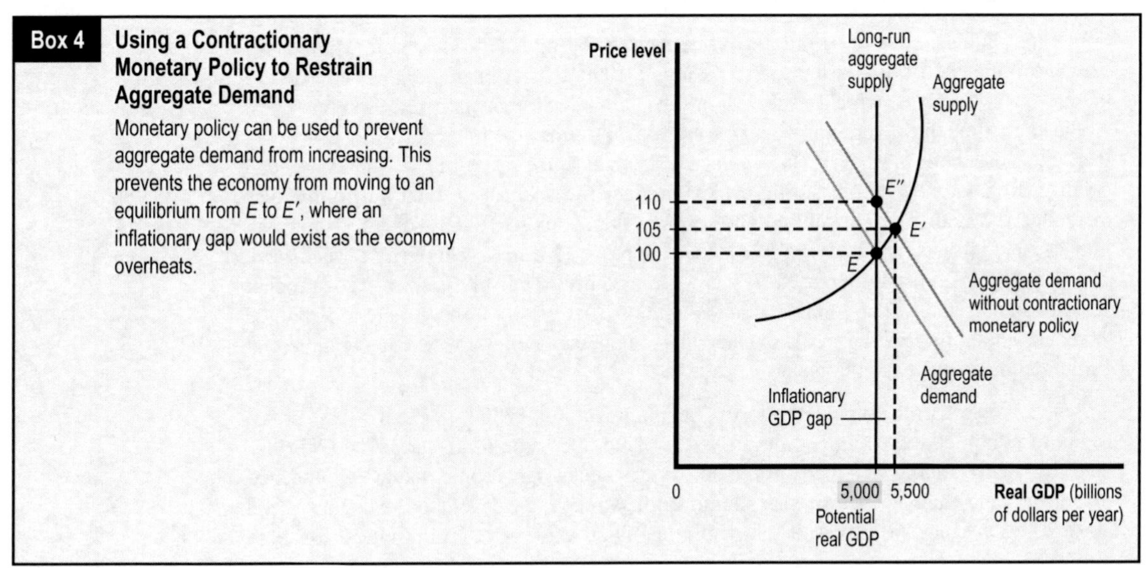

real GDP is at its potential level of $5,000 billion per year and the price level is 100. If aggregate demand increases still further, the economy will move to point E', at which real GDP will increase to $5,500 billion and the price level will go up to 105. Because wages will tend to be fixed, at least in the short-run period of about one year, the increase in the price level will not be matched by increased wages over the year. In the following year, however, wages will start to increase as workers seek to keep up with inflation. The increase in wages will shift the aggregate supply curve inward. The economy will eventually move to point E'' on its long-run aggregate supply curve, at which point real GDP returns to potential real GDP and the price level increases to 110.

To prevent inflationary gaps from occurring, the Fed will have to engage in a contractionary monetary policy as the economy approaches full employment. To do so, it will attempt to decrease the excess reserves available to depository institutions (or reduce their rate of growth) in order to put upward pressure on interest rates as the economy moves to full employment. Monetary policy will be effective in preventing an inflationary gap if it can keep the aggregate demand curve from shifting outward. If monetary policy achieves this objective, the economy will never reach an equilibrium at point E' and will avoid the bout of stagflation that would eventually decrease aggregate supply and result in an equilibrium at E''. In this way the Fed can prevent a wage-price spiral from occurring.

The Fed often tries to restrain aggregate demand from increasing to the point where it overheats the economy. In doing so it hopes to engineer a "soft landing" for the economy by preventing inflation from heating up but avoiding a severe restriction of credit that could cause a recession. However, because precise information about potential real GDP is difficult to obtain along with accurate forecasts of increases in aggregate demand, the Fed has to be careful to avoid "crashing" the economy by tightening too much in a way that causes a recession.

In 1994, for example, the U.S. economy was expanding robustly. Unemployment rates were falling rapidly and, by December, had reached 5.5 percent, down from 6.7 percent in January. In February, the Fed began to tighten the screws on monetary policy. It began soaking up bank reserves, and short-term interest rates began to soar. The Fed was clearly trying to restrain aggregate demand as the economy approached full employment during the year. The Fed continued with a contractionary monetary policy in this way throughout 1994 and the first half of 1995. By the summer of 1995, when the expansion was clearly beginning to run out of steam, the Fed began increasing bank reserves, and short-term interest rates started declining.

Between 1995 and 1998, the federal funds rate fell from a high of 6 percent to a low of 4.75 percent. The Fed began tightening up again in 1999 and 2000, when there were fears the economy would overheat. However, by 2001, it was clear that inflation wasn't a problem and that, in fact, the economy was slowing down considerably. As it became apparent that a recession was approaching in 2001, the Fed eased up and short-term interest rates started falling again. By 2003, the federal funds rate was down to 1 percent, as the Fed was trying to stimulate a sluggish economy. By 2004, the Fed began a contractionary monetary policy, again restraining aggregate demand by reducing bank reserves. Between 2004 and 2005, the federal funds rate was increased steadily from its 1 percent low and, in October 2005, the rate was up to 3.75 percent. The federal funds rate peaked at 5.25 percent in September 2007. Thereafter, when it became clear to the Fed that the economy was starting to contract, the Fed reversed its contractionary monetary policy, and began pumping reserves into the banking system and lowering the federal funds rate.

Money, Real GDP, Prices, and Monetary Policy

4 Earlier in this chapter, we pointed out that monetary policy is an art rather than a science. That may be putting it mildly if we consider the fact that there's great controversy about the way changes in monetary policy and changes in the money stock affect the economy. Economists agree that monetary policy has the potential to influence aggregate demand. However, they disagree about the mechanism through which monetary policy affects aggregate demand and macroeconomic equilibrium. In this section we'll concentrate on the relationship between money and prices in the economy over the long run, when wages and prices are likely to be more flexible than they are over shorter periods.

The major impact of the money supply on real GDP over a short period occurs through the transmission mechanism discussed earlier. Changes in the money supply affect interest rates, thereby affecting investment and other credit-sensitive purchases that, in turn, affect aggregate demand. The long-term impact on the economy of changes in the money supply depends on the relationship between growth in the money stock available, growth in potential real GDP, and shifts in the demand curve for money.

A long-term objective of monetary policy is to adjust the growth of the money stock to accommodate long-term growth in the transaction demand for money. Remember that as GDP grows, so does the transaction demand for money. (See the chapter The Functions of Money.) By doing this, central banks ensure a stock of money and a supply of credit that allow the economy to expand without excessive inflation or recession.

The Concept of Income Velocity of Circulation of Money

Take out a dollar bill from your wallet or purse, and look at it. Unless you've just gotten a nice, crisp, newly printed bill, it's likely to be dirty and worn. It's seen a bit of action. In fact, each dollar of the money stock, in either checkable deposits or currency, is used a number of times each year to make purchases of final products. Therefore, the dollar volume of the final transactions that can be supported by a given quantity of money, on average per day over the year, is a multiple of the available money stock.

The income velocity of circulation of money is the number of times per year, on average, a dollar of the money stock is spent on final products. Because nominal GDP also equals aggregate income in the nation, income velocity also measures the number of times per year, on average, a dollar of the money stock is paid out as income. For example, in 2008, nominal GDP, representing the market value of final products at current prices that year, was $14,264 billion. The average daily stock of currency and checkable deposits that year (M1) was approximately $1,568.9 billion. The $1,568.9 billion money stock supported the $14.3 trillion of aggregate income generated from the final production of goods and services that year. The income velocity of circulation, V, of money is computed from the following formula.

$$\text{Income velocity of circulation} = V = \text{Nominal GDP/M1},$$

when M1 is the average daily stock of currency and checkable deposits held over the year.

In 2008, the velocity of circulation of money was therefore

$$\frac{14,264 \text{ billion}}{1,568.9 \text{ billion}} = 9.1$$

If velocity was about 9, the dirty old dollar in your wallet was involved in nine transactions during the year to purchase final products. The dollar was received as income nine times during the year. Perhaps it was used to buy a greeting card and thus became part of the income of the card store proprietor. Perhaps the card store owner held it awhile but eventually spent it on a cup of coffee at the doughnut shop, when it became income to the shop owner. When a dollar of the money stock is not being used, someone is holding it either as a checkable deposit or as currency.

The Equation of Exchange

The equation of exchange is an identity that shows the relationship among nominal GDP, the money stock, and the income velocity of circulation of money. The equation of exchange is obtained directly from the definition of velocity. Velocity is

$$V = \text{Nominal GDP/M1}.$$

Multiply both sides of the formula for velocity by M1. This gives the following result:

$$(\text{M1})V = \text{Nominal GDP}.$$

Nominal GDP can be expressed as the price level, P, multiplied by the quantity, Q, of final transactions, which is real GDP:

$$\text{Nominal GDP} = PQ = (\text{Price level})\ (\text{Real GDP})$$

If you just remember that money is measured by M1, the symbol M can be used for money to make the equation a little less cluttered. This gives

$$MV = PQ,$$

which is the equation of exchange. Note again that the relationship is an *identity*. The term MV represents total dollar expenditure on the nation's final products over the year. The term PQ represents total receipts from the sale of final products over the year. Because receipts always equal expenditures, the equation is an identity.

Using the Equation of Exchange to Understand Money's Role in the Economy

The preceding analysis of the impact of money on the economy emphasized how changes in money supply can affect interest rates and investment. These short-run effects of changes in the money supply shift aggregate demand, and they can increase or decrease real GDP when it diverges from its potential level in the short run.

Over longer periods, *provided velocity is more or less stable*, changes in the money supply will affect the price level. The classical quantity theory of money is a model of the long-run functioning of the economy, according to which changes in the money stock result in proportional changes in the price level over the long run. We discuss the ideas of the classical economists in the chapter on using aggregate demand and supply analysis. They believed flexibility of wages and prices would ensure the equality of equilibrium real GDP and potential GDP. They also believed that temporary deviations from potential real GDP would eventually be followed by shifts in aggregate supply that returned the economy to equilibrium at full employment.

According to the classical quantity theory of money, the transmission mechanism through which changes in the money stock ultimately affect the economy differs from the mechanism previously discussed. In the short run, when wages and prices may be temporarily inflexible according to the classical economists, increases in the money supply can affect interest rates, investment, and real GDP. In the long run, however, potential real GDP will be equilibrium real GDP and changes in the money stock can affect only the price level. To see this, you can think of Q in the equation of exchange as real GDP, while P represents the price level. If money supply goes up while velocity is fixed, then nominal GDP, which is represented by PQ, must increase. However, because in the long run an increase in M does not affect real GDP, any increase in nominal GDP will be fully accounted for by increases in the price level, provided V is constant. If V is constant, then increases in the growth rate of M will increase the rate of inflation whenever the growth rate of the money stock exceeds the growth rate of real GDP.

For example, suppose the federal government declares that each dollar in checking accounts and each dollar of currency is now worth two dollars. The money stock will double. But if real GDP is equal to potential real GDP, the resulting increase in the dollar value of aggregate demand can't result in more output. There may be a temporary overheating of the economy, but you know that real GDP can't exceed its potential for long without causing decreases in aggregate supply. As you and your friends run out to spend your newly created dollars, prices are sure to rise if quantity supplied can't increase. If velocity (V) is fixed and Q is also fixed at potential real GDP, the equation of exchange shows you that a doubling of the money stock will also double the price level in the economy!

In general, if the economy is already operating at its potential and V is constant, the price level will increase by the same proportion as the dollar amount of money in circulation increases. The increase in the price level increases the demand for money and therefore induces people to hold the larger money stock because, given real GDP, an increase in the price level increases the transaction demand for money. (See the chapter The Functions of Money.) If the price level doesn't change, some other variable, such as interest rates or real GDP, will have to change to induce people to willingly hold the available amount of money. The quantity theory of money, in its crudest form, doesn't consider changes in the interest rate. It also assumes that real GDP is in equilibrium at its full-employment level. Remember that the classical quantity theory of money was developed at a time when the classical economists believed the economy's self-correcting mechanism would work to keep the economy operating at close to full employment. Therefore, the price level must rise to induce the public to willingly hold the larger money stock.

The graph in Box 5 shows how the increase in aggregate demand caused by a doubling of the money stock will double the price level, assuming flexible prices and wages. The initial equilibrium is at point E along the vertical long-run aggregate supply curve. A doubling of the money supply will increase aggregate demand. The new aggregate demand curve will intersect the long-run aggregate supply curve at point E' . At that point, real GDP remains at its full-employment level, *but the price level has also doubled.*

Keep in mind that this conclusion is true only if nothing else changes as the money supply and price level change. This ensures a stable money demand and a fixed income velocity of circulation of money.

Monetary Policy: Implications of the Classical Quantity Theory

If the classical quantity theory is correct, it has some important implications for monetary policy. Suppose the income velocity of circulation is constant. Also assume that, over the long run, wage and price flexibility ensure that real GDP doesn't differ from potential real GDP for long. In a growing economy, for which the assumptions of the classical quantity theory held, stable prices could be maintained if the money stock were allowed to grow at the same rate as potential real GDP. For example, suppose potential real GDP were to grow at an annual rate of 3 percent. In this case, other things being equal, the right side of the equation of exchange, PQ, would also increase by 3 percent annually. Now if V were constant, how much could the money stock increase to prevent the price level from going up? The answer would be 3 percent. What would happen if the money stock were allowed to increase more rapidly than 3 percent? For example, if the money stock were to grow at an annual rate of 10 percent, MV would also grow by 10 percent per year if V were constant. The right side of the equation would also have to grow by 10 percent per year. Because the growth rate of real GDP is dependent on such factors as technological progress and growth in labor productivity, its rate of growth would be unaffected by the

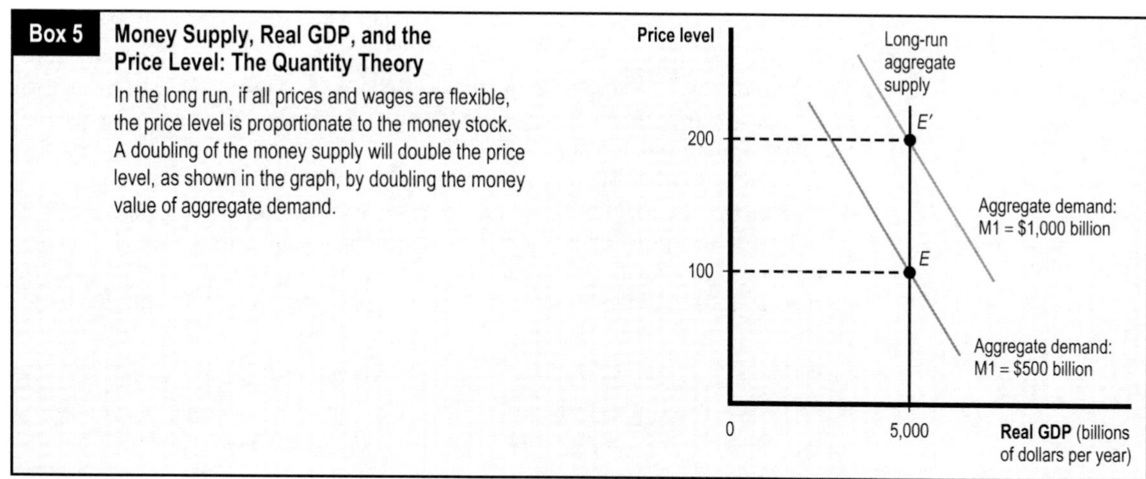

Box 5 Money Supply, Real GDP, and the Price Level: The Quantity Theory

In the long run, if all prices and wages are flexible, the price level is proportionate to the money stock. A doubling of the money supply will double the price level, as shown in the graph, by doubling the money value of aggregate demand.

growth rate of the money stock. It follows that the growth rate of the price level would increase to make up the difference between the growth rate of the money stock and the growth rate of potential real GDP.

Assuming velocity is constant, the classical quantity theory of money implies that over the long run rapid inflation can be caused by growth of the money stock in excess of the long-term growth rate of real GDP. This implies that monetary policy can keep inflation under control over the long run by making sure the growth rate of the money stock does not exceed the growth rate of real GDP over the long run.

However, the income velocity of circulation of money is not constant. In the United States, velocity fell from about 3.5 in 1929 to slightly less than 2 in the mid-1940s. Beginning in 1945, it climbed steadily, reaching a high of 7 between 1982 and 1983. It declined between 1983 and 1984, and, from 1985 to 1994, it fluctuated between 6 and 7. In 1994, velocity was 6.01. Between 1994 and 2000, velocity increased from 6 to 9. By 2005, it was 11.5. However, by 2007 it had fallen to 10.2, and in 2008 it fell still further, to 9.1.

The variability of velocity casts doubt on the simplest version of the quantity theory, which is based on the assumption of fixed velocity. But why does velocity increase and decrease over time? The answer lies in shifts of the demand curve for money in the economy.

The higher the income velocity of circulation, the faster the turnover of dollars as income. Higher velocity means money is being used more frequently to purchase final products and is spending less time as idle cash balances. In other words, given nominal GDP and the level of interest rates over the year, an increase in velocity means the money demand curve has shifted inward. A decrease in money demand is therefore indicative of an increase in the velocity of circulation of money. You can readily see this from the formula for velocity. Given nominal GDP, an increase in V means the quantity of money held on average per day over the year has declined, because V = Nominal GDP/M1. Other things being equal, this implies that the demand for money has declined.

Velocity varies as the demand for money varies. Any change in a nation's financial system that reduces the transaction costs of converting near money to money is likely to decrease the money stock demanded by the public. When such a change occurs, a smaller equilibrium money stock can support a given nominal GDP, and velocity will increase. Technological change in the payment mechanisms of an economy can increase velocity. For example, velocity will be increased by the introduction of a computerized network that allows instantaneous transfer of funds in savings accounts to funds in checkable deposits.

The sharp increase in velocity from 1950 to 1985 can be explained by the many financial innovations that occurred in the United States at that time. One such innovation was widespread use of credit cards, which allowed users to write one check in payment for several purchases made during a month. Many mutual fund accounts allowed easy transfer of investment balances into money market funds that had check-writing privileges. These innovations allowed the public to economize on the money it held. New technology and improvement in management of cash balances by corporations and households has resulted in further economizing on M1 since 1994. Between 1995 and 2005, velocity nearly doubled.

The variability of velocity measured as GDP/M1 will increase with the variability of interest rates. Remember that interest rates are a major determinant of the demand for money balances. When interest rates rise, the opportunity cost of holding money also rises, and individuals economize on their money balances to take advantage of higher yields on such financial assets as money market mutual funds. A lower demand for money means that a lower dollar volume of M1 will be used to conduct transactions. Consequently, a decrease in the demand for money will be associated with an increase in velocity, while an increase in the demand for money will be associated with a decrease in velocity. When interest rates are highly variable, as was the case in the late 1980s, velocity will also be highly variable.

Movements in velocity became much more difficult to predict in the 1980s, when the long-term trend toward increasing velocity was apparently broken. There were highly variable interest rates over the period, leading to increased variability. Since 1995, velocity has increased more steadily and its movements have become more predictable.

Lags in Monetary Policy

The economy is like a big locomotive pulling hundreds of passenger and freight cars. A locomotive pulling such a train cannot be expected to stop on a dime, nor can it be expected to accelerate to full speed quickly. Instead, the engineer has to apply the brakes miles ahead of a planned stop; and acceleration to full throttle can take a long time.

The effects of monetary policy on the economy are a bit like the effects of the throttle and brakes on the locomotive pulling the long train. Monetary policy operates with long and sometime unpredictable lags. For example, when the Fed was trying to stimulate the economy with an expansionary monetary policy in 1991 and 1992 after the recession of 1990–91, the lower interest rates and larger money stock took a long time to translate into increased consumer and investment spending. Also, in 1994, when the economy was approaching full employment, the Fed began increasing short-term interest rates well before macroeconomic equilibrium corresponded to potential real GDP. The Fed knew that aggregate demand would continue to grow before higher interest rates had an effect on the economy. Similarly, by mid-2004, when it became clear to the Fed that the U.S. economy was approaching full employment and that inflationary pressures could mount, the Fed started raising short-term interest rates. Thereafter, it steadily raised its targets for the federal funds rate by one quarter of one percent at each open market meeting.

By June of 2006, the federal funds rate had gone from a low of 1 percent in early 2004 to 5.25 percent. The Fed was clearly trying to restrain inflationary tendencies in the economy before that actually became a problem. The Fed began lowering the federal funds rate in September 2007, when it was becoming clear inflation was less of a problem than a contraction beginning in the fourth quarter of 2007. By December 2008 the Fed had steadily reduced the federal funds rate to zero and had taken other measures to increase bank reserves, resulting in an enormous increase in the monetary base, in an attempt to stimulate aggregate demand. The lags in policy were also in play, as the new reserves were not being lent out and bank excess reserves soared.

The lags in the effects of monetary policy make its use more of an art than a science. Sometimes the Fed makes mistakes by trying to control an inflationary process before it begins; instead of engineering a soft landing, it throws the economy into a tailspin and causes a recession. In other cases, it doesn't act fast enough to control inflation before it begins. The Fed often makes mistakes in policy that could end up "destabilizing," rather than stabilizing, the economy.

Monetarism

5 You may think the variability of velocity over time has rendered the quantity theory of money useless. However, many economists still believe the equation of exchange provides important insights into the way the economy functions and the way monetary policy can affect the price level over time.

Monetarism is a theory of long-term macroeconomic equilibrium, based on the equation of exchange, according to which shifts in velocity are reasonably predictable. Monetarists argue that changes in the money stock are the predominant influence on *nominal* GDP and nominal income in a nation. They maintain that, if predictions about changes in velocity are reasonably accurate, monetary policy can be used in the long run to control the rate of inflation. They believe after adjusting for changes in the rate of increase (or decrease) in velocity, careful control of the equilibrium money stock is necessary to stabilize the economy. If, after adjusting for changes in V, the money stock isn't allowed to grow rapidly enough to accommodate the growth in real GDP, monetary policy could cause a recession. For example, suppose the money stock were to grow by less than the growth in real GDP. If, after adjusting for changes in V, the growth of MV is less than the growth of PQ (which is nominal GDP), growth in nominal GDP will be held back by inadequate availability of money. Typically, except in a severe recession, the price level (P) doesn't fall to allow Q, which is real GDP, to continue growing under such circumstances. Businesses and households won't have enough money to meet their daily requirements for transactions. As they increase their demand for money, the credit supplied to financial markets will shrink, and real GDP growth will fall and may even become negative. This implies that an economic contraction or recession can be precipitated by inadequate monetary growth.

On the other hand, if monetary growth, after adjusting for changes in V, is much faster than real GDP growth, nominal GDP will increase more rapidly than real GDP. Therefore, the rate of inflation will increase. The major conclusion of the monetarists is that, over the long run, the growth rate of the money stock is the major factor influencing the rate of inflation in the economy. They recommend concentrating on the long-term effects of monetary growth. They therefore focus on the impact of monetary growth on the price level.

Suppose the long-term trend of about 3 percent annual growth in real GDP continues. At what annual rate must the money stock grow to prevent excessive inflation? According to the equation of exchange,

$$MV = (\text{Price level})(\text{Real GDP}).$$

If real GDP goes up by 3 percent per year, MV must increase by no more than 3 percent per year to prevent inflation over the long run. If MV increases by less than 3 percent per year, aggregate demand will grow less quickly than aggregate supply, and there will be downward pressure on real GDP and the price level.

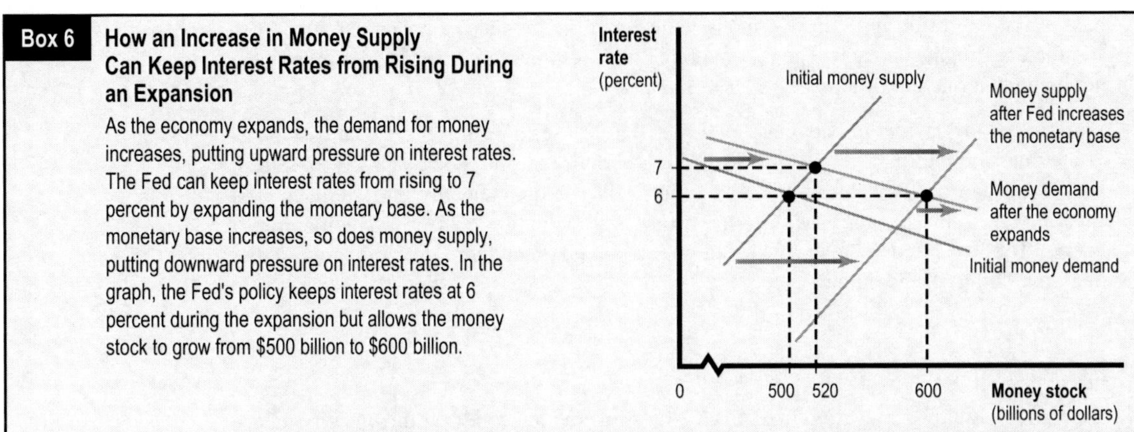

Box 6 How an Increase in Money Supply Can Keep Interest Rates from Rising During an Expansion

As the economy expands, the demand for money increases, putting upward pressure on interest rates. The Fed can keep interest rates from rising to 7 percent by expanding the monetary base. As the monetary base increases, so does money supply, putting downward pressure on interest rates. In the graph, the Fed's policy keeps interest rates at 6 percent during the expansion but allows the money stock to grow from $500 billion to $600 billion.

To prevent excessive inflation, a monetary growth management policy must also predict changes in *V* over the long run. For example, if velocity increases over time (as it did between 1950 and 1985), a 3 percent monetary growth rate will be inflationary because both the increase in velocity and the increase in the money supply will exert upward pressure on the price level over time. A strict rule governing the increase in the money supply can therefore result in inflation if *V* changes unexpectedly. On the other hand, if velocity declines (as it did between 1984 and 1987), a 3 percent growth rate of the money stock will be deflationary. Monetary growth will not provide enough new money to accommodate economic growth. This situation can cause a recession because interest rates will rise unless the price level is downwardly flexible.

Monetarists believe that shifts in velocity are fairly predictable and therefore recommend a rule that allows the money supply to increase within the range of 3 percent to 5 percent per year, depending on predicted changes in velocity.

Monetary Policy in the United States since 1942

6 During the period 1942 to 1951, the Fed pursued policies to keep interest rates at low levels. The federal government had accumulated a tremendous debt as a result of bonds issued to finance the nation's participation in World War II. Up to 1951 the Fed enabled the government to keep its interest costs low by adjusting the money supply in response to shifts in money demand.

When the Fed engages in a policy of keeping interest rates low, it loses its ability to stabilize the economy. It loses the opportunity to influence aggregate demand in the short run through changes in interest rates, and it also gives up control of the money stock because it must adjust the money supply to keep interest rates fixed.

Normally, the demand for money increases as the economy expands because as real GDP increases or the price level rises, individuals demand higher transaction balances. The outward shift in the money demand curve during an economic expansion puts upward pressure on interest rates. To keep interest rates from rising, the Fed must increase the money supply. As shown in Box 6, the increase in the money supply keeps interest rates pegged at a target level, but the equilibrium money stock increases. The increase is likely to add to inflationary pressures just as the economy is nearing full employment. Thus, keeping interest rates at low levels means that the Fed runs the risk of contributing to inflation in the long run by increasing the money supply whenever the demand for money increases. It also loses its ability to stabilize the economy in the short run when it agrees to keep interest rates pegged.

Box 6 shows interest rates rising from 6 to 7 percent during an expansion as the demand for money increases. The rising interest rates dampen the expansion if money supply growth is not increased. By dampening the expansion, the rising interest rates help keep the economy from overheating. However, when the Fed increases the money supply in order to keep interest rates fixed (6 percent in Box 6), the risk of an overheated economy increases.

In 1951 the Treasury and the Fed reached a famous "accord" in which it was agreed that the Fed would have more discretion in influencing interest rates. Subsequently, the Fed sought to keep interest rates within certain bounds and carefully watched bank excess reserves and discount loans as indicators of the availability of loanable funds. Unfortunately, the Fed's stabilization record wasn't very good. When the economy was booming, it engaged in policies that tended to decrease interest rates. When the economy was slack, it engaged in policies that tended to increase interest rates. Rather than stabilizing the economy, the Fed's policies throughout much of the 1950s and 1960s contributed to the severity of cyclical ups and downs of real GDP!

In the 1970s the Fed began to choose monetary growth targets rather than interest rate targets. It sought to control the growth rates of M1 and M2 while keeping short-term interest rates from fluctuating too widely. During this period, whenever an increase in real GDP or the price level caused an increase in money demand, the Fed would react to the resulting upward pressure on interest rates by engaging in open market purchases of government securities. These purchases would increase securities prices, thereby decreasing interest rates. However, the open market purchases tended to increase the money supply, thus getting the Fed off its M1 target. The Fed would then react at the next Federal Open Market Committee meeting to decrease the monetary base. Whenever the Fed missed its target on short-term interest rates, it would increase the rate of monetary growth. This made it hard to control the money stock, which by 1973 was growing at 8 percent per year and putting upward pressure on inflation and nominal interest rates. In 1974 the sharp increase in the price of oil along with high interest rates contributed to a recession.

Between 1974 and 1979 the money supply tended to grow along with the price level during that inflationary period. In 1979, however, the Fed began to engage in policies that sharply slowed the growth rate of bank reserves and M1. Because money demand continued to grow over that period, this decision resulted in upward pressure on nominal interest rates. By the end of 1980, nominal interest rates in the economy were in double digits.

In 1981 the prime rate rose to nearly 20 percent. Given the prevailing inflation rate of 9 percent, the real interest rate paid on prime rate loans in 1981 was at the unprecedentedly high level of 11 percent! The increase in interest rates decreased investment spending sharply and, in 1982, contributed to the most severe recession the nation had experienced since the Great Depression. Apparently, the Fed had reduced the growth rate of M1 too sharply. The basic problem the Fed faced during this period was the familiar one of accurately predicting cyclical increases in money demand that put upward pressure on interest rates.

When the Fed applies the brakes to monetary growth in an expanding economy, interest rates soar. The soaring interest rates can cause a recession, as was the case in 1982. As the Fed restricted the rate of growth of the money stock in 1981, when money demand was still increasing due to a rising price level and still-increasing real GDP, interest rates increased to the double-digit level. This caused a recession, which, in turn, reduced money demand and eventually allowed interest rates to fall.

Box 7 shows the consequences of a monetary policy that adjusts money supply in order to keep the money stock from growing while the economy is expanding. As the economy expands, money demand increases, putting upward pressure on interest rates. If the Fed then reduces money supply to keep the equilibrium money stock from growing, further upward pressure is placed on interest rates. The higher interest rates reduce aggregate demand and can cause a recession.

This case illustrates the often unpleasant effects of pegging the money stock to low growth levels in periods of expansion. The decreased growth rate of the money stock controls inflation over the long run at the cost of risking a severe recession in the short run. However, the bitter resolve of the Fed to halt monetary growth is often necessary to reduce inflation over the long run at the expense of causing a contraction, or even a recession, over the short run.

Inflation was sharply reduced after the 1982 recession, and from 1983 through 1987 the Fed worried less about its effect on the economy. The Fed allowed M1 to grow to accommodate the increased demand for money in an expanding economy. In 1986 nominal interest rates fell sharply, and inflation remained low. Throughout 1986 real interest rates remained quite high by historical standards. In 1986 the Fed engaged in policies that caused real interest rates to fall. By 1987, as the economy approached full employment, fears of inflation increased, and the Fed engaged in policies to increase real interest rates. That increase, combined with the falling international value of the dollar, contributed to a stock market collapse in October 1987.

The economy approached full employment in 1988 and operated at or near full employment in 1989 and 1990. From 1987 to early 1990 money supply growth was sharply curtailed, with M1 barely increasing in 1989. Interest rates increased substantially as money demand grew while the Fed chose to control the growth of monetary aggregates during a period when the economy was expanding. In July 1990, in part because of slow growth in the money supply, the U.S. economy fell into a recession.

Monetary Policy in the 1990s

The recession of 1990–91 and the sluggish recovery that followed was a trying period for U.S. monetary policy. Increases in bank reserves and declining short-term interest rates resulting from an expansionary monetary policy had little effect on aggregate demand. Long-term interest rates remained relatively high throughout 1992 because inflationary expectations remained high.

When the Fed acted to increase bank reserves in 1991 and 1992, short-term interest rates fell. There was a sharp reduction in the return to money market mutual funds and CDs, from around 6 percent to 3 percent and less. As a result, the public shifted assets out of CDs and money market mutual funds and into checking accounts. The public also placed more money in long-term assets whose yields were relatively high, such as Treasury bonds. Because of these shifts in asset demand, the growth rate of M2 fell below what the

Box 7 **Consequences of a Monetary Policy that Keeps the Money Stock from Growing When the Economy Is Expanding**

If money supply is adjusted by the Fed to keep the equilibrium money stock fixed, then interest rates will soar if the economy is expanding. This is because the normal tendency for money demand to increase during an expansion will put upward pressure on interest rates. The soaring interest rates could not only cut the expansion, it could also cause a recession; this was the case in 1982 for the United States when the Fed put the brakes on money supply growth to control inflation.

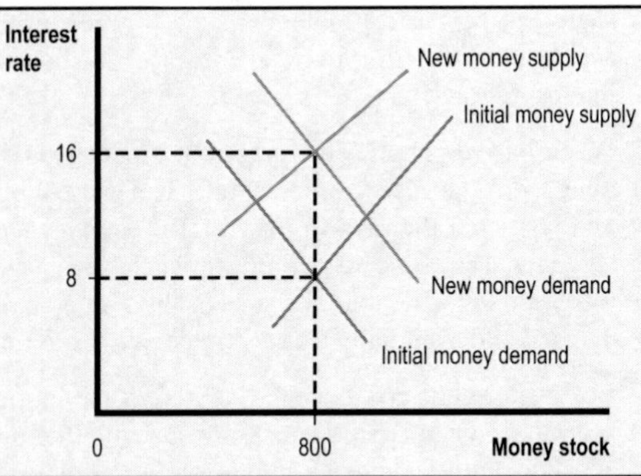

Fed intended to achieve. The increased demand for M1 assets reduced the income velocity of circulation of money, but M1 grew more rapidly than expected. The lagging growth of M2 and the reduced velocity of circulation of M1 made it difficult for the Fed to interpret the results of its policies and to stimulate the economy.

This was complicated by the "credit crunch" that we discussed earlier in this chapter. As banks were pressured to reduce the default risk of their loans and to raise the ratio of owner-supplied capital to assets, they responded by making fewer loans despite the fact that their excess reserves were increasing. They used the excess reserves to purchase government securities instead of using them to supply credit to businesses. Moreover, high business and household debt burdens inherited from the 1980s made it difficult for many to qualify for new loans and reduced the demand for such loans. The demand for real estate credit all but collapsed because of overbuilding in the 1980s.

For all these reasons, the lower short-term interest rates that resulted from the expansionary monetary policy of the late 1980s failed to generate the substantial increase in aggregate demand needed for a vigorous recovery. However, the lower interest rates did reduce debt burdens for many as refinancing of mortgages and corporate debt took place. By early 1993, reduced debt burdens, due in part to lower interest rates, were beginning to increase aggregate demand. As inflationary expectations were also reduced in 1993, a fall in long-term interest rates stimulated a more robust expansion.

By early 1994 it was clear that the economy was steaming at full speed ahead, and in February the Fed applied the brakes. Short-term interest rates rose steadily throughout 1994 as the Fed engaged in open market sales of government securities to reduce bank reserves. By the end of 1994, the U.S. economy was at full employment, and the federal funds rate had increased from 3.05 percent in January to 5.45 percent in December. By mid-1995 the higher interest rates seemed to slow the growth in aggregate demand significantly as car sales and other consumer spending began to decline. At that point, interest rates leveled off and the Fed seemed to be concerned about engineering a soft landing. By July of 1995 it began increasing bank reserves somewhat, and short-term interest rates declined along with the slowdown in aggregate demand. Inflation remained in the range of 3 percent in 1995, and the Fed seemed to think that increasing unemployment was a greater threat to the economy at that time than the risk of any inflationary spirals. From 1995 to 1999, the economy began an unprecedented boom in which it grew with little inflation. The Fed accommodated the boom, keeping interest rates fairly steady and at historically low levels as inflation didn't seem to be a problem.

Monetary Policy Since 2000

In 2000, as fears began to emerge that the economy was overheating and inflation did pick up again, the Fed raised the federal funds rate several times, in an effort to keep inflation down. By the end of 2000, it was clear that the economy was beginning to slow down and the Fed started an expansionary monetary policy. By 2001, it was aggressively lowering interest rates to try to prevent a recession.

After the U.S. economy fell into recession in 2001, the Fed continued its aggressive rate-cutting. As the sluggish recovery continued in 2002 and 2003, the Fed continued an aggressively expansive monetary policy, lowering the federal funds rate to 1 percent during the summer of 2003. In mid-2004, the Fed viewed the risks of inflation greater than the risks of contraction and pursued a contractionary monetary policy. Between 2004 and 2005, upward pressure was exerted on the federal funds rate and, by July 2006, the rate had increased to nearly 5.25 percent. As it became clear to the Open Market Committee that the economy's growth rate was slowing in the last quarter of 2007, the Fed began open market purchases to put more liquidity into the banking system. A series of aggressive cuts in the federal funds rate were then approved, at each Open Market Committee meeting in 2007, and again in the first half of 2008, to stimulate the economy and help avoid a recession. By June of 2008, the federal funds rate had been lowered to 2 percent. The Fed also opened up its discount rate to investment banks hard hit by the subprime mortgage defaults and declines in the value of mortgage-based securities. By easing requirements for lending to these financial institutions, the Fed hoped to add liquidity to the economy and restore the supply of credit

By December 2008, the Fed reduced its target for the federal funds rate to an unprecedented zero! In fact, it was having difficulty maintaining a positive target for the federal funds rate because of a buildup in excess reserves in the banking system, as depository institutions remained reluctant to extend new credit. The demand for federal funds had plummeted, while the supply was increasing. Further, fears of bank failure were increasing the demand for Treasury bills, as holders of large bank balances sought to protect their funds. This bid up the price on Treasury bills and, in some periods, actually pushed the effective yield into negative territory! Long-term interest rates on corporate bonds and mortgages were, however, slow to be reduced, because of remaining fears of default.

Throughout 2009, the Fed remained aggressive in pursuing an expansionary monetary policy. Although it could not further reduce the federal funds rate from its zero level, it aggressively pursued programs to inject liquidity into the economy, through direct lending to investors and non-bank financial intermediaries. As a result of its actions acquiring new assets (mainly, asset-backed securities) used as collateral for loans, the monetary base nearly doubled, from \$820 billion in January of 2008 to about \$1.7 trillion by April of 2009. The monetary base was anticipated to exceed \$2 trillion in 2009, as the Fed aggressively pursued direct lending in credit markets.

As the monetary base increased, fears persisted that the potential existed for an enormous increase in the money stock when the economy eventually recovered. The problem the Fed will face is restraining inflationary pressures once the banks start using their enormous buildup of excess reserves to increase the supply of money and credit, after the economy begins expanding again. To do this, the Fed would have to increase the federal funds rate and reduce the monetary base cautiously, to avoid stalling any future recovery. However, as of 2009, worries about inflation were far off. In fact, many at the Fed were more worried about a deflationary process developing, as the economy continued to contract at a rate not seen since 1983 and during the Great Depression of the 1930s.

Summary

1. Monetary policy consists of actions taken by central banks to influence interest rates and the money supply in ways that affect aggregate demand.
2. An expansionary monetary policy consists of increases in the monetary base or its rate of growth, while a contractionary monetary policy consists of decreases in the monetary base or its rate of growth.
3. An expansionary monetary policy puts downward pressure on interest rates and encourages investment spending by business firms. The increase in aggregate purchases resulting from an expansionary monetary policy puts upward pressure on equilibrium real GDP. An expansionary monetary policy has the effect of shifting the economy's aggregate demand curve outward.
4. The effectiveness of an expansionary monetary policy in increasing aggregate demand depends on the banking system's willingness to extend credit with newly supplied excess reserves and on the responsiveness of investment spending to declines in interest rates.
5. A contractionary monetary policy can prevent an economy from overheating. By increasing interest rates, such a policy puts downward pressure on aggregate demand and aggregate purchases.
6. The income velocity of circulation of money, which is nominal GDP divided by the money stock, measures the number of times each dollar of the money stock is received as income during a year.
7. The equation of exchange is an identity that shows the relationship among nominal GDP, the money stock, and the income velocity of circulation of money. The classical quantity theory of money argues that in the long run money stock changes will affect the price level rather than real GDP, provided the income velocity of circulation of money is stable. According to the classical theory, in the long run the price level in an economy is proportional to the supply of money. In this view, a doubling of the money supply will eventually double the price level.
8. The income velocity of circulation of money has varied considerably in the United States since 1929. Between 1960 and 1985, the income velocity of circulation of money increased as financial innovations reduced the demand for money. Income velocity was very unstable in the 1980s, fluctuating between 6 and 7 from 1985 to 1994. In 1994, velocity was 6.01. Between 1994 and 2000, velocity increased from 6 to 9. By 2005, it was 11.5. However, by 2007, it had fallen to 10.2, and in 2008 it fell still further, to 9.1.
9. Monetarism, a theory of long-term macroeconomic equilibrium based on the equation of exchange, assumes that shifts in the income velocity of circulation of money are reasonably predictable. Monetarists argue that although monetary policy influences aggregate demand, errors in its use prevented its objectives from being achieved in the past. To avoid destabilizing the economy through errors in monetary policy, monetarists advocate steady and predictable monetary growth each year.
10. Shifts in money demand affect interest rates. Money increases during periods of peak economic activity and decreases as nominal GDP declines. Financial innovations that decrease the transaction cost of converting near money into money also decrease the demand for money.
11. Shifts in money demand make it difficult for the Fed to control interest rates and the money supply simultaneously because an increase in the money supply induced by the Fed increases aggregate demand. The increase in aggregate demand increases either real GDP or the price level, which, in turn, increases the demand for money. As the demand for money goes up, there is upward pressure on interest rates and an increase in the equilibrium quantity of money held. Controlling the money supply requires accurate forecasts of shifts in money demand induced by shifts in aggregate demand.
12. When the Fed tries to keep interest rates stable, it allows the money supply to adjust to accommodate shifts in money demand. When the Fed keeps the money supply fixed, shifts in aggregate demand that occur over the business cycle will result in fluctuations in interest rates.

Concept Review

1. Why will the federal funds rate go up if the Fed engages in open market sales of government securities?
2. How does an expansionary fiscal policy increase aggregate demand in the short run?
3. How can a contractionary monetary policy prevent the economy from overheating?
4. Write down the equation of exchange, and briefly summarize the assumptions and implications of the classical quantity theory of money.
5. What is monetarism?
6. Explain why interest rates will soar if the Fed keeps the money stock fixed while the economy expands.

Problems and Applications

1. Suppose the current level of interest rates in the economy is about 8 percent and the Fed believes aggregate demand will decline during the year. How can the Fed counteract the expected decline in aggre- gate demand in a way that will prevent a recession? 1, 2
2. Assume inflation is currently 4 percent per year. The Fed believes an increase in aggregate demand will put upward pressure on the price level during the year. What actions should the Fed engage in to counteract the inflationary pressures in the economy? 1, 3
3. Show how an expansionary monetary policy influences the money supply and the market rate of interest. How are the effects of an expansionary monetary policy transmitted to the economy at large in a way that affects real GDP and the price level? Use aggregate supply and demand analysis to predict the impact of an expansionary monetary policy. 1, 2
4. Explain how a contractionary monetary policy will affect real interest rates and the quantity of investment goods demanded per year. Show how the contractionary monetary policy will affect macroeconomic equilibrium, assuming that the aggregate supply curve is stable. 3
5. Suppose banks held excess reserves made available through Federal Reserve System open market purchases. Under these circumstances, how effective will monetary policy be in stimulating the economy? 2
6. Suppose the demand curve for investment goods is a vertical line plotting investment purchases against the real rate of interest. Under these circumstances, how effective will monetary policy be in eliminating a recessionary GDP gap? 2
7. Assume the economy is at full employment. During the year the money stock is increased by 25 percent. Assuming the income velocity of circulation of money is constant during the year, what will be the impact on the price level? 4
8. Suppose the Fed pursues a monetary policy that allows the money supply to grow at the same rate as the long-term growth rate of real GDP. During a five-year period for which this policy is pursued, the income velocity of circulation of money doubles from 2 to 4. What will happen to the price level over the five-year period? 4, 5
9. Explain why the demand for money will increase as the economy begins to pull out of a recession. Why will interest rates tend to rise as the economy moves into this expansionary phase of the business cycle? How can the Fed prevent the rise in interest rates from dampening the recovery from the recession? Why does keeping interest rates from rising mean the money supply must grow? 6
10. Why are the long-term effects of monetary policy likely to differ from the short-term effects? Why can a policy designed to keep interest rates from fluctuating cause inflation in the long run? 4, 6

Monetary Policy during the Great Depression: How the Fed Prevented the Banking System from Recovering and Allowed the Money Supply to Decline

Much of what you know about the Great Depression of the 1930s may come from reminiscences of older relatives. Whether or not they personally endured the severe hardships and poverty that afflicted large numbers of Americans, the people who lived through those gloomy days can testify to the fear and pessimism engendered by the massive economic collapse.

How did the Federal reserve System respond to this titanic challenge? To state the case tactfully, this was not the Fed's finest hour. Let's look at what happened and what the Fed did--and didn't--do about it.

Between 1929 and 1933, one out of every four workers in the labor force was unemployed. Real GDP fell by one-third over this period, and the price level declined by 25 percent. Investment purchases by business firms were reduced to virtually nothing. The great stock market crash of 1929 wiped out the accumulated wealth of many shareholders, after the market plunged to an 80 percent decline in value.

Because of bank failures between 1929 and 1933, the public held a high proportion of money in the form of currency, rather than bank deposits. Bank failures were common because banks lacked the reserves needed to meet the demand for withdrawals of deposits. The series of bank failures increased the demand for currency, which, in turn, contributed to further bank runs and bank failures. The surviving banks naturally became very cautious in making loans because of their desire to hold liquid assets to meet depositor demands for currency. Banks held high proportions of their assets in excess reserves.

During this period, the Fed allowed the money stock to decline. By not supplying the banking system with reserves to meet the demand for withdrawals, the Fed contributed to bank failures and to the unwillingness of bankers to extend loans. Ironically, during this time of acute economic distress, the Fed failed to fulfill its major function of ensuring the stability of the banking system. The Fed had the power to create bank reserves simply by making loans that would create bank deposits at the Fed. By allowing bank reserves to decline, the Fed contributed to the severity of the Depression and prolonged its duration.

The Fed also contributed to the stock market collapse by encouraging the expansion of credit in 1927. During that year, the Fed had engaged in open market purchases that induced declines in interest rates and encouraged borrowing to speculate on stock prices. When the Fed raised its discount rate in 1929 and started to put the brakes on money supply growth, banks began to call in loans. In the fall of 1929, the stock market collapsed, in part because of the panic selling of stocks to obtain funds to pay off loans.

The decline in the money supply during the Depression contributed to deflation in the price level, but this was insufficient to get the economy's self-correcting mechanism to work. Aggregate production remained in equilibrium at a real GDP level well below the economy's potential.

The monetary policy pursued by the Fed during the early years of the Depression contributed to the severity of the economic decline. The Fed's unwillingness to supply the banking system with reserves undermined the system's integrity. As confidence in the banking system dissolved, the money stock contracted rapidly, contributing to further declines in aggregate demand that aggravated the already miserable economic picture.*

The major lesson learned during the Great Depression is that measures must be taken to stimulate aggregate demand when economic forces contribute to its decline.

*For an excellent historical analysis of the Fed's policies, see Sidney Ratner, James H. Soltow, and Richard Sylla, *The Evolution of the American Economy* (New York: Basic Books, 1979), chap. 22.

Business Brief: Monetary Policy, Real Interest Rates, and the Yield Curve

The most direct effect of the Fed's monetary policy is on bank reserves. A contractionary monetary policy, in which reserves become scarcer, increases the federal funds rate, the interest rate charged by one bank to another for short-term use of reserves. Conversely, under an expansionary monetary policy, the federal funds rate decreases as reserves become more abundant. As the federal funds rate changes, so will other short-term interest rates. However, competition in financial markets will lead to repercussions that will eventually affect long-term interest rates as well.

Interest rates on long-term loans or deposits depend both on short-term rates, and on expectations about future interest rates and future inflation rates. For example, suppose you want to save some money over a two-year period. You can put your money into a one-year CD and then renew the certificate the following year at the going rate of interest, or you can put your money into a two-year CD and earn a certain interest rate over the two-year period.

Suppose the interest rate on the one-year CD is 8 percent, while the rate on the two-year certificate is 9 percent. Typically, in a period of relatively stable prices, longer-term securities yield more than shorter-term securities, because they're less liquid. Depositors and lenders usually want an extra premium for tying up their funds for longer periods of time. If the inflation rate is constant at 5 percent per year, in each of the two years of your CD you'll earn a real rate of interest of 4 percent per year--the 9 percent nominal interest rate less the 5 percent rate of inflation. This rate is higher than the real interest rate of 3 percent you'd earn on the one-year CD each year. If inflation and nominal interest rates are constant over the two-year period, your real interest rate each year on the one-year CD for each period would be the nominal rate of 8 percent less the 5 percent inflation rate, which is 3 percent.

Suppose you expect inflation to heat up next year. To slow it down, you think the Fed will engage in a contractionary monetary policy that will increase nominal interest rates. Under these circumstances, you may be better off putting your money into the one-year CD. With 5 percent inflation, this year you'll earn a real interest rate of 3 percent. If the interest rate on the one-year CD goes up to 10 percent next year and inflation goes up to 6 percent, you'll earn a real interest rate of 4 percent next year. Your real rate of return will average 3.5 percent for the two years. If you buy the two-year CD, in the second year the return will be 9 percent less the 6 percent inflation rate, or 3 percent. Your average return will be 3.5 percent, the same as your return on the one-year CDs. Because you won't get more real interest to compensate for the loss of liquidity, the long-term CD becomes less attractive.

In general, when inflation or short-term nominal interest rates are expected to increase, short-term loans become more attractive than long-term loans. This will increase the supply of short-term credit and decrease the supply of long-term credit, pushing up long-term rates relative to short-term rates.

Given inflationary expectations, the Fed can influence long-term interest rates through the effect of its operations on short-term interest rates. As short-term interest rates rise and short-term credit becomes more attractive, the supply of long-term credit will decrease, and long-term interest rates will rise as well. (These effects will be reinforced by shifts in the demand for long-term and short-term credit, as well as by borrowers who seek to minimize their real interest costs.) In this way, a contractionary monetary policy affects both short-term and long-term credit markets.

When inflation is expected to increase substantially, the "yield curve," which shows how nominal interest rates vary with the time to maturity of a loan, can flatten out. The curve labeled *A* in the illustration below shows a normal upward-sloping yield curve that will prevail when the inflation rate is expected to neither accelerate nor decelerate. The curve labeled *B* shows a flat yield curve, which indicates that long-term rates aren't higher than short-term rates. When this is the case, the general feeling of the financial markets is that inflation is going to accelerate and short-term rates will soon rise. Curve *C* shows an inverted downward-sloping yield curve. This type of yield curve will prevail in the market if it's generally expected that inflation will soon decelerate, and the Fed will be taking actions to lower the federal funds rate and other short-term rates.

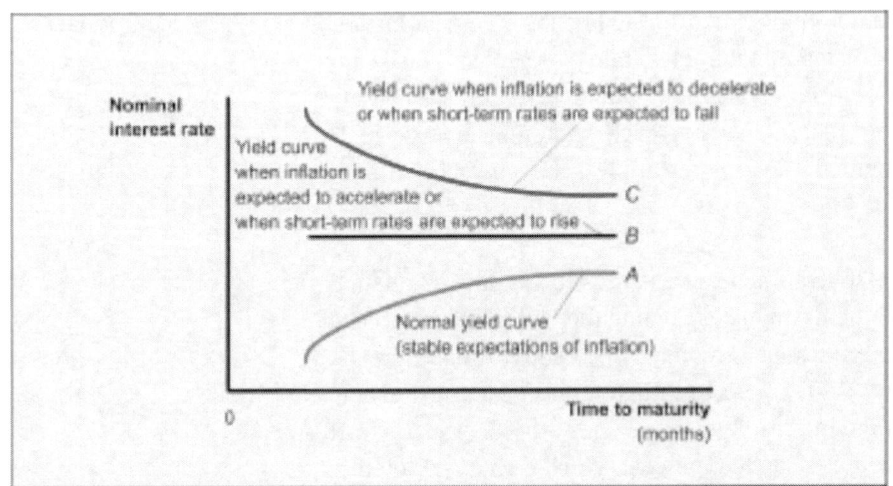

Chapter

32

Stabilization of the Economy through Fiscal Policy

You don't have to be an economist to understand that the federal government has a tremendous impact on the U.S. economy. If you have a job, you know that through its tax policies the federal government affects disposable income, a key influence on consumer purchases. You also know that the federal government is a big spender. In 2008, it spent nearly $3 trillion, which is a bit more than 20 percent of GDP. Retired workers rely on the federal government for their Social Security pensions, and defense contractors and their employees obtain much of their income from federal government purchases. Federal tax and subsidy programs also affect incentives to save, invest, and work.

Government spending and tax policies affect aggregate demand, and the impact of government policies on incentives can affect aggregate supply over time. The federal government has legal responsibility, under the Employment Act of 1946 and the Humphrey-Hawkins Act of 1978, to use its spending and taxing powers to help achieve full employment. The *Council of Economic Advisers* assists the president in recommending policies that maintain economic stability and pursue goals of full employment and low inflation.

In this chapter, we'll examine the impact of the federal government budget on macroeconomic equilibrium. The chapter The Federal Budget, Government Debt, and the Economy zeroes in on the federal government budget deficit to analyze its impact in depth.

Concept Preview

After reading this chapter, you should be able to

1. Explain how expansionary fiscal policies affect the economy and show how such policies can be used to eliminate recessionary GDP gaps.
2. Explain how contractionary fiscal policies affect the economy and show how such policies can help prevent inflation.
3. Show how automatic stabilizers moderate shifts in aggregate demand.
4. Explain how supply-side fiscal policies can affect the economy in the long run and assess the effectiveness of recent supply-side policies.

The Federal Budget and Its Impact on the Economy

When there's a presidential election, one of the biggest issues is always the state of the economy. In the United States we expect the president to pursue policies that reduce cyclical unemployment, keep inflation under control, and ensure adequate economic growth. The president is inevitably blamed for poor performance of the economy and is quick to claim the credit when the economy performs well. Inflation, unemployment, and the rate of economic growth are political issues. Pressure groups and ordinary citizens expect the federal government to take measures to achieve full employment and stable prices.

The use of government spending and taxing for the specific purpose of stabilizing the economy is called fiscal policy. The short-term goals of fiscal policy are to prevent excessive unemployment and to control inflation. Over longer periods, fiscal policy seeks to ensure adequate economic growth to permit improvements in the national standard of living. Monetary policy seeks to help control the cyclical ups and downs of the economy by influencing aggregate demand. Now, you'll see how fiscal policy can be used to stabilize the economy.

The spending and taxing activities of the federal government are influenced by many political considerations, not just those relating to stabilization. Our first step in understanding fiscal policy in the United States is to review the process through which federal government spending and taxes are approved annually.

The Federal Budget

The government budget is a plan for spending funds and for raising revenues through taxation, fees, and other means, and for borrowing funds, if necessary. During the budgetary process politicians, citizens, and government officials propose, debate, and make decisions that affect government spending, taxing, and borrowing.

The budget sets the spending and revenue plan for the federal government's *fiscal year*, which runs from October 1 to September 30. When government revenues raised from taxation and means other than borrowing exactly cover government expenditures during the fiscal year, the budget is said to be *balanced.*

Government spending often exceeds government revenues. A budget deficit is the annual excess of government spending over government revenues. When the budget is in deficit, the federal government must borrow funds by issuing government securities that are sold in credit markets, such as Treasury bills, notes, and bonds. Except for the years 1998-2001, the federal government budget in the United States has been in deficit every year since 1970.

A budget surplus prevails when government revenues exceed government expenditures during the year. When the federal government runs a budget surplus, it can use the excess revenue to pay off some of its debt.

As you undoubtedly know from watching the nightly news, the deficit is a hotly debated political and economic issue. In the chapter The Federal Budget, Government Debt, and the Economy, we sort out the arguments for and against budget deficits. Our goal in this chapter is to examine the general effects of government spending and taxes on macroeconomic equilibrium in order to understand how the government budget can be used to stabilize the economy.

How the Federal Government Budget Affects Aggregate Demand: A Quick Review

As you know, government purchases represent a major component of aggregate demand. Nearly 1 of every 10 dollars spent on the purchase of goods and services in the United States is spent by the federal government. The federal government also makes direct transfer payments to members of households and to state and local governments. These payments, which include welfare benefits, Social Security pensions, veterans' benefits, interest payments to holders of government securities, and grants to state and local governments, constitute sources of income to recipients. Government purchases and transfer payments, other things being equal, add to aggregate demand by increasing disposable income in the United States.

To finance its purchases of goods and services and the payments it makes to individuals and organizations each year, the federal government collects funds through taxation, which accounts for the bulk of federal government revenues. Taxes paid reduce the ability of households and business firms to purchase goods and services for their private use and, therefore, tend to reduce aggregate demand.

The overall effect of the federal budget on aggregate demand depends on the expansionary effect of government purchases or other payments and on the contractionary effect of taxes. When there's a budget deficit, the federal government adds more to aggregate demand than it takes away, because it will spend more on purchases and transfer payments than it raises from taxes. A budget deficit, therefore, indicates the government is putting upward pressure on aggregate demand. The government can use this upward pressure to offset cyclical declines in investment or net export demand, thus employing fiscal policy to prevent the economy from falling into a recession.

The government can *decrease* aggregate demand by running a budget *surplus*. In such cases the government collects more in taxes than it spends. Just as you save when you spend less than your income, the government can save by running a budget surplus. When the federal government spends less than it collects in revenues, it adds less to aggregate demand than it takes away. A budget surplus is, therefore, a contractionary influence on the economy that can be used to offset surges in consumption and investment demand that might cause inflation.

Government borrowing to finance a budget deficit can affect equilibrium in credit markets in ways that indirectly influence aggregate demand. Increased demand for credit by the government can put upward pressure on interest rates. The higher real interest rates can decrease investment purchases. Similarly, when the government runs a budget surplus, its decreased demand for credit can put downward pressure on interest rates. In the chapter The Federal Budget, Government Debt, and the Economy, we examine the impact of the federal budget deficit on financial markets.

Using Fiscal Policy to Influence Aggregate Demand

An expansionary fiscal policy is one under which the government acts to *increase* aggregate demand by adjusting its budget during the year. It can do this by increasing its purchases of goods and services, by increasing transfer payments to individuals and organizations, or by decreasing taxes. Of course, the government can choose to increase aggregate demand by decreasing taxes *and* increasing spending.

Expansionary fiscal policy can be used to increase equilibrium real GDP and to reduce the cyclical unemployment that prevails when the economy is in a recession. This was the remedy proposed by Keynes for an economy in deep recession. Keynes believed that, because the outlook for increased sales would be gloomy in a deep recession, banks would be cautious about making loans and investors would be unresponsive to reductions in interest rates. Keynes' solution was for the government to increase its spending when others wouldn't. To eliminate a recessionary GDP gap, the government would allow its budget balance to shift to a deficit. The resulting stimulus to aggregate demand would then increase aggregate purchases, and, as aggregate production increased, unemployment would be reduced. Once the economy was on course again, the government could reduce spending and let the budget return to balance.

To restrain aggregate demand, the government can engage in a contractionary fiscal policy that will decrease government spending or increase taxes, or both. A contractionary fiscal policy can be used to put downward pressure on the price level, thereby combating inflation in periods when the economy is overheating.

How an Increase in Government Purchases Can Help Pull an Economy Out of a Recession

1 Let's begin our analysis of fiscal policy by examining how an increase in government purchases can increase aggregate demand and eliminate a substantial recessionary GDP gap. In Box 1 the economy is in equilibrium at a level of real GDP equal to $4,000 billion. Potential real GDP is assumed to be $5,000 billion. The economy is therefore experiencing a $1,000 billion recessionary GDP gap. It's also assumed that the economy is currently stagnating in a severe recession, so that it's operating along the flat portion of its aggregate supply curve. Through the use of fiscal policy, the government can increase aggregate demand without heating up inflation during the year.

In our analysis of the multiplier (chapter on Keynesian analysis of macroeconomic equilibrium), we see that less than $1 of autonomous spending, such as government purchases, is required to increase real GDP by $1. Suppose the marginal respending rate in the economy is 0.5. The marginal respending rate is less than 1 because a portion of the increased annual income generated from an initial round of autonomous purchases is used to buy imported goods and to pay taxes. Some is saved. When the marginal respending rate is 0.5, the multiplier for any initial injection of new spending into the economy is

$$\begin{aligned}\text{Multiplier} &= 1/(1 - \text{Marginal respending rate})\\ &= 1/(1 - 0.5) = 1/0.5\\ &= 2\end{aligned}$$

Each dollar of government purchases that's initiated at the beginning of the year will, therefore, ultimately increase real GDP and real income in the nation by $2 as it's spent and respent.

Box 1 How an Increase in Government Spending Can Have a Multiplied Effect on Real GDP

When the marginal respending rate is 0.5, a $500 billion increase in government spending at the beginning of the year increases real GDP by $1,000 billion that year to eliminate a recessionary GDP gap.

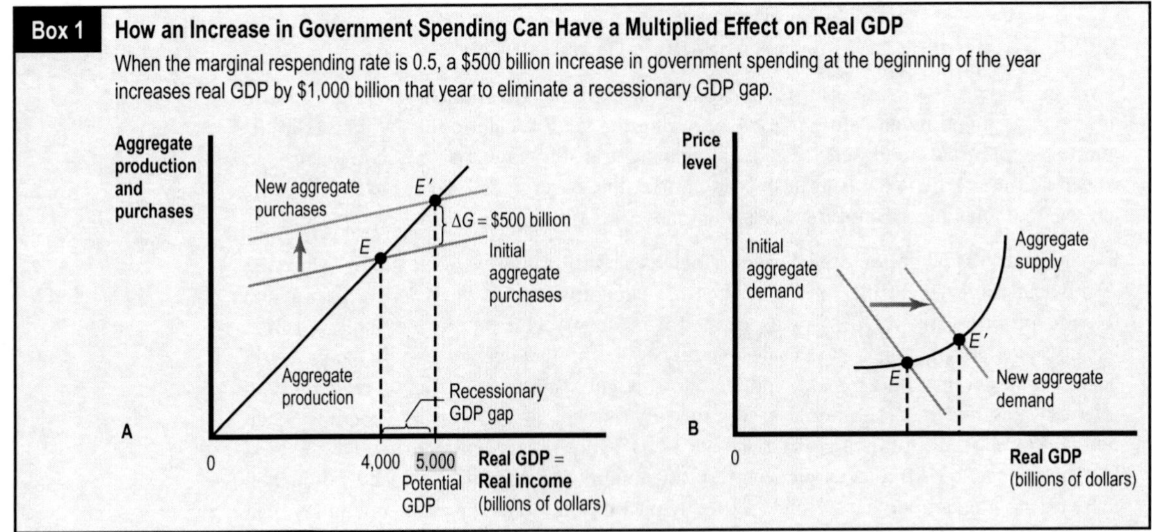

Assuming nothing else changes, G, an increase in government purchases generating \$500 billion in additional business receipts at the beginning of the year, can eliminate the recessionary gap, because the total increase in spending resulting from G will be

$$\text{Increase in real GDP} = (\text{Increase in } G)\ (\text{Multiplier})$$

$$= (\$500 \text{ billion})(2)$$

$$= \$1{,}000 \text{ billion}$$

The graphs in Box 1 show how the expansionary fiscal policy will affect the macroeconomic equilibrium for an economy in a recession. As shown in graph **A**, the economy is initially in equilibrium at point E, where aggregate purchases just equal aggregate production at the current price level. (See the chapter on Keynesian analysis of aggregate purchases for discussion of this graph.) Other things being equal, an injection of \$500 billion of new government purchases shifts the aggregate purchases line upward and results in a new equilibrium at point E'. At that point, real GDP increases to \$5,000 billion as the recessionary GDP gap is closed.

Graph **B** shows that the increase in government purchases shifts the aggregate demand curve outward. It also shows that the expansionary policy has little impact on the price level when the economy is operating in the relatively flat portion of its aggregate supply curve, as is likely to be the case in an economy experiencing a deep recession. Increases in aggregate demand that result from an expansionary fiscal policy are therefore unlikely to contribute to an inflationary process for an economy experiencing a deep recession.

Using Tax Cuts or Government Transfers to Stimulate a Sluggish Economy

A sluggish economy can also be stimulated through a tax cut or an increase in government transfer payments. However, the impact of these measures on aggregate demand is less direct than the impact of an increase in government purchases. Remember that *net taxes* are the difference between government tax revenues and government transfers. In effect, transfers can be viewed as negative taxes. To engage in an expansionary fiscal policy, the government reduces net taxes by decreasing taxes or increasing transfers. In doing so, the government increases disposable income, which results in increased consumer purchases.

It's easy to show that the expansionary effect of a reduction in net taxes is less than that of an equivalent dollar increase in government purchases. When the government makes purchases of \$500 billion, it directly increases business receipts by that amount at the initial stage of the spending increase. However, when the government puts \$500 billion into the pockets of individuals through a reduction in net taxes (either through an increase in government transfers such as Social Security or welfare payments or through a lump-sum refund of taxes to all taxpayers), purchases of U.S. final products will not go up by that amount at the initial stage. Some of the increased disposable income that results from the cut in net taxes will be spent on imported goods, and some will be saved. For example, suppose the marginal propensity to save is 0.2 and the marginal propensity to import is 0.1. This means that 30 percent of the dollar value of the \$500 billion tax cut, or \$150 billion, won't be directly spent on U.S. final products. The initial increase in the purchases of U.S. final products that results from the tax cut will, therefore, be only \$350 billion. The multiplier process thus begins with a \$350 billion injection of new spending rather than a \$500 billion injection, as was the case when government purchases increased by \$500 billion. The \$350 billion initial increase in purchases will then be spent and respent in the course of the multiplier process. Some of the extra income generated in this process will be used to make purchases in the United States, but some will be saved, some will be used to purchase imported items, and some will be used to pay taxes on the extra income. Assuming a multiplier of 2 for the economy, this means the $500 billion tax cut will result in a $700 billion increase in real GDP ($350 billion × 2 = $700 billion).[1]

We can conclude that an increase in government purchases is more expansionary for the economy than a decrease in net taxes of an equal amount. Other things being equal, increasing transfer payments or reducing taxes is less stimulating to the economy than increasing government purchases.

The expansionary effect of a tax cut can also be less than that of an increase in government purchases because households may treat the extra income differently from the way they treat extra income earned. If the tax cut is viewed as only temporary, the proportion saved is likely to be higher for a dollar of reduced taxes than for a dollar of extra earnings.

However, tax cuts have been used with some success to help pull the economy out of recessions. Tax cuts were proposed by the Kennedy administration in the early 1960s to help pull the economy out of a serious recession. In 1964, Congress reduced average personal income taxes by 18 percent. This reduction was widely credited with spurring an increase in consumer purchases that lifted the economy out of the recession. However, in 1975, when President Ford persuaded Congress to reduce income taxes to help increase aggregate demand during a recession, much of the tax cut was apparently used to increase saving, and aggregate demand did not increase substantially.

In 1981, a tax cut designed to increase aggregate supply rather than aggregate demand was proposed by President Reagan and enacted by Congress. In the short run, however, the effect of the Reagan tax cut was to increase the federal budget deficit. The resulting increase in aggregate demand helped pull the economy out of the recession of 1982.

Under the administration of George W. Bush, two major tax cuts were enacted in 2001 and 2003. Both tax cuts lowered income tax rates, and were partially designed to help the economy get out of the recession that began in March of 2001 and help the economy expand more rapidly in the aftermath of the recession. The Economic Growth and Tax Relief Reconciliation Act of 2001 (EGTRRA) substantially lowered income tax rates, and also provided additional tax relief to families with children and to people who save. In 2003, in response to strong pressure from the president to stimulate a sluggish economy, Congress enacted the Jobs and Growth Tax Relief Reconciliation Act of 2003. This legislation accelerated many of the provisions of EGTRRA, to make them effective for 2003 and 2004. It lowered tax rates for these two years, and accelerated the marriage penalty relief for 2003 and 2004, which lowers tax rates for many married couples filing joint income tax returns. The legislation also reduced tax rates applying to capital gains and dividends, and enacted special provisions to encourage business investment.

In 2008, after it became clear that the U.S. economy could be heading into a recession because of reduction in aggregate demand, the president and the Congress acted quickly to enact into law the Economic Stimulus Act of 2008. This law sought to increase aggregate demand by providing tax rebates to most low and middle-income taxpayers. For those eligible for the full rebate, single workers received a $600 rebate on taxes paid or $1,200 if they filed a joint return, provided they had paid at least that much in taxes. A flat rebate of

[1] We have to mention one more complication here. Tax cuts are sometimes a refund of taxes with no change in marginal tax rates, as is assumed in this example of a lump-sum tax refund. At other times, however, the marginal tax rate may be lowered when taxes are cut, as was the case under the Tax Reform Act of 1986. When the marginal tax rate is lowered, the multiplier is increased. Review the Appendix to the chapter Keynesian Analysis of Macroeconomic Equilibrium to see how the multiplier is related to the marginal tax rate.

$300 for single people and $600 for married taxpayers filing jointly was also available, if they had at least $3,000 income from a job or social insurance benefits. The rebates were paid out in the summer of 2008 with a hope they would stimulate consumer spending. Rebates were phased out for taxpayers with relatively high incomes, and the highest income taxpayers received no tax rebates.

Although the tax rebates did temporarily stimulate consumer spending in 2008, they were not sufficient to offset other forces that were decreasing aggregate demand and plunging the economy into a deep recession. As the credit crunch of 2007-2009 and declining asset prices, both for homes and corporate equities, were working to decrease aggregate demand, it was clear the recession that began in the last quarter of 2007 was going to be severe. A financial system that had seized up with the failure of large investment banks and some major depository institutions further decreased aggregate demand, while an aggressive monetary policy pursued by the Fed did not seem to be having significant impact on aggregate demand in 2008. To further stimulate the economy, Congress enacted the American Recovery and Reinvestment Act of 2009 (ARRA). This legislation consisted of a combination of tax cuts of nearly $300 billion, most of which would benefit individual taxpayers, along with other programs designed to inject over $350 billion of new federal government spending into the economy. (See the Principles in Practice Fiscal Policy in 2008 and 2009.)

Equal Increases of Government Purchases and Net Taxes Are Expansionary

The analysis of the two preceding sections can be used to reach a surprising conclusion: An equal increase in government purchases and net taxes has an expansionary effect on the economy. A $500 billion injection of government purchases results in a $1,000 billion increase in real GDP, other things being equal, when the multiplier is 2 for an initial injection of new spending into the economy.

A $500 billion *increase* in net taxes to cover the increased government purchases would result in a multiplied *decrease* in private expenditures because it decreases disposable income. However, the initial reduction in private spending on U.S. goods and services resulting from a $500 billion increase in taxes would be less than $500 billion. This is because some of the $500 billion collected in taxes would have been saved or used to purchase imported goods. Using the same marginal propensities to save and import as in the previous example, a $500 billion increase in net taxes will decrease purchases of U.S. goods by only $350 billion. The remaining $150 billion of the tax increase would have been spent on imports or saved and, thus, wouldn't have added to aggregate demand. The initial tax-induced reduction in spending on U.S.-produced goods and services of $350 billion will then result in a $700 billion reduction in real GDP, assuming a multiplier of 2. Notice that after the multiplier process has been played out, the reduction in real GDP attributable to the increase in net taxes is *less than* the $1,000 billion increase in real GDP attributable to the increase in government purchases. As a result of this increase in government purchases, which is fully covered by the increase in net taxes, there is upward pressure on aggregate demand. The increase in equilibrium real GDP is the multiplier effect of the purchases ($1,000 billion) less the multiplier effect of the taxes (–$700 billion), or $300 billion.

Because the expansionary effect of each dollar of government purchases exceeds the contractionary effect of each dollar of taxes used to finance the purchases, the net effect on the economy of an equal increase in government purchases and net taxes is expansionary. An increase in government spending that is exactly covered by an increase in taxes will increase real GDP. It follows that increased spending adds to aggregate demand, even when that spending doesn't increase the government deficit! Beware, then, of politicians who say that increased government spending won't add to inflationary

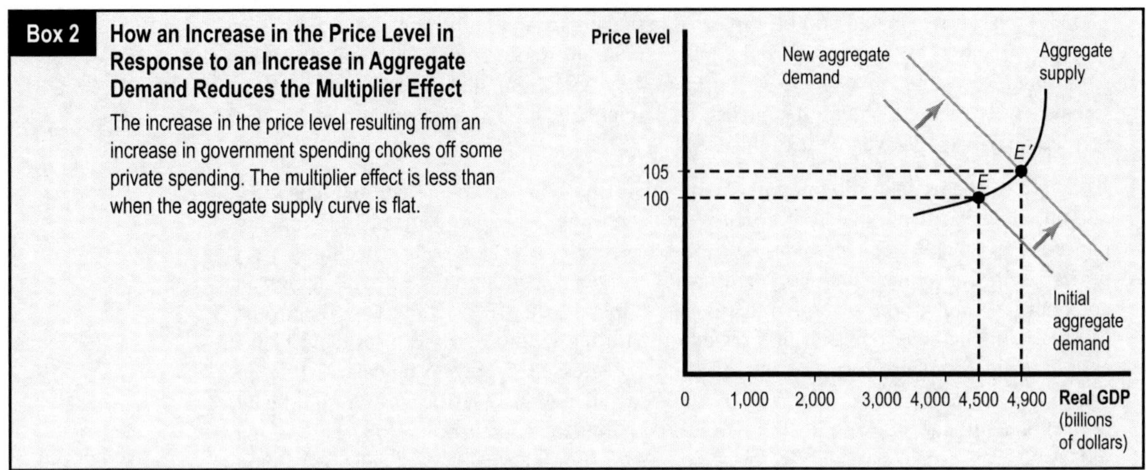

Box 2 How an Increase in the Price Level in Response to an Increase in Aggregate Demand Reduces the Multiplier Effect

The increase in the price level resulting from an increase in government spending chokes off some private spending. The multiplier effect is less than when the aggregate supply curve is flat.

pressures when that spending is fully financed by taxes. Fiscal policies may be expansionary even if they don't increase the deficit.

The Effects of Fiscal Policy on the Price Level

Any expansionary influence on aggregate demand resulting from fiscal policy will increase both the price level and real GDP as the economy moves toward its potential real GDP. The increase in the price level will dampen private spending over the year, and the multiplier effect on the economy will be correspondingly less. The graph in Box 2 shows how the increase in the price level chokes off some private purchases. The economy is initially in equilibrium at point *E*, at which real GDP is $4,500 billion and the price level is 100. The full-employment level of real GDP is $5,000 billion, implying that there's a $500 billion recessionary GDP gap. Fiscal policy is used to shift the aggregate demand curve outward. If the multiplier is 2, a $250 billion increase in government purchases is sufficient to increase real GDP by $500 billion. If there were no increase in the price level, the resulting outward shift of the aggregate demand curve would be sufficient to eliminate the recessionary GDP gap. However, because the price level rises from 100 to 105 as a result of the increase in aggregate demand, the economy achieves a new equilibrium at point *E′*. At the new equilibrium, the price level is 105 and real GDP is only $4,900 billion. The higher prices choke off $100 billion in private purchases. In this case, *more than* $250 billion in government purchases is required to increase real GDP by $500 billion.

The multiplier will be less than that implied by the formulas in other chapters when the price level is responsive to changes in aggregate demand. In addition, there is more risk that fiscal policy will overheat the economy when the economy is already close to its potential real GDP. Fiscal policy must therefore be used with care to avoid starting an inflationary spiral when only a modest gap exists between potential and actual GDP.

The government spending and borrowing required for an expansionary fiscal policy can also affect the level of interest rates in the economy. In the chapter The Federal Budget, Government Debt, and the Economy, we discuss this possibility and its consequences for private spending.

Contractionary Fiscal Policy

Contractionary fiscal policy seeks to restrain aggregate demand by either decreasing government purchases or increasing net taxes. By restraining aggregate demand, a contractionary fiscal policy can help reduce inflation. Such a policy results in a reduction of the federal budget deficit or a movement toward a budget surplus.

The graph in Box 3 shows how a contractionary fiscal policy can help eliminate an inflationary gap or help prevent an economy from overheating. The economy is initially in equilibrium at point *E*, at which the price level is 100 and real GDP is at its potential level of $5,000 billion. If the aggregate demand curve shifts outward due to a stock market boom that boosts household wealth, the economy can reach equilibrium at point *E′* , at which real GDP will increase to $5,500 billion and the price level will go up to 110. If the economy is beginning to overheat in this way, a contractionary fiscal policy can offset the increase in aggregate demand. For example, if the Council of Economic Advisers projects that investment will increase during the year, it may expect a $500 billion inflationary GDP gap like the one shown in Box 3. A reduction in government purchases or an increase in net taxes can offset the expected increase in aggregate demand. Such a contractionary fiscal policy can keep the economy at point *E* and prevent it from moving to point *E′* . If nothing is done to prevent the economy from moving to *E′* , the result may be an inflationary wage-price spiral that eventually moves the economy to point *E″*, at which GDP has again fallen to $5,000 billion and the price level has risen to 115. In other words, fiscal policy can prevent a wage-price spiral from beginning.

Problems in Effectively Implementing Fiscal Policy

Fiscal policy is based on forecasts of shifts in aggregate demand. Unfortunately, such forecasts are often inaccurate. Moreover, the thin line corresponding to potential real GDP is difficult to see in practice. A tax cut or government purchases increase designed to pull the economy out of a recession can easily overshoot the mark and overheat the economy. Stabilization policy is far from being an exact science.

Contractionary fiscal policy often runs into political problems. During the budgetary process, elected representatives oppose cuts in government spending that are likely to reduce their constituents' benefits. Every legislator wants budget cuts to reduce income in someone else's district! For this reason, it's difficult to gain approval for cuts in government purchases and increases in net taxes. On the other hand, expansionary fiscal policies are quite popular. Increases in government purchases and reductions in net taxes provide direct benefits to politicians and their constituents.

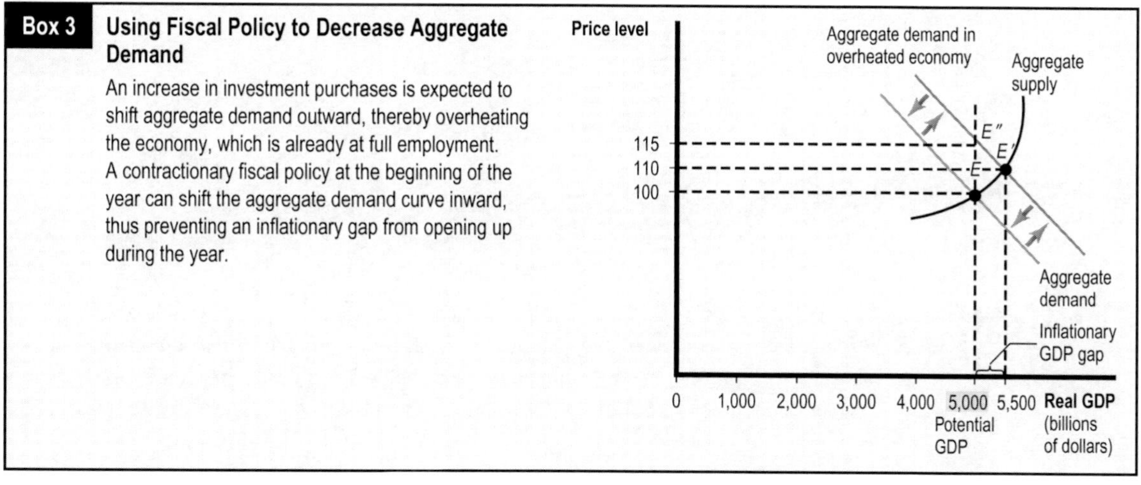

Box 3 Using Fiscal Policy to Decrease Aggregate Demand

An increase in investment purchases is expected to shift aggregate demand outward, thereby overheating the economy, which is already at full employment. A contractionary fiscal policy at the beginning of the year can shift the aggregate demand curve inward, thus preventing an inflationary gap from opening up during the year.

The fact that the government budget has been almost consistently in deficit during both the ups and the downs of the business cycle since 1970 appears to support the idea that there's an expansionary bias to fiscal policy. There's also a temptation for politicians in power to engage in expansionary fiscal policies just prior to major elections, because the party in power is more likely to be reelected during economic upturns than during downturns. In any event, it's clear that, in many cases, fiscal policy takes a backseat to political maneuvering.

Another problem in implementing fiscal policy has to do with its effects on expectations. If participants in credit markets believe that an increase in the government budget deficit will substantially increase inflation, they'll revise their expectations about inflation, which will put upward pressure on equilibrium long-term interest rates. As this occurs, the quantity of funds demanded for private investment will decline, and the fiscal stimulus of the budget will be offset by a decline in investment spending. In effect, increased government purchases financed by borrowing could simply displace private spending without providing any stimulus to the economy. We discuss this complication in the chapter The Federal Budget, Government Debt, and the Economy, when we look at the budget deficit's effect on the economy in greater detail.

Over the years, fiscal policy has had both its successes and its failures. The tax cut of 1964 increased aggregate demand at just the right time and encouraged economic growth. However, during the period 1965 to 1967, when government purchases for the Vietnam conflict were increasing, no tax increase was enacted. Despite a tax increase in 1968, the expansionary fiscal policy pursued by the Johnson administration at that time contributed to a period of inflation when the economy overheated in the late 1960s and early 1970s. A tax increase in 1990, designed to help reduce the budget deficit, was ill-timed—just as the economy was drifting into a recession—and probably made the recession worse and the recovery less robust. However, a tax cut in 2001, meant to use some of the federal government budget surplus that year to finance increases in private income, was timed just as the economy was headed toward a recession. The federal tax cut of 2001 probably mitigated the effects of the recession and helped the economy recover sooner than it would have otherwise. These tax cuts were designed to be permanent, and the resulting decline in revenue in later years contributed, by 2005, to an increase in the federal budget deficit, which was expanding aggregate demand.

Lags in Fiscal Policy Implementation and Effects on Real GDP

Wouldn't it be nice if fiscal policy could be used as a precision tool to keep the economy always at full employment with inflation under control? Unfortunately, any stabilization policy, monetary or fiscal, is difficult to implement flawlessly. There are often problems in timing. For example, as just pointed out, it's hard to determine exactly when an economy is slipping into a recession or beginning to overheat. As a result, there's often a *recognition lag* between the time the economy begins to move away from full employment and the realization by policymakers that such a movement is actually occurring. Economic forecasts are anything but infallible!

There's also an *administrative lag* in implementing a fiscal policy change. Sometimes it takes a year or longer for a major tax cut to be enacted. The tax cut of 1964 was actually three years in the making! Sometimes such lags are so long that the economy's own self-correcting mechanism begins to work before fiscal policy gets a chance to exert an impact.

Finally, there's an *operational lag* between the time a change is made in government purchases or net taxes and the time it takes for equilibrium real GDP to change. The multiplier process isn't instantaneous. It takes awhile for increases or decreases in disposable income resulting from fiscal policy to have an effect on private spending.

Just as monetary policy has its critics (see Stabilization of the Economy through Monetary Policy), so too does fiscal policy. Many critics argue that, because of its expansionary bias and the lags in its implementation and operation, the use of fiscal policy to stabilize the economy often does more harm than good.

Automatic Stabilizers and Cyclical Influences on the Budget Deficit

3 The ups and downs of the economy have an automatic effect on certain government expenditures and revenues. For example, when real GDP falls below its potential value, unemployment increases, thereby increasing government expenditures for unemployment insurance. Also, as real GDP declines, federal tax collections decline because most taxes used by the federal government are collected from labor earnings and earnings from the use of capital or loanable funds. Our earlier discussion concentrated on *discretionary* fiscal policy, which represents deliberate changes in government purchases and net taxes for the purpose of stabilizing the economy. We now turn our attention to the effects of *nondiscretionary* fiscal policy, which consists of changes in government spending and revenues that result automatically as the economy fluctuates.

The magnitude of the budget deficit or surplus is influenced by the inevitable fluctuations of the economy. Budget deficits or surpluses are not under the direct control of policymakers, at least in the short run. Cyclical fluctuations in real GDP and the price level must therefore be accounted for if the government budget deficit is to be predicted accurately.

Automatic Stabilizers

Automatic stabilizers are features of the federal budget that automatically adjust net taxes to stabilize aggregate demand as the economy expands and contracts. When the economy begins to contract, these stabilizers increase transfer payments and reduce tax collections in order to stimulate aggregate demand. When the economy begins to expand, the automatic stabilizers increase tax collections and reduce transfer payments in order to constrain growth in aggregate demand.

A key automatic stabilizer is the federal income tax. As the economy expands, income tax collections rise as income earned increases. Given government purchases, the increased tax collections prevent aggregate purchases from increasing in proportion to the increase in earnings. In a sense, the income tax acts as a damper on private spending as real GDP and real income increase. It slows the growth of aggregate demand and controls upward pressure on the price level when the economy is expanding. This can help slow inflation if the funds are not spent by government but instead are used to reduce the government budget deficit.

Government tax receipts are also quite responsive to changes in business conditions, in part because marginal tax rates increase with income. As national income increases, more people are pushed into higher tax brackets. Therefore, the increase in taxes collected is greater proportionately than the increase in income. Similarly, when a recession causes real GDP and national income to decline, the decrease in taxes is greater proportionately than the decline in real GDP because more people are pushed into lower tax brackets. Their tax bills decline proportionately more than their income does. Corporate profit taxes are particularly sensitive to shifts in the business cycle. Corporate profits typically plummet during a recession, as do receipts from the corporate income tax. The decline in tax collections during an economic contraction prevents aggregate demand from decreasing excessively.

Also included in the automatic stabilizers are programs that increase transfer payments to individuals when the economy contracts and decrease such payments when the economy expands. These increases and decreases don't require acts of Congress or changes in administration policies because most transfers are part of *entitlement* programs that mandate government payments to individuals who meet certain eligibility standards. Because eligibility is based mainly on income and joblessness, government expenditures for transfer programs naturally increase during economic contractions, when unemployment increases and income declines.

Government purchases of goods and services tend to be quite stable over the business cycle. The variation in government expenditures over the business cycle results from changes in transfer payments under entitlement programs. The major entitlement programs that serve as automatic stabilizers are:

1. *Unemployment insurance*. Expenditures for this program increase during recessions, when there are more unemployed workers and longer periods of unemployment. During expansions, as unemployment rates decline, unemployment insurance payments also decline.

2. *Cash assistance welfare programs*. When a recession hits, more people become eligible for programs of cash assistance such as Supplemental Security Income (SSI). Although such programs are designed primarily for people outside the labor force, many of the eligible people manage to find at least part-time work when the economy is healthy. During contractions and recessions, more eligible people must rely on welfare programs for their full support, so cash assistance to the poor increases. During expansions, more eligible people manage to find at least some work, and payments decline.

3. *In-kind assistance programs*. These programs include food stamps and medical care for people with annual incomes below certain threshold levels. As a contraction or recession hits, many workers lose their jobs or suffer reductions in earnings, thus becoming eligible for in-kind assistance programs. Government payments under these programs increase during contractions, thus bolstering aggregate demand, and decline during expansions, putting a damper on aggregate demand.

4. *Social Security pension payments*. During a contraction or a recession, more elderly workers retire and fewer Social Security recipients continue to work. Therefore, government expenditures for pension payments increase. During an expansion, some people forgo part of their pensions to work, which reduces Social Security payments.

In periods when national income declines, all of the transfer programs tend to maintain aggregate demand by automatically increasing payments as the number of eligible people increases. This increases the consumption component of real GDP, which would otherwise decline as earnings fell. During expansions, the transfer programs increase net taxes by reducing transfers as the number of people entitled to benefits declines.

Gauging the Impact of Fiscal Policy

The automatic stabilizers influence the size of the federal budget deficit. Obviously, when aggregate demand declines and the economy is in a downturn, tax receipts fall. However, because of the transfer programs discussed in the preceding section, federal government expenditures tend to increase. Both the decrease in tax revenues and the increase in expenditures contribute to an increase in the budget deficit during recessions. During boom periods, tax revenues increase and transfer payments decline, contributing to a decrease in the budget deficit or to a budget surplus.

To eliminate the cyclical effects of automatic stabilizers on the budget deficit, economists compute the cyclically adjusted high-employment deficit (or surplus), the budget deficit (or surplus) that would prevail if the natural rate of unemployment were achieved. This adjusted deficit is sometimes also referred to as the *standardized-employment deficit*.

The high-employment budget indicates the relationship between government spending and taxes for a given level of government purchases that would prevail if the economy achieved full employment. Receipts and expenditures for the high-employment budget are typically based on an unemployment rate of 5 percent to 6 percent. The high-employment budget is designed to show how much stimulus to aggregate demand the federal government is providing to the economy by setting net taxes equal to the amount that would be observed at full employment.

The graph in Box 4 shows how the federal budget balance can vary with real GDP for the year. The line showing net taxes is upward-sloping. As real GDP increases, so do net taxes. The slope of the curve increases as real GDP goes up, because more people are pushed into tax brackets with higher marginal tax rates. Net taxes also rise with real GDP, because government transfer payments are higher at lower levels of national income than they are at higher levels. Remember that net taxes are taxes paid less transfers received. Government purchases are drawn as a horizontal line because they're authorized at the beginning of the year and, unlike net taxes, aren't subject to cyclical fluctuations.

When government expenditures exceed tax revenues for the year, a budget deficit prevails. When tax revenues exactly equal government expenditures, the budget is in balance. When revenues exceed expenditures, there's a surplus. The graph in Box 4 shows that the lower the level of real GDP realized for the year, the higher the budget deficit. Conversely, the higher the level of real GDP, the lower the deficit. At some level of real GDP, the budget will be in balance, and increases in national income beyond that level will result in a surplus.

Suppose potential real GDP is $5,000 billion. At this high-employment level of real GDP, the deficit is $150 billion. However, if real GDP during the year is less than $5,000 billion, the deficit will be greater because net tax collections will be less. The graph in Box 4 shows that, if equilibrium real GDP is only $3,500 billion, the deficit will be $200 billion.

The actual high-employment deficit or surplus depends on government purchases and tax rates for the year. For example, if government purchases were lower or tax rates were higher, the net taxes curve and the government purchases line might intersect at the point corresponding to potential real GDP. This implies that the budget would be in balance at the higher employment level. If policymakers want to expand the economy, they must choose a fiscal policy that increases the high-employment deficit. Such a policy would either shift the tax revenue line downward or shift the government purchases line upward. The actual budget deficit (or surplus) in a given year depends both on the high-employment deficit (or surplus) and on the cyclical impact of the automatic stabilizers.

Box 4 Cyclical Effects on the Federal Budget and the High-Employment Budget Balance

Net taxes tend to increase as real GDP is higher during a given year. The federal budget tends to be thrown into deficit when real GDP is well below its potential during a year because the increase in transfer payments and reduction in taxes reduce government revenues. Government purchases, however, tend to be fixed during the year. Here, the high-employment deficit is $150 billion when real GDP is $5,000 billion.

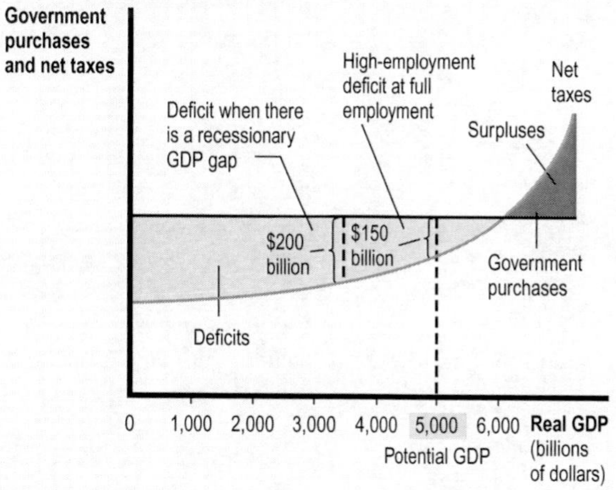

The high-employment budget has been in deficit almost continuously since 1960, indicating that expansionary fiscal policy has been more prevalent than contractionary fiscal policy. The high-employment budget deficit averaged close to 2 percent of GDP from 1960 to 1980 and was approaching 5 percent of GDP in the mid-1980s.

Forecasting the federal budget deficit for any given year is more an art than a science! For example, in 1982, a recession year, the Reagan administration projected that outlays for fiscal year 1983 would be $757 billion, while revenues would be $666 billion, resulting in a budget deficit of $91 billion. However, the president's economists did a poor job of forecasting the intensity of the recession. Unemployment in 1983 turned out to be much higher than expected, and the growth rate of real GDP was –2.9 percent that year instead of the +3 percent projected by the administration! This was complicated by the fact that in enacting the president's proposed budget, Congress cut expenditures less than the president wished. Congress also enacted a larger tax cut than the president requested. As a result, the actual federal budget deficit in 1983 turned out to be a whopping $195 billion, which was over $100 billion more than the amount projected!

In 1992 the Congressional Budget Office estimated that based on a natural rate of unemployment of 5.5 percent, the high-employment deficit was $184 billion, while the actual budget deficit that year was nearly $300 billion! However, in 1994, when the U.S. economy was operating close to full employment, the high-employment budget deficit was only slightly smaller than the actual budget deficit. In 2000, when actual real GDP was estimated to be greater than potential real GDP, the Congressional Budget Office calculated a high-employment budget surplus of $106 billion, which amounted to 1 percent of GDP.

Supply-Side Fiscal Policies

4 Steady and predictable growth in aggregate demand gives business firms an economic environment that fosters investment purchases. Over the long run, however, economic growth depends on growth in aggregate supply. Policies that encourage saving, investment, and increased labor-force participation can increase the economic growth rate in a nation over the long run. Government policies can influence incentives to save, work, and invest by affecting the *net return* to these activities. For example, investment can be subsidized, as it has been in the United States, through credits that reduce the tax bills of businesses investing in new structures and equipment. Government can also affect the net return to these activities through changes in marginal tax rates. Workers, savers, and investors respond to the *after-tax* return they receive. When marginal tax rates on labor, interest, or investment income decline, the after-tax return of working, saving, or investing goes up, providing an incentive to undertake more of the activity.

Supply-side fiscal policies seek to influence long-run growth in real GDP through government subsidies and tax reductions. By increasing investment and work effort, these policies aim to shift the aggregate supply curve for the economy outward at a faster rate than would otherwise be the case. The effectiveness of the policies depends on the responsiveness of workers, savers, and investors to increases in the net returns to work, saving, and investment over the long run. The supply-siders maintain that cuts in marginal tax rates—the tax rates on extra income—will increase both work effort and investment in the long run. They contend that this will increase aggregate supply in the long run, thereby contributing to higher real GDP and lower price levels.

How Supply-Side Fiscal Policies Can Influence Labor Markets

Let's first consider programs designed to increase work effort. The rationale for these programs is that when people decide whether to enter the labor force and how many hours to work, they look at the *net after-tax wages* they can earn. The higher the marginal tax rate, the lower the after-tax wage for additional work.

The graph in Box 5 illustrates supply and demand in the labor market. Initially, the market equilibrium wage is $10 per hour, and *L* hours of labor per year are supplied at that wage. If the marginal tax rate on labor income is currently 20 percent, the net after-tax marginal return to additional work is only $8. This is equal to the gross wage less the marginal tax of 20 percent on extra hourly earnings, or $2.

The labor supply curve can shift when tax rates are changed. Suppose the marginal tax rate applied to labor income is reduced to 15 percent. At the current equilibrium wage, the marginal net after-tax return to additional labor hours will go up to $8.50 (the $10 gross wage paid by employers less the $1.50 tax per hour of work resulting from the 15 percent marginal tax rate). The higher net marginal return to work resulting from the tax cut can attract more workers into the labor force and encourage existing workers to work more hours per year. As a result, the labor supply curve will shift outward and there will be downward pressure on wage rates. In Box 5, as a result of the tax-induced shift in the labor supply, the market wage falls to $9.75 and the equilibrium number of hours worked increases to *L′*. The new equilibrium after-tax net wage is 85 percent of the gross wage, or $8.29.

The effectiveness of the tax cut depends on the increase in labor hours that it causes. If the policy results in more work per year, labor will become more abundant and labor costs will fall, thereby stimulating production in the economy and encouraging growth.

The responsiveness of labor supply to tax cuts can only be estimated. Workers can choose to pocket the increase in net wages and not work any extra hours at all. In fact, estimates suggest that for a large portion of the labor force, wage increases in the past have had little effect on hours worked. Because tax cuts operate mainly through increases in net wages, this suggests that the response to modest tax cuts will be little, if any, increase in work effort. Thus, there is quite a bit of pessimism about the long-run impact of supply-side tax cuts. However, some have disputed this view, arguing that in the past the federal income tax discouraged work effort. For example, an estimate by Jerry Hausman suggests that, on average, married males have worked 8 percent less because of income taxes than they would have otherwise. Hausman's results also suggest that for married women, a 10 percent increase in the net wage resulting from a cut in marginal tax rates would result, on average, in a 9 percent to 10 percent increase in hours worked per year.[2] These estimates are based on past experience.

Box 5 **How Supply-Side Fiscal Policies Seek to Influence Labor Markets**

Supply-side policies seek to shift the labor supply curve outward. By lowering tax rates, the policies increase the net after-tax return to work. If labor supply increases as a result, the market equilibrium wage paid by employers will fall, encouraging them to use more labor hours per year and increase national output.

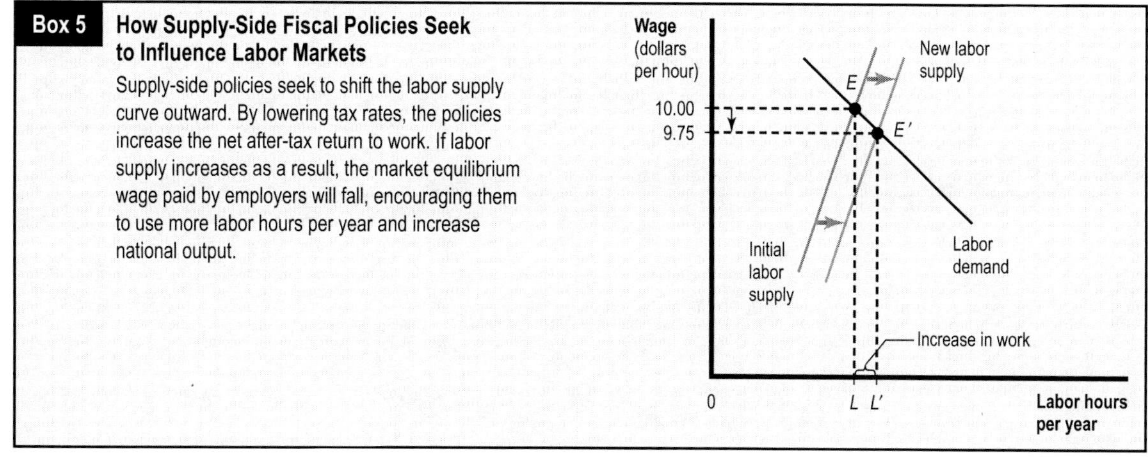

The Impact of Supply-Side Incentives to Save

A reduction in the marginal tax rate for interest income has the same effect in principle as a reduction for labor income. Assuming that savers respond to the net after-tax marginal return to saving, a decrease in the marginal tax rate will increase the supply of saving. This will cause the curve for the supply of loanable funds for the economy to shift outward, as illustrated in Box 6.

Suppose the initial market rate of interest is 8 percent, the gross rate paid by debtors. If savers who supply loanable funds are subject to a 30 percent marginal tax rate, they will earn only 5.6 percent net interest after tax because their net return will be only 70 percent of the interest earned. The marginal tax rate on interest income is typically higher on average than that on labor income because those who earn interest income are generally in higher tax brackets. If the marginal tax rate on interest income were reduced to 20 percent, the supply curve for loanable funds would shift outward because the decrease in the marginal tax rate would raise the after-tax marginal net return to saving from 5.6 percent to 6.4 percent. The higher net return to saving provides an incentive to save more. As the supply of loanable funds curve shifts outward, the market rate of interest falls to 7.5 percent. After the new equilibrium is achieved, the quantity of annual savings supplied as loanable funds to financial markets increases from S to S' dollars per year, and the net after-tax marginal return to saving is 80 percent of the gross interest rate of 7.5 percent, which is 6 percent. At the lower market equilibrium gross interest rate, investment will be encouraged, which will contribute to increased economic growth.

As is the case for reductions in the tax on labor income, the effectiveness of the tax cut in reducing market interest rates and increasing saving depends on the responsiveness of savers to changes in the after-tax interest they can earn on additional saving. Once again, no one knows how responsive savers will actually be to tax cuts. A number of empirical studies show that saver response to changes in interest rates has been virtually nil in the United States.[3] Other studies find that saving is modestly responsive to changes in interest rates.

Box 6 **How Supply-Side Policies Seek to Influence Credit Markets**

Supply-side policies seek to increase the net after-tax return to saving. If this is successful in increasing the supply of saving, loanable funds will become more abundant, thereby putting downward pressure on interest rates and encouraging more investment.

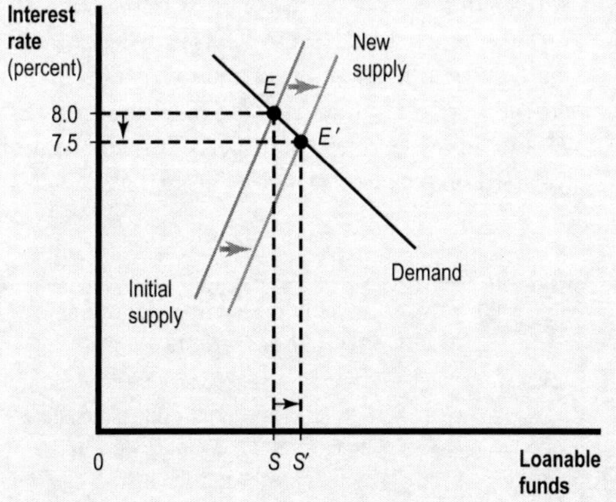

[2]Jerry A. Hausman, "Labor Supply," in *How Taxes Affect Economic Behavior*, ed. Henry J. Aaron and Joseph J. Pechman (Washington, D.C.: Brookings Institution, 1981). Also see James P. Ziliak and Thomas J. Kniesner, "Estimating Life Cycle Labor Supply Tax Effects," *Journal of Political Economy* 107, 2 (1999): pp. 326-359. This research suggests that a 10 percent increase in marginal income tax rates leads to a 0.5 percent decrease in hours worked by prime age males in the United States.

[3]Irwin Friend and Joel Hasbrouck, "Savings and After-Tax Rates of Return," *Review of Economics and Statistics* 65 (November 1983), pp. 537–43.

Under the Reagan administration, a number of supply-side policies sought to encourage personal saving. Two of these policies were

1. *A reduction in the top marginal tax rate applied to income from saving.* The top marginal tax rate applied to nonlabor income was reduced from 70 percent in 1980 to only 28 percent for most taxpayers in 1988. (Some taxpayers, however, were subject to a marginal tax rate as high as 33 percent.)

2. *Special tax treatment of savings placed in individual retirement accounts.* Some taxpayers were able to significantly reduce their taxes by placing some of their savings in special retirement accounts that allowed them to defer taxes on the amounts saved, provided they withdrew no income from the accounts until they retired. Critics of this tax break have argued that it merely results in a shuffling of saving from one account to another without increasing the actual amounts saved per year.

Tax Breaks That Subsidize Investment

A final type of supply-side policy involves tax breaks that directly subsidize business investment. These consist of investment tax credits for new equipment and structures and for research and development. Accelerated depreciation allowances are generous deductions from pretax business income that are allowed when firms acquire new equipment or new structures. These allowances permit firms to recover the cost of capital equipment on their tax accounts much more rapidly than the equipment actually wears out. The more rapid the depreciation allowed for tax purposes, the greater the immediate tax benefit from new investment. For example, suppose a firm subject to a 50 percent marginal tax rate buys a machine that costs $1 million and will last 10 years. If the firm is allowed to deduct one-tenth of the cost of the machine each year ($100,000 per year) for 10 years, the tax benefit of buying the machine will be $50,000 per year. However, if the firm is allowed to deduct one-fifth of the cost of the machine ($200,000 per year) for five years, it will enjoy a tax saving of $100,000 per year for five years. The quicker depreciation enables the firm to get the tax benefit from the machine sooner, providing more incentive to invest. Similarly, an investment tax credit of, say, 10 percent can be deducted from the firm's tax liability as a way of subsidizing investment.

The *marginal tax benefit* of investment is the annual reduction in taxes from each dollar of additional investment. The graph in Box 7 shows how investment demand can be affected by the marginal tax benefit of investment. Normally, a firm invests each year up to the point at which the marginal return to the investment falls to equal the real rate of interest. When investment is subsidized through tax credits or accelerated depreciation, the marginal tax benefit of the investment is added to its marginal return to obtain the full benefit to the firm. The full marginal return to the investment is now

Marginal return to the investment + Marginal tax benefit of the investment,

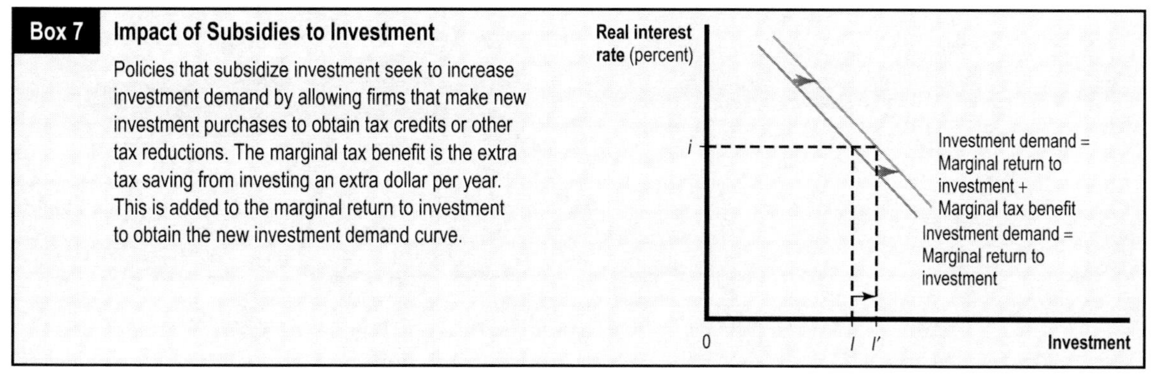
Box 7
Impact of Subsidies to Investment
Policies that subsidize investment seek to increase investment demand by allowing firms that make new investment purchases to obtain tax credits or other tax reductions. The marginal tax benefit is the extra tax saving from investing an extra dollar per year. This is added to the marginal return to investment to obtain the new investment demand curve.
Real interest rate (percent)
i
Investment demand = Marginal return to investment + Marginal tax benefit
Investment demand = Marginal return to investment
0
I
I′
Investment

where the marginal tax benefit is the reduction in tax due per year resulting from investing one extra dollar expressed as a percentage of that dollar. When the marginal tax benefit is added to the marginal return to investment, the investment demand curve shifts outward, as shown in Box 7. Given the market interest rate, *i*, this results in an increase in annual investment from I to I' .

As with all of the other supply-side policies we've discussed, the effectiveness of this policy in encouraging investment and therefore promoting economic growth depends on how responsive investment is to changes in the tax law. In a deep recession, when the business outlook is gloomy, it's unlikely that added tax benefits for investment will have much effect. There's some evidence, however, that over the long run, when the ups and downs of the business cycle average out, subsidies to investment can increase the quantity of new investment goods demanded.[4]

The Short-Run and Long-Run Impact of Supply-Side Policies

The idea behind supply-side tax cuts and subsidies is to shift the aggregate supply curve outward over time. However, it may be a considerable amount of time before the supply curve actually starts moving. Although increases in work effort can shift the aggregate supply curve outward immediately, it takes a number of years before any increased investment adds significantly to the existing capital stock. As a result, it takes a while for supply-side policies to generate an increase in productive capacity for the economy. Meanwhile, unless the tax cuts are balanced with increases in other taxes or reductions in government spending, they will contribute to an increase in aggregate demand.

The graph in Box 8 shows the short-run impact of a supply-side tax cut that is not balanced by increases in other taxes or by a reduction in government spending, similar to the case for the tax cut enacted in 1981. Because the effect of the Economic Recovery Tax Act of 1981 (ERTA) was to increase the federal deficit substantially, it shifted the aggregate demand curve outward. At the time this turned out to be a fine demand-side fiscal policy because the economy was in the depths of a severe recession! As a result, the tax cut contributed to an economic recovery toward the end of 1983. However, the shift in aggregate supply, even after a five-year period, appeared to be slight. ERTA didn't significantly contribute to an increase in saving and investment, and there was no marked increase in work effort. The inflationary tendency was muted in the early 1980s because of the severe recession that prevailed in 1981 and 1982.

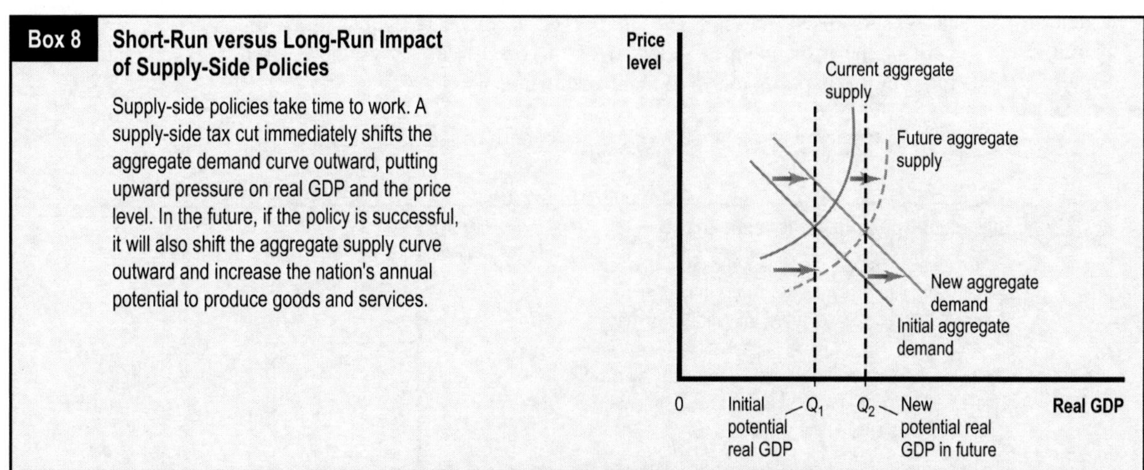

Box 8 Short-Run versus Long-Run Impact of Supply-Side Policies

Supply-side policies take time to work. A supply-side tax cut immediately shifts the aggregate demand curve outward, putting upward pressure on real GDP and the price level. In the future, if the policy is successful, it will also shift the aggregate supply curve outward and increase the nation's annual potential to produce goods and services.

[4]See William R. Hosek and Frank Zahn, "Real Rates of Return and Aggregate Investment," *Southern Economic Journal* 51, no. 1 (July 1984), pp. 157–65.

The graph in Box 8 shows the impact of a supply-side tax cut that increases the budget deficit. The increase in the deficit shifts the aggregate demand curve outward, contributing to a higher price level and a higher level of real GDP. Although the aggregate supply curve and potential real GDP can also shift outward, the magnitude of this shift is likely to be small over a five-year period. As a result, the overall impact of the tax cut and the resulting increase in the deficit is upward pressure on the price level and increases in real GDP. If the economy is close to full employment, the resulting increase in aggregate demand can result in an inflationary GDP gap that overheats the economy and contributes to an inflationary spiral.

Over the long run, say 10 years, further outward shifts in aggregate supply can exert downward pressure on the price level along with upward pressure on real GDP. However, it's unlikely that supply-side policies will result in a significant increase in potential real GDP in the short run. The notion that supply-side tax cuts can increase federal tax revenue is now discredited. The downward pressure of tax cuts on tax revenues doesn't appear likely to be offset by the upward pressure that increases in national income exert on tax collections.

Summary

1. Fiscal policy is the use of government spending and taxing for the specific purpose of stabilizing the economy and encouraging economic growth.

2. The federal government budget represents a plan for spending funds and for raising revenues through taxation, fees, borrowing, and other means.

3. A budget deficit is the annual excess of government spending over government revenues raised by taxes and other means. When a deficit prevails, the federal government must borrow funds through issuance of Treasury bills, notes, and bonds to meet expenses not covered by tax revenues. A budget surplus prevails when government revenues exceed government expenditures during the year.

4. The overall influence of the federal budget on aggregate demand depends on the expansionary effect of government purchases and other payments and the contractionary effect of taxes. When there is a budget deficit, the federal government adds more to aggregate demand than it takes away.

5. An expansionary fiscal policy is one for which the government increases aggregate demand by adjusting its budget during the year. To increase aggregate demand, the government increases spending or decreases taxes. A contractionary fiscal policy restrains aggregate demand through a decrease in government spending or an increase in taxes.

6. When an economy is in deep recession, increased aggregate demand will not put upward pressure on the price level. Under these circumstances, an expansionary fiscal policy can be used to eliminate a recessionary GDP gap with little risk of inflation.

7. A sluggish economy can be stimulated by decreases in net taxes or increases in government spending. A dollar of government spending is more stimulating to the economy than a dollar cut in net taxes because a portion of the tax cut will be saved or spent on imports. Thus, the economy can be stimulated without increasing the budget deficit when government spending increases are fully covered by increases in net taxes.

8. When the economy is experiencing only a mild recession, an increase in aggregate demand through an expansionary fiscal policy is likely to increase the price level. The increase in the price level chokes off some of the multiplier effect. Multipliers for fiscal policy are therefore lower when increases in aggregate demand cause the price level to increase.

9. A contractionary fiscal policy decreases aggregate demand and results in a multiplied decline in real GDP. Contractionary fiscal policies often meet the political opposition of legislators who seek to avoid cuts in government spending or increases in net taxes that would adversely affect their constituents. For this reason expansionary fiscal policies are more likely to be pursued than contractionary fiscal policies.

10. The cyclical ups and downs of the economy affect government tax collections and government expenditures for transfers. Declines in real GDP reduce federal net tax collections as tax revenues go down and transfer payments go up. The opposite holds for the impact of increases in real GDP on the federal budget.

11. Automatic stabilizers are government revenue and expenditure programs that automatically adjust aggregate demand to changes in the level of real GDP.

12. Because of the impact of automatic stabilizers, the federal budget deficit tends to increase during recessions and economic downturns. The cyclically adjusted high-employment deficit gives the budget deficit (or surplus) at some selected level of high employment. The high-employment budget can be used to measure the impact of the federal budget on aggregate demand after adjusting for cyclical influences on the budget deficit.

13. The principles of fiscal policy are to run a high-employment deficit to stimulate a sluggish economy and to reduce the high-employment deficit or run a high-employment surplus to contract an overheated economy.

14. Fiscal policies that encourage saving, investment, and increased labor-force participation can increase a nation's rate of economic growth over the long run. Supply-side fiscal policies seek to influence long-run economic growth in real GDP through government subsidies and tax reductions. The effectiveness of supply-side policies depends on the responsiveness of workers, savers, and investors to increases in the net returns to work, saving, and investment.

15. Supply-side policies that lower taxes to encourage increased work in the long run can increase aggregate demand in the short run and thus put upward pressure on real GDP and the price level.

Concept Review

1. How can the federal government engage in an expansionary fiscal policy?
2. What should the federal government do to its budget if it wants to prevent the economy from overheating?
3. Give some examples of automatic stabilizers in the federal budget.
4. Give some examples of supply-side fiscal policies.

Problems and Applications

1. Suppose real GDP has declined during the past quarter, and the forecast is for a continued decline in real GDP because of a gloomy business outlook. Business investment is expected to plummet next year. As chairman of the President's Council of Economic Advisers, what fiscal policy would you recommend for the coming year? (1)
2. Imagine that estimates indicate of each $1 increase in national income, 60 cents is spent on domestic products, 20 cents is used to pay taxes, 10 cents is spent on imported goods, and 10 cents is saved. The economy is currently in a deep recession, with a $1,000 billion recessionary GDP gap and 15 percent unemployment. How much of an increase in government purchases for the year will be sufficient to pull the economy out of the recession and achieve full employment? (1)
3. If the marginal respending rate is 0.6, calculate the impact on real GDP of a $1 billion reduction in net taxes. How much of a tax cut will get the economy out of the recession with the $1,000 billion recessionary GDP gap discussed in Problem 2? (1)
4. Assume the economy is currently experiencing an $800 billion recessionary GDP gap. A proposal is made to increase transfer payments in order to stimulate aggregate demand. If the marginal respending rate is 0.5, how much must transfers be increased to eliminate the recessionary GDP gap? Use a graph to show the impact on the economy, assuming that the economy operates in the flat portion of its aggregate supply curve up to full employment. (1)
5. Suppose the aggregate supply curve for an economy experiencing a $500 billion recessionary GDP gap is upward-sloping. Use graphic analysis to show that if the marginal respending rate is 0.5, elimination of the GDP gap requires that government purchases increase by more than $250 billion per year. (1)
6. Suppose the price level is downwardly inflexible during the year. If the marginal respending rate is 0.5, calculate the tax increase or the decrease in government purchases necessary to eliminate a $1,500 billion inflationary GDP gap. (2)
7. Imagine the president's advisers propose a budget designed to result in a deficit of $60 billion for the year. In their estimate the advisers assume that the unemployment rate for the year will average 7 percent. Explain why the estimate will fall short of the actual deficit if the unemployment rate each month during the year averages 9 percent instead of 7 percent. (3)
8. Why would a law requiring that the federal budget be in balance every year prevent the automatic stabilizers from operating and thus be likely to destabilize the economy? (3)
9. Suppose a law abolishes taxes on interest income accruing to saving in all forms. Use graphic analysis to show the possible effects of this law on the supply of loanable funds in credit markets and on the equilibrium market rate of interest. Show the impact of the law on investment. (4)
10. The Tax Reform Act of 1986 eliminated the investment tax credit and reduced the tax benefit of accelerated depreciation allowances. Forecast the impact of these changes on investment demand and market interest rates. (4)

Fiscal Policy and the Balance of International Trade

The economy is like a complex computer. A change in one bit of information cascades through it and is processed by thousands of decision makers, who act as the system's "chips." A fiscal policy that generates a deficit can have a pronounced effect on the nation's balance of trade with foreign nations, depending on how interest rates, the international value of the dollar, and other prices respond to information on the deficit.

Let's examine some basic macroeconomic identities for the economy to show how the budget deficit is related to the balance of international trade.

The basic identity between aggregate expenditure and aggregate income can be expressed as

$$C + I + G + (E - M) = C + S + T$$

Aggregate expenditure = Aggregate income.

Net exports, which are measured as (E - M), roughly equal the U.S. balance of trade deficit when imports exceed exports. *Gross domestic purchases* (C + I + G) represent all spending by U.S. households, businesses, and governments on final products, *including* imported products (which are included in the C, I, and G components of GDP).

Gross domestic purchases differ from aggregate purchases of domestic final products (GDP) because they don't include the export sales of U.S. firms, but they do include spending on imports. When domestic spending exceeds aggregate income, domestic spending must also exceed GDP, which is equal to aggregate income.

Because GDP is the amount of final products we produce, it follows that we must import more than we export when we end up spending more than we produce. Therefore, when gross domestic purchases exceed aggregate income, the difference is the balance of trade deficit. This can easily be seen by rearranging terms in the previous identity. Simply move aggregate income (C + S + T) to the left side of the equation by subtracting it from both sides and then subtract (E - M) from both sides, which gives

$$(C + I + G) - (C + S + T) = (M - E).$$

Gross domestic purchases	-	Aggregate income	=	Balance of trade deficit

We can also show that a balance of trade deficit implies that national saving is insufficient to fund gross private domestic investment, and that the difference between investment and national saving is made up by a net inflow of foreign saving into the United States. Simply reduce the previous equation. Because consumption appears as a term in both gross domestic purchases and aggregate income, when we subtract income from spending, consumption disappears, and we get

$$I + G - S - T = (M - E).$$

Now, simply rearrange terms by taking everything except investment over to the right side,

$$I = (T - G) + S + (M - E).$$

The term (T - G) is the difference between net taxes and government purchases. This represents the budget deficit of the government sector when government purchases exceed net taxes. The term S is business and household saving. The sum of the government budget deficit and business and household saving is national saving. When we spend more than we earn, national saving is insufficient to finance gross private domestic investment, and we must borrow from foreigners to make up the difference. The term (M - E) is the balance of trade deficit, which, as we show in the chapter Gross Domestic Product and the Performance of the National Economy, must also equal the net inflow of foreign saving in the United States over U.S. saving abroad:

Investment	=	Government budget deficit	+	Private saving	+	Balance of trade deficit

Because the sum of the government budget deficit and private saving is national saving, and because the balance of trade deficit must equal the net inflow of foreign saving into the United States, we can rewrite the identity as follows:

Domestic investment	=	National saving	+	Net inflow of foreign saving

When fiscal policy increases the government budget deficit in a given year, it contributes to an increase in gross domestic purchases. However, the deficit contributes to a reduction in national saving. Unless there's a corresponding increase in domestic investment or private saving, the net inflow of foreign saving must increase.

The process of adjustment works though changes in interest rates and foreign exchange rates. In the 1980s, a combination of high interest rates and a high international value of the dollar combined to increase foreign saving in the United States as the balance of trade deficit increased in response to the high dollar. In the early 1990s, short-term interest rates fell in the United States, and so did the international value of the dollar, which contributed to a reduction in the balance of trade deficit and a corresponding decline in the net inflow of foreign saving. In this case, the government budget deficit was financed by a combination of a decline in domestic investment and a modest increase in private saving in response to relatively high long-term interest rates. From 2003 to 2005, the federal budget deficit increased and short-term interest rates rose in the United States. The foreign exchange rate of the dollar against other key currencies, such as the euro and yen, which had been falling, stabilized and started to rise slightly in 2005. Foreign saving in the United States remained strong during this period.

Fiscal Policy in 2008 and 2009

Fiscal policy was alive and well in 2008 and 2009, as the U.S. economy plunged into a recession caused, in part, by declining asset values for real estate and corporate equities, and a financial crisis that reduced the availability of credit. In October of 2008, Congress enacted the Emergency Economic Stabilization Act of 2008, in response to the financial crisis. This legislation was primarily designed to provide funds to financial institutions that had incurred losses as a result of the decline in the value of mortgage-backed securities. The Act authorized the Secretary of the Treasury to inject up to $700 billion into the economy, over several years, to purchase illiquid assets through the Troubled Asset Relief Program (TARP) and prop up distressed banks by purchasing their corporate stock, thereby giving the federal government an ownership share in the financial institutions. A sum of $250 billion of the total was made available immediately upon enactment of the legislation, with the remainder to be spent after a detailed plan was submitted by the President for approval by Congress. It was anticipated that the bulk of the spending would occur over a period of two years.

The purpose of the legislation was to prevent the erosion of confidence in the United States financial system, reduce the risk of the failure of depository institutions, and restore the health of other financial intermediaries vital to the functioning of credit markets. The assets acquired by the government under this program could eventually be resold at a later date, thereby offsetting some of the $700 billion cost to taxpayers with future revenue from asset sales. The legislation also increased deposit insurance on individual accounts at federally insured U.S. banks from $100,000 to $250,000. Although the spending authorized by this legislation was primarily directed toward financial institutions, the primary goal was to improve the flow of credit to individuals and businesses, which would stimulate private spending and reduce foreclosures of private homes, so as to prevent further erosion in home values

In early 2009, in the first weeks of the Obama presidency, Congress enacted the American Recovery and Reinvestment Act of 2009 (ARRA). This legislation was intended to stimulate the U.S. economy with a combination of federal tax cuts, increases in transfer payments, such as unemployment insurance benefits, and other social insurance, assistance to state and local governments, and an increase in federal government spending over several years, in such areas as infrastructure (including roads and bridges), education, health care, and energy. Tax cuts were expected to account for $288 billion in lost revenue to the federal government. A sum of $144 billion was allocated for fiscal relief for state and local governments, while $357 billion was allocated to increase federal government spending. Of the total for federal government spending, $89 billion was allocated to infrastructure investment, to be spent on transportation facilities, improved government facilities, including environmental protection and flood control, housing, improved public internet access, and water resource projects.

The increase in federal spending authorized under both these Acts was unprecedented in amount. Combined with estimated losses in revenue, the federal government's budget deficit was expected to balloon into the range of 8 to 12 percent of GDP.

Over the short term, it was generally agreed that the stimulus to the economy from these fiscal policy actions would increase real GDP and employment. However, over the longer term, there was concern that the increase in the federal deficit as a share of GDP could bid up interest rates and reduce private investment. There was also concern that, if taxes were not increased and spending cut quickly enough after the economy recovered, the effects of the package could generate an inflationary process in the future.

Supply-Side Policies: An Assessment of Their Impact

The supply-side approach hit Washington like a storm with the election of Ronald Reagan in 1980. It moved quickly from a slogan to actual policy as President Reagan pushed through the Economic Recovery Tax Act of 1981 (ERTA). This act featured a substantial tax reduction. However, unlike demand-side tax cuts, the ERTA tax reduction was designed to increase aggregate supply. There was a 25 percent across-the-board reduction in income tax rates. ERTA concentrated on reducing *marginal* tax rates, which determine the *extra* taxes that taxpayers must pay on additional dollars of income earned during the year. ERTA's master stroke was a reduction, from 70 percent to 50 percent, in the top marginal tax rate applied to nonlabor income. Finally, there were various incentives designed to increase saving and investment. These included the development of individual retirement accounts (IRAs) that allowed savers to deduct a limited amount of their saving for retirement from their taxable income. Accelerated depreciation rules for business investment reduced tax bills for firms investing in new machinery, vehicles, and structures.

In addition to ERTA, the Reagan supply-side policies, dubbed "Reaganomics," included reductions in spending for Social Security and welfare programs believed to have had adverse effects on work incentives and the reallocation of federal spending to finance a large increase in military expenditures.

Some supply-siders make extravagant claims for the impact of their policies on the economy. Among these claims were the following:

1. The ERTA tax cut would increase tax revenue, because it would encourage increased work and investment that would increase equilibrium real GDP.

2. The budget deficit wouldn't increase substantially as a result of the tax cut. Even if there were an increase in the deficit, its inflationary effects would be offset by an increase in saving resulting, in part, from the tax cut.

3. The supply-side effect of increasing real GDP would put downward pressure on the price level and reduce inflation, at the same time real GDP increased.

Many economists regarded these claims as excessive.[1] However, the economy managed to recover from a serious recession in 1982. Inflation was reduced sharply, and unemployment, although remaining at fairly high levels after the recession, seemed to be less of a problem. The Reagan administration claimed credit for the recovery, and voters affirmed their confidence in the president and his economic policies with an overwhelming landslide reelection in 1984.

How much of the reduction in inflation and the increase in real GDP can be attributed to the supply-side policies? First, let's look at the results in the first half of the 1980s:

1. Actual growth between 1981 and 1985 was 10.9 percent, well below the 19.1 percent predicted by Reagan economists.

2. The economy did recover from the recession of 1982, but many economists attribute this recovery to the increase in the money supply and other policies implemented by the Federal Reserve.

3. There didn't appear to be any significant increase in work effort as a result of the reduction in marginal tax rates.

4. There was little appreciable increase in saving.

5. Federal tax revenues didn't increase as a result of the reduction in marginal tax rates. However, they didn't decrease as much as many non-supply-siders expected, indicating that the disincentive effects of high marginal tax rates aren't negligible. Reductions in tax revenues and increases in federal spending combined to increase the federal budget deficit to over $200 billion by 1986.

Critics of the supply-side policies of the early 1980s contend that these policies did little to shift the aggregate supply curve. These critics argue that the ERTA tax cut provided an increase in aggregate demand between 1982 and 1984 that pulled the economy out of the recession.[2] They point out that the supply-side policies coincided with other important changes that stimulated the economy, such as declining interest rates and declining oil prices. Prices of imported goods also fell during the early 1980s, which contributed to lower inflation.

The budget deficit didn't fall, as many supply-siders had hoped it would. Instead, it increased to record levels. Many economists argued that the large budget deficit kept interest rates at high levels throughout the early 1980s. High interest rates were blamed by many for the reduced investment and increased imports of recent years.

In short, the report card on the supply-side policies of the early 1980s is mixed. There was no significant short-run increase in aggregate supply or economic growth as a result of the supply-side policies.

[1]See Martin Feldstein, "Supply-Side Economics: Old Truths and New Claims," *American Economic Review* 76, no. 2 (May 1986), pp. 26-30.

[2]See Lawrence Chimerine and Richard M. Young, "Economic Surprises and Messages of the 1980s," *American Economic Review* 76, no. 2 (May 1986), pp. 31-36.

Chapter 33

The Federal Budget, Government Debt, and the Economy

The federal budget has a big impact on the economy. Federal spending amounts to nearly one-fifth of GDP, and even small percentage changes in government outlays or receipts can have a major impact on the economy. The federal budget is the government's annual plan for spending for such programs as national defense, roads, social security, health and aid to the poor. The federal budget balance is the relation between revenues and other receipts that finance that spending and the annual outlays for government programs. The balance between federal receipts and revenues can significantly affect aggregate demand. When the government spends more than it takes in from taxes and other sources of revenue, it stimulates aggregate demand. When the government takes in more revenue than it spends, it runs a budget surplus that adds to national saving, but diminishes aggregate demand. The government budget balance can also affect financial markets by affecting the demand and supply of credit and, therefore, affecting interest rates.

In this chapter we will examine the effect of the federal budget balance–either a surplus or a deficit–and the impact of federal government debt on the economy. We will look at the impact of the budget balance on interest rates, future tax rates, spending, private investment, and the price level. Our goal is to clarify the issues regarding deficits, surpluses, and the national debt, and their impact on our economic performance and living standards. We also analyze the consequences of reducing the federal government debt held by the public.

Concept Preview

After reading this chapter, you should be able to

1. Discuss the federal budget balance (surplus or deficit) and how its possible impact on interest rates can influence private investment, economic growth, and macroeconomic equilibrium.
2. Discuss the impact of the national debt on the well-being of current and future generations.
3. Discuss some of the problems involved in measuring the federal budget deficit or surplus.
4. Discuss the concept of Ricardian equivalence of tax and deficit finance.
5. Explain the impact of a federal budget surplus on the economy.

The Federal Budget Balance between Revenues and Expenditures

1 Governments can spend more than is collected from taxes and other sources of revenue through borrowing. By running up the public debt, government can put off the burden of taxation to the future. When government spending exceeds revenues, the result is a budget deficit. Budget deficits have been common for the federal government of the United States since 1960. State and local governments, by and large, are required by state law to keep their budgets in balance and borrow only to finance capital expenditures. Since 1960, it has been common for state and local governments to run modest budget surpluses. However, unanticipated declines in revenue can sometimes result in these governments operating with small deficits, as was the case in 2001.

The U.S. federal government spent more than it collected in taxes and other receipts every year between 1970 and 1998. The resulting budget deficits were, in some years, at levels amounting to 6 percent of GDP. Between 1983 and 1997, the deficit declined as a percent of GDP. In 1998, the federal budget balance was transformed from deficit to a modest surplus. The budget surplus peaked at slightly more than $200 billion in 2000 and then started declining. By 2002, as the effects of a recession and cuts in tax rates enacted by Congress in 2001 were being felt, the federal government was again running a budget deficit of $200 billion, amounting to nearly 2 percent of GDP. Deficits have persisted since 2002, and the federal budget deficit amounted to $455 billion in 2008. The recession in 2008 reduced tax collections and resulted in increases in federal government transfers that year, causing the deficit to increase substantially. The federal government budget deficit was expected to grow a record $1.2 trillion in 2009, as tax collections were expected to further decline and government spending was expected to skyrocket, in part, as a result of the recession, but also as a result in new spending enacted by Congress to try to stimulate the economy. The federal budget proposed by the Obama administration in early 2009, if enacted in full, was expected to increase the federal deficit to $1.75 trillion, or 12.3% of the gross domestic product, a level not seen World War II. A legacy of borrowing to finance federal expenditures is the federal government debt held by the public. In mid-2003 this debt was $3.8 trillion, amounting to 38 percent of GDP that year. By March 2009, the debt had grown to $6.6 trillion and the share held by the public amounted to nearly 50 percent of GDP.

Borrowing by the federal government to finance public expenditures has, therefore, been the rule, rather than the exception, in the United States since 1960. The brief four-year period of federal budget surpluses, between 1998 and 2001, demonstrated that budget surplus, just like deficits, can be used to finance government expenditures or tax rate reductions. A surplus gives politicians the opportunity to fund new programs without increasing taxes or to cut taxes without cutting back on public expenditure. The 1998-2001 federal budget surplus was dissipated over a four-year period, in part, due to a recession and a slowdown in the economy's rate of growth that cut tax collections. However, tax cuts enacted in 2001, along with increased demands for spending for national defense and homeland security, also contributed to the demise of the surplus. If surpluses are allowed to persist, they can be used to pay off and reduce the federal government's debt. Used in this way, budget surpluses increase national saving and make more funds available in credit markets. The increase in national saving could lower real interest rates and contribute to more investment, thereby, increasing the economy's rate of growth.

The graph in Box 1 shows federal government receipts and outlays from 1950-2008. Notice how, during almost all of the period 1965-1998, outlays exceeded receipts and the budget was in deficit. From 1998 to 2001, receipts exceeded outlays, but the deficit returned in 2002. Federal budget deficits are a source of finance for the government through borrowing. Deficits are expansionary. When the government runs a surplus, it is, in effect, saving, and this subtracts from aggregate demand.

Box 1 Federal Receipts, Outlays, and Budget Deficit or Surplus, 1950-2008 (Billions of Dollars)

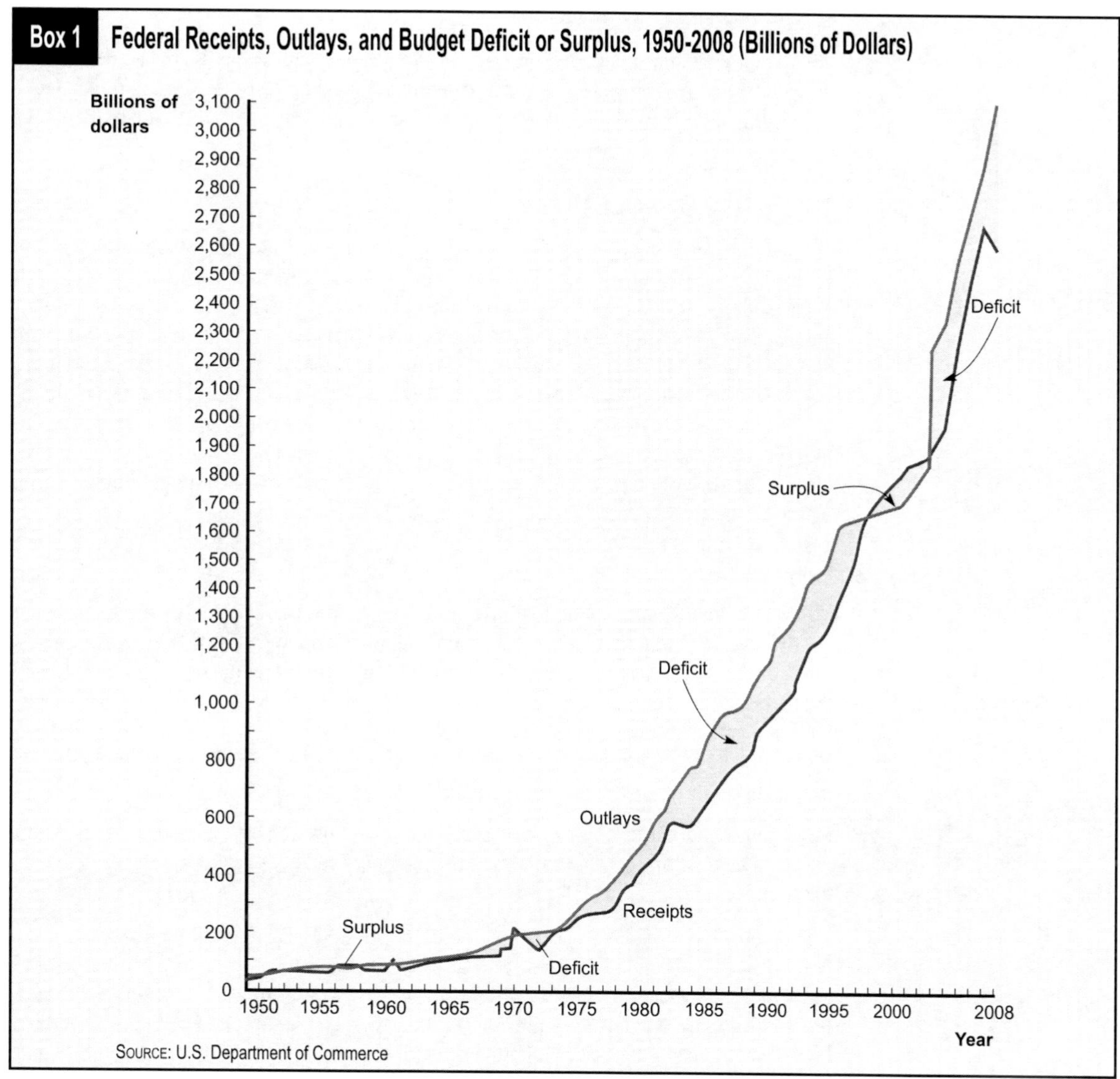

SOURCE: U.S. Department of Commerce

Up until the 1930s, it was viewed as prudent fiscal practice to balance the federal budget each year. However, an annually balanced federal budget rules out any chance for the automatic stabilizers to do their jobs. Balancing the budget can destabilize the economy by decreasing aggregate demand when consumption, investment, and net exports are declining. For example, if the economy experiences a recession, the federal government's net tax receipts will naturally fall. Transfers paid out will increase because payments for welfare, Social Security, and unemployment insurance benefits typically go up during a recession. The decline in income will reduce income tax collections. If the budget is to be consistently in balance, government purchases will also have to decline during a recession to accommodate the decline in tax revenues and the increase in transfer payments.

Similarly, an annually balanced budget prevents the federal government from constraining aggregate demand by running a surplus during periods when the economy is overheated. During a boom period, tax collections naturally rise and transfer payments decline. As a result, net taxes increase during a boom period. If the government were to spend all of the increase, it would add to the already booming aggregate demand and thus aggravate the upward pressure on the price level.

An annually balanced budget therefore contributes to decreases in aggregate demand during downturns and to increases in aggregate demand during upturns. Preventing the budget from ever being in deficit will clearly prolong recessions and may also contribute to their severity.

The Federal Budget Balance

Why all the concern about the balance (deficit or surplus) and the government debt? What, if anything, is wrong with government borrowing as a means of financing its activities? What should be done with a government budget surplus? Should the budget always be balanced, with neither a deficit nor a surplus in any year? In recent years, the federal budget balance has not been a factor in stabilization policy. Instead, issues relating to the size of the federal budget balance or surplus have concerned the long-term effects of the budget balance on saving, investment, the nation's long-term rate of growth, and future living standards. Let's begin with an analysis of the impact of deficits on the economy and look at the federal debt. Then, we will discuss the impact of government budget surpluses on the economy.

Financing Deficits: Money Creation versus Borrowing from the Public

You know what happens when you want to spend more than you earn–you have to borrow the difference. The federal government must also borrow when it runs a deficit. The deficit must be *financed*, which means that somehow the government must obtain the funds to meet its expenditures when its receipts fall short of those expenditures. However, the federal government has a little trick up its sleeve that serves as an alternative to borrowing. It can engage in policies that create new money to pay its bills! At the extreme the federal government has the power to simply *print* new currency to pay its bills.

Financing a deficit by money creation is more expansionary than borrowing from the public. The resulting increase in the money supply is likely to increase the price level over the long run.

The federal government is unlikely to actually print new currency if it chooses to finance a deficit by money creation because, like most households and business firms, it pays for most of its expenses by check. *Monetization of the federal deficit* occurs whenever the Federal Reserve expands the monetary base to finance the deficit. The Fed is prohibited by law from buying new issues of government securities directly from the U.S. Treasury. However, it can still monetize the debt (as central banks in other nations have done) by increasing its purchases of already existing government securities through open market operations. When the Fed does this, it increases the monetary base in the same way it does when it engages in any other open market purchase. (See the chapters on the Federal Reserve System and monetary policy.) Full monetization of the deficit occurs when the Fed increases its purchases of government securities in an amount equal to the deficit, thereby expanding the money supply while the federal government is running a deficit. Because this policy increases bank excess reserves, it's also likely to result in a multiple expansion of checkable deposits.

Monetizing the federal deficit carries a double punch for aggregate demand. First, the deficit contributes to an increase in aggregate demand because it allows an increase in government purchases without a corresponding increase in taxes. Second, monetizating the deficit contributes to an increase in the money supply, which results in downward pressure on the level of interest rates and upward pressure on the equilibrium money stock. The decrease in interest rates and consequent increase in private investment purchase then add further to aggregate demand. Monetizing the deficit is therefore likely to result in upward pressure on the price level unless the economy is in a deep recession.

Because of the inflationary effects of financing a deficit by money creation, the Fed is careful not to monetize the deficit. The federal government borrows by issuing Treasury bills, notes, and bonds. When it borrows from the public, it must compete for available loanable funds with households, business firms, and state or local governments. An increase in borrowing by the federal government to cover a deficit adds to the demand for loanable funds and puts upward pressure on interest rates. Under these circumstances, the Federal Reserve does not intervene to increase its purchase of government securities and therefore does not increase the money supply to finance the deficit.

The effect of borrowing from the public is less expansionary than the effect of directly monetizing the deficit. When the public purchases government securities, a portion of loanable funds available from saving is allocated to make loans to the federal government. When the federal government borrows in this way, there is no increase in bank reserves and no consequent expansion of the money supply. However, the impact on aggregate demand is more expansionary than it would be if taxes instead of borrowing were used to finance the deficit. Borrowing does not reduce disposable income, while taxation does. In effect, borrowing to cover a federal budget deficit postpones the payment of taxes to the future. It also causes the federal government to pay interest on its debt to the people who acquire government securities.

The graph in Box 2 shows the impact on macroeconomic equilibrium of three possible means of financing government expenditures. Suppose federal government expenditures are $1,000 billion per year. If these expenditures are fully financed by tax revenues, the economy is in equilibrium at point E_1, where the price level is 100 and real GDP is $5,000 billion. If, instead, the government runs a $200 billion deficit and borrows that sum from the public, the aggregate demand curve shifts farther outward and the economy achieves equilibrium at a price level of 105 and real GDP of $5,500 billion. If the Fed monetizes the $200 billion deficit, the aggregate demand curve shifts outward still farther, and the economy is in equilibrium at a price level of 110 and real GDP of $6,000 billion for the year. The conclusion is straightforward: Deficit financing is more expansionary than tax financing, but a monetized deficit is the most expansionary of all!

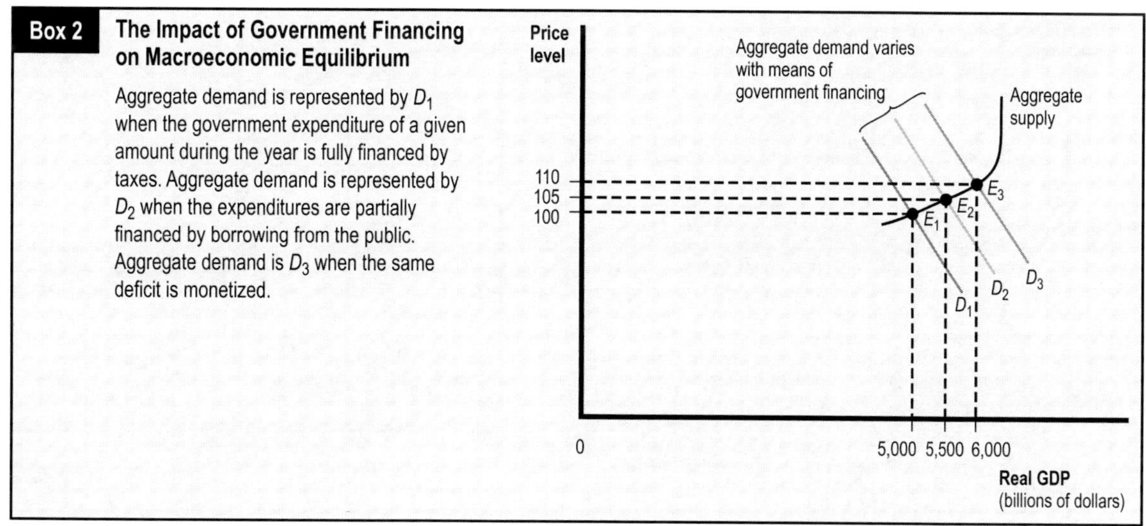

Box 2 The Impact of Government Financing on Macroeconomic Equilibrium

Aggregate demand is represented by D_1 when the government expenditure of a given amount during the year is fully financed by taxes. Aggregate demand is represented by D_2 when the expenditures are partially financed by borrowing from the public. Aggregate demand is D_3 when the same deficit is monetized.

The Crowding-Out Effect

To understand the impact on interest rates of borrowing to cover the deficit, we must examine the impact of deficits on credit markets. The graph in Box 3 shows the credit market for the economy. The demand curve for loanable funds by private borrowers intersects the supply curve for loanable funds at an interest rate of 8 percent. At that interest rate, the amount of loanable funds borrowed during the year to finance consumer durables and business investment would be $900 billion. In other words, if there were no borrowing by the federal government during the year, the market rate of interest would be 8 percent and the equilibrium volume of credit would be $900 billion.

Now suppose the federal government borrows $200 billion from the public to cover its deficit. This represents a substantial increase in the demand for loanable funds. As a result, the demand curve shifts outward and puts upward pressure on the level of interest rates in the economy. The new market equilibrium occurs at an interest rate level of 9 percent for the economy, and the equilibrium volume of credit extended at that interest rate is $1,000 billion. The government's borrowing to finance the deficit has therefore resulted in an increase in the market rate of interest and a consequent increase in the quantity of loanable funds supplied. This analysis assumes that as the government borrows, nothing else changes that might shift the demand or supply curves for loanable funds.

You should notice that the net increase in credit extended through the market is only $100 billion. However, the government borrows $200 billion. Where does the extra $100 billion in funds come from? To find out, go to the curve of the private demand for credit. At the new equilibrium interest rate of 9 percent, the quantity of loanable funds demanded for private investment falls from $900 billion to $800 billion for the year. In other words, the higher interest rate causes private investors to revise their plans and cut back their investment for the year by $100 billion. The crowding-out effect is the reduction in private investment purchases caused by the higher interest rates that result from government borrowing. In this case the crowding-out effect is a reduction in private spending of $100 billion for the year.

The extent of the crowding-out effect depends on the responsiveness of interest rates to the increased government demand for loanable funds and on the reaction of private investors to the higher interest rates. If investment demand is unresponsive to a change in interest rates, the crowding-out effect will be quite small. The crowding-out effect also depends on how responsive the quantity of loanable funds is to increases in the demand for credit. If

Box 3 Crowding Out of Private Investment in Credit Markets

When the government borrows to finance a deficit, the demand for credit increases. The resulting increase in the market rate of interest causes a decrease in private quantity of funds demanded for investment. In this case, $100 billion of private investment is crowded out as a result of government borrowing to finance its deficit.

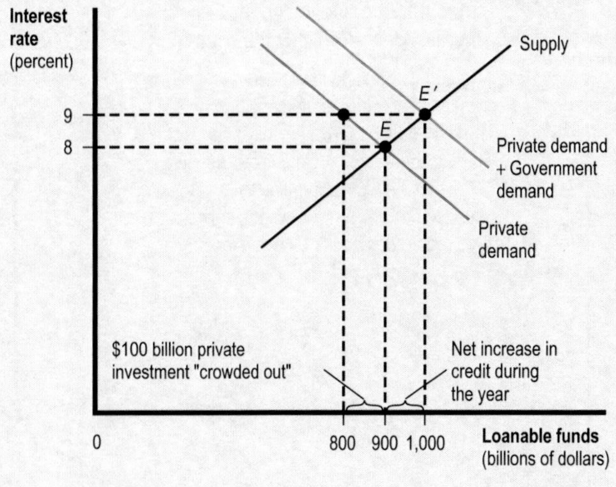

Interest rate (percent)
9
8
Supply
E'
E
Private demand + Government demand
Private demand
$100 billion private investment "crowded out"
Net increase in credit during the year
0
800 900 1,000
Loanable funds (billions of dollars)

the economy is in a deep recession, a substantial amount of excess reserves is likely to be available to the banking system. Under these circumstances, extra borrowing by the government may put little upward pressure on interest rates because the supply of loanable funds curve will be quite flat.

We can conclude that the crowding-out effect is less pronounced during a deep recession than it is when the economy is operating close to its potential. In fact, increased government spending during a deep recession may improve the business outlook, thereby encouraging more investment!

The crowding-out effect dampens the expansionary impact of the federal budget deficit by reducing the private component of aggregate demand. The cutback in private spending then reduces the multiplier effect of an increase in government spending. This implies that the upward pressure on the price level resulting from deficits in an economy close to full employment will be moderated as government spending displaces private investment.

The impact of deficits on interest rates has been a subject of empirical investigation by economists. Some studies have found little impact, which suggests that, on average, the crowding-out effect is small.[1] However, even if the crowding-out effect is small, it remains a matter of concern because a reduction in business investment that continues over a number of years can have serious long-term consequences. Less business investment means that workers will not have as much or as modern equipment with which to work, a situation that will adversely affect their productivity. Thus, if the crowding-out effect causes a decline in investment, the result could be a decrease in the rate of improvement of living standards as worker productivity growth slows down the increase in real GDP per person.

The Deficit and Long-Term Interest Rates

In the early 1990s the chronic federal deficit appeared to be having adverse effects on inflationary expectations, which in turn kept long-term interest rates high. Despite legislation enacted in the 1980s and in 1990 to deal with the deficit, it continued to grow at a rate greater than projected. In 1992, partly as a result of the recession and growing government health care expenditures, it ballooned to 5 percent of GDP. In 1991 and 1992, investors continued to be fearful that the deficit would remain large and difficult to reduce and that it would contribute to an increase in inflation. Consequently, a high "inflation premium" caused long-term interest rates to remain very high even though monetary policy had pushed short-term interest rates down to low levels that had not been seen in nearly 50 years.

The high long-term interest rates necessary to compensate lenders for their fears of inflation were believed to have crowded out private investment. The long-term debt that the government had issued to finance its deficit competed directly with corporate borrowing. Corporate investment stagnated as long-term interest rates increased. In addition, banks found the high long-term rates on government securities a very attractive alternative to business loans. A shift of bank portfolios away from business loans and toward government securities contributed to a "credit crunch" that made it difficult to fund new business. Moreover, the capacity of banks to lend was reduced as depositors reduced their holdings of time deposits and shifted their assets into more lucrative long-term government bonds.

The sensitivity of long-term interest rates to the inflationary effect of increasing the federal deficit is another factor that should be considered before increasing the size of the deficit in an attempt to stimulate a sluggish economy.

[1]See Laurence H. Meyer, ed., *The Economic Consequences of Government Deficits* (Boston: Kluwer-Nijoff Publishing, 1983).

As the deficit was reduced in 1993, 1994, and 1995, long-term interest rates fell significantly. From 1995 to 1999, as the deficit became a surplus, there were further declines in interest rates. Between 2002 and 2005, the deficit reappeared and increased, but long-term interest rates didn't increase significantly, despite substantial increases in short-term interest rates over the same period .Increases in the federal deficits between 2005 and 2009 were not associated with increases in long-term interest rates, but much of that was explainable by the fact that the demand for loanable funds was depressed, due to the recession that began in late 2007.

The National Debt

2 You may not lose sleep over it yourself, but lots of politicians and other people in the United States worry about the national debt. In this section we show how government deficits add to the national debt and examine the consequences of an increased national debt for you and the economy.

The national debt is the dollar amount that the federal government owes its creditors at a given time. It is the cumulative legacy of previous government deficits, and it increases each year that the federal budget is in deficit. When the budget is in surplus, the federal government can reduce the sum of the debt by not renewing government securities that mature. It can also use the surplus to pay off some debt before it matures. In these ways the government can reduce its demand for credit and put downward pressure on interest rates when a surplus prevails.

As of early 2009, the national debt amounted to $11 trillion. About 60 percent of that debt was held by the public, and the remainder was held by the Federal Reserve banks and government agencies. The portion of the national debt held by the Fed and government agencies is debt that the government owes to itself rather than to creditors. Interest paid on this portion of the debt usually returns to the Treasury, thereby increasing government revenues. Similarly, when the debt held by the Fed and government agencies matures, the government itself obtains the funds. Only the net federal debt, the portion of the national debt owed to debtors other than the Fed and the government agencies, represents credit extended to the federal government by the public.

The graph in Box 4 shows the national debt held by the public, as a percentage of GDP, from 1940 up to 2008. The volume of debt began to skyrocket in 1975. Despite the increase in the dollar value of the debt since 1975, the national debt as a percentage of GDP has actually declined since 1950 (when it amounted to 89 percent of GDP), because much of the debt issued to finance government purchases during World War II was retired after 1950. From 1980 to 1995, however, the national debt rose from 33 percent to nearly 50 percent of GDP. From 1995 to 2001, the net federal debt fell, both in dollar amount and as a share of GDP, as budget surpluses were used to retire debt. Since 2001, the debt has increased, as the federal deficit reappeared and grew.

Who Are the Nation's Creditors?

The nation's creditors are the individuals and organizations that hold the net federal debt. When taxes are used to pay off the debt, what really happens is that some people suffer a decrease in income, while those who hold government bonds enjoy an increase in income. In other words, retirement of the debt and payment of interest on the debt transfer income among citizens. However, some of the debt is held by foreigners. (In 2000, for example, about 40 percent of the national debt owned by the public was held by foreigners.) When interest payments are made to foreign holders, a portion of the aggregate income earned in the United States is used to pay the nation's foreign creditors. This could become a

Box 4 **Federal Debt Held by the Public as a Percentage of GDP**

The federal debt held by the public peaked, as a percent of GDP, during World War II. After 1945, the debt declined, as a share of GDP, until the mid-1970s, when increased budget deficit finance pushed it up from a low of 20 percent of GDP to a high of 50 percent of GDP, in 1995. It declined after 1995, as the deficit was reduced and the federal government briefly ran a surplus. By 2007, the federal debt held by the public declined to 31 percent of GDP. However, a sharp increase in the deficit and federal government borrowing in 2008 resulted in the share of the debt in GDP increasing to 43 percent.

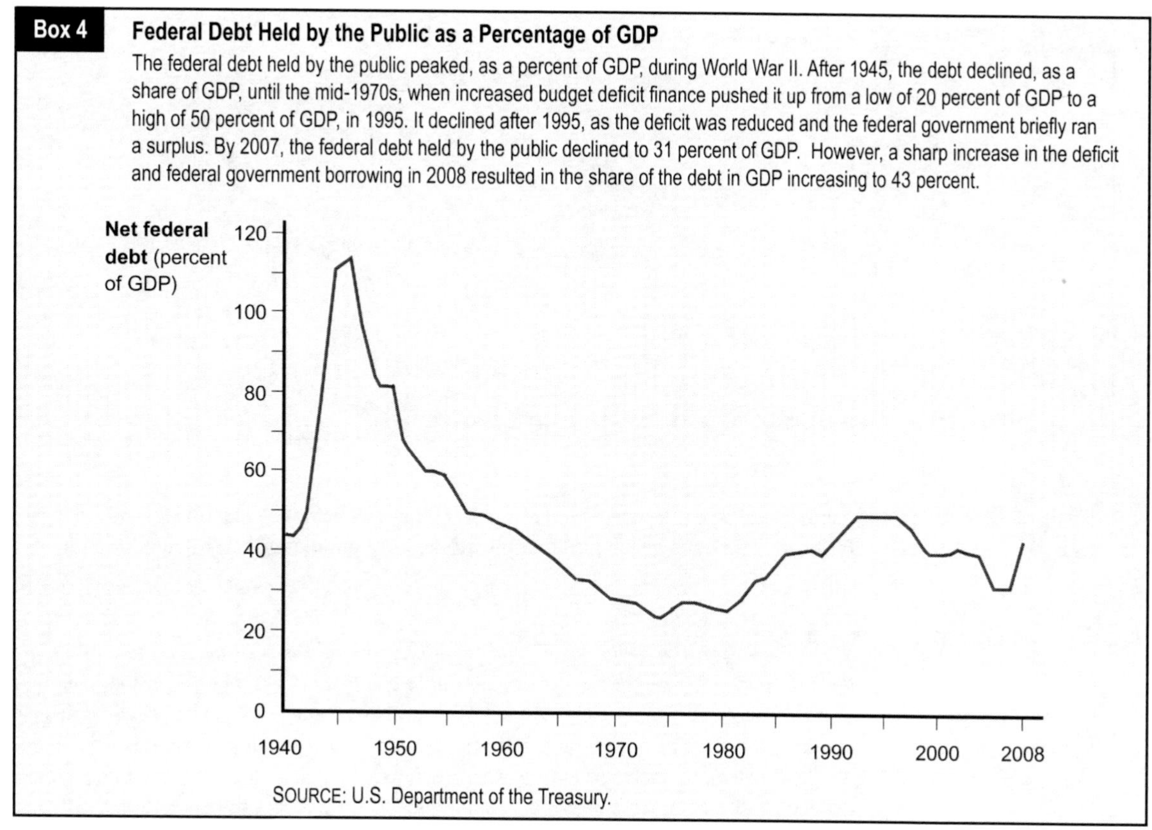

SOURCE: U.S. Department of the Treasury.

contractionary influence on the U.S. economy if the foreign holders don't use their interest earnings to purchase U.S. goods and services.

The portion of the debt the federal government owes to its own citizens is the internal debt. The rest is the external debt, the portion that the nation owes to citizens of other nations. The internal debt is very different from private debt. Payment of interest and principal on the debt doesn't drain income from the nation. As pointed out earlier, payment of interest on the debt redistributes income among U.S. citizens and therefore doesn't directly decrease aggregate demand. However, as the portion of the debt held by foreigners increases, more and more interest is paid out each year to foreign citizens. Payment of interest on the external debt could exert some downward pressure on aggregate demand, contributing to a possible future contraction of the economy.

The chart in Box 5 shows the ownership pattern of the net federal debt in September 2008. As you can see, pension funds, depository institutions, and state and local governments were the major creditors of the federal government. The portion of the debt held by foreigners depends, in part, on interest rates in the United States compared to interest rates in foreign countries.

Burden of the Debt

Will the federal government go bankrupt if it continues to run deficits? There's no need to worry about this because the federal government has a few tricks up its sleeve that are unavailable to a private debtor. First of all, the federal government can pay the interest on its debt from tax revenues. Second, at the extreme, the government can print money to pay off its debt. The risk of default on the debt is therefore virtually nil. Of course, the govern-

Box 5 Distribution of Ownership of the Net Federal Debt, September 2008

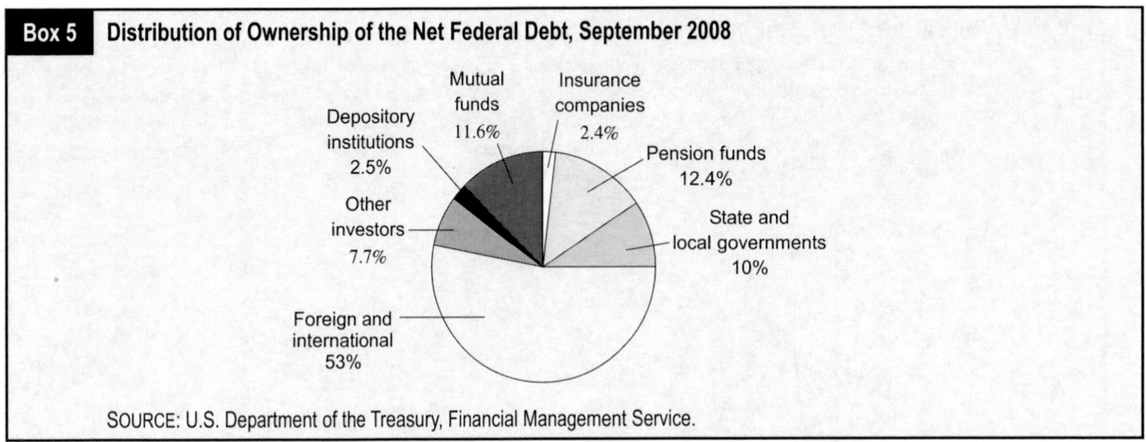

SOURCE: U.S. Department of the Treasury, Financial Management Service.

ment can always roll its debt over by issuing new securities to pay off the ones that mature. However, this involves continued upward pressure on interest rates in credit markets.

Two major burdens result from a larger national debt:

1. *A larger portion of the taxes paid by future generations will be used to pay interest on the debt instead of providing government goods and services.* Interest on the national debt currently accounts for about 11 percent of federal government expenditures. This means that currently 11 cents of each dollar in taxes is used to provide interest payments to holders of the debt instead of such services as roads, defense, and education. If there is no substantial decline in interest rates and the debt continues to grow because of additional deficits, the portion of taxes allocated to interest instead of goods and services will increase.

2. *If the crowding-out effect is substantial, a growing national debt will decrease private investment and reduce the growth rate of private capital stock.* This will decrease economic growth. As the growth rate of worker productivity declines because of a decrease in the growth rate of capital, the growth in GDP per capita will also decline. Therefore, a growing national debt will retard the growth rate of potential real GDP and result in a lower standard of living for future generations.

The burden of the national debt can be offset, however, if taxpayers increase saving in order to pay the higher taxes they expect in the future as a result of the debt. If taxpayers save more in anticipation of the future burden of taxation, the supply of loanable funds will increase. This will put downward pressure on interest rates and offset some of the crowding-out effect. Similarly, if the deficit actually makes real GDP higher than it would be otherwise by making cyclical downturns less likely, it will also contribute to higher savings.

Finally, the burden of the debt can be offset by increased benefits to future generations from government services. The nation may have fewer factories and machine tools, but it may have more and better roads, better schools, and other government projects that increase worker productivity. This outcome is particularly likely if the federal government uses its borrowings to finance long-lasting projects such as roads, dams, and parks. If that is done, higher interest payments and decreased growth of the private capital stock will be balanced by future benefits from government investments.

Measuring the Deficit or Surplus and Its Impact

3 The size of the budget balance provides citizens with information regarding both the state of federal government finances and the impact of the budget on aggregate demand. Interpreting the impact of the deficit or surplus on the economy is quite difficult because the magnitude is influenced by cyclical fluctuations in the economy and by some peculiarities in government accounting techniques. In this section we discuss some of the problems involved in interpreting the meaning of the budget balance and in measuring the impact on the economy.

High Employment versus the Actual Deficit or Surplus

The actual budget deficit or surplus in any given year is influenced by the effects of the automatic stabilizers. When the economy is operating below its potential, the deficit naturally rises. To adjust for the cyclical effects of the automatic stabilizers, the high-employment budget deficit or surplus can be computed. The resulting figure can be used to show whether the federal budget will add to or detract from aggregate demand if the economy is operating at its potential, other things being equal.

For example, in 1991, a recession year, the actual budget deficit was $269.5 billion. In that year the high-employment deficit excluding deposit insurance was only $179.8 billion. The extra $89.7 billion in deficit spending for the year resulted from the cyclical effect of the automatic stabilizers on net taxes and outlays for deposit insurance claims. The recession reduced tax collections and increased transfer payments above the level that would have prevailed if the economy had achieved a 6 percent unemployment rate. In 1995 the U.S. economy was booming, and the total budget deficit that year was actually expected to be *less* than the high-employment deficit because of the effect of the booming economy on tax collections and federal spending.

Remember, when the economy is operating below its potential, a high-employment deficit provides a stimulus that boosts aggregate demand and thus pulls up real GDP. By 1999, when the federal government ran a budget surplus, the Congressional Budget Office estimated, using a 5.2 percent natural rate of unemployment, at high employment, that the surplus was close to zero. Even though the dollar amount of the surplus was $124 billion, the actual unemployment rate was below the natural rate that year. Accordingly, the office adjusted revenues downward and expenditures upward to a recalculated high-employment surplus of only $2 billion that year.

Other Influences on the Size of the Deficit

The size of the deficit (or surplus) in any given year depends not only on the level of employment, taxes, and federal spending but also on the rate of economic growth. The greater the rate of economic growth as measured by the annual percentage change in real GDP, the greater the rate of increase in tax revenues for the year. Federal tax collections are quite sensitive to changes in the growth of both personal and corporate income. Given the tax rates, the greater the growth of income, the greater the growth of the federal government's tax revenues. A higher rate of economic growth is often associated with declining unemployment, which reduces outlays for federal unemployment insurance and federal aid to the poor, further reducing the deficit. When the economy is growing, tax collections tend to increase faster than the rate of inflation.

The sensitivity of federal revenues and outlays to the rate of economic growth complicates budget planning for the federal government. Each year the President's Council of Economic Advisers, the Office of Management and Budget, and the Treasury make assumptions about economic growth during the year and provide analysis in the budget to account for changes in economic conditions. If they overestimate economic growth, as they sometimes do, the actual deficit will exceed the forecast deficit.

The size of the budget deficit, measured in current dollars, is also sensitive to inflation and the level of interest rates in the economy. Other things being equal, inflation tends to increase federal receipts more than federal outlays. As a result, an increase in the rate of inflation tends to reduce the nominal size of the deficit. Other things being equal, increases in interest rates increase the size of the federal deficit because federal outlays for interest payments on the national debt go up.

Sometimes inflation and interest rates move together. Higher inflation can result in expectations of higher future inflation, pushing up nominal interest rates as lenders reduce the supply of loanable funds. When inflation and interest rates rise together, the unfavorable effects of the higher interest rates on the deficit are offset by the favorable effects of the higher rate of inflation.

Which Deficit or Surplus?

Measurement of the federal government's budget deficit is complicated by the fact that some receipts and expenditures of the federal government operate through trust funds that are officially "off budget." The two main government operations treated in this way are Social Security and the U.S. Postal Service. In recent years the Social Security trust funds have run a substantial surplus (in 2005, it was $173 billion), while the U.S. Postal Service has run a small deficit. Even though trust funds are budgeted for separately, their revenues and expenditures affect the federal government's overall borrowing demands on the credit markets. When the Social Security trust funds run a surplus, the surplus is lent to the Treasury and reduces the Treasury's demands on the credit markets.

The *unified budget deficit* is the difference between all federal government expenditures and all federal government revenues, be they "on budget" or "off budget." The unified budget deficit is the best measure of the amount of the funds that the federal government must borrow in any given year. However, from the point of view of measuring the long-term impact of the deficit on the economy, the unified budget deficit has some shortcomings. The net economic effect of the budget depends entirely on the negative saving or *new debt* it generates. Some of the federal government's borrowing has been done to cover the losses of failed savings and loan associations and commercial banks. Such borrowing merely assumes old debt and reflects past obligations of the government that should have been included in past deficits, but were not.

The *NIPA budget deficit or surplus* is the official measure of the federal budget balance in the National Income and Product Accounts. *The NIPA budget balance does not include any transactions that finance preexisting debts, such as outlays for deposit insurance.* The NIPA budget is the best measure of the net new debt (negative saving) that results from a federal budget deficit or positive saving from a surplus. For this reason, the NIPA budget surplus or deficit is most often used to gauge the long-term impact of changes in the budget balance.

Contingent Claims, Inflation, and the Budget Balance

Included in the federal budget are outlays for claims paid under various government-sponsored insurance programs. Among the most well-known of these programs is deposit insurance for depository institutions. The federal government also runs insurance programs for pension funds and for natural disasters such as floods. Ideally, an account for the present value of future payouts under these insurance programs should be established in the federal budget. Each year funds should be set aside for expected future claims on the insurance programs and charged off as an expenditure. Unfortunately, current federal budgeting procedures do not make such charges, and payouts on the insurance funds are charged only as they are actually made. Because of the failure to budget for contingent claims against the insurance funds, current deficits appear to be smaller than they really are, and future deficits appear to be larger. A better budgeting system would use actuarial methods to forecast future payouts under federal insurance programs and budget for those payouts today rather than tomorrow. This system would allow taxpayers to see the true costs of these programs instead of being shocked by large future claims, as was the case with deposit insurance.

When a borrower makes a loan of an interest rate that isn't fully adjusted for future inflation, the borrower can pay off the loan in dollars worth less than those borrowed. Obviously, the federal government, with a very large debt held by U.S. citizens, businesses, state and local governments, and foreigners, can gain substantially from inflation. Inflation reduces the value of the national debt and can be thought of as a tax on those who hold that debt. For example, the 5 percent inflation that prevailed in 1990 reduced the value of the national debt by a whopping $100 billion. Some economists therefore recommend the deficit or surplus be adjusted for inflation each year and this *real budget balance* be used to gauge the effect of the budget.

An alternative to adjusting the budget balance for inflation is simply to gauge its burden relative to gross domestic product. The deficit or surplus as a percentage of GDP shows how much of a burden federal borrowing is *relative to* our aggregate income.

The graph in Box 6 shows how the budget deficit or surplus has varied as a percentage of GDP since 1967.

Box 6 The Federal Budget Deficit as a Percentage of GDP, 1967 - 2008

A deficit is represented by a negative percent of GDP, while a surplus is a positive percent of GDP. Since 1967, the federal government's budget has been in deficit continually, except for the period 1998-2001. The federal budget had a surplus amounting to a bit more than 2 percent of GDP in 1999. By 2002, the surplus was gone and the budget was once again in deficit, with a revenue shortfall amounting to nearly 2 percent of GDP. By 2004, the deficit had increased to 3.6 percent of GDP. The deficit fell as a percentage of GDP between 2004 and 2007, mainly as a result of a rapidly expanding economy during that period. As of 2007, the federal deficit amounted to 1.2 percent of GDP. In 2008, the deficit increased to 3.2 percent of GDP and was projected to grow to 8.3 percent of GDP by 2009. The actual deficit in 2009 could be much higher, depending on how quickly the economy recovers from the recession and how large a federal budget Congress approves for that year.

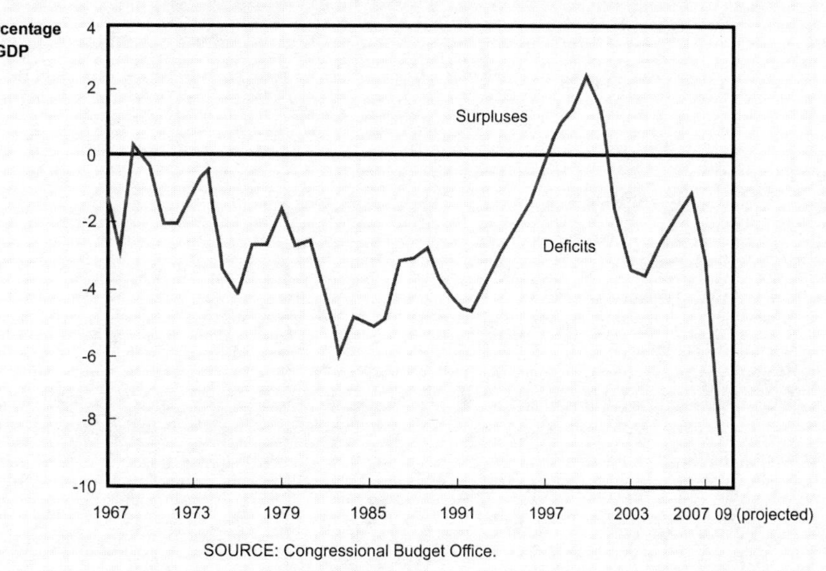

SOURCE: Congressional Budget Office.

Do Deficits Matter? Ricardian Equivalence and the Impact of Federal Deficits on Real Interest Rates

4 The effects of a budget deficit on the economy depend crucially on the impact the deficit has on national saving and real interest rates. According to some economists, because taxpayers know government will have to raise taxes in the future to pay back the funds (and the interest on those funds) it is borrowing today, they will begin saving now to pay their higher future tax bills. Increased government borrowing is therefore offset by a cut in household consumption as taxpayers increase their saving.

David Ricardo (1772 – 1832), a famous English classical economist, was the first to argue that increased government borrowing results in increased saving by forward-looking taxpayers. Ricardian equivalence prevails when an increase in government borrowing to finance a deficit causes a sufficient increase in private saving to keep the real interest rate fixed. Ricardian equivalence implies that the way an increase in government purchases is financed is irrelevant. According to this view, the level of government purchases can affect aggregate demand, but the way government finances those purchases has no effect on the economy. Ricardian equivalence and the irrelevance of the deficit have been advanced in recent years by the American economist Robert Barro.

We can illustrate Ricardian equivalence with a simple diagram similar to the one we used to illustrate the crowding-out concept earlier in this chapter. When the government increases its demand for loanable funds to cover a deficit, the total demand for loanable funds in the economy increases, putting upward pressure on real interest rates. The higher real interest rates crowd out some private investment and adversely affect future generations by reducing the rate of capital accumulation. However, when forward-looking households realize that their future taxes will increase as a result of the increase in the deficit, they begin saving to pay the higher taxes and the supply of loanable funds increases. If they increase their saving exactly enough to pay back the funds borrowed by government, the supply curve will shift just enough to keep real interest rates constant, as illustrated in Box 7. As a result of the forward-looking behavior of taxpayers, there is no increase in real interest rates and no crowding out of private investment. Therefore, saving and investment do not fall as a result of the deficit.

Ricardian equivalence is among the most controversial ideas in modern economics. If, in fact, people behave in the forward-looking manner, the implication is that we should not worry about the size of the federal deficit. While the deficit by itself decreases national

Box 7 Ricardian Equivalence

If taxpayers are forward looking, they realize a deficit means higher future tax bills. As the government increases its demand for credit, households and businesses increase the supply of saving just enough to keep the real interest rate fixed. The increase in the quantity of loanable funds supplied to the credit markets exactly equals government borrowing under Ricardian equivalence. Under such circumstances, a budget deficit has no effect on real interest rates.

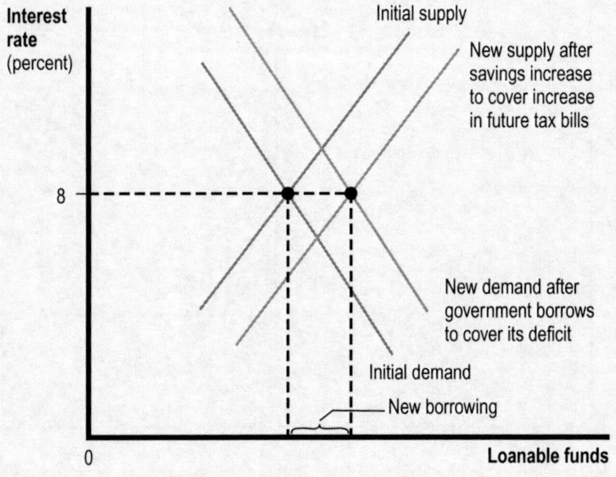

saving, the proponents of Ricardian equivalence argue that it also causes a reaction exactly offsetting its negative effect on saving.

Ricardian equivalence implies that people take future taxes into account not only for themselves but also for future generations. This is because government borrowing for a chronic deficit like the one the United States has experienced since 1970 can rarely be paid off within the lifetime of current taxpayers. Many economists find it difficult to believe that U.S. households are forward-looking enough to save in this way.

There is conflicting evidence on the effect of deficits on interest rates and saving. A number of empirical studies have shown that real interest rates are primarily-affected by the level of government purchases. After adjustment for the effect of increases in government purchases on aggregate demand, variation in the deficit has had little effect on real interest rates in recent years. Other empirical studies suggest that there has been some increase in private saving over and above what occurred as a result of the deficit. However, this research also indicates that the increase in saving has not been sufficient to offset the increase in government borrowing. This research implies that government borrowing has caused consumption and aggregate demand to increase and has put upward pressure on interest rates.

Effect of a Budget Surplus on Credit Markets

When the federal government's budget is in balance or in surplus, naturally there is no need for the government to enter the credit markets as a borrower. A balanced budget or a budget in surplus implies that the market demand for credit is equal to the private demand for credit. However, when the government runs a surplus, it can affect the supply of funds available for private investment in the credit markets.

Box 8 illustrates the possible effect of a surplus used to retire outstanding government debt on the credit market and the equilibrium market interest rate.

If the budget is balanced so that there is neither a surplus nor a deficit, the demand for credit will be equal to private demand for investment. The market equilibrium interest will be i_1. If the government runs a surplus and uses that surplus to retire existing debt, then the supply of credit will increase. By retiring the debt, the federal government exchanges

Box 8 Impact of a Budget Surplus on Credit Markets

An increase in supply of loanable funds results from using a surplus to repay existing federal debt. By repaying the debt the federal government adds loanable funds to the credit markets. The increase in supply lowers market interest rates and encourages more investment.

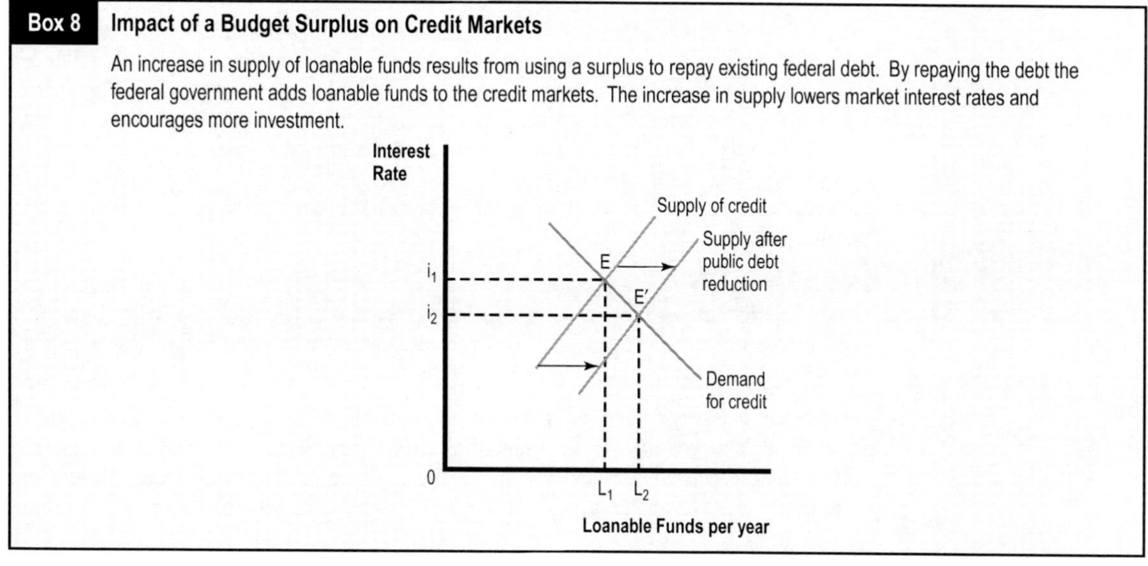

bonds for cash, thereby increasing the supply of loanable funds. Other things being equal, this increased supply of loanable funds causes the market equilibrium interest rate to decline from i_1 to i_2. The lower interest rate increases the quantity of loanable funds demanded for investment and other private borrowing from L_1 to L_2. The increased investment contributes to increases in future worker productivity and can increase future income and living standards.

If, instead of being dedicated to retiring existing debt, the surplus is used as a source of finance for new government spending or for tax reduction, the effects are likely to be different. If the surplus is used for tax reductions, then it supplies funds to consumers as well as investors. If households decide to use the extra funds they receive from tax cuts for consumption instead of saving, then there will be no increase in the supply of funds to the credit markets through saving and no declines in interest rates. Given the meager saving rates of U.S. households (in the range of one percent of disposable income), the most likely scenario for tax cuts is, in fact, increased consumption and no increased saving rates. Because it is saving and investment that contributes to economic growth, many economists and politicians would like surpluses to be used to retire the debt. In fact, some politicians were advocating using the deficit to entirely pay off the government debt over a period of 10 to 25 years.

Of course, other things can offset the potential increase in supply of loanable funds resulting from use of surpluses to retire debt. The Federal Reserve could offset the effects in credit markets with restrictive monetary policy. It is also possible that higher savings rates by government could be offset by lower savings rates by households (although this cannot get much lower), businesses, and foreigners in the United States.

Politics and the Budget Surplus and Reducing the National Debt

Having a federal budget surplus is a great temptation to politicians. The surplus can be used to fund federal government spending or to reduce taxes. Many economists, however, argue that it would be a good idea simply to let the surpluses pile up and use them to reduce the federal government's debt. Eventually, if the surpluses are run for a long enough period, all the debt could be repaid. If this were to be accomplished, it would be the first time since 1835 that the United States government had no debt.

However, there are both costs and benefits to having the federal government move to a debt-free position. There will be both gainers and losers if the debt is paid down to zero. It is good practice to finance certain types of government spending with borrowing. Capital expenditures are good candidates for debt finance. Because public investments, like roads, new government buildings, defense, irrigation, and other capital projects, provide streams of benefits over time to both current and future generations, it makes good sense to borrow to finance their costs. In this way the current generation does not pay the entire bill for a project that will benefit future generations as well. As the interest and principal of the debt are paid off, future taxpayers who will also be beneficiaries of the projects will pay a share of the taxes.

Surpluses will decrease the public debt each year they prevail. The annual reduction in the debt adds loanable funds to the credit markets and can contribute to lower interest rates and increased private investment. Because increased investment means higher economic growth, reducing the debt can make future income higher.

Some debt is always desirable to finance capital expenditures so there is no reason for the debt to always be zero. If we think the best way to raise our national savings rate is through increased government saving, then using surpluses to pay off the public debt is a good strategy. However, we can still run surpluses and not carry it to the extreme of elimination of all the debt. Setting a goal for reducing the government debt to zero represents an attempt to guarantee maximum impact of government on our national savings and therefore benefits future generations to the maximum extent possible. Using the surpluses to lower taxes for current taxpayers represents another extreme. If we were to balance the federal budget every year, the government would neither add nor subtract from national saving. In this case the benefits accrue to current taxpayers. If they use the extra income that results from lower taxes for consumption, then there is no increase in savings and no benefit to future generations.

Summary

1. A federal budget deficit prevails whenever outlays in a given year exceed receipts. When the budget is consistently in deficit, the national debt increases. When government receipts exceed outlays, a government surplus prevails.
2. The federal budget can be financed by the creation of new money or by borrowing from the public. Whenever the Federal Reserve increases the money supply to help the federal government over a deficit, the deficit is said to be *monetized.* Monetizing the deficit adds to aggregate demand directly as the government spends the newly created funds and indirectly as an increase in bank reserves allows expansion of the money supply.
3. The federal budget deficit is usually financed by borrowing from the public. If that is done, the increase in government purchases that are financed by the deficit is paid for by an allocation of saving to purchase government securities. There is no increase in bank reserves. However, borrowing is more expansionary than tax financing because disposable income is not reduced. In effect, borrowing to finance a federal budget deficit postpones the burden of taxation to the future.
4. When the government borrows in credit markets to finance a deficit, it puts upward pressure on interest rates by increasing the demand for loanable funds. The higher interest rates result in a crowding out of investment and a decline in the quantity of loanable funds demanded for investment purposes. The federal budget deficit therefore results in a crowding out of private investment as it causes real interest rates to go up. The extent of the crowding-out effect depends on the responsiveness of investment demand to changes in interest rates. A surplus that's used to retire public debt puts downward pressure on interest rates.
5. The national debt is the dollar amount that the federal government owes its creditors at a given time. The creditors are those who hold government securities and receive interest payments from the government.
6. The net federal debt is the portion of the national debt owed to those other than the Federal Reserve or government agencies.
7. The bulk of the national debt is an internal debt because it is owed to U.S. citizens. When interest is paid on the debt, income is redistributed from taxpayers to debt holders. However, a portion of the national debt is owed to foreigners who have purchased U.S. government securities. When interest is paid on this external debt, income is transferred from U.S. taxpayers to foreigners.
8. The burden of the national debt is the sacrifice U.S. citizens in the aggregate will have to make to repay it. Because the bulk of the debt is owed to U.S. citizens, repayment will make people who receive interest payments better off while making those who pay taxes worse off.
9. Another burden of the national debt is the sacrifices of future government services as more tax revenues are allocated to paying interest on the debt instead of providing government programs.
10. Inflation erodes the real value of the national debt and allows the government to pay off its debt in dollars that have less purchasing power than those it borrowed.
11. Deficits can induce forward-looking taxpayers to increase their saving to pay future taxes. Ricardian equivalence between deficit and tax financing of government outlays prevails when an increase in government borrowing to finance a deficit causes a sufficient increase in private saving to keep the real interest rate fixed.
12. A federal budget deficit decreases the national saving rate because it represents negative saving. Federal borrowing absorbs loanable funds that would otherwise finance private investment. A budget surplus amounts to government saving that can add to the supply of loanable funds and lower interest rates.

Concept Review

1. Briefly discuss the possible impact of the federal budget deficit on the economy and how that impact can vary with the way the deficit is financed.
2. How can the national debt burden future generations?
3. What is the best measure of the federal budget balance's impact on debt?
4. Explain why Ricardian equivalence implies that an increase in the federal budget deficit will not increase real interest rates.

Problems and Applications

1. Suppose a new law is passed that requires the federal government to run a surplus each year until the national debt has been paid off. Explain why such a policy would be likely to destabilize the economy and contribute to recessions when the private components of aggregate demand decrease. 1, 3

2. Suppose the federal government runs a chronic deficit of $200 billion per year and finances that deficit by selling new government securities directly to the Federal Reserve System. Show how, other things being equal, either currency in circulation or bank reserves will increase as a result of this means of financing the deficit. Why would the impact on the economy of this means of financing the deficit be the same as if the government merely printed money to pay its expenses? Why would the impact on the economy be inflationary in the long run? 1

3. Suppose the federal deficit is financed by borrowing funds from the general public. Track the impact of such borrowing on interest rates, private saving, and private investment. Under what circumstances will government borrowing reduce private investment? 1

4. Suppose taxpayers increase the supply of savings as a direct result of the government deficit. Show how, if the increase in the supply of savings is large enough, borrowing to finance the deficit will not affect interest rates and will not crowd out private investment. 4

5. Why is financing government expenditures by borrowing more expansionary than tax financing? 1

6. Suppose both the supply of savings and investment demand are completely unresponsive to changes in the market rate of interest. What will be the impact of a federal budget deficit on consumption, investment, and aggregate demand? What impact will the deficit have on the price level and real GDP if the economy is in a deep recession, so that the economy is operating in the flat portion of its aggregate supply curve? 1

7. How can a large deficit prolong a nation's international balance of trade deficit? 1

8. Suppose that over the years the portion of the net federal debt owned by foreigners increases from 5 percent to 30 percent of the amount outstanding. What is the implication of this change for the future burden of repaying the debt? 2

9. Suppose all of the net federal debt is internal debt. In what sense does repayment of such a debt involve a redistribution of income? Is there a burden of the debt on future generations in this case? In what ways can the burden of the debt on future generations be offset? 2

10. What is the impact of inflation on the burden of repaying the debt and on taxpayers? 1, 2

Policy Perspective: Do We Have More Government Spending Because of Deficit Finance?

The 1994 Republican "Contract with America" emphasized a massive reduction in the scope of government to eliminate the deficit by the year 2002. Did deficit finance in the 1970s and 1980s itself contribute to the growth of government spending?

The level and types of government spending depend, in part, on the means used to finance government. By borrowing instead of using taxes, politicians influence the incentive of voters to vote for increased spending. The success in getting government spending programs approved, therefore, depends on how we finance those programs. Deficits can affect both resource allocation (by influencing the types of government spending) and the overall size of the government sector in the economy. They can also influence prices and interest rates.

By using deficit finance, we can keep taxes lower than they would otherwise be and still enjoy a given quantity and mix of government services. Deficit finance also permits government spending, either for transfers or for purchases of goods and services, without raising taxes. The federal deficits of the 1980s were, in part, used to finance investments in military technology. But much of the growth in federal spending since the 1970s is accounted for by unprecedented increases in transfers--both in-kind and as income support, mainly to the elderly.*

Because borrowing to finance deficits postpones the burden of taxation to the future, it makes sense to use deficits to finance government investments that will provide a stream of future benefits. This is efficient, because taxes will then be distributed among future generations, who will also reap the benefits of such government investments as roads, structures, transportation and communication networks, and environmental protection. Traditionally, nations have relied heavily on borrowing to finance wars and investments in military technology and equipment under the presumption that the removal of a threat to national security will provide future benefits for which future taxpayers should pay.

However, the deficits of the 1970s and 1980s weren't incurred in a period of war or a period of significantly increased national investment in infrastructure. Instead, much of the growth of spending that, in effect, was financed by the deficit was in the form of transfers of income and services (especially medical services) to the poor and the elderly. These federal expenditures mainly financed *consumption* as opposed to *investment*.

The ratio of taxes to GDP remained quite stable during this period, at around 20 percent of GDP, while federal outlays increased to 25 percent of GDP. The growing deficit of the 1970s and 1980s could be viewed as the outcome of a political system that satisfied the demand for increased federal transfer programs in the 1970s (many of which benefited the elderly) and investment in military technology in the 1980s, while preventing federal average tax rates from increasing significantly. It's possible that the growth in transfers couldn't have been approved through the political system if it were financed by increased taxes (or cuts in other types of spending), rather than by borrowing.

*During the 1980s, when federal deficits were increasing as a share of GDP, spending on the elderly continued to grow. See Rudolph G. Penner," Federal Government Growth: Leviathan or Protector of the Elderly?" *National Tax Journal* 44, 1, December 1991, pp. 437-50.

The Social Security Trust Fund Surplus and the Federal Budget Balance

Sweeping changes in the way the Social Security system finances its pensions were enacted by Congress in 1977 and 1983. As a result, the payroll taxes paid by almost all workers in the United States have risen dramatically. In fact, many workers now pay more in payroll taxes to finance Social Security than they pay in income taxes.

The payroll tax collections and taxes levied on the Social Security pensions of certain upper-income taxpayers are used to purchase special government securities issued by the U.S. Treasury. These securities make up two Social Security trust funds, one for old-age and survivors' insurance and the other for disability insurance. When the payroll tax and other Social Security tax collections exceed the payout rate, the Social Security trust funds increase. The extra money purchases more special Treasury securities. The trust funds also grow from the interest paid by the Treasury to the funds.

In the 1970s and 1980s, the Social Security system worked on a "pay-as-you-go" basis. Payroll taxes levied on current workers were used immediately to pay the pensions of retirees. In the 1970s, the Social Security trust fund balance was a mere 15 percent of annual pensions paid. By 1990, the Social Security trust fund balance had risen to more than half of the pension benefits paid.

The trust funds grow steadily now because payroll tax receipts exceed pension benefits paid. The funds will continue to grow and earn interest until the year 2025. Thereafter, their Treasury securities will have to be cashed in to pay pensions, because of a growing proportion of retirees in the population. At that time, the Treasury will have to repay, with interest, the special government securities held by the Social Security trust funds. This repayment could require income and other tax increases if annual pension payments exceed payroll tax and other tax receipts earmarked for Social Security at that time.

What does all this business about the Social Security trust funds have to do with the budget balance? The answer is, "A whole lot." Because any surplus in the trust funds is, in effect, loaned to the Treasury, the surplus in the trust fund account reduces the overall federal budget deficit or increases the surplus. Because of the concern that the funds might be used to finance other government expenditures (or increased Social Security pension benefits), the Budget Enforcement Act of 1990 established new rules that dedicate the Social Security trust fund surpluses to reducing federal debt.

Increases in future income are necessary to prevent higher future tax rates to pay future pensions. The budget rules represent an attempt to make sure that the trust fund surplus will add to national saving, rather than help finance current federal spending programs. If we save more today, we'll have more income in the future, and future tax rates won't have to be increased to generate sufficient funds to pay Social Security pensions at that time.

Chapter 35

International Trade

If you're like most Americans, you enjoy the benefits of consuming products that can't be easily produced in the United States, such as bananas and other tropical fruits. You may also own an automobile, a laptop computer, or a favorite pair of jeans produced abroad. International trade not only permits you to obtain products unavailable domestically, it also permits you to purchase some items at lower prices than would be possible otherwise. The modern global economy requires that domestic businesses compete in international markets. To compete effectively in the global economy, U.S. businesses often must stay on the cutting edge of technology to allow productivity to grow and keep costs down.

In this chapter, we'll examine the process of international trade and show how mutual gains are possible to trading partners. You'll see how international trade contributes to your well-being by allowing an international division of labor and specialized production. We'll also explain why some groups seek protection against foreign competition, and we'll examine who gains and who loses as a result of tariffs and import quotas to restrict international trade.

Concept Preview

After reading this chapter, you should be able to

1. Understand the underlying basis for international trade, the principle of comparative advantage, and the gains in well-being possible from free trade with foreign nations.
2. Show how productivity changes in specific industries can affect their comparative advantage in international trade.
3. Discuss protectionism and analyze the impact on the economy of tariffs, import quotas, and other trade restrictions.

International Trade Theory

In 2008, the total dollar value of U.S. exported goods and services amounted to $1.86 trillion, accounting for 13 percent of GDP that year.. U.S. exports of goods and services provides substantial income for businesses and hundreds of thousands of workers. In 2008, nearly $2.37 trillion worth of goods and services were imported from foreign lands, allowing U.S. businesses and households to enjoy and use materials, supplies, and goods, transports, and banking produced abroad. In 2008 imports were equal to 16.5 percent of GDP in the United States. As you'll see, international trade is a two-way street--not only because it involves exchanges of goods and services among nations, but also because it allows mutual gains to the trading partners.

The Basis for International Trade

1 One basis for international trade is that, through international trade, goods can be obtained that are unavailable or too costly to produce domestically. Another basis for international trade lies in the fact that both human and natural resources vary among nations. For example, the Swiss are noted for their traditional skills in making watches and producing fine chocolate candies. The Italians have long been known for the high quality of their leather goods. The United States is well endowed with timber and coal.

Elsewhere in the text, we discuss the advantages of specialization and the division of labor. Specialization is the use of labor and other resources in a nation to produce the goods and services for which those resources are best suited. Many Japanese workers specialize in the production of automobiles and electronic goods, while many U.S. workers excel in the production of aircraft. The larger output possible from specialization often results in economies of scale that lower production costs still further. International trade is firmly rooted in the gains that are possible from specialization, as well as the gains that can be obtained by acquiring locally unavailable natural resources.

When nations specialize in the production of certain items, their output of those items exceeds the amounts demanded in domestic markets at current prices. The firms can then sell the surplus goods in foreign markets. The foreign currency obtained from these export sales can be used to buy the products of other nations. For example, Italy specializes in the production of wine. By exporting wine, it can gain foreign currency to purchase petroleum products, which it requires as an input into production but doesn't produce domestically in sufficient quantities. Similarly, the United States specializes in the production of wheat, which it exports to Italy in exchange for euros that can be used to purchase Italian wines. China and Russia have sought to encourage tourism as a means of earning foreign currency to purchase goods offered for sale by Western nations.

We Americans are fortunate in that we live in a nation well endowed with both natural resources and a skilled labor force. Our nation's vast and diverse productive capacity means we're less dependent on international trade for such basic resources as fuel, food, and fiber than are other nations. Such nations as Japan and Israel rely heavily on imports of basic natural resources. These nations are under pressure to export goods and services to earn the foreign exchange necessary to finance such imports.

International trade is often opposed by groups that seek to insulate themselves from what they regard as unfair foreign competition. Many people argue that foreign competition is unfair because cheap foreign goods are produced with cheap labor and are heavily subsidized by foreign governments that are under pressure to earn dollars from international trade. Although there are long-run mutual gains from international trade, it's clear that, in the short run, particular groups, such as workers with specialized skills or owners of specialized equipment, can be harmed by increased imports.

The Principle of Comparative Advantage

There are mutual gains from international trade, which means that, on average, citizens in all trading nations gain from exchanging goods in international markets. A simplified example can be used to illustrate the underlying basis for international trade. Suppose two nations both have the capability of producing bananas and wheat. Both nations have the same quantity of natural resources, labor, and capital. The table in Box 1 shows the production possibilities in the two nations when they devote all of their resources to producing either bananas or wheat.

Nation A can produce 20 tons of wheat *or* 20 tons of bananas per year if it specializes in one item or the other. Nation B can produce 5 tons of wheat *or* 10 tons of bananas per year by specializing in one item or the other. Notice that with the same resources nation A can produce more wheat when it specializes in that good than can nation B. Similarly, nation A can produce more bananas when it specializes in production of that item than can nation B. With the same resources nation A can therefore produce more than nation B no matter how it specializes.

A nation has an absolute advantage over other nations in the production of an item if it can produce more of the item over a certain period with a *given* amount of resources than the other nations can. Nation A has an absolute advantage in the production of wheat over nation B in this example because, with the same resources, nation A can produce more wheat by specializing in wheat production than can nation B. In this example nation A *also* has the absolute advantage in the production of bananas because with the same resources as are available in nation B, it can produce more bananas than can nation B.

Another way of interpreting nation A's absolute advantage over nation B in both wheat and banana production is to point out that in nation A each unit of either wheat or bananas can be produced with less input than is needed to produce it in nation B. For example, suppose that the only inputs used to produce wheat are land and labor. Suppose both nation A and nation B have 2,000 labor hours available per year and the same amount of land. When nation A specializes in wheat production, it can produce 20 tons per year with its 2,000 labor hours. The *labor cost* per ton will be

$$\frac{2,\ 000\ \text{labor hours}}{20\ \text{tons}} = 100\ \text{labor hours per ton of wheat}$$

The labor cost per ton of wheat in nation B when nation B specializes in wheat production will be

Box 1 Production Possibilities for Two Nations

Nation A (annual output)	Nation B (annual output)
20 tons of wheat and no bananas	5 tons of wheat and no bananas
or	or
20 tons of bananas and no wheat	10 tons of bananas and no wheat

Opportunity cost	Nation A	Nation B
Each ton of wheat costs	1 ton of bananas	2 tons of bananas
Each ton of bananas costs	1 ton of wheat	0.5 ton of wheat

$$\frac{2,\ 000 \text{ labor hours}}{5 \text{ tons}} = 400 \text{ labor hours per ton of wheat}$$

Given the same quantity of land in both nations, wheat is four times as expensive in terms of labor required per ton in nation B as it is in nation A.

Similarly, just by looking at labor cost, you can see that nation A's absolute advantage over nation B in banana production means it can produce bananas with fewer labor hours per ton than can nation B. The labor cost per ton of bananas in nation A is

$$\frac{2,\ 000 \text{ labor hours}}{20 \text{ tons}} = 100 \text{ labor hours per ton of bananas}$$

In nation B the labor cost per ton of bananas is

$$\frac{2,\ 000 \text{ labor hours}}{10 \text{ tons}} = 200 \text{ labor hours per ton of bananas}$$

Bananas therefore cost twice as much in terms of labor input per ton in nation B compared to nation A.

We can show that nation A's absolute advantage over nation B in both items means that each ton requires less land in A than it does in B. *In general, when a nation has an absolute advantage, it can produce the specific item with fewer inputs per unit than other nations.*

Despite the fact that nation A has an absolute advantage over nation B, we can easily demonstrate that the citizens of nation A can gain by specializing in one of the goods and then trading with nation B to obtain the other. This remarkable conclusion stems from the fact that the gains possible from trade are determined by the opportunity cost of each unit of one good in terms of the other good rather than by the input cost. To see this, begin by calculating the *opportunity cost per unit* of each of the goods in each nation. To simplify the analysis, suppose that each ton of each good involves the sacrifice of a constant amount of the other good in each nation.

Because nation A can produce either 20 tons of wheat or 20 tons of bananas, it will give up the opportunity to produce 20 tons of bananas if it chooses to specialize in the production of wheat. The *opportunity cost* of each ton of wheat is the sacrifice of the bananas associated with the production of each extra ton of wheat. Assuming constant costs per ton of wheat, the opportunity cost of each ton of wheat in nation A is 1 ton of bananas.

A similar calculation can be performed for nation B. Because nation B can produce either 5 tons of wheat or 10 tons of bananas, it follows that it gives up 2 tons of bananas for each extra ton of wheat, assuming constant costs. The opportunity cost of producing a ton of wheat is therefore 2 tons of bananas for nation B.

The opportunity cost of bananas for each of the two nations is calculated in the same way. The table in Box 1 shows that the opportunity cost of bananas is 1 ton of wheat in nation A and 1/2 ton of wheat in nation B, assuming constant costs.

The graphs in Box 2 show the production possibilities curves for these two goods in each of the two nations. The curves have been drawn under the assumption that in each nation there is a constant rate at which bananas are sacrificed for more wheat as resources are allocated from banana production to wheat production. This implies *constant opportunity costs per unit*, meaning that the opportunity cost of each unit of one of the goods in terms of the other is constant, as was assumed in the calculation of Box 1. The main point of the analysis also holds for the case of increasing costs, but the argument for that case is considerably more complicated. Note that the slope of each production possibilities curve

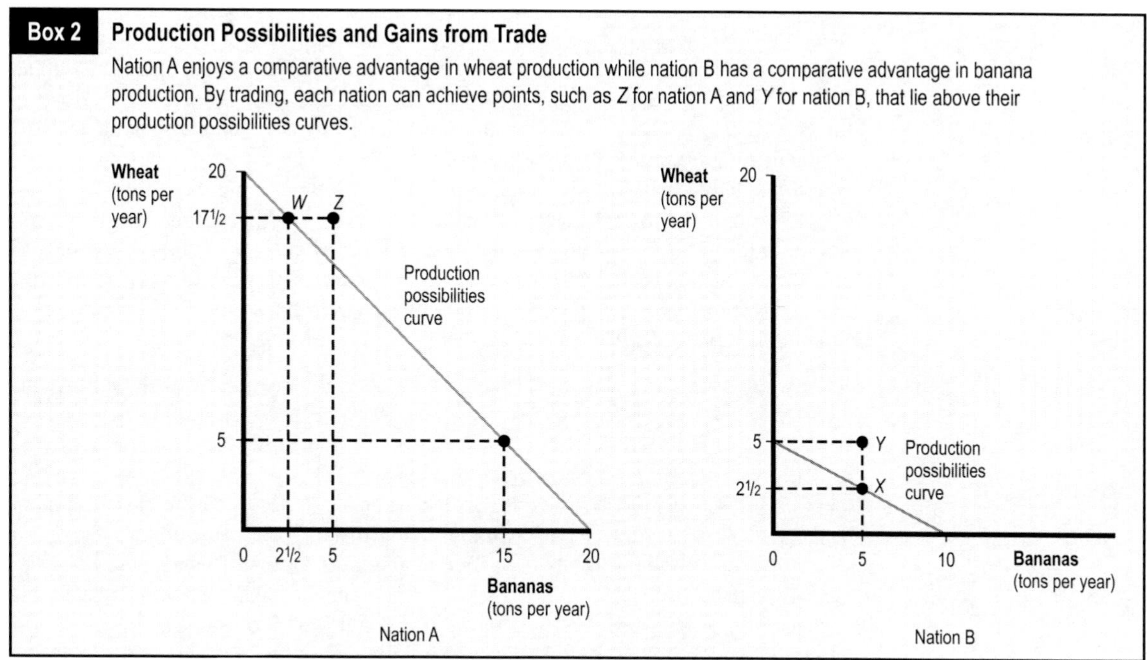

Box 2 Production Possibilities and Gains from Trade

Nation A enjoys a comparative advantage in wheat production while nation B has a comparative advantage in banana production. By trading, each nation can achieve points, such as *Z* for nation A and *Y* for nation B, that lie above their production possibilities curves.

represents the opportunity cost of bananas in terms of wheat multiplied by –1. The slope of the production possibilities curve for nation A is –1, which means each extra ton of bananas produced per year involves the sacrifice of 1 ton of wheat per year. The slope of the production possibilities curve for nation B is –0.5, which means each extra ton of bananas produced per year involves the sacrifice of 1/2 ton of wheat per year.

A nation has a comparative advantage over a trading partner in the production of an item if it produces that item at lower opportunity cost per unit than its partner does. The gains possible from international trade stem from the decrease in opportunity cost per unit of output that is possible when nations specialize in goods in whose production they enjoy a comparative advantage. By specializing, a nation uses its resources to produce items for which it enjoys a comparative advantage. It then exports some of its annual output in exchange for other goods that can be obtained at lower opportunity costs per unit when they are produced by other nations.

Despite its absolute advantage in both goods, nation A is *relatively more efficient in the production of wheat only compared to nation B*. Nation A gives up only 1 ton of bananas for each ton of wheat, while nation B must give up 2 tons of bananas for each ton of wheat. Nation A, however, *is relatively less efficient in the production of bananas compared to nation B* because it must give up a ton of wheat for each ton of bananas if it produces bananas, while nation B has to give up only 1/2 ton of wheat.

Gains from Specialization and Trade

It's easy to show how both nation A and nation B can gain from specializing in the good for which they enjoy a comparative advantage and then trading to enjoy other goods. Suppose nation B uses all of its resources to produce bananas in a given year. By doing so, it will produce 10 tons of bananas per year. Now suppose it offers 5 tons of its production to nation A. What is the maximum amount of wheat that nation A will trade for the 5 tons of bananas? It would cost nation A 5 tons of wheat to produce 5 tons of bananas. If the traders of nation B were skillful enough to extract a bargain like that, they would have 5 tons of bananas to enjoy and 5 tons of wheat. If nation B produced 5 tons of bananas and engaged in no trade, the best it could do, given its production possibilities curve, would be to enjoy 2 1/2 tons of wheat. This would correspond to point *X* on its production possibilities curve in Box 2. By specializing in banana production and trading with nation A, the traders of nation B can enjoy as much as 5 tons of wheat! International trade therefore gives a nation's citizens the potential to achieve points that lie above their production possibilities curve, such as point *Y* in Box 2. Of course, the citizens of nation B would be able to achieve this as long as they received anything more than 2 1/2 tons of wheat for their 5 tons of bananas. If nation A were to trade anything less than 5 tons of wheat for the 5 tons of bananas offered by nation B, the citizens of nation A would also be able to achieve points above their production possibilities curve. *International trade opens up the possibility of gains in world efficiency from resources by allowing mutual gains that would not be possible if each nation attempted to remain self-sufficient.*

It's easy to show how nation A can gain by specializing in wheat. Suppose nation A produced 17 1/2 tons of wheat per year. The graph in Box 2 shows that without trade it could enjoy at most only 2 1/2 tons of bananas per year. However, if nation A specialized in wheat production, it would be able to produce 20 tons per year. It could offer 2 1/2 of these 20 tons to nation B in exchange for bananas. What is the maximum amount of bananas nation B would give up, without being made worse off, to obtain 2 1/2 tons of wheat? Nation B would have to sacrifice as much as 5 tons of bananas to produce that much wheat by itself. This is the maximum amount of bananas it would be willing to exchange for 2 1/2 tons of wheat. If it did give up 5 tons of bananas for 2 1/2 tons of wheat, it would be no worse off. However, if traders for nation A could strike such a clever bargain, nation A would be able to consume 17 1/2 tons of wheat per year and 5 tons of bananas. This would allow nation A to move *beyond* its own production possibilities curve from point *W* to point *Z*. Of course, if nation B gave up anything less than 5 tons of bananas for the wheat, it would gain as well. As you can see, specialization according to comparative advantage allows mutual gains from trade that enable each trading nation to move beyond its own production possibilities curve.

Free international trade allows citizens in trading nations to enjoy consumption possibilities that extend beyond their own production possibilities. Although the simple example we used to illustrate this point is quite abstract, it has great relevance to the world we live in. For example, Japan enjoys a comparative advantage in 35-mm cameras, while the United States enjoys a comparative advantage in aircraft. U.S. workers can gain by specializing in the production of aircraft and other items in which the United States enjoys a comparative advantage. If U.S. aircraft are traded for Japanese cameras, the aggregate output of both these goods can increase. American citizens can enjoy more cameras (because they cost less when purchased from Japan) for any given output of aircraft than would be possible without international trade. At the same time, Japanese citizens can enjoy more aircraft (because they cost less when purchased from the United States) for any given output of cameras.

The Mercantilist Fallacy

International trade benefits all trading nations. What one nation gains in the aggregate from trade is not lost by its trading partner in the aggregate. This point was misunderstood by 17th- and 18th-century advocates of *mercantilism*, a doctrine arguing that nations could increase their power by encouraging exports and discouraging imports. In the 18th and early 19th centuries, gold and silver were used as international currency to settle foreign debts. Nations that consistently ran a balance of trade surplus would require nations with a balance of trade deficit to settle the difference in gold and silver. Nations that exported more than they imported thereby accumulated gold and silver in their national treasuries. The mercantilists mistakenly believed that nations losing gold and silver were made worse off by international trade.

What they didn't understand was that a nation's well-being is not measured by gold, silver, or other commodities in storage. Instead, its well-being depends on the goods and services its citizens can purchase with their available incomes. International trade allows citizens in the aggregate to expand their consumption possibilities beyond their domestic production possibilities. The gains from trade consist of the expansion of consumption possibilities. A nation pursuing policies that encouraged exports but discouraged imports in order to gain gold, silver, or other commodities to hold in storage simply gained purchasing power for the future. If such policies artificially restricted imports, the nation's citizens were deprived of the opportunity to enjoy imported goods that other nations could produce at lower opportunity costs.

Terms of Trade

Trade enables consumers in each nation to gain by obtaining certain goods at lower opportunity cost than would be possible if the goods were domestically produced. To gain from trade, nation B would have to obtain wheat from nation A at any price *below* its opportunity cost of 2 tons of bananas for each ton of wheat. Similarly, to gain from trade, nation A would have to obtain bananas from nation B at a price *below* its opportunity cost of 1 ton of wheat per ton of bananas.

In actuality, prices for goods are determined by world demand and supply. The real terms of trade are the actual market exchange rate of one good for another in international trade. Incentive to trade exists if the real terms of trade are below a nation's opportunity cost per unit of producing a good domestically. The greater the difference between the real terms of trade and the nation's opportunity cost of producing each extra unit of the good it wants to import, the more the nation gains from trade. For example, nation B is better off if the terms of trade allow it to get 1 ton of wheat for 1 1/2 tons of bananas than it is if it has to give up 2 tons of bananas for each ton of wheat. However, nation A is better off if the terms of trade are 2 tons instead of 1 1/2 tons of bananas for a ton of wheat. *When the terms of trade for a pair of goods improve for a nation specializing in one of the goods, they deteriorate for its trading partner specializing in the other good.* However, as long as the terms of trade are less than each nation's opportunity cost of producing each unit, *both nations gain from engaging in specialization and trade.*

Suppose the agreed-upon terms of trade are 1 1/2 tons of bananas for each ton of wheat. It's now easy to show how each nation's *consumption possibilities* are extended beyond its *production possibilities* by international exchange of goods at the agreed-upon terms of trade. Note that the agreed-upon terms of trade can also be expressed as 2/3 ton of wheat for each ton of bananas. For example, if nation A specializes in wheat production and trades its entire annual output of 20 tons of wheat, it will receive 30 tons of bananas in exchange by trading with nation B, which specializes in banana production. By specializing, nation A can consume a maximum of 30 tons of bananas instead of 20 tons. A consumption possibilities curve shows the combinations of two goods a nation can consume, given its resources, technology, and international trade. The graph in Box 3 shows nation A's consumption possibilities curve when it can trade wheat at the rate of 2/3 ton for each ton of bananas. The consumption possibilities curve is not as steep as the production possibilities curve because less wheat must be given up for each ton of bananas in trade than in production. In fact, as shown in Box 4, at the agreed-upon terms of trade, the cost of a ton of bananas to the residents of nation A has fallen from 1 ton of wheat to 2/3 ton of wheat. Thus, bananas are a better buy as imports than as domestic products.

The shaded area in the graph in Box 3 represents the combinations of wheat and bananas that nation A can enjoy when trade is possible at the agreed-upon terms but cannot be enjoyed if nation A tries to be self-sufficient in bananas and wheat. International trade allows consumers of nation A to consume more of *both* wheat and bananas.

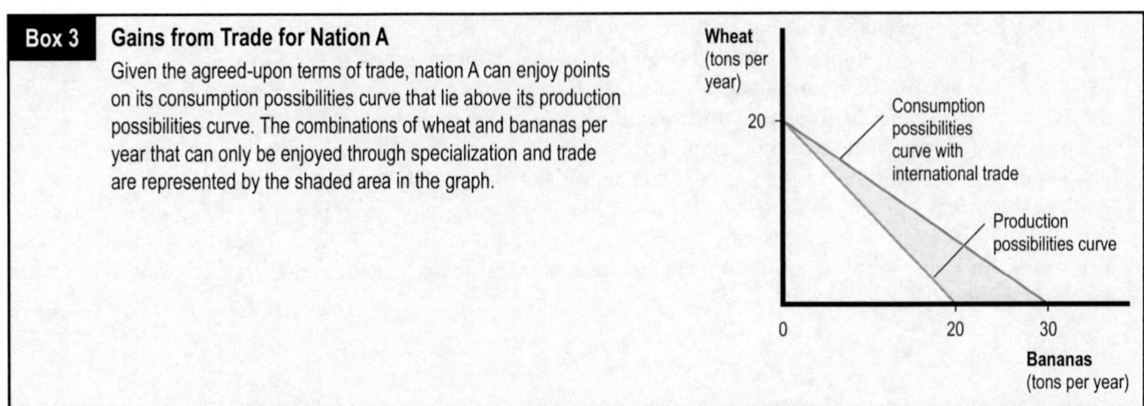

Box 3 Gains from Trade for Nation A

Given the agreed-upon terms of trade, nation A can enjoy points on its consumption possibilities curve that lie above its production possibilities curve. The combinations of wheat and bananas per year that can only be enjoyed through specialization and trade are represented by the shaded area in the graph.

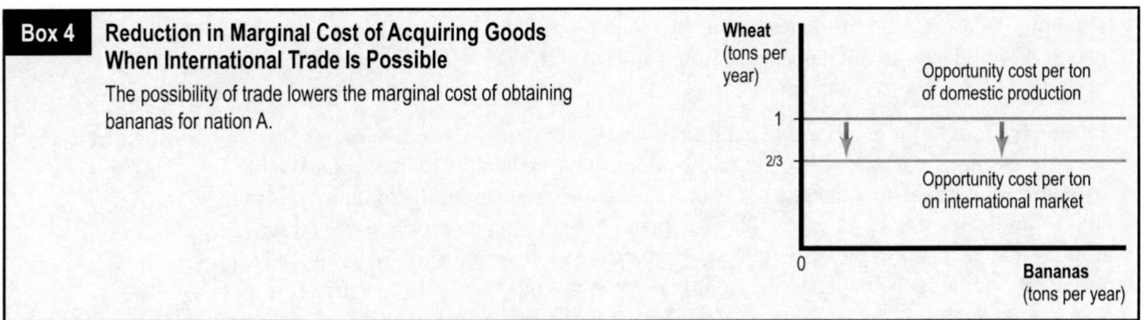

Box 4 Reduction in Marginal Cost of Acquiring Goods When International Trade Is Possible

The possibility of trade lowers the marginal cost of obtaining bananas for nation A.

Similarly, the graph in Box 5 shows how trade shifts nation B's consumption possibilities above its production possibilities. For example, by specializing in banana production and selling its entire annual crop of 10 tons on international markets, nation B can consume 6 2/3 tons of wheat per year. If, instead, it allocates all of its own resources to wheat production, the most it can consume is 5 tons of wheat. The slope of nation B's consumption possibilities curve is steeper than the slope of its production possibilities curve because, as shown in Box 6, international trade decreases its opportunity cost of enjoying a ton of wheat from 2 tons of bananas to only 1 1/2 tons of bananas. The shaded area in the graph in Box 5 shows the combinations of wheat and bananas attainable through trade that would not be attainable if nation B attempted to be self-sufficient in wheat and bananas.

As a result of international trade, citizens in both nation A and nation B have the opportunity to enjoy points on their consumption possibilities curves rather than their production possibilities curves. Given their resource availability, citizens in all nations will enjoy more goods and services when they trade. This is not to say that all people will be better off. As you'll see shortly, international trade can make some people worse off, especially in the short run.

Productivity and Trade

2 The comparative advantage enjoyed by producers of particular goods in a nation can be eroded over time if their productivity growth lags behind that of competing foreign producers. Throughout the 1970s, large U.S. steel firms operated aging plants. Their productivity growth lagged behind that of Japanese firms whose plants were more

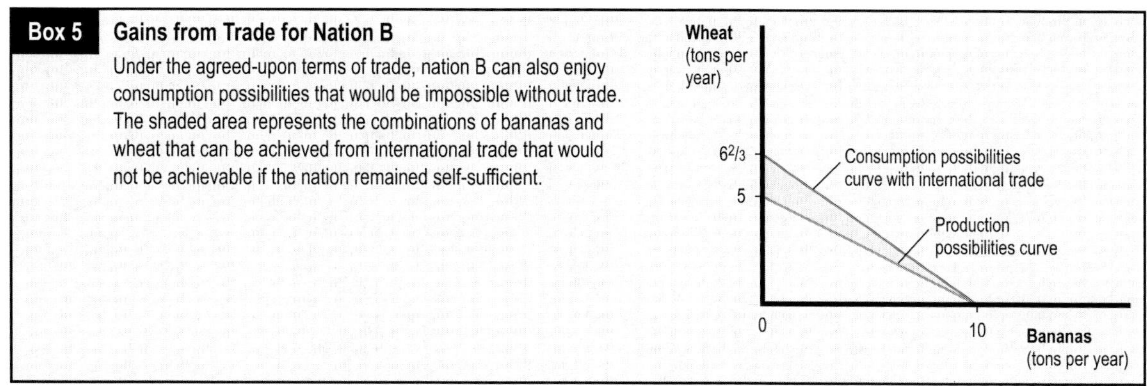
Box 5
Gains from Trade for Nation B
Under the agreed-upon terms of trade, nation B can also enjoy consumption possibilities that would be impossible without trade. The shaded area represents the combinations of bananas and wheat that can be achieved from international trade that would not be achievable if the nation remained self-sufficient.
Wheat (tons per year)
6 2/3
5
0
10
Bananas (tons per year)
Consumption possibilities curve with international trade
Production possibilities curve

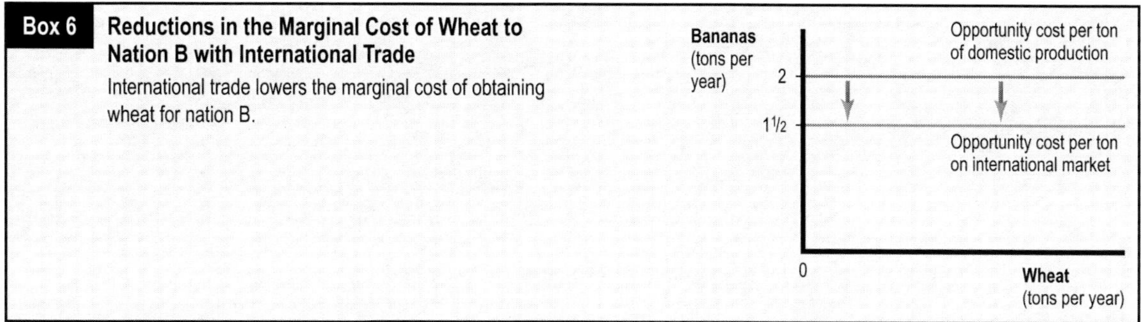
Box 6
Reductions in the Marginal Cost of Wheat to Nation B with International Trade
International trade lowers the marginal cost of obtaining wheat for nation B.
Bananas (tons per year)
2
1 1/2
0
Wheat (tons per year)
Opportunity cost per ton of domestic production
Opportunity cost per ton on international market

modern. As a result, they failed to compete successfully with Japanese firms in international and domestic markets.

Because productivity increased faster in the Japanese steel industry than in the U.S. steel industry, the opportunity cost of U.S. steel rose relative to the opportunity cost of Japanese steel. U.S. steel became less attractive in international markets because Japanese producers were able to sell steel at prices lower than U.S. producers while still covering their opportunity costs.

How to Lose Comparative Advantage in International Markets

In examining the trade process, it's useful to trace out the implications of lagging productivity growth. We can use the analysis of comparative advantage to show how lagging productivity can affect the competitiveness of the U.S. steel industry compared to that of the Japanese steel industry in international markets.

The graphs in Box 7 show hypothetical production possibilities curves for food and steel in the United States and Japan, assuming constant opportunity costs. The initial production possibilities curve for the United States has a slope of –1, indicating that the opportunity cost of each ton of steel is 1 ton of food. The initial Japanese production possibilities curve has a slope of –2, indicating that the opportunity cost of each ton of steel is 2 tons of food.

Initially, the United States enjoys a comparative advantage in steel production because, measured in terms of food forgone, its opportunity cost of each ton of steel is one-half that of Japan. Suppose, however, that, over time in both nations, productivity does not increase in food production but does increase in steel production. Also suppose that the productivity of Japanese firms increases at a faster rate than do U.S. firms. The production possibilities curve will swivel outward and become flatter as productivity growth

Box 7 Productivity Growth and Comparative Advantage

Faster productivity growth in the steel industry in Japan compared to the United States can result in the loss of the comparative advantage in steel production for U.S. firms.

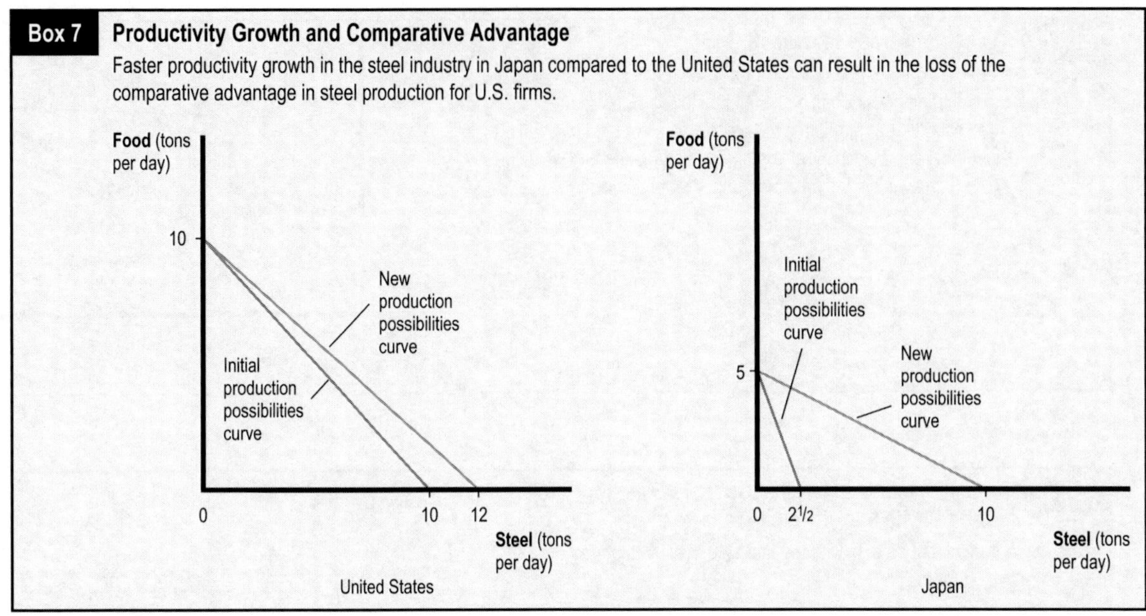

increases. In Box 7 such growth shifts the U.S. production possibilities curve until it intersects the horizontal axis at 12 tons per day. However, steel productivity growth is much more pronounced in Japan, so its production possibilities curve now intersects the horizontal axis at 10 tons per day instead of 2 1/2 tons. Notice that the Japanese production possibilities curve is now flatter than the U.S. production possibilities curve. *The opportunity cost of a ton of steel in Japan has fallen below that in the United States.*

The graphs in Box 8 show that Japan's amazing growth in productivity has reduced the opportunity cost of a ton of steel in that country from 2 tons of food per day to only 1/2 ton. Meanwhile, the low growth of productivity in the United States has merely reduced the opportunity cost of a ton of steel from 1 ton of food per day to 0.83 ton. *As a result of lagging productivity growth, the United States, in this example, has lost its comparative advantage in steel production.* Japan can now produce steel at a lower opportunity cost than the United States. This example teaches an important lesson: An industry that lags behind the times in technology or equipment will lose its comparative advantage in international markets.

Implications of Lagging Productivity Growth

Each nation enjoys a comparative advantage in some products relative to its trading partners. The United States retains a comparative advantage in many products. Moreover, the United States is likely to gain a comparative advantage in the new products it develops.

U.S. manufacturers have been closing obsolete plants and applying improved technology and management techniques that promise to result in future productivity gains. In addition, U.S. research in new technologies, such as superconductivity, can lead to the development of new products in which the nation will enjoy a comparative advantage.

What are the implications for U.S. workers of a loss of comparative advantage in particular export markets? Obviously, workers in such industries as steel and electronics, where comparative advantage has been eroded, will be harmed more than other workers. Keep in mind, however, that all nations enjoy a comparative advantage in some goods. For

Box 8 Impact of Differences in Productivity Growth on Comparative Advantage

Increased productivity growth causes the opportunity cost per ton of steel (in terms of food) in Japan to fall below the opportunity cost of steel (in terms of food) in the United States.

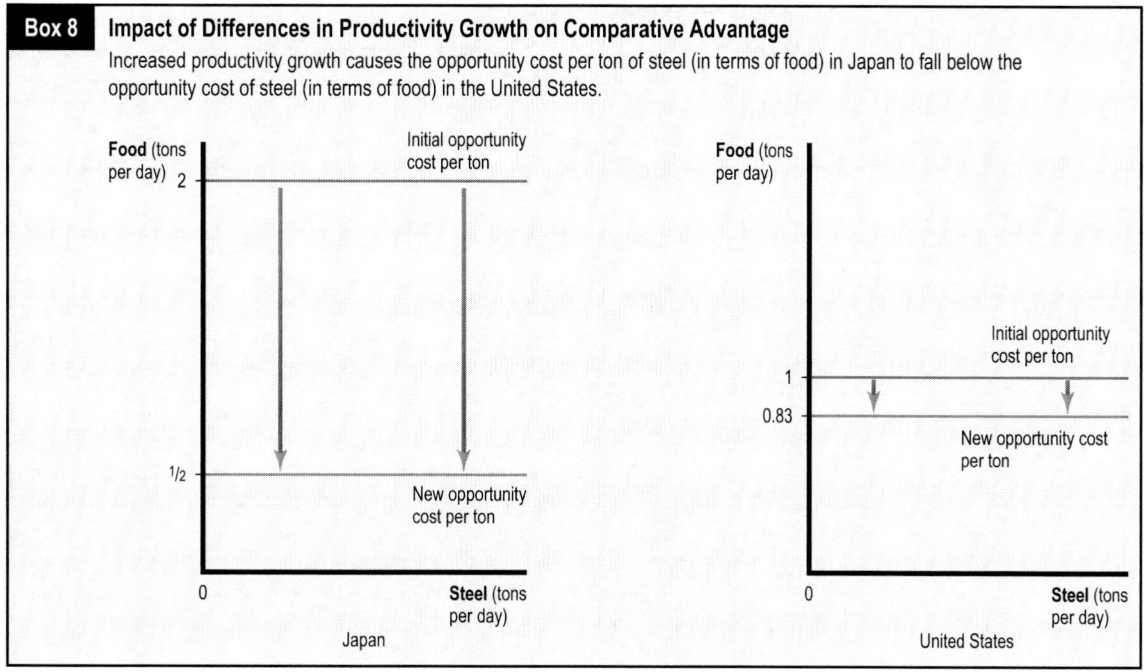

example, notice that in the example from the preceding section the United States will enjoy a comparative advantage in food production relative to Japan when it loses its comparative advantage in steel production. When the opportunity cost of a ton of steel in terms of food in the United States rises above that in Japan, the opportunity cost of a ton of food in terms of steel must fall below that in Japan.

The impact of this adjustment process, however, is bitter medicine for U.S. workers in industries where comparative advantage is being eroded. As a result of lagging productivity gains, their wages will necessarily fall relative to the wages enjoyed by workers in competing nations. For industries in which comparative advantage has been lost, some workers with specialized skills and other owners of specialized inputs will suffer permanent reductions in income. Some of these workers must find employment in other industries. In recent years the U.S. steel and electronics industries have undergone such disruptions. Similar disruptions have occurred in the textile industry, whose lagging productivity growth has caused the United States to lose comparative advantage in international markets.

A key to keeping productivity growth high is adequate investment in new equipment and plants and the development of new products. Business investment in the United States has lagged in recent years, and many economists believe this is the chief cause of the nation's decline in manufacturing productivity.

We can get a rough idea about the areas in which the United States has a comparative advantage by looking at the balance of trade in recent years. The United States has consistently exported more chemicals, aircraft, business and technical services (including advertising, telecommunications, data processing, and accounting), and wheat than it has imported. The United States has consistently imported more automobiles, consumer electronic products, petroleum, and textile products than it has exported, which suggests that we do not have a comparative advantage in the production of these products.

Protectionism versus Free Trade

3 As noted earlier, declines in a nation's comparative advantage caused by declines in its productivity growth inevitably disrupt particular industries. Workers with specialized skills lose their jobs, and owners of other specialized inputs also suffer reductions in income. Some of these workers and owners seek protection from foreign competition because their incomes will be higher if they obtain such protection.

Arguments in Favor of Protecting Domestic Industries from Foreign Competition

The arguments in favor of free trade are covered in the analysis of comparative advantage. Free trade expands a nation's consumption possibilities beyond its production possibilities. It allows higher standards of living by increasing real incomes from available resources. This implies lower prices for goods and services. In this section we look at the arguments *against* free trade and in favor of protecting domestic industries.

1. *National security.* Many people believe that self-sufficiency is necessary for reasons of national security. According to this argument, relatively inefficient domestic industries producing strategically important materials and commodities should not be allowed to go out of business because of foreign competition. A good domestic mix of industries, particularly for food, fiber, steel, and petroleum products, ensures that the United States will not be overly dependent on foreign sources of supply. This will assure stable supplies of these basic goods in the event of an international crisis. The inevitable cost of such protectionism is higher prices for American consumers.

2. *Reducing structural unemployment.* Transaction costs are associated with adjustment to a new industrial mix. For example, you may support protection of the U.S. automobile industry because you think that, in the long run, the United States will be able to produce cars more cheaply than Japan. When the industry is protected in the short run, structural unemployment is reduced. In the long run, consumers won't pay higher prices for cars because a new investment program will result in higher productivity gains and lower prices.

3. *Protecting infant industries.* Protection of a newly established or "infant" industry from foreign competition allows the new industry to expand to the point at which it can enjoy economies of scale. In this case, consumers pay higher prices as a result of protection in the short run, but hope to enjoy lower prices as the new industry achieves productivity gains in the long run. The problem with this argument is that it's difficult to identify an infant industry that will achieve such gains. In addition, protected infant industries often fail to mature to the point where they can be competitive precisely because of the inimical effects of the absence of competition.

4. *Protecting U.S. industries against subsidized foreign producers.* Some governments subsidize exporting firms to enable them to sell their goods at lower prices in foreign markets. These lower prices aren't the result of more efficient production in the exporting country. Because such subsidies cause American industries to go out of business, they give foreign suppliers more control over U.S. market prices in the long run. When a foreign government reduces or eliminates such a subsidy, the price of the imported good rises. Supporters of U.S. protection against such policies argue that there are gains from not letting subsidized goods temporarily disrupt U.S. industries. The chief gain is the reduction in the transaction costs associated with setting up and ceasing operations as foreign subsidies come and go. Another gain is a reduction in the risk that foreign suppliers will acquire monopoly power.

The gains from protecting U.S. industries must always be weighed against the costs to American consumers in terms of higher prices and reduced real incomes. Remember that the gains from international trade are increased consumption possibilities. These gains are mutually enjoyed by all trading partners. The purpose of international trade is not to